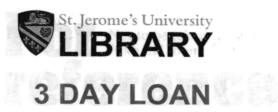

A DICTIONARY OF FAMILY THERAPY

A

DICTIONARY OF

FAMILY THERAPY

JACQUES MIERMONT

English edition edited, expanded and revised by

HUGH JENKINS

Translated by

CHRIS TURNER

Original French text copyright © Payot, Paris 1987
English translation, revised and updated, copyright © Blackwell Publishers Ltd 1995
English translation editorial organization © Hugh Jenkins 1995

English translation, revised and updated, first published 1995
English translation first published in USA 1995

The right of Jacques Miermont and Hugh Jenkins to be identified as editors of this work
has been asserted in accordance with the Copyright, Designs and Patents Act 1988.

Blackwell Publishers Ltd
108 Cowley Road, Oxford OX4 1JF, UK

Blackwell Publishers Inc.
238 Main Street
Cambridge, Massachusetts 02142
USA

British Library Cataloguing in Publication Data

A CIP catalogue record for this book is available from
the British Library.

Library of Congress Cataloging-in-Publication Data

Miermont, Jacques.
[Dictionnaire des thérapies familiales. English]
A dictionary of family therapy / Jacques Miermont; edited,
expanded and revised by Hugh Jenkins; translated by Chris Turner.
Includes bibliographical references and index.
ISBN 0–631–17048–0 (acid-free paper)
1. Family psychotherapy—Dictionaries.   I. Title.
RC488.5.M5313   1994
616.89′156′03——dc20   93–44716   CIP

SEP 0 7 1995

Typeset in 9½ on 11 pt Ehrhardt by Graphicraft Typesetters Ltd., Hong Kong
Printed in Great Britain

This book is printed on acid-free paper

CONTENTS

List of contributors   vi

Acknowledgements   viii

Acknowledgements to the French edition   ix

Foreword to the French edition   xi

Preface to the English edition   xiii

Preface to the French edition   xvi

Introduction   xxxvii

DICTIONARY ENTRIES A–Z   1

Bibliography   441

Index   477

LIST OF CONTRIBUTORS

Pierre Angel   Psychiatrist, Doctor of Psychology, Paris VII. Psychoanalyst, Family Therapist, Centre d'Etude et de Recherche sur la Famille, Paris.

Sylvie Angel   Psychiatrist, Medical Director of the Centre de Thérapie Familiale Monceau. Family Therapist, Centre d'Etude et de Recherche sur la Famille, Paris.

Brian Cade   Family and Couples Therapist in private practice, Eastwood, NSW, Australia.

John Carpenter   Senior Lecturer and Family Therapist, University of Canterbury, Kent. Joint Editor, *Journal of Family Therapy*, UK.

Dominique Christian   Clinical Philosopher, Doctor in Science of Communication, Paris.

Anny Cordina   Clinical Psychologist, Family Therapist, Centre d'Etude et de Recherche sur la Famille, Paris.

Gwyn Daniel   Family Therapist and Director for Training, Institute of Family Therapy, London.

Gilles Errieau   General Practitioner, Paris.

Pierre Garrigues   Neuro-psychiatrist, Doctor of Psychology, Psychodramatist and Family Therapist. Researcher at INSERM, Unite 70, Montpellier, Centre Montpelliérain d'Etude de la Famille.

Martine Gross   Clinical Psychologist and Trainer. Family Therapist, Centre d'Etude et de Recherche sur la Famille, Paris.

Hugh Jenkins   Family Therapist and Director, Institute of Family Therapy, London. Senior Lecturer, Institute of Psychiatry, London.

Annie Lau   Child and Adolescent Psychiatrist and Family Therapist, Child Guidance Clinic, Ilford. Member of the Institute of Family Therapy, London.

Albert Louppe   Psychiatrist, Psychoanalyst and Family Therapist, Centre d'Etude et de Recherche sur la Famille, Rennes. Course Director, University of Rennes.

Guy-Georges Maruani   Psychiatrist. Course Director, Faculté Lariboisière, Paris VII. Consultant in Psychopharmacology at the Institut de Psychiatrie La Rochefoucauld. Director of the *Revue Génitif*, Paris.

Jacques Miermont   Psychiatrist. Director of the Family Therapy Unit at Choisy le Roi. Psychoanalyst and Family Therapist, Centre d'Etude et de Recherche sur la Famille, Paris.

Robert Neuburger   Psychoanalyst, Family Therapist and Director of the Centre d'Etude de la Famille Association, Paris.

Margaret Robinson   Family Mediator and Family Therapist, Institute of Family Therapy, London.

Pierre Segond   Clinical Psychologist, Family Therapist and Study Leader, Centre de Recherches Interdisciplinaires de Vaucresson, Unité associé 412 CNRS, Paris.

ACKNOWLEDGEMENTS

No undertaking of this kind could have been achieved by a single person. It has been one of persistence, detective work and research to confirm and correct entries from the original. It has therefore been a work of collaboration by a number of people to whom I am deeply grateful. First, I wish to thank Jacques Miermont who was tireless in checking on sources and making revisions where necessary. We may not have tracked down every last one but most stones have been dislodged if not entirely overturned.

Next, I wish to pay particular tribute to Chris Turner, the translator. He and I worked closely throughout, rendering the best equivalent that we could in English of technical terms originating from such a broad spectrum of scholarship. Along the way, Chris became something of an expert on the thinking of many of the leading writers in the family therapy field from his prodigious background reading in preparation for this task. With the manuscript completed, came the really detailed work and re-checking of sources, and here I wish to thank the copy-editor, Sue Ashton.

Others have played an important part in the genesis of the English edition. I am grateful to my four Advisory Editors who gave invaluable advice in the early stages: Béla Buda from Hungary; Brian Cade from Australia; Philippe Caillé from Norway who possesses a great understanding of the family therapy field in France; and Louis Everstine from America. While final decisions had to be mine in collaboration with Jacques Miermont, their support was essential and I trust that they will recognize their wisdom here.

Throughout, patiently, and never apparently to be nonplussed by delays, re-schedules and missed deadlines, Blackwell's Reference Publisher, Alyn Shipton, remained unfailingly supportive and understanding. Finally, a number of people helped with typing, but I should like to thank in particular my personal assistant, Elizabeth Furniss, for undertaking the more onerous typing tasks during the editing process.

H.J.

ACKNOWLEDGEMENTS TO THE
FRENCH EDITION

IT would be impossible to mention here everyone whose teaching and support have contributed, directly or indirectly, to the development of the work of which this dictionary is one of the results. We would particularly like to thank Professors Maurice Porot, Didier Jacques Duche, Léon Cassiers, André Feline, Daniel Alagille, Jacques Gagey, Philippe Gutton, Christopher E. Zeeman, Serge Lebovici, Daniel Widlöcher, Michel Soulé, Philippe Mazet, Pierre Fedida, Yves Pelicier, André Julien Condet and Jean de Verbizier; Doctors Rosine Cremieux, Simone Decobert, Paulette Letarte, Danielle Margueritat, Claude Revault d'Allonnes, Marie-Hélène Revault d'Allonnes, Léon Kreisler, Pierre Bourdier, Jean-François Allilaire, Alain Braconnier, Bernard Brusset, Bernard Jolivet, Guy Ausloos, Alberto Eiguier, Robert Barande, Jean-Claude Benoit, Philippe Caillé, Mony Elkaim, Gottlieb Guntern, Carmine Saccu, Carlos Sluzki, Claude Olievenstein, Jean-Pierre Blanadet, Jean-Claude Jany, Martine Charlery, Françoise Premel, Eric Piel, Dider Chartier and Anne-Marie Dubois; and Ophélia Avron, Lynn Hoffman, Louis and Diana Everstine, Georges Allyn, Marcel Boisot, Emmanuel Todd and Mustapha Safouan.

Professor Murray Bowen has granted kind permission to use his genogram symbols.

Professor Paul Watzlawick, Dr Richard Fisch and John Weakland introduced us to an understanding of interactions in medicine and psychiatry, and also brief therapy techniques.

We would particularly like to thank Siegi Hirsch, whose teaching, for the most part oral, has led to much innovative work in training and supervision in the French context; his epistemological openness and great clinical experience have laid the foundations for much valuable work.

Professor Jean-Louis Le Moigne's comments on the manuscript prompted much new thinking and caused us to make a great number of modifications with regard to the interface between general systems theory and the systemic modelling of the family. His encouragement of the work relating to the self-referential calculus has been particularly valuable.

Several lines of enquiry have been explored at the prompting of Professor René Thom. We express our gratitude to him here for the depth and range of his teaching as well as for the interest he has shown in this research; we also thank him for his corrections to the entries dealing with mathematics, catastrophe theory and topologico-semantic models.

We hope that, in presenting some difficult subjects, we have avoided basic errors and accept complete responsibility for any faults which remain and for the lines of argument we put forward.

We would like to thank Catherine Guitton Cohen Adad, Michel Goutal, Laurent Mottron, Marie-José Wagner, Françoise Domenach and Michèle Neuburger for the fruitful encounters they have instigated within the framework of the seminars of the Centre d'Etude et de Recherche sur la Famille. Dominique Miermont, Christian Portelli, Nicole Eckersley, Françoise Couture, Pierre Padovani, Marguerite Leterrier, Alain Ackermans and Chantal van Cutsem, Henri Doussinet, Jean-Claude and Françoise Bouffard, Hugues Gerhards and Michel Gault have improved the text by their suggestions and criticisms.

ACKNOWLEDGEMENTS TO THE FRENCH EDITION

We thank Susan Clot for her bibliographical assistance on the entries 'Psychosomatic illness' and 'Couples', Renée Larbaud and Jean-Jacques Vauchel for their contributions to the entry on 'Marital breakdown' and Alain Laraby and Marie-Hélène Lemaire for their thoughts on the entry on 'Law'.

The preparation of the manuscript owes much to the dedication and patience of Simone Schudy, and Véronique Granier also contributed actively to this aspect of the work. Mrs Michèle Roy, archivist at the Institut de Psychiatrie La Rochefoucauld, and Dr Claude Veil, who built up the library's collection in this area, made it possible for us to undertake bibliographical research into the origin and history of the family therapy movement.

Lastly, the whole endeavour could not have been successfully completed without the kind, active support of Mr Jean-Luc Pidoux Payot, to whom we express our heartfelt gratitude.

G.E.
G.M.
J.M.

FOREWORD TO THE FRENCH EDITION

THE human sciences now have a range of new concepts at their disposal. Their research tools and conceptual apparatuses have been revolutionized and reshaped by the same developments which have overtaken the physical and biological sciences. Fields of application considered inaccessible not so long ago have been explored, marked out and rendered fertile.

In the nineteenth century, madness, that ultimate manifestation of the human condition, was forced from the field of the sacred into that of medicine. For half a century, by way of the concept of the Unconscious, Freud's psychoanalysis restored it to its place of mystery of the soul. With the approaches derived from the study of communications, madness is now perceived as a simple phenomenon, a particular modality of the exchange of information between persons. It is both inside and outside the subject, located in an intermediate region which the key notions of circular causality, interaction, feedback and logical types enable us to construct in principle and in theory. A theory which, distinguishing between the various levels of complexity and respecting their irreducibility one to another, attempts to articulate the brain and thinking, the subject and the group, form and meaning, process and crisis, reason and instinct. Though still in the process of formation, this theory none the less inspires practices, generally referred to as family therapies and/or systemic interventions, which tackle problems of mental illness, delinquent behaviour, psychosomatic illness and drug abuse.

Why a dictionary of family therapy?

First, to draw up a balance sheet of the contribution that has already been made by this new treatment philosophy in psychiatry. Since its initial flowering in the USA in the 1950s, its concepts have been developed, added to and more widely disseminated. Cybernetics, systems theory, information theory and the pragmatics of communication have significantly enriched the behavioural sciences. Crossing the Atlantic, these formulations came up against a psychoanalysis of personal development which, though it was the dominant discourse, was often thwarted in the reality of institutions, its very success having stripped it of its subversive value. European writers have continued the research work of the founders and played their part in establishing a coherent body of theory.

Secondly, because the family is presented, in this approach, as the basic unit of maturation, differentiation and transformation for the human being. The unity in question is a diverse one: anthropological forms of kinship vary widely; in some social structures, care and education is the preserve of the parents, whereas in others it is delegated to third parties; and technology has now burst upon the scene of reproductive biology. Beneath these variations, there is, however, a human core, the reciprocal affective attachment between the child and the adult individuals in its family circle. The lived experience of this provides the foundation for the physical and psychical development of the human being.

The family can thus be seen as prey to a great many contradictions, if not indeed of genuine paradoxes, both biological and symbolic, pathological and creative. In order to deal with these, a number of diverse disciplines have to be called into play: systems theory, cybernetics, psychoanalysis, ethology, ethnology, catastrophe theory, semiotics and linguistics, all with reference to clinical practice as a phenomenon attesting to the great difficulties of existence. Taking the family object as our focus, we have explored these various 'fields' which constitute the obligatory pathways by which the individual connects with society. Given the great proliferation of practices, theories and schools, we felt it necessary to offer an aid to work and thinking which gives an overview of the major currents of thought, the techniques which have been tested out, and the epistemological problems involved.

The dictionary form seemed to us to offer the most effective way of delineating the fields of investigation and mapping their contours. This could, in our view, help to promote a well-informed debate, in order that,

- new techniques of intervention may be outlined without these being reduced to the status of mere procedures to be followed (techniques are necessary, indeed indispensable, but they are not sufficient in themselves);
- new dogmatisms or closed thinking may be avoided: the words chosen are not the only ones possible; they contain a degree of vagueness which reflects the dynamic objects observed;
- new metaphors may be suggested and new contexts for thinking, action and emotion constructed, without which reality is exhausted and practice repeated without being enriched;
- fundamental levels of experience and reasoning may be rediscovered: the family ecosystem is the most widely shared reality in the world. Moses, Oedipus, Buddha, Jesus . . . all so many family stories in the beginning.

There follows from this a critical study of the concept of therapy and, we hope, an extension of the efficacy of the psychoanalytic model, in so far as this means respect for the other person's mental freedom, into situations where it was previously not exploited.

It will be clear to the reader that we are not carrying a banner here for any of the particular factions currently competing for theoretical supremacy in France, relying as they do on the promulgation of exclusive therapeutic myths to the effect that therapists and patients 'tell each other everything' or 'all act together'. Nor are we claiming any better results than other forms of care in psychiatry, which reality would soon show up to be false. Our objective is to recognize that conflict is the precondition for developmental processes, and this applies as much to the therapists' myths as to those of the families they treat.

This book is aimed equally at the student of psychology and the family doctor, the social worker and the psychiatrist, the anthropologist and the biologist, in order to promote a many-sided vision of clinical reality which is most in keeping with our age and best suited to coping with its upheavals.

This project, in which Gilles Errieau, Jacques Miermont and Guy Maruani were the prime movers, has been brought to fruition under the direction of Jacques Miermont. It is the product of research carried out as a team within the framework of the Centre d'Etude et de Recherche sur la Famille (Pierre Angel, Sylvie Angel, Albert Louppe, Martine Gross, Anny Cordina) and the journal *Génitif* (Guy Maruani, Dominique Christian). Robert Neuburger (Director of the Centre d'Etude de la Famille Association), Pierre Segond (President in 1986 of the Association de Thérapie Systémique Familiale) and Pierre Garrigues (researcher at INSERM) have also participated in the work.

Gilles Errieau
Guy Maruani
Jacques Miermont

PREFACE TO THE ENGLISH EDITION

JUST as any meaning attributed to communication is qualified by the context of that communicational sequence, so the publication of a book, in this case a dictionary of family therapy, is part of the context from which it originates. This dictionary is very much the vision of its senior French editor, Dr Jacques Miermont. As such, it reflects a particular perspective on the position of family therapy in France, and how that has been affected by developments in the field worldwide. It draws on a number of important themes, many of which are particular to the French tradition of scholarship and which differ from traditions of the Anglo-Saxon world. It is this which gives it a special interest. In commenting on these themes for the English edition, I echo the words of Freud in his *Introductory Lectures on Psycho-analysis: Psycho-analysis and Psychiatry*: 'I do not aim at producing conviction – my aim is to stimulate enquiry and to destroy prejudices' (Freud, 1929, Lecture 16).

It seems appropriate to begin with a reference to Freud, since so much of family therapy practice, psychiatry and social work in France continues to be influenced by Freud's thought, by Lacan, and by the psychoanalytic world in general. This also represents a significant difference from the direction of mainstream family therapy in the UK, America and other English-speaking countries, especially Australia and New Zealand.

It is appropriate for another reason. With the passage of time we are witnessing something of a new curiosity between systems thinkers and the insights of our 'professional forebears', the psychoanalytic and psychodynamic communities. There is a greater willingness to re-examine some of the truths of the past and to incorporate them into our current understanding without renouncing the important developments brought about in the field of family therapy. The republication in Britain of an expanded edition of *The patient and the analyst* (Sandler et al., 1992) examines important questions about the relationship between the therapist and the patient, applicable in any therapeutic relationship. The importance of this is that the second author, Christopher Dare, is a senior British family therapist who brings together an understanding of the encounter between therapist and patient while working within a family systems framework in his family therapy practice and research. Rather like the offspring in families, there is a realization as we come to professional maturity that our predecessors had skills and useful concepts to offer.

In considering developments in the family therapy field, we might apply our understanding of the importance of context to the question: why was Freud not a family therapist? The answer is both complex and simple. Many of the formal developments in thinking in the twentieth century, including the world of cybernetics, communication theory and general systems theory had not been articulated. And Freud was, like all of us, bounded by his time and a very particular culture, despite his innovative work and the mistakes that he made. It is true that his unwillingness to accept that fathers could sexually interfere with their young daughters set back the treatment of sexual abuse by more than fifty years. It is always easy to criticize with the twenty-twenty vision of hindsight. Despite such justifiable criticisms, he was aware of many of the processes which we take for granted today. It is worth quoting from one passage which demonstrates how ahead of his time he was, even if his theoretical framework did not allow him to make direct use of it. In thirty years' time, I assume that we also will be found wanting for failing to see clearly that which is before our eyes. In his twenty-eighth and final introductory lecture, 'The analytic therapy', Freud writes:

> Psycho-Analytic treatment is comparable to a surgical operation . . . [H]ow many surgical operations would be successful if they had to be conducted in the presence of the patient's entire family poking their noses into the scene of the operation and shrieking aloud at every cut. In psycho-analytic treatment the intervention of the relatives is . . . one which we do not know how to deal with . . . Anyone who knows anything of the dissensions commonly splitting up family life will not be astonished in his capacity of analyst that those nearest to the patient frequently show less interest in his recovery than in keeping him as he is. When as so often occurs the neurosis is connected with conflicts between different members of a family, the healthy person does not make much of putting his own interest before the patient's recovery. (Freud, 1929, pp. 384–5)

The last two sentences could have been written by almost any 'systemic' thinker of the late twentieth century.

Much of Freud's work shows a systemic understanding of the nature of resistance, of the importance of context, and of how by starting with a clearly defined model, in this instance a medical model of surgery, certain courses of action are precluded by that framework while others are actively encouraged. Whereas in current family therapy writing, more and more attention is rightly being given to the contexts of practice in order for specific clinical skills to be effective (Carpenter and Treacher, 1993), Freud was more preoccupied with clearing the ground of noxious influences which could interfere with psychoanalytic treatment. For Freud it was a matter of either/or, while systemic thinkers address the both/and, influenced initially by the writings of Bateson (1972, 1979). Freud is modest in acknowledging his lack of skills necessary to deal with interventions by relatives. Whatever his shortcomings in the light of current developments, Freud demonstrated: courage in pursuing his explorations of the human mind; a willingness to challenge accepted beliefs; a commitment to stimulating enquiry to push back the boundaries of knowledge; and a self-critical capacity. These are all qualities that the serious student needs today as both theoretician and practitioner.

In this dictionary, Jacques Miermont highlights issues arising from a juxtaposition and comparison of psychoanalytic and systemic points of view. As both a clinician and leading thinker in the field in France, he executes challenging conceptual leaps, drawing on theories from other intellectual fields of enquiry both to inform and expand the theory and practice of family therapy. The original Introduction will help the reader to use the text to its fullest benefit. This volume also makes available family therapy material not easily obtainable by the non-French-speaking reader, drawing on a rich vein of French thinking and scientific endeavour not normally addressed in the Anglo-Saxon world.

Miermont and his colleagues draw on the field of mathematical models and symbols to explicate their understanding of our world. In this way they show how developments in family therapy in particular and in psychotherapy in general can be conceived as part of the broader mainstream of intellectual thought. A field of thought not widely developed in Britain outside the world of mathematics is René Thom's work on catastrophe theory (Miermont and Neuburger, 1989). Complex in its explanation, some of these ideas help make sense of discontinuous shifts in human behaviour, introducing the reader at the same time to a different level of intellectual rigour. The challenge is to set alongside this thinking, material which will be familiar to the student of family therapy and to explore how theory and practice illuminate and inform each other through alternative theoretical lenses.

A dilemma in preparing this English edition was the extent to which the specific French character should be maintained. This, after all, is part of its difference. I have respected Dr Miermont's wish that the French character should be maintained and the psychoanalytic–systemic tension held. This produced some problems in how to render examples which were very context bound to the original and how to find titles to some of the articles which would resonate with the English language reader. It may be that the bringing together of frameworks, cultures and models had not been entirely seamless. This also raised the question of how much additional referencing to make. A text which originated in one of the English-speaking countries would not have drawn on the Francophone field to the extent that this does. Therefore it seemed wise to be sparing in adding references which appeared first in the English language except where it was felt this would specifically enhance the original. The same held true for including additional articles, especially where those topics were already covered by Simon et al. (1985) or Walrond-Skinner (1986). Where there were important omissions, articles have been commissioned, including some from Miermont. Some of the original French contributions have been modified, and their meaning made more explicit. Where in the original I felt that some minor contributions did not add to the overall coherence of the volume, they have been deleted, and in some instances where I could not be in reasonable agreement with the original text I have added material to provide what I trust will be a greater balance to the whole.

Hugh Jenkins

PREFACE TO THE FRENCH EDITION

TOWARDS A THEORY OF COMMUNICATION

In 1956, Gregory Bateson, Don D. Jackson, Jay Haley and John H. Weakland published 'Towards a theory of schizophrenia', an article which gradually assumed the status of a major paradigm in understanding psychopathology; the writing of this dictionary some thirty years later is still an echo of this work. Several epistemological principles were laid down in this article which, even more than the ideas presented, revolutionized the approach to mental disorders and, in fact, suggested another vision of human experience.

On the one hand, postulated Bateson, communication is the social matrix in which psychiatric symptoms are registered (to paraphrase the title of Ruesch and Bateson, 1951); on the other hand, it is legitimate and fruitful to approach the world of psychosis with an anthropologist's eye and with no preconceptions, and to observe how schizophrenics exchange information with those around them with the same curiosity, respect and desire for objectivity as an ethnologist in a strange society whose language, behaviour and customs he or she must gradually decode. Bateson and his team discovered that the 'being-in-the-world' of the schizophrenic described by the phenomenologists was not an immanent property but the result of a process. This process is permanently at work in implied relations with others. In other words, there is no schizophrenic ontological modality, but a schizophrenic mode of communication. How does this mode become established? Following his line of reasoning, Bateson replies: like a culture, by a process of learning. And the site of this learning can only be the human institution which is allotted the task of teaching the child the ways of society, namely the family.

The idea that the child's first relations can determine its development was not new in 1956. On the contrary, Bateson and Jackson spontaneously integrated into their description the contributions of Freudian and post-Freudian culturalist psychoanalysis, as developed in the USA by Harry Stack Sullivan, Erich Fromm and Frieda Fromm-Reichmann. This is why they tended, at the beginning, particularly to emphasize the role of the mother in the construction of the schizophrenic's psychical reality. However, by insisting on the fact that what they were concerned with was not a phase of affective and mental development but a form of communication still being actualized in the present, they marked themselves off from psychoanalysis and opened up a great many new paths. Let us mention some of these here not merely for historical interest but because they represent dimensions which the family therapist encounters and uses today.

That 1956 article by the Palo Alto team is usually identified as the moment of break and conceptual reorganization because it introduces the *double bind* hypothesis. This was formulated by Bateson after Haley had suggested that the symptoms of schizophrenia were an expression of an inability to discriminate between *logical types* or, in other words, *between levels of communication ranked according to their degree of abstraction*, in reference to the theory put forward by Whitehead and Russell in their *Principia mathematica* of 1910. For his part, Jackson contributed his idea of *family homeostasis*, that is, of a constant internal state of the family milieu seen as an organism subject to external dynamic forces. This idea was itself taken from the model of the brain proposed by Ashby (1952), a psychiatrist who had become first an electroencephalographer and then a cybernetician in his concern to eliminate all notions of subjectivity, and who imported the main principles of the physiology of Claude Bernard and Cannon into the scientific approach to human behaviour. Weakland and Haley completed this key article by developing the analogy between the effects of hypnosis and schizophrenia.

In substance, according to the double-bind hypothesis, the future schizophrenic *learns not to distinguish the different levels of maternal messages* and, for example, is led to confuse real feelings (one logical type) and simulated feelings (another logical type). The schizophrenic must systematically distort his or her perception of the signals of metacommunication and does not develop a capacity to classify the different registers of communication and to pass from one to the other. Thus he/she does not differentiate between the concrete and the metaphorical, as is required in humour, art or play. Admittedly, as Watzlawick noted in 1963, the hypothesis of levels of learning had been developed long before the double-bind theory and had been explored independently in the 1940s by Hull, Bateson and Harlow. What was fundamentally new in the study of psychosis, however, was the demonstration of an 'interactional pattern', a sequence of interchanges between several persons rather than either an individual intrapsychic disposition such as Bleuler's 'ambivalence' and Freud's 'projection' or a particular family structure as was being pursued by many of the other founders of family therapy in this same period.

A NUMBER OF INITIATIVES

Bowen (1978b) saw the family as the unit of illness and treatment and the patient's psychosis as the symptom of an active process in which the whole family was involved. Three generations or more were required for schizophrenia to appear when the succession of immaturities and retrograde attachments had reached the point where the emotional divorce between the parents was matched by a symbiotic relationship between the mother and the potential patient.

Lidz et al. (1965) stressed what might be the equally harmful role of certain fathers, the difficulty certain parents had in forming a couple – and, as a result, forming couples that were often lame or schismatic – and the blurring of boundaries between generations. Ackerman (1958) observed that families tend to form factions which enter into emotional warfare. A certain equilibrium is brought about within those families by the emergence of a scapegoat and/or healer through shared unconscious mechanisms of persecution and reparation.

The work of Wynne et al. (1958) was close to that of the Palo Alto team since it established that the thought disturbances of the schizophrenic derive from the internalization of the characteristics of family organization. The family style, which was confirmed in the projective testing of members of the family other than the patient, accounts for the degree of fragmentation and indeterminacy of the schizophrenic's thinking. The patient invests the stereotyped complementarity of family roles – secured by relations of so-called 'pseudo-mutuality' in which all divergence and progress are excluded – as a necessary condition of reality.

Subsequently, other American writers added further insights. For example, from a psychosociological perspective, Florence Kluckhohn (1953) and John Spiegel (1968) placed the emphasis upon the interiorization of social roles within the family, on conflicts of cultural values and on the psychopathological risks when a mechanism of role distortion gains precedence over adaptive modification. Boszormenyi-Nagy showed that children are 'parentified' in order to respond to the unconscious need of one or both parents for a symbiotic relationship which, at adolescence, will prevent them from achieving autonomy, in spite of their apparent attempts at emancipation. All the writers quoted here accompany their reflections with proposals for therapy and their theoretical intuitions are supported by analyses of clinical material.[1]

Now, the impossibility of identifying double binds in a specific, naturalistic way, far from destroying the credibility of the Palo Alto hypothesis actually secured its place as a paradigm. Just as the hypothesis of the unconscious enabled Freud to integrate and transcend many of the features of the culture of his day, the double-bind hypothesis enabled the Palo Alto school not only to extend to psychiatry the epistemological advances achieved by the basic sciences in the first half of the twentieth century (indeterminacy, relativity, complexity, circularity), but also to provide an ultimate conceptual framework for the empirical research of practitioners whose theoretical propositions always remained asymptotically related to the double-bind theory. As a model, the double bind was all the more convincing for being an image not an experience. A great many writers were to refer to it, though many did so erroneously, taking it to signify a conflict of meaning, whereas in fact it denotes a conflict between meaning and communication about meaning.

None the less, in the United States, such diverse authorities as Arieti, the editor of the *American handbook of psychiatry* of 1960 and Szasz, the opponent of the 'myth of mental illness' (1961) both felt the need to refer to double binds. The reason was that 'Towards a theory of schizophrenia' presented, in a remarkably integrated way, a synthesizing and innovative account of what were then the various contemporary tendencies in psychopathology. Let us now turn to these and examine their legacy.

THE CYBERNETIC REVOLUTION

Like other revolutions, the cybernetic revolution was heralded and prepared long before by various movements which combined to produce a radical change then separated out in a new order. The prophet was, without doubt, Alfred Korzybski, the first of those fallen aristocrats of *Mitteleuropa* who, with a number of Jewish *Wunderkinder* fleeing Nazism and some New England engineers, were in at the inception of cybernetics. From Paris, it is difficult to be certain that the first relatively confidential editions of Korzybski's books, *Manhood of humanity* (1921) and *Science and sanity* (1941),[2] do indeed contain what he later claimed they did, but he acknowledged his debt to the work of Bertrand Russell and of Whitehead for the formulation of his main thesis, namely the demolition of the so-called Aristotelian structure of language which reviewed the subject-predicate structure of language as the result of the attribution to 'nature' of 'properties' or 'qualities' whereas the 'qualities' are in fact originated by our nervous system. Usually, only the first premiss of non-Aristotelian semantics is remembered. We would do well, however, to remember all three:

1   A map *is not* the territory.
2   A map does not cover *the whole* territory.
3   A map is self-reflexive (in language we can talk *about* language).

This brings us back to the theory of logical types but also to other principles which I here summarize or infer:

- our nervous system includes in its functioning ineffable non-verbal levels;
- these are affected by the verbal level (and vice versa) through the similarity of structure of the relations;
- the verbal level is 'time-binding', that is, it accumulates experiences registered by the species;[3]
- verbal thinking limits our degrees of freedom of thought, which the solipsistic position of the mathematician and the mystic transcends thanks to the endo-perception of visual or kinaesthesic mechanisms;

- there is an endless circularity between perception and language;
- abstraction is a danger if one is not aware one is abstracting;
- a *functional*, rather than a zoological or mythological, approach views man as an 'organism-as-a-whole-in-an-environment'.

It was by focusing on *the concept of function* that three different sources were to unite to give birth to cybernetics and computing (which would share a common history between 1948 and 1952).[4]

The *theory of automata* was based on the Turing machine (1937), which was capable of performing any operation so long as it was reduced to a series of alternatives in binary logic. If the list of inputs is known, then the list of outputs is known from the correspondence table of its functions. Thus McCulloch (a psychiatrist) and Pitts showed in 1943 that a finite automatic network – such as was constituted, in their view, by the nervous system – could perform all the cognitive functions.

In drawing up the plan of the first real computer in 1945, von Neumann was to refer to the neuronal logical organization they had postulated in what was a kind of quest for an artificial brain. Von Neumann, who had created 'game theory', invented the computer by replacing the arithmetical logic of the Pascalian machine with an information-organizing programme, of which calculation was now a mere by-product.

Wiener had already introduced the notion of complexity of behaviour in 1942, in place of the notion of complexity of internal structure. McCulloch and Pitts's network of neurons was, similarly, a model, intermediate between brain and mind, which was unconcerned with whether or not it could possibly be represented in neurophysiological terms. Wiener's disciples Weaver and Shannon, who formulated the mathematical theory of communication (1949), in fact conceived information as a quantity merged entirely with signals.

This physicalism of *information theory* was only overcome because studies on artificial intelligence gradually discovered that information is what calculation is practised upon and, hence, the manner of calculating may influence the form of the result. This idea had already been broached by Wiener in 1948 in his attempts to combine communication and control, and it was to undergo two rather opposing courses of development. One was Ashby's *homeostat* (1952) which claimed to prove that two or more articulated sub-systems are able to arrive spontaneously at equilibrium by randomly searching through all their possible configurations and maintaining the record of the effective configurations in the form of stochastic processes. Though he disagreed with this approach and criticized its reductionism, von Bertalanffy, with his general systems theory, remained a prisoner of it to the extent that, for him, variations in the environment played the role of an external sub-system contributing to homeostatic regulation.

The other line of development was that of von Foerster's *non-trivial machines*. He took the view that there was no information in the outside world. Information is determined, rather, by the calculation carried out by the machine as a function of the inputs and of its previous internal states. His disciple, Maturana, was to use the term 'autopoiesis' to refer to the processes of coupling between the environment and the organism and between the organism and the nervous system.[5]

All in all, then, the cybernetic revolution provides yet further exemplification of the two traditions in the making of automatic machines since the fourteenth century:

- the quest for mastery of time, as with clepsydrae or water-clocks, which rely upon analogic means of regulation;
- the quest for mastery of movement, as with springs, which rely on programming and calculations.

There is some relevance in asking which cybernetic type each family therapist tends towards.

THE PRAGMATICS OF COMMUNICATION

The theory of the double bind is steeped in the philosophy of Oxford and Cambridge. From the *Summa theologica* of William of Occam in the Middle Ages to the *Principia mathematica* of Russell and Whitehead, there is a tradition – onto which Wittgenstein's *Tractatus logico-philosophicus* is also grafted – of 'supposition' which subordinates semantics to pragmatics, i.e. to the assumption of intersubjectivity. In the act of communicating, an organism may be regarded as handling one tool (verbal or other) in order to engrave the representation of facts, aptitudes or priorities in another.

The inventors of the double bind were in the same tradition when they asserted that the schizophrenic has difficulties in assigning the correct mode of communication to:

- messages he/she receives from others;
- messages he/she utters or sends by non-verbal means;
- his/her own thoughts, feelings and perceptions;

and that the schizophrenic is particularly unsuccessful in manipulating the signals of the class whose members assign logical types to other signals.

In 1963 Bateson and his colleagues clarified their thinking further. They stated that perhaps the most important aspects of their work had not been fully appreciated in their original article on the double bind in 1956. For them this was a framework for a general communicational approach to study a wide range of human, and even animal, behaviours, of which schizophrenia was a major example. There is never a message in isolation, but rather in real communication there are two or more messages, of different levels, and often channelled by different means such as voice, tone, movement and context. Bateson and colleagues were not merely contenting themselves with replying to the seven questions on human communication posed by Ruesch (1953),[6] but were anticipating developments in ethology, linguistics, microsociology and anthropology which were to lead to the vast range of sciences of communication.

Non-verbal communication[7] is, obviously, to be found primarily among animals. Bateson studied it in otters and was to study it in dolphins without achieving the same intellectual breakthrough as in psychiatry. In the wake of Tinbergen and Lorenz (and Darwin after 1872), Eibl-Eibesfeldt was to attempt to establish that a code of signalling exists that is common to all humans. This code relates to expressive movements of the face and body. It has been set in place by phylogenetic ritualization, but it may be implemented differently as a function of varying cultural sequences. For example, partly hiding one's face with one's hand indicates embarrassment. Eibl-Eibesfeldt has gone so far as to speak of a homology of facial expressions among the primates. He has thus set himself against Birdwhistell who takes the view that there are no expressions independent of culture and learning. Eibl-Eibesfeldt (1975, p. 467) finds, by contrast, a '*superposition* of a few invariable components' which 'yields a relatively complex and *variable expression*'. The fact is that if there is universality of schizophrenic discordance, there must indeed be universality in the concordance between emotion and expression.

Birdwhistell (1981) has none the less attempted to prove that communication by the moving body (*kinesics*) is an interactional behaviour and, as such, cannot be dissociated from the lexical and vocal context in which it occurs. Hall (1976), basing himself upon research into social space as bio-communication (or, put more prosaically, research into the distance and volume of air between individuals) concludes that cultural ritualizations intervene to determine this, not biological ritualizations. In his view, *proxemics* depends upon the syntactic structure of language as first cultural determinant, a position in line with the writings of Sapir, Whorf and Chomsky.

Hall (1976) believes that in life, the three dimensions of code, context and meaning are three facets of a single fact. He also maintains that the level of the context determines the overall nature of the communication which represents the basis for all other behaviours (including symbolic behaviour). Perhaps Leach (1972) provides us with a halfway house solution between these advocates of the interactive context[8] and the biologists of behaviour who, with Lorenz, feel that man's expressive movements result from a process of reduction and rearrangement of instinctual sequences in his social behaviour. He suggests, in fact, that, in a private context, action rituals are essentially metaphorical while the proxemics are loose, whereas, in a public context, action rituals are metonymic, referring on to a cultural coding in language form, an utterance. He quotes the diagram drawn up by Lane (1970) illustrating the fundamental structuralist hypothesis which may be extended as here.

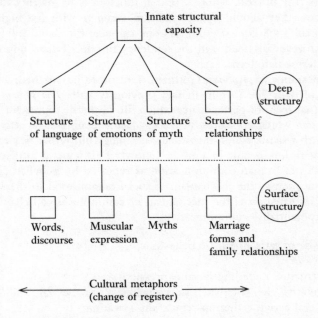

This may be so, but what is the situation where mental patients are concerned? The limit case is represented by autistic children who, as Tinbergen and Tinbergen (1972) have confirmed, release a behaviour of fear and withdrawal as soon as they feel they are being looked at, which is already an interaction.[9] Grant had claimed that schizophrenics use the same vocabulary of non-verbal communication and the same internal logic of behaviour as other individuals, but that the ambivalence and great anxiety, the side-effects of medication and the hierarchies of dominance which are established in an institution through aggression, contribute to making the communicational repertoire more rigid and restricted. Posture, facial and bodily gesture only degenerate into stereotypes because they are inappropriate to a new communication context.

Now Goffman (1961) had already noted that a psychiatric asylum (which he equates with a totalitarian institution) implies a constraint of the patient, that is, the requirement to display a particular behaviour and participate in a particular universe. Defence then consists in manifesting a primary behaviour of adaptation to the official rules and a secondary behaviour of adaptation to the clandestine life of the institution, that particular form of absenteeism which involves maintaining one's distance not from an activity, but from a prescribed person. It is interesting to note that for three years, operating as a scrupulous anthropologist, Goffman observed the daily practice of the social distance which separates the patient from those who designate him/her as one, without drawing any other conclusion than that to leave the hospital or to be comfortable living in it, mental patients have to show themselves satisfied with the place that is organized for them. Moreover, that the hospital must also confirm the professional roles of those who impose the conditions of the setting. Now, Bateson and his team, themselves operating as ethnologists in a neighbouring asylum at the same time as Goffman, brought back from that experience a theory which, slowly but surely, exploded the asylum (and I am not referring here to the reference which anti-psychiatry will make to Bateson and Goffman, but to the new epistemology which, situating mental illness in the structure of family interactions, renders completely invalid the prolonged internment of the actual symptom-bearer). Moreover, Goffman quotes Bateson twice: once to take cognizance of his observation that the asylum personnel remain socially integrated in the outside world and once in connection with a text about the middle members (the nurses), whose essential function is to instruct the lowest level (the patients) how they should behave in their contacts with the highest level (the doctors) (Goffman, 1968 edn, p. 108). As one can see, the 'hand' of Bateson shows through here (however discreetly) in the tendency to reject binary oppositions and to introduce an intermediate term.

After the appearance of *Asylums*, Goffman went on to pursue his research into the microsociology of daily life (begun in fact previously with *The presentation of self*). Exploring first that form of performance which life in public represents, and then the *rituals of interaction* which crystallize in face-to-face encounters, he attempted to promote a model with was not about individual psychology but rather was concerned with relational rules with link people in a group context. This logic of interaction concords with the systemics of human communication as reported by Scheflen (1972). He described communication as the mechanism of social organization in the same way that transmission of information is the mechanism of communicative behaviour where all behaviours are (potentially) communicative.

- vocal, linguistic or para-linguistic behaviour;
- kinesic behaviour:
    body movements, including facial expression;
    neuro-vegetative elements, such as the colouring of the skin, the dilation of the pupil, visceral activity, thermo-regulation, sweating;
    posture;
    bodily non-language sounds;
    tactile behaviour;
    territorial or proxemic behaviour;
    artifactual behaviour, including dress, cosmetic usage, use of ornament etc.

CONNECTEDNESS

Let us return from California to Oxford, by way of the discovery that words can be acts. As early as 1940, Collingwood had affirmed that *every assertive utterance is in fact interactive* since it is a reply to a question which, even if it has not been directly put, is present in the context. The canonic example is the following utterance: 'he has stopped beating his wife' which is, in fact, a reply to a whole series of questions stated or unstated.

Austin (1962) observes that questioning, threatening, promising and ordering are also speech acts, like assertion, and he constructs a particular locutionary category termed *performative utterances*. An utterance is performative if it describes a present action on the part of the speaker which is accomplished by virtue of the utterance itself. An example might be 'I declare this session open' or 'I promise to come.' However, the performative is only possible by virtue of the subjectivity of discourse introduced by the pronoun 'I' and the present indicative which presupposes reciprocation on the part of the receiver of the message and, therefore, intersubjectivity. 'I am lying' is not, in that case, a paradoxical self-referential utterance, whereas '*I congratulate you*' is. In other words, *the product of speech is intersubjectivity*.

Another way of looking at communication was, at the same time, to extend that study of 'the performative' to the whole human race and the entire planet. In *The Gutenberg galaxy* (1962), Marshall McLuhan declares that: 'The interiorization of the technology of the phonetic alphabet translates man from the magical world of the ear to the neutral visual world' (p. 18); 'the interiorization of media such as *letters* alter[s] the ratio among our sense and change[s] mental processes' (p. 24); 'The new electronic interdependence recreates the world in the image of a global village' (p. 31); 'The stage has been cleared of the archetypes or postures of individual mind, and is ready for the archetypes of the collective unconscious' (p. 244). In other words, the *product of the electronic media is the interconnection of unconsciouses*.

In the preface to the 1976 edition, McLuhan prophesies that the left hemisphere of the brain will be dislodged from its position of pre-eminence, the electronic environment liberating the right-hand hemisphere from its 2,500 year-long enslavement. For Watzlawick (1978a), this is also the objective of psychotherapy, or, at least, its instrument.[10] It remains to be seen how all the theoretical hypotheses referred to here have succeeded in translating themselves into practical means for coming to the aid of individuals and families who are suffering, first of all, from psychosis and, subsequently, from other forms of mental affliction.

'HERE AND KNOW'

It is the virtue of this bad pun that it condenses the two principles which presided over the progressive elaboration of a therapeutic strategy derived from the communicational approach. These were, on the one hand, the 'here and now' of the psychotherapist's inspiration, caught up as he or she is in the *system of interactions* and, on the other, the knowledge of mental functioning derived from the experience of psychoanalysis and hypnosis. The article 'Towards a theory of schizophrenia' is also revealing in this regard since two of the case-studies reported are taken from Milton Erickson and Frieda Fromm-Reichmann.[11] The authors of that article deduced first of all that certain sequences of communication, produced with the aid of hypnotic technique or of the affects involved in transference, could be arranged into therapeutic double binds. How, then, were they to explain that double binds – like speaking by allegory and fable – could at certain times give rise to schizophrenia and at others provide a means of treatment?

The subsequent careers of the Palo Alto pioneers perhaps provide the beginnings of an answer to this question. Gregory Bateson left for Hawaii to observe attempts at communication with dolphins. He never received the academic recognition that was his due and became a kind of intellectual guru to the ecologists. Don D. Jackson died suddenly while director of the Mental Research Institute, where he practised and taught 'psychotherapy conducted conjointly with families'. Jay Haley left Palo Alto and the MRI for Philadelphia where he worked alongside Salvador Minuchin at the child guidance clinic. As first editor of *Family process*, he rejected the double-bind concept, replacing it with that of logical paradox. Haley was fascinated by Milton Erickson and his gift for metaphorical communication. Advocating a 'strategic psychotherapy', he emerged as one of the principal leaders of family therapy. John Weakland stayed at Palo Alto, concerning himself with psychosomatic medicine and pop culture and, together with Richard Fisch, he developed the Brief Therapy Centre where practice is based on the idea that the responses patients have found to their difficulties in fact constitute the real problem and obstacle to change.

In the outer circle, Virginia Satir, a social worker, became the great marriage guidance enthusiast at the Esalen Institute and the great trainer in family therapy. A large number of eminent family therapists in all parts of the world were students of hers. William Fry, Irving Yalom and Jules Riskin pursued careers as psychiatrists, and it was to fall to Paul Watzlawick,[12] who had joined the MRI in 1961, to spread the word. As chief author of *Pragmatics of human communication* (written in 1966, but appearing only after the death of Jackson, 1967), a book dedicated to Bateson, 'our mentor and friend', he produced a formal exposition, that was brilliant, didactic and erudite, of the clinical findings of Erickson and Jackson and laid down a veritable axiomatics for a new psychiatry, which was anchored in cybernetic epistemology and took on other forms of pathology apart from schizophrenia.

In spite of being fashionable in the 1960s, it does not seem that family therapy, the handling of paradoxes and verbal hypnosis, or the committed systemic approach, became durably implanted among psychiatrists in the USA, who were more attracted by classic psychoanalysis and/or drug-based psychiatry. By contrast, non-medical psychotherapists, excluded from these two approaches, were more willing to commit themselves to it. The medical hierarchy was undoubtedly shaken by the emergence of a technique that was accessible to all professionals working in the field of relationships. In a kind of chiasmus, Europe took up the torch, gradually giving family therapy's methods and style of thinking a place within the official psychiatric landscape. It must be said, however, that, in France, they were not working in a total desert.

THE FRENCH CONTEXT

The fact is that, just as d'Alembert could say, speaking for the Encyclopaedists, that 'we had ancestors under Louis XIV', today's French family therapists can say that they 'had ancestors before Bateson'. In this field, as in many others, the true precursor was René Laforgue who, with his idea of a family neurosis, put emphasis upon the neurotic complementarity of the parents in the formation of the child's character, and even of his/her symptoms.[13] His 'superego' – when one limits its scope to the family set of individual superegos – is not far from the later formulations of 'family unconscious' or 'family myth'. One could, similarly, re-cast Laforgue's (1936a, b, 1939) account of the articulation of family identifications on the axes of *captativity* or *oblativity* in terms of mutuality and sacrifice. However (even though his thesis of 1920 was devoted to the affectivity of schizophrenics), he did not have sufficiently open access to the clinical treatment of psychoses. The fact remains, none the less, that his notion of *scotomization*, rejected by psychoanalytic orthodoxy because it opened the way for manipulation of the real situation rather than the interpretation of phantasies, may seem highly pertinent to describe certain intrafamilial attitudes of non-perception of messages by their intended receiver. And he certainly had a general influence on the generation which followed him, which was orientated towards child guidance.

And who, in 1938, wrote the following, under the heading 'Family complexes in pathology' (subtitled: 'determination of psychosis'):

> Moreover, a disposition of the family group *en vase clos* tends to intensify the effects of summation characteristic of the transmission of the ego-ideal, as we have pointed out in our analysis of the Oedipus; however, whereas, there, it normally exerts itself in a selective sense, here these effects run in a degenerative direction.
>
> If the aborting of reality in the psychoses derives, in the last instance, from a biological deficiency of the libido, it also reveals a derivation of sublimation in which the role of the family complex is corroborated by the convergence of many clinical facts?

Who, but Jacques Lacan (1938), in his contribution to the *Encyclopédie française*, then published by Larousse. He made reference, moreover, to Legrand du Saulle who, as early as 1871 (*Du délire des persécutions*) was describing disturbances of communication within the families of psychotics: 'any serious observer will note among the parents of the alienated some very frequent peculiarities. They can be seen, for example, making false assessments of the most undeniable facts, excusing any and every failure of reason or justifying the most outrageously obvious delusional acts. They are suspicious, defiant, inconstant, elusive and disavow their own actions at will.'

André Green who cites this quotation in 1957 in his work on 'the family milieu of schizophrenics', goes even further back into the past, to Moreau ('of Tours') who observed, in respect of the family members' commitment to the delusional ideas of the patient, that 'it is very difficult to recognize in others errors which exist in a virtual state within oneself, anomalies of understanding to which we are ourselves in some way subject' (1859). Green takes advantage of this to ignore the article by Lacan (1938) completely, even though he was to become his pupil (as he was later the pupil of Jean Delay and Henri Ey). Though he accords proper recognition to Manfred Bleuler and his school (Klaus Ernst, Sechehaye), he does not seem aware of the publications of the Palo Alto group or at least he does not refer to them, even though he provides a very complete bibliography of studies relating to the parents of schizophrenics.[14]

However, in 1954–5, actually at Sainte-Anne, in Delay's department, Lacan, in his seminar, missed no opportunity to speak of cybernetics:

> All that until then had been numerical science becomes combinatory science. The more or less confused and accidental movement in the world of symbols is arranged around absence and presence. And the seeking for laws of presence and absence will lead towards the establishment of binary order which leads to what we call cybernetics. (Lacan, 1954–5, p. 345)

It might be said that a first conjuncture favourable to the emergence of family psychotherapies in France was allowed to pass by at this point, and one might regret that French psychiatry did not grasp the historical opportunity, being no doubt too divided between social psychopathology and psychoanalysis to bring the two together and map out a new field of enquiry. Moreover, a great conceptual rivalry had arisen with the triumphant emergence of chlorpromazine and the defining of the precise scope of neuroleptics. It was in the same number of *Encéphale* of 1957 in which Green's work appeared that there was an article by Deniker, 'Hibernothérapies et médicaments neuroleptiques' which forms the cornerstone of psychopharmacology. Deniker acknowledged his debt to Laborit's idea of a 'uniformity of organic responses to aggression' in the wake of Reilly's research into the malign syndrome, René Leriche's investigations into the role of 'sympathetic irritation' and Hans Selye's work on stress reaction. He explains how, just as Laborit had worked on hibernation, he and Delay (among others) had, in 1952, tried out chlorpromazine as a means 'for achieving a quelling or interruption of the reactional processes which, in certain cases, may constitute the substratum of the illness, if not the illness in its entirety'. And this achieved the successful results which are so well known in the treatment of psychoses, excepting melancholic depression.

It seems to me essential to point out clearly here that the chemotherapeutic revolution in psychiatry emerged in France on the same epistemological base as that on which the cybernetic revolution (and, we should add, the spread of drug addiction) developed in the USA. That base was the ideas of homeostasis, control, the 'nervous machine' and levels of regulation. For the first, phenothiazine (from which promethazine and chlorpromazine were derived) had been waiting, since being synthesized in 1883 by Bernthsen, for someone to have the idea of using it to modify the working of the neurovegetative system.

In what is admittedly a later text, but one that is faithful to his initial thinking, Laborit (1978) reveals the similarities and differences between his conceptions and those of Bateson. He notes that between each level of organization, each regulator is transformed into a servo-mechanism by a command from its regulatory system. This takes information from outside the regulated system. He noted that human ecology not only draws attention to observing inter-individual relations through language, but also to how those relations are organized on the basis of experimental knowledge, from the levels of molecules to neuronal pathways, resulting in human behaviour in social contexts.

This engineering mentality had to be present, from the 1950s onwards, for the psychiatry of the second half of the twentieth century to be invented, whether we are thinking of neuroleptics or family therapy. That is why it is virtually pointless to search out other glorious forerunners such as the psychoanalyst John Leuba, who announced in 1936 to a French-speaking conference, in a paper on 'the neurotic family and family neuroses', that 'it is not necessarily the person who makes the lives of those around him impossible who needs to be treated.' Or, again, such as Paul Sivadon and R. and J. Mises who, as early as 1954, published in *Evolution psychiatrique* some remarkable thoughts on a clinical case entitled 'Le milieu familial du schizophrène'. They quote Rosen, Sechehaye, Bettelheim and Hill and, from France, Schweich, take from Despert the idea that the ambivalence and anxiety of the mother has a counterpart in the passivity of the father, and state that the most noteworthy factor is the immaturity of the mother. Sivadon et al. (1954) describe how a style of relationships is established, characterized by both absence of affect and presence of tyrannical attachment. They go on to stress the harmfulness of particular pathogenic family structures, including the actual or functional absence of the father, the presence of grandparents or aunts in the home and the absence of siblings. They suggested that techniques should be developed, especially those of group psychotherapy, believing that only if the mother's affective attitude could be modified would there be any chance of maintaining therapeutic improvement in the patient, who they characterized as being the son.

After having fleetingly thought in terms of interaction, they return to a more classic mode of reasoning, proposing to investigate whether the pathogenic conditions are encountered with particular frequency. As we can see, a psychiatrist as creative and as sensitive to the relational, environmental and social dimension as Sivadon, was on the verge of discovering that disturbances of family communication were consubstantial with schizophrenia three years before Green was writing, but he ran up against the same problem: the lack of a suitable tool for their description (logico-mathematical language).

This failure is probably to be explained by the fact that it was impossible for French psychiatrists, the direct heirs of the French Revolution and hence of Pinel, Esquirol and Parchappe, to imagine change in any other way than through public institutions or, failing this, through the creation of philanthropic institutions. Moreover, unlike in the Anglo-Saxon world where the individual is the ultimate source of legality, in France, a land governed by Roman law, the law of 1838 related from the outset to the patient and his family. The result was that the urgent task at that moment of psychiatry's history was to knock down the walls of the asylum, in the hope of then involving the family in efforts at 'readaptation', the great watchword of the time.[15]

Let us not forget that the movement of liberation of attitudes towards mental patients with the adoption of methods of collective psychotherapy and active methods of social reinsertion had preceded the introduction of chlorpromazine (which was now added to the other biological treatments, electric shock therapy, insulin treatment, sleep cures and, at times, lobotomies, which were already being practised). Sivadon (1983) describes how, after some important and original experiments were carried out at St Alban with Balvert and Tosquelles, and at Fleury-les-Aubrais with Daumezon, the

Centre de Traitement et de Réadaptation Sociale (CTRS) was born in 1948 at Ville-Evrard. This was followed by further centres at Villejuif with Le Guillant and at Bonneval with Henri Ey. The CTRS showed that it was possible to change the hospital institutional atmosphere without reliance on new drugs, and that therapeutic progress could still be made.

The wartime experience in France had been terrible. A Nazi-inspired policy, aimed at ensuring atrocious living conditions for the 120,000 mental patients interned in France, had caused the death of half of them by starvation or cold. By contrast, a number of chance events which had led to the destruction of asylums or collective escapes had shown that well over a third of the 'chronic patients' released in this way had managed to get by, to survive and to fashion a new existence for themselves. The reduction in psychiatric morbidity (particularly in the number of suicides) also proved that there was a subtle equilibrium between individual and collective madness, and that alienation was a social behaviour. The experience of captivity, deportation and the Resistance was too overwhelming for those psychiatrists who had gone through it to tolerate a supposed watertight barrier being established once again between the mental patient and the normal person.

ANTI-PSYCHIATRY, AN EMBARRASSING RELATIONSHIP

The debate in Europe was directed mainly against institutions. In 1961, Michel Foucault published *Folie et déraison: histoire de la folie à l'âge classique*. There, to his own question 'How did our culture come to give to madness a sense of deviation and, to the patient, a status which excludes him?', he replies: 'The mental patient in the nineteenth century is the person who has lost the use of the freedoms conferred upon him by the bourgeois revolution (Foucault, 1954). 'Man only became a "psychologizable species" at the point when his relationship to madness was defined by the inner dimension of moral assignation and guilt' (Foucault, 1962). From the abridged edition, translated into English as *Madness and civilization*,[16] we shall retain simply this thesis: 'the constitution of madness as a mental illness, at the end of the eighteenth century affords the evidence of a broken dialogue ... The language of psychiatry, which is a monologue of reason about madness, has been established only on the basis of such a silence' (Foucault, 1961, pp. xii–xiii).

The same year, 1961, saw the appearance in the United States of *The myth of mental illness* by Thomas Szasz, who endeavoured to demonstrate that hysteria was not a mental illness, but games people play with each other and themselves, which are arbitrarily deemed pathological by psychiatry for socio-historical reasons.[17] And 1961 also saw Gregory Bateson's presentation of the autobiographical narrative of a nineteenth-century madman, John Perceval, in which Bateson clearly sets out what was to be proclaimed as the major premiss of British anti-psychiatric therapy:

It would appear that once precipitated into psychosis the patient has a course to run. He is, as it were, embarked upon a voyage of discovery which is only completed by his return to the normal world, to which he comes back with insights different from those of the inhabitants who never embarked on such a voyage. Once begun, a schizophrenic episode would appear to have as definite a course as an initiation ceremony – a death and rebirth – into which the novice may have been precipitated by his family life or by adventitious circumstance, but which in its course is largely steered by endogenous process ... What needs to be explained is the failure of many who embark upon this voyage to return from it. Do these encounter circumstances either in family life or in institutional care so grossly maladaptive that even the richest and best organized hallucinatory experience cannot save them? (Bateson, 1961, p. xiv)[18]

It was also from this British tradition of respect for others – including their eccentricities – that the great ferment was to come. In 1960, R. D. Laing published *The divided self* and, notably, in 1961, *Self and others* in which he took up cudgels against the psychiatriac and psychoanalytic establishment. In their studies of the families of schizophrenics from 1958 onwards, Laing and Esterson did not look, in seeking to understand and model their functioning, to the concepts of the Palo Alto school, with which they were familiar and which had grown out of the native soil of British philosophy, but to Jean-Paul Sartre's concepts of the dialectic of totalization.[19] In *Sanity, madness and the family* (1964), Laing and Esterson 'set out to illustrate by eleven examples that, if we look at some experience and behaviour without reference to family interactions, they may appear comparatively socially senseless, but that if we look at the same experience and behaviour in their original family context they are liable to make more sense' (1970 edn, p. 12). Their method of interviews with the families of schizophrenics does not claim to be therapeutic,[20] but attempts to make schizophrenia socially intelligible.

The stakes in this debate are important and it can by no means be regarded as outdated by a family therapist today, since what we are seeing here is nothing less than the debate between the Bleulerian conception of schizophrenia (only the 'secondary', social symptoms are accessible to therapy) and an ontological conception of schizophrenia (the schizophrenic is the person who fails to assume our common alienation, consubstantial with man as social being). Laing and Esterson (1970 edn, pp. 19–22) write:

> Each person not only is an object in the world of others but is a position in space and time from which he experiences, constitutes and acts in his world . . . it is precisely each person's *perspective* on the situation which he shares with others that we wish to discover . . . In other words, we are interested in what might be called the family *nexus* . . . [They continue] . . . if one wishes to know how a football team concert or disconcert their actions in play, one does not think only or even primarily of approaching this problem by talking to the members individually. One watches the way they play together . . . [in Sartrean terms] . . . what happens in a group will be *intelligible* if one can retrace the steps from what is going on (process) to who is doing what (praxis).

The group is *not* to the individual as the whole is to the part. The group is not a mechanism, unless its action is constituted as such by the praxes of each of its members. These aphorisms of Laing's indicate precisely in what sense his anti-psychiatric approach is not a systemic one.

Another theoretical endeavour in this same vein is Gilles Deleuze and Félix Guattari's *Anti-Oedipus* (1972). Though they succeed in introducing schizo-analysis as a grid for deciphering the fluxes of production in the cultural superstructures – not far removed in this from the systems of thought developed by Baudrillard and Lyotard – and though they hit the mark in saying that it is not Oedipus which explains neurosis, but neurosis which explains Oedipus,[21] they are in no way convincing as regards the links between capitalism and schizophrenia.

THE OFFSHOOTS

Psychiatry was shaken. For reassurance, two conferences were called. The first at Montreal (5–8 November 1969) brought together some of the most eminent French, British and American psychoanalysts and some of the great names in family therapy under the chairmanship of Green and Arieti (for the proceedings, see Doucet and Laurin, 1971). The result was a series of brilliant papers, but a dialogue of the deaf. The return match took place in Paris between 23 and 26 February 1972. Everyone who was anyone in the world of psychiatry and psychoanalysis was present (for the proceedings, see Chiland and Becquart, 1974). All theoretical aspects and therapeutic endeavours were discussed, but Palo Alto was strangely elided. Only Green, who compared it with British anti-psychiatry, criticized it for denying 'unconscious intrapsychical organization. The entire clinical picture is interpreted in terms of perturbations of *interpersonal* processes exclusively, whose origins are in the family *nexus*.' Watzlawick was to retort, in a brief unprogrammed intervention that 'learning to communicate means learning what one is not supposed to see, what one is not supposed to think, what one must not hear, what one must not say . . . The question of the suppression of the symptom is a logical taboo within psycho-dynamic theory, not because human nature imposes that limitation, but because the theory does not allow any other conclusion.' Henri Ey had opened the conference by defining psychosis as a 'sickness of reality'. Watzlawick countered that reality is merely what a sufficient number of people agree to call real and that we are accustomed to accepting to be so.[22] The future was to confirm the correctness of these shafts to the extent that the spread of the Palo Alto theory was to bring about a new therapeutic reality, which was to find its recognition, initially, in Italy.

The Lausanne seminar (11–13 October 1973) devoted to the issue of the families of schizophrenics, and sponsored and published by *Evolution psychiatrique* (1975, no. 2), brought proof of this. There were at Bordeaux (Bargues, Demangeat) and at Lausanne (Kaufmann, Masson) teams who no longer balked at using the 'schematic' concepts of the theories of communication and family interaction and received into psychotherapy families viewed as single organisms. Furthermore, there was at Milan a team which – inspired by the works of Bateson (1972) and Harley Shands (1971) and by regular contact with Paul Watzlawick – was engaged upon discovering the missing link between the application of the theory of logical types to human communication and the creative intuitions of a Rosen or an Erickson. Mara Selvini-Palazzoli who was director of that team had already given much thought to the problems of context and meta-context in couples and families, but the 'discovery' of counter-paradox as a therapeutic tool occurred when, with Luigi Boscolo, G. F. Cecchin and G. Prata, she became aware that the greatest obstacle to communication with families was her own linguistic conditioning. Through Shands, the Milanese rediscovered the lessons of Whitehead, Russell, Korzybski, Sapir and Whorf, as the title of the 1973 article 'The barrier of linguistic conditioning in the family therapy of the schizophrenic (Proposals for a new epistemology and methodology)' tells us. In order to circumvent that barrier, they took up the following positions: language is not reality; living reality is circular and language is linear and moralistic.

To be able, without contradicting oneself, to arrive at the paradoxical prescription of the symptom of the index patient, one has to resort to 'positive connotation', i.e. to approving all the behaviour of the family members as interactions tending to reinforce group cohesion, i.e. homeostasis. The family metacommunicates to the therapists that the definition of the relationship is anathema for the homeostasis of the system. The therapists then do exactly the opposite of the demand for change by reinforcing the homeostasis (which requires a patient – a subtle paradox). 'Provisional prescription', from the first session, is used to this end, followed by the establishment of an analogical *family ritual*, which is more action than verbalization (Selvini Palazzoli, 1975).

The other major contribution of the Milan team was the demonstration of the efficacy of systemic family therapies in cases of anorexia nervosa, permitting autonomous status to be given, for the first time, to the so-called communicational specificities of the families of psychotics (Selvini Palazzoli, 1974). From that point on, family therapies were exported as of right into other fields of pathology, including drug addiction, alcoholism, psychosomatic illnesses and child abuse. There had, admittedly, already been a degree of study of family interactions, but systemic family therapeutic interventions only took off after the work of the Milan school.[23]

The rest of the history of family therapy merges with that of the rivalries between the various leaders who have emerged and the different groups they have formed by proselytism or mutual recognition. The major (and repetitive) debate consists in determining what dosage of the intrapsychic each therapist injects into the system and, in a sense, in replying to the question: 'does one treat an individual by way of his family or does the individual provide a pretext for treating the family?'[24]

SOME WAYS FORWARD

Basically, family therapy has contributed a theoretico-practical efficacy adapted to the theories of understanding of our time, of which it is a consequence and a cause. New questions are now emerging following the disappearance of the analytical method in its own deconstructive frenzy (Morin, 1980b): 'What is a subject? What is alienation? What is a phenomenon?' The systemic approach, used concretely in situations where suffering families and therapists meet, obliges us to regard the world and people differently:[25] circularity, complexity, 'nexiality', indetermination. The Kantian real-in-itself no longer oppresses us, but appears as the sum-total of the discoveries to come:

- the discovery of our mental processes, in particular thanks to the localizations of the symbolic in its belonging to two adjoining levels of reality;
- the discovery of socio-historical processes translated into the forms which kinship relations take on over the generations.

I shall illustrate this conclusion by two little verses:

(1)   Speech produces intersubjectivity,
      intersubjectivity produces consciousness,
      consciousness produces speech.

(2)   The subject is alienated in production,
      Production is alienated in culture,
      Culture is alienated in the subject.

Guy Maruani
December 1986

NOTES

1   The success of the double-bind concept may perhaps derive from the favourable reception which Kurt Lewin's interactional psychology had been accorded in the United States in the 1930s. Applying the model of the dynamics of forces, Lewin proposed a vector psychology based on the representation of the play of the various emotional tensions and forces within the life-space and the social field. Similarly, Jacob Levi Moreno attempted, with his notion of roles and psychodrama, to link individual behaviour and interaction within the social group. The ground was prepared for a theory of psychical extra-territoriality to be established.

For a reasoned account of the various contributions to the development of family therapy, the reader is referred to Jackson and Satir (1961), which contains a bibliography of forty-five titles. Jackson and Satir, two Palo Alto pioneers, acknowledge as ancestors Freud, for his study of the Schreber case (1911), Rubin for his initial genetic research into the families of schizophrenics, Moreno for his attempts at group psychotherapy with hospitalized patients, Sullivan for his insistence that, as the patient's new family, the hospital team should behave differently from that expected by the schizophrenic from experience of his or her own family, Kasanin for the emphasis he puts on the parent–child relation as a specific aetiological relationship in schizophrenia, Hallowell for stressing the social and cultural elements in psychosis, Ackerman for proposing that the family be considered clinically as a unit and, lastly, Richardson, the title of whose book is eloquent: *Patients have families* (1945). They reject any connection with the work of Flugel (1921), whose *Psychoanalytic study of the family* merely aimed to arrive at a better knowledge of the sick individual. In their view, only Ackerman and the Palo Alto group transformed their practice in such a way as to treat the family as a set of transactions before Bowen hospitalized and treated five families in which there was a psychotic member. They pay homage to the great 'dynamic' psychiatrists, Eugen Bleuler, Adolf Meyer and Manfred Bleuler but, curiously, they do not refer either to Rosen or Searles whose contribution Watzlawick was later to acknowledge.

We may note that Howells's tome on family psychiatry (1968) already contained some 1,071 indexed bibliographical references. Naturally, given this accumulation of material, this dictionary does not claim an exhaustive bibliography. An excellent historical account of family therapy and a selection of titles can be found in Winkin (1981).

2   For Korzybski's work, see his *The role of language in the perceptual processes* (1951). I shall, however, emphasize here the extraordinary advantage that therapists would derive from adopting *non-Aristotelian extensional methods* for 'dealing with dynamic realities with static means'. For example, the transcription of a session with the Martin family, consisting of a couple and three children and two therapists would be written as follows, being modified as one went along:

1930 Martin 1 (in his armchair)	1938 + Martin 2 (wringing her hands when she speaks)	1960 + Martin 3 (standing with no definite position)
1966 + Martin 4 (in the middle of the room)	1968 + Martin 5 (swaying about on his chair)	
1945 + Doctor X 1 (holding the microphone)	1951 + Doctor Z 2 (smoking a cigarette)	

Key:
year of birth
name
position in the family (father, mother, children) or team (position concretely observed)

3   We are not far here from the conception of mind, as understood by Bateson.

4   I am indebted, in these brief notes on the history of cybernetics, to the contributions of Philippe Breton, *Pourquoi a-t-on inventé l'ordinateur?*, Pierre Levy, *Perception ou reconnaissance de forme?* and Pierre Livet, 'Les ambivalences de la cybernetique: l'absence du symbolique' a paper delivered at the Fourth Conference of the European Association for the Study of Science and Technology ('Senses of science') held at Strasbourg, 29 September–1 October 1986. The classic founding texts are: Rosenblueth (1943); McCulloch and Pitts (1943); von Neumann and Morgenstern (1944); and Weaver and Shannon (1949).

5   The following are extracts from the contributions of these two researchers to the Royaumont colloquium of 1972 (Morin and Piatelli-Palmarini, 1972), quoted as a metaphor to enable us to imagine how psychotherapy functions, i.e. the coupling of a cultural reality between the family and the therapists! ' "The environment" is the representation of the relations between "objects" and "events". Since the calculation of relations of equivalence is not unique, the results of these calculations, namely "the objects" and "the events" are not unique either . . . This explains the possibility of having an arbitrary number of different (culturally determined) realities, but each of which is coherent in itself. Since the calculation of relations of equivalence is made on primitive experiences, an external environment is not an obligatory condition for the calculation of reality' (von Foerster, 1972, pp. 139–55). 'The problem of the cultural unity of man does not come down to a problem of learning a single and valid cognitive approach to an objective reality, but, on the contrary, that of forming a common behavioural field dependent on the subject which defines a common reality dependent on the subject' (Maturana, 1972, pp. 156–80).

6   The seven questions (Ruesch, 1953) were: (1) What are the limits and the context of communication agreed by the observers? (2) Who is the sender? (3) To whom is the communication sent? (4) What is the message content sent and the content received? (5) What methods of communication are used? (6) How? What are the metacommunicative clues? (7) What is the result of the exchange of messages?

7   For a coherent bibliography, see Hinde (1972).

8   In 1957, Gisela Pankow had a long discussion at Rosen's seminar in Philadelphia with 'Dr Bird Vijssel' [sic] who told her he could not follow Bateson (?) since 'there are no more actions, there are only interactions'.

9   Jules Henry, an anthropologist and student of Margaret Mead, has attempted to develop the notion of *family culture*, an idosyncratic expression of the dominant general culture, to which will be added the dynamic sum of the – relatively stable – interactional types between the n members of the family (given by the formula $2n - n - 1$). Before launching into the observation of daily life, he had armed himself with two ideas (Henry, 1961). These were that psychosis appears partly as a variation in the child's adaptation, which variation exceeds the organism's tolerance in a particular culture, and that the (parents') interventions which adversely affect the learning capacity of the child are likely to be the most harmful, just as is any other action which could undermine the child's confidence in its abilities to discriminate correctly. From Henry's direct observations, he derived only the perception that 'psychopathogenic' parents probably attack the innate mechanisms producing homeostasis by distorting buffer behaviours (such as the infant's cries aimed at signalling hunger) by inappropriate responses (such as bringing a rattle or solid food). Thus, on the way, Henry had forgotten the concept of interaction and fallen back on accusing the parents, even though one might just as well say that the psychotic child perturbs the capacity of the adults who have him/her in their charge to become parents, by his or her innate inability to emit adaptive signals. Which reminds us, if we needed reminding, that it is theory which orientates observation or, alternatively, that to observe well, one must not believe in theories.

10   Family therapists' attachment to visual techniques (one-way mirrors, closed circuit television, video recording etc.), in contrast with the listening which is dominant in psychoanalysis, can no doubt be explained in part by these aphorisms of McLuhan's, in so far as the visual is geared to movement and automatically involves the right

hemisphere of the brain. These paths opened up in the field of 'neuro-cultural research', continuing the investigations of Innis and McLuhan, are being explored in a lively manner by, among others, Derrick de Kerckhoue at Toronto, Vilem Flusser at São Paulo and Baudoin Jurdant at Strasbourg. A CIP/IRCAM conference (*Nouvelles technologies et mutations des savoirs*, Paris, 24–26 October 1986) covered this same area of research.

11   The cases referred to were written up in other publications where many further details may be found; see Erickson (1939). Frieda Fromm-Reichmann died in February 1957 shortly after the appearance of the article on the double bind. She worked at Chestnut Lodge along lines laid down by the culturalist psychoanalysis of Harry Stack Sullivan. In that clinic for the privileged, the entire medical personnel had undergone analysis, which at the time was a luxury. The account of the therapy referred to by Bateson was written in novel form by Hannah Green (pseudonym) under the title *I never promised you a rose garden* (London: Gollancz, 1964).

The influence of psychoanalysis on the Palo Alto group is a delicate matter. Bateson never disavowed Freud and his theory of dreams, for example, was the psychoanalytic one. Haley rejected the dogmatism of the Freudian unconscious and, with Jackson, broke down into their component parts the communicational mechanisms of the transference. But Watzlawick, trained in Jungian psychoanalysis in Zurich ('centuries ago', as he puts it), very often borrows clinical examples and therapeutic procedures from psychoanalysts.

The Palo Alto team does not seem to have been greatly influenced by Karen Horney or by the ego psychology of Hartmann, Loewenstein and Kris. On the other hand, Watzlawick does acknowledge his indebtedness to John Rosen, the promoter of 'direct analysis' in whose department he worked. Like Scheflen, he admires the intuitive and often non-conscious way in which Rosen provides the patient with the missing metacommunication in respect of his/her symbiotic dependence on a rejecting parent, for example by buying the delusional patient who thinks he is the Pope an airline ticket for Rome. Watzlawick also refers to Harold Searles, whose study of the interaction between the schizophrenic and his/her mother has become a classic: 'the child's own desire for individuation may be experienced by him as a desire to drive the mother crazy . . . this part of [the mother] which ostensibly tries to drive the child crazy – tries, in actuality, to help the child become an individual . . . Thus both participants tend unconsciously to perpetuate a symbiotic relatedness with one another', a mode of relatedness which Searles describes as extremely immature and unhealthy, but highly gratifying (Searles, 1959). Searles practised for several years at Chestnut Lodge.

12   The varied nature of Watzlawick's cultural background is no doubt one of the reasons for his ability to grasp the significant elements in a context. To the question, 'How many European languages do you speak?', he replies, 'I don't speak Albanian' and his ability to conduct a conversation with several people simultaneously in English, French, German, Italian, Spanish and other languages is impressive. It must be remembered that Palo Alto is not so legendary in the United States as it has become in Europe. In 1981, Watzlawick confided that more of his books had been sold in Holland than in the United States! On the publication of his book *The language of change* (1978a), which deals with the cognitive strategies of the two cerebral hemispheres, I suggested the hypothesis that this was for him a sublimation of his dividedness between Europe and the USA (*Evolution psychiatrique*, 1981, 46 (1): 237–41). In Ruffiot's view, however, Watzlawick is essentially the disciple and vulgarizer of the Anglo-Saxon philosophy of pragmatism of William James, C. S. Peirce and J. Dewey (*Génitif*, 1981, 3: 13–22). Whatever the truth of this, thanks to his talents as a writer, the countries of Latin culture have been given a clear access to a complex body of work.

13   It was while reading Laforgue (1936a) that Jackson, some fifteen years later, had his initial idea of family homeostasis: 'Laforgue mentioned that at a significant point in his (female) patient's therapy her sister (with whom she lived) became severely depressed. He attributed the sister's difficulty to a manifestation of the same unfortunate genetic structure that had caused his patient's schizophrenia. He did not note that the sister's depression was coincident with a sudden improvement in his patient' (Weakland and Jackson, 1958).

14   Green's thesis, 'Le milieu familial des schizophrènes', dates from 1957. The articles inspired by it appeared under the joint authorship of Delay and Deniker in *Encéphale* in three separate numbers, in 1957, 1960 and 1962. Neither the bibliography of the thesis nor that of *Encéphale*, updated to 1962, mention Lacan's article, which did, admittedly, remain entirely forgotten for many years. In 1962, Green drew attention to Bateson and his school in a review of Jackson (*The etiology of schizophrenia*, 1960), and also Whitaker (*The psychotherapy of chronic schizophrenic patients*, 1962).

Green outlines his method, situated somewhere between individual psychotherapy and statistical research, for studying and defining the family constellation, showing the 'clear presence of *conflictual nodes* which have studded the personal history of the schizophrenic'. In his view, 'the configuration', i.e. the articulation of the various roles within the domain of the family unit and their reciprocal relationships 'is marked by *the symbolic annihilation of the father*'. He concludes that there is 'a need to concern oneself very closely with the patient's parents, either through individual interviews, or within a group therapy context – with or without the patient – which must 'lead to an adequate reorganization of hospital assistance'.

15   This would give rise to a great range of things, institutional psychotherapy, the right to health for all and 'sectorization' among others.

16   Initially, however, the French psychiatric establishment dismissed this as a trifling work and accorded it no more importance than it had to André Breton's remark in his *Nadja* of 1928 (p. 161): 'You have to have never entered an asylum not to know that they *make* madmen there, just as they make crooks in the reformatories.' Astonishingly, it was from the philosophical and literary milieu that the best appreciation of Foucault's essay was to come, in the form of Jacques Derrida's article, 'Cogito and the history of madness': 'The unsurpassable, unique, and imperial grandeur of the order of reason . . . is that one cannot speak out against it except by being for it' (Derrida, 1978, p. 36); 'The expression "to say madness itself" is self-contradictory' (1978, p. 43). But Derrida adds that, since Descartes, reason knows that it can only philosophize 'in the confessed terror of going mad . . . And the cogito of the schizophrenic (and of family therapy) would thus be 'the others think, therefore I am.'

17   Let us note that Etienne Trillat, who has nothing but scorn for Thomas Szasz, whom he calls 'Thomas the Impostor', concludes his book *Histoire de l'hystérie* with the words 'Hysteria is dead, as we know . . . What is the use of the private theatre of the hysteric when we are all part of a public theatre?' (1986).

18   This notion is so strangely close to Laing's idea of the 'metanoiac voyage in discovery of oneself, with its natural revolutionary potentialities' (*Recherches*, Enfance aliénée II, December 1968) that we must see in it either the result of a borrowing by Laing from Bateson during his stay in the USA in 1962 (when he also met Birdwhistell, Goffman, Jackson, Scheflen, Speck, Wynne and others) or the influence on the two men of Timothy Leary's psychedelic doctrine and the fashion for LSD.

19   *Reason and violence* (Laing and Cooper, 1964) is entirely devoted to the ontological thought of Jean-Paul Sartre and its objective of dissolving existentialism in a Marxist philosophy with human dimensions. In *Psychiatry and anti-psychiatry* Cooper (1967) radicalized the position, endeavouring to demonstrate that, since primary alienation is ontological and Sartrean (and economic, Marxian alienation is secondary), the very definition of schizophrenic mental alienation is an act of violence. He was later to go on to advocate *The death of the family* (1970) as the sole tactic of liberation, from 'alienation, in the sense of a passive submission to invasion by others, originally the family others' (1972 edn, p. 11).

20   Given this position, how is a therapy to be established? Laing proposes that no diagnosis be applied and that the subject be allowed to experience his/her metanoiac voyage in a place where the carers are merely assistants. However, the Kingsley Hall experiment, as reported by him, by David Cooper and by Mary Barnes, also included the use of neuroleptics and individual psychoanalytic sessions. Moreover, in the film *Family life*, inspired by their work, the psychiatrist behaves more like a Kleinian analyst than a travel agent.

The other great anti-psychiatric project, the Psichiatrica democratica movement of Franco Basaglia brought about the closure of psychiatric hospitals in Italy (Law 180). Having conflated ontological alienation with social alienation (through the idea that the segregative psychiatric institution was merely a mirror of the class struggle), Italian anti-psychiatry got the mental patient thrown out on to the street and delivered up to the 'free play of social relations' which it had precisely wished to transform by making psychiatry everyone's business. For exactly opposite motives, namely the political rejection of solidarity and the attendant fiscal burden, the American administration let a great number of chronic patients out of the psychiatric hospitals to walk the streets of its great cities, homeless and without families (cf. the *Synapse* symposium of June 1985, New York).

21   One feels like adding: 'Some family!'

22   In his hilarious essay, 'The painted word' (*Harper's Magazine*, April 1975), Tom Wolfe shows how a remark by an art critic Hilton Kramer, is revealing of the construction of social reality: 'Realism does not lack its partisans, but it does rather conspicuously lack a persuasive theory. And given the nature of our intellectual commerce with works of art, to lack a persuasive theory is to lack something crucial – the means by which our experience of the individual works is joined to our understanding of the values they signify'.

23   Modified to be appropriate to the particular situation; see, for example, Kaufman and Kaufman (1979); Cancrini (1977); Signer et al. (1982).

24   We may again take our inspiration here from Sartre, who, in his study of Flaubert (1971), writes: 'The point is that a man is never an individual; it would be better to call him a *singular Universal*; totalized and hence universalized by his age, he re-totalizes it by reproducing himself within it as Universal singularity by the singular universality of human history, singular by the universalizing singularity of his projects.' Sartre offers an aetiology: 'disturbances have their origins at the difficult level where every discourse is a man and every man a discourse. It assumes a bad insertion of the child into the linguistic universe, or, in other words, into the social world, *into his family*.'

But, it will be objected, is there any evidence for this responsibility of the family context in the fabrication of a 'singular universal' bearing mental disturbances? In fact, we have no real epidemiological studies since the variables are far too numerous, the assessment criteria too ambiguous and since it is, for example, impossible to constitute healthy or normal control families for experimental purposes. Nevertheless, retrospective studies have attempted to measure the impact of the parents' neuroses on the children's health (cf., for example, Hare and Shaw, 1965). In spite of a bibliography of sixty-one titles, a compilation on the children of depressed parents comes to no general conclusions, other than that the children are to some degree at risk (Guedeney, 1986).

The attempts that have been made to live in the households of psychotic children (Henry, 1961) or schizophrenic adults (Stoleru, 1979) are more exciting. It seems from these that the observer is very quickly threatened by the projective identifications created and that an attitude of intrafamilial therapy would assume the pre-existence of a flexible intersubjectivity which is precisely what is lacking. In these conditions, the evidence has to be found for each individual family and there is never any certain proof.

25   What has been the itinerary of the group that has written this dictionary? From diverse clinical practice, pursued over many years, there emerged, beyond an initial shared commitment to psychoanalysis among some of the contributors, a common questioning into the contribution of communication theory. Jacques Miermont has played a pioneering role in the study of etho-anthropology, systems theory, the theory of mathematical models of morphogenesis and of semiotics as a framework of thinking for psychotherapies and family therapies in France. Robert Neuberger was the first to formalize methodological differences of demand in psychoanalysis and in systems-based family interventions. Pierre and Sylvie Angel opened the first family therapy centre in Paris specializing in the problems of drug addiction. Pierre Segond found a place for the family-theoretic approach in the prevention of delinquency. All were trained by Siegi Hirsch and have in turn trained many family therapists. Guy Maruani has applied Palo Alto concepts to clinical reality: interaction in the prescription of lithium, paradoxical messages in termination of pregnancy, levels of communication in carcinogenesis, and the placebo effect in psychiatric institutions. Gilles Errieau has theorized the systemic principles at work in general medicine.

INTRODUCTION

A therapist is neither an artist nor a scientist. And yet the therapist's activity involves both art and science. The therapist knows how to negotiate a way between knowledge and skill, and appreciates what he or she must not try to explore. Thus, somewhat contradictorily no doubt, the therapist must know the contexts in which it is best not to intervene as well as the points where it is proper to do so. The therapist has to act locally, while, at the same time, thinking globally enough for what he or she is doing to be pertinent.

Family therapy arose out of problems of clinical practice in psychiatry, linked to the pragmatic dead ends in which certain practitioners found themselves in their daily reality; it emerged as a response to inextricable problems. It established a connection between the semiology of the body and mind, on the one hand, and the modes of behaviour, emotion and thinking of suffering family microcosms, on the other, by creating events that were singular in time and space and, at that level, modifying the spontaneous development of the family.

Thus therapists are born without knowing that they are therapists, caught up, beyond their desires to care and cure, in the necessity of performing therapeutic acts, without necessarily knowing 'theoretically' all the relevant parameters which contribute to the accomplishment of such acts.

The relationship between clinical experience and theoretical elaboration is not a linear one; it is one of counterpoint, rather than one-to-one correspondence. Intuition and empirical attitudes are often a bulwark against the hubris of a preconceived knowledge, which is too open or too closed. Therapeutic action and thinking often seem simple to the observer, but it is a simplicity which is not as simple as it seems, even if it ultimately connects with common sense.

The object of this dictionary relates, on the one hand, to the dynamics of family processes confronted with symptoms which are perceived as a problem, either within or outside the family, and, on the other, to the nature of the changes which occur spontaneously or artificially. We are not, therefore, presenting here a general theory of the family. But it has seemed necessary to describe the maximum of variables which cast light upon the family; hence the importance of comparative work within ethology, linguistics, ethnology and sociology, and across these various disciplines. The field opened up in this way requires a conceptual armature and poses questions which cannot be resolved in terms of isolated prior models: the field of metasystems, as a meta-psychological generalization, requires:

1   A marking of the *genetic terrain* (identification of the phylogenetic, sociocultural and ontogenetic time-scales, an analysis of the multi-axial organizers of the individual, the family, the social units).
2   A marking of the *economic terrain*, describing the material quantities and the quantities of energy and information required for the life and survival of persons and groups and the structures of the interchanges associated with these.
3   A marking of the *terrain in topological terms*, accounting for the positions of the family systems in relation to wider systems, the static and dynamic positions of the various partners in relation to one another, the modes of connection which link them together and the territories and boundaries produced as a result.

4   A marking of the *terrain in dynamic terms* which shows the potency, if not indeed the violence, of the biological and cultural forces which underlie the individual and collective movements and which clash in the physical and symbolic renewal of the generations.

5   A marking out of the *terrain in structural terms*, which permits a differentiated study of family typologies from the ethological, anthropological, psychoanalytic, ethnological, symptomatic and morphological angles.

In this context, classic metapsychology is at once too broad and insufficient. Too broad because certain refinements made necessary by the analysis of the neuroses or borderline states lead to ever more sophisticated theoretical elaborations which move outside the field of family therapy properly so-called, if they do not indeed lead to the inappropriate application of concepts out of context. And insufficient, since systems of metacommunication involve the meta-biological and the meta-sociological as much as the meta-psychological. Thus, for example, medical drugs have to be integrated into the field of study, as 'partners' having their levels of efficacy, their semiotic function and their own dynamic, while being manipulated, in a specific way, by the family unit.

This is why we have attempted here a *comparative study of models*. A model may be understood as the representation of a system. It is a kind of table, a grid of reading and intervention which focuses the object of study, without becoming conflated with it. A model can only really be evaluated if it is compared with other models, from which it is differentiated.

Clinical practice is a set of models. It serves as a practical reference point to guide action and thinking. It is medical, psychosomatic and psychiatric clinical practice. It is also the clinical treatment of social behaviour disorders. And it is also psychoanalytic, systemic, cybernetic and catastrophist clinical practice. Clinical practice cannot, in and of itself, serve as the authority for its own action; the self-referential character of clinical case studies interrogates the theories and models which they justify: a psychodynamic model will produce psychodynamic 'results'; a transgenerational model will produce transgenerational 'results'. All therapists show results, rapid if the therapy is defined as brief, or deep if the therapy accepts regressive movements. Only through outside observers is it possible to evaluate the nature of the changes effectively obtained.

The medical, psychoanalytic and systemic models clash, mutually restrain one another, work together, and, no doubt, also generate other models. But the models cannot of themselves claim to be the necessary and sufficient legitimation of clinical activity. It then seems necessary to outline: (a) *family models not centred on clinical practice*. (Is the fact of keeping a grandparent in the household a legitimate datum of cultural anthropology, a pathological phenomenon or a situation of affective solidarity?) And (b) *methodological models not directly centred on the family*. (Are not the methodologies used in clinical practice merely falsified borrowings from more serious theories? Do results exist in family therapy, which, in turn, have an impact on the epistemological horizon of our age?)

In doing this, this dictionary is inevitably incomplete, making its own choices and leaving many paths to be explored. We have tried, on the one hand, to give an account of what is accepted knowledge and, on the other, to leave sufficient openness to the current theories which remain, both in clinical and epistemological terms, in conflict and flux. Respect for therapeutic processes requires, in our view, an intellectual attitude of open questioning, both as regards theories which are utilized and information which is useful. Hence our desire to produce a kind of 'work in progress'. The reader is consciously requested to make the effort to affirm his or her autonomy of thought and action.

Through examining blocks and pragmatic realities of various kinds (slips, parapraxes, dreams, jokes, neurotic symptoms etc.), Freud discovered the determinism of certain unconscious mechanisms, namely the paths which connect neurosis and normality. From this a first coherent theory of the family was derived, starting with the description of infantile sexuality and the Oedipus complex. The theorization of the psychical apparatus rests on the theory of representation. Word-representations and thing-representations enter into relations of synergy and antagonism in the articulation of the psyche's primary and secondary processes.

Now, it appears clearly, in clinical practice with families, that the nature of interactions and of interpersonal events has considerable weight in the structuring and organization of representations. That practice leads to the recognition of the existence of founding myths which are different from the Oedipal myth.

The family, as semiotic, therapeutic, psychoanalytic and systemic field, only became an object of science with the identification of certain determinisms concerning the pathology of behaviour and relationships. The means of access to these determinisms are not of the same nature as they are for persons apprehended solely at a psychical level. A 'family' allows the differentiation–confusion of the individual and social levels of human identity.

Bateson clarified the circular determinism governing human interactions by the exploration of zones of continuity between normality, psychosis and behavioural disorders. Relationships are subject to contextual learning, determining the categories of play, humour, delusion, phantasy, dream, nightmare and the real. The modes of communication, conscious and unconscious, voluntary and involuntary, are detectable by means of signals, which Bateson calls 'mode-identifying signals'. Hence the interest of semiotics, so long as it incorporates the findings of medical semiology, comparative ethology and differential ethnology.

The analysis of family interactions brings to light another type of determinism: the determinism linked to the position of individuals one to another. This connects up with Aristotle's formal causality. Just like the animate beings from whom they emanate, behaviours have a complex form, deriving from conflicting flows, expressing themselves in the opposition between the temporal movement of evolution and the forces opposed to that movement. The manifest expression of these conflicts may be appraised as emotional shock waves (Bowen, 1978a). The family thus creates a genuine morphogenetic landscape.

Whether we are speaking of the schizophrenic, the delinquent, the alcoholic, the psychopath, the paranoic, the drug addict, the anorectic, the psychosomatic or the cancer patient, we find that the individual personality is, in these cases, separated from itself, leaving split-off parts to develop on their own. Paradoxically, such a process leads to the necessary recognition of the inseparability of the persons in family and social interaction.

A state of affairs thus exists which is to some degree reminiscent of quantum mechanics. When an individual is divided up in this way, split in him/herself (individual is the Latin equivalent of 'atom'), there exists an uncertainty in the perception of personality/interaction. If one knows the position or the structure of the personality, one loses sight of the dynamics of the interaction and therefore its specificity. If, on the other hand, one knows the relational dynamics, one loses sight of the position taken up by the individual, and therefore his/her structure. Hence the antinomy which exists between psychoanalysis and systems theory. This has a knock-on effect on the way therapeutic responsibilities are understood in the two approaches: the psychoanalytic point of view will tend to see resistance to change as coming from the system itself; the systemic point of view will tend to think that the resistance comes rather from a bad epistemology on the part of the intervenor.

The forms which change may take are not infinite, unless one holds out the hope of magical action or, which comes to much the same thing, displays irresponsibility as regards the therapeutic framework which is supposed to mark out the course of change. There is an emergent quality in real change, which moves from the quantitative (more or less of the same thing) to the qualitative (something else). A qualitative change most often takes on a paradoxical character, defying common sense. The paradox is not so much an explanation as a statement that has to be elucidated. Elucidation makes it possible to understand its meaning: the point is not to eliminate paradoxes, but to make them more functional.

Two theories attempt to find solutions to logical, semantic and pragmatic paradoxes: theories of self-referentiality and the theories arising out of topology (theory of the universal unfolding, catastrophe theory, theory of morphogenesis).

The *theory of self-referentiality* stresses the discontinuity of phenomena, the function of chance and noise in the emergence of the new, the indeterminate aspects in the evolution of reality. Far from seeking to eliminate the confusion of logical levels, self-referential models are based on a calculation where the operator is its own operand, the content its own container. The indeterministic character of the model is well suited to accounting for processes linked to disorders of autonomy in which the alienation of persons and groups is prevalent.

Catastrophe theory seeks, by contrast, to found a determinist epistemology on the basis of the primacy of the continuous. Within this perspective, certain archetypal changes occur in an orientated linearity, with a beginning and an end (elementary catastrophes). Other changes are dependent upon phenomena of recurrence, of cyclical return, both periodic and aperiodic (generalized catastrophes). The deterministic character of the model makes it possible to envisage, at least asymptotically, the conditions for – and possibility of – free will on the part of the persons and groups in a state of suffering. Catastrophe theory is a deep model of analogic phenomena, and therefore of semantic phenomena.

Change in therapy can be evaluated in terms of these two types of catastrophe: the improvement of a perturbed state, or the disappearance of a problem, can be registered on a gradient dynamic, as formalized in elementary catastrophes. The repercussions 'at a deep level' and in the more or less long run, lead to ramified effects, either by successive waves, or by fragmentation, as described in generalized catastrophes. A topological analysis of this kind completes the circular–finalistic models of cybernetics by stressing the importance of formal causality. The position of each member of a family has an influence on its overall morphology and creates a semantics of communication, without this being the effect of a purely material or efficient mechanistic causality of either a linear or a circular type.

The concept of family is ambiguous, oscillating constantly between the individual and the collective, the natural and the cultural, the practical and the theoretical, the perennial and the new, the determinate and the indeterminate, the predictable and the unpredictable, the established and the unestablished. Around this ambiguous concept, other concepts gravitate which are themselves no less ambiguous: therapy, instinct, self, unconscious, system, catastrophes. We have attempted to give the reader information on these concepts that is as accurate as possible. It turns out that some terms travel badly, changing meaning completely as a function of the situations in which they find themselves. Others, by contrast, were designed to travel between disciplines. These are not the easiest to define, since they require a launch-pad and a sufficient energy and structural stability to maintain their semantic value during the course of their voyage.

We have thus attempted to induce different levels of reading. First, the *theoretical and clinical thinking* of those who founded family therapy. The thought of *Bateson* is developed along the following path: double bind; diachronic and synchronic axes of a therapy; maps; territory; schismogenesis; alienation; context; context-markers; eidos, eidonomy; cognitive epistemologies; ethos, ethonomy; immanence; alcoholism;

schizophrenias; stochastic processes; redundancy; learning; algorithm; heuristics; genetics and the family; mind; information; phantasy; play; acculturation; power; mode-identifying signals; metacommunication systems; game theory; theory of logical types; semantic unit of mind; evolutionary survival unit. *Jackson*: circularity, circular; family rules; family systems; homeostasis; provocation, crisis provocation; quid pro quo. *Erickson*: hypnosis, hypnotherapy; metaphorical objects. *Haley*: couples; metagovernor; therapeutic strategies and tactics; power; re-framing; perverse triangles; hypnosis, hypnotherapy. *Ferreira*: split double bind; family myths. *Watzlawick*: agreement and disagreement; reality, the real; digital (or numeric) coding; analogic coding; change; messages; pragmatics of communication; self-fulfilling prophecy; reality, the real; brief interactional therapy; interactional typologies of the family.

  The psychodynamic model is covered as follows. *Laforgue*: scotomization. *Lidz*: coalition; marital schism; marital skew. *Ackerman*: adolescence; principle of complementarity; scapegoat. *Wynne*: adolescence; alignment; boundaries; collective cognitive chaos; meta-binding; pseudo-hostility; pseudo-mutuality; reciprocal victimization and rescue. *Whitaker*: absurd. *Stierlin*: adolescence; delegation, delegate. *Racamier*: paradoxicality. *Ruffiot*: family psychical apparatus. *Eiguer*: family organizers.

  Bowen's theory of the family system is developed in the following entries: alcoholism; coach; coalition; couples; de-triangulation; differentiation of self; family emotional oneness; family life-cycles; family projection; family systems; genogram; interlocking triangles; shock waves; sibling position profiles; triangles.

  Minuchin's structural model: affiliation or joining; alignment; boundaries; detouring; disengaged families; enmeshed families; family maps; family structures; locus; mimesis; morphogenetic or structural typologies of the family; psychosomatic illness; restructuring.

  Boszormenyi-Nagy's contextual therapy: ethics; exploitation; fairness; indebtedness; ledger; loyalty; merit; multi-directional partiality; multi-laterality; parentification; relational stagnation; scapegoat; trust.

  Selvini Palazzoli's systemic model: anorexia nervosa; data gathering; neutrality; positive connotation; ritualization, rituals; systemic hypothesis; triadic questioning.

  Andolfi's provocative model: provocation, crisis provocation; tasks, prescription of tasks.

  Elkaim's model: assemblage; bifurcation; dissipative structures; family self-referentiality; networks; singularities.

  Caillé's model: family self-referentiality; metasystems, metasystems of intervention; model of the systemic model.

  The contributors to this dictionary suggest other paths. *Neuburger*: clan; demand; 'nothing plus 10 per cent' paradox; rituals of belonging; supervision; symptoms. *Angel and Angel*: adolescent suicide; children of survivor parents; drug addiction; prescribing (medical) drugs. *Segond*: legal context; sucking-in by the system; systemic modelling and intervention; therapeutic double binds and multiple binds. *Miermont*: actuogenetic landscape of the family; actuogenesis; ancestral relation; family actant; family catastrophes; family maps; family self-referentiality; family passions; family self-belonging; oscillators; relational archetypes; residual relations; self-referential calculus; self-referential coupling; transgenerational memories. *Miermont and Garrigues*: familiodrama in training and therapy. *Maruani*: anti-theatre; mesnie; sociogenetics of family schisms; sofa-bed syndrome. *Miermont and Maruani*: psychosomatic double binds. *Christian*: acoustic feedback.

  Several trajectories are possible depending on the goal sought by the reader. The clinician could usefully start out with the *psychopathological entries*: alcoholism; anorexia nervosa; child abuse; children of survivor parents; delinquent acting out; delirium; dementia; drug addiction; incest; indications and contraindications for the use of family therapy; infantile autism; legal context; mourning; paranoia; prescribing (medical) drugs; psychosomatic illness; schizophrenias; violence etc.

More *technical entries* are available to the therapist: absent member manoeuvre; abstinence, rule of; affiliation or joining; brief interactional therapy; contrary injunction; co-therapy; data gathering; demand; familiodrama; family doctor; family rules; family–therapeutic institution differentiation; family therapies; free association; genogram; hypnosis, hypnotherapy; index patient; interpretation; manipulation; metaphorical objects; neurolinguistic programming; positive connotation; prescription; provocation; psychodrama; psychosomatic medicine; restructuring; ritualization, rituals; rituals of belonging; sculpting; singularities; sociodrama; supervision; systemic hypothesis; systemic modelling and intervention; tasks; therapeutic abstention; therapeutic double binds and multiple binds; therapeutic strategies and tactics; therapeutic styles; transference; triadic questioning.

The *theory of clinical practice* is more specifically developed in the following entries: adolescence; alienation; change; coalition; couples; demand; differentiation of self; double bind; evolutionary survival unit; family catastrophes; family life-cycles; family psychical apparatus; family myths; family organizers; family systems; family typologies; interactions; ledger; map and counter-map of a family system; marital breakdown; metapsychology; 'nothing plus 10 per cent' paradox; paradoxes; paradoxicality; parentification; perverse triangles; pragmatics of communication; read-write memories; semantic resonances; semantic unit of mind; triangles; training; unconscious, the; unit of change etc.

Considerable space is given over to *etho-anthropological aspects*: acculturation; agonistic behaviour; alethic (modalities); alienation (mental, familial, therapeutic); attachment behaviour; becoming accustomed; behaviourism; calumny; deculturation; deixis; deontic (modality); disclosure; domestication; ecosystem; ethology; evolutionary survival unit; family ethnology; family ethology; functional circle; gatekeeper; habituation; humour; imprinting; instinct; institutions; law; learning; misunderstanding; multi-channel communication systems; nostalgia; pseudo-speciation; reality, the real; scandalmongering; secrets; semantics of communication; semiotic square; sexed behaviour; shifters; social organization; speech acts; symbol; syntax of communication; territory.

The *psychoanalytic conception* is developed in the entries: psychoanalysis; metapsychology; abstinence, rule of; free association; interpretation; transference, countertransference; family psychical apparatus; unconscious, the; family unconscious; identification; projective identification; foreclosure; scotomization; transitional objects; alpha and beta elements; splitting, individual and family; law; narcissism; family organizers; paradoxicality; psychodrama; phantasy; dreams; reality, the real; true self; psychoanalytic–phantasmatic topologies of the family etc.

Systemic modelling is developed in the following way: cybernetics (Wiener, Ashby, von Foerster); general systems theory (von Bertalanffy, Le Moigne, Morin); family systems, algorithm; heuristics; black box; artificial codes; analogic coding; digital (or numeric) coding; messages; holographic memory; fuzzy sets; multi-level hierarchies; tangled hierarchies; holism; homeostasis; information; feedback; machines, trivial and non-trivial; read-write memories; redundancy; communication systems; metacommunication systems; paracommunication systems.

The *theory of self-referentiality* (Gödel, Spencer-Brown, Varela) is dealt with in the following sequence: self-organization; autonomy and heteronomy of a system; family self-referentiality; circularity, circular; self-referential calculus; paradoxes; tangled hierarchies; incompleteness theorems etc.

For greater ease of understanding *catastrophe theory modelling* (Thom, Zeeman, Petitot), this theme can be approached in the following order: topological space; ball, sphere; dynamic systems; force fields; attractors; universal unfolding; connectedness; structural stability; elementary catastrophes; generalized catastrophes; singularities, chreod; vectors; relational archetypes; semantic resonances; semantics of communication; deixis; fractals; symbolic reference; family catastrophes.

Lastly, the worried reader might begin with the entry on humour!

This is not an exhaustive list. In the body of the work, the paths linking the different concepts are various and do not solely follow the foregoing subdivisions. Some zones of passage are broad and obvious; others are more tenuous or, indeed, more hazardous.

If the concept of the family is, then, ambiguous, the elimination of the ambiguity is ensured, in this comparative study of models, by practice: a practice which shows that a therapist is neither an artist nor a scientist.

Jacques Miermont
Paris, 9 November 1986

A

absence See RESIDUAL RELATIONS, RELATIONS OF ABSENCE OF ABSENCE.

absent member manoeuvre Finding that a member of the family is absent from a session poses tactical and methodological problems for the therapist. Depending upon the model used, the nature of the context and the point in the development of the therapy, the absence of a person will be interpreted either as a form of resistance or, by contrast, as the establishment of a spontaneous change in the family, with a view to creating new BOUNDARIES.

The motive may be one of resistance to change. The absent member manoeuvre is observed when a member of the family is not present at a given session, particularly at the beginning of the therapy, even though he or she is expected. This absence – or these absences – have been seen to express a particular meaning: they are, more or less, an attempt by one part of the family to preserve its present system and mode of functioning. The absent person will delegate the persons present in such a way that the therapist does not have the means to evaluate the situation or bring about progress.

In other cases, the absent person will be notable by his/her very absence. Some patients (alcoholics and paranoiacs) have a way of getting themselves talked about behind their backs, of getting everyone else to gang up on them and of orchestrating scandal about themselves. It then falls to the therapist to evaluate how much the value of the absent person should be acknowledged. The therapist has to support not only the persons who are present and absent, but also the system, if it appears particularly dysfunctional. It is, in fact, this dysfunction which, in spite of everything, ensures the survival of the totality. Where that dysfunction is threatened, in the name of a therapeutic ideal, there is a risk that the family will break the contract prematurely.

Finally, in other cases, certain persons – or certain subgroups – will end their participation in a process of therapy when their presence is no longer so necessary. This may either occur spontaneously or in response to the explicit request of the therapist. At this point, it will be advisable to structure transgenerational boundaries or the boundaries which limit the NUCLEAR FAMILY and the extended family. This may then lead to the parental couple consulting the therapist on their own, not for therapy as a couple, but in order to consolidate the alliance between the two parents.

(See also COALITIONS; MANIPULATION; PRAGMATICS OF COMMUNICATION; TRIANGLES.)

P.S. & J.M.

abstinence, rule of The rule of abstinence (Freud, 1915) is a psychoanalytic principle according to which the analysand must avoid substitutive satisfactions for his or her symptoms as much as possible. For their part, analysts must refuse to play the roles which the analysand tends to impose upon them. A corollary of the rule of abstinence is the psychoanalyst's recommendation to the analysand that he or she should not take important decisions during the treatment. This principle may be compared to the prescription of no change (see PRESCRIPTION), as defined in systemic therapies.

Instead of satisfying the libidinal demands made by patients, the dynamics of the analytic treatment tends to defer any immediate response, in order to enable a work of interpretation to take place. A rule of this kind is proposed by Ruffiot (1981b). This consists of confining the role of the patients and their families to the use of language alone. The function of the therapists is to listen and interpret, with the aim of re-establishing the activity of thought and enabling phantasy to circulate. Family members will therefore receive no advice or immediate pragmatic solutions. As for the therapist, he or she makes no claim to immediate understanding, or to a superior symmetrical or complementary position (see SCHISMOGENESIS) and thus renounces the illusion of omniscience and omnipotence.

The rule of abstinence has been debated within the framework of individual psychoanalysis by Ferenczi (1920, 1926), and in part re-adjusted by his method of *active technique* (see also Sabourin, 1985). It has in fact been observed that with narcissistic pathologies, the technique of strict abstinence merely increases the patient's affective deficiencies and sense of emptiness. Writers like Winnicott (1971) and Masud Khan (1974) have established individual forms of therapeutic games, which are particularly creative and inventive in their various ways.

In family therapy, one encounters the problem of families inundated by a flood of words or completely silent, who wait for the therapist to engage with them, to express his or her demands, to make explicit the contexts in which he or she is intervening. Various authors have advocated the use of PSYCHODRAMA, SOCIODRAMA or FAMILIODRAMA. It then becomes important to tailor the techniques of intervention to the pathology encountered and the different stages of therapeutic action.

Recourse to institutions by the most disturbed families necessarily involves the *de facto* imposition of alienating roles upon medical practitioners and social workers who may activate the dysfunctional interactions generated by the family systems concerned, which these systems can no longer control. The more grave the pathology, the more family pressure is inevitable. It is therefore essential to take account of this frantic enactment by the members of the family and indeed to prescribe it (see PRESCRIPTION) and encourage resistance to it (see HYPNOTHERAPY), rather than attempt to destroy it at all costs.

(See also AFFILIATION; FREE ASSOCIATION; INFORMATION; INTERPRETATION; SYSTEMIC HYPOTHESIS; TRANSFERENCE.)

J.M.

absurd, psychotherapy of the   The expanded exploration of apparently absurd propositions is proposed by Whitaker (1973) as a way of overcoming pathological family situations dominated by boredom, the status quo and continual aggression. When dealing with violently aggressive families, elements of absurdity serve as a means of moving from a 'rational' attitude to tactics which reduce the aggression by establishing a craziness that is a source of creativity in the therapeutic space. Such a technique was later taken up by Andolfi and Angelo (1980) (see PROVOCATION) and Elkaim et al. (1980) (see DISSIPATIVE STRUCTURES) as a controlled use of positive feedback in family systems invaded by death-laden forms of regulation. Thus the work of subversion here no longer involves bringing out the individual desire of the neurotic patient by techniques of pure empathy, but granting families permission to 'think madly' and accompanying them as they do so (Miermont, 1982a). This supposes that the therapist provides the patients and families with a therapeutic space that has sufficiently safe boundaries (hence the interest in modelling in terms of catastrophe theory, Miermont, 1982b).

Whitaker (1973) offers several clinical examples, from which the following is a short extract. A woman is talking to the therapist about her husband:

Wife: I can't stand my husband.
Therapist: Men are pretty difficult. Why haven't you divorced him? Why not try an interim boyfriend?
Wife: But I love him.
Therapist (expanding the absurdity by pressing on): Of course, that's why you'd have an affair – to prove your love and to stimulate his love till it equals yours.

Wife: But I love my kids.
Therapist (pressing on with the escalation of the absurdity): Well if you do, you should make a sacrifice by leaving them so they'll learn that father also loves them.
Wife: But he'll neglect them.
Therapist: Then you can prove your love of them by suing him for child neglect.

The patient will then seek to put an end to this absurd escalation by pointing out to the therapist that his or her propositions are mad or stupid. The therapist will insist on the perfectly logical and necessary character of these deductions, by demonstrating the change-activating value of what at first glance may appear absurd.

A therapeutic attitude of this kind thus seeks to increase the complexity of the system rather than re-establish an order made up of boredom and jammed routines. Madness is no longer considered pathogenic in itself, but as absurdist theatre, as a source of creativity in search of appropriate contexts.

(See also ANTI-THEATRE; DISSIPATIVE STRUCTURES; FAMILY CATASTROPHES; PROVOCATION.)

J.M.

abuse   See CHILD ABUSE.

accommodation   See AFFILIATION.

acculturation   A word formed from 'culture' and the Latin prefix '*ad*' meaning 'movement towards', denoting cultural *rapprochement* between two social groups: clans, ethnic groups, nations etc. The term is thus synonymous with cultural contact, cultural change or with the interpenetration of civilizations. It corresponds to a process of dynamic interaction between different cultures and has to take into account the conflictual aspects this engenders, as well as the global situation in which contact occurs (Bastide, 1990). The characteristics of this process have been seen by Bateson (1972) as connected with the phenomena of SCHISMOGENESIS.

MYTHIC ACCULTURATION/JURIDICAL ACCULTURATION

Classically, a distinction is made between mythic acculturation and juridical acculturation (Alliot, 1968). *Mythic acculturation* refers to the transmission of myths from one people to another. The mythic level corresponds to the homeostasis which founds cultural groups and therefore tends to maintain the values and belief systems of the past. At this level, there is a direct, immediate access to absolute values. *Juridical acculturation* refers to the transmission of LAWS from one people to another. It can thus lead to the overall transformation of the system of laws of a given society. The juridical level describes the evolutionary movement of societies in their attempts to establish rudiments of their security in the present. It corresponds to an indirect, mediated approach to absolute values, whether these be religious, scientific, philosophical or moral.

These two levels of acculturation are in a state of permanent tension and conflict. Whether they wish to or not, at times of cultural contact between two civilizations, the initial cultures 'form part of a single set' (Balandier, 1971, 1974; see also the Batesonian definition of SCHISMOGENESIS). The dominant culture may thus generate a position of passive resistance, which is liable to last for as long as is necessary. Though ethnology mainly lays emphasis on the transition from myth to law (the dominant societies planning acculturation from a 'civilizing' perspective, Bastide, 1990), the family-theoretic approach is more often confronted, at the level of family micro-systems, with interplay between these two registers. The goal of a process of family therapy might be the creative establishment of new systems of acculturation for a given family.

ACCULTURATION AND FAMILY ALLIANCES

We shall assume that acculturation already exists in the way in which two family systems of the same generation permit (or do not permit) the engendering of new family units in the following generation. The alliance between the two families of origin rests upon a set of reciprocal interactions. Similarly, the work of therapists when confronted with a family requesting aid supposes a whole process of cultural adaptation on the part of the therapists towards the group they are meeting; that group also reacts to the therapeutic contact. These phenomena of acculturation lead to the putting into question of personal and group identities.

The pathology of acculturation is particularly clearly defined in families with schizophrenic transactions (see SCHIZOPHRENIAS), paranoiac reactions (see PARANOIA), families confronted with problems of DRUG ADDICTION and in cases of ADOLESCENT SUICIDE attempts (Philippe and Davidson, 1981).

FAMILY ACCULTURATION/SOCIAL ACCULTURATION

For drug-taking, the link with drugs as metonymy for the 'new culture', which breaks with the parents' culture of origin, seems clear (We may observe that young North African immigrants smoke hashish in an addictive way unlike their fathers who smoked cannabis on festive occasions.) The use of drugs thus forms a part of a set of behaviours that are ordeals to which the adolescent submits as rites of passage into the dominant culture. The adolescent girl, torn between the norms

of family behaviour ('the way they do things back in the home country') and the norms of social behaviour (at school, in the factory, at the office, at university), has recourse to massive intoxication through medical drugs and another form of risk-taking in the shape of pregnancy followed by abortion. Drug addiction, suicide attempts and terminations of pregnancy are thus symptoms furnished by society. Where schizophrenia is concerned, the conflicts are not so much over SOCIAL STATUS as over FAMILY ROLES, in particular as these are defined by the FAMILY MYTH.

Taking up the ideas of Kuckhorn, Spiegel (1968) distinguishes between *formal roles*, which in cases of conflict are subject to distortion, and *informal roles* liable to dislocation. However, what are the respective parts played here by the forces constraining one to adapt to a constantly developing environment and the need to maintain a family – and indeed cultural – identity? Indeed, Margaret Mead (1957) said that in an urbanized world, 'Nature is what one's fathers had, as opposed to what one's sons invent . . .'. Nevertheless, each patient may be considered as a link in a continuous long-term historical process which involves a specific subculture. Mendell and Fisher (1956, p. 173) add: 'The patient is a product of group disorganization.' Acculturation is thus used at times to explain the anomie of families, at times to justify their attachment to the values of their tradition, and at times to explain their willingness to assimilate to the dominant values. In fact, acculturation seems to be as much a creator of suffering as a condition of creativity. Minuchin (1967) described this when working with the families of the black and Puerto Rican ghettos of North America.

A study by Cohen and Emerique (1979) on a carefully defined population located the points of family suffering normally found in situations of acculturation among migrants who have no possibility of returning to their countries of origin, forced by the reality of their situation to pass through some major life-changes in a few short years:

1 Disappropriation of their former status (which can to some extent be protected against by the formation of a ghetto).
2 Loss of paternal authority.
3 Formation of 'vertical' mother–son and father–daughter couples.
4 A confusion of inciting messages, promoting the emergence of transgressive social behaviour.

SYNCHRONIC AND DIACHRONIC ACCULTURATION

Miermont (1979c) has emphasized the distinction between *synchronic acculturation*, i.e. the confrontation between diverse human groups at a given point, and *diachronic acculturation*, i.e. the progressive transformation of a group as a function of scientific and technological development. It seems that each form of acculturation derives support from the other, but that each may give rise to a specific pathology. Maruani (1985b) finds that: the first generation, which is struggling to be accepted and to survive, is prone to somatic illnesses and acute psychotic episodes; the second generation, which wants to be integrated and to succeed, is prone to psychosomatic illnesses (high blood pressure, coronary disorders, cancers) and to mood disorders (depression, alcoholism); the third generation, which wants to re-find its lost or imaginary roots, is prone to schizophrenia or to interminable psychoanalysis.

Basing themselves upon the hypothesis of Green (1970) of a complementary negative replica of the structure of the preceding generation, Gear and Liendo (1981, p. 165) have advanced a model of family semiotic structure that is particularly pertinent for describing psychopathological disturbances in families where the process of acculturation occurs in a dysharmonic way in the parental couple: 'Not only does each of the parents do to the other what he or she says that the other does, but also both unconsciously impose an ethical normative code on their child which is the opposite of the code which governs their own actions.' The third generation thus takes up the values of the first together with the roles (though these are reversed between the two sexes) of the second, the semantic and Oedipal mirrors combining their effects.

(See also DECULTURATION; LAW; MYTH; VIOLENCE.)

J.M. & G.G.M.

acoustic feedback Relations between a couple are modified profoundly when a commitment is made to a third party, whether this occurs through the common event of marriage, the birth of a child or merely by the signing of a contract (regarding accommodation, a bank account etc.). The change arises because, as soon as it takes concrete form before a witness, the project of 'remaining the same for one another' assumes the status of a commentary on the situation, the status of enforced metacommunication, mobilizing the images that derive from the families of origin of each of the partners (Maruani, 1985c).

The electro-acoustic phenomenon of 'feedback' provides a good metaphor for this. As is well known, this produces a whistling noise when a microphone and a loudspeaker are at a particular distance from each other. This effect of acoustic oscillation is due to the looping of a self-sustaining circuit of metacommunicational commentary on to the initial sound: the sound enters the microphone, comes out of the speaker, is picked up by the microphone which sends it back again to the speaker and so on. The oscillating circuit is only set up if a sound is emitted, but once the whistling has been triggered, the nature of the sound no longer has any

effect upon it. The whistling sound will depend on the system formed by the volume of the room in which the equipment is sited, the types of equipment involved and, most importantly, the distance between the two.

Marriage may be something like a couple's acoustic feedback. It sets up a circuit of oscillation (a commentary on the relationship) which may remain silent or lead to behaviour which had previously been harmonious being affected by 'interference'. For example, the couple's sexuality may be fully developed (logical level 1) when the decision to conceive a child poses the question of sexuality as a means of handing on the name and property (logical level 2). This may then either obstruct or enhance the mutual understanding between the couple. In certain conditions which are beyond the intentional control of the protagonists, only breaking the circuit makes it possible to re-establish the requisite distance.

(See also COUPLES; FAMILY SELF-REFERENTIALITY; MARITAL BREAKDOWN; OSCILLATORS; THEORY OF LOGICAL TYPES.)

G.G.M. & D.C.

actant, actor See FAMILY ACTANT, FAMILY ACTOR.

acting out In psychoanalysis, acting out corresponds to a break in the flow of FREE ASSOCIATION and to the impulsive realization of a scenario which is not able to be structured in the form of a fantasmic representation. Instead of following a process of rememorization, the patient unleashes a form of unrepressible behaviour, frequently presenting an aggressive or erotic dimension, a behaviour which may be displayed either in or outside therapeutic sessions.

As Freud states: 'The patient does not *remember* anything of what he has forgotten and repressed, but *acts* it out. He reproduces it not as a memory but as an action; he *repeats* it, without, of course, knowing that he is repeating it' (Freud, 1914c, p. 150). Elsewhere he notes: 'We think it most undesirable if the patient acts outside the transference instead of remembering. The ideal conduct for our purposes would be that he should behave as normally as possible outside the treatment and express his abnormal reactions only in the transference' (Freud, 1938, p. 177). However, the eruption of acting out can be the start of an experience from which the fantasmic elaboration of a failing or absent representation becomes possible.

In family therapy, the pressure to act is often very strong on the part of the patient and his/her relatives. The tendency towards repetition, far from producing isolated incidents, is the beginning of the work, starting from mental images which are already remembered.

Everything takes place as if the enactment of interpersonal exchanges was itself the necessary way without which fantasmic elaboration would be impossible. Most often, far from being able to treat the psychical representation directly, family therapists deal with daily life events, that is, they actualize them. This actualization can take place within or outside the therapeutic sessions when therapists come to talk about the problems presented to them with the various professionals who are involved with the patient.

As Bateson discusses in his essay, 'A theory of play and fantasy' (in Bateson, 1972), transference is distinguished from real love and hate by signals which indicate the psychical frame within which it is possible to talk during a psychoanalytic session. Usually the frames of reference are seriously absent in spontaneous psychotic interaction. The ritual of family sessions with a therapist serves as a frame of reference by which 'acting out' is transformed through semiotic acts and support for the elaboration of mental material. As Haley (1963, p. 156) underlines:

To the individually oriented, a symbolic statement is not only a metaphor about internal conflicts, but conflicts in relationships are said to be metaphoric expressions, or 'acting out' of an internal drama. Quite the reverse is true of the family point of view; external conflicts induce inner ones which reflect them.

(See also ACTION; DELINQUENT ACTING OUT; FAMILIODRAMA IN TRAINING AND THERAPY; PLAY; PSYCHODRAMA; SCULPTING.)

J.M. & P.S.

action Action is a fundamental operator of systemic interventions and the site of numerous paradoxes. The most fundamental of these concerns a-pragmatism, a shock symptom in its unbearable dimension of apparent absolute inactivity. In fact, such inactivity seems to correlate directly with hyperactivity in the surrounding milieu.

Family therapy involves action in several ways: at the point when therapy is seen to be indicated; in meetings between the family and the therapist; in the prescription of TASKS or RITUALS; in the paradoxical action imposed by the symptoms; and in meetings between several therapists. Action brings out the effect of ideological positions and, where circumstances are favourable, enables these to be regulated. An important part of therapeutic action involves the accommodation of various therapeutic points of view in their concrete effects.

Here the systemic conception of therapeutic action connects up with Goethe's Faust: 'In the beginning was the deed.' The arrangement of the conceptual and material aspects of the therapeutic framework is marked by this PRAGMATIC dimension of communication.

It seems as if, in the case of families struggling with psychosis, criminal acts or behavioural disorders, the application of concrete aspects of reality enables individuals to be located and localized in their situation and makes it possible to create new spaces and hence new frontiers. These topological re-adjustments are not confined to the observable manifestations in terms of which they are defined. They are accompanied by a re-organization of the systems of representation and an activation of the phantasy lives of the various protagonists involved. 'We perceive only operations, that is to say, only acts' (Valéry, 1973, p. 562).

(See also ACTING OUT; ACTIVATION; ACTUOGENESIS; AGONISTIC BEHAVIOUR; ATTACHMENT BEHAVIOUR; BEHAVIOURISM; CYBERNETICS; ETHOLOGY; FAMILIODRAMA; GAZE; INSTINCT; MAP; PERFORMATIVES; PLAY; PSYCHODRAMA; REALITY; SEXED BEHAVIOUR; SOCIODRAMA; SPEECH ACTS; TERRITORY.)

P.G. & J.M.

activation and de-activation of systems mediating behaviour A process leading (a) to the setting in motion of systems of behaviour and the spatio-temporal realization of sequences of action which have until now been inhibited or prohibited, and (b) to the interruption of sequences that have become inopportune or dangerous.

Activation and de-activation of a behaviour enable one to transform the definition which may be offered of REALITY. This is distinct from ACTING OUT. Confronting family protagonists with one another, in the presence of a third person (or several others) who take on the function of a protective barrier providing security, obliges one to structure the interactions and manage one's interventions as a function of the goals one is seeking to attain.

In certain cases, it is necessary to allow a process of communication to unfold without over-hasty or untimely metacommunicative commentary, at a point where the family group, not having any solid basis for communication, has habitually been swept off into a process of metacommunicative escalation. In other cases, the expression of thoughts, phantasies and dreams gives one leave to activate mentalized behaviours which can stand in place of violent, if not indeed lethal, instances of 'acting out'. In yet other cases, the need arises to activate certain acted sequences of behaviour where expression through phantasy proves either impossible or completely unstructured. One may then envisage the PRESCRIPTION of tasks or rituals, either within the session or outside it, starting out from the elaboration of desired scenarios, in which the distinction can be made between scenarios in thought (preliminary to phantasmatic activity) and acted scenarios (along the lines of projects of family distancing which are apparently simple, but which must be carried out with caution where there are serious cases of psychosis).

(See also ACTION; ACTUOGENESIS; PRAGMATICS OF COMMUNICATION.)

J.M.

actualizing family transactional patterns   In the structural model, the techniques of actualizing transactional patterns constitute, along with the techniques of 'joining' and of 'restructuring' one of the three main intervention strategies. The three categories can be conceptualized as follows: (a) the creation of transactions including enactment and task setting within the family interview; (b) joining the family's transactional patterns, including tracking, accommodation and mimesis; (c) restructuring the transactions in the session, including system recomposition, symptom focusing and modifying the family's structure (Aponte and van Deusen, 1981; Minuchin and Fishman, 1981).

In *structuring*, the therapist organizes the sequence of his or her transactions with members of the family to modify their habitual transactional patterns. For example, with a woman whose views are ignored by the family, the therapist may show him or herself attentive to her opinions and judgements, striving to enable her in this way to take up a position complementary to his or her own and abandon her previous transactional mode.

In *enacting transactional patterns*, the therapist uses the material of the session to bring the members of the family to transact, in the therapist's presence, some of the ways in which they naturally resolve conflicts, support each other etc. 'He can . . . create family scenarios by directing certain family members to interact with each other in a clearly delineated framework. The instructions must be explicit, such as, "Talk with your father about that." ' (Minuchin, 1974, p. 141).

Assigning tasks, during the session or outside it, differs from enacting, in that precise parameters are prescribed which make it possible to highlight – or facilitate the discovery of – certain transactional patterns that would not naturally have developed in the ordinary flow of family transactions.

(See also AFFILIATION; BOUNDARIES; FAMILY STRUCTURES; STRUCTURAL FAMILY THERAPY.)

A.L.

actuogenesis   Along the same lines as epigenesis in embryology (the development of tissues), we may think of 'actuogenesis' as the actualization in the present

of behaviours (Leyhausen, 1974); actuogenesis is the result of what is happening to an individual at a given moment. It is the ACTIVATION or de-activation of behaviours at a particular instant. Actuogenesis has therefore been re-examined from the perspective of self-referential processes (Miermont and Gross, 1985; Miermont, 1986a).

Actuogenesis is influenced by biological, psychical and social parameters. It is thus distinct from the phylogenetic and ontogenetic aspects of the history of each behavioural unit. *Phylogenesis* corresponds to the evolution of species, which is itself dependent upon the collective fate of the individuals who go to make it up, as a function of the survival context (natural selection, sexual selection, cultural selection). *Ontogenesis* corresponds to the development of the individual, who is dependent him or herself on the individuated destiny of his/her various phylogenetic and cultural bases (families, ethnic groups, nations).

On a diachronic level, actuogenesis is the product of phylogenesis and ontogenesis, and thus cannot be reduced to either. There exists an autonomy of behaviour which actualizes itself in a given context and which makes it impossible to predict behaviour solely on the basis of the elements of the individual or collective past. On a synchronic level, actuogenesis is the product of transformations of the surface structures by the deep structures.

This product is the simplification of a complex question. The levels of evolution and change within the individual and the human species are established on the basis of demographic units of varying sizes, running from the family unit through the various identities (ethnic groups, nations, supranational entities) which become institutionalized in the course of history. Actuogenesis is the result of terrestrial, biological, psychological and social events occurring at every moment.

For example, the *phylogenetic parameters* are the biological properties of the organism, its morphological characteristics (form of the skeleton, variations of the teguments etc.), certain behavioural characteristics (instincts, rituals, propensity to learn). The *ontogenetic parameters* are certain biological and morphological variations as a result of nutrition (height, weight), cultural factors acquired through upbringing and education, and belonging to a language community, ethnic group or a particular family. In actuogenesis, the resulting product may not always be the work of a single, specific parameter. Each level retroacts upon each other, over variable time-scales. But it does happen that certain degrees of autonomy of behaviour free that product from phylogenetic and ontogenetic constraints: these latter begin to oscillate, leading to an impulsion toward spontaneity, creativity and free will. The ontogenetic and phylogenetic levels then become confused: the individual is then the whole species of which he or she is a part; the species becomes the individual unit it contains.

The autonomy of actuogenesis may be expressed symbolically using the SELF-REFERENTIAL CALCULUS. On a diachronic level, there is an oscillation between ontogenesis and phylogenesis:

$$AG = \overline{\boxed{OG \mid PG}}$$

AG = actuogenesis
OG = ontogenesis
PG = phylogenesis

On a synchronic level, there is an oscillation between SURFACE STRUCTURES and deep structures of behaviour.

$$AG = \overline{\boxed{SS \mid DS}}$$

AG = actuogenesis
SS = surface structure
DS = deep structure

In effect, the production of the act in its spontaneous dimension is, to a certain extent, 'freed' from its ontogenetic and phylogenetic parameters, which lose their value as distinguishing marks as they oscillate in a wider context of action. Such a liberation from phylogenetic and ontogenetic constraints may be considered the generator of processes of symbolization. Actuogenesis is what brings the real (see REALITY) into being.

(See also ACTUOGENETIC LANDSCAPE OF THE FAMILY; INSTINCT; LEARNING; SYMBOLS.)

J.M.

actuogenetic landscape of the family When the family group presents itself to a therapist, a 'total' spectacle occurs, which is seen, heard and felt. Bodies, voices, gestures, gazes and words are the reflection of a landscape within which all the members of a family move, as do all the therapists concerned. Each person has greater or lesser degrees of freedom in the exploration of the landscape, as a function of their position, their particular strength and the constraints imposed by the 'lie of the land'. This landscape only truly appears in the activation of exchanges, and gives rise, in its turn, to a dynamic that lends itself to interaction and determines each person's capacities for action. Kinaesthetic perceptions (movements) and coenesthesic perceptions (internal integration of perceptions) reveal the constraints of the territory thus traversed, through images, phantasies, affects and thoughts.

On entering the room where therapy is to take place, the members of the family and the professionals concerned create an implicit and explicit hierarchy with regard to positions adopted in the group and abilities for thinking, acting and feeling. The INDEX PATIENT may, for example, take the chair which the therapist would spontaneously have taken. Or again, the patient

may find him or herself left standing, without an allotted place. All the members of a family move within an interactive landscape which determines the nature of their exchanges.

The unfolding of interactions leads to the identification of profiles of behaviour, of speaking and remaining silent, which may be interpreted in terms of the ETHOS and EIDOS of the family (emotive and intellectual group norms). The elucidation of these may in some cases be facilitated by role-playing games, by SCULPTING, by elaborating GENOGRAMS and leads to the staging of a true FAMILIODRAMA.

In other words, behaviours are organized in sequences that are more or less coordinated with one another. Their integration leads to an overall configuration which may be apprehended as the symbolic representation of the landscape presented by the family. However, verbal and non-verbal behaviours are not only clearly identifiable sequences; they give rise to relational flows whose intensity modifies the degree of freedom enjoyed by the therapist. There may thus be a distortion between what an outside spectator perceives of a session and the overall impression of the therapist *in situ*. The therapist is thus led to modify certain trajectories and certain boundaries, and to allow other landscapes to be glimpsed. He or she cannot, however, totally change their structures or create them out of nothing.

(See also ACTUOGENESIS; FAMILY MAPS; FORCE FIELDS.)

J.M.

admission of impotence, recognition of failure When faced with the challenge presented by certain patients and their families, demanding more and more interventions, different therapists, technical input and commitment, and insisting on yet further 'impossible missions', but in fact rejecting every form of change, it becomes absolutely essential to acknowledge, in a general (institutional and familial) consensus, that none of the efforts currently being undertaken can offer any improvement and may indeed appreciably aggravate the initial situation without resolving the problem or problems they are supposed to be solving.

This admission of impotence may be regarded as a therapeutic attitude or as an epistemological preliminary, necessitating a genuine work of elaboration among therapists. The alcoholic's bottle, the schizophrenic's apragmatism, the anorexic's orgiastic asceticism and the anti-social loyalty of the delinquent are then to be evaluated as points of no-return, as 'potential wells' (Thom, 1989) which cannot be got rid of and which it is, however, impossible to climb out of. It is then up to the family and the therapeutic personnel to attempt to define the minimal result that is to be obtained from this admission, which comes down to taking the view that all the medical and therapeutic efforts made so far are to be considered null and void (meta-therapeutic or para-therapeutic dimension).

It may, however, also appear that one has exhausted all the possible 'therapeutic' models in all they have to offer strategically and tactically. In which case, it is essential that one should know not to intervene, or that one should learn to prescribe THERAPEUTIC ABSTENTION for the system requesting attention.

J.M.

adolescence In Western societies, adolescence is often regarded as a stage in personality development which is characterized by the formation of identity. It is a period of life in which 'crises' frequently occur, which bear witness at one and the same time to conflictual readjustments internal to the subject and the random play of interactional processes between the adolescent and his or her family. Family therapists follow Ackerman (1962) in seeing the adolescent's disturbances as distress signals which reflect the chaos of his/her family, society and culture.

Very often the adolescent patient is made a scapegoat by the whole of the family group. The young person takes upon him or herself the greater part of collective guilt and his/her symptoms represent a fixation point: only conflicts concerning the adolescent command the family's attention.

Many family therapists have described family characteristics in terms of the particular difficulties of the adolescent. Among others, we may cite the following pathologies to which specific studies have been devoted:

- school phobias;
- suicide attempts (see ADOLESCENT SUICIDE);
- psychosomatic disturbances (see PSYCHOSOMATIC ILLNESS);
- psychotic manifestations (see INFANTILE AUTISM; SCHIZOPHRENIAS);
- criminal behaviour (see ACTING OUT).

The concept of FAMILY LIFE-CYCLES has made it possible to cast light on the problems of separation at adolescence (Haley, 1973, 1980). Thus the transgenerational rules of the different family systems of origin find themselves reactivated by the children's moves towards independence. The difficulties of the adolescents come into resonance with the fact of the grandparents entering the last phase of their lives. The parents are confronted with a double separation: the separation from their children ('the empty nest') and mourning their parents. These transitions in the life-cycle bring with them a number of internal and interactional readjustments.

It has been observed that the procedure by which the children gain their independence varies as a function of the FAMILY MYTHS of each of the parents. Certain families are not good at accepting their child's reaching post-adolescence and fear too early a separation, a projection of their own process of gaining independence. Others, by contrast, maintain rules of dependence, the coming of independence reactivating a process of anticipated mourning. Clinical observations in fact reveal the importance of the repercussions of the processes of children gaining their independence on the dynamics of the family. Stierlin (1981) describes three modalities of separation:

1 In the first case, a *very close bond* keeps the adolescent within the orbit of the family. The parents and the adolescent prove incapable of redefining their relations on new bases. Few members of these families are ready to confront the pain, comparable to that of a bereavement, which separation brings on.

2 In other cases, separation occurs in the mode of *rejection*. The adolescent is discredited and expelled from the family unit: these brutal breaks occur more frequently in disunited families.

3 The third mode is that if *delegation*: the adolescents enjoy a margin of limited autonomy, but they must accomplish missions which often overwhelm them. For example, a particular adolescent must fully satisfy the family's expectations in terms of social success, while another will be given the mission by one of the parents of attacking the other.

Separation problems are considered by Wynne (1965) as an excellent sign that the family therapy approach is indicated. He advocates a preliminary evaluation of the family dynamic made in conjoint interviews. During these sessions, the principal factor that has to be evaluated is the level of ambivalence and confusion on the part of the parents and the adolescent when the question of the young person's departure is raised. The revelation of interpersonal bonds of a symbiotic type and of intrusive parent–child relations usually justifies pursuing the therapeutic process. The families in which mechanisms of projective identification (which Wynne called 'trading of dissociations') predominate generally derive benefit from family therapy, since the collective suffering is great while at the same time none of the members of the family is prepared to acknowledge that he or she presents any king of psychopathological problem. The same is true of families which have to deal with an acute psychotic episode in an adolescent. According to Wynne, intensive family interviews can induce a modification of the levels of pseudo-mutuality and pseudo-hostility, and a re-casting of interpersonal distances.

The credit for having described the particular characteristics of 'counter-transference' in the treatment of families with adolescents must go to Stierlin (1975). The multiplicity of levels at which conflicts between missions and loyalties are situated often baffles the therapist, who runs the risk of departing from his or her position of neutrality. He or she faces several possible pitfalls.

First, the therapist risks the trap of taking the side of the patient 'who has been made ill by his family'. In this case, without wishing to do so, the therapist is adhering to a linear conceptualization which sees the adolescent as the innocent victim of pathogenic parents. This is to underestimate the enormous power which the adolescent enjoys in the position of consenting victim: in this role, he or she is a constant representation of the failure of the parents both emotionally and in their role in his or her upbringing and hence increases their guilt. A therapeutic strategy of this nature accelerates the escalation of mutual aggression between adolescent and parents.

Secondly, the same is true when the therapist serves as mouthpiece for the 'rebel' adolescent by de-coding, in a reductive way, the young person's behavioural disturbances (risk-taking behaviour, for example) as manifestations of opposition. In so doing, the therapist misses the transgenerational dimension of the symptom (frequent fascination of the parents for deviance) and its latent signification: in fact, above and beyond the immature forms of protest the adolescent is adopting, he or she is working him/herself ever deeper into a logic of dependence. The forging of a secret alliance with the adolescent patient is something mainly done by young therapists who, in spite of themselves, are re-playing within the context of the family interviews the failed stages of their own process of separation–individuation. Recourse to CO-THERAPY and to SUPERVISION appreciably reduces the risks of such harmful inflections of the course of the therapy. Conversely, older therapists tend to place themselves in open alliance or in competition with the adolescent's parents. These two attitudes, if they are repeated, increase the risk that the therapist will be disqualified, either by the adolescent or by the parents.

(See also ANOREXIA NERVOSA; DELEGATION; DRUG ADDICTION; INCEST; TRANSFERENCE.)

P.A. & S.A.

adolescent suicide   Suicide among adolescents will be viewed here solely from the perspective of the interactional approach. The phenomenon is one which represents a major public health preoccupation. In France, it is the second highest cause of adolescent mortality after accidents.

When dealing with a suicidal patient, it is advisable to try to ascertain the ultimate objective of their action in terms of their life-contexts: for whom and for what are they seeking to sacrifice themselves? Several pilot studies (Davidson and Choquet, 1981) indicate that the number of young people making suicide attempts in a year is between 3 and 5 per cent (in a ratio of three girls to one boy). Family factors, which are brought out by a psychosocial approach to the suicidal adolescent, play a very significant role.

THE FAMILY CONTEXT

It has been observed that, among those attempting suicide, family break-up is significantly more frequent than in a control population. There is also a higher frequency of pathological family antecedents. The existence of forebears attempting suicide, suffering from mental illness or alcoholism is found among 50 per cent of persons attempting suicide. Family alcoholism is a factor which differentiates, in a statistically significant way, between those attempting suicide for the first time and recidivists.

Particular difficulties are found at the level of intrafamilial relational problems, independent of the matrimonial status of the parents, as has been shown by a study carried out by the Institut National de la Recherche Médicale (Davidson and Angel, 1978). We may note that the percentage of young people attempting suicide who enjoy good family relations is low. In the families of those attempting suicide, paternal authority is exercised in a manner that is regarded as unsatisfactory by 59 per cent; 39 per cent find it excessive and around 20 per cent find it inadequate. Some 43 per cent identify an absence of affection or hostility on the part of the father and 30 per cent on the part of the mother.

Snakkers et al. (1980) have attempted to highlight the intrafamilial factors which either restrain or facilitate the suicidal act. One phenomenon has attracted the attention of these clinicians: a lapse in a parent's responsibilities (generally through a depressive episode) seems to be an important element in the accumulation of the significant factors leading to the suicidal behaviour. At the first collective interview, they note a consensus between parents and children to find causes outside the family for the suicide attempt.

Flavigny (1980) also takes the view that the family approach is the first phase of psychiatric action: suicidal acts by children almost always fit into a context of problems relating to major developments. Severe intrafamilial relational pathology aggravates the prognosis very appreciably. In most family situations, an adolescent's suicide attempt creates a state of tension, if not indeed of crisis. It sometimes happens that various members of the patient's immediate circle will take part in the therapeutic process and agree, with seeming interest, to attend the interviews proposed by the clinicians. The communicational dysfunction between the adolescent and his/her family seems intense. The adolescent's assessments of parental attitudes towards him/her are largely negative.

Stierlin (1979) has observed that there is a risk of attempting suicide when three orders of factors coexist at the level of the adolescent's relations with his/her circle (factors which could be detected by that circle):

1 Increasing exhaustion of the threatened subject and a growing sense of being exploited and abandoned, a feeling which, however, is neither accepted nor communicated to his/her closest relatives.
2 Deep feelings of solitude, abandonment, impotence, despair or distress, which the person concerned strives to conceal.
3 A desire for punishment and vengeance directed both against others – among whom feelings of crushing guilt will be aroused by the suicide – and against his/her own self.

FAMILY INTERVENTIONS

Very often, however, in the immediate aftermath of the suicide attempt, the adolescent, guilt-ridden as a result of the impact of his/her act, tries to suppress or deny the intrafamilial efforts to relate to him/her which, before the attempt, were a source of painful experience. The obvious content of the adolescent's comments may at times be marked by an excessive over-valuing, if not indeed idealization, of his or her parents' behaviour. All discrepancies between the parents' value system and his/her own are denied. In what they say, these young people thus tend to present the clinician with a picture of excellent family harmony to which their attempted suicide dramatically gives the lie.

Meeting the family – the parents and brothers and sisters or the important people in the young person's circle – frequently enables one to make various observations, most particularly: (a) that one or more of the family members present serious psychopathological disorders (alcoholism, recurrent depressive states etc.); (b) that this type of behaviour fits into a long-standing conflictual family dynamic. In some families, one or more of the members have already tried to put an end to their lives, are threatening to do so, or have actually committed suicide. The adolescent's suicide attempt appears in this case as a learned behaviour and, in some cases, one that is, unconsciously, positively regarded by the close circle.

The first family interview offers an opportunity to evaluate the reaction of each of the members to the young person's cry for help. Very often, one finds in the parents the same attempt at concealment or denial of conflicts, by systematically playing them down, as one found in the adolescent. The minimization of the psychological or somatic disorders presented by the adolescent over the months and weeks preceding his/her suicide attempt is also frequent. The parents will often seek an alliance with the therapist, especially where

they are in opposition to, or have broken with, their child. They set a trap for the clinician: 'Tell us why he did this . . . it'll be easier for him to tell you.' To offer any sort of response, however rudimentary, is to run the risk of disqualifying oneself, both with the adolescent, who often wishes to remain secretive about his/her act or denies all meaning to it, and with the parents themselves, who see any attempt at explanation as a criticism. By contrast, bringing the family members to take part in understanding what was going on between them at the point where suicide was attempted and placing the emphasis on the relational aspect of that behaviour rather than on the intrapsychic conflicts underlying it, is, in some cases, to lay the basis for the prevention of a subsequent attempt, as described in the work of Hollis (1987).

(See also ADOLESCENCE; ALCOHOLISM; INCEST; VIOLENCE.)

P.A. & S.A.

adoptive families　See PROCREATIVE FAMILIES, FOSTER FAMILIES, ADOPTIVE FAMILIES.

affect　See AGONISTIC BEHAVIOUR; ALIENATION; ALIGNMENT; ATTACHMENT BEHAVIOUR; DOUBLE BIND; EIDOS; ETHOS; FAMILY MYTHS; FAMILY SYSTEMS; FUSION; HUMOUR; INSTINCT; INSTITUTIONAL MYTHS; LOVE; METAPSYCHOLOGY; MOURNING; RESIDUAL RELATIONS; SEXED BEHAVIOUR; SYMBOLIC REFERENCE.

affiliation or joining　In individual development (ontogenesis), affiliation is the ritualized behaviour which develops during the earliest months and is distinct from ATTACHMENT BEHAVIOUR. Described by Bretherton (1974), Bretherton and Ainsworth (1974) and discussed by Lamb (1976), affiliation behaviour is more electively orientated towards the father figure and its substitutes. It is characterized by the following features: smiling, looks, vocalizations and laughter. It develops gradually on the basis of mechanisms of imitation and contributes to the establishment of processes of identification.

The ritual of affiliation or 'joining' is used for therapeutic ends (Minuchin, 1974): the therapist is led to join in, to some extent, with the mode of organization and style of the family, so that the latter will accept him/her more openly and therapeutic change can be brought about. This 'affiliation' may be directed towards the family as a whole (mainly in the early stages of therapy) or towards certain sub-systems, as a function of the various strategies or tactics brought to bear at particular points.

Together with the creation of transactions and restructuring, operations of joining are one of the three main intervention techniques in structural family therapy, as elaborated by Minuchin (1974). They place emphasis on the need for the therapist to choose the attitude he/she is going to adopt towards the family, avoiding the trap of false neutrality. They seek to respond to the double objective of creating the therapeutic system and preserving the therapist's position as leader within that system. Joining the family is a necessary condition for restructuring techniques to be effective. It embraces the 'actions of the therapist aimed directly at relating to family members or the family system' (Minuchin, 1974, p. 123). 'Accommodation', 'tracking' and 'mimesis' are the three main techniques of such affiliation.

ACCOMMODATION

As is well known, for Piaget (1976), the equilibration of cognitive structures begins with dialectical pairing, accommodation and assimilation. In the sessions, the therapist makes personal adjustments, such as adopting the linguistic peculiarities of the family. This is done with a view to forming an effective alliance with the family. What is involved here is a style of intervention calculated to realize a therapeutic alliance and to find resonances with the familial ETHOS. The therapist thus affiliates him/herself with the family by fitting in with its habitual relational models and respecting its rules and its customary channels of communication. For example, in a couple where the father seems to be the spokesperson, the therapist goes through him initially in order to establish contact with the mother.

The notion of accommodation also covers the idea of active confirmation of the family or of the specific traits of an individual or family subgroup by the therapist.

TRACKING

In this technique, the therapist 'follows the content of the family's communications and behaviour and encourages them to continue. He is like a needle tracking grooves in a record. In its simplest form, tracking means to ask clarifying questions, to make approving comments, or to elicit amplification of a point' (Minuchin, 1974, p. 127). He or she therefore follows the content of communications rather like the free association model of psychoanalytic therapists.

MIMESIS

For Minuchin, within every human relationship there exists an inevitable degree of MIMESIS between the participants. The therapist may use this natural process as a way of getting close to the family.

The therapist joins the family system, then, taking on the style and content of its communications and adopting, for example, the tempo, vocabulary, tone and even certain gestures of the family members. He/she may also, in order to stimulate the creation of the therapeutic system, share in certain personal experiences with the family. Thus, for Minuchin (1974, p. 128), 'The therapist is like the family members in all the universals of the human condition. Therefore, situations will always arise in which they have common experiences. The therapist can emphasize these to blend with the family in a mimetic operation.' Affiliation techniques thus enable the therapist, by adopting an active attitude, to become an 'actor in the family drama', by lessening the distance between himself and the family.

(See also BOUNDARIES; FAMILY STRUCTURES.)

A.L., P.S. & J.M.

aggression See AGONISTIC BEHAVIOUR; INCEST; TERRITORY; VIOLENCE.

agonistic behaviour All activity relating to combat, appeasement or retreat is *agonistic* (from the Greek 'agonistikos', meaning 'relating to struggle in games and discussion'). Aggression relates to an attack upon another's physical or psychical territorial integrity. It presupposes a limitation of the living space of the victim of the aggression, an intrusion into that space, if not indeed the complete destruction of the individual concerned.

In animals we can make a distinction between intra-species aggressive behaviour (establishment and defence of territory, sexual rivalry) and inter-species aggressive behaviour (search for food, predation). These two forms of aggression are interdependent. Intra-species aggressive behaviour appears in species that are capable of inter-individual recognition and equipped to establish relations with certain individuals and to reject those felt to be outsiders. But there also exist forms of collective aggression by one community of conspecifics against another.

In man this distinction is transformed as an effect of PSEUDO-SPECIATION. Man draws up cultural boundaries, establishes new personal and collective territories with the aid of ever more elaborate MAPS. The symbolic levels of VIOLENCE and of agonistic behaviour have not put an end to direct violence. In some ways they have exacerbated it, by virtue of the possible confusion between maps and territories. Man has become a universal predator: a predator towards all other species and towards the members of his own species in warfare.

We may distinguish between:

1 Levels of aggression: phantasy, playful exchange, threat, provocation, verbal aggression, physical aggression, lethal aggression. Phantasy patterns signifying the nature of the aggression also fall into this last category.

2 Forms of aggression: interpersonal, intrafamilial and social aggression; collective, clan, social and group aggression; the interaction of aggressive behaviour may produce the phenomenon of scapegoating.

3 Functions of aggression: aggression in the search for food, territorial aggression, aggression in the effort to establish hierarchical differentiation, the aggression of rivalry and competition, sexual aggression, legal and illegal aggression.

THE PHYLOGENETIC BASES OF AGONISTIC BEHAVIOUR

For Lorenz and his school, inter-individual aggressive behaviour rests upon a phylogenetic base. In the evolution of species, every form of inter-individual recognition and of interpersonal contact goes together with the existence of aggressive behaviour. The aggressive dimension is particularly evident in the establishment of a couple, which is obliged to learn to ritualize its exchanges and to elaborate appeasement behaviours through a phenomenon of BECOMING ACCUSTOMED. Acts of aggression assume a typical form within a given species. They have an instinctive, spontaneous character and are released by autonomous centres (internal oscillators), but are also dependent upon internal and external stimuli. Indeed, they are expressed as part of appetent behaviours and therefore of forms of learning dependent on family and social contexts. This means that the interactive point of view cannot be reduced to the study of a syntax of individual and collective behaviours. It has been the merit of the objectivist school (Lorenz, Tinbergen, Huxley) that it has identified the semiotic structure on which the transition from aggressive behaviours to appeasement behaviours, greeting ceremonials and friendly and loving behaviour is based. These last mentioned are a secondary channelling of the crude aggressive sequences, in a manner typical of RITUALIZATION. A greeting ceremonial depends for its expression on partly modified aggressive sequences being expressed: the aggressive movement may be directed towards a fictive conspecific; it includes 'mock aggression', in which there are indications to show that what is happening is not real aggression.

SEMIOLOGY AND ONTOGENESIS OF AGONISTIC BEHAVIOUR

Children spontaneously develop aggressive acts and, in some cases, also rituals of appeasement or threat, or games which deflect the aggressive intention from its goal and reduce the intensity of the direct charge of aggression. All these acts are absent to a particularly high degree among autistic children.

Threatening behaviour

The signals indicating threatening behaviour are: open mouth, high-pitched or intense vocalizations, clenched fists, pronation of the hand, index finger pointed towards the person being threatened, arms spread wide, head thrust forward, upper body thrust forward, sudden forward movement, blows which are 'pulled', arms thrust out toward the person under threat.

Aggressive behaviour

The signals indication aggressive behaviour are taken from among the following: blow with the hand or fist, kick, hair-pulling, tugging at clothing, shaking, pulling or pushing till the opponent falls, seizing an object without being asked, snatching an object from someone's hands, hitting someone with an object, throwing an object at another person, pushing someone against a wall.

Bonding and appeasement behaviour

The main signals indicating bonding and appeasement are: smiling, inclining the head to one side, inclining the trunk to one side, shaking the head, supination of the hand, lightly touching, offering gifts, caressing, kissing, taking someone's hand, putting one's arm around someone's neck, assuming the squatting position, clapping, vocal exchanges, bending one's legs, tapping, rotating one's trunk, hopping about on the spot, turning halfway or right around.

Fear-withdrawal behaviour

The main signals indicating fear-withdrawal behaviour are: arm raised for protection, leaning back of the head, drawing back of the trunk or limbs, drawing back the whole body, shedding tears after interaction, flight.

During development, threat and aggression may also be expressed verbally. The child, when put in contact with adults and other children, develops a whole series of signals. These signals structure profiles of behaviour and play a role in the identification of the modalities of communication. They determine the nature of the relations established and produce effects of social hierarchization. The position within a hierarchy is related to the nature of family relations (Montagner, 1978).

PREDATORY BEHAVIOUR

Not content with systematically preying upon the animal species that are necessary to him, man also preys upon other men and has become a kind of universal predator. He takes up again, both on the level of the real and the symbolic, the phylogenetic techniques of predation: ambushes, traps (and the use of lures), and hunting singly or in groups. Human predation is both biological and symbolic. Predatory behaviours determine the form of intra-group and inter-group aggression, as well as the ritualization of that aggression (licit and illicit rivalries).

Not only does man consume other species, but he

kills other men, imprisons them and seeks to submit them to his rule. He incorporates the image, thinking and emotions of others into himself. This function of universal predator poses the problem of war and violence at all levels of society. Violence and warfare are directly related to the birth of identity, the construction of territories on various levels of symbolic organization. They are a by-product of economic constraints. It is evident that the techniques of predation reappear in the phenomenon of war, though this is certainly not reducible to a purely phylogenetic analysis. War is a complex ritual which has been modified over the course of history. It plays a considerable role in the formation of national identities, the establishment of collective territories and of laws to which the citizens of those territories are subject.

PHANTASIES OF AGGRESSION

To the extent that humanity is more a meta-species than a real species and processes of pseudo-speciation have occurred within it (see also DOMESTICATION), the distinction between intra-species and inter-species aggressive behaviour is to a certain extent abolished. More precisely, confusions appear in the hierarchical levels between these systems of behaviour on the one hand and the 'objects' towards which they are directed. Only through phantasy activity can a reorganization and structuring of aggressive behaviour be achieved in man. Through the superego, social prohibitions can be interiorized. These are passed on to the child in the course of his or her upbringing. On the level of psychical representations, Freud emphasized the relationship of anaclisis between the sexual instincts and the instincts of self-preservation (the search for food). Each stage of psychosexual evolution (oral, anal and phallic) has a characteristic tone and mode of aggression.

The family theoretic approach shows that the distinction between phantasy activity and the activation of agonistic behaviour is far from being as clear-cut as it might appear. Phantasy activity has the function of enabling aggressive drives to be worked out mentally. To take another aspect, it is Bowlby's view (1969–80) that actual threats uttered in childhood and really aggressive behaviour are of crucial importance in the generation of anxious attachments or of various behavioural disturbances. Family therapy seems particularly to be recommended when phantasy organization no longer fulfils its role as a shield against excitation or when it can no longer be distinguished from other modes of communication. It is also necessary when the mechanisms regulating aggression degenerate into pure violence, for want of territorial, material and psychical space.

INTRAFAMILIAL AGGRESSION

The family is the site of the primary experience of aggressive behaviour, both as regards its direct expression and the channelling of such behaviour. These experiences have repercussions in the socialization of the child and the hierarchical position he/she will occupy within his/her age group. In interaction, agonistic behaviours lead to the creation of TRIANGLES and COALITIONS.

Intra-generational aggression
Conjugal aggression can be thought of as part of a reciprocal definition of roles and tasks. Each partner, seeking an ideal complement to, or a reparation of, an idealized parental *imago*, comes to blame the other for not adequately fulfilling the expected functions. In a sense, war begins within the conjugal couple: it is in intimate relationships that violence is most intense (Pennachionni, 1986). The couple is thus under pressure from the more or less successful systems of alliance between the families of origin and from the relations established with the children.

Phenomena of *fraternal rivalry* are expressed differently depending on the anthropological structure of the family concerned (see NUCLEAR FAMILY). Fraternal rivalry may express itself in the effort to win parental affection. It is structured as a function of the positions of the brothers and sisters in relation to one another (age difference, ordinal position in the family), depending upon the nature of the forms of intra-conjugal aggression and the material and psychical space available to each person within the family group.

Transgenerational aggression
The *aggression of parents towards their children* takes various forms, as a function of the development and degree of maturity of the child. It expresses itself:

1 *At the moment of weaning* (primary separation from the mother).
2 *With educative intent* (learning of limits, establishment of material and phantasmatic territories). The total absence of aggressive response on the part of the parents often leads to an increase in the aggressive potential of the child. Violence is normally born out of the incapacity to ritualize the child's spontaneous aggression and the inability to draw up personal security boundaries for all the partners in the relationship.
3 *By distancing* in the transition from adolescence to the adult state. This transition is a particular source of conflict. It may assume a pathological form in the schizophrenic double bind by a confusion of the levels of autonomization. It is very often at this point that the mother tries to push her child from her while, on another level, the child maintains a symbiotic relation which exacerbates the attempt at distancing.

With *children's aggression towards their parents* the typical experience of bi-generational conflict is the

Oedipal confrontation. It is a characteristic feature of the Oedipal structure that it brings phantasies of love and aggression together in a triangulation of relations between the child and his/her parents. It stabilizes psychical representations and enables conflicts to be mentally hierarchized. Phantasies of aggression enable the child mentally to work through threatening, aggressive and predatory behaviours. In adolescence, a dramatic swing may occur: the adolescent actualizes his/her revolt and expresses his/her aggressive tendencies more or less directly and violently. This actualization may come to grief for various reasons, preventing the maturing experience of adolescence from occurring. The parents may be afraid of this confrontation, which is no longer merely a phantasy conflict, but has consequences in reality in which their own future and that of their child is concerned. This confrontation may in some cases take on an aggravated character and lead to schizophrenic episodes or to the parent-beating syndrome (see VIOLENCE).

Multigenerational aggression may break out at moments of conflict between parents and grandparents over the children; this aggression may express itself directly in the form of an attack by a child on a grandparent or a grandparent on a child, leading possibly to the creation of PERVERSE TRIANGLES. The extreme form of such aggression comes with the psychotic explosion, the structure of the parental couple being unable to cope any longer with the vertical affective encroachments.

SUPRAFAMILIAL AGGRESSION

Interpersonal social aggression
Where acts of aggression take place that society condemns, the legal system or psychiatry are often called upon to intervene. Such forms of behaviour appear from the socialization of the child at school onwards or when the young adult enters the world of work. Family and network therapies thus function most often at the interface of exchanges between family groups and wider social groups.

Family–society aggression
This runs in both directions. Society seeks to protect itself from certain intrafamilial abuses and to control the modes of thought and action of family systems (see ALIENATION; FAMILY ETHNOLOGY; INCEST). Conversely, some family groups may be opposed to the institutions of a given society and even seek to subvert them.

Clan and inter-group aggression
The defence of territories is a significant factor at all levels of social organization. Clans, ethnic groups, classes, churches, nations and multinational enterprises seek to defend their identity and also fall prey to many confrontations, which are sources of historical violence. These have been analysed by Bateson (1972) in 'Culture contact and schismogenesis' from the angle of symmetrical and complementary SCHISMOGENESIS.

(See also ATTACHMENT BEHAVIOUR; DOUBLE BIND; IDENTIFICATION; LAW; LEVELS OF COMMUNICATION; LOVE; MAPS; MIMESIS; RECIPROCAL VICTIMIZATION AND RESCUE; SCAPEGOAT; SEXED BEHAVIOUR; TERRITORY.)

J.M. & P.G.

agreement and disagreement Processes by which two or more persons come to define together, explicitly or implicitly, the nature of their exchanges. These presuppose a process unfolding over time where rituals of personal encounter are synchronized. From a formal point of view, the definition of agreements and disagreements bears on the different hierarchical levels of communication: index and order, content and relationship (see PRAGMATICS OF COMMUNICATION) and contributes to the organization and disorganization of conscious, preconscious and unconscious phantasmatic resonances. From a semantic point of view, agreement is based on instinctual, representational and phantasmatic resonances which are, to a large extent, not conscious (see SEMANTICS OF COMMUNICATION).

CONTENT AND RELATIONSHIP

Looking for areas of agreement and the recognition of points of disagreement within a couple or a family is a useful means of identifying the nature of communication, as well as possible dysfunctions within it (see INTERACTIONAL TYPOLOGIES OF THE FAMILY). It will be noted that forms of pseudo-agreement or pseudo-disagreement exist which do not stand up long against the test of reality.

In a couple, a discordance may arise between the *content* and the *relationship* aspects of communication, so that a disagreement may emerge at the relationship level, while agreement persists at the level of content; thus, for example, 'we agree on everything, but I can't allow you to have the last word.' Conversely, there may be agreement about the relationship, whereas there seems to be total disagreement about the content: in this case, the couple will give the impression of not agreeing about anything, while a deep mutual understanding exists between the two quite openly to display opposite points of view (Watzlawick et al., 1967, see PRAGMATICS OF COMMUNICATION). In other situations, the members of a family will define themselves as 'very united', though their bodily, intellectual, emotional and phantasmatic resonances will result in a chaotic disorganization of interactions.

COUPLING OF RESONANCES

In the situation analysed here in this abstract way, the couple or group involved will have the wholly subjective impression either of being or of not being on the same wavelength, of vibrating to the same emotions, of being either in phase or not. In every ritualized exchange, the synchronization of gestures, of nods of the head, of rises in the tone of voice or of styles of thinking, speaking and feeling leads to the periodic repetition of events, making it possible to regulate and define the nature of the exchange.

In clinical practice, the arrival of a child (particularly of the firstborn) or the death of a close relative completely transforms the rhythms of encounters and hence the periodicities set in place by the partners and their own parents; in effect, the slow periodicities of life-cycles cut across the micro-synchronizations of daily life and destroy the pre-existing phantasmatic harmonies. Depending on the quality of boundaries and the nature and intensity of resonances between generations, chaotic interactions may appear, which destabilize the habitual rhythms of life by modification of the system's ATTRACTORS.

The phenomena of agreement and disagreement which ensue will have effects upon the therapeutic and institutional systems consulted. Two approaches to intervention are then possible:

1 One may seek to stabilize the boundaries within which the chaotic regime has established itself, which presupposes that the therapists first manage to 'come to an agreement among themselves' or to 'dramatize' the disagreements which exist among them, in so far as these are induced by the family system (see PLAY).
2 Or one may give a stimulus to new frequencies with a view to bringing about a meta-stable state (change, far from the equilibrium state).

(See also ANALOGIC CODING; COALITIONS; DIGITAL CODING; DISSIPATIVE STRUCTURES; OSCILLATORS; PERVERSE TRIANGLES; SEMANTIC RESONANCES; TRIANGLES.)

J.M.

alcoholism, alcoholics   If one considers alcoholism as the excessive, repeated and prolonged consumption of alcoholic drinks or as the 'intermittent or permanent intake of alcohol leading to dependence or bringing about harmful effects' (Davis et al., 1974, cited by Ades, 1985) there is no ambiguity in the definition of an alcoholic. An alcoholic is an individual who has lost her/his freedom of consumption in relation to alcohol, towards which he/she now has only a stark alternative: abstinence or inebriation.

From an interactional point of view, the alcoholic is seen as protecting his/her family from intolerable levels of anguish, anxiety or depression. Further evidence of this is given by the frequent decompensation of one or more members of the family when the alcoholic stops drinking. An example of positive feedback may be identified when the patient's spouse re-stocks the house with alcohol or, in spite of herself, encourages her husband to go out to places where lots of drink is to be had.

Family therapists took an interest in this pathology at a very early stage, and family therapy has proved to be very strongly indicated as a treatment. None the less, it needed various different currents of thinking to play their part in the conceptualization of models for social and family theoretic approaches to this symptom, which is extremely common in Western countries.

ALCOHOLIC PERSONALITY AND/OR SOCIAL ENVIRONMENT?

The excessive drinker and the alcoholic
The alcoholic is incapable of regulating his/her alcohol consumption; the only alternative is 'all or nothing', abstinence or inebriation. He/she is thus distinct from the *excessive drinker* who is very largely determined by social and cultural circuits, and uses alcohol as an integration ritual, as a drug to quell his/her anxiety and reduce his/her inhibitions or simply to conceal his/her misery (even though he/she suffers the toxic effects of alcohol on the nervous system, liver and glands). The excessive drinker stops when his/her required intake is reached.

Sociofamilial factors
A study carried out by Sieber (1979) on 84 young men seen at the ages of 19 and 22 shows that alcohol abuse is related more to sociofamilial factors (the low social status of the father, poor relations with the parents, poor socio-professional integration) and to other forms of abuse (excessive smoking, cannabis) than to personality factors. The only common feature observed among future excessive drinkers was greater emotional lability, while in other studies common factors of impulsiveness and individualistic tendencies have been found. The initial nexus of alcoholism therefore emerges: to young people who find socialization difficult, the collective mentality offers alcohol as a means of integration, and even, in some cases, prescribes it (it is well known that alcoholism often begins during military service).

Admittedly, the frequency and the qualitative and quantitative character of drinking varies a great deal from one individual to another. Nevertheless, in general it takes the form of a habit. Repeating forms of behaviour at regular intervals, which we usually call habit formation, is doubtless a major vital process. It extends and economizes the adaptive capacities on which Bateson (1972) lays such emphasis. Alcohol dependence only makes its appearance where there is a prior drinking habit. And that habit is a social effect.

First, at the *macrosystemic level*. In 1956, the mathematician Ledermann studied the frequency of the distribution of alcohol consumption in France (the average was around 30 litres of pure alcohol per year). It emerged that two-thirds of consumers in France drank less than the average and one-third more than the average. Ledermann showed that there was mathematical co-variance between average consumption and excessive consumption, where the latter was established by a disorder of the liver or nervous system. He concluded that average consumption and excessive consumption are represented by statistical values which are not independent and that a variation in one brought about a variation in the other. Nahas (1982) extended this model to other addictive drugs. In other words, this means that it is necessary for there to be a risk of serious toxicity for a small percentage of the population, before the majority is able to find pleasure.

Secondly, at the *microsocial level*. It is obvious that the family environment plays a fundamental role in alcohol consumption habits. Children brought up in a milieu where alcohol is freely available in large quantities, regarded as normal or even viewed in a positive light are certainly under threat of becoming alcoholics at an early age, but they particularly acquire a potential for later alcoholism through the familial ritualization of drinking. Nevertheless, when one or both parents are alcoholics, though their offspring tend to imitate them, that imitation seems to end at the point where the parents' behaviour is perceived as extreme. Harburg et al. (1982), in a study covering 1153 people, found that the children of parents whose alcoholism was associated with major interpersonal problems or with loss of social status, did not follow their behaviour, any more than did the children of abstemious parents. It would appear that experiencing the rigidity of abstemious parents only taught an 'all or nothing' attitude and that witnessing alcohol-related problems produced a protective aversion. It is the children of moderate drinkers who most willingly copy the attitudes of their parents.

The multiplicity of roles which devolve upon the child of alcoholic parents often places him or her outside any intergenerational demarcation lines. As parent substitute for his or her younger brothers and sisters, marital substitute in coalition – and an Oedipal complicity – with the non-alcoholic parent, or victim of the incestuous violence of the alcoholic parent of the opposite sex, he or she tries desperately to stand out against the break-up, which is always imminent, of the couple, for which he or she is the go-between, counsellor and family therapist. This is very often to the detriment of the child, though on occasion it helps to advance his or her maturation (Pilat and Jones, 1985). This adaptive result does not seem particularly probable, however, when the child is physically maltreated. There are lines of descent in which, at each new generation, the ex-battered child of a 'drinker' beats his children in his turn, in a context where alcohol has some part (91 per cent of cases in a sample of 51 children who were victims of physical abuse according to Behling, 1979, who stresses that this is a specific sub-category and that in no sense is alcoholism alone sufficient to cause maltreatment of a child).

The social and familial factors, which are clear to see in the case of the excessive drinker, do not, then, explain how he/she becomes transformed into an alcoholic, except in so far as they suggest a specific personality type characterized by impulsiveness, by phobic traits in men and hysterical narcissistic traits in women, or, as some writers believe, a metabolic predisposition.

Drinking habit and drink dependence

The transition from a drinking habit to drink dependence remains a perplexing problem. It seems plausible that we should be able to describe it better by reinserting it into the complex and hierarchic sequence of processes that determine our behaviour. The first stage in this is the perception of reality which, in this case, is a sum of communicational indices. Drawn from the environment, these indices depend on a deterministic coding. More precisely, they correspond to biological constraints and also to symbolic necessities. The former are connected to the genetic programme and the latter to different levels of cultural learning. As with the consumption of other drugs, the drinking of alcohol introduces radical modifications into the vast system of behaviour and its regulation. It profoundly re-defines the perception of the environment, in both its sensible and symbolic dimensions. It is radically distinct from habitual adaptive behaviour and leads to the perception of an environment seen as constraining and imposing alcoholism. The paradoxical result is that chronic alcoholism is experienced as alienating by those around the alcoholic whereas he or she constantly invokes his or her autonomy. The alcoholic counters our repeated denials by insisting on his or her freedom to be dependent. While a drinker generally adopts an analogical form of behaviour towards alcohol, the alcoholic adopts a binary form (no alcohol or never enough alcohol).

Since the social and the somatic confront one another here, the transition occurs in *catastrophist mode*. In the movement from the one to the other we see in the alcoholic a brutal inversion of the sense of regulatory mechanisms. In biology, the regulatory mechanisms identified generally function in an agonistic–antagonistic mode. When one process is accelerated, there is a parallel braking process. Out of this conflictual equilibrium there emerge possibilities of gradual, fine regulation. By contrast, in alcoholism, where Bateson (1972) uses the metaphor of failing brakes, in 'Cybernetics of "self": a theory of alcoholism', we would suggest that there is also an accelerator jammed down as far as it will go.

The alcoholic system

There thus emerges the *outline of an alcoholic system*. Under certain constraints upon consumption, which are (represented as) individual and social, the habitual drinker becomes dependent. Clinical experience teaches that this alcoholic behaviour is then definitively acquired. In practice, the alcoholic will only be able to adopt one of two attitudes: abstinence or drunkenness. For a long time he/she will oscillate between these two attitudes, arousing at best incomprehension among those around him/her who are abstainers or light drinkers.

Therapists know the following stage, which seems just as disconcerting, very well. Spontaneous attempts to wean him or herself off alcohol alternate with severe relapses. Intoxication and abstinence oscillate at a lesser frequency, but one that is comparable with that seen in chronic intoxication. Therapists are not therefore in a comfortable situation. Pharmacology does not offer them any adequate model of biochemical dependence, though it is probable, however, that this also plays its part.

Therapies that are psychoanalytic in inspiration run up against other logical 'binds':

1 Drinking alcohol is normal in Western countries (where psychoanalysis is widely practised). The psychotherapist cannot avoid it, being him or herself sometimes a prudent drinker.
2 The watchword of a well-conducted analysis is 'become oneself'. Bateson (1972) shows us how much this paradigm is doomed to failure in the case of the alcoholic in 'Cybernetics of "self": a theory of alcoholism'.
3 The psychoanalytic relationship is built on transference. The relationship with the alcoholic should then lead the psychotherapist, sooner or later, either into a dionysiac fusion with him/her, or to abstinence. Otherwise, the therapist will find him or herself in a situation of powerlessness.

Associations of ex-drinkers

This leaves the associations of ex-drinkers. The paradoxes here seem no less acute. These associations are viewed with suspicion by institutional medicine and they reply in kind. Yet it is they who obtain the best results. When an alcoholic backslides, they explain to him/her that this offers him/her the source of a cure. The cabbalistic tradition gives the same numerical value to Yain (the Hebrew word for 'wine') as to Sod, which means 'secret'. The Roman tradition adds *in vino veritas*. For alcoholics, the truth and the secret are that 'alcohol is stronger than we are'. What is the point of fighting against its seductive power? Better rather to fear it and flee from it, to deify it rather than defy it. The alcoholic is initiated into this truth by a former drinker turned prophet. This stage is indispensable for the complementary fusion with the community of ex-drinkers in which the therapeutic effect is achieved. This belonging

to a community constitutes a matrix for the re-learning of new inter-individual regulations. Thus an astonishing social process is accomplished, whose meta-logic – of a religious type – has nothing paradoxical about it. Moreover, Jung (1964), who was so sensitive to the role of collective myths in the structuring of personality, had, in his own day, played a decisive role in the birth of Alcoholics Anonymous, referring to 'the thirst for union with God' as the meaning of the symptom.

Bateson (1972) proposes a model of the therapeutic action of Alcoholics Anonymous, which was to develop very significantly thanks to its co-founders Bill W. and Dr Bob Bateson (1972) offers a detailed conceptualization of this group model in his article 'Cybernetics of "self": a theory of alcoholism', and suggests:

(1) that an entirely new epistemology must come out of cybernetics and systems theory, involving a new understanding of mind, self, human relationship and power; (2) that the addicted alcoholic is operating, when sober, in terms of an epistemology which is conventional in Occidental culture but which is not acceptable to systems theory; (3) that surrender to alcoholic intoxication provides a partial and subjective short cut to a more correct state of mind; and (4) that the theology of Alcoholics Anonymous coincides closely with an epistemology of cybernetics. (Bateson, 1972, p. 280)

Bateson analyses the stages in the Alcoholics Anonymous process stressing certain points, such as the basic position of the alcoholic towards alcohol; and the alcoholic's attitude of pride which gets him/her into a process of symmetrical escalation. The use of the 'theology' of Alcoholics Anonymous enables the alcoholic to modify his/her symmetrical relation by allowing him/her, through putting a complete halt to his/her addiction, to move to a complementary position. The starting point for this epistemological change is the admission that the bottle will always remain stronger than the alcoholic.

Bateson is, however, cautious in his analysis, admitting the existence of several modalities of alcoholic behaviour, which vary in relation to the specific practices of different civilizations and cultures. It is therefore desirable to work out an appropriate therapeutic epistemology for each case. This model of change will be largely taken into account by the different therapies, as also will be the social structures which they engender.

Bateson's stroke of genius is to offer us here a pertinent epistemology with which to approach this illness, an illness of which the subject is cured as soon as he understands that he is suffering from it. As for therapists, against the normal run of their practice, their strategy will have to be to ally themselves with the sick part of the person they are attempting to treat.

ALCOHOLISM AND FAMILY THERAPY

Alcoholism and family micro-systems

The United States has been in the vanguard of treatment here, as in all forms of systemic practice. Forms of family therapy have developed in response to various clinical observations: the fact that alcoholic patients' symptoms often reappeared on their return to their homes; the complexity of the family ties of alcoholic patients with their families of origin; the interaction of patients in their relations with their spouses. These practices take place in a different register from that of the associations of ex-drinkers (see above).

It was in fact as long ago as 1937 that Robert Knight showed the role of family factors in the aetiology of alcoholism. He described the impact of a dominating mother and a passive father. The family approach did not, however, begin to develop until the 1950s, the period in which systems theory began to gain currency. Interest was then directed towards the study of alcoholics' marriages, and group techniques were set in place for the wives of alcoholics. The symptom of 'alcoholism' was no longer conceived solely in intra-psychic terms but entered the interfactional field and the first forms of treatment for alcoholic families were established. Various authors wrote on the subject. In addition to Peter Steinglass (1979), we can mention Ewing and Fox (1968) who showed the role of alcoholics' wives in maintaining the status quo; the passive dependency needs of the husbands reciprocally encouraged the attitude of their wives. Davis et al. (1974) and Steinglass et al. (1977) see alcohol abuse as fulfilling adaptive functions which reinforce one another and strengthen the drink habit.

It is crucial to take account of the different levels of functioning of the couple, of the families of origin and of the psychic processes if one is to set in place a coherent therapy.

Systemic models of alcoholic families

Two Anglo-Saxon writers have devoted particular attention to this pathology. Like the majority of clinicians who have worked with this type of family, Murray Bowen (1978a) puts the emphasis on the high level of anxiety he perceives. The excessive use of alcohol appears to palliate this symptom. He draws on his theory of the DIFFERENTIATION OF SELF to explain this behaviour: the alcoholic marries a wife of the same degree of self-differentiation, with very strong relations with her family of origin. The alcoholic is very attached to his mother, but adopts a 'super-independent' position. He thus denies his relational needs, a denial reinforced by his wife and children. He becomes isolated and his anxiety is relieved by the consumption of alcohol. Bowen also describes another interactional pattern relating to alcoholism among young adults: they remain very attached to their parents and more particularly to their mother and are incapable of managing their personal lives. They take to drink early, thus affirming a *pseudo-independence*. Their denial mechanisms enable them to function in this way. These cases might be regarded as similar to what we shall see to be the interactions within the families of drug addicts (see DRUG ADDICTION).

David Berenson (1976) identifies five major difficulties in the treatment of alcoholics and their families:

1 The trap of causality: like the patient, the therapist tends to privilege a particular order of causality, whether biological, psychodynamic, sociological etc. It is by freeing oneself from an over-reductive, linear mode of thinking that one becomes more effective.
2 The plurality of contextual levels has to be kept constantly in view, in order for a hierarchy of modes of intervention to be established.
3 The alcoholic's sense of responsibility and that of those around him has to be appealed to, with correspondingly less appeal being made to the patient's will.
4 The therapist's renunciation of the position of saviour enables him or her to avoid becoming trapped in an endless game with the patient and his family.
5 One must clarify the objectives that are to be attained. The effectiveness of the therapy can be evaluated in terms of abstinence and of behaviour within the family and the socio-professional milieu. Therapeutic choices are difficult to make. The therapist's not focusing upon the alcoholic behaviour brings with it as many risks of failure as an over-exclusive preoccupation with the symptom.

One other observation must be added here: alcoholism is often at the root of VIOLENCE within the family.

Therapeutic interventions

We shall in fact distinguish between various familial approaches:

- couple therapy;
- family therapy taking in the nuclear family;
- multiple family therapy;
- network therapies taking into account the community environment.

Sometimes, clinicians will adopt various joint approaches (for example, marital and family therapy etc.), the better to deal with the complexity of the problem. There are considerable differences between the different schools (structural, strategic, psychoanalytic etc.) as regards the rhythm of sessions and their length.

In Europe, the family therapy of alcoholics has developed only very gradually and group therapy approaches have generally predominated. We should, however, mention the contribution of Cassiers (1982), who analysed the family function of alcoholism. Following Bateson, he observes that it is in the field of ethics or morality that the most paradoxical 'knot' often appears in these families. He remarks that, not only the alcoholic, but very often those close to him/her at one and the same time maintain the most classic moral ideals and yet fall most lamentably short of them. The alcoholic thus seems a constant witness to the fact that classic morality, understood in a particular way, is absurd and unsustainable, but has to be sustained all the same. Such family systems adopt reasoning of the 'all or nothing' type: if you become attached to your partner, you lose or reject your parents; if you are in conflict on a particular point as a couple, the whole of the life of the couple is at stake. This all or nothing dialectic makes such families particularly fragile; they cannot manage their conflicts, their sexuality or their anxiety. According to Cassiers, the therapist's task perhaps consists in making it appear to the different members of the family that, though behaviour is, as such, relatively unambiguous, the ideas and the desires which underlie it are many and varied.

(See also INCEST; SYMPTOMATIC AND/OR AETIOLOGICAL TRANSACTIONS.)

G.E., P.A., S.A. & G.G.M.

alethic (modalities) The semiotic modality, as defined by Greimas and Courtes (1979), of ontological necessity ('having-to-be') and its structural oppositions on the SEMIOTIC SQUARE which are impossibility ('having-not-to-be'), possibility ('not-having-not-to-be') and contingency (not-having-to-be).

For Greimas and Courtes (1979), the semiotic square is a basic semiotic structure which describes the inter-human modalities of communication in linguistic terms. A sign is structured within a system in which it may be opposed to its absence, to its opposite or to the absence of its opposite. The alethic modalities (from the Greek 'aletheia': truth, as opposed to error or lying) produce the indispensable social conditions ('having to be') for veridiction or truth-saying. This latter relates to the system of oppositions structuring the relationship between being, appearing, non-being and non-appearing.

In Greimas's semiotics, 'having to be' is one of the possible predicates (the predicate is a syntactic function, corresponding normally to the verb or the verbal syntagm) of utterances of state or of doing. A modality is what modifies the predicate. 'Utterances of state' correspond to the person's being and identity and hence to his/her legal or official status, while 'utterances of doing' correspond to his/her acts, to the style of relations he/she actually produces at the pragmatic or cognitive level and thus to his/her social or semi-official status. On the semiotic square, utterances of state produce the following structure: being, appearing, not

being, not appearing; while utterances of action produce the following structure: doing, doing passively, not doing, not doing passively.

It seems a good idea to take these semiotic modalities and re-situate them in the context of familial and social processes; in practice, so far as alethic modalities are concerned, each person in a family is faced with the following choices of identity:

- positive: having to be something or someone;
- negative: having not to be something or someone;
- contingent: not having to be something or someone;
- possible: not having not to be something or someone.

These choices take their orientation, to a greater or lesser degree, from FAMILY MYTHS. In a particular familial and/or social context, one has to be brave, obstinate, alluring, athletic, hard-working, modest, boastful, artistic etc. In some other context, the myth will be able to impose behaviour which is, for preference, possible or contingent. In this case, the fact of 'having to be' or 'having not to be' something or someone will be proscribed.

These alethic modalities will be more or less consonant with the DEONTIC MODALITIES of 'having to do'. It will not be possible to recognize certain actions as authentic if they come from a person whose identity is not in keeping with the action in question. A child may act as the family's 'therapist', even when his or her identity does not permit of his or her being recognized as such. The construction of his/her identity may, similarly, be impaired by tasks which exceed his/her competence.

The transition from alethic modalities to deontic modalities (and vice versa) corresponds to profound changes in the economy of a person and the groups to which he or she belongs and by which he or she is recognized. Carrying out a corpus of actions to their end leads to a modification of the identity of the person in question. A 'therapist' child may thus end up becoming an authentic therapist.

Conformity with the operant myth is perceived within the group which shares in that myth as grounding 'true', authentic – and, indeed, model – behaviour. It may, on the other hand, be perceived as inauthentic by outside observers. In moments of crisis, the accepted alethic modalities may be put in question, creating conflicts of a more or less open character between parents, children, social workers and therapists.

On a psychoanalytic level, these semiotic modalities are the linguistic reflection of the agencies of the superego, the ego ideal and the ideal ego, as well as the narcissistic organization of the personality. On the level of the PRAGMATICS OF COMMUNICATION, the alethic modalities depend on the symmetrical, complementary and reciprocal regulation of interpersonal or inter-group exchanges (see SCHISMOGENESIS). If 'having-to-be' leads to the imperative of the affirmation of identity, the complementary lower position leads asymptotically to the position of non-existence, 'having-not-to-be'. These modalities of exchange are fundamental in determining the familial EIDOS and ETHOS, the values advocated and prohibited, professional and affective choices and choices of love–object.

In schizophrenic transactions, one observes a complete break between the deontic modalities and the alethic modalities of communication: each protagonist is urged to have-to-do, though he is never the person he should be for his attempt-to-do to be accorded consideration (see DISQUALIFICATION).

(See also MANIPULATION.)

J.M.

algorithm An algorithm is a finite series of rules to be applied to a finite quantity of data in a finite number of stages in a determinate order, to arrive at a certain result and to do so independently of the data and without indeterminacy or ambiguity.

For Bateson, feelings and emotions are the outward signs of precise and complex algorithms, regulating the relations between self and self, and self and others: love, hatred, fear, confidence, anxiety, hostility etc. are then seen as the superstructures of behavioural algorithms, abstractions of models which come into play in relationships. These algorithms form part of broader HEURISTICS, the procedural rules of which are more open.

A very simple numerical algorithm is the one which lays down the procedure to be followed for adding two numbers together: adding the units together, writing down the figure for that sum, possibly carrying one etc. A mathematical formula is an algorithm. A recipe is an algorithm. There is an algorithm for finding the way through a maze, though it is admittedly not very effective; it consists in exploring all the paths at each different point. A computer programme is nothing but an algorithm written in a language that is understood by the computer. An algorithm does not simply solve an individual problem, but a whole class of problems which differ only in terms of data while being governed by the same prescriptions.

ALGORITHMS AND THERAPY

Every therapeutic framework, psychoanalytic cure or systemic intervention possesses an algorithmic aspect constituted by the theoretical corpus, rules and spatio-temporal dispositions upon which it is based. This algorithmic aspect is necessary, but by no means sufficient. The obligatory complement to the algorithm is the heuristic (i.e. the set of rules and procedures not leading in any certain fashion to a sure result).

The theory, setting and modes of intervention (INTERPRETATION; PRESCRIPTION; POSITIVE CONNOTATION; RE-FRAMING etc.) which flow from these are forms of algorithmic endeavour. In particular, the model proposed by Selvini Palazzoli et al. (1978) involving the search for a hypothesis concerning the function of the symptom and the positive connotation of that function, constitutes, at least in theory, an algorithm for solving problems. The same goes for BRIEF THERAPIES, which set themselves limited and circumscribed objectives in solving a precise problem.

By contrast, clinical practice and therapy themselves are far from algorithmic endeavours. The personal style of therapists, their clinical intuitions, the risks taken with regard to what they see as the dangers involved, and their own ways of gathering and interpreting information constitute a series of heuristics which enable one to develop a distinctly more acceptable approach to the COMPLEXITY of the different levels, whether individual or familial.

THE LIMITS OF ALGORITHMIC PROCEDURES

The theory of algorithms runs into difficulties with the comprehension and modelling of complex problems. What are called 'the most complex' problems are those for which no algorithms exist. The existence of an algorithm describing the development of a system is synonymous with a knowledge of how that system is determined. It presupposes a total mastery of the many variables, their interactions and the effects of a variation in any one of them. It gives a predictable character to the phenomenon that is to be elucidated.

However, like any living system, the family has the capacity to adapt to the chance events which assail it, to assimilate these by modifying its structure and thus to bring about the emergence of something new. And it is, among other things, because the system is partly indeterminate, and therefore non-algorithmic, that it can integrate the disturbances which affect it and transform them into meaningful experiences.

NATURAL AND CULTURAL PROGRAMMES

In speaking of innate behaviour in animals, the term 'programme' is frequently used to designate behavioural sequences triggered by specific stimuli or particular situations. The hierarchies of systems which mediate instinctive behaviours (Tinbergen, 1947) set in action algorithmic programmes of very great complexity in the higher animals; these programmes enable the animal to combine hereditarily coordinated sequences, learned sequences and movements varying as a function of context. The specific feature of instinctive behaviours is that they are characterized by internally autonomous excitation and impulsion (Lorenz,

1978b). In vertebrates, the algorithmic programmes of the instincts are broken down into individual operations and, as one reaches the higher mammals (cetaceans, primates), these programmes form part of increasingly sophisticated heuristic procedures.

In man, by virtue of self-domestication (see DOMESTICATION), these behaviours are re-framed, regulated and hierarchically ordered by specific cultural and family structures; they are not thereby destroyed, however, since man also reproduces as a biological organism, since he cannot be the product of purely biological or cultural conditioning and since his behaviour is subject to spontaneous impulses. However, an immense number of programmes and variants underpin this spontaneity and 'flexibility' which may, at meta-levels of expression generate an impression of producing chance phenomena. For Bateson, 'the heart has its algorithms' or, to paraphrase Pascal, its reasons which are unknown to reason.

The 'programmatic' aspect of human interaction has been particularly emphasized by Scheflen (1973a) in the fields of ritual, ceremony, courtship or simple conversation. Interactions are made up from 'programmes' which evolve and are transmitted culturally. Each culture elaborates particular modes for eating, bathing, fighting, courtship etc. Knowledge of these programmes is transmitted from generation to generation. Not just verbal behaviour, but all modes of behaviour are codified and structured by cultural programmes which to some extent inaugurate traditions. According to Scheflen (1965), if we come from a certain region, we will not only speak the dialect of that region, but, up to a point, we will move, sit, walk, make gestures and pull faces, eat, court and mow our lawns in the way the people of that region have learnt to.

The relations between the various modalities of communication (linguistic, kinetic, neurovegetative, tactile, proxemic, vestimentary etc.) also obey very precise algorithms which are dependent on the cultural context: for example, according to Scheflen (1965), our heads and eyelids (or sometimes our hands) are slightly lowered with the pitch fall of a declarative and raised with the pitch rise of a question; though these algorithms are indispensable in the identification of courtship, friendship and working behaviours or when making therapeutic prescriptions, they are insufficient to establish free and open interactions. The application, to the letter, of pre-established therapeutic schemas very rapidly produces results contrary to the desired aims. In every living exchange, algorithms are concretely integrated into heuristic procedures; where they are not, they remain mere skeletons, empty of meaning.

(See also ENTROPY; ORDER; RANDOMNESS; STOCHASTIC PROCESSES.)

M.G. & J.M.

alienation (mental, familial, therapeutic) A basic motif which leads family systems to present as patients and to request assistance. Alienation concerns the relation between the familiar and the strange, the familial and the social, as it exists in every human person who is individuated and socially situated.

The first sense of the word 'alienation' is a legal one and it is practically synonymous in the legal context with the word 'transfer'; by this process, an 'alienating' individual transmits a property or right, for payment or otherwise, to another individual. The transfer is the act by which this person transmits that property or that right to another. Alienation concerns a transference of a heritage, which normally moves out of one family system to become the property of another social system. In this sense, alienation is a loss of 'having' and is normally accompanied by an increase in 'being'.

Alienation may be understood, then, from a systemic point of view, as the transference of a material and spiritual heritage which leaves the sphere of family reproduction to be offered to an outside social institution. Such a carrying over enables the social institution to be stabilized and reproduced, by the construction and autonomization of the personality. Every institution rests on a mechanism of family alienation. To change social organization, it is necessary to destroy existing family systems and to replace them with others.

Alienation depends on the social body intruding into the family and functions as one of two poles upon which narcissism is structured, enabling TRANSFERENCE to occur. Alienation in fact presupposes the impact of social institutions on the family group, whereas transference leads to the displacement of family experiences into the social body.

Mental alienation suggests the disorder of a man who has become psychically alien to himself, those nearest to him and to society (a break in the symmetry where the recognition of human identity is concerned). He thus loses all familiarity with the things of society. In this sense, mental alienation is a disturbance of alienation, signifying loss of reason.

PSYCHOPATHOLOGY OF ALIENATION

Mental alienation is essentially defined both as loss of being (identity disorder) and loss of having (disorder of the mental capacities). We may thus distinguish between:

1   *The organized alienation of the psychotic*, which leads ultimately to forms of alienation which are either productive or in deficit; the family approach to such problems shows that the deficit dimension is wholly relative and that, conversely, a family dynamic exists which is associated with it. Alienation manifests itself here in the predominance of territorial disturbances: the INDEX PATIENT has no stable place anywhere; he or she seems deprived of his or

her inner sphere, thinking, emotional activity, and personal action.

2   *The de-structured alienation of the sufferer from dementia,* who is confronted with a simulation of psychosomatic death. Here again, the analysis of the family and social contexts leads us to relativize what classic diagnostic activity tended to regard as fixed (see DEMENTIA).

3   *The alienation of the desire of the neurotic* which Freud captured in the famous formula, *Wo es war soll ich werden* ('Where id was, there ego shall be').

This psychopathology of alienation must be re-situated in terms of a wide variety of contexts: bio-ethological, psychoanalytic, familial, social and therapeutic.

BIO-ETHOLOGY OF ALIENATION

Alienation seems to be correlative with any relation in which the question of the same and the other arises. To this extent, there exists a biological, ethological level of the appearance of the phenomenon: the relation to the congener, the predator–prey relation, the male–female relation and the parent–child relation are only made possible if an individual accepts that he or she must devote part of him/herself to simulating the properties of the organism which stands over against him/her as other or as complementary. Every gain in autonomy is thus derivative of the development of the alienation of a part of oneself by organisms outside oneself.

ALIENATION AND AUTONOMY

It will be evident that there is, in this way, an oscillatory coupling between phenomena of autonomy and alienation (see SELF-ORGANIZATION). There is no autonomy without alienation, no alienation without autonomy. The less autonomy there is, the less alienation (Bettelheim, 1966–67). The systems which totally suppress alienation also totally suppress autonomy (Zinoviev, 1980–81, 1981). If one entirely relieves a patient who is diagnosed as schizophrenic of his alienation, he is left completely dependent upon his therapists. The more he shows how cured he is, the less likely he is to detach himself from those treating him; and every manifestation of autonomy will be perceived as a clear indication that the psychotic state is still not overcome; it is necessary, then, to re-frame the very concepts of illness, therapy and cure.

ALIENATION AND TRANSFERENCE

The interdependence of alienation and transference may be demonstrated schematically as follows:

1   *Transference* is what gives a content to alienation. It is a movement which runs from the familial towards the extrafamilial and social.

2   *Alienation* is what gives body and consistency to the transference.

It is an institutional appropriation of the 'familiar' qualities which enable autonomization to occur in relation to the familial and by introjection of the alien (compare, for example, schooling and its disturbances).

Transference in psychoanalysis will come to refer to the carrying over of representations and emotions from one part of the personality to another and from one person to another. In its classic description, it presupposes that the distinction between the familiar and the alien is acquired, the transference being the vehicle of a movement of familiar psychical representations towards alien psychical representations. Transference neurosis is the prescription of a particular alienation from the family, with the analysand investing his or her time, money and person with a third party from outside.

The senses of the terms 'alienation' and 'transference' thus have aspects in common. Both involve a distortion connected with a transferring. They are, to some extent, two complementary parts of the same reality. The difference between them concerns what is transferred and the person who receives what is transferred. In the case of transference, psychical representatives and affects are involved which are carried over on to a person external to the family of origin such as a doctor, priest, teacher, artist or even a psychoanalyst when a 'transference neurosis' is established. In the case of alienation, the distinction between the subject–predicate system does not operate due to the undifferentiation of self which follows from this.

Alienation determines the narcissistic side of the personality; it is the capture of the self by an alien object; in alienation, the nature of what is transferred is the opposite or reverse of a representation or emotion since what is involved is a behavioural movement, an unrepresentable praxis, if not indeed a set of movements which prevent, occult or inhibit the representation or the affect in the target person or group. Instead of representing the object to itself, alienation merges with it.

Alienation and transference are also essentially different in nature: whereas with transference, the movement is directed outwards from the family circle, mental alienation initially affects a member of the family; it is only in a second phase that the alienation will be transported outside the family and on to a group of people. If then, within the transference (or its neurotic form), the distinction between the familiar and the alien seems acquired, and seems to serve as a support for the displacement of representations, mental alienation rests on a kind of radical confusion between the familiar and the alien which originates within the family, before going on to be directed towards an external organization. The greatest sense of alienation sometimes overtakes the member of the family who is the most committed to its ideals.

FAMILY ALIENATION BY SOCIAL MACRO-SYSTEMS

Sociopolitical and economic constraints sometimes weigh so heavily that they lead to family break-up. Some family systems do not have the resources to survive the pressures imposed on them by the wider 'social macro-system'.

Family alienation may equally be concerned with the diversion of an inheritance or the appropriation of family property by the state, the Church or by other authorities. Property, which in theory would have devolved to the descendants, is diverted towards an outside association. The alienation of family property consists in gifts made by families either within the donor's lifetime or in his will. Alienation is clearly distinct from spoliation since it presupposes the active and consenting participation of the person alienating the property.

Goody's (1983) view is that the Church strengthened the possibility of alienation of family property by legislation as a counter to ancient successorial strategies based on adoption, marriage between cousins, the taking of many wives or concubinage, union between relatives and the remarriage of divorcees. Such an attitude emphasized the fundamental importance of the nuclear family by eroding the rights of collaterals and extended kin groups.

The paradox of the transition from sect to established Church may be formulated as follows: every revolution, whether religious, technocratic or ideological, seeks to break the existing family system; each form of social organization which results from such a revolution seeks to control the family system which ensures its survival. Social and religious institutions constitute the spiritual emanation of kinship systems, while also seeking in their turn to transcend and control them.

THE PHILOSOPHY OF SOCIAL ALIENATION

As Guitton Cohen Adad (1982) reminds us, alienation, from Hobbes onwards and particularly in the work of Rousseau, was to become the crux of the social contract. Contractual alienation is in effect 'the loss or giving for the good of the general will of a natural right in exchange for peace and security. A contract which constitutes the origin of political power, a contract of association, not of subjection, a contract which is the founding act of institutions. The concept represents a considerable historical step: the transition from a state of nature to society' (Guitton Cohen Adad, 1982, p. 29). Alienation is thus seen in a positive light, for the loss to which it gives rise, enables us, in exchange, to enter into institutionalized society and thus makes civilization possible. Then, with Hegel, alienation as loss

of having is re-situated at the opposite pole: alienation as loss of self. Religious alienation is denounced by Hegel as 'voluntary dispossession by relinquishment of Being' (Guitton Cohen Adad, 1982, p. 29).

Finally, with Karl Marx, alienation is the taking from the worker of his labour power; instead of bringing him a return, the worker's labour power simply goes on adding to the wealth of Capital to which he or she, as a worker, has no possible access (theory of surplus value).

On the one hand, the production process incessantly converts material wealth into capital, into the capitalist's means of enjoyment and his means of valorization. On the other hand, the worker always leaves the process in the same state as he entered it – a personal source of wealth, but deprived of any means of making that wealth a reality for himself. Since, before he enters the process, his own labour has already been alienated [*entfremdet*] from him, appropriated by the capitalist, and incorporated with capital, it now, in the course of the process, constantly objectifies itself so that it becomes a product alien to him [*fremder Produkt*]. (Marx, 1867)

Alienation thus arises in the very process of capitalist exchange, which establishes strict equivalence between use value and exchange value. 'One of the parties to the exchange sells his labour power, which the other purchases. The first party receives the value of his commodity, the use of which, as labour, is alienated to the second.' We may observe here that in this sense, the schizophrenic, in his non-insertion into the social tissue of work and exchange, categorically refuses alienation thus defined, only to fall into an even more redoubtable alienation. (Paul Lafargue, the son-in-law of Marx, in his *Le droit à la paresse* [*The right to idleness*] had pushed the paradoxes associated with enslavement by work to their extreme theoretical consequences by producing a 34-page tract whose very slimness was perfectly in keeping with the theory!)

The interest in communication theory stands in a direct line of descent from the Marxist tradition of the sociology of knowledge and/or theories of alienation, in particular the question of the TANGLED HIERARCHIES. If Marx's hypothesis in *The German ideology*, that 'the production of ideas, of conceptions, of consciousness, is at first directly interwoven with the material activity and the material intercourse of men, the language of real life' is accepted, that hypothesis is valid for defining its own status as a superstructural effect. As a science, a sociology of knowledge is its own object and, as the product of an authour, its constitutive elements are also bound to the experience of an individual. Now, this individual dimension of production very soon made it possible to point out the relativity introduced by the fact that 'opinions, affirmations, propositions and systems of ideas are not judged as such, but in relation to the experience of the person who expresses them. This means that the specific character and experience of the subject influences his opinions, perceptions and interpretations.'

It is in this way that alienation will be assimilated with false awareness. This concept, the product of Hungarian Marxism, is, as its own begetters admit, a particularly complex one. More precisely: when people have a type of consciousness such that they believe that they are acting in keeping with their real interests, but in practice they are acting *against* those interests, then one can say that they have a *false consciousness*. Now this type of functioning may also extend to an entire class: for example, an entire class may have a *false consciousness* where it does not analyse its role within a given society. False consciousness has to be seen in relation to a theory of society and the conflicts that arise within it. Lastly, there is the false consciousness of the ideologues. The problem concerns, among others, the intellectuals who produce the ideologies of the dominant classes, i.e. the scientists, writers and all who mould public opinion through the mass media.

PARADOXES INVOLVED IN OVERCOMING SOCIAL ALIENATION

Problems begin, of course, when it comes to knowing who can claim to perceive the false consciousness of others and, possibly, seek to transform it. (The question also deserves to be posed in so far as the distinction between false and TRUE SELF suggested by Winnicott (1960a) is concerned.) The work of a writer like Zinoviev is indubitably fascinating when it comes to elucidation the paradoxes connected with the systematic conquering of alienation, as this has been attempted in Communist societies. It should be compared with the contribution of Bateson which, all in all, constitutes a similar unveiling of the processes of so-called Western societies.

The articulation of the concept of false consciousness with a conception of society as conflictual makes it possible to cast a particular light on the approach of family therapists in general and of Bateson in particular, even though they remain prudent in their noble desires to see a generalized overcoming of alienation.

Going along with all of Bateson's teaching was the rumour which he himself reported: 'There's something behind what Bateson says, but he never says what it is.' This thought is reminiscent of the Zen Buddhist tenet that enlightenment comes when the disciple realizes that there is no secret, no ultimate answer and therefore no point in continuing to ask questions (Watzlawick et al., 1967, p. 244). In an epistemological investigation into his own thinking, this hidden element was run to ground by Bateson when, reflecting upon the complementarity of induction (based

on experimental 'data') and deduction (based on certain fundamentals), he stressed the chronic absence of the deductive dimension in a great deal of scientific research.

> The would-be behavioural scientist who knows nothing of the basic structure of science and nothing of the 3,000 years of careful philosophic and humanistic thought about man – who cannot define either entropy or a sacrament – had better hold his peace rather than add to the existing jungle of half-baked hypotheses. (Bateson, 1972, p. 27)

Bateson's ultimate aim is to arrive at a presentation of the processes by which the relations between men are ordered. A study of the detailed mechanisms which did not take account of the surrounding context could be of no long-term interest. According to Bateson, an analysis of interpersonal relations which was not reinforced by an account of the complex machinery underlying it could not enjoy our confidence.

Zinoviev (1980) has done for large groups what Bateson conceptualized for family ecosystems. Thus, for example, a guaranteed right to work has led to identifying all those whose labours are not officially listed as 'idlers'; and as 'workers' all those who perform no work but remain faithfully at their official posts. What people are in reality forced to do comes to be classified as voluntary work. Building paradise on earth unfailingly means making a hell of every tiny detail.

The solution to the question before us is not, then, where spontaneously one might have expected it.

> The longer that a society of a given type exists, the harder it becomes to change its type granted the given human material and the conditions of its existence. Attempts to change the type usually end in the collapse of the community itself or a return to an earlier regime with certain changes that take account of altered circumstances. (Zinoviev, 1981)

For his part, Bateson has shown in what respect the schizophrenic's family is an organization of immutable stability, maintained by the self-abnegation of each of its members. To aspire to modifying such an unalterable entity is a mistake that is made too often. The very attempt to overcome alienation is itself the problem which aggravates the solution already found by the patient and those around him.

Among such notions as biological alienation, social false consciousness, the alienation of desire (Freud), the individual false self (Winnicott) and the terrible, alienating self-maintaining effect of all attempts at overcoming alienation (Zinoviev, Bateson), in what way is the communications-based approach to family and social systems a viable alternative? Without believing it possible to provide an exhaustive answer to this formidable question, we shall endeavour to outline a few elements of a provisional response.

THERAPEUTIC ALIENATION AND THE OVERCOMING OF ALIENATION

In family therapy the same problem arises: 'alienation' is overcome by prescribing group therapeutic alienation. Alienation (alien, other, strange) rests upon a process of exchange, if not indeed of theft, as in the myth of Hermes, in which that character steals Apollo's cattle and ends up as the god of ambiguous communication, trade . . . and thieves. (On the interest of the Hermes myth as a tool for analysing communication, see Miermont, 1982a, and MYTH OF HERMES.) Hence the interest of the communication model with regard to delinquency (theft of property, physical despoliation) and psychotic and psychosomatic illnesses (theft of thoughts, feelings and acts in 'mental automatism' leading to the theft of the imaginary, the wearing down of the subjective sphere, the loss of personal and family territories).

On the family systems level, alienation has been the subject of a great deal of research, including Neuburger (1982), Miermont (1983) and Benoit and Roume (1986). The object of study here is the family system. More specifically, the term 'alienation' will be used to describe the confusion which arises within the family between the familiar and the strange. 'Strangeness' very often seizes hold of the person who, within the family, is the most family-orientated member. Freud (1919) described all the paradoxical nuances of the troubling strangeness of what he termed the 'uncanny', which cause a sense of terror to well up out of the most intimate and primitive core of the familiar: 'Many people experience the feeling [of the uncanny] in the highest degree in relation to death and dead bodies, to the return of the dead, and to spirits and ghosts' (Freud, *Standard Edition*, vol. 17, p. 241).

Alienation makes it difficult, if not indeed impossible, to locate a property or quality in one particular person rather than another: phenomena of non-separability can be observed which render transference paradoxical, split or splintered, the source and aim of emotional and cognitive movements being indeterminate.

The only way to recover one's bearings where there is pathological alienation is to identify the structure of the family, together with the way its dysfunctioning has succeeded in manifesting itself within the institutions involved and among the therapists consulted (see MAP AND COUNTER-MAP OF A FAMILY SYSTEM).

In fact, groups of therapists are liable to fall prey to processes of alienation; institutional meetings are a double-edged weapon in which mutual and reciprocal aid between therapists may quickly turn into the disqualification of any enterprise, if that mutual aid has no concrete purchase and if no one takes any precise individual responsibility. In this respect, the alienation of the therapist is the mirror of family alienation, which should be regarded as a source of information concerning the state of the family under consideration. There is an oscillatory coupling between the properties of AUTONOMY and alienation which makes them inseparable from one another.

Machines and the mechanistic play a role in overcoming man's alienation (freeing him from the stereotypical thoughts and actions associated with slavery and bondage). The paradox is that the schizophrenic is reduced to simulating mechanistic and slavish attitudes. To attempt to free oneself from mechanistic constraints, one has first to recognize their existence, and indeed their functional necessity.

The identification of phenomena of therapeutic alienation is a first step in the resolution of problems concerning the most serious forms of psychosis. Three levels of communication may be taken into account in the family-theoretic approach to schizophrenias: familial alienation, 'institutional' alienation and, if possible, the confrontation between – and disentangling of – the familial and social levels of alienation:

First level
schizophrenia = familial alienation – – – therapy = 'institutional' alienation

Second level
institutional schizophrenia – – – – family therapy

Third level
differentiation of familial and therapeutic organizations

The *first level* is self-evident; the schizophrenic seems totally alienated, while therapeutic activities seem the indispensable condition for the questioning of the autonomy of the family.

The *second level* is to some extent the other side of the coin: schizophrenic manifestations are first and foremost exacerbated, last-ditch attempts by the patient and his family to gain autonomy from their families of origin. In this respect, every form of therapy comprises a dimension which is all the more alienating for not being identified as such. Daumezon and Bonnafe (1946) used to argue very forcefully that therapies brought on an artificial illness preferable to the natural illness. The psychoanalytic model of the transference neurosis is an example of this. So far as psychosis is concerned, the process of alienation includes a collective dimension in which several therapists are caught up (or not, as the case may be). It will be noted that a disengagement is possible if the therapists place themselves in a meta-therapeutic or para-therapeutic position.

The *third level* only exists in relation to the existence of the first two; it involves the recognition of self-referential mechanisms at work in familial schizophrenic processes; alienation and autonomy become opposite polarities in a state of continual oscillation. These manifestations appear and disappear, giving an impression of vagueness and indeterminacy at the clinical level. Therapeutic activity consists of distinguishing between the categories of the familiar and the alien, both for the families and for the therapeutic organizations.

(See also BECOMING ACCUSTOMED; DELEGATION; DIFFERENTIATION OF SELF; DISQUALIFICATION; DOUBLE BIND; FAMILY SELF-REFERENTIALITY; IMPRINTING; LEDGER; NARCISSISM; QUID PRO QUO.)

J.M. & D.C.

alignment   Term employed by Wynne (1961) to indicate the experiencing of a reciprocal community of interests, attitudes or values occurring between certain members of a family. Such alignments generally occur between two or more members of the family and, mostly, do not concern the family as a whole, except when the family itself aligns against the therapist.

A distinction is made between intrafamilial alignment and systems of interfamilial alliance, which are created by the meeting of two families of origin, leading to the establishing, if not indeed the legal creation, of a new family. In the real situations one meets in clinical practice, conflicts may exist between alignments experienced at an intrafamilial level and alliances established at an interfamilial level, which may lead to genuine misalliances. For Wynne, the concept of alignment may be defined as 'the perception or experience of two or more persons that they are united and that in this sector of their experience, they have positive feelings toward one another.' This is, then, an essentially emotional experience.

From a structural point of view, the notion of alignment covers a wider field. Aponte (1976) sees alignment as 'the union of a member of a system with another or his opposition to that member in the execution of an operation'. Alignment becomes one of the three basic structural dimensions of family transactions. In *Psychosomatic families*, Minuchin et al. (1978) describe three modalities of alignment which may lead to psychopathological disturbances: the *stable coalition*, which unites two members of a system in a rigid, exclusive way against a third; *detouring*, which seeks to diminish the stress arising between two members of the system by designating a scapegoat as the source of the tensions between them; and *triangulation* in which two members of the system who are opposed to one another attempt to ally themselves with a third party. Boszormenyi-Nagy (see Boszormenyi-Nagy and Spark, 1973) considers that the state of equilibrium

between reciprocal obligations and merits is more significant in the impact of alignments on family life than the structural aspects or the lived experience.

(See also COALITION; PERVERSE TRIANGLES; TRIANGLES.)

A.L. & P.S.

allegation   See DEMAND.

alliance, misalliance   See ALIGNMENT; COUPLE; FAMILY ETHNOLOGY; LOYALTY; MARITAL BREAKDOWN.)

alpha and beta elements   Alpha and beta elements are abstract concepts formulated by W. R. Bion (1962, 1963, 1965, 1970) to cast light upon the object of psychoanalytic research outside the frame of the psychoanalytic session. These concepts are just two among several theoretical tools which Bion elaborated to assist the analyst in his thinking. These include the theory of functions (in particular the alpha function), the grid for understanding the mechanisms of thought, transformation and invariance and so on.

The theory of alpha function concerns the study and understanding of the capacity to think and disturbances of that function. It postulates that there exists within the personality a function which transforms sensory impressions into alpha elements. This latter, unlike the impressions of perception, may be employed in new transformations, stored away or repressed. Alpha elements correspond to sensory impressions which, when transformed into images, serve in the formation of dream thoughts, unconscious thought in the waking state, dreams, memories and representations.

Untransformed sensory impressions are known as beta elements. They play no role in thinking, dreaming or remembering. They constitute a kind of anti-thought, are experienced as 'things in themselves' and most often are expelled by projective identification. They are in a sense disconnected from the rest of psychical life.

Alpha and beta elements are not directly observable in clinical reality. Alpha elements make contact between the conscious and the unconscious and play a similar role to sleep. They protect the phantasies of external reality and make contact with it from the reality of the inner emotions. Mental states in which there is no difference between the conscious and the unconscious, between being asleep or awake, would be characterized by a proliferation of beta elements or a 'screen of beta elements'. Alpha elements are the basis of a normal relation with reality and the inner and outer worlds, while the beta screen is characteristic of the psychotic 'link'. Following this model, when the faculty of thought is seriously disturbed, this is a result of the alpha function having failed to produce alpha elements. Instead, beta elements predominate and these are unable to form links with one another. Alpha elements appear to be synonymous with the phantasmatics specific to each individual subject. Phantasies allow those elements to be contained which otherwise would be expelled by projection. Alpha elements, like phantasmatization, are what enables the ego to fulfil its role as mediator and defensive pole, and its roles of binding, managing conflict and adaptation to reality.

Is it possible to use these notions, which were essentially conceived to provide an account of psychical activity, to define the nature of family processes? Alpha elements would enable the family system to retain its cohesion and its integrity, to regulate itself in the face of disturbances, to make it possible for different individual goals to coexist within the system and to transform both internal and external elements in such a way as to enrich family behaviour as a whole, thus increasing the flexibility of its regulations and the complexity of the system. Beta elements would, on this hypothesis, be the events within family dynamics which the regulative system cannot integrate and which reappear in the actions of a particular patient, whose role would be to try desperately to transform the unrepresentable into alpha elements or to expel it. At the extreme limits, one might see the effects of these elements in the total disconnectedness of disengaged and exploded families in institutional systems (see Ausloos, 1980).

(See also PHANTASY; PROJECTIVE IDENTIFICATION.)

M.G.

anachronistic plagiarist   See INSTITUTIONAL MYTHS.

analog–digital/digital–analog converters   The CYBERNETIC theory of coding presupposes the possibility of transcribing units of information into different coding systems (analog and digital) by means of converters. The relations between the central nervous system and the vegetative nervous system or between the right and left brain, presuppose transcriptions of information between codes, as do the structure of MYTHS, rites, DREAMS and PHANTASIES. This 'mechanistic' point of view will be supplemented by the morphogenetic theory of SYMBOLIC REFERENCE which demonstrates the biological connections between PREGNANCES (in the analog domain) and SALIENCES (in the digital domain).

The manner in which dreams take into account conditions of representability, as described by Freud, is a complex example of digital–analog transcription, although it probably also depends upon procedures connected with HOLOGRAPHIC MEMORY. Similarly,

RITUALIZATION is based on a conversion of analogic behaviours into a digital frame which resolves the ambiguity of the relationship. Depending upon whether the transcription occurs towards the individual or towards the collective, we may distinguish two systems of conversion:

1   Centripetal converters (individuation)
    (a) analog–digital: obsessional symptom, phantasy
    (b) digital–analog: hysterical symptom, dream
2   Centrifugal converters (socialization)
    (a) analog–digital: rites
    (b) digital–analog: myths

The term 'converter' is to be understood here not so much as a real object, but rather as an artificial distinguishing tool used subjectively by the therapist. It makes possible an assessment of what are the prevalent coding systems and the disturbances of inter-code translations in a given communication. It can be used to seek out modifications of the therapy. One may ask patients to quantify the intensity of their fear or obsession and to say what percentage figure would have to be reached for them to regard their symptom as bearable. Similarly, one may ask the various members of the family to estimate 'numerically' the intensity of the anxiety in circulation or to quantify the distribution of power, self-sacrifice or selfishness, for example, among them. In other cases, by contrast, one will seek to transcribe into analog terms messages overloaded with digital expression, and to transfer on to a metaphorical or non-verbal plane conversation which is too digitalized and by that token rendered ineffective.

(See also ANALOGIC CODING; ARTIFICIAL CODES; DELIRIUM; DIGITAL CODING; MESSAGES; PRESCRIPTION.)

analogic coding   Analogic coding is based on the use of continuous physical magnitudes to establish a relation of denotation, which is more or less a relation of likeness, between the semiotic structure of the referent and the material supports of the code. Thus the analogic representation of the value 5 may be achieved by a comparison between two heights or two electrical intensities, one of which is five times greater than the other etc. Similarly, imitating the miaowing of a cat, drawing it in outline or simulating its gait all amount to using analogic coding to indicate the referent 'cat'.

The properties of such a coding are its:

- resemblance between code and referent;
- equivocal, ambiguous character: tears may signify joy or sadness;
- immediate and motivated aspect;
- high intrinsic semantic content;
- low level of direct syntactic differentiation;

- continuous 'plus or minus' functioning, by measure of information;
- use of a previously deformed image to indicate negation;
- order of the relation aspect.

Approximation to precision and detailed counts are achieved by using ANALOG–DIGITAL CONVERTERS. Only a minimum of salient features containing a likeness are needed to give meaning to an analogic message. But it requires a maximum of imprecise signals for a decoder to change the semantic value of an analogic message.

On the psychical level, analogic coding is akin to the primary processes of thought and thus to unconscious representations (perceptual identity, principle of non-contradiction, free-flowing energy, tendency to seek discharge, mechanisms of condensation/displacement governed by the pleasure principle).

The continuous physical magnitudes which may serve as material supports for analogic coding are temperature, quantity of liquid or electricity, intensity of an electrical potential or of illumination, length of distance, quantity of force or work. We find the equivalent of these in clinical practice: the warmer or colder tone of a message; liveliness of exchanges; variations on a continuum of interpersonal distances and spaces; intensity of vocalizations and gestures; the fluid or resistant character of interactions; the measurement of the forces present etc. These continuous entities are abstract entities of the same nature as a segment of a line, or a disc being shifted through an angle, or indeed the speed or acceleration of a rotating axle. The slide rule, a car accelerator pedal, an alcohol or mercury thermometer, a tensimeter or a wind tunnel are analogic devices.

The characteristics of the analogic machine are found at various very different levels of the organization of and communication between living organisms. The vegetative nervous system, which regulates heartbeat and respiration continuously, the contraction–dilation of the bronchi and the secretion in particular quantities of a great many substances seem, overall, to function in terms of analogic principles of coding and regulation. Though opposite in their effects, the orthosympathetic and parasympathetic systems are not opposed in the synergy–antagonism correlation of their effects. The major processes of the metabolism (anabolism, catabolism) follow continuous curves which are interdependent and are similar from one organism to another. These analogic visceral phenomena should be seen in relation to the great emotional and instinctive phenomena, on the one hand, and to their semantic activation in communication, on the other. Emotions such as fear, threat, aggression, anger and affection reveal themselves in a whole continuum of attitudes from which certain salient features stand out.

There is therefore a very close link between relational contexts (of which family interactions are the prototype) and the biological processes of regulation of interacting organisms. It is in this way that it will be possible to find correspondences between psychosomatic or psychotic dysfunctions or behaviour disturbances and the family and institutional contexts in which they arise.

It is tempting to regard analogic coding as synonymous with non-verbal communication. This seems at first to offer a clear conception, but it is soon contradicted by a number of counter-examples: non-verbal emblems have a digital dimension, while the words of everyday speech may be used in a richly analogic fashion (in his film, *High anxiety,* Mel Brooks put up the following sign to describe the psychiatric clinic where the action takes place: 'clinic for very *very* nervous people').

(See also DIGITAL CODING; MESSAGES; RITUALIZATION.)

J.M.

analogy, analog See ANALOG–DIGITAL/DIGITAL–ANALOG CONVERTERS; ANALOGIC CODING; ARTIFICIAL CODES; ELEMENTARY CATASTROPHES; FRACTALS; GENERALIZED CATASTROPHES; HOLOGRAPHIC MEMORY; MESSAGES; METAPHORICAL OBJECTS; PRAGMATICS OF COMMUNICATION; SEMANTICS OF COMMUNICATION.

ancestors Forebears, now dead, who played a part in the reproduction of the generations. The ancestor is thus in the position of progenitor in relation to the descendants who form a family lineage, these latter more or less possessing his/her characteristics, qualities or faults. There is, however, a qualitative leap in the position of ancestor which excludes it from the systems of kinship which establish the difference between what is 'family' and what is not. Beyond three generations back (great grandparents), it seems that forebears are no longer universally considered as close relatives. Hence the cult of ancestors and the appearance of illnesses or exceptional virtues in cases where it seems possible that their spirits may return to visit someone among the living.

The modern analysis of TRANSGENERATIONAL contexts often runs up against serious gaps in information about a person's origins; Racamier (1984) observes that the schizophrenic is 'suspended in a time without duration'. He or she would seem to have no history, neither a personal history nor a history of his/her family, culture and race. Now the schizophrenic, as soon as one sees him/her in connection with his/her family, seems desperately to embody ancestral functions which have disappeared or have not yet appeared; beyond simply taking into account the systems of interaction between persons ranging over three or four generations, it may be useful to consider – to some extent as an abstract fiction – the ancestral function or functions bearing the genetically and/or culturally transmitted characteristics of the group under consideration; this ancestral function seems to affect the INDEX PATIENT – the point of fragility and rupture in the family system – more or less directly. The newborn child is the bearer to a certain extent of the ancestral values of the families of origin. Such a view may enable us to avoid a moralizing assessment of the reciprocal action of grandparents, parents and children upon each other.

(See also ANCESTRAL RELATION; FAMILY CATASTROPHES; GENOGRAM; TRANSGENERATIONAL THERAPIES.)

J.M. & P.S.

ancestral relation From the point of view of formal logic, Bertrand Russell defined the ancestral relation of a term, y, to another term, x. Such a relation implies that y possesses all the properties of its ancestor x, this latter being related to the former by finite relations of descendance. This amounts to saying that y belongs to the hereditary class to which x belongs, a hereditary class of a term supposing that the successors of the successor and, by extension, all the successors of that class belong to it.

The total family of a number is the set of its ancestors and descendants, its forebears and its posterity. If numerical series are identified and defined in this way, it also emerges that genealogical series – i.e. the succession of generations – are subject to rules and paradoxes of the same nature. The origins of the family (multiple levels of ancestral relations) and the apparently infinite succession of generations concretely engender antinomic situations. Is there an origin and an end to these successions? If a point of origin, O1, is defined for the reproduction of the family system, it will always be possible to go back beyond this to a point of origin, O2, which precedes O1. And if an end, E1, is set to these successions, which is supposed to be the last term, there is a risk that another term, T2, will appear after it, itself to be followed by T3 etc. We may symbolize the ancestral relation using the SELF-REFERENTIAL CALCULUS. We have, in effect:

$$\text{AR} = \boxed{\text{P} \mid \text{GP}}$$

where AR is the ancestral relation, P the parental relation and GP the grandparental relation.

Religions, ideological systems and FAMILY MYTHS provide responses to these questions. So-called primitive societies have identified the ancestral language aspect of illness, which bears witness to origins forever lost and beyond the reach of knowledge: some children are perceived from the outset as ancestor-children (in Nathan, 1985a). However, the quest for origins is endless. This is not merely a human, transgenerational matter (even if Bowen, 1978b, has attempted to extend his model of the pathogenics of schizophrenia to ten generations). It also stretches across the animal and plant species and into the inorganic, mineral world and the origins of the world: questions which the great collective beliefs, both mythological and religious, seek to resolve and which are posed within each family.

There is a 'beginning of the world' and 'end of the world' position in the challenge which the psychotic and his/her family throw down to the succession of the generations, as if the irreversible deposits of history were, at each moment, forgotten or destroyed.

(See also TRANSGENERATIONAL MEMORIES; TRANSGENERATIONAL THERAPIES.)

J.M.

anchor, anchoring and disanchoring An anchor is defined by Bandler and Grinder (1979) as the stabilization and crystallization of a typical form of psycho-sensory experience, leading to a constant pattern of response and interaction in a person. The anchoring phenomenon may be compared with the coupling of perceptual resonances in respect of the various sensory systems: auditory, visual, kinaesthetic, tactile, gustatory. The 'madeleine' experience is an 'anchor' for Proust (Cayrol and de Saint Paul, 1984) and his readers. A look, a knitting of the eyebrows, an expression, an intonation may anchor the person in a positive or negative way around anchoring points, ensuring sufficient redundancy for stable relations to be established.

In the life of a couple, for example, anchoring points are liable to accumulate in the moments of tension in the life of each partner; instead of serving as points of attraction and articulation, the anchors end up rigidifying interactions. The essential character of therapeutic action consists in modifying the anchoring systems, by judiciously selecting the type of experiences that have to be disanchored and the moment at which this is to be done.

(See also NEUROLINGUISTIC PROGRAMMING.)

J.M.

anorexia nervosa A psychosomatic syndrome which mainly affects adolescent girls. It comprises:

1 Increasingly drastic restriction of food intake, connected with a fear of putting on weight.
2 Weight loss, the somatic consequences of which may put the patient's life in jeopardy.
3 Primary amenorrhoea (menstruation does not occur at puberty) or secondary amenorrhoea (interruption of menstruation after its appearance).

In so far as it is a dramatically urgent condition, such a disorder requires recourse to multiple therapeutic strategies, which may in some cases appear mutually contradictory: hospitalization, individual approach, family approach. The mode of comprehension of the disorder is necessarily interdisciplinary: ethological, psychoanalytic, systemic, catastrophe theoretic. The increase in the prevalence of food-related disorders of the anorexia nervosa or bulimia type thus causes the clinical practitioner great concern. Hilde Bruch (1979) points to determinants of a psychosociological order to explain the recrudescence of alimentary disturbances.

MULTIPLICITY OF AETIOPATHOGENIC HYPOTHESES

Barthes (1970) suggests that food is not merely a collection of products which can be subjected to statistical or dietetic studies. It is also at one and the same time a system of communication, a corpus of images, a protocol of customs, situations and behaviour. The meal is increasingly losing its socialization function and ceasing to be governed by the traditional rules (solitary eating, eating in small, fragmentary groups etc.). Certain authors (Fischer, 1979; Collonge, n.d.) have established parallels between the anorexic's behaviour and the development of eating practices: inflation in the number of slimming diets, food sectarianism (vegetarianism, macrobiotic diets) and the use of the hunger strike as a form of political protest. We may also note the absence of anorexia nervosa in traditional societies. This is a symptom which seems to push to the limits the Western dissociation between biological and cultural reproduction, by inhibiting the former and exacerbating the latter. The patient seeks to maintain an ideal, disincarnate feminine image, free of any internal or external taint.

Since the nineteenth century (Lasegue and Falret, 1877), various pertinent descriptions have been offered of *eating disorders*. A great number of studies, both psychiatric and psychoanalytic, have proposed aetiopathogenic hypotheses and laid down various prescriptions for therapy (Brusset, 1977, 1985). On an individual, metapsychological level, Kestemberg et al. (1972, p. 213) describe a process of *hunger orgasm*, 'where nonsatisfaction of hunger produces an intense organic pleasure raised to its acme, as though, at the deepest level, not even that of the drives, but that of instinct, perversion were at work, supplying a satisfaction to nonsatisfaction.'

ETHOLOGICAL HYPOTHESIS

From an ethological perspective, Demaret (1979) suggests the hypothesis that the girl who becomes anorexic possesses mechanisms which cause her to struggle against her mother, while paradoxically seeking to separate from her. The restriction of her own food intake is seen as going together with an increase in the attention she pays to her siblings from a position of alimentary altruism. Being unable to confront her mother, the anorexic comes instead to adopt an oppositional stance to her milieu by using the only means at her disposal, namely rejecting the common meal and adopting a pattern of snack feeding, akin to 'vagabond feeding', which is opposed to the family's normal pattern of commensalism. Such an attitude on the part of the patient seems to be particularly well suited to conditions of famine. The anorexic would thus seem to be indicating, symptomatically, that her family group is in a famine situation. It is the mismatch between this signal and the real situation of the family which enables us to hypothesize that there is displacement of a family conflict here.

Vagabond feeding is seen in certain higher animal species: when an animal discovers a large quantity of food, it only eats a small part of it, then moves off, develops other activities and returns periodically to consume the food in small amounts. Other animals eat in groups, a form of behaviour known as *commensalism* (lions, social predators); the dominant animals eat first, ingesting large quantities of food at one go. Other species such as baboons use both modes of feeding depending on the circumstances (Bilz, quoted in Demaret, 1979). Demaret stresses the extent to which the anorexic is caught up in paradoxical hyperactivity, 'bingeing' on intellectual and sporting activities, while engaging in under-feeding behaviour.

MODELS BASED ON CATASTROPHE THEORY

Zeeman (1980, 1985) has suggested a model for understanding anorexia nervosa in terms of CATASTROPHE THEORY. According to his hypothesis, the normal periodic cycle of transition from the consumption of food to satiety is exaggerated. Consumption of food becomes bulimia, if not indeed grossly animal gluttony (the dehumanized side), while satiety becomes fasting, if not indeed a behaviour of spiritual disembodiment (the angelic side). These two extremes could then be inscribed on a cusp catastrophe.

Zeeman's model offers an explanation of the development, increasingly observed in clinical practice, of 'cured' ex-anorexics who settle into an oscillation between phases of eating restriction and phases of bulimia, the 'intermediate' solution consisting in short periods of bulimia, followed by spontaneous or induced vomiting. The great danger is then that of hypokalaemia, which sometimes brutally reveals a state which had previously passed unnoticed by the professional and family entourage.

The dynamics of the HYSTERESIS could conform to one of the two classic relational games in the feeding of children.

1 The *'yes-but-no'* game
   'Eat your soup!'
   'I don't want to.'
   'Then go to bed.'
   'I'm hungry!'

This game is observed from the earliest months of life right up to adolescence; in general, the mother occupies the superior position, which consists in regarding eating as a purely voluntary effect relating to the necessities – and a recognition of the merits – of communal life (she becomes, moreover, violently hostile when without any difficulty a third person gets the child to eat hungrily). The child occupies the inferior position which consists in only being able to eat if he or she feels a physical need to do so, while referring to contextual effects as releasing or inhibiting the need.

2 The 'Jewish mother' game
   'Eat up, son/daughter!'
   'I'm not hungry any more.'
   'Eat it up for me. Do you want me to warm it up/ add some salt/make you something else/cut up your food/feed you each mouthful myself/bring the food to your bedroom?'

The child occupies the superior position of the sovereign who, by the mere performance of what is in the end a natural function, holds the key to the mother's happiness, but runs the risk of losing his or her autonomy and, in any case, his or her idiosyncratic motivations. He or she develops a behavioural tactic of manipulating the mother's mood, but also of denying his/her own individuality.

Nevertheless, such games only lead to anorexia/ fasting where a family meal is taken or a meal involving at least two persons. Let us remember that the family meal is *a ritual tied to daily life* (Lemaire, 1986), forming part of the household habits which lie 'at the root of the social construction of all family reality' (Kaufmann, 1986) which 'ensures the transmission of traditional values while contributing to change by a slow but irreversible modification of rites' (Sjögren, 1986). In this respect, the family meal is a good indicator of family cohesion and adaptability (Olson et al., 1980), in particular in families of migrants (Serrano and Dipp, 1986), whose eating habits are undergoing change. On the other hand, in conditions favouring meals in an anonymous collective ('the lonely crowd') or where a person living singly is concerned, the only possible game is that of anorexia/bulimia in which the subject occupies the two positions by turns. We have here a good example of the sociogenetic process of MARITAL SCHISM leading to the symptom of an individual subjected to the tensions of ACCULTURATION.

DISORDERS OF FAMILY RELATIONS

Almost all clinical practitioners lay the main emphasis on a disturbance of intrafamilial relations. The mother–child relationship has been described by Hilde Bruch (1979) among others, who insists on the fact that the mother, incapable of deciphering the child's messages, privileges the 'food' response and does not teach the child to discriminate between hunger and satiety. Food thus becomes the essential regulator of the dyadic mother–child relations.

Selvini Palazzoli (1974) agrees with Bruch in stating that the mother has not shown herself receptive to the primordial movements and signals of the child and noting that the whole set of pathogenic interpersonal experiences produces paralysing feelings of ineffectualness, which invade the thinking and activity of anorexia patients. In a second phase of thinking, it has been the overall functioning of the family unit that clinical psychologists have focused upon. In 1978, after some years of research using the methodology of systemic therapy, Selvini Palazzoli et al. described specific features which characterized these family structures.

1 The mother is fixated on a latent homosexual plane. Similarly the father has profound passive tendencies, which may be masked by counter-phobic mechanisms; he often has an obsessional character structure.
2 Sadomasochistic relationship between the parents. It is common to observe the most glaring sadistic behaviour in the father, while the mother knows how to exert her influence behind the scenes and manages to be highly castrating in spite of her apparently submissive attitudes.
3 The index patient is subordinated to the needs of the mother, and deprived of any relationship with the father, who, for his part, accepts and reinforces that isolation.
4 The system that is set up in this way prevents the index patient from differentiating herself from the mother and from successfully elaborating a solid Oedipal experience.

Each of the marriage partners remains extremely attached to their family of origin. Following Sperling, Selvini Palazzoli et al. (1978) stress the bad influence of grandmothers in the families of anorexics. Fearing conflict, the partners restrict their exchanges to the minimum necessary for resolving the problems of daily life. The rites associated with eating occupy an important place in family transactions and the anorexic is rarely the only one in the family to accord a great deal of attention to food (one member of the family may be on a diet, another may have food 'fads').

Minuchin et al. (1978) also describe certain specific features of the families of anorexics:

1 In these families, the children play a preponderant role and often engage the greater part of the parents' interest.

2 The child grows up in an atmosphere in which she feels constantly under observation. She ends up being completely preoccupied with the need to present a good image of herself and to attain perfection. She has constantly to please her parents in order to feel pleasure for herself and the negative feedback she receives makes the situation within the family an increasingly inextricable one. No autonomy is possible.

3 The parents have recourse to feelings of guilt and shame as educative principles.

4 The adolescent's body is a subject of controversy within the family and weight represents the chief reference point of the discussions. In these families, eating is not done for pleasure but to satisfy the needs of a body whose functioning is a first-order concern.

5 The boundaries between the family and the outside world are difficult to cross. The relations with peers are precarious and the closest ties are formed within the family itself.

6 Within the family, the barriers between the generations are hazy and poorly defined. To the extent that puberty is in abeyance, the prevalent symptoms (anorexia, weight loss, amenorrhoea) may be interpreted as a refusal, in the case of the female patient, of femininity, an expression of a radical refusal to identify with her mother.

While according great importance to the drive aspects of anorexia nervosa, Brusset (1977) brings out the paradoxical dimension of that behaviour. The eating restriction represents both a call for help and a show of aggression towards the family environment. The demand which the anorexic maintains analogically by flaunting her massive weight loss, is denied by her actual words, which loudly protest her well-being. Clinically, one also observes the thinking and action of the father being disqualified, the children having no possibility of expressing their grievances, and the whole family group expressing itself emotionally and intellectually *en bloc*.

Most current research has freed itself from linear mechanisms of thought and incorporates various different levels of analysis and methodology. Systemic modelling has made it possible to bring out certain of the functions of this pathology, which have been seen as compromise solutions for keeping the fragile family equilibrium protected from conflicts that would be too massive. Several writers (Caillé et al., 1979; Elkaïm, 1979a; Caillé, 1985) attest to the effectiveness of family therapy in cases of anorexia.

(See also ELEMENTARY CATASTROPHES; TRANSACTIONAL TYPOLOGIES OF THE FAMILY.)

P.A., J.M., S.A. & G.G.M.

anthropological typologies of the family See FAMILY ETHNOLOGY; NUCLEAR FAMILY, EXTENDED FAMILY.

anti-theatre The theatre has become caught up in processes of self-reverberation and has, with the work of Luigi Pirandello, Eugène Ionesco and Samuel Beckett, become fragmented, giving rise to the development of an anti-theatre.

THE SCHIZOPHRENIAN THEATRE OF IONESCO

David Cooper, who coined the term 'anti-psychiatry', gives as an example of alienated family relations Eugène Ionesco's 'anti-play' *The Bald Prima Donna*. 'A man and woman meet apparently as total strangers. They gradually discover that they have shared a train compartment, a house, a bed, a child. They conclude in amazement that they are one and the same family' (Cooper, 1967, p. 37). Cooper adds, 'Families of psychiatric patients who are called schizophrenic exhibit this sort of alienation and estrangement in a particularly intense form.'

It must be said that the dialogue in this play provides numerous illustrations of the logical peculiarities which the Palo Alto school identified as occurring in the genesis of schizophrenia in children incessantly subjected to such a climate of nonsense. In other words, what produces gales of laughter in the theatre is what, by the same unconscious process, produces anxiety in the future schizophrenic.

The double bind
We have an example of a double bind in the following excerpt:

Mrs Smith: . . . Is she nice-looking?
Mr Smith: She has regular features, but you can't call her beautiful. She's too tall and too well-built. Her features are rather irregular, but everyone calls her beautiful. A trifle too short and too slight perhaps. . . .

The double bind consists in the simultaneous sending of two absolutely contradictory messages, on condition that the signifiers in opposition are not of the same nature. Thus, for example, the mother who is referred to as a 'smoocher' kisses her child to show him affection, but does so in such a repetitive way that she stifles him. Or the father will tell his son that the son is allowed to criticize him, but his physical expression will show that he does not tolerate such criticism. Mr Smith's tirade will only have the status of a double bind if his interlocutor cannot escape from it (this is the case, in theory, for the audience) and if it is accompanied by gestures that are out of phase with it, expressing first desire, then indifference and, lastly, greed.

Negation by mirroring

Mary: I have just spent a very pleasant afternoon. I went to the pictures with a man and saw a film with some women. When we came out of the cinema we went and drank some brandy and some milk and afterwards we read the newspaper.

Mrs Smith: I hope you spent a very pleasant afternoon. I hope you went to the cinema with a man and drank some brandy and milk.

Mr Smith: And the newspaper!

In this case, accession to the status of subject is impossible since every act is presented not at the expression of an autonomous will but as the echo of a desire on the part of the Smiths who are Mary's employers.

Negation by short-circuiting

In this case, the negation of the subject's psychical reality takes the form of a satisfaction of his (supposed) desire even before he shows it with a 'Mother knows best what's good for you' (cf. Ionesco, *Jacques or obedience*): Father to son: 'Not ugly enough! Not ugly enough! Have you had a good look at her? Have you got eyes in your head? . . . You don't know what you're talking about.'

Talking beside one another

There is no real articulation of the parental figures who live, not together, but side by side.

Mrs Smith: A motor car travels very fast, but I'd rather have a cook to cook the dinner.

Mr Smith: Don't be a silly goose, kiss the conspirator instead.

Mrs Smith stresses the practical aspect of the conversation. She tries to keep the lines of communication open by giving neutral information, statements without an author. Mr Smith, by contrast, by his surrealistic remarks, attacks semantic conventions and, from that point, puts his interlocutor in a state of uncertainty as to her place as receiver of messages. Laing (1965) gives this process the name MYSTIFICATION, while Sluzki et al. (1967) term it transactional DISQUALIFICATION. Is it any surprise that what Laing (1970) calls the 'knots, tangles, impasses, disjunctions, whirligigs, binds' of communication give rise to the ambivalence, mental automatism, depersonalization and discordance of the schizophrenic?

Ionesco's theatre, an anti-theatre of the absurd, illustrates in the form of caricature this absence of the use of language for the purpose of conveying meaning to another person and helps us to understand the schizophrenic's powerlessness to master the symbolic register.

PIRANDELLO'S 'THEATRE IN THE THEATRE'

With his 'theatre in the theatre', Pirandello draws on all the various aspects of the paradox of representation to show that theatre is life or, at least, that interpersonal reality is merely a convention. His plays are so many PSYCHODRAMAS in which the obsessional mechanism of staging actors playing at staging a play is attacked by the logic of communication in the here and now.

The hierarchy of levels of communication (level of affects, of gestures, verbal level) converges in fact towards the emergence of a single reality. This is decoded and interpreted by individuals in function of the symbolic context that is theirs, but the levels of spectacle are merely an intellectual construct. They certainly cannot have a series of markers attached to them indicating that 'this is play' once an original marker has been put down to this effect when the spectator has settled into his chair and the flesh-and-blood actors have begun to act.

In other words, there is no representation of representation. There is not more than one logical level of representation (short of combining theatre and cinema): there are levels of narrative. Reality in its synchronic dimension is one and indivisible; in its diachronic dimension it is established through dialogue and hence through the speeches of the various participants and the reciprocal effects of speeches and narrative. Once that is recognized, reality is undecidable. Everyone has his or her own truth or, in other words: 'Right you are (If you think so).'

One has only to read through the titles of Pirandello's plays to see that, in his view, identity is merely a form of alienation (for example, *Tonight we improvise; When someone is somebody; To find oneself*) and that, on the other hand, madness is an attempt to find identity in the face of the lies of others (*Henry IV* provides the fullest illustration of this). With the rupture effected by 'theatre in the theatre' defeating obsessional defences, and the hysterical strategy of identification with the other's desire also leading to disaster (*La Signora Morli, una e due* [*Signora Morli, one and two*], *The doctor's duty, The rules of the game* and *As you desire me*), this interpersonal abrading of the neurotic mechanisms (particularly within families, as it happens) leaves no alternative but psychosis. This takes the form, in fact, of paranoid delusion, the only available register of certainty in the face of the 'naked masks' presented by one's interlocutors (*La ragione degli altri* [*Other people's reason*], *It's only a joke, O di uno o di nessuno* [*Either somebody's or nobody's*], *Each in his own way; Dream, but perhaps not; No one knows how*).

Half a century after the stunning impact which the discovery of *Six characters in search of an author* made upon him, the thinking of Henri Ey, as expressed in his last book, still bears the mark of the Pirandellian dialectic of person and character. 'This is to say that psychopathological being does not constitute a radically heterogeneous situation in respect of the organization of being, but that it is constituted by an eluding of the order of that organization' (Ey, 1977). Jean-Paul Sartre did not have far to go after Pirandello to have the characters of his *In Camera* opine that 'Hell is other people.'

(See also FAMILIODRAMA; SOCIODRAMA.)

G.G.M.

artificial codes and systems of coding Coding is an artificial/symbolic representation of a MESSAGE. Its formal definition derives from problems of tele-transmission (Weaver and Shannon, 1949), computer construction (Wiener, 1975; von Neumann, 1979) and, more generally, from artificial systems of information processing (Simon, 1969; Newell and Simon, 1972).

Coding is defined by Bateson in 'Redundancy and coding' (1972), as the substitution for an organism of internal events for external events, so that the internal events take the place of the external events. Coding may then be apprehended as a first level of representation. This substitution is a transformation of spatial patterns into temporal relations and of temporal patterns into spatial relations. Certain codings which result from this are common to elementary organisms, to animals, machines and men. There are:

- *sequential systems of coding* (analogic, digital, iconic), which are capable of reciprocal transcription (see ANALOG–DIGITAL CONVERTERS);
- *simultaneous systems of coding* (HOLOGRAPHIC MEMORY), in which the spectrum of information is distributed from each element of the code to the totality of the referent and from the totality of the code to each element of the referent.

The structure of signs presupposes relations between codes, between codes and messages, and between messages (indices, icons, symbols). ANALOGIC CODING is essential to characterize the relationship aspect of communication, while the content of communication is chiefly taken care of by DIGITAL CODING (Watzlawick et al., 1967; Bateson, 1972). Analogic coding is of a higher logical type than digital coding, while digital coding is of a higher order of organization than analogic coding (Wilden, 1972). Holographic memory ensures a simultaneous conjunction of these two levels: each part of the content resembles the totality of the relationship; each part of the relationship is represented in the totality of the content. This appears in the figures of rhetoric: metaphor, metonymy, oxymoron, catachresis etc.

THE CYBERNETIC MODEL

The construction of artificial machines capable of processing information had to resolve a first great dilemma regarding the nature of the code that was to be used to represent the referent, and to carry out operations. Though traditional machines tended mainly to use analogic coding, based on the perceived resemblance between the referent and its representation, the present-day computing revolution was made possible by the choice of von Neumann to use basically numerical or digital coding, based upon a discrete, discontinuous relation between the referent and its representation. This did not, however, put an end to the construction of analogic machines; moreover, the smallest machine of relative sophistication is based on a hierarchical integration of ANALOG–DIGITAL and DIGITAL–ANALOG CONVERTERS.

Courtship behaviour, the attitude of the lover, and care given to children or the sick form part of the types of behaviour and thought which can be interpreted in terms of these two modes of coding by an observer or a therapist. The empathic function, based on the appreciation of perceived resemblances, calls, preferably, for analogic coding. But precise deciphering, the authentic or inauthentic value of the message is identified by a system of digital coding. We may note at the outset that this 'identification', this 'interpretation', is the result of a personal and subjective involvement of the person globally integrating the sense of the message. This global integration presupposes a structure of coding which is no longer merely bi-univocal (digital) nor equivocal (analogic), but multivocal (the hologram).

THE HOLOGRAPHIC MODEL

The referent 'cat' may be represented by a drawing which resembles it more or less closely or simulates its mewing or its feline movements (analogic coding). By contrast, one might write the word 'cat' which, as Bateson rather wittily observes, does not 'miaow' (digital coding). However, in speech acts or even in writing, meaning is only possible thanks to an overall conjunction between the elements of a semantic field and the total field. The intonation with which the word 'cat' is pronounced may recall 'miaowing'. Similarly, the hissing sound 'ch' in the French word *chat* may analogically recall the animal's threat signal. It is in this way that a word contains a part of the information distributed over the word and the contexts to which it is related, just as it is part of its own overall semantic spectrum.

The figures of rhetoric thus possess a high holographic content: metaphor (e.g. hazy thinking), metonymy (e.g. a glass of water), oxymoron (e.g. the black sun of melancholy), catachresis (e.g. a plastic glass, a divan for the family) etc. call upon information 'distributed' and 'degenerated' between the literal and the figurative aspects (Pinson et al., 1985).

(See also COMMUNICATION SYSTEMS; DEIXIS; ICONS; INFORMATION; METACOMMUNICATION SYSTEMS; MULTI-

CHANNEL COMMUNICATION SYSTEMS; PARACOMMUNICA-
TION SYSTEMS; SYMBOLS.)

J.M.

assemblage   Defined by Elkaim (1986, 1987a) as the
set created by the different elements intersecting in a
particular situation. These elements may be genetic,
biological, linked to family rules or sociocultural aspects. What determines blockage or change in a particular situation is the nature of the assemblages in
play.

A system is habitually described as made up of
individuated elements in interaction; now, even if that
system is something other than the mere sum of its
elements, these latter are most often still conceived as
separate biological entities, bounded by their skins.
Mony Elkaim throws into question the very concept of
individual; what happens to us cannot be limited to
our cutaneous envelope: the symptoms of an anorexic
patient does not belong to her as her own: it is an
assemblage of genetic, biological, identificatory,
phantasmatic, mass-media, cultural and social elements.
That asssemblage changes as the patient's life-context
changes, causing the symptoms to appear or disappear
over time.

(See also ANOREXIA NERVOSA; COMPLEXITY; GENERAL
SYSTEMS THEORY; SINGULARITIES; SYMPTOMS.)

J.M.

attachment behaviour   Described by John Bowlby
(1969), in the light of the findings of ethology, psychoanalysis, psychology and cybernetics, as an instinctive bonding behaviour which the child deploys from
birth towards persons encountered in his/her environment. It becomes structured and differentiated in the
course of existence, while being subject to normal or
pathological perturbations which modify its expression
(anxious attachment, grief reactions and depressive
states).

The foreseeable result of attachment behaviour is
the attainment or maintenance of the proximity of a
preferred person. The prototype of this behaviour is
the attachment behaviour of the infant to his or her
mother and/or her substitutes. It plays a part in the
survival of the individual in a very great number of
species. This behaviour, the basis of family bonds in
adulthood, when a couple is formed, is structured within
the family through the establishment of TRIANGLES,
which are connected to sexual and generational differences. This leads to the creation of extrafamilial bonds,
which comprise an essential condition for the achievement of personal autonomy and the reproduction of
family ties.

STRUCTURES AND FUNCTIONS OF ATTACHMENT
BEHAVIOUR

This behaviour is regulated as a function of the goal to
be attained, is auto-adaptive and distinct from feeding
and sexual behaviour. It is an instinctive behaviour
which is released autonomously and reacts to signals.
On the level of its manifest expression, it thus comprises call signals (smiles, vocalizations, cries and skin
contact) and movements towards other persons (non-
nutritive sucking, clinging, crawling, locomotion). It is
set, temporally, in a hierarchy of rhythmic inscriptions
of presence/absence which becomes more complex with
the maturation of the child, and, subsequently, of the
adolescent and adult. Periods of presence and absence,
of contact and of distancing, are set in place. Attachment is formed on the basis of interaction between
neurophysiological systems and relational systems.
Within this perspective, the processes of IMPRINTING,
BECOMING ACCUSTOMED, HABITUATION and phobic reaction are to be taken into account.

Attachment behaviour fulfils a number of functions:
protection from danger (physical dangers, predators,
strangers); the maturation of love and friendship behaviours; the stabilization of relations by the construction of systems for representing those relations; and
the development of a sense of security and the evaluation of dangers. Attachment behaviour unfolds under
the influence of mother–child relations. It presupposes
a quantitative and qualitative availability of the mother,
her capacity to appease her child and to leave him/her
alone as his/her needs permit.

PATHOLOGY OF ATTACHMENT BEHAVIOUR

Attachment comprises a system of attaching, a system
of rooting and a system of acquisition of stages of
freedom in the establishment of relations. The pathology
of attachment thus concerns *rooting* itself, the *forming*
of the bond, and also the distending, if not indeed the
breaking, of the bond (Louttre du Pasquier, 1981).

Bowlby has described an *anxious attachment* linked
to the experience of the mother being available in an
insufficient or unstable way, to anxious attitudes on
her part or again to more or less repeated separations.
Bowlby here connects with Freudian theory which
regarded anxiety as a signal expressing risk of a loss
of the love object. In cases where the loss of the love
object is actually experienced, mechanisms of mourning, separation and depression are set in place.

(See also AGONISTIC BEHAVIOUR; COALITION; IDENTIFI-
CATION; LEARNING; SCHISMOGENESIS; SEXED BEHAVIOUR;
TRIANGLES.)

J.M. & P.G.

attitudes, conscious and unconscious   An attitude
is a set of factors which mediate information and the

control of conscious and unconscious behaviours. It is simultaneously:

1 The posturo–gestural disposition of the body of the human person in interaction.
2 The psychological disposition which orders information and gives it meaning on the basis of rules and which makes a choice from among the possible responses according to selection criteria, which leads to the actualization of certain tendencies.
3 The conscious and unconscious availability for action and the enactment of behaviour.

There is an interesting convergence between the way attitude is defined within the framework of cognitive psychology, which derives from American behaviourism, and within experimental psychology, which draws its inspiration from Soviet reflexology. For the former school, an attitude is what influences our behaviour in a way that is not consciously decided, which is acquired by imitation and which is impossible to force (such as the love of classical music, for example). For the latter, an attitude (or, more precisely, *ustanovka*) is a set of models of orientation structured by experience between stimulus and response and capable of being modified through use; driving a car is a good illustration.

Whatever sense of the concept one accepts and whether one limits oneself to the classic definition of 'a state of preparedness on the part of the subject for perception and action' or to that of a mental image in Piaget's sense, the attitude of the therapist during the session will appear to be an essential determinant of the relationship; once that is accepted, it is clearly a factor to be evaluated, orientated and exploited.

We may thus distinguish between the attitude of the therapist(s) and the attitude of the family members in a clinical situation. The *attitude of the therapist* is an active disposition which forms the relational framework that is received by the patient; though acquired by IDENTIFICATION, both implicit and explicit, with the therapist's teachers and trainers, it reveals itself in a spontaneous way. It is made up of behavioural elements which, by unconsciously transmitting meanings by pictogrammic communication, may bring about a favourable change in the symptoms presented. The *attitude of the members of the family* reveals to the therapist(s) the ordered hierarchies of their posturo-gestural and linguistic behaviours, as well as their mutual influence upon one another.

The flexible adaptation of behaviour results from variations in the state of consciousness and oscillations in the capacity to perceive one's own attitude and that of others at every moment. Attitudes are both conscious and unconscious. It is also necessary, however, to distinguish between variations in levels of vigilance. In hypnotic states or in REM sleep (sleep with dreaming activity), there is a state of consciousness, even though vigilance is very much diminished. Conversely, the state of vigilance may be high even though the individual may be totally unconscious of his/her actual situation. These variations in the state of vigilance and the state of consciousness are unequally distributed among the family group and the therapeutic group, both within and outside the sessions.

There results from this a *grammar of attitudes*. A distinction has been made between active and reactive therapists depending on whether they tend to lead and initiate, or to follow and track in relation to the members of the family. Very often, the index patient is the indicator of the considerable distortions which exist within the family as regards the family's action–reaction exchanges. Ideally, the same therapist must be capable of being at times *active* and at times *reactive* depending upon the situation, which presupposes on his/her part a basic attitude of attention to others and to the metacommunicative phenomena transmitted at an unconscious level.

The therapeutic sub-system may be assisted by *auxiliary memories* (see READ–WRITE MEMORIES): note-taking, tape or video recording, extemporaneous *prise de conscience* by the interruption of the session and meeting with co-therapists and supervisors etc. It is important that the clients should be informed of the context in which these 'auxiliary memories' are being used.

Attitudes are made up of metacommunicative and paracommunicative elements (see METACOMMUNICATION SYSTEMS; PARACOMMUNICATION SYSTEMS): thus the therapist may direct his or her remarks personally to one member of the family, speaking to him and looking him in the eye, while in fact he or she is really trying to address these remarks to all the other members of the family. It is, similarly, of importance to decode the circuits of ocular, gestural and linguistic communication within the intrafamilial exchanges, and their levels of congruence or incongruence.

It is very often in occupying oneself with things that have no apparent objective connection with the therapeutic situation that the greatest potential lies. There is a risk of a brutal breaking-off of the relationship if such activities seem in contradiction with the attitude displayed; a risk of an abreactive upsurge of emotion if these activities maintain a logical status as part of that attitude; and a possibility of a positive change if, by accompanying the group in its defensive and mythical positions, they enable the patient and the family to achieve metacommunication. In this way, the symptom loses its function without having been approached head on. As examples of such practices, we may cite allusive remarks, techniques of confusion or disinformation, the use by the therapists of METAPHORICAL OBJECTS (manipulation of toys, changing places, moving about).

(See also BEHAVIOURISM, ETHOLOGY; FAMILY ETHOLOGY.)

G.G.M. & J.M.

attractors, strange attractors   An attractor, A, is a compact set (almost every trajectory is dense in A) of the phase space of a DYNAMIC SYSTEM:

- A is invariant: every function of A is equal to A;
- A is situated within a domain, B, the neighbourhood of A, which constitutes its basin of attraction: every point belonging to B tends towards A.

The attractor, A, is therefore a geometrical manifold (point, curve, surface, volume etc.) of the phase space towards which the representative points of the system tend asymptotically.

The phase space of a dynamic system is the reference space, whose axes of coordinates define the position and velocity of the representative points of the system. A phase trajectory is any curve of the space representative of the evolution of the system. The total set of trajectories is the phase portrait of the system.

A *punctual attractor* (or punctuation) is the reflection of a stationary situation (STATIC or PSEUDO-STATIC form of the system), corresponding to a gradient dynamic. A *periodic behaviour* is associated with a limit cycle, which is characterized by its amplitude and its period. Interference between several cycles forms attractors of r frequencies, representable on a torus Tr, such that $r \geq 2$. The cycles governing the rhythm of the life of a couple or a family are thus regulated by periodic attractors, but also by aperiodic attractors.

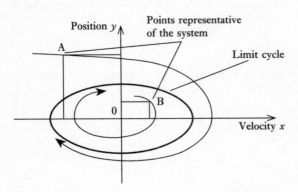

Periodic attractor of a dynamic system (oscillating movement).

Strange attractors appear for certain particular functions. A dissipative dynamic system (which expends a certain quantity of energy) may become chaotic when a dimension of the phase space is greater than or equal to 3. Strange attractors with complex forms appear when the phase space of the system has a fractal dimension (see FRACTALS), i.e. when the dimension d is such that $2 < d < 3$.

Perturbation in couples or families could be the product of an appearance of strange attractors, bringing about chaotic relations. Certain interferences in life-cycles might thus bring about sudden breaks in exchanges. An excitation – even a minimal one – may enter into resonance with a frequency of great amplitude (for example, the conjunction of a family celebration and the death of a grandfather at the very moment of the ceremony, triggering off an acute psychotic episode in, say, his eldest daughter, the age difference between the grandfather and the eldest daughter corresponding more or less to the age of the child for whom the ceremony was being held). Similarly, quasi-periodic regimes arise in couples who do not succeed in synchronizing their actions (for example, when one partner puts off a positive behaviour expected by the other partner); such regimes bring about the appearance of completely de-synchronized relations, which leads to a more or less complete destabilization of interactions. In other cases, 'turbulence' will be observed in the children in families where the relation between the parental couple is too static.

So far as families with schizophrenic transactions are concerned, it is not clear that one can construct the phase space representative of the system with a finite number of dimensions, i.e. that one can have an overall representation of the system.

(See also AGREEMENT AND DISAGREEMENT; BEHAVIOURISM; ELEMENTARY CATASTROPHES; FAMILY CATASTROPHES; FAMILY LIFE–CYCLES; GENERALIZED CATASTROPHES; INFORMATION; OSCILLATORS; RELATIONAL ARCHETYPES; SEMANTIC RESONANCES.)

J.M.

autism   See INFANTILE AUTISM.

autonomy and heteronomy of a system   It is commonplace to represent systems in general and living systems in particular in terms of a dialectic between two complementary, and in part contradictory, characteristics: autonomy ensures a coherence in the system's own definition of itself, in the establishment of initiatives and spontaneous impulsions and the differentiation of a specific identity (the 'self'); heteronomy leads to justifying or invalidating the coherence of the system from outside, to rendering its autonomy functional, and, in certain cases, to modifying its structure.

We thus see standing in opposition to one another here two polarities in the structuring of systems: we shall therefore, following Varela (1979), give a description of heteronomous and autonomous structures, bringing out the distinct properties of each:

The logical basis
- heteronomous structures are based on a correspondence between two or more elements;

- autonomous structures are based on the coherence of these elements.

Type of organization
- heteronomous structures are characterized by inputs and outputs, as well as by the transference of information from inside to outside and vice versa;
- autonomous structures are characterized by organizational closure and by a feedback of behaviour which ensures its informational coherence ('eigenbehaviour').

The mode of interaction
- heteronomous structures operate on the basis of instructions relating to the internal representations they have of the outside world; they are thus heteroreferential and presuppose the existence of internal images that are isomorphic or at least homomorphic with external objects;
- autonomous structures operate by constructing a world of meaning which makes the internal and external aspects of their components indistinguishable; they are self-referential (see FAMILY SELF-REFERENTIALITY, based not on approximate representations producing a 'likeness' but on solipsistic and autistic co-actions).

Historicity
- heteronomous structures pursue optimum adaptation, as a function of the properties of the environment, and fit themselves into the mould provided by that environment;
- autonomous structures are creationist; they have a natural motion, drift or course which transforms organism–environment relations into a phenomenon of co-emergence or co-evolution.

Epistemology
- heteronomous structures are eternalistic, reflexive and objectivistic;
- autonomous structures are nihilistic, impulsive and subjectivistic.

Varela (1979) has emphasized the necessity of a shifting between these structures. However, the precise articulation between these two systemic polarities still remains to be worked out. We shall merely content ourselves with noting here that there is no autonomy without dependence. As Morin points out:

Every closure upon oneself corresponds to an opening up. It might even be said that nothing is more open than the living being that is a subject. Nothing is more dependent in so many ways upon the world around it. Nothing has so much need to know the outside world. And the more developed it is, the more it is dependent. It is the higher animals that are ceaselessly driven by need, lack, thirst and hunger. . . . (Morin, 1980b, pp. 275–6)

(See also ALIENATION; SELF–ORGANIZATION.)

J.M.

autopoesis   See FAMILY SELF-REFERENTIALITY; SELF–ORGANIZATION.

axes of a therapy   See CONJUNCTION OF THERAPEUTIC AXES.

B

ball, sphere In a metric space (with distance), the closed ball B, with centre O and radius R is the set of points M such that $d(OM) \leq R$. The points M such that $d(OM) < R$ form the open ball $B°$. The set $B–B°$ is the perimeter sphere such that $d(OM) = R$.

The ball of dimension 2 is the disc. The ball of dimension 1 is the segment. The sphere of dimension 2 is the normal sphere. The sphere of dimension 1 is the circle. The sphere of dimension 0 is the pair of points.

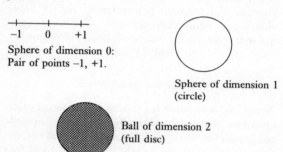

Sphere of dimension 0:
Pair of points –1, +1.

Sphere of dimension 1
(circle)

Ball of dimension 2
(full disc)

For Thom (1981b, p. 60), to the extent that it is individualized, a living organism, a human being, is topologically a ball: 'The only salient forms appropriate for receiving a pregnant form are individuated forms', corresponding topologically to balls with distinct surfaces. If, then, the ball is representative of the properties of biological bodies, the sphere provides a model of the milieu within which organisms develop within the environment. It evokes the 'territory', spaces as they are mentally introjected and conceived by the organism's internal milieu or mentally projected and realized in the outer milieu. The notion of sphere may thus evoke that of physical and psychical territoriality. An animal establishes around itself a hierarchy of spheres defined by critical distances of flight or attack. From a psychosociological point of view, we may speak, then, of psychical spheres, spheres of influence etc.

We may thus distinguish between the internal and external milieu of the organism, and its environment (see diagram). The frontier between environment and milieu corresponds to the limit of mutual influence between the organism and the contexts in which it has its being; the milieu is that part of the environment which affects the organism, psychically or physically. This frontier is both external and internal (only the external frontier can be represented here). The frontier between the internal and the external milieu corresponds to the physical boundary of the organism.

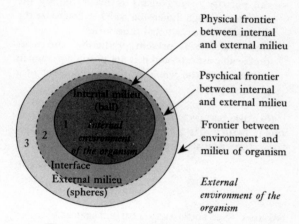

The organism, its milieu and its environment.

Zone 3 corresponds to a zone of biological influence between the organism and the external milieu, without there being any psychical modification (conscious or unconscious) of the organism. Zone 2 corresponds to the zone of the environment which the organism psychically takes into account (by introjection, projection etc.). This zone is an intermediate space, an interface in which the milieu is both internal and external. Such a zone may be represented as a non-orientated figure. From two dimensions upwards, non-orientated figures exist in which there is continuous passage between inside and outside: in two dimensions, the Moebius strip, in three dimensions, the Klein bottle. Jacques Lacan proposed an 'ontological' theory of the subject on the basis of the sphere with a cross-cap (a figure with an orientated and a non-orientated part).

What is useful about topology is that it enables us to structure the spaces on which TANGLED HIERARCHIES in the differentiation of individual, family and society are inscribed, and this resolves a certain number of psychical or relational paradoxes. Such a model enables us to realize that COMMUNICATION THEORY cannot be reduced to a psychological analysis of interferences between the organism and its external milieu. The frontier between the environment and the organism's milieu corresponds to the borderline of interaction between organism and environment. The internal environment is made up of one part (the inner milieu) which affects the physical or psychical functioning of the organism and one part which does not interfere with this.

This model is necessarily reductive. It does not take into account the organizational complexity of behaviours and systems of interaction which would require a multidimensional space in which D ≥ 4 dimensions if the temporal dimension is to be taken into account. The description of behaviours and interactions exceeds the current capacities of mathematical formalization. At best we can offer some suggestions:

- the polarity of organisms is decentred by the attractors of high dimension which characterize the dynamics of interactional trajectories;
- these trajectories present predictible and non-predictable aspects, and it is not possible to remain in control of the whole of the development of a given situation.

(See also DISTANCE; ELEMENTARY CATASTROPHES; ENTROPY; FAMILY MAPS; MAPS; METAPSYCHOLOGY; TERRITORY; TOPOLOGICAL SPACE; TRANSITIONAL OBJECTS.)

M.G. & J.M.

barriers See BOUNDARIES, LIMITS, BARRIERS.

becoming accustomed 'Becoming accustomed' (or habit formation) is the individual (ontogenetic) acquisition, complementary to IMPRINTING, which enables reciprocal and selective parent–child recognition to take place; once achieved, this acquisition is not modifiable by trial and error (see LEARNING). The phenomena of habit formation appear very early on in the life of the child, but they also operate in adult life and even in old age, both in 'normal' and in pathological ways (the individual becoming accustomed to his or her family ecosystem, the old person becoming accustomed to his or her habitat, the drug addict becoming accustomed to his or her drug).

ONTOGENESIS OF 'BECOMING ACCUSTOMED'

For Lorenz (1973, 1978b), 'becoming accustomed' (or habit formation), is the behavioural process in which key stimuli can trigger an action only when presented within the context of an overall, complex configuration of perception. 'Habit formation' thus stands opposed to HABITUATION in which overall perception inhibits the effect of the key stimulus. In habit formation, for a particular behaviour to be released, a connection between the key stimulus (or stimuli) and the perception of the figure in its totality is required. This does not mean that the range of these configurations (overall perceptions) of complex stimuli is substituted for the initial key stimuli; these latter must remain present within the context of the configurations to trigger the behaviour in question. There exists therefore an increase in initial selectivity which leads to the ability to learn to recognize persons.

The process of 'becoming accustomed' is in effect complementary to imprinting properly so called, in so far as it enables the child (and reciprocally the adult in relation to his/her child) to select once and for all the individual organism on which their ATTACHMENT BEHAVIOUR (and parental behaviour) will bear. The addition of multiple activation conditions for the initial attachment behaviour, while not removing the need for the initial key stimuli, also becomes imperative for this behaviour to be released in satisfactory conditions.

It is in this way that the human infant moves from a behaviour pattern in which he or she is reacting to very vague, arbitrary and general key stimuli (connected with typed indices or 'sign Gestalts': forehead, eyes and nose, or even between two and six points in the middle of a round shape, a marked difference between the shape of the face and the surrounding background, the categorial perception of certain vocal, olfactory or tactile patterns) to the selective recognition of his/her mother as a person (Spitz, 1965; Bowlby, 1969; Allyn, 1974; Vidal, 1976a).

PATHOLOGY OF 'BECOMING ACCUSTOMED'

'Becoming accustomed' is a process of acquisition which cannot be modified retroactively by means of rewards or aversion (see LEARNING). Once the child has become imprinted on and accustomed to the detailed and holistic perception (see HOLISM) of his or her mother and father, the pleasant or unpleasant experiences attaching to them cannot further put into question the nature of the process thus acquired, and therefore the identity of his or her perceived and recognized parents. We are not, then, dealing here with a learning process that is modifiable by conditioned experiences of a trial-and-error kind. This has certain consequences, both for pathology and therapy:

The transition from the local releasing stimulus (in psychoanalysis the 'part object') to the more sophisticatedly selective recognition of a person as totality (the total object) is liable to a wide range of blocks, inhibitions and splittings; in the autistic individual (see INFANTILE AUTISM), this transition seems completely impossible, any human forms only being apprehended so as to be systematically avoided thereafter.

In DRUG ADDICTION or ALCOHOLISM, the total form seems to be accepted, but it seems to stamp the experience with affective deprivation so far as the initial objects are concerned, and this has marked depressive consequences. At the stage when the changes of adolescence occur, with the cracks this creates at the most fragile points of individual and family structures, we find systems of habit formation which are pathological, in that the substitutive object (the artefact represented by the bottle, the syringe and their contents) never matches the 'compact' and limited satisfaction afforded by the initial object; the short-circuit which ensues sets in train an escalating process of positive retroactions (supra-normal allurement effect of the substitutive drug substance).

From a therapeutic point of view, disconnecting from the lure of addictive substances cannot be obtained by simple de-conditioning techniques. This requires the re-establishment of specific inter-human bonds (the re-establishment of familial interactions, the setting up of specialist associations, Alcoholics Anonymous etc.), the correct balancing of which in terms of time and space should be strictly assessed and monitored.

J.M.

behaviourism, behaviour therapy Behaviourism is based on the analysis and manipulation of environmental factors which modify a higher form of behaviour. Its object of study is operant conditioning, i.e. the positive and negative reinforcements which the actions of the environment exert upon a given behaviour, as a function of trial-and-error learning. The behaviour therapy which results from that study seeks to isolate the dependent variables, the 'contingencies of reinforcement', and act explicitly on the environmental factors capable of eliminating an unwanted symptom or of giving rise to a desired behaviour.

'Behaviourism is not the scientific study of behaviour, but a philosophy of science regarding the subject-matter and methods of psychology' (Skinner, 1969). In actual fact, behaviourism has influenced a great number of sciences (psychology and linguistics through the work of Leonard Bloomfield in particular), as well as the arts (the American thriller).

Behaviourism was initially associated with the reflex model and the stimulus–response schema. B. F. Skinner made a thoroughgoing critique of this latter. Such a schema omits to consider the action of the environment on the organism after a response has been produced. Skinner suggested that the stimulus–response schema should be supplemented by the addition of the model of *operant reinforcement*. By re-afference – a circular reflex – the response modifies and renews the original stimulus. The *operant* is the class of responses on which the presentation of a reinforcement depends. The action of the milieu on the organism operates as a function of the variations in rate of response, forming the dependent variables. (By contrast, in this model, stimuli, internal motivations, emotions are independent variables.) An increase in the rate of response can lead to either a *positive reinforcement*: the appearance of consequences, e.g. rewarding of a child for producing desired behaviour; or a *negative reinforcement*: the disappearance of consequences, for example, the punishment of a child for producing behaviour that was not desired.

Bateson (1978) has shown that experimental double binds can be produced in dolphins by making a contradictory and incoherent series of reinforcements for a sequence of exercises demanded of the animal (for example, by successively rewarding and punishing expected behaviour; or by rewarding the expected behaviour, but doing so with a delay); after a certain period of confusion and perplexity, the animal will eventually invent sequences involving a degree of novelty and unexpected behaviour. However, in the same circumstances, dogs are incapable of such an inner revolution.

Several models of family dysfunction can be derived from behaviourist theories.

THE DYADIC MODEL

This model stresses the possibility of falling into an aggravated cycle of reciprocal reinforcements: parents who give a child a lot of negative reinforcement run the risk of the same kind of attitude coming back to them from the child (Gordon and Davidson, 1981). The same is true where there is an excess of positive reinforcement.

In a couple, it may be observed that one of the most effective factors involved in maintaining relations in a fixed state is connected with aperiodic negative reinforcements (Skinner, quoted in Jackson, 1965b). In such a situation, one partner will, in a random manner, defer the response which is a source of pleasure for the other partner and which he/she expects to occur within a certain time. In such a case, even if this deferring partner is apparently in a complementary lower position, he/she takes power in the definition of the relationship. The disturbances in the organization of the couple which result from this may be interpreted as being connected with the appearance of strange ATTRACTORS within the phase space of the conjugal system.

The advantage of such a model is that it centres on units of behaviour such as can be perceived and monitored, both by the members of the family and by the therapists. This therapeutic attitude is particularly useful when dealing with persons with weak powers of phantasmatic elaboration or ones who indicate clearly to the therapist that such a phantasmatic investigation is an epistemological error for the resolution of their problem. In these cases, one very often sees a total confusion between imaginary perception and the perception of reality.

TRIADIC AND SOCIAL MODELS

These models focus interest on certain limited and localized aspects of the interactions between parents, grandparents etc. The important thing is to recognize that behavioural disturbances may occur in a child in families with or without conjugal discord. 'The simple presence of marital discord in these families may or may not be causally related to the child's problems' (Gordon and Davidson, 1981, p. 522).

It has been the merit of American behaviourism (together with European objectivistic ethology) to stress the importance of the environment in the structuring of behaviour, and the advantage of sequencing the problems to be treated. Skinner shows that, in dealing with psychotic behaviour, it may be preferable to act on the life-context of the patient rather than on his/her internal structuring. The aim is then to create true *environmental prostheses*.

Skinner (1971) criticizes non-directive therapies. He acknowledges that they have some value, in so far as the mere fact of caring for someone is reinforcing, but

> The fundamental mistake made by all those who choose weak methods of control is to assume that the balance of control is left to the individual, when in fact it is left to other conditions. The other conditions are often hard to see, but to continue to neglect them and to attribute their effects to autonomous man is to court disaster. (Skinner, 1971, p. 99)

If, then, the so-called non-directive therapies free the patient from harmful contingencies, it is only because the ethical, religious, political and educational contingencies permit this. All weak methods of control can therefore be said to run the risk of therapeutic irresponsibility.

> The freedom and dignity of autonomous man seem to be preserved when only weak forms of nonaversive control are used. Those who use them seem to defend themselves against the charge that they are attempting to control behavior, and they are exonerated when things go wrong. Permissiveness is the absence of control, and if it appears to lead to desirable results, it is only because of other contingencies. Maieutics, or the art of midwifery, seems to leave behavior to be credited to those who give birth to it, and the guidance of development to those who develop. . . . (Skinner, 1971, pp. 99–100)

We shall simply note here that the psychoanalytic and systemic models are not non-directive techniques. Moreover, an integrative ethology of behaviour has to take into account the very structure of these autonomous behaviours, and their dysfunctions. The fact that one does not act directly upon conditions that cannot be transformed directly should not be taken to indicate that one is ignorant of them, or that one can act directly upon them. It is by submitting to constraints that the sportsman or the artist gains in autonomy and freedom. Furthermore, behaviourism only takes into account linear and circular causalities. It leaves out of account the appreciation of formal causalities, the morphogenetic fields to which individuals and groups are subject. Though the study of the FORCE FIELDS that are present

does not make it possible to change their nature, it does lead to our identifying the critical points where positive, negative or neutral changes are likely to occur.

From a psychoanalytic point of view, autonomy is built up from processes of incorporation–projection, projective identification and identification; i.e. from the reciprocal influences of the internal and external environments, which are prerequisites for the structuring of desire. Behaviourism does not take into account the influences of the organism upon its environment (including other organisms and their own internal environments). It does not take into account the organism's impulse-generating mechanisms, its creative dimensions and therefore its universal properties. A fundamental – integrative and nuanced – critique of behaviourism and classical ethology is offered by Lorenz in *Evolution and modification of behaviour* (1965).

All study of behaviour cannot be reduced to behaviourism. An anthropo-ethology remains to be constructed which is not reduced either to a mere interspecies comparative study, or to a stimulus–response and operant-conditioning analysis.

(See also BECOMING ACCUSTOMED; CATASTROPHE THEORY; ETHOLOGY; FAMILY ETHOLOGY; HABITUATION; IMPRINTING; INSTINCT.)

J.M.

belonging See RITUALS OF BELONGING (OR MEMBERSHIP), RITUALS OF INCLUSION.

bifurcation A point of bifurcation is a critical value of the parameters of a system from which a new stationary state of a system may appear. Deriving from the Latin '*bifurcus*', meaning forked, bifurcation presupposes a choice between several outcomes which are a priori difficult to predict; once the set of critical points has been reached, there are states of the bifurcation set which become inpossible to cover.

The notion of bifurcation, first theorized from a mathematical point of view by H. Poincaré (1854–1912) (see Poincaré, 1963), has been utilized systematically by Thom (1972) in his theory of ELEMENTARY CATASTROPHES to study the discontinuities which may arise where there are continuous perturbations of one or more parameters of a DYNAMIC SYSTEM. In this model, for every value of the parameters there are one or more corresponding stable states. These are stable forms of the bifurcation. The values of parameters for which the system will 'hesitate' between several possible states and, at the slightest perturbation, jump suddenly towards one of them form the bifurcation set and describe a determinate and structured geometrical configuration of the loci in space–time at which change is possible. In fact, Thom distinguishes between *conflict catastrophes* and *bifurcation catastrophes*:

- conflict catastrophes are shock wave surfaces separating the different domains where attractors are in competition;
- bifurcation catastrophes describe situations of conflict between attractors, at least one of which is no longer structurally stable. Each bifurcation singularity engenders conflict catastrophes in its neighbourhood (see ELEMENTARY CATASTROPHES).

It will be up to the therapist, therefore, to identify the ACTUOGENETIC and MORPHOGENETIC landscapes of the family system and to seek to modify the parameters which may modify the bifurcation set, thus bringing about a change at the critical or singular points (see SINGULARITIES) reached by the system.

The work of Prigogine (1980) on the thermodynamics of non-equilibrium states shows that 'far from' the usual equilibrium, bifurcation points appear beyond which the fluctuations affecting a system will no longer tend to bring it back towards an earlier state, but rather to amplify themselves by virtue of positive feedback processes, thus enabling the system to reach a new equilibrium state. This may in turn give rise to new instabilities and new bifurcations towards other possible states. On the other hand, for the same critical value of the parameters, different bifurcations are possible, depending upon which fluctuation has been amplified, and this occurs in a random manner.

Taking up the work of Prigogine, a number of family therapists, such as Elkaim et al. (1980) suggest that we should be attentive to the perturbations and singularities of family dynamics, even when these are difficult to perceive, which, when amplified, could take the family system far enough from its usual equilibrium, thus giving it the possibility of a transition to other stable states and other modalities of functioning. In such a process of destabilization, the therapists, being open to the emergence of singular elements which are not necessarily understood in terms of their own explicative map, will accompany the family system in an escalation of non-equilibrium states, constituting a series of successive bifurcations of its figures or regulation.

(See also ATTRACTORS; EQUIFINALITY; SENSITIVITY TO INITIAL CONDITIONS; SINGULARITIES.)

M.G.

black box The inaccessible part of a system, of which only the inputs (control variables) and outputs (behaviour variables) are visible. The 'black box' is a concept, not a real object. This concept is a universal modelling tool. It enables us, by construction, to put black boxes inside one another, like Russian dolls. To learn how a black box functions, it is more pertinent to play around with it than to seek to open it.

The concept of the black box describes the opaque character of the complex systems being studied. An individual person, a family or a social organization are only apprehended as complex systems by the examination of inputs and outputs, and by the variations existing in the state of outputs as a function of the variations tried out in the state of inputs.

The understanding of the functioning of black boxes can be clarified in part by virtue of the distinction between trivial and non-trivial MACHINES, on the one hand, and by CATASTROPHE THEORY and the theory of SINGULARITIES on the other.

SYSTEMIC MODELLING OF A BLACK BOX

For Ashby (1956), black boxes are not to be understood as real objects. Real objects can be modelled as black boxes which only deliver up some of their properties of the observer thanks to transducers or ANALOG–DIGITAL CONVERTERS.

The concept of black box is therefore indissociable from the experimenter acting upon the box and allowing himself to be affected by it. A *coupling* phenomenon exists between experimenter and black box, produced through the feedback which connects the two together (Ashby, 1956). The recognition of the properties of the system occurs over time, by describing the values of the state of the inputs and the values of the state of the outputs, together with their differentials. One will thus obtain, though in a qualitative manner, the values or VECTORS of the black box, as well as their temporal trajectories (see FORCE FIELDS).

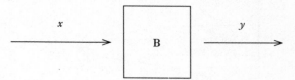

Elementary diagram of a black box (B): x, input variables; y, output variables, such that $y = f(x)$. (In catastrophe theory, x represents the control variables, y the behaviour variables.)

When confronted with a black box, two opposing attitudes are possible:

1 *The systemic attitude* consists in playing with it, hovering around it, connecting it up with other similar or complementary black boxes. Hence the importance in therapy of the role-playing games and artificial simulations of real situations.
2 *The analytic attitude* consists in attempting to open the black box, break it up and perhaps to come upon other smaller boxes, whose opacity may be reinforced by the very fact of the previous manoeuvre (Thom, 1980b).

The two attitudes have their advantages and disadvantages. The systemic attitude may be more dynamic, respecting the state of construction under examination. The risk here, however, is that one may take a superficial view of the situation, remain content with crude, general results, or even, indeed, reinforce the resistances of the system by a 'cutting' perception and intervention. (There is, for example, a risk of a '"wild" prescription of symptoms', through ignorance of the history and the structure of the sub-systems.) The analytic attitude has in its favour a prestigious scientific and efficacious past. It enables one to identify the qualities of the system with precision, but it has a sorcerer's apprentice character. The breaking up of a black box into its component parts (particularly when this is a very disturbed family) may lead to potentially irreversible explosions of energy. The method of FREE ASSOCIATION, outside the relevant contexts, may also become a 'wild' method.

The figures of regulation of a living system may be modelled on the basis of ELEMENTARY CATASTROPHES in cases where one may postulate that the behaviour variables are finite in number. Catastrophes have survival value. They change the state of a system in order to maintain its structural stability. Behind the apparent discontinuity and the apparent illogicality of DOUBLE BINDS, one may thus postulate the existence of continuous curves which ensure the regulation of the symbolic boundaries of the system. When the system can no longer cope with change, a catastrophe, in the usual sense of the term, occurs and this breaks up the system.

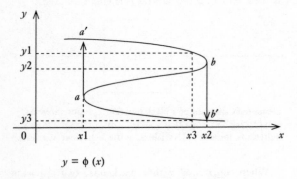

$$y = \phi\,(x)$$

Catastrophe theoretic modelling of the black box. For the input value $x3$, there are two stable values, $y1$ and $y2$, and an unstable value, $y3$.

THE BLACK BOX AND PSYCHOPATHOLOGY

The configuration of the black box under consideration will depend on the observation protocol and interpretive system employed. In psychoanalysis, the couch–armchair arrangement excludes direct visual contact so far as is possible. That method relies upon use of language based upon the structure of the alphabet (the insistence of the letter, puns, signifiers, jokes etc.). Focus on language reveals another level of psychic structure and all the snares of the audiovisual world. Face-to-face therapeutic situations, by playing upon the register of positions, postures and the multisemic attitudes of the members of a family engaging more or less directly with the therapist, bring other semiological forms to the fore and function with other black boxes. For the child, drawings are what reveal the psychoaffective positions of each member of the family, so long as they are never interpreted as doing so.

For writers like Maurel et al. (1983), the concept of black box is seen as revealing ultimately the radical inadequacy of the Batesonian model. However, could one resolve to leave the box intact?

> We shall never agree to abstain from attempting to open this box on the pernicious pretext that it might contain something, perhaps even explosives! Bracketing out 'the intrapsychic', which goes along with putting the patient in a black box, is admittedly consistent with American behaviourism. But we reject it. (Maurel et al., 1983, p. 55)

This opinion, which is quite widely shared, calls for critical discussion.

On the one hand, it classifies the 'psychical apparatus' proposed by Freud as an intrapsychic black box which is thus seen as having been opened. It also implies that, in analysing the internal productions of schizophrenic patients, the handling of explosives would in this case be beneficial. The most common clinical experience shows that every attempt at the 'classic' psychoanalysis of psychotic patients forces us, in the cases that turn out fortunately (i.e. the ones which do not end in fatalities), to reinforce neuroleptic and/or institutional therapies with the greatest haste. It was one of the virtues of the Freudian model that it recognized the field of psychosis as a concrete limit to its practical pertinence.

On the other hand, though psychoanalysis has opened up certain black boxes of the psyche, the preconscious and unconscious phantasy contents never reveal the internal or external mechanisms which produce them. The problem of schizophrenia is precisely connected with a recognition of maximum psychic opacity and impenetrability. We shall note here that in the most disturbed family systems, the decomposition of the family black box into 'intrapsychic' black boxes does not necessarily illuminate the situation any further. Schizophrenic impenetrability marks the limits of a decomposition of a system into its smallest elements.

For Eiguer (1983), the recognition of phantasy activity could be seen as making the box transparent. Now, when that phantasy activity is sufficiently stabilized (which is precisely not the case in great psychotic outbursts), it is merely the representational reflection of the drives or instincts, which Freud stresses remain inaccessible as such. The affect has no psychical representations itself. In other words, even in classic metapsychology, the unconscious systems of motivation (*Triebe*) are recognized as black boxes inaccessible to introspection or to a verbalized conscious awareness. Psychoanalysis – and this goes for both individual and group analysis – seeks to work here only on systems of representation. Only ETHOLOGY enables us to identify the black boxes on which the systems of representation are based, while at the same time remaining aware that this cannot be reduced to the stimulus–response model of BEHAVIOURISM. Systemic modelling attempts to recognize the phenomena of communication as they emerge in the nascent state, the enactment of processes not yet constituted as phantasy scenarios, in order to permit phantasy organization and the understanding of the mind which organizes the functioning of the system.

THE FAMILY AS BLACK BOX

There are two means of access to the properties of the black box according to Ashby (1956): first, the *study of regularities, repetitions and redundancies*. When faced with schizophrenic transactions, delinquent behaviour and apparently perverse and shocking attitudes, it is necessary to identify the structurally stable forms which are attempting to preserve the survival of the system by giving it a solid structure, which provides a basis for memorization (without, however, giving one's approval to the moral value of such behaviour). Paradoxically, the identification of those forms which seek to repeat themselves and to rigidify, and indeed their prescription and stabilization, is likely to lead to a release of the most troubling pathological aspects. A symbiotic relationship between a mother and her 35-year-old child will only disengage itself from the apparently most 'incestuous' and dangerous aspects if the vital functions of the symbiosis are recognized, respected and indeed technically controlled. This gives rise to a 'canonical representation' of the system, and of its singularities.

Secondly, the *comparison between several black boxes of the same kind*. The recognition of inaccessible states, such that there exists no 'manipulation' of inputs, x, which acts in such a way as to enable one to obtain a state of outputs, y. This is particularly clear in learning processes. It then becomes necessary to study not the individual in the process of transforming him/herself, but the group (or groups) within which one or more other individuals will make comparative study possible. The family system here appears as a system of interpersonal differentiation *par excellence*, both for the members of the family system under consideration and for the therapists. It is, for example, possible to envisage multiple family therapies in situations in which the internal state of the family system is particularly inaccessible (see FAMILY THERAPIES).

ISOMORPHISMS AND HOMOMORPHISMS OF BLACK BOXES

Two black boxes are isomorphic if their canonical representations are identical, i.e. if there exists a strict equivalence between two black boxes. By contrast two pendulums, one of which beats at a frequency of half the other, are not isomorphic but homomorphic. Homomorphism corresponds therefore to a partial isomorphism. For example, the resonances existing between the individual psyche of a person and the family group to which he/she belongs are homomorphic rather than isomorphic. If one adopts such a point of view, the psychical resonances of a small child are obviously simpler than those of his two parents, if not indeed resonances produced by their communication. The simplest psyches are to be found in children, who are seeking to structure their identity in relation to appreciably more differentiated systems than their own. By contrast, the adolescent is supposed to interiorize the system of his family of origin sufficiently to free him or herself from it, to criticize it and, possibly, to reproduce it. The resonances between the various members of the family and the whole system will become isomorphic. Complexity is then likely to flip over from the family system to the individual who is likely to be leaving it. There then exist dangers of destruction of the family boundaries by interference or ACOUSTIC FEEDBACK.

(See also FAMILY PSYCHICAL APPARATUS; FAMILY SYSTEMS; GENERAL SYSTEMS THEORY.)

J.M.

boundaries, limits, barriers   The study of family boundaries is a way of identifying one of the essential properties of a family system, of its sub-systems and its relations with the environment and with other family and social systems. The boundaries or limits are the outer envelopes of physical or psychical material or fictive territories (Wynne et al., 1958; Lidz et al., 1965; Minuchin, 1974).

Boundaries are determined by the rules governing the establishment of relations. Their function is to distinguish between inside and outside, to protect and differentiate between sub-systems and to make possible exchanges with surrounding sub-systems and systems. Boundaries may be visible or invisible, permeable, impermeable or semi-permeable, rigid or flexible, enmeshed or disengaged, functional or dysfunctional. There are thus intra/inter-individual, intra/inter-dyadic and inter/intra-triadic boundaries. These relate to the parent–children system, the conjugal system and the grandparents–children system, as well as nuclear and extended families and interfaces with other social structures.

This notion also refers to material and imaginary lines drawn in a family group. Part of therapeutic work consists in aiding the family either to define or redefine its limits or to change the limits operating within it. The therapist also assists the family either to reinforce these limits or to make them more flexible as a function of the family situation (for example, when the children are penetrating into the parents' territory too much, Minuchin, 1974).

There are several possible approaches to the identification of boundaries: metapsychological or psychodynamic (Bion, 1961; Skynner, 1981), metasystemic–transgenerational (Bowen, 1978a; Kerr, 1981) and morphological–structural (Wynne et al., 1958; Minuchin, 1974).

We have first to make an important distinction: one of the parameters of the definition of a family is the territorial parameter. The *domus*, house or *oikos* (which gives us the terms ecology and ecosystem, the term 'family ecosystem' being virtually a pleonasm) defines a normally stable space, limited by internal and external boundaries. The product of the materiality of the *oikos* is not purely material. It presupposes that a great range of skills has been historically, multigenerationally and institutionally laid down, which in themselves define, in a general sense, what the spirit of a home should be. But the members of a concrete family will, in their turn, be defined by that ecosystem, adapt to it more or less, inhabit it, transform it, work the texture of its walls, doors and openings into personal and group representations. In family therapy, it may then possibly be pertinent to ask the members of a family to describe these territories and these boundaries and the way they move within them, invest them and possibly quarrel over them. One then discovers different points of view for describing the psychical and communicational nature of the boundaries under consideration.

METAPSYCHOLOGICAL–PSYCHODYNAMIC APPROACH

In the first Freudian topography, the psychical apparatus is thought of as being made up of several systems of representation. The boundary between the perception–consciousness system and the preconscious system allows exchanges of representations to occur unceasingly, while keeping the representations not immediately necessary for mental activity unconscious for as long as is necessary. By contrast, the boundaries between the unconscious system properly so–called (though made up of thing-representations) and the preconscious and perception-consciousness systems are much more closed, though the levels of permeability depend on the synergistic or antagonistic character of the functionings of the various systems. Though closed towards the interior, the unconscious system permits exchanges between one unconscious and another, which

entails the need for permeable interpersonal boundaries. Now, the more a person is autistically closed upon him or herself and this is coupled with impenetrable thought mechanisms, the more trans-personal invasion of systems of thought there is.

In a group psychoanalytic perspective, Skynner (1981, p. 49) writes that: 'the family therapist must stand at the *boundary* of the family and the community or the *boundary* between the individual and the family, avoiding identification with one or the other side.'

METASYSTEMIC–TRANSGENERATIONAL APPROACH

At the heart of this perspective we find the distinction between self and non-self as this is structured both in ontogenesis and as it is transmitted in a differential manner from one generation to another. The continued variation of undifferentiation over three to ten generations would lead, in Murray Bowen's words (Berger, 1978) to autistic or schizophrenic catastrophe. The more weakly boundaries are established between self and others, the more powerful the forces of collective cohesion, preventing a true distancing between each person. This brings about a fusion or undifferentiation of emotional, perceptual and intellectual systems, leading to purely subjective and unrealistic assertions about oneself and others.

A paradoxical self-sustaining process may then set in, in which anxiety increases the fusion of the emotional–intellectual systems which, in turn, strengthens the forces of collective cohesion and these themselves increase the fusion of the emotional–intellectual systems. In other words, fusion comes about as a result of suffering and itself creates further suffering. An invasion of the material territories of the various family members may then be observed, each person thinking and feeling in the other's place, hounding each other into intimacy by the continual transgression of proximal distances. This is accompanied by a variety of pathological manifestations, such as somatic conversion, behavioural or eating disorders.

MORPHOLOGICAL–STRUCTURAL PERSPECTIVE

For Minuchin (1974, p. 53), 'The boundaries of a subsystem are the rules defining who participates and how.' They determine who takes part in carrying out an operation and the respective roles in its execution. The function of boundaries is to protect the differentiation of the system and its members by making possible both the acquisition of interpersonal skills within the autonomous sub-systems and contacts with the outside. Depending upon the differentiation and permeability of boundaries, families may be ranked on a continuum running from an enmeshed extreme where boundaries are diffuse to a disengaged extreme where they are hyper-rigid (see DISENGAGED FAMILIES; ENMESHED FAMILIES).

In a functional family, depending on the needs of the system and the stages of family life, boundaries may be more or less enmeshed or disengaged, thus enabling a harmonious balance to be achieved between feelings of autonomy and a sense of belonging. The functioning at the two poles, enmeshed or disengaged, points, however, to 'zones of possible pathology' when mechanisms of adaptation to family stresses are called for.

The family system differentiates itself and discharges its functions by means of a division into sub-systems. Several sub-systems are detectable within a family: dyads such as husband and wife, or mother and child constitute sub-systems. Sub-systems are formed by generation, sex, interest, function or role, creating a number of boundaries with a variety of different qualities.

The establishment of boundaries stimulates the differentiation of the system. Each family sub-system performs specific functions and formulates specific demands upon each of its members. The development of personal competence acquired in these sub-systems depends on the degree of autonomy which each sub-system manages to achieve by protecting itself against interference from the other sub-systems. For example, the learning of a certain complementarity between spouses requires that the couple be free from excessive interference on the part of the in-laws and also by persons from outside the family. When family therapy takes place, the husband and wife may have sessions in which they are received as a sub-system in the absence of the children or grandparents. If they continue to speak only of parental transactions, without speaking of their conjugal transactions, they reveal the existence of an ineffective transgenerational boundary, which is being continually crossed. In cases of psychosis, these generational boundaries are completely permeable, thus bringing about an invasion by multigenerational forces and leading to a rigidification of intra-personal and horizontal interpersonal boundaries. The death of a young child may lead to a real defensive wall being built up between the marital partners.

Harmonious family functioning is a product of a clear definition of the boundaries of the sub-systems. These boundaries must be both well defined to enable the members of the sub-system to discharge their functions, while retaining sufficient permeability to permit regular contacts between the members of the sub-system and the outside. Thus the development of the capacity to negotiate with one's peers, which is learned among siblings demands relative non-intrusion on the part of the parents.

The distinctness of boundaries within a family is a useful parameter for assessing family functioning. Certain families withdraw into themselves to develop their own family microcosm and, as a consequence, undergo an exaggerated increase in the quantity of exchanges and concern among the family members. Interpersonal distances are reduced and boundaries become confused. The undifferentiation of the whole family system may easily restrict its adaptive capacities in times of stress. Other families establish excessively rigid boundaries: communicational exchanges between sub-systems become difficult and the family protection functions are diminished. These are two extreme modes of structuring of boundaries which Minuchin (1974) terms respectively 'enmeshment' and 'disengagement'. These terms refer to a transactional style and a preference for a type of interaction, not to a qualitative difference between the functional and the dysfunctional.

Rigid functioning over a long period may lead to various forms of pathology. A highly enmeshed mother–child sub-system (perpetuating the first symbiotic phases of the relationship) generally excludes the father, who becomes extremely disengaged. The autonomy of the children is then diminished and this may constitute an important factor in the development of symptoms. Individuals belonging to enmeshed sub-systems or families are penalized since their intense sense of belonging brings with it a weakening of their tendencies to achieve autonomy.

Individuals belonging to disengaged sub-systems or families function autonomously, though they have a faltering sense of independence: they lack a sense of loyalty and belonging and they are not capable of deriving benefit from relative interdependence or requesting support and help when they need it.

Thus a family system which is situated at the outer limit of disengagement tolerates a great diversity of individual variation in its members. By contrast, outward signs of suffering in one of its members do not get through the over-rigid boundaries. It is only at a very high level of symptomatology that the family mobilizes its capacities for mutual aid. In cases of extreme enmeshment, we see, by contrast, each person's behaviour having an immediate impact on the others and a massive overrunning of the boundaries by the difficulties that arise, which are then echoed throughout the other sub-systems.

These two styles of relationship are at the origin of family tensions when adaptive mechanisms are called for.

- The *enmeshed family* responds to the slightest modification of context with excessive rapidity and intensity (Hoffman, 1975).
- The *disengaged family* tends not to react, even where a response would seem to be needed. The therapist often functions as a boundary-builder: he or she seeks to clarify fuzzy boundaries and makes breaches in boundaries that are too impermeable. The assessment of the functioning of the family sub-systems and their boundaries enables the therapist to establish a structured diagnosis of the family and to orientate his/her therapeutic interventions.

ELASTIC BOUNDARIES

This term expresses the idea that the family's relational boundaries create a resistance by continuous deformation, rendering the perception of the situation hazy, amorphous and confused (Minuchin, 1974). Such boundaries may be marked out mentally with RUBBER FENCES, which are most often encountered in families where transactions are rigidified and difficult to grasp. The term 'rubber fence', which was coined by Wynne et al. (1958), refers to the impression of an elastic boundary which the therapists bounce off without ever being able to gain access to the family system in question.

GENERATIONAL BOUNDARIES

Within families that are functioning adequately, these are invisible lines, between parents and children or between children separated by a substantial age difference, which are respected. In other words, the children stay in their roles as children and the parents in their roles as parents. The children do not play the parental role and do not become parental figures, nor do they usurp the roles that traditionally fall to the parents. For example, a child does not have to be her own mother's mother.

(See also BALL, SPHERE; DISTANCE AND ORGANIZATION OF TERRITORY; ELEMENTARY CATASTROPHES; FAMILY PSYCHICAL APPARATUS; FORCE FIELDS; FRACTALS; MAPS; METAPSYCHOLOGY; PARENTIFICATION; PARENTIFIED CHILD; TERRITORY; TOPOLOGICAL SPACE.)

P.S., J.M., P.A., S.A. & A.C.

brain damage As a complex cybernetic model of the relations between the brain, thinking and the person comes to be developed, many authors, beginning with Luria (1963), have emphasized the advantages of a multidimensional approach to the care of the victims of brain damage (particularly of traumatic lesions) and the treatment of the psycho–organic sequelae.

As early as 1963, Serrano and Wilson defended a combination of individual psychotherapy, chemotherapy, pedagogy and family therapy for brain-damaged children. There has since been criticism of the pseudo-diagnosis of 'minimal brain damage', too easily applied in the United States to hyperactive children who are unable to tolerate frustration and have low attention spans, and the intensity of whose behavioural disturbances is very often modified by bringing into proper perspective their real intellectual functioning and the values of the parents. In cases where there clearly are lesions, a family attitude that is stimulating and not hyper-protective and does not deny the handicap, seems to be a powerful lever for compensatory cognitive acquisitions.

So far as the adolescent and young adult who are victims of serious head injuries are concerned, from the deep coma phase onward, a mobilization of the family through a straightforward process of information-gathering about the injured individual and his/her milieu makes it possible to promote a triangulation which prevents the patient in neuro–intensive care from being reduced to a body. In the undifferentiated wakefulness phase, ritualization and enhancing the sensory and affective environment make it possible to combat the sense of dislocation. In the phase of recovery of attention, helping the injured individual in the process of self-organization requires the active involvement of the family, and this may sometimes occur in the family home (Pheline, 1986).

Head-injury patients suffer both from cognitive deficits (reduction in capacities of concentration, inability to cope with simultaneous inputs of information, memory difficulties, confusional states) and from behavioural disorders (passivity, impulsiveness, emotional lability). They thus go through a long mourning period, though often the mourning is impossible on account of the partial persistence of the lost function (Lesser et al., 1986).

The psycho–organic syndrome may be corrected by care incorporating:

1 A cognitive re-education which takes account of the basic disturbances of orientation, activation and interest. The personal computer is a powerful aid in this.
2 A readaptation to interpersonal microsocial tasks through participation in a peer group, for example in a specialist day care centre.
3 Family therapy aimed at moving the patient out of the regressive role which was initially necessary for his/her survival but which his/her diminished capabilities have since perpetuated. Placing the family in a position as witness to the cognitive progress made is a very important element in this (Ben-Ishay et al., 1985).

The variable configuration of our neuronal structures enables that absorption of information which becomes an integral part of ourselves to take place, and the partial and one-sided knowledge each person has of the world and of himself is inscribed in a dynamic and evolutive way in his neuronal circuits. (Pheline, 1986, p. 1258)

G.G.M.

brief interactional therapy The brief interactional approach developed out of the work of the Gregory Bateson research project, set up in 1952, to look at the paradoxes of abstraction in communication. The project also included John Weakland, Jay Haley and William Fry Junior. Don Jackson, a psychiatrist who was developing ideas on family homeostasis (Jackson, 1975), joined the project a couple of years later. During the course of the project, some members made frequent visits to consult Milton H. Erickson to discuss aspects of hypnosis and therapy and to receive supervision on their cases. His approach was to be an important inspiration (Haley, 1973, 1985; Erickson et al., 1976; Erickson and Rossi, 1979; Rossi, 1980). Also of importance was the work of Norbert Weiner on cybernetics, the science of communication and control in systems (Wiener, 1948).

Jay Haley defined brief/strategic therapy as follows:

Therapy can be called strategic if the clinician initiates what happens during the therapy and designs a particular approach for each problem . . . [the therapist] must identify solvable problems, set goals, design interventions to achieve those goals, examine the responses he receives to correct his approach, and ultimately examine the outcome of his therapy to see if it has been effective. The therapist must be acutely sensitive and responsive to the patient and his social field, but how he proceeds must be determined by himself. (Haley, 1973, p. 17)

In the literature, the terms brief therapy and strategic therapy have often been used as synonyms. More recently, however, the term 'strategic therapy' has become associated with the structural/hierarchical approach developed by Haley and Madanes (Haley, 1961, 1976, 1980; Madanes, 1981, 1984), and thus will be dealt with under its own section (see STRATEGIC THERAPY). There are other brief approaches to therapy associated, for example, with the psychoanalytic tradition (Malan, 1976) and behaviourism (Lazarus and Fay, 1990). These are not the concerns of this section.

In 1958, Don Jackson founded the Mental Research Institute (MRI) in Palo Alto, California, where he was joined by John Weakland, Jay Haley, Jules Riskin, Virginia Satir and Paul Watzlawick. Its purpose was to study the implications of cybernetics, the circular view of causality and feedback loops, with 'the concept of information, that is, of order, pattern, negentropy' (Watzlawick and Weakland, 1977, p. xii). In 1966 Richard Fisch began the MRI brief therapy project which was subsequently to have a profound effect on the development of brief interactional approaches.

In 1974, the project published the book *Change: Principles of Problem Formation and Problem Resolution* (Watzlawick et al., 1974) and the paper 'Brief therapy: focused problem resolution' (Weakland et al., 1974). These works contributed profoundly to the rapid spread of interest in brief approaches. The project has continued to refine its ideas about therapy, concentrating less on theory and more on the pragmatics of brief,

problem-focused therapy (Fisch et al., 1982). The implications of the interactional view have been further examined by Watzlawick and Weakland (1977).

One of the project's most influential ideas was the notion that many problems develop from, and are maintained by, the way that quite normal difficulties come to be seen and are subsequently tackled. Guided by reason, logic, tradition or 'common sense', attempted solutions have often been applied (which can sometimes include under-reaction and denial) which have had little or no effect or, alternatively, can be seen as having exacerbated the situation. A problem evolves and becomes entrenched as more of the same solutions, or classes of solutions, lead to more of the same problems, attracting more of the same attempted solutions, and so on. This leads to the development of a vicious circle that locks the difficulty into a self-reinforcing, self-maintaining pattern. As Weakland et al. comment:

We assume that once a difficulty begins to be seen as a 'problem', the continuation, and often the exacerbation, of this problem results from the creation of a positive feedback loop, most often centering around those very behaviours of the individuals in the system that are intended to resolve the difficulty. (Weakland et al., 1974, p. 149)

Chronicity is seen as the persistence of a repeatedly mishandled difficulty. No inferences are made about underlying pathology, be it at the individual or family level. No purpose or function is attributed to symptoms. The focus is primarily on process, on repetitive sequences of behaviour. Fisch et al. comment that;

people often persist in actions that maintain problems inadvertently, and often with the best of intentions . . . They follow poor maps very carefully, and this is quite expectable for people who are understandably anxious in the midst of difficulties. Belief in such maps also make it hard to see that they are not serving as effective guides. . . . (Fisch et al., 1982, pp. 16–18)

Another important contribution was the drawing of a distinction, based on the theory of logical types (Whitehead and Russell, 1910–13), between *first-order* and *second-order* change. The former is described as 'one that occurs within a given system which itself remains unchanged', and the latter as 'one whose occurrence changes the system itself' (Watzlawick et al., 1974, p. 10). Attempted solutions often tend to fall within the former class (i.e. changes that do not make a significant difference to the functioning of the problem system), whereas second-order change is seen as a change of change (i.e. a difference that makes a difference).

Therapy is thus focused on the 'attempted solutions', on preventing or even reversing the usual treatment that is seen as having served to exacerbate the situation. The assumption is that, once the feedback loops maintaining the problem are blocked, a greater range of responses (second-order changes) becomes available. In contrast with the conventional wisdom, 'If at first you don't succeed, try, try again', Fisch et al. suggest that, 'if at first you don't succeed, you might perhaps try a second time – but if you don't succeed then, try something different' (Fisch et al., 1982, p. 18). They go on to sum up their approach as follows:

> If problem formation and maintenance are seen as parts of a vicious-cycle process, in which well-intentioned solution behaviors maintain the problem, then alteration of these behaviors should interrupt the cycle and initiate resolution of the problem – that is, the cessation of the problem behavior, since it is no longer being provoked by other behaviors in the system of interaction. (Fisch et al., 1982, p. 18)

Thus 'less of the same' can lead to 'less of the same', and so on.

Re-framing is another central technique in brief therapy, arising out of its constructivist view of how each person's reality is evolved. Watzlawick et al. (1974, p. 95) define re-framing as changing 'the conceptual and/or emotional setting or viewpoint in relation to which a situation is experienced and to place it in another frame which fits the "facts" of the same concrete situation equally well or even better, and thereby changes its entire meaning'. It is also seen as important to 'think small'. Weakland et al. remark:

> We contend generally that change can be effected most easily if the goal of change is reasonably small and clearly stated. Once the patient has experienced a small but definite change in the seemingly monolithic nature of the problem most real to him, the experience leads to further, self-induced changes in this, and often also, in other areas of his life. That is, beneficent circles are initiated. (Weakland et al., 1974, p. 150)

Important to the approach is a careful analysis of the patient's position about therapy and about change and also a concern that the therapist maintains a position of maximum manoeuvrability. The patient position seen as the most optimistic is where a person clearly defines themselves as a client. As Fisch et al. (1982, p. 97) explain, 'such a definition includes three elements: (1) "I have been struggling with a problem that significantly bothers me." (2) "I have failed to resolve it with my own efforts." (3) "I need your help in resolving it."' Where a person comes to therapy reluctantly or under duress, it is seen as important that the therapist respect that position and not try to talk the person into therapy. The therapist might acknowledge the validity of the person's cautiousness or antipathy and warn

them against too quickly making a decision about therapy, or even warn them against entering therapy at all.

Central to the maintenance of a position of maximum manoeuvrability is that the patient should always need the therapist more than the therapist needs the patient. Where therapy is primarily guided and maintained by the therapist's enthusiasms, ideals, agendas and goals, the patient is likely to remain unhelped or become helpless, indifferent or oppositional. Alternatively, when the patient attempts to impose restrictive conditions about who is to be seen, where and when, about what subjects are taboo, through 'secret' communications, and sometimes through intimidation, it is important to find a way of respectfully avoiding the 'trap'. Almost inevitably a 'one-down', non-confrontational position will be taken by the therapist. An important dictum is 'never argue with the client'.

The interview in brief therapy is used to gather information and to develop the kind of rapport necessary for the development of a cooperative relationship (Rosenthal and Bergman, 1986). Frequent use of tasks and directives is made, to be carried out between sessions. A client or family will often be given ideas about, or even instructions requiring, specific changes in behaviour. Brief therapists must therefore develop skills at influencing people and maximizing the likelihood of directives being accepted or carried out. Often it is recommended that changes be avoided or delayed. The use of paradoxical directives has been an important and controversial aspect of the approach.

Also of importance in the development of brief approaches has been the work of Steve de Shazer and his colleagues at the Brief Family Therapy Center, Milwaukee (de Shazer, 1985, 1988, 1991; de Shazer et al., 1986; Berg, 1991; Berg and Miller, 1992) (see SOLUTION-FOCUSED THERAPY). Another early figure of importance is Richard Rabkin whose unique style is demonstrated in *Strategic Psychotherapy: Brief and Symptomatic Treatment* (Rabkin, 1977). He comments, 'Patients attempt to master their problems with a strategy which, because it is unsuccessful, the therapist changes. All the rest is commentary' (1977, p. 5). He uses a chess analogy, dividing the stages of therapy into the opening, the midgame and the endgame (see also Rabkin, 1980).

After the follow-up of ninety-seven cases, Weakland et al. reported success in 40 per cent, significant improvement in 32 per cent, and failure in 28 per cent of cases. The average number of sessions was seven (Weakland et al., 1974, p. 164). In the MRI project, a limit of ten sessions is fixed. Other brief therapists fix no specific limits. However, de Shazer reports an average number of 4.7 sessions (de Shazer, 1991, p. 57). Using a follow-up procedure similar to that used by the MRI group, he found that 65.6 per cent met their goals, while 14.7 per cent made significant improvements. Both groups reported that for most of their respondents no new problems had developed (i.e. symptom substitution) and also that improvements were often reported in other areas of their patients' lives.

Brief approaches appear to have an extremely wide applicability. Stanton (1981, pp. 368–9) lists a wide range of problems that have effectively been treated, from straightforward behavioural difficulties, delinquency, marital problems up to serious neurotic and psychotic disorders. Brief therapists tend to have no particular client selection criteria. As Stanton points out, therapists using this approach 'are less likely to reject particular kinds of problem families than they are to shun situations where the context of the situation permits little or no leverage' (p. 369).

Greenberg (1980, p. 320) cautions 'the assumption is made that because the therapy is brief it is simple to carry out.' He continues:

Therapists new to the format often familiarise themselves with the literature then hurriedly attempt to apply brief principles and techniques without the particular information needed for assessment and treatment. Also, the novice team tends to attempt 'cookbook interventions' that are primarily based on descriptions from the literature. . . . (Greenberg, 1980, p. 320)

The brief interactional approach has been criticized for being superficial, for being manipulative (Treacher, 1987), and for showing little interest either in the inner world of the client or in the sociopolitical context (Luepnitz, 1988; Flaskas, 1992). Several writers have begun to address these criticisms (de Shazer, 1991; Kleckner et al., 1992; Cade and O'Hanlon, 1993).

(See also BRIEF THERAPIES; ETHICAL ISSUES IN FAMILY THERAPY; INTERACTIONS, FAMILY INTERACTIONS.)

B.C.

brief therapies The Palo Alto school resurrected certain lines of enquiry abandoned by Freud when he established the model of the standard cure, testing out active and varied techniques of intervention and exploring, in paradoxical mode, the recourse to HYPNOSIS and, therefore, to induced variations in the subliminal levels of consciousness. In this perspective, data-gathering at the first interview is centred on a certain number of principles: defining precisely the nature of the present problem; studying in what way it may be approached and treated; indicating the objective(s) of treatment. It is then necessary to centre observation on the most specific details and on the external behaviour of the patient and his or her environment. The state of the patient's ideas and feelings is useful, but it is so in conjunction with the description of his or her behaviour.

One often encounters unsatisfactory responses of two types. First, there is the extremely vague or over-

general response, such as 'we can't seem to communicate' or, referring to an internal state that is difficult to express with precision: 'I feel on edge, I don't feel right in myself' or 'I don't feel fulfilled.' In such cases, the therapist has actively to seek out the precise nature of the context to which these statements refer such as, give an example of bad communication, find out exactly what the patient would have to do to feel fulfilled etc. Secondly, there are precise responses, but ones that come all in a great rush, indicating that 'nothing is right' and pouring out an endless catalogue of problems. The therapist's reply must then be: 'which is the greatest problem, the one you would like to see solved first?' When two difficulties are equal in importance, the therapist may lean upon one of them to resolve the other as a priority (Haley, 1976).

The plan of treatment revolves around three basic axes:

- what is the problem?
- what have you done, up to now, to try to solve it?
- what is the minimal element which would enable you to begin to see a solution to this problem?

Various difficulties obviously constitute a hindrance to the resolution of the problem thus posed:

We assume that once a difficulty begins to be seen as a 'problem', the continuation, and often the exacerbation, of this problem results from the creation of a positive feedback loop, most often centring around those very behaviours of the individuals in the system that are intended to resolve the difficulty: the original difficulty is met with an attempted 'solution' that intensifies the original difficulty, and so on and on. (Jackson and Yalom, in Watzlawick and Weakland, 1977, p. 281)

Some patients appear intent upon thwarting the efforts of all therapists, in spite of their intense demand for assistance. This often appears as a point of no return in the families of psychotics, where recourse is had to a whole series of therapists, each of whom is disqualified in succession. The attitude of the therapist or therapists may then consist in indicating to the patient or the family group that it is not possible to find a solution to the problem posed in spite of all the efforts already made and that the treatment can at best help them to put up with the situation as it is. Just as, in the treatment of alcoholics, the bottle is regarded as always being the stronger force, come what may, so the voices, the apragmatism and the absence of all initiative, thought or emotion are accepted as realities for the psychotic patient which therapy cannot overcome.

We may note that in *Change: principles of problem formation and problem resolution*, Watzlawick et al. (1974) lay down an average of seven hours treatment time per case. That average is challenged by a more recent approach, the background or which is also in Chomskian and Batesonian computer-based models, with NEUROLINGUISTIC PROGRAMMING, which stands on the margins of therapeutic activity.

Finally, the work of de Shazer (1982, 1984, 1985) has proved effective in reversing the more traditional problem-focused approach by emphasizing clients' abilities and working from a solution-focused starting point.

(See also CONJUNCTION OF THERAPEUTIC AXES; FAMILY THERAPIES; HYPNOSIS; THERAPEUTIC STRATEGIES AND TACTICS.)

J.M.

C

calumny A structure of communication leading to the spreading of false and malevolent information about a third person who is placed in the position of victim.

Calumny may in some cases have performative effects within a family, in that it leads to someone being designated a victim or scapegoat. This PERFORMATIVE UTTERANCE will be the more effective if it is relayed by powerful informational media, within or outside the family. As Machiavelli pointed out (in his *Discourse on the last decades of Livy*), the remedy against calumny is democratic accusation.

For example, Revel (1977) describes the process by which the thoughts of an author can, in all good faith, be disqualified by a series of opponents to theses of which it is less a question of refuting than of ignoring or disinforming. Revel summarizes the arguments used in this way:

First stage: I am read 'with great interest'.
Second stage: I speak from 'no particular standpoint'.
Third stage: I am not to be taken seriously, being only a pamphleteer who 'flogs a dead horse', which means that the dangers of totalitarianism are only humbug.
Fourth stage: I am a plagiarist.
Fifth stage: I am in the maw of the Ministry of the Interior, which no one can disprove, and which constitutes a serious breach of trust for an intellectual.
(Revel, 1977, p. 249)

One could, all things considered, and whatever the fundamental position that each is at liberty to adopt with respect to the totalitarian social system, unpack the structure to which this relates and which is found in microcosm in families:

1 We are listening to you with all our attention.
2 What you are talking about does not exist.
3 What you say quite frankly is crazy, everyone agrees; the voices, the threats and the insults which warn you of the dangers of the total system are pure and simple madness.
4 What you say is just what everyone else says.
5 What you are moved to say stems from your own inner rules, rules which until now we have managed to eliminate completely (since all rules are iniquitous).

Calumny is a modality of communication which relates back to the mythical organization of the family group under consideration, in the same way as SCANDALMONGERING, DISCLOSURE, SECRETS and NOSTALGIA.

(See also FAMILY MYTHS; FORGETTING; INSTITUTIONAL MYTHS; MISUNDERSTANDINGS.)

J.M.

cancer The systemic modelling of cancer (or, more precisely, of cancers) may involve three levels:

1 The level of the appearance and development of the illness in an organism as a disorder of biological communication.
2 The level of the modification of the family rules induced (or reflected) by one of the members falling ill with cancer.
3 The level of the specific doctor–patient interaction which is formed with this disease, which has weighty connotations in the social imagination.

Let us briefly comment, first of all, upon this last point and state that cancer has, in the neo-industrial period, taken over from plague in the Middle Ages or tuberculosis in the nineteenth century as the chief object of anxiety, as the collective focalization of the fear of incurable disease, of the body falling foul of an evil force directed by the whim of chance (or a transcendent power).

As therapeutic advances are made, cancer has become less of a taboo subject, but it often remains unnameable for two reasons: on the one hand, its cause or causes are still shrouded in mystery (for example, the incontestable epidemiological arguments demonstrating the part played by tobacco in respiratory and digestive cancers do not prevent anyone from smoking, since they prove that tobacco plays a role but not that it is the ultimate agent); its causality being mysterious and its prevention uncertain, one may always hope to escape it and see its manifestation as a sign rather than an effect. On the other hand, cancer fulfils a function as a representative of the return of what our society fiercely represses, namely old age and death. Given this situation, the doctor–patient relation is contaminated by notions of chance and irrationality which open the way up to charlatanism or to glorification. Whether he or she wishes to or not, the serious doctor ensnares his or her patient in a form of doublespeak:

- 'it is an illness like any other, there's no need to be so afraid';
- 'regular surveillance is essential; we can never say someone is actually cured'.

Apart from the greater frequency of certain hormone-dependent cancers running in certain families, for many years nothing was said about the *family dynamic* of the disease. Much greater attention has been paid either to general psychosocial factors, such as life-style, habitat, alcoholism, degree of stress etc., or to individual personality factors, with the aim of finding a standard profile of the future cancer sufferer, or a psychosomatic explanation linked to the vagaries of the development of the illness (long latency period, phases of sudden decompensation and, in some cases, total spontaneous regression of the tumour).

Stierlin et al. (1986) provided an excellent résumé of the work done in this direction at the same time as publishing the first study on the psychotherapy of the families of cancer patients. Before going over their article in broad outline, let us recall that Freud (1856–1939) fought for sixteen years and through thirty-three operations against a cancer of the jaw, before asking his doctor to help him to die by giving him an overdose of opiates. The first of these operations was carried out at more or less the same time as Freud's favourite grandson, Heinerle, was having his tonsils removed. When this grandson died a few months later, it was the only occasion that Freud was seen to shed tears. Afterwards, he was unable to enjoy life any more: 'It is the secret of my indifference – people call it courage – toward the danger to my own life' (Jones, 1957, p. 550). Let us also remind ourselves that Gregory Bateson (1904–80), the third son of an eminent biologist, and a man who, after the tragic death of his two elder brothers, had had all his father's hopes placed in him, had, when it was thought that he was afflicted with a terminal cancer, summoned his daughter to his side for a month in order to write a book which would be his intellectual testament; in fact, an unexpected remission of more than a year occurred, giving us the book *Mind and nature: a necessary unity*.

These two stories allow us to put into perspective the propositions of Stierlin et al. (1986). In their view, the families of cancer patients belong variously to the three types of psychosomatic families:

1 For the majority, *bound families* (equivalent to the enmeshed families of Minuchin, 1974). These are families united by reciprocal concern, the absence of internal boundaries contrasting with the rigidity of the barriers put up against the outside world, and family-conserving processes of DELEGATION perceived as unquestionable obligations.

2 In a third of cases, *split families*. Transgenerational coalitions seem to be the only way to overcome the contradictory feelings of idealization and violent belittlement, to overcome disappointed hopes. Only care for the sick member (or the addict or delinquent) interrupts the family arguments.

3 More rarely, *dislocated families*, characterized by reciprocal isolation and lack of care, absence of loyalty, sudden turnabouts in bonding and rejections. 'Many children in these families have been conceived before marriage in order to cement the couple and gain acceptance for it, in spite of the prejudices of their families of origin. Most often, after the birth, however, the child very soon becomes a burden' (Stierlin et al., 1986, p. 49).

In these three contexts, 'the subjects suffering from a psychosomatic illness essentially present themselves as men for whom it is particularly difficult or has been made difficult to individualize themselves against those who are important reference persons for them' (Stierlin et al., 1986, p. 51). Blocking up their energy in life programmes involving persistent overwork, they find themselves in a 'frozen' relational environment, with no way out other than 'the feeling of no longer being at home in their own bodies and no longer being desirable' (Stierlin et al., 1986, p. 53). And cancer often occurs when a decisive change comes about in the family situation.

In the face of the failure of the supportive psychotherapies proposed to bring relief from invasion by the illness (and designed additionally to prevent transmission of the destructive pattern of functioning to the next generation), Stierlin et al. eventually contented themselves with positively connoting the mental shield of the cancer patient in family interviews integrated into the framework of medical treatment. Applying Selvini Palazzoli and colleagues' (1978) technique of apparently paradoxical interventions and circular questioning, they thus enabled an exchange and a liberating dialogue to take place within those families. This is no doubt what in her naïve and unreflected manner Simonton (1984) is also advocating. Like Fritz Zorn in his autobiographical story, *Mars*, she emphasizes the negation of feelings on the part of the cancer sufferer, the revelation of the illness as 'a shock leading everyone really to find themselves' and the need for the attitude of the family to sustain the patient's will to be cured. She suggests that, in order to share in the hope, the family members assist in the visualization of the illness, and that the health of the family as a whole be seen as impaired and potentially restored by tasks carried out as a team during therapy.

Basing her work upon the research of Bahnson (1978) at Philadelphia, which established very high rates of correlation between conditions of depression and lack, on the one hand, and certain reactions of the immune system on the other, Denise Morel (1984, pp. 179–81) introduced a psychodynamic and psychosomatic model of carcinogenesis, recognizing:

- a *basic situation* of coldness and family insecurity, compensated by 'clinging on to a key object, denial and the profound repression of conflicts';
- an *intermediate solution* of social over-adaptation, anxiety and depression which are not mentalized in cases of stress but combatted by tobacco, alcohol, overwork and self-medication;
- a *triggering by a trauma* of loss or abandonment, the absence of the key object leading to a collapse of the vital narcissistic equilibrium.

The various hypotheses summarized here seem convincing for adult subjects who fall victim to cancers of the lung or breast. However, is the process the same for the children and adolescents who develop malignant tumours? Does family structure play a significant role? In reading the literature on this subject, the most striking feature seems to be the way in which, when the diagnosis is announced, during treatment and subsequently, families tend to come to *resemble the model of the bound family*, overprotecting the patient while officially denying the degree of seriousness and handicap in his or her presence. The consequence is that, when cured (cf. Carton et al., 1984), there is every likelihood that the former cancer patient will become a hyper-adapted individual, never accepting that he or she may be tired and displaying a strong sense of duty, i.e. the very model of the individual prone to cancer.

Guyotat (1985) has established a parallel between the breakdowns of homeostasis which occur within families upon the diagnosis or amelioration of a psychosis or a cancer. Exchanges may be set up between these two diseases to maintain the balance of the family LEDGER. He sees this as an effect of what he terms *narcissistic filiation*, which is to be compared with the phenomenological observations of Tatossian (1977) and the rather Lacanian formulation of Guir (1983).

Guyotat (1985, p. 696) rightly draws attention to:

the mechanisms of projection associated with the phenomena of communication of thought. The psychotic projects his own thought contents on to those around him and feels he is a victim of the thought processes of others. I think this also occurs in those around cancer patients in a pre-terminal phase and also as remote after-effects to a dramatic case of cancer.

Another feature in common with psychosis is *secrecy*: 'it is always something which is hidden from someone else, but this someone else has to exist. This relation is established by signs; it is infra-verbal.'

The quantity of writing devoted to the question of how the diagnosis of cancer is to be revealed to the patient will be well known to the reader.

(See also SYSTEMIC MODELLING OF CARCINOGENESIS.)

G.G.M.

canonical representation of the family system
See FAMILY SYSTEMS; GENERAL SYSTEMS THEORY.

cardinal values, ordinal values The *cardinal values*, which may be defined as ends in themselves – freedom, peace, solidarity etc. – serve as foundations for the body of laws. *Ordinal values*, which may be defined as the means to be employed – such as work, family, country, health – constitute the corpus of rules. Following Lewin (1935), we may take the view that values are internalized parents.

This articulation between means and ends is delicate and often disturbed. We have seen catastrophic periods of social conflation of these two levels ('*Travail, Famille, Patrie*' replacing the cardinal values '*Liberté, Egalité, Fraternité*' on the façades of French town halls). And one often finds, in respect of preventive medicine, the highly regrettable reduction of cardinal solidarity to ordinal health.

However, a particular clinical curiosity merits our attention in this connection. Many studies conducted in the USA, Hungary and south-east France have revealed a peculiar phenomenon: that users of chemical prostheses (alcoholics and drug-abusers) typically rank values differently. That is to say that, when asked to arrange in order of importance eighteen ordinal values (being polite, brave, honest, loving, ambitious etc.) and eighteen cardinal values (peace, security, love, joy etc.), we see two different phenomena: the population as a whole lists these various items in a very homogeneous way (varying only by two or three degrees) so far as the ordinal values are concerned; by contrast, when it comes to cardinal values, there is a very marked difference of evaluation between the users of toxic substances and a control population. The users of toxic substances overvalue within the cardinal values those which are of a personal type (love, inner harmony, self-respect) at the expense of social values (national security, freedom, peace). These elements should concern every family therapist, in so far as the family has traditionally been the site where these systems of ordinal and cardinal values are passed on.

(See also ALCOHOLISM; DRUG ADDICTION; FAMILY, HISTORY OF THE; FAMILY RULES; VALENCE.)

D.C.

catastrophe theory See BALL, SPHERE; DYNAMIC SYSTEMS; ELEMENTARY CATASTROPHES; FAMILY CATASTROPHES; GENERALIZED CATASTROPHES; RELATIONAL ARCHETYPES; TOPOLOGICAL SPACE; UNIVERSAL UNFOLDING.

causality See ALGORITHM; CHANGE; CIRCULARITY; COMPLEXITY; ELEMENTARY CATASTROPHES; EQUIFINALITY;

FAMILY ORGANIZERS; FEEDBACK; FORCE FIELDS; GENERALIZED CATASTROPHES; GENETICS AND THE FAMILY; HEURISTICS; HOMEOSTASIS; MACHINES; MYTH; ORDER; PUNCTUATION SEQUENCES OF EVENTS; RANDOMNESS; RITUALIZATION; SELF-ORGANIZATION; SENSITIVITY TO INITIAL CONDITIONS; STATIC, PSEUDO-STATIC AND METABOLIC FORMS; STOCHASTIC PROCESSES; STRUCTURAL STABILITY; SYMPTOMS; SYMPTOMATIC AND/OR AETIOLOGICAL TRANSACTIONS; UNCERTAINTY PRINCIPLE; UNIVERSAL UNFOLDING.

change Change is at the centre of all internally coherent therapeutic activity. Freud showed that the paradoxes of change are directly connected with the problems of the resolution of the TRANSFERENCE neurosis in the treatment of neurotic patients. Bateson elaborated a theory of change in behavioural pathology, on the basis of contexts of LEARNING.

If change in the case of neurosis relates essentially to the status of 'psychical representatives', where madness and delinquency are concerned, change presupposes an epistemological re-framing, a new way of defining reality (see ALIENATION; REALITY). We thus arrive at a double paradox: *plus ça change, plus c'est la même chose* and, conversely, *plus c'est la même chose, plus ça change*. If the former paradox corresponds to the spontaneous attempts at change made by a system, the prescription of the status quo is, by contrast, based on the second paradox.

The question of change is at the centre of the Freudian revolution. The analytic experience consists in overcoming the opposition to change that is expressed in the neurotic symptom (see Widlöcher, 1970). It makes it possible to concretize life elements which would not have been able to be realized in other contexts. It is in this way that Freud was able to study the different resistances which arise as obstacles to therapeutic change: three resistances originate in the ego: the resistance of repression, the resistance of transference and the resistance arising from secondary gain; a fourth resistance derives from the id (the resistance of the unconscious) and a fifth from the superego (sense of guilt and need for punishment).

Change occurs, in psychoanalysis, in the movement of transference. The transference neurosis, as actualization of childhood neurosis, is in effect both:

- in the service of resistance by the repetition of the neurotic style of object choice with the analyst; and
- the lever of therapeutic change, by the reactivation, in a new context, of these old repetitive patterns.

The PRAGMATICS OF COMMUNICATION generalizes this observation to other symptomatic situations, and even accentuates it. Watzlawick et al. (1974) distinguish between first-order and second-order change. In first-order change, there is a *quantitative* modification of the parameters of the system, within limiting values, without any perturbation occurring in the organization of the system. In second-order change, there is a *qualitative* modification which transforms the state of the system in a discontinuous manner. There then occurs a change in the manner of change.

The analysis of family systems thus brings out other types of resistance which appear at other levels of organization:

- a collective non-differentiation of selfs, leading to disturbances of the processes of thought, making it difficult to define the problems to be resolved;
- systemic family–society alienations, interpersonal disqualifications or mystifications, pathological manipulations leading to therapeutic conflicts;
- biological FORCE FIELDS underlying the behavioural systems of interactions and therefore the emotive systems;
- cultural force fields, bringing with them social and institutional pressures and leading, usually to a series of secondary gains (self-maintenance of vicious circles of assistance–dependence);
- FAMILY MYTHS leading to dysfunctional FAMILY RULES.

The Palo Alto school notes that, very often, the solution advanced to attempt to solve the problem is itself the problem. Thus couples end up in rigidified relationships when they repeatedly attempt to inject more of the same to resolve a difficulty. It then becomes a genuine problem. Pathological jealousy may thus be considered as the product of a relationship in which one member of a couple seeks to know everything about his or her partner, while the other is then left with no solution but to conceal a great deal of information which he or she would otherwise have been able to reveal quite easily (Watzlawick et al., 1974).

As to the nature of the discontinuity introduced by second-order change, several interpretations emerge. For those who adhere to the theory of logical types (Bateson, Watzlawick), second-order transformation is purely paradoxical, discontinuity being, to some extent, considered an absolute: 'the logical levels must be rigorously separated if we do not wish to fall into paradox and confusion' (Watzlawick et al., 1967). If first-order change is based essentially on negative feedback, second-order change would, by contrast, be a product of positive feedback, which, by the amplification of deviations, would lead to the self-organization of new structures.

For his part, Bateson (1958, pp. 295–6) writes:

Equations of first order (in x) denote uniform velocity; equations of second order (in x^2) imply acceleration; equations of third order (in x^3) imply a change in acceleration; and so on. There is moreover an analogy between this hierarchy of equations and the hierarchy of Logical Types; a statement of acceleration is *meta* to a statement of velocity.

And he also writes, 'It is not, in the nature of the case, possible to predict from a description having complexity C what the system would look like if it had complexity C + 1' (p. 302).

It is in this field that qualitative mathematics has progressed most in the formalization of the changes of state of structurally stable systems. The theory of UNIVERSAL UNFOLDING, the discovery of ELEMENTARY CATASTROPHES, FRACTALS and SELF-REFERENTIAL CALCULUS offer profound alternatives to the THEORY OF LOGICAL TYPES.

Catastrophe theory demonstrates the forms that are assumed by levels of structurally stable change. It enables us to discover the existence of an inaccessible continuity behind sudden catastrophic changes (see the cusp in ELEMENTARY CATASTROPHES). Above all, it adds to our knowledge in two ways:

1 Structurally stable forms of change are complex, but obey severe topological constraints.
2 The morphological properties of these elementary and generalized catastrophes (see FRACTALS) were completely beyond the scope of the theory of logical types. Discovering them has produced a solution to certain paradoxes.

For therapists, the difficult thing is to evaluate the level of tension, bearable by the system, which will permit a satisfactory meta-change to take place on the basis of prescription of the status quo. Very often, when individuals or families consult a therapist, the system is already confronted with positive feedback which has caused it to fragment and has set in place strange ATTRACTORS (see DYNAMIC SYSTEMS; SEMANTIC RESONANCES). The self-organizing capacities of the system are not sufficient to re-establish its autonomy. The prescription of the status quo cannot then simply be a therapeutic tactic, but must rather be a strategic attitude. Just as a fracture can only be healed by being immobilized and set in plaster, the fragmentation involved in certain psychotic states requires appropriate techniques of restraint (spatial constraints), the results of which can only be appreciated over a sufficient timescale (temporal constraints). In cases of schizophrenic transactions, the prescription of rest and of the status quo is not just a matter of a few days or a few weeks.

(See also BRIEF INTERACTIONAL THERAPY; BRIEF THERAPIES; EVOLUTIONARY SURVIVAL UNIT; FAMILY SELF-REFERENTIALITY; GENERALIZED CATASTROPHES; HYPNOSIS; INSTINCT; SEMANTIC UNIT OF MIND; STATIC, PSEUDO-STATIC AND METABOLIC FORMS; UNIT OF CHANGE.)

J.M.

channels of communication See GATEKEEPER; MULTI–CHANNEL COMMUNICATION SYSTEMS.

child abuse Situations of risk in which one or more children in the same family may be maltreated, leading, for example, to the presentation of child abuse, are a difficult problem to assess and resolve. Social workers, doctors and the courts are, however, often confronted with such situations, though the symptoms take different forms: straightforward neglect leading to the child being deprived in physical or psychological ways; various forms of bodily injury which may end in the child's death; sexual abuse; or psychological maltreatment, which may oscillate between attitudes of pure and simple rejection and subtle forms of alienation through one or other of the parents bringing a child or adolescent 'under their influence'.

Families in which abuse occurs are, naturally, very diverse and the prognosis will vary depending upon whether the parents acknowledge their responsibility in the situation. Masson (1981) distinguishes two major subgroups: first, families in which the abuse is a sign of a temporary crisis, the family having shown, in other respects, that it can function more harmoniously; and, secondly, chronically and transgenerationally disturbed families, with repeated poor levels of care and aggressive behaviour, among which Masson distinguishes two sub-categories:

1 Chaotic families with transgenerational repetition of relational breakdowns and, sometimes, of abuse. The parents themselves suffer from a past in which they were placed in care or experienced deprivations of various kinds and expect relief and reparation of their distress from their children, who can only disappoint them in this impossible task. Hence the aggressive reactions which ensue.
2 Families whose structure remains intact but which is characterized by the persistence of alliances with privileged figures in the previous generation fixed in a sort of PERVERSE TRIANGLE between the grandparents and the young parents. This makes it impossible for the latter to form a conjugal and parental alliance of the kind that is indispensable for the protection of the children. These young parents are often children chronically PARENTIFIED in their families of origin, which, from time to time, suck them back into old alliances.

Systemic intervention may be of great help in such situations and this is the case at two levels of intervention. First, it may facilitate the analysis of the functioning – often incoherent and contradictory – of the many professionals already involved in the situation (courts, paediatricians, home helps, psychiatrists, social workers, teachers etc.) who often see the situation in different – if not indeed opposed – ways, and either become involved in conflicts about how it can be resolved or remain totally ignorant of one another. As stressed by Masson (1981), medical personnel, triangulated by the different members of the family, are placed in coalitions with sub-systems and tend to take over and play out between themselves a conflictual scenario which has as its model the unresolved family conflict.

In a second phase, systemic intervention may be a resource in dealing with and treating the problem. As an indispensable preliminary to this, a precise evaluation of the risks run by the victim(s) must be made and a decision taken as to whether the children need to be temporarily or permanently placed in residential care or foster homes. For this purpose, a 'functional intervention team' must be set in place, comprising multiple professionals who are able to work as a team when the case is being taken up. This is always a serious and difficult matter and it therefore requires a high level of training on the part of the team members and 'relationships in which they mutually value and recognize each other's skills'. It is possible to begin family therapy in such cases where there is a hope of creating new modes of transaction within the family. This may apply even where the child is temporarily placed in care. Such hope may be based on several criteria: interest shown by the parents in the child placed in care; the gradual establishment of a bond with one of the professionals involved and regularity of attendance at the meetings arranged with them (even if they openly criticize the function of such meetings or even the actions of the courts in their case); the appearance of a phase of cooperation after an initial phase of opposition; the identification of affective resources which may yet be mobilized; the possibility of a change in transgenerational relations.

(See also INCEST; LEGAL CONTEXT; VIOLENCE.)

P.S.

children of survivor parents In the light of psychoanalytic and systemic theories of the family, it is possible to formulate a number of hypotheses on the functioning of families of survivors, basing ourselves in this regard on the observation of Jewish families who had at least one family member deported. The repercussions of these ordeals and mourning processes on the first post-war generation represent major psychological effects.

THERAPEUTIC INTERVENTION

Kestenberg (1974) relates the treatment of an apparently psychotic adolescent girl, whom it became possible to cure when the analyst had overcome the resistance of her parents, who refused to relate what they had lived through during the holocaust, and the resistance of the daughter against listening to their account. The adolescent girl's behaviour was linked to the unconscious desire to sacrifice herself in the place of a lost relative. This same theme appeared in other cases analysed by Kestenberg which she sees as being connected with deep-seated guilt among those who survived.

As a result of his experience in Child Guidance at Tel Aviv, Rosenberg (1974) acquired the conviction that the children of survivors have no distinct psychopathology and that the differences that may be observed have to be attributed to the personalities of their parents. This clinician makes a distinction between two types of 'survivor parent':

1 Those who neglect the emotional needs of their children and are obsessed by the need to feed them and to spare them the hunger and privations they themselves had known in Europe.
2 Those who identify almost completely with their child as he or she is growing up and who relive their childhood through their offspring or believe in an identification with their own deceased parents. They lack emotional maturity and use their children to fulfil their own narcissistic needs.

Rakoff (1966) and Trossman (1968) have described other problems experienced by the children of concentration camp survivors. These include exaggerated protection on the part of their parents, excessive hopes and a particular type of cultural conflict: parents want their children to blend in to the culture in which they live and want them to be a link between themselves and other people, but, in spite of this, they also want the children 'to remember' that they are continuations of themselves and of the family which disappeared. This type of family interaction seems to be prevalent among survivors of the camps, but Aleksandrowicz (1974) did not encounter this in Israel. Parents studied there had less need to ask their children to be a kind of living memorial to their tragic destiny and that of their deceased family. In that country, this function has been taken over by the state itself.

The clinical treatment of such families leads us to offer some hypotheses regarding the processes involved. The premature death of the grandparents – the guardians of tradition – in dramatic circumstances, reinforced their idealized position. All conflict concerning the adolescence of the deported parents is suppressed for the following reasons. During the pre-war years, these families, most especially those in Poland, were subjected to pogroms and the rise of anti-semitism. These real external dangers pushed interpersonal conflicts within families into the background. Even the parent–child conflicts which were able to emerge have been erased from memory and have not been passed on to the following generation, in order to preserve a mythical image of the grandparents. And, lastly, these conflicts were seen as insignificant by comparison with the intensity of suffering subsequently endured.

REPERCUSSION OF FAMILY TRAUMAS

History has, therefore, imposed brutal separations which are often premature in relation to the degree of independence of the adolescents. We observe the later effects of this during their own children's separation phase. Two maturational processes may be observed in these adolescents.

First, some young people expressed a wish to leave the family home at an age when they could cope with living independently. These departures were not possible without massive conflict, which left behind a great burden of guilt. It is, in fact, painful for these adolescents living in very despotic family milieus to become individuated and to form object relations which do not respond to the ideals of the family. The fact of these young people leaving home reactivates the excessive number of mourning processes experienced by the parents while also demanding of them a reorganization of their conjugal relations.

A defensive compromise has often been met with. It consists in keeping secret from the parents for a long time all the life–choices which may be a source of conflict. It is difficult to oppose victim–heroes on a permanent state of alert. In effect, these families still fear a renewal of the persecutions. History has, in fact, shown them the repetitive phenomena of anti-semitism though these have not been on the scale of the holocaust. Moreover, these fears are not unjustified if one takes into account recent events and the existence of neo-Nazi political groups.

Other adolescents only separated from their families by making choices that were strictly in conformity with their parents' wishes. Their low level of individuation often led them to choose partners of the same level of undifferentiation in relation to their families of origin (see DIFFERENTIATION OF SELF). This second type of attitude reinforces the myth of family harmony by cancelling out generational conflicts.

In certain cases, beyond this pseudo-harmony, a collective anxiety shows through. In such cases, we meet a typical form of family organization centred upon a member suffering psychosomatic problems or neurotic symptoms of a phobic nature. In order to lighten these sufferings, the index patient (one of the parents) leads a life without risk and puts pressure on the other members of the family to become part of the same defensive system. Thus, this reorganization enables the patient to reduce his or her symptoms by diminishing his or her stress. One particular feature of the behaviour of these parents is a hyper-protective attitude which is expressed in the compulsive need to feed their children to excess, since they themselves have suffered privation during certain periods of their life. According to Klein (1970), many of the children of survivors – and particularly the firstborn – eat too much and suffer from food-related disorders. Further, the missions with which the children have been entrusted relate not only to the choice of marital partner but to modes of investment in which the wartime experience plays a part. Some children have chosen trades or professions which their parents had wished to pursue, but had been unable to learn or to study as a result of historical circumstances. Other parents put pressure on their children to choose a *useful* profession in periods of such tragedy.

In almost all the families, past and present dangers are essentially seen as emanating from outside and constantly act to reinforce family cohesiveness. By imposing a permanent reorganization of family bonds in order the better to fight against a hostile environment, the reality of persecution deflects the forms taken by reciprocal identifications. After the holocaust, the great difficulty consisted in performing the task of mourning that was both individual and collective. Traditional family and community rites reinforced these families' sense of belonging to an ethnic group. These collective rites both made the work of individual mourning easier and modified the normal work of mourning of adolescence. The children of survivors have often been used to symbolize the lost members of the family, a fact marked quite patently in children being given the forenames of ancestors who died in the holocaust. Repressed aggressiveness, linked to the humiliations and the human losses of the holocaust, seems to have been one of the factors producing chronic depressive states and the sinistrosis alluded to above.

COLLECTIVE ELABORATION OF FAMILY HISTORY

The various pathologies encountered in these families frequently seem to connect with the major traumas of their past histories. Even if we do not encounter any specific intrafamilial form of relational organization, it often seems right to suggest psychotherapeutic work at the family level. The aim of this approach is to assess the impact of the tragic events experienced by the survivors and to gain a detailed insight into the particular nature of the work of mourning which is specific to each family, while at the same time respecting the homeostasis of the group. Family interviews of this kind enable us to bring out the FAMILY MYTHS, to see what missions are assigned to the various children and to perceive their reactions as delegates. By involving all the members of the family, the transgenerational approach promotes better individuation in each member of the group. One of the therapeutic factors seems to us to reside in the elucidation of what the family's experience has been and the collective elaboration of its history which the family can successfully carry out for itself.

P.A. & S.A.

choice of partner See ATTACHMENT BEHAVIOUR; COUPLES; FAMILY ORGANIZERS; IMPRINTING; MARITAL BREAKDOWN.

chreod A chreod ('obligatory path', from the Greek *chreon*, necessity, and *odos*, path) is a canalized trajectory which acts as an attractor for neighbouring trajectories: a chreod thus delimits a morphogenetic field possessing structural stability, having a beginning in time and being irreversibly orientated on the temporal axis. A chreod may formally describe a canalized nonverbal or verbal behaviour, i.e. the morphogenesis of processes of RITUALIZATION at different levels of communication.

The term 'chreod' was proposed by Waddington (1957, 1975) in embryology and was adopted by Thom (1972) as a topological description of semantic morphologies (support of the signified). It makes it possible to describe, in the most general manner, those forms endowed with meaning such as are canalized in natural and cultural rituals, in the form of words and grammars, in the movement of the great currents of thought and action. Chreods are capable of generating successor chreods in a hierarchical sequence subject to the passage of time.

(See also HOMEOSTASIS; SEMANTIC RESONANCES; SEMANTICS OF COMMUNICATION.)

J.M.

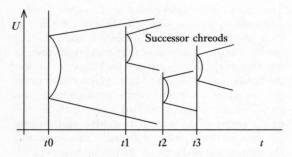

Schematic model of semantic chreods. *U*, open space of *n* dimension; *t*, time dimension.

circular questions A technical ploy advocated by Selvini Palazzoli et al. (1980), circular questions, or

'mind-reading questions' following Haley (1963), are used positively to connote the homeostatic tendency of the family system. It consists in addressing oneself directly to a family member by asking him/her to think for another person as though this were a natural thing to do. For example: 'Mrs X, what does your husband think of your son's taste in music?' (and not: 'What do you think your husband thinks of your son's taste in music?').

The structuralist perspective of Salvador Minuchin is opposed to this systematic perspective, seeking rather to work towards a delimitation of individual boundaries. 'Family members should speak for themselves. They should tell their own story. Family members should not tell what other members think or feel ... Two members should not discuss a third who is present without his participation' (Minuchin, 1979, p. 16.)

It is never right to induce instabilities in a patient and it is therefore best to avoid putting mind-reading questions to subjects suffering from mental automatism. On the other hand, using this technique to bring out the state of mental undifferentiation of those in the patient's close circle may be very effective.

(See also DATA-GATHERING; TRIADIC QUESTIONING.)

G.G.M.

circularity/circular, linearity/linear The linear/circular opposition describes a complementary polarity of interactions:

- the linearity of the chain of discourse ('my son is taking drugs', 'our daughter is behaving scandalously in public');
- the circularity of infra- and para-verbal exchanges (mutual influencing, through FEEDBACK, of interpersonal behaviour).

Circularity describes a temporal sequence of succession of states connected together by a relation of causality, in such a way that the last state of the sequence reacts back upon the initial state, thus forming a loop. This return to the initial point in fact determines a cycle which repeats itself periodically in time. The relative reversibility of the system goes together with the temporal irreversibility of the process. Circularity is a basic property of living organisms. Jackson (1957) and Watzlawick et al. (1967) have observed its effects in family interactions in clinical practice.

The property of circularity in closed systems has been tested by the simulation on artificial machines of certain properties of living organisms. It corresponds to a linear causality of the type A–B–C ... N, such that the outcome N of the process retroacts, also in a linear fashion, on the origin A of the process under consideration. This circular determinism is the functional basis of self-organized systems. In fact, circularity is an approximation since the influence of time modifies the state of the circular series, even in imperceptible ways, during the succession of FAMILY LIFE-CYCLES. Moreover, the regulation of each cycle is itself dependent upon a great many other circles, arranged in the form of TANGLED HIERARCHIES.

In family therapy, circular questioning is an interview technique which enables one to take account of circular causality, of the family's feedback to the information solicited about relationships and of the differentiation of the members of the family. The technique consists in inviting each participant to express his or her point of view on the relationship that exists between two other members of the family. What is involved here is the investigation of a relationship between two people as it is seen by a third person. This technique sets off a whirl of responses which bring out a great deal of information about the various triadic relationships (Selvini Palazzoli et al., 1978).

To the extent that psychological 'events' seldom occur all at one time, but extend over a certain period

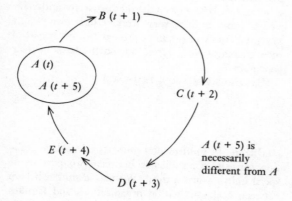

$A (t + 5)$ is necessarily different from A

and are tangled up with enormous complexity, this circular model is often more appropriate than the one which artificially abstracts events from the complex temporal order of their succession. Bernard pointed out as early as 1865 in *An introduction to the study of experimental medicine*, that the determinism of living organisms was 'harmoniously graded' (p. 87) and that it rested upon phenomena which 'each determin[ed] the other' and combined 'for a common final object'. He went further indeed and recalled that the ancient emblem accurately represented life as 'a closed circle formed by a serpent biting its own tail . . . In complex organisms, the organism of life actually forms a closed circle, but a circle which has a head and a tail in this sense, that vital phenomena are not all of equal importance, though each in succession completes the vital circle' (p. 88).

In practice, *circular determinism* introduces indeterminacy. It is of a nature that each element influences

all the others, by producing a self-defined distinction between the living organism and its environment and therefore between an 'inside' and an 'outside' (Pichot, 1983). This determinism leads to an 'internal coherence', an active process in dynamic equilibrium with the 'external coherence', ensuring the articulation of the organism with its milieu. This self-definition implies a turning back upon itself, ensuring internal autonomy and external dependence. Now this turning back upon itself, the product of the interaction of all the parts, is dependent upon the linear passing of time (Pichot, 1983). Each element, e, of the living being, V, is determined by the remainder $(V - e)$ of the circular entity thus defined. However,

since the determination of e by (V − e) requires a certain time, one cannot say that the living being, V, is its own determinism (and its own finality) at time, t, but that the living being, V, at time, t, determines the living being V at time t + dt. Hence it follows that, considered at a specific instant, the living being does not have perfect, internal coherence since it does not have a perfectly circular determinism; time introduces a functional deficiency into it. (Pichot, 1983, pp. 19–20)

The circularity of the living being is therefore *pseudocircular*: it is a temporally deferred circularity; each cycle creates the existence of a state which maintains itself by changing and which changes by maintaining itself. Hence the fundamental antinomy of every living process, which produces repercussions upon each action of therapeutic change: *plus ça change, plus c'est la même chose* and, conversely, *plus c'est la même chose, plus ça change.*

Circularity is a *cybernetic model*, which artificially simulates a property of living beings, by displacing the traditional materialism/spiritualism opposition. The term 'circular' is therefore an interesting metaphor if one considers it a consequence of a self-looping linear determinism, which maintains the identity of an internal/external difference (being or state), by changing (bifurcation), and which changes by returning to the starting point (recurrence).

Circularity is an *approximate metaphor*, having more pragmatic than theoretical value. It has more of a descriptive than an explicative value, since it combines in dynamic fashion the notions of recursiveness, return to the starting point and interdependence of the parts in a whole. It is the vehicle of those paradoxes which arise as a result of the irreversible flow of time. The linear scansion of events may in some cases produce an epistemological error, when a scapegoat or an index patient is identified as the 'cause' of all ills. The 'punctuation of the sequence of events' (Watzlawick et al., 1967), however arbitrary and falsifiable it may be, is the ultimate recourse which permits a minimal definition of reality. The solution lies not so much in the negation of linear determinism as in the prescription of its multilinear or pseudo-circular consequences.

(See also CYBERNETICS; HOMEOSTASIS; PUNCTUATION OF SEQUENCES OF EVENTS.)

J.M. & M.G.

clan In certain primitive societies, the clan is the reference organization, whatever the age of the subject, and this is so at the expense of the conjugal family. A clan is organized around a totem. This is not the mythical ANCESTOR, but its representative or, one might say, its signifier. In fact, even when the totem is a real element, for example an animal, it often bears a different name from the usual one. The totem is the group organizer, the emblem. Its nature – whether animal, vegetable or geographical – is of little importance. It creates a common bond among a certain number of subjects whose belonging to the group is not dependent upon inter-individual relations, nor even on family bonds, but on their relation to the common totem.

The system of totemic thinking is radically distinct from family kinship. In fact, family kinship situates the subject in a relationship of filiation (at least three generations) and permits the creation of new family units. Totemic kinship binds the individual directly to a mythical ancestor through the totem, thus bypassing a generation, namely that of the parents. It has even been thought at times that some societies have no understanding of the role of the father in conception. In reality, it is his importance that is denied. This 'flattening out' or reducing of his importance means that, in a certain sense, all those in the clan group are 'brothers', whatever the family relationships between them. It is not that there is no difference between the clan members, but this is more a hierarchical matter than one relating to filiation. The bond in the clan is more a bond of AFFILIATION than of filiation.

(See also ANCESTRAL RELATION; RITUALS OF BELONGING.)

R.N.

closed systems In contrast to an OPEN SYSTEM, a closed system does not exchange matter, energy or information with the outside world. A closed system cannot have the property of EQUIFINALITY, its final state being determined in an irreversible way by the initial conditions. The structure of a closed system is essentially synchronic. Every complex system has zones of openness and closure.

The psychical FAMILY ORGANIZERS of childhood are structured during the sensitive periods of maturation; they close themselves to certain features of the environment, and the child is, therefore, led to make some necessarily irreversible choices. A distinction will be made between the open system/closed system alternative, which is based on the distinction between organism and environment, and the perspective of operational closure which describes the SELF-ORGANIZATION of the overall system. A FAMILY SYSTEM may be dysfunctional by excess of closure or openness, and this may have a subsequent impact upon the operational closure of its organization.

(See also GENERAL SYSTEMS THEORY.)

P.S.

coach An expression used by Bowen to describe his own transformation from psychoanalyst into family therapist: 'from couch to coach'. In this view, the family therapist must function as an active agent, supporting his clients and encouraging them to make changes within the family. The family therapist will also be able to have recourse to a 'coach' to assist him in exploring his own family system (supervisor, therapist's therapist). Thus, many family therapists advocate that family therapists should themselves undertake a certain amount of personal work on their own FAMILY SYSTEMS (family of origin or present family) as part of their training (work carried out on the basis of their genograms).

(See also SUPERVISION; TRAINING.)

P.S.

coalition A fundamental property of triads, a coalition consists of an alliance between two persons or social units against a third. We may distinguish here between coalitions within organizations and families and coalitions between families and institutions. Alliances are based on the establishment of an AGREEMENT between two members of the triad, while the third party finds himself in a state of disaccord with the others.

It is a tendency of a dyad to seek out a third party to make up a triangle, hence forming a triad. The tendency of a triad is to divide and form a coalition of two of its elements against the third. This tendency is related to differences of hierarchical ranking between each of the elements concerned and to the degree of influence (or force) which each exerts on the two others. The phenomenon can be observed not only in organizations, but also in families, and in interactions between families and organizations (such as the psychiatric, medico-educative or judicial institutions). The theory of coalitions has been particularly closely studied by Theodore Caplow (1968). The study of triads and coalitions rests on the following postulates: 'in a set of linked triads, a coalition partner in one triad may not be an opponent in another' and 'in a set of linked triads, an actor who is offered a choice between incompatible winning coalitions will choose the winning coalition in the superior triad' (Caplow, 1968, p. 59).

COALITIONS WITHIN ORGANIZATIONS

Within an organization each person occupies a position linked to their *status* (designated by the legal framework, see SOCIAL STATUS, LEGAL STATUS), their *role* (a designation that is linked to a reciprocal consensus, see FAMILY ROLE, SOCIAL ROLE) and their *function* (homeostatic regulation of – or force for change exerted on – the system). There is thus a difference between them which relates to hierarchical status and the real distribution of power.

Let us assume a hierarchy between A, B and C, such that $A > B > C$ (A may be the director of an institution, B a supervisor, C a nurse; or else A is a senior surgeon, B a middle-ranking hospital doctor, C a young houseman, or yet again A may be a doctor, B a nurse, C a nurse assistant etc.). We may distinguish between three types of coalition:

1 *The revolutionary coalition* is based on the winning coalition of B and C over A who is their superior in rank.
2 *The conservative coalition* is based on the winning coalition of A and B which respects the established order of rank.
3 *The illegitimate coalition* is based on the coalition of A and C against B.

FAMILY COALITIONS

These have a fundamental dilemma at their base:

- the desire to form winning coalitions with partners of a different generation or sex;
- the existence of opponents who have one characteristic in common with at least one of the partners in the coalition.

The Oedipus complex can be seen as a way of resolving this dilemma.

We may distinguish between primary triads (parents/children) and secondary triads (grandparents, parents/children, brothers/sisters, uncles etc.)

Primary triads

Caplow (1968) reveals the existence of three types of family:

1 *Patripotestal families*: Let A be the father, B the mother and C the child. We then have $A > B > C$ and $A > (B + C)$. It is then impossible to form a revolutionary mother–child coalition against the father.
2 *Equipotestal families*: The father and mother have more or less the same power in relation to their

child. When the child grows up, the mother–child coalition may be able to stand up against the father's autority. Conflicts, whether gentle or furious, may often break out, but there is in that case quite a lot of flexibility in the establishment of coalitions, depending upon each person's aptitudes and registers.
3 *Matripotestal families*: The father does not recognize this feminine authority, but he is relegated to the position of C. When the child is small, the mother–child coalition (A–B) is revolutionary. When he grows up, it becomes conservative, but maintains the father in the peripheral position of a 'parasite'.

Secondary triads

These enable us to study grandparents/parents/children, brothers/sisters/parents, couple/mother-in-law and uncle/parent/nephew triads.

1 *The grandparent/parent/child triad*. We shall simply note here (following Dorrian Apple's study quoted in Caplow, 1968, pp. 96–8) that the grandchild/grandparent relationship is only established on a level of affectionate equality if the grandparents no longer exert their authority over the parents (see NUCLEAR FAMILY, EXTENDED FAMILY).
2 *The brother/sister/parent triad*: Most often sibling relationships are based on a rivalry which looks to the intervention of one or both of the parents to strike a compromise. When the parental coalition is particularly strong, a sibling coalition may emerge. When one of the parents clearly dominates the other, we see a coalition emerge between the children and the weakest parent. When the parents are more or less equal in force, then sibling rivalry is stronger with each child seeking to take advantage of the changes that develop as regards relations of authority within the parental couple (Caplow, 1968).
3 *The husband/wife/wife's mother triad* is the most explosive and the most frequently avoided in all cultures by the creation of a cold relationship between the son-in-law and mother-in-law. According to Caplow (1968), 'avoidance of the mother-in-law' makes it possible to maintain bonds between the three protagonists, while preventing them from forming a triad. In reality, this triad rests upon two strictly incompatible coalitions: the husband–wife coalition, on the one hand, and the mother–daughter coalition on the other. When this latter wins out, it may lead to the break-up of the COUPLE.

FAMILY–INSTITUTION COALITIONS

When confronted with the symptomatic difficulties which they encounter, families will seek to consolidate an organization which cannot meet its own needs by making calls upon various 'specialists': lawyers, educators, psychiatrists, social workers etc. The advantage of the systemic model is that it identifies the family–institution mappings which result from this. Revolutionary, conservative and illegitimate coalitions now come to be formed in relation to a third person external to the family system. Work on FAMILY–THERA-PEUTIC INSTITUTION DIFFERENTIATION may then lead to a more specific clinical understanding of the family's functioning.

FAMILY COALITIONS MET WITH IN CLINICAL PRACTICE

From a clinical point of view, the enmeshed super-imposition of triads leads to more or less structurally stable conflictual forms. One thus finds:

1 *Functional parental coalitions*: term used by Lidz (1970) to describe a husband and wife who both discharge their respective parental roles in a way that is mutually agreeable and satisfying to each of them. However, these 'satisfying' roles may not necessarily be satisfactory for the well-being of the children. The conjugal coalition is the most pregnant one within the family, being open to all the other channels of communication and roughly equivalent to each of them in importance.

2 *Schismatic coalitions* (see MARITAL SCHISM): in the schismatic family, the marital coalition is relatively weak or absent and one finds solid alliances reaching across generations and sexes taking its place (e.g. alliances between father and daughter, mother and daughter, mother and son etc.). In another category of schismatic family, the intergenerational relationships are between father and son or mother and daughter, with other effective channels of communication being virtually non-existent (Lidz et al., 1965).

3 *Skewed, distorted, asymmetrical coalitions* (see MARI-TAL SKEW): one member of the family is relatively isolated from the others who constitute quite a cohesive coalition or unit (Lidz et al., 1965).

4 *Generation gaps*: coalitions in which the marital couple and their offspring form relatively cohesive units with little or no interaction across the generational lines.

5 *Pseudo-democratic coalitions*: all the communication channels in the family seem to be of more or less equal importance to the conjugal coalition. There is little hierarchy and weak differentiation between the conjugal coalition and parental roles.

6 *Disengaged families*: in this case, no one is part of a coalition. Each member of the family is cut off from all the others and each only accords very little importance to positive interaction or the sense of belonging to a family unit.

7 *Enmeshed families*: here there is a total seamless coalition between all the members of the family and every action, feeling and/or thought of any

member sends a shock wave through the family system. Hoffman (1975) has described this very clearly, while Minuchin (Minuchin, 1974; Minuchin et al., 1978) has articulated the clinical and treatment implications for highly enmeshed families.

(See also AGREEMENT AND DISAGREEMENT; ALIGNMENT; CO–THERAPY; MAP AND COUNTERMAP OF A FAMILY SYS-TEM; SCHISMOGENESIS; TRIANGLES.)

J.M. & P.S.

codes SEE ANALOGIC CODING; ARTIFICIAL CODES AND SYSTEMS OF CODING; DIGITAL (OR NUMERIC) CODING.

cognitive epistemologies Epistemology, 'the science of science', has striven since its inception in the nineteenth century to eradicate the paradoxical reduplication inherent in its project. It is located within the different sciences according to their particular methods, being concerned with the study of the postulates rather than the results of those sciences. However, complexity arises when it studies the human sciences and enquires into cognitive phenomena: cognitive epistemology becomes the science of itself, or the epistemology of the sciences of cognition (Le Moigne, 1986b).

From a more general point of view, Bateson defines epistemology as perhaps 'the study of the ecology of mind' (1972, p. 372), i.e. the way in which we acquire knowledge, by contrast with ontology (which corresponds to the being of things, persons and the world). An epistemology will be erroneous if it is based on a wrong choice of units of MIND or units of survival (see EVOLUTIONARY SURVIVAL UNIT). Families secrete epistemologies which are more or less appropriate for the transmission of their values and the perpetuation of the lives of their members.

The first reaction to the problem of epistemology was to reduce the processes of the act of knowing to the states of consciousness of the knowing subject (the position of 'psychologism'). Though it is still to be found in the minds of certain clinical practitioners, its influence has been historically diminished by the dual critique which has come from theories of alienation and from phenomenology. The founder of this latter school, Husserl, argued that there was a necessary distinction to be made between the subject as an object of study for psychophysiology and the subject of knowledge. From this he deduced the need for an epistemology that was not derived from the scientific act in itself and thus one that was based, as he saw it, upon the essence of things.

He laid the ground for his approach with the hypothesis of an original 'universal/general essence', the EIDOS (though what he meant by this was different from what Bateson meant by it), to which one could have immediate access, provided that certain rules for the direction of the mind had been applied (the 'reduction'). All this echoes the Freudian elaborations upon the idea of a 'proton pseudos hystericon'. The importance of Husserl's philosophical development for the family therapist derives from the conceptual proximity of this eidos to the holistic entity which is the paradigmatic foundation of the systemic approach. Hence the importance for the therapist of the critiques which were levelled against that elaboration of the eidetic. We may consider, first, Bachelard's critique, which rejects the aspect of transcendence, then that of Heidegger who thought that one cannot discover a ground 'outside the proposition' as a place where the 'metaphysical' and the 'primordial' would meet and upon which the explanation of a proposition on being would be revealed. However, the most important critical movement was to come from the abandonment of that approach and its replacement by internal epistemology, i.e. reflections on the work of closure, of loops and the self-referential.

Such a work of closure leads to a reconsideration of the self as a unity connected to itself, to others and to the environment (auto- and hetero-reference). The concepts of true and false self suggested by Winnicott (1952) are based on a prior de-centring which is connected with the 'therapeutic' evaluation of the ontology and epistemology of persons as a function of their life-contexts.

As an anthropologist, Bateson was to emphasize cultural relativism, showing the diversity of possible ontologies, not all of which are equally true. Similarly, epistemological errors may arise, which correspond to a mistaken identification of the ecological units that are pertinent in a particular environment: intra- or inter-species conflicts; the 'ecology of bad ideas' (1972, p. 459): the idea of power corrupts (though power does not). Furthermore, the idea of therapy is prone to generating illusions and to corrupting the very use of therapeutic processes, which, whatever formal science may say, are to be found everywhere. It may lead to: (a) thinking and acting with a view to a purely conscious goal, without taking into account the totality of the system (which is something that raises the question, *ipso facto*, of the importance of unconscious processes); (b) attributing the whole of a problem to a single member of the family ecosystem on which one is dependent. The reciprocal accusations of the various protagonists are all the more intense in that the pain and the fact of deflecting blame in this way lead to relational impasses.

(See also DIFFERENTIATION OF SELF; FAMILY SELF-REFERENTIALITY; HOLISM; POWER; SELF; SELF-REFERENTIAL CALCULUS; TRUE SELF, FALSE SELF.)

D.C.

collective cognitive chaos An expression used by Wynne (Wynne and Singer, 1963; Wynne, 1965) to refer to a mode of communication in which each person seems to be expressing themselves normally while the exchange between the persons gathered together has, in fact, no sense. This communication is accompanied by a permanent oscillation between fusion and distancing, attachment and detachment, without it being possible for an adequate distance to be maintained between the partners. All the members of the family are incapable of extracting themselves from the chaos, metacommunicating about it or interrupting it. Chaos of this kind goes together with difficulties in the establishment of coherent emotional distance. One of the therapeutic objectives will be to change this mode of family functioning when it is present by progressively focusing upon the possible meaning of certain exchanges. This focusing is effected through the regulation of interpersonal distances and the structuring of the thoughts and emotions exchanged.

(See also BOUNDARIES; ORDER, DISORDER; OSCILLATORS; RANDOMNESS; STOCHASTIC PROCESSES.)

P.S.

collective interviews, conjoint interviews See CONJUNCTION OF THERAPEUTIC AXES; CO-THERAPY; EVOLUTIONARY SURVIVAL UNIT; FAMILY–THERAPEUTIC INSTITUTION DIFFERENTIATION; MAP AND COUNTER-MAP OF A FAMILY SYSTEM; METABINDING; MULTI-LEVEL HIERARCHIES; SEMANTIC UNIT OF MIND; SOCIAL ORGANIZATION; SUPERVISION; SYSTEMIC MODELLING AND INTERVENTION; TANGLED HIERARCHIES; THERAPEUTIC DOUBLE BINDS; UNIT OF CHANGE.

communal individuals: basic and complex units This is a distinction proposed by Alexander Zinoviev (1981). By definition, human beings may be defined as 'basic' communal individuals. It is a fundamental principle that they try not to act to their own detriment and seek to prevent others from harming them. The biological evolution of humans has led them to take their place within communal life. This derives from the existing social situations and positions.

A 'complex' communal individual is made up of two or more persons on condition that,

• this group of people relates to the environment as a unit;
• this unit distinguishes between the functions of a governing group and a group that is governed;
• there is a division of functions among the individuals who are governed.

Basic communal relations include relations between the individual and the group of which he or she is a member, the relations of the group with the individual, relations between individuals within the group. Derivative communal relations concern relations with individuals outside the group or relations with society as a whole. These relations are of two types: domination–submission (of which the command–subordination relation is an example) and coordination.

(See also ASSEMBLAGE; EVOLUTIONARY SURVIVAL UNIT; MULTI-LEVEL HIERARCHIES; SCHISMOGENESIS; SEMANTIC UNIT OF MIND; TANGLED HIERARCHIES; UNIT OF CHANGE.)

J.M.

communication If the basic axiom of the PRAGMATICS OF COMMUNICATION is that one cannot *not* communicate, there is a corollary to this, which very quickly becomes embarrassing: when communication is everywhere, it ends up being nowhere; communication no longer exists. We have therefore to state the original axiom more specifically: one cannot *not* communicate at one level of reality or another. Such an axiomatics is based, therefore, upon a theory, which does not seek to explain the total set of phenomena in play in a particular communication. The concept is at risk of degrading rapidly, in fact, if the circumstances of communication are not specified, together with the call signs or symptoms.

Without seeking to define what is or is not a communication, we are proposing here to lay down limits: a communication between two persons rests upon:

- the establishment of RITUALS;
- the elaboration of MYTHS;
- a process of co-memorization (see READ–WRITE MEMORIES).

(See also COMMUNICATION SYSTEMS; COMMUNICATION THEORY; FAMILY SELF-REFERENTIALITY; META-COMMUNICATION SYSTEMS; PARACOMMUNICATION SYSTEMS; PATHOLOGICAL COMMUNICATION; PRAGMATICS OF COMMUNICATION; SEMANTICS OF COMMUNICATION; SYNTAX OF COMMUNICATION.)

J.M.

communication systems A 'communication system' is defined as the interaction between a source and a destination, exchanging a MESSAGE transformed into a signal by a coding system through a channel which may possibly be disturbed by noise. The definition proposed by Weaver and Shannon (1949) covers transmission without interaction. A general communication system of this kind is based on:

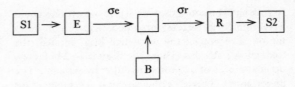

Schematic diagram of a general communication system after Weaver and Shannon, 1949: S1, information source; S2, destination; E, sender; R, receiver; B, noise; σe, signal; σr, received signal.

1 The exchanging of a message transformed into a signal by way of a channel.
2 The signal, via the channel, makes possible the connection between a source and a destination.
3 The source transforms the message into a signal by way of a sender.
4 The destination transforms the message into a signal by way of a receiver.
5 The transmission of the signal in the channel is more or less modified by noise.

This description is of interest in studying the quantitative aspects of information, but it very soon appears inadequate for describing the slightest effective and qualitative communication process between several persons. Even if one looks at living organisms that are low on the evolutionary scale, this definition does not enable us to understand the way two or more homo- or hetero-specific populations interact when confronted with the same or with connected ecosystems. Now 'there are no good receivers which are not also senders' (Cloutier, 1978), entering into contact with similar structures, transforming one another reciprocally in the course of time.

CO-EVOLUTION OF COMMUNICATION SYSTEMS

We shall note here that the animal kingdom has, following a variety of different evolutionary axes, managed to construct systems for sending and receiving messages which are largely analogous if not indeed isomorphic as regards their functional structuring. These systems form circuits with an internal coherence which goes beyond a purely individual analysis of the organisms under consideration. The visual system is directly hooked up to the morphological appearance of conspecifics and co-evolving organisms. Moreover, such a system sends as much as it receives. The olfactory and gustatory systems lead to the differentiated recognition of multiple chemical substances (glandular secretion of pheromones) which are also sent and received reciprocally. Acoustic systems make possible differentiated exchanges of calls, indicating distress, threat, sexual advances etc.

Every individuated organism possesses internal feedback in which its perceptual systems influence its transmission systems. This produces self-informing circuits and enables hierarchized meta-systems to be built up which simulate the morphological and behavioural properties of the co-organisms encountered in the ecosystem. One of the basic functions of the psyche is to simulate the characteristic features of prey, predators, parents, children and sexual partners in so far as these ensure the survival of the individual, its kin group or its species. This self-referenced loop has the peculiar characteristic of anticipating the more or less limited number of possible responses of the co-organisms encountered.

SYSTEMS OF METACOMMUNICATION AND PARACOMMUNICATION

Moreover, noise, which is capable of disrupting the exchange of the message under consideration, may itself assume the status of a signal by virtue of the metacommunication properties of complex communication systems (see METACOMMUNICATION SYSTEMS; PARACOMMUNICATION SYSTEMS). We may thus distinguish between:

- the 'containers' of communication: metacommunication and paracommunication;
- the 'contents' of communication: categories, modalities and tonalities of communication: disclosure, misunderstanding, secrets, forgetting etc.;
- containers and contents may transform one another.

(See also ARTIFICIAL CODES; ANALOGIC CODING; DIGITAL (OR NUMERIC) CODING; FEEDBACK; HOLOGRAPHIC MEMORY; PRAGMATICS OF COMMUNICATION; SELF-REFERENTIAL CALCULUS; SEMANTICS OF COMMUNICATION; SYNTAX OF COMMUNICATION.)

J.M.

communication theory Communication, conceptualized as the 'social matrix of psychiatry' by Ruesch and Bateson (1951), becomes an entity which can be studied as a general system for the modelling of human relationships and as the focus of therapeutic intervention. Communication can be understood from several points of view:

1 *Phenomenological viewpoint*: communication occurs when events which take place at a given time or place are closely connected to events which happen at a different time or place (Weaver and Shannon, 1949; Miller, 1978).
2 *Hermeneutic viewpoint*: communication is the interpretation of an event made by the observer of the interaction of two organisms $\Omega 1$ and $\Omega 2$ (von Foerster, 1960).

3 *Cognitive self-referential viewpoint*: communication is the representation (internal) of a relation between oneself (an internal representation of oneself) and another (von Foerster, 1960).
4 *Constructivist viewpoint*: communication occurs by a process of coupling, of the intersection and construction of the world (Elkaim, 1989, pp. 90–1).
5 *Ecosystemic viewpoint*: communication is the manner in which one MIND influences another. It is the system of reference by which the phenomena of transference and counter-transference occur as affective and cognitive expressions of this influence.

Many questions arise from these different definitions. In which way can an event occur in space and time? Can it be integrated psychically in an objective or subjective way? Is it possible to distinguish the reality of the phenomenon from its interpretation? How can a self-referential point of view of an individual or an individuated group (that is, having the capacity to define a 'self' with a real identity) adjust itself to the points of view of much larger systems?

These questions lead to a certain number of paradoxes. In studying the exchanges between man, animal and machine, cybernetics and then the science of cognition prompts the study of properties in common which link organisms and objects that permit exchange. The facts of communication come from the worlds of science and art to make an action meaningful by the use of information. 'Communication' relies on the activation of one or more COMMUNICATION SYSTEMS. Communication systems can be interpreted in terms of messages received and transmitted, certain messages being organized in parallel – (paramessages), others being organized in a hierarchical manner (meta-messasges) (see PARACOMMUNICATION SYSTEMS; METACOMMUNICATION SYSTEMS).

SOCIAL COMMUNICATION

Demailly and Le Moigne (1986, p. 303) define social communication in the sense of 'proposing a representation' as, and by, a system of 'treatment of information':

1 *Principle of limitation*: each person has only a limited capacity for the treatment of information, and will restrict his/her exchanges as a function of that capacity.
2 *Principle of rationality*: social communication is the confrontation of space and problems which are produced by individuals.
3 *Principle of inference*: social communication is where heuristics develop.
4 *Principle of economy*: a treatment system for effective information must be economical and intelligent. It must in some way provide a volume of information less than it has ingested at the start; it must include strong enough mechanisms of indexation which can

filter and select information. It must include models which, beyond the storing of information, allow problems to be resolved, solutions to be evaluated and decisions taken.

5   *Principle of qualitative change*: social communication has undergone a qualitative leap. This is the shift from a time of scarce information to a time of excessive information with rapid reproduction of data. Memories are information based and the transmission of information has accelerated.

Social communication relies on the conjunction of memory and information processing which evolve in parallel following varied traditions and interests that are ultimately in opposition, and which continue to pose problems for their adjustment and mutual synchronization.

TRANSMISSION, COMMUNION, QUANTITY, QUALITY

The theoretical field involved in the thinking on communication, and its own field of application, may be represented graphically by two cones joined at their apices (isomorphic with the figure proposed by Thom, 1980b; see Costa de Beauregard, 1980, p. 66). The 'neck' of the hourglass represents the particular quality of the figure in question, and is occupied by the calculations of Weaver and Shannon (1949) relating to the quantity of INFORMATION contained in a message. The retrospective of these calculations reveals the work of Maxwell and Boltzmann as their closest neighbours, then, by levels, all Western knowledge and reflections upon knowing, including both Claude Bernard and Pascal, E. Gallois and Heraclitus. The question of the nature of this explanatory principle which attempts a 'total explanation of the world' by defining itself as the epistemological keystone will be echoed by its field of application. Appearing first in cybernetics, then in biology and in systemic psychological approaches, it opens up ever wider to the point where it implodes. Now, that keystone, that unique point where multiple traditions and multiple objects of study meet, is in itself ambiguous.

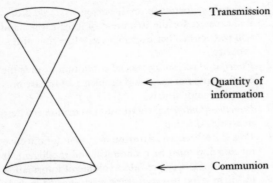

Graphic representation of the paradigm of communication.

In its transitive form, to communicate means to transmit, i.e. to assist a linear displacement or change. In the intransitive sense, by contrast, it means to be in relation; not in this case to send elsewhere, but to keep here, to introduce circularity. Weaver and Shannon's (1949) mathematical model, which has come to be viewed as the central element of the new paradigm, is linear in nature. The essence of that model, as von Foerster (1960) has pointed out, is that the message in question is to be sent from a point A (the sender) to a point B (the receiver) like a commodity or substance circulating in a tube which can be fed out in slices or 'bits'. The channel or link is, for its part, of a minor 'ontological nature'. It is a *vade mecum* with no autonomous existence. In no way, however, can the basic exclusion of the intermediary figure, the channel, the transducer, be justified from a heuristic point of view. It was indeed on this reified element, the channel, that the study of communication and its quantification was to bear initially, in the form of information theory.

However, the other dimension of the word 'communication' – communion and the communal – was to be developed simultaneously by the cyberneticians (see Wiener, 1975). The processes of FEEDBACK in effect introduced this notion of CIRCULARITY and led to the notion of GENERAL SYSTEMS THEORY which was defined by von Bertalanffy (1947). Weaver and Shannon (1949), in their linear causality-based thinking were, by contrast, to focus on noise, to compare and differentiate information and uncertainty, chance and organization.

SEMIOTICS OF COMMUNICATION

The semiotic conception of communication (see SEMIOLOGY) makes the distinction, within the framework of a general theory of language (Carnap, 1942, 1956, 1964; Morris, 1946), between syntax, semantics and pragmatics. Syntax can be seen as leaving out of account meaning and the users of meaning, in order to study the structures of the relations between expression (grammars). Semantics leaves these structures and their users out of account, to focus its attention on meaning effects, i.e. the significations of the concepts which result from them. As for pragmatics, it can be seen as being concerned with the users of language and the way they wield language in the context of such general events as arise in the history of the language users. Pragmatics is concerned with the information which is not in the text of the discourse, but which has to be known for the text to be comprehensible. This is to say that pragmatics, semantics and syntax are part of the same whole, even if it is necessary to separate them out for the purposes of study.

In Léo Apostel's (1967) view, pragmatics presupposes a theory of action and a theory of sets of actions. Since it cannot be closed upon itself, pragmatics can only be dependent on the definition that is given of

The figure in the image contains the following labels:

Transmission

Quantity of information

Communion

action, whether that definition be, for example, behavioural, psychological or sociological. There would thus be as many possible forms of pragmatics as there were initial definitions. Such a point of view runs the risk of leading, sooner or later, to the pure and simple disappearance of pragmatics, if no account is taken of the co-texts or contexts defined by the systems of metacommunication.

In the preface to their *Dictionnaire de la sémiotique*, Greimas and Courtes (1979, p. v) remark:

either the problematic (of pragmatics) is an integral part of the theory of language, and then the translation of its contributions into a semiotic form is self-evident or pragmatics is merely, according to its own definition, a non-semiotic appendage of semiotics, using heterogeneous categories – of a psychological or sociological order, for example – and it cannot then claim a place in a dictionary of semiotics.

In the view of these two writers, the pragmatic modalities of discourse are merely one of the aspects of the cognitive dimension, relating to the cognitive competence of communicating subjects. For example, manipulation, conceived as the action of one human being upon others, is structured in language by the factitive structures: 'make . . . be', 'make . . . do' and the structural variations of these on the semiotic square ('not make . . . be', 'make . . . not be', 'make . . . not do' ('prevent') etc.). Such an approach represents an undoubted advance in terms of conceptual clarity, but it is necessary to confront this semiotic structure with real situations of manipulation. The aspect of magnification or even caricature introduced by pathological situations (relations between a schizophrenic, his/her family, institutions; relations between the alcoholic, the bottle and the alcoholic's spouse etc.) becomes an indispensable source of information. To a lesser degree, such facts are pinpointed in the 'psychopathology of everyday life' analysed by Freud or in the oddities of daily communication as described by Bateson, Watzlawick and Haley, for example. There also follows from these an etho-linguistics of performative, gestural and linguistic acts (Austin, 1962; Searle, 1969; Benveniste, 1979–80; Berrendonner, 1981; Recanati, 1981; Cosnier et al., 1982).

It is, however, imperative that we recognize that language, as a general semiotic system, cannot self-validate itself to explain medical, psychoanalytic, ethological, ethnological and family semiotics as we observe them, in clinical practice. Furthermore, this new approach investigates the tensions, distortions, congruities and incongruities that arise between the semiotics of language, the semiotics of speech, the semiotics of the body and that of its non-linguistic movements. The semiotics of communication thus urges the de-centring of language from itself as subject of study.

Conversely, the PRAGMATICS OF COMMUNICATION necessarily directs interest back again towards the study of 'human cognitive capacities' and the 'mental structures which serve as their vehicles' (Chomsky, 1980, p. 47), as well as the simulation of these capacities in machines as explored in artificial intelligence. Such a study goes beyond the bounds of language and concerns many other human activities. In effect, as Chomsky (1980, ch. 2) writes, 'the linguistic system is just one of the many cognitive systems which are combined in the most intimate way at the level of the effective use of language.' To cite only a few, these include: differentiated recognition of complex forms, non-linguistic thought processes, specific behavioural strategies and tactics such as love, work and play behaviour.

CYBERNETICS OF MAN–ANIMAL, MAN–MACHINE AND MAN–HUMAN ECOSYSTEM COMMUNICATION

The CYBERNETIC paradigm is based on a dual movement according to Bateson in 'Cybernetic Explanation', (Bateson, 1972):

1 The contexts of study proceed by progressive extensions (in the macrocosm or the microcosm). In the face of an incomprehensible situation, it is necessary to take some distance from it, to change perspective (de Rosnay's metaphor of the 'macroscope' is pertinent here).

2 The informative, communicational value proceeds by progressive restraints. Explanation of a cybernetic type functions in a negative way by evaluation of differences. The cybernetic model functions by simulation of the REDUCTIO AD ABSURDUM proof. An outcome in family therapy is not so much a positive outcome as a diminution of negative effects.

There is a dual, hardware (quality and quantity of information-processing media) and software (quality and quantity of organization of the information and symbols to be processed) aspect in the structuring and memorizing of the information to be communicated.

The essence and *raison d'être* of communication is, for Bateson, the creation of REDUNDANCY, of meaning (see the SEMANTICS OF COMMUNICATION), of a model of what is predictable, of information and of the reduction of chance by 'restraint'.

MULTI-SENSORY, MULTI-CHANNEL AND MULTI-MEDIA COMMUNICATION

Multi-sensory, MULTI-CHANNEL SYSTEMS OF COMMUNICATION (Cosnier et al., 1982): coenaesthesis ensures a coherent translation between systems of perception. There is a perception of the three-dimensional character of space which is shared by kinaesthesia, skin contact, sight and hearing (Poincaré, 1963). It follows from this that there are parallel systems of communication (see PARACOMMUNICATION SYSTEMS) whose para-messages either function synergistically or antagonistically at the same levels of complexity.

Multi-contextual (Bateson, 1972), multi-media (McLuhan, 1964) systems of communication: where the media and contexts transform each other mutually. Phylogenetic acquisition and ontogenetic learning correspond to the self-referential interiorization of hetero-referential properties encountered in the environment. These metasystems which provide information, in advance, of the possibilities of meetings with co-organisms are, in effect, the products of learning processes that become increasingly hierarchized as one moves up the evolutionary scale (metacommunication systems).

Human language is a ritualization, if not indeed a meta-ritualization, which simulates animal, vegetal and mineral communication. If there is no metalanguage (Wittgenstein, 1921; Lacan, 1966), this is because human language is in its essence a metalanguage simulating all possible forms of metacommunication.

There is, therefore, a process of co-evolution in which interpersonal and intrapersonal communication are in conflict. The more complicated communication becomes, the more the organism develops internal mechanisms for simulating the functional circles of the organisms which are of interest to it in terms of its life or survival. The capacity to elaborate imaginary scenarios, phantasies, dreams, daydreams and games makes it possible to test out the properties of the external world either in imagination or in reality.

Communication thus appears structured in multiple levels, combining aspects of linear scansion and circular recursivity. In a certain number of cases, that communication cannot be reduced to the separate analysis of the properties of the interlocutors; the more the scansion of facts appears linear and irreducible to the equally linear but opposing version of the partner, the more strikingly apparent the emergent quality of the system. The singularity of the communication is then no longer comprehensible in terms of isolable personality structures and it becomes all the more necessary to recognize the underlying or 'overlying' processes of circularity.

SOCIAL COMMUNICATION AND SYSTEMS FOR THE TREATMENT OF INFORMATION

Demailly and Le Moigne (1986, p. 303) define social communication in the sense of 'proposing a representation' as, and by, a system of treatment of information:

1   *Principle of limitation*: each person has only a limited capacity for the treatment of information, and will restrict his/her exchanges as a function of that capacity.

2   *Principle of rationality*: social communication is the confrontation of space and problems which are produced by individuals.
3   *Principle of inference*: social communication is where heuristics develop.
4   *Principle of economy*: a treatment system for effective information must be economical and intelligent. It must in some way provide a volume of information less than it has ingested at the start; it must include strong enough mechanisms of indexation which can filter and select information. It must include models which, beyond the storing of information, allow problems to be resolved, solutions to be evaluated and decisions taken.
5   *Principle of qualitative change*: social communication has undergone a qualitative leap. This is the shift from a time of scarce information to a time of excessive information with rapid reproduction of data. Memories are information based and the transmission of information has accelerated.

It may be noted that social communication relies on the conjunction of memory and information processing which evolve in parallel following varied traditions and interests that ultimately are in opposition, and which continue to pose problems for their adjustment and mutual synchronization.

(See also GENERAL SYSTEMS THEORY; SYNTAX OF COMMUNICATION.)

J.M. & D.C.

complementarity   See COMMUNICATION THEORY; COUPLES; PRINCIPLE OF COMPLEMENTARITY; SCHISMOGENESIS.

complexity   The first definition of complexity can only be a negative one: complexity is what defies simple description in everyday language. Unlike the complicated, however, the complex often gives an appearance of simplicity. A simple unit is a unit which is apprehended as elementary, non-reducible, isolable from its environment, easy to perceive and define. 'The "very complicated" may not be "very complex" and the "very simple" (a particle) may turn out to be very complex' (Le Moigne, 1986a, p. 49).

Complexity is a property attributed to a model by an observer. He or she may therefore evaluate it using the information necessary to express that model. Complexity leads us to the problem of intelligence, which may possibly be modelled as an artificial act (Le Moigne, 1986a). Organization, in Morin's (1980b, pp. 40–6) sense is complex, being based upon an organized and organizing process.

Thus a sufficiently complex system may give a supreme appearance of simplicity. Conversely, a sufficiently simple system leads to questions that are open and not calculable by ALGORITHMS. A schizophrenic process will appear relatively simple if one considers certain levels of action: that of internment in an asylum, prescription of sedatives, intervention with the family. It will become extremely complex as soon as one takes into account the levels of description: neurophysiological, psychoanalytic and systemic.

COMPLEX SYSTEMS AND OPENNESS TO THE RANDOM

A simple system, for example a gas, may be thought of as being made up of elementary units, all of them similar and unorganized, with little interaction between them, the whole being characterized by the sum of the characteristics of the individual units. A causality may be regarded as simple if the cause and effect can be easily isolated and connected together. What is simple excludes the uncertain or the ambiguous. In effect, the complexity of a phenomenon reveals itself to the observer by its character of uncertainty, unpredictability and irreproducibility; that is, its essentially unforeseeable nature. This uncertainty of prediction has to do with the complication of the elementary units and the interactions between those units. To this must also be added the variety of the elements, the totality being organized into hierarchical internal levels, and the variety of interactions. The various elements and levels are themselves connected by a great variety of links, producing a high density of interconnections and very specific behaviour in complex systems. This behaviour, which is difficult to predict, derives from the LAW OF REQUISITE VARIETY of the system under consideration. The paradox is that complex systems also have properties of self-reproduction, of SELF-ORGANIZATION and that they possess predictable behaviours. The most complex systems are the 'receptive structures' that are most open to events (to randomness, accidents, perturbations etc.). Their determinism predisposes them to identify, receive and transform events that arise in an apparently random manner. Complexity increases with the number and diversity of the elements, the rise in the number of catastrophes of regulation, and the number of dimensions of the structurally stable attractors of the system. A system will be the more complex for its being able to integrate chance events and, thence, potentialize its internal dynamism. The question thus arises whether that capacity is itself the product of chance or whether it implies the existence of a systemic determinism which has to be sought out.

SYSTEMS, SUB-SYSTEMS, METASYSTEMS

The perception of complex systems in organizations of living or inanimate matter usually leads to the following observation. The study of the system under consideration shows that the elements which make it up can themselves be analysed in terms of systems, which are then called sub-systems, or sub-sets, or elements of the system. The same reference system will be integrated into larger systems, of which it will become a part as a sub-system or element of these 'metasystems'. Within the limits of the infinitely small and the infinitely large, represented by elementary particles on the one hand and galactic super-clusters on the other, a great number of hierarchical organizations are to be found. The more or less arbitrary way these are divided up determines scientific specialisms or fields. This cosmogonic structuring has in part replaced one of the functions traditionally fulfilled by mythological activity. One of the limits of the systemic model is that it never tells us what the boundaries are at which we must halt for the resolution of a given problem. Moreover, in what ways do the infinitely large and the infinitely small connect with one another? Complex hierarchical systems imply the image of a pyramidal stratification, in which complexity is evenly spread across all the levels, but relativized by virtue of the relations which exist between the levels; neurophysiological and neurobiological analysis leads to models which in some cases may be highly sophisticated, but which suddenly become much more simple, if not indeed elementary, when we pass on to the plane of psychological analysis. Similarly, individual and group psychoanalysis have described a hierarchical functioning of the psychical apparatus and have led to ever more elaborate and complexified theoretical models, and yet certain phenomena studied in this way take on a much less opaque – not to say obscure – appearance when the analysis starts out from the specific form of organization of the family system (see BLACK BOX). Similarly, the analysis of larger cultural groups enables us to intervene in certain problems which arise repeatedly within family groups, but which are only intelligible and offer scope for the necessary leverage at the suprafamilial level (NETWORKS; Elkaim, 1979a, b).

PROPERTIES OF COMPLEX SYSTEMS

The tree-shaped structure of complex systems presents a certain number of characteristics, functions and qualities which are fully documented by Simon (1969): stability of assembly in cases of destabilization, economy in the transmission of information, break in the relationship between the complexity and size of the system.

Stability of Assembly

Let us imagine, writes Simon (1969), a watch made up of ten thousand pieces. Two watchmakers follow a totally different plan to assemble it. The first constructs the watch using no intermediate unit between each piece and the completely constructed watch. The second proceeds by stages making functional and structural units at intermediate levels: ten stable sub-assemblies of around one thousand pieces each, themselves made up of ten stable sub-assemblies of one hundred pieces, then ten sub-assemblies of ten pieces. The first watchmaker will be forced to make his watches one by one. If he is interrupted in the work of assembly, he is forced to start again from scratch. The second watchmaker, by contrast, will have at his disposal a certain number of stable sub-assemblies which will not be destroyed if he is interrupted or has to move to some other activity. Simon points out that the assembly of a large-scale hierarchical system may proceed from the bottom upwards, by successively putting together sub-systems, as in the preceding metaphor, or from the top downwards by the successive break up of units and the emergence of sub-units. Uexküll (1956) perceived this distinction between the centripetal organization of artificial machines like a watch and the centrifugal organization of living organisms. Thom (1972, 1980b) pursues this distinction, suggesting the hypothesis of an organizing centre in living systems and their development in terms of the UNIVERSAL UN-FOLDING of a germ expressing the 'logos' of the system under consideration.

Yet is man not, in his very being, subject to the pull of these two opposing forces – the centrifugal and the centripetal – as is envisaged in the theory of SPLITTING in psychoanalysis? However this may be, the organization of the psyche, the family and institutions would be unthinkable without a complex hierarchization of their constituent parts. If this were not the case, the slightest perturbation of the system in question would lead to its complete disintegration. The schizophrenic explosion shows precisely the disintegration of hierarchical levels and the existence of multiple sub-systems in abeyance, which only recover a relative stability by the re-establishing of internal–external family connections.

Economy in the transmission of information
In a complex hierarchical system, a stable unit does not require the whole of the information present and more or less available. It is enough, at a first approximation, for information to circulate as much as possible between the members of the unit in question, while the necessary pertinent information may be limited, sequenced, reduced to a number of precise details and/or general features depending on specific needs. One cannot, in fact, have a clear view of several hierarchical levels that are far removed from one another. Though prescribing drugs may be seen, for example, to have clear effects both as regards the modification of the patient and at the level of family organization, that act of prescribing will obscure to some degree the understanding of the dynamics of the family interactions. Conversely, the same therapist working on that family dynamic will not be able intelligibly to manage the administration of drugs in cases where this is necessary

for several members of the family. Drugs will become symbolic substitutes, independently of their action on the psychobiological plane. In the field of therapy, therapists have to evaluate the quantity and quality of pertinent information to be communicated, as a function of the types of intervention under consideration.

Break in relationship between complexity and size of systems
Depending on the point of view adopted, each level of the hierarchy will appear simple or complex. The lower levels are no less complex than the upper levels. Stepping back to acquire sufficient distance for the perception of an apparently complex form makes it possible to simplify the problem. The study of family systems or political systems is no more complex than the study of physiological or psychical systems even though they are on wider or 'higher' levels of the hierarchy. Though the totality of all these systems obviously appears hypercomplex, ordering them into levels of perception and action has a simplifying function.

Change of level may possibly lead to a clarifying of a situation that otherwise would be experienced as confused or incapable of resolution. In this sense, even if responsibility and sum total of knowledge increase as a person rises to the higher-ranking positions in a company, army or nation, that increase is in no sense linear and is certainly not exponential. Rising to a higher level of the hierarchy simplifies certain actions and reduces certain constraints and tensions, since the systems at the level from which one has come become sub-systems which are now perceived as relatively simple elements. This 'disengagement' makes it possible to gain access to the higher level of complexity starting out from a simplified perception of the sub-sets.

(See also ASSEMBLAGE; DYNAMIC SYSTEMS; FAMILY SYSTEMS; GENERAL SYSTEMS THEORY; MULTI-LEVEL HIERARCHIES; MODEL OF THE SYSTEMIC MODEL; ORDER; PRESCRIBING (MEDICAL) DRUGS; RANDOMNESS; SOCIAL ORGANIZATION; STOCHASTIC PROCESSES; TANGLED HIERARCHIES; TRANSGENERATIONAL MEMORIES.)

M.G. & J.M.

compounding of errors In the face of certain difficulties of existence and the inability to find satisfactory solutions, it is sometimes the case that the attempted solution increases the degree of distress instead of reducing it. Examples of this might be having a baby to save a marriage, adopting a child to reduce the other children's sense of loneliness (Haley, 1963; Bloch, 1973; Watzlazwick et al., 1974; Hoffman, 1981).

Such an attitude might seem to be akin to the gambling tactic of doubling the stakes in an effort to 'recover your losses', to the policy of the ostrich burying its head in the sand or to the behaviour of a simpleton who dives into the water to get out of the rain. 'Symptom prescription' in this case would consist in pushing what are apparently aberrant attitudes to the point of absurdity and amplifying the movements of the system which take it into a far-from-equilibrium state (see DISSIPATIVE STRUCTURES).

We should, however, question to what extent we are justified in putting matters this way. Starting out from a procedure with 'scientific' connotations (learning by trial and error), we have come to a clearly moralizing conclusion here, and we are running the risk of leading therapists into passing value judgements on the clients who consult them. Although the therapist should certainly take account of his or her subjective assessment, this should be relativized within the internal dynamics of the treatment.

(See also ABSURD, PSYCHOTHERAPY OF THE; PROVOCATION; SUPERVISION.)

P.S. & J.M.

conflict See AGONISTIC BEHAVIOUR; BIFURCATION; COALITION; DOUBLE BIND; ELEMENTARY CATASTROPHES; FAMILY LIFE-CYCLES; FORCE FIELDS; RECIPROCAL VICTIMIZATION AND RESCUE; RITUALIZATION; SCAPEGOAT; TEACHING OF SYSTEMIC APPROACHES; TRIANGLES; VIOLENCE.

conjunction of therapeutic axes A therapeutic action is decided upon on the basis of certain criteria and choices which it is possible to locate in terms of the conjunction of the axes structuring the action in question:

• diachronic and synchronic axes;
• individual and collective axes;
• surface and deep axes;
• actual and potential axes;
• strategic and tactical axes;
• regressive and progressive axes;
• analytic and holistic axes;
• sub-systemic and meta-systemic axes.

(See also ACTIVATION AND DE-ACTIVATION OF SYSTEMS MEDIATING BEHAVIOUR; FAMILY SYSTEMS; GENERAL SYSTEMS THEORY; HOLISM; PRINCIPLE OF COMPLEMENTARITY; PSYCHOANALYSIS; SURFACE STRUCTURES; THERAPEUTIC STRATEGIES AND TACTICS; UNCERTAINTY PRINCIPLE.)

J.M.

connectedness, connected spaces The connectedness of a space is a topological property which indicates that one cannot find two parts of the space which are disconnected and which, when reunited, reconstitute the space in its entirety; or, to put it another way, two points of a connected space may always be joined by a path of that space.

A coherent definition of a system presupposes that the parts comprising it are connected to one another by linked paths, whether material or conceptual. The pathology of systems is often attributable to a loss of pertinent connections between their functional sub-units.

For Thom (1972: 2nd edn, 1977, p. 81), a system is the content of a domain of SPACE–TIME. A domain of space–time is nothing other than a connected open set. This approach may at first sight seem too vast. In fact, it formalizes the notion of linkages between the elements of a system and exchange with the outside. In effect the property of a space of being connected implies that, in one way or another, the elements of that space are linked and that it would not be possible to extract parts from it without affecting the others. It expresses the non-summability of the parts in relation to the whole.

Connectedness characterizes the space constituted by the relational fabric in a natural group such as the family, the couple or institutions. This connectedness is not merely material and physical (since two living beings are corporally separated), but is also of a fictive, psychical nature. It is expressed through bonds which unite the various members of the family. Therapists are often led to define the system they will be receiving in terms of the various levels of family connectedness:

1 Spatiotemporal connectedness of persons living under the same roof, or living apart, but maintaining other forms of proximity.
2 Generational and transgenerational connectedness: sub-systems such as the sibling group or the parental couple constitute connected components, in which the bonds are a function of the family positions, roles and myths imposed by the figures of regulation. Invisible loyalties and the ledgers in which the accounts of legacies and merit are kept make explicit a 'historical' connectedness.
3 Emotional and phantasmatic connectedness, which implies including in the system mythic personages, ANCESTORS or a dead brother etc., whose positions are embodied in one or more members who become depositories of hidden bonds, but which continue to live on in the form of invisible loyalties.

(See FAMILY MYTHS; GENERAL SYSTEMS THEORY; LOYALTY, SYMBOLIC REFERENCE; TRANSGENERATIONAL MEMORIES.)

M.G.

constructivism An EPISTEMOLOGY, or rather a set of epistemologies, in the science of observing–observed systems, which asserts the importance of relationship in the act of knowing and seeks to provide an alternative to realism and idealism. Knowledge is based on a process of reflective abstraction which gives access to the concrete by experiences of consciousness, which structure mental models whose reliability is then tested by experience. In constructivism, knowledge is not so much an object – given quite independently of the subject who 'discovers' or 'observes' it – as an active project in which the subject–object distinction is a relative one.

In order to know the world, one must know oneself. Constructivism postulates an interaction between the world, which governs the process whereby organisms come into being, and the activities of organisms which elaborate models of the environment. Reality is neither a pure state independent of the observer, nor a pure product of cognitive representations. It is a developing construction which links a community of observers/actors to the ecosystem and enables us to specify the distinction between the real, the potential, which may be actualized, the virtual, which is accessible, and the fictive, which is unreal. The knowledge of the process of knowledge becomes a decision-making process, a question of making a finite choice, in circumstances of potentially infinite regress, of the perception of oneself by oneself. The cognitive procedure could thus be said to be based on a multiplicity of open choices; within a constructivist perspective, several systems, though mutually incompatible, may have a coherence of their own and may not be regarded as contradictory. Constructivism seeks to explain the processes of cognition and the constraints which limit our cognitive capacities.

We may distinguish between several constructivist epistemologies: the intuitionist constructivism of L. H. J. Brouwer; the genetic constructivism of J. Piaget; the self-organizing constructivism of H. von Foerster; the systemic constructivism of E. Morin; the engineering constructivism of H. Simon; the radical constructivism of E. von Glaserfeld; the aesthetic constructivism of N. Goodman; the pragmatic constructivism of P. Watzlawick; and the symbolizing constructivism of J.-L. Le Moigne.

Historical background

The history of constructivism is an eclectic one, reaching back to the origins of Western philosophical thought. Its influence has fluctuated over time, ebbing in periods when there was recognition of the ontological primacy of the object as an entity existing independently of the knowing subject:

1 Realism regards truth as a discovery of the properties of the universe as they objectively exist, independently of their representation. On this view,

what is represented is the thing which exists independently of representation, external to consciousness and determining representation.

2 Idealism regards truth as the perfect match between the subjective representation and the world apprehended phenomenally. Phenomena are the whole of reality. Reality is identical to the knowledge we have of it and a reality of which we had no representations would have no existence.

Plato is a realist in so far as, for him, a reality exists which is independent of the perception we have of the world. But he is also an idealist, in so far as the Ideas are more real than tangible beings which are merely their reflection or image.

Constructivism puts the emphasis, rather, on the way man produces knowledge. Such a point of view is expressed in sceptical thinking, being found, for example, in the writings of Montaigne: 'The conviction of wisdom is the plague of man' ('Apology for Raimond Sebond', *Essays*, Book 2, ch. 12). This mistrust of absolute knowledge is accompanied by an expression of the need for self-observation: 'I study myself more than any other subject; that is my Metaphysics, that is my Physics' ('Of experience', *Essays*, Book 3, ch. 13). Or again: 'Of philosophical opinions, I more readily embrace those which are most solid, that is to say, most human and most our own; my words, in keeping with my actions, are mean and humble' (*Essays*, Book 3, ch. 13). Knowledge is a matter of incorporation, of impregnation. It is movement and stands opposed to the ontological principle which founds Descartes' philosophy: 'I think, therefore I am.'

Going beyond the 'being' of the Cartesian *cogito*, constructivism conceives truth as an active pursuit. Giambattista Vico, a Neapolitan philosopher born in 1668, eighteen years after the death of Descartes, was to propose an alternative to the ontological philosophy of the French philosopher: *'verum ipsum factum'* [the truth is the same as the made] or, alternatively, 'truth and action are convertible'. Whereas Descartes seeks to describe the knowable world after the model of geometry, Vico insists on 'the caprice, fortuitousness, chance and hazard' which govern human affairs. Vico states that primary, infinite truth rests in God since He is the prime mover; man thinks fundamentally in two dimensions, whereas the world was created in three dimensions. God's truth would be an assembly, a model in three dimensions, whereas human truth would be 'what man comes to know as he builds it, shaping it by his actions' (*De antiquissima Italorum sapientia*, ch. 1, s. 1). Human knowledge, being able to apprehend only the extremity of things, could only produce a flat likeness of them. For Vico, even mathematical theorems are constructions: 'We demonstrate things geometric by the act of making them.'

For John Locke (1632–1704), knowledge is the

perception of a match or mismatch between our ideas expressed in a judgement. It is based on an actual and real existence which matches something of which we have an idea in our minds (see *An essay concerning human understanding*, 1690). Locke stresses the 'limits of our faculties, our definitive ignorance of the intimate essence of things'. George Berkeley (1865–1753) was to criticize Locke's doctrine of abstract ideas. Minds which perceive and the ideas perceived by them are all that exist: *esse* is *percipi*. To exist is to be perceived or to perceive, or to wish, i.e. to act. The object and the sensation are one and the same thing and cannot be detached from one another. Real things are the ideas imprinted on our senses by the Maker of Nature and these are distinct from the ideas provoked by our imagination. Moreover, one may only confront ideas with ideas, not with anything else. Berkeley rejects the idea of infinite divisibility, arguing that every magnitude must be made up of a finite number of visible minima. A space cannot be greater than any given space: what one has an idea of must be something given; the thing cannot be bigger than itself.

For David Hume (*An enquiry concerning human understanding*, 1758), though impressions are innate, ideas are not. The problem is one of knowing how to get from ideas to knowledge. We reason by association of ideas, on the basis of analogical inferences which proceed by resemblance, contiguity and relations of cause and effect learnt from experience. These connections between ideas come to seem stable to us through the habit which forms from the repeated observation of causal relations. It is only our imagination which allows us to believe in the existence of bodies which are permanent and distinct from ourselves.

According to Immanuel Kant (*Critique of pure reason*, 1781–7), knowledge does not give access to reality in itself, but to the objects of experience which are given to us by means of sensibility and are thought through the understanding; the understanding is 'the faculty of rules', whereas judgement is the faculty for subsuming under rules, i.e. for deciding whether a thing is or is not subject to a given rule. It is only by uniting that the understanding and the sensibility can determine objects in us. 'Thought is the act which relates given intuition to an object' (*Critique of pure Reason*, 1973 edn, p. 264). As for reason, it is the 'faculty of principles'.

INTUITIONISM AND FORMALISM

The intuitionism of the Dutch mathematician L. E. J. Brouwer is based on mental constructs which do not themselves constitute the object thus constructed. Possessing a limited, finite intelligence, man has only an abstract representation of the infinite, the experimental conditions of existence of which have to be specified. These latter are apprehended in different ways by the formalist and intuitionist schools of mathematical thinking, which propose different interpretations of infinite sets. These sets are an abstraction from the properties inherent in the higher cognitive systems which are capable of modelling the difference between the finite and the infinite, the continuous and the discontinuous. The human psyche, in representing itself, conceives the possibility of distinguishing between numerically limited and unlimited collections. The totality can be apprehended as a part of itself. It all comes down, then, to the question of the status of such a totality.

An infinite set possesses the paradoxical property of being reflexive: it is possible to create a one-to-one correspondence (mapping) between an infinite set and one of its own parts or subsets. For the formalist school (Bolzano, Cantor), an infinite set is *really* equipotential to one of its own subsets. The infinite is an *actual infinite*. For the intuitionist school, an infinite set is not a finished entity but a series of choices, linked to a process of growth in which only the initial segments of the series are known. The infinite is a *potential infinite*. The intuitionist denies any reality to a representation (even a virtual one) of actual infinity. The principle of the excluded third – 'A proposition is either true or false and there is no other alternative' – is not valid in the construction of infinite sets, in that one encounters situations where infinite series have properties which cannot either be validated or refuted by using a known algorithm. The possible is only accessible by means of a method of construction that can be put into operation in a predictable future. The infinite falls outside forms of material representation (causality) or logical representation (excluded third). 'Intuitionism . . . recognize[s] mathematics as an autonomic interior constructional mental activity which although it has found extremely useful linguistic expression and can be applied to an exterior world, nevertheless neither in its origin nor in the essence of its method has anything to do with language or an exterior world' (Brouwer, 1975, vol. 1, p. 551).

THE CONSTRUCTIVISM OF JEAN PIAGET

According to Piaget, intelligence, as a mode of exchange of the human organism with the environment, is constructed in a fashion analogous to the biological mechanisms of the development, regulation and structuring of the organism itself. For Piaget, that 'construction' is the outcome of the differentiatory interaction of the knowing subject (logico-mathematical operations) and the known object (figuration), by the assimilation of environmental data and a pre-adaptive accommodation to the external milieu on the part of the subject, which leads to a circular, stage-by-stage transformation of the organism by the environment (internal milieu) and of the environment by the organism (external milieu).

Far from being inscribed a priori in the nervous system or in thought, the structures of knowledge are constructed by the development of successive levels, by a process of *reflective abstraction*: starting out from a lower level of activity, the elements constitutive of these activities are projected on to a higher level, forming a reflexive structure, which is a point of departure for new constructions. Each level, once transcended, gives rise to an ontological realist point of view.

For Piaget (1967b), the notion of object is not innate or given 'ready made in experience', but is constructed gradually. In the earliest stages, the child has no sense of the permanence of substances or of spatial organization. During the stages which follow, the child discovers the beginnings of a permanence of objects by means of gripping movements. The object as permanent substance, an invariant product of a group of movements, is acquired only between 12 and 18 months. The representation of absent objects only appears at 16–18 months. 'Intelligence organizes the world by organizing itself' (Piaget, 1967b, p. 311). We may accept that intelligence organizes the world by organizing itself so long as we recognize that the world organizes the very conditions in which intelligence appears (Miermont, 1993).

RADICAL CONSTRUCTIVISM

For the biologist and philosopher Humberto Maturana (1987), scientific statements are dependent on a subject but do not need a language of objects. The operations required for experimentation consist of successive stages: (a) distinguishing, (b) constructing a hypothesis, (c) computing, (d) demonstrating. An observer is a system the components and properties of which allow it to make the four operations required for observation. Scientific theories, though dependent on a subject, are not subjective. They are valid within a community of observers united by the act of carrying out operations which validate or refute theories.

Following Kant, Ernst von Glaserfeld established a distinction between metaphysical and constructivist realists. For metaphysical realists, a thing is true if it corresponds to an independent, objective reality. For constructivist realists, reality is a functional adaptation, which no longer even requires an isomorphic relation between the object and its representation. From the *radical constructivist* perspective, E. von Glaserfeld (1984, pp. 20–21) opposes the radical constructivist's theory of adaptation or 'fit' to the metaphysical realist's theory of correspondence or 'match'. It is not, he argues, that organisms adapt to reality; reality simply limits what is possible. For radical constructivism, knowledge does not reflect an 'objective' ontological reality, but an ordering and organization of a world constituted by our experience.

The world, as we perceive it, is only a more or less viable, more or less reliable construct. What we call (individual, social, ideological or scientific) reality is already an interpretation elaborated in and by communication (cf. Watzlawick, 1976). Where the realist position seeks a correspondence between the world and representation, the constructivist position prefers a fitting adaptation. Reality does no more than limit what is possible, annihilating what is not fit to live. Constructivism criticizes the ethological position which argues that the morphological and behavioural structure of organisms can serve as a basis for understanding the objective world. In von Glaserfeld's view, the environment can be held responsible for the extinction of non-viable organisms, but never for their survival. For the constructivist approach, the environment is a creation of the organism. 'The environment, as we perceive it, is our invention' (von Foerster, in Watzlawick, 1984, p. 42). We may note here that Lorenz does not advocate recourse to metaphysical realism, but to its opposite, hypothetical realism, according to which all knowledge is based on the interaction between the knowing subject and the object of knowledge, both of these being regarded as real. Lorenz rejects the vicious circle of SELF-REFERENTIALITY, the circular reasoning by which one might be able, like Baron von Munchausen, to pull oneself up by one's own hair.

ECOSYSTEMIC CONSTRUCTION AND RECONSTRUCTION

Psychical reality and the status of phantasies
The question of the reality of sexual trauma is at the very heart of the psychoanalytic approach. Is that 'reality' reducible to events which objectively took place during the subject's childhood or is it dependent on the subject's personal psychical sensibility, which may possibly be reactivated, or indeed revealed, by the random events of existence? So far as the pathology of hysteria is concerned, Freud opts for the hypothesis of a psychical reality, a reality which is, admittedly, dependent on the conditions of the subject's experience, but is registered in the specificity of his/her fantasy organization. This perspective implies an oscillation between the impact of traumas experienced in reality and the zones of fragility of the psycho-affective organization, which may vary from one subject to another. It has to be acknowledged that some people succeed in structuring themselves on the basis of infantile experiencees which may appear particularly arduous, whereas others react very keenly to situations perceived as relatively anodyne. Moreover, the refusal to accept frustrations, prohibitions, authority or conflict in the family milieu may amplify the sense of trauma which is felt at the slightest relational difficulty instead of allowing it to be psychically integrated. Put bluntly, the Freudian theory takes the following form: 'Freud saw through the "lie" of hysterics. Frequent

seduction by the father is a "fantasy"' (Marie Bona-parte, quoted in Masson, 1984, p. 112). Freud aban-doned the hypothesis of a real childhood trauma with the observation that, if it were true, 'the father, not excluding my own, had to be perverse' (Masson, 1984, p. 108). Seduction is, first, a game acted out between parents and children before becoming an experience of discovery between the sexes. Everyone necessarily plays their part in it. The absence of the reality of this game is often the sign of a dysfunction. Pathological phe-nomena appear when the game of seduction is no longer a game during childhood, and when it remains a sterile game in adulthood.

The difficulty arises from the tendency to seek to generalize the psychoanalytic hypothesis to situations to which it is not relevant. Children often react very keenly to scenes of violence between their parents, to their threats to leave, to intense affective involvement in their conflicts or even to physical confrontations between them (with a possible failure to distinguish clearly between violence and rape, sexual penetration and bloody assault: 'frightening, violent, explosive scenes which can affect the victim's entire later life' (Masson, 1984, p. 117). In other cases, children are actually subjected to sexual abuse, maltreatment, as-sault and battery, producing experiences which actu-ally prevent them from effecting a proper fantasmatic organization of inter-human violence. Suffering may be regarded as a sign of the reality principle, which escapes the constructions that may be put upon it and is only tolerable in a ritualization of interactions.

Delirium

From a positivist point of view, DELIRIUM is a disorder of belief which has to be eradicated in so far as that belief radically contradicts the positive experience we have of reality. For a constructivist, delirium may be understood as a signal of a mythic subversion within a suffering ecosystem, overwhelmed by its homeostatic and homeorhetic capacities.

Delirium can only be legitimately accepted in an artificial arrangement in which the viability of the eco-system within which it finds expression is recognized: this is the project of family therapies. Delirium is a dereistic reconstruction which seeks to palliate the fragilities of the individual and community self (pa-thology of autonomy). The themes of delirium usually centre on an attempt to recognize and/or repair a nar-cissistic wound: poisoning, bodily transformation, physi-cal or psychical invasion, remote-control, certainty that one is being persecuted, megalomaniacal constructions. There is, in this case, a disequilibrium between the processes of centring on oneself (self-determination) and de-centring (regulation of the boundaries of as-similation and rejection of objects constitutive of the subject) which normally attend the emergence of autonomy.

What is called reality is based on a consensus within a community of the distinction between form and con-tent, essentials and details, in respect of the semiotic systems governing social exchanges. There has to be agreement concerning the non-verbal codes referring to emotional invariants (joy, sadness, anger, fear, anxi-ety etc.) and the linguistic codes peculiar to each cul-tural community. The formation of these codes depends on two different levels of abstraction (Korzybski, 1951). It is essential that the abstractions which preside over the constitution of signs (formalization) be accepted without question by the partners to the exchange.

Bringing together a family for therapeutic ends forms part of a cognitive project: it enables the family to be distinguished as an autonomous ecosystem, hypo-theses to be formulated by a process of THERAPEUTIC ABDUCTION (by identifying the regularities and sing-ularities of the persons and their organization), new cognitive procedures to be generated, and the basis of this new knowledge (meta-knowledge) to be tested. Delirium becomes the voluntaristic expression which questions the rituals, myths and epistemes of the fam-ily group and the therapeutic team. The therapeutic project seeks to get beyond the classic opposition be-tween reality and madness. The aim is not so much to reveal a pre-existent hidden truth as to make the rela-tions between the present construction of reality and the complex elaboration of the delirium evolve.

CRITIQUES OF CONSTRUCTIVISM

'Constructivism is the projection of the subject–object interaction' (Le Moigne, 1992). In the epistemological conceptions based on the project → subject/object in-teraction, the criteria of absolute truth disappear. The distinction between internal and external cohesiveness then emerges, the testing out of which enables us to check which systems of adjustment 'fit'. But the test which allows us to verify cohesiveness is, in fact, more rigorous and dynamic than that of 'matching the truth'. It proceeds by inquiry, the logical forms of which in-stitute a control which leads to the production of war-ranted assertions (Dewey, 1938).

A perspective of this kind leads to an autonomic conception of knowledge which establishes an equiva-lence between knowing and 'knowing how'. Learnt knowledge relates to the fixing of constants which are able effectively to modulate internal behavioural mech-anisms. Learnt knowledge relates entirely to these mechanisms and is, therefore, akin to 'knowing how'. Knowledge becomes indissociable from the particu-larities of the knowing subject, which happens to be the human being (Tabary, 1991). Knowledge bears solely on relations and processes, not on substances or primary structures.

For Paul Watzlawick (1984), the question of what the reality is which is constructed by constructivism has no meaning. Constructivism does not create a reality that is independent of us. There is, for him, neither interior nor exterior, object nor subject. The radical distinction between subject and object disappears. The interpretation of the world in terms of opposing polarities is merely an invention of the subject who, by his/her descriptions, reveals his/her own characteristics. Reality, for the constructivist, is ambiguous in the extreme. It is indeterminable, except for the fact that it puts constraints on the models we construct. To admit, as E. von Glaserfeld (1984, p. 39) does, that 'the "real" world manifests itself exclusively there where our constructions break down', is tantamount to accepting the importance of reality as knowledge/apprehension/intuition of the limits of all forms of knowledge. If the real functions as a constraint, as a limit to certain forms of self-construction of the world, this means that the real re-emerges at a point where it was presumed to have been totally eliminated. The real, defined here by contrast with that which is modelled or constructed, no longer refers to static, immutable entities but to active-reactive systems of evolutive control.

The question which then arises concerns the status of relations and processes if these are not regarded as part of a structurally stable universe. Radical constructivism seems to consider only one of the possible alternatives: that the organism transforms the environment in which it lives. And yet the converse is also true: if man is 'stardust', it is because he is made from the stars; in the prey–predator cycle, we may, from an ontogenetic point of view, stress that the predator creates a model of the prey, but from a phylogenetic viewpoint, the opposite is true: the predator shapes its actions as a function of the constraints imposed by the structures of the prey (Thom, 1992). From an ethological point of view, the territory structures the morphological and behavioural regulations of organisms, to the extent that it provides vital resources. The organism may then be defined as a map-making emanation of its territories; the organism is itself the invention of the world in which it lives; the map is a more or less precise representation of territories, organisms and maps. In other words, realism is an idealism of the pre-established, pre-constructed world which, unlike constructivism, rejects the emergent quality of the interactive communication between the observer and the observed.

Conclusion

Reality is what is accepted as legitimate by the human community, it is recognized by an experience of shared consciousness and is normally indicated by the experience of a certain degree of suffering, a quantum of unpleasurable affect. The notion of infinity gives us an idea of reality independent of our present knowledge: this is always potentially specifiable in part and never accessible in its totality. There is undoubtedly a whole host of phenomena independent of the representation we can have of them. We may represent to ourselves the fact that a great quantity of events is not representable, or lies outside our knowledge or beyond our understanding. What is known can thus be seen as a matter of choice, as a function of the demands imposed by life or survival.

Reality is something which can be perceived by several different pathways, it being possible to cross-check between these (Harthong, 1992, p. 233). The notion of an object or thing arises out of a subjective congruence in the comparative evaluation of the various means of investigation, a large number of which are employed by persons other than ourselves. Thus Tabary (1991) stresses that, within a constructivist perspective, the validation of knowledge cannot be based on truths, but only on coherence between all the acquired knowledge. Knowledge does not so much progress by the discovery of an immutable truth as by the validation of hypotheses subject to increasingly drastic refutations. In this way, constructivism substitutes the criterion of 'rigour', 'correctness' or 'rightness' (Goodman, 1992) for that of truth. This criterion is only viable within a conception of a multi-dimensional world, where rightness is rooted, in circular fashion, in 'correct' worlds, which impose adequate restriction and radical relativism, and prevent the existence of an absolute meta-level (Handjaras, in Goodman, 1992). Such a position is reminiscent of the Buddhist vision of two truths, these being conventional truth – or the truth of the daily usages of the world – and an ultimate truth, which is not absolute truth, but ultimate in the sense that there is no truth beyond it: only Nirvana, which cannot be assimilated to, or subsumed, under, the concept of truth. Truth is neither an end nor an object (Allyn, 1993).

Constructivism, by its nature, cannot methodologically refute realist or idealist positions by exclusion. When confronted only with itself, like all 'isms', it becomes an ideology, which has constantly to be rectified by the operators of RITUALIZATION and of the episteme. As more than just an alternative, it leads to the adding and combining of epistemologies congruent with the needs and constraints of interdisciplinarity (Le Moigne, 1993). By widening the field of cognition, it forces us to implement new methodological procedures. Not all constructions are equivalent or interchangeable; a construction is the more viable the less it runs up against the obstacles of reality. But how are we to know whether our construction is not merely a flight of fancy? We run the risk of reducing illness, and psychical suffering in particular, to an imaginary disorder. Treating patients cannot be equated with playing with the ideas we have of the illness. Similarly, if the world is our invention, how are we to avoid solipsism? What is the nature of the structure or structures common to subjects who might be seen as content to observe themselves observing others? Biological evolution has put millions of years into testing the most viable cognitive procedures. Constructivism and realism only seem capable of explaining themselves in their indissoluble interdependence.

(See also COMPLEXITY; INCOMPLETENESS THEOREMS; MYTH; REALITY.)

J.M.

context The analysis of context concerns the study of the circumstances and situations in which a living being interacts with its environment. The project of objectivist ethology (Tinbergen, 1947; Lorenz, 1954) was to re-situate the behavioural analysis of living beings by taking into account the natural ecosystem in which they live. An isolated chimpanzee, a 'brain' or a 'human being' do not exist and are merely abstractions in search of semantic life and survival contexts.

In proposing a human eco-etho-anthropology, Bateson (1971, 1972, 1979) laid down the premises for the study of human contexts. All complex learning is indissociable from the contexts, both internal and external, in which it occurs. Moreover, certain paradoxical messages tend to transform the contexts within which they are emitted.

Jumping into one's mother's arms, caressing her, saying 'I love you' or 'I want daddy to go away so the two of us can be together' is a behavioural sequence which may possibly be one that promotes maturation in a pre-pubescent child. The same sequence between a 45-year-old adult and his mother will appear as incestuous, if not indeed schizophrenic, conduct. It is the analysis of the context which makes it possible to differentiate between the two.

In Bateson's view, every form of experience or learning occurs in a context possessing specific formal properties. It is the specific characteristic of the human species to have multiplied contexts in terms of an open series of metacontexts which may extend to infinity. Now conflicts may exist between contexts and metacontexts. In the above example, the transformation of puberty *ipso facto* changes a game into a fundamentally realizable sequence, if, for one reason or another the mother and child have not been able to broach this question in time. If a mother has always forbidden the child's sexual games, but cannot give up stereotyped maternal conduct, she and her son will be caught up in a system in which it will be impossible for him to be considered 'normal'. The appearance of apparently sexual behaviour directed towards her will then appear as a disturbance in the learning of the contextual and metacontextual levels of a given situation.

Within this perspective, every exchange between persons presents itself in terms of contexts and meta-

contexts of learning. The context, conceived as metamessage, classifies the message, but is not situated at the same level. There is a hierarchy in learning contexts (Bateson, 1972, pp. 216–19). The human species is continually causing the contexts and metacontexts in which its adaptation occurs to develop.

Psychotic, psychosomatic or delinquent disorders reveal the existence of metacontextual confusions between the individual, his or her family and society. The forms of action and utterance 'are parts of the ecological sub-system called the context' (Bateson, 1972; 1973 edn, p. 309).

(See also CONTEXT MARKERS; DOUBLE BIND; LEARNING; LEGAL CONTEXT; SEMANTICS OF COMMUNICATION.)

J.M.

context–content syndrome A type of marital relationship described by Hogan (1963) in which one partner pays attention solely to the content of verbal communications, both in matters concerning them and matters concerning others. The other partner, by contrast, pays greater attention to non-verbal communication, both where he or she – and others – are concerned. In this case, the first partner is 'content-centred', the second 'context-centred'. In such a syndrome, gaps necessarily arise in the communication between husband and wife.

(See also AGREEMENT AND DISAGREEMENT; COUPLES; MARITAL BREAKDOWN; PATHOLOGICAL COMMUNICATION.)

P.S.

context markers According to Bateson (1972), CONTEXT may be considered a collective term which indicates to the organism the range of options from which to make its next choice. An organism responds differently to the 'same stimulus' in different contexts. In human life, signals exist, the function of which is to classify contexts. It is this source of information that is called a 'context marker' (Selvini Palazzoli et al., 1978).

At the human level, there are context markers which allow differentiation between a theatrical and a real drama; a boxing match and a fight to the death; a placebo treatment and a pharmacologically real treatment. Such markers are signs which allow the differentiation between context and metacontext, and thus the classification of the nature of the lived experience.

(See also DOUBLE BIND; ECOSYSTEM.)

P.S.

contextual model See ETHICS; INDEBTEDNESS; LEDGER; LOYALTY; MERIT; MULTI-DIRECTIONAL PARTIALITY; MULTI-LATERALITY; TRUST.

Contraindications for the use of family therapy
See INDICATIONS AND CONTRAINDICATIONS FOR THE USE
OF FAMILY THERAPY.

contrary injunction A particular style of formulation of warning or advice, generally with a predictive
connotation, issued by parents to their children. Warn-
ings or advice of this type most often achieve the opposite of the desired aim, which seems to be to help
their children to avoid getting into various kinds of
trouble. This type of transaction has been described by
Ausloos (1983) as relatively frequent in families containing a delinquent child.

The injunctions concerned are of the following type:
'I hope you're not going out again tonight' or 'If you
go on like that, you'll end up in jail!', or, more subtly,
'you aren't really an addict, but you're going to end up
as one if you carry on like that', or, lastly, 'all these
parties . . . they always turn into orgies'. The formulation of these evaluative statements confers upon them
the inevitability of predestination and indicates that
the person making them feels a sense of implicit dis-
couragement about the possibility of doing anything at
all to prevent the negative prediction from coming to
pass. These ambiguous injunctions would seem to relate back to dysfunctional transgenerational patterns of
prohibition perpetuated from generation to generation
(with a tragic destiny or inevitability). They might also
be interpreted as a kind of delegation disguised as an
apparent moral prohibition ('I'd have liked to have
done that, but I couldn't; it wouldn't be so bad if you
could do it!') as if, according to Ausloos (1983), in
order to prevent this forbidden desire in the parents
becoming embodied in the child, it had to be both
stated in precise terms and at the same time forbidden.

(See also DELINQUENT ACTING OUT; LEGAL CONTEXT;
LOYALTY; SPLIT DOUBLE BIND.)

P.S.

co-therapy Often a central element in the framework of family therapy, co-therapy creates an inter-
systemic relationship (family system and therapeutic
system) in preference to a dyadic patient–therapist
relationship. It is a procedure which fits in to a therapeutic protocol that aims to grasp the interrelation of
individuals rather than simply taking into account the
psychical dynamic of the individuals themselves. The
co-therapy relationship means much more than the
mere utilization of several therapists instead of just
one. As has been shown in the case of the family group,
the relationship between the therapists represents more
than a mono–therapeutic intervention and more than
the sum total of separate interventions. It is in itself a
dynamic entity which, above and beyond the interventions of each of the partners in the therapeutic action,
creates favourable conditions for change and for the
implementation of strategies adapted to each family
group (Walrond-Skinner, 1976; Bowen, 1978a).

Processes of co-therapy can be distinguished from
processes of SUPERVISION. A co-therapy may thus be
taken to designate several professionals working conjointly. Such a process presupposes an alliance between therapists distributed over several positions:
family therapist, attending psychiatrist, general practitioner, institutional teams.

FORMATION OF THE TEAM

A co-therapy team may be made up of two therapists,
or more, and the members may or may not be of the
same sex. They sometimes have different professional
backgrounds. While accepting the basic principles of
family therapy, they often adopt varying theoretical
positions, so far as therapeutic strategies and detailed
modes of intervention are concerned, depending upon
their individual styles. Very often, necessities imposed
by the constraints under which such work is undertaken imply a confrontation between the therapists
pursuing a family approach and the therapists who
intervene on other levels. In a co-therapy relationship
involving a sharing of responsibilities, it is often in the
therapists' interests to formulate a definition of the
reciprocal roles played by each at the outset. Therapeutic work consists just as much in setting coherent
boundaries between the workers as in working with
the family as a whole.

ADVANTAGES OF CO-THERAPY

Recourse to co-therapy in the treatment of family groups
enables tasks to be divided up in a way that would be
impossible in the case of a therapist working alone.
Each therapist is in a position to respond in his or her
own way to the various demands formulated by the
members of the family. The presence of two therapists
and the reference to a relationship developing between
them offers the family greater diversity and a greater
wealth of possibilities in the processes of identification,
alliance of opposition. The therapists may divide between themselves the dual function of participant/
observer.

The co-therapist makes it possible for the therapist,
who, as often happens, is 'swallowed up' by the family
system, to step back and avoid counter-transference
feelings which would nullify his or her neutrality. He
or she is able to cast a new light on matters and to
analyse the therapist's function within the family system. This often means that the conduct of interviews
can also be modified towards greater flexibility and a
better tailoring to the specific difficulties of each
family, by means of the extemporary treatment of

inter-transference phenomena and ALIENATION. When, for example, the index patient in a family is schizophrenic, one of the therapists may choose to accompany the psychotic in his or her processes of thought, while the other therapist observes and reflects on the interactions produced within the family group. It is often useful too to distribute roles between the co-therapists when there are very young children in the family. The mode of communication which is most important for these children is essentially non-verbal or iconic in nature (see ICONS), while the parents often accord most significance to linguistic or symbolic exchanges (see SYMBOLS). One of the therapists will be able to play with the children while the other will remain attentive to the interactions between the adults.

Lastly, co-therapy provides direct assistance to the therapists in the face of the vicissitudes of the therapeutic enterprise, particularly when the situation is highly complex and family functioning very rigid.

DIFFICULTIES INHERENT IN CO-THERAPY

In spite of the many advantages, the establishment of a co-therapy relationship is a difficult undertaking. The family's attempts to divide the team constitute one of the most common obstacles. Families frequently tend to divide the team into 'good' and 'bad' therapists. This process may be used in a constructive way to aid the family members to test out their feelings against reality, but, in certain cases, the team finds itself sorely tried by the family's constant disqualifications.

The second difficulty encountered by the co-therapy team is created by the problem of leadership. In order to distribute therapeutic functions in an effective and non-pathological manner, the difficulties inherent in leadership have to be carefully thrashed out at the level of overall strategy. In a coherent co-therapy relationship, the leadership functions are shared in a complementary manner.

However, the family will often tend to designate one therapist as leader and the other as auxiliary therapist, as a function of its own defensive needs. In this case, it is important for the later course of the therapy that the co-therapists do not allow themselves to be trapped in the roles which the family has assigned to them. If such difficulties are not overcome, the co-therapy relationship degenerates into a competition to appear the 'best' therapist.

A newly created team may encounter the opposite problem to that of disconnectedness or leadership conflicts. The co-therapists may be so concerned to avoid these problems that they become fused together in what Bowen (1978a) would call an 'undifferentiated ego mass' (see FAMILY EMOTIONAL ONENESS). Just as the parents may sometimes fuse so closely that the children feel excluded from their relationship, the family may have the painful sense of being excluded from the intimate and harmonious relationship between the therapists. In such a context, the family tends to fall back to exclusive and dysfunctional positions and to inhibit further the capacity for each of its members to achieve greater independence. Walrond-Skinner (1976, p. 121) suggests that it will reduce their 'capacity for growth'.

Finally, in co-therapy, the therapists must constantly reckon with their transference and countertransference feelings towards the family which deflect both the functioning of the family system and of the therapeutic system. Rubinstein and Weiner (quoted in Walrond-Skinner, 1976) have described the phenomenon of 'double transference'. The complex transactional experience that is set up by co-therapy produces the phenomenon of *transferring the transference*; the co-therapist or the family are then used as intermediaries. One of the therapists may, for example, experience negative transference feelings towards a mother, because she evokes in the therapist memories of his or her own difficult relationship with his/her mother. He or she may express this feeling towards his/her co-therapist, who then becomes the recipient of the colleague's 'transferred transference'. Similarly, a transference experienced in relation to one's co-therapist can become transferred to a member of the family group. However, if the channels for continuing dialogue between the therapists remain open, and if consultative help is available (see SUPERVISION), the source of these reactions can usually be traced and they can generally be prevented from having a negative effect on the subsequent course of the therapeutic process.

CO-THERAPIES, MONO-THERAPIES AND POLY-THERAPIES

In certain cases a single family therapist may conduct the treatment of a family, so long as he or she has adequate experience, is sufficiently responsible for his or her actions, and so long as the disturbances presented do not reach levels of alienation that are too intense. He or she will then be able to have recourse, when the need is felt, to consultative help, whether this is available as direct supervision or as a deferred consultation.

In other cases, a group of therapists may be needed to respond to the problems which arise for the family group. The problem posed is less one of an obligatory family co-therapy, than a need for the articulation of simultaneous therapeutic interventions including the administration of psychotropic drugs – perhaps to several members of the family – the psychotherapy and psychoanalysis of one or more members or institutional therapy. In these 'heavy' cases, it becomes necessary to find the correct dosage of the different conjoint interventions and to find the contexts in which the therapists are coherently coordinated.

(See also ALIENATION; FAMILY–THERAPEUTIC INSTITUTION DIFFERENTIATION; MAP AND COUNTER-MAP OF A

FAMILY SYSTEM; METABINDING; PRESCRIBING (MEDICAL) DRUGS; THERAPEUTIC DOUBLE BINDS; TRANSFERENCE.)

P.A., S.A., A.C. & J.M.

counter-transference See TRANSFERENCE, COUNTER-TRANSFERENCE.

couples The human couple will be viewed here essentially in the specific context of the family system which produces it and the family system it reproduces. Within this perspective, certain difficulties, crises and even break-ups experienced by couples will be considered not only as a function of the personality structures of the partners, but also of the 'specific personality' of the couple and of the transgenerational tensions, both with the preceding and subsequent generation, to which it is subject. Data from ethology and ethnology show that the structure of the couple – the male–female differentiation and the distribution of roles – correlates with the nature of caring behaviour towards children and with the representation of the partners as regards their social power.

CHOICE OF LOVE OBJECT, PARTNER, SPOUSE

From a psychoanalytic point of view, the choice of a spouse is a matter of object choice, i.e. the psychical act of selecting a person or a type of person as love object (Laplanche and Pontalis, 1967). This choice of love object is effected in two interdependent modes (Freud, 1914a):

1   *Narcissistic object choice*, in which the object is chosen as a function of the subject's relationship to him or herself in one aspect or another. In this case, the love object must be what one is oneself, what one has been or would like to be, or a part of oneself.
2   *Anaclitic object choice*, in which the object is chosen along the lines of the relationship between the parents and must reproduce, either in reality or in phantasy, the experiences of feeding, care, protection and prohibitions.

Within this dual choice, the transgenerational structure of the partner's family also intervenes, either in the form of a search for structural isomorphism or in the form of a search for complementarity and a compensatory reparation of what is lacking in one's own family system.

The choice of partner is an organizer of family relations (Eiguer, 1983; see FAMILY ORGANIZERS). In the very earliest stages of the choice of love object, a process of idealization of the partner is in operation, which makes it possible, by splitting, not to take into account all their imperfections and to keep these away from conscious perception, by mechanisms of denial. Some couples even manage to restrict their sexual life to a limited sphere, which preserves these conditions of idealization of the love object and makes it possible to resist depressive positions (Lemaire, 1979).

Sager (1976) and Hirsch (1981) stress that, when two partners meet, there are three contractual levels in play. First is the *conscious contract*: 'I like you because you are like this or that.' Secondly, there is the *preconscious contract*: 'It's true that I like you, but (non-verbalized metacommunication) once we are married, your friends won't come to the house any more and we're not going to your mother's for dinner.' Conflict may then arise after about a year. Thirdly, there is the *unconscious contract*: this is connected to each person's survival positions and, therefore, to the destructive desires of the real man and woman which no longer correspond to the highly cathected and idealized image of father, mother, brother or sister which have to be safeguarded at all costs. Conflict may arise in such cases on average seven years into life together; this initial contract is unconsciously broken by one partner or the other, who has achieved social recognition or gained greater emotional independence. Similarly, the birth of children breaks this unconscious contract and shatters the bonds established over many years with the parents of these new parents who have themselves to become grandparents: 'Similarly, everyone accepts intellectually that a child one day has to go to school, or enters puberty or adolescence but living through these things can break the unconscious contract' (Hirsch, 1981, p. 8). For Hirsch, there are innate factors in living together which one day suddenly confront each of the partners with their unresolved problems.

Lemaire (1979, p. 65) analyses in detail the way in which choice of partner operates.

> In the conjugal type of choice, corresponding to an acknowledged or unacknowledged intention that the relationship shall be a lasting one, the choice of main partner is intimately linked to the person's defensive organization; the partner's personal characteristics are selected with a view to reinforcing the defence mechanisms whose aim is to block off the partial drives and, most importantly among these, the ones which remain alien to the drive system as a whole.

The chief factor in such a choice is the partner's ability to preserve him or herself from the partial drive which he/she has carefully isolated. By contrast, in non-conjugal forms of sexual life, such as flirtations or brief affairs:

> the hedonistic aspect and the pursuit of direct instinctual gratifications is the exclusive objective, or at least

by a long way the most important; what is required of the Object in that case is that they be essentially a means of satisfaction, and if they do not respond to this, the relationship breaks off immediately. (Lemaire, 1979, p. 66)

Moreover, Lemaire shows that the psychoanalytic understanding of the choice of a partner is only possible if one takes an overall view of the processes set in play within the dyad. Taking over Wynne and colleagues' (1958) concept of a TRADING OF DISSOCIATIONS, he shows that the choice of partner depends not only on the organization of each person's personality, but also on the dyadic structure which develops around the latent or patent similarities of the members of the couple. Within this perspective, each of the partners tends to attribute to the other the characteristics of his/her personality which he/she feels is negative. It is therefore frequently the failings of the object which underlie the choice of love object, all the more so as the subject often feels vulnerable in the same area.

Two opposing rules seem to govern the choice of marriage partner: *homogamy* (like attracts like) and *heterogamy* (opposites attract). The results of research into this question are contradictory. On the sociological plane, similarities between the partners generally win out over differences, so far as social class, ethnic group etc. are concerned. By contrast, it has proved more difficult to devise a pertinent methodology to identify the relevant psychopathological factors.

Some writers, including Winch (1958), argue that, by virtue of an homogamy of social characteristics, a choice of potential partners is defined at the outset, but the final selection seems, by contrast, to be based upon a heterogamy of motivations. More precisely, Winch stresses the complementarity of needs as the formative factor in most couples. This seductive hypothesis has been widely contested, by Murstein (1961, 1971), Tharp (1963), Jacobson and Matheny (1962) among others. These writers find rather that similarity of clinical characteristics predominates among normal couples, while complementarity is the general rule among neurotic couples.

According to Willi, (1982), the similarity and opposition hypotheses are not necessarily mutually exclusive, since it might be the case that the 'opposite' personality simply represents an opposite pole of the other's personality. The two sayings could therefore be combined: 'the opposites of likes attract.'

In his analysis, Willi calls upon the concept of *collusion* which designates:

an unacknowledged shared game between two or more partners, in which they keep the fact of their playing it secret from each other. The game is based upon the existence within each of them of a deep conflict of the same kind which has not been resolved. The

fundamental unresolved conflict is expressed in different roles which gives rise to the impression that one of the partners is exactly the opposite of the other, whereas what are actually involved are merely polarized variants of the same behaviour. (Willi, 1982, pp. 69–70)

Collusion involves each of the two partners in its progressive and regressive forms, but, in the behaviour of each towards the other, one shows the progressive side and the other the regressive side of the same theme. Is this collusive complementarity a product of personality structure or does it only appear after a period of reciprocal adjustment? Willi (1982, p. 175) speaks here of an 'interaction personality'. Each person behaves in a different manner depending on the partner with whom he or she is interacting. This 'personality' interacts with the corresponding adaptation process in the partner. The 'interaction personality' is the result of a destructuring linked to a partner and to a situation in which what was previously latent becomes manifest, and what was manifest passes into the background.

Basing himself upon sociocultural mythology, Maruani has defined three *archetypal couples*:

- paranoid/hysterical;
- anaclitic/obsessional;
- perverse/schizoid.

The first combines a dark and fiery type of man with a devastating beauty (cf. Clark Gable and Vivian Leigh in the film *Gone with the Wind*) but may also occur in the form: intellectual full of bookish humour/ravishing idiot. The second brings together a passive, dependent and impulsive subject with a great degree of oral fixation and a person dominated by *ananke*, i.e. driven by a sense of duty and order. This is the inspired artist (or scatter-brained scientist) and 'no-nonsense' housewife pairing. The third form combines the abiliity of one of the partners to stage phantasy scenarios and the apragmatism of the other, who is trapped in daydreams and indifferent to acting them out.

Each archetype has its particular formula for degradation and pathology. The first goes wrong either by the wife becoming a feather-brained flirt and the husband brutal and possessive or by the husband turning into a selfish Don Juan and the wife into a rejected, nagging figure.

In the second couple, the man slides easily into playing the good little boy between frenzied bouts of drinking and sexual violence, while the woman becomes sharp-tongued, frigid and bitter. Or alternatively, the husband is the model bureaucrat with his neatly ordered attaché case and the wife a spendthrift addict, hooked on cocaine, tranquillizers and/or designer clothes.

The third model leads to the man becoming a handyman type, who never puts down his drill, an avid reader of pornographic magazines and the mental torturer of a wife who is incapable of getting out of her dressing gown and filling in a social security form; or, alternatively, the wife being a nymphomaniac and the husband taking the line 'She's cheating on me, but I don't want to know about it.'

In a 'systematic', less naturalistic manner, Gear and Liendo (1984) have elaborated a *typology of dyads*, which, in their view, always divide up as follows:

1 The authoritarian dyad, made up of a sadistic agent and a masochistic subject.
2 The demagogic dyad, made up of a masochistic agent and a sadistic subject.
3 The disengaged dyad, made up of a sadistic inadequate and a masochistic inadequate.

Not every marital conflict is a collusion, but it can become so. One is dealing with a process of collusion, when, in a marital conflict, the two partners engage in a stereotyped ritual of struggle which absorbs a large part of their energy. Willi (1982) states that in couple therapy, 'the object is not to render the basic themes of collusion ineffective, but to arrive at a balance which will work in a free and flexible way.' The dynamics of the couple requires that a lasting balance be created in the relationship between the two people. However, though starting out from a freely oscillating middle position, that balance may swing into a situation of disequilibrium in which the partners become fixed, for one another, in extreme and rigid positions. The healthy (median) position uses the themes of collusion for reciprocal enrichment:

1 The narcissistic position is used to confirm to the partner that he or she is a clearly delimited self.
2 The oral position to establish exchange in which there is give and take.
3 The sado-anal position to establish a solidarity without constraints.
4 The phallic position to achieve a reciprocal complementarity, each person retaining the identity of their sex.

THE COUPLE FROM THE PERSPECTIVE OF COMMUNICATION THEORY

Following Bateson (Haley 1963, 1971, 1973; Sluzki et al., 1967; Watzlawick, 1967; Lederer and Jackson, 1968), the Palo Alto school has further decentred the perspective to problems arising within couples by employing the concepts of symmetrical, complementary and reciprocal relations, which are seen as underlying the SCHISMOGENESIS that is constitutive of the establishment of interpersonal and inter-group contacts. Such an approach rightly insists on the specific aspects of the relationship, which are not strictly reducible to the personality of each partner, in which the influence of *cultural contacts* and *systems of alliance* plays a part.

We shall note here the necessary existence of points of view which cannot be adopted simultaneously, but which are none the less both necessary. This is a situation which recalls the indeterminacy principle in quantum physics (where the position of an elementary particle and its velocity cannot both be known at the same time). Either one adopts the viewpoint of the dynamics–systemic perspective of the relationship and one loses sight of the parameters of the personality structure of the partners, or one adopts the structural–psychoanalytic viewpoint of character and personality and loses sight of the dynamic context in which the people under consideration are functioning.

Lederer and Jackson (1968) have attempted to describe viable conjugal relations by defining reciprocal schismogenesis as being parallel in nature. They thus distinguish between: *symmetrical conjugal relations*, where the partners have the status of contestants in a competition for equal achievement (aiming to be as good as the other, to do as much as the other in all fields etc.); *complementary relations*, where one of the partners takes responsibility for the other, obeying them in every particular (there is a lesser degree of this, in which each partner simply has completely separate areas of control within the relationship); and *parallel relations* in which the partners alternate between symmetrical and complementary relations, combative and accommodating attitudes, depending upon the possibilities offered and the needs at any particular moment.

Harper et al. (1977) have suggested that parallel interactions should be seen as being at different levels of abstraction from symmetrical and complementary interactions. In fact, it would doubtless be necessary to distinguish the process of (symmetrical, complementary and reciprocal) schismogenetic differentiation from the domains of regulation which organize it.

The existence of *parallel, convergent* and *divergent trajectories* will then become apparent. If it is necessary for the attitudes of the partners towards one another to possess a certain parallelism, in order to guarantee the regulating boundaries of the couple, the schismogenesis of the couple will become symbolic within the family if convergent strategies win out over divergent strategies. If divergent strategies predominate, it will only be possible for the symbolic function to be performed by some third party (the problem of divorce, for example). In the case of schizophrenic transactions, one might say that there is perfect parallelism between the partners, but that no real complementary or symmetrical differentiation ever takes place. Symbolic schismogenesis then becomes transformed into schismatic marital relations (total absence of complementarity, see MARITAL SCHISM) or skewed marital relations (total absence of symmetry, see MARITAL SKEW). This can be seen in families with schizophrenic transactions where the fact of the couple coming under pressure must not be seen as a marital conflict, but as a parental conflict over the index patient.

THE COUPLE AS A SYSTEM OF RULES

Every couple lives by rules that are established at the beginning of the marriage (see FAMILY RULES). These rules must be flexible and must allow for development and change. Haley (1963) distinguishes three types of rule:

1 *Explicit rules* arrived at by the partners by common agreement (this is akin to the conscious contract, see above).
2 *Implicit rules*, which are not verbalized in a manifest way, but which none the less produce metacommunicative effects (akin to the preconscious contract).
3 *Transactional rules*, which are denied by the partners themselves but which appear clearly to the observer (akin to the unconscious contract).

Haley states that 'the process of working out conflict over rules becomes a set of metarules, or rules for making rules' (Haley, 1963, p. 123). In cases of conflict, it may be these meta-definitions that are the bone of contention. We can therefore see several types of disagreement (see AGREEMENT). These are:

• disagreements over the rules which are creating disorder within the life of the couple;
• disagreements over who must set the rules;
• the most serious difficulties are connected with attempts to reinforce inadequate rules, which may be mutually incompatible.

What is established in the alliance between the marriage partners serves as a basis for their relations and constructs the FAMILY MYTH. This is eminently paradoxical: 'When a man and woman decide their association should be solemnized and legalized with a marriage ceremony, they pose themselves a problem which will continue through the marriage: Now that they are married are they staying together because they wish to or because they must? (Haley, 1963, p. 119). This paradox is at the heart of the dual nature of the couple: intimate and private on the one hand, public and social on the other.

Jackson (1965b) has suggested that the term *quid pro quo* be used to describe the marital contract, which provides the basis for the family myth and generates rules between the two partners. Each person gives something and expects to receive something in exchange. The important thing here is the common, shared definition which each person gives of the relationship thus established. From the beginning of their exchanges,

there is a relationship that has been specifically created between the alcoholic and his wife, the brutal husband and his long-suffering wife, the 'babyish' woman and the 'doting father'. This emergent quality of the couple can only be seen if one focuses exclusively on the structure of the individual personalities. Conversely, when one adopts the perspective of the structural analysis of personality, the dynamic dimension of the specificity of the couple tends to disappear. The incompatibility of these two points of view may be regarded as an individual–relationship indeterminacy principle. This theoretical principle forces us into a practical methodology which alternates between the two positions.

THE COUPLE AS MULTIGENERATIONAL TRIANGULATIONS AND DIFFERENTIATIONS

During the years 1955–75, Murray Bowen developed a global theory of marriage and the problems experienced by couples. That theory implies that the behaviour of each person is the product of a long process which has developed over several generations. Pathologies of behaviour are at once predetermined and self-engendered. Bowen attaches great importance to the history of the FAMILIES OF ORIGIN in his efforts to assist the members of a couple in difficulty. His therapeutic protocol is based partly on the notion of DIFFERENTIATION OF SELF. Each individual operates on an emotional plane, an intellectual plane and a plane of feeling. The differentiation he manages to make between these three levels of operation is the guarantee of a clearly defined individuality.

For Bowen, every relationship is triadic. A dyadic system may function during periods of calm, but it rapidly becomes unstable in cases of conflict and calls for the participation of a third party. This third-party function helps the dyad to overcome stressful situations, if the third person maintains his/her own level of differentiation. This is the role of the therapist when he/she accepts a couple as his/her patients. Marriage is generally an alliance between two partners who share the same level of differentiation. The lower the level, the more fusional the couple and the greater the risk of the relationship being pathological. The pathology of the couple manifests itself in the form of irresolvable conflicts and often expresses itself through the presence of symptoms in one of the partners. Projection mechanisms frequently make for the emergence of corresponding pathologies in the children. In other cases, the process leads to MARITAL BREAKDOWN and the break-up of the couple.

COUPLE THERAPIES

In a systemic perspective, the couple therapist accords greatest importance to the study of interactions between the members of the couple, rather than the study of the specific characteristics of each of the partners. Every form of behaviour is analysed in terms of its impact on the marital dynamics and on the ecosystem in which the couple is located. Whatever theoretical perspective the therapists adopt (whether psychoanalytic, behaviouristic, etho-anthropological or systemic), certain *common objectives* may be identified (Lemaire, 1979).

- the definition of problems;
- the clarification of needs and desires, within the framework of the marital relationship;
- the redefinition of the nature of the couple's difficulties;
- the acknowledgement by each partner of his/her contribution to the couple's dysfunctioning;
- the modification of models of communication, rules of operation and styles of interaction;
- an increase in the capacities for mutual aid;
- a decrease in coercive or culpabilizing attitudes.

Other objectives have less priority:

- increasing cooperation between the partners to resolve their difficulties;
- establishing a positive professional relationship between the couple and the therapist;
- modifying the analysis of individual needs within the couple;
- increasing the capacity for expressing emotion and for listening of each of the partners.

The advocates of systemic intervention treat the couple as a sub-system of the family system. By examining the difficulties of couples and symptom-formation, Gurman (1978) suggests that marriage should be regarded as a process of defining relations between the partners and as a struggle for power and control. Conflict, which may be manifest or latent, is produced by dysfunctional communication between the partners. Preserving a balance between desires and constraints is an underlying necessity. Most of the agreements required in the formation of a couple are tacit agreements. Only some preliminaries are discussed before marriage. A number of rules for the functioning of the couple form part of the heritage of each of the partners and depend to a large extent of the rules in force in their families of origin. Crowe (Crowe and Ridley, 1990) has developed a systems approach to marital therapy based on a model of reciprocal negotiation.

Haley (1963, pp. 117–50) advocates conjoint couple therapy in the following cases:

- when one of the partners presents a symptomatology which cannot be treated outside the context of the couple;

- when it is not likely that individual therapy will be successful with the patient on account of the inadequate amount of material provided;
- when the couple is in a crisis period;
- when the symptoms presented by one of the members coincide closely with conflictual situations within the life of the couple;
- when curing a patient is likely to cause the appearance of symptoms in the partner or lead to a change of such a kind that divorce seems inevitable.

Caillé (1985) has attempted a new approach to couples, by having recourse to analogical language, by combining the use of conjoint interviews with the couple with individual interviews and by prescribing tasks. The protocol was initially employed in work with groups of five couples, but its use has expanded to cover therapy with individual couples. This technique, which calls on a systemic epistemology, is thus located at the interface between individual psychotherapy and couple therapy work.

Caillé shows how, during therapy, a METASYSTEM OF INTERVENTION is created. This involves a combination of three elements: the contest of intervention, the model of organization of the system that is being treated and the behaviour/messages of the therapist. Caillé proposes a rigorous codification of the protocol governing the sessions, which are not usually more than ten in number. The object is to gain a picture of the organizational model of the couple by distinguishing:

1 *The phenomenological level*, by creating living statues. During the first session, each partner is asked to sculpt the body of his partner and his/her own body in terms of what he/she sees as being the real relations which determine their interactions.
2 *The mythical level*, by establishing a phantasy picture during the second session, the SCULPTING is orientated towards the symbolic understanding of the relationship, above and beyond daily exchanges.

A common session then makes it possible to confront the difficulties which each partner encounters from wanting to change the situation and never actually being able to. The last session (generally the tenth) allows the therapist to declare the situation to be a confused one, without implying that it could be clarified, and then to suggest that a gap of sixth months be allowed before a possible fresh consultation.

Richter (1970) proposes a brief couple therapy model (lasting around two weeks at two hours per day). The central idea is to give fresh momentum to the partners, whose marital conflicts are often long-standing. The object is to improve the couple's self-curative capacities. Beforehand, two tests are carried out, one bearing on the various psychosomatic disorders, the other on the relationship between one member's perception of the couple and that of his/her partner. A detailed preliminary assessment is then made:

1 Are the two partners capable of verbalizing their own psychological problems?
2 Does each recognize his/her share of the responsibility and is he/she ready to find a solution to the common conflict?
3 Is each of the members of the couple strong enough to stand this therapy which, through its intensiveness and intensity, produces deep changes?
4 The therapist has to satisfy him/herself as to the absence of characteristics of a paranoid nature before beginning the treatment.

In conclusion, we may note that a poly-axial model leads to a nuanced and varied use of contexts of intervention. As well as interviews with the two partners, couple therapy may include individual interviews, interviews with the previous generation or even lead to multiple therapies. Conversely, certain family therapies, which are focused on the difficulties of a particular child or adult index patient, will be able to include the presence of the parental couple, without it being possible to define the work carried out – or to be carried out – in such treatment as couple therapy.

(See also COALITION; FAMILY ETHNOLOGY; FAMILY ETHOLOGY; FAMILY SELF-REFERENTIALITY; SEXED BEHAVIOUR; UNCERTAINTY PRINCIPLE.)

P.A., J.M., S.A., M.G. & G.G.M.

crisis intervention A state of crisis in a family is usually a moment at which a homeostatic equilibrium, which has lasted for a certain amount of time, is readjusted. This is normally linked to a change of phase in the FAMILY LIFE-CYCLES. In this sense, a crisis is the opposite of a pathological state, as its aim is to avoid a catastrophe. It is a singular moment which, in the more felicitous cases, enables new definitions of the various members of the family to develop, both for each other and for themselves.

It does, however, happen that a phase of open crisis may appear suddenly and possibly for the first time in a family, accompanied by unusual symptomatic reactions on the part of one or more of its members of such intensity that they come to the attention of one or other of the social systems of assistance or care or social control (the reception of a general hospital, general practitioner, police, preventive health care teams etc.)

MODELLING OF CRISES IN TERMS OF CATASTROPHE THEORY

As Thom (1976a) points out, there are few visible morphological signs when a crisis breaks out in a person. Though 'function' may be affected, 'structure' is, for its part, normally intact. Though catastrophes often lead to a clearly visible phenomenon, an observable and nameable discontinuity, crises often have a latent, subterranean character which is difficult to apprehend or to put a name to.

Though crises bring about a perturbation of a quantitative type (first-order change in Bateson and Watzlawick's conception), catastrophes correspond to a qualitative change (second-order change). The crisis is essentially a subjective process, connected with a state of consciousness. It reflects a threat to the life of the organism, which becomes aware of the risk of its own disappearance. In fact, the crisis seems to function as the possible transition from a physical catastrophe to a psychical catastrophe: 'For the individual, the crisis is a "psychical catastrophe" which often makes it possible to avoid the physical or physiological catastrophe which it presages' (Thom, 1976a, p. 38). Such a process already exists at the level of the species, which is apt to simulated the relations it maintains with its biotope. The micro-unit of evolution that is the family is probably an essential transmission belt between the phyletic, sociological and individual planes. The solutions it is apt to set in place to resolve the crisis may be bad solutions, leading to particularly aberrant stationary states.

CRISIS AS ALARM SIGNAL OF THE FAMILY GROUP

Such a reaction should not then be underestimated, but, on the contrary, appreciated as an *alarm signal*, which calls for a rapid intervention with the family ecosystem if only by the organization at an early date of an exploratory family interview, which will complement – in order to give it meaning and open up perspectives for resolving the problems – any urgent measure which may have been necessitated by the intensity of the crisis. In actual fact, the crisis constitutes a fertile moment where the best chances exist for positively readjusting a system and helping it to reassess the rules by which it usually operates and which this crisis has shown to have failed, whether the crisis was foreseeable or one that occurred accidentally in the family life-cycle.

This 'crisis intervention' appears to be particularly indicated in cases of the first appearance of a warning symptom, whether this be a case of running away from home, an overdose (revealing drug addiction), a suicide attempt etc. The attitude adopted by the various agents who have to intervene in such crises too often still consists of setting in train linear modes of intervention that are highly individualized and centred on the index patient, thus leading to a fragmentation of the problem.

MODES OF INTERVENTION WITH SYSTEMS IN CRISIS

If several members of the family are directly involved and taken into treatment urgently, there is a danger that the interventions will themselves be fragmented and uncoordinated, if not indeed downright contradictory, the various practitioners not being aware of each other and merely repeating the one-sided, split versions of each member of the family. It would seem that all energies are directed at such moments towards ending the crisis, towards snuffing it out as quickly as possible, as though only the negative and dangerous aspects of such a moment were taken into account. The only priority, in such an approach, which coincides with the desire and 'aspiration' of the family itself, would seem to be to re-establish the prior state of equilibrium and 'calm', whereas the proper way to proceed would be to grasp the opportunities offered by the temporary disequilibrium produced by the crisis within the system. The goal ought then to be to promote the establishment of new rules and new, less rigid equilibria and to allow each person to become individuated, and to do so through work with the family which may be relatively brief or which may lead to a perspective of longer-term family therapy.

Even if it proves necessary in the moment of crisis itself, no emergency placement of an index patient should occur without it being accompanied by work carried out with the family system as a whole (this may be laid down as a necessary precondition for responding to the request for assistance) in order to assess the meaning, probable duration and detailed forms of such a measure. Moreover, the placement should be re-framed as aiming at the temporary relief of the problems of the family and the patient and not as a punishment or a sanction against the deviance of an individual to be 'straightened out' or 'cared for'. Within such an approach, one is also aiming to assess the resources of the family system in question, its more or less long-term capacities for readjustment and, in a sense, to keep the crisis in being – in a controlled way – in order to keep the system on the alert and actively to mobilize it for the resolution of the problematic situation that has to be confronted, instead of seeking to protect it at any price (even at the cost of relapse or backsliding) by stifling the crisis too quickly and providing easy reassurance by absolving the family system of responsibility. The precipitating of crises in therapy is essential for change to occur which supports the view that therapeutic interventions at the point of crisis should not be focused primarily on damping down (Jenkins, 1989b).

The development of crisis centres (such as already exist in some countries) and the intensive training of multi-disciplinary teams for this type of intervention, together with the sensitization of the various social referral agencies to the possibility of using the crisis as a fertile moment, should form an integral part of any policy of preventive health care or preventive social action.

(See also FAMILY CATASTROPHES; FAMILY CRISIS; INSTITUTIONS; PROVOCATION.)

P.S. & J.M.

crisis provocation See PROVOCATION, CRISIS PROVOCATION.

cybernetics Defined by its creator, Norbert Wiener, as 'the entire field of control and communication theory, whether in the machine or in the animal' (1975, p. 11), cybernetics (from the Greek, *kubernetes*, steersman) is concerned with the regulation of – and communication between – living organisms and artificial systems. Louis Couffignal (1972) adds to this definition that it is 'the art of ensuring the efficacy of action'. Abraham Moles (1986) completes the formula, calling cybernetics 'the generalized science of organisms, irrespective of their physical nature'. In fact, the project of cybernetics is to combine the art and science of self-governed systems possessing activity and finality, which are capable of reproducing themselves. It has served (a) as a model for the conceptualization of behavioural systems in ethology, such as Bowlby's theory of ATTACHMENT BEHAVIOUR, for example; and (b) as a founding paradigm enabling Bateson and his followers to discover paradoxical communication in human interactions, both normal and pathological, leading to the theory of the DOUBLE BIND.

In his inaugural work, Wiener examined a number of problems: time series, INFORMATION, statistical mechanics, non-linear feedback and oscillations, the analogy between the central nervous system and the computer, Gestalt and universals, the cybernetic conception of psychopathology, learning and self-reproducing machines, and cerebral oscillators (electro-encephalograph waves) as self-organized systems. Wiener shows the difficulty that theoretical logic runs up against: 'All logic is limited by the limitations of the human mind when it is engaged in that activity known as logical thinking' (1975, p. 125). It is the virtue of cybernetics that it offers a methodology which does not create a dichotomy between action and thinking, knowledge and skill, art and science. It is at the heart of the contemporary problem, which concerns man at the crossroads of biological evolution and the revolution of information technology.

A basic concept is that of *self-reproducing machine*: 'The machine is not only a form of material, but an agency for accomplishing certain definite purposes. And self-propagation is not merely the creation of a tangible replica; it is the creation a replica capable of the same functions' (Wiener, 1975, pp. 177–8). The

Freudian metaphor of a mental apparatus is not so far removed from such a perspective. And there can be no doubt that the family possesses psychical spaces limited by boundaries organized in terms of certain goals, which are potentially capable of reproducing themselves. The problem here is that not all of the family organization can be understood in purely psychological terms. It is also connected to the fact that the family psychical space is not necessarily constructed on the lines of the topographies as Freud constructed them in seeking to provide a METAPSYCHOLOGY of the human person.

Within this perspective, cybernetics makes it possible to model, on the basis of artificial or theoretically possible MACHINES, systems which are subject not to efficient or formal causes, but to final causes. The mutual influence of several variables does not merely occur in the form of linear sequences, but produces a tangle of feedback of a circular kind, which (a) either regulates the equilibrium of the system as a function of the goal sought, on the basis of an uneven number of elements of negative feedback (systems in a state of equilibrium were studied by what is known as the *first cybernetics*); or (b) amplify the divergences, by explosion or blocking, on the basis of an even number of negative feedback elements, or of positive feedback (the amplification of divergences, far from the equilibrium state, has been studied by 'the second cybernetics', Maruyama, 1968).

The father of cybernetics raised the same objection against orthodox Freudian psychoanalysis as has ultimately come to be levelled against the subsequent fate of his own model: a refusal to allow divergences of opinion, mechanicism, reduction of man to an automaton, the closed character of systems, contempt for the individual in the name of a fetishized, mechanized ritual. It has, however, been one of the essential virtues of cybernetics that it has provided the first steps towards the deterministic explanation of the finality of self-regulated organisms.

(See also ANALOGIC CODING; ARTIFICIAL CODES; DIGITAL (OR NUMERIC) CODING; FEEDBACK; HOMEOSTASIS; MESSAGES; OSCILLATORS; PARADOXES; SELF-ORGANIZATION; SELF-REFERENTIAL CALCULUS; STRANGE LOOPS.)

J.M.

cycle of hysteresis   See ELEMENTARY CATASTROPHES; INFANTILE AUTISM.

D

data gathering   When dealing with families confronted with high levels of confusion and chaos, it is sometimes necessary actively to seek out differences – even minimal ones – which will convey information, at the point where the spontaneous perception of the participants is swept away by movements of maximum non-differentiation.

The school of Mara Selvini Palazzoli has developed techniques for collecting information which make it possible to take account of circular causality and family feedback and to provide the information necessary for the elaboration of hypotheses on the FUNCTION OF THE SYMPTOM for the family system. In this model, the family is questioned,

1   *About behaviour in specific interactions* in specific circumstances, and not in terms of feelings or interpretations. For example: Andrew's sister is asked, 'When Andrew starts to get violent, what does your father do?' 'How does your mother react to what he does (or doesn't do)?' 'What do you do?'

2   *About differences in behaviour*, and not about a person's intrinsic qualities. For example:

Mother: 'The children are really annoying!'
Therapist: 'What is it that they do which makes them so annoying?'
Mother: 'They're always bothering their father, even though they know he's working.'
Therapist: 'Which of them does that worse, the older child or the younger one?'
Mother: 'The older one.'
Therapist to younger child: 'And who gets angrier at your brother, your father or your mother?'
And so on.

3   *About how they would rank on a scale a specific behaviour or a specific interaction between several members of the family.* For example: 'Rank the various members of the family according to the frequency of their going out. Begin with the one who goes out most.' This method is a source of important information on family interplay and often reveals interesting divergences in the rankings produced by the different family members.

4   *About changes in relations before or after a precise event.* For example:

Therapist to son: 'In your opinion, did your father and brother fight more before your mother fell ill or after?'

Son: 'After. Dad's a lot more edgy. It's when mum's got a headache that he tries to calm himself down.'

5   *About differences in relation to the supposed function of the symptom.* For example:

Therapist: 'If one of the children had to stay at home and not get married who do you think would be the best one to do that, for your mother?'

6   *About feedback reactions to the symptom.* For example: The therapist asks how each person reacts to the symptom. The model is triadic: one member of the family is asked to describe how another reacts to the symptom, and how yet another reacts to that reaction. (See also CIRCULARITY; SYSTEMIC HYPOTHESIS; TRIADIC QUESTIONING.)

M.G.

'deadly embrace'   See STALEMATE.

deculturation   The failure of processes of diachronic ACCULTURATION tends to leave in existence some of the traditional values of the group of origin. These then come into sharp conflict with the new behaviour which arises as a result of the forms of family life having undergone great change. The outcome may be termed deculturation to the extent that, in the absence of norms mediated by the example of the parents, violence becomes the only symbolic expression which produces real effects. Three examples, from among the many available, will illustrate this.

In Japan, ancestral pressures on the eldest son, on whom all duties fall and who is under a great obligation to preserve the honour of his lineage, remain intact even though, as a result of the disappearance of large families (which have largely been replaced by couples with one or two children) almost all boys in urban situations find themselves in the position of eldest son. Given this state of affairs, the need to succeed at school is such that, from the age of five onwards, 'model' children no longer have any leisure time to themselves. They are victims of the obligations which go with the role of eldest son without having any of the advantages of that position. Japan has the highest rate of child suicides and the highest rate of educational qualifications among its adolescents.

In Black Africa, the creation of great urban agglomerations alongside the reshaping of the countryside to conform to the needs of cash-crop rather than subsistence agriculture has broken down traditional family structures which were of a communal type. In the city, 'the child is no longer the child of the group. He has to cope with competition and loneliness' (Koudou, 1983). Failure at school and delinquency among adolescents are the heavy price paid for the attempt to employ the European educational model before the model of the nuclear family has been solidly established.

Carrer (1983) explains the frequency of alcoholism in Brittany, in spite of the fact that it is not a wine-producing region, by the psychological matriarchy inherited from the Celtic culture which is not counter-balanced by the symbolic class of fathers.

According to Mitscherlich (1969, p. 299), the whole contemporary world is threatened with a deregulation of instincts by the gradual disappearance of the paternal figure: 'Mass society with its demands for co-operative work excludes the kind of creation on which the individual stamps his own mark and creates a gigantic army of competing jealous brothers.'

(See also DRUG ADDICTION; FORECLOSURE; SCHIZO-PHRENIAS; VIOLENCE.)

G.G.M.

deep structures See SURFACE STRUCTURES, DEEP STRUCTURES.

deixis An act of designation, bringing together an informant and a person receiving the information, a referent (the mediate or 'dynamical' object, referred to by C. S. Peirce, see Peirce, 1935) and a signified object (Peirce's 'immediate' object). The referent and the signified object are connected together – and subsequently detached from one another – by means of an index or deictic performing that act which consists in showing and denoting something by means of a sign (demonstration). The presentation of the mother to the child in the imprinting process is a deixis; pointing out an object with one's finger and naming it for another person, or a mother's gaze accompanying that of her child on to a third object are also deictic acts. Deictic messages are illustrators (Ekman, 1977, 1985), forms perceived and verbalized as a function of particular contexts.

In ontogenesis, the deictic function begins developing in the child at birth, in the form of the contact connecting him or her to his/her immediate circle. At this stage, deixis functions in the designation of the child's forename by one or both parents, the first SHIFTER which anticipates the potential personality of the child.

At the outset, the information is essentially the family system and the person informed is the child; in the process of IMPRINTING, if we consider the child's point of view, the dynamic object is the person of the mother on which the maternal representative is based. This maternal representative, the immediate object of the sign so constructed, is indicated from the very earliest days by the various features and multi-sensory key stimuli on which the construction of the maternal pattern is based: skin contact (the way the mother holds the child or breaks off inter-corporal connection) and the mother's smell, taste (milk, sweetness), voice (which addresses the child with a purpose, calls the child by his/her first name) and face all possess key stimuli, abstract and distinct, salient features which trigger off the child's attachment to a real woman. This proto-typical deixis is in fact reciprocal, the child also being an informant and the family system a 'person informed' about the newcomer and the systems of relationships which ensue. In fact, the mother and the immediate circle of the family will come to recognize the existence of the newborn through the indices he/she emits. The newcomer assuming his/her place in the family system is not therefore the pure product of a unilinear action, but presupposes a reciprocity of multi-linear effects.

In a second phase, once the 'parent' and 'child' deixis has been established (or indeed that of the grandparents or various substitutes), a deixis is set in place which allows *the non-verbal to be designated in a certain way for the child by the verbal*. The hereditary motor coordination of the child pointing its index finger towards an object, in the presence of a close relative, bears witness to this. The child expects the relative to name that object, which is suddenly now localized in time and space and associated with a symbolic verbal index which Jakobson (1957) terms a 'shifter'. Peirce had already observed that the index is connected in time and space with the individual object of which it is the trace, and with the senses and memory of the person for whom it serves as a sign. Thom (1972) seeks to define this spatiotemporal anchoring of deixis in an even more detailed way. A circuit of eye contact between the mother (or father or other person in the child's circle) and the child (or, if this is lacking, a purely tactile contact, as among blind people) focuses the pointing of the mother's and/or child's index finger on the object that is to be named. The adult then introduces a word to name the object in question. Though the linguistic sign appears largely arbitrary on the individual level, it is *socially motivated* (de Saussure, 1906–11). In fact, it turns out to be carried along by a socio-familial trajectory which is collectively motivated in a profound sense. In Thom's view, the 'pregnance' of the mother on the child can be regarded as being diffused by contact with the objects abutting upon the mother's person in a double projection which is both temporal (synchronization) and spatial (the co-localization of the name that is pronounced and the dynamic object perceived and experienced). Secondarily, the word, once localized and connected, has the ability to *exfoliate*, thus leading to the apparently arbitrary character of the linguistic sign. A whole pathology of psychosis (INFANTILE AUTISM; SCHIZOPHRENIAS etc.) might be studied in the light of disturbances of deixis (Mottron, 1983).

See also DELIRIUM; ICONS; SEMIOLOGY; SYMBOLIC REFERENCE; SYMBOLS.)

J.M.

delegation, delegate The interplay of centripetal and centrifugal forces which characterizes delegation is already present in the original ambiguity of the Latin verb *delegare* which means both 'to send' and 'to entrust with a mission'. Delegation is based on the bond of loyalty which unites 'delegator' and 'delegate'. Processes of delegation have been particularly closely studied by Helm Stierlin (1977a).

Delegation gives a direction and a meaning to our lives. It is the anchorage point of the obligations which are transmitted to us over the generations, and is the expression of an indispensable and legitimate relational process. As delegates of our parents, we have the possibility of proving our loyalty and our honesty and fulfilling missions which do not just have a directly personal sense, but also a supra-individual meaning. However, it can happen that processes of delegation become pathological.

INTERRUPTIONS TO THE DELEGATION PROCESS

Three types of disorganization of the delegation process can be observed. First, the various missions which a subject is given may sometimes clash with the talents, resources and needs the delegate possesses as a function of his or her age. He or she will not then have the requisite maturity to assume these missions. In such cases, the psychosocial development of the delegate is disturbed.

Secondly, the tasks he or she is given by one or more 'delegators' turn out to be incompatible and produce a 'conflict of missions'. The delegate thus finds him or herself polled in several directions at once. For example, a girl may be entrusted with the mission of being virtuous, while at the same time being expected to take on the secret sexual aspirations and perverse desires of her mother.

Thirdly, 'conflicts of loyalty' towards parents may arise: the delegate is then exposed to paralysing feelings of guilt when he or she lets down one parent-delegator in serving another. *Bound delegates* must carry out missions which keep them constant prisoners within an affective perimeter controlled by the family. For example, the delegate may have a secret mission to continue the life of a dead brother or sister and thus spare the parents the necessary work of mourning. *Rejected delegates* are subject to intense pressures. In fact, those who have always suffered from parental coldness and lack of interest often persuade themselves that they will only be able to win their parents' esteem by accomplishing the missions entrusted to them with unbounded perfectionism and devotion.

THERAPEUTIC IMPLICATIONS OF THE DELEGATION MODEL

It is possible, on the basis of this model, to set in train a particular therapeutic strategy which essentially focuses upon the index patient. This person can often be seen as an exploited delegate. He/she is attempting faithfully to fulfil missions which are beyond him/her and/or mutually irreconcilable and, at the same time, trying to turn round against his/her parents the violence that they have inflicted. He/she first assumes the role of victim towards his/her parents. By accomplishing this mission, he/she ensures their psychological survival. He/she discharges them of all fear, shame and guilt since it is he/she who is the sick person and the failure, not them. The index patient performs the function of a catalyst of a family therapy process from which all the members profit. Yet it is precisely in playing the victim role assigned by the family that the delegate finds his/her opportunity for revenge. The mere fact that he/she presents symptoms, that he/she defines him or herself as sick and disturbed, constitutes living proof of the failure and perversity of the parents and the patient is thus able to make them feel guilty or throw them into a panic. The therapist must make every effort to show as much understanding towards the parents as to the delegate and must start out from the principle that all parents wish to be loving and good, but that they are also the children of their own parents.

Therapy sessions often reveal the severity of the disappointments, frustrations, traumas and prejudices from which the parents have suffered. This is a heavy burden which they hand on to their offspring, to whom they entrust the mission of obtaining reparation. These latter have to provide their parents with the satisfactions they lacked in their own childhood. This is why, in order not to blame these parents, one has to take account of the transgenerational perspective of legacies and merit.

TRANSGENERATIONAL PERSPECTIVE OF LEGACY AND MERIT

Legacy

This concept, proposed by Ivan Boszormenyi-Nagy (Boszormenyi-Nagy and Spark, 1973), represents a transgenerational extension of the principle of delegation. The term delegation also evokes a bond extending over several generations, a commitment or even an obligation to make oneself answerable to someone. Certain legacies are accompanied by a conflict of loyalty and a mission of reconciliation in which not only several generations, but also family clans, in very profound opposition, may participate. Ivan Boszormenyi-Nagy and Spark (1973) speak of a legacy of split LOYALTY. The tragic story of Romeo and Juliet is a notable example of this.

Merit

According to Boszormenyi-Nagy and Spark (1973), the dynamic of family relations is determined by a MERIT account; gain or a sense of gain is seen as the expression of a motivating force, which plays a role similar to that played, in individual-centred psychodynamic theory, by drives or needs. The fact of receiving the legacy (or not) has repercussions upon the 'state of the merit account' of each member of the family. The sense one has of being treated justly or unjustly, of being in the right or having a goal in life is determined by that state.

The idea of a merit account conjures up the sense of a constraint operating across the generations, the aim of which might be the following: everyone must produce accounts of their present and past merits and, at the same time, demand a similar action on the part of other members of the family. The therapeutic objective consists in defining the legacies and the registers of assets and including them in therapeutic transactions in order to re-balance the ledgers.

(See also LEDGER; TRANSGENERATIONAL MEMORIES; TRANSGENERATIONAL THERAPIES.)

A.L.

delinquent acting out Can be broadly defined by reference to the classic sense attributed to it in psychopathology and criminology. It consists in impulsive acts which may be merely delinquent (thefts) or at times criminal (rape, murder etc.) or, yet again, self-destructive (suicidal acts). Such acts are the externalized expression of partially conscious or totally unconscious representations, marking the failure of an internalized phantasmatic conflict between the agencies of the id and the superego and becoming visible in its effects on family and social systems. In spite of the numerous theoretical and clinical difficulties which the various specialists run up against, it is possible to suggest the following lines of exploration.

Acting out may be considered as a *signal for help*, a signal all the more pressing for being so dramatic and one which, for all its being centred on the symptom—child, none the less represents a request for help for the whole family (Boszormenyi-Nagy and Spark, 1973,

p. 376). It calls for a multi-level, individual, familial and social reading. On the individual plane, it can be understood as an instinctual gratification of sexual and aggressive behaviours, questioning the failing superego functions of the family system, and, subsequently, of the substitutive institutional systems. On the family plane, it appears as the expression of the unconscious delinquent tendencies of the parents, who are inhibited by long-standing prohibitions that are no longer adapted to their lives. On a transgenerational plane, it may possibly reveal an *invisible LOYALTY* (Boszormenyi-Nagy and Spark, 1973) to a character whom the family has come to consider as being beyond the pale, whose memory it revives, though without anyone being aware of this. On a social plane, it questions the grounds of ethics, of collective power and of the arbitrary authority of institutions. The social body is concerned, then, not so much with an INDEX PATIENT, as with an index family.

Acting out is thus the testing out in reality of a FAMILY MYTH which no longer fulfils its homeostatic function. Thus, as Ausloos suggested (1977, p. 181), 'acting out in the adolescent (apart from its individual, social, cultural, institutional, spatial and circumstantial aspects) may be considered as the expression through action in the outside world of a family secret that cannot be verbalized within the family.' It might be said to be revealing the secret without disclosing its meaning, its repetitive character lying in this perpetually unsatisfied quest for meaning.

It then appears as the *expression of a transgenerational conflict*, in so far as the delinquent will exploit the moral transgressions which have been perpetrated over several generations within his family ecosystem to emerge explosively in the social context. In this sense, the delinquent act is the expression of a hidden demand for justice and an attempt at meeting that demand. In his or her position as SCAPEGOAT, the delinquent takes upon him/herself a negative identity, leading to an implication of negative loyalty towards his or her family of origin (Boszormenyi-Nagy and Spark, 1973).

(See also CONTRARY INJUNCTION; LEGAL CONTEXT; SPLIT DOUBLE BIND; VIOLENCE.)

J.M. & P.S.

delirium A mode of belief which is unshakeable and directly contradicts the definition of reality validated by the social consensus at a given point. Delirium is a product of the faculty of judgement. It expresses a non-legitimated way of connecting together one's ideas, which are perceived socially as false, and one's behaviour, which is experienced as producing subversive effects that may in some cases be dangerous to oneself or to others. Classically, a distinction is made between the delirium experience (acute attack) and chronic delirium. In the delirium experience, the patient lives out his or her delirium; in the chronic delirium, he or she lives off his or her delirium.

A delirium may be shared (delirium à deux, collective delirium, Lasègue and Falret, 1877). Freud describes it as an attempt at a cure and it can be interpreted as revealing a particular disturbance in the structure of interactions. It acts out in reality, within a given family group the following semiotic utterance: 'It is crazy to believe, think or say x or y.' By definition, delirium cannot be self-defining. The statement 'what I am telling you is a product of delirium' is a paradox of the same type as that of Epimenides on lying. Fully constituted delirious activity cannot be apprehended through self-perception. This is why it is possible for a delirious patient to believe in good faith that it is the others who are mad. Conversely, a person who defines him or herself as mad is not necessarily so (at least if one is looking at the very moment in which he or she makes the statement). The paranoiac (see PARANOIA) or the delirium sufferer of a jealous, megalomaniac, erotomaniac or interpretative type is habitually in the grip of signals which preserve his or her delirious convictions regarding reality. The jealous delirium sufferer will base his beliefs upon clues given out by his wife in a totally involuntary way. Certain triggers, which are linked to transgenerational or synchronic loyalties, are carefully hidden and encrypted and function as embedded manipulations. Watzlawick et al. (1967) quote the example of a possible matrix of jealous delirium: an individual X, whom another individual Y trusts implicitly, threatens Y with something which would make him, X, unworthy of trust.

Another possible definition of delirium which contrasts with – or reinforces these – arises from the systemic definition of language. In delirium, the idiosyncratic arbitrariness of the sign is in search of a social system that is lost and/or yet to be constructed, of which the patient's family, the smallest psychosocial unit, is the vehicle. Whereas phantasies and dreams throw into question the relation between signifier and signified on the plane of individual perception, delirium throws that relation into question on the plane of the inter-group definition of signs. As an activity, delirium puts into question, at every moment, the systems of collective belief that have developed. In this sense, delirium is a family and/or social myth which can find no legitimate place either in time or space. It marks a disorganization of the systems of inter-code transcription at the level of ANALOG–DIGITAL/DIGITAL–ANALOG CONVERTERS and writing to HOLOGRAPHIC MEMORY.

(See also ARTIFICIAL CODES; DEIXIS; DREAMS; FAMILY MYTHS; LEVELS OF COMMUNICATION; MYTH; PHANTASY; REALITY; SCHIZOPHRENIAS; SEMIOLOGY.)

J.M.

demand Two complementary aspects can be distinguished in the concept 'demand'. Demand is something continually manifested by every individual, underlying the fact that he/she addresses him/herself to other subjects, that he/she speaks and communicates. This demand does not necessarily expect a response which might meet the need it expresses. It seems that the fact of not having one's demand met by a response enables the subject to perceive something lying beyond demand, namely desire, which is indeed sexual, and yet no more reducible to sexuality than demand is reducible to a need (Lacan, 1966). This demand to demand, in other words this state of demand may – and this is its second aspect – have a demand for help or for therapeutic attention as its content. That demand may be an individual one, in the sense that the subject expressing it suffers on his or her own account and relates this to a personal symptom. This represents an indication for the subject to seek the assistance of a psychotherapist.

By contrast, other instances of demand take the form of parents complaining on behalf of a child or a wife on behalf of her husband. Here the suffering experienced by the person emitting the demand does not relate to themselves, but to a member of their family group. A mother suffers on account of her son who is presenting a particular symptom or a husband on account of his wife for one reason or another. In this situation the elements of the demand are fragmented. The person expressing the demand is often the one suffering the most. He or she is suffering from another's symptoms and, in certain extreme cases, this latter person may not be experiencing any discomfort whatever from the symptoms which the complainant alleges are present and he or she may not therefore express any personal demand. Cases like these are often the product of a general malaise within the family group, such as latent crises, for example. Employing an individual approach towards the person to whom symptoms are attributed seldom bears fruit. A systemic family approach seems more adequate, ultimately enabling conditions to be restored in which individual demand can be expressed by the members of an alienated group, within a logic of self-belonging, leaving them free to use this possibility or not in terms of an individual approach.

Lastly, there are other cases (which are particularly frequent and require the intervention of a great number of professionals from the legal system, social services, or the medical and psychiatric services) in which demand is expressed mainly on the part of society. Families in these cases are termed 'unwilling', meaning that they are extremely reticent to accept any type of mobilization or spontaneous challenge. The function of systemic intervention in these cases is to improve communication between the family group and those intervening on society's behalf (social services, psychiatrists etc.). Alternatively, within *disengaged families*, the apparent engagement of a particular member is based upon a considerable amount of delegation of responsibility to the various 'specialists' called upon, though these are merely disqualified the more for seeking only to respond to the most superficial level of the 'demand'. In these cases, it is in the interest of the therapists or those working with the family to make explicit the constraints under which they are operating in respect of the demands which their professional responsibilities impose upon them. They may then come to an assessment of their own demand, their own difficulties in responding individually within a complex situation. Such an attitude leads to an evaluation of the degrees of involvement to which the family may respond, if it is assisted in the task.

(See also DEONTIC MODALITY; LEGAL CONTEXT.)

R.N. & J.M.

dementia Family therapists who have worked on the pathology of old age have thrown into question the notion of dementia, which is seen by definition as a prisoner of:

- the anatomo-clinical model;
- its irreversible course;
- its classification as organic pathology.

1 *The anatomo-clinical model*: The refinement of histopathological methods and an increase in the number of tomo-densimetric examinations reveals the somewhat doubtful dependability of the anatomo-clinical correlation.

2 *The notion of irreversibility*: The paradox of the diagnosis of dementia is of the same order as that relating to schizophrenia. If, by definition, dementia is an irreversible condition, every clinical case which improves is then redefined, a posteriori, as pseudo-dementia. In addition, the longer the period of hospitalization, the greater the probability of a diagnosis of dementia being made.

3 *The idea that the condition is organic*: If this notion of an organic basis is partly thrown into question by the the unreliability of the anatomo-clinical correspondence, the latest DSM III classification (American Psychological Association, 1987) reveals an ambiguity. In spite of the authors' concern to keep to a description 'systematically free of any hypothetical etio-pathogenic reference', they consider that, 'in the absence of such evidence, an etiologic organic factor can be presumed.'

In order to escape the presuppositions built into the diagnosis of dementia, Maisondieu (1985, 1986) proposes that it be replaced by the term 'thanatoses', relating the behaviour and mental states associated with dementia to a questioning centred upon the fear of death: 'This death of the mind is merely the product of the fear of death.' He writes of a situation which looks like a negative variant of the mirror phase: 'One fine day, the ageing man sees the cruel truth. He becomes aware of this wrinkled face that is his own, which he had only been vaguely aware of before' (Yankelevitch, 1982, p. 215). This mirror-effacement may then take him into the field of thanatosis, between social death and real death. Yves Colas (1984, p. 28) echoes this definition, describing dementia as a 'presence-absence which places those around them in a double-bind situation: the patient can be seen as choosing to die psychologically while remaining alive.' Dementia may then be perceived as an excessive deployment of the rational faculties with the aim of not seeing one's own ageing or thinking of one's own death which is 'a moment that defeats all further speculation' (Dumas, 1982).

In a study of the pathology of old age, Cottet (1984) makes a similar observation. By the confusion of signs of ageing and signs of illness, 'ageing as a phenomenon of degradation of the mental and physical individual is made made logically impossible since it is viewed as the mark of an intolerable illness' (1984, p. 12). The patient, then, is placed in a position where it is impossible to grow old and thus to die naturally.

Some of these authors consider that most families of dementia sufferers are families in which there is a high degree of complementarity, or ones in which identification of roles is clearly established. The elements of the system are so identified with their personas that they end up losing the substance of their being, and become mere puppets or non-entities. They are nothing but what they do, and when they have nothing to do, they become nothing, or, in other words, demented.

The dementia sufferer takes on the status of 'human wreck', a mere empty casing with no social or family role. Such a status enables him or her to face up to the aggravation of death-laden aggression within the couple or the family, which is re-awakened by the loss of roles and the degrading of rituals. The ageing couple is then trapped in a fearsome impasse: to attack his or her partner in order to survive, to die separated from his or her partner.

On the therapeutic level, efforts ought to be made therefore to 're-situate death as a normal stage in the continuous development of the family' (Colas, 1984, p. 29); that is, to recognize the inevitable fact that human life is finite. A therapeutic triangulation makes it possible to halt the escalation of the aggression–guilt cycle and to temper the symmetrical escalations with which the hospital teams are confronted, being inevitably impotent in the face of death, but often also being caught up in the patient's rejection of contact. Maintaining contact, in a modulated fashion, with those close to him or her can to some extent offset the effects of waning or defunct family rituals, by permitting other alternatives to the usual therapeutic omnipotence, which always finds itself faced with the following antinomy: struggling at all costs against death; or refusing to accept its approach by denial.

A.L. & J.M.

deontic modality Modality of communication in which the action/inaction opposition is overdetermined by the 'have to'/'not have to' opposition. The following system of oppositions results (Greimas, 1979):

- having to do: prescription;
- having not-to-do: prohibition;
- not having to do: optionality;
- not having not to do: permission.

Though PRESCRIPTION and prohibition seem to be semiotic structures that can be clearly circumscribed, the polarity of not-having-to 'do' or 'not do' leads, in the PRAGMATICS OF COMMUNICATION, to a whole series of PARADOXES. These cannot be reduced to a mere play of language, but put into question the relations – of congruence and incongruence – between verbal and nonverbal communication or, more exactly, between actions and words.

(See also DEMAND; SEMIOTIC SQUARE.)

J.M.

depression See MOURNING, DEPRESSION, MANIA, MELANCHOLIA.

detouring For Minuchin (1974), detouring is the situation in which a conflict between parents is transformed into either a mother–child or a father–child conflict as a way of maintaining the illusion of a harmonious relationship between the parents, even at the expense of their child.

(See also FAMILY PROJECTION; PERVERSE TRIANGLES; TRIANGLES.)

P.S.

de-triangulation According to Bowen (1978a), in disturbed families the members do not arrive at agreement on a basis of reciprocity, but in actual fact a third person intervenes between two others either as an intermediary or buffer or by introducing a certain confusion between them. Bowen calls this process 'triangulation'. De-triangulation is the process by which

this state of affairs is overturned, bringing people to communicate on a one-to-one basis, by responding instead of reacting.

(See also COALITION; PERVERSE TRIANGLES; TRIANGLES.)

P.S.

deutero-learning or learning II See LEARNING.

diachronic and synchronic axes of a therapy Determine the coordinates parameterizing the temporal relation set in play in a therapy. The *diachronic axis* is concerned with the history of the patient and/or those close to him/her. The *synchronic axis* is concerned with the present circumstances assailing the patient, and seeks to orchestrate differently the relations which this latter maintains, at a particular moment, with those around him.

Starting out from its basic treatment model for neurotic patients, psychoanalysis has built up a model based upon the diachronic quest for memorized representations of conflicts. The transference neurosis makes possible a reactivation of the infantile neurosis, by leading to regressions that are sufficient to enable a reorganization of ontogenetic processes to occur. There exists, therefore, a reorganization of the individual history, as a function of the modifications of positions appearing in the lineage of the analysand. It goes without saying, however, that these reorganizations occur in the here-and-now of the sessions (re-synchronization of these diachronic events). The success of the cure depends on the relationship which exists between the infantile events, such as it has been possible to memorize them, and the analysand's capacity to transform them in the relational dynamic which comes to be established with the analyst.

Bateson (1958), upon coming into contact with the Iatmul people of New Guinea, clearly identified the limits of such a therapeutic procedure in dealing with non-neurotic patients:

It is likely that while for some patients the administering of a diachronic view is curative in its effects, for others this treatment may only accentuate their maladjustment. For these latter, it is possible that the administering of a synchronic view would be curative and give them a complete and realistic understanding of themselves. The dangers of psycho-analysis when administered to schizoid patients may indeed arise simply out of the preoccupation of such patients with destiny and the inevitability of historic accident. A sense of contemporary process is perhaps a necessary corrective to an over-developed sense of personal history, and *vice versa*. (Bateson, 1958, pp. 181–2)

Moreover, Bateson distinguishes between *internal schismogenesis* and *external schismogenesis*, each of these being capable of reinforcing the other in cases of maximum loss of social adaptive behaviour: 'Here we have two forms of schismogenesis to consider: first a probable schismogenesis between the patient and his friends, and secondly a possible schismogenesis *within* the personality of the patient' (1958, p. 182).

The therapeutic approach towards families which results from this is thus based, initially, on the synchronic gathering together of several members of a single collectivity who are involved in vital relations of belonging, filiation and consanguinity. The demand formulated may explicitly be that they forget all that is past and accept the need to resolve their concrete problems in an extemporaneous manner. In conflicts within couples, in psychotic catastrophes, and in 'acting out' which takes the form of criminal behaviour or drug abuse, all reference to the past takes on a negative connotation, since it may lead to an exacerbation of the sense of guilt. Such situations seem to indicate the need for a redefinition, for a continual return to the starting point. The goal of therapy may be to achieve the re-emergence of a diachronic dimension where this had seemed totally impossible.

(See also FAMILY THERAPIES; SCHISMOGENESIS.)

J.M.

diachrony See ACCULTURATION; DECULTURATION; DIACHRONIC AND SYNCHRONIC AXES OF A THERAPY.

differentiation of self The study of the process of differentiation of self starts out from the supposition that the family is an active system constantly undergoing transformation, a complex organism which becomes modified in the course of time in order to ensure the continuity and psychosocial growth of its members. This process, in its dual aspect of continuity and growth, enables the family to develop as a 'system' and, at the same time, the individuals who make it up to become differentiated. Many authors have attended to the study of the differentiation of self as one of the basic functions acquired by the individual in the context of his belonging to a family (Winnicott, 1952, 1960; Whitaker and Malone, 1953; Searles, 1965; Bowen, 1978a).

DIFFERENTIATION OF SELF AND FAMILY INTERACTION

Once individuals have it confirmed to them that they belong to a sufficiently united family group, they can progressively develop their individual selves. In fact, each individual must become decreasingly essential to the functioning of his/her family of origin in order to be able to separate from it and create in his/her turn a new family system by assuming different functions. This transition from a fusion/differentiation stage to a differentiation/separation stage is determined not only by biological stimuli and by the mother–child psychological unit (Mahler, 1968), but also by the full range of interactions within a wider reference system such as the family.

The structural unit which contributes to determining the individual autonomy of each person is the triangular relationship between parents and child. The third element, represented in turn by each of the three, forms the point of reference for all transactions between the other two. In an exclusive dyadic relationship, no differentiation is possible. Neither of the two individuals can determine in relation to whom it will be possible to effect differentiation. Even in situations in which, apparently, the relationship is dyadic – for example in families in which only one of the parents is present – each nevertheless belongs to a vast network of relations which includes the families of origin, themselves made up of many relational triangles.

In order to become differentiated, each individual must mark out and expand a personal space in his/her exchanges with the outside world. In this way identity is defined. This can only assert itself if the individual tries out new relational modes which enable him/her to vary the function he/she assumes in the sub-systems to which he/she belongs, without thereby losing a sense of continuity.

The capacity to move from one place to another, to participate and separate, and to belong to various sub-systems makes it possible to assume functions usually performed by others, to exchange certain tasks, accomplish new ones and thus express increasingly differentiated aspects of oneself. This process requires the family to be able to cope with the phases of disorganization which are necessary if it is to abandon the position of equilibrium it had arrived at in order to acquire a more appropriate one.

The family thus passes through moments of instability during which the cohesion–differentiation relationship is modified. During the development of the family group, through an exchange of behaviour/information, each individual acquires a specific identity and particular functions. The modification of the functions of one of the members implies the simultaneous transformation of the complementary functions performed by the others. It lays down the character of the process of individual growth and the continual reorganization of the family system throughout its lifecycle.

This development does not always take place in these conditions. It may happen that the rules governing a family group deny the AUTONOMY of the members of the system and prohibit their individualization. Each individual is condemned always to behave in a way imposed by the system. The individual is alienated in the function assigned to him (see ALIENATION).

If the function designates the set of behaviours which, within a relationship, satisfy the respective demands of both parties, it is clear that it may, depending upon the families, take on a negative or POSITIVE CONNOTATION. In the latter case, each individual gradually acquires a differentiated image of him/herself, and of the others and of him/herself in relation to the others. Each person knows he/she can always share his/her space with other people's space, without thereby feeling forced to live on their terms. For an encounter to be mutually enriching, it must not be experienced as an intrusion, but must be based on a real exchange and on each person giving and receiving in their turn.

By contrast, the function takes on a negative connotation when it is assigned in a rigid and irreversible way, or when it stands in contradiction to a biological function as, for example, in the case where the function of the father is allotted to the son. The result is a progressive alienation of the most involved individual, to the detriment of his self and his own personal space. The situation becomes pathological when the process tends to become frozen in a rigid, irreversible way. This type of relationship is characterized by the absence of clearly marked interpersonal boundaries.

The consequence is an inability to move freely in relations of intimacy and separation. The intrusion into someone else's personal space and the simultaneous loss of one's own space may then become the only form of relation possible. The more this mode of relating gains in importance, the more rigid the system becomes. The vital necessity only to live as a function of others sterilizes exchanges, wipes out the boundaries of intimacy and reduces each person's personal space until it merges with the space of interaction. In these conditions, it is not so much the need to differentiate oneself which poses a problem – that is too ambitious a project as yet – but rather the danger that someone else will obtain their autonomy at the expense of the others. In such a system, respect for the basic rule prohibits 'leaving the field'.

DIFFERENTIATION OF SELF ACCORDING TO MURRAY BOWEN

For Bowen (1978a), the imprint of the family is so crucial that the degree of individual autonomy may be assessed very precisely during childhood and its development in the future history of the subject predicted by basing oneself upon the degree of differentiation of the parents and the emotional climate prevailing in the family of origin.

The concept of differentiation of self characterizes persons in terms of the degree of fusion or differentiation of their emotional and intellectual functioning.

Those with the greatest degree of fusion are those who present the most severe difficulties and, by contrast, those who reach the highest level of differentiation are those who have the least severe difficulties.

To describe affective attachments within the family which are too constraining, Bowen has used the term 'undifferentiated family ego mass' (see FAMILY EMOTIONAL ONENESS). He proposes a scale running from 0 to 100 in which 0 represents the lowest possible level of human functioning and 100 the score to which man might aspire. He also proposes the concept of a 'pseudo-self', a product of excessive emotional pressure, together with the concept of a solid self. Each person presents varied and possibly variable levels of pseudo-self and solid self. Similarly, the levels of differentiation of the self may vary within the same person depending upon the circumstances, making it possible for the emotional, intellectual and feeling systems to click into – or out of – gear.

Low level of differentiation of self: 0–25
These people live in a world dominated by emotions and by subjective and instinctive expression, which it is impossible for them to differentiate from the facts of objective reality. They are incapable of constructing projects and waste their lives in day-to-day struggles. Their reactions and behaviour are strictly regulated by the continual and contradictory fluctuations of their emotional perceptions. They grow up remaining appendages of their parents. This group presents the most serious health problems and has the greatest difficulties entering socioprofessional life.

Average level of differentiation of self: 25–50
The existence of these subjects is still guided by their emotional systems, but their styles of life are more diversified than at the lower levels. They do manage to work through their feelings and rise above elementary emotional reactions. Their mode of life takes greater account of what persons outside the family think.

Higher level of differentiation of self: 50–75
Persons within this range possess a sufficient basic differentiation for the two systems, the emotional and the intellectual, to operate at the same time, without one having the upper hand over the other. The result is the expression of feelings, which are the product of nuanced affects correlated with elaborated representations. In periods of calm, these persons use logical reasoning to assert beliefs, principles and convictions. They also succeed in dominating their own emotional systems in situations of anxiety and panic, while at the same time allowing themselves to be invaded by their emotions in the appropriate contexts (love-making, aesthetic experiences etc.). Persons with differentiated selves manage to refer, when they express themselves, to what they think and believe. By contrast, persons with weak differentiation of self can only register what they feel and

what they are experiencing, without achieving any distance from it.

Access to social life presupposes the learning of codes appropriate to particular situations, a process akin to that undergone by the actor, who is able to slough off his immediate subjectivity to develop a broad register of expression. Diderot, in his day, drew attention to this is as the 'paradox of the actor' (see FAMILY ACTANT).

TRANSGENERATIONAL UNDIFFERENTIATION OF SELVES

For Bowen (1978a), marriage is usually a functional association between partners at the same level of differentiation of self. This differentiation itself draws upon the models of parental childcare and upbringing. It is revealed at the point when the individual leaves his nuclear family and attempts to lead an independent existence. One then often finds that the adolescent or young adult reproduces the style of life and differentiation which his family of origin has led him to accept.

It then becomes possible to hypothesize that, over at least three generations, this differentiation of self will be subject to continuous positive or negative variations. In a family, the child with the least differentiated self will choose a partner with an equally undifferentiated self; if the partners of this new couple have children, one of these runs the risk of building up a self that is even less differentiated. For Bowen, autistic or schizophrenic pathology can be seen as the expression of minimal differentiation, the product of an increasing undifferentiation of persons over several generations. We might think of this as a catastrophe jump in which a gradual multi-generational disorganization of intellectual and feeling systems leads to an apparently sudden and unforeseen break and to exclusion in mental illness. The goal of treatment would then be to assist patients in freeing themselves from the excessively burdensome emotional constraints with which some families weigh down their members, through enabling the person to learn relational codes and by activating the resources for simulation and play that are inherent in all social life.

(See also DELEGATION; INFANTILE AUTISM; NARCISSISM; SCHIZOPHRENIAS; SELF; SPLITTING; TRANSGENERATIONAL MEMORIES; TRANSGENERATIONAL THERAPIES; TRUE SELF, FALSE SELF.)

J.M., A.C., P.S. & P.A.

differentiation of self scale See DIFFERENTIATION OF SELF.

digital, numeric See DIGITAL (OR NUMERIC) CODING; MESSAGES; PRAGMATICS OF COMMUNICATION.

digital (or numeric) coding Digital coding is based on the use of discrete physical magnitudes, producing a character of discontinuity between the material support of the code and the perceptible appearance of the referent. There is thus a break in the symmetry between the code and what it designates. Thus the number 5 is not five times larger than the number 1. The lack of resemblance is even clearer in binary numerals. Similarly, the word 'cat' bears little resemblance to the animal to which it refers.

The properties of digital coding are:

1 Absence of resemblance between the code and what it represents.
2 Its bi-univocal character: the term-to-term relation between an element of the code and its referent, which makes it precise by convention.
3 Its mediate, arbitrary aspect (barrier between signifier and referent).
4 Its capacity for syntactic differentiation.
5 Its low level of intrinsic semantic evocation.
6 Its discontinuous functioning in an all or nothing mode, by discrimination.
7 Its symbolization of negation and of distinctive oppositions.
8 The function of indication of content.

Modification of the tiniest coded detail may totally change the sense of a digitalized message for an observer. For a semantic value to appear, the bi-univocal correspondence between the referent and the code has to be made explicit, and the totality of the discriminant elements of the coding have to be present.

At the level of the psyche, digital coding is comparable to the secondary processes of thought, and thus to preconscious representations (thought-identity, distinction between opposites, bound energy, limited and controlled flows of energy, logical reasoning based on the reality principle through deferring of immediate satisfaction).

A great number of devices can achieve this 'all or nothing' functioning artificially: electromagnetic relays, lamps, diodes, transistors, ferromagnetic coils or the valves of hydraulic circuits. Their equivalent is to be found at very different levels of the organization of living organisms: the genetic code, the neuron, the linguistic sign and the mathematical symbol are, at a first approximation, digital codes. As may be seen, each digital unit is situated at an immediately higher level in the hierarchy than the previous one, at the maximum level of specialization permitted by that unit; the neuron is the most specialized cellular form the genetic code can programme; the linguistic code is the form of neuronal organization which separates the human being most radically from the other animal species; as for the mathematical symbol, it is the most digitalized signifier possible.

The digital system of coding will hence possess the opposite qualities and failings to those of the analogic system. It is theoretically more precise, but the least error will render the intended result totally incomprehensible; a single modification in the arrangement of the code totally modifies the quantity to be calculated or the sense of the information that is to be transmitted (for there is little that a 'cat' and a 'car' have in common, while, by contrast, reproduction of a cat's miaowing only has to be done quite approximately for the message to be understood). This amounts to saying that digital coding is easily falsifiable and indicates directly a value and its opposite. But it does not allow one to say what that value is. It can be observed that a collection of neurons or an assemblage of words is capable of generating transcodings with analogic effects. F. de Saussure (1906–11) indicated many years ago that the linguistic sign was arbitrary for the individual, but that it was socially motivated and subject, by that token, to transformations as an effect of analogic processes.

(See also ANALOGIC CODING; ANALOG-DIGITAL/DIGITAL ANALOG CONVERTERS; ARTIFICIAL CODES; MESSAGES; RITUALIZATION.)

J.M.

disagreement   See AGREEMENT AND DISAGREEMENT.

dis-alienation   See ALIENATION; FAMILY–THERAPEUTIC INSTITUTION DIFFERENTIATION; PRESCRIPTION; THERAPEUTIC DOUBLE BINDS AND MULTIPLE BINDS.

disclosure   One of the modalities of transmission of information that is generative of family and social myths. It is characterized by the imparting of an excess of true information to someone else and is to be distinguished, on the level of semiotic modalities, from CALUMNY; MISUNDERSTANDINGS; SCANDALMONGERING; and SECRETS.

This excess of the true information, directed towards another, may have therapeutic or pathogenic effects. The divulging of a secret presupposes that a therapeutic context exists. Giving out true information in the wrong conditions may have particularly destructive effects. Three pathological cases are found:

First, the parental couple disclose all their (sexual, child-rearing) difficulties to their children. Therapeutic action will then consist of attempting to reconstruct barriers, in enabling the parents to recover a sufficiently private space for dialogue leading to the rediscovery of an adequate degree of intimacy. It may then be necessary to suggest that the parents attend sessions where the children are not present.

Secondly, a patient in an institution terrorizes all the medical staff. The meetings may be used as a place for developing the phantasmatic resonances generated by the patient's psychotic action. Therapeutic action will consist of channelling this 'phantasmatic haemorrhage'. Here again, just 'making a patient speak', or seizing hold of the scattered fragments of his or her destroyed FAMILY MYTH and then divulging this content to all comers is not sufficient to constitute a therapeutic act. The re-establishing of certain secret zones is the very pre-condition for a restoration of systems that are often under great pressure and somewhat impaired.

Thirdly, apart from the ethical questions which are often difficult to resolve, the making of video films of families for purposes of clinical presentation, use in training or at conferences creates situations which cannot be totally anodyne in so far as the process embarked upon is concerned, even if the family gives its assent or explicitly calls for it to be shown on television.

(See also INFORMATION; MOURNING; NOSTALGIA; REALITY; VIDEO.)

J.M.

disengaged families   In 'disengaged' families, variations in the behaviour of one family member do not affect the behaviour of the others. Disengagement is the exact opposite of family 'enmeshment' (see ENMESHED FAMILIES) and is principally found in underorganized families (Aponte, 1976), where there may be high levels of delinquency. For example, in an enmeshed family, parents will be extremely upset if a child will not eat his dessert, whereas the parents in a disengaged family may not feel concerned if their children steal the money to buy lunch (Minuchin, 1974).

(See also BOUNDARIES; COALITION; DELINQUENT ACTING OUT; DIFFERENTIATION OF SELF; FAMILY TYPOLOGIES; LEGAL CONTEXT; SYSTEMIC MODELLING AND INTERVENTION; VIOLENCE.)

P.S.

disengagement   See DISENGAGED FAMILIES.

disinformation   See FAMILY MYTHS; INFORMATION; THERAPEUTIC STRATEGIES AND TACTICS.

disorder   See ORDER, DISORDER.

disqualification   An interactive process which consists in discrediting either the content of a person's utterance or the person him or herself or what that person does, or the context in which the utterance or action occurs. In the most disturbed transactions, disqualification bears upon all these levels at the same time. In a psychoanalytic perspective, disqualification corresponds to a disorder of primary NARCISSISM.

(See also DOUBLE BIND; SCHIZOPHRENIAS.)

J.M.

dissipative structures Forms of organization brought to prominence through the work of Prigogine's team (see Prigogine and Stengers, 1979) in the field of the thermodynamics of far-from-equilibrium states. The use of these structures in systemic clinical practice has been suggested by Elkaim et al. (1980).

When dealing with certain families in rigid transaction, at certain points in the therapy, it may be necessary to accentuate the crisis, if not indeed to provoke it, in order to amplify the evolution of the family system far from the state of equilibrium, as the only means to recover effective means of regulation and change.

THERMODYNAMICS OF IRREVERSIBLE PROCESSES

The state of equilibrium is the state of maximum ENTROPY towards which an isolated system evolves. In a state of equilibrium, a system is no longer crossed either by fluxes or forces; it is inert. All its energy is dissipated and the production of energy per unit time falls to zero and the irreversible activity linked to this entropy production ceases totally.

The stationary state which may be attained by an OPEN SYSTEM differs from that equilibrium. In effect, such a system may exchange matter and energy with the outside world and the variation of entropy no longer expresses itself solely as a function of the irreversible processes of which it is the site, but also as a function of exchanges with the outside world. This constant contribution from the environment renews the energy which the system dissipates as time goes on. In a nonequilibrium stationary state entropy production per unit time never falls to zero and the system is kept constantly active in production and destruction.

Prigogine and Stengers (1979) show that the stationary states of a system differ very appreciably depending on the distance separating them from equilibrium. Close to equilibrium, the stationary state is characterized by a minimum of entropy production and the state of equilibrium itself is merely a particular stationary state for which that minimum is zero. Not far from equilibrium, a system tends towards stable, predictable behaviour, maintaining a minimum rate of irreversible activity compatible with the exchanges which supply it. Evolution towards equilibrium and towards a stationary

state are similar. Irreversible activity does not fall to zero in the stationary state, but does not prevent an equifinal evolution, independent of the conditions peculiar to the system.

Prigogine and Stengers' key finding is that the stability of these stationary states is no longer ensured once the system is sufficiently far from equilibrium and becomes the site of non-linear processes. By nonlinear processes, we mean self-referential phenomena such as the involvement of a product in its own synthesis, phenomena which constitute the classic mechanisms of regulation and metabolic functioning and which are the rule in living systems. Possibilities of instability exist when these two conditions are combined (far-from-equilibrium and non-linear processes). A system will be termed unstable if certain of the fluctuations, instead of regressing, may become amplified, invade the whole system and cause it to evolve towards a new regime which is qualitatively different from the stationary states defined by the minimum of entropy.

Beyond a certain critical threshold, the stationary state becomes unstable and a new order is established which corresponds to what has become a gigantic fluctuation. This new regime state constitutes a dissipative structure, the term expressing the association of the ideas of order and waste, and articulating the fact that the dissipation of energy, which is generally associated with disorder, becomes a source of order when far from equilibrium.

Dissipative structures appear beyond the point of instability and may be sustained oscillations, spatial structures or transitions between multiple stationary states. Several dissipative structures are possible for a single critical threshold. This variety of possibilities introduces an irreducible element of uncertainty. The state towards which the system evolves depends on the nature of the fluctuation which destabilizes it and amplifies it to the point where it produces one of the possible states. Fluctuation is what, in the intrinsic activity of the system, escapes control and expresses the difference between the system as an 'overall entity', which may be defined, and the individual processes which make up the activity of that entity. In this sense, one may speak of 'system choice'.

One is led to distinguish between the states of the system at which all individual initiative, all singularity and all difference is condemned to insignificance and the zones of BIFURCATION in which a minute deviation from normal behaviour will be a source of crisis and renewal and will be capable of transforming the state of the system. The more rapid the communication within the system, the less chance there is that a fluctuation will become dangerous for the state of the system, since the environment of a fluctuating region tends to damp the deviation as soon as it is informed of it.

FAMILY INTERACTIONS FAR FROM THE STATE OF EQUILIBRIUM

In the approach to social and family systems, dissipative structures may constitute an important theoretical tool for conceptualizing change. Elkaim et al. (1980) ask what might be the means for destabilizing a family system and bringing it to a critical point to create a context allowing the 'dangerous' singularities, i.e. the singularities rich with other possibilities, to be amplified. He stresses the importance for the therapist of taking care that perturbations which only play a barely perceptible role and which are not necessarily included in his theoretical grid can have their chance. Therapeutic work then consists in attempting to identify and block the feedback loops which lead the family to the damping of differences and to immunization against its own fluctuations, to allow it to test out other loops while remaining open to the appearance and proliferation of possibly strange singular elements.

POSITIVE CONNOTATION of non-change may encourage the amplification of a deviation by preventing the triggering of figures of regulation and by sustaining a confusion that allows the system to ignore changes which are beginning. Parents who know everything about the psychical life of their child prevent him/her from growing up and the family system cannot adopt new modalities of functioning more adapted to growth, rather than give up total control of the adolescent. Adolescence as amplification of a deviation invading the system is then strictly forbidden, since it threatens the HOMEOSTASIS of the system.

(See also ASSEMBLAGE; SINGULARITIES.)

M.G.

distance and organization of territory The study of interpersonal distances or 'proxemics' concerns the whole range of observations and theories relating to the use of space by man (Hall, 1966). We may regard the human being as surrounded by a series of invisible BALLS, SPHERES, the dimensions of which can be measured. These include spheres of intimacy, spheres of personal distance, spheres of social distance and spheres of public distance. These spheres are an expression of the modes in which territories are constructed. We shall here postulate the existence of a family level regulating instinctive proto-cultural distances and constructing the arbitrary distances characteristic of the culture of which the family in question feels itself a part.

The clinical study of distances between family members, the position of the INDEX PATIENT and the places assigned or assumed by the therapists must take account of the multiple variables which are involved in this 'setting in place'.

STUDY OF HUMAN PROTO-CULTURE

This must take account of the two proxemic levels:

1 *The prehistoric level* expresses the biological past of humanity and the homological structures which have been transformed as a function of the evolutionary contexts.
2 *The infra-cultural level* takes into account current underlying structures which are only actualized in specific cultural manifestations but recapitulate prehistoric biological forms.

STUDY OF SPACING IN ANIMALS

This shows that there are concentric spheres determining security and flight distances, together with critical attack and sexual contact distances.

1 *Flight distance*: the distance beyond which an animal will flee if approached by a conspecific. This distance is reduced in domestic animals, but is probably accompanied by the construction of an internal distance leading to defence mechanisms in man: repression, isolation, denial etc.
2 *Critical attack or copulation distance*: this distance is even nearer to the animal's bodily boundary than the flight distance.
3 *Personal protection distance*: this corresponds to the normal distance between two conspecifics without contact. This personal distance is greater for dominant animals than for dominated ones. We find it in humans, with personal distance increasing with accession to a dominant hierarchical level.
4 *Family distance*: the distance beyond which the animal loses contact with its near relatives.
5 *Social distance*: the distance beyond which the animal loses contact with its group.

STUDY OF DISTANCE IN HUMANS

These distances become more complex in nature in the human species as a result of human self-domestication, which increases the number of artificial protection spaces and modifies interpersonal distances as a function of cultural norms. Inter-human distances may in part be regulated and modified by the construction of internal spaces (imaginary spaces, phantasy constructions). We may thus distinguish:

1 *Close and far phase intimate distances*: the former include the sexual act and fighting; the latter are subject to great cultural variations (see INTIMACY).
2 *Close and far phase personal distances* (Hediger, cited in Hall, 1966): these provide a protective sphere which is relatively constant and may be regarded as a spatial continuation of the skin-ego (Anzieu, 1985) which regulates interpersonal spacing.

3 *Close and far phase family distances*: members of the same family have forms of proximity and intimacy that are peculiar to that family depending upon status and role. There is, however, a distance beyond which the sense of family membership is lost. It is necessary here to integrate the time dimension into the pure notion of distance or separation.

4 *Close and far phase social distances*: these distances are met with in informal meetings, in institutional exchanges etc. Far phase social distance allows an individual to isolate him or herself from other individuals in his or her presence without being impolite (Hall, 1966). It varies a great deal between cultures.

5 *Close and far phase public distances*: these distances come into play when there are very hierarchized relationships and when individuals belong to different hierarchical levels (important politicians etc.). Access to a higher hierarchical level normally increases far phase distance.

VARIATIONS OF FAMILY DISTANCE

Variations as a function of age
Family distance varies between birth and adulthood and provides the human self with a distance within which to feel security and control through attachment behaviour. We encounter pathological phenomena when the margin for manoeuvre between the flight distance (or critical distance) and the family distance is insufficient or non-existent. In certain cases, the mother or father literally intrude into the close phase intimate distances of their child. In other cases, personal distances are, by contrast, extremely distended. One also encounters oscillations between intrusive and distended relations.

Variations as a function of pathology
In psychotic manifestations, arbitrary forms of distance are frequently lost, ignored or destructured. The patient is often reduced to bringing critical distances and flight distances into action, and playing matters out at an ethological level by taking metaphors literally (e.g. a hebephrenic patient attacking anyone who literally 'treads on his toes'). More often, the more a patient is considered mentally ill or alienated, the more he or she is excluded from the family circle and the more he or she is spontaneously set apart or finds him or herself flanked by two or more members of the medical staff. The identification and adjustment of these interpersonal distances is one of the basic elements of family therapies. There are, in this regard, many approaches for the regulation of distances and they vary a great deal between the various therapeutic techniques.

(See also AGONISTIC BEHAVIOUR; BOUNDARIES; DOMESTICATION; POWER; SOFA-BED (SYNDROME); SPACE–TIME; TERRITORY; TOPOLOGICAL SPACE.)

J.M.

domestication, self-domestication Domestication is the general and hereditary extension of the morphological and behavioural characteristics of the species, probably by virtue of the existence of contexts in which natural selection does not operate. It is based on the modification of the natural territories of the undomesticated species, the introduction of artificial protection barriers, which render the 'pure' properties of the morphologies and behaviours of the undomesticated species less useful.

Humanity, as a species, has broken down the rigidity of stereotyped, instinctual behaviours by a phenomenon of self-capture and self-domestication. The family is probably the privileged site where these multiple barriers become established. By virtue of this fact, man acquires degrees of freedom from his instincts, which then have to be resituated in cultural learning contexts.

Domestication is characterized by morphological and behavioural changes. *Morphological changes* include slackening of the connective tissues; decreased muscle tone; tendency to fatten; shortening of the extremities; shortening of the base of the skull; increase in genetic polymorphism (great variety in height, weight and morphological characteristics of individuals). *Behavioural changes* include the decay of instinctive behaviours, which are blown apart, become fragmented and divide up into individual units, subsisting in the form of traces or exacerbated, hypertrophied phenomena (generalized catastrophes). Thus the hypertrophy of the instincts of mating and feeding in man (which is particularly played upon in some advertising) is the characteristic feature not of a wild species, but a domesticated one. In other cases, however, these instinctive behaviours are not very greatly developed. 'Bestiality' is a specific feature of domestication, leading to great morphological and behavioural conflict between individuals.

Domestication is based upon three factors:

1 The '*endogeneous stimulus-production* of some instinctive motor patterns is open to considerable *quantitative changes*, leading either to tremendous hypertrophy or to utter disappearance' (Lorenz, 1954, vol. 2, p. 235).

2 Quasi-total loss of the specific selectivity of the innate releasing mechanisms. Releasing in the domestic species occurs through a number of simpler excitations.

3 A sometimes total independence of certain types of instinctive behaviour which, though fused together in the wild species, in some cases become completely separated. A behavioural difference between the wild and the domestic duck is that in the latter, the instinctual acts of love (formation of a long-term, monogamous couple) are dissociated from acts of copulation.

Domestication leads to the phenomenon of neoteny, i.e. the preservation into adulthood of characteristics which, in the wild form, belong to the early stages of development. This may lead to the newborn's rapid development being inhibited (Bolk's 'process of foetalization' taken up by Mendel in *La révolte contre le père*, 1968). Neoteny, which is already present in the lower apes, becomes marked in primates and is of considerable significance in man. This physiological, endocrine 'backwardness' is matched by a similarly extended period of openness to learning processes. Self-domestication corresponds in man to the social establishment of his own boundaries or frontiers by means of language barriers and institutions.

(See also DISTANCE AND ORGANIZATION OF TERRITORY; ETHOLOGY; FAMILY ETHOLOGY; INSTITUTIONS; LEARNING; PSEUDO-SPECIATION.)

J.M.

double bind The 'double bind' theory was developed by Bateson et al. (1956) to account for the communication effects that are characteristic of schizophrenic disorders. The double bind involves:

- a learning to learn (deutero-learning);
- concerning trans-contextual communications;
- connecting together persons in a situation of inter-dependence;
- with a shared threat to survival;
- in a nexus of constraining messages which are logically connected and yet antinomic;
- which prevents any decision being taken;
- including the decision to escape the threat to survival.

The initial version of the theory comprises six indispensable parameters, relating to the mother–child configuration, or even the father–mother–child configuration as prototype:

1 *At least two persons*, including a mother and her child who are caught up in a relationship with life-or-death implications of the 'persecutor–victim' type; other persons, such as the father and/or other siblings may figure alongside the mother expressing the same attitude of imperative injunction towards the target child.

2 *A traumatic experience* which is repeated in a recurrent and regular way, based essentially on the perceived experience of punishment and the threat of abandonment and definitive exclusion.

3 *A primary negative injunction*, expressed verbally, calling upon the victim 'to do' or 'not do' so and so, in a context of aversive learning, from which any possible reward is apparently excluded: 'If you do x, you will be punished.'

4 *A secondary negative injunction*, commenting upon the first in such a way as to oppose it completely, and reinforced like the first by punishment and/or the expression of signals which directly threaten survival: 'If you do not do x, you will be punished.' This second injunction thus contradicts the first at a more abstract level, though it is expressed in a concealed way, most often on a non-verbal plane, and there is never any possibility of its being stated explicitly.

5 *A tertiary injunction*, which prohibits the target child from escaping from the field. 'If you do not obey x and the opposite of x, you will be punished.' In fact none of the protagonists can really escape from the relationship, the 'victim' doubtless lacking the internal and/or external resources to find a way out. Moreover, this level of injunction, which also includes a commentary on the other two, comprises not only aversive learning, but also promises and rewards of a regressive kind.

6 *A possible concealment of the 'booby-trapped' messages*. The complete set of ingredients no longer needs to be present once the 'target' individual has become accustomed to seeing his or her universe in terms of self-contradictory messages from which there is no question of escaping.

Thus, for example, a mother may write several letters to her son who is in hospital in an acute critical state (catatonia with loss of all independent motor activity and serious somatic disorders), in which she says:

- do you want to sit the exam which takes place in a week's time?
- it is very important for your future;
- it will mean your father will have to make great financial sacrifices;
- and you have practically no chance of passing given how difficult it is;
- and you cannot decently envisage taking up any less worthy career;
- and this first hurdle, though a formidable one, is the easiest by comparison with those that will come later;
- to understand this, you only have to take a good look at your father who has had to make his own way in the world.

Such a message runs the risk of calling forth a linear scansion of events, even though the parents and child concerned are in the same – sinking – boat. The structure of this type of message can be seen to be akin to the structure of the law in Kafka (see LAW) or the theatre of Ionesco and Pirandello (see ANTI-THEATRE).

The concept of double bind is based on a COMMUNICATION THEORY derived from Whitehead and Russell's *theory of logical types* (1910–13). This theory implies the existence of *hierarchical levels*, thus leading to a separation of the various levels to which the various elements and sets belong, the parts and the whole which unites them, the members of a class and the said class by which they are designated. On a strictly logico-mathematical level, a whole series of PARADOXES arises when a set of elements is an element of itself or when a class belongs to itself or again when a totality is identical to one of its parts. On the level of the PRAGMATICS OF COMMUNICATION, the authors observe that the discontinuity between the members of a class and the class itself is frequently and inevitably breached: psychology is not logic (Bateson, 1972, p. 174). Schizophrenic pathology might thus be seen as the negative, pathological expression of this rupture between hierarchal levels of messages. The double bind theory is based on the analysis of LEVELS OF COMMUNICATION, the recognition or misrecognition of the possible falsification of the signals which make it possible to identify these modes (which Bateson calls MODE-IDENTIFYING SIGNALS), and also on the study of the processes which make the learning of the cognitive and affective dimensions of social relations possible.

This communication theory includes a theory of cultural learning which makes it possible to discriminate the modes of exchanges as a function of context. The double bind could be seen as a disturbance of deutero-learning (see LEARNING), i.e. a disturbance of the capacity which makes it possible to learn to learn. The sets of arrangements which may possibly produce pathological double binds (arrangements for learning social relations) could depend on supra-individual genetic characteristics shared within the family group encountering contexts of contexts that are mutually incompatible.

At the level of the clinical encounter with schizophrenic communication, considerable distortions appear in fact between the emotive experience which really occurs between the mother and her child (even when he or she has become an 'adult') and the discursive manner in which the two will 'agree' to speak of it. If the child derives a pleasant inner feeling from contact with her, his or her mother will be able to persuade the child that he or she is in fact feeling discomfort, if not indeed hatred (by PROJECTIVE IDENTIFICATION). The schizophrenic then learns not to distinguish between the levels of the messages emitted by his mother, by those in his close circle and by him or herself. Above all, though, he or she learns not to distinguish that lack of distinction.

We shall note here that Bateson has correctly observed that, in everyday life, normal persons continually mix up modes of exchanges: humour, 'kidding', witticisms and play are based precisely upon an equivalence between messages that are usually identified as different or as having no obvious relation between them. The creative transformation of social rules presupposes more or less complex entanglements of logical levels. This is only made possible, however, because the linguistic distinction between metaphorical and literal use is maintained intact. In the schizophrenic, by contrast, metaphors and rhetorical figures in general are not labelled. It does in fact happen that schizophrenics seek desperately to actualize or realize a metaphorical expression taken literally, as if to preserve its lost foundation.

EVOLUTION OF THE CONCEPT

Since its initial description in 1956, the theory of the double bind has given rise to many developments, modifications and critiques. The theory has met with a destiny which has, to say the least, been paradoxical. The authors of it were awarded the Frieda Fromm-Reichmann prize in 1961–2, but as a theory, it remains either ignored, severely criticized or totally transformed by many psychoanalysts (see PARADOXICALITY). Its main author, Bateson, was to abandon the field of psychiatry and psychotherapy to devote himself first to the study of dolphins and then to the general development of the mind. One of his most eminent co-authors, Haley, was to come to regard the double bind as one of those theories, alongside organicist or psychodynamic theories, which 'handicap therapists', and to advocate that it simply be dropped and the term 'paradox' restored. Conversely, some writers were to extend its use to cover a great number of concrete situations, whether pathological or not, while others used it as a therapeutic tool in contexts where treatment was impossible. Yet others were to attempt to 'get beyond it' by integrating it into wider theories, on account of the fact that the theory of logical types had been abandoned (even by its creator, Bertrand Russell), having been rendered obsolete by a great deal of work by 'fundamentalist' scholars, beginning with Gödel and his INCOMPLETENESS THEOREM. How did all this come about?

First of all, there was a first experimental disappointment when the attempt was made to test out the scientific objectivity of the concept. How many double binds were there in a particular sequence of interactions, or a particular therapy session? The more effort made to track them down and entrap them, like butterflies in a net, the more they fluttered away, as if by some miracle. And the further one was from potentially operational and therapeutic situations (as in an asylum), the more they settled in, wantonly, functioning in that case as defence systems against any change.

Then came a second experimental disappointment. Some experts succeeded in collecting them and indeed in identifying them in situations involving delinquency, neurosis, creativity and everyday life. But the problem of specifying the difference between schizophrenic, therapeutic, sociocultural and creative double binds still remained. So far as SCHIZOPHRENIAS were concerned, a cure only appeared to be asymptotic and indeed it was not even certain that it could be achieved. If one accepts the model in all its force and pertinence, we even have to admit that, as in the case of the alcoholic's bottle, the family double bind will always remain the strongest. In this respect, the pragmatics of communication is close to Bleuler's theory of schizophrenia as a process that is irreversible without *restituo ad integrum*, but one that is compatible, in its basic structure, with a social life and an absence of perceptible symptoms, apart from the incidental signs which are often not tolerated, but can be reversed. If that was the case, then what purpose did the new theory serve?

These two disappointments relate to a misrecognition of the field of action in which this particular paradigm operates. This paradigm, as Bateson (1972) made clear in his essay 'Double bind' of 1969, questions the processes of *reification* and *quantification* of structures of behaviour as these are perceived by the mind. Double binds in a relationship cannot be counted in the same way as tables and chairs. As Bateson points out, the observer has to be 'so-minded' for him to be able to 'see' or perceive this type of relationship.

In fact, the identification of double binds *ipso facto* involves the observer in the very object of his description. Far from denying the value and reality of the relational processes involved, the theory of the double bind leads us to question not the relation to the object, but the *impossible splitting* of the subject, with which the observer will find himself confronted. What must be questioned is not the pure quantity of messages exchanged, but the quality of communications as apprehended by the observer; not madness as a residue of sickness, but as an index of a transcontextual disorder and as an appeal to the observer for a re-definition of the accepted contexts; not a 'cure' by adaptation to an aberrant situation from which there is no way out, but a prescription of symptomatic SINGULARITIES which can generate new systems of meaning. The observer we are speaking of here is not necessarily one single person, but a system of therapists such as the family seeks to define and create.

A second modification occurred in the initial view of the theory, this time relating to the persecutor–victim couple. Schizophrenic communication is characterized by a split between being and appearance in the veridictory modes of communication (see SEMIOTIC SQUARE). What is 'displayed' does not correspond to what 'is'; the mother (or parents, brothers and sisters) 'display' persecutory behaviour, while the child identified as the patient 'displays' behaviour appropriate to a victim. These arrangements of simulated display of attitudes (which are indispensable in any communication) here no longer mesh with an underlying identity. Such simulated communication arrangements do, however, have an indispensable vital function in inter-human exchanges.

A third point has also emerged. Though the double bind realizes itself in ontogenesis, the difference which exists between the creative use of socially desirable *transcontextual gifts* and the confrontation with *transcontextual confusions*, that are unbearable both for the family and for society, may very well derive from family singularities expressing the clash between biology and culture.

Watzlawick (1963) points out that the double bind is not a product of *contradictory injunctions* (like a traffic light that is simultanously showing red and green), but from *paradoxical injunctions* (like a sign bearing the legend 'Ignore this sign' or a sentence which reads 'Please do not read this sentence'). A contradictory injunction enables us to make a choice, even if the two terms of the alternative have equally pernicious consequences. A double-binding paradoxical injunction rules out even the possibility of a choice, since the two antinomic terms imply one another. To try to make a choice in that case is, at one and the same time, to select the alternative one had thought one was eliminating and hence to be unable to escape from this fascinating bond. The statement 'It is forbidden to forbid' is paradoxical, but it only becomes a double bind if it is impossible for two or more persons to step out of such an exchange of messages. An example of a therapeutic double bind, provide by Watzlawick (1963), might be 'If you want this prescription to have its full effect, then whatever you do, don't think of a blue monkey at the time of carrying it out!'

The question which then arises concerns the very structuring of space and time: what is this reality which is described as supervening 'at the same time'? And what is this multi-contextual space (MAP–TERRITORY; REALITY–PHANTASY; DREAM–NIGHTMARE; SYMBOLISM–DELIRIUM) in which informational deficits have the character of a dead-end, an impasse? To recognize the paradoxical character of the double bind was simply to describe, with a precision and a pertinence which the West had lost at the time, a factual state of affairs in inter-human communication. Yet the paradox merely points up a limit to explanation. It reveals that a phenomenon has been identified where understanding breaks down. In this respect, the *counter-paradox* is merely the therapeutic system passing back to the family system the acceptance of the therapeutic system's own limits. In itself, it is neither an explanation nor really a solution, but an opening up.

The concept of double bind may usefully be compared with the concept of '*mystification*' proposed by R. D. Laing. It is a generalization, on the level of the structuring of symbols, of the observations of Kurt Goldstein (1934) concerning the abnormal alternation of opposite effects (in the ambiguous oppositions between figure and ground, for example) when the parts of an organism are isolated, whether this occurs artificially or pathologically. The fluctuation of antagonistic effects resolves itself into a stable and continuous process where there is more active participation on the part of the whole organism. The double bind could be interpreted as a failure of adjustment of two phases in oscillation. There thus exists a distinct clinical difference between abnormal alternating phenomena and normal rhythmic operations. One can see therefore that in respect of functions of symbolization, it is not the individual, but the family immersed in its social communities that has to be regarded as the whole organism. So far as the double bind is concerned, the fact of taking into consideration the family as a whole and sustaining its regulatory mechanisms, leads to the violently antagonistic aspects of the signals exchanged being transformed into more regular and more functional rhythmic oscillatory processes.

TOWARDS NEW INTERPRETATIONS?

The double bind has given rise to a number of new developments, both from a theoretical and a practical point of view. From a theoretical point of view has come: (a) an extension of the number of antinomic messages: n-binds, multiple binds; (b) a formalization of the SELF-REFERENTIAL CALCULUS; and (c) the study of the topological properties of the variables in conflict (cycles of hysteresis of ELEMENTARY CATASTROPHES). From a practical point of view we have: (a) a refinement of clinical descriptions (simple bind, SPLIT DOUBLE BIND; THERAPEUTIC DOUBLE BIND); and (b) a diversification of the modes of approach to family groups and social networks.

(See also METABINDING; MYSTIFICATION; PSYCHOSOMATIC DOUBLE BINDS; SYMPTOMATIC AND/OR AETIOLOGICAL TRANSACTIONS; SYMPTOMS.)

J.M.

dreams, nightmares, sleep and the waking state
It was from dreams that Freud (1900) discovered the major part of the determinisms governing the primary processes of thinking. Dreamwork operates by condensation or displacement of representations and affects, and by considerations of representability (unconscious thoughts in rebus form). In the classic psychoanalytic perspective, the dream is essentially the realization of an unconscious desire, most often transfigured by defensive counter-cathexes.

Our dealings with dream activities, as these are apprehended in waking memory, suggest that we are right to re-question this 'royal road' leading to the discovery of the unconscious. What in fact becomes of the unconscious and preconscious in a family in schizophrenic transaction in which each person lives a nightmare reality, no longer sleeps at night and only has dreams presaging imminent catastrophe? How is the slightest

desire to be located where the absence of rules has passed totally beyond even 'rulelessness' or where the apparent consensus is that the index patient should be sacrificed?

We know that dreaming is one of the basic activities of the infant. Rapid-eye movement (REM) – or 'paradoxical' – sleep, which reflects dream activity, is the first to appear in embryogenesis (it exists in the premature baby of six months), whereas slow-wave sleep becomes synchronized more slowly and gradually. However, REM sleep only occurs within the context of slow-wave sleep. In the newborn child, the first smiles appear in paradoxical sleep. In the infant, the absence of synchronization of the two parts which contribute to the establishment of slow-wave sleep shows that the distinction between sleep, waking, dream and hallucination is less clear cut than in the adult. Thus, Lebovici and Soule (1970) has been able to advance the hypothesis, following Freud, that the infant hallucinates the maternal object before even being able to perceive it distinctly.

Sleep appears to be an absence of behaviour, whether differentiated or general, as in the state of vigilance. But this paradox is merely apparent since it is accompanied by electro-encephalographic activity. One might more correctly say that sleep is a behaviour which simulates the absence of behaviour. Within this first paradox a second arises, which is known indeed as 'paradoxical sleep', the subjective expression of which is dreaming. Dreaming is the perception of carrying out motor activity without there being any such activity (Pichot, 1983). Dream activity is, in effect, a reaction *in vacuo*, which is accompanied by an inhibition of motor coordination. When this inhibition is artificially removed, higher animals (the higher vertebrates, at least, such as cats) set in train their instinctive behaviours (predation, sexuality) during the paradoxical phase of sleep. In other words, paradoxical sleep is a hallucination of an instinctive behaviour, the impression of its realization, without its direct activation. Such an observation confirms the Freudian hypothesis that the dream is a realization of desire. The dream is thus a behaviour which simulates, for the dreamer, the realization of a fictive behaviour, and one which occurs within the context of a behaviour which simulates, for the observer, the absence of behaviour. Pichot (1983) rightly emphasizes that sleep possesses all the characteristics of an instinctive behaviour. It is released in an autonomous fashion, cyclically, and is also dependent upon internal and external stimuli functioning by difference. Sleep presupposes a sufficient state of tiredness, a state of inner calm and the absence of over-intense internal stimuli; moreover, its spontaneous rhythmicality is influenced by the nyctheremeral rhythm. Sleep and dreams are thus particular RITUALIZATIONS, which are addressed essentially to the individual's self.

In Freud's view, in *The interpretation of dreams* (1900),

dreams carry on the occupations and interests of waking life. Their paradox is that they treat problems which are important for the dreamer by only gleaning what are apparently insignificant details from the day's residues. However, their structuring is regulated by the dreamer's overall relational context: that context varies depending on whether he or she has to face up to a known ordeal or if there is love-interest developing or if he or she senses a situation of imminent catastrophe in family and social relations.

Thus only the waking state can re-frame oneiric activity. That re-framing is precisely in question when a *nightmare* occurs, where the intensity of what is dreamed prompts an urgent return to the waking state and short-circuits slow-wave sleep. But the re-framing is destroyed when oneiric delusions or hallucinatory experiences occur. The nightmare functions as a state of alert in respect of a threat concerning family or social reality; it seeks to stabilize an unstable reality.

Some therapists seek to draw out the dream activity of the various members of a single family. In a relatively active way, the therapists will ask them explicitly what they have dreamed of since the last session. 'As reproductions, admittedly with secondary revisions, of primary hallucinatory activity, [dreams] enable the therapists to grasp the functioning of the family psychical apparatus which precisely has its deep origins in an hallucinated thought, a dream thought' (Ruffiot, 1981a). Clinical experience shows that the appeal to dream activity may be a nuanced one and that it may be adapted to the situations encountered. It may be incorporated into other modalities of intervention which are likely to produce varying levels of vigilance (see HYPNOSIS). It may be connected with the activation of psycho- or sociodrama, with relational interplay or with the definition each person gives of the others' behaviour. In some more disturbed families, one finds an almost epistemological or ideological refusal to make use of psychical material. This often goes together with a confusion regarding what activities have been dreamed, realized, phantasized, hallucinated or experienced. These various modalities of communication are then poorly differentiated and do not succeed in becoming structured in distinctive oppositions. One of the essential functions of therapy is, then, to attempt to re-establish spaces for dreams, daydreams, thought, emotion and action.

(See also PRAGMATICS OF COMMUNICATION; PSYCHO-ANALYSIS.)

J.M.

drug addiction The spread of drug addiction throughout the world has caused considerable concern particularly since the mid-1960s. Studies on the families of drug addicts have mainly been concerned with the use of heroin. The tensions which can typically be seen between drug addicts and their environments are not without their effects on the development of knowledge relating to addiction. Various different teams have undertaken research on this subject.

INTERACTIONAL MODELS

We shall begin with the work carried out in America, particularly by Stanton and co-workers (Stanton et al., 1974–8, 1978; Stanton, 1977; Stanton and Todd, 1981). Stanton works within a dual – structural and strategic – perspective and adopts a rigid model, setting the families very precise objectives which they must achieve in a number of stages. For example, he fixes a date for the addict to come off his or her drugs, in order to help the family to prepare itself for this change. In his 'brief therapy' model (3–5 months), he assigns the parents the task of helping their child to find work and independent accommodation. During the various sessions, the therapists attempt to restore the parents' place on the hierarchical scale and try to consolidate the generational frontiers.

One of the first goals to be achieved consists of involving the 'peripheral' parent and in clarifying the inextricable nature of the intrafamilial bonds. Stanton at no point abandons complete control of the interview to the family, for fear of seeing the addict take on responsibility for all the family's difficulties, thus reinforcing homeostatic mechanisms. He notes that, usually, after the disappearance of the symptom, marital tension increases. Couple interviews are then proposed.

There are several criticisms of this therapeutic model:

1 The approach allows too little place for the creativity of families and does not take into account the diversity of family configurations.
2 The therapies are essentially centred on the symptom, the disappearance of which is programmed to occur 'in the short term' without sufficiently taking into account the place of the symptom in the economy of the family.
3 The clinician is only interested in the 'here and now', completely leaving out of account the transgenerational perspective.

This model is therefore very different from the one we adopted in Europe several years later. It seemed important to us to distinguish, from the outset, between families which included recreational users of drugs and the families of heroin addicts.

In this type of problem, we must remember Doctor Claude Olievenstein's formula: drug-taking is the product of an encounter between a substance, a personality and a sociocultural moment. To this we have added the family parameter. Though, in effect, users have no problem coming off minor drugs, regular use does often indicate difficulties. Some families consult a therapist for problems of minor drug use when in fact depressive symptomatology or other symptoms such as apragmatism or inhibition are the main problems. These families, who are generally very insistent in their request for treatment, usually benefit from a conjoint family therapy approach.

When we look at the families of heroin addicts, we can identify sequences, bonds and interactions specific to these families even if a typological classification does not seem wholly pertinent (see FAMILY TYPOLOGIES). There is, in effect, no single and pathognomonic family profile of drug addiction, but common features are found in many family constellations. Some of these traits are observable in other pathological family systems (see ANOREXIA NERVOSA; DELINQUENT ACTING OUT).

SPECIFIC CHARACTERISTICS

Family blindness
There is a latency period between the point when the young person begins drug-taking and the point when the family identifies that behaviour, the family being most often informed of it by a third party. In fact, the family's blindness connects with a mechanism of denial which is shared by all members of the family group. This blindness may be compared to the blindness one finds in the families of sufferers of anorexia nervosa.

Denial of life-threatening character of behaviour
The life-threatening character of the young person's behaviour is denied by the family group as a whole. The risk to life, which is always present, is rarely faced up to consciously by family members.

Family pathologies
Many studies have shown that psychotropic drugs are frequently used by these young people. At an early stage, psychotropic drugs are included in the system of family communication and used to regulate conflicts. One also finds frequent psycho-pathological episodes in the parents: depressive states, sometimes with suicide attempts, ALCOHOLISM and severe neurotic decompensations. We should note, moreover, the frequency of suicidal behaviour within the extended family and also the overconsumption of psychotropic drugs by the parents. One also finds a serious degree of pathology at the sibling level, in particular risk-taking behaviour, acts of delinquency, eating disorders and suicide attempts.

Transgenerational transgressions
The transgenerational approach to families has enabled the great number of trangressions that are repeated from one generation to another to be brought out. These are also families in which one finds an absence of generational frontiers. The 'real marriages' in the family are those between mother and son, father and daughter, leading to quasi-incestuous relations (see incest; PERVERSE TRIANGLES).

Acculturation and deculturation
Phenomena of ACCULTURATION and DECULTURATION play an important role when there has been no proper integration of a cultural rupture. This may be a cultural gap between generations (parents in relation to their families of origin or second generation immigrant children), but there are sometimes major cultural rifts between the father and the mother. These factors contribute to reinforcing family dysfunction. There is a frequency of premature deaths in these families and inadequate processes of mourning, which contribute to aggravating depressive mechanisms.

THERAPEUTIC INTERVENTIONS

Integrating these different levels of analysis, the systemic modelling of the families of heroin addicts has developed greatly in Europe and, most particularly, in France (Angel et al., 1982–3). Though writers in the English-speaking world have developed various types of family approach, drawing on multi-family and group therapies, in Europe efforts have generally been confined to an approach inspired by the techniques of one or other of the schools of family therapy (structural, strategic, analytic, Rome schools etc.), depending on the background of the therapist. The interval between the sessions varies depending on the nature of the demand and the problem posed. It may be between one week and one month.

Particular technical adjustments have to be made when, as in approximately 50 per cent of cases, one is dealing with single-parent families. Structuring the interviews already represents a therapeutic reference point for the family. The designation of the young person as the family's only sick person usually goes back a long way and we have to focus on understanding the meaning of that stigmatization. The *first phase of therapy* focuses on the here and now, as close as possible to the family's demand and to the symptom. It is during this period that the therapists attempt to 'join' the family, i.e. to create a climate of confidence by reflecting on the meaning of the addict's behaviour within the framework of his or her family organization. During these first sessions, the team must show competence in regard to drug addiction. If it does not, it will quickly be disqualified. Various points are raised systematically, such as planned withdrawal, relations with other specialist institutions, the problem of money etc. The *second phase of therapy* is centred on the history of the family. This is the transgenerational work and it is concerned with identifying the repetitive patterns found over several generations. In the last stages of treatment the addict learns to place him or herself in the complex pattern of his or her genealogy and progressively rediscovers his or her roots.

It seems essential to us that siblings should participate in the interviews. This is, on the one hand, preventive work so far as the brothers and sisters are concerned, since some of them may acquire the same symptom. It is also a work of therapy, since many of the siblings have grave psychological difficulties.

The family approach cannot be seen as the sole approach to be taken in respect of a symptom as complex as drug addiction and it must be included within a range of therapeutic modalities. In the United States, it has emerged that, over the past fifteen years, most of the centres dealing with drug addicts (detoxification, post-cure centres, medium stay) have also been doing work with families alongside this. Institutions in most of the countries of Europe are now following the same path.

(See also CARDINAL VALUES; DELEGATION; DIFFERENTIATION OF SELF; PRESCRIBING (MEDICAL) DRUGS; TRANSGENERATIONAL MEMORIES; VIOLENCE.)

S.A. & P.A.

drug prescription   See PRESCRIBING (MEDICAL) DRUGS.

dynamic systems   The theory of dynamic systems enables us to develop a dynamic point of view in communication systems and to recognize the importance of the FORCE FIELDS to which the members of a group in interaction are subject. Family processes, which are products of interaction between consanguine and affiliated persons, can thus be grasped in terms of dynamic systems. In such processes, biological and cultural forces are led to interact, to enter into conflict, to tend towards limit points.

DEFINITION OF A DYNAMIC SYSTEM

Let F be a system considered as a TOPOLOGICAL SPACE. Let U be the control space. The phenomenological appearance of the state of the system varies if the point which represents the system meets a closed space, K, in U, termed by Thom (1972, pp. 335–43) the *catastrophe set*. That topological space will have several properties. It will have properties of *differentiable structure* (Euclidian space of n dimensions, i.e. R^n, also called a *differentiable manifold*: this is a set of multi-dimensional maps, differentiable or integrable, completely covering the space of the system under consideration). This manifold enables us to study the accidents and regularities of the system, the critical points and the points of bifurcation, appearing for precise values of the derivatives of order 1, 2 . . . or n (see also FAMILY MAPS). There will also be *dynamic properties*: this manifold possesses a dynamic, defined by a vector field X (qualitative evaluation of values possessing a direction and an intensity: see FORCE FIELDS).

The STRUCTURAL STABILITY of the system, together with the changes leading to the maintenance of that stability, are provided, in dynamic models, by ATTRACTORS, conceived as limit sets towards which the points of the system tend asymptotically. In static forms, the attractors are point attractors, resulting in a gradient dynamic; in metabolic forms, the attractors may have complex forms and may be recurrent (limit cycles, and may even lead to meta-stable states – strange attractors). The more complex the system under consideration, the greater the number of dimensions of its attractors. In the event of simplification or degradation of the system (generalized catastrophe such as schizophrenia, psychomotor handicaps, the birth of a backward child etc.), the number of dimensions of the attractor diminishes.

THE FAMILY AS DYNAMIC SYSTEM

Such a model leads to recognizing the members of the family as actants in a morphology subject to formal, topological constraints: the family inscribes itself in a spatiotemporal domain, structured like an ensemble of open and closed sets. Each actant occupies a particular position and is subject to tensions which prevent it from modifying its trajectory at will. The trajectories to which the actants are subject tend towards basins of attraction which may be in conflict one with another. The conflict between several attractors is symbolized by the minimum potential of the system under consideration.

Above and beyond the effects of efficient – linear or circular – causality, the effects of formal causality are thus recognized, linked to the characteristics of boundaries, the configuration of territories, the intensity of the forces in conflict, the position of the different persons in the system and the shock waves which ensue.

In families in schizophrenic transaction, one very often finds considerable distortions in the material organization of the living territory. The number of beds is inferior to the number of persons making up the family; some 'beds', some living spaces are not differentiated (SOFA-BED SYNDROME described by Maruani, 1982a). It is entirely as though the presence of some members of the family were merely a statistical presence, subject to random variations in the system's evolution. Receiving a family of this kind into 'family therapy' amounts to creating or recreating structurally stable attractors and re-establishing psychical spaces, an indispensable condition for the redefinition of coherent material spaces.

(See also ELEMENTARY CATASTROPHES; FAMILY CATASTROPHES; GENERALIZED CATASTROPHES; SHOCK WAVES; UNIVERSAL UNFOLDING; VECTORS.)

J.M.

E

ecosystem, family ecosystem In its initial sense, the ecosystem defines the level of organization of nature, within which individual organisms constitute fundamental elements of interaction (Tansley, 1935). The ecosystem is thus a physical system, subject to the ordinary constraints of all physical systems.

In a secondary sense, the family ecosystem (from the Greek *oikos*: place, niche, house, habitat) describes a doubling up of the biocenosis or ecological niche on itself. By simulating the constraints and dangers of the biocenosis, as well as the riches it has to offer, the family ecosystem enables the offspring to learn about the conditions of life and survival in the mineral, vegetal, animal and social environment.

The living individual is never isolated in an ecological niche. Intra- and inter-specific systems of behaviour co-evolve with the natural resources and the climatic conditions. As Bateson (1972, p. 406) points out, animals and plants 'live together in a combination of competition and mutual dependency'. This is also true if we look at human society and all the population subgroups which characterize it. In humankind, culture becomes an ecosystem in a full sense, enabling all the previously separate ecological niches to be explored, transformed and unbalanced. A disequilibrium often appears through the appearance of an exponential curve: the destruction and/or anarchic proliferation of one or more species. This 'explosive character' of living beings carries with it a risk of extinction or disappearance, but the absence of this characteristic is a certain guarantee of elimination (Bateson, 1972).

When dealing with a complex ecosystem, a frequent epistemological error is to think that a conscious goal which has to be attained will enable us to short-circuit the totality of co-evolving processes which inevitably lie beyond the scope of consciousness. 'Each additional step towards increased consciousness will take the system farther from total consciousness' (Bateson, 1972, p. 408). Now this error is often committed by the members of a family confronted with a system pathology:

in the field of psychiatry, the family is a cybernetic system of the sort which I am discussing and usually when system pathology occurs, the members blame each other, or sometimes themselves. But the truth of the matter is that both these alternatives are fundamentally arrogant. Either alternative assumes that the individual human being has total power over the system of which he or she is a part. (Bateson, 1972, pp. 413–14)

This connects up with René Dubos's famous formula: 'Think globally, act locally.'

For Bateson, ecology has two faces to it, a *bioenergetic* face and an *informational* face. The two units involved are not necessarily in accord, since their limits are not necessarily identical. The bioenergetic unit manages the economics of energy and materials. It is a unit bounded at the cell membrane, at the skin or at the boundary between conspecific individuals, at the frontier of the family ecosystem. One arrives at the balance of the exchanges through an additive-subtractive budget of energy or resources for the given unit. This produces a construction of territories and a building up of agonistic behaviours, enabling boundaries to be established and maintained.

The informational unit budgets information, negentropy, hierarchization and the quality of memories etc. Budgeting here concerns the pathways which maybe or are taken, together with the probabilities of certain events occurring. The resulting budgets are, in Bateson's view, fractionating and not subtractive in character. The boundaries imposed on the budgeting of information must not cut the relevant pathways. By virtue of the fact that the unit of mind is not bounded at the frontier of the skin, the family or the institution, the 'ecology of ideas' (a metaphor Bateson takes from Vickers, 1968) ensures that mind lives on in our collective memory of the dead.

(See also FAMILY SYSTEMS; GENERAL SYSTEMS THEORY; MIND; TRADING OF DISSOCIATIONS.)

J.M.

eidos, eidonomy The eidos or eidonomy is defined by Bateson (by opposition to ETHOS or ethonomy) as the norm of thought of a structured cultural group, i.e. the type of mental operations governing that group's common structure of thought. It corresponds to the normalization of logical systems of thought and of the intellectual systems which constitute the personality of individuals within a given culture. The eidos is thus the set of ideas and presuppositions which serve as common referents for a cultural group.

Bateson (1958) proposes the eidos/ethos distinction in *Naven*, in order to be able to locate, through contact with foreign cultures, the relation which exists between thought structures and pragmatic reality. The general set of intellectual processes typical of a culture contributes to creating common features in the cognitive apprehension of reality. There is a connection between cultural structure and a culture's eidos in the same way as there is a connection between affective functions and its ethos. This presupposes the preliminary study of the fragments of the cognitive structure of the culture. This term may be seen as related to that of 'intellectual system' proposed by Bowen (1978a) or to 'ideology'.

This concept, together with that of ethos, has been both criticized and advocated by its creator (see Bateson, 1972, pp. 47–61). He demonstrates the danger of reifying these concepts or of burdening oneself with abstractions which have close synonyms in everyday parlance and yet he also asserts the impossibility of operating without them if we are to have a chance of analysing concrete phenomena.

(See also COGNITIVE EPISTEMOLOGIES; FAMILY SYSTEMS; LOVE; MIND.)

J.M.

elastic message An expression used by Ausloos (1983) to refer to a type of communication that is frequently encountered in certain families (chaotic families, for example) by which a member of the family – often the father – seems to allow an adolescent to leave the family, whereas in reality he keeps him or her solidly bound to it.

Unlike the DOUBLE BIND, this is not a self-contradictory message, but it is one that is only apparently logical: 'after everything we've done for you, if you're not happy here, then you can go. But don't count on me to give you a penny.' The much more serious message implied here is: 'I am withdrawing all my affection and esteem.' There is no absolute contradiction in the propositions, but it remains difficult to take up the suggestion to leave, since, for want of the practical resources required, the adolescent will not actually be able to adopt this solution. In this type of situation, true breaks are rare and separation is difficult (Ausloos, 1983).

(See also SPLIT DOUBLE BIND.)

P.S.

elementary catastrophes Catastrophe theory (Thom, 1972; Zeeman, 1980) seeks to describe the morphology of the discontinuities which occur in the development of living and non-living processes. The description of these morphologies was made possible by the demonstration of theorems of differential topology (theory of UNIVERSAL UNFOLDING). It has led to the formalization of processes of change of state, both in the so-called 'hard' sciences (physics, chemistry etc.) and in the 'soft' sciences (psychology, sociology,

psychiatry etc.). It has enabled new properties of dynamic systems to be recognized, along with processes of regulation, STRUCTURAL STABILITY and change in living beings. It has made possible a new examination of individual, familial and social processes.

An elementary catastrophe, in Thom's sense, corresponds to the appearance, at a particular moment, t, of a discontinuity of the morphological appearance in the development of a trajectory or a space perceived as continuous before or after the catastrophe. Catastrophe theory makes it possible to envisage the description of the development of complex systems (which have a number of control parameters that is immense, if not indeed infinite), by effecting mathematical simplifications justified by the projection of these multiple parameters into the four coordinates of SPACE–TIME.

We shall thus suppose a system the state of which is described by n internal variables and by p external parameters. This system will possess a potential F, a function of the internal variables, governing the system in the following manner: for every value given to the external variables, the state of the system characterized by the internal variables places itself on a local minimum of the potential function F. The minima of the potential F define the stable local regimes or, alternatively, ATTRACTORS of the system (points or spaces within the control space towards which the system tends asymptotically).

For certain values of the external parameters, several minima of the potential may coexist. There are then two or more attractors in conflict. The slightest perturbation of the external parameters will lead the system to 'jump' abruptly into one of the stable states. This sudden change of behaviour is termed a catastrophe. When there is a situation of conflict between local stable regimes, the system is determined as a function of the 'rule of delay' or 'Maxwell's law' (see FAMILY CATASTROPHES for possible examples in family therapy).

The *rule of delay* stipulates that the system will remain on a stable equilibrium until the final moment where this disappears: the change only occurs when the representative point of the system reaches the bifurcation set. *Maxwell's law* states that the internal variables move at each moment towards a global minimum of the potential and not a local minimum. But both these rules lead to the consideration of 'catastrophe' values, the exceeding of which by the external parameters implies a discontinuous transformation of the internal variables and a change in the morphology of the system.

An elementary catastrophe is characterized by a polynomial function, or singularity, with characteristic algebraico-topological properties. An internal space x and a control space u may thus be distinguished (see the examples of the fold and the cusp below). An elementary catastrophe is characterized by:

- the germ of the function or organizing centre: $f(x,0) - (r, 0)$;
- its UNIVERSAL UNFOLDING (that is to say, the supplement of the set of structurally stable deformations of the germ considered, parametrized by u: let $f(x,u) = 0$ be that set);
- the set of critical points (the derivative $fx(x,u) = 0$, describing the configuration characteristic of the genesis of the form);
- the BIFURCATION set: the image of the critical curve in the control space; crossing that curve may bring about a discontinuity in state.

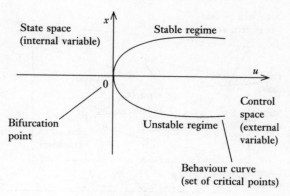

Fold catastrophe.

The term 'catastrophe' signifies a sudden change of behaviour when there are very gradual and continuous perturbations in the external parameters, but also a general type of system in which such changes occur. An elementary catastrophe includes such a structure.

It will thus be possible to describe, from its topological properties:

1 *A control space*, i.e. the space of the values which the external parameters, which are also known as 'control parameters', may take (in which the bifurcation set is located).

2 *A state space*, i.e. the space of values that the internal variables characterizing the state of the system may take (corresponding to the set of critical points).

3 *A response space*, known also as a 'behaviour space' whose points represent the possible states assumed by the system (corresponding to the universal unfolding of the singularity under consideration). These various spaces may be of several dimensions.

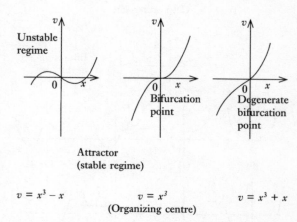

$$v = x^3 - x \qquad v = x^3 \qquad v = x^3 + x$$
(Organizing centre)

Universal unfolding $v = x^3 + ux$ of the singularity $v = x^3$ (fold catastrophe).

The fundamental result of the theory of elementary catastrophes is that, for a number of external parameters less than four, and any number of internal variables, there are only seven forms of elementary catastrophe to which all the forms of discontinuity encountered in natural processes may be reduced by combination. These seven forms are morphologies that are stable and distinct topologically. Moreover, though one may imagine more complicated potentials or increase the number of internal variables, except in very unusual cases the sets of catastrophes will be combinations of these seven sets. The processes of morphogenesis, morphostasis or morpholysis are thus, to a large extent, independent of the nature of the substrate under consideration.

THE SEVEN ELEMENTARY CATASTROPHES

1 The fold
The organizing centre of the function contains a bifurcation point which may either degenerate or give rise to a stable attractor and an unstable attractor in the universal unfolding (see diagram). The control space is of one dimension. The bifurcation set (values of the external parameters for which a discontinuity is produced) is a point. The state space (set of critical points, internal variable of one dimension) is a parabola.

The stratum of the fold corresponds to the RELATIONAL ARCHETYPES of death, birth, beginning and ending etc. Similarly, the archetypes of the boundaries and limits of a system are generated in this way.

2 The cusp
The cusp corresponds to the description of systems whose potential depends on one internal variable and two external parameters. The organizing centre is parabolic in form (a point attractor, structurally stable) (see diagram); the universal unfolding causes two point attractors, which are structurally stable, to appear, one of which is captured by the other depending upon the position of the representative point of the system in the set of critical points. The set of critical points is a cusp (behaviour surface): for example, fight or flight behaviour. The bifurcation set is a parabola: the control surface provides a visual representation of two stable regimes in conflict, namely a bimodal conflict (example: expression of aggression/expression of fear).

113

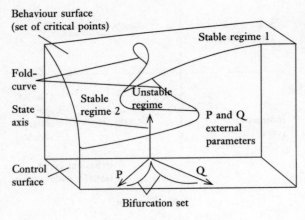

Cusp catastrophe.

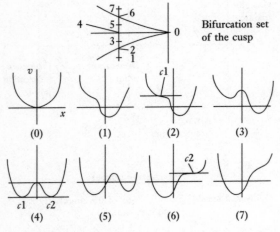

Universal unfolding $v = x^4/4 + ux2 + v$, of the singularity $v = x^4/4$ (cusp catastrophe).

The cusp singularity appears at the point 0 of the bifurcation set and is a semi-cubical parabola (0). The universal unfolding causes two attractors to appear, $c1$ and $c2$, expressions of two stable regimes of the cusp catastrophe. Stages (1)–(2)–(3) and (5)–(6)–(7) describe a *bifurcation catastrophe*, in which one of the attractors is captured by the other. Stages (3) and (5) which converge towards (4) describe a *conflict catastrophe*, in which two attractors have the same minimum potential.

Zeeman (1980) describes the five fundamental properties of the cusp:

1 *Bimodality* (conflict between two forces).
2 *Divergence* (bifurcation between a simple state and the creation of an alternative).
3 *Sudden jumps* (opposition of a slow and a fast dynamic in the process of change).
4 *Inaccessibility* (the zone of the fast dynamic is improbable, unstable).

5 *The hysteresis cycle* (cyclical journey across the cusp, with periodic return to the starting point: it may be observed in autonomous circuits, organs, instincts, symbolic processes and certain symptoms).

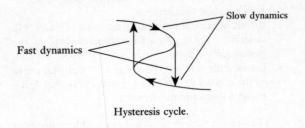

Hysteresis cycle.

The cusp corresponds to the archetypes of emission and capture (predation, identification, reproduction). It defines the non-pathological regulation of a situation of conflict between two opposing tendencies when this situation is realized in space–time (see INTIMACY).

3 The swallow-tail

The potential depends on three external parameters and one internal variable. The behaviour space is of dimension 4; the control space generates a bifurcation set of dimension 3, having precisely the form of a swallow-tail (see diagram); in the view of Petitot-Cocorda (1983), this corresponds to the morphology of the SEMIOTIC SQUARE as defined by Greimas and Courtes (1979). The semantic archetypes would be those of an actant perishing: to spit, to sparkle.

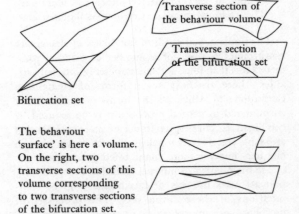

The behaviour 'surface' is here a volume. On the right, two transverse sections of this volume corresponding to two transverse sections of the bifurcation set.

The swallow-tail catastrophe.

4 Butterfly

The potential depends on four external parameters and one internal variable. A catastrophe of this kind might be seem to be at the organizing centre of the archetype of communication: source–message–receiver (see RELATIONAL ARCHETYPES). It brings into play two situations of bimodal conflicts overlapping one with the other. We may thus formalize the catastrophe of biological and psychical child–parent reproduction by differentiating between the processes of identification and parentification (see FAMILY CATASTROPHES).

5 Umbilics

Umbilics depend on two internal variables (singularities of co-rank 2). Their description is much more intricate, since they are not wholly representable within the four dimensions of space–time. We can only approach an understanding of them by means of successive 'sections'.

1 The hyperbolic–umbilic is the organizing centre of the morphology of breakers: the crest of a wave, the appearance of a fashion, the invasion of – if not indeed engulfment by – an ideology.

2 The elliptic–umbilic is the organizing centre of all the organs and instruments which come to a point (thorns, swords, intrusion, jets of liquid etc.).

3 The parabolic–umbilic of co-rank 2 (two internal variables) and of co-dimension 4 (four external parameters) is the most difficult to describe. For Thom (1972), it generates the bi-sexed morphologies (phallus and feminine receptacles), the collision of a point with a surface, the formation of lip, of jaws closing etc.

All these singularities may serve as starting points in the semantic construction of reality (see SEMANTICS OF COMMUNICATION). Other catastrophes of a higher level of complexity seem to defy all formalization, but have without doubt considerable importance in evolutionary processes.

(See also DYNAMIC SYSTEMS; GENERALIZED CATASTROPHES; SYMBOLIC REFERENCE.)

M.G. & J.M.

enmeshed families Transactional style in which there is no clear differentiation between the various family sub-systems. The behaviour of one member spreads contagiously to all the other members of the family instead of remaining confined within the sub-system in which it arose.

Alternating over-protection of and over-investment in a child affects the relationships of the two parents and the child with all the other members of the family. Enmeshment is at one end of a continuum the opposite pole of which is 'disengagement' (see DISENGAGED FAMILIES) (Minuchin, 1974). This style of functioning is common in psychosomatic families (Minuchin et al., 1978; Dare et al., 1990).

(See also BOUNDARIES; COALITION; FAMILY TYPOLOGIES; PSYCHOSOMATIC ILLNESS; PSYCHOSOMATIC MEDICINE.)

P.S.

entropy, negentropy There are at least three approaches to defining entropy: it can be defined within the theoretical framework of thermodynamics, statistical theory and information theory.

THERMODYNAMICS

Entropy is defined in the second law of thermodynamics (Carnot, 1850, in Prigogine and Stengers, 1979, p. 136) which states that in a closed system, the quality of energy degrades in an irreversible way, while its quantity remains constant. Energy is not destroyed, but it becomes unavailable for performing work. It is the irreversible increase in this unavailability of energy for work which is measured by a magnitude known as entropy (from the Greek *entrope* signifying the 'action of turning round, change of disposition, of feelings'), and it therefore represents a qualitatively irreversible change of a system that is, ideally, reversible. 'The world's energy is constant. The world's entropy increases to a maximum' (Clausius, 1865, *Ann. Phys.* 125, 353). Negative (or positive) entropy now refers to the quality of the different possible actions within a system. Instead of describing ideally reversible closed systems, contemporary thermodynamics will, by contrast, seek to take as its point of departure the irreversible phenomena inherent in any dissipation of energy, which lead therefore to the so-called DISSIPATIVE STRUCTURES.

STATISTICAL THEORY

This discovers an equivalence between entropy and disorder. In its degraded form, energy leads the system into a state of maximum disorder. Between disorder and probability there is a mathematical relationship which expresses the fact that an ordered, organized state of a system is highly improbable. Within the framework of statistical theory, the second principle of thermodynamics becomes: 'left to itself, a closed system tends towards a state of maximum disorder, a state of the highest probability which has maximum entropy.'

INFORMATION THEORY

Léon Brillouin established an equivalence between negative entropy (which he termed 'negentropy') and information (Brillouin, 1949, 1950, 1956). The lower the likelihood of its occurrence, the greater the information contributed by a message or an event. This last property is expressed by a relationship formally identical to the one which connects together probability and negative entropy.

These concepts have been used a great deal in the approach to living systems outlined by von Bertalanffy (1981): the living system is an open system; it is the introduction of negative entropy or negentropy which enables it to increase its level of organization and order. It may fight against the disintegration due to an increase in entropy and renew its energy and organization by drawing these things from its environment; it can only subsist and develop with and by exchanges with its milieu.

The environment does not, however, contribute only order. It is a source of perturbations and random events and thus of disorder. This disorder both threatens the living system and enriches its COMPLEXITY. The increase in order contributed by the openness of the system and negentropic exchanges expresses itself in the establishment of increasingly numerous homeostatic responses. A system displaying such organization is, in the extreme case, 'mechanized', rigid, reduced to its homeostatic mechanisms. Bateson stresses this idea that the negentropic contribution reduces the flexibility of a system. He defines this latter as 'uncommitted potentiality for change' (1972, p. 472) and observes that a system reaches a maximum of flexibility when it displays a maximum of entropy.

The flexibilty of a living system and, in particular, of a family system, resides in its capacity to disorganize itself, to reduce the constraints upon it in order to liberate a 'potentiality for change' when all homeostatic responses have proved inadequate. A living system like the family may change its own homeostatic mechanisms and effect second-order changes and is thus capable of interpreting exchanges with the environment either in the sense of a rigidification of its responses and an increase in order and redundancy, or in the sense of disorganization which, in spite of the increasing entropy it brings with it, does not bring about the disintegration of the system, but leads rather to a possibility of its being reorganized at a higher logical level, to increased flexibility and to complexification.

This potential that living systems have for managing the complementarity between order and disorder and taking perturbations and transforming them from within is a property which cannot wholly be described in terms of entropy and negentropy, but requires the introduction of concepts of a higher logical level such as that of SELF-ORGANIZATION or categories (see MULTI-LEVEL HIERARCHIES) which could take account of morphogenetic phenomena of organization and disorganization.

(See also COMMUNICATION THEORY; INFORMATION; ORDER; RANDOMNESS; SOCIAL ORGANIZATION; STOCHASTIC PROCESSES.)

M.G.

epistemology, episteme The epistemology of a person or group is the state of its knowledge as formed into an expressible, communicable doctrine. The episteme corresponds to the procedures by which knowledge is elaborated.

In interactions, the episteme is an operator of access to knowledge, distinct from and complementary to ritual and mythic operators. The episteme has an individual and a collective side to it, each unit of life or survival generating a specific episteme which is irreducible to the episteme of each individual person.

A person's episteme corresponds to his or her capacity to understand a given situation, to reason on the basis of that situation and assess that attitudes to be adopted as a function of that understanding and the reasoning to which it gives rise. The episteme is, thus, the cognitive aptitude, conscious and unconscious, of an individual who is able to make mental connections between apparently unconnected phenomena and establish distinctions from closely related phenomena, on the basis of experiences he/she derives from contact with others, with the world of objects and with him/herself. The episteme is, therefore, the disposition which enables a person to distance him/herself from the effects of RITUALIZATION and MYTH. Whereas the ritual allows events to emerge, the episteme corresponds to the procedures which take account of the whole range of phenomena which show themselves to consciousness or are registered as engrams in the unconscious. Similarly, if ritualized activity enables us to answer the question 'what?' and mythic activity essentially seeks answers to the question 'why?', epistemic activity is focused, first and foremost, on the question 'how?'

Epistemic activity relates to living beings and to things. From the moment he or she comes into the world, the human infant has preconceptions regarding the objects he/she is likely to meet in his/her sensorimotor field: an object must have a certain 'substance' which we cannot pass through; the various parameters which enable us to identify its form must change in an invariant manner. The infant is also expecting to encounter, by way of specific stimuli, living persons, who will take him/her in their arms, and rock, feed and speak to the child. In a complementary way, the parents, grandparents, sisters and brothers and professionals involved with young children have a series of preconceptions about the infant. These preconceptions make the establishment of spatiotemporal schemata possible which give a periodic rhythm to interactions. Bringing the newborn into the presence of his or her close family leads to the confrontation of 'personalities', which necessarily leads to adjustments, experiences, modifications and the maturing of reciprocal attitudes. It seems that the family and social environment usually possesses a capacity for comprehending situations which is superior to the episteme of a lone individual.

The family episteme and the social episteme seem indispensable in the differentiation of the individual and the enriching of bonds. Since the human being lives from infancy in groups, he or she develops a knowledge of the processes which go on in them. Conversely, every family or social organization creates its own culture, its own modes of knowledge and understanding of the surrounding world, as indeed it develops specific representations of itself. In families where members display cognitive disorders and significant mechanisms of reality distortion, recourse to the family group represents a way of developing capacities of personal and interpersonal knowledge.

This socio-epistemic function finds expression in a corpus of images, sentiments and words which correspond to what Jérôme Bruner calls 'popular psychology'. By contrast with what happens in myth, the episteme introduces refutability or correction into the very interior of the fictive system which enables knowledge to be theorized. This proceeds by trial and error, theoretical scenarios being built up as a function of their capacity to be refuted or modified by experience.

Epistemology corresponds to the formalization of the episteme as social doctrine. If the episteme corresponds to the spontaneous forms of intuition and knowing generated by the various levels of familial and social organization, the group epistemology is knowledge formed into a corpus that can be shared communally. A person's epistemology may thus be opposed to his/her family's episteme or that of the groups to which he/she belongs socially. Similarly, the episteme of a society, at a given point, is more or less in harmony with the epistemologies running through or structuring it. We might therefore observe that the epistemology of psychoanalysis or systems theory corresponds, to a greater or lesser degree, with the episteme of a particular human individual or group.

Gregory Bateson sought to modify the study of epistemology. Traditionally, epistemology is the theory of knowledge, the study of the nature of knowing. This is linked, in philosophy, with ontology, the study of being. In other words, epistemology may be regarded as access to a knowledge productive of meaning. Bateson distinguishes between local *epistemologies*, which relate to personal knowledge, and 'capital-E' *Epistemology*, which is the type developed by the great religious, philosophical and scientific systems. There are two great Epistemological traditions and they do not have the same relationship to the testing of facts. There is the tradition of the monotheistic religions, the Marxists and a large part of biologists, for whom a defective or ill-founded Epistemology may have lethal consequences (hence the appearance of the distinction between orthodoxy and heresy) and that of essentially Asiatic religions (Hinduism and Buddhism) which do not seem to regard the question as being of importance. Bateson opts for the former tradition, while believing none the less that a religion worthy of our age – which would have to be based on immanent hypotheses – still remains to be constructed.

A correct epistemology in Bateson's terms has to do with the distinction, suggested by Jung, which allows us to relate *pleroma* (the play of forces, impacts, flows, i.e. the TERRITORY) to *creatura* (where are played out

those 'differences which make a difference', information and description, i.e. the MAP). Far from leading to Cartesian dualism, which separates mind from matter, this distinction allows us to apprehend the two jointly, in a complementary, complex relationship.

(See also COGNITIVE EPISTEMOLOGIES; COMMUNICATION THEORY; CONSTRUCTIVISM; FAMILY MYTHS; THERAPEUTIC ABDUCTION.)

J.M.

equifinality One of the properties of open systems demonstrated by von Bertalanffy in his *General systems theory* (1947). If open systems achieve a stable state, then, unlike the state of equilibrium achieved by isolated systems, this stable state is independent of the initial conditions and the pathways that have led to it. For von Bertalanffy, equifinality is an aspect characteristic of the dynamic order in organismic processes. He cites many examples, including the development of a normal organism from a complete or divided ovum, or from the fusion product of two whole ova, the achievement of a particular final height from different initial heights and after different paces of growth.

The property of equifinality is a *law of unpredictability*, since the present state does not allow one either to deduce the history of the system or to predict its future. At the same time, however, one can predict that it will arrive at its goal. An open system tends towards a stable state, but may begin by taking a direction opposite to that state by phenomena of 'overshoot' and 'false start'.

This tendency towards a characteristic final state and the homeostatic maintenance of that state are based upon circular causal chains and upon mechanisms of regulation. At the basis of the equifinal behaviour of living organisms, social systems or machines built by man lies the concept of FEEDBACK introduced by cybernetics.

The systemic modelling of the family has largely been inspired by von Bertalanffy's thesis, and research in this area has consisted, among other things, in applying concepts like TOTALITY, equifinality and HOMEOSTASIS to therapeutic work with families, together with their interactions with the other systemic levels (physical, biological, psychical, social etc.). This approach is chiefly able to account for stability, for phenomena of self-regulation and equifinality, but it throws no theoretical light on change, which is, however, the essential axis of clinical work. More recent work has thrown into question once again the idea of equifinality in living systems and has enabled us to take into account the capability which these systems possess for adopting new regimes through global restructuring.

For the theorists of SELF-ORGANIZATION, living systems are self-referential systems, the most eloquent example of which is the genetic programme which requires for its reading and execution the products of its own reading and execution. The self-referential system is a system which makes itself. Similarly, in the realm of communication, there exist self-performative utterances. Within this perspective, only artefacts can display goal-directed behaviour because they are input–output systems. Now this input–output schema cannot be applied to the description of living systems, for which the choice of an input is always arbitrary, the input, whatever it may be, always being determined by the rest of the system.

The apparent convergence towards a future order and the teleological behaviour of living systems could be seen as connected with the existence of fixed points and limit cycles equivalent to stable states and oscillations, observed when the process which consists in reinjecting its own production into the system is reiterated to infinity. They study of very simple self-referential systems shows that such a system may possess several fixed points or even several limit cycles and that it is sensitive to initial condition. The fixed point or the limit cycle arrived at depends upon the point of entry chosen.

The apparent equifinality of living systems can thus be explained: with each fixed point may be associated a connected set, which we may term a 'basin of attraction' which is the set of all the entry points and the trajectories which lead to it. In such a basin, equifinality can be verified at every point. This is emphasized by Stengers when she shows that the sense given to the term 'open' led von Bertalanffy to study systems whose openness does not prevent the system having a certain stability. The 'open systems which function in a stable manner . . . are precisely those whose equifinal state resembles the equilibrium state. The openness of the systems does not prevent our understanding them in a way that is similar to how we understand isolated systems.'

The existence of several basins of attraction, the 'multi-stationarity' of self-referential systems, accounts for the stability of living organisms in certain conditions, as well as their capacity to adopt new states, and to effect a transition from one fixed state to another, as soon as one takes into account the field of non-equilibrium states with its bifurcations, amplifications of singularities and symmetry-breaking.

(See also ATTRACTORS; CIRCULARITY; DYNAMIC SYSTEMS; FAMILY SELF-REFERENTIALITY; FAMILY SYSTEMS; GENERAL SYSTEMS THEORY; HOLISM; LINEARITY; OSCILLATORS; PHASE SPACE; SENSITIVITY TO INITIAL CONDITIONS; STRUCTURAL STABILITY; UNIVERSAL UNFOLDING.)

M.G.

ethical issues in family therapy The essence of all family or systemic therapies is an understanding of people in terms of their relationships with others: an individual is always considered as a member of a social group, usually, but not necessarily, the family. The family, in turn, is considered as a system in interaction with other systems, such as the neighbourhood, school, work and health and welfare agencies. In practice, however, the focus of the therapist's interventions has typically been on the family group, although, it must be said, family therapists seem to be well aware of variations in the definition and understanding of what constitutes 'the family'. A number of ethical issues are raised when seeing people through this lens.

Some critics (e.g. Reiger, 1981; Kingston, 1987) have argued that family therapy has over-focused on the family and that historical and sociological influences have too easily been ignored. Thus families can inappropriately or disproportionately 'take the blame' for behaviours which are caused or strongly influenced by wider social and structural factors: inner-city delinquency is one example. The French writer, Jacques Donzelot in his book *The policing of families* (1980) characterizes professionals who intervene in families in order to educate them or to repair faults as, 'technicians in human relations'. He argues that interventions into families construct the entities they are supposed to treat. In other words, family therapy does not just treat families, it also constructs families and family problems, so that therapists see dysfunctional families with problems in their structure and hierarchy, families with communication problems, psychosomatic families, and so on. What family therapists fail to see is the impact of social disadvantage and exploitation: poverty, class, gender, age, race and disability. An ethical objection to family therapy itself is, therefore, that it colludes with such oppression rather than confronts it. At its worst, family therapy can be seen as an instrument of state control, both holding families responsible for creating problems and for caring for its weaker members (Carpenter, 1992).

A systemic perspective, in itself, brings an awareness of the consequences of change which might be overlooked or ignored by an individual therapist. Thus, Papp (1983) sees change within a system as being not a solution to a single problem (removing the symptom or freeing the oppressed) but rather as a dilemma to be solved. 'Change extracts a price and raises the question as to what the repercussions will be for the rest of the system. To ignore these repercussions is to act out of . . . ecological ignorance' (Papp, 1983, p. 11).

Therefore, although it is usually individuals who are referred, family therapists typically assume that their 'client' is the family as a whole. An individual's symptoms or problems are seen as evidence of a family system in difficulty, a system that is not adapting to stress from within or from external pressures. The solution lies not in simply curing the presenting problem of the individual but in helping the family members to find new patterns of meaning and behaviour, with the most positive outcomes for all. Thus, many family therapists consider it a professional ethic that they should act in order to promote the good of the family as a whole, and not necessarily in the primary interests of the individual who was referred. This might be contrasted with the requirement on, for example, a social worker to act as an advocate for his or her client if in conflict with his or her family. It is to take up a moral position, because there is no requirement that the therapist treat all family members equally. A family therapist might, therefore, insist that all members of the family attend for therapy and withhold treatment if they do not. He or she might allow a family member to remain distressed rather than attempt to rescue them, so that the other members, rather than the therapist, accept responsibility for helping resolve the problem. He or she might use techniques which intensify the effects of the symptom or, in the structural model, 'unbalance' the family system by taking sides, supporting one member and attacking another. Such actions would be justified on the grounds that, in the long term at least, the best interests of the family are in the best interests of the individual, and vice versa. On the other hand, the autonomy of the individual and his or her rights to privacy and self-determination are apparently violated.

An emphasis on individual autonomy and rights within families is, of course, a Western position. It is important to recognize that in many other cultures the rights of the individual come second to those of the family group, an ethic which many Western therapists find difficult to accept. This example highlights the fact that family therapists inevitably work with a set of beliefs and values about the family, although these are rarely made explicit.

Feminist therapists have argued that these models of the family, and hence of therapy, have often been blatantly sexist. For example, Goldner (1985) pointed out that many family therapists convey confusing messages to 'over-involved' mothers, asking them on the one hand to 'step aside' and on the other requiring them to ensure that the family comes to, and stays in, therapy. An assumption about the respective roles of men and women in parenting – that they should both be involved – leads to women's further oppression.

Feminist family therapists (e.g. Perelberg and Miller, 1990) have challenged their colleagues to recognize the structured inequalities in family life and to confront oppression based on gender. In so doing, they have raised questions about the moral concerns of therapy and highlighted the values of therapists and the potential abuse of power. The feminist critique of family therapy strongly contests the notion that the therapist can somehow be value free, or 'neutral'. The Milan Approach advocates that therapeutic neutrality is maintained towards different points of view, different members of the system, and even towards the outcome of the therapy itself. The therapist's stance is, instead, one of 'curiosity' (Cecchin, 1987). However, a neutral position in the face of inequality and injustice is literally amoral – without morals. As MacKinnon and Miller (1987) contend, the position of neutrality ignores issues of power in families, and ignoring the abuse of power is in effect to condone it. If, for example, a therapist does not tackle the matter of violence in a family, the message he or she conveys is that its use is acceptable. Many would agree that this was unethical.

The same ethical danger arises from the use by family therapists of Maturana and Varela's (1988) contention that instructive interaction is impossible since an organism's response is structurally determined. As Jones (1993) observes, this has been interpreted by some to mean that the therapist has no responsibility for the family's response, and even that all action and intentionality on the therapist's part is futile. Jones points out, 'this then leads to an amoral stance where the therapist feels free to do anything whatsoever – or nothing – on the assumption that it is up to the client to make what they will of the interaction' (1993, p. 148).

In contrast to this radical constructivist position, others have considered that therapists can all too easily influence their clients and that the process of therapy can consist of the imposition of the therapist's own value system, and worse. Jeffrey Masson, discussing the abuse of power in family therapy claims, 'What is silently apparent in psychotherapy in general is made loudly clear here. The therapist knows best and in family therapy can abandon any pretence of modesty and boldly give orders' (Masson, 1988, p. 251). While family therapists might object that Masson is merely caricaturing the more directive approaches (e.g. structural and strategic family therapy), the question of power is not so easily avoided, particularly because power is exercised through the way in which the therapeutic relationship is structured. Thus, for a client to receive a service, he or she has to accept the therapist's definition of the problem, to accommodate to the therapist's particular way of looking at things and to accept his or her way of working. Jones notes that although a number of writers have consciously attempted to 'shed' power, for example by using the notion of 'co-construction', a power differential exists if only because one is seeking help from the other and, 'The therapist is less likely to abuse this power if she acknowledges its presence than if she believes her own propaganda' (Jones, 1993, pp. 155–6). It still seems uncommon, for example, for clients to be offered choices about their therapist(s) and ways of working, including the use of video and screens. (To be asked to 'consent' is different from being given a free choice.) Similarly, clients rarely seem to be given information about the range of therapeutic approaches available and asked for their preference.

While restricting choice is not necessarily unethical,

effectively excluding clients because they do not conform to strict rules violates the principles on which public services are supposed to be based. Further, as Walrond-Skinner has remarked, the 'rules' for the conduct of family therapy, the more public atmosphere associated with video cameras and screens, 'may provide a very strong magnetic pull on the narcissistic tendencies of the therapist. Choice of venue, length of treatment, the use of "demonstration interviews" with expert therapists and well-known consultants may all be dictated more by the narcissism of the therapist than the needs of the family' (Walrond-Skinner, 1987, p. 6). A clear recognition that therapy must first and foremost meet the needs of clients is essential for ethical practice.

The methods of strategic therapy, and in particular the use of paradox, have been open to ethical debate on the grounds that they involve trickery and manipulation (e.g. Whan, 1983). Watzlawick et al. (1974, p. xv) attempted to counter this charge by claiming that our behaviour in the presence of another cannot avoid being a communication about the relationship and cannot fail therefore to influence that person. However, as Collier, a philosopher, points out, this is to confuse influence with manipulation: manipulation occurs when a person's actions are controlled by getting them to misunderstand the situation. Manipulation violates what moral philosophers call 'autonomy', the power to base one's actions on a reasonable awareness of oneself and others, something which most of us value. 'The harm involved in the violation of someone's autonomy', concludes Collier, 'is not merely either the deception or consequences of it adverse to their interests, but that the agent is compromised in their actions by a false belief about something close to their heart' (Collier, 1987, p. 124).

Lindley (1987), another philosopher, observes that strategic therapy covers a large range of interventions, many of which do not violate autonomy. For example, duplicity is not intrinsic to the paradoxical injunction to an insomniac to perform complicated boring tasks at night, since there is no reason in principle why the client could not think up and adopt this solution him or herself. Instructing clients to carry problematic behaviour to extremes can, Lindley argues, be seen as a form of communication akin to the use of metaphor which, while not superficially true, carries a clear communication at a deeper level pointing out the absurdity of the client's position.

On the other hand, Lindley considers that deceptions, such as lying to the family about the views of the supervision team, are difficult to justify. He quotes a published case study where the therapist used a strategy in which whenever the client put herself down, the therapist would criticize her a little more, irrespective of whether he thought the criticism reasonable. When challenged by the client, the therapist stated that she could depend on his honesty. Lindley contends that this was a serious violation of her autonomy: although the goal of therapy was achieved, 'imagine how she would react to the discovery that he had been deceiving her all along' (Lindley, 1987, p. 117).

Treacher (1987) remarks on the use of the analogy of the battlefield in many descriptions of strategic, including early Milan, approaches. If therapy is seen as a power struggle, then all manner of unethical practices can be justified. Further, even if the problem is removed, the family is not allowed to gain any understanding or control over the processes which caused it in the first place. It seems reasonable to ask whose needs are being met: the family's, or the therapist's needs for power and control.

In family therapy, the grosser forms of self-gratification by therapists, including sexual exploitation, which are evident in individual psychotherapy (Masson, 1988) are less easily available. However, Walrond-Skinner (1987) warns that the therapist's counter-transference may lead him or her to exploit the family or its individual members at an unconscious level. 'The need to be helpful, avoid hostility, be nurturant, controlling, potent, act as a rescuer . . . may all lead the therapist to collude with pressures . . . to act out sexual attraction or punitive impulses' (1987, p. 2). This consideration raises the question of whether family therapists should have to undertake work during training on understanding their own families of origin and procreation. Such a requirement has been proposed in draft guidelines for the training criteria for qualified family therapists in the UK, which further propose that candidates for qualification demonstrate that they can use various forms of supervision to 'develop awareness of the personal contribution their unique combination of values, experience and skills enables them to make to the therapeutic process' (CRED [Association for Family Therapy, UK] 1992).

The development of training criteria is one approach to promoting an awareness of ethical issues in family therapy. Thus, the CRED guidelines also propose that candidates should have an appreciation of the social, political and institutional context of families and family therapy. They also require adherence to the (UK) Association for Family Therapy's code of ethics. However, as they stand, the guidelines do not insist on a study of ethical issues per se.

Ethical codes have been developed as part of the professionalization of family therapy. As Zygmond and Boorhem (1989) comment in relation to the Code of Ethical Principles of the American Association of Marital and Family Therapy (AAMFT), codes can set rules about professional conduct (e.g. rules about confidentiality and not claiming competence when it is not possessed) and advance general principles (e.g. to promote the welfare of families and individuals), but they are not much help in resolving the kinds of ethical dilemmas posed above. They cannot say what should be done when, for example, the needs of family members conflict. Nevertheless, codes of ethics may have some value in setting standards of professional conduct, particularly for family therapists who do not have a basic professional affiliation (e.g. as a nurse or psychologist) and in protecting clients from unethical practice. (According to Engelberg and Symansky, 1989, breaches of confidentiality are common causes or professional liability claims against family therapists in the USA.)

Zygmond and Boorhem (1989) have proposed a framework for 'ethical decision making' in family therapy. This considers ethical rules (codes) and principles (e.g. autonomy, fidelity and justice) and proposes that ethical principles must be upheld unless they are mutually conflicting; for example, a promise to keep confidentiality (fidelity) versus protecting an abused child (justice). If principles are in conflict, Zygmond and Boorhem recommend recourse to asking first whether the proposed action can be 'unambiguously applied to all similar cases', i.e. 'If I or my family was in a similar situation, would I want my therapist to make this decision?' Secondly, they advise taking the action which produces the least amount of avoidable harm to all concerned, even if this limits possible benefits. The answers to these questions are, of course, matters of judgement, and judgements are made on the basis of beliefs and values. The task, therefore, is perhaps for family therapists to be much more explicit about their beliefs and values and to be prepared to discuss these both with families and with society in general.

(See also CONSTRUCTIVISM; ETHICS; FAMILY SYSTEMS; GENDER; LAW; PARADOXES; STRATEGIC THERAPY; STRUCTURAL FAMILY THERAPY; SYSTEMIC WORK WITH INDIVIDUALS.)

J.C.

ethics In the contextual model, the concept of ethics does not refer to a definition of good and evil or a series of moral rules, but the necessity of preserving the equilibrium of intrafamilial exchanges according to a law of reciprocity, taking into account the interests of the group and each of its members (Boszormenyi-Nagy and Spark, 1973). It is based on realities of an existential nature and is connected to the notion of survival, somewhat in the manner of a law of the jungle. The concept of ethics is closely connected to the notion of justice. An attempt to resolve family difficulties is termed ethically valid or invalid, depending upon whether it obeys or is subject to the principle of FAIRNESS.

(See also ETHICAL ISSUES IN FAMILY THERAPY; LAW; LEDGER; LOYALTY; TRUST.)

A.L.

ethnicity in family therapy A core definition of culture has been offered by Leighton (1981) as follows: 'Culture consists in the knowledge, values, perceptions and practices that are (1) shared among the members of a given society; (2) passed on from one generation to the next.' The components of a culture are interrelated in such a way as to constitute a whole that governs the functioning of the pertinent society. Culture directs the behaviour of individuals within the group, enabling the group to survive.

In cross-cultural family work we need to address the areas of tension at the interface between the therapist and the family from a different ethno-cultural and racial background. These will be:

- differences in race;
- differences in symbolic and belief system;
- differences in family structure and organization;
- differences in language and communication.

RACE

Here one needs to consider both conscious and unconscious racial attitudes and also the fact that different racial tensions exist between different racial groups. For example, the historical experience of slavery has led to attitudes based on the master/slave dynamic in the tensions between American whites and blacks. Over generations this has led to a lowering of self-esteem in vulnerable clinical populations, with the influence of negative racial stereotypes perpetuating feelings of learned helplessness and uselessness. It is important that this paradigm, based on the Afro-Carribean experience, not be applied indiscriminately to all non-white groups, e.g. Chinese and Vietnamese. It is important, however, to be aware of power disparities between the therapist and the client family.

DIFFERENCES IN SYMBOLIC AND BELIEF SYSTEMS

The cultural and religious traditions of a group organize the perception of experience, give shape and form to myths and beliefs, and determine the limits of appropriate behaviour and family roles. The symbolic belief system of the group also provides explanations of health and illness, definitions of normality and deviance, and guidelines for how to be acceptably deviant within a recognized pattern (Lau, 1990).

Value orientations that are culturally determined organize the individual's view of the proper relationship between self and context. Differences in basic assumptions between the Western and Eastern views of self (Lin, 1986; Rao, 1986) are as follows; the Western view emphasizes independence, self-sufficiency, assertiveness and competition, clear and direct verbal communication, while the Eastern view emphasizes interdependence, harmony and cooperation in relationships, with more emphasis on non-verbal and indirect communication through the use of shared symbols.

Embedded in the system of cultural meanings for traditional societies is the central role of religious beliefs. Family therapy and the understanding of family systems have developed largely in an areligious, secular context, with the erosion of the authority of the Church in contemporary Western society. In religious communities, the authority of religious teaching cannot be discounted by the family therapist. For example, adherence to the principles of the Halacha is a central tenet of individual and family life for Orthodox Jewish communities, and the Rabbi wields considerable personal and community authority. Similar powers are invested in the Imam by Muslim communities.

FAMILY STRUCTURE AND ORGANIZATION

Value orientations determine structural relationships; hence family organization following the ideal of the pre-eminence of the group would be along extended family lines, with a primary emphasis on connectedness. For example, in the traditional Chinese family an important organizing principle is filial piety, where loyalties to parents take precedence over loyalties to spouse and children. Families will need to be located along a continuum between the traditional, hierachical family with adherence to extended family values and the Western, contemporary, egalitarian family.

In the non-Western European family there are important differences in the construction of 'family' as a concept and the role of the individual within the family. The importance given to interdependence and the need to preserve harmonious family relationships has given rise to structures that do not conform to Western European norms; for example, extended family groups within the same household. Life-cycle transitions are managed in the context of different rules with regard to authority, continuity and interdependence. In the traditional Asian or Oriental family, relationships are hierachical between the sexes as well as between the generations. Authority is invested in grandparents or the most senior male members; elder siblings have authority over younger siblings, and responsibility for their welfare. The presence of the aged provides continuity and a link between the generations. Where kinship systems are highly structured, kinship terms delineate the individual's place in the family, including duties and expected obligations, within a system of mutual dependence. Where religion is an important organizing factor, as in Islam, strict religious guidelines may exist for sex-role behaviour including the ideal of segregation of the sexes, particularly after puberty.

DIFFERENCES IN IDEAS OF INDIVIDUAL AND FAMILY COMPETENCE

Current definitions of family competence used in research into family functioning, e.g. the Timberlawn study of working-class black families in America, are based on nuclear family norms. They do not include, for example, the concept of a network of reciprocal obligations characteristic of ethnic groups with highly structured kinship systems (Lau, 1988). It is important to clarify ethnocultural differences in competence for individuals throughout the life-cycle, as this has implications for expected stage-specific family tasks.

For example, the competent adolescent from a traditional, non-Western European extended family background is one who will have been prepared to meet his/her obligations to the family, which often include the obligation to look after one's parents and younger siblings. Within the family he/she will have been socialized to know the importance of being dependable, and to be expected to have a behavioural repertoire which includes respectful behaviour to one's elders, and strategies for the diffusion of tension and avoidance of conflict within the immediate and wider family.

Other issues to do with individuation and separation, as well as distance regulation, will be negotiated differently. Preparation for leaving home is an important difference for adolescents from different ethnocultural groups (Lau, 1990). There are also differences in stage-specific family tasks. For example, where arranged marriage is an expected event in the family life-cycle, the wider family has to provide a facilitating environment for stabilizing and nurturing the relationship between the couple, particularly in the first year of marriage. There are also gender differences. The new wife moving into a joint household must invest emotionally in the relationship with her mother-in-law and sisters-in-law, and work out power relations within the female network. Competence in these tasks is vital towards ensuring her survival in the new family.

The Afro-Carribean extended family functions by different rules compared to the extended families of Asia and Africa. Functional relationships are not necessarily defined by formal kinship (Littlewood and Lipsedge, 1982; Lau, 1990). Contemporary studies of the American black family find a heterogeneity of structure and function. Particular strengths have included role adaptability, strong kinship bonds, a strong religious orientation and church affiliation, and strong orientation towards work and achievement (Hill, 1972).

LANGUAGE AND COMMUNICATION

Proper assessment of family needs, vulnerabilities and strengths is difficult where language presents a barrier to communication. If an interpreter is used, he/she needs to be familiar with the therapist's theoretical and conceptual base otherwise important information may be screened out. There may also be differences in expected modes of communication. The Western-trained therapist's expectation of clear, direct verbal communication and confrontation is often at variance with styles where direct communication and confrontation are avoided because this may lead to loss of face within the family group (McGoldrick et al., 1982). Therapeutic goals may differ. A preferred direction of change for families from traditional hierarchical backgrounds will be towards a process of integration, rather than towards differentiation and increasing separation of the individual from his/her family (Tamura and Lau, 1992). This has potential for conflict for therapists and their supervisors from a different value orientation. Acceptance of these differences in norms implies the use of different therapeutic strategies, with different aims; for example, diffusing and containing conflict rather than amplifying it.

A therapist from a similar ethnocultural background may well find it easier to engage the family, and be more prepared to take on the cultural material in a way that facilitates therapeutic change. Weiselberg (1992) describes work with Orthodox Jewish families in which the therapist was able to engage with the family in trading religious metaphors. Lau (1988) has described work with a Chinese family using a cultural ritual that facilitated commitment to change.

Conflicts in mixed marriages

Intergenerational conflict in families with a mixed racial/cultural background may be compounded by the child's sense of confusion regarding racial or ethnic identity. Where the parental sub-system has a poorly maintained boundary, with ineffective emotional containment, the child or young person's frustrations may give rise to a wide range of deviant behavioural disturbances. There may be parental conflict over which family cultural traditions, rituals, values and loyalties are more important; cultural differences in the expected roles of spouses, including kinship obligations, may not have been resolved. The child or young person may end up being triangulated in the parental conflict, or expected to make up for the losses incurred by the parent of ethnic origin in the process of immigration. The young person will end up being unable to resolve the racial diversity in his/her background; it becomes a source of adversity instead of strength.

Guidelines for family assessment

1 What belief systems and values (including religion) influence role expectations, define and set limits of appropriate behaviour?
2 What are the structures relevant to authority and decision-making in the family? Are there formal kinship patterns? What key relationships have important supportive and homeostatic functions? What is the relevant family network to be worked with?
3 What are the stage-specific developmental tasks at different life-cycle stages for this family? How does this family negotiate life-cycle transitions, continuities and discontinuities with the past and present? What are traditional solutions and mechanisms used for conflict resolution and to what extent does the family use them?
4 How is the living unit organized to enable essential tasks to be performed?
5 What activities, including family rituals of ethnocultural and religious origin, maintain and support structural relationships? What traditional networks supported and enabled traditional family tasks to be performed? Which of these networks or rituals have been lost?
6 What are significant stresses and losses arising from the family's own experience, from the environment of origin, or from adaptation to host country? What racial or cultural factors confer advantage or disadvantage in the host culture?
7 The clinical hypothesis must take into account the meaning and function of the disturbance for the family, the cultural group, and the wider community.
8 Therapeutic interventions must engage the authority structure in the family and be congruent with the family's world view. For example, it is important to enable the identified client and his/her family to work out the right balance of separation/attachment consistent with family and societal norms. It is often helpful to reframe the problem within a developmental context, in order to make it more manageable.

Existing therapeutic techniques and methods can be successfully used in work with ethnic minority families, providing the therapist is sensitive to the importance of respecting cultural rules and prepared to modify his/her clinical approach. Ethnic minority families respond more readily to therapists who are directive and assertive (Tseng, 1975; Jung, 1984; Rao, 1986; Tamura and Lau, 1992) as this conforms to traditional expectations of the learning process. Structural family therapy with its emphasis on problem solving in the present has been described as highly successful with Chinese families in the USA (Jung, 1984), where the therapist works on modifying communication patterns while supporting parents' traditional beliefs. Gestalt-type work and sculpting was described by Lau (1988), including the use of metaphors and family rituals (Scheff, 1979; Levick et al., 1981; Peseschkian, 1986). Wolin and Bennett (1984) link the importance of maintenance of family ritual to the continuity of family heritage. All these strategies attempt to mobilize strengths and assert competencies within an ethnocultural context.

A.L.

ethological typologies of the family See FAMILY ETHOLOGY.

ethology Ethology is the comparative biological study of behaviour, as a function of species, individuals and the ecosystems in which they live, survive and evolve. The term ethology, created in 1854 by Geoffroy Saint Hilaire, was first used in its present sense in 1910 by Heinroth (Konrad Lorenz's mentor). It has been popularized by the so-called objectivist school (Lorenz, Tinbergen) which stands in opposition to the empiricist school (Lehrmann, Hinde). Ethology is distinct from behaviourism to the extent that it is a semiotic biology of behaviour based on the comparative study of individuals and species and the analysis of the semantic contexts in which they live and survive. Ethology is concerned with the differences in behaviour which, as much as morphological differences, characterize a species. But it goes further and shows in what way morphological and behavioural differences influence each other reciprocally.

Ethological thought has influenced psychoanalytic thinking (Freud, Hermann, Spitz, Bowlby). It was at the centre of Gregory Bateson's preoccupations and the innovations he introduced. More recently, various schools of human ethology have appeared (Eibl-Eibesfeldt, Montagner, Cyrulinck, Gervet, Vidal, Garrigues, Miermont etc.).

The comparative method is based upon bringing analogical and homological characteristics into relation.

HOMOLOGICAL PROPERTY OF A CHARACTERISTIC

A characteristic is homologous with another characteristic if it is related to it by virtue of dependence on a common ancestral characteristic. In the comparative study of species or the cultural evolution of symbols, this property stands opposed to analogy. An example of a homological series is the upper member of the mammal, which is a flipper in the whale, a wing in the bat, a foot and a hoof in the horse, an arm/forearm and prehensile hand in man. Though the functioning of the computer is profoundly analogous to human thinking, it is practically devoid of any homological trajectory. The numerical or digital computer is deeply analogous to the ten fingers of the hand (these latter having served in many cultures as a system of counting and calculation). However, the nature of its components has no connection whatever with the distal extremity of the upper member of a tetrapod.

ANALOGICAL PROPERTY OF A CHARACTERISTIC

A characteristic is analogical across two or more species when it possesses an isomorphic functional structure (visual system, attachment behaviour etc.). It is based on the phenomenon of convergent evolution. In a given context, selection pressure will produce similar functional systems in species which may possibly be very dissimilar. Examples of analogical series include, for flight, the wing of the butterfly, the fly, the bat, the aeroplane, the microlight; for the analysis of light, the eye of the insect or of man, the lens of the camera, the microscope or the telescope.

It is not unknown for convergent evolution to appear in the case of two homologous species. The resemblance between them is then very great and may lead to their being confused (from a systemic point of view, this phenomenon is reminiscent of the equifinality of certain open systems).

DEGREE OF RELATEDNESS

The degree of relatedness between two species depends upon: (a) the relationship between the number of homologous and the number of analogous characteristics; (b) the relative speed of transformation of the characteristics within each of the groups under comparison. The family may be studied from this angle. Comparative work between species or within the human 'meta-species' is only of interest if it combines this dual – homological and analogical – aspect of systems of behaviour.

(See also ATTACHMENT BEHAVIOUR; BECOMING ACCUSTOMED; DOMESTICATION; FAMILY ETHOLOGY; HABITUATION; IMPRINTING; INSTINCT; LEARNING; PSEUDO–SPECIATION; RELATIONAL ARCHETYPES; RITUALIZATION; SEXED BEHAVIOUR.)

J.M.

ethos, ethonomy Ethos (or ethonomy) is defined by Bateson, by opposition to EIDOS, as a norm of behaviour of a given cultural group. It consists of a system of attitudes possessing normative value through the organization of the instincts and emotions of individuals. The ethos of a given culture is arrived at by abstraction from the total mass of its institutions. The content of affective life may change from culture to culture, but the underlying sub-systems – or ethos – may be repeated continually. An ethos is manifested through the valorization of certain affective dispositions and typical emotional emphases, based upon a grid of emotions that are permitted, recommended, tolerated or forbidden for a given human group.

The study of the ethos of a culture is a necessary preliminary to the study of its pragmatic functions. What is involved is an 'obscure emotional content', yet one which reflects a state of mind, the general tone of a community. A group of intellectuals may speak with mild cynicism, impose a relaxed style or, by contrast, assume a serious tone. Austerity or humility, pride and theatricality, boastfulness etc. are all so many psycho-affective attitudes which may be made obligatory or prohibited. The differential organization of these into a system determines the ethos of a given group. The traditional African ethonomy of the mother–child relationship is based on bodily closeness; the mother's breast is the child's first 'plaything'. By contrast, the Western ethonomy is based on separation, on apartness, on the sexualization of all bodily contact.

Misunderstandings may therefore exist between one cultural ethos and another. Bateson thus distinguishes between the ethos of masculine and feminine identities, which is variable in different civilizations and countries. And we may even find the same ethos across different cultures. 'Ethos' is thus close to the concept of 'emotional system' proposed by Bowen (1978a). Bateson (1958) has shown how the ethos of a culture may (or may not) promote schismogenetic mechanisms (which are absent in Bali, for example), even though such an explanation, based on the 'ethological' model, is incomplete.

(See also MODE–IDENTIFYING SIGNALS.)

J.M.

evolutionary survival unit By definition, an evolutionary survival unit, or unit of evolution, can only be appreciated from the relationship an organism maintains with its environment (Bateson, 1972). Now, the environment is itself made up, in large measure, of populations of heterogeneous organisms, as well as populations of similar organisms (the phenomenon of co-evolution).

The family and social organizations may be viewed as fundamental survival units for the human being. In coping with conditions which make its situation precarious, the survival unit runs the risk of rendering any change impossible. For a change to occur, it is necessary to carry out re-framings, in order to discover wider units of mind.

KIN SELECTION

In many animal species, we find a reduction in the reproduction of certain individuals with a view to promoting the reproduction of other related individuals. Hence the hypothesis, already advanced by Darwin, that natural selection might operate not at the level of a single organism, but at the level of the family.

This theory was revived by Hamilton et al. (in Wilson, 1975). Networks of individuals linked by kinship cooperate within a given population. They deploy

altruistic behaviour towards one another and this behaviour increases their degree of genetic adaptiveness as a whole, even if the behaviour reduces the adaptiveness of some members of the group. Wilson (1975) has ventured the hypothesis that there are variable units of selection: individual selection, kin selection, inter-demic selection (groups made up of several kin units). He sees selection mechanisms as operating on units such as these (increase or diminution in the number of certain units as a function of their adaptability). Without having to subscribe here to all the theses of sociobiology, we may advance the view that man, as a pseudo-species, is called upon to adapt himself biologically, within certain limits, to the constraints of his own culture. It is, moreover, not illegitimate to suppose that some altruistic or sacrificial behaviour within a family (refusal, on the part of the index patient, to marry or take a particular job) have a survival value for the group and are, to some extent, underpinned by biological factors. The essence of therapeutic action consists, not in denying the importance of biological regulation, but in playing on the learning capacities of the family group which is confronted with equally critical survival alternatives.

SURVIVAL UNIT

We may take it that a minimum survival unit may be made up of a mother and her child, while the biological father is not present in such a unit. We may, more fundamentally, define the nuclear family as the minimum unit of survival for a given individual. Now, such a unit can only evolve in interaction with other broader units.

Reduced to its survival function alone, a unit is a minimum system of non-change, taking a static or pseudo-static form; its boundaries are rigidified, its semantic functions disappear, its relationships become petrified or are reduced to their 'institutional' canvas. Conflicts appear when there is too poor a fit between a SEMANTIC UNIT OF MIND (which has remained localized, for example, in the grandparents or the collateral families) and an evolutionary survival unit left to its own devices. When a survival unit is threatened in its existence, it may be incapable by itself of finding the conditions for its development and change. It is necessary for the intervenors or therapists to try to define which group UNIT OF CHANGE will make it possible to re-establish a fit between units of mind and evolutionary survival units.

J.M.

exploitation The notion of exploitation, in its broad sense, covers the idea of a disequilibrium in mutual exchanges within the family. Boszormenyi-Nagy and

Spark (1973) have described many forms of exploitation. In pathological PARENTIFICATION, for example, the parents may keep down a child by asking more than is due of him or her or by entrusting a function of responsibility to the child. A family member may also be exploited by not being allowed, as an effect of 'a non-receptive attitude', to repay his/her debt. The concept also covers a structural form of exploitation in which a relationship develops without balanced mutual retribution, thus penalizing both parties.

(See also DELEGATION; ETHICS; LEDGER; MERIT; PARANOIA; TRUST.)

A.L.

extended family   See NUCLEAR FAMILY, EXTENDED FAMILY.

extended kinship networks   See NETWORKS.

eye contact   See GAZE, EYE CONTACT AND POSTURO-GESTURAL EXCHANGES.

F

failure See ADMISSION OF IMPOTENCE, RECOGNITION OF FAILURE.

fairness According to Boszormenyi-Nagy and Spark (1973, p. 54), fairness 'can be regarded as a web of invisible fibres running through the length and width of the history of family relationships, holding the system in social equilibrium throughout phases of physical togetherness and separation.' The principle of fairness, which is multi-personal and systemic, but above all ethical in nature, and which is based on existential imperatives, governs interpersonal exchanges within the family in accordance with the norm of reciprocity, a 'mechanism involved in the maintenance of any stable social system' (Boszormenyi-Nagy and Spark, 1973, p. 56). Respecting this principle is a precondition for establishing a climate of TRUST within a group or family.

(See also CHILD ABUSE; DELINQUENT ACTING OUT; ETHICS; INCEST; LAW; LEDGER; SYSTEMIC MODELLING AND INTERVENTION; VIOLENCE.)

A.L.

false self See TRUE SELF, FALSE SELF.

families of origin This expression refers to the respective families in which the father and mother of the NUCLEAR FAMILY (made up of parents and their children) were themselves born and brought up. Every individual human being possesses a family of origin, whether or not he is married or has children (and is therefore integrated into a current nuclear family or into a non-officialized lineage). In other words, every person was, in the last analysis, born in a particular family.

In some cases, however, even this obvious rule is not confirmed by the facts. This occurs not so much where children have clearly been abandoned, since they can be put out relatively easily to adoption, but in cases where children have been received into a great number of foster families in succession and the parents have only put in a very intermittent appearance. We then see conflict situations arising between the various protagonists: the authorities responsible for fostering (the social services, the foster family), the natural parents, and the therapists and social workers who are called in to assist in compensating for this lack of emotional support. This state of affairs gives rise to what Bridgman (1986) has called 'multiple parenthood families' and we may acknowledge, as Bridgman does, that, in this situation, inter-institutional and interfamilial conflicts cannot be avoided and must therefore, rather, be managed.

P.S. & J.M.

familiodrama in training and therapy 'Familiodrama' can be defined as the process of staging the family dynamics. It is based on the amplification of events of a serious or violent nature within a framework in which relational interplay wins out over both direct 'acting out' or the achievement of awareness of unconscious phantasies (access to unconscious phantasies being impossible in this case through the method of FREE ASSOCIATION). The therapist is then 'the producer of the family drama' (Andolfi and Angelo, 1980).

Familiodrama might be seen as generating the processes that occur in PSYCHODRAMA and SOCIODRAMA, as these latter have been brought out by the work of Moreno (1934–70). In familiodrama, there is a dynamic oscillation between individual identity and social identity, between the psychic dimension and the collective belief, of which the family ecosystem is the transmitter–receiver: (a) differentiation of the individual psyche on the basis of family processes; (b) structuring of collective ideologies (EIDOS), pragmatic organization of emotional systems (ETHOS) on the basis of that psychic differentiation.

The dynamic of family life-cycles is based on the adoption of roles – and changes in those roles – which accord more or less well with the real age of each person involved. The capacity to enter into role-playing games makes it possible to mobilize the members of a family and to change points of view not in a purely intellectual way, but through active emotional participation. Just as SCULPTING makes a crystallization of the static and dynamic aspects of interactions possible, so familiodrama makes it possible to play out a dramatic exaggeration of relational nodes by the temporal deployment of conflictual situations. What is involved is, so to speak, an artificially created staging of these.

When familiodrama is used in therapeutic interventions, the dual polarity of the family approach – psychodramatic or sociodramatic – comes up against another polarity which is also in question: therapy for the patient with his family, as against therapy for the family as a group immersed in a much wider social system. Satir (1972) developed this approach both in her clinical practice and training programmes.

In groups in which TRAINING in family therapy is being carried out, it is the family which becomes the subject that is activated dramatically, to the extent that it confronts the individual and the group either synergistically or conflictually. If psychodrama unfolds '*in situ*, i.e. everywhere the subject happens to be' (Moreno, 1965), familiodrama attempts to make the family act freely as and when things come into the minds of the protagonists. A family therapy training group is, however, also part of a sociodrama, whose subjects of study and dramatization are the families of the therapists and the families they encounter in their work contexts.

(See also ANTI-THEATRE.)

J.M. & P.G.

family actant, family actor   Within families, interaction is based upon two different modalities of action, which are necessarily effected by all the members of the family, whether they are placed in an active or a passive position. We may distinguish between the family actor fulfilling a role and the family actant, fulfilling a family function.

The *family actor* is the person who plays a role, whether or not this is recognized by the other actors, and whether or not it corresponds to his or her status (father, mother, child). The action is here what is offered up to perception; it is essentially 'salient', easy to see on a video recording or in a written account. The paradox of the actor is that, like Diderot's play-actor, in order to express all the subtlety of his or her emotions, it is necessary that he or she does not feel them directly, but is able to play with them.

The *family actant* is the person who, above and beyond the roles that are played, fulfils the efficient functions demanded by the system (protection, generation of terror, homeostasis etc.) In this case, the action is 'pregnant' and often difficult to see in a superficial evaluation. It can only be assessed then by the – more or less delayed – results which it produces in the style of life (ETHOS) and the mode of thinking (EIDOS) of the family. The paradox of the actant is that the action here draws on an internal dynamic: the more intensely it is felt and carried out, the less it is capable of being acted.

Therapists are themselves confronted with this double movement of actors and actants. An excess of actors in a clinical situation, brings about a multiplication of non-efficient 'salient forms', while an excess of actants leads to an accumulation of invasive 'pregnant forms'. It is possible to use the synergic and/or conflictual confrontation of these movements and the varying of the relationship between them as a therapeutic lever.

For the distinction between salient and pregnant, see PROCREATIVE FAMILIES; SYMBOLIC REFERENCE.)

J.M.

family catastrophes   Appear as a necessary extension of 'the catastrophe of the individual' as defined by Kurt Goldstein (1934). The regulating functions of the organism do not stop at its bodily or psychical form. In this perspective, the DOUBLE BIND could be seen as the limit expression of a 'fragmented' symbolic figure of regulation, seeking the continuous path which links two opposing values (the cycle of hysteresis), from the cusp catastrophe, being the simplest, onwards (see ELEMENTARY CATASTROPHES).

It is possible to consider family systems from the angle of catastrophe theory (Miermont, 1982b; Cauchois, 1985). Certain family catastrophes become predictable, to a certain extent, if one is able to connect the symptoms to the underlying continuous dynamics (absence of sufficient physical or psychical territories for each of the members, excessive intensity of conflicts etc.). From a therapeutic point of view, modelling in terms of catastrophe theory permits of a morphological representation of processes of change.

When such a representation is not developed, or is not possible, then it is at the moment when one least expects it, and when all the favourable conditions for positive progress seem to have been met, that an unstoppable reverse appears, a long-nurtured balance collapses and, in short, a catastrophe in the ordinary sense of the word occurs. The subjective perception of catastrophes varies as a function of the point of view adopted. A catastrophe is to be distinguished here from a FAMILY CRISIS.

Serious family pathology thus reveals failings of spatiotemporal inscription in a sufficiently well-constructed and organized physical and psychical territory on the part of related groups (see, for example, the SOFA-BED SYNDROME). Identifying family–therapeutic institution interactions, bringing together in ritual fashion several members of the same family in a circumscribed time and space, amounts here to seeking out the topological constraints to which persons and groups are subject and modelling the socializing function of family interactions on the material and spiritual planes.

ELEMENTARY AND GENERALIZED CATASTROPHES AS MODELS OF INTERPERSONAL RELATIONS

Elementary catastrophes

Elementary catastrophes provide a representation of changes of state in systems confronted with a conflict between point attractors. The situations described are essentially linear ones, in which a transformation of a state A into a state B can clearly be identified. The rules of delay (perfect delay) and of minimum potential (Maxwell's convention, see ELEMENTARY CATASTROPHES) are of clinical interest.

The rule of delay explains how a conflict situation may be maintained for a long time in a stable regime while the antagonistic forces are acting beneath the surface. The catastrophe comes about quite some time after all the conditions have been fulfilled for its occurrence. The formation and break-up of a family, and peace and violence within a family, only arrive at stable regimes when the critical point has been reached and the fast dynamic, which precipitates the system on to the other slope of the conflict (see 'cusp' under ELEMENTARY CATASTROPHES), takes over. It is the same with certain therapeutic changes. These can only be envisaged when the system has proceeded far enough in its trajectory along the cusp without any untimely attempt having been made to precipitate the anticipated change (this explains the notion of 'prescribing the status quo').

The rule of minimum potential indicates the position which the attractor of the therapeutic system must assume in the dynamic space in which the patient, his family and the intervenors from the various institutions are situated. For the metasystem of interventions to function, its attractor has to be situated in a basin of attraction whose minimum is inferior to that of the institutions prescribing the treatment to be followed or intervening conjointly.

Sexuality, reproduction and predation have been interpreted by Thom (1972, pp. 294–303) as elementary catastrophes (cusp catastrophe); these catastrophes have a metabolic character which the various family members find more or less easy to integrate into their psychical organization.

In the case of the cusp catastrophe, *the slow dynamic* created by the stable attractors of the system corresponds to *strategies of appetence*: the predator is alienated in imagination by the prey, as simulated psychically; the attitudes of seduction and courtship are produced by the tension which exists between allurement and flight; similarly, biological reproduction is based on the junction/disjunction between parent and child actants.

The *fast dynamic* corresponds to *consummatory sequences* characterized by the capture of the prey by the predator, the structuring of the couple or the separation of the child organism from the parent organism.

One may also, if one is seeking to take account of conflicts over three generations, represent the sequence of family cycles in terms of the *butterfly catastrophe*. The stable attractors here are those of the child, the parent, the grandparent and the ancestor. Two cycles of hysteresis interlock (see diagram).

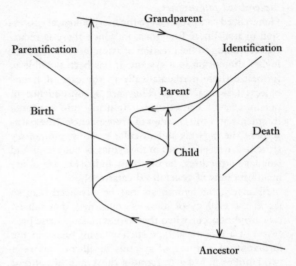

Model of family catastrophes in terms of the butterfly catastrophe.

Model of family catastrophe in terms of butterfly catastrophe

The catastrophe of biological birth (the parent begets a child) comes into conflict with the symbolic catastrophe of reproduction (the child becomes a parent: phenomenon of identification). The catastrophe of biological death comes into conflict with the symbolic catastrophe of parentification (the parent becomes a grandparent).

Within this model, it will be observed: (a) that there is continuity between the parental and grandparental functions: it does happen, for very diverse reasons, that grandparents raise their grandchildren with the parents being excluded; and (b) that the child is in a relation of continuity with the ancestral functions: the child-as-king, the ideal child and the ancestral child (who may be authenticated as such out of fear of assuming – or incapacity to assume – the parental function). By a regressive movement (ebbing of energy due to a blocking of cycles), he may jump catastrophically into the position of grandparent (the stakes then being parentification or death).

These behaviours thus 'run wild' when their cyclical repetition and coupling are caused to fail. The birth of a disabled child, the appearance of autistic or schizophrenic behaviour are the expression of GENERALIZED CATASTROPHES of a catabolic type. Entry into adulthood, marriage, the birth of a child or the death of a beloved individual will produce emotional ruptures, shock waves (Bowen, 1978a) which sometimes spread far from their points of origin. Verbal and non-verbal communications are, in this same way, marked by the linear punctuation of events. In this sense, the linear chain of spoken discourse reflects the sequence of transformations between actants.

Generalized catastrophes

Generalized catastrophes are the morphological expression of non-linear functions, in which there is recurrence, leading to the creation of attractors of a lower or higher dimension in a system. It has been possible to formalize these mathematically in the case of fractal objects (see FRACTALS). They are a consequence of phenomena of CIRCULARITY. Splitting into scattered fragments and the creation of arborescences (the pathways of the nervous and vascular systems, pulmonary structure, decision-trees in the syntax of behaviour and language structures, family trees and GENOGRAMS) are manifestations of generalized catastrophes.

Similarly, the hypothesis may be advanced that, so far as the ecology of ideas is concerned, generalized catastrophes occur when there are schismogenetic processes of a reciprocal type such as come about in the formation of couples, of systems of alliance between two families in order to found a third, and of cultural contacts in general (see SCHISMOGENESIS). In this perspective, schismogenetic reciprocity can be seen as the terminal phase of the differentiation of two groups which are in contact.

NATURAL, TECHNOLOGICAL AND ECONOMIC CATASTROPHES

Unemployment, social tensions, war, natural cataclysms and traffic accidents also have considerable traumatic effects on family organization. They destroy metabolic forms, reducing them to STATIC or PSEUDO-STATIC FORMS (hence the impression of rigid transactions).

These catastrophic perturbations have an effect on the perception and definition given to reality. Some family collapses are more or less anticipated by a particular family member (at the level of dreams, nightmares or phantasies). It is, then, a somewhat dubious practice to interpret these mental elaborations as the expression of unconscious desires. Such interpretations are akin to 'wild' interpretations since they do not respect the contextual constraints to which the families are subject.

What was merely phantasy, if not indeed nightmare, becomes reality, while certain fundamental aspects of reality in effect disappear and assume the character of a phantasy scenario. The fractures caused by all these accidents lead to the appearance of rigid axes (static or pseudo-static forms, functioning as read-only memories) around which family relations may be reorganized and some secondary gains may be acquired (pensions, invalidity benefits, preferential aid to the disabled).

CATASTROPHE THEORY MODELS OF THERAPEUTIC PROCESSES

Depending upon the level of suffering, appropriate therapeutic responses (including, possibly, THERAPEUTIC ABSTENTION) will have to be found. In approaching this matter, therapists are confronted with an oscillation between the everyday and the theoretical meanings given to the term 'catastrophe'. To the extent that it studies structurally stable changes which are generative of new morphologies, the catastrophe theory vision of reality leads to perceptions and strategies complementary to the analytic and systemic methodologies. The method itself involves transforming natural catastrophes into theoretical ones. The therapist's objective is certainly not to impose the models he has constructed himself, in his own head, either implicitly or explicitly, but rather to enable families and patients to discover the theoretical, ludic and phantasmatic dimensions of their own catastrophic adventures (Miermont, 1982b). Similarly, modelling in terms of catastrophe theory enables one to appreciate, in a qualitative way, the static, pseudo-static and metabolic forms which characterize systems in which semantic exchanges take place (see SEMANTICS OF COMMUNICATION). Thus, for example, Cauchois (1985) has shown how light may be cast on the phenomena involved in SCULPTING by introducing a catastrophe theory perspective.

(See also ANCESTORS; IDENTIFICATION; PARENTIFICATION; TOPOLOGICAL SPACE; UNIVERSAL UNFOLDING.)

J.M.

family crisis A period of tension and conflict which arises periodically in the life of every family and which may be the effect of a change which the family has undergone, or the consequence of a therapeutic intervention. Every crisis entails a disruption of the temporary homeostasis of the family system, and thus a need to reorganize interrelations and the discovery of new rules of family functioning. A crisis most often occurs at the time of changes forced upon the family by transitions in its life-cycle (see FAMILY LIFE-CYCLES).

In the history of a family, one can distinguish 'predictable' crises (for example, adolescence, the parents' retirement) and 'unpredictable' ones which, by that very token, are all the more traumatic (deaths, unemployment, illness affecting one or more members of the family). It is often when a family is overwhelmed by a crisis which it cannot manage to surmount that it may seek out a therapist or be referred to one by a third party. CRISIS INTERVENTION may constitute an important and fruitful moment, either at which to sort out the levels of problems presented – while at the same time avoiding 'taking over responsibility' for these, since this itself can become a new problem – or to begin family therapy, couple therapy or individual psychotherapy.

(See also PROVOCATION.)

P.S.

family doctor This is a position traditionally occupied by the general practitioner, who is allotted the task of providing primary health care and is thus well placed to observe the interrelations between pathology relating to aggression from the patient's milieu, pathology relating to biological maturation and pathology relating to the vicissitudes of affective investments. Paraphrasing Bateson, we may wonder whether our conception of medicine changes when we accept that illness appears in 'an infinite regress of contexts linked to each other in a complex network of metarelations' (Bateson, 1972, p. 237).

Let us here attempt to illustrate with a number of examples how this systemic approach relates to what is conventionally referred to in Britain as 'general practice'. The reader is also referred to Asen and Tomson (1992). Three preliminary remarks are necessary:

1 Cybernetics has been defined as 'the art of ensuring efficacity of action' (Couffignal, 1972), which, for us, would mean the art of optimizing our therapeutic procedure.
2 When one speaks of cybernetics, of systems and interaction, we should accept that all these terms belong to the same conceptual approach.
3 We are so well trained to reason in terms of linear causality, that it is very difficult, even when speaking of cybernetics, to get out of thinking along those lines.

In the systemic model and systemic intervention in general medicine, I have attempted to distinguish between three levels of increasing generalization.

FIRST LEVEL OF INTERVENTION

The first and simplest level concerns the concept of a general medicine embracing all aspects. Let us take as our example a young woman who sees her doctor for fainting fits. This consultation enables the doctor to gather a certain amount of data about her, some of which will not be medical in the classic sense of the term. She is twenty-eight, married with two children and her marital situation is difficult. She works as a secretary. She has more than two hours of travel by underground each day. She does not eat in the morning before going out. She does not eat dairy products, nor does she eat much meat or fish and therefore gets little protein. Lastly, she works in a north-facing office. The examination reveals good, bilateral reflexes.

She is seen for a second consultation. It is noticeable that her blood pressure varies considerably with changes of position. Her sugar and calcium levels are a little low. The rest of the somatic examination is normal.

There are several ways of interpreting these fainting fits. Looked at from the organic point of view, they will be labelled crises of tetania or hypoglycaemia or even crises of orthostatic arterial hypotension. From the psychological point of view, it would be tempting to place the label of neurotic personality on her. If one takes up a feminist position, one might say that she is alienated both by men – her husband and her boss – and by her children. If one takes a political point of view – and why should there be any objection to this? – one would say that this patient is a victim of the society in which she lives.

The doctor who saw this patient first sorted out the various elements, by which I mean the social sub-system: her family situation and work situation; the lifestyle sub-system: housing, transport, eating habits; the sub-system and relational context with husband and children and the patient's own psychological history; the somatic sub-system: the biological parameters, blood pressure etc. Clearly, this list is not exhaustive since the doctor's aim is to understand her demand in all its complexity. Is it misguided to believe every complaint is polysemic?

At a second stage, the doctor proceeded in the following way:

He avoided radical advice of the type: 'You should change jobs, move house, divorce your husband, take a lover, leave your husband to cope with the children on his own etc.', i.e. suggestions that she should make a violent break.

He set in train not a totalizing treatment, but a variety of single actions all running in the same direction, i.e. towards the establishment of good doctor–patient relations, reasonable prescription of medication, a short period off work, all of which are solutions which relieve the excessive tensions in each of the sub-systems.

He did not aspire to avoid all possible binds, but avoided creating new ones, as might be done, for example, by requesting that the patient undergo non-essential medical exploratory tests; he thus avoided pseudo-solutions themselves becoming the problem.

He was aware of the necessary response time, i.e. aware that some time would elapse between setting these measures in train and the straightforward amelioration of the symptom. One of the consequences of such an understanding will be that this mechanism is explained to the patient and treatment is not changed without solid reasons for doing so. We might refer, here, to the concept of hysteresis (see ELEMENTARY CATASTROPHES).

He was attentive and flexible in working toward his ultimate goal, which was a lasting change in the patient's state.

Now, has not this practitioner intuitively applied a certain number of the rules formalized by systems theory?

1 Identification of elements and secondary sub-systems.
2 No violent break in feedback loops.
3 The combination of single, individual actions.
4 Taking binds into account.
5 Respecting response time.
6 Flexibility and patience to achieve objectives.

I believe this systemic intervention may be very effective for treating a certain number of patients. There is another very precise, very everyday problem, which is the dilemma of hospitalizing an old person. Here again, we know by experience that hospitalizing old persons often results, shortly, in their death. Now, one might suppose that if the person goes into hospital, this is because they have to go there and that that is possibly why they ultimately die. It is not, however, quite so clear. We even have the opposite impression at times, namely that what has occurred in these cases has been the breaking down of a precarious ecological balance. In this connection, let us quote the following remark by Ashby, which is cited by Bateson (1972, p. 472):

> any biological system . . . is describable in terms of interlinked variables such that for any given variable there is an upper and a lower threshold of tolerance beyond which discomfort, pathology and ultimately death must occur . . . When, under stress, a variable must take a value close to its upper or lower limit of tolerance, we shall say, borrowing a phrase from the youth culture, that the system is 'up tight' in respect to this variable, or lacks 'flexibility' in this respect.
> But, because the variables are interlinked to be up tight in respect to one variable commonly means that other variables cannot be changed without pushing the up-tight variable. The loss of flexibility thus spreads through the system.

If we generalize this definition to relational and social variables, we can certainly sketch out a theory of old age.

Here, lastly, are two other examples which are commonly met with in medical practice. In intensive care, it is not just a single parameter that is controlled, such as cardiac rhythm, renal function or respiratory rhythm, but the whole set of parameters, since it has been observed that these parameters are interdependent and that there is no point – indeed that it could be dangerous – to correct the anomalies in one parameter, without paying great attention to the consequences and to the development of the others. In the same way, in therapy, we very often begin treatments where the dose will gradually be increased, since to begin at a high initial level would result in violent secondary effects, feedback, the halting of the treatment and thus overall failure of the therapeutic measures. This first type of systemic reasoning represents a first stage, though, for most doctors, the approach is doubtless still to see a particular illness as being explained by a particular single cause.

SECOND LEVEL OF INTERVENTION

The second level of systemic intervention is complementary. It consists in not being preoccupied solely with what an individual is complaining of as an individual, but setting the complaint and the individual back in his or her social and family system.

Let us take as an example a woman of 76 who had been operated on for cataracts more than two months before. The surgical result of the operation was good and the surgeon was happy with his work, but in spite of this she was only recovering her sight with difficulty. Her husband and daughter were very worried by her state. The daughter had a very interesting personality, was a dynamic individual and played a part in all spheres of her parents' lives. She decreed that her mother had to be stimulated. But the more she stimulated her, the less her mother could see. This went on until the woman had a fall and returned to the hospital with a broken leg. Within three weeks it became evident that, on the one hand, the mother seemed in remarkably good spirits in an environment which was hardly such as to generate a sense of great well-being and, on the other, she made substantial progress with her sight within this short period. She subsequently went home, where the progress ceased and her sight deteriorated once again. Her daughter had undertaken not only to re-develop her mother's sight, but also to make her walk. It is clear that at such moments, the systemic approach demands not that one pay attention to the mother, who can be left to her own devices, but that a change of attitude be negotiated with the daughter. This is what was done. The outcome seemed promising. The only problem then was that the daughter tended to be too concerned about her father.

THE THIRD LEVEL

Lastly, the third level of systemic or interactional modelling consists in an even more thoroughgoing generalization, since it includes not only what the patient is complaining of, with its various parameters, and the family system in which the patient lives, but also the doctor, if not indeed the medical system. What is at stake here is the importance of the situation occupied by the doctor concerned in the organizational structure of the health system. He or she is the only person whom the medico-social institution grants the right to involve him or herself in everything and to approach things as a whole.

Let us here quote two research projects undertaken by the *Société Française de Médecine Générale*. The first consisted in studying what were the factors affecting subsequent development when idiopathic high blood pressure is discovered in a patient. It emerged that one of the important factors in the subsequent development of the disorder was the figure given to the patient at the time when the hypertension was discovered.

The second piece of research, which was also into high blood pressure, relates to its treatment. When a new drug was being tested with sufferers from this condition, a clear correlation was found between commitment to that treatment at the end of six months and the blood pressure figure given to the patient at the end of the first three weeks of the treatment. These two studies strongly suggest the presence of interactional mechanisms.

More basically, beyond rituals, is not the practice of medicine always based on the interaction between the subjectivity of the patient and that of the doctor? I have, for example, attempted to understand in cybernetic terms the classic sequence described by Balint (1957) of the general practitioner vainly repeating to the patient: 'There's nothing seriously wrong with you', and finding that the more he tries to reassure, the more his patient complains. If we accept with Baillet (1982) that it is not up to the patient to learn his job as a patient, there are only two solutions: either the doctor learns to handle the techniques of paradoxical psychotherapies or he joins a Balint group. In both cases, the doctor–patient relation will have undergone a second-order change.

GENERAL MEDICINE AND PSYCHOTHERAPY

In general practice, psychotropic drugs in general, including those which are the most difficult to handle, represent the first response to a request for assistance of a psychological nature. At first sight, this seems to run counter to the idea of general practice being a relational practice. The matter is not, however, quite so clear cut and we shall look again here at the question of psychotherapy in general medicine. This has its limits, as we can intuitively sense, whatever the personal competence of the general practitioner concerned.

First, in the patient's eyes, the general practitioner occupies a certain position in the organizational structure of society and the health service. That position is not the specific one of the psychotherapist who is not expected, in theory, to solve all a person's pathological problems.

Secondly, he or she responds to a request for treatment by a therapeutic act, which is, literally, in prescriptive form and most often in the form of a written prescription. In this way, he or she is in fact involved in dealing, in a nuanced fashion, with a complex situation, not in exploring a level of regulation. Moreover,

he or she is often the *family* doctor and maintains a lasting relation with the family. Can he or she establish a privileged relationship with one of the members of the family without modifying his or her function as family doctor? This point is described in some detail by Graham (1991).

Lastly, as a doctor who deals with the body, he or she has occasion to examine, i.e. to touch (in reality) the said body. How can he or she then attempt, without running some risk, to make interpretations which have to do with the imaginary?

This leaves two questions that are worthy of exploration. What attitude must the general practitioner adopt when the patient requests his or her point of view on an ongoing psychotherapy? One should be extremely prudent here, which means most often listening but giving no reply. The risks of error appear far greater than the probability of making some apposite intervention. What is to be done where the prescription of psychotropic drugs and psychotherapy occur together? The distinction made between the role of the psychotherapist and that of the general practitioner can easily be resolved by the latter taking on the prescription of psychotropic drugs.

In conclusion, it seems important that during psychotherapy, the psychotherapist should maintain a dialogue with the general practitioner who will often provide him or her with important somatic and sociological information.

(See also PARADOXES; PRESCRIBING (MEDICAL) DRUGS; PSYCHOSOMATIC DOUBLE BINDS; PSYCHOSOMATIC ILLNESS; PSYCHOSOMATIC MEDICINE; THERAPEUTIC DOUBLE BINDS.)

G.E.

family ecosystem See ECOSYSTEM, FAMILY ECOSYSTEM.

family emotional, intellectual and affective systems See AGONISTIC BEHAVIOUR; ATTACHMENT BEHAVIOUR; DIFFERENTIATION OF SELF; EIDOS; ETHOS; FAMILY MYTHS; FAMILY PASSIONS; FAMILY SYSTEMS; HUMOUR; INSTINCT; LOVE; LOYALTY; METACOMMUNICATION SYSTEMS; METAPSYCHOLOGY; MOURNING; PARACOMMUNICATION SYSTEMS; SEXED BEHAVIOUR; UNCONSCIOUS, THE.

family emotional oneness An expression used by Bowen (1978a) to describe the whole constellation of attitudes, feelings, values, beliefs and rules which a family emotional system represents. In families with schizophrenic patients, 'family relationships alternate between overcloseness and overdistance. In the closeness phases, one family member could accurately know the thoughts, feelings, fantasies, and dreams of another family member' (Bowen, 1978a, p. 105). Every area of ego functioning is involved in the 'fusion of selfs'; one member could become physically ill in response to emotional stress in another family member. The same process is described by Reiss (1971) as 'morbid consensus, by Boszormenyi-Nagy and Framo (1965) as 'intersubjective fusion' and by Singer and Wynne (1965) as 'cognitive chaos' (SEE COGNITIVE CHAOS).

(See also DIFFERENTIATION OF SELF; FAMILY–THERAPEUTIC INSTITUTION DIFFERENTIATION.)

A.L.

family ethnology The human family appears to be a universal given, which varies in its manifestations from one ethnic group to another. The comparative examination of these forms, which are subject to multiple variations as a function of historical and social contexts, enables us to appreciate more fully the nature of certain parameters which have pathogenic effects upon the destiny of the individual. It also enables us to avoid immediately perceiving certain forms of family organization, which may appear quite distant from the present 'norm', as 'pathological'. For Robert Lowie (1969, p. 68):

Biologically, every community must rest on the family, – the group comprising a married couple and their children. But biological and sociological necessity need not coincide. It does not follow that the biological family must exist as a unit differentiated from the rest of the social aggregate of which it forms part.

One universal trait does, however, exist:

regardless of all other social arrangements, the individual family is an omnipresent social unit. it does not matter whether marital relations are permanent or temporary in nature, whether there is polygyny or polyandry or sexual licence; whether conditions are complicated by the addition of members not included in *our* family circle; the one fact stands out beyond all others that everywhere the husband, wife and immature children constitute a unit apart from the remainder of the community (1969, p. 71).

We might question the way that biology and sociology are placed in opposition here. Social facts have been anchored in biological reality for millions of years. But one fact is certain. The sociological definition of the family (see SOCIOGENETICS OF FAMILY SCHISMS), by seeking to validate it purely from the outside, threatens its existence and universality.

Claude Lévi-Strauss (1983, p. 60) defines the family group by delineating the aspects that are fundamentally in conflict with society:

the restricted family is no more the basic element of society than it is its product. It is more precise to say that society can exist only in opposition to the family while respecting its constraints: no society can maintain itself through time if women do not give birth to children; and if they do not benefit from male protection while carrying, nursing, and raising their children; and, finally, if precise sets of rules do not exist to perpetuate the basic pattern of the social fabric throughout the generations.

For Lévi-Strauss, not only does society not seek to honour the family or perpetuate it, but it constantly mistrusts it and contests its 'right to exist as a separate entity' (1983, p. 61). Society seems, to him, to be constantly attempting to confine the 'restricted family' to a limited duration and to detach the persons making it up as elements who have to be moved around, recombined and re-associated in many different ways. While being obliged to 'come to terms with' the family, which is an essential condition of its own reproduction and survival, society is not especially accommodating towards it. From this perspective, society is essentially seen as a fact of culture, while the family is regarded as the product of natural exigencies to which society is forced to submit. The most important thing is to identify the systems of kinship and alliance and the marriage rules determined by the society which ensure a continual work of destruction and reconstruction of this labile and relatively uncertain form that is the family.

Lévi-Strauss does, however, consider that there are two joint foundations to family structure. On the one hand, there is a natural, biological foundation which is evident in the instinct of procreation, maternal and paternal instincts, affective and sexual bonds between man and wife. On the other hand, there is an absolutely essential cultural foundation, which marks man off from all other animal species. A human family can only be founded by an alliance or contractual accord between two families who agree to a man and a woman respectively being separated off from them, to become the married couple.

A paradox then appears in this perspective. Though societies in general (unlike our own and some others) do not pay much regard to the 'elementary' family (the so-called nuclear family), they put a very high price on the *conjugal state*. This contradiction has to be considered alongside another of Claude Lévi-Strauss's observations: 'The conjugal family thus predominates at the two ends of the scale on which one can arrange human societies according to their degree of technical and economic development' (1983, p. 40). Within this kind of cycle, we can see in human history a long series of extreme positions around the axis of monogamy:

We have seen that when the family fills a tenuous functional role, it tends to descend even below the conjugal level. In the opposite case, it is effective above that level. So far as it exists in our societies, the conjugal family is thus not the expression of a universal need and is no longer inscribed in the depths of human nature: it is a halfway measure, a certain state of equilibrium between patterns that are in opposition to one another and that other societies have positively preferred.

A new paradox then appears. If the conjugal family is not the expression of a universal need, how are we to explain the nature of the biological, natural foundations of the family mentioned above (procreation, parental care, conjugal fidelity)? Moreover, a great number of polygamous families (whether polyandrous or polygynous or both) are only so to a limited degree. There may be, for example, a hierarchical difference between the first wife and the others; and in genuinely polygamous societies, only a minority of men in fact have access to several women (1983, p. 45).

The paradox we are speaking of takes on an even more spectacular form when mention is made of the Nayar, a group living on the Malabar coast of India:

the men, engrossed in war, could not establish a family. A purely symbolical ceremony, marriage did not create permanent ties between spouses: the married woman had as many lovers as she wished; and the children belonged to the maternal line. Family authority and property rights were exercised not by the ephemeral husband – a negligible person – but by the wife's brothers. Since land was cultivated by an inferior caste, subservient to the Nayar, a woman's brothers were as completely free as her insignificant husband to devote themselves to military activities. (Lévi-Strauss, 1983, p. 41)

The question posed by such a limit situation is the following: why then a symbolically monogamous marriage? Who makes a value judgement on the significance or otherwise of a social role or status? That the husband should be conspicuous by his absence and 'insignificance' is a particularly effective manner of founding a symbol, the content of which asserts itself all the more strongly for having seemed to have been wholly emptied out. In this regard, the situation of today's one-parent families seems an even more extreme – and symbolic – position.

In fact, Lévi-Strauss recognizes a 'model reduced to a few invariable properties' that are found in families throughout the world:

1 The family originates in marriage.
2 It includes the husband the wife and the children born of their union, forming a nucleus around which other relatives can eventually gather.
3 The members of the family are united among themselves by:
  (a) Legal bonds.
  (b) Rights and obligations of an economic, a religious, or some other nature.
  (c) A precise framework of sexual rights and prohibitions, and a variable and diversified group of feelings such as love, affection, respect, fear, and so on. (1983, p. 44)

Fourthly, all societies make a distinction between *de facto* and legitimate unions.

The reduced model proposed here is effectively an ideal model, a kind of fictive monster which is rarely complete and perfect in reality. If one adds in the various accidents – divorce, concubinage, death, discord or an indifferent level of mutual understanding – then this reduced model appears as one that is too complete to be realized often or for long. We can say, then, that monogamous marriage is predominant and, furthermore, that it is regarded most highly in primitive societies and in our own. It is not, however, an attribute of human nature, since forms of union differing in all possible ways from this relatively prevalent model are found.

Lévi-Strauss suggests a hypothesis to account for this fact. Since the family is an emanation of natural forces, any cultural attempt to counteract those forces would incur a relatively heavy price (violence, murder, suicide, various disorders). The most archaic societies do not have the material resources to free themselves from natural pressures, while our present societies, having understood that 'one can overcome nature only by submitting to its laws' (Bacon, quoted by Lévi-Strauss, 1983, p. 61) respect there pressures and constraints better. Here again we find a curious paradox, since monogamy appears both to be a reference that is non-natural – since it can be transgressed, avoided or even eliminated – and one that is all the more natural in that its indirect effects make themselves felt in no uncertain terms when they are forgotten or denied.

(See also ALIENATION; COUPLES; FAMILY ETHOLOGY; INCEST; NUCLEAR FAMILY; SOCIOGENETICS OF FAMILY SCHISMS.)

J.M.

family ethology Family ethology enables us to arrive at a comprehensive view of the phylogenetic origins of the family structure and its ontogenetic functions in the perspective of a comparative study of different species. The aspects studied include care for offspring, protection from natural dangers and predators and learning of the social constraints applying to species living in a co-evolutionary relationship. It leads us to recognize the great diversity of family forms, as well as the biological and physiological underpinnings of social activity. The bodily presence of the conspecific has fundamental biological effects which contribute to the creation of the psyche and the differentiation and recognition of oneself and others.

Within this perspective, we shall recognize the importance of analogies (identical functional constraints) and homologies (common origins of certain semiotic structures with possibly different functions, depending on species and groups). Such recognition is the optimal attitude to adopt to prevent human destiny simply being reduced to this identification of analogical and homological features.

Family ethology enables us to understand some of the pathogenic and therapeutic dimensions which relate to the co-presence of various members of the family, while taking account of the ecosystem in which life takes place. While FAMILY ETHNOLOGY studies the variations and oppositions which distinguish the different human family systems structured by myths, family ethology enables us to grasp the relations between history and pre-history, between invariant universals and systems of cultural variation, by insisting on the hierarchized and interdependent aspect of the levels of biological and symbolic regulation.

PHYLOGENETIC ORIGINS OF THE FAMILY

Jacques Gervet (1986) shows that the mere co-presence of two conspecifics caught up in the same intersensory field modifies their physiology and behaviour. Cyrulnik (1991) states that children suffering from affective dwarfism, presenting with a diminution of the rate of growth hormone and an impairment of deep slow-wave sleep, have usually been subject to early affective deprivation. The artificial and ritualized re-establishment of an adequate relational context triggers an increase in the rate of growth hormone and leads to the re-establishment of normal size, so long as the therapeutic intervention occurs before the age of around 14 or 15. The results of such interventions are corroborated by family therapy work in other pathological contexts.

The family, understood as a structure resulting from the establishment of privileged social bonds between the parent organisms and their offspring, is an ancient phylogenetic creation. Though virtually non-existent in invertebrates, it seems to have appeared, according to Lorenz and Eibl-Eibelsfeldt (in Lorenz, 1978a) in the first fish to have a complete skeleton, teleost fish (some 350 million years ago). In insect societies, there is great diversity in the form of attention accorded to the young and its degree of intensity. Such variation correlates weakly with the degree of complexity of social organization. By contrast, in vertebrate societies, there is a strong correlation between the quantity and quality of parental care and the complexity of social organization. Parents' behaviour has a profound influence on the development of their offspring and this is particularly true for mammals (Wilson, 1975).

A close phylogenetic relation exists between the appearance of the inter-individual bond in the first vertebrates, a bond constitutive of non-anonymous group relations, and the existence of behaviour of caring for the young as carried out by the parental couple. The family so defined is the structure within which the personal differentiation of the partners in the parental couple occurs and also the personal differentiation of the young. The 'cohesion of the couple taking care of its offspring' (Lorenz, 1978a) might thus be seen as the 'phylogenetic prototype which gives rise to the personal bond and the formation of the group'. As for the group itself, it presupposes the individualized, selective recognition of the members who make it up, independently of the place where they meet. This personal identification of each conspecific in a group stands opposed to what Lorenz calls the 'anonymous band' in which all the individuals are undifferentiated and simply lumped together in what seems to be an even more primitive social form than the family group structure (though it is also one that is present in man, as can be seen in the flows of human beings in public transport or in crowd movements etc.).

One of the basic differences between these two types of association concerns the behavioural structure underlying the existence of personal bonds. In fact, the more these are elaborated and differentiated, the more the conduct of the individuals possesses a morphology of intra-species aggression (AGONISTIC BEHAVIOUR). The constitution of the bond rests, on the one hand, on the existence of threat mechanisms and mechanisms of intra-species aggression which ensure distancing and territorial limits between conspecifics and, on the other, on the existence of mechanisms of channelling, reorientation and inhibition of direct expressions of aggression. The phenomena of ritualization give rise to processes of BECOMING ACCUSTOMED and appeasement of partners, who are induced to form personalized bonds of a more or less lasting character.

The family thus enables the young to be protected from outside dangers (climatic excesses, predators, hunger) and from intra-species dangers (social violence, interpersonal aggression). However, it also allows defensive strategies and tactics to be formed that are, to varying degrees, adapted to the life conditions of the group (social LEARNING). Ethological analysis thus enables us to recognize the instinctive behaviours of parent–child and child–parent attachment, the possible inhibitions of those behaviours and the many differentiated structures which enable bonds to be established:

IMPRINTING, HYPNOSIS, imitation, IDENTIFICATION (Cyrulnik, 1983, 1989).

STRATEGIES OF REPRODUCTION AND CARETAKING BEHAVIOUR

The comparative study of species enables us to re-situate more precisely the sense and genesis of family morphologies, by demonstrating the complex relations which exist between the biological structure of living organisms, their sexed and sexual strategies and the caretaking behaviour they show towards their offspring. We shall refer the reader here to Günter Vogel and Hartmut Angemann's *DTV-Atlas zur Biologie* (1967), Edward O. Wilson's *Sociobiology* (1975) and R. Schappi's (1984) excellent work of synthesis.

Paternal and maternal care are based on genuine reproductive strategies, imposing a list of duties on each of the partners. Sexual reproduction is based, fundamentally, on the difference between the sexes. This difference enables genetic material to be end-lessly recombined and permits an infinite variety of slightly differing individuals and the 'invention' of new species. This recombination of bisexed species is based on *anisogamy*, i.e. on a dissymmetry between male and female organisms.

The male emits a great number of gametes, which are small and mobile; the female emits a small number of gametes which are large and immobile and rich in nutrient materials. The female thus contributes more 'information' than the male, since she also contributes epigenetic information which is almost totally absent from male gametes (apart from their degree of viru-lence). This biological distinction has considerable morphological and behavioural effects which will in-fluence the structure of the sexed and sexual bonds between males and females and the nature of the care-taking behaviour directed toward the young.

Two broad types of reproductive strategy exist in bisexed animals. From the point of view of the genetic population there are in sexed animals two main types of reproduction, resulting in different selection pro-cesses depending on the constraints of the ecosystem (Wilson, 1975; Schappi, 1984). These kinds of selec-tion rely on two different reproductive strategies, known respectively as strategy r and strategy K.

The r strategy is a *quantitative strategy*: produce the maximum number of young, in order to make up for the losses due to the conditions of the biotope: this corresponds to the strategy of colonizing species, whose habitats are unstable biotopes. The K strategy is a *qualitative strategy*: produce a small number of young, but surround them with a great deal of parental care; we find this strategy in sedentary species whose habi-tats are stable biotopes.

However, above and beyond these differences, the ultimate strategy of species seems to be to get the partner 'stuck with' the offspring and then 'desert' whenever possible. Such a general attitude will have variable effects depending on the morphology and re-productive behaviour of each species.

Two systems of sexual relations ensure sufficient proximity of the fertilizing male to his progeniture: monogamy and polygyny (several females for a single male, all under his control). These are indeed the sys-tems most often met among bisexed animal species. These behavioural strategies seem to ensure a certain level of certainty of paternity for the male, not on a rational plane of psychical representations, but at a ratiomorphic level of organization of behaviours be-tween sexual partners (elementary maps of relations and territories). Monogamy is thus more common in fish and birds than in mammals. In these latter, there is an asymmetry in the reproductive strategies of males and females. The male seeks to fertilize a maximum number of females: he is a fertilization specialist; the female seeks essentially to rear the young; she is a child-rearing specialist.

COMPARATIVE STUDY OF FAMILY STRUCTURES IN DIFFERENT SPECIES

Family structures evolve as a function of the very con-ditions of biological reproduction.

External fertilization
External fertilization without copulation. In fish, this follows the laying of eggs. A characteristic of this kind explains the greater percentage of exclusively parental behaviours in fish species: once the female has spawned, the male must stay by the eggs since his semen is very labile. The female then carries out a strategic with-drawal after spawning. External fertilization enables the male fish to establish a behavioural continuity be-tween his act of fertilization and his caretaking behav-iour. This behavioural continuity has the advantage of assuring him about his relationship of paternity to the offspring (though at the level of unconscious ratiomorphic processes, of course, and not of symbolic representation which is impossible in this case).

Fertilization of amphibians: this varies a great deal between species and this variation is accompanied by an equal variation in parental caretaking behaviour.

Internal fertilization
Internal fertilization with copulation in vertebrates whose development begins on land (sauropsida: rep-tiles, birds and mammals) was made necessary by these species' abandonment of the aquatic environment.

In *birds*, the two orifices, male and female, are sim-ply applied to each other. Laying occurs rapidly and is followed by incubation, which may in some cases be shared by the male and the female. This symmetry in parental duties is accompanied by monogamy (92 per cent of current bird species are monogamous). When the list of parental duties becomes asymmetrical, polygamy and polygyny replace monogamy and, unlike in fish, evolution occurs by paternal care falling away. In monogamous birds living in colonies, the male keeps the female under surveillance. The territorial instinct further increases the male's 'certainty' of paternity.

In *mammals*, gestation replaces incubation and renders the dissymmetry in parental care fundamental. Suckling at the maternal breast further accentuates the division of labour, prevents the male from playing an early feeding role and ensures that his role will be the specialist one of protecting the group and defending the territory. Thus the number of monogamous species in mammals is not higher than 4 per cent. Most often, we find: (a) an asymmetry between the sexes which runs counter to monogamy (tendency to polygyny); (b) heightened competition between males for access to females with a hierarchy of dominance among males; (c) an intensification of mother–daughter bonds and the creation of matrifocal and matrilinear clans (in which females are related over several generations, Schappi, 1984). Paternal care is only found in mammals (chiefly among some species of carnivores and primates which are the most social species) where the male has sufficient *certainty of paternity*.

ANTHROPO-ETHOLOGY OF FAMILY STRUCTURES

The human species takes this dissociation between sexual and reproductive behaviour to the extreme. Within a family, the 'list of duties' becomes the 'ledger of merit and indebtedness'. Thus family structures vary within the human race itself in proportions unparalleled in any other species (see FAMILY ETHNOLOGY). These variations go together with characteristics peculiar to humanity:

- fertility cycles in women are no longer seasonal, but continuous;
- the female figure becomes an object of visual attraction (one that is particularly exploited, as a metonymic attractor, by contemporary advertising);
- several families are integrated into a single community, whether diachronic (families of origin) or synchronic (clans, tribes etc.);
- the structuring of exchanges between the sexes obeys kinship rules laid down by the different cultures and civilizations;
- the exacerbation of the K and r strategies of reproduction as a function of socioeconomic conditions (with risks of extinction in the overdeveloped countries and risks of overpopulation, famine and violence in the poorest countries).

In man, sexual dimorphism is naturally moderate. But cultural traits appreciably accentuate or attenuate the differentiation depending upon the particular habitat or culture (just as the human skin is supplemented by clothing in all cultures, which may very from the extreme covering that enables tropical temperatures to be maintained even at the North Pole to the emphatically dimorphous quasi-nudity found in the Tropics).

Above and beyond symbolic beliefs, the question of paternal participation in reproduction arises in all human societies. As we have seen, only two forms of society help to encourage certainty of a direct participation on the father's part. These are egalitarian monogamous societies and patriarchal polygynous societies (see FAMILY ETHNOLOGY). For Schappi (1984), post-industrial Western society accentuates the symmetry of the monogamous couple by dint of the neolocality of the couple, which prevents the dominance of one of the families of origin (the experience of MARITAL BREAK-DOWN demonstrates that the persistence of traditional family systems clashes directly with present legislative provisions). In addition, bottle-feeding turns the 'breast' into an object to be symbolized, which therefore becomes something distinct from the actual physical breast. It becomes dispersed and disseminated on to transitional objects, losing its natural function as a source of food and play (which is, by contrast, present in African societies, for example). Gestation still remains the prerogative of the woman, even if the phantasy of the male giving birth is promoted in some sections of the media, giving rise to the myth of perfect symmetry between the sexes. Finally, the control of ovulatory cycles further accentuates this male–female symmetry. All these features taken together lead to sexual monomorphism, as underlined by unisex fashion, by both parents carrying babies stomach-to-stomach and by an 'egalitarian' division of roles and the sharing of caretaking and child-rearing tasks.

FAMILY ETHOLOGY AND SOCIAL HIERARCHY

Montagner (1978) describes what are effectively *child behaviour profiles*, which seem to depend on family factors and which lead to the establishment of hierarchies in relations between children. These profiles are the conjunction of essentially non-verbal ritualized signals, allowing an exchange of messages on the nature of the relation. From this he derives a triple opposition: dominant–dominated, appeasing–aggressive and timid–expansive, which leads to the following behaviour profiles:

Aggressive dominant: predominance of behaviours of open aggression over behaviours of bonding and appeasement. Aggressive dominant types are not very attractive nor are they much followed or imitated. They rapidly change activity and are constantly seeking competitive situations. Submissiveness and acts of appeasement are always short-lived behaviours which do not become organized in elaborate sequences. Boys are two to three times more likely to display behaviour of this kind than girls.

Leadership: predominance of bonding and appeasement. These behaviours are linked together in complex sequences which produce: approaches and offerings from other children; channelling of the threat of aggressive children. Their threat behaviours are clear and unambiguous and are seldom followed by openly aggressive behaviours. When these do occur, it is as a reaction to the aggression of an attacking child.

Dominant with fluctuating behaviour patterns: variation between leadership behaviour and aggressive dominant behaviour from one week to another.

Dominated with leadership mechanisms: homogeneous sequences with much bonding and appeasement behaviour (30–40 per cent of girls). These have a power of attraction and lead to imitation.

Timid dominated: many fear, withdrawal and flight behaviour patterns and frequent calls made on the attention of adults.

Aggressive dominated: these are isolated, take little part in collective activities and competitions, make virtually no offerings and rarely display bonding or appeasement behaviour. Unpredictable aggression. Like the aggressive dominant types, they have few long homogeneous behavioural sequences.

Dominated with weak range of gestures (withdrawal): little bonding, appeasement, threat or aggression behaviour; they remain apart.

These behaviour profiles seem directly connected to family relations and are modified to a certain extent (mainly before the age of three or four) when these relations themselves evolve. The maternal figure seems to be of great significance in the expression of these manifest variations, but the mother's attitudes are themselves influenced by her relationship with the father.

The mother of an aggressive dominant child is likely to have a closed, rigid attitude to the child; she is impatient and hurried; she threatens him physically and verbally, grasps him sharply by the arm or the shoulder, slaps his hands, cheeks, bottom or head. She does not listen to the child, but keeps a close watch on him to make sure he is not doing anything he is not supposed to. She only notices the attitudes of the child which displease her. Her child-rearing is based on prohibitions, respect for authority and the need for constraints.

The mother of a child with leadership mechanisms listens to her child, and establishes multi-channel dialogue (mime, gesture, touch, words, smells etc.). There is very little threat and aggression; rituals of offering, bonding and appeasement are foregrounded; the child is greeted in a sequenced way which involves crouching down to the child's level, hugging, speaking softly, taking the child by the arm. Maternal behaviour is stable. The mother is not continually making demands on the child's attention, but leaves it to occupy space freely. The child's profile may change if the mother is away for more than a week when the child is small. It then becomes more threatening, with the balance of its behaviour leaning towards acts of aggression.

The mother of a leader child with fluctuating behaviour patterns also displays fluctuation in her attitudes. There is an oscillation (daily/weekly) between rituals of appeasement and rituals of threat, and this depends on the prevailing conditions. The prolonged absence of the father, or shows of aggression on his part, coincide with the variations in maternal behaviour that are registered.

The family of a dominated child with a leadership profile turns out, from the point of view of hierarchical relations, to have a mother who is subordinate to the father's decisions. He is the one who actually prescribes (though not coercively) the way in which the child will be looked after, brought up, taught manners and even, in some cases, how the child will be fed. However, rituals of appeasement, bonding and greeting predominate over aggressive behaviour.

The mother of a dominated fearful child appears overprotective (which can in fact be connected with excessive PARENTIFICATION), anxious, attentive to the physical and physiological state of the child; offerings, appeasement, fear and worry appear in succession; she is afraid to let him play outside the confines of the family space; movement and communication are thus subject to significant limitations within the family.

The aggressive dominated child is either 'hustled', hurried or intellectually hyperstimulated in his family milieu, in an effort to turn knowledge to profitable account as quickly as possible. Such intellectual stimulation may be produced in milieus where there is below average income or in intellectual milieus (teachers).

The mother of a very withdrawn child does not exteriorize her behavioural profile. She does not express open aggression, but her behaviour is smothering and repressive, though she also 'forgets' to perform certain caretaking activities (changing the child when he soils himself etc.). The principles of upbringing seem rigid and the mother herself seems very much dominated and smothered by her husband.

This interactional model draws attention to the non-verbal aspects of interaction among children and between children and their parents. It makes use of ordinary descriptions of group or family relations such as might be made by novelists or in common parlance. It establishes an analogy with the hierarchical systems of animal societies. The phylogenetic and biological foundations of this organization of human relations are not, however, demonstrated. The risk therefore exists of these observations and discoveries being separated from broader contexts and the self-referential effects inherent in any 'objective' observation of man by man not being taken into account. It would, for example, be to some extent a subjective deviation to wish to make all children into appeasing leaders. The family ecosystem and styles of behaviour which characterize it, have also to be studied in terms of the family EIDOS or, in other words, of the mental structures which define its norms of thought. In no sense should there be an attempt to substitute for the operational family myth, which organizes and orientates the instinctual dynamics and emotive systems (jealousies, seizures of power, relational hierarchies etc.). Though it is, then, necessary to take into account the structuring of non-verbal sequences, this is not sufficient in itself. The singularity of each family can only be apprehended by recognition of – and respect for – the family rites and myths which enable it to defend and organize itself.

(See also ACTUOGENESIS; ETHOLOGY; HABITUATION; INSTINCT; MULTI-LEVEL HIERARCHIES; RITUALIZATION; STRANGE LOOPS; TANGLED HIERARCHIES.)

J.M. & P.G.

family, history of the   The family nucleus, to which systemic therapists devote attentive care in the course of their clinical practice, is not a timeless entity. The family has a history. And this is even truer of family functioning. That history is, in terms of the evolution of human societies, at least in appearance a very rapidly changing one.

Adopting a historical perspective on the family leads us to a constitutive and conflictual identification of its various parameters. The relative importance of each of these parameters varies with the period that is under consideration (Flandrin, 1984):

- topographical: the *domus*, the house, the *oikos*, the home;
- symbolic: transmission of the patronym and/or matronym, filiation:
- dynamic: persons living together 'for better or for worse';
- genetic: genealogical relatedness, by consanguinity and marriage;
- economic: the community of interests.

The whole of the Christian West has put the child at the centre of the family. Byzantine representations of the Virgin and Child appear as early as the sixth century (Goody, 1983). Until the Middle Ages, children were depicted with the same features and clothing as adults. They are simply smaller in size. Or rather, if they are adultified – if not indeed parentified – they are then portrayed as founts of wisdom and as guardians of the ancestral values which need to be perpetuated. The Virgin and Child are symbols of the idealized representation of the mother–child relationship. In the eighth century, the Madonna was depicted giving the Child the breast, an encouragement to mothers to breastfeed their children and a reproach to those who

delegated that task to a wet nurse. In the fifteenth century the Child appears in iconography in reality and not as an idealized figure. At the same time, we also see intimacy coming to the fore as something to be valued. The seventeenth century is the age of a balanced relationship between the family and the social dimension. The child developed social and personal virtues, a capacity for integration and integrity, in a balanced way.

The family was progressively to distance itself from society. The social display of emotion between parents and children would develop and the sphere of intimacy, the private zone, was to grow. If the traditional family was 'a ship held fast at its moorings' (Shorter, 1975, p. 3), solidly tied down on all sides to the wider social systems, the modern family has been torn away from those moorings, and comes to abandon relationships with distant relatives and to drop the notion of lineage. While the nineteenth century saw a shift from honour to happiness, the extended family gradually became reduced, closed in on itself and the sites of social entertainment (cafés, clubs etc.) would gradually come to emerge as being in competition with – and antagonistic to – the family. The family, now wholly separate from the social field, from the world of roles and statuses, was to become the strictly delineated field of intimacy, of emotion and of personal development, to the detriment of the social qualities of integration. Effects of dress, for example, which used to punctuate family micro–ceremonies visually (meals, outings) have disappeared. Gone is the 'sailor-suit'. The whole family, assuming the guise of joggers, now dress in the same way. The distinguishing marks of daily life are disappearing and the therapist is often called upon to intervene when only verbal transactions remain possible within the family, a potential site of speech occupied by mute beings.

The thesis that the development of the nuclear family is a recent process does not, however, seem to stand up to historical examination (see, for example, Todd, 1983, 1984, 1990). Beyond appearances, systems of family organization, as well as the attendant ideologies, continue to do their work and may well lead astray the therapist who is in too great a hurry to look for 'pathogenic factors'.

(See also FAMILY ETHNOLOGY; NUCLEAR FAMILY; TRANSGENERATIONAL MEMORIES.)

D.C., J.M. & G.G.M.

family interactions   See INTERACTIONS, FAMILY INTERACTIONS.

family life-cycles   A concept proposed by Reuben Hill and Evelyn Duval in 1948 (see Cuisenier, 1977), describing the succession of phases which a family unit passes through, from its formation to its disappearance. The notion was taken up again explicitly in the 1970s with the contributions of Satir (1972), Haley (1973), Minuchin (1974), Bowen (1978a) and Carter and McGoldrick (1980).

Although the term is widely criticized by psychosociologists, it seems in fact to be unanimously accepted by family therapists of all schools, though admittedly it is interpreted and understood in various ways. The concept of cycle is useful because it introduces both the notion of return and perpetuity, and the notion of irreversibility and temporal bifurcation. Family life-cycles thus make it possible to describe the development of the family over time, the return of periodic phases over several generations and the effects of transformation/permanence which each return involves. Such cycles are correlated and regulated by other cycles: the inter-individual micro-cycles of daily life, economic, political, social and religious macro-cycles. These enter into resonance with the cycles of the earth (nycterohemeral, the seasons etc.).

These adjustments between cycles lead to a self-regulating model which would remain merely superficial if it attempted to establish the existence of a standard cycle, but which becomes of practical value if it enables us to study the particular cycles of each family system encountered. The phases under consideration may be studied from various angles.

DESCRIPTIVE, EVENT-CENTRED, PHENOMENOLOGICAL VIEWPOINT

Cycles of natural reproduction: characterized by RITUALS of interpersonal encounter:

- 'unattached' single adolescents;
- rituals of seduction, formation of a couple (including the developmental phases of that couple: one encounter only, intermittent or stable, with varying time-spans, ending with separation or death);
- act of sexual reproduction originating from that meeting/encounter;
- birth of one or more children;
- the development of the child or children, who themselves become 'unattached' single adolescents;
- death of a grandparent, parent or child;
- rituals of seduction;
- formation of a couple;
- act of sexual reproduction etc.

Cycles of cultural reproduction: characterized by established rites of passage (secular and religious ceremonies), relating to:

- the child: ceremonies and festivities relating to the birth;
- the adolescent: communal rites of passage to the adult state;
- the couple: engagement, civil or religious marriages, sealing (or not) the symbolic alliance between the families of origin;
- the end of the couple: divorce or death;
- the end of life: ceremonies for the dying, funerals.

These cycles are themselves the product of many – cultural and religious – traditions with their own life-spans and their own periodicities.

The enforced interference of these two cyclical processes leads to a more or less successful psychical integration, on the individual, familial and social planes.

PSYCHOANALYTIC AND SYSTEMIC VIEWPOINTS

These two points of view enable us to apprehend the formation, transformation and repetition of FAMILY MYTHS. The family is the site where periodic and aperiodic cycles, of varying nature, produce their precipitate: the micro-cycles of everyday life, with the periods of encounter between parents, grandparents and children, crystallize and transform the cultural macro-cycles established by human cultures. It is in this way that we are in a position to evaluate:

1 The singular points of emergence of the psychical organizers of each of the children, of their resonances with the surrounding context and of the tolerance levels of the family system in relation to them.
2 The moments of the symbolic handing on of material and spiritual values, of the powers of the grandparental to the parental couple, of transmission of the heritage.
3 The constitution of sexual, professional and cultural identities and potential obstacles to these.
4 The dates of occurrence of illnesses, deaths, abortions, divorces etc. The symptoms then function as indices of interferences between cycles which may or may not be synchronized. The phenomena of parentification – both normal and pathological – or of ancestor–children, reveal this cyclical return of forgotten ancestral functions.

SOCIOLOGICAL VIEWPOINT

Family life-cycles enter to a greater or lesser extent into resonance with the waves in which society as a whole is reproduced. This leads to the study of the processes of flow of successive cohorts, and age stratification (Hill, 1977). A shock wave will tend to invade the family system, which is more or less receptive to this external influence, at the same moment: formation of the couple, reproduction, death etc. Historical cohorts comprise age groups which, for example, fought in the Algerian War, or went through May '68, or were part of the information technology revolution. There are also marriage, birth and death cohorts; shock waves of births within an age group and so on.

HISTORICAL VIEWPOINT

Historians and sociologists have stressed the dangers of promulgating a 'normal', if not indeed normalizing, cycle of family life. Françoise Lautman (1977, p. 189) writes, for example:

> The principle of dividing up the course of domestic life using categories based on length of marriage and presence or age of children may be criticized for leading to measuring the real against an ideal type of family. Beneath the deceptive appearance of realism and flexibility, and of taking account of lived reality and the possible variations of membership of a particular type of family organization, according to the time of their specific development at which the families being studies are situated, the theory conceals the constraining notion of the normal family.

Similarly, Hervé Le Bras (1981, p. 10) points out that currently

> it is not a new form of family cycle that is taking shape, but rather a form of human relations which is precisely beyond the grasp of the family: attachment between individuals without, however, forming a family, the attachment of a mother to her child without the father being necessary. All these experiments are necessary and full of promise, because the development of the nuclear family is now blocked and cannot provide a variety of adaptations and behaviours. Thus the family life cycle, which appeared two centuries ago, may not be destined for a very long history.

THERAPEUTIC VIEWPOINT

The tracing of family life-cycles is able to provide pertinent semantic information, as a function of the nature, occurrence and periodicity of the symptoms presented. This tracing is in no sense a piece of cold, distant, objectivistic research on the part of the therapist; it forms part of the very dynamics of the therapy and is based on a perception of causality that is not linear but, rather, circular (see CIRCULARITY) – or more precisely, pseudo–circular – and formal. The therapeutic intervention itself proceeds in a cyclical manner, and thus produces specific phenomena of interference. It leads to the perception and modification of the morphogenesis of the family.

What is of interest in the therapeutic approach to family systems is precisely that it questions the established foundations of the family and does not reduce it to a purely phenomenological dimension. It is indeed the way in which individuals define their reciprocal attachments (choice of partner) which provides the basis

of the constituents of family systems. There are in existence bonds, following unconscious trajectories (Eiguer, 1983), fibres and invisible loyalties (see LOYALTY; Boszormenyi-Nagy and Spark, 1973) and therefore transgenerational memories, the archetypes of which are realized in a cyclical manner.

The paradox of individual freedom and personal growth has to do with the fact that both these things depend on the degree of success of insertion into the groups to which one belongs and the ability to participate in the development of one's group: as Haley (1973) points out, the arrival of a child increases the independence of the young couple from their families of origin, if they are at least able to make a deeper commitment to the family system, which is the only way to make it develop.

We can see therefore that there are conflictual versions of the family which relate back to certain ideal models. The *individualist model* is prepared to destabilize any family structure in the name of individual desire. Though it is of great service with regard to neurotic inhibitions and the sense of unconscious guilt linked to the Oedipal structure, it sometimes, paradoxically, enables mythic renewals to occur, which are at the origin of new families. It is, however, catastrophic in the face of the conflagrations of schizophrenia, or the realities of delinquency, drug addiction etc.

The *familialist model* will seek out the spatiotemporal constraints within which it is best to situate oneself for the morphology of family systems to be respected and for personal desire to assume meaning. Such a model cannot be equated either with the institutionalized ideal of the family, nor with the pseudo–subversive model of the individual free of all constraints. Such a model is the only dis-alienating approach for patients confronted with psychotic, psychosomatic and delinquent 'behavioural disturbances'. The danger of this model might be that it would lay down new 'systemic' norms, offer a new ethic and trap 'cohorts' of normal subjects or patients in new straitjackets of thinking or action.

Bombs and PROVOCATIONS may in some cases be placed inside deeply disturbed family structures, on condition that the healthy forces of the family group under treatment be consolidated. We shall suggest here that it is often in the name of an ideal, unattainable family, that all the failings are produced which depart from what is supposed to be the norm. Incest, adultery, homosexuality, divorce and abortion, not to mention suicides and murders, are cyclical events which may possibly be interpreted as invisible loyalties (see LOYALTY) to ideal persons or families.

Family life-cycles must be considered protean. With the existence of single-parent families and multiple marriages, not to mention early deaths, the 'ideal' family made up of mummy, daddy, children and four grandparents (including aunts and uncles together with their own offspring) is, rather, the exception (Le Bras in Soulé, 1980). For the therapist it is the particular form of the cycle that is of importance, much more than the ideal archetypes.

(See also FAMILY CATASTROPHES; DIFFERENTIATION OF SELF; MENETIC THEORY; OSCILLATORS; RELATIONAL ARCHETYPES.)

J.M. & A.L.

family maps A technique of graphic representation developed by Minuchin (1974) for understanding the structure, modes of relation and transactions of a family. It involves both a family history and a diagram of the organizational pattern in order that the therapist may more easily understand the complex material gathered together by the family.

This family map takes account of the development of each member of the family, including the nuclear family, the families of origin of each of the parents, the extended kinship network and the original potency of the transmission of this authority down through the generations. This enables the therapist to determine the zones of adaptive functioning of the family and to diagnose the dysfunctional zones. Moreover, an understanding of the family map helps the therapist to define the therapeutic objectives that are to be pursued. Parallel with this map – and to make it easier to read – the therapist may also draw up the GENOGRAM of the family in which only the relations of kinship between generations are shown (a kind of family tree).

'A family map is an organizational scheme. It does not represent the richness of family transactions any more than a map represents the richness of a territory' (Minuchin, 1974, p. 90). In the structural model, it nevertheless makes it possible, at the cost of great simplification and through a schematic representation of boundaries, alignments and the distribution of power to organize the material from the session in a way that is useful for setting objectives and evaluating the therapeutic process.

(See also BOUNDARIES; DISTANCE AND ORGANIZATION OF TERRITORY; MAPS; TERRITORY.)

P.A. & A.L.

family memories See TRANSGENERATIONAL MEMORIES, FAMILY MEMORIES.

family myths The term 'family myth' was proposed by A. J. Ferreira (1963) to describe defensive attitudes of thought on the part of the family group with provide internal cohesion and external protection. The family myth is thus a FAMILY ORGANIZER which fulfils a homeostatic function that is all the more desired when the group in question is experiencing suffering, difficulty or crisis and is threatening to transform itself or is in danger of becoming dislocated or even of disappearing. A family myth relates to a series of beliefs created and shared by all the members of a family group. It is constituted in relation to the family's ETHOS and RITUALS. The family myth is thus the meaning that the domestic unit (see HOME) seeks to give to each person's actions, thoughts and emotions, though that meaning may be in contradiction with these actions, thoughts and emotions. In fact, the content of the myth develops independently of the distortions which may possibly exist between the type of belief and the doings of those who share it.

FAMILY MYTHS AS QUEST FOR MEANING

We may note here that Ferreira (1963, 1966) plays on the ambiguity of the word 'myth' in English, understanding this at times as a mythological narrative and, at others, as a collective illusion (as in *The myth of mental illness* by Thomas Szasz, 1972, who denies the existence of mental illness). Thus the family myth, which is first defined as a system of organized beliefs shared by all the family members and attributing specific complementary or symmetrical roles to them gradually becomes a psychopathological trait, a set of false beliefs, concealed rules of daily behaviour and interactions frozen in a PSEUDO-MUTUAL form. The homeostatic function it performs degenerates into group defence, *folie en famille*, which is, in some cases, handed down from generation to generation, determining choice of partner or even the status of reality. The family are 'overburdened by their own mythology' (Ferreira, 1966 in Watzlawick and Weakland, 1977, p. 53). Now what myth is concerned with is not proof, but belief. The question of its truth only arises as a function of the position adopted in relation to it. If one participates in the myth from inside, it necessarily expresses something true; if one defines it as myth, then one succeeds in distancing oneself from its content. The use one makes of contemporary scientific knowledge – which concerns each person within his or her family and the groups to which he or she belongs – is necessarily mythic in nature. And neither psychoanalysis nor the pragmatics of communication are exceptions to this assertion, which is itself part of a mythology. It is in this way that the myth of Oedipus transforms itself into a complex that is operative in the analysis of neurotic patients.

Anthropologists like Lévi-Strauss (1973) or Leach (1972) accept that the myth is a narrative about origins, transmitted in such a way as to convey a set of directives as to how one is to make best use of the reality of things around one and give an everyday meaning to the group's social customs. With industrial civilization and urbanization, the mythic function has increasingly been transferred to the education provided by the school and the media, to the detriment of direct verbal exchanges between ancestors and their descendants. However, in spite of a highly unstable environment, families still preserve some anecdote or significant object or photographs which act as a basis for the construction of a myth which has an intimate bearing upon their identity.

The more intense the pathology of one or more of the protagonists, the more the family myth will be called upon to attempt to re-establish the figure of regulation of the group. The family myth is an image for internal consumption. It is distinct from the external façade which the family attempts to present. It describes the identified roles and acknowledged attributes of each member in transactions and effects a consensus between all the family protagonists, who will thus preserve its character as something sacred, tabooed, implicit, and which is not to be disclosed, revealed or modified, however much it may seem to outsiders to represent a falsification. Family myths ensure the stability of the group's cohesion, by giving rationalized explanations for the behaviour of individuals within the family, while concealing their motivations and the irrational aspects which direct such behaviour. So long as a family myth functions as such, it cannot become the subject of any metacommunication; it brooks no commentary or critique, whether this comes from someone familiar or an outsider, since it is supposed to be the operant system of explanation. Paradoxically, however, it only comes to be defined as a 'myth' in an internal/external mythology, a discourse about myth made necessary by the pragmatic and/or therapeutic approach to family and social groups.

EXPRESSION OF FAMILY MYTHS

Among the main general themes met with, we shall note here the myth of *family harmony* ('we are a very united family') and the myth of *unlimited sharing of information* ('we tell each other everything'), while at the opposite pole, themes of *family negation* will appear (families perceived as non-existent, terrifying or detestable: 'communication is completely impossible', 'he never talks', 'he's mad' etc.). These themes may be combined, as if to ratify the disruptions of logic the system has to deal with. In fact, every family group will build up, in a characteristic manner, idiosyncratic mythologies which will be based upon the genetic, cultural and historical SINGULARITIES of the various members.

This construction appears at the point when the couple first forms, during their courtship and seduction rituals, and it emerges in the way they define the reality of their relationship, the activities they seek to engage in together, the types of intra- and extrafamilial

relations (preferential relations with a particular relative or friend) and what behaviour is allowed, tolerated or prohibited. In more fortunate cases, the couple succeeds in creating a mythology which is the product of the joint mythologies handed on by the systems to which they respectively belong. The arrival of a child or children (or, indeed, the absence of children) will to some extent put this first mythological definition in question; it will then be modified, completed or, on the other hand, impoverished and rigidified. In fact, this shared definition of the behaviour, attitudes, thoughts and feelings of each member of the group is something derived from MULTI-GENERATIONAL TRANSMISSION both biological and cultural. As a function of a great many variables, this definition will be called forth by the very many random events imposed by FAMILY LIFE-CYCLES.

Family myths do, in fact, define a family identity, so far as choices of profession and decisions in affective and sentimental matters are concerned. They assign FAMILY ROLES and statuses to each member, more or less independently of their talents or desires and their actual accomplishments. Thus a particular member will be placed on a pedestal, recognized as a genius, a madman, as hateful, devoted, or selfish, or as the DELEGATE for a particular mission or as a SCAPEGOAT etc. The group consensus is, of course, shared also by the bearer of the role or status concerned.

FAMILY ROMANCES OF ORIGINS AND COLLECTIVE IDEOLOGIES

On an individual level, the family myth is structured by the existence of particular prevalent defence mechanisms in the group members: repression–isolation (myths of Oedipal rivalry and confrontation), denial–idealization (myths of harmony) and projection–identification (myths of shame, disculpation, redemption etc.). In this respect, the family myth is distinct from the family romance, which is a construction produced by the phantasizing of an individual concerning the possible extrafamilial origins – of a more or less ideal kind – of that individual. The less diversified such mechanisms and the less they operate at the individual level, the more intensely will the family mythology make its effects felt. Similarly, any behaviour on the part of a group member which is perceived by the rest of the group as incompatible with the family myth, will trigger the ACTIVATION, either explicitly or implicitly, of a mythic form of expression, and will lead to feedback being set up which re-establishes family HOMEOSTASIS by inhibiting or de-activating the behaviour concerned, even at the cost of producing symptoms.

On a suprafamilial level, family myths are influenced by the great INSTITUTIONAL MYTHS transmitted by the collective interfamilial and extrafamilial units of the surrounding society (types of conjugal or sexual relations, relations between work and leisure, success and wealth etc.). It is also the case that these great collective myths are moulded, perpetuated and modified as a function of the structuring of the family and the preferred modalities of communication of that entity (endogamy/exogamy, hierarchy/equality, communality/nuclearity etc.).

FAMILY MYTH AND STRUCTURE OF COMMUNICATION

From the point of view of psychopathology, family myths make their effects felt in the way they structure the transmission of INFORMATION. The family myth expresses the way in which the group differentiates and selects semantically pertinent information. It depicts exchanges of information in so far as these are transmitted by excess or lack, directed towards oneself or others, bearers of positive or negative values, and creating effects of truth or falsehood (all of which gives a matrix of four distinctive features). Therapists will thus be confronted with secrets, confusions, disclosures, scandal, slander and confidences in the presence or absence of a particular person concerned. If some information will thus, unbeknown to a particular protagonist, be totally concealed from view, other information will, by contrast, be laid before a particular subgroup or before the group in its entirety. In this respect, the myths of the consulting family will enter into resonance with the family myths of the therapists themselves. The product which results may be considered an artificial neo-mythology enabling reorganizations to be made in the symbolic semantisms of the family.

(See also EIDOS; FAMILY SELF-REFERENTIALITY; MODEL OF THE SYSTEMIC MODEL; MYTH; MYTH OF HERMES; NARCISSISM; SEMANTIC RESONANCES; SEMANTICS OF COMMUNICATION; TRANSGENERATIONAL MEMORIES.)

J.M. & G.G.M.

family organizers The creation of a family is based on a certain number of organizers, which are both material and spiritual, physical and psychical, individual and social, natural and cultural.

Organizers of the MORPHOGENETIC LANDSCAPE of the family include:

1 Ancestral function: these manifest themselves in biological, ethnic, religious and political characteristics.
2 Temporospatial functions: we can distinguish here:
   (a) the historical and geographical trajectories of the families of origin and of the current family;
   (b) the nature of the habitat ('*oikos*' or '*domus*');
   (c) the organization of time.
3 The distribution of tasks, the anchoring in work:
   (a) socio-professional identity;
   (b) housework, the management of the assets.

4 The nature of systems of alliance of the families of origin:
   (a) the transmission of the family name (matrilinear, patrilinear or composite);
   (b) the real nature of the parental couple, above and beyond the mere biological parents (single-parent, two-parent, nuclear or communal families);
   (c) the articulation of the nuclear, extended and clan sub-systems and the structure of the systems of religious and ideological belief;
   (d) the transmission of authority and heritage.

Etho-anthropological organizers include:

1 The family's rites and rituals: seduction rituals, ceremonies surrounding births, marriages and deaths, the centripetal functions of children etc. (see RITUALIZATION).
2 The founding MYTHS of the family group: social and INSTITUTIONAL MYTHS, the myths of the families of origin, the organizing myths of the couple or the parent who is bringing up the child or children (see FAMILY MYTHS).
3 Family memories, which organize transgenerational transmissions, and are the product of biological and cultural factors (see READ-WRITE MEMORIES).

Ontogenetic organizers: it seems essential to distinguish between the structuring of the individual person, that of the family group and that of the metafamilial social group. This distinction is the condition for identifying the isomorphisms that are required for the articulation of these various levels.

The organizers of the individual psyche have been identified by Spitz (1959) as a veritable embryogenesis of the ego:

- the smile: this lays the ground for interpersonal recognition, the shared elation connected with meeting and constitutes the starting point for attachment behaviour (Bowlby, 1969–80);
- the fear of strangers: this phenomenon, which is connected with the constitution of imprinting on maternal objects, marks the primary differentiation between familiar and strange objects;
- the acquisition of 'no': this marks the child's ability to differentiate itself, by the use of speech, from those around it. It marks the possibility of defining AGREEMENT or disagreement, the true and the false, and thus the principle of contradiction inherent in the secondary processes of thinking – in short, the possibility of asserting and of asserting oneself.

The psychical organizers which structure an artificial, non-family group according to Anzieu (1975a) include:

- the circulation of group illusions;
- the constitution of imagos;
- the structuring of primal phantasies.

Anzieu (1975a) makes a number of observations:

- a group cannot have a sex; only individuals have a sex;
- psychical organizers are not the same in individuals as they are in the group;
- the Oedipus complex is the unconscious organizer of the family; it is not a group organizer. Groups use the Oedipus complex as a pseudo-organizer;
- the psychotherapeutic group resembles a simple group, i.e. a non-family group, more than it resembles a family;
- a phantasy is as much an organizer of a group as it is a disorganizer.

For the psychical organizers of the family group, Eiguer (1983) describes three family organizers more specifically:

1   The choice of partner, on the basis of object relations (Oedipal, anaclitic or narcissistic) at the point where the love relationship is established, and the sharing of unconscious objects.
2   The familial self, made up of three sub-organizers: the inner world, the sense of belonging to the family group and the family ego ideal.
3   Shared phantasies, leading to phenomena of inter-phantasmatization specific to the given family (Anzieu, 1975a).

For his part, Ruffiot (1979) finds that the families of schizophrenics lack true Oedipal structuring.

Clinical experience shows that setting up adequate safety barriers leads to the actualization of structuring confrontations between the patient designated as schizophrenic and his/her parents. Such a process is only possible if one respects the idiosyncratic character of the family myth of the family one is treating. In other words, if one respects the personal way that the family members define their version of the myths which constitute and pervade them.

(See also TRANSGENERATIONAL MEMORIES.)

J.M.

family oscillators   See OSCILLATORS, FAMILY OSCILLATORS.

family passions   The confusion of boundaries between nature and culture, between the individual and the collective and between the familiar and the strange makes intra- and interfamilial space the site where passions unfold or may even be said to be unleashed, passions whose intense, urgent character shows itself in symptoms.

Therapists are no more protected from passion, being themselves members of many real and emotional families, whose exclusiveness is at times merely a way of arriving at the identical through difference. The recognition of these various 'family passions' (Maruani and Miermont, 1981) and the necessary re-framing which makes it possible to get them back into proper proportion, are the guarantee that the therapeutic interchange is indeed a matter of personal reciprocity.

J.M.

family projection   Process by which a problem experienced by one or both parents is transmitted to one or more of their children. A transmission of this kind occurs when the parents are focused on their children rather than being centred on their own difficulties. The illusion of harmonious marital relations is thus maintained, at the cost of transmitting symptoms or suffering to the child, who then takes on the role of INDEX PATIENT (Bowen, 1978a).

(See also COALITION; TRIANGLES.)

P.S.

family psychical apparatus   Defined by Ruffiot (1981b) as an intermediate, ternary, mediating space between internal psychical reality and external social reality. It might be seen as the matrix of all group psychical apparatuses. Ruffiot (1981b, p. 29) sees a psychical apparatus being constructed in an 'obscure and undifferentiated psychical zone of the different members of the family groups'. He conceives it as a fusion of psychical spaces open to communication. Within the family psychical apparatus, the strange or alien is not recognized as alien.

This concept is a prolongation of Freudian hypotheses according to which mental activity can be described in metapsychological terms, revealing a 'psychical apparatus' or *Seelische Apparat* made up of several systems of representation functioning in both a synergistic and an antagonistic manner (see METAPSYCHOLOGY; UNCONSCIOUS). Freud (1938) wrote that, 'We have arrived at our knowledge of this psychical apparatus by studying the individual development of human beings' (*Outline of psychoanalysis*, p. 2). What we know of it is its somatic origin in the nervous system and also the conscious acts of which we have direct knowledge. The rest is unknown and requires hypotheses. Among these hypotheses, Freud proposes that of a psychical apparatus which is localized, has spatial extension and is made up of a number of parts. According to Ruffiot, the function of the family psychical apparatus is to contain the individual psyches. It is seen as the ALPHA function of the mother, i.e. the capacity for reverie, which is shared by all the members of the family, being the sum of the alpha functions of each. Ruffiot bases this assertion on early observations of infants which show the intensity of their dreaming activity, during which the first smiles appear.

The concept of a family psychical apparatus leads to a two-pronged – psychoanalytic and systemic – process of critical thinking:

PSYCHOANALYSIS

For Freud (1938), the psychical apparatus is localized within the brain or nervous system; it has a somatic origin and possesses spatial extension or a topology. The unconscious is something collective deposited in the individual memory. By definition, the psychical apparatus is structured to simulate family and social relations. In this sense, it is the emanation of the representation of these. But just what might the topology of the familial and social objects containing the psyche be? What are their frontiers, the elements and sites of their constituent parts?

It is Bettelheim's view (1982) that '*Seelische Apparat*' for Freud was synonymous with 'soul apparatus'; it is able to transmit and transform a determinate energy and to differentiate itself into systems and agencies (Laplanche and Pontalis, 1967). Pollak-Cornillot (1986) rightly draws attention to the multiple meanings of the term '*Seele*' depending on context. It is used by Freud as the equivalent of mind, the mental, the psychical, as well as the soul.

SYSTEMS THEORY

The word 'apparatus' is synonymous with system, 'a set of elements which combine toward a single goal while forming a whole' (*Petit Robert* dictionary definition); it is also, however, an artificial system of observation and execution; the term 'psychical apparatus' is therefore a systemic description, hierarchized and structured, which is ideally suited to the activities of the human spirit. This 'apparatus' influences family and social groups, but is in return influenced by them. What structures and contains this 'psychical apparatus' is bio-sociological and therefore depends on multiple external factors. The distinction between MAP and TERRITORY is necessary here or, put in other terms, between the representation one has of familial and social groups and what characterizes them in reality.

It is thus worth making the fine distinction between the foundations of the individuating psyche which have collective repercussions and the foundations of the mind or spirit of individuals, families and societies (such as we find in the expressions 'the spirit of a family' or 'the spirit of an institution') which in their turn influence the personal psyche.

(See also family systems; FAMILY UNCONSCIOUS; ISOMORPHISM; METAPSYCHOLOGY; PSYCHOANALYSIS.)

J.M.

family resemblance It is through the question of family resemblance that genetics is apprehended in popular epistemology.

Physical resemblance, which is immediately detectable, is the first to be mentioned. Character traits are added to this to give the subject his or her place within the family (forenames have an analogous function):

- as a 'throwback' ('He/she's the spitting image of X');
- as an 'operator' (splitting the maternal and paternal sides of the family);
- as a mutant ('It makes you wonder where he/she comes from').

In fact, no one procreates his or her own type: 80 per cent of the phenotype is individual (and not the simple sum of the two halves of the parental genome) on account of polygenic heredity, which leaves room for the specific combination of the effects of heterozygotic genes and the effects of the environment, random or selective. Moreover, even in homozygotic twins, the expressivity of the same gene varies in different milieus.

That is why we now resort to multifactorial models of genetic analysis, such as the one advanced by Debray and Lalouel in 1981, to explain family resemblance, bringing in phenotypic homogamy (choice of partner), Mendelian genetic transmission, cultural transmission and the effects of sibling pressure. Reference may also be made to Maruani's sociogenetic model (1982a) and to writings on FAMILY MYTHS. It has, in fact, often been observed that adopted children begin to resemble their adoptive parents through motor identification and the way of using the same facial and gestural code for expressing the same emotions.

This question of family resemblance and of the twin and the double doubtless has its roots in the fraternal relationship which mobilizes affects of FUSION and persecution to the most intense degree. The Marx Brothers and the Beatles provide a light-hearted illustration of this (Maruani, in Soulé, 1980).

(See also GENETICS AND THE FAMILY; GENETICS AND PSYCHOPATHOLOGICAL HEREDITY; SOCIOGENETICS OF FAMILY SCHISMS.)

G.G.M.

family role, social role   A role is the set of behaviours of a given person which is expected by other persons of the same social unit. It defines 'an area of obligations and constraints that corresponds to an area of conditional autonomy (Boudon and Bourricaud, 1982, p. 308). The concept of role is a fundamental one in the sociology of the family and the sociology of social organizations.

Whereas family roles are occupied and transmitted, with more or less appropriateness, as the position of each member of the family develops, social roles most often presuppose the learning of specialist knowledge and skills. In this sense, family roles are much less formalized, a priori, than social roles.

A family role is an abstract, universal and normative model of the biological, cultural, generational, sexual and sexed status of a member of the family in relation to the overall system of reciprocal roles. A role can only be defined, therefore, in a system of oppositions in relation to other roles: father, mother, husband, wife, son, daughter, half-brother, sisters, grandmother etc. Such roles are subject to biological constraints but presuppose complex social learning processes, for which the family provides the crucible (Jackson, 1965a, b). A family role is also a particular behaviour which presuppose an interpretation of the normative role and corresponds to behaviours actually realized by each member of the family; a mother is supposed to take care of her children and to see that they are fed; she may also tell them stories without being particularly obliged to do so. Role behaviour is situated in a margin between what is a duty and what is forbidden (Cazeneuve, 1976).

In the dynamics of interaction, every role will be an expression of the expectations or demands directed towards each member of the family by the other members. In the broad sense, the social role governs the way a given member of the family behaves (Ackerman, 1966). For a person, the range of roles he or she effectively performs determines his or her social status, whereas the range of roles which are legitimately attributed to that person determines his or her legal status. A parentified child may have the social status of a parent without having that legal status.

Jackson (1965b) criticizes the concept of role on the grounds that it is too individual-centred and does not take sufficient account of the relational aspect which plays its part in interchanges between individuals. Moreover, in his view, to speak of roles amounts to considering the arbitrariness of culture as a norm to which each person either conforms or does not. Jackson offers an alternative, preferring to speak of FAMILY RULES. The more rigid the family relations, the more difficult it is for each member of the family to move into the expected roles. It is even more difficult to move out of one's own position and to play the roles of others. This failure to conform to the norms of expected roles is often perceived in a negative way by observers outside the family. It is possible through POSITIVE CONNOTATION to achieve a therapeutic re-framing of behaviour that is apparently outside the norm. When faced with psychotic transactions, therapists may even stage their own relational difficulties and play on the way they fall short of fulfilling their own roles. The relaxation of positions within the family game will come from an invitation made to the family to participate in this process of questioning and accept their failing to live up to roles which are often totally idealized and disembodied.

(See also FAMILIODRAMA; LAW; PLAY; PSYCHODRAMA; SOCIAL STATUS.)

J.M. & P.S.

family rules   This is an expression used by Jackson (1965b) to refer to a certain number of rules which control family life. He writes (1965, pp. 23–4) that 'The observation of family interaction makes obvious certain redundancies, typical and repetitive patterns of interaction which characterize the family as a supraindividual entity.' Family relations are governed by various hidden and generally unconscious rules which define the rights and duties of each person and ensure the maintenance of the HOMEOSTASIS of the family system. These rules are implicit laws, tacitly accepted by all the members but rarely verbalized. It is this system of rules on which the family draws in its interactions. They govern the relational structures of the family and imply mutual expectations of each other by the family members.

Family homeostasis is thus sustained by a set of rules specific to each family. These rules are meant to preserve the system's equilibrium. To question them directly is to put the system in danger. It does, however, become essential to change the rules which control the family's functioning at different stages of growth, as marked by such events as weddings, births, children starting school, adolescence etc. and defining FAMILY LIFE-CYCLES.

The rule is an element that is, consciously or unconsciously, shared, can be put into words and enables behavioural, emotional and phantasmatic accord to be achieved between the partners in a marital or familial relationship. It is the relational expression of the superego or of the 'symbolic' in the Lacanian sense. The concept of rule, however, stresses the specificity of a singular relationship and appears particularly appropriate for evaluating a system of communication between marriage partners or among members of a family. The establishment of rules may usefully be re-situated in relation to the laws pertaining to the family and society in general (see LAW).

Examples of family rules include:

- the parents' bedroom door must remain closed;
- there is no talking during meals;
- it is the mother who manages the budget;
- only the father starts discussions at mealtimes;
- you must never talk about your feelings;
- if you talk about your feelings, you have to do so self-mockingly;
- you can confide in your elder sister or your mother, but not in any other member of the family.

Another, more complex, example is when the eldest daughter is said to be incapable of speaking for herself. This rule will become manifest every time she tries to open her mouth, since she will then be interrupted or disqualified: 'She doesn't know what she's saying.' Again, the rule might be that the father and mother must never express disagreement. In this case, conflicts will probably be expressed through the children. When, at adolescence, the question arises of the children leaving home, the parental couple will have to face up to changing this rule. If they do not succeed in so doing, the system is in danger and the adolescent may produce worrying behaviour in order to delay the possibility of his or her departure and so protect the system.

Many schools of systemic family therapy hypothesize that the function of the symptom is to protect the family system, threatened by an imminent and necessary change to its family rules which have been adequate up to that point, but are now shown to be unsuitable as a result of growth.

(See also COUPLES; DOUBLE BIND; FAMILY MYTHS; QUID PRO QUO; REALITY; SOCIAL STATUS; SYMBOLS.)

M.G. & P.S.

family sculpting   See SCULPTING, FAMILY SCULPTING.

family self-belonging   When a family is forced to incarnate the myth of the ideal eternal family, it sets in play the paradox of relations of self-belonging, which may be described as follows: 'All the members of the family are devoted to others to their own detriment; they must not belong to themselves, they must be excluded from themselves.'

The FAMILY SYSTEM which results from this is then subject to an infinite oscillation between antinomic positions. Either, as a system or a group, it belongs to itself and the consequence will be that it does not belong to itself; the more it seeks its own identity, the more it will be dispossessed of it; the more it seeks to include its properties, the more these will escape it; in other words, the more the system seeks to devote itself to its members, the more it will alienate them. Or this

system does not belong to itself, breaks up, explodes and invades multiple institutions one after another or all at once and also many therapists. As a consequence, this system will belong to itself: its members will have a sense of existing for themselves, of becoming autonomous, of taking possession of their bodies and psyches. This is made possible if the institution or institutions repeat the structure of the family system by maintaining maximum autonomy for the patients by allowing the minimum of liberty (the 'ideal' limit being confinement in an asylum or, better, in an isolation cell). Therefore, the more the family system is alienated through resort on many occasions to therapeutic institutions, the more autonomous it will be and the more comfortable it will be in its identity and self-belonging. This then brings it back to the first alternative (Miermont, 1984c, 1986a, b).

This connects with a remark made by Douglas Hofstadter. If God helps all those who help themselves, the Devil helps those who do not help themselves. The question then posed is: does the Devil help himself? This is a question which, ultimately, confronts every therapist.

(See also FAMILY SELF-REFERENTIALITY.)

J.M.

family self-referentiality   Describes the capacity of a family group to define its identity, to find within itself a representation of its totality, to enable its members to respect that representation; it thus leads to the reproduction of the family identity by the creation of new groups which ensure that the heritage is carried forward. Such a creation presupposes an operational closure guaranteeing the internal coherence of the system, which can only appear through the acceptance of an external coherence and therefore an opening up to hetero-referenced parameters (alliance between two families), thanks to a schismogenetic process (see SCHISMOGENESIS).

Self-referentiality is thus susceptible of two possible tendential developments: (a) excess of closure, leading to activities with no purchase on the real, with no connection to external influences and ending in a degradation of the potentialities capable of creating and reproducing the system; (b) excess of openness, leading to a hyper-dependence with regard to the external milieu and an inhibition of the system's capacities for self-organization, if not indeed their fragmentation.

A LITERARY EXAMPLE OF SELF-REFERENTIALITY

In his *Dictionary of received ideas*, also known as *The catalogue of fashionable opinions* (1850), Flaubert presents the following little example of an escalating self-referentiality:

Negresses: hotter than white women (See Brunettes and Blondes)
Brunettes: are hotter than blondes (see Blondes)
Blondes: hotter than brunettes (see Brunettes)
Redheads: (See Blondes, Brunettes, White Women and Negresses)

There is no entry for 'White Women'. If one wishes for more detail, one comes upon a laconic item, but one that is open to infinity: 'Woman . . .'.

THE SELF-REFERENTIAL SYSTEM AND FORMATION OF THE HUMAN COUPLE

Self-referential mechanisms ensure the very reproduction of the human couple, which may be studied from an ethologico-phantasmatic angle in the light of the reactivation of the infantile sexual stages. Three oscillating polarities may be described:

1 Attachment–detachment polarity: the oscillation then occurs between auto-eroticism and narcissism; or, alternatively, between phantasies of intra-uterine elation, which are present in periods of amorous involvement, and objectalized phantasies of the breast, which are present later (Eiguer, 1983). This polarity is prevalent among the most regressive and symbiotic couples (prevalence of orality).
2 Mastery polarity – abandonment of territorial representations: in this case the oscillation occurs between phantasies of retention/conservation, in the choosing of a partner, and phantasies of expulsion/evacuation in the regulation of distances between partners (couples invaded by anal-sadistic relations).
3 Phallic polarity – symbolic of social representations: the oscillation produces an alternation between seduction phantasies, present at times of amorous involvement and castration, present at intimate critical moments (couples invaded by questions of hierarchical standing and Oedipal rivalry).

These three polarities are more or less balanced out in the formation of every couple. The foundation of the couple could thus be seen as resting on the vibratory motions of these three oscillators. These oscillators derive from a great number of eco-systemic factors: material, transgenerational, ethnic and religious conditions, etc.

RITES, MYTHS AND MEMORIES

One may then seek to differentiate between three registers which, in a wider sense, interfere. The function of the first, the *register of rituals*, is to synchronize and harmonize behaviours, emotions and thoughts. Within a given framework, RITUAL is based upon the identification of indices which make it possible to dispel the ambiguity involved in the present relationship and therefore to define the facts which arise from every inter-subjective relationship. Where the therapeutic ritual or *metasystem of intervention* is concerned, Caillé (1985) proposes that we should speak of a 'phenomenological level' which he distinguishes from a 'mythic level' (see MODEL OF THE SYSTEMIC MODEL): this phenomenological level is based on the gathering of information about the way in which the family members perceive the events which concern them.

Secondly, the *register of myths* (explored by Ferreira, 1963; Stierlin, 1977; Caillé, 1985) makes it possible to explore the family system's modes of defence in an overall way. As the founding unit of the family, the couple re-elaborates on its own account a system explaining its origins, the surrounding world, politics, sexuality and love, religious, sporting, artistic and scientific practices (Miermont, 1982a). As Caillé (1985) points out, the mythic level is located in an intuitive manner by a labour of abstraction and technical research (see MYTH).

Thirdly, the *register of memories* appears at the centre of communication and makes it possible to isolate the ritual and mythic levels. One might even say that 'to communicate is to co-memorize' (Le Moigne, 1988, pp. 18–19). Such a register corresponds to the set of hierarchical, de-activated, hyper-activated, cryptic or lost memories which organize SECRETS; incomprehension, MISUNDERSTANDINGS, regrets and indiscretions within the family and among the therapists. These memories are structured by the interference between rites and myths. These are individual and group memories, historic and a-historic, emotional and cognitive, phylogenetic and ontogenetic, conscious and unconscious memories. They are dependent upon the media in which they are stored and the contexts which reactivate them. The spoken word does not create the same effects as a written text or a video recording. A statement has very different meanings when made in conversation between two persons, during a family celebration or in a therapeutic session with the family. Therapeutic work tends to recombine these hierarchies of memories differently, which is the only way to bring into being more harmonious relational rituals and more appropriate mythological theories (Miermont, 1982a).

FAMILY OSCILLATORS

In each of the family's systemic spaces there are oscillators, generating vibratory phenomena, situated in frontier zones of the sub-systems, which generate the relative autonomy of each space in relation to the adjacent – underlying and overlying – levels (Miermont, 1984c). These autonomous oscillations are regulated by internal and external variables. The vibratory phenomena create resonances which take on a semantic value when they are coupled on identical frequencies (see SEMAN-TIC RESONANCES; SEMANTICS OF COMMUNICATION). It is in this way that the family group is able to possess its own level of autonomy leading to the reproduction of structures of interaction and their succession, above and beyond the disappearance–emergence of particular real families. One may thus speak of SELF-REFERENTIAL COUPLING. The emotional and cognitive systems of the various members of a family where there is suffering may appear completely disjoint, antinomic, and as having no relation between one another. Therapeutic activity then consists in creating zones where these opposed points of view can come together, in order to make them alternate in a continuous fashion.

According to Caillé (1985, p. 59), it is a necessary precondition of the self-referential process 'that the two perceptions – the phenomenological and the mythic – which the system has of itself should succeed each other alternately, in a kind of validating oscillation'. The system succeeds in achieving autonomy and in creating itself to the extent that the self-referential process functions: for example, the apparently opposed perceptions which the two members of a couple may have succeed in alternating in a functional way and hence ensure the autonomy of their relationship.

Family self-referentiality probably fulfils its functions of ensuring autonomy, generating spontaneous impulses, developing persons, renewing generations and transmitting values all the better when it operates silently, not revealing its machinery and yet being subject to a whole series of internal and external regulating influences.

Schizophrenic disturbances arise from an implosion/explosion of the self-referentiality of the family, which leads to the appearance of a 'racing' of activities functioning without any purchase on reality. When self-referentiality becomes the prevalent, unresolved question, the pathology of relations is no longer comprehensible in terms of individual genesis; the family group becomes a single body, the family becomes one person, the index patient comes to embody the whole system's generator of autonomy. Psychotic disturbances, identified as autism, auto-eroticism, rocking or swaying, incessant stereotypies, ambivalence and ambitendency, removed from their operational contexts, bring startlingly to light the existence of dysfunctional self-referential processes. Stierlin (1977) stresses that every child must realize that he or she is the site of a causality emanating from him or herself, that he or she is a centre of initiative and responsibility, and that his or her own wishes and actions have a value and an importance and that they count with those around him or her. Disorders relating to the development of autonomy predispose to a sense of omnipotence and encourage the appearance of hallucinatory, interpretative, delirious activity. They go together with the existence of a disjointed alternation between absolute relational proximity and infinite interpersonal distancing (see INFANTILE AUTISM).

The self-organizing capacities of the family may be considered as compensations to which the system has recourse when its economy is threatened by deformations or infractions (Cauffman and Igodt, 1984). The neutralization of perturbations is effected by adapting the structures but leaving the organization invariant. The processes which produce the relations which characterize the specific organization of the family remain intact. Only the structure varies, leaving these processes to continue to form a self-productive network. Let us take as an example a mother falling ill. The family system produces a compensation, which may be that the grandmother will temporarily replace the mother in the organization of household chores. This process becomes a perturbation in its turn if that grandmother forms a coalition with the children against the father, or permanently takes over the mother's role after she has recovered.

THERAPEUTIC SELF-REFERENTIALITY

Family therapists come into relation with family autopoesis by concrete interference with its organization and its unity. That structure is modified as a result of the perturbations thus engendered. However, the compensations produced when deformations deriving from the system itself arise may in their turn become perturbations which necessitate a new adaptation of the structure. Therapeutic intervention may thus be considered a new self-referential coupling: family self-referentiality and the self-referentiality of the therapist enter into resonance with one another (for a complementary model, see SELF-REFERENTIAL CALCULUS). 'The therapist constructs the world he is supposed to be describing' (Mony Elkaïm, Brussels Congress, April 1986). It is in effect by way of the 'unique and singular bridge' created with the family that the therapist organizes the therapeutic system (family therapist) starting out from his or her own reference points (see SINGULARITIES). That 'potential space' (Winnicott, 1971) obeys specific laws in which more than one logic may co-exist. The therapeutic team becomes a source of perturbation for the family, which produces compensations that become perturbations for the therapists. The system formed by the therapeutic team compensates the family system and hence perturbs it again. It is this sequence of 'perturbation–compensation–perturbation' between two autopoietic systems which might be designated by the term self-referential coupling, or reciprocal structural coupling (Cauffman and Igodt, 1984). One may regard the family as having been dragged into a spiral of perturbations which have imposed themselves as a 'pathological' structure (the symptoms). The self-referential coupling between therapeutic team and family system brings the pathological structure to adapt itself to the perturbations caused by the therapists.

For Guitton Cohen Adad (1987), the therapist draws upon four factors which interact in the time and space of the session:

- the narrative of family reality;
- the perception of digital and analog communication;
- the emotional impact connected with that perception and the distortions it engenders;
- a modelling constructed on the basis of established bodies of theory, generating his or her 'model of growth'.

The connection between these various logics makes it possible to define (a) the significant interactions, by the therapist's punctuating activity, and (b) the gap which invariably appears between the image perceived by the members of the family and the image recreated within the domain of therapy.

The impulse created in this way from interactions causes events to occur (Bompart, 1972–86) which are decisive within the session itself (Guitton Cohen Adad, 1987) and which function as the seeds of other psychical events, both collective and individual.

(See also ACOUSTIC FEEDBACK; FAMILY MYTHS; FAMILY SYSTEMS; GENERAL SYSTEMS THEORY; OSCILLATORS; PERFORMATIVES; SELF–ORGANIZATION; SYMPTOMATIC AND/OR AETIOLOGICAL TRANSACTIONS.)

J.M.

family splitting   See SPLITTING, INDIVIDUAL AND FAMILY.

family spokesperson   The regulation of the flow of words, the quality of the comments uttered or exchanged and the tenor of unconscious metacommunications may in some cases be controlled by a person playing the role of spokesperson for everyone, thus expressing resistance to any form of over-violent intrusion into the family system.

In certain families, a member may thus be delegated to keep the conversation going, express grievances or general discontent, give the impression of monopolizing attention and deflect the therapist's interest. In families where there is great suffering, the spokesperson may literally invade the whole space of the sessions. Such an attitude reveals the possible complementarity of mutually shared roles, for example within the conjugal couple. Depending on the therapeutic approach, it will either be possible to achieve a greater balance between speakers by using active techniques (Erickson, 1981) or to produce this as a change occurring in a more 'spontaneous' way in the course of the therapeutic process itself.

(See also MANIPULATION; SCAPEGOAT; SPEECH ACTS.)

J.M.

family structures   This is an expression used by Minuchin (1974) and the school of structural family therapy to refer to the transactional structures and family roles – both implicit and explicit – which govern the family over time. Family structure is highly resistant to change and the therapist's attempts to bring about change in that structure are often countered by open appeals to family loyalty, as well as by hidden fears and guilt-inducing manoeuvres which constrain family members – and often the therapist – to maintain the structure rather than change it. The details of that structure can be apprehended through the CANONICAL REPRESENTATION of the system in question.

For Piaget, a structure is a system of transformations which comprises laws by its nature as a system (and not by virtue of the properties of the elements) and which is preserved or enriched by the play of its transformations, without these having their effects outside its boundaries or calling on external elements. Thus, briefly, a structure comprises the three characteristics of totality, transformation and self-regulation. The character of totality has to do with the existence of laws of composition which bind the elements of the structure and play a structuring role. There is, therefore, a duality in the notion of structure; it is both structured and structuring.

In the domain of family and social relations, Lane (1970) takes the view that there is in man 'an innate mechanism, genetically transmitted and determined, which acts as a structuring force'. In his view, human beings and society bear within them predetermined processes influencing the range and nature of the rules governing human relations.

The notion of structure refers, in human relations, to regulative codes which manifest themselves in operational models through which people enter mutually into relation to fulfil certain *functions*, actualized in specific actions termed *operations*. On the family level, the obligation a father imposes on his daughter to return home at a given time when she asks his permission to go out, for example, is an operation which actualizes the function of the maintenance of a certain discipline within the family. The range of structures used by a family in the realization of these functions is just as unique as the psyche of an individual.

For Minuchin (1974, p. 51), family structure is 'the invisible set of functional demands that organizes the way in which family members interact. A family is a system that operates through transactional patterns. Repeated transactions establish patterns of how, when and to whom to relate and these patterns underpin the system.' He describes three structural dimensions in family transactions that are present in all interchanges. These are the notions of BOUNDARIES, alignments (see AFFILIATION) and POWER. 'The boundaries of a subsystem are the rules defining who participates, and how' (Minuchin, 1974, p. 53). They thus determine who takes part in an operation and who is excluded from it. For Aponte, alignments are 'the combination or opposition of members of a system in the realization of an operation'. Lastly, power may be defined as 'the relative influence of each member in the way an activity develops' (Aponte and van Deusen, 1981).

In the structural perspective, family structure must be apprehended in the wider context of the ECOSYSTEM, certain functions, such as the upbringing of children being shared between the family and the wider structure that is society. That structure, must, moreover, adapt itself, through a certain number of transformations, both to the stresses related to its members' contacts with the outside world and to the stresses of the normal transitional periods met with in the course of its natural development. This necessitates the determination of new boundaries, new alignments and a new distribution of power. The family structure is, then, an OPEN SYSTEM and one capable of transformation.

(See also STRUCTURAL FAMILY THERAPY.)

A.L.

family systems There are many definitions of the family system, depending on the level of modelling (biological, psychological or sociological) and the systemic properties taken into consideration (set-theoretic, interactive, hierarchical, topological etc.). In therapy, the family has been defined as a system on the basis of two types of investigation: synchronic and diachronic.

The *synchronic*, beginning with Bateson and with Jackson, Haley and Watzlawick, stresses the therapeutic effects relating to recognition in the here and now of interactions between several members of a single family, producing homeostatic circuits regulated by positive and negative feedback.

The *diachronic*, beginning with Bowen and Boszormenyi-Nagy, recognizes the importance of multigenerational transmission and differentiation, transgenerational invisible loyalties, emotional equilibria and disequilibria producing effects over what may possibly be very long time-scales.

SET-THEORETIC DEFINITION OF THE FAMILY SYSTEM

From a clinical, immediate point of view, the family system is a set of persons with common characteristics linked by specific interactions. Three forms of more or less superimposed group stratification may be distinguished: these influence each other dynamically:

1 Group of persons linked by consanguinity, filiation or alliance, gravitating around parental-filial relations (see GENOGRAM).

2 Group of vitally concerned persons, involved directly in a problem, reacting physically and psychically in response to a symptom or an incapacitating illness to a close relative who is one of their own; sharing an identity, handing on a name, having projects which share a common 'spirit', understanding certain ideas, phantasies, myths, beliefs, spiritual beliefs.

3 Groups of persons in linear and circular interaction. Each person influences the other members of the group and is influenced in return. But the group itself, as a system, produces effects which act on persons and their interactions. There is an 'emergent quality' of the system, irreducible to the properties of the sub-systems making it up.

The set-theoretic definition requires that the elements of the system under consideration be specified: are we dealing with persons, individuated organisms or psychical units? These elements are themselves made up of sub-systems as has been brought out in the Freudian topographies (unconscious, preconscious, consciousness; id, ego, superego) and are themselves part of larger systems: extended families, clans, tribes, social organizations.

TOPOLOGICO-DYNAMIC DEFINITION OF THE FAMILY SYSTEM

Two other specific considerations should be taken into account here. On the one hand this relates to the structure of the space and time within which the system moves and, on the other, the nature of the pathways or connections which join the individuated spaces.

The topological point of view in effect brings out the fact that individuation is linked to the appearance of boundaries delimiting units (Thom, 1988, 1989). A system is then defined as a portion of space contained within a box B, where the walls of the box may be material or fictive, traversed by flows of matter, energy or information going into or coming out of the box (see also DYNAMIC SYSTEMS). Very often, the box is a BLACK BOX the nature of which can only be apprehended from its inputs and outputs. In this perspective, the family will be defined as the content of a space limited by the intersection of many material and fictive walls: the bodily limits of the organism, the psychical apparatus, the architectural and spiritual structure of the home. These different strata determine TERRITORY and BOUNDARIES characterized by topological properties (BALL, SPHERE, tori etc.). These spaces must be considered as having multiple dimensions, projecting themselves into the four dimensions of space–time. Let us give a few details here of the nature of the intersections and the interlocking of family architecture.

Material boxes provide outer walls for the concrete territories of the family: the 'nest', *domus, oikos*, house, domain, apartment: 'the people who live under the same roof'. But also the media provide long-distance connections: telephone, letters, visits etc. The flows to be considered are, for example, centripetal movements arising from geographical origins, from the interlocking with families of origin (extended family) as well as the centrifugal movements of persons moving out of the bounded area of the family to integrate themselves into social organizations: school, work etc.

Fictive boxes: these boxes are characterized by limits and qualitative differences which are apparently not local and therefore abstract. The connectedness of bonds of kinship, filiation and alliance determines relational boundaries; the distinction between persons who are regarded as familiar and those considered as outsiders gives rise to barriers of varying degrees of invisibility, with intrusions giving rise to reactions of withdrawal or fear. The position of each as a function of age, sex and place in the succession of generations creates the construction of phantasmatic scenarios. Superimposed upon this domain, the family identity is marked by the patronymic or matronymic name, the cultural values, religion, modes of thought and belief, emotional (ETHOS) and intellectual (EIDOS) group norms (Bateson, 1972).

The projection of these forms into space–time sometimes gives rise to confusion, conflict, uncertainty, shock waves, rifts and the collapse of previously stabilized systems. Family therapy is particularly confronted, like psychoanalysis, with the management of parameters that lie outside space–time and the projection of these into space–time.

FUNCTIONS AND GOALS OF FAMILY SYSTEMS

Considering the family as a general system of human individuation and reproduction, the following may be considered as family systems on which a therapeutic intervention is possible: (a) the smallest, indivisible social units which reproduce themselves ensuring the survival, protection and education of the children; (b) which are also constitutive of human groups 'which have a history' (diachrony) and which make history (synchrony).

Family therapies deal with precisely such units, which are veritable functional EVOLUTIONARY SURVIVAL UNITS, that develop and have common goals – both explicit and implicit – over a continuous period. In this sense, the family is an organism the characteristics of which are identifiable over several generations, irrespective of the individuals directly involved. Family systems are thus radically different from artificially created groups which are based on a relatively precise goal (psychoanalytic groups, institutional groups etc.).

Ashby (1956) defines the canonical representation of a system as the set of equations which, for each variable in a system, gives a function of the present values of the variables and of all the other necessary factors: this relates to the standard, 'canonical' form to which all descriptions of a dynamic system may be referred.

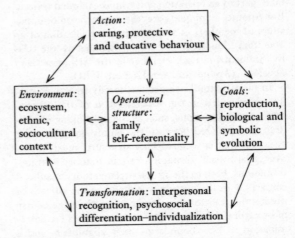

Canonical representation of the family system (after the definition of the general system given by Le Moigne, 1977; see GENERAL SYSTEMS THEORY).

A family system is characterized by *roles* (archetypal action), *social statuses* (relational position) and legal statuses (institutional position) determining a set of functions of more or less operational variables (veritable family processors, structured along the lines of RELATIONAL ARCHETYPES): husband, wife, child, parent, grandparent etc. The operational character depends on the biological maturity and the way in which these statuses and roles confirm or invalidate that biological maturity (function of psychical integration and cultural evolution). These variables are therefore invested with positive, negative or neutral values. The canonical representation of a given family will attempt to account for all the peculiar and typical characteristics permitted by the system under consideration. Thus the degrees of PARENTIFICATION and infantilization will be evaluated, as will the differentiation or undifferentiation of the sexes etc. In a foster family, the role of parent will be predominant whereas the status will be ambiguous and the legal status limited. In an adoptive family, the legal status and function may be soundly based, whereas role and status may possibly be overinvested.

SYNCHRONIC VIEWPOINT OF THE FAMILY SYSTEM

The synchronic point of view shows the importance of effects of interaction in the here and now. It identifies phenomena of:

1   Family HOMEOSTASIS (Jackson, 1957): the attempt to maintain equilibrium, which may be achieved by one member of the family falling ill.

2   TOTALITY: a change in the behaviour of one member of the family will influence all the other members.

3   *Non-summativity* (see HOLISM): there is an emergent quality which arises out of the interaction between two or more persons.

4   EQUIFINALITY: in the evolution of a system, the same consequences may have different origins. Within this perspective, schizophrenia cannot simply be considered as being linked to an infantile trauma, but must be seen as a mode of interaction which manifests itself in particular interactive contexts.

5   Multi-level HIERARCHY: the family system possesses hierarchical centres of representation, decision-making and organization.

DIACHRONIC VIEWPOINT OF THE FAMILY SYSTEM

This includes the family emotional, intellectual and affective systems: SENSITIVITY TO INITIAL CONDITIONS.

For Bowen (1978a), the emotional system of the NUCLEAR FAMILY describes the patterns of instinctual functioning operating within a family over one generation. Some patterns of interaction between parents and children reproduce the patterns of previous generations and will be reproduced in generations to come (emotional system of the extended family, social emotional systems). The diachronic point of view stresses transmission effects related to prehistory and history and to the sensitivity to initial conditions created by the evolution and transformation of living organisms and sociocultural symbols. For Bowen, the family system is thus made up, not only of the feelings and perceptual attitudes of the immediate family, but also of those of the extended family, the social and work environment and other societal institutions, as well as of factors intimately related to family homeostasis.

The *emotional system* is the one directly in touch with the instinctual levels of behaviour: reproduction, sleep and the control of function effected by the vegetative nervous system. It is profoundly rooted in the phylogenetic past. In man, it is usually in relation with the intellectual systems.

The *intellectual system* is dependent on the cerebral cortex and involves the capacity to think, reason and reflect. It is, in its development, incredibly more recent in phylogenetic terms and it is responsible for the passage from prehistory to history and presides over cultural evolution. The more the emotional and intellectual systems are fused, the more the individual will be under the influence of the emotions of the groups of which he or she is a part.

The *affective or feeling system* is thus the product of the emotional and intellectual systems. It opens out onto the more elaborated levels of psychical representation.

FAMILY SELF-REFERENTIALITY AND CIRCULARITY

The diachronic–synchronic opposition is rendered dialectical by the CIRCULARITY of interactions. The paradox is, in effect, that the return to the starting point of a circular reaction is always deferred in time. Conversely, the anticipation of a result influences the attempt to bring it about. To understand disturbances of FAMILY SELF-REFERENTIALITY, it is the conjunction of several different factors – prehistoric, transgenerational, ontogenetic and anticipatory – that has to be grasped.

(See also FAMILY CATASTROPHES; GENERAL SYSTEMS THEORY; SELF-REFERENTIAL CALCULUS; MACHINES.)

J.M. & P.S.

family–therapeutic institution differentiation
Serious disorders of family organization (schizophrenias, autism, drug addiction, anorexia nervosa, delinquent behaviour) are the expression of a group conflict in search of therapeutic and educative organizations on which this conflict will try to map itself. The therapeutic institutions themselves become implicated in alienations of varying degrees of intensity, which affect the identity of the professionals involved and the structure of their own interactions. The differentiation of therapeutic interventions relating to the resolution of complex problems necessitates, therefore, the modelling of multidimensional systems.

The question before us, then, is why the existence of several levels or dimensions arises in the construction of information-bearing structures. The mathematical metaphor which follows provides the first stages of an answer. Consider the following problem: how can four equilateral triangles be made with only six matches? So long as we remain in a two-dimensional universe, there is obviously no solution. The answer emerges suddenly as soon as we add an extra dimension into our reasoning, moving from a simple surface to a volume.

The addition of extra dimensions thus increases the number of shapes and therefore of informational possibilities, with an economy of materials. Changes in psychotherapy often come about through the addition of extra dimensions in the reorganization of arrangements which, in other respects, remain unchanged in quantity and quality. We can increase the number of dimensions either by playing upon the spatial dimension (gather together a whole family in a specific space presumed to be therapeutic, which is different from the family's usual space and from the hospital), or by playing on the temporal dimension (prescription of the status quo, seriation–oscillation of antinomic alternatives).

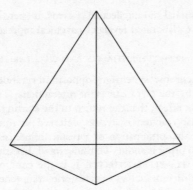

Multidimensional model.

The modelling of these polyhedral structures is obviously just a static approximation of the underlying dynamic processes. The tip of the pyramid will thus represent the 'organizing centre' of the morphology under consideration: the home for the family, the therapeutic institution for the organization of the treatment that is proposed. This organizing centre can be considered as a space with dimensions, the number of which may exceed the four dimensions of space–time.

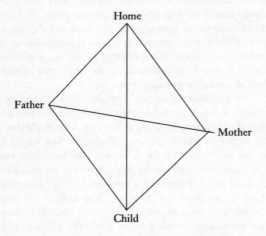

Schematic representation of the family system.

From the birth of a child on, there is an interweaving of systems of intervention (therapeutic and social systems, family of origin systems etc.). This interweaving produces alienation phenomena which, paradoxically, ensure the autonomy of the family system under consideration. The more each person's self is constituted, the more that structure is integrated psychically, the more it is isomorphic with the family and social systems to which it belongs (the, apparently chaotic, fractal construction of reality).

In pathological cases, alienation leads to the systems dispossessing each other reciprocally of their organizing

centres: the institution becomes the family, the family becomes a pure therapeutic or social system. A minimal amount of detection work comes in here to try to find the point of view of the therapeutic metasystem (collective interviews, case conferences).

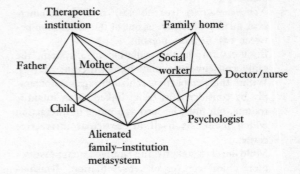

Example of reciprocal alienation of the therapeutic and family systems.

The therapeutic function (family therapeutic metasystem) can only intervene at the lowest level of potential in a differentiating identification of the positions of each person in the system. Family therapy is only possible if the therapeutic, institutional and family spaces are disentangled. Even if the continues to request outside aid, the family group has to recreate adequate protective barriers. In other situations, several intervention pyramids will come into the model, leading, for example, to network therapies.

By taking into account these multiple dimensions, it becomes possible to respond, in a more appropriate way, to the questions posed by the most overdetermined of symptoms. One is able to differentiate the logical levels which are normally perceived as antinomic (double binds, n-binds) when they are actualized in reality.

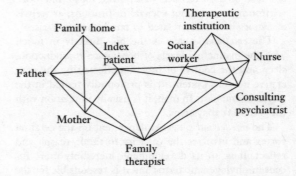

Differentiation of the institutional systems in family therapy.

However, these schemas can only be viewed as static canvases which take into account neither the complex hierarchical articulations between levels nor the dynamic, metabolic, conflictual aspects of situations that are encountered in reality.

(See also ALIENATION; DYNAMIC SYSTEMS; FRACTALS; INSTITUTIONS; MAP AND COUNTER-MAP OF A FAMILY SYSTEM; NETWORKS; THERAPEUTIC DOUBLE BINDS.)

J.M.

family therapies In the strict sense, family therapies are psycho-therapeutic and/or socio-therapeutic treatments of families which present difficulties relating to one or more patients recognized socially as being ill. The conjunction–disjunction of the psychical and social aspects is, in part, reflected in the divergences of points of view between the psychoanalytic and (socio-)systemic models, without it being possible to remain for very long – either as practitioner or as theorist – within a purely dichotomous and exclusive style of action or thinking on this topic.

In a broader sense, the term refers to a set of practices and theories in which individual, family and social problems are posed, independently of factors belonging purely to the realm of medicine: behavioural disorders, delinquent acts, family and social violence, inter-institutional or transcultural confrontations etc.

This is to say that the term 'therapy' may here produce some confusion if not indeed create, of itself, a formidable obstacle to a true process of maturational change coming about. From time to time, recourse is had to other terms, which themselves generate other disturbances and paradoxical confusions (see NETWORKS; PRAGMATICS OF COMMUNICATION; PSYCHOANALYSIS; SYSTEMIC MODELLING AND INTERVENTION; THERAPEUTIC DOUBLE BINDS).

In the strict sense, the term 'therapy' seems to indicate the objective to be attained: treating the sick persons with their families, treating the family which has fallen ill in the form of one of its members and/or its environment. In practice, to talk too hastily of family therapy may have negative PERFORMATIVE effects and undermine the process which is to be set in place by short-circuiting the goal to be achieved. In effect, the strictly therapeutic dimension of an intervention can only be evaluated once the process has ended and, where possible, through a consensus arrived at between persons within the family group and sufficiently qualified, neutral observers, who may be external to the system of intervention itself.

Moreover, it appears that pertinent interventions on family communication relate to the meta- and para-therapeutic dimensions and can in no way supplant the purely therapeutic and medical systems of intervention, though they do bring out and regulate the therapeutic potentialities inherent in family communication. It is, none the less, true that family therapy can be rigorously seen to be indicated in certain cases, and

this may possibly be integrated into more wide-ranging treatment interventions, while at the same time going beyond them (see TANGLED HIERARCHIES).

As an entity, 'family therapy' is traversed by many apparently contradictory currents: psychoanalytic, systemic, behaviourist, gestaltist, ethological, sociological etc. Family therapy presupposes preliminary work to establish what is indicated and contraindicated. From this a wide variety of practices follows, and we can give a brief list of these here:

1 *Cooperative therapies*: individual treatment of several members of the same family by different therapists, with organization of a structured collaboration between these various therapists and ordered combination between them (also linking in psychoanalytic models and institutional therapy).

2 *Psychoanalytic therapies*: based on psychodynamic models (Ackerman, 1958) include the experiential (Whitaker and Keith, 1981); intensive family therapies (Boszormenyi-Nagy and Framo, 1965); therapies based on the presence of two generations, INTERPRETATION of the TRANSFERENCE, FREE ASSOCIATION, the RULE OF ABSTINENCE (Ruffiot, 1979; Eiguer, 1983) and exploratory therapies (Wynne, 1980).

3 *Transgenerational* (Bowen, 1978a) or *contextual* (Boszormenyi-Nagy and Spark, 1973) *analytic–systemic therapies*.

4 *Therapies of a communicational-systemic bent*: conjoint family therapies developed in the 1960s by Don Jackson, John Weakland and Virginia Satir; structural therapies (Minuchin, 1974); strategic therapies (Haley, 1973); provocative therapies (Andolfi, 1980; Elkaim, 1987a); problem-solving BRIEF THERAPIES (Watzlawick et al., 1974); systemic therapies (Selvini et al., 1978; Hirsch, 1980; Hoffmann, 1981; Caillé, 1985); family therapies extended to families of origin and collateral families, in so far as these have close emotional relationships with the nuclear family.

5 *Multiple family therapies* (Laqueur, 1976): several families (up to five or six) are brought together at the same time, often around a common problem, in video-taped sessions. These may last for 60–75 minutes and are conducted by two therapists, with several observers.

6 *Crisis therapies* (Langsley and Kaplan, 1968): to respond to acute crisis situations in certain families. The treatment lasts around three weeks and the therapists are available around the clock to respond to calls from the family.

7 *Family therapies in the home*: the therapists travel and conduct sessions in the family home. This approach is necessary in families of low socio-economic level which are difficult to mobilize, at least in the early stages. This work in the home

may be limited to one session or a few. It enables the therapists to take into account the real ecological situation and life-context of the family (Bloch, 1973). In all families, additional information can be gained by the therapist undertaking home visits.

8   *Multiple impact family therapies*: a team works both with isolated members of the family and with various combinations of family members for intensive periods, usually lasting two or three days. The therapists centre their attention on the family system and work to change it throughout this intensive period (MacGregor et al., 1964).

9   *Individual therapy* with temporary orientation on to the family to discuss the best orientation to give to the treatment.

10 *Simultaneous or parallel therapy*: the same therapist treats one or more members of the same family but sees each member individually.

11 *Social network therapies* (Speck and Attneave, 1973; Elkaim, 1979b): which involve not only the immediate family, but also the members of the extended family, neighbours, work colleagues and all the others who may be of some assistance to the disturbed family and who have an emotional or functional significance in the life of the index patient (some of the alternative practices of antipsychiatry come close to this model).

FAMILY INTERVENTIONS WITH A PROPAEDEUTIC OR EDUCATIVE AIM

Just as psychonalysis has made it possible to decentre the understanding of neurotic phenomena, by exploring what is not a strictly medical space, interventions with families have led to the discovery of dimensions in which the doctor–patient relation is only one aspect of the problem. Madness cannot simply be reduced to a mental, biological, psychological or sociological illness. It is a particular modality of communication which questions REALITY and the real and the functions of the best-established collective MYTHS.

Families confronted with delinquent acts or families requiring socio–educative aid may benefit from interventions whose function is not metatherapeutic, but meta-educative or metapropaedeutic (relationship to the LAW: see also LEGAL CONTEXT; SYSTEMIC MODELLING AND INTERVENTION).

The diversity of the practice that actually takes place often cuts across the monolithic character of theoretical – or what might even be termed 'ideological' – divisions. We shall simply note here that certain types of systemic intervention make it possible to delimit what may possibly belong to the sphere of therapy and what definitely lies outside it. The set of mental illnesses is, fortunately, not isomorphic with the set of

states of madness, just as 'delinquency' cannot strictly be classed as an individual or social 'illness'.

(See also BEHAVIOURISM; FAMILY ETHOLOGY; METASYSTEMS; THERAPEUTIC STYLES.)

J.M.

family typologies   The identification of family typologies puts in the hands of the therapist grids for reading and intervention. If some of these are directly centred on clinical practice, others enable him/her to step back and reflect upon that practice. There are as many family typologies as points of view adopted. We here outline ANTHROPOLOGICAL, INTERACTIONAL, TRANSACTIONAL, MORPHOGENETIC OR STRUCTURAL and PSYCHOANALYTIC–PHANTASMATIC typologies of the family.

The advantage of typologies of this kind is that they offer a meta-reading of the facts observed and a space for thinking about these that lies beyond the merely phenomenological. There is, however, a danger of confusion between psychiatric and psychoanalytic symptoms or between psychiatric and systemic symptoms. Furthermore, who, in reality, could arrogate to themselves the right to define a normal family or even to say that another is 'pathological' because its behaviour, transactions, phantasies and modes of thinking are shown to be singular? Contextual, circular, multidimensional analysis aims to avoid over-hasty judgements made on the basis of stereotyped moralistic positions.

A coherent typology either attempts to respect as closely as possible the most up-to-the-minute nosological differentiation, in order that a true evaluation of the effects of therapeutic interventions can be made, or else it abjures all diagnosis. In the latter case, it is better for this not to be re-introduced at some later stage, with its labels of family perversion or psychosis, for example, since this would then only increase confusion.

J.M.

family unconscious   It is essentially around this concept – and that of FAMILY PSYCHICAL APPARATUS – that the distinction between family therapists who define themselves as psychoanalytic and those who define themselves as systemic has come to be made. For the former, there is an unconscious specific to the family group, and it is not so much topographical as dynamic:

The family unconscious is no longer, as is thought, in some obscure region of the brain of the family members. Nor is it something that slips out in certain unfortunate instances of symbolic expression or in a lapsus during an exchange between persons. It is in the very weft of discourse; it is the canvas which governs its deepest, most fundamental expression. (Brodeur, 1980, p. 113)

For the latter, there is an unbridgeable gap between logical levels: the total set of the elements of a system is more than – and other than – the sum of the elements making it up (see THEORY OF LOGICAL TYPES). The family level cannot be reduced to the sum of the individual alienations. This level of family ALIENATION is subjected to systemic modelling, preserving what is specific to each person: dreams, phantasies, which belong to the register of the individual approach. Freud himself distinguished between the phenomena of individual identification and the collective level of unifying empathy (*Einfuhlung*).

It is, therefore, very difficult to seek to extrapolate the concept of family unconscious from Freudian thought. Thus Freud writes, in *Moses and monotheism*, 'It is not easy for us to carry over the concepts of individual psychology into group psychology; and I do not think we gain anything by introducing the concept of a "collective" unconscious. The content of the unconscious, indeed, is in any case a collective universal property of mankind.'

(See also FAMILY SYSTEMS; FAMILY THERAPIES; GENERAL SYSTEMS THEORY; INCOMPLETENESS THEOREMS; ISOMORPHISM; MULTI-LEVEL HIERARCHIES; PARADOXICALITY; RELATIONAL ARCHETYPES; TANGLED HIERARCHIES; UNCONSCIOUS, THE.)

R.N.

feedback The feedback loop is a particular interaction between a system and its environment during which information concerning the outcome of an action is fed back as an input into the system in the form of data. The concept was developed in the 1940s and forms part of the basic conceptual armoury used by CYBERNETICS in its approach to regulation and communication in machines and living creatures. The discovery of the information loop required by a goal-seeking system to correct any action, or negative feedback, was made by Wiener in 1949 who subsequently extended this discovery to take in living organisms. Then, under the aegis of Bateson (from 1952 onwards), the Palo Alto school verified its operation in inter-human communication.

NEGATIVE AND POSITIVE FEEDBACK

Let us assume a system with inputs and outputs. Inputs are the data which the system receives and which are produced by the influence of the environment. Outputs arise from the action of the system on the environment. In feedback, a part of what comes out of the system is reintroduced into the system in the form of information about what has come out of it.

Two types of feedback exist, negative and positive. The dynamics of change of a system, its growth and development (homeorrhesis) is based on positive feedback. The re-establishment of equilibria, self-preservation, regulation and stability are based on negative feedback (HOMEOSTASIS). *Positive feedback* is the feedback in which the information reintroduced at the entry point contributes to facilitating and amplifying the system's response. Its effects are cumulative and have a transformative function. In the case of *negative feedback*, this information acts in a sense opposite to the previous results. It reduces the gap between what comes out of the system and a given norm and thus has a regulatory function. The effects of negative feedback stabilize the system. In the former case, there is exponential growth or diminution of a 'deviation': in the latter, there is re-establishment of an equilibrium.

Negative feedback leads to adaptive or goal-seeking behaviour, i.e. behaviour which seems to tend towards a goal: maintenance of a particular level, temperature or concentration etc. In some cases, the objective is established by the system itself. The system secretes its own finality: keeping an organism alive, maintaining a family system in spite of various disturbances. In other cases, this has been assigned by men to machines: automatisms and servo-mechanisms. In a negative loop, any variation towards 'more' entails a correction towards 'less' and vice versa. There is regulation, and the system oscillates around a position of equilibrium which it never reaches. The thermostat is a simple example of regulation by negative feedback. It is the prototype of the cybernetic system. Living creatures obviously differ from cybernetic machines; the number of perturbations to which machines may retroact is finite and programmed. Amplification by positive feedback is generally fatal to them. By contrast, living organisms can regulate themselves, even when they are subject to fluctuations that are both unforeseeable and infinite in number and are capable of bringing out something new where there is risk of breakdown. Negative feedback thus appears as an attempt to correct a disturbed system and re-establish its previous equilibrium. For example, a child will take on the role of 'patient' in an attempt to re-establish the equilibrium of the family group by giving the parental couple an opportunity for a new level of communication. Negative feedback also works to preserve the status quo or maintain family homeostasis.

Positive feedback leads to divergent behaviour, indefinite expansion, or total block. More creates more and there is a 'snowball' effect. Examples include the chain reaction, demographic growth, the proliferation of cancer cells, symmetrical escalations, marital conflicts, power struggles etc. Less creates less, there is a 'downward spiral' effect, the amplification of a reduction. Examples include economic depression, business bankruptcies, the successive decompensation of all the members of a family etc. Thus positive feedback left to itself may lead to a breakdown of the stability of the system or its destruction by explosion or by implosion with all its functions coming to a halt. For a system to be able to maintain itself in a stable state over time, positive loops have to be controlled by negative loops.

FEEDBACK AND FAMILY SYSTEMS

Within the framework of family therapy, the concept of feedback makes us recognize that input data introduced by each member of the family lead to output data that are more complex and centred on the family system. The 'outputs' of a family system have to be analysed in their specificity since they produce an emergent quality that is irreducible to the analysis of the individual inputs. Without denying the importance of psychical factors in the construction of the family organization, the way in which the organization of the family system has repercussions on the psychical activity of each of its members will also be recognized. The analysis of positive and negative feedback makes it possible to change and modify certain types of feedback perceived as inducing disturbances at the level of system organization.

Take, for example, a mother scolding her daughter. In doing this, she attacks the daughter, 'parentifying' her, in order to settle a score with her own mother. The terrified child strikes a deep emotional chord with the father who resolutely takes her side and will not have his wife seek to exert her authority in this way. The father will then take his own mother's side, still being emotionally dependent upon her. Dispossessed in this way, the mother has hysterical crises and assumes the status of 'sick person' of the family. These crises terrify the child even more and she will 'decide' to be brought up by her grandmother with the active support of her father, a decision which brings on even more intense maternal crises. The mother's symptom thus secures a compromise between the family's homeostatic tendencies and its tendencies to change. Such a situation can be modelled from a cybernetic point of view, by studying the inputs and outputs of the system, the negative and positive feedbacks and the TANGLED HIERARCHIES which result.

Positive feedback makes it possible to orientate the family towards new modes of behaviour by making the previous structures of behaviour untenable. It is often used to counteract negative feedback through the introduction of a crisis-inducing mechanism, with a view to provoking therapeutic change and preventing the family from maintaining the status quo (Bloch and La Perriere, 1973; Haley, 1973; Jenkins, 1989b).

(See also CIRCULARITY; FAMILY SYSTEMS; GENERAL SYSTEMS THEORY; PARENTIFICATION; PERVERSE TRIANGLES; PRESCRIPTION ; PROVOCATION; PUNCTUATION OF SEQUENCES OF EVENTS; STRANGE LOOPS; SYMPTOMS; TRIANGLES.)

M.G. & J.M.

feedback loops See FEEDBACK; STRANGE LOOPS.

field See FORCE FIELDS, VECTOR FIELDS, MORPHOGENETIC FIELDS.

force fields, vector fields, morphogenetic fields A 'field' is a space determined by a gradient, within which one may construct restricted forms. Field theory was proposed by Kurt Lewin (1936, 1939, 1947b) in the perspective of a topological psychosociology. A field presupposes a geometrical representation of the person, the family and groups, made up of internal dynamic sub-systems coexisting alongside one another; the result of these sub-systems is itself connected up with neighbouring intra- and interpersonal systems.

These systems are under tension, subject to synergistic or antagonistic forces. The field of operation of a person or group of people is more or less fluid or rigid. The greater the fluidity, the more the difference in tension between neighbouring systems diminishes. The maintenance of a difference in tension between partial systems, whether individual or familial, depends on a sufficient rigidity of the milieu. In this perspective, the rigidity of psychotic systems is a means of defence against too great a fluidity of interpersonal tensions (diffusion–invasion of affects, thoughts and emotions, leading to a non-differentiation of the neighbouring systems). The immuring or distancing of a family member does not eliminate the state of fluidity–rigidity of the system.

Lewin's 'topological' theories have been contested from two quarters. On the one hand, mathematicians have criticized them for their lack of rigour and their arbitrary character, while, on the other, psychoanalysts have attacked them for making little reference to unconscious processes. The profound intuitions contained within these theories do, however, deserve to be reconsidered, both as historical preliminaries to the dynamic understanding of family and social systems and because they cast a complementary light on the theory of the DOUBLE BIND (theory of antagonistic gradients).

A family or social field is the result of co-present entities, connected together by channels of COMMUNICATION, differentiated by BOUNDARIES or barriers, structured in sub-systems and supra-systems. 'One of the fundamental characteristics of the field is the relative position of the entities which are parts of the field. This relative position represents the structure of the group and its ecological base. It also expresses the fundamental possibilities of movement within the field' (Lewin, 1935, p. 246). The dynamic analysis of the field depends on an understanding of the distribution of forces which drive the protagonists within the field under consideration. The concept of 'phase space' will be used to describe the quantitative or qualitative development of an isolated property, in terms of a system of coordinates (see ATTRACTORS; DYNAMIC SYSTEMS). The result of the forces in conflict produces a gradient dynamic which leads normally to a quasi-stationary state of the interrelated systems.

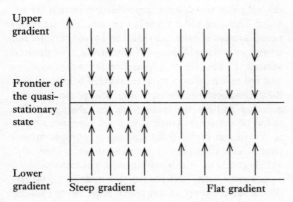

Gradients of resultant forces, quasi-stationary state (adapted from Lewin, 1951).

This quasi-stationary state explains the extent of such a field's resistances to change. Before one can hope to obtain a transformation, it is necessary to identify (at least intuitively, as therapists) the nature of the forces present and the possible morphology of the development of the gradient dynamic. Just as a sailor assesses the state of the sea and the force and direction of the winds, a therapist must seek out information relating to the conflictual dynamics of the persons before him or her: degree of mobility or fixity of gaze, of attitudes, of oculo-gestural exchanges and styles of speaking; above all, the emotional and intellectual state of the therapist is a basic indication, to be placed in relation with the – real and phantasmatic – position which he/she happens to have in the field of interactions. He/she will thus be able to appreciate the levels of aggression, seduction, provocation and threat which weigh, differentially, on each of the members of the group.

As early as 1947, Lewin identified the importance of SCAPEGOATS in groups in an atmosphere of aggressive autocracy. The fact of being attacked or attacking corresponds to a quasi-stationary regime, which will suddenly get out of equilibrium when its tension has reached a critical point. He thus noted phenomena of circularity in interactions, namely here the close relation between attacking and being attacked. Let there be two scapegoats, A and B, in a group:

the attack of A against B increases B's readiness to attack; the resultant attacks of B raise A's readiness etc. This would lead to a continuous heightening of the level of equilibrium for A, for B, and for the group as a whole. This holds, however, only within certain limits: if the attack of A is successful, B might give in. This is another example of the fact that the change of a social process which results from the change of the force field determining the level of equilibrium may in itself affect the total situation in the direction of a further change of the force field. This example can, of course, be regarded as a case of non-equilibrium which corresponds to a constellation of forces away from the present level. (Lewin, 1951, p. 214)

We thus see the existence of a circular causal process, which breaks down at a certain level of disequilibrium and results in a change of linear type. Such a change of state will be interpreted as an ELEMENTARY CATASTROPHE.

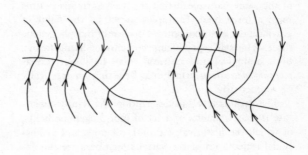

Catastrophe jump of a gradient dynamic (after Bruter, 1974).

Vector fields (see VECTORS) are mathematical tools, the importance of which relates to their property of being able to generate curves representing the temporal development of such a dynamic system. Such fields will here be conceived in a qualitative perspective. In family therapy, it will be possible to appreciate the historical trajectories of family groups, or the members of a single family, as the result of opposing dynamic tendencies (economic or cultural constraints etc.). Similarly, the extent of the psychical and somatic impairments of INDEX PATIENTS leads to the induction of centrifugal movements in the persons directly involved; such facts lead to the recognition of considerable dynamic pressures to which the patients and their close relatives are subject. It will be possible to consider the emotional forces which possess a direction and an intensity as the results of a vector field.

A vector, in a space of n dimensions, is defined by

its components on *n* Cartesian axes. The set of *n* components enables us to describe a length and a direction of the vector. On each occasion that several parameters describe a phenomenon at a given moment, it is possible to use a vector field to represent the development of the parameters over time.

A vector field defined on a differentiable manifold (representing the 'mapped' states of the system) is a correspondence which at every point of the manifold connects up a vector belonging to the tangent plane to the manifold at this point. The points of the manifold for which this vector is zero constitute the SINGULARITIES of the field, in such a way that the stable elements of a dynamic system and, in particular, the stationary points, are determined by the singularities of the vector field. A differentiable manifold on which a vector field is defined and which possesses one or more attractors, constitutes a dynamic system.

Force fields are vector fields which guide the movement of the objects that are sensitive to this field. To say that an object is subject to a force is to say that it has been possible, at a particular moment, to observe a modification in the morphlogy, internal structure or the trajectory of the object under consideration. Forces of the same nature exerting themselves in space–time form a force field. Examples might be the fields of gravitational, electromagnetic, nuclear or morphogenetic force. The self-reproducing currents of living forms, both biological and cultural, may be conceived as *morphogenetic fields*, which may be acting synergetically or conflictually.

The various levels of description of a family constitute the components of a set of morphogenetic fields, of which the historical, cultural, religious and professional trajectories of the various members are the expression. Various authors have pursued the exploration of field theory in family therapy, Howells (1979) by defining a vector therapy, Stierlin (1977) by distinguishing between centrifugal and centripetal patterns and Stanton (1981) by describing a geodynamic balance of the family process.

On an *inter-individual plane*, relations are regulated by coalitions and exclusions, which are expressions of positive or negative vector fields of greater or lesser intensity; conflicts between vectors running in opposing directions may appear, leading to the upsurge of emotional shock waves or of sudden changes, which may lead to breaks that are perceived as catastrophic. Cultural forces play the role of channelling the pressure exerted by the development of children. The Oedipus complex, in its direct and inverse aspects, describes a prototypical mode of ambivalent conflict, in which the child may be attracted to or repelled by the same parent, while in each case experiencing the opposite feelings towards the other parent. Beyond the hetero-sexed structuring – and the stabilization of phantasy registers – which usually results, a great

number of family situations appear in which the various fronts or alliances are not so 'ideally' structured. It is possible that the men or women will band together against the other group, or a particular man will take up the position of the paranoid person hated by everyone, or a 'transgenerational marriage' will be established between a husband and his own mother etc. At that point it becomes useful for the therapists, to attempt, in terms of their own perceptions of the system under consideration, to understand the dynamic of the forces present and the way in which it will be possible for the fields thus created to enter into resonance with the symptoms presented.

On a *transgenerational plane*, the currents of biological, religious and cultural reproduction stretch far beyond the individual (or even nuclear familial) consciousness of each individual and place persons and groups in dynamic fields with centrifugal or centripetal vectors. Families with schizophrenic transactions reveal the existence of centripetal vortical fields of which the patient becomes the attractor, both for those around him/her and for the institutions and therapists. So-called DISENGAGED FAMILIES seem, by contrast, subject to centrifugal vector fields leading to multiple investments. The discovery of invisible loyalties (see LOYALTY) reveals the burden of unconscious transmissions over a great many generations and leads to a postulation of the existence of long-term movements running through persons, families and societies (see ACCULTURATION). Making a geometrical representation of these currents for a patient and those around him/her means to attempt more clearly to perceive the lines of force of the system and the intensity of the dynamic conflicts resulting from it, in order to appreciate at what point and at what moment it is most opportune to intervene.

(See also GATEKEEPER; POWER; TOPOLOGICAL SPACE; TRANSGENERATIONAL MEMORIES.)

J.M. & M.G.

foreclosure Foreclosure is a mechanism which is at work in psychosis. The concept was developed by Jacques Lacan, building upon the Freudian concept of 'repudiation' (*Verwerfung*). Foreclosure occurs when a fundamental signifier (the phallus, the Name-of-the-Father etc.) has never come into the place of the Other (structural site of the unconscious signifying chain, subject of the strategy of games, witness to truth effects) and is called there in 'symbolic oppposition to the subject' (Lacan, 1966, p. 217).

The lack of a fundamental signifier throws into question the whole of the signifying structure. The absence of the 'Name-of-the-Father' in this place of the Other opens up a breach into which imaginary reshapings of the signifier cascade, until a stabilization of signifier–

signified relations appears in the delusional metaphor. This fundamental signifier is then 'unleashed into the real'.

The Name-of-the-Father reduplicates in the place of the Other the very signifier of the symbolic triad, in so far as it constitutes the law of the signifier. This place of the Name-of-the-Father has to be reserved by the mother in the promulgation of the law.

Lacan stresses the 'ravaging effects' of a father placed in the position of legislator or a father who presumes to embody the LAW. More than any other, he is then exposed to appearing unworthy, inadequate and even fraudulent, thus excluding the Name-of-the-Father from its position in the signifier. These 'ravaging effects' may extend as far as dissociation of the personality when a falsified filiation arises and when the constraints imposed by the entourage work to sustain the lie (Lacan, 1966). Therapeutic action with families does, however, show that psychosis cannot merely be reduced to a linear relation of falsification (short of turning the therapist into a moralist). In psychotic systems, falsification is most often stunningly obvious and impossible to remove. It appears more as failed falsification, an inability clearly to demarcate truth from falsehood. Such a falsification disorder seems to be the result of effects of a disintegration of interactions rather than their cause. It does in fact seem necessary to avoid the purely linear and moralizing position, which would say: 'if he's mad, it's because his parents didn't tell him the truth or spun him stories about his origins.' But who can say he never tells such 'stories'? And, in similar vein, we know a child's lying lays the ground for his acquiring the definition of truth.

It is here, precisely, that Lacan rapidly dismisses the idea of 'a meticulous enumeration' (1966, p. 217) of the features of the schizophrenic's 'entourage' (à propos André Green's, 1957, thesis), both from the point of view of anamnesis and of a real encounter with the patient's milieu. He branches off towards the structural analysis of President Schreber's delirium, concealing more even than Freud himself the specificity of schizophrenic relations, to stress the predominance of the paranoid structure. Similarly, the only thing he refers to in Niederland's analyses (1959), which were further discussed by Schatzman (1973), is the linear perception of Schreber's father's imposture. However, only the reconstitution of family exchanges would enable us to understand on what real foundations the signifier operates or does not. For if the signifier is unleashed into the real, the fact is that the real, precisely, is the operator of the unleashing, as constitutive of the morphology of the signified.

It will also be noted that the word 'foreclosure' implies an irreversible process. What is foreclosed cannot be 'repaired'. Which means that attempts to 'reinject fatherness' or reinforce the couple or 'transplant' the foreclosed signifier generally prove fruitless,

as Chemama (1983) has noted in relation to the position adopted by Dolto regarding psychoses.

We may possibly compare this concept with certain systemic hypotheses. In so-called psychotic families, there is no founding MYTH, properly speaking, at the level of the parental couple. A founding myth is usually to be found at the origin of the constitution of new marital groups: it is developed out of the myth contributed by each of the members making up the couple. Following a process of 'negotiation', a common myth is derived. It is clear that such a process does not take place around a table, but rather with the aid of certain forms of analog communication. In psychotic families, it is as though no such negotiations had taken place, the original myths remaining intact, completely separate, and inoperative. In other words, it might be said that no family has come about, if we take 'family' to mean a group structured by a common myth. The psychotic group is structured in an entirely negative way, with external myths and medical myths. If we pursue this hypothesis, it seems clear that one cannot repair something which has never existed. By contrast, we may assume that the partners in such a grouping may decide at a particular moment to constitute a family.

(See also ALIENATION; FAMILY MYTHS; LAW; NARCISSISM; PARANOIA; REALITY; SCHIZOPHRENIAS; TRANSGENERATIONAL MEMORIES.)

J.M. & R.N.

forgetting A mishap or accident of communication which may possibly occur in the structuring of certain FAMILY MYTHS. It is characterized by a lack of information directed towards oneself, which may possibly have consequences on the plane of wider interactions. It is possible to imagine a whole semiotics of forgetting which relates to different psycho-pathological interactions.

FORGETTING BY EXCESS OF SUPPRESSED MEMORY: REPRESSION

Freud was the first to reveal the full importance of forgetting and of parapraxes, discovering the process of repression of unconscious representations which continue to be active. Repression appears quite particularly in the hysteric who 'suffers from reminiscences' relating essentially to the Oedipus complex. In this sense, the analysis of the Oedipus complex appears as the identification and prescription of a particular family myth.

FORGETTING BY PARTIAL AMNESIA

This is met with in head injury, but is also brought about experimentally when electric shock treatment is prescribed. It generates a radical break in the continuum of personal experience, creating a 'blank' in the system of memorization of affects and representations.

In a different form, the severely mentally handicapped engender mechanisms of forgetting around them: or they are, rather, the expression of a deficiency of family and social memory. Hence the difficulties of developing an approach to these problems, where, paradoxically, an excess of intervention and care very often alternates with wholesale abandonment.

FORGETTING BY AMNESIC SIMULATION OF THE INTERRUPTION OF COMMUNICATION

It is possible for other family myths to be based upon forgetting: thus, for example, the myth according to which 'one mustn't dwell on one's past, but always look to the future'. A case of hebephreno-catatonic schizophrenia shows a patient taking this assertion of his father's literally, to the point of forgetting all the events, important or otherwise, that have preceded the moment when he is asked the least significant question.

(See also CALUMNY; DISCLOSURE; INFORMATION; NOSTALGIA; SCANDALOMONGERING.)

J.M.

foster families See PROCREACTIVE FAMILIES, FOSTER FAMILIES, ADOPTIVE FAMILIES.

fostered children See PROCREATIVE FAMILIES, FOSTER FAMILIES, ADOPTIVE FAMILIES; SYSTEMIC MODELLING AND INTERVENTIONS.

fractals, fractal objects Fractals describe the properties of certain complex DYNAMIC SYSTEMS, both linear and non-linear, in which there is recurrence (such as the regulation of the growth rate of a population that is far higher than its stable equilibrium state). The basic property of fractal objects is self-similarity which occurs in all the fractional dimensions of the object under consideration. Fractals were discovered by the mathematician Benoît Mandelbrot (1975).

The field of fractals constitutes a new geometry which studies the most immediate natural forms (the earth, the oceans, the sky), artificial forms and abstract objects in their most irregular and fragmented aspects. Numerous examples of fractals can be found in the world of living organisms: the alveolar structure of the lungs, the convolutions of the cerebrum, the increasingly delicate arborescences of the vascular and nervous systems, systems of symbolic representations, the boundaries and hierarchies of human systems, the flows

of turbulence in communication channels etc. Every fractal object is characterized by its degree of irregularity and fragmentedness, which is known as its fractal dimension.

Brownian motion, the most elementary form of pure chance, is a continuous curve of two dimensions and is, in fact, the simplest possible fractal curve. Many of the most interesting fractal objects are, however, of a dimension intermediate between one and two or between two and three etc. 'It is thus reasonable to say of certain highly irregular plane curves that their fractal dimension is intermediate between 2 and 3 and, ultimately, to define dusts on a line the fractal dimensions of which are between 0 and 1' (Mandelbrot, 1975). We therefore see curves appear which do not extend to infinity, but in which a distance between any two points on them is infinite. A figure of a dimension between 1 and 2 is more 'slender' than a surface and 'bulkier' than an ordinary line.

Fractal sets (Julia sets, Mandelbrot set) occur from the point where non-linear dynamic systems enter a situation of extremely simple and general feedback. An example might be the following recurrent function:

$$x_n + 1 = x_n^2 + c$$

in which x is a variable and c a complex number.

We may represent this by the following diagram:

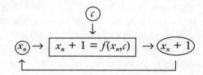

Or $x0$, $x1 = x0^2 + c$; $x^2 = x1^2 + c$ etc . . .

We thus have the sequence $x0 \rightarrow x0^2 \rightarrow x0^4 \rightarrow x0^8$. Depending on the values of $x0$ (fixed or variable) and of $c \neq 0$ (fixed if $x0$ is variable, variable if x is fixed), we obtain the Julia sets and the Mandelbrot set respectively. These sets possess the property of self-similarity, their structure repeats itself in identical form but with great variation in its dimensions. Julia sets vary a great deal as a function of the fixed choice of c: the figures produced may be connected or may be clouds of points; this gives us clouds, branches of foliage, sea-horse tails, showers of sparks after a firework etc. We thus arrive at imaginary cartographies, at depictions of planets or organisms, psychedelic images which can considerably enrich our representation of objects in reality (Peitgen and Richter, 1986).

To generate fractal irregularity, it is necessary to have recourse to chaotic phenomena, to chance. Two degrees of order in chaos then emerge: the Euclidian order and the fractal order. The geometry of nature is, to a large extent, chaotic and can only be represented on a first approximation by the usual Euclidian forms and the manipulation of these using differential calculus

(Mandelbrot, 1975). It then becomes necessary to specify the type of chaos one is studying: 'Between the field of uncontrolled chaos and the excessive order of Euclid, we now have a new zone of fractal order.' In fact, fractal objects are pseudo-chaotic objects rigorously organized in terms of sophisticated laws of combination (Douady in Peitgen and Richter, 1986).

The analysis of fractal objects demonstrates that the dimensions of a territory that is represented will vary as a function of the unit of measurement adopted; the perimeter of the coast of Brittany is not the same when measured from a satellite (in tens of kilometres) as it is when measured out in human paces or by a centimetre rule. Furthermore, a phenomenon that is regular in appearance at a macroscopic level will have a chaotic, irregular appearance if the resolution for the observer is much greater.

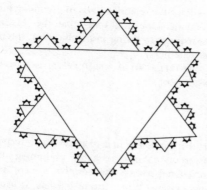

Example of a continuous non-differentiable curve with internal consistency: 'snowflake'-shaped Koch island.

In this way attention directed towards the psyche, towards the person within a group situation or towards the family considered as a micro-social unit, will lead to apparently different points of view, leading quite properly to opposite conclusions all of which do, however, have access to a certain level of reality. A chaotic and irregular boundary seen close up will appear smooth and regular from a sufficient distance. It is all the points of view integrated together that will give a coherence to an object that has been studied in reality.

This difference in unit of measurement, which characterizes the status of MAPS and related representations, is a pragmatic preoccupation of every therapist confronted with apparently totally irreconcilable points of view within a single family, the difficulty being to know the appropriate unit of measurement by which the intervention will be appraised.

(See also BOUNDARIES; FAMILY MAPS; GENERALIZED CATASTROPHES; INFORMATION; TERRITORY.)

J.M.

free association The rule of free association is the basic technical rule laid down by Freud and Breuer (1895) in the psychoanalytic treatment of adult neurotic patients. The analyst instructs the analysand to express verbally all that he is feeling and thinking, without attempting to select and without leaving out those emotions and representations perceived as improper, insignificant or irrelevant.

As Laplanche and Pontalis (1973, p. 179n), point out 'obviously the rule of psychoanalysis does not urge the subject to speak in systematically incoherent terms, but simply to avoid making consistency a criterion of selection.' Though this rule is fundamental in the structuring of classic psychoanalysis, it seems it must be modified to meet the specific circumstances in therapeutic situations which move away from that protocol. We shall note that the rule cannot be prescribed in situations dominated by an absence of demand, narrative incoherence, absence of preconscious structuring of representations and affects and inability to modify how one speaks to adapt to different persons and groups. Freud himself noted that the fundamental rule did not get the analyst very far in child analysis or with adults who are still very much dependent on reality conditions imposed by the presence of their parents (see TRANSFERENCE).

Ruffiot (1981b), who advocates its use in family therapy, calls at the same time for oneiric expression in an active form in the sessions. Many writers have recourse to techniques of psychodrama, sociodrama or active techniques, which were suggested as exceptional measures by Freud, but were later developed into a model by Ferenczi (1920). In fact, what becomes an exception in one context may become the rule in another.

In family therapy, the point is not so much to attempt to tell or express everything as to learn the contexts in which it is desirable, conceivable or indispensable to express oneself in a particular way. In dealing with the most disturbed families, rather than free association, one might lay down the opposite rule and call on subjects to dissociate thoughts, actions or emotions, in order to create spaces of security marked off by BOUNDARIES.

(See also ABSTINENCE, RULE OF; AFFILIATION; CO-THERAPY; DATA GATHERING; INTERPRETATION; SCHIZOPHRENIAS; SYSTEMIC HYPOTHESIS.)

J.M.

function of the symptom, the It is noteworthy that symptomatic behaviours often arise at moments when it becomes necessary to adapt or change rules that have been in force until that point, but have now become obsolete as a result of development brought about by growth. Events such as the birth of a child, a child starting school or reaching adolescence make it essential that the rules, the homeostasis and the relations between the family members be re-defined, together with the pattern of family life. When the system feels threatened by the possibility of a change of rules, a symptom may appear in order to maintain the status quo or to protect the system from any danger.

It then frequently appears that the function of the symptom is to resolve a conflict between HOMEOSTASIS and homeorrhesis. It protects the present operation of the system and serves to prevent a threatening change to the FAMILY SYSTEM. In spite of the pain it causes, it brings with it benefits for each of the members. It represents the best solution the family system has found to ensure its survival.

(See also FAMILY LIFE-CYCLES; FAMILY RULES; PRESCRIPTION; SYMPTOMS.)

M.G.

functional circle   The setting in place of the subject–object structure, which von Uexküll (1956) suggests is characteristic of the semantic organization of the animal world.

The subject–object relation is based upon a long phylogenetic history. von Uexküll (1956) proposes the concept of functional circle to describe the animal relationship between the inner world of the subject and the objects characteristic of his environment. From the simplest to the most complex animals, a more or less successful self-referential sufficiency exists between the inner world of the organism and its environment. Simple animals objectivate a simple environment; complex animals objectivate a complex environment. The 'animal' level of biological organization lays the ground for a subject–object relation: the 'animal subject grips its object in the two claws of a pincers – a perceptual claw and an active claw'. For an animal, an object will be a vehicle of perceptual and active characteristics. For an animal subject, an object may be a more complex animal (for a tick, it may, for example, be a mammal). Usually several functional circles are structured in a hierarchical relationship to one another.

Object relations become peculiarly complicated if one considers the development of the human child. For Winnicott (1963), the object is at the outset a subjective phenomenon and, as such, enables one to experience omnipotence. In a second phase, this 'subjective object' becomes an object that is perceived objectively. In communication, the object becomes transformed and the subjective is then perceived objectively, to the extent that the child abandons omnipotence as a living experience. On this point, Winnicott identifies a paradox which, in his view, must be left as a paradox: the object is created for the infant, and not simply found – 'A good object is no good to the infant unless created by the infant' (1963, p. 181) – and yet, in order to be created, the object must be found by the infant.

But one might add that the found object in its turn creates the infant. Similarly, in the human adult, the relationship between two or more persons itself becomes the object and subject on which the protagonists – or third persons – establish activo-perceptual functional circles; it is in this way that a relationship may become a subject capable of capturing one or more of its members as object. At the height of schizophrenic transactions, the relationship is not susceptible of objectivation, either by the members of the family or by the various professionals who intervene. It generates conflicts of interpretation and is the subject of communication, without being able to bring the participants into 'subjection' by putting them into positions where they are purely 'ruled by their passions'. A group conflict then exists regarding the definition to be given to the relationship. This break in the symmetry of inter-subjective relations leads to pseudo-symmetrical escalations. One might say that the relationship does not manage to 'bring into subjection' the objects it brings together.

(See also RELATIONAL ARCHETYPES; SEMANTICS OF COMMUNICATION.)

J.M.

fusion   Fusion is the first phase of any interpersonal or inter-group contact; it is the preliminary to any differentiation between the emotive system and the emotional system. When fusion persists, it leads to a non-differentiation of selfs and produces symbiotic relations. The BOUNDARIES thus created are enmeshed ones.

The emotive and intellectual functioning of every person is characterized by a greater or lesser degree of fusion or differentiation. Bowen (1978a) suggests that we assume the existence of a continuum between these two extremes, thus giving us 'a scale of DIFFERENTIATION OF SELF'. In the case of fusion, the intellect is totally submerged by emotivity. Existence is then determined more by the emotive process and by what 'is required to make one feel alright in oneself' than by beliefs or opinions. Bowen takes up arms against the view that differentiation of the intellectual system is synonymous with intellectualization and that the free expression of all feelings is the highest form of self-realization. In fact, a weakly differentiated person is wholly enslaved by his or her feelings. His or her efforts to achieve well-being by means of a close emotive relationship may increase fusion which, in its turn, increases his or her alienation from others.

(See also COUPLES; FAMILY EMOTIONAL ONENESS; FAMILY SYSTEMS.)

P.S. & J.M.

fusional postulate This is a term used by Hochmann (1971) to describe an underlying, but fundamental rule of operation within the family where relations are so symbiotic that any possible differentation between members is excluded. For example: 'We are all identical, we all think and feel in the same way; we are perfectly transparent to one another.'

(See also FAMILY EMOTIONAL ONENESS; FUSION.)

P.S.

future See SOLUTION-FOCUSED THERAPY.

fuzzy sets The concept of 'fuzzy set' was introduced by Zadeh (1965) to provide a mathematical solution to the problems of formalization of approximate, vague or imprecise situations. The concept makes possible the consideration of situations in which relations of membership or inclusion are not absolute, but have an imprecise character.

In classic set theory, an element either belongs or does not belong to a given set. The classic theory is based on binary logic in which the law of the excluded middle prevails. The theory of fuzzy sets is based on the fundamental concept of membership, but the compromise proposed by Zadeh (1976) introduces the notion of a gradual membership running from non-membership to total membership:

Almost the whole of human knowledge and interaction with the outside world involves abstract constructions which are not sets in the classical sense of the word but rather fuzzy sets, classes with indeterminate boundaries in which the transition from membership to non-membership is gradual rather than sudden. Almost all the logic of human reasoning is not the classical two-valued logic, but a logic of fuzzy truths, fuzzy connections and fuzzy rules of deduction.

These concepts permit a better approximation in clinical practice, linguistics etc. They make it posssible to formalize situations which defy binary logic.

As with ELEMENTARY CATASTROPHES and FRACTAL objects, it is the basic idea of *continuity* which is of interest. Membership of a social group cannot be treated as a precise concept. The theory of fuzzy sets introduces the possibility of formalizing partial membership or membership of multiple sets. It also complements the theory of logical types. In clinical situations, do we not see transitions that are continuous rather than sudden between the different logical levels of communication? If we examine in a practical way the CHANGES in the style of interactions obtained through family therapy, then we notice that the transition from pint-order change to second-order change comes about through very small changes. Qualitative leaps are not always to be seen. Further to this, the notions of fuzzy logic, which make provision for a continuity of values between true and false could offer us a means of formalizing the paradoxical phenomena of communication.

(See also QUANTIFIERS, RITUALS OF BELONGING; THEORY OF LOGICAL TYPES.)

M.G.

G

game theory Game theory is a mathematical tool which serves in the analysis of human social relations, starting out from the mathematization of the concept of utility. Game theory concerns itself not so much with PLAY itself, but rather with the rules of games and the individual 'plays' allowed by those rules. This theory, which was introduced by von Neumann and Morgenstern (1944), has principally been applied to decision-making strategies in economics. It is currently one of the most fertile sources of the application of mathematical methods in the human sciences.

THE THEORY

A game is a mathematical object formalizing a conflict between two or more persons known as 'players'. In other words, it is a situation which they judge in terms of contradictory preferences and which they may influence, if not in its outcome, then at least in certain parameters. Two types of game may be envisaged:

1 *Games in the inessential form* in which the power of decision is wholly and exactly shared between the players. The rules of the game entirely specify each player's scope for action and the set of players as a whole has no particular power, even to take partial decisions. Games such as go, chess, draughts or bridge are practically the only decision-making models in which these conditions are perfectly fulfilled.
2 *Games in the essential form* in which the players are obliged to cooperate or to form coalitions for a game to have a meaningful outcome (i.e. an outcome within a limited period of time). In this type of game, the point is to define a distribution of gains as a function of each player's scope for breaking cooperation.

Game theory directs its attention to the more precise study of this type of game and its objective is to analyse the power relations deriving from the strategic interdependence of the players. That is, how each of them will use the share of decision-making power which the rules of the game allow them. The analysis of game situations may be approached from two different points of view: the normative and the descriptive. The normative approach attempts to describe the optimal strategies of the players if any such exist. We should note that in most cases such an optimal strategy (one which ensures certain victory) does not exist. The theory provides no infallible response to the question 'How should one play?' It can at best define a 'prudent' and a 'sophisticated' course of action when no optimal strategy exists and the players may anticipate their competitors' moves. The descriptive approach does not seek to answer the question 'How should one play?' but rather the question 'How will the players play?' The answer to this question depends crucially on the mode of communication between the players. In this connection, game theory defines several concepts of equilibrium corresponding to the various modes of exchange of information. In all the game situations envisaged, each player is attempting either to maximize a certain value which we shall call the player's 'gains' or, on the other hand, to minimize another value which will represent his or her 'losses'.

GAME WITH A WINNING STRATEGY

Example 1

In the following game, each player has a choice between three possible strategies, A, B and C. The rule of the game, i.e. the distribution of payments as a result of the strategies chosen, is formalized in the following table, which represents the gains and losses of player 1.

Strategies/of player 2 of player 1	A	B	C	Maximum losses of player 1
A	−2	5	−3	−3
B	−1	0	−1	−1
C	−3	2	−2	−3
Maximum losses or minimum gains of player 2	−1	5	−1	Value of game: −1

A 'prudent' strategy is a strategy which minimizes the losses incurred or which maximizes the guaranteed minimum gains. Let us consider player 1. If he plays A, he risks losing −3; if he plays B, he risks losing −1 and if he plays C, he risks losing −3. It is thus in his interests to play strategy B which minimizes the maximum loss incurred.

Let us consider player 2. If he plays A, he will win at least 1 (loss of −1 for player 1). If he plays B, at worst he will gain nothing and if he plays C, as with strategy A, he will win at least 1. The prudent strategy for him is to maximize the minimum guaranteed gains. This player thus has two prudent strategies, A and C.

The payment being the same for the prudent strategy of player 1 and the prudent strategies of player 2, since in each case player 1 ensures a minimal loss of 1 and player 2 a maximum gain of 1, the game has an outcome. We say the game has a value, namely that of the payment obtained when the players play their prudent strategy. This situation only arises, however, when the minimum of the maximum losses incurred by the first player is equal to the maximum of the minimum gains guaranteed to the second player. In many cases, this does not occur and the prudent strategies are then not the optimal strategies.

Each of the players then attempts to anticipate the other's choice and to play a better strategy. This is what is called a 'sophisticated' strategy and it may lead to an endless game since each player may, in his or her turn, try to anticipate the behaviour of the other.

Example 2: No optimal strategy: oscillations
Each player has two possible choices and the payments are as follows:

	A	B	Min. gain
A	0	3	0
B	2	1	1
Max. loss	2	3	

Player 1's prudent strategy is B since it minimizes losses. At worst, he or she will gain 1, whereas with strategy A, he or she risks gaining nothing at all.

Player 2's prudent strategy is A, since it minimizes his or her losses: at worst he or she will only lose 2, as opposed to losing 3 with B. He or she can, however, anticipate that player 1 will play his/her prudent strategy B and it will then be in player 2's interest to play B also so as only to lose 1.

Player 1 anticipates the behaviour of 2 and plays A to win 3 rather than 1. Player 2 anticipates the behaviour of 1 and also plays A so as not to lose anything, etc.

Example 3: The Prisoner's Dilemma
This is one of the most famous examples in game theory. Two prisoners interrogated separately each have two options. They can either admit to a crime or accuse the other prisoner. The one who accuses the other prisoner goes free and the accused man serves twenty years in prison. If, however, they both accuse each other, they receive a ten-year penalty. If both confess, they get only a five-year sentence. More generally, this game represents a situation in which each player has to choose between a peaceable strategy and an aggressive strategy (here confessing = peaceable attitude, accusing = aggressive attitude), in which peace (peaceable A, peaceable B) is preferable to open warfare, but in which the surprise attack (using the aggressive strategy when the other player is peaceable) pays off. This situation may be formalized as in the following table:

	P2 confesses	P2 accuses
P1 confesses	5, 5	20, 0
P1 accuses	0, 20	10, 10

Each square on this table represents an outcome to the game. The two numbers represent the respective penalties meted out to prisoners 1 and 2.

It is in the prisoner's interest – and this therefore is his or her prudent strategy – to accuse the other prisoner, since in that case he or she is only risking ten years at worst instead of twenty with the peaceable strategy. The game has an equilibrium point if both players adopt aggressive strategies and this corresponds to the situation of open warfare. Such an outcome is not, however, satisfactory from the viewpoint of their general interest since the outcome if both were peaceable is strictly preferable for the two players (they would each receive five-year penalties). This is precisely where the dilemma lies. For a player who is not entirely certain of the peaceable intentions of his or her partner, the use of the aggressive strategy becomes imperative in the name of his or her individual interest, but the common interest clearly urges that everything should be done to arrive at the peaceable outcome.

APPLICATIONS OF GAME THEORY TO INTERPERSONAL RELATIONS

To bring out the contrasts between the Balinese cultural system and any kind of competitive system, Bateson (1972), in 'Bali: the value system of a steady state' takes a von Neumann type game and then considers the modifications which have to be made to it to describe the Balinese system more accurately. He proposes the hypothesis that social organizations are comparable to the systems of coalition in theoretical games.

In an abstract game, the players are motivated by the maximization of one value. Their strategies are determined by the rules of the game. Bateson notes the points at which human societies diverge from the games of von Neumann's theory.

1 The players in the theory are intelligent from the outset, whereas in society, human beings learn.
2 The value to be maximized is neither a single nor a simple one in mammals. An excess of a substance which may be necessary for survival may be just as harmful as a lack of that substance. Human games are multidimensional, not maximizing.
3 In game theory, the number of moves in a game is postulated as finite. The strategic problems of individuals have a solution in a limited temporal context. Games end and may be recommenced from scratch with the slate wiped clean. In society, life is not punctuated in this manner.

4 Theoretical players are not affected either by death or boredom.

Bateson emphasizes, however, that in spite of a multidimensional and non-maximizing system of primary values, human beings may find themselves in situations where they will strive to maximize certain values (money, power, esteem, prestige etc.). He proposes the hypothesis that Balinese society seeks to maximize the overall stability of the village rather than any individual simple variable. If one envisages a system made up of identical players and an umpire whose task is to maintain the stability of the system and who, to that end, has the power to modify the rules of the game, it is clear that such an umpire will find him or herself constantly in conflict with the players whom he or she prevents from maximizing their advantage to maintain the stable collective state.

To improve the model, it is sufficient to conceive the umpire as the village assembly made up of all the players. The players then have an interest in maintaining the stability of the village, i.e. preventing the maximization of every individual variable which, if excessively increased, would produce an irreversible change. This is quite clearly in conflict with individual competitive strategies.

Bateson also uses game theory to develop a circular model of transactions in the families of schizophrenics. More specifically, he uses game theory in the essential form, i.e. in which coalitions between players are essential if the game is to have a definite outcome.

For there to be a coalition, there have to be at least three players. Two of them – it does not matter which – may join forces against a third. Each of the three possible coalitions is stable. In effect, the player excluded from the coalition can do nothing against the other two. Bateson points out that things are quite different in a five-player game since there is then a much wider range of options. The possibility then arises of games within the game and of rule changes while the game is in progress. Four players may form a coalition against the fifth, but none of these five possible four-player coalitions is stable. In effect, each of the four allies will seek to increase his or her advantage, which will cause him or her to seek out a privileged ally within the coalition of four and form a sub-coalition with that person. That situation amounts to a model of two against two against one. The lone player may then attempt to associate with one of the two two-person sub-coalitions to form a three against two model. In this three against two system, it will be to the advantage of the three to get one of the other two players on their side to obtain a surer advantage. This, however, brings us back to the four against one model which will, in turn, break up into two against two against one, and so on.

For Bateson (1972, p. 211), this model is reminiscent of what goes on in the families of schizophrenics.

No two members seem able to get together in a coalition stable enough to be decisive at the given moment. Some other member or members of the family will always intervene. Or, lacking such intervention, the two members who contemplate a coalition will feel guilty *vis-à-vis* what the third might do or say, and will draw back from the coalition.

In game theory, at least five players are needed to arrive at this type of instability or oscillation. But human beings seem gifted at producing this kind of instability, even when there are only three of them.

I want to stress that in such a system, the experience of each separate individual will be of this kind: every move which he makes is the common-sense move in the situation as he correctly sees it at that moment, but his every move is subsequently demonstrated to have been wrong by the moves which other members of the system make in response to his 'right' move. The individual is thus caught in a perpetual sequence of what we have called double bind experiences. (Bateson, 1972, p. 211)

The major difference between human beings and von Neumann's theoretical game-players is learning.

The players in the dance which I have described [the von Neumann game] could never *experience* the pain which human beings would feel if continually proven wrong whenever they had been wise. Human beings have a commitment to the solutions which they discover, and it is this psychological commitment that makes it possible for them to be hurt in the way members of a schizophrenic family are hurt. (Bateson, 1972, p. 212)

Picking up on Bateson's analogy between schizophrenic transaction and game theory, Miermont and Angel (1983) have advanced the hypothesis that the schizophrenic game is a game over three generations involving seven players: the four grandparents, the two parents and the index patient.

The schizophrenic process would seem to become active and manifest as the various players from the initial matrix disappear. The patient who is recognized as schizophrenic would seem to embody as ancestor, totem or prophet, an antinomic combinatory of bygone players, who were the creators of the initial matrix. The shadow of that multiple combinatory of unstable games would seem to hover behind the current situation with five players (who are not necessarily the original ones) or three-to-four players, or even two players (the mother and her schizophrenic). Moreover, a sufficient number of therapists with multiple skills would normally have come to the rescue, especially when the number of survivors from the initial situation has diminished dangerously. What is then required of these therapists is that they accept the principle of symmetrical games, i.e. games in which their only scope for action is to make up part of the numbers, to be able to permutate therapeutic roles, functions and attitudes. (Miermont and Angel, 1983, p. 91)

(See also PLAY; REALITY; SCHIZOPHRENIAS.)

M.G.

gatekeeper Channel theory was first suggested in psychology by Lewin (1951, pp. 174–87). How do consumer goods (provisions, household goods) arrive in the family home and how are they used? Who controls their production or purchase? Who decides how they are distributed or who gets first choice? Gatekeepers regulate the incoming and outgoing flows of goods in a family.

In relation to foodstuffs, two essential channels contribute to the arrival of food on the table: the buying channel and, in some cases, in our societies, the gardening channel. It is important to know who, in a family, controls a particular type of goods, both of everyday consumption and of non-habitual consumption. On the simple level of food, we may look at the psychology of the 'gatekeeper' who regulates essential, secondary or luxury foods, as well as those foodstuffs which are prohibited or disliked. If the children do not have a role in such regulation, their anorexic or bulimic behaviours, as well as their refusal to eat certain foods (and indeed all foods in serious cases) reveal the possibility of conflicts between the marriage partners, if not indeed of transgenerational conflicts. We may note here that the intervention of a third party (doctor, psychologist or therapist) in such a situation is likely to modify the rate of circulation of a particular consumer good, if not indeed to modify the systems of control and decision-making of the 'gatekeepers' of a particular channel (Lewin, 1951).

(See also FORCE FIELDS; LAW; MULTI-CHANNEL COMMUNICATION SYSTEMS.)

J.M.

gaze, eye contact and posturo-gestural exchanges
Gaze is defined as the action of staring someone in the eyes or between the eyes or in the upper half of the face. When the gaze is reciprocated, one speaks of visual contact. This is, normally, of brief duration and corresponds to only one-third of the time spent watching others. For the establishment of reciprocal interaction, it needs to be maintained in a labile fashion and is broken off in a relatively subtle way in a mixture of voluntary and involuntary behaviour.

GAZE AND DEIXIS

Gaze seems to intervene at several levels while remaining dependent on other constituents of signalling/reception (Feyereisen and de Lannoy, 1985, pp. 133–44):

- establishment of contact, sign of attraction or power/intimidation;
- stabilization/equilibration of interaction, in joining (see AFFILIATION) behaviours;
- indication of the motivation to interact;
- information-gathering.

Communication by gaze is a powerful deictic (see DEIXIS). From its first month, the infant catches the mother's gaze, follows the trajectory and direction of her eyes and fixes its own gaze on the object designated in this way by the mother. Similarly, gaze is a powerful indicator of the emotions a person is expressing and triggers, in its turn, emotions of the same nature. Nothing is more frightening than the visual perception of a terrified gaze (a device used successfully in so many horror films), more frightening even than the direct perception of the terrifying object itself. Conversely, a tender, loving gaze from the mother triggers smiling and babbling behaviour on the part of her infant.

Unilateral and reciprocal gazes are integrated into every spoken communication. They vary a great deal between cultures. In interaction, the speakers determine the meaning to be given to the gaze. Speaking and silence seem to be coordinated by visual contact. The spontaneous nodding of the head when one's interlocutor is speaking maintains the RITUALIZATION of the exchange of words.

SEMANTICS OF GAZE

There is a whole semantics of gaze (Cook, 1977). This semantics rests on the interaction of natural and cultural codes. Hatred, love, flirtation, shame and friendship are expressed in differentiated expressions of the direct and reciprocal gaze. Courtship and flirtatious behaviour tend to make use of visual exchanges where acquiescence is less compromising than verbalized acquiescence. The dilation of the pupils has a seduction value and increases sexual excitation. Hatred quite frequently expresses itself through active avoidance of all visual contact with the other person in one's presence. Goffman (1963, quoted in Cook, 1977) terms this 'civil inattention'. By contrast, the lover's gaze is usually intense, frequent and exchanged reciprocally. A sense of shame causes the head and the eyes to be lowered.

Cook has shown how much the purely non-verbal

perception of visual expressions and facial signals can be deceptive. The interpretation presumed by the interlocutor often turns out to be different from the real interpretation which is confirmed when the person speaks. Conversely, the authentically felt attitude (of real aversion or profound love) may only be revealed in 'micro-momentary' changes which are only perceived in a frame-by-frame analysis and are undetectable in normal interaction.

Exchanges of eye contact by partners who have been married for many years appear to be rarer in harmonious couples than in others, in so far as they seem to reserve eye contact only for positive expressions of sympathy (Noller, 1980; quoted in Feyereisen and de Lannoy, 1985, pp. 187–91).

PATHOLOGICAL AND THERAPEUTIC VISUAL COMMUNICATION

Locating visual contact within a family, as well as the visual contact between members of the family and the therapist, is of great semiological and therapeutic interest. Establishment of contact normally occurs through gazes meeting, being stabilized and being averted.

Modifications of the process of seeking visual contact are to be found among autistic and schizophrenic patients. The absence of gaze or visual contact seems linked to withdrawal behaviour. When conditions are made favourable, such patients recover a normal gaze. Autistic withdrawal – whether we are speaking of childhood or schizophrenic autism – might be linked to a sensory over-stimulation, forcing the patient to establish a protective barrier from any human form which is perceived as intrusive (see INFANTILE AUTISM; SCHIZOPHRENIAS). The sense of being spied upon or observed, leading to pathological mental automatism, often goes together with particularly intrusive unconscious observation behaviour on the part of the parents, this being established without the patient realizing it (and the parents themselves not being aware of it, though it is in fact uncontrollable).

In consultation and therapy, eyes often converge on the index patient to objectivate him or her, examine him/her from head to foot, describe his/her odd behaviours. He/she, in turn, seems caught in a position where he/she solicits such behaviour on the part of those close to him/her and the therapists. By contrast, as soon as an inter-subjective linguistic exchange occurs, one finds that the index patient is spontaneously ignored and that particular interest is directed towards the therapists. The therapeutic modification of the positions of the family members in relation to the index patient leads to the restoration of sequences of normal spoken and oculo-gestural exchanges.

(See also AGONISTIC BEHAVIOUR; ATTACHMENT BEHAVIOUR; SEXED BEHAVIOUR.)

J.M. & P.G.

gender　The importance of gender has only been highlighted in the family therapy field in the past ten years. Feminist critics have pointed to the fact that systems theory is gender blind and, in so being, tends covertly to support social systems and beliefs about gender roles which buttress the patriarchal structures that are oppressive to woman.

Rachel Hare-Mustin, who was one of the first practitioners to draw attention to the importance of gender (1978) has argued, in a later paper (1987), that prejudices about gender can be categorized as 'alpha' and 'beta'. Alpha prejudices are those that overemphasize gender differences and thus create descriptions of masculinity and femininity that become objectifying and normative. She classifies psychoanalytic theory as an example of alpha prejudice. Systems theory comes into the category of beta prejudice by ignoring gender difference as a context for understanding human relations.

Among the reasons for this 'gender blindness' could be that:

1　The most prominent practitioners of family therapy in its early years were white middle class and male and thus less inclined to challenge oppressive social structures.

2　Systemic ideas and practice arose partly in reaction to reductionist views of behaviour and that included ideas of emotional experience being mediated through gender.

3　The move from the intrapsychic to the interactional view involved describing human relationships in terms of systemic rules, structures and informational systems which left no room for the subjective experiences of gender (Watzlawick et al., 1967; Bateson, 1971, 1978; Hoffman, 1981).

4　Strong ideological belief in family strengths and resources led to a denial of inequality within the family, which meant that generational difference (as an 'acceptable' power difference) was emphasized at the expense of gender (Goldner, 1988).

5　Family therapy offered a robust therapeutic model of change which was empowering to both male and female practitioners and led to an overemphasis on instrumentality at the expense of expressiveness and empathy which were experienced by practitioners as passive and ineffective (Walters, 1990).

FEMINIST CRITIQUES

Feminist critics of family therapy have emphasized in particular the extent to which therapists have treated the family as if it were a closed unit and have thus not explored the wider system of societal beliefs and inequalities within which the family is embedded, one of the foremost among them being patriarchy (James and McIntyre, 1983; Goldner, 1985, 1988).

The systemic concept of circularity, when applied to relationships between men and women, e.g. that oppressor and victim are participants in an interactional system around violence or abuse, can imply that the participation is based on equality. This fails to pay attention to the power differential which includes physical strength and differential access to resources.

Family therapists have been criticized for taking on board uncritically societal assumptions about men's and women's roles, e.g. that women should hold prime emotional responsibility for children. This has led to therapy which implicitly or explicitly blames the mother and which places less expectation on men to change. These criticisms have been made in relation to the different models of family therapy as follows.

Structural family therapy, as a model of the family which places particular emphasis on the restoration of parental authority, often in practice leads to the therapist aiming to support men's authority and diminish the power of the mother. Minuchin's therapeutic work has been particularly criticized for this because he often attributes children's problems with emotional development to over-closeness with their mother and disengagement from their father. In aiming to 'bring the absent father in to the family', the woman's expertise and competence may be seen as a threat and ignored or undermined (Minuchin, 1974; Minuchin and Fishman, 1981; Walters et al., 1988).

Strategic therapy, by emphasizing the therapist's power and by focusing on the problem at the expense of its history, context or meaning, can lead to interventions that, however creative, radical and effective in solving problems, are essentially conservative because they do not question assumptions or explore context. They may implicitly accept men's agenda for therapy which is more likely to be at a 'first-order' level of solving a problem, rather than women's, which is more likely to be at a 'second-order' level of changing relationships (Burck and Daniel, 1990).

Milan systemic therapists have primarily been criticized for appearing to believe in the neutrality of a therapeutic domain in which the gendered values and assumptions of the therapist are not constitutive. By acting as if the therapist treats all interactions as equally useful information, including violent or abusive behaviour, the crucial dimension of power is underplayed and thus the therapist can easily play a part in colluding with oppressive practices (Goldner, 1985, 1988; Luepnitz, 1988).

It is important to point out that all of these criticisms are made about the way therapists have generally used the theoretical framework; they are not inevitable criticisms of the models themselves. The following section describes how feminist thinkers have addressed the relationship between gender and family therapy.

ISSUES FOR A GENDER-INFORMED FAMILY THERAPY

Theory

Conceptualizing gender has been challenging to systemic thinking in three main areas:

1. Because gender is a, if not *the*, basic constitutive element of human experience (Chodorow, 1978; Gilligan, 1982; Goldner et al., 1990) the challenge is to incorporate gender into the theory without resorting to reductionist thinking, which renders systemic thinking useless as a conceptual tool.

2. Focusing on gendered experience challenges systemic thinkers to find new definitions of subjectivity (Leupnitz, 1988; Goldner, 1991b; Burck and Daniel, 1993).

3. The issue of power which has been a fundamental and unresolved debate in family therapy is clearly crucial (Dell, 1989).

Theoretical Integration

Whereas the systemic approach has largely failed to incorporate gender into its theoretical framework, there has been much rich cross-fertilization with feminist theorists in the fields of psychology (Baker Miller, 1976; Chodorow, 1978; Gilligan, 1982), linguistics (Spender, 1980; Cameron, 1985; Kristeva, 1986) and social anthropology (Mead, 1935; Eisler, 1988; Perelberg and Miller, 1990). These theorists have, in different ways, challenged the hegemony of academic disciplines to reveal their ordering though gender. Chodorow and Gilligan, in particular, have developed an account of psychological growth that addresses female experience. This has led to a crucial understanding and validation of women's experience that has informed the therapeutic process and challenged theorists and practitioners to take account of the development and experience of women as well as of men. Feminist linguists have brought the same critique to language, demonstrating its gendered base.

However, particularly in the context of postmodernist ideas (Hare-Mustin and Maracek, 1990; Nicholson, 1990; Goldner, 1991b), there has been a critique of this way of presenting women's experience as if it represented a unitary truth, and instead a focus on a multiplicity of experiences and a recognition of the different contexts for black and gay women (Hooks, 1982).

Subjectivity

Some feminist family therapists (Leupnitz, 1988; James, 1991) have argued that the systemic approach, with its basis in cybernetics, cannot provide an adequate theoretical model for understanding gender and subjectivity. They believe that object relations is a more promising theory for family therapists because it has a conceptualization of gender. There is a longer tradition of feminist therapists using psychodynamic approaches (Eichenbaum and Orbach, 1982; Irigaray, 1985; Benjamin, 1988) while maintaining a critique of many aspects of Freud's thinking. However, there is also much fruitful connecting of psychoanalytic and systemic approaches (Goldner et al., 1990) and much scope for the development of constructivist and social constructionst approaches to subjectivity. These theories focus on how our understanding of ourselves is constructed contextually, through relationships, language and societal beliefs about gender (Burck and Daniel, 1993).

Power

While the issue of power has been a crucial marker for feminist critiques of family therapy, there have been some important developments that have taken the debate further than the sterile question of whether power exists or not. Bateson's position that power is an epistemological error and cannot exist in the human world, when taken as a statement about *belief* in power, comes close to the position taken by many feminist writers critical of patriarchal values (French, 1986; Eisler, 1988). Understanding power as a constitutive as much as a repressive force (Foucault, 1980) has provided a means of understanding power systemically because it allows for an understanding of different levels of participation in oppression through relationship to the dominant narrative. Much creative and gender-sensitive therapy has developed from this theoretical framework (White, 1989). Feminist writers such as Goldner, who have been particularly influential in the field of family therapy, emphasize the importance of crossing boundaries and argue for maintaining the creative tension between psychoanalysis, developmental psychology, feminism and systemic thinking. There is much scope for further work in this area.

Clinical practice

In the past ten years there has been a large body of literature on feminist-informed family therapy (Braverman, 1987; Goodrich et al., 1988; Walters et al., 1988; McGoldrick, 1989; Durrant and White, 1990; Perelberg and Miller, 1990; Jones, 1991). Walters et al. (1988) have outlined principles of feminist-informed family therapy which include the need to empower women, to recognize that the personal is political, to challenge existing norms and to think about the different meaning of interventions for men and for women.

While structural therapists such as Marianne Walters would approach these issues directly and often prescriptively, other approaches informed by strategic or Milan systemic models would take a more questioning stance and focus more on dilemmas of change (Burck and Daniel, 1990, 1993, 1994; Papp and Silversten, 1990; Jones, 1991). Constructivist approaches to therapy focus on challenging fixed beliefs about gender including, crucially, those of the therapist and team.

Some of the most important and innovative work using a feminist and family systems approach has been in those areas of practice most challenging to therapist neutrality, i.e. violence and sexual abuse. Goldner et al. (1990) use an approach to therapy with couples in which the man is violent which, as well as dealing directly with the issues of men's responsibility and women's safety, also 'unpack' the gendered beliefs and experiences of the couple.

The work of Jenkins (1990) has been particularly influential in addressing issues of responsibility for violent men, using Michael White's ideas about identifying restraining beliefs and highlighting unique outcomes (White, 1988, 1989). Similar approaches have been used in working with perpetrators and survivors of sexual abuse (Durrant and White, 1990).

Teaching

Increasing numbers of training establishments in the USA and UK include gender as a core curriculum component, although a survey by Coleman et al. in 1990 revealed that many training institutes paid no more than lip service to the subject. This in part reflects a dilemma around whether the subject should be taught separately or integrated into the curriculum at every level. In turn, this reflects a continuing and much wider question of whether gender is still seen as a somewhat marginalized 'women's issue' or as a core and crucial dimension of relational experience. As such, it needs to involve much more attention to men's experience, not as the benchmark for all experience, nor only in relation to extremes of behaviour such as violence or abuse but as a construction of self within a patriarchal context (Mason and Mason, 1990; Segal, 1990). Connected with this, there is a challenge to the field not to isolate and thus reify gendered experience but to connect it to other forms of social inequality, marginalization and oppression.

G.D.

general systems theory Following Ludwig von Bertalanffy (1947), general systems theory defines a system as 'a complex of elements in interaction', such that:

1 The elements are sub-systems (or processors) which can also be broken up into smaller units, while the system is a sub-system of a larger metasystem (complex systems contain hierarchized systems embedded within them: see COMPLEXITY).
2 The interaction between elements or between systems and sub-systems is provided by negative and positive FEEDBACK, an expression of the circular causality which ensures the HOMEOSTASIS and homeorhesis of the system.
3 The system is OPEN or CLOSED, depending upon whether or not it permits exchanges of matter, energy and information with its environment.
4 Most often, the internal working of the system cannot be known; it forms a BLACK BOX and only the inputs and outputs can be perceived.

5   The black box is a morphology deployed in space–time.

As defined by Hall and Fagen (1956, p. 18), a system is 'a set of objects together with relations between the objects and between their attributes'. Watzlawick et al. (1967, p. 120) stress that, in this definition, 'objects are the components or parts of the system, attributes are the properties of the objects, and relationships "tie the system together"'. This set-theoretic definition appears inadequate since it does not specify the structure of the set in question, the way in which the elements are selected and the specific properties of the set.

Le Moigne (1977) points out that this is the theory of the general system as much as a general theory of systems, as is shown by the name originally given to it by von Bertalanffy, *General System Theory*. The advantage of this reversal of perspective is that it shows that that model, in its operational relevance, does not claim to be exhaustive, but rather localizes an object, so to speak, one essential property of which is to be general. For Le Moigne (1977), 'the theory of the general system is the theory of the modelling of (natural or artificial, complicated or complex) objects, with the aid of that artificial object gradually fashioned by the human thinking which L. von Bertalanffy proposed to call the General System: the system is a model of a general nature.'

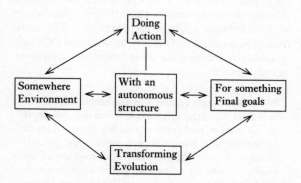

Canonical representation of the general system according to Le Moigne, 1977.

The elementary and fundamental processes act within a triple frame of reference: *form, space* and *time*. Their role is to deal with exchanges and transformations of matter, energy, information and symbols by the constitution of memories. The set of the constituents of the system is organized in the form of tree-structures (hierarchies) and feedback (Le Moigne, 1977). Such a system is an active, structured object, developing in an environment in relation to certain final goals. It oscillates between three poles: the genetic (origin and development), the ontological (its identity, its being) and

the functional (what it does). This system is not, as such, in nature, but in the minds of men. It possesses a function of representation. It is traversed by flows and creates dynamic fields. It is made up of at least one processor (sub-system within the system, or organs) generating momentum and activity. It is self-organizing and sets its own final goals.

The black boxes of the system can be studied from the perspective of their topological properties: every black box is bounded by more or less opaque walls; spatiotemporal interaction between the internal elements or between the black boxes presupposes connected pathways, whether material or psychical (Thom, 1983a). Certain parts of the system thus define the distinction between inside and outside (orientated topological spaces: see BALLS, SPHERES); other parts of the system move continually from the inside toward the outside and vice versa (non-orientated topological forms, see TANGLED HIERARCHIES).

Following the example of von Bertalanffy, systems theory has been applied in psychology and psychiatry (see in France the work of Audisio, 1978; Marchais, 1983; Wiener, 1983). Now, most often in the description of the various hierarchical levels, the family level is curiously occulted, as if it could be reduced either to the level of individual analysis or to that of the social body as a whole. General systems theory takes on its real dimensions in the human sciences when the family unit is perceived as a necessary level of articulation between the individual and society.

(See also CIRCULARITY; COMMUNICATION SYSTEMS; CYBERNETICS; DYNAMIC SYSTEMS; ELEMENTARY CATASTROPHES; FAMILY SELF-REFERENTIALITY; FAMILY SYSTEMS; HOLISM; MACHINES; METACOMMUNICATION SYSTEMS; MULTI-LEVEL HIERARCHIES; OSCILLATORS; PARACOMMUNICATION SYSTEMS; SELF-ORGANIZATION; SELF-REFERENTIAL CALCULUS; STRANGE LOOPS; SYMBOLS; SYSTEMIC MODELLING AND INTERVENTION.)

J.M. & M.G.

generalized catastrophes   Unlike static or pseudo-static forms, which are solely subject to a gradient potential, metabolic or organic forms (living beings, family and social systems) or mineral forms (galaxies, movements of the earth or atmosphere), which are subject to cyclical return, fall prey to generalized catastrophes when certain perturbations destroy the homeostatic restraints of their boundaries. To put it another way, their figure of regulation is destroyed (Thom, 1972).

On a phenomenological level, generalized catastrophes are of various types: filament, tubular, laminar, bubble, lump and arborescent catastrophes. Generalized catastrophes occur in metabolic forms, whether animate or inanimate. Metabolic forms are characterized by attractors of more than one dimension and have a circular, periodic character. The evolution of the system is thus subject to the phenomenon of recurrence. The trajectory of the fibre dynamic of the system returns close to its starting point. It thus cuts through the initial space an infinite number of times. The dynamic of the attractor of a metabolic form, to the extent that it possesses periods of its own, is capable of entering into resonance with similar metabolic forms. It is thus a 'significance carrier' (Thom, 1972).

A generalized catastrophe occurs through the destruction of the recurrence of this fibre-dynamic, by virtue of a perturbation which exceeds the possibilities of regulation of the system. In this sense, death and psychosis are generalized catastrophes of a catabolic type. Other generalized catastrophes are anabolic: genealogical arborescences, the explosion which occurs in the acquisition of language forms where each word becomes the object of a kind of locally circumscribed IMPRINTING process or process of BECOMING ACCUSTOMED.

It has recently become possible to formalize certain generalized catastrophes. The sets of ramified catastrophes have led to the mathematical understanding of FRACTALS or fractal objects. Most often, however, recourse to intuition is needed here, all the more so in that a great number of living phenomena are dependent upon systems in which there is recurrence. So far as behaviours are concerned, one would have to look for such forms in the PHASE SPACE which describes the inputs and outputs of the particular BLACK BOX under consideration. The more complex a DYNAMIC SYSTEM, the greater the number of dimensions of its ATTRACTOR. In a generalized catastrophe of the catabolic type, the initial attractor is destroyed, leaving the field to attractors of fewer dimensions. In the case of generalized catastrophes of the anabolic type, the resulting attractor is of a greater number of dimensions. It is probably only the living dynamic which is the site of generalized anabolic catastrophes.

(See also CHREODS; FORCE FIELDS; FUNCTIONAL CIRCLES; SEMANTIC RESONANCES; SEMANTICS OF COMMUNICATION; STATIC, PSEUDO-STATIC AND METABOLIC FORMS; VECTORS.)

J.M.

genetics and the family So far as heredity is concerned, it is not perhaps inappropriate to recall the fact that the great English biologist William Bateson, who introduced Mendelian theories into Great Britain was the first to use the term 'genetics' in its current sense. His son, Gregory Bateson, named in honour of Gregor Mendel, was to discover a new approach to psychopathology by re-evaluating the relations between adaptation and evolution. 'Trouble arises precisely because the "logic" of adaptation is a different "logic" from that of the survival and evolution of the ecological system' (Bateson, 1972, p. 309).

Like other animal species, the human race is subject to the laws of natural and sexual selection. At the same time, however, it gives the impression of escaping them, of being free from them, much as birds or aeroplanes seem to be free of the constraints of gravity. The diversity of kinship systems, both elementary and complex, means humanity is in some ways disengaged from the highly elaborate order of biological regulation. Kinship systems deal with universal biological data (Héritier, 1981): the existence of two sexes; the succession of generations as a result of procreation; the order of succession of births within a single generation, which distinguishes the elder children from the younger. This universal biological fact may seem 'simple' and 'banal' in the eyes of that particular writer, but the nature of neurotic and psychotic symptoms reminds us that the biological order in question is by no means so simple.

Not only does Bateson not hesitate to describe the negative aspect of schizophrenic disturbances, he clearly emphasizes this negative side by affirming the importance of genetic factors in the constitution of the schizophrenic double bind. Such a double bind corresponds to a complex LEARNING disorder. It even seems that this disorder concerns the very mechanisms responsible for certain basic forms of the learning of socialization, as these are manifested in the PRAGMATICS OF COMMUNICATION. Admittedly, what is involved cannot be mere Mendelian transmission in which there is a one-to-one relation between genotype and phenotype. The criterion of hospitalization is clearly by no means sufficient to enable us to distinguish those patients suffering from genetic defects:

> We cannot simply assume that the hospitalized members carry a gene for schizophrenia and that the others do not. Rather, we have to expect that several genes or constellations of genes will alter patterns and potentialities in the learning process, and that certain of the resultant patterns, when confronted by appropriate forms of environmental stress, will lead to overt schizophrenia. (Bateson, 1972, pp. 229–30)

Bateson goes further. The disorder concerns the genetic endowment which usually enables the subject to modify the environment by his behaviour, as in the case, for example, of mathematicians, musicians or humourists who are able to mould their natural and human environment to fit their inner dispositions. In a similar way, the environment of the schizophrenic is perfectly adapted to his or her symptoms, with the one qualification, however, that this schizophrenic disposition is a mark of substantial individual and group suffering. Bateson here proposes the hypothesis that while the patient displays manifest schizophrenia, there is latent schizophrenia in some of those close to him or her – most often the parents. This 'latent' schizophrenia (the manifest form of which may be regarded as a mere caricature) is, in Bateson's view, itself dependent upon genetic factors. Bateson is not simply 'dangerous' here; he is not merely handling traditional explosives but an arsenal which has implications for the survival of the species (or, at the very least, the notion of species)! We shall have to take this into account in the assessment we make of our activity as family therapists. Not only does Bateson call on us not to bury our heads in the sand, but he exhorts us to construct the appropriate contexts so that the *expression* of the very worst – of collapse, of cybernetic disorder, of alienating de-humanization, of incapacity to differentiate between the various systems of communication, and of the impasses generated by the antinomies of thought and action – can be recognized, explored, technically simulated and worked on, this being the only way in which they may at some point be overcome.

(See also EVOLUTIONARY SURVIVAL UNIT; GENETICS AND PSYCHOPATHOLOGICAL HEREDITY.)

J.M.

genetics and psychopathological heredity   For a long time, the only family model drawn upon by psychopathology was that of heredity. After a period in which, by contrast, those who argued for the psychogenesis of mental disorders repudiated any genetic contribution, the orientation today is towards interactive models in which the subject's history is seen as playing a part in bringing out and selecting constitutional predispositions.

Admittedly, very often the only arguments advanced in favour of genetic theses were of the order of FAMILY RESEMBLANCE, with destinies taking the place of physical features. As a consequence, they were open to the same criticisms as to the validity of comparing phenotypes. Let us attempt, however, to sum up what is currently known for the two groups of major psychoses.

SCHIZOPHRENIA

In 1979, Cassou and colleagues wrote that there was no scientific proof of any kind of a genetic contribution to schizophrenia, and they also pointed out that it was equally impossible to demonstrate the absence of any genetic effect. Nevertheless, we find a high level of concordance of the diagnosis of schizophrenia in twins where these are monozygotic (two-thirds of cases) and a much lower level in dizygotic twins (one-sixth of cases). However, the concordance is never total, even when all other factors are equal; and rates of concordance fall almost by half when monozygotic or dizygotic twins are brought up by different families.

Some authors conclude from this that schizophrenia is inheritable, arguing that its polygenic penetrance is connected with a gene-milieu interaction function (Debray et al., 1979). Inheritability is not, however, a property of the genes, but a measure of their deviation from the average of a clearly delimited population. For the genetic polymorphism that is the support of the predisposition to schizophrenia to be maintained constant within a population in spite of the low rate of reproduction among schizophrenics, the milieu must select the bearers of genes that predispose towards it, i.e. these genes must confer an advantage.

In other words, we arrive at yet another paradox. It is because the conditions of modern life encourage the survival of schizophrenic inheritability that the rate of schizophrenia in our population does not diminish even though individually the subjects predisposed to it are disadvantaged (Serre et al., 1979). However, genetic does not mean inevitable and the influence of lived experience remains preponderant in a subject's development. Indeed, we may go further and say that genetically programmed potentialities acquire dynamic intelligibility from the perspective of familial and social interactions (Miermont and Angel, 1982).

MANIC-DEPRESSIVE PSYCHOSIS

It is impossible to advance any definitive findings regarding the modes of transmission of manic-depressive psychosis on the basis of studies of families and twins. According to Mendlewicz (1981), in bipolar psychoses a dominant heredity exists which is connected with the X chromosome, though we also know of cases of father–son transmission, and he also argues that there is great genetic heterogeneity for unipolar depressions. In all cases, the risk of morbidity is increased for the members of the family of a proband (10–15 per cent as against 2–4 per cent for the population as a whole). Winokur (1974) has suggested that a gene is necessary for endogenous depression, which in women is also sufficient to bring about mania, whereas in men mania requires a second gene that is not connected to sex, a gene which, if absent, would make men vulnerable to alcoholism as a way of 'artificially' provoking states of mania. Let us add three further comments in reference form.

First, Andreasen and colleagues (1986) studied the family antecedents of 566 probands diagnosed as suffering from major unipolar depression (melancholia) and 2,942 of their first-degree relatives. They found no evidence of a higher frequency of family histories of thymus disorders in the relatives of subjects considered to be suffering from endogenous depression than in those suffering from non-endogenous (or what we would call reactional) depression. This tends to prove the emptiness of this distinction between depressions and therefore of any genetic theorization based upon it.

Secondly, Roy (1985) observed that in 300 cases of non-endogenous depression, an early and prolonged separation from the mother or father (which is significant when compared with a control group) is found in the subject's history. Thirdly, the heads of more than 5,000 families were interviewed every year in the USA for fifteen years (Elder, 1985). It was deduced from their accounts that the circumstances in which an event occurs, the way it is interpreted and the impression of control individuals possess are much more important in determining the affective consequences of that event than its mere nature. In other words, it is the context which determines whether or not an event constitutes MOURNING for a subject, with the attendant risk of depression or mania, and that context has much more to do with the family than with genetics.

(See also BECOMING ACCUSTOMED; DOUBLE BIND; GENETICS AND THE FAMILY; HABITUATION; IMPRINTING; INSTINCT; LEARNING; SCHIZOPHRENIAS.)

G.G.M.

genogram A genogram is a map that provides a graphic picture of family structure over several generations and gives a schematic representation of the main stages in the family life-cycle together with the attendant emotional processes. The standard repertoire of symbols was established by Murray Bowen (Carter and McGoldrick, 1980). It includes:

1 Names and ages of all family members.
2 Exact dates of birth, marriage, separation, divorce, death and other significant life events.
3 Notations, with dates, about occupation, places of residence, illness, and changes in life course, on the genogram itself.
4 Information on three or more generations.

The main symbols used by Murray Bowen act as a tool enabling the family members and therapists in training to modify and achieve greater exactitude in the perception they have of their own family systems, as well as their own positions within those systems.

Before intervening with a family, Bowen would hold an assessment interview in which he sought to establish the names, ages and activities of all the family members over three generations, as well as the main events both happy and unfortunate which have affected the family: dates of births, marriages, separations, changes of occupation or place of residence, deaths etc.

Male ☐ Female ○ Death ⊠ or ⊗

Marriage: Husband on left, wife on right ☐—○

Children: Listed in birth order beginning on the left with the oldest

Example: First child (daughter) ☐—○—○ Second child (son) ☐—○—☐—○

Common variations

Living together or common-law relationship ☐--○ Marital separation ☐—○ Divorce ☐—○

Miscarriage or abortion ☐—○ Twin children ☐—○—○○ Adoptions or foster children ☐—○—☐☐

The main standard symbols used in Murray Bowen's genograms (reproduced by kind permission of the author).

During family therapy, use of the genogram becomes a dynamic tool. The remembering of certain events does not follow a linear and direct logic of information-giving, but may possibly unleash intense emotional processes. The more the family system is confronted with serious pathology (for example, schizophrenia), the more difficult it is to raise the transgenerational dimension without eliciting fierce resistance. Most frequently this resistance is expressed in the statement that 'X or Y's symptoms have nothing to do with our history.' It also happens that the family history is subject to various taboos or silences, the slightest mention of the past being experienced as an explosive risk to the present system. Such defensive processes reveal the intensity of the emotional ruptures with which the system may have been confronted. As with any therapeutic action that is effective, the handling of the genogram, within the dynamics of a family therapy or a training group, presupposes a nuanced appreciation of the points where the persons and group in question are fragile.

(See also DIACHRONIC AND SYNCHRONIC AXES OF A THERAPY; FAMILY PSYCHICAL APPARATUS; FAMILY UNCONSCIOUS; LOYALTY; LEDGER; TRANSGENERATIONAL MEMORIES; TRANSGENERATIONAL THERAPIES; UNCONSCIOUS, THE.)

J.M.

grief See LOSS AND GRIEF.

H

habituation Habituation is a decrease in, and possibly even disappearance of, instinctual reaction resulting from the repetition of a releasing stimulus. It is equivalent to a mechanism of acquired desensitization, for example enabling the organism, when confronted with a potentially predatory form, not to release the flight reaction when the repeated presence of the form in question has not turned out to be predatory. It only requires a small modification of that form, however, for the reaction to be released once again (Lorenz, 1973, 1978b).

'The teleonomy of habituation resides in the fact that only certain stimuli subject to this process lose their efficacy, whilst the release threshold of all the other stimuli releasing the same reaction remains unchanged' (Lorenz, 1978b, p. 321). Habituation goes together with a complex associative phenomenon, since only a perceptual combination of highly differentiated stimuli inhibits the initial instinctive reaction. It is only when this combination is present that wild chimpanzees or gorillas allow themselves to be approached by man.

Habituation is thus one of the foundation stones of learning mechanisms. It shows that instinctual behaviour can be inhibited or redirected by a very elaborate perceptual configuration even in animals relatively low on the evolutionary scale. It is the converse of BECOMING ACCUSTOMED, which, for its part, only releases an instinctual reaction as a function of a differentiated perceptual pattern.

The human infant initially reacts to a very wide range of sensory stimuli (various noises, visual perceptions etc.). A noise which may apparently be inaudible to an adult because he or she is so used to it, attracts the child's attention. In psychopathology, the more undifferentiated the self (thus the more caught up in the instinctual emotional systems), the more the person reacts to the slightest stimulus by going on the alert, or even by anxiety and panic. The *qui vive* sweeps away boundaries. In a clinical situation, a psychotic patient thus reveals him or herself to be incredibly sensitive to a whole series of signals which pass totally unnoticed by those around him or her. This observation is confirmed by the statements of therapists who point out to the patient and to those close to him or her how hypersensitive he or she shows him or herself to be.

In fact, it is a precondition for a clinical interview with a psychotic patient that the therapist has convincingly shown that his or her intentions, both conscious and unconscious, will not aggravate the state of the patient, who already feels he/she is against the wall. The slightest lapse in the unconscious attitude of the clinician (or relations between family members and among the clinicians themselves) is immediately perceived as a source of danger.

(See also IMPRINTING; INSTINCT; LEARNING.)

J.M.

hatred See AGONISTIC BEHAVIOUR; FAMILY SYSTEM; LOVE, HATRED, KNOWLEDGE, INDIFFERENCE.

heredity See GENETICS AND THE FAMILY; GENETICS AND PSYCHOPATHOLOGICAL HEREDITY.

heteronomy See AUTONOMY AND HETERONOMY OF A SYSTEM.

heuristics Describes a form of reasoning which leads in a plausible, though not certain, manner to a stated result which is itself not certain. Heuristics are to be distinguished from the ALGORITHM which leads with certainty to a stated result. There may be systemic modelling without algorithms, where there are heuristics. Heuristics are based on decision-making trees, characterized by the lopping off of unusable branches.

Modes of reasoning which, for example, reduce the scale of the fields of research involved in a particular problem are defined as having heuristic power. These may be selection procedures or, in science, 'concepts' or 'theories' that are likely to bring to fruition strategies with a sufficient success rate in fields that are too complex to be totally explored.

The heuristic search is thus the opposite of the algorithmic calculation. This latter is ideally possible when one is dealing with variables of linear functions, the dynamic relationships between which can be represented by linear difference equations (see Simon, 1979). When dealing with non-linear systems, heuristic procedures, though apparently less certain, reveal themselves to be more profound and, most importantly, more effective.

The concept of heuristics was restored in 1945 by the mathematician Polya, through his reflections on the forms of reasoning actually deployed in problem-solving (one makes stabs at the problem, tries things out, looks for analogies, sets oneself intermediate goals etc.). One thus uses reasoning without, for all that, performing 'deductions'. Polya was to go on to do a great deal of work on 'plausible reasoning'. Like the algorithm, the heuristic is programmable. It was upon this observation by Newell and Simon (1972) that the development of artificial intelligence was to be based.

Like the mother in Winnicott's theory, the heuristic approach seeks 'good enough' solutions, by modelling the world that is to be studied and by posing demands for structural elucidation that are much weaker than the rules laid down in linear decision-making. The heuristic search makes it possible to find solutions that are satisfactory without necessarily being optimal. In practice and in theory, the possible situations where optimal solutions can be found are very rare. The optimum can only be defined when we are in prior possession of an algorithm enabling us, in theory, to determine it. The heuristic approach deals with problems of the combination of different factors for which there is no effectively calculable solution, even using very large computers: 'It is an especially powerful problem-solving and decision-making tool for people who are unassisted by any computer except their own minds, hence must make extensive simplifications in order to find even approximate solutions' (Simon, 1969: 2nd edn, 1982, p. 35). The heuristic search can be applied to the processing of numerical and non-numerical information through the establishment of qualitative procedures. It functions by generating hypotheses and testing them.

Some problem-solving programmes have been designed independently of the precise objectives to be achieved. These programmes have several knowledge fields to manage, which may possibly be independent of each other. The job of the programme will be to test out the interest of a concept. It may be the case that a concept is interesting, for example, if it is intimately linked to other equally interesting concepts, or if examples – and not necessarily immediate ones – are found to justify it. The example will itself be interesting if it is a 'limiting' example, i.e. if it only barely satisfies the definition of the concept. Such a programme will normally have a set of several hundred heuristics with which to construct examples for practical application. Selectivity in trial-and-error decision-making procedures is part of heuristic research: certain paths are explored first, others are systematically eliminated by 'scanning through' procedures.

Like every individual who has to practise and conduct research in the 'human sciences' field, the family therapist is caught between two fires. Therapeutic activity needs a protective ring thrown around it. Therapists may tend to search for precise algorithms, which are often described as 'technique', or pre-established

programmes of intervention in treatises on family therapy. In so doing, they run the risk of missing the point of the therapeutic process which, by its essence, cannot be strictly codified and often arises from an 'accident' occurring in the established protocol at a deep strategic level. A literal application of interview techniques soon leads down blind alleys, of the kind explored in Flaubert's novel *Bouvard and Pecuchet*.

This shows the importance of – if not indeed the necessity for – a heuristic approach, both in the modelling of the family system and in the interventions which may be carried out. Only very rarely can human situations be dealt with by an algorithmic approach, since they are complex, ambiguous, involve a multiplicity of criteria etc. In practice, you have to 'invent' a solution you had not thought of rather than apply a method leading to a strictly predefined result.

If, then, a number of concepts in the human sciences are fuzzy ones, whose origins are confused and which, in combination, give rise, as Bateson rightly reminds us, to a conceptual fog, they none the less enable us to engage in heuristic reasoning. The concepts of 'ego', 'anxiety', 'the unconscious', 'instinct', 'goal', 'mind', 'family', 'self', 'fixed action model', 'intelligence', 'stupidity', 'maturity' etc. doubtless should not be taken too greatly to relate to fixed entities. And yet they still have great heuristic value. Thus, when it remains aware of its limits, the heuristic approach shows itself to be distinctly more respectful of reality than is an endless quest for algorithms.

(See also ABSTINENCE; FREE ASSOCIATION; INTERPRETATION; PRESCRIPTION; SYSTEMIC HYPOTHESIS.)

J.M.

holism From the Greek *holos* (meaning 'which forms a whole, is entire'), refers to those theories which affirm that the whole is more than the sum of the parts. Watzlawick et al. (1967) thus state that 'the analysis of a family is not the sum of the analyses of each of its members.' The family unit thus possesses an 'emergent quality' irreducible to the personal qualities of the members who make it up. A rider must, however, be added to this statement: in some cases, the member of a totality is greater than a fraction of the whole. Thus Morin states: 'a system is more, less, other than the sum of its parts. The parts are less, possibly more, but in any case other than what they were or would be outside the system' (Morin, 1977, vol. 1).

The most nuanced description of the relations between the elements that make up an organism in its entirety is at the heart of Claude Bernard's thinking in *An introduction to the study of experimental medicine* (1865). The properties of bodies do not derive solely from the properties of their constituents, but also from the manner in which they are arranged. 'Moreover, as we know, it happens that properties which appear and disappear in synthesis and analysis cannot be considered as simple addition or pure subtraction of properties of the constituent bodies' (Bernard, 1966 edn, p. 140). The mere dissociation of the parts from the whole thus causes the phenomena to disappear by the destruction of relations. Whether it is a question of elements of organic matter or of people isolated from their social, institutional environment, the appearance of characeristic properties only arises from the union of isolated elements. The union of these elements 'though distinct and self-dependent . . . expresses more than addition of their separate properties'. But Claude Bernard none the less remains prudent, since acknowledging the importance of relations and the quality attaching to the totality must not distract the observer, researcher or clinician from the analytical properties of the components, on pain of introducing an extreme scientific regression. Analytic and synthetic methodologies are, therefore, two approaches running in opposite directions, but they provide necessary correctives to each other in relation to the – scientific, clinical or therapeutic – objectives being pursued. Though they cannot merely be reduced to these two elementary axes, the psycho–pharmacological, psychoanalytic and familio–socio–systemic approaches are the expression of this necessary tension and these constraints.

The system of a living organism, simple or complex, is never at rest, but in a permanent state of excitation. In a complex living organism, any stimulation at a particular point will produce changes throughout (Goldstein, 1934). That is why the concepts of reflex and INSTINCT are, in Goldstein's view, to be criticized. Their isolation is in itself a pathological or experimental artefact which, in reality, is always integrated into a global activity. But the question which then remains is the following: what are the limits to this 'throughout' and where does the 'organism as a whole' end? An organism living in isolation is as much an artefact as the reflexes or instincts one is seeking to analyse. Every organism is part of a population unit or an EVOLUTIONARY SURVIVAL UNIT and it is in a global fashion that these are themselves affected by change, as, for example, when medication is prescribed for, or psychotherapy undertaken with, one of the members making up that unit. We may go even further. This notion of totality relates not only to human systems.

Another example is that of the so-called 'moiré phenomena', which are optical effects produced by superimposing two or more lattice patterns. In this way, we reach a complexity which could never be accounted for on the basis of the elements taken alone. And even if it is principally around the workings of the brain that thinking about totalities which are irreducible to their component parts has been reactivated, these 'beats and moiré phenomena' (Bateson, 1979, p. 79) open up a space for interpretation that is much wider and, in Bateson's view, includes, among other things, 'poetry, dance, music, and other rhythmic phenomena' (1979, p. 80).

Moreover, all clinical practitioners have encountered drug-users who, by taking a knock-out dose, attempt a wildcat recourse to totality, an attempt which results from a failure of elaboration in metonymic-metaphoric play and an inability to integrate the constituent emergence of a totality (individual, family, nation) beyond its component parts.

The fact that holism is based on the differentiation of, and interaction between, parts shows it to be heir to yet another tradition, that of the 'structural historicism' of Lefebvre and a whole range of post-Marxist writers who, by associating the problem of the irruption of totality with that of transition between the continuous and the discontinuous, throw an epistemological bridge over to CATASTROPHE THEORY. This 'holistic' style of thought is, however, sometimes reduced to a third-rate mysticism based on a few snippets of Eastern philosophy, such as: 'What the soul designates as reality as such is the unity of all things, the "Great All"', which, when taken out of context, are about as meaningful as the statement that 'Everything is in everything else and vice versa', as the French humourist, Pierre Dac, would say. Thus, to base one's practice upon holistic interpretation means understanding the precariousness of the equilibria between multiple and shifting hierarchies (Gurvitch, 1962). What is involved is an increased degree of complexity, which requires the adoption of specific strategies in the approach that is to be taken towards it: framing games, reflection on TANGLED HIERARCHIES, working out the nature of antagonisms, articulation of maps to territories and construction of reality.

For want of such a complex holism, one may observe the effects of a wildcat holism, for example in the search for a globalization of the phenomenological categories of space–time without first studying the drastic constraints to which forms are subject in their spatiotemporal inscription. Such as inscription (territory) is one of the three basic anthropological axes, alongside self-maintenance (i.e. nutritional constraints) and the reproduction of the species (essentially, the sexual urge).

(See also GENERAL SYSTEMS THEORY; HOLOGRAPHIC MEMORY; MULTI–LEVEL HIERARCHIES.)

D.C., J.M. & G.G.M.

holograms, hologramorphism See HOLOGRAPHIC MEMORY.

holographic memory, holoscopic memory Holography, invented by the Hungarian physicist

Dennis Gabor in 1947, is a system of information-processing such that a hologram element is an extract from the spectrum of an object distributed over the whole hologram: each part of the object is represented in the totality of the hologram and each part of the hologram represents the totality of the object. Hologramorphism describes a fundamental property of the functioning of memory which is reminiscent of the SELF-REFERENTIAL CALCULUS.

After the invention of the hologram by Gabor, its application in physics was made possible by the use of the laser by Leith and Upatnieks, and its application in neurophysiology by Karl Pribram and Christopher Longuet Higgins. Hologramorphism is based on a FRACTAL property of the processing of information, which completes the cybernetic description of systems of codification.

A hologram element is an extract from the spectrum of the object, distributed over the whole hologram. Each point of the object is memorized in the whole hologram; each point of the hologram contains information on each point of the object and thus on the whole object (Pinson et al., 1985). Thus if the hologram is broken, the entire object will appear in each broken fragment of the hologram, but it will be fuzzier than before.

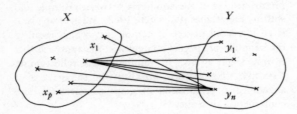

The modelling of a highly holographic representation of an object: almost every point x_p of the object X is represented by the quasi-totality of hologram Y. Almost every point y_n of hologram Y represents the quasi-totality of object X.

The hologram shows the existence of non-localizable phenomena of memorization. The holographic structure of communication functions in the recognition of shapes, the representation of mental images, and the understanding of language. In the figures of rhetoric, a word contains the semantic spectrum of a set of words in a circular fashion. It is thus difficult to extract a word from its semantic field. Information is, therefore, 'distributed' and 'degenerated': an error does not have the same importance here as in algorithmic logics or even in heuristic logics. There is no error at a precise point: nothing is, strictly speaking, wrong, but nothing is, strictly speaking, true either.

The interest of holographic modelling for family therapy lies in the fact that the SYMPTOM is at one and the same time a totality representing every element of the context and an element in the totality of the context. A singular feature in the family's functioning may reveal a property of the whole group. Each family member possesses a holistic representation of his or her family system, while the family system is distributed and 'degenerated' information about each person. Family therapy is the more necessary where the holographic representation of the system is fuzzy and indistinct. The unfolding of a course of therapy is part a sort of defining process: each session represents the totality of the course of therapy, while the whole of the therapy is more or less present in each session. Only the complete unfolding of the therapeutic process ultimately provides a precise representation of the family system. Cade (1985) uses the holographic metaphor in describing his approaches to therapy.

(See also ALGORITHM; ANALOGIC CODING; ARTIFICIAL CODES; DIGITAL (OR NUMERIC) CODING; FUNCTION OF THE SYMPTOM; HEURISTICS; MESSAGES; MYTH; RITUALIZATION; SEMANTIC SPECTRUM OF THE PROPER NAME; SYMPTOMS; TRANSGENERATIONAL MEMORIES.)

J.M.

home As Maurice Porot (1954, pp. 10–11) points out, in addition to the essential persons (father, mother and child), the family only takes shape around an essential 'fourth person', the home.

> The chance coming together of a man, a woman and a number of children selected at random does not make a family: the home, which is based above all on the parental couple, is a spiritual, living being with a past, a present and a future that profoundly influence the relations established between the constituent elements.

This symbolic personage ensures reciprocal solidarity of roles and normally enables the child to find love, acceptance and stability, which are the preconditions for a sense of security. The home therefore functions as a centre of attraction, allowing a sufficient convergence of relational movements towards the material and spiritual centre of the family. The home is to some extent the entity that makes it possible to resolve, with greater or lesser degrees of conflict, the following paradox. From an affective point of view, reality, even when hidden, has much more influence on the child than appearances; the parents must demonstrate that the appearance of unity of their points of view regarding the upbringing of the children is more than mere appearance, even though they are not able to avoid conflicts over the decisions that have to be taken.

Porot describes three forms of pathological home:

1 Non-existent homes: the couple is not formed as such, even if the partners live together.

2 Unstable homes, with the existence of acute latent misunderstandings giving rise to a great number of evasive solutions and the search for compensations.
3 Broken homes.

There is, however, no such thing as a perfect home. The home may suffer from being too ideal just as much as from failure to meet ideals. The multiple and opposed constraints to which it is subject may thus hinder its birth, development, transformations, reproduction and disappearance.

(See also ATTRACTORS; COUPLES; DYNAMIC SYSTEMS; FAMILY–THERAPEUTIC INSTITUTION DIFFERENTIATION; FAMILY MYTHS; FAMILY SYSTEMS; FORECLOSURE; MARITAL BREAKDOWN; MESNIE; MYTH OF HERMES.)

J.M.

homeostasis, homeorhesis Homeostasis refers to the stabilization of the state of living organisms by the maintenance of the various physiological variables within constant limits (regulatory mechanisms). Its complement is *homeorhesis*, which describes the stabilization of the flows of organisms, the stabilization of their temporal trajectories and thus their time-extended course of change through the non-linear fluctuation of physiological variables (Waddington, 1975; see also CHREOD).

Though Cannon introduced the concept of homeostasis in 1929, many years after it was first prefigured by Claude Bernard (1865) ('constancy of the internal milieu'), it seems that its general application to systems only became apparent with the writings of Wiener (CYBERNETICS in which homeostasis is associated with negative FEEDBACK), von Bertalanffy (1947) and Weiss (see Piaget, 1976).

Don Jackson (1957) was the first to identify the homeostatic mechanisms at work in family groups. Psychotherapeutic action undertaken with an isolated individual creates feedback within the other members of the family system which leads, possibly unknown to them, to an attempt to return to the initial state. In flexible family systems (where the symptomatology is, essentially, neurotic), this attempt will take into account the context and the temporal evolution of the family; in rigid systems, the slightest attempt at change causes possibly lethal outbursts which reinforce the status quo and the 'outside SPACE–TIME' aspect of the system.

The classic homeostasis of the system is achieved with the aid of negative feedback. A homeostatic system is an OPEN SYSTEM, maintaining its structure and functions by means of a multitude of dynamic equilibria controlled by independent regulatory mechanisms. Such a system reacts to every change arising from the environment or every random perturbation by a series of modifications running in the opposite direction. The ultimate goal of these modifications is the maintenance of internal equilibria. The evolutionary capacities of the system depend upon positive feedback, which pushes it apparently a long way from the initial equilibrium state.

The idea of family homeostasis sums up the tendencies of the family system to maintain its coherence, stability and security within its physical and social environment. Homeorhesis describes the trajectory of its transformations over time, the time-extended course of the flows that traverse it.

HOMEOSTASIS, HOMEORHESIS AND FEEDBACK

The way this notion is used reveals an ambiguity in its definition: homeostasis refers both to an *end*, the existence of a certain constancy in spite of changes, and a *means* to arrive at that end: regulatory mechanisms, negative feedback loops which mitigate the repercussions of a change and tend to bring the system back to, or keep it in, a stable state. The cybernetic approach describes the family as an open system maintaining itself in a stable state by the play of two antagonistic and complementary forces, family homeostasis and the capacity for change (homeorhesis), the balances between these forces making it possible for the family to modify itself without losing its identity and finality as a viable context for its members.

Negative feedback and homeostasis thus appear as an essential condition of survival for complex systems. Apart from a homeostatic tendency, living systems do, however, possess a property for evolving toward higher degrees of organization, i.e. a capacity to adapt themselves, to self-organize. This capacity to evolve depends upon positive feedback loops and leads to homeorhetic processes. During the system's encounter with random perturbations from the environment (events, mutations, 'noise' etc.), the *positive feedback* enables the system to seek other stationary modes of functioning, increases the number of action options, accentuates differentiation and enriches the 'palette' of responses to the possible forms of aggression from the environment and therefore leads to an increase in the complexity of the system. Homeostatic and homeorhetic phenomena introduce a dynamic vision by bringing duration and irreversibility into the nature of phenomena, causality becoming circular, leading, by virtue of the temporal dimension, to periodic cyclical structures (Thom, 1983c).

FAMILY HOMEOSTASIS AND HOMEORHESIS

Systemic modelling of the family has brought out these two essential – homeostatic and homeorhetic – properties (the maintenance of identity going hand in hand with the capacity to adapt to change). The complementarity between homeorhesis and homeostasis has led to a distinction being introduced between rigid family systems and others. In rigid systems, relationships are virtually crystallized in 'stereotyped roles, to the detriment of new and differentiated experiences and information which are experienced as too threatening to the family equilibrium' (Andolfi et al., 1979, p. 26). Personal space is denied in deference to the homeostatic ideal. The cybernetic approach to families has created techniques aimed at frustrating that ideal (see PARADOXES; POSITIVE CONNOTATION) which assume that it is sufficient to reduce homeostasis to give rein to the capacity for change.

Catastrophe theory and non-equilibrium thermodynamic models produced further development in this field, putting greater emphasis on change and its morphogenetic and dynamic properties. The hypothesis common to the two models is that stability responds to an extremum principle: states which are stable and where homeostasis functions are those which render extreme a particular function of the parameters of the system and the constraints to which it is subject. Structural instabilities only occur if the external parameters cross a critical threshold. The point is no longer to thwart homeostasis, but to attempt to push the system beyond a critical threshold into a zone of instability where any little internal fluctuation will be able to become amplified, forcing it to pass beyond its limits and to reappear in a different state.

Family homeostasis is underpinned by a set of rules specific to each family. It is the range of the family system's negative feedback when it is faced with perturbations which constitutes this set of operational rules. When faced with imminent change (the birth of a child, departure of an adolescent, a death etc.), the family system will activate its homeostatic tendency by seeking to find out whether the risk of change does not imperil its mythical and spiritual identity. The more that identity is threatened, the more rigid the negative feedback will become. In the most disturbed families, the basic therapeutic strategy consists in reinforcing that identity, which is the only way of adding positive feedback to that system and with it the prospect of homeorhetic transformations.

Homeostasis derives from several logical levels. On a first level, homeostasis resides in the way the family has organized itself to ensure its survival. One may then suppose the existence of family rules, which are kinds of implicit laws tacitly accepted by all the members of the family, which divide up functions, roles and tasks, manage interactions etc. The identity and specificity of the family reside in the set of rules which express the conception the family has of itself. On a second level, the notion of homeostasis is associated with the existence of regulatory processes whose function is to preserve and confirm the validity of the rules in order to ensure the maintenance both of the family's identity and of its specificity. A third level loops on to the other two and supposes the existence of meta-rules

indicating how far the rules can change to enable the system to adapt itself to the environment or individual exigencies without its being threatened with destruction. The meta-rules are, then, homeostatic processes which manage the homeorhesis–homeostasis complementarity. We find this same paradoxical reasoning in the use of the notion of regulation. What regulates the regulation of the system, if not its own regulation? The use of the concept of homeostasis reveals its profoundly self-referential nature.

If one views the family as a self-organizing system, the homeostasis–homeorhesis antagonism coincides with an *information-gathering structure* which chooses from the environment, both internal and external, those events it will be able to integrate into itself in order to change itself. An event only assumes meaning for the family system after having been compared and integrated with what constitutes the conception the system has of itself. The systems described as rigid have a narrower selection structure. Rather than being continuous, evolution occurs in a discontinuous fashion. It breaks down the figure of regulation and leads to a painful destabilization leading to therapeutic intervention. Bateson defines the flexibility of a system as a maximum of 'uncommitted potentiality for change (1972, p. 473) and the capacity to take on the greatest possible number of new elements as a means of enriching one's structure.

(See also CYBERNETICS; FAMILY SYSTEMS; GENERAL SYSTEMS THEORY; SELF-ORGANIZATION; STRUCTURAL STABILITY; UNIVERSAL UNFOLDING.)

M.G. & J.M.

homology See ETHOLOGY.

hubris Excessiveness, wantonness, violence (for example, the proud insolence of the suitors of Penelope, the wife of Ulysses) describes the pretension to succeed one day or another in bringing off a relationship with a 'difficult' partner, even at the price of death. Hubris is not a psychical attribute inherent in persons but 'a function in this type of relationship in which symmetry increases hubris and hubris symmetry' (Selvini Palazzoli et al., 1978, p. 29).

(See also SCHISMOGENESIS; SCHIZOPHRENIAS; SYMPTOMATIC AND/OR AETIOLOGICAL TRANSACTIONS.)

J.M.

humour According to Freud, *Jokes and the relation to the unconscious*, 1960a, the essence of humour resides in the fact of sparing oneself unpleasant or painful feelings connected with the situation in which one finds oneself, to make way for a joke which rises above the affective tension and enables one to free oneself from it. On the economic level, humour corresponds to a saving in the expenditure of affect. The humorous attitude may be directed either against others or against oneself.

Humour differs from the comic in so far as it involves an elevated, sublime dimension. This dimension would seem to be connected with the triumph of narcissism, which victoriously affirms the invulnerability of the ego. It enables the pleasure principle to be affirmed and the claims of reality denied. 'Its fending off of the possibility of suffering places it among the great series of methods which the human mind has constructed in order to evade the compulsion to suffer – a series which begins with neurosis and culminates in madness and which includes intoxication, self-absorption and ecstasy' (*Standard Edition*, vol. 21, p. 163).

The value of humour has to do with the fact that it succeeds in *maintaining psychical health*, while affirming the victory of the ego over reality, and the satisfaction of the pleasure principle. One can see why this particular mode of communication with oneself and others should be one to be pursued as one of the possible solutions to pathological suffering. Freud further states that 'A joke is . . . the contribution made to the comic by the unconscious . . . In just the same way, *humour would be the contribution made to the comic through the agency of the super-ego*' (*Standard Edition*, vol. 21, p. 165; Freud's emphasis). By hyper-cathecting his superego, the person in a sense prescribes the symptom to it, alters its reaction and obliges it to become full of solicitude towards the ego.

Humour arises out of the confusion of irreconcilable logical levels that are suddenly brought together ('Towards a theory of schizophrenia' in Bateson, 1972). It has its basis in a condensation of apparently incompatible modalities of communication and emerges at the point where the classification of these modalities is dissolved and re-synthesized. Following André Breton (1939), we may distinguish between *l'humour d'émission* (voluntary humour) and *l'humour de réception* (involuntary humour), this latter being closely related to the expression of madness itself. If we further admit consideration of the nature of the channel utilized, and thus the structure of the medium, the voluntary and involuntary aspects of humour are usually regulated by one another. Thus the apparently unmotivated wild laughter of a schizophrenic patient may acquire meaning in the restoration of family communication. In other words, the appreciation of humour defies any clear signposting of the modalities of communication. It varies as a function of persons, situations and cultural codes.

J.M.

hypnosis, hypnotherapy   Hypnosis is a state of subliminal consciousness occurring spontaneously in animals and man as a vital reaction in moments of extreme danger and/or in response to a violent physical or psychical trauma. Hypnosis is not used as such in family therapy though many techniques have been borrowed from the innovative hypnotherapist, Milton H. Erickson. This American psychiatrist in fact re-thought the use of hypnosis, introducing innumerable modifications into the trance-inducing techniques and recasting the conduct of therapy. Erickson was wary of theoretical constructs and he devoted the greater part of his activity to developing new modes of intervention which attracted the attention of some of the pioneers of family therapy, especially Jay Haley (1973). Watzlawick et al. (1974) and Everstine and Everstine (1983) have demonstrated the usefulness of hypnotherapy for dealing with a variety of conditions: detoxification, physical pain, violent family crises, and 'accompanying' terminal cancer patients. It is chiefly contraindicated for depressive states.

The induction of the trance is based on self-suggestion on the part of the patient. It is based on finding a framework that brings about a sense of well-being, by the systematic elimination of negative linguistic injunctions and the reinforcement of the subliminal state by positive formulations (suppression of words indicating negation, pain and aversion).

The considerable body of work produced by Erickson is based on a particularly creative and inventive use of hypnotherapeutic techniques in which paradoxical injunctions play a very large part. These techniques have since been developed in important ways in family therapy. Erickson's clinical work was essentially patient-centred, but he attached great importance to contextual factors and, in particular, to the family context. In certain cases, he involved one or more members of the family in the hypnosis sessions. His therapeutic action was based on certain precepts.

OVERCOMING RESISTANCE

Far from being combatted, resistance is in fact accepted, if not indeed encouraged. The therapist redefines all the patient's attempts at opposition as cooperative behaviour. The therapist views resistance as an expression of the personality of the patient and therefore to be respected. To a patient doubting the possibility of being hypnotized, he or she will say, 'Why not show that it is possible?' and, in alliance with the patient, he or she will adopt a defiant attitude. In family therapy, it is common to find that a member of the group will not speak, even when invited to do so. In such a situation, Erickson will tend to solve the problem by forbidding that person to comment. Seldom does the silent person respect such an order for long and it is more than likely he or she will try to have his/her say.

BINDS AND DOUBLE BINDS

In the definition of the bind, Erickson states that the point is to present one or more options to the patient. In fact, whatever the patient's choice, it will be directed towards a therapeutic goal. In the case of a DOUBLE BIND, the options offered to the patient are situated beyond his or her conscious choices and his or her capacities for voluntary control. As examples of binds we may cite the following questions put to the patient:

Do you want to go into a trance now or later?
Do you want to go into a trance seated or lying down?
Do you want to reach a light, average or deep trance?

In Erickson's view, according to Haley (1973), double binds make it possible to mobilize unconscious processes in many ways. He will sometimes address the following injunction to the patient: 'If your unconscious wants you to go into a trance, your right hand will rise of its own accord. Otherwise, the left hand will rise' (Haley, 1973, p. 26). Whether the answer is yes (right hand) or no (left hand), the trance has in fact already been induced. If, after a few minutes, the patient does not move his or her hands, the therapist can add a second double bind:

Since you are sitting peacefully and there has still been no hand signal, you can ask yourself whether your unconscious wouldn't prefer not to make any effort at all as you go into a trance. It may be more comfortable for you not to have to move or speak to yourself or bother to keep your eyes open. (Haley, 1973, p. 26)

According to Erickson, this type of intervention, in association with other techniques, constitutes a means of bringing on the trance and exploring the patient's responsiveness.

USE OF WORDPLAY, METAPHOR AND SYMBOLS

Erickson resorts to wordplay to help the patient free him/herself of over-rigid constraints and reach new levels of meaning. The metaphor or analogy is used to facilitate the development of insight or new levels of consciousness during the therapeutic transaction. Thus, as Watzlawick (1978a, p. 62) reports, in a case of frigidity, Erickson sometimes asks the patient to imagine in the tiniest detail how she would set about defrosting her refrigerator. At no point does the therapist mention the patient's sexual problem. The figurative language reduces the effects of the censorship and constitutes a sort of 'reverse' dream. Unlike the dream, which is a *passive* expression of internal conflicts, recourse to dream language is, in Erickson's work, an *active* intervention.

TECHNIQUE OF CONFUSION

This is indicated in the case of patients whose preferred method for avoiding psychotherapeutic engagement is intellectualization. Erickson deluges the patient with long complex formulas or banal truism. Only the conclusion is comprehensible and the patient, intellectually overwhelmed by the torrent of words he has just heard, will tend to cling on to the last part of the therapist's intervention.

FORESTALLING OR ENCOURAGING RELAPSE

When a patient proves over-cooperative and too rapid a cure seems likely to be leading to a relapse in the near future, Erickson takes the improvement into account, but suggests to the patient that he or she should experience a relapse. The only way for the patient to pick up the challenge is not to relapse. To justify his attitude, Erickson explains to the patient: 'I want you to go back and feel as badly as you did when you first came in with the problem, because I want you to see if there is anything from that time that you wish to recover and salvage' (Haley, 1973, p. 31).

USE OF SPACE DURING THE INTERVIEW

Erickson accords importance to the way the members of a family arrange themselves in his consulting room, believing that how they do so provides information on the family dynamic. To emphasize certain roles, highlight a symptom or an alliance, Erickson at times changes the various positions of each of the members of the family group during the session. Other techniques, such as prescribing the SYMPTOM, PROVOCATION or RE-FRAMING have largely been inspired by Erickson (Malarewicz and Godin, 1986).

All these modes of intervention may be grouped, as Haley does, in the framework of strategic therapies, which he defines as follows:

In strategic therapy the initiative is largely taken by the therapist. He must identify solvable problems, set goals, design interventions to achieve those goals, examine the responses he receives to correct his approach, and ultimately examine the outcome of his therapy to see if it has been effective. (Haley, 1973, p. 17)

Credit must also go to Haley (1958) for having proposed an interactional approach to the phenomena of hypnosis. The modes of communication between therapist and patient are analysed, taking into account the way each of these protagonists defines their relationship. And mechanisms of the 'double-bind message' type are brought out, as are the styles of response of the patient.

Where depressive states are concerned, hypnotherapy is contraindicated to the extent that it confronts the depressed patient all the more starkly with the distance that separates him or her from the well-being – which is at the centre of hypnotic action – that he or she feels will never be re-attained. The strategy adopted towards the depressed patient is the reverse. The experience of distress must be prescribed, rather than acting as though it could be emotionally cancelled out. Therapy then proceeds through a ritualization of an aggressive agent directed against the depressed patient.

(See also PRESCRIPTION; THERAPEUTIC DOUBLE BINDS; THERAPEUTIC STRATEGIES AND TACTICS.)

P.A. & J.M.

hysteresis See ANOREXIA NERVOSA; ELEMENTARY CATASTROPHES; INFANTILE AUTISM.

I

icons   The icon is a sign which refers to the object it denotes through resemblance to one or more of its properties. The icon as a sign therefore possesses the character which makes it signify, even if the denoted object is not present or does not exist in reality (Peirce, 1935).

Iconic communications have a number of characteristics. Being based on the primary process of thinking, they have a timeless, spaceless aspect, but are realized in effects of simultaneity and ubiquity. They have no code-markers, since there is isomorphy between the nature of the message and the analog structure of the coding. They have no way of indicating simple negation: 'organisms say the opposite of what they mean in order to get across the proposition that they mean the opposite of what they say' (Bateson, 1972, p. 114). Phylogenetic rituals are essentially based on iconic communication; for a dog a signal of greeting may be baring its teeth to the point where fighting does not take place, thus indicating: 'we are not going to fight.' In man, the handshake is a sign that he has no weapon in his hand. Courtship rituals are similarly founded upon this presentation of aggressive messages which are channelled away from their normal aggressive ends. To allow a certain degree of play into pathological communications is also to re-orientate potentially dangerous interactions into therapeutic neo-rituals.

(See also AGONISTIC BEHAVIOUR; ARTIFICIAL CODES; ANALOGIC CODING; HOLOGRAPHIC MEMORY; MESSAGES; PLAY; RITUALIZATION; SEMIOLOGY.)

J.M.

identification   In Freud's conception, identification is not merely imitation, but appropriation, assimilation of properties, qualities, functions and positions existing in another person. In families with pathological transactions, the processes of PARENTIFICATION, failure of DIFFERENTIATION OF SELF and ALIENATION will win out over structuring identifications. Similarly, the defectiveness or absence of certain parental positions will prevent the constitution of coherent representations capable of being internally assimilated in a stable form.

Following Freud's inaugural observations, the process of identification has been very extensively studied in psychoanalysis (see, for example, the works of Klein, 1921–45; Winnicott 1958; Lacan, 1966; Laplanche and Pontalis, 1973; Florence, 1984; Widlöcher, 1986). The field opened up by family therapy further enhances the findings contained in these works through the observa-

tion of specific disorders relating to the nature of interpersonal relations within the family (psychosis, delinquency etc.).

PRIMARY AND SECONDARY IDENTIFICATION

Primary identification, as distinguished by Freud, is direct and immediate in the life of the child. It occurs prior to any object cathexis. As a product of the ego ideal, it takes family imagos from personal prehistory – the father, and also the mother, grandparents and siblings – as its object. It serves as an attractor for *secondary identifications*, which are produced by experiences one has with characters from family life. The father and mother then become objects of love and rivalry. Identification is not simply imitation, but appropriation of qualities external to oneself. In the Oedipus complex, it consists in taking the parent of one's own sex as a model in order to make a conquest of the other parent. It sets in place an 'as if', by reference to a common unconscious element constituted as a phantasm. It therefore allows disengagement from attachments to the first objects of love and aggression. It is identification which permits us to speak of a 'plurality of psychical persons'. It enables conflict to be structured in the form of internalized, polysemic representations (Widlöcher, 1986), and infantile, Oedipal cathexes of the parental imagos to be abandoned. Ambivalence towards the object becomes unconscious, roves over several strata, and reinforces masculine and feminine roles and the psychical interplay between them. Identification makes it possible to bring two contrary positions together into a single subject position. As Widlöcher in fact points out, unconscious identification never relates to persons but to roles.

IDENTIFICATION AND LOGICO-PRAGMATIC PARADOXES

For Jean Gillibert (in Goutal, 1985), the Oedipus complex is itself based on a double-bind: ' "Do as I do", the father says to his son, but "don't do as I do" (i.e. do not take my wife).' Identification is thus based on the pragmatic assumption of a set of logical paradoxes:

- being like/not being like;
- doing like/not doing like;
- taking another's place/taking one's own place;
- appropriating another's qualities/appropriating one's own qualities;
- communality of representation/disjunction between 'the person identifying' and 'the person being identified with'.

Jacques Lacan (1961–2) pointed up how identification lies at the heart of the paradoxes concerning the self-membership of classes which are not members of themselves (see PARADOXES; THEORY OF LOGICAL TYPES). Lacan reminds us of a basic opposition between Russell and Wittgenstein. If, for the former philosopher, A = A, for the latter, what is equal between the first appearance and the second precludes the notation A = A. In Lacanian theory, the object a is to some extent conceived as representative of all the other letters of the alphabet:

> We can do one of two things; we shall either list the other letters of the alphabet from b to z, in which case the letter a will represent them unambiguously without, for all that, including itself; it is, however, clear on the other hand that, representing these letters of the alphabet as a letter, it comes quite naturally not to enrich the series of letters – I shall certainly not use that expression – but to complete it, in the place from which we have withdrawn, excluded it, and the simple fact is that, if we start out from the fact that a – this is our starting point where identification is concerned – is fundamentally not a, there is no difficulty here; the letter a within the parenthesis in which are oriented all the letters which it comes symbolically to subsume is not the same a and yet at the same time is the same. (Lacan, 1961–2)

Lacan thus proposes a first model to get beyond the paradoxes inherent in processes of identification, as these appear in logical positivism's formulation. He thus distinguishes between the two planes of enunciation and the utterance, defines the structuring of the subject by identification with the signifier and comes ultimately to that 'elastic logic' that is topology. But other paradoxes remain to be resolved in the construction of the *familial and social real* as phylogenetic foundation of the psychical organization in ontogenesis, and of the morphology of the signified. In this sense, family therapy is the 'psychotherapy of the real' to use Elkaim's expression (1989, p. 90).

It is thus essential to take into account the effects the real inflicts upon the imaginary and the symbolic, by the play of family and social interactions. Moreover, the paradoxes also concern the *object* of identification. From the imprinting process onwards, the individual identifies with the class to which the object presented to him belongs. The child begins by identifying at least as much with the family system as with the persons who make it up. The more that system is perceived as uncertain, endangered or de-structured, the longer identification will remain in suspense, its development blocked. Throughout his life, the individual identifies not only with formal units of life and survival (the groups and SOCIAL ORGANIZATIONS on which he depends for his existence, Simon, 1945–7); but also on units of MIND which may possibly extend beyond instituted groups (artistic, religious, scientific, sporting communities etc.)

FAMILY FACTORS

Disorders of identification

Disorders of identification may be associated with a variety of factors: (a) mimetic disorders (absence of internal endowments, absence of identificatory figures); (b) disorders of family organization, roles and statuses; (c) family identity disorders; (d) symbolization disorders (transition from the experience of the real to phantasy elaboration); and (e) territorial disorders (internal and/or external topographical constraints: positions within the group, the nuclear or extended family, absence of place).

In every family, the child comes to identify with the healthy or pathological aspects of the personality of the parents and of the interactions between them (Lidz et al., 1965). Parents will offer models of identification which will become 'incorporable' if they are not totally conflictual and mutually exclusive and incompatible. This presupposes reciprocal recognition and esteem between each partner, which is itself only possible if the family of origin systems have permitted this recognition. Thus the self-esteem of each parent is reinforced by a play of reciprocal recognition. The difficult question, on the level of psychical work, is this passage from 'personification' to the unconscious integration of roles. Primary identification disorders are signs of a failure to assume one's place within a lineage and a failure in the transition from prehistory to history; secondary identification disorders are signs of difficulties of finding one's place within society.

Identification and delinquent transactions

Schouten et al. (1974) find that a consciousness deviating from the norm corresponds, in delinquent adolescents, with problems of identification. The father's exemplary value can only function if he is sufficiently present. Disorders relating to paternal presence are of various types.

Frequent changes of partner to some extent indicate that the family norm is to accept no continuous and enduring parental norm. It is not easy to form a structuring identification with a transient adult, whose status with the mother is not necessarily clear. The father may be physically present in the family, but mentally elsewhere, by dint of the constraints of his work and/or his personal disinvestment from the family. In other cases, he is actively excluded by the mother as a symbolic function and may indeed be perceived in his family as a failure, or as a violent or irresponsible man.

It will become more difficult to question family norms, at adolescence, if the identificatory models of childhood have been insufficient or indeed themselves deviant. The 'quasi-absent father' thus brings about a defective identification on the part of the son, if not indeed an opposition to any form of identification, by rejection of the principle of authority. The father who is socially a failure also runs the risk of having his son loyally follow him into identificatory failure.

Identification and schizophrenic transactions

Lidz et al. (1965) note the disturbances of identification in patients designated as schizophrenic, in relation to the family context. Often, before the appearance of mental disorder, they note a brief period of identification with the dominant parental figure, who is usually the most disturbed parent. But where the parents maintain odd, grandiose or megalomaniacal beliefs within relatively restricted limits, the patient for his or her part, is confronted with beliefs running to limitless excess. He or she can only caricature the generalized bad labelling of attitudes, feelings and thoughts which circulate within the group by identifying with the distorted or schismatic features of the interactions.

In Lidz's view, there is also a weakness in the identificatory processes of those close relatives who are of the same sex as the patient designated schizophrenic. Identificatory fragility thus seems to relate to the sexed identity of the family members, and is also found in siblings of the same sex as the index patient.

(See also AGONISTIC BEHAVIOUR; ATTACHMENT BEHAVIOUR; DEIXIS; FORECLOSURE; LOVE; NARCISSISM; PARADOXES; PARADOXICALITY; PERFORMATIVES; PROJECTIVE IDENTIFICATION; FAMILY ROLE; SCHIZOPHRENIAS; SEXED BEHAVIOUR; SOCIAL STATUS; THEORY OF LOGICAL TYPES.)

J.M.

immanence For the Scholastics, who in an action distinguish between the subject of that action and its object, and *immanent action* is one that remains wholly within the subject (for example, seeing). It is the opposite of a *transitive action* which, for its part, modifies the object (touch etc.).

Systemic modelling, which has taken over the tradition of epistemology, together with the complexification of subject–object relations and the interrelation between these two things, have thrown this notion into question. Since the Scholastic period, however, the notion has itself evolved and is now not so much the opposite of transitive action (which would be directed toward the outside), as of what comes from outside. What is immanent is defined as what is not the effect of an external action, but of an 'internal' logic. One speaks of 'immanent' justice. There then arises the question of the interferences between a system and its context (or its 'outside', its margin).

The place of the family therapist has particularly come in for questioning and has brought back on to the agenda discussions within moral philosophy around the question of immanentism. When one speaks of reasons of the heart or the sense of shared experience as a means of access to the spirit of the family, for example, the debate is re-opened. 'Reality is not made up of distinct pieces juxtaposed; everything is in everything; in the tiniest detail of nature or science, the scientist finds all of science and all of nature; each of our states and our acts envelops our whole spirit and the totality of its powers' (Le Roy, quoted in Lalande, 1985). The discovery of the hologram, which, in breaking, reconstitutes totalities and reproduces the whole in every part, and of homeostatic processes maintaining stability within family systems, gives fresh impetus to all these questions.

The Kantian opposition between immanence and transcendence (which implies that the two lie on a continuum) does not operate here, in so far as every living system, in particular every human system, has within it an immanent transcendence, a self-surpassing principle (a theme expressed, for instance, by the Zen tradition in the formula 'become what you are', but what you are is someone who 'is compelled to become' and whose identity is changed). Recourse to the notion of immanence therefore presupposes a particular attention to the – strategic – definition of the agent of the projected activity: the individual, the family, the group including the therapist.

(See also HOLISM; HOLOGRAPHIC MEMORY; MAIEUTICS; TRANSFERENCE.)

D.C.

impotence See ADMISSION OF IMPOTENCE, RECOGNITION OF FAILURE.

imprinting Imprinting is the acquisition in the course of the development of a higher vertebrate of the characteristics of the object upon which certain acts bear that are directed towards its fellow creatures. This acquisition is distinct from a learning process since, unlike such a process, it cannot be unlearned or can only disappear gradually. These instinctive acts may be varied in their nature: bonds with parents, offspring, companions, sexual bonds. Konrad Lorenz (1978a, b) stresses that in natural living conditions, innate schemata and schemata acquired from a fellow creature form a functional unit. Vidal (1976a, p. 34) points out that imprinting 'determines both the reaction that consists in approaching familiar objects and simultaneously – or subsequently – the reaction which consists in the avoidance of unfamiliar objects; there is a structuring of differentiated responses towards different objects.'

ETHOLOGICAL DEFINITION OF IMPRINTING

Following Lorenz, we may define imprinting in terms of a series of factors:

1   Acquisition of the pattern of the object, which triggers the instinctive bonding reaction, during a short and precise critical period.
2   Impossibility of forgetting after this sensitive period; this aspect of irreversibility contrasts with the phenomenon of learning in which what has been acquired can be forgotten.
3   There may exist a different form of imprinting for different types of behaviour at different stages of development: filial, sexual or 'companionship' behaviour.
4   The object of the imprinting determines a supra-individual identification of the features of the species to which the object belongs.
5   Imprinting develops types of behaviour which are not yet developed in the organism (filial, sexual, parental and companionship behaviour).

The imprinting phenomenon was originally described by Whitman (1919) and Heinroth (1910) who discovered it in birds which left the nest soon after birth; it was later conceptualized by Lorenz. It remains an open question whether it is possible to infer its existence in man, even though the process of fixation described by Freud seems very closely related to it. For Lorenz (1978b), there exists a stark opposition between birds and mammals on this point. He noted that young birds who have grown up away from their own kind are unlike all the small mammals studied in this respect in that they do not recognize fellows members of their own species with whom they are placed in contact. Many authors (for example, Allyn, 1974; Vidal, 1976a) have criticized the idea of a very narrowly demarcated critical period. Thus, in higher mammals, the hypothesis has been proposed that there might be optimal or sensitive periods, the temporal limits of which might be more elastic than in birds which leave the nest early. In many cases, what is involved seems to be less an irreversible process than simply a stable preference, leaving some possibility of later modification of the object of preference.

IMPRINTING, ATTACHMENT AND SEXUAL CONDUCT IN MAN

For his part, Bowlby (1969) stresses the similarities observed between attachment in mammals and phenomena observed in human young in so far what will become a preferred figure is concerned (see ATTACHMENT BEHAVIOUR). Thus, in the human child we can see:

1   The range of stimuli which release social responses is initially wide, but becomes progressively narrowed down and is ultimately restricted to a select group of effective stimuli.
2   Attachment to a person becomes stronger as the experience of social interaction with that person is richer.
3   The aptitude for discriminating faces and voices normally follows periods in which the child is looking and listening attentively. Exposure to attachment figures during certain optimal periods no doubt plays its part.
4   Once attachment has been achieved, the child shows a marked preference for attachment figures and separation from them has specific effects.
5   The acquisition of schemata of familiar persons is accompanied, around the age of eight or nine months by a movement of withdrawal and by crying in the presence of strangers.

A great quantity of data suggests that the human child acquires psychosensory schemata at an early stage, which are integrated into affective movements of instinctive searching for bonds. These include the preferential recognition of a particular smell, voice and face. A similar process probably also plays a part in the maturation of sexual behaviour.

On the basis of a survey carried out among 2,769 Israeli couples in which each partner had been brought up on the same kibbutz, Shepher (1971) postulated the hypothesis of 'negative sexual imprinting': except for thirteen of the couples, none of those surveyed had played 'closely' with their partner during childhood. The more detailed study of the exceptions is instructive. In each case, one of the children had been away from the other for a sufficient period of time before the age of six. The emergence of the sexual instinct during childhood is accompanied by a learning of the class of persons to whom the later sexual objects must belong, with the precise object on whom imprinting is achieved being excluded. Now this neither eliminates forms of regulation belonging to other levels (symbolic, familial and social) nor infringements of the rule (see INCEST).

MICRO-IMPRINTING IN THE ACQUISITION OF LANGUAGE

Through deictic phenomena, the child is not content merely to acquire the gestural, vocal, olfactory patterns of those around him/her. He/she also 'engrams' the phonological system of his/her parents' language, then its vocabulary. It is precisely as though the process of imprinting were extended and exploded into a multiplicity of micro-imprintings, localized in the acquisition of each word, in the circuit of naming connecting together the child, the objects he or she discovers and his or her parents who provide the linguistic expression for them (Thom, 1983a). The tendency every person has of reifying words and concepts could be connected with this archaic process, which is the basis of all acquisition of the connections between signifier and signified.

PATHOLOGY AND IMPRINTING

Certain aspects of pathology may be correlated with the properties of imprinting

1   The shift from the local feature to the overall configuration seems to be of significance in autistic pathology. The autistic individual perceives the local stimuli of human schemata, but will have nothing of their higher level integration (Mottron, 1986).
2   Shifts from individual features to features typical of the class to which they belong. The schizophrenic patient is apt to play on confusions of level between a differentiated person and the class to which he or she belongs.
3   Existence of critical points. It seems probable that there are singular points or SINGULARITIES which may be interpreted as embryological, psychical, familial and social 'organizers' (see FAMILY ORGANIZERS) and which have, in spite of everything, an irreversible fixation function. The quality of the fixation, however (even in perversions), probably refers back to a fixation/confusion of schemata belonging to biological and symbolic levels.
4   Articulation of imprinting with BECOMING ACCUSTOMED, HABITUATION, phobic reactions to traumatic experiences etc. The quality of early experiences will in part determine the style of relation which the individual will be likely to establish later on in their social relations.
5   Phenomena of auto-imprinting. Such phenomena have been observed experimentally in cocks deprived of any recognizable pattern during their ontogenesis (Vidal, 1976b). These observations may be compared with clinical findings of self-directed behaviour (auto-eroticism, self-mutilation) in patients presenting serious forms of autism and/or associated encephalopathies.

(See also IDENTIFICATION; SEXED BEHAVIOUR; SHIFTERS.)

J.M.

incest   Incest will be defined here as the enactment of sexual relations between same or opposite sexed persons (at least one of whom is post-pubertal) within the family. A distinction is made between intergenerational incest (father–daughter or mother–son) and intragenerational brother–sister incest. A distinction must also be made between incest as an endogamous, intra-nuclear practice, which is a form of violence and

sexual abuse by an adult on his children violently prohibited in all cultures, and certain endogamous sexual object choices which are encouraged but strictly regulated in certain cultures (e.g. brothers and sisters in Ancient Egypt, frequent marriages between the children of two brothers).

Incest, as a behavioural disorder, corresponds to an enormous violation of trust, which is the usual foundation of family life (Everstine and Everstine, 1985). Such sexual abuse is the expression of very high levels of anger, mistrust and fear in the internal and external environment of the family: 'sexual assault is an assault on the ultimate territorial boundary, one's skin . . . The involuntary penetration of this very primitive boundary causes the victim to experience a sense of not feeling whole' (Everstine and Everstine, 1989, p. 68).

Psychosociological understanding of the family leads us to appreciate that the incest taboo, structured by the Oedipal myth, is very regularly flouted to a statistically significant degree (between one in 300 and five in 100 families according to surveys by Pierre Strauss). Sexual abuse thus appears as the first cause of maltreatment of children and violence against minors.

A systemic formulation of the family leads to a differentiation of plans of intervention. Some of these necessitate that apparently opposing paths be followed simultaneously, while also demanding emergency action.

A distinction will be made between:

1   *Incestuous phantasies*, revealing the psyche as Oedipally structured, functioning as founding myths of neurotic psychical organization.
2   *Para-incestuous acts*, which stage a symptomatic drama of behaviours not issuing in genuine sexual abuse in reality, but questioning seduction rituals performed out of context, as for example where a mother and adult son seduce one another, but act as if the son were still an infant (psychotic transactions), revealing a traumatic violence on the psychical level.
3   *Incestuous acts*, actually carried out in reality, defying the efficacy of psychoanalytic approaches and calling for appropriate multi-focal professional interventions, as in sexual abuse work.

GENUINELY INCESTUOUS FAMILIES

In an incestuous family, confusions of role and generation connected with the existence of PERVERSE TRIANGLES come to light. As Everstine and Everstine point out (1983, 1985), the child or adolescent who is subjected to an incestuous act must simultaneously play what are usually antinomic roles: lover and child of one of the parents; parent of the parent who is not sexually involved. This also implies a distortion of the temporal parameters, since time is both suspended and speeded up. The child is pushed toward complex sexual relations beyond his or her age, which speeds up time while, on the other hand, the nature of these relations is so overwhelming that they prevent the progress of certain important aspects of personality development (Everstine and Everstine, 1985).

Mother–son incest seems infinitely rarer than father–daughter incest. It is almost always accompanied by some form of backwardness or psychosis in the son. Father–daughter incest is present in the histories of 40 per cent of under-age prostitutes, and is more common where there is paternal alcoholism (Strauss, 1985). A first constant emerges here: the complete dissymmetry between father–daughter and mother–son relations.

Scherrer (1985) distinguishes between:

- *despotic incest* (abuse of all the daughters by the father);
- *amorous incest*, with some degree of 'consent' on the part of the daughter;
- *self-punitive neurotic incest*: father who is abandoned by his wife and is passive and incapable of winning another woman, 'falling back' on to one of his daughters, while at the same time seeking to be punished socially for this.

TREATING THE INCESTUOUS FAMILY

The problem must be defined as clearly as possible, taking into account the different levels on which appeals for intervention are made. Accusations made by the children deserve a hearing, since they are nearly always well founded. Just as there is a simultaneous confusion between several levels in family roles, the therapeutic approach requires simultaneous interventions that are apparently contradictory since they must take antinomic messages into account: the child must be protected, from the abusing parent and possibly the family, but the family ecosystem as a whole must also be protected and supported. It is not always either necessary or even desirable to separate the members of an incestuous family (Everstine and Everstine, 1985). There is a double therapeutic danger: therapists acting as accomplices of the family and not accepting moral sanctions, and therapists repudiating the family on moral grounds.

Therapeutic sessions must work on distinct sub-systems:

- with the entire family, with a view to restoring the integrity of the group;
- with the parental couple, where appropriate, with a view to re-working the sexed positions of each of the partners;
- with the child alone, in order to enable him/her to structure his/her emotions and secret thoughts;
- with the child and non-abusing parent;
- with the sibling sub-system.

Secret internal coalitions, and absence of trans-generational boundaries and the erecting of a wall within the marital relationship are found within such families. The sexually uncompromised parent may play an active part in the appearance of the symptom; he or she neglects his/her role as protector of the child and maintains the *de facto* separation from the spouse by refusing any shared bodily pleasure and adult sexual satisfaction. One pattern that is often met is that of an immature mother refusing to have any sexual relations, delegating her role as wife and mother to her daughter, and of an alcoholic father, obsessed by sexuality and morality, who is shy and has withdrawn into a paranoid position.

Useful references on work with sexual abuse and the family include Mrazek and Kempe (1981); Pierce and Pierce (1985); Bentovim et al. (1988); Glaser and Frosh (1988); Jenkins (1989a).

CRITICAL RECONSIDERATION OF INCEST THEORIES

These facts oblige us to reconsider the classic positions regarding the incest taboo, the structuring of the Oedipus complex and the mechanisms of natural and cultural regulation that are in play.

For Needham (1971), incest prohibitions do not constitute a class of homogeneous social phenomena. In this regard, he takes a radically opposite position to that of Claude Levi-Strauss, for whom 'the prohibition of incest is culture itself'. We may note, then, on this point, that anthropologists are far from being in agreement as to how to define the general anthropological laws which would 'explain' the incest prohibition. The Lacanian explanation in terms of the Symbolic, which has curiously been taken up by Vidal (1985) as excluding biological forms of regulation which, none the less, seem probable, has a marked air of tautology about it. The great many infringements of this prohibition, observed daily by social workers, psychiatrists etc. will thus be explained by a symbolic failing, while the symbolic order will explain why, in general, the father does not sleep with his daughters and the mother with her sons. We shall here advance the hypothesis that there are several layers of prohibition, both biological and symbolic; confusions are possible within the definition of parental and sexed roles (the myth of OEDIPUS plays, from start to finish, upon these confusions). There would thus be multi-hierarchical forms of regulation (phenomena of negative imprinting, of natural and cultural structuring of distances of intimacy, of see-sawing between the familiar and the strange at adolescence, with possibilities of recursive loops between levels, which may, however, fail in their missions). To say of the incest prohibition that it is either innate or acquired is, then, to pose the question in simplistic terms. The inhibition of that instinct is no doubt also related to the existence of numerous feedback loops, which may possibly operate on several levels at the same time (Miermont, 1978b).

What would have to be explained is both the relatively general character of systems of genuinely endogamous prohibitions, the necessary variation of these systems of prohibition in man depending on cultures and the regular transgression, if not indeed the collapse, in reality, of these systems, in families with particular destinies.

(See also ATTACHMENT BEHAVIOUR; CO-THERAPY; FAMILY–THERAPEUTIC INSTITUTION DIFFERENTIATION; IMPRINTING; INTIMACY; LAW; METABINDING; MULTI-LEVEL HIERARCHIES; PHANTASY; REALITY; SEXED BEHAVIOUR; SYSTEMIC MODELLING; THERAPEUTIC DOUBLE BINDS; VIOLENCE.)

J.M.

inclusion See RITUALS OF BELONGING (MEMBERSHIP), RITUALS OF INCLUSION.

incompleteness theorems The incompleteness theorems demonstrated by Gödel (1931–6) relate to number theory. They are a response to Russell's theory of logical types, a response definitively excluding the possibility of any formalization of a sufficiently powerful mathematics being internally consistent and complete. The theorems, which are based on a self-referential coding, lead to propositions which assert the impossibility of their own validation within the axiomatic framework within which they originate.

At the beginning of the century, set theory, then still in its infancy, produced a multitude of contradictions and paradoxes. The axiomatics of set theory was still vague and paradoxes were generated by self-referential set-theoretic definitions such as that of the set whose elements are the sets that are not elements of themselves.

Many variants of this paradox of self-belonging are to be found. These paradoxes produce the same effect as that of Epimenides the Cretan and the point they have in common is self-reference. In this context, it was felt important to found a 'healthy' mathematics without paradoxes and, more importantly, without self-referentiality. In response to this need, Russell and Whitehead produced their *Principia mathematica*, which, together with the THEORY OF LOGICAL TYPES, forms part of a project aimed at eliminating self-referentiality completely from logic, set theory and number theory. Self-referential propositions are prohibited. The only legitimate propositions are ones relating to 'objects' of a lower logical level.

Moreover, the project of *Principia mathematica* was to establish a mathematical formalization of reasoning

which would have made it possible to remove all ambiguity surrounding the validity or invalidity of a demonstration. In this sense, it was a meta-mathematical enterprise, laying down rules of procedure. It remained to be proved, however, for the absolute security of the mathematical arguments which would be based on this meta-mathematics, that the methods of *Principia mathematica* did cover the totality of mathematics. In other words, that every mathematical proposition could be deduced from *Principia mathematica* (*completeness*) and, moreover, that these methods would not lead to contradictory results (*consistency*).

Hilbert (see Hilbert and Ackermann, 1928) and his school undertook to prove 'rigorously' (i.e. using the rules of reasoning of *Principia mathematica* itself!) that the *Principia mathematica* constituted a theory that was both consistent and complete. Gödel (1931) published his two incompleteness theorems and put an end to the work of Hilbert. The first of his theorems showed the incompleteness of *Principia mathematica* and reintroduced self-reference in spite of Russell and Whitehead's intentions of banning it altogether. The second proved that it was impossible for a theory to validate itself.

GÖDEL'S FIRST THEOREM

'No formal theory of arithmetic can be both finitely presentable, consistent and complete.'

What is a complete theory?
A *formal theory* is made up of a language and a set of propositions known as axioms. The language of a theory is a set of signs or symbols. The *propositions of a theory* are sequences of these symbols obeying very precise syntactic rules.

The *axioms* are propositions given at the outset which, with the language, constitute the theory. Theorems are propositions which can be deduced from the axioms by a series of stages using very precise rules of deduction. When a proposition is a theorem, one also says that it is demonstrable or deducible. To verify whether an assertion is a theorem of a theory, it has first to be 'translated' into a proposition, i.e. expressed in the language of the theory using its symbols and syntactic rules.

What is a finitely presentable theory?
A theory is termed finitely presentable if it either has a finite number of axioms or has an infinite number of axioms but there exists an explicit rule enabling an effective list of these to be drawn up.

What is a consistent theory?
The notion of consistency in fact covers two distinct notions: formal (or syntactic) consistency and semantic consistency. The *formal consistency* of a theory is equivalent to its internal non-contradictoriness. A proposition and its negation cannot both be theorems, i.e. demonstrable on the basis of the axioms of the theory.

A theory is *'semantically'* consistent if a part of the real world exists of which it is the formalization. There then exists a real interpretation of the symbols, axioms and theories which makes these latter true. The part of reality which correctly interprets the theory is called a *model*. It is a fundamental result that semantic consistency entrains formal consistency. If, then, a theory is the formalization of a part of reality (semantic consistency), it is necessarily non-contradictory (formal consistency). The converse is not always true. There are theories which are formally consistent (non-contradictory from the internal point of view) which are not the theory of any model.

What is a complete theory?

For its part too, the notion of completeness covers a formal (syntactic) notion and a semantic notion. The two definitions of completeness are, however, equivalent. If a theory is complete from the formal point of view, it is so from the semantic point of view and vice versa.

From the *semantic point of view*, a theory is termed 'complete' if all the true assertions in a part of the reality (model) which interprets it are theorems, i.e. propositions provable from the axioms of the theory. This means that the theory 'covers' the part of reality it claims to formalize. All that is true in reality then finds its theoretical justification.

From the *formal point of view*, the notions of truth and falsehood are devoid of meaning and the propositions of a formal system are merely correct or incorrect syntactically. Truth and falsehood only appear in the (semantic) confrontation with an external reality.

When one speaks of consistency or completeness without further qualification, it is always in relation to an external reality. Thus we are always dealing here with the semantic properties of a theory. To speak of (semantic) completeness or (semantic) consistency only has meaning in a relationship to reality. It will, for example, be more correct to speak of the completeness of the familio-systemic or socio-systemic approach than of the systemic approach in general.

Generally speaking, when faced with an incomplete theory, one may either extend the theory by stating new axioms or limit the part of reality (the model) one is attempting to formalize to obtain a more rigorous interpretation of the theory. These two ways of 'completing' a theory amount to extending the theory or making reality more adequate to it, depending upon whether the primary object of study is reality (the Platonic point of view) or the theory (formalist point of view).

The definition of formal completeness introduces the notion of decidability. A propositon of a theory is decidable in that theory if either that proposition or its negation is a theorem of the theory. A theory is said to be (formally) complete if all its propositions are decidable, i.e. if there are no undecidable propositions, a proposition of which one cannot say whether it or its negation is a theorem. The proof of Gödel's incompleteness theorem consists in exhibiting, for every consistent theory, a true assertion, which, when formally stated, cannot be proved.

The proof of such a proposition confirms once and for all the incompleteness of every finitely presentable and consistent formal theory, including the *Principia mathematica*, for, in a complete theory, every true assertion must be a theorem. A complete theory is supposed to reflect all reality and to possess a theorem for each truth. As soon as we find even a single truth which cannot be expressed as a theorem, the theory is incomplete. The proposition highlighted by Gödel bears some similarity to Epimenides' paradox. The statement 'What I am saying is false' is replaced by a proposition which says, more or less, 'I am not provable.' The first difficulty in constructing such a proposition arises from the fact that propositions in the language of number theory relate to the properties of whole numbers, not to propositions themselves. To get around this difficulty and legitimately construct a meta-proposition, Gödel employed a numerical coding of syntax. To each symbol, s, of language, a positive integer, $ng(s)$, was appended and this is known as the *Gödel number* of s.

Thus every proposition has a Gödel number and every whole number is the Gödel number of a sequence of symbols of the theory. A proposition concerning the properties of a number may therefore also be interpreted as concerning the properties of the proposition encoded by the number as a Gödel number. Every number acquires two meanings, the first numerical, the second residing in the coding of a proposition.

It was with the aid of this coding that Gödel succeeded in writing a syntactically correct formal proposition in the language of number theory which referred to itself and said of itself, in natural language, 'I am not a theorem.' Once this proposition has been constructed, it is very easy to demonstrate that if theory T is consistent, then this proposition 'I am not a theorem' is in actual fact not a theorem and that, moreover, it is not decidable, since its negation too is not a theorem.

The beauty of the demonstration is that it leads one to see a distinction between the true and the provable. Gödel's proposition says 'I am not provable.' It is true since one can demonstrate that it is not provable and it is, however, non-provable because it is true. There is no paradox here, only a necessary conclusion that no finite and consistent theory can claim to 'cover' all assertions and, in particular, all the assertions that relate to it. Moreover, the essence of the demonstration of this incompleteness theorem shows how vain was *Principia mathematica*'s ambition totally to eradicate self-referentiality since Gödel's proposition, constructed with the methods of the *Principia*, powerfully reintroduces it.

GÖDEL'S SECOND THEOREM

This theorem leaves Hilbert's project in tatters and, referring to it, Hilbert described the whole meta-mathematical enterprise as a 'fiasco'. If a theory, *T*, is a theory with a finite number of axioms, the formalizations (formal propositions translating an assertion) of the assertion '*T* is consistent' cannot be deduced within *T*.

A proof of the consistency of a theory therefore always exceeds the scope of the principles which can be formalized within the theory. This is what the second Incompleteness Theorem expresses in a formal way. Thus, the *Principia mathematica* cannot demonstrate its own consistency, any more than can any other theory. This does not mean, however, that the *Principia* must be thrown away. Gödel's theorems do not state that a proof of consistency is impossible, only that one cannot be found without either going outside the framework of the theory or using a less-powerful theory. The best course would be to demonstrate consistency on the basis of a less-powerful theory, since otherwise the question of the consistency of the theory used for the demonstration would arise as a further problem. Now, Gödel's work shows that any formal system sufficiently powerful to demonstrate the consistency of the *Principia* is at least as powerful as the *Principia* itself.

We have to give up the idea of the whole of 'reality' (all models) being covered by a single consistent and finitely presentable theory. The *Principia mathematica*, in so far as it summarizes and codifies a set of methods which cover the field of classical mathematics, is sufficient for most questions. However, given the impossibility of a material proof of consistency, we can no longer regard that work as the ultimate justification of mathematical theories. The horizon is opened up for new and surprising theories, increasingly capable of formalizing the real world.

A LITTLE EPISTEMOLOGY

When a theory turns out to be incomplete, i.e. when the parts of reality it claimed to formalize interpret none of its axioms and theorems, two options arise, depending on the objective being pursued. If the goal being aimed at is the formalization of a complex reality, one may attempt to extend the theory, naturally taking care to maintain intact its precious consistency so that it describes a larger part of that reality. If, on the other hand, the aim is to know what part of reality is correctly and 'completely' formalized by the theory concerned, one will attempt to 'reduce the model', to limit the claims of the theory to a 'smaller', more local reality.

Extending the theory

Extending the theory is the approach which most corresponds to usual scientific practice and is, *par excellence,* the Platonic approach. One sets out from the hypothesis that reality exists and has to be studied. New theories arise to approximate closer and closer to the same reality. To study the way in which theories expand to become more and more 'complete' is to study the axioms and theorems of a 'meta-theory'. These state how a theory is to be elaborated and summarize the rules governing the elaboration of a particular theory. A meta-theory is, in a sense, a theory of theories. The statement of Gödel's Incompleteness Theorem is a 'meta-theorem'. Epistemology, the *Principia mathematica*, Freudian metapsychology, general systems theory and systemic modelling are all examples of meta-theories. Gödel's second theorem – 'A theory cannot demonstrate its own consistency' – leads to the idea that the consistency of meta-theory such as the *Principia* could be demonstrated in a meta-meta-theory.

If psychoanalysis and most of the theories of psychical functioning are meta-theories, where then are the theories? Taking a dream, for example, the 'interpretation' of its latent content is a theory of which the dream is the model. However, the work of Freud, in particular his *Interpretation of dreams*, with its axioms – displacement, condensation etc. and the rule of free association for inferring new interpretations – forms a meta-theory enabling 'theories' of each element of the dream to be developed. Similarly, when the proponents of systemic modelling draw up hypotheses which they then attempt to verify, they are constructing a theory of the model presented by a particular family reality. However, the hypotheses are not developed simply anyhow. A meta-theory, the corpus of concepts which constitutes the systemic approach, lays down the conditions that are to be respected in drawing up the hypotheses: circular formal causality, non-summativity of the family system, respect of homeostasis etc. Psychoanalysis and systemic modelling are generators of theories.

Reducing the model

The second possibility on offer when a theory reveals itself to be incomplete in respect of a reality it cannot formalize 'completely' is to limit our expectations where that theory is concerned and circumscribe more narrowly the part of reality which the theory claims to formalize. This is a relatively uncommon measure which must not be confused with the dishonest common variant of it which consists in distorting reality so as to make it fit or, in other words, of 'bending the reality to meet the theory'. This measure is, in fact, akin to the formalist philosophy which sets out from the hypothesis that there is no reality other than that formalized by our axiomatic systems.

Reducing the claims of a theory by taking a smaller part of REALITY as a model is different from a distortion or a denial. Now if, in mathematics, there is only one reality (arithmetic, for example), this is by no means the case in the other disciplines, and, particularly, in the human sciences. There, reality is merely the perception of reality. There is no longer just one reality, but as many realities as persons perceiving them (Watzlawick, 1976), so that, when one is dealing with a complex human reality where theoretical endeavours are incomplete or wholly absent, the stroke of genius consists not in reducing that reality (which, it must be admitted, offends against our scientific megalomania and our Platonism), but in making our perception perform a qualitative leap and ascribing to the same observed facts a different semantic reality. It is worth our while to linger a moment over what is implied in the possibility of giving several different meanings to a single 'reality' in this way.

When reality depends on the perception one has of it, it is, quite obviously, multiple. It is then better to refer to the object of perception as the 'observed facts' and reserve the term 'reality' for a particular perception of a set of 'observed facts'. Now, is one perception among other possible perceptions anything other than a theory about the 'observed facts'? A theory of which we become aware only when we abandon another 'perceived theory'. Thus, what we call reality and seek to formalize is already a theory in relation to which our later formalizations are meta-theories. For example, it was a mark of the genius of Bateson that, among other things, he transformed the perception of schizophrenia. Until that point, the development of (meta)theories on schizophrenia was guided by a perception of the condition as a mental illness. That perception amounted to an implicit theory of schizophrenia. By resituating the schizophrenic in the communicational context of his family, Bateson changed the perception and, in the process, changed the implicit theory, opening up possibilities of new (meta)theories such as that of the double bind. The change of perception leads necessarily to new hypotheses, new (meta)theories (re-framing).

We may therefore distinguish between several levels of theorization:

Level 0: Observed facts: 'reality' in the sense of a single reality.

This is inaccessible except in the case of mathematical abstraction.

Level 1: perception of observed facts, implicit theory, low level of consciousness, interiorized dominant ideology, habits of thought.

Level 2: Elaboration of theories relating to what we perceive. High level of consciousness. Examples: the interpretation of a dream or a hypothesis about the function of a symptom for a particular family system.

Level 3: Meta-theories indicating the rules to be respected in elaborating the theories of level 2. Examples: systemic modelling, metapsychology, *Principia mathematica,* logic etc.

In the two alternatives proposed for pushing back the frontiers of incompleteness, the intellectual difficulty resides in the logical levels immediately above and below that of the process of theorization itself. In the first alternative, the object is to conceive a meta-theory (level 3) which makes it possible to extend the existing theories or to develop new ones. In the second, the object is to re-frame the observed facts, to change the implicit theory represented by our particular perception of these facts (level 1).

We may note, in this regard, that animals have extremely rigid 'theories' concerning what they perceive, whereas human beings have flexible theories but rigid meta-theories. It is in fact very difficult for us to develop new meta-rules when we have to change our theories.

INCOMPLETENESS THEOREMS AND (META)THEORIES OF PSYCHICAL REALITIES

Gödel's theorem only applies to theories that are sufficiently powerful to formalize 'almost' the whole of arithmetic. Less ambitious theories may, for their part, be finitely presentable, consistent and complete.

When one abandons mathematics for the human sciences, one notices that there exist, there again, theories which are a formalization of a small part of psychical reality, and which may then have a claim to consistency and completeness in respect of that small part. As an example of this type of conceptualization, we may cite theories of behaviour, the psychology of perception etc.

Systemic modelling and psychoanalysis are theories which aspire to formalize practically the whole of inter- and intrapsychic life. It seems very reasonable to assume that they thus fall within the ambit of Gödel's theorems, particularly the second theorem. These theories cannot demonstrate their own consistency. Nothing allows us to say that no empirical result, no psychical fact will ever come along to invalidate them. Gödel's first theorem also reminds us that there very certainly exist realities which do not fall within the scope of psychoanalytic or systemic theory and which require an understanding extending beyond the methods of those theories.

As regards psychical life, the incompleteness theorem consigns any attempt to produce a universal theory of psychogenesis to certain failure. This has not, however, prevented long debates taking place on the subject of the universality of the Oedipus complex.

Hilbert's ambition to prove the completeness and consistency of the *Principia mathematica* on the basis of its own axioms may be compared with the schizophrenic phantasy of 'self-begetting' as described most notably by Racamier (1980):

the subject becomes his own father, short-circuiting the primal scene and castration, and this traps the schizophrenic in an all-powerful, vertiginous paradox. This paradox, central in the life of the schizophrenic, concerns the mutual existence of self and object, decreeing that each of these shall only be by not being.

Though not wishing to push the analogy too far, we may state that a formal system becomes self-validating, short-circuiting the notions of the non-provability of basic axioms and incompleteness, trapping the theory in a fantastic paradox as soon as it claims to be both complete and consistent. In effect, in such a formal system, the distinction between the true and the provable disappears. Gödel's proposition 'I am not provable' becomes 'I am not true' and we fall back into the clutches of the paradox of Epimenides the Cretan.

RENOUNCING COMPLETENESS

Gödel's extraordinary finding, that one must give up the quest for completeness in mathematics, may be compared with Freud's discovery that one must give up primary narcissistic representations (see NARCISSISM). This, the basis of the concept of 'symbolic castration', is very well described by Leclaire (1975):

No life is possible – as life of desire or of creation – if we stop killing the marvellous child which is ever being re-born within us. A marvellous child who, from generation to generation, reflects the desires and dreams of the parents . . . For each of us there is always a child to kill and mourning to be done – and continually re-done – for a representation of plenitude.

The error which consists in losing interest in a theory because it is incomplete has its counterpart in the confusion between our first death, that of primary narcissistic representation, which we have to pass through in order to live, and our second, organic death. There are close similarities between the behaviour of the researcher who, when faced with a complex reality, develops theories for which he or she seeks maximum completeness and the parental 'compulsion to ascribe every perfection to the child . . . The child shall have a better time than his parents . . . The child shall fulfil those wishful dreams of the parents which they never carried out' (Freud, *On narcissism: an introduction, Standard Edition*, vol. 14).

That person has wisdom who knows how to give up the quest for completeness for his theoretical productions in spite of the desperate hope of attaining it. Freud also writes: 'The development of the ego consists in a departure from primary narcissism and gives rise to a vigorous attempt to recover that state.'

(See also GENERAL SYSTEMS THEORY; PARADOXES; PSYCHOANALYSIS; SELF-REFERENTIAL CALCULUS; THEORY OF LOGICAL TYPES.)

M.G.

indebtedness   The notion of indebtedness is one of the elements of the theory of the family LEDGER. Debts comprise all those things which a family member has received from the others. For repayment to be valid on the ethical plane, Boszormenyi-Nagy and Spark (1973) insist that the real 'debtor' must be involved and not a substitute.

(See also DELEGATE; LOYALTY; TRANSGENERATIONAL MEMORIES; TRANSGENERATIONAL THERAPIES.)

A.L.

index patient   This term refers to the member of the family for whom a request for treatment is made by one or more family members and/or by professionals who have been forced to intervene (Selvini Palazzoli et al., 1978). The 'patient' becomes the carrier of the symptom (illness, madness, delinquency, disability), who will coincide more or less with the diagnosis/es of the specialists in society who are qualified to pronounce people ill, disturbed or deviant. Contrary to appearances, the 'therapy' of the family in no case allows one to bypass this moment when the social body recognizes an individual as a patient, identifies him or her as suffering and attempts to isolate the nature of his/her disorder. Understanding and intervention on the plane of family communication is both secondary to a technical indication and is likely to RE-FRAME the various interventions made in a technical and specialized mode.

The systemic model enables one to decipher anew the patient's symptoms. The symptomatic behaviour of an individual is perceived as the product of a family dysfunction. It is one or more symptoms that will be the focal point of the consultation. The patient recognized as such by all the members of his family crystallizes the difficulties of the group. From a systemic point of view, the symptoms presented by the index patient have to be located in the relational contexts in which they occur. They provide a compromise solution, by making it possible to maintain a threatened HOMEOSTASIS and by signalling the existence of a state of suffering. Such a function gives the index patient a not inconsiderable power: the power to bring the family together around his or her difficulties, a coming together which simultaneously reflects the risk of disunity.

It is a paradoxical fact that the symptoms of the index patient bring the family to the consulting room and this marks a failure to maintain the family's equilibrium. Some therapists believe that symptoms break out in a family when it is blocked at a certain level in the development of the FAMILY LIFE-CYCLE.

SCAPEGOAT OR VICTIM

The index patient is to be distinguished from the family SCAPEGOAT or victim. Some families find themselves confronted with multiple illnesses. The family scapegoat is not necessarily the family member who is recognized as the most ill or who is suffering the most. Thus the father may be the 'scapegoat' of intra-family violence without being designated as patient. A particular 'intellectual' child may be regarded as 'worrying' by comparison with brothers whose handicap is patent and almost reassuring.

Nor is the 'index patient' necessarily the family member who is the most 'ill'. A child of normal height in a family of dwarfs who derive their livelihood from their handicap may possibly be perceived as failing to fulfil the family's peculiar destiny. An adolescent who commits delinquent acts is normally the bearer of a socially unacceptable symptom, but to designate him or her a 'patient' would be an abuse of medical or social power.

A Down's syndrome child, suffering from profound encephalopathy and grave dyshormonia, creates a designation which corresponds to the degree of family suffering inherent in the recognition of that irreversible state. Far from necessarily implying a possibility of treatment on the level of the injury or handicap itself, the essence of the pathology thus recognized obliges one to mourn the lost normal child, and the feelings of guilt, both conscious and unconscious, with which the family and the professionals concerned are faced (unconscious phantasies of death, for example) must also be taken into account. On the family plane, the symptom, in its historically dated and irreversible character is one of the rigid elements of reality which the family must reckon with and from which it can derive support, the symptom effecting a re-ordering at the mythological level (rituals of visiting, modification of distances between husband and wife, brothers and sisters etc.). A poorly understood 'family therapy' could at that point aggravate a problem or create extra suffering. It is none the less the case that nuanced interventions between 'specialists' and family members are able to resolve certain questions with an economy of means.

The designation of the 'patient' is thus a focus for multiple conflicts, both within the family and between the various specialists consulted. There are, in a sense, battles between the family members who are themselves specialists and the social specialists who are at home with diagnoses, examinations and various kinds of intervention. The therapeutic attitude has to be very different in each case, depending on the nature of the designation. And the levels at which therapeutic changes can be envisaged have to be appreciated. It is only when this is done that it will be possible to appreciate the articulation of the family's static and metabolic forms, or, alternatively, the levels at which the designation will have to be stabilized or, by contrast, mobilized.

ROLES, FUNCTION AND POWER OF INDEX PATIENT

One of the essential roles of the index patient is to preserve the family's operating rules. The function of designating an index patient makes possible the avoidance of greater suffering by localizing the source of all the group's difficulties in linear fashion. In a system where every other form of designation has become impossible, the recognition of a patient thus provides a minimum DEIXIS. Designation normally concerns one member of the family at a time, even if other members present serious problems. Families may in some cases change designation over time; an improvement in a patient may lead to the appearance of a decompensation in another member. It is commonly found that when a problem is isolated from its context, the family's interactional rules are not modified, but may indeed be accentuated and bring about the appearance of a new symptomatology.

By virtue of the place he or she occupies, the index patient often wields enormous POWER over the family: he or she controls its relations with others and serves as an intermediary in all relationships within the family. His/her symptomatic behaviour, which reflects his/her own individual suffering and that of the family group, procures a certain number of advantages: all the members of the family are in agreement that only the index patient requires treatment and, very often, in the early stages, that consensus is confirmed by the socially empowered specialists (judges, social workers, psychiatrists etc.). Most often, this agreement conceals an inability to confront the real conflicts inside the family and the life-threatening dangers – real and phantasized – which might ensue from so doing.

The patient's function as homeostatic regulator within the family renders his or her presence indispensable. The 'oddity' and apparent absurdity of his/her behaviour provide a more than plausible justification for the way the others are 'forced to be' and for the impossibility of breaking down the merciless control each exerts on the other.

In families in rigid transaction, the fear that one of the members of the family may withdraw from the game creates a high degree of emotional tension and induces each person to exert very tight control over the others. This emotional tension may reach such a pitch that it becomes an incentive to change. However, when these families make up their minds to undergo therapy, this does not mean that they are ready to re-examine the established relations between their members. In actual fact, behind the manifest rigidity of their transactions, chaotic, invasive, undifferentiated phenomena are concealed, relating to the emotional, intellectual and feeling systems of all the protagonists and leading to the perception of a danger of an even more serious outburst. The symptomatology of the index patient expresses, then, the double aspect of the message the family is addressing to the therapist: on the one hand, this is a call for help to achieve change; on the other, it is a request not to question the principles by which it functions. The family makes the implicit demand that there should be no challenge to the definition of the index patient as 'the person who is ill'. The paradoxical character of the family's message can be resolved so long as the therapists are aware of the multidimensional nature of the competing FORCE FIELDS to which the family ecosystem as a whole is subject.

THERAPEUTIC STRATEGY

The therapist's role is to keep as close as possible to the family's demand, i.e. to the symptoms presented by the index patient, the better to understand the implicit rules of the system. Any overhasty redefinition of interactions in fact runs the risk of increasing the family's resistance. One must strive to understand the meaning of the designation, especially in families in rigid transaction. This also applies to the definition given by the various persons in positions of institutional responsibility who are involved in the situation. If the index patient loses his or her place too soon, or too openly defies the compromise which his/her designation as index patient has made possible, then an implicit collusion may appear between institutional and familial homeostases. The family therapists must, therefore, integrate into their models of change the morphogenetic constraints which weigh on all the parties involved. It is thus necessary to be explicitly cautious with regard to any excessively spectacular improvements and to anticipate a relapse if such improvements occur.

See also DELEGATION; DEMAND; DOUBLE BIND; RECIPROCAL VICTIMIZATION AND RESCUE; SYMPTOMS.)

S.A., P.A., A.C., J.M. & P.S.

indications and contraindications for the use of family therapy Family therapy is indicated for a certain number of behavioural disorders, revealing the limits (but not the obsolete character of) chemotherapeutic, psychoanalytic and sociotherapeutic treatment interventions, which may be pursued jointly with family therapy. PSYCHOSOMATIC ILLNESS (asthma, epilepsy, enuresis, encopresis, etc.), disorders of eating behaviour (ANOREXIA NERVOSA, BULIMIA, ALCOHOLISM,

DRUG ADDICTION), psychotic disturbances (SCHIZOPHRENIAS, PARANOIA), medico-legal behavioural disorders (CHILD ABUSE, INCEST, parent abuse, DELINQUENT ACTING OUT, family VIOLENCE etc.) are all situations in which it seems pertinent to consider the relationships between the structure of the family ecosystem in question and the personality, and between that structure and wider systems.

From a practical point of view, the problem never arises in a direct, linear manner. A whole complex trajectory of recognition and social designation necessarily occurs beforehand. The type of therapy indicated will thus depend on several factors:

1 Intensity of the symptoms presented.
2 Ability of the therapeutic and socio-educative organizations to evaluate their levels of competence and delegation.
3 Degree of mobilization of the social unit concerned to deal with the specific problem.
4 Quality of the desire and capabilities of the 'designated' family therapist(s): depending upon their personal aptitudes, their individual commitment and their own history, they will respond to certain types of transactions with more or less experience and skill. The indication for family therapy is thus arrived at by a process of mutual recognition between the 'prescribing' professionals and the therapists whose help is sought.
5 Quality of the joint institutional interventions. In the most difficult cases, work with the family can only be carried out in concert with other forms of specialist intervention, which poses the problem of the joint organization of care.

HOSPITAL ADMISSIONS

With hospitalized patients, one cannot expect explicit formulation of a demand for treatment as a group to come from the family. We may, however, assume that the fact of the patient being hospitalized does, in a sense, express a request for treatment, the family handing over to the hospital the task of providing adequate care. Family therapy is presented as an offer made to the family on the part of the institutional service or services directly concerned with the family's problem(s). It is presented as a gift from the institution which decided that this particular form of therapy was indicated (Eiguer, 1983). It is an example of an exchange between the family and the hospital: between a family which has handed over or is handing over a patient to the hospital and the hospital which is offering a family therapy. It is a key moment which stamps the interactions between the family and the institution that is providing the care as being characterized by reciprocity. The acceptance of this offer is, for certain families (and for the institution), a long process of work.

JUDICIAL INTERVENTIONS

A similar problem appears for families facing problems with the law. The judge, who has to rule on the fate of the child or adult in difficulty, is often faced with contradictory demands for both retaliation and reparation. Given its situation, the family of the 'designated delinquent', seldom requests aid, but rather signifies, by the intensity of the socially intolerable symptoms, the nature of the family's suffering. In dealing with cases of child abuse, father–daughter incest or theft, antinomic demands arise which require a combined response: protection of the most threatened individual persons and social units, and an attempt to understand and act on the ecosystems which are, in this way, signalling their acute suffering.

PRACTICAL MODALITIES

In reality, the decision that family therapy is indicated often involves great conflict within the very group of persons who are empowered to take it. The more intense and acute the family's suffering, the more intense the conflict and the more difficult it is to assess it and work it out within the institutions concerned. In the first phase, these conflicts will play themselves out on an intra-institutional and inter-institutional basis. It may be all the more urgent to decide what therapy is indicated, if the conflict is violent and impossible to resolve within the institutional frameworks directly concerned. In other words, the approach to the family may be a joint one, with the problems being worked through in one institution or in several. In other cases, family therapy should be seen to be indicated when a number of different practitioners encounter a shared impression of confusion and incomprehension of what is at stake, when they run up against insistent repetition of symptoms and a sense of life-and-death risk. Most often, the demand seems to come more from the therapists and the social work professionals than from the family. It is necessary, then, to grasp the semiotic structure of the messages in play, both in their semantic, syntactic and pragmatic aspects and in their intellectual and affective dimensions: in the first phase, the information to be transmitted to the family is that the specialists have a problem which they cannot solve alone, without the family's help. In the second phase, the nature of the conflicts between the therapists will possibly serve as a metaphorical tool to be highlighted to the family. This focus on the institution–family and institution–institution dimensions differs from the focus for indications and contraindications described by Walrond-Skinner (1978).

See also INFANTILE AUTISM; CO-THERAPY; DELIRIUM; DEMAND; DEMENTIA; FAMILY DOCTOR; FAMILY–THERAPEUTIC INSTITUTION DIFFERENTIATION; FAMILY THERAPIES; LEGAL CONTEXT; METABINDING; MOURNING; NETWORKS; PSYCHOSOMATIC DOUBLE BINDS; PSYCHOSOMATIC MEDICINE; SUPERVISION; THERAPEUTIC DOUBLE BINDS; THERAPEUTIC STYLES.)

P.G. & J.M.

indifference   See LOVE, HATRED, KNOWLEDGE, INDIFFERENCE.

individual splitting   See SPLITTING, INDIVIDUAL AND FAMILY.

infantile autism   Infantile autism, as described by Kanner (1942) is characterized by:

- *primary disturbances*: autistic withdrawal, corresponding to an extreme inner solitude and a compulsive quest for sameness.
- *secondary disturbances*: psychomotor, alimentary, linguistic and behavioural disturbances.

At the level of interaction, infantile autism expresses itself as a breakdown of the figures of regulation of proximity and distance in the establishment of bonds.

We thus find disturbances of communication, such as:

1   A fundamental disorder, which takes the form of an incapacity to establish normal relations with persons and react normally to situations from the outset of life.
2   A failure to assume an anticipatory posture preparatory to being picked up.
3   Linguistic disorders
   (a)   Muteness or a delay in acquiring language.
   (b)   Where it is possible for normal language structure to be acquired, its use for receiving and imparting meaningful messages is impossible.
   (c)   Rote memory is highly developed, enabling objects to be named; but their use is inappropriate and characterized by immediate or delayed repetition (delayed echolalia).
   (d)   Absence of pronoun inversion: the child refers to him or herself in the third person; 'I' and 'you', which are SHIFTERS of reciprocity at the linguistic level, are not used.
4   Fear of any movement or change; fear of incompleteness and a quest for sameness.
5   Withdrawal from human relationships, pursuit of mechanical contact with objects.
6   The maintenance of good intellectual potentialities.

Kanner (1942) points to a dual aetiological polarity, crystallizing in the psychical state of the child: 'The child's own psychological structure resulting from inherent factors and the parent – child relational dynamics must be regarded as the main determinant of later development' (Kanner, quoted in Berquez, 1983). Similarly, in his first communication on the subject, Kanner gives an account of the characteristics of the family group. The members of the family, the parents and grandparents are highly intelligent, with marked obsessional tendencies and an inclination to abstraction and social success in the literary, scientific and artistic fields. The expression of emotions is, however, almost non–existent and affective relations are 'formal', 'cold' or in some cases downright non–existent. Experience with socially under–privileged families, or families unconcerned with intellectual values, shows, however, that autism is not restricted to one social or intellectual group.

There is the particularly appropriate expression coined by Soulé (1977) 'the child who came in from the cold'. It is advisable not to rely on a purely psychogenetic hypothesis, which inevitably leads to aggravating the parents' sense of guilt or even of shame, but rather to recognize the setting in place of *pathogenic reverberating circuits* which are sometimes structured at a very early stage and which are in danger of increasingly impairing the personalities of the child and the mother' (Soulé, 1977, pp. 81–2). In this way, one can reverse the point of view which instinctively tends to treat the mother's desire as the source of the problem, and adopt the point of view of the child: 'How I drove my mother mad. The story of a twelve month old child' (Soulé, 1977, p. 82).

The innate and acquired factors leading to autism are therefore no longer to be considered from a merely individual, but from a collective point of view. The parents' despair amplifies a psycho–affective position already characterized by emotional distancing and depressive reactions which have been present for many years and over several generations. Bowen (1978b) suggests that there many have been a non–differentiation of self over several generations, which may thus lead to breaks in the emotional systems. A de–structuring of the systems of METACOMMUNICATION results. The hierarchies of these systems collapse and the systems themselves disintegrate, rendering indistinguishable the order and message, analog and digital, salient and pregnant aspects of human interactions.

The cognitivist explanation insists on the incapacity of autistic children to decode social stimuli. However, as Mottron (1983) rightly points out, even though it is genetically programmed, there is nothing to show that the diffusion of a release of an effect by a physical characteristic that is present at birth, when a living form is recognized in its totality with a particular apparent outline, cannot be interrupted in the course of ontogenesis by a variety of processes. Among these processes, family morphologies probably play quite a considerable part.

The autistic child finds him/herself caught up in a network of transgenerational espionage, becoming the double or triple agent of the definitional impasses of love, hatred and indifference, the double or triple agent of the two emotional systems of the families of origin. He or she then has to fulfil an impossible mission of decoding/encoding the incompatible and impermeable emotional definitions of each family of origin. In this way, he/she becomes a keystone supporting the edifice of three or four generations (Dessoy, 1985). In this type of family, Selvini Palazzoli et al. (1976) draws particular attention to the intensity and the possessiveness of the ties which bind the parents to the grandparents. No re–definition of the myth is possible at the parental level, since the grandparents themselves are caught in a situation where it is impossible for them to delegate the slightest degree of authority, nor is any definition of affective relations possible at that level. In being put in the position of unloved and unlovable child, one particular autistic child described by Selvini Palazzoli enabled her maternal grandmother to obey the imperative 'to love the unloved' in the family. In a family therapy involving two index patients (the father, a pantophobic, and his autistic daughter, the three other members present being the father's mother, his wife and his eldest son), one of the father's mother's main concerns was her son's possible impotence, on account, as she said, of the medicines he was taking. During the therapy, when an inventory of the results obtained was drawn up, the father was able to state that he had realized that he had children.

From an ethological point of view, Tinbergen and Tinbergen (1972) stress that autistic withdrawal testifies to an unresolved conflict of motivation in the establishment of a tie to another, which is connected with the constraints of the family environment. Every establishment of a bond between conspecifics of evolved species involves a conflict between attraction and withdrawal, between approach and avoidance tendencies. This is particularly marked even in the normal child. There are varying degrees of opening up depending on the nature of the channel utilized. When confronted with a stranger, the normal child is both attracted and intimidated, seeking eye contact and being wary of it. For a distressed child, words are more troubling than looks, looks more troubling than touch. As he or she grows up, this is reversed. In the adult (particularly the Westernized adult), touch is the level of maximum opening up and/or intimacy.

A clinical approach to the child consulting with his family can be seen to ensue from this. It is not in the practitioner's interest to address himself directly to the child. It is necessary for him to affiliate with the the parents (see AFFILIATION OR JOINING). Feeling that the therapist has established a relationship of confidence with his or her parents, the child may then him or herself seek to approach the therapist. It is important for the therapist to adapt to the rapid emotional changes of the child and to respect his or her fluctuating moves of approach and withdrawal. A preferential mode of making contact is to accompany the child in his or her activity, in play if such exists and to spread this to the whole group. Usually, the child will first seek bodily contact, then fixing with a stare, and lastly linguistic exchange. The therapist should adjust his or her own actions to those of the child: touching without looking at the child when the child touches him or her; laughing with the child; looking at the child briefly when the child seeks eye contact; speaking can only begin very gradually in a step-by-step ritualization of the relationship.

For the infant, there are SYMBOLIC REFERENCES between the cutaneous, vocal and visual signs exchanged with the mother and her substitutes. But a mere look from the mother (or the tone of her voice or her bodily attitudes) may be the expression of the ambience of the whole family system; it may reflect the static, deep state of intrafamilial exchanges. The autistic child will flee every signal indicating terror or emotional confusion, saving him or herself by 'catching on to' dehumanized configurations.

By comparison with normal children, autistic children emit more than they receive, present a great deal of stereotypy, show little aggression, little play and more attachment behaviour (Garrigues et al., 1973). Paradoxically, however, this attachment is not orientated and not ritualized. What is involved here is approach behaviour which reduces distance without establishing contact, whether this be skin, eye, sound or verbal contact; it takes on the form of a social avoidance and avoidance of the eyes. These non-orientated attachment behaviours occur more often in the presence of adults than in the presence of children of the same age. Dominant in their attitudes are behaviours of fear-withdrawal and active avoidance behaviours.

Several writers (e.g. Berquez, 1983; Dessoy, 1985) argue strongly that there is an all-or-nothing alternation of position in such situations, giving the impression of a quantum break between two oscillating polarities:

1 The polarity of unitary integration (stable symbiotic position) leading to the establishment of close contact (unstable dynamic position of nearness).
2 The polarity of absence of contact (position of stable rupture) leading progressively to the establishment of a 'setting aside' (unstable dynamic position of the relation of distancing).

For Dessoy (1985), fusion with a parent involves an experience of unity which is so powerful that it imposes itself upon the whole of the family. Similarly, the experience of apartness brings in its wake the total absence of relationship and contact which also imposes itself on the whole family. The absence of connection

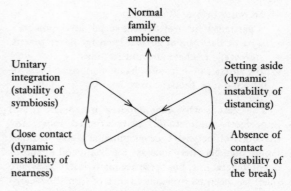

Cycle of dynamic hysteresis of the relations of nearness and distance in a normal family (after Dessoy, 1985).

Quantum break in the relational dynamics of a family with autistic transactions (after Dessoy, 1985).

between these two tendencies leads to the separate coexistence of a totally open universe alongside a totally closed one. The system by which an alliance is formed between the two families of origin has not worked. There is a continuing variation upon a single family theme to the exclusion of the other. Each partner, at the level of the parental couple, instead of actualizing the two themes of the families of origin by re-creating them and, in critically and conflictually surpassing them, transforming them, maintains intact his or her myth of origin without any connection with the other. The autistic child is both a creature of fusion and of rupture, half apprehended by each of the two families of origin. This can be seen in clinical situations in which a mother presents with her child (who may be an adult) and clearly indicates the exclusion of the father. In these cases, this exclusion sets the seal within reality upon the presence of absence and of rupture.

FORMAL CLASSIFICATION

While a systemic perspective on infantile autism, drawing on the work of Bowen and others, as above, is useful in understanding some of the interactional processes, especially from a clinical point of view, a brief diagnostic description of infantile autism is of importance. Much of the recent work on infantile autism has been carried out by Rutter (Rutter, 1985; Lord and Rutter, 1994). He defines infantile autism as a pervasive developmental disorder, the diagnostic criteria being (Rutter, 1985, p. 545):

- an onset before 30 months;
- a particular form of deviant social development;
- a particular form of deviant language development;
- stereotyped behaviours and routines;
- the absence of delusions, hallucinations and schizo-phrenic-type thought disorder.

The reasons why some children are autistic is still imperfectly understood. As mentioned above, the existence of pervasive developmental delay in other family members may increase the likelihood in subsequent generations, but there are many instances where there has been no previous history of formal developmental delay or psychiatric history in family members. If one accepts the above, then treatment will need to be predominantly behavioural, wherever possible taking place in the home, working with the parents and siblings, often with a family that would otherwise not have come to the notice of the mental health professions. Work will need to include help in how to handle the child and to help him or her reach his or her potential; helping the parents grieve the loss of the healthy child they never had (Jenkins, 1986); helping parents with their own guilt over producing a child with developmental delay; helping parents have appropriate time for their other children and for their own marital relationship. It may also include genetic counselling should the parents be considering a further pregnancy.

In work with families with a child who is autistic, the diagnosis of autism may be less important than that of mental handicap where this is the predominant factor inhibiting the child's psychological and intellectual development. A diagnosis of autism may have less stigma in the minds of the parents, but be less important in terms of clinical management and treatment.

(See also ALIENATION; DEIXIS; DOUBLE BIND; FAMILY SELF-REFERENTIALITY; PRAGMATICS OF COMMUNICATION.)

J.M. & H.J.

information The term 'information' is an outstanding example of a vague, all-purpose concept. Yet it is particularly useful, in the PRAGMATICS OF COMMUNICATION, when one wishes an exchange to remain as ambiguous and open as possible.

Notwithstanding the polysemic nature of the term, we may date its introduction into the field of science to the work of Norbert Wiener in 1948 (see Wiener, 1975) and Weaver and Shannon (1949) and, in the human sciences, Ruesch and Bateson (1951). As the titles of these works indicate, it is the field of communication which provides a contextual reference for information (see COMMUNICATION SYSTEMS).

Bateson put forward the founding statement: information is a difference which creates or produces another difference. Or, alternatively, a difference which 'makes a difference'.

CLINICAL VALUE OF CONCEPT OF INFORMATION

In family therapy, information should be grasped in its twofold dimension: quantitatively and qualitatively.

Information as distinctive unit of communication system
Social and FAMILY MYTHS are built up out of structural oppositions which are at work in any clinical situation. In this perspective, it is possible to generalize the systems of opposition advanced by Lévi-Strauss (1973). The distinctive traits which enable these oppositions to be created operate on a continuum based on the following four axes:

- oneself – others;
- excess of information – lack of information;
- true information – false information;
- positive information – negative information.

An exchange of information can thus be symbolized by a representative point situated in a four-dimensional space. Calumny or slander, for example, would appear as an excess of false and negative information about another person.

For certain communications, oppositions registered on a given axis may be situated around a mean value, or may oscillate. One may also simplify the description and take only two axes into account. If we do not take into account the truth–falsehood and positivity–negativity dimensions, we shall have a simplified matrix in which there are excesses or lack of information, either in relation to oneself or to others:

Lack of information about oneself: individual defence mechanisms of repression, isolation, displacement, disavowal, projective identification, foreclosure etc.

Lack of information about others: SECRETS, censorship, exclusions, excommunications, disinformation, mix-ups, MISUNDERSTANDINGS etc.

Excess of information concerning oneself: narcissistic disorders, unconscious feelings of guilt, hypermnesia, *idées fixes*, obsessional ideas, invasion of secondary processes of thought by primary processes, NOSTALGIA etc.

Excess of information concerning others: DISCLOSURE, SCANDALMONGERING, CALUMNY etc.

The structuring of exchanges of information is dependent upon many factors, personal, interactional and transgenerational. They are an expression of the management of conflict, whether individual–individual, individual–group, group–individual or group–group conflicts.

Seeking out pertinent information
The information sought by the attending psychiatrist and the social worker in direct contact with the family is not of the same type as the information with which the family therapist works. An excess of information requested by the 'specialist' or provided by the family may serve as a resistance to the development of an

ongoing process. From a qualitative point of view, there are thus many different semantic fields. The quality of an item of information depends also on the decision-trees relating to the nature of the information one is trying to reveal or conceal (see HEURISTICS).

The concept of information enables us to manage extremely diversified levels of exchange, which do not involve prejudgement of the specific nature of each interaction realized. The nature of the symptoms in effect imposes adequate responses. One cannot adopt the same approach in consultations with a family in schizophrenic transaction, a family with a member suffering from severe brain damage and a family faced with a crisis posed by an adolescent.

In every dynamic interaction, because of semantic unity (see SEMANTIC UNIT OF MIND), the information given and the information received are indissociable. To request information from a family is to give information regarding the nature of what one is doing. Not to give information is, none the less, to impart information and may, indeed, amount to prescribing a different way of communicating.

Depending upon the individual case (the different families' epistemological aptitudes and self-definitions) and the particular point in an intervention, it seems necessary to work either on the introspective aspects (thoughts, emotions, feelings, dreams, nightmares, phantasies etc., which presupposes that these are sufficiently structured and labelled as such) or on the exteroceptive aspects (perception of the behaviour and attitudes of others, activation of play sequences, of curiosity, working out GENOGRAMS, SCULPTING etc.) of the various family members.

Properties of exchanges of information
The more intense the failure of DIFFERENTIATION OF SELF, the more necessary it is to activate and structure the symptomatic behaviour of the family. From a pragmatic point of view, we shall therefore note the following entanglements:

- to seek information is to give information;
- to give information is to receive information;
- to receive information is to lose other information;
- to lose information is possibly to find other information.

Information and group units
The quantity and quality of information varies according to the units and sets one looks at: Wiener (1975) has already noted that a group may have more group information or less group information than its members. Such a finding implies different therapeutic strategies: schizophrenic transactions reveal considerable information defects so far as family organization is concerned.

The psychoanalytic model, which is introspective, addresses itself to situations in which the quantity and quality of information is sufficiently psychically integrated. The systemic model, which is centred more on externalization, makes it possible to objectify behaviour, and previously ignored or inaccessible sequences of behaviour, and therefore to structure phantasy activity.

Morphologies as media of information
With regard to morphologies as media of information, we shall distinguish between the following:

One-dimensional, linear and orientated morphologies (which are, in this respect, isomorphic with the one-dimensional and irreversible flow of time). The signifying chain of language is the most manifest example of this in human exchanges; this linearity lends itself to long-distance transmission of information and, by virtue of redundancy, dependability in the transmission of messages is quite high. On the other hand, there is relatively low semantic density, whereas errors of representation of significations are quite frequent (cf. all the semantic traps of language which prepare the ground for neurotic symptoms). In terms of transmission of knowledge, the model is transmission by books, speeches, lectures etc.

Multi-dimensional, non-linear morphologies with tangled orientations: if spatial extension is limited, the transmission of information only being possible by direct contact, or by diffusion into a restricted space, the semantic combinatory is much richer, even if errors of transmission over distance are more frequent. As regards transmission of knowledge, this will take place by sensitization and TRAINING in small groups. In the communicational approach, we see here the importance of simulations of real situations through the medium of ROLE PLAY, sculpting and the deployment of phantasmatic resonances induced by family systems. The importance of these multidimensional morphologies appears most particularly in the pragmatics of communication. It is not sufficient to give purely verbalized information for there really to be pertinent exchanges of information: 'to tell everything' about oneself may then be the surest means of not really talking about oneself. The multidimensional information communicated is of the order of the resistance met with to the disclosure of information which might appear obvious or banal; the identification of that resistance, occasioned by individual defence mechanisms and family and collective myths, is often the pertinent information which has to be processed in the appropriate manner.

HISTORICAL ORIGIN OF SCIENTIFIC CONCEPT

It was Norbert Wiener who coined the formula, which has since become so celebrated (with its reference to the words of Cabanis and Gall), that 'The mechanical brain does not secrete thought "as the liver does bile",

INFORMATION

as the earlier materialists claimed, nor does it put it out in the form of energy, as the muscle puts out its activity. *Information is information, not matter or energy. No materialism which does not admit this can survive at the present day'* (Wiener, 1975, p. 132, emphasis added). However, differentiating information from matter and energy is one thing, defining it another. The term in fact refers to a number of situations, in which there is great complexity of meaning. This has to do with its 'semantic instability' which perhaps contributes to its present success as a focal point for multivocal or ambiguous communications.

Though Einstein established the precise mathematical equivalence between matter and energy, $E = mc^2$ (where E = energy, m = mass, c = the speed of light), there still remained the task of differentiating both quantitatively and qualitatively between information, on the one hand, and matter and energy on the other and also of studying the mathematical equations involved. In fact, information arises out of transformations of matter made possible by transformations of energy. If the brain's energy reserves run out, the processing of information by the brain is rapidly and irremediably brought to an end. Information is directly dependent upon material modifications made possible by expenditure of energy, even though these transformations occur at very different levels from those established by Einstein's formula. By contrast, a surfeit or insufficiency of information in a system may produce material outbursts with considerable releases of energy, of which inter-human violence is a constant example.

For the purposes of studying communication processes, they have been divided into three levels (Weaver and Shannon, 1949):

1 *A syntactic level*: this is a technical level, enabling the accuracy of the transmission of symbols to be evaluated (see SYNTAX OF COMMUNICATION).
2 *A semantic level*, enabling the precision of the transmission of desired meanings to be determined (see SEMANTICS OF COMMUNICATION).
3 *A pragmatic level*, enabling the effect of the transmission of a message to be determined, and with it the influence which it has on the protagonists who are communicating, and thus its meaning (see PRAGMATICS OF COMMUNICATION).

The classic theory of information, advanced by Weaver and Shannon (1949) is a resolutely quantitative theory, being situated at a technical level and limited to a particular type of situation in which information is transmitted from a sender to a receiver by way of a channel. In itself, it does not make it possible to resolve the semantic and pragmatic problems. However, these two latter levels are strictly derivative from the first, which therefore becomes a necessary preliminary object of study in the investigation of informational phenomena. Though information is not synonymous with 'meaning' (Miller, 1978) nor even of 'signification' (Wilden, 1972); it is an imperative condition for the appearance of signification and meaning.

MATHEMATICAL STUDY OF QUANTITY OF INFORMATION

Quantity of information is a measure of the number of choices possible when faced with several alternatives. Roughly speaking, *the unit of information* – the 'digit' or 'bit' (binary digit) – corresponds to the elementary operation which enables a choice to be made between two possible alternatives. The quantity of information in a system is therefore the number of bits, i.e. the number of binary choices which have to be made to select the required element from among the set of elements that are to be excluded. This measure of freedom of choice corresponds therefore to a diminution of indecision.

Quantity of information is measurable by Shannon's formula:

$$H = - (p_1 \log p_1 + p_2 \log p_2 \ldots + p_n \log p_n) = -\Sigma p_1 \log p_1$$

in which p_1 corresponds to the probability of occurrence of the symbols used in messages and Σ is the sum of the probabilities of occurrence of n independent symbols, where the probabilities of choice between these is $p_1, p_2, p_3 \ldots p_n$. Shannon's formula shows that the quantity of information depends on several variables: the product of the probability of occurrence of a certain number of elementary messages and the logarithm of that probability; and the sum of all the products of the probability of messages and their logarithms. Shannon's formula thus answers the question: given a finite set of symbols, if one wishes to send a selected sequence from one point to another, what, leaving aside interference from the channel of communication, are the constraints imposed by the system of symbols itself?

At first sight, this question seems aberrant and was regarded as such until 1949. How was it possible to speak of information without referring to the level of signification, arrived at through the articulation of signifier and signified? How was it possible to leave out of account the relational aspect, both on the side of the hearer and the sender (whose rhetoric took such pains to achieve affects) and of the channelling, transmitting medium, which intervenes in the communication to the point where it becomes the only speaker (McLuhan and Fiore, *The medium is the message*, 1967) and rapidly then proves to be the only entity present: 'It is not merely that the message implodes into the medium, but there is, in this same movement, an implosion of the medium itself into the real, an implosion of the medium and the real, in a kind of hyperreal nebula in which even the definition and distinct action of the medium can no longer be identified' (Baudrillard, '*Médianalyse*', no. 1, p. 12).

Shannon does, however, attempt this step and achieves an unstable equilibrium between information and disinformation, which makes it possible to quantify the predictability of a message without paying any regard to its content. The epistemological status of the mathematical theory of information is related to the characterizations by Prigogine and Stengers (1979) of DISSIPATIVE STRUCTURES. It thus reflects the body of work from which it was developed, namely thermodynamics.

We have seen that information is associated with a transformation of matter, which is itself made possible by an expenditure of energy. Now this expenditure is itself connected to the ENTROPY of the system under consideration, entropy corresponding to the state of greatest probability of the micro-states of the system, or, to put it another way, to the maximum disorder of the system. In effect, the lower the probability of the occurrence of a message or event, the greater the information introduced by that message or event. In other words, information measures the negative of the system's entropy, which is also termed *negentropy*. At the same time, however, even more information will be introduced where the choice between two alternatives is equiprobable. In this perspective, information corresponds to an increase in entropy in the context in which the informational system is located and to a diminution of entropy (negentropy) in the local system in which the information appears.

Intuitively, Shannon's equation corresponds to the following properties. Information correlates very closely with the set of messages between which it distinguishes; it does not apply to isolated messages, but takes account of the overall situation in which the alternatives are posed; it permits a precise quantitative determination of the message retained as against the messages excluded. As Weaver and Shannon stress, 'this word *information* in communication theory relates not so much to what you *do* say but rather to what you *could* say' (1963 edn, p. 8). The quantity of information contained in a message is the higher where the number of possible alternatives is the greater.

Information is a stochastic concept (see RANDOMNESS; STOCHASTIC PROCESSES) since it concerns an ordering of statistical events: the greater the freedom of choice between equiprobable events, the higher the quantity of information.

In reality this freedom of choice will be limited by two phenomena: the first concerns the REDUNDANCY of messages. The second concerns the noise which becomes superimposed on the signal.

Redundancy is not determined by the free choice of the sender, but by the rules of stochastic occurrence of the symbols. The grammars of languages, the rules of psychical functioning and the circuits of family regulation are based on specific, idiosyncratic hierarchies causing repeated events which are the less clearly perceived for being inevitable and obvious. Redundancy leads to the appearance, within a system of symbols, of a greater probability of occurrence of certain messages, or, more exactly, of certain material supports of messages. Though the resulting repetition diminishes the absolute quantity of information conveyed, it does in fact increase the dependability of the transmission and, to a certain extent, prevents noise and transmission errors from falsifying at every turn the information that is transmitted or is to be transmitted. In fact, a system of totally equiprobable messages would simply be indecipherable.

As regards *noise*, it is a consequence of the very definition of information. If information measures freedom of choice and increases with the equiprobability between several uncertain choices, noise is a factor which potentially augments the quantity of information. In this regard, the distinction between signal and noise supposes a subjective choice in the system of observation and reception; it is relative to the metasystemic levels under consideration. By changing metasystem, it will be possible for a signal to be transformed into noise, and vice versa.

The quantity of information increases in arithmetic progression (by addition) when the number of elements increases in geometric progression (by multiplication); this is conveyed by use of the logarithmic function. This gives us the equation: $\log(a.b) = \log a + \log b$.

If we take the example of a dictionary, the quantity of information it contains is then equal to the number of binary choices necessary to find the word being searched for: the logarithmic function indicates that quantities of information increase by addition when the quantities of words contained in a dictionary increase by multiplication. There is more information if selection is from a set of fifty standard messages than if it is from only twenty-five. In this case, the number of messages has doubled. The quantity of information to add to the system is a logarithmic function of 2. The choice of an item among fifty is therefore:

$$\log_2 50 = \log_2 2.2.5 = \log_2 2 + \log_2 25.$$

We may then envisage a transmission of information along a channel with noise which may be carried out at an infra-representative and statistical level. Let us take as an example the relationship which may exist between two dependent variables, in a given population, such as the relationship which exists between the heights of fathers and their daughters. It is possible, on the basis of Quastler's work (quoted in Atlan, 1972) to define the quantity of information transmitted from one series of variables of this kind to another (see diagram).

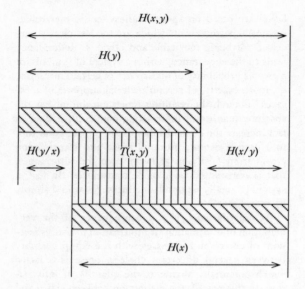

Relationship between heights of fathers and daughters.

$H(x)$ = the number of binary symbols which enable us to define x: uncertainty as to the source or quantity of information of the input message (heights of the fathers).

$H(y)$ = the number of binary symbols which enable us to define y (heights of the daughters): uncertainty as to the reception or quantity of information of the output message.

$H(x,y)$ = the number of binary operations which enable us to define the system made up of x and y.

$T(x,y)$ = the number of binary operations common to the definitions of x and y: the quantity of information transmitted along the channel (information really transmitted from fathers to daughters).

$H(x|y)$ = the number of binary operations which enable us to define x when y is given: the quantity of information: the quantity of input information when there is a determinate ouput, or equivocation (degree of uncertainty of the heights of the fathers when the heights of the daughters are known).

$H(y|x)$ = the number of binary operations which enable us to define y when x is given: quantity of output information when there is a determinate input, or ambiguity (degree of uncertainty as to the heights of the daughters when the heights of the fathers are known).

Ambiguity and information correspond to the 'noise' component of the signal. If we look at the relationship between the heights of the fathers and the heights of the daughters, on the basis of the conditional probability which makes it possible statistically to know the heights of the one from the heights of the other, it emerges that the heights of the fathers 'communicate' 'information' about the heights of the daughters, and

vice versa. Such a transmission is obviously not a transmission of representations, but a transmission of probable information.

The measurement of information cannot be reduced to the study of a linear, one-dimensional channel either. In so far as this is the case, information is a product of the formal properties of these transformations, and this has led Thom (1983b) to write that information, from a quantitative point of view, corresponds to the scalar measurement of the topological complexity of a form. From a more general point of view, it is necessary to recognize the topological complexity of the form, both on the spatial and temporal planes. We may define the spatial complexity of a system in terms of how many parameters one requires per unit of volume to specify the spatial structure of the system. Similarly, the temporal complexity of a system presupposes that the quantity of information produced by the system per unit of time and volume is known. Every system will be represented by a PHASE SPACE (or, alternatively, configuration space of the system), the number of dimensions of which corresponds to the number of parameters (or variables) necessary for apprehending the system. As a function of the temporal development of the system, the points defined on the phase space will describe trajectories which will be accumulated on ATTRACTORS that are to a greater or lesser degree stable. The dimension of the attractor is a FRACTAL dimension (not 2 or 3, but, for example, 2.37 or 2.5): it is a measure of the probability which gives the density of trajectory, which corresponds, on the phase space, with the information dimension of the object under consideration.

QUALITATIVE APPRECIATION OF INFORMATION

This leads to several paradoxes:

First paradox: information is at one and the same time increase of entropy and negentropy, depending on whether one looks at the metasystem or the system. Every living organism reduces its entropy by increasing the entropy in its life or survival system. For Thom, Shannon's formula:

is a relation which links the rarity of initial conditions of an unstable process to the topological complexity of the resulting situation (or of the set of resulting positions of the stabilisation of initial instability). This formula expresses the relation between the initial instability of some stochastic event, and the geometric complexity of the set of all situations which may arise after stabilisation of the instability. It is in this way that information is linked to an 'obscure' kind of causality. (Thom, 1983, p. 284)

Second paradox: it appears that noise itself may have the value of a signal in the appearance of certain redundancies in the noise itself, leading to a metacommunication with regard to the initial signal. Conversely, this original signal loses its signalling function and acquires the nature of noise if it ever arrives at such repetitions that it is emptied of its informational content. Such a modification occurs when one changes scale, point of view, or systemic level.

Third paradox: following on from Simon's thinking, the problem that is often posed is not one of accumulating information, but of ordering it and concentrating human attention upon it. The question therefore is one of making profitable use of the information. Similarly, Thom indicates that 'every quantitative model supposes that reality first be divided up qualitatively' (1980, p. 19). The quality of information depends upon the nature of the decision-trees which hierarchically manage access to memories and the ability of these to relay the pertinent information. There is a relationship of complementarity between this process and that of disinformation, which is all the more effective where it bears upon complex informational systems. In information-rich systems, one of the most effective ways to disinform is to put out the maximum quantity of information while at the same time obscuring the differences indicating what information is semantically pertinent. A sophisticated system of disinformation is so constructed that:

> even its instigators can no longer draw a line between fact and fiction. Here it is interesting to note that it is not so much intentional deceit that is at work as an inability to know the truth because of the social conditions in which information functions and of the state of affairs to which information refers. (Zinoviev, 1981: 1984 edn, p. 274)

Bateson rightly points out that *information is a difference which makes a difference, which produces another difference.* When such a difference propagates itself and becomes transformed into forms that are successively modified in a circuit, Bateson then speaks of an *elementary idea.* For there to be information, it is necessary that two – real or imaginary, material or fictive – entities are marked by a difference, which belongs, properly speaking, to the connection which joins them together. Now, it is equally necessary that the 'news' of their difference should be representable as a difference within another entity which 'processes' information, whether it be a brain, several brains or one or more computers. The two initial entities, as such, are not known: information is here a *difference between two uncertainties.* Every attempt to differentiate the elements of a system amounts to increasing the information one has about that system. But the problem soon becomes complicated since, even in simple cases, it is necessary to distinguish between the signal transmitted down the channel and the noise which covers and, to a greater or lesser extent, degrades the signal. It

remains therefore to evaluate the quality of the differences transmitted and produced by information between one system and another.

The 'fractal' quality of information leads us to make the following remarks: the modelling or representation of an imagined 'space' cannot simply be content with highly individualized levels or with absolutely clearly perceived dimensions. All semantically pertinent information presupposes an itinerary that runs in between such levels. For example, the categories of individual, person, family and group are less clear-cut than they seem here (as are the relations between drug therapy, psychotherapy, family therapy and sociotherapy). Moreover, the map, as constructed and read by the mind, modifies the territory covered. Though the territory is not the map, this latter to a large extent defines the scale on which the territory is approached and the instruments used to explore it. Depending on the map employed, the look of the territory – and hence its exploration and dimensions – may change its appearance quite radically.

(See also COMMUNICATION THEORY; PUNCTUATION OF SEQUENCES OF EVENTS; SELF-ORGANIZATION.)

J.M. & D.C.

instinct In the narrow sense, an instinct is an act, or even an innate motor pattern, i.e. a pattern coordinated in a hereditary manner, thus conforming to a phylogenetic adaptation (acquisition by all the members of a particular species). In this case, we speak of instinctive acts. In higher organisms, instinctive behaviour patterns alternate with sequences which vary in response to changes in the environment, such as taxes, individual acquisitions etc. There are also instinctive learning processes in bees, for example. In a wider sense, instinct is an elementary unit of behaviour, typical of the animal world, made up of an appetitive behaviour possessing an autonomous centre of excitation, an innate releasing mechanism (IRM) and a consummatory behaviour. From the vertebrates upwards, certain hereditary coordinations become inaccessible to direct expression and act to mediate sequences of acquisition or even LEARNING sequences. Certain releasing mechanisms are also acquired individually. In the case of these, we speak of instinctive behaviour.

In the most general sense, instinct corresponds to the hierarchical integration of many instinctive behaviours, which combine to perform a variety of functions: recuperation (sleep), predation/feeding, protection against danger, sexuality, reproduction, the knowledge instinct (or epistemophilic drive). We speak in this case of systems of instinctive behaviour or emotional systems. Instinct is an innate competence or a competence which determines its own acquisition procedures, which are also shared by the conspecifics of a single species. It is therefore a supra-individual semantic unit of communication, produced by a phylogenetic adaptation. Just as the skeleton cannot be dissociated from the muscles and nervous system, so instinctive behaviour patterns cannot be dissociated from individual systems of learning which potentialize them or repress them as a function of family and cultural norms.

The term 'instinct' is a problem, not the solution to a problem. Suppression of the concept does not suppress the problem that is posed, but creates new ones. The concept is criticized both by 'analytic' thinking (since it makes reference to the explanatory principle of the goal-directedness and autonomy of behaviour, see for example Bateson, 1969) and by 'holistic' thinking (since it breaks up behaviour into component parts in an arbitrary manner, by singling out an entity created by the artifices of observation, whereas this can only be one part of the overall reaction of the organism, see for example Goldstein, 1934).

Instinct is an organ of behaviour, endowed with individual autonomy and supra-individual expression. It allows us to conceive that the unity of the organism does not stop at its bodily envelope. Such a semantic unit is regulated as a function of the goal to be achieved (predation, copulation, reproduction etc.). This unit generates the autonomy of the movements of animated living beings, as well as specific affective actions and reactions, towards goals of self-preservation and reproduction. Certain goals are inhibited by hierarchically higher goals. Such units are secondarily channelled and reorientated in phylogenesis to semiotic ends, thus forming the prototypes of the systems of representation (RITUALIZATIONS, which, by re-presenting, stand in for a sequence which has itself become latent). DO-MESTICATION, and even self-domestication, deeply modify the structure of instinctive behaviours by bringing about what are often substantial behavioural variations, which do not appear in species in the wild.

INSTINCT AND/OR DRIVE?

We shall not make a sharp distinction here between 'instinct' and 'drive' for the following reasons. First, in *animal ethology*, Lorenz hesitated between *Instinkt* and *Trieb*, choosing *Instinkt* or, more precisely, *Instinkthandlung* (instinctive behaviour pattern):

I am compelled to return to the term 'instinctive behaviour pattern' because the word 'drive' (*Trieb*) has recently been taken up in circles in which there is an obvious trend towards denying the existence of the very thing which we understand under that word. In order to avoid confusion with the (in my opinion) aberrant drive concepts of American behaviourists and psychoanalysts I am forced to drop the German term in favour of the Latin one. (Lorenz, 1954: 1970 edn, p. 194)

For Lorenz and his school, instinctive behaviour patterns are easy to identify both in animals and in man.

Secondly, in *psychoanalysis*, Freud mainly used the word '*Trieb*', which has been variously translated as 'instinct' or 'drive'. The argument put forward by Laplanche and Pontalis (1973) that Freud reserved the term '*Instinkt*' for animals and '*Trieb*' for humans, thus creating a semantic opposition between the two is contradicted by the first sentence of the 'Three Essays on the Theory of Sexuality': 'The fact of the existence of sexual needs in human beings and animals is expressed in biology by the assumption of a "sexual instinct" [Geschlechtstrieb], on the analogy of the instinct of nutritition, that is of hunger' (Freud, *Standard Edition*, vol. 7, p. 135). Moreover, from an excellent study by Michèle Pollak-Cornillot (1986), it emerges that Freud most often translated the French word 'instinct' as '*Trieb*', though he also used the Latin word '*Instinkt*', thus showing that he attached greater importance to the polysemy of the signified than to the letter of the signifier. There is thus a movement back and forth between narrow and broad meanings of concepts which only imperfectly cover the reality they describe. To abandon them totally, however, would amount to the complete semantic scotomization of a stubborn reality!

Thirdly, in *everyday language and in literature*, the term 'instinct' is semantically much richer and more general than that of 'drive' (which is a neologism dating from the early part of this century). Instinct is both impulsion and attractor; to do something by instinct means that a structured skill is at work, with intuitive psychical participation. This is not, in any sense, to reduce man to an animal – unless the great majority of characters in classical literature could be said to be reduced to animals.

Lastly, the terms 'instinct' and 'drive' can be seen as no different in their explanatory power; at best they make possible an approximate definitional handling of a reality man shares, in part, with the animal world.

DEATH INSTINCT OR DEATH OF INSTINCT?

Freud has described in detail this boundary zone between the somatic and the psychical called instinct or drive. The Freudian description of the *Trieb* was confirmed, in its non-representable aspects, by Lorenz and the so-called 'objectivist' school (Tinbergen, 1947; Lorenz, 1954, 1966, 1973, 1978a, b; Eibl-Eibesfeldt, 1967). Freud postulated the death instinct as the basis of the activity of thinking (see his letter to Einstein, 1932). This turning around of the question of instinct in man is the basis of his specific capacities for autonomy, in which the partial death of the instinct plays an integral part: only what is living can be killed. Man has integrated the instinctive levels of organization of his behaviours into symbolic and intellectual systems and systems of feeling. But, fortunately, he has not suppressed the morphological reality of his instinctive components or, in other words, his ability to feel (even elementary) emotions, to feed, to mate, to reproduce biologically (no more than he has suppressed the existence of the skeleton, joints and muscles, reflex systems and short-term memory or irreversibly acquired features). A large part of appetitive behaviour, or releasing mechanisms and consummatory activities is, admittedly, dependent upon complex learning processes, but may satisfy elementary instinctive activities.

INSTINCT AS ORGAN OF BEHAVIOUR AND LEVEL OF LEARNING

An instinct is the behavioural equivalent of an organ for all 'deracinated' organisms which possess mobility (animals). It supposes the articulation of rigid and flexible patterns. It is a level of learning that is not susceptible of modification by the individual; it is, in a sense, a read-only memory, modified only by the species. The emergence of flexible patterns which can be modified by the individual, is to be found in the most highly evolved insects like bees, which are capable of instinctive learning. An increase in levels of learning correlates with the appearance of vertebrates. These learning processes themselves have the family ecosystem as their matrix, thanks to the caring behaviour directed towards their offspring by parents. There is as much difference between the instincts of invertebrates and vertebrates as there is between the instincts of the higher mammals and those of man. However, to reject by definition the application of the concept of instinct to man ultimately brings with it more difficulties than advantages. It is a specific characteristic of higher organisms that they can inhibit (HABITUATION), accentuate (sensitization, see SENSITIVITY), simulate (PLAY, learning, MIMESIS) or repress (inhibition) certain complex instinctive behaviours. Instinctive behaviours have to do with the emotional systems as described by Bowen (1978a). If the instinct is the phylogenetic prototype of autonomous behaviour, the existence of the self presupposes the autonomous integration of the full range of autonomous behaviour. The more differentiated the self, the more able it is to regulate the emotional systems by bringing into play the intellectual, conceptual and affective systems.

PROPERTIES OF INSTINCTIVE BEHAVIOURS

Autonomous and heteronomous motivation

Its motivation is autonomous (it is the prototype of autonomous behaviour); that autonomy is ensured by oscillating nerve centres which generate impulses and the spontaneous occurrence of the behaviour associated with it. In other words, behaviour is both determined and yet unpredictable as regards the precise moment when it will spontaneously be released.

Its motivation is also heteronomous: its release depends both on that internal autonomy and on stimuli from the internal milieu (hormones, nerve circuits) and the external milieu (releasing stimuli). Contrary to the reflex pattern of stimulus–response, the instinct is an integrated behavioural unit that is both active and reactive, autonomous and heteronomous. When external stimuli are lacking, instinctive behaviour is none the less released.

Articulation of fixed patterns (coordinated hereditarily) and acquired patterns

The fixed patterns are instinctive acts properly so-called: they are present essentially in the consummatory part of the instinct. In man, suckling, non-nutritive sucking, the search for contact, the infant's smile, eye contact with raising of the eyebrows, flirtatious attitudes, and certain threat, salutation and appeasement signals are movements which need no learning to be emitted and understood.

In vertebrates, these patterns are coordinated with patterns that may be modified in response to changes in the environment: without memorization, taxes (orientations regulated in terms of a goal to be achieved), or with memorization. The foundations of individual learning are based on phenomena of sensitization, habituation, BECOMING ACCUSTOMED and IMPRINTING. Learning is thus based on procedures that are phylogenetically adapted, and; hereditary coordinations thus serve as metasystems orientating and channelling modifiable patterns.

Concatenation of appetitive behaviours, innate/acquired releasing mechanisms and consummatory behaviours

Appetitive behaviour allows the organism to seek out the conditions in which consummatory behaviour is to be released: the search for food, for a sexual partner, for a companion, for a rival, for territory marking. So long as the key stimuli have not been encountered in reality, the animal remains in a state of excitation. The most primitive forms of appetence are *motor agitation, disordered locomotion*. These increase the chances of meeting up with the sought-after releasing stimulus. Such agitation behaviour is probably a behaviour of last resort and we also find it in man. Appetitive behaviours are the framework within which all behaviour of acquisition and learning regulated by rewards has developed.

The *innate/acquired releasing mechanism* is the system of perceptual association which enables the relationship between appetitive and consummatory behaviours to be regulated.

Consummatory behaviour enables the instinct to be satisfied by feeding, copulation, care for the young, nest-building etc. Initially a consummatory behaviour was essentially made up of instinctive behaviour patterns. In vertebrates, these are articulated to taxic movements enabling the animal to orientate itself within a space as a function of the characteristics of that space.

In higher mammals, consummatory behaviours are modifiable by learning, through the handing on of certain 'traditions' (some primates have, for example, learned to put salt on sweet potatoes). It may be noted here that a regulative cycle causes the final consummatory act to re-act back on the initial appetitive behaviour, thus transforming the very nature of the instinctive behaviour.

Hierarchical systems of behaviour

As Tinbergen (1947) has described, instinct, as a global behaviour, corresponds to the hierarchical integration of several appetitive behaviours, innate/acquired releasing mechanisms and consummatory behaviours. A consummatory behaviour may serve as appetitive behaviour for a subsequent link in the chain. The object of the main appetitive behaviour may very well not be fulfilled in the consummatory act which terminates the behaviour. Hunting dogs will seek to kill their prey without necessarily devouring it afterwards.

AVATARS OF INSTINCTIVE BEHAVIOUR IN HUMANS

In man, appetitive behaviours are split up into increasingly smaller segments. These do not eliminate the structure of instinctive acts, but re-order them into a number of symbolic systems of autonomy. Now, these latter are based on complex appetitive behaviours, on releasing mechanisms for certain activities and on consummatory behaviours: a sports match, a concert or a museum visit are collective consummatory behaviours, products of high-level learning, which are based on long self-sustained appetitive behaviours.

Being looped back upon themselves, appetitive behaviours become in effect their own ends (goal-inhibition): either (a) *pathologically*, as for example in anorexia nervosa, described in psychoanalytic terms as an 'orgasm of hunger' (Kestemberg et al., 1972) the consummatory act is released in the very movement of self-sustained appetence; or (b) *in a creative manner*, as in sublimation or the achieving of a high degree of mystical fulfilment.

The sexual instinct is itself a multi-hierarchical emotional system, made up of appetitive and consummatory behaviours, of fixed, rigid patterns, hereditarily coordinated (instinctive movements) and patterns that are open to the nature of the environment (taxes, strategies and tactics by which appetitive behaviours are organized). By instinct we understand here a complex and specific behavioural morphology, produced by autonomous internal centres of excitation and activated by internal and external stimuli. The release of such behaviour may occur spontaneously. In order fully to unfold, the sexual instinct requires an activation of all its components in childhood experience or play. It presupposes a multiplicity of tangled levels or organization of biological, hormono-physiological and neuro-physiological systems.

(See also AGONISTIC BEHAVIOUR; ATTACHMENT BEHAVIOUR; LOVE; SEXED BEHAVIOUR; STATIC, PSEUDO-STATIC AND METABOLIC FORMS.)

J.M.

institutional myths, social myths   Just as families are bearers of systems of shared collective belief, which ensure the internal cohesion of their operation and provide protection from other groups, so too are the organizations of contemporary society (schools, the army, the judicial system, medicine, the state etc.). Every institutional micro-system (the mental hospital, classroom or socio-educational service) secretes its own levels of mythic organization.

One of the possible founding myths of any social organization is the radical difference between its functioning and the functioning of any sort of family and the elimination of anything explicitly reminiscent of the families to which the protagonists belong. In other cases, by contrast, the appeal to 'familialism' will be *de rigueur*. The mythic foundation of the institution is secured by the (theoretical and/or practical) interchangeability of persons as a function of their levels of competence. This is achieved either by the existence of rules of co-optation (reciprocal personal recognition) or, by contrast, of hierarchical advancement based on no personal factors, but simply on selection of the most skilled (competition).

The institutional myth controls the nature of an organization and the regulation of exchanges between the various persons within it. It will deal, for example, with the equivalence and interchangeability of everyone's fields of competence or, on the other hand, the formal recognition of personal identities, rejecting any confusion of roles. It will decree the meaning of the recognized and implicit hierarchies or state the need to have no hierarchy at all. It will regulate horizontal exchanges and the gangways between the different levels of the hierarchy. It will formalize the importance or irrelevance of meetings within a 'democratic' or an 'autocratic' vision. It will specify the centres of power, decision-making and responsibility, together with how such things are concentrated or delegated.

The great collective myths of our societies regulate access to work ('the labourer is worthy of his hire') and which sexual relationships are seen as permissible, tolerated or forbidden. They also regulate values, prohibitions, and which transgressions are both encouraged and at the same time frowned upon (alcoholism) and which are very violently prohibited (drug abuse). In some other cultures, alcoholism is totally forbidden, while hallucinations or catatonic expression are tolerated or even highly regarded. Similarly, institutional myths govern the structuring of space and time in interpersonal and social relations. These grand bodies of myth make use of the ideological and political structures of society, and these latter, of course, also depend on family structures (Todd, 1983), at the same time as making their influence felt on family systems, and being particularly called upon when these latter are malfunctioning significantly.

Lastly, other myths ensure the transmission of knowledge and power, by enabling TRANSGENERATIONAL MEMORIES to be registered, along with collective historical memory. We shall note, in this regard, that myth tends to produce considerable distortions in the construction of memories. In the reproduction of scholarly institutions (or perhaps we should say scholastic ones), a phenomenon exists which we might term the reproduction of the anachronistic plagiarist. An anachronistic plagiarist is a thinker or an academic or creative writer who has the ability to copy the thinking of his successors. For such a plagiarist, the mark of the highest art is to be able to carry off such a performance posthumously. Among others, Marx and Freud have recently excelled in this sphere.

(See also EVOLUTIONARY SURVIVAL UNIT; FAMILY MYTHS; MYTH; RITUALS OF BELONGING; RITUALIZATION; SEMANTIC UNIT OF MIND; SOCIAL ORGANIZATION; UNIT OF CHANGE.)

J.M.

institutions An 'institution' will be understood here as the process of structuring of social relations as established by law, custom and habit. The institution is the performative realization of the law (see LAW; PERFORMATIVES). The process of institution is found at the various different levels of social groups: persons, families, social organizations, nations etc. The concept of institution does not itself enable us to determine at what level of organization this structuring of the relations between individuals, families and collectivities intervenes. Although, for example, the family may be considered an institution, it cannot merely be reduced to one, since it is the outcome also of processes of interaction which may possibly come into conflict with instituted norms.

From a general point of view, the social institution which is the guardian of identity is what might be called the ideology of a collectivity (Erikson, 1968, p. 133; see also ETHOS; EIDOS). More precisely, the judicial and psychiatric aspects of social institutions will be dealt with here, in their conflictual relations with the family as an institution. What are in play here are the limits which society aims to impose on the systems of behaviour and belief of the individuals who make it up.

The contemporary crisis of institutions has expressed itself, in the field thus defined, in various attempts at 'de-institutionalization'. Family therapies have emerged as one of the means for coping with the institutional transformations which are destabilizing family systems and with the crises which confront the judicial and psychiatric institutions as a result.

ETYMOLOGY AND DEFINITIONS

The term derives from the Indo–European root 'stha', 'to be standing'. In Greek, 'istemi', 'to make to stand' is found in 'episteme': science, knowledge and, literally, 'the taking of a position upon' (for a detailed study of the meaning of this word and its history, see Maurel et al., 1983).

In Latin, 'instituo' means (a) to place within, implant; (b) to set up, dispose, establish; (c) to arrange, prepare, begin; (d) to establish, institute, found; (e) to organize something which exists, to ordain, regulate. We shall note here the initial topographical dimension – 'to place within' – and the way an act of this type is repeated in the psychiatric institution (putting the madman in an isolation cell, into a 'chemical straitjacket' or into a sufficiently structured institutional network where the family has failed to do so, within an even wider framework established by the law). The therapeutic approach to the family is a way of taking over this containing function, either to prevent hospitalization or to accompany it and to offer an attenuation of the potentially pathogenic effects of *parentectomy* (Hirsch, 1980).

We shall also note the self-referential dimension: to institute someone, in the legal sense of appointing them as one's heir, or to institute an order or a law etc. is effected by a performative speech act (see PERFORMATIVES; SPEECH ACTS). By uttering that performative, the person instituting something (or someone) creates a new situation, which is imparted to that thing or person in such a way that what is imparted lies outside the power of that thing or person and outlasts it/them.

> The institution must tend to combine production and reproduction, genesis and transmission, and, moreover (and here we part company with 'orthodox' definitions of institutions), it can only fulfil that task of production–reproduction if it adds to it the opposite task of – at least potentially – killing off what it produces and reproduces. (Barel, 1985, p. 100)

In their extreme and conspicuous aspects, the judicial and psychiatric institutions seem to be based on the exclusion from normal society of deviance in behaviour or thought and on inclusion (or enclosure) in places of confinement. Paradoxically, the prison and the asylum are sites where society stands revealed to itself, where it marks out its own limits at every moment. Paradoxically, the 'parentectomy' produced by confinement only functions to exacerbate the original conflict. As Benoit (1984, pp. 57–8) writes, with reference to the psychiatric institution:

every hospital practitioner can confirm the following systemic law: beyond the gates of the hospital to which a schizophrenic has been admitted, there waits a family. It remains in constant – more or less open – conflict with the institutional team and it delegates correspondents to keep up the confusion that is already present within the team that has to deal with the schizophrenic's ambiguities. In fact, the matter of a patient gaining or regaining autonomy concerns a great number of people and his symptomatology may even oscillate as a result of what is happening to people thousands of miles away.

CHEMOTHERAPIES, PSYCHOTHERAPIES, INSTITUTIONAL THERAPIES, FAMILY THERAPIES

The psychiatric institution is defined by Jean-Claude Benoit as *hyper-homeostatic* and by Philippe Caillé as *hyperstable*. It seems to lack the mechanisms necessary for its renewal, having only one option, the maintenance of the status quo or disappearance. Benoit (1984) emphasizes the paradoxical injunction which society establishes at the site of madness: 'You must cure the mentally ill and you must keep them locked up.' Now, the containing functions of the psychiatric institution incontestably have a therapeutic dimension. However, as in all therapy, there are iatrogenic risks involved. The degree of the institution's hyperstability is relative to the level of tension tolerated by the surrounding society. Furthermore, this hyperstability has to cope with the inertia imparted by family life-cycles and the profoundly repetitive goals of the systems of family reproduction (far beyond their appearance of dynamic change).

In Caillé's view, the medical personnel in psychiatric institutions are very dependent on the positive opinion which the patients have of their stay and the assistance received in such institutions. The systemic model poses a challenge as regards the value of those medical staff who do not subscribe to it and who continue with the usual pattern of work. The impossible alternative seems to be as follows: either a number of persons define themselves as family therapists and are officially regarded as such by the whole of the service, in which case the risk is that the other medical personnel will feel devalued and excluded from the dynamic dimension of the treatment, or, alternatively, everyone is brought in to a 'systemic revolution' within the institution and the risk then arises of a complete confusion between the levels of institutional therapy, chemotherapy, psychotherapy and the levels of family therapy. Therapeutic competence is transformed into ideological collusion and the illusion of a shared theory.

The debate may be different in nature, first, if the family therapists succeed in conveying to the rest of the team that their routine is no more extraordinary than anyone else's and should confer no higher status upon them; and, secondly, if mutual recognition of one another's skills is achieved in practice. The prescription of medicines, nursing care (intensive nursing in the most serious cases) and institutional meetings will doubtless be very effective in this regard. Furthermore, other alternatives complement the chemotherapeutic, institutional and psychoanalytic inputs: therapeutic units, crisis centres, day centres, residential centres etc. It seems reasonable to assume that, in the most difficult cases, family DOUBLE BINDS are the expression of a demand for polytherapy. But the institutional collectivization of therapies produces a substantial risk of resistance to the indication of family therapy and to its being carried out. This takes us back to the paradox which often appears when the question of a patient's discharge from the institution arises. If the patient asks to leave, his or her psychotic defences which are adapted to social reality will be perceived as the prolongation of his or her morbid state and efforts will be made to delay his/her discharge. If, however, he/she stops asking to leave the institution (being, in a sense, cured within the asylum), the view will be taken that he/she has to be made autonomous (which he/she has precisely succeeded in achieving within the institution) and will be urged to leave as soon as possible.

This presupposes that the levels of organization of care for – and intervention with – the index patient and the family be differentiated: it is not advisable for the institutional therapy of one or more patients from a family and family interventions properly so-called to be wholly conflated, nor should they be totally separated. An airline pilot cannot at the same time be an air traffic controller, nor can an airport director monitor the flight plan of every aircraft over its entire course. It seems problematic to have the same person take on the two tasks for very long, like some sort of demiurge (especially in cases where there are several identified patients). For such a dual task to be possible, however, it is necessary for each of the intervening therapists to concert their actions with the others, depending on the particular needs, and for a hierarchical organization of levels of intervention to be established. When this is done, it becomes possible to envisage family therapy treatment for schizophrenics.

It will be noted that these two therapeutic spaces, the institutional and the familial, form a TANGLED HIERARCHY. Family therapy forms part of the arsenal of therapies; it is one possible element in the make-up of the institution. The institution can protect and structure families which have suffered fragmentation. Conversely, the family context of the index patients re-frames the institution as a part of their adventure, the only possibility they have of freeing themselves from it at a later date (this part may be integrated in a positive way or in a projective form, in which the bad is expelled).

Though the contrary is often asserted, institutions

can cope with novelty, on condition that the new element does not threaten the basic homeostatic functions of life and survival. The pharmacological, psychoanalytic and so-called institutional therapy revolutions have succeeded in changing the institutional landscape, where the figures of regulation and the inertia factor of the institution have been respected. Repetitive behaviour and rigid interactions have to be seen as STATIC or PSEUDO-STATIC FORMS which have their rationale and their functions. Change arises not so much through freeing up what has become fatally rigid as by discovering contexts in which metabolic forms can articulate themselves to existing structures. The organization of care thus need not be reduced to its institutionally accepted aspects.

In this regard, the use of the term institution as synonymous with 'organization of care' or 'therapeutic intervention' is, in itself, a symptom. Where family therapy is concerned, any coherent project must take account of the feedback which the coordination of care will inevitably generate in respect of this specific organization of work. This assumes an adjustment to other specialist activities. What is required is the complementing of established hierarchies and ideological horizons by mutually recognized skills and effective performance.

(See also CO-THERAPY; FAMILY–THERAPEUTIC INSTITUTION DIFFERENTIATION; INSTITUTIONAL MYTHS; METABINDING; MULTI-LEVEL HIERARCHIES; PRESCRIBING OF (MEDICAL) DRUGS; SELF-ORGANIZATION; SOCIAL ORGANIZATION; SUPERVISION.)

J.M.

interactional typologies of the family Interactional family typologies may be subdivided into two groups:

1 The typologies which establish a one-to-one correlation between the psychiatric – or forensic – symptomatology and the nature of the transactions. Interactions become stabilized into schizophrenic, anorectic, psychosomatic, addictive or delinquent transactions (Ferreira, 1963; Haley, 1967; Bateson, 1972, pp. 242–9; Minuchin, 1974; Jackson, 1977; Weakland, 1977; Selvini Palazzoli et al., 1978; see TRANSACTIONAL TYPOLOGIES OF THE FAMILY).

2 The typologies which try to generalize and objectify the clinical intuitions of earlier typologies, taking into account the possibility of a polysymptomatology in certain families, of a potential family suffering in families with no symptoms, and linking the characteristics of these families to certain specific parameters of interactions (Riskin and Faunce, 1970 in Watzlawick and Weakland, 1977).

ONE-TO-ONE TYPOLOGIES

These typologies lie at the basis of the discoveries of the Palo Alto school and the epistemology which resulted from those discoveries. It is the virtue of these that they established a dynamic bridge between certain diagnoses of an essentially static character, which traditionally led to an unfavourable prognosis, and entirely new possibilities of dynamic amelioration. This has led to a radical transformation of the relations between psychotherapies and sociotherapies through the family approach. A schizophrenic symptom, an anorectic behaviour, a paranoid character or delusion, a delinquent act etc. may thus be linked to systems that have a relational meaning (SEMANTIC UNIT OF MIND) and modified by a group intervention of those systems (UNIT OF CHANGE).

MORE COMPLEX TYPOLOGIES

Many writers (Laforgue, 1936a; Wynne et al., 1958; Lidz et al., 1965; Jackson, 1977) have noted the polysymptomatic aspect of the most disturbed families, where interchanges of disorders take place between the various members of a single family in an effort to maintain the homeostatic equilibrium of the group. What is one to do then in those family situations in which the patient is schizophrenic (or a self-mutilating autist), truly signalling that help is needed, and has gravitating around him a mother in a saintly position, a father oscillating between positions of paranoia and obsessional uncertainty, who is alcoholic into the bargain, and sisters presenting more or less compensated hysterophobic symptoms?

Riskin and Faunce (in Watzlawick and Weakland, 1977) suggested a family typology based on the following parameters, situated on an assessment scale:

- clarity/obscurity of linguistic interchanges;
- topic continuity/discontinuity;
- commitment or lack of commitment;
- agreement/disagreement;
- intensity of affective variations as family members communicate with one another;
- who talks to whom, who interrupts whom?
- friendly, indifferent, attacking quality of the relationship.

As a result, these writers came up with a classification into five types of family.

Multi-problem families
In these families, verbal exchanges are the least clear and are characterized by irony, sarcasm and laughter. Speakers change topic suddenly, reflecting the intense rivalries existing between them. Comments are of the 'mind-reading' type, with one person speaking for another. Each person is highly committed to their own

wishes and feelings and seldom in agreement with the ideas and beliefs of the others. The atmosphere is essentially unfriendly. The score in these families was highest for formal prohibitions of the 'behave yourself' type. The most frequent interactions were of the child-to-child type, parent-to-parent and parent-to-child interactions being minimal. There is a total absence of mutual emotional and moral support. Riskin and Faunce conclude that such families do not provide models for learning clear modes of communication or effective cooperation.

Constricted Families

These families are extremely, even compulsively, clear. Though they speak in complete sentences, they make sudden, frequent and inappropriate changes of topic. The tone is relatively depressive and unfriendly. Their jokes have a highly intrusive character and do not produce laughter. The parents seem on very good terms, and the children speak to the parents, but the parents tend only to speak to the children to criticize them. The children do not talk among themselves. All these families function by attacking at least one member as a scapegoat. Comments of the 'behave yourself' type are very infrequent. In fact, the children behave badly and no limits are set to them.

Families with Official Child-labelled Problems

These families do not speak clearly on account of frequent interruptions. They very strongly disagree, without balancing this with agreement. Only one person in the family changes topic frequently. Jokes are rare and the demand for good behaviour is high on the part of the parents. Moral support is non-existent, as is open aggression. The atmosphere is relatively muted, depressive, argumentative and tense and no encouragement is expressed. Personal commitment is avoided by recourse to a target person within the family. Parent-to-parent and child-to-child interactions are average, parent-to-child and child-to-parent interactions a little less frequent. One person speaks appreciably more than the others without being spoken to very much by them.

'QUESTIONABLE FAMILIES'

The atypical or 'questionable' nature of these families seems to be connected with the nature of the study itself. They cannot be seen as normal families, by virtue of the existence of at least one patient, 'somatic' or otherwise. That person's illness cannot, however, be related to the parameters of the study.

NORMAL FAMILIES

These families are in the high-medium range of clarity, and show an average level of unclarity. Humour and jokes are present. A topic is worked through to its natural resolution. Though there is an average level of disagreement, levels of agreement are higher and go together with positive support. If expression of anger is possible, there is a low score for aggression. Anger is most often expressed between children and from children to parents, parent-to-child aggression being minimal. There is slightly more intragenerational than intergenerational interaction. Differences are respected and there is great deal of information-sharing, but there is relatively little expression of strong opinions.

(See also SYMPTOMATIC AND/OR AETIOLOGICAL TRANSACTIONS.)

J.M.

interactions, family interactions An interaction is a dynamic sequence of exchanges of several messages between at least two persons. Interactions have a specific character that is irreducible to the personality structure of the actors.

The concept of interaction appears both in a psychodynamic perspective and in systems theory. A family interaction describes the way in which the members of a family are connected, how they communicate with one another and each play their roles. This interaction is the central object of attention of family therapists, to the extent that they find they are themselves caught up in the peculiar interactive games of the family.

Depending upon the type of family and the style and training of the therapist, stress will be placed more on what is shown or on what is said. In the former case, within a psychodynamic framework (Box et al., 1981), the approach will be centred more on imaginative, phantasy or oneiric activities. The accent will then be put on the inter-phantasmatic, inter-oneiric or inter-transferential aspects of interactions. In the latter case, the approach will perhaps seem more communicational, behavioural and ethological. In that case, the talk will be of complementary, symmetrical, reciprocal, parallel, divergent or convergent interactions, within the framework of the study of SCHISMOGENESIS.

In practice, this distinction will perhaps appear somewhat forced, or will not correspond to the real strategic choices that have to be made. In certain situations where the family is very greatly disorganized, one finds incoherence of phantasmatic organization, an absence of 'labelled metaphors' (Bateson, 1972, pp. 101–25). It is necessary in such cases to establish or re-establish boundaries, to lay down rules and not to allow oneself to be totally invaded by the potency of the diffusion of family pregnances. In other situations, it is preferable to activate interpersonal, phantasmatic and oneiric resonances in communication, so long as these are sufficiently well constituted, to arrive at a better integration of the psychical levels of symbolization.

(See also COMMUNICATION SYSTEMS; FAMILY ROLE; FAMILY RULES; FAMILY SELF-REFERENTIALITY;

METACOMMUNICATION SYSTEMS; PARACOMMUNICATION SYSTEMS; PRAGMATICS OF COMMUNICATION; PUNCTUATION SEQUENCES OF EVENTS; SOCIAL STATUS; SYMBOLS; SYMPTOMATIC AND/OR AETIOLOGICAL TRANSACTIONS.)

P.S.

interlocking triangles The term used by Bowen (1978a) to describe the way in which the members of a family form themselves into a series of triangles which interlock. The therapist must take into account all these triangles and the ways in which they interlock and try to differentiate them or, to use Bowen's own expression, to 'de-triangulate' the family through the therapeutic process.

(See also COALITION; DE-TRIANGULATION; FAMILY—THERAPEUTIC INSTITUTION DIFFERENTIATION; PERVERSE TRIANGLES; TRIANGLES.)

P.S.

interpretation In psychoanalysis, interpretation is the procedure whereby a latent meaning is brought out of the manifest discourse of the patient and those close to him. It takes place, necessarily, within a prescriptive setting, of which the following elements are part: the rule of ABSTINENCE; FREE ASSOCIATION, analysis of the TRANSFERENCE.

It thus becomes a psychoanalytic technique when it arises in a communication which has meaning-value, resulting from the activation of the psychoanalytic process. Interpretation is only operative when it is accompanied by the lived experience of an analysis, by a particular experience of resistance and a particular experience of transference.

In psychoanalytic family therapy the act of listening calls up a circulation of phantasies at the preconscious and unconscious levels of the psychical activity of the family members. Interpretation is thus only operative if the differentiation of the primary and secondary processes of thinking is sufficiently well established. Or, in other words, if the primary processes have not totally invaded the secondary processes.

For his part, Eiguer (1983) distinguishes between various types of interpretation:

1 *Associative interpretation*, completely distinct from conjoint institutional treatment. The therapists in this case give no information regarding the interventions of the other medical personnel. They maintain a discreet listening attitude and do not leave the room. Their chief aim is to connect together the possibly contradictory affects of the patient and those close to him or her.

2 *Centripetal interpretation*: The blandest, most anecdotal remarks and accounts of present events are re-centred on current transferential phenomena.

3 *Re-balancing*, seeking to avoid excessively individualized interpretations.

4 *'Concertina' interpretation* (differentiation–synthesis–deeper exploration of the interphantasmatic field):
   (a) concerning, first, the differentiated aspects of each member of the group (narratives, affects, phantasies), and what each person conveys that is peculiar to him/her;
   (b) then focusing upon the particularities each person conveys about the common organization;
   (c) leading finally to the elucidation of inter-phantasmatic scenarios (of seduction, intrusion etc.).

5 *Interpretation of transference phenomena*, in which the therapist makes explicit the nature of the positions or attitudes of the various family members towards him or herself.

The problem of the status of interpretation arises when interpretative mechanisms of the psychotic, perverse or delinquent type are prevalent in a situation. In such cases, the tendency to interpret is already caught up, within the family interactions, in 'runaway' phenomena. One here finds damage to the very structuring of the modalities of communication, which obliges the various practitioners involved to achieve a structuring of the exchanges between them and to restore these exchanges to the family members. Moreover, as Watzlawick et al. (1974) observe, mutational change usually precedes awareness through insight, rather than the other way about. The concept of interpretation may usefully be compared with that of SYSTEMIC HYPOTHESIS.

(See also METAPSYCHOLOGY; MISUNDERSTANDINGS; NARCISSISM; PARADOXICALITY; PSYCHOANALYSIS.)

J.M.

intimacy Intimacy is bound up with the conjunction of two ethological forces, i.e. two flows relating to animal and human modes of intra-specific and extra-specific relations:

1 Defence of territory, which prompts an individual to drive any conspecific out of the territory it has appropriated.

2 Sexual attraction which, by contrast, causes an individual to approach another, and to come as close as possible.

The strangeness of this articulation derives from its consequences, which unfold in space and cannot simply be registered on a plane surface: to represent it, we need to have recourse to a three-dimensional geometry (see diagram 1).

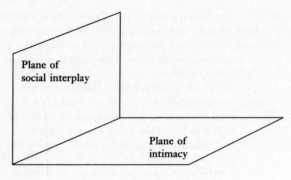

Diagram 1

A second peculiarity is that the form which the meeting of these two interests determines is called a 'saddle', a term borrowed from French terminology relating to the art of pottery, which is, *par excellence*, an art of morphogenesis. I have a little slab of soft clay; if I press evenly on the centre and the outer edges, my slab will flatten and its surface area will increase, but it will remain quite flat. If, rather, I only press in the centre without increasing the circumference, the edges will gradually rise to form a bowl. Hence the reference, above, to the potter's art. If now I press around the outer edges, i.e. if I increase the circumference in relation to the surface, I get that form of saddle, which will cause me astonishment. I am in fact going to imagine that the surface on which my various interests meet, the territorial and the sexual (those which guarantee my social integration), is going to be subject to an analogous treatment. One side in particular, that of meetings, is going to be multiplied systematically. If I initially had a flat rectangular surface, gradually, the

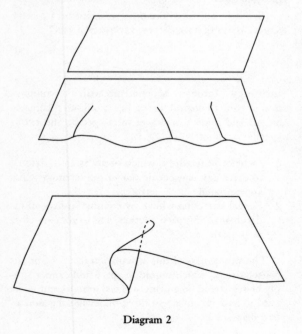

Diagram 2

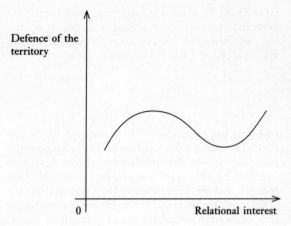

Diagram 3

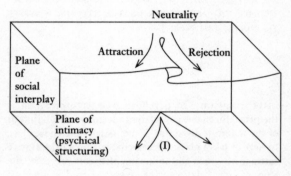

Diagram 4

shapes will become more complicated, will become furrowed and will suddenly fold (see diagram 2). From the point when this fold appears, it is no longer possible to speak of the phenomenon on a single plane: what I must describe is three-dimensional, situated in space. The representation which offers itself to my thinking is no longer a simple curve drawn between two axes (diagram 3), but a three-dimensional representation (diagram 4). Quite clearly, if this phenomenon were reduced to the strict plane of intimacy, it would become absolutely incomprehensible: we should then see a zone of indecision (I) where either aggressive behaviours or seduction manoeuvres would suddenly manifest themselves. This type of pathogenic situation is well known. It is, for example, the ordeal to which every institution that is organized around human relations rather than technical skills subjects its members: it is the effect of an abuse of power on the part of those exercising guardianship.

(See also AGONISTIC BEHAVIOUR; BOUNDARIES; DISTANCE AND ORGANIZATION OF TERRITORY; ELEMENTARY CATASTROPHES; FAMILY CATASTROPHES; HOME; INSTITUTIONS; LOVE; MAP; POWER; SEXED BEHAVIOUR; SPACE–TIME; TERRITORY.)

D.C.

invisible loyalties See LOYALTY, SPLIT LOYALTIES INVISIBLE LOYALTIES.

isomorphism Denotes structural identity: two sets (algebraic, topological etc.) are said to be isomorphic if there is a one-to-one correspondence in which the relations characterizing the structure remain invariant. Thus we speak of an isomorphism of a set S, with law of internal composition T, towards a set S', with a law of internal composition T', where there is a one–to–one element-by-element correspondence f from E to E' in which the laws of internal composition T and T' also correspond.

To express this more rigorously let x be an element of the set S and $f(x)$ *the* element of E' corresponding to x;

let y be another element of the set S, and let $f(y)$ be the element of E' corresponding to y;

let xTy be the element of E which is the result of the composition T of the elements x and y, let $f(xTy)$ be the element of E' corresponding to xTy;

Because of the fact that f is an isomorphism and therefore causes not only the elements but also the internal laws of composition to correspond, it follows that:

$f(xTy) = f(x)T'f(y)$, which is to say that $f(xTy)$, is the element corresponding to the composition xTy internal to E is the same as the element resulting from the composition internal to E of the elements $f(x)$ and $f(y)$.

We may write this formally as $f(xTy) = f(x)T'f(y)$

There is an important qualitative difference between a mere bijection and an isomorphism. With a bijection, the elements of one set correspond to those of another element by element. Additionally, however, with an isomorphism, the isomorphic sets have the same structure. In effect, the properties conferred on the first set by its law of internal composition are found in identical form in the second set. That is to say that we can be sure that the law of internal composition of the second set confers upon it the same structure and properties as the first set. For example, if an internal law confers on set E a group structure (associativity, neutral element, symmetrical element), every set isomorphic with E will also have a group structure.

In the human sciences, bijections are often confused with isomorphisms and it even happens that any form of correspondence is (sometimes wrongly) termed an 'isomorphism'. Hofstadter et al. (1980) attempt to draw a distinction between 'prosaic isomorphisms' and 'exotic isomorphisms'. The prosaic isomorphism is merely a correspondence element-to-element, i.e. a bijection. The 'exotic' isomorphism is a correspondence not element-to-element, but between the relations that exist between the elements and the elements of the target

set. Such a correspondence is not, properly speaking, an isomorphism but a bijection, and a bijection not between the elements of the two sets, but between the elements of two quite different sets, made up of the relations existing within each of the initial sets.

FAMILY ISOMORPHISMS

Two families made up of the same number of persons are isomorphic since the internal law which designates the father, mother and children has properties which are found in both. If we now examine the set formed by the family rules of a particular family, this is obviously a metasystem *vis-à-vis* the family system and it obviously follows that between two such metasystems of family rules, there will only very rarely be an isomorphism, since each family system derives its specificity and coherence from an original and unique system of rules. The atttempts at family typology made by some therapists are aiming to seek out isomorphisms between the sets of transactions characterizing families which include a schizophrenic, a delinquent etc. To establish a classification or a typology of families which divides them into 'families in schizophrenogenic transaction' or 'families in delinquent transaction' is to attempt to show an isomorphism not between two or more families containing a sick member, but between two or more sets of relations and interactions which seem to have the same structure. It was the discovery of isomorphisms existing between different sets of relations necessary to life that enabled von Bertalanffy to propose a GENERAL SYSTEMS THEORY.

FAMILY SYSTEM AND FAMILY UNCONSCIOUS

There is a regular debate between, on the one side, the advocates of the systemic family approach and, on the other, those who espouse the psychoanalytic approach concerning the concepts of collective unconscious and FAMILY UNCONSCIOUS, and, more generally, the pertinence of extending the concepts of the unconscious to human groups. In effect, the concepts which make it possible to explore the object of psychoanalysis – i.e. the human subject – cannot be appropriate for exploring a set of subjects such as the family, whose relations transcend the mere juxtaposition of its members. As a concept, the family unconscious cannot belong to psychoanalysis since psychoanalytic concepts are of a logical level that characterizes the human subject, an element in a system, whereas the concepts of collective or family unconscious are of a logical level characterizing a global entity, a system. Up to what point can what relates to the member of a class be placed in the same set of concepts as the class itself?

Moreover, psychoanalytic family therapists utilize the concepts of group psyche and collective and family unconscious as a matter of course in their theory of clinical practice. They base these concepts on the experience acquired with small groups and the phenomena that arise in them. This enables them to suppose an isomorphism between the individual unconscious and an entity which transcends the unconscious of each of the group members, which is referred to as the collective unconscious.

ISOMORPHISM BETWEEN PSYCHICAL APPARATUS AND FAMILY

Does an isomorphism exist between the structure of the psychical apparatus and that of the family? If so, is this an isomorphism between the various elements that make up the unconscious (the repressed elements) or does that isomorphism relate to the relations that pertain between these elements (ego, id, superego etc.)? If this 'isomorphism' exists, is it truly an isomorphism or rather a mere correspondence, i.e. a relationship in which the structure is not preserved?

We may attempt to come at these questions by way of an analogy from the field of mathematics. Real numbers, i.e. rational numbers (those which can be represented in the form of fractions), and the irrational numbers form an infinite continuum which is most often represented by the infinity of points making up a straight line. It has been demonstrated, quite remarkably, that a hierarchy of infinities exists. In effect, the set of whole numbers is also infinite, but the infinite number of elements of that set is not the same as the number of elements making up the set of real numbers.

When one looks at the sub-set of the set of real numbers constituted by all the real numbers between 0 and 1, we find that they are infinite in number. One might think that, since this is a sub-set, the infinite number of elements of the sub-set is smaller than the infinite number of the elements in the whole set of real numbers. However, this is not the case at all, since it

has been demonstrated that it is the same infinity in each case, so that, in reality, there are exactly as many numbers included between 0 and 1 as in the complete set of all the real numbers! To prove this result, Cantor (1932) demonstrated the existence of an isomorphism between the sub-set of the real numbers between 0 and 1 and the set of all real numbers.

From this result we may draw the following conclusion: there may be parts of a whole which possess the same number of elements as the whole and the same structure. The analogy I wished to stress is the following: it is possible that certain parts of the collective unconscious may be isomorphic with the individual unconscious and that, in particular, each subject bears within him or herself, in his/her unconscious, collective representations belonging to a heritage which founds our culture. The collective unconscious is here approached in its Jungian sense: 'a universal psychical foundation of a suprapersonal nature which is present in everyone' (Jung, 'The archetypes and the collective unconscious').

It is also highly probable that within each member of a family there are representations not only of the relations which bind them to the other family members, but also of the relations between the other members, of past or ancestral relations, myths and family secrets dating back several generations and a whole array of elements belonging to no individual as their own, but to the family collectively. The same argument may be applied to any human institution with a history and internal coherence.

(See also FAMILY PSYCHICAL APPARATUS; FAMILY SYSTEMS; FAMILY UNCONSCIOUS; FRACTALS; INCOMPLETENESS THEOREMS; METAPSYCHOLOGY; RELATIONAL ARCHETYPES; SELF-REFERENTIAL CALCULUS; THEORY OF LOGICAL TYPES; UNCONSCIOUS, THE.)

M.G.

J

jealousy Jealousy always involves two or more persons, may be covert, and where it involves three people may result in a denied coalition (Minuchin, 1974) or in perverse triangles (Haley, 1967) or it may equally well be overt. In all instances, there is a competitive component between one or more persons for a third party's attention or affection. Jealousy may be expressed by open behaviour or by withdrawal of interest (Box et al., 1981, pp. 91–2) as in when different family members compete for the attention of the therapist. In psychodynamic terms we may view jealous behaviour as acting out of primitive phantasies where the individual strives to possess that which is forbidden. In systemic terms jealous behaviour can be viewed as part of the attempt to re-define relationships, to regain ascendancy in a disadvantaged situation, or to deal with dilemmas over intimacy perhaps in a situation where the desired relationship can never be fulfilled and so actual disappointment need never be faced. Jealous behaviour may be an attempted solution (Watzlawick et al., 1974), to reassure the individual that he or she is the most favoured one.

Following Haley (1976), a symptom may be viewed as both a communication about the need for change in a relationship and an indication of the danger of change. In relationships characterised by high levels of fusion and poor differentiation (Bowen, 1978) jealous behaviour is more likely to be displayed where family members have difficulty in expressing their needs directly.

See also COMMUNICATION; DIFFERENTIATION; FUSION; SYMPTOMS.

H.J.

joining Joining is described by Minuchin (Minuchin, 1974) as key in accessing the family's structure: 'The therapist's data and his diagnoses are achieved experientially in the process of joining the family' (Minuchin, 1974, p. 89). The structural family therapy model pays particular attention to the activities of the therapist as actor and agent for change. 'In order to join the family, [the therapist] emphasizes the aspects of his personality and experience that are syntonic with the family's. But he also retains the freedom to be spontaneous in his experimental probes.' (p. 91).

Whereas joining receives particular importance in the description of Structural Family Therapy, it is a process which if not addressed in all approaches to therapy within the different theoretical frameworks, will result in therapeutic impasse, and at worst, in failure. Thus, near the other end of the therapeutic continuum, in Milan Systemic therapy, the therapist maintains a position of neutrality and avoids allying with any individual or aspect of change. The therapist must still through circular questioning and addressing the beliefs which organise family relationships and behaviours, 'join' with each person present, except that the process is implicit or covert unlike structural therapy.

Joining is not a once for all activity. It is part of the process from beginning to end of therapy, although it may be more overt at the start. It is part of the ongoing feedback between therapist and family.

See also CIRCULAR QUESTIONING; MILAN SYSTEMIC THERAPY; STRUCTURAL FAMILY THERAPY; FEEDBACK; NEUTRALITY.

H.J.

K

kinship Kinship relates directly to our understanding of 'family'. Kinship is defined as 'the sharing of characteristics or origins' (OED, 1990). Stone (1979) defines family as 'those members of the same kin who live together under one roof' (p. 28). It was also especially important for the aristocracy in England, since it allowed members to make special claims in terms of loyalty, obedience or support. Kinship provides a wider definition of blood ties and relationships by marriage than those who may live together at any particular time.

One of the most influential surveys in the UK since the Second World War was that undertaken by Young and Wilmot: Family and Kinship in East London, (Young and Wilmot, 1962). Here the researchers, both sociologists, studied families, 'the oldest of our institutions' (p. 11) and the effects of building new housing estates on family life. Elizabeth Bott (Bott, 1968) in her study also looked specifically at kinship networks. Of working class families she writes that: 'The elementary family does not stand alone; its members keep up frequent and intimate relationships with parents and with at least some of the siblings, uncles and aunts, and cousins of the husband and wife. But, at the same time, it is quite clear that kinship does not provide the basic framework of the total social structure as it does in so many small-scale primitive societies, even those with a bilateral kinship system of the same basic type as that found in Western Europe.' (p. 116). This contrasts strongly with the complex kinship systems described by Bateson in Naven (Bateson, 1958). Current preoccupations of social scientists, politicians, and family therapists, among others, are to what extent we in the western world are seeing the breaking down of traditional kinship networks, due in part to rapid industrialisation, social mobility and new work practices. In addition, the nature of the family with many new forms evolving, would seem to further bring into question previous structural arrangements. Included in these changes are homosexual and lesbian 'marriages', single parenting by choice, open communal arrangements, and a high and increasing divorce rate where in the UK and USA the rate for divorce approaches one in two marriages, and where marriage as an institution is not seen as necessary for a planned stable relationship. All these changes mean that traditional expectations of kinship are being tested to the limit, and new ones experimented with, without a tradition on which to rely in times of instability. It might seem that the work of social constructionists (McNamee and Gergen, 1992) would be more in tune with current changes in family and social organisation than more clearly defined therapeutic approaches which rely on explicit models of normal family functioning (Minuchin, 1974).

See also STRUCTURAL FAMILY THERAPY.

H.J.

knowledge One of the concerns of therapists is to understand the world as experienced by their client. Bateson (1972) addresses this problem both directly and indirectly in much of his work. It is fundamental to how humans make sense of the world around them: 'Philosophers have recognised and separated two sorts of problem. There are first the problems of how things are, what is a person, and what sort of world this is. These are the problems of ontology. Second, there are the problems of how we know anything, or more specifically, how we know what sort of world it is and what sort of creatures we are that can know something (or perhaps nothing) of this matter. These are the problems of epistemology.' (Bateson, 1972, pp. 313–14). The problems of epistemology were the greater for Bateson, and those to which he devoted more of his time. In his essay, 'Pathologies of Epistemology', (Bateson, 1972, pp. 478–87) he examines further the problem of how we know and the implications of epistemological error, since 'in spite of very deep error, [t]he erroneous premises, in fact, work.' (p. 479).

The question of knowledge, and how we know, has been especially important in approaches to therapy which address the belief systems of family members, as in Milan Systemic therapy, (Selvini et al., 1978; Campbell and Draper, 1985). Questioning approaches based on feedback, and which rely on introducing new information for their effect, access the client's belief systems, their epistemology, how they know their world, and how introducing difference may begin the process of change, (Tomm, 1987a, b, 1988).

Influential in some current thinking in the family therapy field is the work of the French philosopher Michel Foucault. In particular, the relationship between knowledge and power and the role of the therapist is considered. (Hoffman, 1992; Madigan, 1992; Luepnitz, 1992).

See also CIRCULAR QUESTIONS; FEEDBACK; INFORMATION; MILAN SYSTEMIC THERAPY.

H.J.

L

lack of complementarity So-called symmetrical escalations may arise, in a couple, from an inability to regulate interactions through complementary relations (see SCHISMOGENESIS). These 'patterns of family role complementarity' (Ackerman, 1958, 1966) refer to the relations between roles that are apportioned out or shared within the family.

According to Foley (1974), there are five causes of lack of complementarity in marriage. These are:

1 *Cognitive divergence*: a member of the family does not know what is demanded of him or her.
2 *Divergence of aim*: a member of the family has objectives which conflict with those of the other partner.
3 *Difference of position*: one partner is a victim of the other by virtue either of his/her age or sex.
4 *Instrumental difference*: a partner possesses something (money, prestige or a quality) which confers upon him or her a power which the other can in no way possess.
5 *Difference at the level of values*: the values of one partner conflict with the values of the other.

(See also COUPLES; MARITAL BREAKDOWN.)

P.S.

law A system of rules which apply in a mandatory fashion to everyone; the regulative function to which living and non-living beings are subject.

On the social plane, it is the putting into words and symbols of institutional regulations. The social law regulates the behaviour of those who find themselves subject to it. It decrees the statuses and normative roles and the rights and duties of each person. Everyone is bound to comply with it and it is the expression of the general will (with all the paradoxical consequences that go with totality).

This system may be imposed by practice, custom or tradition without laws actually being promulgated or passed by a centralized legislative power; in such cases, we speak of natural law. It may also be formulated and promulgated in terms that are recognized as authentic and unquestionable by a society's supreme authority.

On the family level, the law defines the level of parental authority, the lineage and clan systems (the transmission of the name, of property, spiritual values and identity), the responsibility of the marriage partners, succession strategies, how children are to be raised, licit and illicit moral practices and what marriages are permitted, forbidden or recommended as preferable in a society (Goody, 1983).

The set of laws is constituted as a corpus at a different hierarchical level from that of rites or family rules. We may thus distinguish between a tendency (habits and preferences), a rule (implicit or explicit structuring of interpersonal relations) and a law (a natural and/or cultural collective norm which applies to everyone). The body of laws is based on the cardinal values (the ends in themselves: freedom, peace, solidarity) whereas the corpus of rules is made up of the ordinal values (the means: work, family, fatherland, health).

It is in this conflict between the polarities of family rules and social laws that the dialectic between law and transgression plays itself out. Symptoms are an expression of the impasses of this dialectic (the gap between visible and invisible loyalties, between legality and legitimacy etc.).

Etymologically, 'autonomy' (*auto-nomos*) is the law possessing the power of recurrence, the law which maintains itself.

LAW AS NATURAL AND CULTURAL FUNCTION

The fact that laws are expressed at various different levels leads either to the discovery of absolute rules or to the prescription of edicts that are more or less relative to a given society.

In the former case, we may cite the *laws of nature*; the law becomes an object of science when the relation between two or more variables is stated in a mathematical function: gravitation submits all living bodies to the law $F = mg$ (whereas intuition might have expected $F = mv$). The flight of a bird takes implicit account of this, whereas the design of an aeroplane takes it into account explicitly.

There are also *social laws*, which are the contradictory products of the regularities imposed by nature and of prescriptions that evolve with civilization (see INSTITUTIONS); the biological and cultural foundations of laws are many and varied (the law of the prohibition of incest or the laws instituting physical and psychical territories, for example); here again, we find implicit and explicit levels of regulation. In *The spirit of laws*, Montesquieu (1748) writes:

Laws, taken in the broadest meaning, are the necessary relations deriving from the nature of things. In this sense, all beings have their laws: the divinity has

LAW

its laws, the material world has its laws, the intelligences superior to man have their laws, the beasts have their laws, man has his laws. (*The spirit of laws*, 1989 edn, p. 1)

As a rationalist, Montesquieu believed in the existence of a primal Reason and that the laws describe the relationship of human beings with that Reason, as well as the relations between human beings themselves.

'Objectivist' ethology (Lorenz, Tinbergen) tends to argue that there are natural laws which govern the formation of the couple and the family. Wickler (1971) goes so far as to describe the factors which constitute the 'natural laws of marriage':

- behaviours which ensure the couple's cohesiveness;
- social feeding, kissing;
- the feminine chest as container of the relation (the psychoanalytic 'breast');
- the silhouette of the child;
- the mother–child relationship: the human child is neither nidicolous nor nidifugous; the child is secondarily nidifugous or, more exactly, matricolous;
- the pseudo-sexualization of society (sexual simulation of social relations; see SEXED BEHAVIOUR);
- the matrimonial bond, a complex component of behaviours derived from the mother–child relation and from sexed and sexual behaviours;
- sexual behaviour is linked to social behaviour and to hierarchy. Modifications of behaviour bring about transformations of the morphological structure and vice versa.

Such a model is obviously not sufficient to cover the whole range of problems raised by the laws laid down by men. Machiavelli wrote several centuries ago:

All writers on politics have pointed out, and throughout history there are plenty of examples which indicate, that in constituting and legislating for a commonwealth it must needs be taken for granted that all men are wicked and that they will always give vent to the malignity that is in their minds when opportunity offers. That evil dispositions often do not show themselves for a time is due to a hidden cause which those fail to perceive who have had no experience of the opposite; but in time – which is said to be the father of all truth – it reveals itself. (*The discourses*, pp. 111–12)

For Machiavelli, the law restrains men in circumstances which otherwise would make them bad. The law is thus, theoretically, a moral violence imposed upon all which prevents an even greater violence, the physical violence which everyone is in danger of using against others. It thus enables us to manage a relationship of forces. If we acknowledge that violence is at the centre of family and social interactions (see VIOLENCE), the law and its failings (whether by its excesses or its shortcomings) and the transgressions which ensue, will be at the heart of the questions posed by the relations between families and societies. So far, then, as specific laws are concerned, those which govern the relations between people in society, they appear linked to two states of war inherent in the nature of social man. The state of war consists in seeking to impose one's law on others by force, either as one nation on another, or as an individual on a social group. We might add that the state of war is already present and already regulated within the family group.

LAW, JUSTICE, EDUCATION AND MENTAL ILLNESS

Montesquieu (1748) later defines the laws of education:

The laws of education are the first we receive. And as these prepare us to be citizens, each particular family should be governed according to the plan of the great family that includes them all.
If there is a principle for the people taken generally, then the parts which compose it, that is, the families, will have one also. Therefore, the laws of education will be different in each kind of government. In monarchies, their object will be *honour*; in republics, *virtue*; in despotisms, *fear*. (1989 edn, p. 31)

There is a contradiction between the law defined as a general system and the socio–educative law, a particular system of inscription in the social body. Penal law, the law of inheritance and the laws of divorce are written laws. In France, by contrast, the right of '*assistance éducative*' is not a written right (Amiel et al., 1985). In educative matters, there are few general laws of conduct, few specific laws and these refer back to custom and practice. The right of '*assistance éducative*' is mediated through direct contact between the court and the family. The law which provides a basis for the educative relation is a specific law. It is, then, for the court to evaluate the link between unacceptable behaviour and customary norms. The judge establishes the shift from customary social norm to legal social obligation (Amiel et al. 1985). Such a judgment should, however, be subtle, if we compare the development of French law by comparison with the Anglo-Saxon system.

Roman law, from which French law derives, is inquisitorial and contradictory, with a prior investigation of the evidence; it is the Public Prosecutor's Department (the judge) which has to prove guilt. Anglo-Saxon law is adversarial law; based on precedence: each side presents its evidence at the time of the trial. In current French penal law, the accent is increasingly being placed on the oral or properly speaking the 'accusatory' character, based on the 'principle of contradiction'; on the over hand, divorce by mutual consent also reduces the starkness of the opposition between the two systems outlined above.

Judges are themselves subject to the law, as indeed are psychiatrists and mental health professionals. To give two examples. First, in France the law of 1838 concerning the insane (*les aliénés*) governs the confinement in specialist establishments of persons who are a danger to themselves or to others. Voluntary committal is based on the paradox of a 'voluntary' request by at least one close relative of the patient, when the patient refuses treatment. Compulsory committal occurs by direct decision of a representative of the social authorities (prefect, mayor etc.).

Secondly, article 64 (the code of 1910) is based on the request made by society upon a psychiatrist to pronounce on the existence (or otherwise) of criminal responsibility in 'distorted persons': 'There is neither crime nor misdemeanour when the accused was in a state of madness at the moment of the action or was under the power of a force which he could not resist.' It will be noted that this particular point takes no account of historical, personal and family factors and that it is based on a reading at one single moment of what is, in fact, a complex situation.

However this may be, judges and psychiatrists are forced into certain actions towards individuals and the families to which they belong. In this, the law operates as the expression of an imperative demand upon them on the part of the social body. It is, effectively, the converse of the psychoanalytic 'request', where the individual makes the request for treatment. In the most extreme cases, the 'demand' here seems to come from the professionals of the psychiatric world (see DEMAND).

LAW AND DESIRE

From a psychoanalytic point of view, the father, the bearer of the law, sees his authority generated in the act of separation and de-fusion of the mother–child dyad. There is a displacement of the incest taboo (oral law) on to the societal-collective: written documents, rules, laws etc. (Amiel et al., 1985). The law is thus the very precondition of desire.

'It is well-known that the only universal social law is that of exogamy which defines, in a way that varies between cultures, the prohibition of incest, and that the horror attached to the transgression of that law is comparable to the degree of destructive hatred that founds it' (Noel and Soulé, 1985, p. 28). Thus, in psychoanalytic theory, it is the paternal function to separate the child from the mother, a separation which functions as a law for the father, the mother and the child. That category of law is to be distinguished from the laws of society, while it does, however, serve as a prototype of the prohibitions which structure the personality.

For Lacan (1966, p. 277), 'The primordial Law is therefore that which in regulating marriage ties superimposes the kingdom of culture on that of a nature abandoned to the laws of mating. The prohibition of incest is merely its subjective pivot . . . This law, then, is revealed clearly enough as identical with an order of language.' But, conversely, is it not the 'law plain and simple' that forbids incestuous unions? Though the French penal law no longer represses 'endogamy', civil law still forbids marriage in certain cases (Laraby, 1983). The contemporary identification of incestuous families (see INCEST) shows that the articulation between social laws and psychical laws is far from simple, even when mediated by language effects.

Where perverse structuring is met with, we find a refusal of natural and cultural laws. For the fetishist, there is a denial of the difference of the sexes (natural law of the anatomical difference between the sexes), a transgression of the laws as laid down and a challenge to established social forms. The perverse subject acts out his law against all comers. The mother of the perverse subject is often described as phallic-castrating, not having succeeded in symbolically integrating the paternal phallus.

LAW AS DOUBLE BIND

No one has explored the DOUBLE BIND on which the organization of justice and the law is based more thoroughly than Kafka in his short story 'Before the Law'. This is also taken up again, this time in the form of a parable, by the priest who addresses Joseph K. in the cathedral shortly before his execution in *The trial*.

In the penultimate chapter of *The trial*, Joseph K. tells the priest in the cathedral that he trusts him and that he believes he can speak openly with him. The priest replies that he is deluded about the Court and this particular delusion is described in the writings which preface the Law.

A door-keeper stands on guard before the door leading into the Law. One day, a man asks permission to enter. After saying no, the door-keeper replies that it is possible, but not at the moment. He even adds that the man can try and get in without his permission, since he seems to wish to do so so intently. He warns him, however, that he, the door-keeper is powerful and that he is only the lowest of the guards. In every hall there stand guards more powerful than the last, so that he cannot even bear to look at the third of these. The man persists with his claim, seeks to bribe the door-keeper with gifts, which he takes, not out of venality, but so as to keep the man from feeling he has left something undone. The man grows old and his sight gradually darkens, yet he stays by the door, wearying the guard with his questions. On the verge of death, he tells of his astonishment that no one else has come to request entry. Then the door-keeper bellows in his ear: 'No one but you could gain admittance through this door, since this door was intended only for you. I am now going to shut it' (*The trial*, 1953, p. 237).

Though the man in the parable dies a natural death, Joseph K. is condemned and stabbed to death, guilty of being not guilty, not guilty of being guilty. In fact, *The trial* begins as follows: 'Someone must have been telling lies about Joseph K., for without having done anything wrong he was arrested one fine morning' (p. 7). But if Joseph K. knows he is not guilty or if it is said that he is not guilty, he does not even know the law of those who arrest and condemn him. He is in principle not guilty before a law whose guiding principle he does not understand.

The double bind structure is clearly apparent here: a life-or-death risk connects Joseph K. and the men who belong to the Court and he receives antinomic messages, all equally threatening, to which he has no option but to respond. The priest is the prison chaplain: ' "That means I belong to the Court," said the priest. "So why should I make any claims upon you? The Court makes no claims upon you. It receives you when you come and it relinquishes you when you go" ' (p. 244). And yet the door-keeper's message seems to be the opposite of this. He threatens the man if he transgresses the order not to enter *now*. Unlike the guard, who is forced to remain at his post, the man in the parable is free to go where he wants. He can stay by the door all his life: all that is forbidden is the Law that is personally destined for him. But how can he free himself from a Law he does not know? Thus, for Joseph K., it is impossible either to enter or not to enter. Either he transgresses against the door-keeper's threats, risking his life in the process, in order to gain admittance to the Law, or else he risks his life by falling under the jurisdiction of the law which relates to him as a particular individual, but of which he knows nothing.

The adage 'ignorance of the law is no defence' is well known, but no one can have access to the law individually, without social mediation. Kafka's law is an abstract law, with no precisely defined rules. It is totally detached from the family structures which might give it body and from their homeostatic and homeorhetic regulation. These structures no longer fulfil their function of protection and DEIXIS (signalling of the real stakes and dangers); they seem, in fact, to have exploded. The halls and doors guarded by the 'door-keepers' seem neither to contain nor to have content. We do not know what Law is being spoken of, nor what it relates to. From where do the priest – and, *a fortiori*, the door-keeper – derive their authority? Upon what is their power exerted? What does one risk by entering the Law and what does one risk by simply going on one's way? What are the initial stakes in this process of intimidation? Is the number of rooms finite or infinite? The 'power of the law' operates in the form of a blind and absurd violence, by way of a symbolic process of self-engendering referring only to itself. Hence the imaginary boundless terror of the father–son relationship, dispossessed of its protective functions

as a result of a failed or impossible transgenerational transmission.

RULES AND LAWS

The law is different from a rule (see FAMILY RULES) in the same way as a set is different from the elements that go to make it up. At the same time, however, a limit-element ensures identity between the rule and the law. Rules are, to some extent, regulative processes which give substance to the law. By that token, therefore, there are possibilities of confusions of logical level between rules and laws. Hence the transgressive tensions between families and societies (see, for example, DELINQUENT ACTING OUT; DRUG ADDICTION; INCEST).

A *rule* may be implicit or explicit, verbalized or non-verbalized, but it is possible for it to be verbalized and it is, precisely, recognized as 'regulating' the relationship between two or more persons; it is the systemic equivalent of the Freudian '*superego*' or the Lacanian '*symbolic*'. As a concept occupying an intermediate position between the biological origins of the superego and the Lacanian transcendental law, it places the emphasis upon the degrees of freedom of the conjugal and familial space in the face of individual desires and social demands. The concept of rule seeks to define a meta-level specifying the singularity of an exchange, not a general and abstract psychical property (a once-and-for-all 'role'). The rule is immanent, restricted and is produced by ritualization, the interplay of communication and the family myth (Baudrillard, *On seduction*; see also the application of these ideas in Baltat and Smagghe Floc'h, 1980).

The *law* has a transcendental, universal status, when it is laid down or promulgated. Its transcendence is, however, a relative, metasocial rather than a metaphysical transcendence. Whereas a rule breaks down, a law is transgressed. The law imposes its order upon family systems, whereas the set of family rules exerts pressure on collective beliefs and ideologies to transform laws. We can see this from the way the laws governing family relations have developed. In Ancient Rome, the *paterfamilias* had the power of life or death over the members of his family. During the Middle Ages, the father had the right to beat his wife and children. Today the status of head of household does not devolve solely upon the father.

Though rules are developed, the law, as the general set of rules, is created. The hypothesis we are proposing here is that law specified in this way is the sum of multiple levels of regulation. We find it on the various planes of biological regulation of the reproduction of living species; stating it symbolically, in human language, is not necessarily sufficient to prevent its being transgressed. Action on family communication enables us to re-establish, to a certain extent, the symbolic foundations of human language.

(See also CARDINAL VALUES; GENDER; LEGAL CONTEXT; LOYALTY; PERFORMATIVES.)

J.M.

law of requisite variety The notion of variety, which is closely connected with that of COMPLEXITY, is at the origin both of the stability of a system and of the possibility of its evolving towards levels of increasing complexity. The variety of a system is the number of possible different behaviours which that system is able to exhibit at a given moment.

It is the very great variety of forms of regulation which enables HOMEOSTASIS to be established and maintain itself. The more complex a system, the more the METASYSTEM of forms of regulation must also be complex in order to offer a response to external perturbations. This is what is expressed in the 'law of requisite variety' proposed by Ross Ashby in 1956. The regulation of a system is only effective if it is based on a system of control that is at least as complex as the system itself.

However, when the system can no longer reach a previous state of equilibrium, either because of over-rapid growth or because of a series of random perturbations originating in the environment, it seeks new stationary states by allowing negative and positive feedback loops to come into play. These latter, amplifying the slightest divergence, accentuating differentiation and increasing the possibilities for interaction are real generators of complexity by dint of the extra variety they produce. The new stationary state adds new properties to the system: there is a qualitative leap, a new threshold is crossed and new realities emerge.

Generating variety thus leads to increasingly flexible adaptation, the emergence of new properties and new levels of organization. It is this which materially brings about evolution within a system towards increased complexity.

(See also ATTRACTORS; DYNAMIC SYSTEMS; STATIC FORMS.)

J.M.

learning One of the modalities of information processing which leads to the modification of systems of thought, action and feeling, by trial and error, as a function of data received from the internal and/or external environment. It is based upon various different forms of memory which incorporate data which may in some cases be transmitted from one generation to another. Learning is what enables us to acquire unconscious and preconscious automatisms as a result of experiences gained in familial and social interaction.

It is distinct from: (a) the processing of information without storage of the processed data action; (see HOMEOSTASIS; INSTINCT); and (b) adaptive behaviour modifications acquired individually, without secondary transformation as a response to their success or failure (see BECOMING ACCUSTOMED; HABITUATION; IMPRINTING; etc.), corresponding to Bateson's zero learning.

Learning is a key concept for the understanding of the structural processes which go on within a family; it enables us to explain the effect and limits of therapeutic actions. The family ecosystem is the societal acquisition of vertebrates (phylogenetic acquisition) which creates the basis for inter-individual social relations. The family enables related organisms to give aid to their progeniture, to develop the differentiation of inter-individual recognition, to promote the acquisition and maturation of the rituals of love, friendship and aggression. For the child, it determines what is encouraged, permitted, tolerated or prohibited in a given social environment. The family is thus the context produced by phylogenesis and transformed by the cultural tradition which enables the children to learn about their life and survival contexts. Learning takes place by means of hierarchized and structurally differentiated memories (see READ–WRITE MEMORIES), permitting the existence of transgenerational traditions which are to a large extent unconscious, and structured on the plane of systems of PARACOMMUNICATION and METACOMMUNICATION.

The higher forms of learning have not eliminated the short-term forms of information processing or the irreversible acquisitions of ontogenesis, such as imprinting, 'becoming accustomed', habituation etc. At most, they incorporate these into symbolic systems. Phylogenetic acquisitions (see INSTINCT) are far from being devoid of meaning; certain SEMANTIC UNITS are only intelligible in terms of groups or populations. There is thus both a biological and an ecosystemic approach to genetic disturbances.

The articulation of instinctive acts and acquisitions that are not modifiable by trial and error have a part in the construction of the organizers of the psyche and the family (see FAMILY ORGANIZERS); they lead ultimately to primal repression and are at the root of the phenomena of fixation described by Freud (imprinting, 'becoming accustomed', facilitation by practice, sensitization, habituation, post-traumatic phobia etc.) inaccessible to behaviourist therapies working by deconditioning (see BEHAVIOURISM).

A certain level of ALGORITHMIC and HEURISTIC programming causes the individual's instinctive acquisitions to tip over into a delegation to symbolic systems. This presupposes hereditary coordination procedures which are sufficiently powerful to allow this delegation to take place. The more sophisticated the learning, the more it goes together with capacities for unlearning which are connected with the use of labile memories of various sorts and the recourse to modalities of repetition (psychotic stereotypy might be seen as the waste side-product of this). Culture might therefore be seen less as what is left when you have forgotten everything as what is not left when you have learnt everything.

The basic building blocks of individual learning are: curiosity (which lasts a lifetime in humans), exploration, play, forgetting and repetition. These parameters are at the heart of every therapeutic process.

For Lorenz (1973), the minimal requirements for learning to take place are:

1 *Genetic capacities for open programming.* These capacities must be quantitatively and qualitatively sufficient to permit a non-chaotic open programme, leading to manifold adaptive modifications, thus offering scope for trying out varied and apparently random pathways.
2 *Differentiated memory capacities, enabling behavioural trials to be memorized*; certain memories must allow for the information which is to be transformed to be rapidly deleted, while others permit the information that is to be conserved to be stabilized (see READ–WRITE MEMORIES).
3 *Sufficiently reliable receptor mechanisms and machinery for the comparison of the information gathered and tested.* Lorenz writes that the receptor mechanism 'must achieve a function similar to that of the innate releasing mechanism'.

From this, Lorenz is led to postulate the existence of 'innate teaching mechanisms'. For one or more sub-systems within a learning system to be susceptible of greater or lesser degrees of variation, it is necessary for the other sub-systems to be sufficiently stable and resistant to modification for the whole system to cope with the modifications introduced by learning, without the overall identity of that system being lost. Such sub-systems may either be internal to the individual under consideration or shared with other organisms with which the individual interacts.

For Bateson (1972), apart from the zero level, there are four levels of acquisition and learning.

Zero learning

Such learning permits of no correction once the modification has been made; one might understand this as 'species specific drive action', the product of numerous hierarchized sub-units incorporating appetent and consummatory behaviours. Zero learning is therefore already a system of acquisition articulating instinctive acts, taxes and motor and/or perceptual associative sequences which have been stabilized during ontogenesis: once the acquisitions made possible by imprinting, 'becoming accustomed', sensitization, facilitation of movement by practice and post-traumatic flight have been made, these last a whole lifetime and cannot be modified by techniques using trial-and-error processes. This does not mean, however, that they are not integrated into contexts which will engender, where necessary, considerable modifications concerning their importance, value and significance.

Learning I

This assumes a change in the specificity of the response; it is possible for the organism to revise its choice within the framework of a set of possibilities which, for their part, remain fixed and unchanged. Classic Pavlovian conditioning is based on a mechanism of positive conditioning by reinforcing the trials which result in success; it is therefore elementary, level-one learning and is no doubt much more complex than a mere reflex reaction.

Learning II or Deutero-learning

This corresponds to 'transfer of learning'. The organism involved in this learning ends up acquiring information about the learning itself and is likely to modify that learning as a function of the information acquired. What is involved here, then, is a change which comes about in learning I. This change concerns the set of possibilities from which the choice is made, or it presupposes the carrying over into another context of learning made in a past context. For Bateson, the description of human character (dependent, mad, hostile, passive, playful, canny) is a way of punctuating human interaction in relation to the context of contexts in which habitual interactions take place. This is then a form of learning which the individual learns about his/her successive learning processes. Similarly, TRANSFERENCE phenomena in psychotherapy and double-bind phenomena will appear as 'learning about learning' about systems of relating within the family and society. In both cases, a meta-context will modify the modifications introduced by the initial context. One of the paradoxes is no doubt that the hierarchically superior learning processes cannot modify the stabilized data of zero learning, but can only transform the contexts of their expression.

Learning III

This has to be regarded as a rare phenomenon, a change in a change, which 'does from time to time occur in psychotherapy, religious conversion, and in other sequences in which there is profound reorganization of character' (Bateson, 1972, p. 272). We might cite as examples here the change brought about by transference in psychoanalysis, or those which occur in curing the alcoholic of his/her addiction, rehabilitating the delinquent or opening up a person to a successful sublimation.

Learning IV

This would be a change in Learning III, but it has to be seen as little more than a mental horizon which it is impossible to encounter in any individual on earth.

Perhaps we are here running up against the very constraints inherent in the human mind's learning processes, if not indeed against the limits of a model based solely on the theory of logical types. The fixed, 'self-referential' point of learning phenomena is in fact the following: *unlearning to unlearn*.

Let us note, in conclusion, that we can observe the importance of the relations between learning and family systems from two complementary perspectives: (a) the clinical perspective and the observation of DOUBLE BINDS; and (b) the anthropological perspective, which reveals that the degree of literacy is connected with the age of women at marriage and therefore of their degree of emancipation and their own level of education.

(See also SYMPTOMATIC AND/OR AETIOLOGICAL TRANSACTIONS.)

J.M.

ledger Every family keeps a record in the family 'ledger' of what each of its members may expect to receive and what they owe. The 'family heritage', which is multigenerational in essence, being handed down from one generation to the next, defines a specific configuration of rights and obligations that are incumbent on the individual and which he/she must conform to if he/she is to be loyal to his/her family (Boszormenyi-Nagy and Spark, 1973).

THE FAMILY AND ITS ACCOUNTS

Originally, 'ledger' is a term from book-keeping and accountancy and specifically from double-entry book-keeping. In that system, as soon as an entry exists in one account, a contra-entry is made in another. The daily accounts are kept in subsidiary journals and all the subsidiary journals are brought together in a central journal. The general ledger contains a historical record of all transactions, with all the accounts recorded there in terms of debits and credits. The balance of the general ledger is necessarily equal to the balance of all the journals. From an accounting point of view, the whole is strictly equal to the sum of the parts.

Boszormenyi-Nagy and Spark (1973) propose the ledger metaphor to describe the nature of the exchanges between a child and its parents or, alternatively, between the NUCLEAR and the extended family. Thus the extended family, a significant context for Boszormenyi-Nagy and Spark, functions according to a principle of dynamic FAIRNESS. To conform with this principle, each individual must 'give' as much as he or she 'receives'. The repayment of debts occurs through the accumulation of MERIT. How the individual fulfils his or her obligations, on the one hand, and the state of the balance between debts and merits, on the other, constitute the two components of the family 'ledger'.

LEGACIES AND MERITS

The 'account balance' of the family members is continually changing. When a baby comes into the world, he or she of course owes nothing to anyone. By contrast, he or she is owed everything. As the child grows up, however, his/her natural rights decrease at the same time as what he/she owes increases, since the child will be increasingly capable of giving in his/her turn. There is therefore a relative tendency to inversion of the relation between each individual's rights and obligations throughout his/her life.

Since the concept of 'ledger' is closely related to the notion of multi-laterality of family relations, no member of the family can judge the state of equilibrium of the ledger on his/her own.

UNBALANCED ACCOUNTS

It is in fact inevitable that the accounts will be unbalanced and in every functional family there are oscillations around an equilibrium point, which is determined as a function of the state of multi-lateral relations established by each member of the family. In dysfunctional families, the balance of accounts and merit may lose its flexibility and mobility and take on a fixed, rigid character which encourages the development of psychopathological disorders.

REVOLVING SLATE

In this contextual model, when it has not been possible for accounts to be settled between two family members, there may be an attempt at a 'settlement' by an 'innocent' third party, e.g. a spouse or a child, acting as a substitute for the 'debtor' or 'creditor'. It is argued that it is this phenomenon which gives rise to the transgenerational transmission of symptomatic behaviour. This process is ineffective as a way of re-balancing accounts because it is invalid on the plane of ETHICS, but it is none the less, as Boszormenyi-Nagy and Spark (1973) emphasize, 'the main factor in marital and family dysfunction'.

(See also EXPLOITATION; LAW; LOYALTY; RELATIONAL STAGNATION; TRANSGENERATIONAL MEMORIES.)

A.L.

legal context A number of people involved in the earliest beginnings of family therapy in the USA were non-medical social workers (Satir, 1967; Hoffman, 1981), which is one of the novel aspects of this current of therapy in relation to other forms of psychotherapy. The arrival of the model in Europe did not change this, in spite of the fact that the context for psychotherapy is somewhat different. In France it remains the relatively privileged domain of medical practitioners and their institutions, while in the UK family therapy has gained its greatest number of adherents from workers in child and adolescent psychiatric services and from social work practitioners.

MODELLING THE EDUCATIVE CONTEXT IN FRANCE

There is little need to emphasize the fact that for some 15 years, in France, the systemic approach has enjoyed an increasing degree of success, without any noticeable setbacks among the diverse groups of social workers, psychologists, welfare workers, nurses, and those who work with the handicapped. The development of this approach in part filled a gap caused by the absence of a reference model in this particular area of work and to some extent it dispelled the sense of disappointment produced by failed attempts to apply other models, failures which were in fact more attributable to the difficulties of the working context and insufficient account being taken of it than of the intrinsic invalidity of those models.

A large number of social workers perform their functions under a mandate from the courts dealing with minors or a childcare order from the Social Services Department; these two types of mandate are sometimes combined in a single form of intervention or embroiled in the complex jumble of multiple measures which families with a variety of problems generate. This *de facto* and *de jure* situation has two consequences:

1   The social worker is 'mandated' for a given period to fulfil a certain objective, which means that he/she has an obligation to fulfil the mandate conferred upon him/her by a legal or administrative authority within a given time and is answerable to that authority for the performance of his/her mission.
2   The index patient(s) (whose names figure on the Judge's Order) are bound to conform to the execution of this mandate (even if that obligation is, in some cases, though not in all, more of a symbolic order than backed by any threat of enforcement in reality).

A further difficulty is to be found in the fact that, in spite of a great diversity of individual features in the families within this 'client group', we are none the less dealing here in the majority of cases with families which are suffering but isolated, families emotionally and economically deprived and, most importantly, families which do not openly express a desire for therapeutic aid, at least in any clearly decipherable verbal mode. We may say that this demand exists at least partly in what the family reveals by its symptoms and its suffering, but that the suggestion that psychological or educative aid is required seems more easily decodable in the analogic register of a-social or anti-social, extra- or intrafamilial 'acting out'. In very few cases do social workers deal with people who are motivated and who clearly express a demand for therapy. That demand is most often, when they first take up a case, conveyed by the agencies of social control and thus by the Juvenile Magistrate who plays both the role of referent and 'translator' of the expression of that demand.

FAMILIES WITH MULTIPLE PROBLEMS

Such families are also in receipt of multiple forms of assistance. Because they are families with multiple problems, their referral for a systemic interactive form of therapy could occur in respect of a number of different possible index patients, depending on the particular moment and the specialist nature of the services dealing with their case. Thus the same family might be called upon to take part in family interviews as a result of:

- a child protection consultation, where a young child has been identified as neglected;
- a family placement consultation for the two children preceding the last-born, who have been subject to repeatedly reported violence from the father;
- a detoxification centre, on account of the father's alcoholism;
- a district psychiatric consultation, on account of the mother's depression;
- a specialist consultation on account of an adolescent son's drug addiction;
- an educational orientation consultation on account of a child's absenteeism from school or repeated cases of running away from home or stealing.

Listing the many ways of access to treatment structures in this way emphasizes the importance of an overall view and global intervention, taking the family as a semantic unit of survival, stability and change. In this context, it is always relevant to note that a particular family is in a position where it is dealing with the legal system rather than another institution, that the Juvenile Magistrate has him/herself chosen to intervene in the problem, or one of the family members has appealed to him/her to do so. Contrary to often expressed fears, recent clinical experience would tend to show that the context of mandates and obligations imposed by the legal system within which care is administered in these cases is not incompatible either with the possibility of a gradual emergence of a more elaborate request for aid (and one for which responsibility is assumed by the family) or with the therapeutic effect of systemic interventions in the form of family interviews, without needing to 'announce that one is engaging in family therapy' (Selvini Palazzoli et al., 1980a).

LEGAL DISTINCTION BETWEEN THERAPEUTIC AND EDUCATIVE INTERVENTION

The LAW makes the very pertinent distinction between what is of the order of *'care'* or *therapy*, on the one hand (this latter being outside its scope, except in the case of dangerous alcoholics and drug addicts, for whom the law provides the possibility of a 'treatment order' as an alternative to penal sanction) and *educative intervention*, on the other. It falls to the Juvenile Magistrate to prescribe and monitor this latter. One of the advantages of the judicial framework, by comparison with that of the administration or health service, is that it enables, both by the seriousness it gives to matters and by its guarantee of adversarial debate, a precise specification of the respective roles, functions and powers of those concerned.

Without going in detail through the legal provisions concerning the scope and powers of the legal system as it relates to minors, though there are in fact few statutes applying to this area in France, we shall merely cite in passing the two principal laws:

- the Ordinance of 2 February 1945 (Penal Code) relating to juvenile delinquency;
- the Law of 4 June 1970 (Civil Code) concerning parental authority which, in its articles 375 et seq. defines the conditions under which young people in physical and moral danger are to be protected and the organization of the educative assistance that is to be given to them.

More than the letter of the text, it is the spirit of this legislation (a similar form has been adopted in many European countries) which we must emphasize here. Where juvenile delinquency is concerned, educative measures are to be the rule and recourse to penal sanctions the exception. As regards protection, clearly the measures taken can only be educative ones. In every case, the Juvenile Magistrate 'must always endeavour to gain the family's backing for the measures proposed' (Henry and Pical, 1984).

This brief résumé of the legislation relating to minors will perhaps enable us better to grasp that an intervention based on a family approach from a systemic perspective within the field of rehabilitation is not incompatible with the presence within this context of a Juvenile Magistrate. There are, however, two conditions to this.

1 It would be wrong to turn a blind eye to the legal context and the reference to the law; this must rather be integrated into the work with the family, as a vehicle of meaning and a structuring factor.
2 Work must be centred on the problematic interaction between parents and child, taking as the starting point the patient designated by the judge (who

can only be a juvenile). One must know how to fix precise limits both as regards time and as regards the problems to be tackled in the course of this family intervention. It may be appropriate to recommend therapeutic treatment of the same order or of a different level (individual therapy of one of the parents, for example, but offered only if they ask for it) within a context other than the judicial one.

THE LEGAL CONTEXT IN THE UK

Whereas there are similarities between other countries and France, there are also differences. In the UK the juvenile justice system has moved, albeit slowly, towards a more collaborative approach in working with families. The Children Act 1989 was a landmark piece of legislation which enjoins professionals to work with all family members and others who have a responsibility for the child to ensure that the interests of the child are paramount. The legislation refers to the rights of the child and the responsibilities of parents and other adults. While this should always have been good practice for social workers and others in the mental health field, it was not always clearly supported in legislation. As is often the case in the UK, imaginative legislation is not accompanied by the release of funds to implement it adequately.

Some of the dilemmas for family therapy work in the context of the legal system are highlighted by Crowther and her colleagues (1990), while the wider impact on families of deprivation and multiple agency involvement is described by Jenkins (1990). Looking at the legal system in Britain, Minuchin (1984) describes something of the experience of the disempowered family member in the face of the legal system, and the responsibility on the professional to take this into account when attempting to understand the often seemingly irrational and unpredictable responses of those caught up in judicial processes. Scotland has its own legal system, and for many years there has been the practice of the Children's Panel. This attempts to remove an adversarial approach when dealing with young people in trouble.

The challenge for family therapists is to find ways of incorporating this awareness into practice. In the USA there has been a move away from the practice of family therapy in the public service and into private practice. To some extent a similar move is occurring in the UK as pressures on social service and mental health service systems make them more market-led and less client-responsive. An emphasis on rationing services and on servicing the courts make it more difficult to provide preventative and therapeutic services.

(See also DELINQUENT ACTING OUT; DEMAND; DRUG ADDICTION; ETHICAL ISSUES IN FAMILY THERAPY; EVOLUTIONARY SURVIVAL UNIT; FAMILY THERAPIES; INCEST;

PROCREATIVE FAMILIES; SEMANTIC UNIT OF MIND; SYMP-
TOMATIC AND/OR AETIOLOGICAL TRANSACTIONS; SYSTEMIC
MODELLING AND INTERVENTION; UNIT OF CHANGE;
VIOLENCE.)

P.S. & H.J.

legal status   See SOCIAL STATUS, LEGAL STATUS.

levels of communication   Systems which provide
the basis for the definition of truth, for systems of
belief, for 'having to', 'making' and 'being able to' do
or be are organized according to various levels or
modalities of communication.

   Various different types of modal structures, organizing semantic categories, can be distinguished: certain
predicates such as 'have to', 'be able to', 'believe' organize modal utterances concerning states ('being') or
actions ('doing'). As a result, various modalities appear: from 'to have to' come the *alethic modality* (from
the Greek for truth or reality), 'to have to be' (necessity), and the *deontic modality*, 'to have to do' (prescription); and there are also the *epistemic modality*,
'to believe to be', and the *veridictory modality*, 'to know
to be'. For our guidance as therapists, two modalities
can be added that are complementary with the epistemic
and veridictory modalities, the *mythic modality*, 'to
believe to do (or be done)', and the pragmatic modality, 'to know how to do'.

   Thus both 'doing' and 'being' are modalized by different values. 'Wanting to', 'being able to', 'having to',
'knowing how to', 'believing' and 'making' are all so
many ways of semantically qualifying an identity or
an activity. Greimas and Courtes (1979) propose an
elementary logico-semantic organizer, the SEMIOTIC
SQUARE, which enables the semiotic structures underlying all language to be defined. There follows from
this a logico–cognitive definition of power, manipulation, knowledge, truth, duty and belief as these can be
described in terms of semio–linguistic structure, independently of the internal/external referents that may
possibly be denoted.

   (See also COMMUNICATION SYSTEMS; DELIRIUM;
DREAMS; MODE–IDENTIFYING SIGNALS; PHANTASY; PLAY.)

J.M.

limits   See ADMISSION OF IMPOTENCE; BALL, SPHERE;
BOUNDARIES; CHREOD; DIFFERENTIATION OF SELF; DIS-
TANCE; DOMESTICATION; ELEMENTARY CATSTROPHES; EVO-
LUTIONARY SURVIVAL UNIT; FAMILY–THERAPEUTIC
INSTITUTION DIFFERENTIATION; FAMILY PSYCHICAL APPA-
RATUS; FRACTALS; INCOMPLETENESS THEOREMS; MAPS;
MULTI–LEVEL HIERARCHIES; RITUALIZATION; SEMANTIC
UNIT OF MIND; SPACE–TIME; SYMBOLIC REFERENCE;

TERRITORY; THERAPEUTIC ABSTENTION; TOPOLOGICAL
SPACE; UNIT OF CHANGE.

linear, linearity   See CIRCULARITY; DEIXIS; ELEMEN-
TARY CATASTROPHES; INFORMATION; SYMPTOMS; SYNTAX
OF COMMUNICATION.

locus   The determination of the 'locus' in the family
ECOSYSTEM is, together with the identification of the
problem, one of the stages in the assessment phase in
the STRUCTURAL MODEL. The locus may be defined as
the set of the structures of the system connected to the
problem. Structural family therapists speak of a primary locus, a secondary locus and a tertiary locus.

   The *primary locus* brings together the members of
the sub-systems or systems whose interrelations give
rise to the problem. Aponte and van Deusen (1981)
distinguish between the 'bearers of the problem' who,
being unable to fulfil certain functions, are frustrated
in their aims, and the 'constitutive participants' whose
relations with the 'problem bearer' are disturbed.

   The *secondary locus* covers the active environment
of the problem which sustains the appearance of the
difficulties and perpetuates them. It plays a role in
reinforcing the problem.

   The *tertiary locus* is the passive environment, the
crucible in which the problem takes shape, but it has
no impact upon its development. In a play, the actors
would be the primary locus, the stage-hands the secondary locus and the audience the tertiary locus.

   It must be noted that the notion of locus refers to
the totality of elements of the family or ecosystem
affected by the problem in the present and contributing to its continuance. It does not relate to what it was
in the past that gave rise to the current difficulties.

   (See also EVOLUTIONARY SURVIVAL UNIT; SEMANTIC
UNIT OF MIND; UNIT OF CHANGE.)

A.L.

logical types   See DOUBLE BIND; FAMILY SELF-
REFERENTIALITY; INCOMPLETENESS THEOREMS; MULTI-
LEVEL HIERARCHIES; PARADOXES; SCHIZOPHRENIAS;
SELF–REFERENTIAL CALCULUS; STRANGE LOOPS; SYMP-
TOMS; TANGLED HIERARCHIES; THEORY OF LOGICAL TYPES.

loss and grief   Death is never an individual event.
Different cultures at different times have endeavoured
to explain the significance and the impossibility of accepting death. Rituals have evolved to help the individal,
family or community cope with the impact of losing a
member, and myths (Ferreira, 1963; Byng-Hall, 1973)

can become powerful factors in maintaining the influence of previous generations in the present. Those charged with the responsibilities of helping at the time of death and afterwards – shaman, priest or therapist – vary according to culture and beliefs. Where losses through death are not satisfactorily mourned, the impact on current and future generations can be serious. A systemic perspective and a life-cycle framework are useful in understanding the processes involved and in providing support and healing. Effective ways of helping to understand loss are essential for the current and future mental health of family members, whether the point of contact is with families who are facing the imminent death of a member, have recently lost someone, or have been unable to resolve previous bereavements. How individuals and families adjust and re-adjust to loss is one of the central dilemmas of human life.

Only individuals die yet, except in the most exceptional circumstances, every death affects more than the individual. How loss is experienced will, for example, be mediated by gender, age at the time of the loss, the family's life-stage, ethnicity, the possibility of appropriate cultural or religious rituals, economic stability and how losses have been dealt with in the past.

A working definition of loss is proposed as:

> The disappearance of a significant object or attribute which has high physical, emotional or psychological survival value for the individual(s) concerned. This is the person's subjective experience of the loss, since loss of a particular object or attribute for one person may have a different value for another. The relative effect(s) of loss will be mediated by time and circumstance. (Jenkins, 1986, pp. 97–8)

How a family experiences death will impact both immediately, and in the long term. Death, trauma, or severe loss can freeze families, in the same way it can individuals, in a particular developmental phase.

STAGES OF GRIEVING

The stages of grieving have been described variously by different writers. A useful framework is the following:

- numbness, lasting from a few hours to a week perhaps interrupted by outbursts of extreme anger, distress, denial and a preoccupation with the loss;
- yearning and searching, lasting months or even years, characterized by a period of intense inner struggle where awareness of the death conflicts with a desire to recover the lost person and the lost family structure;
- a reorganization phase, with feelings of hopelessness where the individual is aware of the discrepancy between his/her inner model of the world and the world as it is;

- a phase of greater or lesser degree of reorganization with the development of new sets of assumptions which include establishing a new personal identity, greater acceptance and an increased ability to look towards the future without denying the past and the loss (Bowlby-West, 1983).

It is only when under stress that the family system's ability to cope is tested and when there is likely to be symptomatic occurrence, signalling that the family's coping abilities are being pushed beyond their normal limits. Where there is no stress there is unlikely to be significant symptomatology, so that absence of symptom(s) is not necessarily a sign of health. The pre-existing characteristics of family and social systems will largely determine how members will cope when stressed and faced with loss. This will be related to past history and the nature of current external and internal events and relationships. Bowen (see 1978a, pp. 467–528) states that the lower an individual's levels of differentiation, the less able is that person to share anxiety-provoking thoughts without becoming severely distressed. It is then more likely that under stress, dysfunctional patterns will develop and recur. A systemic analysis offers a framework for understanding the impact of loss from a contextual perspective, while retaining a focus on the individual (Jenkins, 1989d).

IMPLICATIONS FOR THERAPY

The therapist should evaluate the interrelationships of age of death of the deceased, the life-cycle stage(s) of the family (Lewis, 1976; Carter and McGoldrick, 1989), significance to the family system of the dead member (Lindemann, 1944), and the degree of disruption caused by the death to current life. Key factors are the timing of the death or serious illness in the life-cycle, the nature of the death or serious illness, the openness of the family system, and family position of the dead family member (Herz, 1980). The only aspect which professional intervention can affect is the relative openness of the family system. The family system through the FAMILY LIFE-CYCLE is a powerful and useful diagnostic framework (Gleser et al., 1981) and one which can usefully suggest ways in which the clinician may intervene. Where possible, early intervention is likely to facilitate effective mourning and reduce the likelihood of long-term emotional and psychological difficulties (Paul, 1967; Bowen, 1978a, pp. 321–35; Acworth and Bruggen, 1985).

RESEARCH

Research indicates that early loss of a parent is likely to affect subsequent mental health (Parkes, 1965a, b; Birtchnell, 1970a, b; Brown et al., 1977). Where there has been significant failure to mourn early loss, psychiatric breakdown may be a linked consequence

(Lieberman, 1978). The lessons for therapy are that active mourning for the dead member are the most effective (Paul, 1967; Black, 1981; Lieberman and Black, 1982; Gelcer, 1983). The literature on stress is also useful in this field (Garmezy and Rutter, 1985).

OTHER LOSS

While death is the most extreme example of loss, other experiences evoke similar feelings and processes. In these case, a 'bereavement' framework for professional help provides an effective model for practice. Examples of different kinds of loss include: loss of home (Fried, 1962); physical illness (Lask, 1982; Ferrari, 1983); ageing (Berezin, 1965; Weisman, 1970); incest (Gutheil and Avery, 1977; Pittman, 1977; Furniss, 1983); handicap (Black, 1982).

(See also ACCULTURATION; ETHNICITY; FAMILY SYSTEMS; GENDER; INCEST; MOURNING, DEPRESSION, MANIA, MELANCHOLIA; MYTH; RITUALIZATION; SELF.)

H.J.

love, hatred, knowledge, indifference Love is normally or ideally what cements relations within the family (Porot, 1954). Coexistence under the same roof and ties of blood or affiliation are not in themselves enough to build a HOME upon. Knowledge, love, hatred and indifference are the differential polarities which structure the emotional systems within a family.

Though there is an invariant aspect in these fundamental affective oppositions, it appears that their differentiation is very largely an effect of the experience drawn from events lived through within the family of origin. Rather than propose here what might be a definition and *a fortiori* a 'theory' of what these terms convey, it is more important to identify the manner in which the various members of a family will invest these emotional aptitudes in relation to one another and the way they will conceive the categories thus created (see FAMILY MYTHS; FAMILY SYSTEMS). Love, hatred, knowledge and indifference are more or less united or split (phenomena of neurotic ambivalence, psychotic ambitendency); it is with their integration that the elaboration of transference processes begins (see TRANSFERENCE).

MODALITIES OF PROCESSES OF LOVE

The term 'love' here conveys a variety of different values: love between husband and wife, brotherly love, parental love, filial love, extrafamilial and extraconjugal love and love of oneself. The polarities of love are intrafamilial, interfamilial and extrafamilial. The various different psychoanalytic theories have particularly explored this dimension of family relations and their psychical integration. Though *transference is above all a love story*, it is not always constituted in such a

way that it can be analysed. In the gravest cases, the most pressing task is to attempt to re-establish the contexts in which it can be constructed or reconstructed.

AFFECTS AND EMOTIONAL SYSTEMS

Affective dispositions are thus organized in systems of oppositions, taking their lead from the initial family configurations. Processes of love are subject to multiple conflicts. Some of these break out in reality, others are structured on phantasmatic planes and yet others can be more or less flexibly re-cast between these various planes:

- narcissistic love, object love;
- love, hate, knowledge, indifference;
- love, sexuality, Oedipus complex.

Fromm (1942) emphasizes the different characteristics of love in the case of different objects. He writes of love between equals in brotherly love, the complementary love providing care and ensuring survival in maternal love; and the differentiation, separation and conflictualization functions of paternal love.

Bion (1965, 1970) suggests that a distinction should be made between three emotional modalities based on the relations H, L and K, where K signifies 'x knows y', L 'x loves y', and H 'x hates y'. It seems necessary to add to these the relation I, of indifference or ignorance, which may be established with the birth of a child and lead, either to the child's being expelled from the family or to its being kept within the family, but misrecognized by it. Knowledge, love, hatred and indifference are the signs by which we express the forces of attraction or repulsion or the neutral forces which take hold of the various members of the family; it then becomes helpful to track down the forms and forces of family interactions, by studying the FORCE FIELDS (directions, intensities and variations) underlying the trajectories of the various persons involved.

Phenomena relating to love possess both a qualitative and a quantitative dimension. The parents of psychotic children often complain of not having been loved themselves. Now, the absolutely essential precondition for working out conflicts is to be able to recognize feelings of hatred and permit their expression within a therapeutic setting capable of guaranteeing the physical and psychic integrity of the various family members.

THERAPY AND EMOTIONAL SYSTEMS

Questions then arise in therapy: how is one, as a parent, to cope with the knowledge, love, hatred and indifference etc. of one's own parents. Similarly, how do grandparents come (or not) to love their grandchildren: love for the unloved from a grandparent (Selvini Palazzoli et al., 1978) can lead to transgenerational paradoxes which a child will come to embody in a form of sacrificial altruism. One may then attempt to identify two aspects:

1 To determine in what way the family members perceive and describe the nature of these emotional relations between them (coalitions, alliances, ruptures, passions).
2 To determine in what way the therapists receive and interpret the displays of love, hatred and indifference in the family system under examination. Hatred very often appears as a resentment, often very difficult to overcome, that is connected with a love relationship that has been thrown over or betrayed, a resentment that is lived out within the operational closure of the family group. One of the roles of therapy is to mark out the exit routes from these emotional impasses.

(See also ABSURD; ALIENATION; FAMILY–THERAPEUTIC INSTITUTION DIFFERENTIATION; IDENTIFICATION.)

J.M.

loyalty, split loyalties, invisible loyalties Loyalty, a central concept in the contextual family therapy of Boszormenyi-Nagy and Spark, is defined as a

motivational determinant which has self-other dialectical, multipersonal rather than individual roots . . . its real nature lies in the invisible fabric of group expectations instead of manifest law. The invisible fibres of loyalty consist of consanguinity, maintenance of biological life and family lineage on the one hand and earned merit among members on the other. (1973, p. 52)

Loyalty is a mark of belonging to a group and therefore manifests itself both as a group characteristic and as an individual attitude.

Loyalty, as an individual attitude, goes beyond mere identification with the group. To be a loyal member of the group implies internalizing the spirit of its expectations and complying with its internalized injunctions. Failure to live up to the demands of loyalty leads to feelings of existential guilt which constitute a system of secondary regulative forces which play a part in maintaining the homeostasis of the family system.

The development of loyalty is determined by the history of the family group, the type of justice in force within it and its myths. The nature of each of the group members' obligations depends on his/her emotional disposition and his/her position in respect of the family LEDGER, which recapitulates what each member of the family owes to – and may expect to receive from – the others.

In families, as in other groups, the most basic loyalty is aimed at ensuring the survival of the group itself. As a consequence, the power of that loyalty, which is usually concealed, may only reveal itself when situations occur in which the very existence of the family is at risk or when there is a danger that one of its members may break away.

Over the succeeding generations, vertical loyalties, directed towards the previous or following generation may come into conflict with horizontal loyalties to companions, brothers and sisters or to one's peers in general. The establishment of new relationships, particularly through marriage or the birth of children, creates new loyalties. The more rigid the initial system of loyalty, the more severe the conflict will be for the individual: 'Who will you choose? Me? Him or her?'

SPLIT LOYALTIES

Boszormenyi-Nagy and Spark define the concept of *split loyalties* within a family as the consequence of contradictory demands placed upon the child by its parents. In responding to these demands, the child can only be loyal to one of the parents by being disloyal to the other. The existence of a parental conflict does not in itself bring about split loyalty. The essential factor is the unconditional involvement of the child in that conflict and the demand that he or she take up a position in regard to it. This conflict of loyalty may then given rise to the development of symptomatic behaviour.

Loyalty, as a duty to safeguard the group, may necessitate the emergence of pathological behaviour in one of the members of the family. A child's delinquent behaviour or anorexia may, for example, achieve the effect of preventing a change which the parents feel to be dangerous.

Adults who have not adequately worked through their emotional separation and guilt feelings may remain unconsciously overcommitted and loyal to their families of origin. Their children may then be used as substitute objects of gratification for the parent's unmet dependency, aggressive or sexual needs. The parents may even attempt to pay off their indebtedness to their own parents by martyr like, guilt-producing giving to their children. (Boszormenyi-Nagy and Spark, 1973, p. 272)

This type of *invisible loyalty* may connect the symptom-bearer to more or less distant relatives, if not indeed to dead antecedents. It is possible, for example, that the loyalty of a delinquent individual may in fact amount to keeping faith with a relative whom the family may have treated as an outcast. In such a case, loyalty would be conforming, in a sense, to a cryptic moral code and functioning as a reminder of an ethics which was not allowed a place within the family.

(See also ETHICS; FAIRNESS; TRUST.)

A.L.

M

machines, trivial and non-trivial The concept of 'machine' was elaborated by Turing (1937, 1950) in developing an approach to the symbolic description of the operations which occur in logic. A concept of this kind, which is the basis of the theory of automata, prefigures the study of the logical structure of computers by formalizing the notion of ALGORITHM. The distinction between trivial and non-trivial machines was developed by Heinz von Foerster (1985). The trivialization of a system consists in reducing it to the model (machine) that has been made of it.

Trivial and non-trivial machines can be formal means of grasping living systems. The trivial machine is a machine that repeats without error. Any relation between a stimulus and a response remains self-identical (algorithm). The non-trivial machine is a machine which is so complex as to prevent an analytical knowledge of its operation. It is a BLACK BOX.

```
                  ┌──────────┐
          x       │          │      y
Input  ─ ─ ─ ─ >  │          │  ─ ─ ─ ─ >  Output
                  │          │
                  └──────────┘
```

What goes into the machine belongs to an alphabet of inputs, what comes out of it to an alphabet of outputs. The function F is a univocal relation between the input and output alphabets. Each input has one output attributed to it and one alone. This is the model of logical thought and of many concepts in physics, the logic of behaviour etc. The philosophical idea underpinning classical determinism is that nature is a trivial machine. For Skinner (1969), the organism is a trivial machine. The trivial machine also provides a model of Aristotelian syllogistic thinking.

Model	x	F	y
Physics	Cause	Law of nature	Effect
Behaviour	Stimulus	Organism	Response
Logic	Minor premiss	Major premiss	Conclusion
Formalism in abstract machine terms	Input	Transference function	Output

Trivial machines can be completely determined from the moment one knows the transference function correspondence table. They can also be completely determined by the analysis of inputs and outputs. They are, therefore, analytically determinable. They are independent of the past and are predictable. Scientific explanations tend to transform the world into trivial machines in order to determine it and to be able to make predictions.

A non-trivial machine also possesses an alphabet of inputs (cause, stimulus, perturbation, minor premiss etc.) and an alphabet of outputs (effect, response, compensation, output, conclusion etc.). However, the non-trivial machine also possesses an internal state and a state function, together with a transference function. The transference function which determines the output depends not only on the input but also on the current internal state of the machine. The state function determines the new state of the machine and also itself depends on the input and the current state of the machine. The output – and the new internal state – are determined by the current internal state and the input.

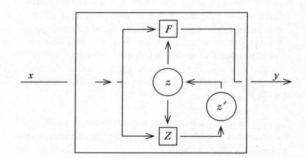

Non-trivial machine: x = input; $y = f(x)$ = output; $z' = Z(x,z)$ = new state; z = current state; F = transference function; Z = state function.

Non-trivial machines can be determined if the transference and state function tables are known. They are, however, analytically indeterminable since it will never be possible, even with the aid of a detailed analysis of the inputs and outputs to reconstitute the operation of the machine. A single input may not give the same output if the internal state has changed between the two observations. Moreover, the non-trivial machine depends on the past and is not predictable. Human beings, families, systems and living organisms do not behave like trivial machines. Many institutions seek to 'trivialize' individuals in order to render their behaviour predictable.

The concept of the non-trivial machine enhances that of the BLACK BOX. If one accepts the hypothesis of organizational closure, a living system then comes to be seen as an interactive closed network which may, in von Foerster's view, be modelled by a non-trivial machine functioning recursively, i.e. responding indefinitely to the 'stimuli' which it emits itself. Such a system may then reach a state of self-sustaining behaviour or, alternatively, an ATTRACTOR or a fixed point, made up either of a particular state or of oscillations between two or more states.

This model accounts for the apparent equifinality which prevails around these extraordinarily stable fixed points. In the neighbourhood of these points, whatever the initial conditions, the process which consists in the system making itself on the basis of its own production leads to an identical result. However, a system modelled by a non-trivial machine may arrive at several 'fixed points', depending upon the input which it chooses to reiterate *ad infinitum*.

When a family consults a therapist, its particular functioning, the laws specific to it and its myths etc. are akin to self-sustaining behaviour, being the product of the recursivity it has generated and on which it has fed in constituting itself. The therapeutic system/family system encounter may lead the latter to open itself to or select new 'events' which constitute an 'input' that is able to destabilize the limit cycle in which it finds itself trapped, and, by a process of recursive amplification, to trigger the emergence of another fixed point which may, temporarily, be the self-sustaining behaviour of a new system: the family–therapist system.

(See also FAMILY SYSTEMS; GENERAL SYSTEMS THEORY; HEURISTICS; OSCILLATORS; SELF-REFERENTIAL CALCULUS.)

M.G.

maieutics Initially referred to the pedagogical method employed by Socrates, by which his interlocutors were enabled to discover the knowledge they possessed without actually knowing that it was within them. He associated this method with the profession of his mother, that of midwife (*maias*), a calling which exemplified the technical function in Greece, the midwife's role being to attend at a moment of creation and be an auxiliary to that creation: 'The craftsman actually makes the thing, but he does so, as a craftsman, without a perfect knowledge of its eidos, i.e. its purpose. Only the user possesses that competence' (Vernant, 1965, p. 216).

Now, with industrial civilization, this technical function became hypertrophied and autonomous to the point where production gradually became the ideal and use a secondary matter. This process of autonomization enabled a form of technological thinking to develop, which was built upon the notion of abstract work. Newtonian

mechanics was to represent the high point of that form of thought.

The whole of the Western world's conceptions were changed by this development, particularly the field of psychology. In that sphere, the interpretation in terms of forces, energy, gears and flows (of libido) was adopted and the present age has seen this development reach fulfilment with the introduction of technology into human reproduction (see the article, 'Nouvelle genitalité', *Génitif*, 1985). The transformation wrought here consists not so much in the accumulation of artificial means as in the substituting of new ends. It is not parents who create and produce any longer; it is obstetricians.

At the same time, an opposite movement is occurring, with the appearance on the scene of therapists who are putting this maieutic function back at the centre of family systems. Abandoning the productivist model (energy, conflicts, 'working through' etc.), they have in fact succeeded in re-establishing a status for the psychologist as someone who serves a user (whether it be an individual or a group), based on a teleological strategy which connects both with Socratic tradition and with contemporary work on disimplification. The 'reflecting team' model of Andersen (1987) would seem to draw on the Socratic position.

(See also BEHAVIOURISM; HOLISM; IMMANENCE.)

D.C.

mania See MOURNING, DEPRESSION, MANIA, MELANCHOLIA.

manifold See DYNAMIC SYSTEMS.

manipulation A corollary of the fundamental axiom advanced by the theorists of the Palo Alto school, 'one cannot *not* communicate' (Watzlawick et al., 1967, p. 49). The result of this is that one cannot not influence others in exchanges. In other words, 'one cannot not manipulate'.

Pathological transactions, whether they manifest themselves as sadomasochistic, paranoid or schizophrenic, in fact mark a failure of manipulation, which breaks out into the open, leads to ineffectiveness of action and signals a disturbance of the organization of relations. In effect, any normal administrative process is based on 'the art of "getting things done"' (Simon, 1945–7, p. 1) and therefore on manipulation.

MORPHOLOGICAL STRUCTURE AND INTERACTION

On the phylogenetic plane (evolution of species), a great number of species divide up the anterior relational field into two distinct and complementary territories, the one determined by the action of the head and the other by the action of the facial organs and of the extremity of the forelimbs (Leroi-Gourhan, 1964). From the vertebrates upwards, one can distinguish the species in which the forelimbs serve exclusively for locomotion and those in which they serve the anterior relational field. Man belongs to the latter category. Thus predation, caretaking, attachment and sexual behaviour are differentiated by the development of this anterior relational field and by way of multiple communication signals. The brain–hand relation appears as a functional sub-structure for symbolic activities, from the simplest to the most sophisticated. Manipulation is thus the behavioural and symbolic emanation of this morphological disposition. It is from the higher primates onwards that the hand assumes such importance in the manipulation of objects, in exchanges with conspecifics and in self-centred behaviour (auto-eroticism). Chimpanzees are aware of manipulating the relationships that exist between them. In man, a large amount of the manipulation takes place unconsciously.

SEMIOTICS OF MANIPULATION

On the plane of semiotic analysis, manipulation is a modality of communication characterizing the way men act on other men (Greimas and Courtes, 1979), which is expressed linguistically in the phrase 'having something done' and its opposites on the semiotic square (having something not done: prevention, not having something done: non-intervention, not having something not done: *laissez-faire*). Manipulation has effectiveness of action as its goal. It is therefore the expression of the dimension of power and hierarchy inherent in every human inter-relationship: parents have their children do lots of things; at other points, they let them do as they wish or they don't let them do as they wish, or alternatively they let them not do as they wish. A great many paradoxes arise out of the pragmatic articulation of these various polarities.

PATHOLOGY OF MANIPULATION AND THERAPEUTIC MANIPULATION

The way a schizophrenic's parent intervenes to modify the treatment of the child or to supervise his/her psychotherapist reveals a dysfunction in the capacity to act effectively on an interaction. On the level of behavioural disorders (alcoholism, drug addiction, schizophrenia, psychopathy etc.), we shall thus find considerable distortions in the manipulatory dimension of behaviour. It is where manipulation seems at its crudest and most obvious that it is in fact least effective, and that it reveals a *failure of authority* (it being possible to define authority as 'the power to make decisions which guide the actions of another' (Simon, 1945–7, p. 125).

From a communicational point of view, every therapy is also an artificial manipulation (whether it be pharmacological or psychoanalytic) and, in the happier cases, a manipulatory learning process enabling patients and those close to them to gain an effective purchase on the relationship.

(See also ABSENT MEMBER MANOEUVRE; ABSTINENCE, RULE OF; FREE ASSOCIATION; INTERPRETATION; PRESCRIPTION; PROVOCATION; THERAPEUTIC ABSTENTION.)

J.M.

map and counter-map of a family system
Process by which a family system impresses the peculiarities of its functioning and dysfunctioning upon one or more institutional teams independently of the individual psychical capacities of the therapists to attempt to understand and resolve the problem as isolated individuals.

The psychoanalysis of family groups led to the recognition of inter-phantasmatic, inter-transferential and inter-countertransferential processes operating in the members of the family as well as among the various therapists and professionals consulted (Ruffiot, 1981b; Eiguer, 1983). Similarly, Wynne (1978) has described the existence of METABINDING arising among therapists, leading to confusions, misunderstandings and misconceptions regarding the respective actions of each. In this way, disagreements and even conflict may arise among therapists, and genuine therapeutic ALIENATIONS may also be produced. In cases where the specificity of communication overrides intrapsychical, transpersonal action and leads to the creation of family and institutional MYTHS, it will be possible to describe a transformation of the therapeutic space, Y, by the family space, X. This transformation is then akin to a mathematical function in which Y is a function of X. Such a function is called the map of a source space on to a target space, the source space here being the family, X, the target-space, Y, the domain of the specialist professionals (made up in some cases of an institution or set of institutions). In practice, a better understanding of the family problem is often to be had from studying the characteristics of the particular map under consideration than by simply collecting information directly transmitted by the family. In effect, the map of the family system concerns a multidimensional NETWORK of communication which cannot be studied until it is deployed. The professionals most directly concerned in the approach to the family under consideration will be able, by evaluating the effects of this mapping on their own communications, to judge what the systemic modality of their intervention with members of the family system should be: educative–propaedeutic–didactic (see LEGAL CONTEXT; SYSTEMIC MODELLING AND INTERVENTION; LAW), therapeutic, cathartic (see SACRED) or MAIEUTIC (see also BEHAVIOURISM).

The 'complement' of this mapping of the family system on to the therapeutic system is an inverse map or counter-map which is orientated from the therapeutic system towards the family system (see, for example, the therapeutic attitudes of accommodation and AF-FILIATION or joining). The problem is complicated by the fact that, on the one hand, the family system awaiting attention is not necessarily requesting a specifically systemic approach and it may see itself – and act – entirely as therapist to the INDEX PATIENT and the many institutional professionals; conversely, what is called the therapeutic (medical, institutional, psychoanalytic and communicational) system, by the fact of its own functional and organizational weaknesses, may be induced to enter pathologically into the open breaches in the family system. The identification of such alienating impulses is one of the preliminary conditions for finding solutions to the problems concretely posed.

(See also FAMILY–THERAPEUTIC INSTITUTION DIFFER-ENTIATION; TRANSFERENCE.)

J.M.

maps The concept of map is quite close to that of representation in psychoanalysis. It corresponds to the location system which the person possesses internally in order to orientate him or herself in space and time and is an asymptotic simulation of the TERRITORY, though it remains, however, fundamentally distinct from this.

The three principles of the non-Aristotelian semantics of Korzybski (1941, 1951) are the following:

- a map is not a territory;
- a map does not cover the whole territory;
- a map is self-reflexive: a map is a map of maps, in the same way as, in language, it is possible to employ language about language.

Bateson, in 'Form, substance and difference' (see Bateson, 1972, pp. 423–40), thus specifies that a map is a *representation of representations*, which therefore refer on necessarily to an 'infinite series of maps'. If the map is never the territory, this is because the territory is a '*Ding an sich*', a thing-in-itself, on which no purchase is possible. The process of representation will always filter it to such a degree that the mental world will only be a series of maps of maps *ad infinitum*. Thus all 'phenomena' are literally 'appearances'.

It is then possible to make semiotic distinctions in terms of the relations between the territory and the map: in primary processes, map and territory are confused; in secondary processes, they are distinct; in play, they are both confused and distinct (Bateson, 1972). The map appears as the expression of representations, while the territory is what the definition of reality is based upon.

Maps are structured as a function of specific topological properties. Thus, for Thom, the analysis of the human mind can be apprehended on the model of differential geometry and the topological constraints associated with it. This is not without its consequences where the analysis of reality is concerned. A sphere cannot be covered with a single map; two hemispheres are necessary. The blank 'flaps' left between the parts of these maps obey topological laws of map changes (diffeomorphisms). Euclidian space is described, by definition, from a single map which corresponds to one point of view. To reconstruct a global object, one must have topological laws of map changes which make it possible to take in a multiplicity of points of view. It will be noted, moreover, that the description of FRACTAL objects leads to the discovery of intermediate zones between the absolute order of Euclidian geometry and total chaos. The structure of mineral, biological or psychical objects is only smooth at a first approximation.

(See also BALL, SPHERE; FAMILY MAPS; METAPSYCHOLOGY; PLAY; REALITY.)

J.M.

marital breakdown Marital breakdown is dependent on biological factors and personal psychodynamic factors, as well as on familial and social factors. It brings with it a certain number of consequences for the FAMILY LIFE-CYCLE and modifies the triangulations provided by society, out of a concern for the protection of minors. Divorce is equivalent to a legalization of separation. The problems of couples breaking up have always existed in all societies. However, the social status granted to that problem varies a great deal depending upon the period and the culture.

As Padovani et al. (1986) point out, 'a couple lasts not so much by its capacity to withstand the erosion of time as by its ability to produce something new.' The break-up of couples is increasingly frequent; for France in 1985, the divorce rate was one couple in three and, for Paris, the figure was one in two. Figures for the UK are similar, with a higher divorce rate for re-marriage. In spite of the spirit of the times, which tends to represent such break-ups as normal, we must note the importance attaching to phenomena relating to the MOURNING of the love object and the internal and external, normal and pathological repercussions which result from this (Padovani et al., 1986). We shall here seek to maintain a distinction between the problems of a couple or the break-up of a couple and parental problems related to the pathology of one or more children.

PSYCHODYNAMIC FACTORS IN PLAY IN MARITAL BREAKDOWN

Many psychoanalytic studies (see, for example, Eiguer, 1983; Padovani et al., 1986) draw a distinction between three types of organization of couples and three different modalities of dysfunctioning.

The neurotic couple

The dysfunctions of these couples crystallize around sexual difficulties: confrontations revolve around jealousy (the phantom rival serving as ideal unconscious model) and phallic rivalry; Oedipal, homosexual and pregenital desires lead to the de-erotization of the conjugal bond. Similarly, a transition from the status of husband/wife to father/mother may come to overshadow the couple's relationship as man and woman. The phantasmatic weight accorded to the children is not without its part in that process. Pregenital attachment links then come to the fore. In extramarital relations, a partner may be chosen who is at the opposite extreme from the legitimate partner (Padovani et al., 1986).

The anaclitic couple

This is based on identifications with part objects, as these are elaborated at the various sexual stages of childhood. Object choice is based on fear of the loss of these partial satisfactions. The resolution of conflicts occurs not so much through attempts at elaboration in speech as by the intervention of a third party (parents, friends, children) and by projection into external conflicts.

The narcissistic couple

This brings psychotic mechanisms of thinking and relating into the foreground: these lead to interactions in the form of domination–overwhelming, control–contempt, projective identification–interpretation and fusion–annihilation.

These various types of organization are in fact preferential polarities dependent upon biological and sociocultural factors. One may thus describe parameters operating in several dimensions at once and leading to dangers of the marital bond becoming fragile and breaking.

TOPOLOGICO–DYNAMIC FACTORS WHICH ENCOURAGE
MARITAL BREAKDOWN

McGoldrick (1980) describes a set of factors which predispose to risks of destabilization, or even breakdown, of couples.

1 Formation of the couple shortly after a significant loss, by defence against too painful a process of mourning.
2 Formation of the couple out of a desire to be distanced from one of the families of origin.
3 Difference in the backgrounds of the families of origin: in terms of religion, education, social class, ethnic group or age of partner.
4 Constellation of incompatible sibling groups.
5 Too small or too great a distance between nuclear family and family of origin.

6 Financial, physical, emotional or intellectual dependence on the extended family.
7 Marriage before twenty or after thirty.
8 Having known each other for more than three years or less than six months before marriage.
9 Family and friends not present at marriage.
10 Woman pregnant before first year of marriage.
11 Limited relations with siblings and parents.
12 Negative perception of one's childhood or adolescence.
13 Unstable marital or family patterns in the extended family.

PSYCHOSOCIAL FACTORS CONTRIBUTING TO
ESTABLISHMENT AND BREAKDOWN OF MARITAL BOND

These factual parameters have to be seen in relation to the contractual form on which the couple is based. Where the basis of the private–public interface of the couple is concerned, a paradox exists: once the couple has been officially recognized, do the partners continue to love one another because they wish to or because they have to (Haley, 1963; see COUPLES)? The breaking off of the relationship will not have the same effects depending on the nature of its basis. Roussel (1986, 1989) stresses that marriage and divorce are two elements of a single reality, the matrimonial model.

Roussel distinguishes four types of marriage:

1 *Traditional marriage*: its basis is a strong institution, whose ultimate purpose is the survival of individuals and where the surrounding society intervenes very little. Divorce is then exceptional.
2 *Alliance marriage*: the institution serves as a framework for affective solidarity; society only carries out the formal education of the children; divorce is then a *divorce-as-punitive-sanction* in which the judicial systems plays a preponderant part and where the sense of shame of the partners – who have been 'judged' and 'stigmatized' by society – is dominant. The economic consequences are serious, particularly for the woman.
3 *Fusion marriage*: the institutional dimension here is virtually a mere formality and is supplanted, as regards the real basis of the marriage, by intense affective solidarity. Society provides a range of services, including taking care of the children during the daytime, alongside their formal education. Divorce then becomes a *divorce-as-failure*, a serious psychical event, in which feelings of guilt and anxiety are dominant. There is then a tension between the formal law and the actual practice of the courts.
4 *Associative marriage*: the alliance between the partners is no longer in any way based on a legally sanctioned contract. That contract changes as the desires of the partners change. A large proportion of the functions is, in this case, taken on by society, which looks after the children, gives advice, provides

a wide range of services and therapies etc.; divorce becomes a *dissociation divorce* which is relatively less painful on the personal level. The role of the legal system is relatively limited in such cases.

PATHOLOGY OF MARITAL BREAK-UP

Therapeutic interviews

A divorcing couple is often seen as a counter-indication to therapy and/or met with as the result of a 'couple' therapy. However, a consultation often makes it possible to clarify the partners' intentions to separate, even when the initial demand might have been for couple therapy. That consultation usually takes the form of a few sessions of short – or even very short – duration. In some cases, it enables reciprocal movements of violence and hatred to be attenuated, through projection on to the therapist consulted of what is experienced as the failure of all therapy. Interviews may also serve to allow divorced parents to deal with certain of their children's problems in conditions of sufficient neutrality. It is right that the systemic interventions here should define the nature and stakes of the interviews and not seek to reactivate the dynamics of the couple, by stressing, for example, the parent–child conflicts which have to be clarified.

Break-ups between clans

In other cases, one finds veritable wars between families of origin, with more or less total disqualification of one of the partners' status as a relative. Some families even go so far as to refuse to let the partner who is excluded from the 'clan' have the children or even visit them. The FAMILY PASSIONS which arise as a result bring into play transgenerational settlings of account, making interventions on the part of the judicial or socio–educative agencies particularly difficult. These latter become the focus of the various passions in play, establishing substitutive triangulations which are, themselves, often in conflict one with another.

The civil courts, which deal with matrimonial affairs, are then brought into play. In Paris, 85 per cent of divorces are by mutual consent. Of the remaining 15 per cent, in 10 per cent the partners accept a compromise and 5 per cent refuse any compromise, making it necessary for the judge to pronounce on the case. We may note that even in divorces by mutual consent, problems often re-emerge two or three years after separation, once the 'euphoria' of the break has passed.

In the most extreme cases, an acute transgenerational problem arises. The partners are then placed in extremely infantile positions and become very much dependent upon the will of a grandparent who arrogates to him or herself virtually all decision-making power (this is very often the grandmother).

In women, one often finds a poorly resolved adolescent crisis; choice of partner is made in a mode of provocation to their own mothers, with whom they refuse to identify. In men, affective immaturity is dominant, with a very strong bond with their mothers and an inability to cope with frustrations within the couple. The arrival of children functions as a detonator, threatening the narcissistic fragility of the partners and rekindling power struggles on the generational level. Identification with the parents is either too strong or too weak. Grandfathers then often reinforce, passively and implicitly, the powers of the parent/guardian of the children.

MOURNING FOR THE COUPLE

The dimension of mourning is a fundamental one in divorce. And that mourning is all the more difficult for being multiple and contradictory. It is multiple because the couple, the partner and, often, the children too, are lost. It is contradictory because one must both resolve to forget the other and to maintain relations, generally for the sake of the children, but sometimes for the management of property. Generally, this process takes three years.

When they have to deal with depressive affects, men and women do not react in an identical way. As a general rule, men take flight, while women protest. We must, however, distinguish between the successive phases of the process, particularly where divorce is a result of one of the partners forming a new sexual relationship. In the elation arising from falling in love, that partner will not understand the jealousy of the other partner, whose happiness he/she persists in desiring (Alberoni, 1979). The abandoned party first responds to this denial of aggressiveness by anger and reprisals, then accuses – and even reproaches – him- or herself for the good memories he/she has. The 'loser', to reconstruct an individual identity, needs a commentary, a metacommunication (see ACOUSTIC FEEDBACK) to triangulate the relationship, by doing justice to it, which is, unfortunately, something legal proceedings rarely do. The 'lost party', when he/she emerges from his/her period of adulterous *innamoramento* also needs judgement to be pronounced so that he/she can be unburdened of his/her sense of guilt. This is why various writers have suggested procedures of symbolic intent to make up for the painful lack of social rituals of divorce.

For example, Kaslow (1986) organizes a divorce ceremony as part of a role-playing game for the divorced; in France, the AFCC has set up 'divorcing/divorcee groups' (Colin, 1984; Lesourd, 1984); in the United States, the Group for the Advancement of Psychiatry suggested in 1980 that the work of family therapists should consist in urging ex-partners to negotiate and compromise, in order that resentments will not be offloaded onto the children and that, for their benefit, the network of interaction with the families of their two parents will be maintained as much as possible.

(See also FAMILY MYTHS; FAMILY SELF-REFERENTIALITY; GENOGRAM; TRANSGENERATIONAL MEMORIES.)

J.M. & G.G.M.

marital schism 'Schism' is the term applied to a split within religious believers or the members of an organized group, who subsequently come to subscribe to different authorities. The term is used by Lidz et al. (1956), Wynne et al. (1958) and Schaffer et al. (1962) to define relationships characterized by 'a chronic failure to achieve any degree of complementarity between the marital pair' (Walrond-Skinner, 1986, p. 304) and within the family.

It is also used to indicate a family relationship characterized by an excessive attachment to the parental home on the part of the children. The function of such an attachment is, in reality, to delay or prevent the threatened dislocation of the marital pair. In cases of this kind, the actions of the child/children represent genuine rescue manoeuvres.

(See also MARITAL SKEW; RECIPROCAL VICTIMIZATION AND RESCUE; SCHISMOGENESIS.)

P.S.

marital skew Term employed by Lidz et al. (1956), Wynne et al. (1958) and Schaffer et al. (1962) to refer to the type of asymmetrical relationship in which a strong and a weak personality find themselves thrown together. In this skewed, uneven, 'oblique' situation, whereas the 'strong' partner seems openly to dominate the relationship, it is the 'weak' or dominated partner who permits him or her – sometimes in a concealed way – to do so.

On a morphological level, this skew leads to a fissure in the marital relationship which makes any attempt to move apart or become closer very delicate. Alongside marital schism, Lidz sees it as one of the forms in which couples are structured in families with schizophrenic transactions.

(See also COALITION; MARITAL SCHISM.)

P.S.

mediation: systemic approaches Mediation as a method of intervention has emerged during the past fifteen to twenty years and is still developing. The objective of child-centred mediation is to assist the separating or divorced couple to come to agreement regarding arrangements about their children, and in comprehensive mediation, financial matters are also included (Fisher, 1992). There is still no clear distinction between conciliation and mediation, although

because of confusion with the word 'reconciliation', mediation is now more generally used.

As mediation has evolved recently and takes place on the boundaries of law and other forms of intervention, it has been important to clarify the principles on which it is based: that the couple voluntarily involve themselves in the process, that the primary goal is to come to agreement regarding arrangements for their children's residence and contact with each parent, and perhaps also relating to financial matters and the matrimonial home. The process is confidential (i.e. legally privileged) and not reportable to the court, or to any other person without the express permission of the couple. The confidentiality boundary is broken only if there is some evidence of child sexual abuse.

The mediator is impartial, working to an explicit contract in assisting the couple to make their own decisions; and is in charge of the process, acting as educator, clarifier or organizer but remains impartial. The tasks are clear, concrete, and focused on external data and not on inner meanings, the mediator using only overt techniques which empower the couple. While there may be a therapeutic spin-off, this is not the prime intention. The expression of feelings, usually strong and negative at the early stages of mediation, are kept to a minimum. The mediator has some understanding and respects the legal processes in which the couple may also be involved. The practice of mediation can be stressful for the mediator because of the high level of conflict, particularly in the early stages of the process.

It could be argued that the theories on which the models of mediation are based are on a continuum which range from a negotiations model (Coogler, 1978), which is fairly legalistic and comprises industrial relations negotiation, to a more systemic model (Haynes and Haynes, 1989) which combines negotiations management with questioning techniques based on those of Tomm (1988). However, the family systems model which is most congruent with the principles of mediation is the social constructionist model (Hoffman, 1988, 1992; Robinson, 1991, 1993). Family therapy techniques which are compatible with the principles of client autonomy in mediation are re-framing, diversion, embedded suggestions, circular and future questioning; those which are not compatible include many structural techniques and those which use paradox, confusion or trance.

As the divorce law in the UK is adversarial, the partner who wants a divorce must prove that the marriage has irretrievably broken down and that his/her spouse has been guilty of one of five faults, the most commonly used being behaviour, adultery, desertion, two years' separation (if the couple agrees) or five years' separation (if the other partner does not consent), in order of frequency. The law is linear rather than systemic and lawyers are appropriately concerned with the rights of their individual client. As their task is to get the best deal for their clients, lawyers are understandably critical of therapeutic techniques which they consider undermine the autonomy of clients (Roberts, 1988). Proposals for what is known as 'process divorce' are on the Lord Chancellor's parliamentary rolling programme ('Looking to the future: mediation and the grounds for divorce', 1993), whereby either partner can be awarded a divorce in a year, during which arrangements regarding the children and finance are agreed. This would encourage couples to seek mediation, although these proposals are politically controversial.

The organizations presently concerned with training mediators are the National Association of Family Mediation and Conciliation Services and the Family Mediators' Association. The former initially trained only social workers and counsellors, although it has now moved into training people who demonstrate appropriate attitudes for mediation, including lawyers, and are steadily accrediting trained mediators. They are also now providing comprehensive mediation in some services.

The Family Mediators' Association trains lawyers and counsellors who co-mediate in comprehensive mediation, and although mediation is inexpensive in comparison to legal costs, it is still beyond the financial reach of many clients. Different models of comprehensive mediation are now being developed, which are less lawyer-intensive. This is important because of the reduction of legal aid in the UK. There is also concern because, following the implementation of the Child Support Act 1991 (in April 1993), officers of the Department of Social Security will gradually take over the arrangements for child support according to a very complicated formula from which the only appeal procedures are to another officer, or to a tribunal rather than the courts as at present.

The process of mediation involves a limited number of interviews, not usually more than five or six, though for comprehensive mediation this may rise to ten or twelve. Although the couple mediating may initially be seen weekly, for two or more sessions, later in the process sessions are more spread out; and where the conflict is at first very high, mediation may take as long as a year. In some services there are two mediators who co-work, although in others the mediator works alone, perhaps with a colleague behind a one-way screen. In comprehensive mediation in the UK at present there are usually two mediators co-mediating, one of whom is a lawyer who joins at least some of the sessions. In North America, lone mediators undertake both child-centred and comprehensive mediation. Parents need to be seen together so that they can become involved in the negotiations, although early in the process, they may be seen separately in shuttle mediation. The first stage is to distinguish the areas of disagreement or conflict and these are usually displayed on a flip chart.

The order in which the issues are negotiated depends on the style of the mediator and the couple. The mediator may suggest that they try out some of the proposals which have been discussed, before coming to agreement and these are then reviewed, clarified and perhaps agreed subsequently and in some detail, for instance detailed arrangements for contact. If the couple is able to reach full or partial agreement on the issues, then in child-centred mediation a brief note is usually sent to each of the parties' lawyers, indicating in outline the agreements reached, in a memorandum of agreement. The lawyers can negotiate these into legally binding documents or present them in court. For comprehensive mediation the memorandum of agreement is much more complicated, though at present it is unclear how these will be affected by the Child Support Act 1991.

There has been some debate about whether the children themselves should be involved in mediation and some principles seem to be emerging. First, both parents should agree that the children should be seen and it is made clear that the children also have a right to confidentiality. Secondly, the children should be interviewed according to the principles of the Children Act 1989 in the UK, in particular that their welfare should be the paramount consideration, and according to their age and stage of development. Thirdly, the children's right to have their views taken into account does not amount to them making the decisions. This is the responsibility of their parents, or if they cannot, then it is the court who should do so. Because of the confidentiality of the mediation process, mediators are not prepared to provide assessment reports to the court, as information gained during interviews with children is only fed back to both parents with the consent of the children concerned, according to the principles of the Children Act 1989.

(See also CIRCULARITY; LAW; PARADOXES; STRUCTURAL FAMILY THERAPY; SYSTEMIC APPROACH.)

M.E.R.

melancholia See MOURNING, DEPRESSION, MANIA, MELANCHOLIA.

memories See READ–WRITE MEMORIES, READ–ONLY MEMORIES, BULK MEMORIES AND AUXILIARY MEMORIES; TRANSGENERATIONAL MEMORIES, FAMILY MEMORIES.

menetic theory Froussart et al. (1985) have, under this heading, attempted to work out a grammar of the organization of family time. Basing themselves on the epistemology of dynamic systems presented by Mairlot

(1982), they consider the '*mene*' (the age at which an individual marries, accedes to parenthood or dies) as a word the subject will use in a '*menetic sentence*' for the scansion of his or her life. Thus the age gap between spouses or between parents and children will have the status of temporal FAMILY ORGANIZERS regulating 'inputs' and 'outputs' in the dynamic system of alliances, births and deaths, which is thus kept invariant. Bovet and Schmid (1985) also point out the repetition of instances of MOURNING in the genealogies of schizophrenics.

(See also RESIDUAL RELATIONS.)

G.G.M.

merit The accounting unit of the family LEDGER and may be defined as the benefit derived from contributing to the well-being of others.

(See also FAIRNESS; LOYALTY.)

A.L.

mesnie An old French word (*L'Information grammaticale* no. 27, October 1985) which means, first, the 'community of relatives living under the same roof (see HOME); secondly, the group of relatives and workers 'who work the same piece of cloth'; and, lastly, the company of a person of high rank (and also the pieces of a chess set).

In the agricultural world, the production unit was the family, but by virtue of a high infant mortality rate and low adult life expectancy, the *mesnie* brought together persons from several generations, who had failed to inherit, either as a result of their position in the family or of re-marriages, as well as any servants there might be. In today's world, quite opposite social factors (the individual as production unit and increased life expectancy) produce a similar situation, i.e. the coexistence under a single roof of adults (except for the aged) and children who, as a result of births outside wedlock, divorces, co-habitation and various other short-term relationships between couples, only live with at most one of their biological parents at a time, and therefore live with their parents in intermittent fashion. This produces a problem for family therapy: should the biological family or the mesnie be taken as the unit to be treated? The worldwide success of the television series *Dallas* and *Dynasty* bears witness to the extraordinary prevalence of these questions of filiation and transmission. What is today's view of heredity and inheritance can be translated into the language of pop culture as 'Is it your name or your behaviour that makes you a true Ewing? Is it money or love? Is it blood or oil? Your father or your mother?' Even Molière was not averse, in his day, to revealing secrets of ignoble

birth as a way of ending plays that were veering towards tragedy on a comic note. *Dallas* and *Dynasty* draw on this same '*Deus ex machina*' and do not hesitate to put incestuous passions within the 'mesnies' of American millionaires on the screen. These are today's small-screen Atridae.

(See also FAMILY PSYCHICAL APPARATUS; FAMILY SYSTEMS.)

G.G.M.

messages A message is a set of signals produced and transmitted from a sender to a receiver by means of a system of coding and de-coding. The message is what the receiver of the signal understands, as coded and produced by the sender. The structure of the message depends on the system of *codification* (which enables meanings to be transcribed), on *redundancy* (which conveys signification) and on the *analogic function* (which creates meaning effects). The message and the codings that make it up are concrete entities such as have effects in speaking and other behaviour, whereas the signifier and the signified, making up the signal are abstract entities.

CODE AND MESSAGE

A message requires a code if it is, first, to be expressed and, secondly, to be intelligible. Examples of codes might be linguistic systems (English, French) or a particular iconic system (the Highway Code, a code of etiquette etc.) or a more general system of information processing (analogic code, digital code). Codes (C) and messages (M) refer to one another in a circular fashion (Jakobson, 1957, p. 132). This occurs in four ways:

- a message about a message (MM): for example a quotation in a linguistic statement;
- a code referring to another code (CC): a proper name refers to the bearer of that name;
- a message referring to the code (MC): for example, a self-referential statement such as 'the word "language" forms part of the English language' or '"the weather is fine" is a sentence';
- a code referring to a message (MC): the SHIFTERS and, more generally, all DEIXIS.

REDUNDANCY

Bateson (1972, pp. 101–25) interprets REDUNDANCY as an organism's ability to reconstruct the whole of the message from one part of it. It is what makes it possible to distinguish a signal from 'noise'. Redundancy here is synonymous with structuring and signification of the message. It operates on the plane of phylogenesis, since the morphology of an organism reveals the external environment in which it evolves. It functions also on the plane of learning, when the repetition of certain messages creates an effective transformation of the model of perception and action. In both cases, the sense organs themselves become bearers of messages. Similarly, in certain cases, the message increases the redundancy of the world by integrating into the signalling the relations between organisms and therefore a part of the messages which organisms exchange with one another: to express danger from a predator, potential prey may simulate for each other the fear and aggressiveness which a predator inspires in them. This mechanism is typical of the 'μ function' of metacommunication. Now, in man, two different layers of message exist:

1 *Kinetic, protolinguistic messages* which are present in the animal world and which man has developed to a higher degree. These are essentially cases of analogic communication. They correspond to the affective, unconscious and involuntary portion of messages. They are not very effective in eliminating ambiguity from messages.
2 *Linguistic messages*, the origin of which is related to analogic communication, but which are 'digitalized' (Bateson, 1972, pp. 387–401) or 'exfoliated' (Thom, 1972, p. 310) on the plane of the structure of the signifier. Verbal signifiers are in fact very poor at communicating affects, by virtue of their all-or-nothing precision.

THE ANALOGIC FUNCTION

Analogic reasoning reveals a link between two representations merely by virtue of a resemblance. The question which then arises is whether or not the analogy is a legitimate one. The theory of artificial systems of information processing is a theory based on an analogy between animals/men and machines. Catastrophe theory reveals the dangers of superficial resemblances in the elaboration of theory of analogy. Two messages may have the same topological structure while being apparently very dissimilar. On the other hand, two messages which appear alike may have a dissimilar topology.

(See also ANALOG-DIGITAL CONVERTERS; ANALOGIC CODING; ARTIFICIAL CODES; COMMUNICATION SYSTEMS; DIGITAL (OR NUMERIC) CODING; HOLOGRAPHIC MEMORY; MULTI-LEVEL HIERARCHIES; PRAGMATICS OF COMMUNICATION; RITUALIZATION; SEMANTICS OF COMMUNICATION; SYNTAX OF COMMUNICATION.)

J.M.

metabinding   Wynne (1978) employs the term 'metabinding' to describe the set of double binds to which therapists, therapeutic teams and nursing/psychiatric personnel are subject when they are in contact with a psychotic patient and/or his or her family.

Such a phenomenon leads to what are sometimes considerable distortions in communication between the various professionals involved in a particular pathological situation so that, although they meet every day, the practitioners most involved in the situation no longer manage to exchange pertinent information about a patient. Or, alternatively, theoretical conflicts come to predominate. In some cases, even, practitioners find themselves in an awkward position as regards their own actions and convictions as a result of the contexts of intervention in which they are operating (hospital, outpatients' department, family consultations etc.). Such phenomena cannot be avoided in practice. And, in fact, they deserve the greatest attention, since they reveal the particular character of the dysfunctions of the suffering family group. The ability to identify these, and to accept that it is these one has to manipulate, is a condition *sine qua non* of any coherent therapeutic activity.

(See also CO-THERAPY; DOUBLE BIND; MAP AND COUNTER-MAP OF A FAMILY SYSTEM; PARADOXES; SUPERVISION; THERAPEUTIC DOUBLE BINDS.)

J.M.

metabolic forms   See STATIC, PSEUDO-STATIC AND METABOLIC FORMS.

metacommunication systems   In higher organisms, every system of COMMUNICATION includes 'metasystems' made up of hierarchies of signals and MESSAGES which communicate on the communication or about the communication. Some systems of metacommunication, called 'μ function' of communication by Bateson, seem to be the prerogative of mammals. The 'speech' of higher animals seems to bear essentially on the 'relationship' between self and others, between self and environment or between the self and itself without real identification and denotation of the things related. In humans, the faculty of denotation radically modifies the phenomena of metacommunication and reduces the frequency of the appearance of paradoxical communication.

DEFINITION OF A METACOMMUNICATION SYSTEM

Metacommunication systems are the product of hierarchies of communication systems. These hierarchies are largely unconscious and have great importance in determining the command aspects relating to the meaning of a relationship. They are based upon the capacity to represent to oneself not only the receiver's figure of regulation, but also the sender–receiver relation. These unconscious stratifications are perturbed or even completely disorganized, caught in all or nothing alternatives, in schizophrenic transaction.

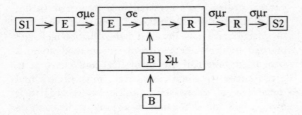

General metacommunication system: S1, source of information; S2, destination; E, sender; R, receiver; B, noise; $\Sigma\mu$, metasystem of communication; σe, signal; σr, received signal; $\sigma\mu e$, metasignal; $\sigma\mu r$, received metasignal.

The morphological appearance of an animal possesses numerous indices metacommunicating its status as prey, predator, conspecific, sexual partner or rival for another animal. It goes without saying that these metacommunicative signals are situated on very different planes, some of which correspond to supra-individual semiotic strata acquired either in the context of phylogenesis or in the cultural context of human history.

Mood indicators (joy, sadness, fear, dread, aggression etc.) are the product of a long phylogenetic evolution to which the processes of RITUALIZATION bear witness. Though re-framed by a great range of cultural variations, they are none the less present in man, continuing, on the plane of the expression and recognition of emotions, the invariant and universal dimensions which attach every man to humanity. Each culture necessarily gives rise to a commentary on these emotional universals (see SYNTAX OF COMMUNICATION).

However, it is a specific characteristic of man that he does not necessarily respond automatically to mood-indicating signs. The human being is capable of recognizing any sign as a signal, referring on to other signals in a sign system. Signals are thus metacommunicative signs which mask, amplify, transform, falsify, represent or repeat the signals indicating or releasing emotions.

METACOMMUNICATIVE FUNCTIONS OF LANGUAGE

Similarly, the slightest linguistic utterance – even a 'denotative' one – metacommunicates about the cultural origin of the speaker and gives a necessarily metacommunicative sense to that relationship in which a speaker denotes something for someone or for him or herself. If simple words can never convey the same message as gestures, they define either implicitly or explicitly a frame which metacommunicates about: gestures, voice, intonation, ideographs, kinetographs, and so on in the act of speaking; manuscripts, printed matter, and books in written messages. In the same way, a metacommunicative message defines 'either explicitly or implicitly, the set of messages about which it communicates, i.e. every metacommunicative message is or defines a psychological frame' (Bateson, 1973 edn, p. 161).

Verbal communication operates on several levels of abstraction beginning with the basic linguistic metacommunication that is denotation: 'The weather's fine', 'This is a table' etc. It permits metacommunications on the μ function (which is itself already metacommunication): 'I was joking', 'This is play', 'I didn't want to annoy you' are metacommunications on already complex metamessages. However, a metacommunication of a particular type concerns language itself, namely metalinguistic utterances properly so-called: 'the word cat has no fur and cannot scratch'. There is thus a possible distinction between the *metacommunicative system* ('I am joking', 'This is play') and the *metalinguistic system* ('This sentence without a verb', 'The word "arbitrary" is arbitrary').

PARADOXES CONNECTED WITH METACOMMUNICATION

Some paradoxes occur when contextual confusion arises between several levels of metacommunication. Saying 'This is play' immediately creates an uncertain state concerning the nature of the exchange. The linguistic sign was identified as arbitrary by de Saussure, but is the word 'arbitrary' arbitrary? It is, in so far as it is a linguistic sign, but, by the same token, its content is no longer arbitrary, because necessarily arbitrary etc. And can someone say of himself that he is deluded? If he can, he is no longer deluded; if he cannot, he is deluded etc. An example of paradoxical communication cited by Watzlawick et al. (1967) is a sign saying 'Ignore this sign.'

Such paradoxes arise from (a) a confusion between signals and metasignals, sent and received (σe, σr, $\sigma\mu e$, $\sigma\mu r$), on the one hand, and between the system (Σc) and the metasystem of communication ($\Sigma\mu$), on the other; and (b) a contradictory feedback in an infinite loop between them.

The stratifications of metacommunication are essentially laid down in individual or supra-individual unconscious memories. In other words, it would be necessary to specify what unconscious level one is seeking to address. Hence, metacommunications within a family correspond to unconscious metacommunications which may be varied: religious rituals, ethnic codes, father–son, daughter–grandmother relations setting in place metacommunicative messages indicating the sacred, a particular ETHOS, a family style, rivalry, friendship or hostility etc.

Metacommunication systems are akin to ritualization phenomena on the one hand and to CHREODS on the other. On a topological plane, the semantic archetype which characterizes them corresponds to a BIFURCATION catastrophe in which an attractor, A1, degenerates and is captured by an attractor A2. For example: play (attractor A2) takes the place of combat (attractor A1) which is no longer portrayed as such.

(See also ELEMENTARY CATASTROPHES; MESSAGES; MODE-IDENTIFYING SIGNALS; PARACOMMUNICATION SYSTEMS; PLAY; PRAGMATICS OF COMMUNICATION; RESIDUAL RELATIONS; SEMANTICS OF COMMUNICATION; UNCONSCIOUS, THE.)

J.M.

metagovernor A term used by Haley (1963) to refer to the therapist during family therapy when he or she is, or may be, the concealed controller of the family system at a point when a therapeutic development is about to occur. 'If a therapist is going to change the "setting" of a family system, he must become a metagovernor of the system' (Haley, 1963, p. 174).

For Haley, the description of family regulation does not fit with a simple homeostatic systems model, but implies 'two levels of governing process':

(a) the error-activated response by a member if any member exceeds a certain range of behaviour, and
(b) the attempt by family members to be the metagovernor, i.e. the one who sets the limits of that range.

It is at this metagoverning level that the control problem enters the picture because the governing process at this level will manifest itself as a struggle by each family member to be the one who determines the limits of the behavior of the others. An additional complexity is the existence of subsystems within the family which govern one another' (Haley, 1963, p. 160).

The therapist's position is necessarily self-contradictory. He or she must belong and not belong to the family system; he or she must absorb the nature of the conflicts without implying any partisanship. The therapist must behave as if directly involved but separate from being intimate with the family. The therapist becomes an absent–present family member whose actions aim to produce a lasting effect on the family, while having only temporary contact. The more the therapist attempts to influence the family, the more he or she will become included in the system which unleashes resistance to change, 'The interventions of a family therapist are paradoxical in nature and are, in fact, surprisingly similar to the tactics family members use with one another' (Haley, 1963, p. 177). But there is a difference between the behaviour of the therapist and family members: 'The therapist is protective, but he also permits the family to work out problems independently' (p. 178).

Especially with schizophrenic patients and families, the quality of the interchange becomes 'play-like' (pp. 114–15). In such situations, 'it is necessary to persuade or force the patient to respond in such a way that he is consistently indicating what kind of relationship he has with the therapist instead of indicating that what he does is not in response to the therapist' (p. 102).

(See also CHANGE; FEEDBACK; HOMEOSTASIS; METASYSTEMS; MILAN SYSTEMIC THERAPY; STRATEGIC THERAPY; THERAPEUTIC STRATEGIES AND TACTICS.)

J.M. & P.S.

metaphor See ARTIFICIAL CODES; METAPHORICAL OBJECTS; SYMBOLIC REFERENCE.

metaphorical objects, metaphorical language Rhetorical figures or tropes are not simply pure linguistic effects. They take on substance in the genesis of interactions and it is from such interactions that they emerge into the world of language. 'Taking things literally' most often occurs with violence, in delinquent or psychotic acting out.

It happens that family therapists use material or symbolic objects as supports for faltering metaphors. Language itself is capable of being taken as a metaphorical object, offered as such to the family group. These metaphorical objects may be considered as a symbolic and technical emanation of the TRANSITIONAL OBJECTS described by D. W. Winnicott.

METAPHORICAL LANGUAGE

Metaphor is frequently employed in everyday language, as a means of representing reality and the objects around us. We must remember that the metaphor is a rhetorical figure: it is a use of language which consists in a transference of meaning and truth from a concrete term into an abstract context, by analogic substitution. The signification of a metaphor varies as a function of the context and connotations associated with it.

As Bateson (1972, pp. 101–25) points out in his metalogue, 'What is an instinct?', metaphor compares things without stating the comparison: 'When a metaphor is labelled a metaphor, it becomes a comparison.' As his daughter puts it, 'If I say you are like a pig, it's a comparison; and if I say you are a pig, it's a metaphor.' By contrast with the dream, the metaphor puts the emphasis on the concept by masking the relationship of comparison. In dreams, the concept is masked, being figuratively represented by the terms of the comparison, without the identification of the elements that are being associated.

Watzlawick (1978a) stresses how rich the oriental cultures are in similes and metaphors, as is shown by innumerable Russian, Armenian, Jewish, Arabic and, especially, Far Eastern stories. This is a figurative language whose structure is archaic. Erickson (1979) is an important figure in the area of the therapeutic use of metaphor. His teaching provided the basis for many family therapists to learn to use this kind of language (for example, Whitaker; Haley, 1973; see HYPNOSIS). To enable patients to modify their functioning, he offered them metaphors closely related to their symptoms. He never proposed interpretations, but communicated through metaphorical language. Members of families in therapy often employ metaphors to express their emotions or to signify a relational situation.

Symptom as metaphor

The symptom itself may be considered as a metaphor. The patient and the family attempt to reconcile contradictory demands in an equivocal SYMBOL. It seems as if the symptom as metaphor were succeeding in reconciling what is in reality opposed, and that, by crystallizing the opposition, it were fixing that reality.

The symptom often becomes the point at which elements converge which may be very distant from one another. Different situations are superimposed, condensed and express themselves through the same symbol. The symptom may therefore lose its specific determinations. Originally, it bore witness to a determinate form of discomfort, but once it has become a symptom, it expresses itself in all circumstances. Only the personal and family history of the patient will be able to reveal its meaning (Andolfi et al., 1982). Nicolo (1980) describes

this therapeutic procedure as a process of common recodification carried out by the therapist within the family system. He re-binds the broken threads between signifier and signified. The use of metaphorical language mobilizes the family and creates a therapeutic context which opens up possibilities of a mediation between the content of a symbolic language used by the index patient and its understanding by the family.

Various options are open to therapists. They can either use the metaphors expressed by one of the family members, knowing that these have often arisen out of the family culture, or they can suggest a metaphor or picturesque story in order to allow the family to work on this new content. It is a remarkable effect of such use of metaphor in therapy that it amplifies the imaginative and creative potential of the family. Lastly, SCULPTING may be regarded as a form of metaphor belonging to the prelinguistic, posturo-gestural register.

The metaphorical object

By assigning a metaphorical signification to them, the therapist may also use the material objects which seem appropriate for representing the family's behaviour, relations, interactions or rules. This technique, which is chiefly used by the Rome school (Andolfi et al.,

1982) requires an excellent relationship between the therapist and the family members, since it may be experienced as aggressive or felt to be beside the point if it is not proposed in a favourable context.

Starting out from the redundant interactions of the family or the symptoms presented by the index patient, the therapist suggests an object as a means of communication. He or she is thus no longer the centre of attention of the family group: that place is now occupied by the metaphorical object as if it contained some secret that had to be deciphered (Angelo, 1979, in Andolfi et al., 1982). The visual and sensory information relating to that object accentuates the contrast between its literal and symbolic significations and therefore reactivates the symbolic function. An object will be the more effective where it brings to mind certain details of the family situation or certain characteristic features of the index patient, who is trapped by having taken certain key expressions literally in his/her symptoms. It will serve as a lever for modifying the representation the family has of itself and its relations with its various environments.

(See also FAMILIODRAMA; FUNCTION OF THE SYMPTOM; PLAY; PRESCRIPTION; SYMPTOMS; TASKS.)

S.A., P.A. & A.C.

metapsychology   The body of theory elaborated by Freud on the basis of the psychoanalytic treatment of neurotic patients to describe mental activity, the organization of psychical representations and the relations which these maintain for a subject between biological–somatic activity, on the one hand, and family and social relations, on the other. It postulates the existence of a 'psychical apparatus' made up of systems of thought and emotion having their own mode of functioning and articulated to one another.

In Freud's conception, the psychical apparatus presupposes a successful integration on the level of the individual psyche, of family and social hierarchies and their levels of censorship (neurotico–normal structure of the personality). This 'apparatus' presupposes the organization of instinctive and/or 'drive' behaviour into representations. Mental representations have a dual aspect: there is an affective, non-representable part (quantum of affect: *Affektbetrag*) and a cognitive part associated with them (the *Vorstellungsrepräsentanz* or 'ideational representative'). Freud proposes an intersystemic model of the psyche, by distinguishing between several points of view: the economic (quantum of affect), the dynamic (forces in conflict), the topographical (topographical representation) and the genetic (the theory of stages of infantile sexuality).

He constructs two different topographies which are complementary. The first topography describes the processes of thought, the systems which produce and differentiate them (preconscious, unconscious, perception-consciousness) and the relations between these processes and the levels of consciousness. The second topography describes agencies which bring together the biological, psychological and sociological levels of mental representations (id, ego, superego). Lacan (1966) proposed that this conceptual edifice be completed by building a structural model and by enunciating a sort of third topography, which might indeed be called a topography of the subject made up of the categories of the symbolic, the real and the imaginary (the symbolic would in some sense be comparable to the superego, the imaginary with the ego and the real with the id).

The first topography is based on the distinction between the preconscious, unconscious and perception-consciousness systems. A certain quantity of cathexis, 'cathectic energy' starts out from a purposive idea and follows the associative paths this has selected. A distinction must be made between the nature of the discharge of energy in the different systems: this is direct and rapid in the unconscious system (free energy), but delayed and contained where the preconscious system is concerned (bound energy).

The preconscious system is an 'unconscious' in which representations may reach consciousness in the form of *word representations*. Many thoughts abandoned by conscious thought continue their course without attention being focused on them. However, the desire to recall these to consciousness does not encounter any insurmountable obstacle. The preconscious system is based on the secondary processes, whose objective is to arrive at thought-identity. Transfers of energy here concern small quantities: energy is bound. It is structured as a function of the evolution of the perception-consciousness system on the basis of the reality principle (see REALITY). Such a system allows for contradiction between opposing values. It is characterized by the existence of negation and the oppositions/distinctions which ensue from this.

The unconscious system: representations can in no case come into consciousness (Freud, *The interpretation of dreams*). It deals with *thing presentations*. The energy cathecting these representations is termed free energy and this tends toward rapid discharge. It corresponds to the pleasure principle and, on the ontogenetic and phylogenetic levels, precedes the organization of the preconscious system. Associations of ideas are based on the search for identity of perception. These representations may possibly bear on word presentations and therefore use words as things (as in slips, parapraxes, jokes or even schizophrenic breakdown and completely re-cathect the preconscious system of word representations). It is based on the absence of contradiction, the absence of 'no'; the distinction between opposing values does not exist in the unconscious system.

The perception-consciousness system: this system makes it possible to localize the attention on a number of representations at a given single moment. For Freud, the state of consciousness is a transitory, labile state, restricted by the very focused orientation of attention. Furthermore, the unconscious of one person may react to the unconscious of another, bypassing consciousness.

Now, there is here necessarily a second subdivision which Chomsky (1980) has identified. The barring from consciousness may indeed be due to an active – or even hyperactive – censorship. The inaccessibility in that case derives from a particular relation of forces between opposing representations. Other unconscious processes may, however, be inaccessible for structural reasons. There is an analogy here in computing. The applications software which determines the normal functioning of the computer is not accessible, without totally halting any actual use of the computer. Such accessibility is only possible in certain cases, using special procedures, specialized languages and a particular type of programming. In other cases, accessibility is absolutely impossible, since the rules of procedure have been placed in read-only memories (see READ-WRITE MEMORIES). There is thus a change in systemic level to be found here, bringing with it a change in the structural organization of memory systems.

The second topography is based on the distinction between three agencies: the id, the ego and the superego.

The *id* corresponds to the instinctual activities of the personality. It is essentially unconscious (in the sense of the first topography) and is based on the articulation of innate and acquired mechanisms. It is the psyche's energy reserve and it is out of it that the ego and superego are differentiated.

The *superego* corresponds to the structuring of prohibitions and social demands and is fashioned out of experiences of contact with the parental superegos. Though derived from a differentiated part of the id, it constitutes an agency that is antagonistic to that of the id. It is, to a large extent, unconscious and, in part, preconscious. It performs the functions of self-observation, self-criticism, and provides a sense of an ideal and of moral conscience.

The *ego* is the mediating agency which manages the antagonistic and synergistic movements which arise in the id and the superego. It is a factor of psychical binding and corresponds to the defensive polarity of the person (defence mechanisms). It is at once a source of adaptation and a site of synthesis and enticement. It is partly unconscious and partly preconscious.

The *structural topology* of Lacan (1966) offered a new perspective on the organization of the psyche, through the registers of the imaginary, the symbolic and the real.

The *imaginary* is essentially the sphere of activity of the ego. The ego is then conceived as constituting the relation to the image of one's fellow human beings on the basis of the 'mirror stage'. In this perspective, the ego, far from being the 'reasonable' agency of the personality, is what is at stake in the interplay of phenomena relating to illusion and the 'lure', as revealed by the ethology of releasers and IMPRINTING. In this perspective, the DOUBLE BIND corresponds to an escalation of imaginary productions, which can no longer be mediated by the symbolic register.

The *symbolic* is, for Lacan, the register of the signifying chain, the structure of which is provided by language. This represents a reversal of the classic Freudian theory, since, if 'the unconscious is structured like a language, then language is more related to the preconscious of the first topography and the superego of the second topography.

The *real* is irreducible to the symbolic-imaginary anchoring of reality, but is connected to the other two registers in ways described by the topological figure of Borromean knots. It is distinct from reality properly so-called and corresponds to the Freudian id. The Lacanian topography thus leads to a decentring of the psyche from the inside towards the outside. Or rather, Lacanian theories explore the topologically non-orientated zones of mental activity in search of an ontology of the psychical subject in which the inside is conjoined with the outside (Moebius strip, Klein bottle, cross-cap etc., see TANGLED HIERARCHIES).

METAPSYCHOLOGY, METACOMMUNICATIONS, METASYSTEMS

This Lacanian decentring is further extended in the model proposed by Bateson and his school. What in fact happens, they ask, before and beyond psychical processes themselves? Metapsychological description then runs up against what lies beyond the grasp of the psychological level of the organization of mental processes. There is a common structure between ANALOGIC messages and primary processes and between DIGITAL messages and secondary processes, which is clearly identified by Watzlawick et al. (1967). However, the fields explored, the levels of description and the technical means employed are no longer the same. If we accept the distinction suggested by the study of MULTI-LEVEL HIERARCHIES, we are dealing with two abstract models, situated on two distinct strata. One explores the physical and material conditions of the coding and processing of information, together with the consequences of these things on the plane of communication, i.e. the very possibility of structuring representations and affective interactions. The other explores the psychical functioning permitted by the articulation of different types of representations to one another. It presupposes that affects are sufficiently organized, as well as the passage from referent to sign: hence the importance accorded by Freud to the ideational representative of the instinct or, by Lacan, to the signifier. The represented or the signified are either supposed pre-given (Freud) or strictly dependent upon the signifier (Lacan).

There are a great number of unconscious levels (the biological unconscious, the information-processing unconscious) which cannot be grasped by metapsychology. Conversely, this latter explores the space of ontogenesis (the development of the individual) which lies outside the scope of the analysis of phylogenesis (development of the species), on the one hand, and the analysis of communication between man, animal and machine on the other (see CYBERNETICS).

METAPSYCHOLOGY AND CATASTROPHE THEORY

It is one of the virtues of CATASTROPHE THEORY that it has rehabilitated the principle of theoretical research into meaning; the morphology of the signified is not purely dependent upon the order of the signifier. Beneath the appearance of the discontinuities of the system, it is possible, in many cases, to rediscover the trajectories or continuous spaces from which the system has emerged or towards which it is seeking to move. From that point it becomes conceivable to propose a solid foundation which connects together, for example, phonetics and phonology (Petitot-Cocorda, 1985); it also becomes conceivable, however, that we may reconsider metapsychology in the light of Thom's concepts of 'pregnance' and 'salience' (see SYMBOLIC REFERENCE). The affect is a particular form of pregnance, whereas representation is of the order of salience. As Petitot-Cocorda (1985b, p. 219) points out, 'In our opinion, a large part of Freudian metapsychology (conceived as an anthropological ethology) may be interpreted ... as a theory of the way the symbolic relays pregnance and, weighted with "unconscious", interferes with the cognitive.' It does, however, seem difficult to concur with this author when he asserts that there is: 'a correlation between the fact that man is "without instincts" and the fact that he is a speaking being', even if it seems obvious that 'Human "ethology" (sexuality, aggression etc.), far from being an immediate (instinctual) consequence of a distribution of innate pregnant forms, is, by constrast, *subordinated* to the random and individuating course of free pregnance.' There seems no doubt that this goes for the great majority of higher animals. The position of subordination cannot be equivalent to a position of pure and simple disappearance. In Freud's view, at any rate, the affects might be 'reproductions of very early, perhaps even pre-individual, experiences of vital importance' (*Standard Edition*, vol. 20, p. 133). And he adds: 'I should be inclined to regard them as universal, typical and innate hysterical attacks as compared to the recently and individually acquired attacks which occur in hysterical neurosis and whose origin and significance as mnemic symbols have been revealed by analysis. (*Standard Edition*, vol. 20, p. 133).

Metapsychology could derive a new impetus in the light of the processes in play in family therapy. The need would then arise for a combination of several points of view. The object would be, in confronting family and social systems, the interaction between the biological and the symbolic, and interactions between animals, man and machines, to develop meta-models which incorporate metabiological, metapsychological, metafamilial and metasocial data. Hence the importance of METACOMMUNICATION SYSTEMS which may be explored:

- from the genetic or diachronic point of view: see ACTUOGENESIS; FAMILY LIFE-CYCLES; FAMILY ORGANIZERS; MORPHOGENETIC TYPOLOGIES; SHOCK WAVES; TRANSGENERATIONAL MEMORIES etc.
- from the economic point of view: see LEDGER; QUID PRO QUO; TERRITORY.
- from the dynamic point of view: see ATTRACTORS; DYNAMIC SYSTEMS; FORCE FIELDS.
- from the structural, synchronic point of view: MAPS; spatial and temporal BOUNDARIES of the family group conceived as an indissociable entity.

(See also AGONISTIC BEHAVIOUR; ATTACHMENT BEHAVIOUR; INSTINCT; LEARNING; LOVE; PSYCHOANALYSIS; SEXED BEHAVIOUR; UNCONSCIOUS, THE.)

J.M.

metasystems, metasystems of intervention Every general system comprises:

- hierarchical levels regulating movement upwards or downwards;
- horizontal or transverse relations within each level;
- TANGLED HIERARCHIES in which the higher and lower levels regulate each other reciprocally.

A system is therefore at the same time also a metasystem.

Caillé (1985) proposes the term 'metasystem of intervention' to describe the type of action undertaken with a family, a network or an institution.

(See also FAMILY SYSTEMS; GENERAL SYSTEMS THEORY; METACOMMUNICATION SYSTEMS; MODEL OF THE SYSTEMIC MODEL; MULTI-LEVEL HIERARCHIES; PARACOMMUNICATION SYSTEMS; SYSTEMIC MODELLING.)

J.M.

Milan systemic therapy An important development in the therapeutic approach originated in Milan on the original work of Selvini Palazzoli and her colleagues. Since its early days there have been several changes in the group, and the original four workers have subsequently parted, with members following different developments. Significantly, the original workers were psychoanalysts, which led to a particular blend of therapeutic abstinence with regard to directing the client about future behaviour, while also integrating elements of their own forms of indirect directiveness, influenced by a greater emphasis on therapist activity.

Of particular interest is the relationship between the therapist and client, whether individual or family. Haley has written persuasively on this, especially in terms of control and the definition of the therapeutic relationship:

it is of crucial importance that the therapist deal successfully with the question of whether he or the patient is to control what kind of relationship they will have. No form of therapy can avoid this problem, it is central, and in its resolution is the source of therapeutic change. (Haley, 1963, p. 19)

The question of power and control is one which has preoccupied the Milan group and its successors ever since. Haley addresses some of the paradoxes of the therapeutic relationship: 'The crucial aspect of non-directive therapy from the point of view offered here is the fact that the patient cannot gain control of the psychoanalyst's behaviour. If a therapist both directs and denies he is directing, he will be in control of the relationship' (Haley, 1963, p. 71). It is to the therapeutic paradoxes common to all patient–therapist relationships that Haley addresses himself in this early text, and one which is central to an understanding of the developments of the Milan group.

Dissatisfied with the outcome of work with anorexics, Selvini Palazzoli published *Self-starvation* (Selvini Palazzoli, 1974). At this time she and her associates, Prata, Boscolo and Cecchin, immersed themselves in the writing of the MRI group in Palo Alto, emphasizing communications theory (Watzlawick et al., 1967), general systems theory (von Bertalanffy, 1968), the work of Gregory Bateson (Bateson, 1972), and the importance of cybernetic thinking (Wiener, 1948). The revolution in thinking that this represented for the field of therapy should not be underestimated. An interest in interpersonal processes, in patterns of behaviour, in rules of interaction beyond the awareness of the particpants in the 'family dance'; an interest in ritual, myths, the scripts which individuals and families play out in the interests of maintaining some form of familial integrity, and the 'sacrifices' that are performed in the pursuit of this became the *leitmotif* for the group.

In 1980 a seminal paper was published, 'Hypothesizing–circularity–neutrality: three guidelines for the conductor of the session', in which Selvini Palazzoli et al. (1980a) described the formal stance of the therapist wishing to practise within their famework. The third position of neutrality is of particular interest, echoing as it does in many ways the formal stance of the psychoanalytic therapist's apparent neutrality towards the material generated by the patient. The formal activity of hypothesizing proved to be a powerful tool in developing and maintaining a systemic perspective as regards the meaning of the symptom, while the emphasis on circularity guided the therapist to observe the recursive nature of interaction in the room between family members, and between family and therapist.

As often happens with new ideas, there was both scepticism in some quarters, since this challenged the proactive stance of many developments so far in the field, and especially in North America with a more action orientated life-style, and an uncritical adherence to these ideas by early acolytes. The stance encouraged by the Milan associates as they came to be known was rather like that of a scientific investigator who generates a hypothesis which is then rigorously tested, refined, abandoned should a more plausible one emerge, and where the therapist is less concerned about establishing a strong personal connection with the patient than in unravelling the 'dirty games' of the family around the symptom. Of course, if the therapist does not make a strong connection with the patient, change is unlikely to occur. The difficulty arose in the way in which the ideas communicated played down the importance of the therapeutic encounter in preference to emphasizing the power of the conceptual structures on which the ideas stood: 'In truth, *if the method is correct, no charisma whatsoever is needed*' (Selvini Palazzoli et al., 1978, p. 11).

In 1978 the first major text on Milan systemic therapy was published in English, introducing a new model for working with families 'in schizophrenic transaction' (Selvini Palazzoli et al., 1978). The language used is powerful: 'in the moment in which we attempt to formulate a therapeutic intervention, we force ourselves to transcend language, considering what we see in the circularity of its here and now, as the pivot, the nodal point of the momentary equilibrium of the opposing factions' (Selvini Palazzoli et al., 1978, p. 137). This highlights both the interest in circularity, in pattern, in current process, while at the same time the language of power and force, imposed by the therapists on their own thinking, is also used.

Without the advances made by the work of this group, family therapy would not have developed the range it has today. One of the ways in which their thinking also potentially set back the field, however, was in the insistence on the power of the system over the individual. '*The power is only in the rules of the game which cannot be changed by the people involved in it*' (Selvini Palazzoli et al., 1978, p. 6). At the time, the truth of this was seductive, and there remains a sense in which this statement cannot be challenged. The difficulty was that with the enthusiasm of converts,

many therapists would no longer see individuals, or even families if one member was absent. Part of the difficulty stemmed, inevitably as with all new developments in the field of thought, in the followers becoming more orthodox than the originators (Jenkins, 1985). It also potentially encouraged clinicians to avoid addressing issues of violence, gender inequality and abuse (Glaser, 1991).

What this group enabled clinicians to do was to challenge the received shibboleths of psychotherapy, and to have available a range of techniques with a coherent theoretical framework to inform practice. Rather than treating an individual as 'depressed', 'schizophrenic', 'alcoholic', the therapist could begin to think of the patient as 'showing depression' more or less so in different contexts of time and place. The struggle between patient and family, and between therapist and patient/family was redefined in terms of communication patterns, of attempts to define and redefine the nature of relationships, of power, in ways which helped the therapist to become 'meta' to these 'games' and so become less inducted into the same incapacitating processes which the family brought in the first instance to treatment. Goldner has addressed many of these issues in her work in respect of gender, power and violence in relationships and in therapy (see Goldner, 1985, 1988, 1991a,b; Goldner et al., 1990).

There have been many developments by the original group since these early publications. They have described the dynamics of the referral process for example (Selvini Palazzoli et al., 1980b). When the original group split, Boscolo and Cecchin focused more on training, while Selvini Palazzoli has drawn around her different teams at different times. In 1988 she published a useful paper on work with the individual (Selvini Palazzoli and Viaro, 1988), and more recently she has become interested in a much more proactive approach to families with a psychotic member (Selvini Palazzoli et al., 1989), developing further her ideas of 'dirty games'. Gone is the strategic stance of neutrality. The therapist takes a strong position as regards putting parents in charge, often using the 'invariant prescription', similar in many ways to formal structural approaches to therapy (Minuchin, 1974).

The original ideas have been developed in a number of areas. Penn (1982, 1985) developed her thinking around the ways in which questions can be constructed so as to have greatest therapeutic impact. Tomm (1987a, b, 1988) has taken these ideas futher and developed a series of frameworks, emphasizing the power of formulating questions which in different ways introduce new information into the 'system'. Boscolo and Cecchin (Boscolo et al., 1987) describe their more recent ways of thinking and working, and Cecchin has updated his ideas on the original 1980 paper on hypothesizing (Cecchin, 1987). Boscolo (Boscolo and Bertrando, 1992) has described his ideas about time and its reflexive nature between past, present and future, also addressed by Jenkins and Asen (1992) in their paper on systemic work with individuals. Some of the ideas of the time of the system were originally discussed in *Paradox and Counterparadox* (Selvini Palazzoli et al., 1978), but rather in terms of understanding the system's (the family's) particular stage and pacing.

Other writers who have further developed theory and technique from the early ideas of Selvini Palazzoli and her colleagues include Hoffman (1985), who discusses the tensions between an epistemology based on power as in the work of Haley (for example, Haley, 1976, 1980) and Bateson's view that belief in power comes from an incorrect epistemology. Campbell and Draper (1985) bring together practitioners from a variety of settings to describe therapeutic applications different from those first described by the Milan group. Campbell and his colleagues have since developed their own practice in relation to training (Campbell et al., 1988) and to consultation (Campbell et al., 1989). The dilemma of how to address problems of violence and remain within a systemic perspective have been raised by Dell (1989), while Glaser (1991) has discussed some of these issues from a practical perspective in the child abuse field.

The impact of the original Milan systemic model of therapy continues to exert an important influence on the field, especially with current interest in constructionism and narratives in therapy. Its influence will continue to be felt for a long time to come.

(See also ANOREXIA NERVOSA; CIRCULARITY; COMMUNICATION; CYBERNETICS; FAMILY RULES; GENDER; GENERAL SYSTEMS THEORY; MYTH; NEUTRALITY; PARADOXES; RITUALIZATION; SYSTEMIC HYPOTHESIS; VIOLENCE.)

H.J.

mimesis, mimicry   (a) A term referring to the technique employed by a therapist to adapt him or herself to the style of a family and thus to consolidate the therapeutic alliance: for example, joking with a jovial family, beginning the dialogue slowly with a family which expresses itself slowly and gradually (Minuchin, 1974; see also AFFILIATION). Such an attitude is an indispensable condition for establishing contact and for the possibility of creating a reciprocal representation of relations.

(b) Mimesis is, in fact, one of the foundations on which the representation of reality is based in Western culture (Auerbach, 1946). It has been systematically analysed by Girard (1978) in a general theory of mimetic desire and the scapegoating process.

Mimetic desire takes its lead from a model desire. It chooses the same object as the model, abandoning the initial object of its desire. Such a desire is therefore based on a rigorous symmetry between the mimetic partners, leading to paroxystic rivalries which are only regulated by the designation of a scapegoat. In man, mimesis seems to go beyond a criticial threshold which is not normally reached in animals in the expression of their instincts and needs. The explosion of mimetic desire is thought to arise out of multiple 'symbolic remodelling' which leads to the human ability to recognize another as an alter ego. It is in this way that, in the master–disciple relation, a mimetic desire is set in place. Even if the master encourages imitation, he is surprised, as the incarnated model, by the competition to which he is subjected. The more the disciple imitates the master, the more the latter feels betrayed. The disciple then also feels betrayed and humiliated.

Mimetic desire is a desire for appropriation. In converging on the same object, mimetic desires block one another. All mimesis bearing upon desire leads ultimately to conflict. The paradox of a desire of this kind is that it seeks not what resembles it, but what is different, while at the same time investing the same object; now, 'the more desire seeks the different, the more it comes across the same' (Girard, 1978, p. 361). This movement has an essentially contagious aspect. 'If desire is free to settle where it wants, its mimetic nature will almost always drag it into the impasse of the double-bind.' The unchannelled mimetic impulse hurls itself blindly against the obstacle of a competing desire; it invites its own rebuffs and those rebuffs will in turn strengthen the mimetic inclination (Girard, 1972, p. 148).

(See also DOUBLE BIND; IDENTIFICATION; SCAPEGOAT.)

J.M. & P.S.

mimetic desire   See IDENTIFICATION; MIMESIS; 'NOTHING PLUS 10 PER CENT' PARADOX; PARANOIA.

mimicry   See MIMESIS, MIMICRY.

mind   According to Bateson (1972, 1979), mind is immanent and impersonal. Bateson proposes a cybernetic version of the ecology of ideas, while emphasizing its conjunctural and prospective character. This perspective maintains openness towards a renewal of contemporary epistemologies and scientific mythologies.

In *Mind and Nature*, his intellectual testament, Bateson (1979) attempts to describe mind in terms of six criteria. He states:

1   A mind is an aggregate of interacting parts or components.
2   The interaction between parts of mind is triggered by difference, and difference is a non-substantial phenomenon not located in space or time; difference

is related to negentropy and entropy rather than to energy.

3 Mental process requires collateral energy.

4 Mental process requires circular (or more complex) chains of determination.

5 In mental process, the effects of difference are to be regarded as transforms (i.e. coded versions) of events which preceded them.

6 The description and classification of these processes of transformation disclose a hierarchy of logical types immanent in the phenomena. (Bateson, 1979, p. 92)

For Lorenz (1983), the human mind is the product of collective human thinking, made possible by syntactic language and its transgenerational cultural transmission. The psyche, a subjective emotional experience, is much older. We find agreement between Freud and Lorenz on this point. Both recognize the existence of a psyche in the higher animals, akin to the human psyche, and acknowledge that the human psyche is an invariant of humanity. It will be useful to contrast Bateson's theory of mind with that of the mind (*Seele*) and/or psychical apparatus of Freud, on the one hand, and René Thom's theory of symbolic reference, on the other.

Such a description in fact produces the following points of conflict:

1 CATASTROPHE THEORY shows that transformation processes do not necessarily pass through systems of coding, but through breaks in categorial perception, the morphogenetic invariance of which is described in elementary and generalized catastrophes.

2 The limitations of the THEORY OF LOGICAL TYPES have become apparent both in the fields of logic and mathematics (INCOMPLETENESS THEOREMS; SELF-REFERENTIAL CALCULUS) and in the field of psychology (see Bateson's theory of the DOUBLE BIND).

3 A theory of pure mind is in danger of leaving out of its purview the biological underpinnings of the psyche in terms of instincts and/or drives. The family is at the crossroads of this conflict between the individual soul and the supra-individual mind. Freud, Bowen and Lorenz, when they speak of drives, emotional systems or hereditarily coordinated behaviours, are describing phenomena which underlie the mind's activation and/or may possibly pose an obstacle to its development.

4 If the concept of mind is to be a heuristic one, it can only be considered an approximate description of reality and not a definitive reality.

(See also ARTIFICIAL CODES; ELEMENTARY CATASTROPHES; FAMILY PSYCHICAL APPARATUS; METAPSYCHOLOGY; PARADOXES; PARADOXICALITY; SEMANTIC UNIT OF MIND; TOPOLOGICAL SPACE.)

J.M.

miracle questions   See SOLUTION-FOCUSED THERAPY.

misunderstanding   A divergence of interpretation among two or more persons of a message shared between them. Either the same words are employed to refer to different referents or different words are used to refer to a single referent. The appearance of a misunderstanding in an interaction may be interpreted as the effect of a family or social myth. In this respect, it is of the same order as the discovery of a SECRET, a DISCLOSURE of information or the displaying of a nostalgic attitude (unfinished MOURNING).

Jackson has shown that the initial contract which leads to the formation of a couple is based on what he calls a QUID PRO QUO. Each element in the trade-off is set against an equivalent element. The development of the relationship may lead to the initial quid pro quo being transformed into a thorough mix-up. Though one can easily take the view that the outcome of a process of therapy may lead to a clarification of MESSAGES and the facilitation of exchanges between people living together continually, the ideal quest for the dissipation of all misunderstandings doubtless has its origins in a quite other form of MYTH. A positive therapeutic outcome may be achieved when an initial misunderstanding comes to be transformed into a misunderstanding that is more tolerable for all concerned.

(See also CALUMNY; FORGETTING; INTERPRETATION; NOSTALGIA.)

J.M.

mode-identifying signals   The development of COMMUNICATION SYSTEMS has led to the description of systems which denote other communication systems. Laughter, dreaming, humour, threatening, intimidation, sacraments, figures of style, smiling, phantasy and play etc. are so many modes of communication which are differentiated by 'differences making differences' (information) with the status of signals. This differentiation is based on a double biological and cultural development leading to a double homological drift (see ETHOLOGY).

A *friendly* signal is based on derivation from a threatening signal from which one or more features are missing. We see this in the 'triumph ceremonial of the greylag goose'. We may also cite handshaking which 'symbolically' denotes an absence of weapons in the hand. (The refusal of the outstretched hand by schizophrenics shows their avoidance of METACOMMUNICATION SYSTEMS.)

PLAY denotes the absence of a fictive fight (the indicating signals are, here, silent, non-vocalized laughter, the alternation between the positions of attacker and defender, the existence of 'blows' not really delivered).

Threats and intimidation (see AGONISTIC BEHAVIOUR) denote a future risk of aggression. That risk is akin to play to the extent that a fictive behaviour is displayed, but it is distinguished from it by the calculated imminence of its possible actualization.

Display and deception are manifestations elaborated over many years by the higher birds and the mammals. Dramatization is a basic property of affective attachment behaviour and sexual behaviour.

HUMOUR rests, in its explosive aspect, on the destruction/synthesis of a mode of communication, condensing the metaphorical and literal levels of communication.

Appeasement behaviour, based on smiling and welcome signals (see Montagner, 1978), has a particular importance in therapeutic contacts; in pathological cases, there is a whole area of fine tuning in visual contact and the careful establishment of verbal contact, making it possible to avoid clastic explosions.

Bateson greatly stresses the importance of *sacraments* (see SACRED) which, at the other extreme from metaphor, phantasy and dreams, achieve the embodiment or re-embodiment of a symbol, a 'visible sign of an inward and spiritual grace'.

Though the infant's smile is an integral invariant of the attachment relation, such a signal may be simulated to many different ends: advertising, manipulation of friendship, the frigid smile etc. That falsification can be detected from details. It may be unconscious and/or involuntary, be directed towards oneself and/or others (see PSEUDO-HOSTILITY; PSEUDO-MUTUALITY; PSEUDO-SPECIATION; TRUE SELF; for a thorough study of the semiotics of lying, see Ekman, 1985). For a general discussion of posture in mode-identifying signals see Scheflen (1973).

It is one of the characteristics of human beings to juggle continually with the endlessly readjusted, transformed, abolished and recreated hierarchy of the levels of communication denoted by these metacommunicative signals. One observes, in the moments of catastrophic transformation of a family (violent accidents, psychotic catastrophes), sudden modifications in the detection of reality-identifying signals. The nightmare loses its function of alerting the psyche, reality becomes a nightmare, the maddest idea becomes reality, whereas one part of reality is forever out of reach, through the building up of a phantasy of an irremediably lost situation. In these cases, it has not been possible for the preventive function of the PHANTASY (psychical elaboration of the catastrophe) to come into operation.

(See also DOUBLE BIND; REALITY; RESIDUAL RELATIONS; RITUALIZATION; SEMANTICS OF COMMUNICATION; SCHIZOPHRENIAS.)

J.M.

model of the systemic model A clinical construct suggested by Caillé (1985): the model of the model is based on the distinction between the phenomenological and the mythic levels. It corresponds to the family's self-representation model.

As a METASYSTEM of intervention, the *phenomenological level* is based on the gathering of information relating to members of the family, on the nature of the symptom and on the circumstances in which it appears and disappears. The phenomenological level is the sum of the descriptions each person makes of the events as they occur.

The *mythic level* cannot be approached directly; speech acts and verbal comments indicate more by what they conceal than by what they state. The perception of such a model occurs in an intuitive way, on the basis of analogic indices, spatial positions and their possible modifications, and techniques which may at times be used (PRESCRIPTION OF TASKS; SCULPTING; TRIADIC QUESTIONING etc.). The mythic level is the signification or meaning which everyone attributes, directly or indirectly, to what happens.

The phenomenological and mythic levels are the creators of a self-referential process (see FAMILY SELF-REFERENTIALITY), in so far as the perceptions they generate are apt to succeed each other in time, in an oscillatory movement, in such a way that they validate one another. Caillé (1985) takes the view that the advantage of the model of the model is precisely that it prevents our falling into the problem of the incompatibility of models or ending up in a sterile struggle between models (that of the model of the person requesting aid against the therapist's model). The discovery of the model of the model makes it possible to reintroduce its own specificity into the system, thus creating a perturbation which instigates change. The model of the model must, in effect, be understood as information modelled by the therapist, but deriving, both in its content and its form, from the system itself. It perturbs and disturbs by its isomorphism, which does not allow the symmetrical escalation to occur which usually happens in confrontations between rival models.

R.N. & J.M.

morphogenetic fields See FORCE FIELDS, VECTOR FIELDS, MORPHOGENETIC FIELDS.

morphogenetic or structural typologies of the family Minuchin (1974) distinguishes between two opposed polarities in the structuring of family systems: DISENGAGED FAMILIES and ENMESHED FAMILIES. These polarities are dependent on multiple parameters: the quality of boundaries and territories, the nature of inputs and outputs on the material, energy, informational and organizational levels.

QUALITY OF BOUNDARIES

BOUNDARIES, demarcation lines of territories, may be rigid flexible, enmeshed, non-existent or impassable etc. A dysfunctional system may have rigid, impermeable external boundaries and non-existent or totally permeable internal boundaries. The apparent rigidity perceived from outside goes together with the near-total absence of internal rules: beds shared by mother and daughter, father and son, brothers and sisters etc.

QUALITY OF INPUTS–OUTPUTS

Psychotic families, in rigid transaction, are subject to distortions in the structuring of inputs and outputs (systems that are open/closed in respect of exchanges of matter, energy, information or organization).

The *material level* may be understood in its every-day meaning: the conditions of socioeconomic life, the ability to meet material needs and to create wealth varies greatly from one family to another. Some families seem completely reliant on assistance, all the adult members being unable to work and meet their needs (external economic problems, internal problems of collapse of identity); one finds such situations both in disengaged families with children in care and in enmeshed families with one or more psychotic or psychosomatic patients.

The *energy level* relates to the ability of the family system to give each of its members a sufficient potential for action. The birth of a child places considerable energy demands on the mother (postpartum depression). In time of crisis, energy tends to be liberated and to invest itself in new directions. In the face of the anxiety relating to the expression of the crisis, it often happens that the redeployment of energy is contained or blocked, preventing the system from evolving towards new equilibria. Psychotic (and, more generally, all seriously ill) patients are confronted with blocked situations in which conflicts bring about energy diminution of such a kind that the slightest attempt at activity ends in almost immediate exhaustion (the most obvious symptoms are refusal to attend school, apragmatism, tiredness) and/or the depressive decompensation of one or more family members.

The *informational level* reveals the quantitative and qualitative nature of the transmission of information. Some families are completely closed to any internal or external information. Internally, it can be observed that children and parents have no sense of where they stand in the genealogical line. Alternatively, they may know this intellectually, but the nature of transgenerational emotional ruptures is such that the mere uttering of the knowledge brings them a considerable degree of affective suffering and threatens to blow the family system apart. Externally, there is then a refusal of all change arising from external developments. The cost of ACCULTURATION being too great to bear, some families remain fixed in codes of communication, modes of thought and ways of expressing feelings which date back several generations.

Other families, by contrast, only exist through an attitude of openness to the outside world, through friends and other family groups, a tendency to adopt foreign children etc. This openness may enable them to regulate internal tensions by functional triangulations. It may, however, be the case that such an attitude has to do with the misrecognition or avoidance of a more serious internal dysfunction, as a result of the disqualification of the family of origin of one – or both – of the partners. Marital conflicts are sometimes fuelled by differences of ETHOS within the families of origin with regard to this.

The *organizational level* relates to the degree of complication or complexity of systems, the articulation of natural functionings and artificial simulations, the nature of the media employed:

- levels of autonomy and heteronomy of family systems and sub-systems;
- internal coherence–external coherence and the way these are balanced out;
- nature of the coalitions (absence/presence of dyadic coalitions, normal and pathological triangulations);
- structuring of communications (secrets, disclosure, disinformation, confusions etc.).

(See also FAMILY SELF-REFERENTIALITY.)

J.M.

mourning, depression, mania, melancholia Mourning is a psychological process, both conscious and unconscious, triggered off by the loss of an object of attachment (see ATTACHMENT BEHAVIOUR). It is accompanied by a sense of affliction and is a kind of psychosomatic 'healing of the wound' connected to the process of detachment. It corresponds to the emotional working through which occurs when one loses someone one loves (the breaking of the bond established by attachment behaviour). Depressive disorders most particularly necessitate the combination of apparently contradictory logics and polyaxial strategies (Widlöcher, 1983). Mania and melancholia correspond to disorders in the regulation of the thymus, far from the limits of the equilibrium state.

MOURNING, DEPRESSION, MELANCHOLIA

Freud (1915) suggested that a relatively clear distinction should be drawn between mourning and melancholia.

In mourning, reality testing shows that the object no longer exists; it is a conscious loss. However, whereas in mourning, it is the world which seems impoverished, in melancholia, it is the ego that is impoverished. There is a loss of the sense of self-esteem which is not usually found in normal mourning. In melancholia, too, the object is lost as an unconscious love object. The wound is open, and the melancholic begins to treat him or herself as the lost object which is to be suppressed. On a metapsychological plane, melancholia thus marks the unconscious loss of the love object; as for mania, this could be seen as the triumph of the ego in the face of this misrecognized unconscious loss.

A great number of psychoanalytic works have taken this inaugural study as their starting point, either to accentuate the distinctions made there or to suggest that mourning and melancholia lie on a single continuum; pathological mourning might then be seen as the exaggeration of a normal process (Bowlby, 1980).

Bowlby (1980) distinguishes between four phases of mourning, which are found, with variants, in children and in adults:

- phase of numbing, distress and anger;
- phase of yearning and search for the lost figure (moments of disbelieving the loss);
- phase of disorganization and despair;
- phase of greater or lesser degree of reorganization.

These four phases manifestly have phylogenetic foundations, since Lorenz (1935–54) and van Lawick-Goodall (1970) describe similar reactions in greylag geese and chimpanzees. The formation and destruction of bonds have in fact common biological finalities in a great number of species, the study of which reveals analogical and homological similarities (phenomenon of convergent adaptation, see ETHOLOGY). The mourning reaction is a psychosomatic reaction of healing over-restoration of attachment behaviour.

The mourning reaction is usually accompanied by a deep sense of affliction, by sadness and tears, though these may be inhibited to a greater or lesser degree. It takes several years for such a reaction to wear off. The periodic reappearance of the pain is common, and is triggered off by the least reminder of the lost person.

In the case of the mourning of a child suffering from a mortal illness, mourning begins at the point when the doctors announce that the outcome will be fatal. It has an anticipatory character, but usually sets in place attitudes of disbelief and desperate attempts to alter the outcome. The loss of a child produces considerable disturbances, both in each parent and at the level of conjugal and family relations. It is not rare for the marriage to collapse and depressive or psychosomatic decompensations by one or other of the partners are frequent. The mourning ordeal of each of the partners then falls out of synchronization. This is particularly clear-cut when one of the two reacts with manic defence. It then becomes advisable for the couple to receive therapy, allowing each partner to develop his or her own way of going through the process of mourning and/or depression while avoiding either of the partners taking the other's attitude as a form of misrecognition or rejection of the painful situation. Bowlby shows that there are numerous common features between the mourning connected with the loss of a spouse and that connected with the loss of a child. The aftermaths of the two are, however, very different. Spouse to spouse, sibling to sibling, parent to child and child to parent bonds (to which we also have to add the many subtypes due to sex differences) represent different types of affectional bond. Reactions to loss, whether of object or of function, have been reviewed by Jenkins (1986).

DEPRESSION AND MANIC-DEPRESSIVE PSYCHOSIS

The breaking of affectional bonds may be the product of a breakdown of internal or external circuits, or both. A so-called 'reactional' depression, the onset of which can be understood in psychological terms, is not without its biological, psychosomatic effects in the depressed person. Conversely, a so-called 'endogenous' depression, which is related to a dysfunctioning of internal mood regulation, comes into resonance with the family and social contexts and produces specific structures of communication.

For Widlöcher and his school (1983), the array of actions at work in depression reveals a general slowing down of behaviours, whether these have to do with ideational, verbal or motor activity. The melancholic freezes up, 'plays dead'. The slowing up involved in depression thus appears as a response with its own intentionality and adaptive purpose.

One can only make sense of a large part of that intentionality by understanding family interactions. The family approach then provides an indispensable therapeutic context to the establishment of a coherent drug therapy (Seghers, 1982, 1984). There is even a paradox here. The more prevalent the endogenous factor, the more the external contexts and the sociofamilial environment must be studied if the circumstances of its emergence and the dynamic of the disorder are to become intelligible. The shock waves, which radiate out from the triggering event, may affect various members, of the family, who may possibly be distant from one another, and this effect may only occur several months or years later. These triggering factors which it would be incorrect to term the psychological 'cause' of the melancholia, may be a marriage, a death or becoming unemployed etc.

MANIC-DEPRESSIVE FAMILIES

Manic-depressive families are most often of above average socioeconomic status (Bolton Finley and

Wilson, 1951). Such families suffer great collective pain when one of their number undergoes an acute manic-depressive episode. They are confronted with an intense narcissistic wound and with emotions of anguish, guilt and shame. They become embroiled in the concealment of transgenerational secrets concerning suicides and episodes which have afflicted one or more of their forebears (Seghers, 1982, 1984).

Some individuals in the family are particularly idealized and placed on a pedestal. Such families are subject to intense and extreme emotions which are of the order of emotional HUBRIS. When a patient is hospitalized, the members of the family make their presence felt very strongly and are highly committed emotionally to the problem. The therapists run the risk of being 'muzzled' by secrets and caught in METABINDINGS if the family is not apprehended as an entity which is worthy of hearing and respect. It is all the more tempting to disqualify the index patient in so far as he or she is mute, prostrate and caught up in the inertia of the slowing-down process. Delirious self-accusation does, however, fulfil a function of attraction, cohesion and cementing of the whole group. The various family actors are trapped in positions of heroism and boundless devotion, in positions of martyrdom, guaranteeing that separation will be impossible (Seghers, 1982, 1984). In fact, difficulties in adequate separation and individuation are made impossible and become transmitted from generation to generation. Bolton Finlay and Wilson (1951) point out the existence of a dominant (matriarchal or patriarchal) figure who maintains sustained pressure on the entire group in such a way that children, who may be adults, are controlled by invisible family forces and inhibited in their individual initiatives (Byng-Hall, 1973). The weakest members of the group feel guilty about the deeply hostile feelings which keep them, despite themselves, impotently in their positions.

From a therapeutic point of view, the combination of drug therapy and a family therapy approach on the basis of hospitalization, has a structuring function so long as the responsibilities of the various interventions are clearly distributed (Seghers, 1982, 1984). Bowlby (1980) stresses the immense value for a person in mourning to have someone available who can provide emotional support. The narcissistic restoration of the functions of the various family members may assist them in this task, by enabling them to divest themselves of their defensive counter-attitudes. Such families evolve by qualitative leaps, in a stage-by-stage development, and display a considerable capacity for readjustment and reorganization.

IMPOSSIBLE MOURNING, RELATIONS OF ABSENCE OF ABSENCE

The existence of impossible mourning may be observed when there is a pathology of the forming of relationships or within the existing web of relationships, which is particularly the case in families with psychotic transactions; this pathology may be interpreted as linked to the establishment of relations of absence of absence (see RESIDUAL RELATIONS; Miermont, 1986a).

Thus the existence of paradoxical relations will be noted, these being linked to the multiplication of gaps/lacunae in affective relations over several generations. One then finds a de-activation of emotive systems and the existence of schizoid positions, leading to transgenerational breaks which are very difficult to deal with clinically, and which go together with all the paradoxes of 'non (non (communication))' and DOUBLE BINDS.

(See also GENETICS AND THE FAMILY; GENETICS AND PSYCHOPATHOLOGICAL HEREDITY; LOSS AND GRIEF.)

J.M. & P.G.

multi-channel communication systems   In mammals, the sense organs become organs for the transmission of messages about relationship (Bateson, 1972). This metacommunication will be called the μ-function of messages. The shape of the eyes or mouth, the coloration of the facial skin, the movements of the 'tactile' body (respiration, tone of voice, posture) become messages indicating the contexts of a relationship.

The interconnection of the various sensory and motor channels produces an equivalence class which structures the experience of the four dimensions of space–time starting out from the parental imagos. These imagos are constructed by the integration of tactile, olfactory, gustatory, acoustic, visual and coenaesthetic experiences. The intersensory analysis of multi-channel communication systems has been proposed in France by Corraze (1980) and Cosnier (Cosnier et al., 1982; Cosnier and Brossard, 1984).

Saint Augustine (quoted by Todorov, 1977) classified signs according to various different criteria: mode of transmission, origin and usage, social status, the nature of the symbolic relation and the nature of the designatum, in particular whether it was a sign or a thing. So far as the mode of transmission is concerned, one fundamental feature is occulted, the effects of which still continue to be felt in the majority of semiotic studies: 'Among the signs by means of which men express their meanings to one another, some pertain to the sense of sight, more to the sense of hearing, and very few to the other senses' (Aristotle, quoted in Todorov, 1977, p. 45). Such a prior supposition has led to a very disembodied view of transmission, setting up at the outset an opposition in which the referent is essentially verbal.

THE FOUNDING DIMENSION OF TOUCH

The description Aristotle gives of the psyche (*De anima*) has not been bettered in this regard. In his study of the various senses and animal survival, Aristotle comments that no non-stationary body possesses a soul without being endowed with perception: 'If, then, it is to have perception, the body must be either simple or mixed. Simple it cannot be, as it would then lack touch, which it must have . . .' (Aristotle, para. 434b, 1986 edn, p. 218). The preservation of animals is, in effect, strictly dependent on touch, which enables the animal to flee dangerous contacts and to approach the contacts needed for life. Only tactile sensation and taste, which is derived from it, enable the animal to flee certain animals, to be in contact with other animals and to feed on 'what nourishes', 'a tangible body'. 'This makes it clear that it is the deprivation of this sense (touch) alone that leads to death in animals. Just as it is impossible for anything that is not an animal to have this sense, so there is no other sense that something must have to be an animal except this one' (para. 435b, 1986 edn, p. 220). The other senses which permit of perception 'at a remove' only become vital ones in the animals 'that travel' (Aristotle, para. 434b, 1986 edn, p. 219). We can understand, then, why touch comes to the fore in all communication with the very gravely ill or seriously handicapped. In such relationships, words and looks come with difficulty and only appear as something secondary to the relationship. It is the care given to the body which gives the words and things exchanged their authenticity. In the medical model, in which symptomatology is a basic discipline, one observes how often inhibitions or phobias attach to techniques of physical observation (such as palpation, sounding by percussion, or mobilization). Now, auscultation and visual perception are also indicative modes of communication, which can be put into words. They are, however, also modes involving the coming together of two bodies, in which effects of contiguity remain very much present, and are thus poles apart from purely digital communication.

In their exploration of infantile psychosexual stages, Freud (1910–24), Abraham (1916, 1925) and Klein (1921–45) discovered the phantasmatic simulations which may be very elaborate and occur at a very early stage, underlying the learning of metacommunication. The dimension of touch is focused on the *representation* of the (oral, anal and phallic) erogenous zones. These are the zones of the body which ensure the contiguity between inner and outer bodies. Aristotle, too, stressed that, in the dissolute individual, touch was directed not towards the whole of the body, but to certain of its parts, relating to food, drink and erotic pleasures.

The newborn baby's first contact, upon leaving the mother's womb, is by skin contact. Skin contact is thus the first form of possible connection in interpersonal relations. It will later make possible the stabilization of the co-localization of the protagonists in rituals of approach and contact (handshakes, embraces, the various forms of kissing, with affectionate, friendly or sexual connotations); rituals of intra-family welcome and departure, for example, which connect with the various forms of the ritualization of the absence of aggression and therefore of the establishment, for example, of familiar, familial, friendly, sexual or love relations.

Ethologists have studied the rough games played by children and even between children and animals. And what parents are not familiar with tickling games with their children or 'incy-wincy spider' etc.? Several levels of distanciation – or even complete breaking-off of contact – do, however, exist. We shall here recall the 'clinging instinct' extensively studied by Hermann (1943) and its human viscissitudes ('the grasp-loosing catastrophe'). Similarly, Freud's 'Fort-Da' game (the toy thrown away and then pulled back by the child) is already a very highly elaborate symbolic expression of separation: a to-ing and fro-ing between material contact and separation and the integration of psychical contact. The sense of modesty or decency seems to be a reaction which varies greatly between different cultural codes. There thus exist close connections of a tactile–visual–muscular coenaesthesia type and connections at a distance of the olfactory–acoustic–visual type.

Even in relations at a distance, like hearing and sight, the receptive person is 'touched' by 'pregnant' messages. Marshall McLuhan (1964) greatly stressed the tactile aspect of many media, such as television, for example. At what level does this contact function? What is its biological or phylogenetic basis? Thom (1989, p. 50; 1990b, p. 57) emphasizes that there are two types of communication, by contact (contiguity) and by similarity. In his view, the psychical functions exfoliate out from relations of contiguity. Psychical contact becomes the basis of all relationship. Whether one is speaking of pre-linguistic or linguistic communication, they are based on foundations of *position and co-localization*. The psychism is the organ which makes it possible to superimpose stratifications of contact in the absence of real, material, body-to-body contact. The other sense organs – of smell, taste, hearing and sight – are themselves based on processes of physical closeness.

In other words, phonetic letters and figures are like cast-off bodily extensions which have fragmented and detribalized man. Numbers are an extension of our most intimate and interrelating activity, the sense of touch (McLuhan, 1964, p. 118). Where writing functions as an acoustic abstraction of sight, number presupposes a visual abstraction of touch. 'Perhaps *touch* is not just skin contact with *things*, but the very life of things in the *mind*' (McLuhan, 1964, p. 119).

Taste

Taste is a form of communication which is so self-evident that it seems not to exist as such. The infant does not take long to make the distinction between sweet milk and foods he or she dislikes. As with the sense of smell, taste intervenes in the most radical way to define what is familiar and good and differentiate it from what is strange, bad or dangerous. Food choices connect with the variously 'civilized' forms of predation (from cannibalism to symbolic predation). These form the substance of intrafamilial culinary rituals which differentiate cultures from one another.

Conflicts of eating behaviour bring about considerable modifications in the structure of communication. Feeding rituals may thus lead to genuine 'conflicts of rituals' of which certain eating phobias are the expression. Similarly, there exists an ethology of the alcoholic, anorectic, bulimic or heroin-addicted person. That ethology is indissociable from communication with the life and survival ecosystem (families, institutions etc.).

SMELL

The human sense of smell determines *olfactory spheres*, the meaning of which varies between cultures. There are extremely early and reciprocal olfactory imprintings between mothers and their babies and also between the various members of a single family. These 'involuntary' secretions are a first form of recognition, the unconscious character of which is such that it is practically impossible to describe in what respect the smell of one person can be distinguished from another. Our verbal representations are practically impotent to describe the configuration of these hormonal forms of communication. The inability to put this into words does not, however, eliminate the intuitive recognition of the odour of close and familiar persons.

A great proportion of olfactory communication is, however, artificially prescribed by culture. Depending on the culture and the individual, spontaneous odours will either be accepted or masked by 'deodorants'. Perfumes are simultaneously 'supra-normal lures' in the ethological sense and highly elaborated and metaphorized signals which play a role in forming cultural and personal identity. The olfactory spheres play a part in the working out of interpersonal distances. Olfactory communication is also, to a large extent, used in the development of metaphor. In French, for example, one either can or cannot *'sentir'* [stand (the smell of)] someone. The processes of incorporation–introjection mean that the good and the bad object refer directly to the question of smell and taste.

AUDITORY AND VISUAL COMMUNICATION

Auditory and visual communication is at the forefront of human communication, to the point that part – and doubtless an important part – of tactile, gustatory and olfactory communication has been 'transported' or transmuted into the acoustic or scopic spheres. The very importance of this area of communication means

that we really ought to examine it at length here (see GAZE; SPEECH ACTS).

The spoken word is obviously a fundamental medium of the human species, one of its chief characteristics (though not the only one). Human language probably came about as a result of the prolonged interaction between the mother and her child. But there are pre-linguistic, para-linguistic, musical and pictorial acoustic transmissions which may be structured in a manner completely contrary to the structures of the verbal apparatus. Moreover, the acousticoscopic synthesis of language (the *'langue'*–*'parole'* opposition, and that between verbal and written transmission) is relatively recent in human history and not universal. As McLuhan (1962, p. 620) points out, 'The world of the Greeks illustrates why visual appearances cannot interest a people before the interiorization of alphabetic technology.' The tribal world might be said to be essentially acoustico-tactile; Greek geometry and art can be seen as being based on muscular–tactile intuitions of reality. Now, the separation of the visual and the tactile cannot occur purely and simply through the fact of handwriting. It required the massive and stereotyped intervention of written characters that were uniform and repeated.

INTERSENSORY STRUCTURING

Territoriality and intersensory programming
The comparative study of cultures (Hall, 1966, 1968) reveals the existence of an unconscious perceptual matrix specific to each cultural group. The sensory world of an American is not that of a Frenchman or an Arab. Each culture reacts differently to smells, maintains eye contact in a particular way and lays down different norms for what interpersonal distances are to be or how one listens to an interlocutor. The interconnection of channels of perception and emission creates a veritable 'territorial apparatus', the characteristics of which are acquired by the child through contact with his or her family system. Personal, family and social TERRITORIES are thus structured in a totally non-conscious manner and affect the definition of social reality.

Importance of media in structuring multi-channel systems
McLuhan has successfully demonstrated the extent to which the medium also determines the structure of multi-channel interchanges: the voice, the written word, the telephone, the television, the telegram, newspapers, letters, books and festivals are messages in themselves, independently of their content. Similarly, the media used in therapy determine the nature and meaning of the process set in train. A verbal interpretation is not the same in nature as a prescription by letter, or an unguarded remark behind the one-way mirror or a family interview in a doctor's consulting room in a hospital.

(See also DEIXIS; DISTANCE AND ORGANIZATION OF TERRITORY; MAPS; PERFORMATIVES; REALITY; SHIFTERS; VIDEO.)

J.M.

multi-directional partiality The term Boszormenyi-Nagy and Spark (1973) apply to the therapist's ability to adopt the position of each of the family members and even that of an absent member. The therapist is neither a neutral umpire, nor someone who stands 'above the fray'. He or she actively takes the side, during the therapy, of each of the family members, being guided in that task by his or her empathy and sense of fairness. This implies that he or she gives each person the sense of being someone important, someone who counts and whose desires he or she is trying to understand, while at the same time letting each person know that he or she is trying to support everyone in the family. Such a concept may be compared and contrasted with the concepts of NEUTRALITY and 'siding' with.

For Boszormenyi-Nagy, the therapist must plead the case of each of the members of the family in turn, both of the nuclear and the extended family, including deceased members. He must therefore show partiality, but must do so with everyone, both avoiding an attitude of 'benevolent neutrality' and refusing to join any pre-existing coalitions. This multi-directional partiality is the precondition for restoring mutual trust within the family and for maintaining the credibility of the therapist, both of which are necessary if a therapeutic process is to be engaged. An attitude of this kind is, therefore, different from the models proposed by Minuchin (1974) and Selvini Palazzoli et al. (1980a).

(See also AFFILIATION; ALIENATION; TRANSFERENCE.)

P.S. & A.L.

multi-generational transmission See DIFFERENTIATION OF SELF; RITUALIZATION; TRANSGENERATIONAL MEMORIES.

multi-laterality For Boszormenyi-Nagy and Spark (1973), assessment of the balance of the LEDGER must be based on multi-lateral criteria, i.e. in the appreciation, in terms of debts and MERITS, of the whole set of significant relations for each of the members of the family. Therapy must therefore take into account all the family members who may potentially be affected by it and the possibility of including them in the sessions must be foreseen in the initial contract.

(See also MULTI-DIRECTIONAL PARTIALITY.)

A.L.

multi-level hierarchies One of the basic properties of complex general systems, extensively studied by Mesarovic et al. (1970). These writers propose a distinction between several types of hierarchical level:

- level of description and abstraction: stratified hierarchies (modelling);
- level of complexity of decision-making: multi-layer hierarchies (intervention);
- level of organization: multi-echelon hierarchies (organization).

From this there follows a general theory of the coordination of these three basic systemic levels: modelling, intervention and organization.

The human mind, the family system and social micro- and macro-organizations have a hierarchical internal structure and are themselves hierarchically ordered; the family system, which is apparently at an intermediate hierarchical level between the individual and the collectivity, is the compulsory crossing point between the two; the nature of family interactions determines the positions an individual will take up within the social hierarchies (see FAMILY ETHOLOGY).

Certain entities, individual personalities, family groups or social structures are borderline entities which afford the possibility of movement from one level of the hierarchy to another.

IMPORTANCE OF HIERARCHICAL SYSTEMS

Organizations which function on a purely symmetrical or egalitarian basis very soon end up in exhausting conflicts, if not indeed inevitable explosions. The most visible signs of this on the organizational level are the appearance of SCAPEGOATS, of heroes set on a pedestal, or internal and external exclusions. Hierarchies afford the possibility of operational economy in the division of tasks, a diversification of decision-making processes, through a more or less nuanced RITUALIZATION, arrived at by mutual consent, between the dominant and the dominated. As ethological studies show (Rushen, 1982), the dominant–dominated couple is not strictly dyadic, but is based on triangulations and coalitions. The dominated position is not purely negative, but leads to the organization of diversified TERRITORIES. This shows how necessary it is not to reduce hierarchies to the level of power alone, as Louis Dumont has pointed out on the macro-social plane (see below).

Thus, in view of the conceptual difficulty of apprehending general multi-level hierarchical systems, it seems necessary to specify several basic types of hierarchy. The urgent need to do so is felt in clinical practice and therapy, if one takes into account:

- the levels of modelling: psychopharmological, psychoanalytic and holistic;

- the levels of intervention: chemotherapeutic, psychotherapeutic, family-therapeutic, sociotherapeutic and psycho-pedagogical;
- the levels of organization: between modelling and intervention, between therapeutic techniques and between established realities and open processes.

Theory of logical types or theory of categories?

It has proved impossible, by means of the THEORY OF LOGICAL TYPES, to model:

- the concrete and specific differentiation between types of hierarchy;
- the existence of elements affording a connection between different levels;
- the structure of the transitional zones between levels.

It is possible to formalize evolutive hierarchical systems on the basis of the *mathematical theory of categories* (Ehresmann and Vanbremeersch, 1986). If we have a system defined by elements and by the relations uniting those elements, that system will be represented by a category whose objects model the components and whose 'arrows' model the relations between them.

We may then define a hierarchical system as a category whose objects are dividied into several levels 0, 1, 2, ... p of increasing complexity, such that each object of level n is a *limit object* of a system of connected objects of level $n - 1$. A limit object is thus an object which possesses the properties of level $n - 1$, but which represents objects of level $n - 1$ at level n.

Theory of multi-level hierarchical systems

Mesarovic et al. (1970) propose a distinction between three interconnected hierarchical levels:

Stratified hierarchies: description and abstraction: systemic modelling
In an enterprise transforming products, Mesarovic et al. (1970) distinguish between three strata: the stratum of the physical process of transformation of material and energy into finished products; the stratum of information processing and control, and the stratum of the general economics of the enterprise. Similarly, a computer can be represented, on a descriptive plane, on a two-strata basis: physical operation (interrelation of the components which make up the hardware) and strata of mathematical operations (the programming which makes up the software). Similarly, a higher living organism can be represented in terms of three strata:

1 *Biological*: this stratum gives rise to the basic embryological distinction: endoderm, mesoderm, ectoderm. The interaction between these thin layers leads to the hierarchization of cellular, tissue

and organic levels; the systemic ordering of the embryological layers thus organizes the great vital functions: of morphological coherence, metabolic and anabolic–catabolic exchanges, and immunological differentiation. Confusions of logical levels could be at work in disorders of regulation (see SYSTEMIC MODELLING OF CARCINOGENESIS).

2 *The stratum of mental functioning*: this level manages the hierarchies of representation (representations of representations), memory storage, modalities of access to the various levels of memory, on the basis of the primary and secondary processes.

3 *The stratum of membership of groups*: 'individuals' are defined on the basis of the groups of which they are members: family units, social units which are themselves defined by distinction with neighbouring groups in the ecosystem.

Multi-layer hierarchies: levels of complexity of decision-making: systemic intervention
Mesarovic et al. (1970) remind us of the fundamental dilemma involved in any decision process: when the decision time comes, the making and implementation of a decision cannot be postponed. A postponement itself constitutes a decision. If it is impossible to grasp all the parameters of a situation, the thinking process has to be prolonged and further information sought out.

Multi-layer hierarchies correspond to algorithmic and heuristic procedures. Within decision-making, we may thus distinguish between the self-organizing hierarchies layer, the learning and adaptation hierarchies layer and the selection hierarchies layer.

Systems of human behaviour are, typically, multi-layer systems:

1 Autonomous oscillatory centres providing impulses towards action (instinct), towards representation (desire) and towards symbolization (social inscription).

2 Levels of activation of representations held in memory; the stratum of mental functioning is multi-layer. Freud identified the hierarchical structure of mnemic representations in the hysteric: this produced the description of the unconscious, preconscious and perception-consciousness systems, on the one hand, and the agencies of the id, the ego and the superego on the other. Defence mechanisms (repression, isolation, denegation, denial, projection etc.) ensure a hierarchization in the evocation of memories, and in acting out, if not indeed the appearance of acting out. It has proved possible to illuminate these latter by the theory of stages of infantile sexuality and the organization of the concomitant characterial strategies. One of the functions of the psychoanalytic cure is to rearrange the hierarchical relations between these agencies: '*Wo*

Es war, soll Ich werden' (Where id was, there ego shall be).

3 The complexity of the decision-making is a crucial problem in the case of behavioural disorders: there are several levels on which urgent action may be required, including the organic (risk to life), psychical (loss of self-identity), familial (collective suffering, with interpersonal threat to life) and social (danger posed by certain persons or families, threatening the identity of broader social units). Decisional conflicts ensue between several levels of organization. In the face of an organic danger, which persons in the family or the society are best suited to decide on the right option? Or when confronted with a threat to the family, the 'sacrifice' of which person would be the most economical solution to ensure the survival of all? When faced with a sacrifice of this kind, what will be the level of maximum solidarity which makes it possible to get beyond the sacrificial position?

Multi-echelon hierarchies: levels of organization: systemic organization

Systems are made up of sets of interacting sub-systems. Some of these sub-systems have decision-making functions. The decision-making units are arranged hierarchically, so that some of them are influenced and controlled by others (Mesarovic et al., 1970, p. 49). As these authors point out,

> it should be stressed again that there is no one-to-one correspondence between strata, echelons and layers. Tasks for more than one echelon can be defined by using the model from the same stratum, while the decision problem on a given layer can be distributed through several echelons; furthermore the task for an echelon can contain elements of the problems from more than one decision layer. (Mesarovic et al. 1970, p. 52)

Now, when faced with a complex symptomatology, the systems to be apprehended are multi-echelon systems. Modelling these systems presupposes several strata and the procedures of integration/decision-making are based on several layers. To take one example, Freudian metapsychology is thus a theory situated on a stratum, but made up of multi-layer hierarchies (the different topographies) on the basis of what is initially a single-echelon analysis (the classic individual psychoanalytic cure). Extrapolations to family, group and ethnic echelons have been made subsequently. The level of organization is most often left out of account in family therapy: how are we to conceive the articulation between modelling and intervention, between psychoanalysis and a holistic approach, between chemotherapy and psychotherapy, between institutional levels, with a view to achieving certain goals? The question remains, to a great extent, an open one.

THE FAMILY SYSTEM

The FAMILY SYSTEM is a multi-level hierarchical system if one takes into account:

- *the family strata*: biological levels of bonding, reproduction and differentiation; symbolic and mythic levels;
- *the family layers*: FAMILY SELF-REFERENTIALITY; adaptive transformation (care, protection, upbringing); deciding of cultural, spiritual and religious orientations;
- *the family echelons*: the family organization is structured on the basis of the difference between the sexes and the generations and differences of age. Authority relations are organized on the basis of the distinctive positions, which are variable across the different anthropological systems of kinship, occupied by parents, grandparents, children, men–women, father–mother, brothers–sisters etc.

The family system thus enables the individual to become differentiated and to move out into the wider society. It makes it possible to divide up tasks in terms of FAMILY ROLES and SOCIAL STATUSES, both as these are ideally represented and as they are embodied in concrete persons. The grandparents have a fundamental role to play here in the development of alliances between the families of origin and in the possible cohesion – or destruction – of the marital and parental couple.

FORMS OF SOCIAL ORGANIZATION

Dumont (1966) has proposed a distinction in SOCIAL ORGANIZATION between (a) societies which make a show of hierarchy and play down equality and the politico-economic field (caste system in India); these lead to the creation of a 'collective man', a society-man; and (b) societies which emphasize equality and the politico-economic field and play down hierarchy (the Western system); these lead to the creation of an 'individual man'. It is the virtue of such an analysis that it shows that hierarchical systems are not necessarily bound to power, but that they may give rise to a disjunction between status and power (this may be seen as similar to the distinction made above between strata and echelons).

Hierarchies within micro-organizations and those within macro-organizations probably do not function in an identical way. However, whether we are speaking of the army, medicine, the church, business enterprises or the state, we cannot deny the presence of hierarchical echelons in the organization of inter-human relations, some of which seem invariant, if not indeed universal (see Handy, 1985).

FAMILIAL AND SOCIAL CREATION OF THE PERSON

Family and social systems are also hierarchically related one to another; these hierarchies are TANGLED ones, the nature of the entanglements evolving as a function of the unfolding of FAMILY LIFE-CYCLES. Each systemic unit possesses its own hierarchical structure which is distinct from the structure of the other levels. Social hierarchies cannot be reduced either to the structuring of the individual psyche or to the organization of family systems. But every unit under consideration can, up to a certain point, 'simulate' the hierarchical functioning of the other levels and this is a precondition for passing from one system to another. Pathology may possibly signify limits to the functions by which one level simulates another.

It might be postulated that a system reveals itself to be 'totalitarian', 'rigid' or 'closed' when its organization becomes essentially mono-hierarchical. Once an organization gains in COMPLEXITY, it is led to diversify the quantity and quality of its forms of hierarchical precedence, as well as to build up cross-connections.

(See also COALITION; COMMUNAL INDIVIDUALS; FAMILY PSYCHICAL APPARATUS; GAME THEORY; GENERAL SYSTEMS THEORY; MIND; POWER; STRANGE LOOPS; SYSTEMIC MODELLING AND INTERVENTION; THERAPEUTIC TACTICS; TRIANGLES.)

J.M.

mystification   A term employed by Laing (1965) to describe a manipulatory manoeuvre which occurs with great frequency in the families of schizophrenics. The term 'disorientation' refers to the process by which the feelings of a child are denied by its parents to the point where the child begins to lack confidence and, as a consequence, does not succeed in basing itself on its own perceptions. It follows that individuals may become schizophrenic by virtue of having their experience invalidated, or of elastic boundaries or of manipulatory manoeuvres.

(See also MANIPULATION.)

J.M.

myth   A system which explains the origin of the world, plants, animals, men, marriage, the family and death. It is thus a true story for those who share in it and a fiction for those who are excluded from it or study it from the outside (Eliade, in Bonnefoy, 1981). In seeking to give a meaning to origins, to life, death and actions, it is part of the SEMANTICS OF COMMUNICATION.

Our aim here is not to give an exhaustive definition of myth, nor even to limit ourselves to setting out the many conceptions relating to what is a particularly complex and fuzzy mode of thought and exchange, both on the level of content and on that of the boundaries separating it from other types of expression (the folk tale, the novel, religion, knowledge, ideology etc.). Our object is not so much to place ourselves on the plane of the objective and retrospective history of myths – or of their anthropological or psychoanalytic interpretation – as to attempt to identify, switching constantly between the subjective and the objective, the mythopoeic function as realized in contemporary microsystems (families, institutions) and as it projects itself towards the future.

Although *mythos* was originally synonymous with *logos* (the spoken word) and *epos* (the meaning of connected discourse), Durand (1969, 1979) distinguishes it from the spoken word and discourse to the extent that it escapes ultimately from the linearity of the signifying chain of language and conveys an irrational and overdetermined polysemantism, which makes it akin to the dream. It is a kind of collectively shared waking dream which combines a one-dimensional linear narrative with a multi-dimensional and non-linear semantic morphology. It thus appears as an attempt to transform synchronic values, interlarded and filled out with swarms of symbols, into diachronic discourses capable of being conveyed in time and space over some distance.

In this respect, its orientation is directly contrary to that of the dream, since the latter re-transforms – in the form of a rebus – for personal internal use, linear verbal sequences of the secondary processes of thinking into overdetermined syncretic representations of the primary processes (condensation, displacement, considerations of representability – Freud). On a cybernetic plane, the myth may be seen as functioning as a centrifugal ANALOG-DIGITAL CONVERTER (the 'myth of the hero' regulating collective, interpersonal relations); on the biological plane of SYMBOLIC REFERENCE, it corresponds to a salience which invests itself collectively in a pregnance. A dream may be retranscribed into verbal language to rediscover the latent content behind the manifest; conversely, the myth as narrative is supposed to have regulating effects on the non-verbal communications of those who share in it. What makes the dream akin to myth is the way in which there is conflict in each between desire and prohibition, rule and transgression, and the conscious and unconscious feelings of shame and guilt connected with these types of conflict, as they arise between the sexes and the generations (Freud).

One of the functions of myth, with connects it with RITUAL, is to differentiate between the various units of population (see EVOLUTIONARY SURVIVAL UNIT). Hence the importance, recognized by Lévi-Strauss (1973), of the system of opposition of a single version in different geographical areas. What is interesting in the study of myths from the point of view of the PRAGMATICS OF COMMUNICATION is to perceive them in their operative functions, both within the complex structures of contemporary societies and at the level of family and social microsystems. The relevant mythopoeic units should no longer be studied like fossils, but are to be apprehended in the dynamism of the natural–cultural contexts in which they take on meaning: in family groups, social organizations, spiritual families and in the cultural bases of civilization.

Myths are systems of transmission and hierarchization of information which structure the functions of memory and forgetting. This information is conveyed by the stories grandparents tell their grandchildren and parents tell children about their own parents. This mythopoeic function is reactivated over three generations, but can transmit unconscious attitudes whose historical origins may be more or less lost. The prototypical domain in which myths are conveyed, re-actualized and transformed is the family group; FAMILY MYTHS ensue from this and recognizing these and formulating an approach to them requires special strategic and tactical procedures. Byng-Hall (1973) describes the functions of family myths from a clinical perspective, and later (1986) developed his concept of family scripts. These concepts come from the original work of Ferreira (1966).

On a general level, myth is not merely the discursive unfolding of a ready-made narrative. It involves the uttering of redundant, repetitive sequences which constitute multiple layers, the arrangement of which provides rhythmic, melodic scansion (Durand, 1969, 1979). In so far as this is the case, myths structure the modalities of communication for the family group. Repetition lays bare the structure of the myth (Lévi-Strauss, 1973) by enabling conscious and unconscious psycho-affective schemas to be memorized. The myth effects a semantic synthesis, making what are over-determined and possibly contradictory explanatory themes into something confluent and isotopic (Durand, 1969, 1979).

(See also ARTIFICIAL CODES; MYTH OF HERMES; INSTITUTIONAL MYTHS; TRANSGENERATIONAL MEMORIES.)

J.M.

myth of Hermes Hermes, who was the son of Zeus and Maia, the youngest of the Pleiades, was the god of thieves, brigands, traders and travellers. As messenger (*aggelos*), he accompanied souls to Hades. He made paths, set up signposts and marked out space. Being situated at the doors and windows to homes, he was to be found in those places where change happens, where man is in motion from the inside towards the outside. He was thus present when seduction, marriage and reproduction occur.

From originally being a thief, he came to be seen by men as the founder of the exchange of goods and words. He is, literally, the one who invented language and speech. As the god of ambiguous communications, he is their interpreter and the architect of their transformations.

HERMES ACTS ON THREE INTERCONNECTED PLANES

On the first plane, he is a newborn who is at once a brigand, thief, corrupter and deceiver with words, and a cunning, ingenious individual, pushing to the extreme – and right from birth – the depraved nature of the human being in communication with others.

Secondly, he is a skilful technician, exerting a civilizing influence in all spheres. He is a handyman of genius, transforming oak bark into shoes, wiping out the tracks left as he passes, making a lyre out of a tortoise-shell and inventing the pan pipes. He manages to transform the rustling of animals into the basis for friendly and profitable exchange with Apollo, to change lies into truth, savagery into domestication and crude fire into reproduction.

On a third plane, he is the one who effects passage between the various levels, the interpreter of the gods. His protectress is Mnemosyne, Memory, the mother of all the Muses: 'he is the interpreter, or messenger, or thief, or liar or bargainer; all that sort of thing has a great deal to do with language' (Socrates, in Plato, 'Cratylus', *The Dialogues of Plato*, trans. B. Jowett, Clarendon, Oxford, 1892, p. 351).

THE GOD OF CHANGES OF STATE

As the bearer of unexpected messages, Hermes is the god of changes of state, of transitions, of contacts between elements that are alien to one another (Kahn, 1978). 'Hermes passes!': this was how the Greeks greeted the sudden occurrence of silence within a conversation, a more or less embarrassed or extended silence, which gave the participants pause for thought and modified the modality of the communication. As such, it is the equivalent of our expression 'An angel passes.'

TRANSITION FROM NATURE TO CULTURE

On the very day of his birth, he unties his swaddling bands and goes off to steal twelve cows, a hundred heifers and a bull which belong to Apollo (Grimal, 1951). He makes them walk backwards and wipes out the tracks they make with branches from which he makes sandals. He also makes a lyre from a tortoise-shell. He tries to corrupt an old man in order to prevent him from reporting what he has seen with his own eyes. He then goes from one lie to another when Apollo, in anger, pursues him, threatens him with death and tries to reveal his guilt before Zeus. The latter is amused and shows a degree of admiration for the ingenuity of his latest son. He calls on him to give back the cattle to Apollo, but the latter, seeing the lyre, offers to accept it in exchange for his livestock.

GUARDIAN OF HOMES

It is thus by way of a heinous crime that Hermes comes to accede to the status of immortal god, whereas by his birth he was only a demi-god. In becoming wholly a god, Hermes was to become, with Hestia, the divinity closest to humans. And he was to fulfil a function complementary to hers. In the centre of the home, Hestia ensures its perpetuity and fixity. Her name refers simultaneously to the essence and existence of things. Hermes, situated at the level of doors, keyholes, at the limits to properties and the boundaries of land presides over exchanges between the home and the outside. This Hermes, termed 'ithyphallic' (relating to the erect phallus), takes the form of an ancestral sculpture which is met with in the most varied civilizations. It is made up of a pillar carved in stone representing a bearded man. At the front are carved genitals showing an erect phallus and the figure has its back turned to the building that is being guarded. For Wickler (1967), it recalls the posture of the old-world primates (the most highly evolved) which mount guard also by turning their backs on the territory they are protecting: their erect penises have a threatening function and they give the alarm as soon as danger arises. Such a myth offers an illuminating metaphor for the transition from savage behaviour to DOMESTICATION and civilization.

(See also FAMILY MYTHS; HOME; INSTITUTIONAL MYTHS; INTERPRETATION.)

J.M.

N

narcissism A term used by Freud (1914a), in reference to the myth of Narcissus. Insensitive to the many feminine passions he aroused, Narcissus fell in love with himself when he saw his own image in the pool of a spring. The various different versions of the myth either say that Narcissus allowed himself to die or that he committed suicide out of despair at his passion. Narcissism is thus a mythic polarity based on an excess of information about oneself (see FAMILY MYTHS; INFORMATION; NOSTALGIA).

In psychoanalysis, narcissism refers to the love directed toward 'oneself' (primary narcissism) or toward one's own image (secondary narcissism). This 'oneself', not yet structured into a differentiated image, refers us back to the paradoxes of FAMILY SELF-REFERENTIALITY. It is constitutive of self-esteem and the capacity for sublimation.

Narcissism will be considered here chiefly in its relations to family constellations, in a sense which marks the difference between transference neuroses, borderline states and full-blown psychotic states. The more primary narcissism is concerned in the pathology, the more will transference phenomena be subject to chaotic distortions, by virtue of the prevalence of processes of family and social alienation.

RECAP OF HISTORY

The human being has two original sexual objects: him or herself and the woman who nurses him/her. Freud thus distinguishes between two types of libido: *ego libido* (narcissistic libido) and *object libido*: the more the one is employed, the more the other becomes depleted. The opposition between narcissistic libido and object libido connects up with the opposition suggested in this volume between ALIENATION and TRANSFERENCE.

According to Freud, the study of narcissism provides an introduction to ego psychology. Access to this is gained through the study of paraphrenias (SCHIZOPHRENIAS) and PARANOIAS. 'Just as the transference neuroses have enabled us to trace the libidinal instinctual impulses, so dementia praecox and paranoia will give us an insight into the psychology of the ego' (*Standard Edition*, vol. 14, p. 82). Thus, until 1924, Freud was to term the psychotic states (paranoia, schizophrenia, melancholia) the 'narcissistic neuroses', though he did subsequently modify his theory of narcissism and came to reserve the term 'narcissistic neurosis' for melancholic states alone. The concept of narcissism was to be further relativized by the opposition between

Eros (the life instincts) and Thanatos (the self-preservation instincts – the death instincts).

The study of narcissism gave rise to a great many developments within psychoanalysis (Lacan, 1966). In more recent years, it has mainly been studied in connection with pre-psychotic or 'borderline' states (Kohut, 1971; Bergeret, 1974; Green, 1983; Widlöcher, 1983a, b). In our view, it remains important, however, to distinguish between the 'narcissistic transference' (Kohut, 1971) encountered in 'borderline' patients and the narcissistic disorders experienced by subjects with clear psychotic pathology and their close relatives.

PRIMARY NARCISSISM, SECONDARY NARCISSISM AND THE FAMILY CONSTELLATION

Primary narcissism is a postulated original state that is paradoxical in nature. The child invests its libido in a space of progressive differentiation of the ego, in contact with the family and its circle. Now, this ego narcissism will be recognized as a *secondary narcissism* in the second topography. Primary narcissism will then be regarded as corresponding to a part of the libido of the id; it is said to be connected to an anobjectal disposition, a total absence of relations with the persons around the subject. This is archetypally paradoxical and sends us back to the first axiom of the PRAGMATICS OF COMMUNICATION: one cannot not communicate. It will be possible to clarify the paradoxes inherent in this study of primary narcissism by the distinction between AUTONOMY AND HETERONOMY OF A SYSTEM, as well as by the study of the DIFFERENTIATION OF SELFS.

Secondary narcissism is based on a narcissistic object choice, by a secondary re-direction of libido towards an ego that is already constructed as an object (for example, homosexual love). The object choice is thus made along the lines of oneself as person, once that person has been differentiated as such. Desexualized narcissistic libido could be displaced onto the agencies of the id and the ego. In secondary narcissism, the ego is thought to capture as its object the libido which is diverted from external objects in this way.

Primary narcissism is a *transgenerational attractor:* it accounts for the paradox of the immortality of an as yet unborn ego; the affectionate attitude of parents towards their children corresponds to the revival and reproduction of their own narcissism which they have long since abandoned:

At the most touchy point in the narcissistic system, the immortality of the ego, which is so hard pressed by reality, security is achieved by taking refuge in the child. Parental love, which is so moving and at bottom so childish, is nothing but the parents' narcissism born again, which transformed into object-love, unmistakably reveals its former nature. (Freud, *Standard Edition*, vol. 14, p. 91)

In other words, the relation which synchronizes instinctive ATTACHMENT BEHAVIOURS and caring behaviours sets in train the paradoxes of primary narcissism, by the progressive differentiation of the ego. The ideal ego and the superego as interiorized simulations of kinship relations seek to realize themselves from one generation to another.

[the ego ideal] . . . has the most abundant links with the phylogenetic acquisition of each individual – his archaic heritage. What has belonged to the lowest part of the mental life of each of us is changed, through the formation of the ideal, into what is highest in the human mind by our scale of values. (Freud, 'The ego and the id', *Standard Edition*, vol. 19, p. 36)

We suggest the hypothesis that RELATIONAL ARCHETYPES are the expression of this narcissistic lack of distinction between ego and non-ego, which corresponds to the indissociable part which enables two or more persons to form a bond within a relationship. If, for one reason or another, this part is damaged, the persons in the relationship cannot either unite or separate.

NARCISSISM, SCHIZOPHRENIA, PARANOIA

Unlike the ego, auto-eroticism exists from the outset. In Freud's view, schizophrenia corresponds to the withdrawal of libido from persons and things in the external world, without the substitution of other object in phantasy. One can see the importance for such patients of hypochondriacal delusional ideas, dysmorphophobias and a painful fascination with their own image in the mirror. When this substitution occurs, it seems to appear secondarily, as an attempt at a cure, which undertakes to restore libido to the object. The delusion of grandeur is thus the expression of secondary narcissism constructed on the basis of a primary narcissism.

Paranoia marks a frustration of satisfaction in the field of the ego ideal. For Jacques Lacan, paranoiac alienation arises at the point where the specular 'I' veers over into the social 'I'. The end of the mirror phase inaugurates, through identification with the imago of one's fellow human being and the drama of primordial jealousy, the dialectic which, from that point on binds the 'I' to socially elaborated situations.

NARCISSISM AND ACTUALIZATION OF SPECULAR REALITIES

Lacan has shown the importance of the mirror stage as a dramatic event, constitutive of the subject's identification with his or her inverted image as he/she perceives it in the mirror, at around six months, in a jubilatory manner. The pregnance of this form inscribes the mental permanence of the 'ego', while prefiguring its alienating dimension. 'The notion of the role of spatial symmetry in the narcissistic structure of man is essential for laying down the foundations of a psychological analysis of space' (Lacan, 1966, p. 122).

Racamier (1978) describes the process of *narcissistic seduction*, in relations between the schizophrenic and his/her mother. The two partners are interchangeable and between them there reigns an exacerbated omnipotence and 'the infinite peace of spaces devoid of conflict' (Racamier, 1978, p. 935). Eiguer and Litovsky de Eiguer (1981) speak of *narcissistic induction* and even of *narcissistic perversion*, when the subject causes feelings, actions or reactions in others, or inhibits them. In a sense, he or she uses a magic power, as a sort of 'malefic prestidigitator' influencing, in a *passage à l'acte*, the psychical state of those around him.

In ontogenesis, the jubilatory assumption of narcissistic relations establishes itself when the child 'spontaneously' takes over complex attitudes which he/she perceives in his/her parents; the specular function plays itself out in family interactions: the 'oneself' is constructed out of parts external to the bodily unit. The play of resemblances, of reciprocal IMPRINTINGS creates that space in which mimetic reduplication makes possible the recognition and transmission of what is learnt. One may thus speak of a veritable family mirror. At this point, it becomes necessary to recognize symmetrical specular relations and asymmetrical specular relations.

THERAPEUTIC SPECULAR INTERACTIONS

Now these foundational events may not have been actualized in reality. Play on specular interactions then becomes an essential therapeutic axis in the activation of family interactions. Therapeutic work is not centred solely on the narcissistic image the subject has of him or herself; in family therapy, it is of value to seek to modify the reciprocal narcissistic images which the index patient and those close to him/her have of each other. Haley (1973) does not hesitate to centre the attention of certain patients on their own appearance in the mirror and to seek to modify it actively, rather than await a hypothetical spontaneous modification of that appearance.

In this perspective, the one-way mirror and the VIDEO emerge as tools with specific effects, METAPHORICAL OBJECTS playing a supporting role in narcissistic readjustments for family groups where there is suffering.

The two-way mirror, like any mirror, restores the original experience of the mirror stage: perception of oneself in an inverted form, which is not that perceived by others. But the image is diffused behind the mirror in an objectifying manner. It serves to sift out verbal and visual signals. *Video*, by contrast, objectivates the voice (what one perceives of one's own voice does not correspond to what others hear) and the visual appearance in a non-inverted form. In therapy or training, work can be undertaken on these comparisons, distances or even distortions.

(See also ALIENATION; FORECLOSURE; MIMESIS; REALITY; SELF-REFERENTIAL CALCULUS; TRANSGENERATIONAL MEMORIES.)

J.M.

negative feedback in the family system See CYBERNETICS; FEEDBACK; HOMEOSTASIS; MULTI–LEVEL HIERARCHIES; STRANGE LOOPS; TANGLED HIERARCHIES.

negentropy See ENTROPY, NEGENTROPY.

networks A family or social network is the set of pathways, material and fictive, connecting persons together in an informal, spontaneous way. It corresponds to the principles which connect individuals to the non-institutionalized channels of exchange and communication in a given society.

Three different hierarchical levels of networks may be distinguished:

1 At the broadest and most abstract level: the network of all humans communicating at a given moment in the whole world.
2 The network of humans communicating together in terms of a community identity.
3 At the most immediate and the most elementary level: the network of family exchanges in a nuclear family.

In France, networks, within restricted groups, have been studied by Anzieu and Martin (1968). In terms of fundamentals, a useful contribution to the analysis of networks is made by topology, graph theory and systems analysis (Attneave, 1976). Speck and Attneave (1973) define an extended kinship network, including in their family therapy all the persons involved in the family's functioning, i.e. the grandparents, aunts and uncles, together with all the friends and neighbours, along with the nuclear family. As Elkaïm points out (1979b, 1987b), networking practice is 'a "transversal" practice, which seeks out, outside the official stratifications (institutions, affects etc.) the praxic levers of a situation.' It thus leads one to situate oneself at the pertinent group level where the conflict, of which the symptom is the expression, is played out.

The notion of network has been studied in a sociological perspective by many writers (e.g. Bavelas, Jeavitt, Luce, Flament quoted in Anzieu and Martin, 1968). A distinction is made between chain, circle and radial networks, as well as 'all circuits' networks. Though it is the case that the persons in a position of centrality have the maximum influence on the functioning of the group, the most satisfied group is the one which communicates in a circular configuration. This is, however, the least effective in terms of accomplishing a task. We shall note here that in the most disturbed family systems, all the conflicts are concentrated on the index patient (radial network), whereas a conflictual narcissistic elation is realized in the form of a circular network. This is particularly clear in hospitalized patients, the focus for the family members and for the members of the therapeutic team during collective interviews. The more the patient is alienated in the institution, the more he/she will be spontaneously placed among the medical personnel and away from the family. The beginnings of a 'release from alienation' appear when he/she manages to find a place, during the interview, on his/her family's side and when a topological and psychical differentiation is created between the family and the therapeutic team.

The concept of network has been applied in a most thorough way in the field of family therapy by Speck and Attneave (1973). Their work is focused on persons who, in reality, exchange in a significant way in the apparently informal interface between the family group and related social groups. Such a therapeutic attitude is particularly appropriate in situations where the members of the close family may be 'intimate strangers', while profound ties have been formed in real life contexts. For Attneave, 'It saves time and often induces changed behaviour more efficiently than merely discussing the projections and fantasies about these others' (quoted in Guerin, 1976, p. 220). Elkaïm has pointed out the advantage of opening out narrow individual and family levels by integrating the pertinent sociopolitical contexts. This leads to the discovery of new forms of expression in the face of contradictions connected with official codings.

Rather than considering the family unit as a well-defined, well-delimited unit (a risk which may be maintained by the protocol of training schemes seeking definitively to formalize 'standard cures' or systematic supervision behind one-way mirrors where the family is sent away if all the members are not present), network therapies attempt to take into consideration the connections between the family under consideration and friends, neighbours and work colleagues who may possibly be involved in the problem at a particular moment.

Individual meetings may then be arranged in groups and sub-groups, as therapeutic needs dictate. Attneave proposes a mapping of the family network in which the aim is, with the participants, to define:

- people living in the same household;
- those who are emotionally significant;
- casual and functionally related persons;
- persons geographically distant or seldom seen.

Such a map will thus attempt to produce a visual representation of spatial distances and to mark the positive and negative VALENCES of relations. Negative valences (persons detested, rejected or hated) are as important as those marked with a neutral or positive valence. The individuals who know each other are connected by lines, by 'pathways' which gives the map a spider web appearance. Some individuals focus a particular interest on their own person, whether this be positive (hero, saint, opinion former, patriarch etc.) or negative (INDEX PATIENT, SCAPEGOAT) in nature.

As Attneave emphasizes, the act of mapping one's own network triggers intense resistances and emotions, as does the act of drawing up one's own GENOGRAM. It is only of value if it is part of a process in which a therapist who is capable of assessing its dynamic is involved.

Speck (1987) points out the existence of several phases in network interventions:

1 A *retribalization* phase, the tribe being the traditional unit of problem-solving in societies not touched by the industrial revolution. It is the task of the intervenors to restore the functionality of the tribal unit of the individual concerned.
2 A *polarization* phase which leads to the formation of sub-groups in conflicting positions (generational conflicts, male–female conflicts, power conflicts etc.).
3 A *mobilization* phase of the activists of the tribe, enabling support to be given to the various members of the family concerned.
4 A *resistance and depression* phase.
5 A *breakthrough* phase when the objectives of the network are achieved;
6 A sense of plenitude, exhaustion and *termination* phase.

Networking techniques may be used either as modes of intervention in the general population and in training with multi-disciplinary teams (social workers, nurses, midwives, psychologists, residential social workers, psychometricians, general practitioners and medical specialists; see, for example, Benghozi et al., 1986). Such techniques may be of assistance to the professionals who have to intervene to respond to complex demands or problems, such as high-risk pregnancies, drug addiction, requests for hostel places, children in danger, requests for placement, dangers of eviction, problems of physical and psychical health etc. (Benghozi et al., 1986). Whereas, spontaneously, the various intervenors have to work in a totally isolated way,

without being able to grasp the overall configuration of families, clans or ethnic groups, identifying the networks created between the persons making a demand and the intervenors permits a better grasp of the context. It is then possible to perceive the nature of the groups in a state of suffering, to differentiate the problems and the bonds formed and to clarify the responses required.

(See also EVOLUTIONARY SURVIVAL UNIT; MULTI-LEVEL HIERARCHIES; SEMANTIC UNIT OF MIND; TANGLED HIERARCHIES; UNIT OF CHANGE.)

J.M. & P.S.

neurolinguistic programming The terms 'neurolinguistic programming' or 'very brief therapy' coined by Bandler and Grinder (1975) correspond to a combination of three factors.

First, 'neuro' refers us to the importance of systems of sensorimotor interconnection, sensory windows on the world provided by our sense organs: the observation of the synergies and antagonisms between the systems of visual, auditory, olfactory, tactile and gustatory emission and perception brings about a more or less consistent kinaesthetic and coenaesthetic anchoring. These various systems are at least as paracommunicative as they are metacommunicative. They do not cover the whole range of the continuous spectrum of resonances of the internal and external world. Sensory experience is conceived as the primary reference experience.

Secondly, the term 'linguistic' indicates an emphasis on the polyvalent human tool which enables the world of experience to be modelled and represented. It is therefore a secondary experience. In this perspective, transformational grammar is regarded as a representation of language, as, therefore, a representation of a representation, i.e. a metalanguage.

Thirdly, 'programming' (which, like 'problemsolving', has already been used in Batesonian models) derives from a model based on computing. We are constantly programming automatic decision trees in our psycho-affective strategies and tactics. Our central and peripheral nervous systems and our bodies can be conceived as hardware, the use of which can be modified depending upon the software used.

Neurolinguistic programming is centred on very brief therapeutic interventions, by separating out visual–kinaesthetic or auditory–kinaesthetic patterns. Since 1976, its creators have been able to treat phobias in ten minutes and depressive states in a few sessions (Cayrol and de Saint Paul, 1984). This approach combines:

- the transformational linguistic model: tracking down, through branching tree patterns, the deep structures beneath the surface structures;
- taking into account the interactional synchronicities in every relation;

- the multi-sensory anchoring of every structuring (or destructuring) learning process, whether relating to taste, smell, sight, hearing or body movement.

In his preface to Bandler and Grinder's (1975) book, *The structure of magic*, Bateson writes:

We did not see that these various ways of coding – visual, auditory etc. – are so far apart, so mutually different even in neurophysiological representation, that no material in one mode can ever be of the same logical type as any material in any other mode. This discovery seems obvious when the argument starts from linguistics . . . instead of starting from culture contrast and psychosis, as we did. (Bandler and Grinder, 1975, pp. x–xi)

Though such a displacement may have interesting consequences for the refinement of interview techniques and in the 'pursuit of excellence' as an improvement of the results of psychotherapy, it remains problematic *vis-à-vis* the most serious conditions or, at least, *vis-à-vis* those which are most enmeshed in a polyaxial organization of treatment.

(See also ANCHOR; GAZE; PRAGMATICS OF COMMUNICATION; SURFACE STRUCTURES; SYNTAX OF COMMUNICATION.)

J.M.

neutrality Selvini Palazzoli et al. (1980a), describe neutrality as a basic therapeutic attitude to be observed towards the various participants in a family group. As such, it goes together with hypothesizing (see SYSTEMIC HYPOTHESIS) and CIRCULARITY. Neutrality consists in not getting oneself definitively tied into a coalition with a member of the family, which may lead to *de facto* opposition to one or more of the other participants. More precisely, neutrality is the specific pragmatic effect of the therapist's overall behaviour on the family.

The therapist may feel sympathy or antipathy. Neutrality does not have to do with his or her intrapsychic attitude, but is a consequence of the shifting alliances which the therapist strikes up with each member of the family system. The therapist's successive alliances lead him or her to ally with everyone and no one, in order positively to connote the system of which all are necessarily part. A characteristic indication of a failure of neutrality occurs when one of the family members can say to another: 'you see, I told you, the gentleman (or lady) has understood the situation perfectly!' At bottom, neutrality is not at variance with techniques of AFFILIATION or joining, or temporarily and provisionally siding with one family protagonist or another (see MULTI-DIRECTIONAL PARTIALITY), even if such attitudes may at first sight appear to contradict each other.

Cecchin (1987) has further developed this original thinking, adding the position of therapeutic curiosity, which enhances the therapist's ability to maintain an active position of engaged neutrality.

(See also COALITION; MILAN SYSTEMIC THERAPY.)

M.G. & J.M.

nightmares See DREAMS, NIGHTMARES, SLEEP AND THE WAKING STATE.

noise See COMMUNICATION SYSTEMS; ENTROPY; INFORMATION; ORDER; RANDOMNESS; SELF-ORGANIZATION; STOCHASTIC PROCESSES.

non-voluntary families Many families referred to psychiatric and social welfare agencies do not come of their own free will. Someone else has decided that they should attend because one or more family members is deemed to be at risk, either to him or herself, or to put others at risk. Families referred by the courts, by a social worker to tertiary agency or by a school to a specialist service will be a non-voluntary referral. The referral may have the strength of the courts and be a mandated referral, or be a referral where not to comply would be viewed by the referring agency as not wishing to cooperate and therefore as being resistant. In all such instances, the family members will think that they have little or no choice and must at least be seen to cooperate, even if they have no intention or expectation of needing to change.

In these instances, the family is the 'client' and the referrer is the 'customer', i.e. in the sense of being the person(s) with the greatest investment in change occurring. Selvini Palazzoli et al. (1980b) have addressed the problems of the referring person whose agenda must always be taken into account when accepting a referral from a third party. Others have also addressed these issues (Treacher and Carpenter, 1982; Carpenter et al., 1983).

Many therapists maintain that when working under such constraints, and especially where the therapist is employed in an agency which has a role which is defined primarily as one of social control or protection or of medical containment, it is not possible to be therapeutic or systemic. This is a limited view of what is possible. The therapist who uses the powers invested in him or her or in the agency as a way of challenging the family to take stock of the implications of its actions and for taking responsibility for changing, or not changing, will find that many more options open up for useful and effective therapeutic work. By challenging the family or individual members to see the consequences of their actions; by asking what the family think would be the response of the senior manager in a social services department, or of the magistrate or judge in the courts, or the mental health tribunal in a psychiatric setting, and of then helping them to choose what is their desired outcome, a different and more collaborative working relationship can often be developed.

(See also DEMAND; SYSTEMIC MODELLING AND INTERVENTION.)

H.J.

nostalgia   For Lévi-Strauss (1969, p. 454), nostalgia is a particular transmission of the information which marks a mythic activity and which stands in structural opposition to DISCLOSURE, SECRETS and FORGETTING. It corresponds to an excess of INFORMATION directed towards oneself and is related to narcissistic phenomena.

On the family plane, nostalgia is the mythic expression of depression and of melancholy, i.e. the quest for a family narcissistic object which is impossible to attain. Nostalgia thus marks the existence of unconstituted object relations and unresolved MOURNING. It appears, for example, with great force at moments when young psychotic patients experience particularly explosive reverses in their love lives, reverses in which the whole family may come to participate with mingled fascination and repulsion.

(See also CALUMNY; FAMILY MYTHS; NARCISSISM; SCANDALMONGERING.)

J.M.

'nothing plus 10 per cent' paradox   This is a particular paradoxical mode of communication which is mainly to be observed in families with psychotic transations. The index patient's requests for help, whether implicit or explicit, are met by offers of help on the part of the relatives, in a symmetrical relationship. The relatives show themselves ready to 'do anything' for their patient. Attentive observation reveals that this offer is contentless and does not correspond to any concrete proposition.

This paradox was described by Neuburger (1981) as a transgression of the rule that applies at auctions, where some kind of figure must be put on the bid at the outset and where bids with no figure attached are prohibited. Similarly, the request for aid on the part of the patient is equally devoid of pragmatic content. Requests for, and offers of, aid can continue to infinity without the least change occurring: 'Nothing' (direct offers and requests) 'plus 10 per cent' (10 per cent of nothing!).

(See also DOUBLE BIND; PARADOXES.)

R.N.

nuclear family, extended family   On the clinical level, the term 'nuclear family' refers to the family unit made up of the parents and their children. The term 'extended family' describes those members of the family (grandparents, uncles, aunts, nephews etc.) who both (a) belong to the same family (by alliance, filiation) as the symptom bearer; and (b) are in affective, intellectual proximity and have a lived involvement with the symptom bearer. These notions refer in fact to implicit or explicit conceptual models, which may be identified from a perspective of comparative anthropology.

In anthropology, the nuclear family is in fact regarded as being made up of two parents and their children living in the same home. The married children never live with their parents in the nuclear family cycle. Marriage marks the point of separation between the generations. It may, however, occur that a grandparent comes to live in the home of one of his/her children.

Extended families may be of two types: the *stem family,* in which a single couple from among the children remains with the original couple to continue the line and perpetuate the family property; and the *patriarchal family,* in which several married couples live under the same roof as the original couple.

These distinctions, which were established in the nineteenth century by Le Play, have recently been recast through a comparative analysis of the broad types of family structure that are met with throughout the world (Todd, 1983). They may be seen as having connections with the major religious and ideological systems of belief which operate on a 'meta' plane in relation to the family institution.

From the perspective of comparative anthropology, it is appropriate, following Todd (1983), to distinguish between seven family systems and an eighth group which does not constitute a structured family system. These systems can be distinguished from one another by the absence or presence of three distinguishing features.

1   *Endogamy/exogamy:* marriage taking place for preference within or outside the family line. The endogamous model is that of Islam, the exogamous model that of Christianity. Endogamy is not to be understood as incestuous behaviour, but as preferential marriage within the clan; it is not a rule, but a tendency.
2   *Authority/liberty:* maintenance of transgenerational authority within the family of origin after marriage or, conversely, delegation of that authority to the nuclear family. The authoritarian model of family relations assumes that children will continue to live with their parents after marriage. The liberal model assumes that they will leave their parents at adolescence and form an independent household. Authority is not understood here in the sense of

physical violence; it is even opposed to it, since authoritarian families often prohibit any corporal punishment.

3 *Equality/inequality in relation to inheritance*: if the family's possessions are equally shared, we may speak of an egalitarian model. When the inheritance goes to one or other of the descendants, to the exclusion of the others, the model is inegalitarian. The authoritarian family transmits its inegalitarian values and an egalitarian social practice. Nuclear and communal families transmit egalitarian values and an inegalitarian social practice.

We may distinguish between several family structures.

EXOGAMOUS FAMILY STRUCTURES

No marriage between the children of two brothers.

Exogamous nuclear families

Exogamous nuclear families subtly propagate the individualist model and a questioning of power. There is a liberal variant (absolute nuclear families) and an anarcho–military variant (egalitarian nuclear families, based on the motto 'liberty–equality–fraternity').

The absolute (inegalitarian) nuclear family is characterized by:

- the absence of precise rules of succession: the 'will' then assumes great importance since it alone determines the distribution of the family heritage;
- married children not living under the same roof as their parents;
- the absence of marriage between the children of two brothers.

This model is typical of the Anglo-Saxon world.

The egalitarian nuclear family is characterized by:

- equality between brothers, defined by rules of succession;
- married children not living under the same roof as their parents;
- the absence of marriage between the children of two brothers.

It is typical of northern France, northern and southern Italy, central and southern Spain, central Portugal, Greece, Romania, Poland, Latin America and Ethiopia.

Exogamous extended families

The authoritarian exogamous extended family (inegalitarian, Le Play's stem family) is characterized by:

- inequality between brothers so far as rights of succession are concerned; the inheritance is passed on to one of the children; the others either choose a

military career or a religious vocation or marry outside the family;
- the married heir living under the same roof as his parents.

This is a typical model among the Germans, the Jews and the Japanese, and also for the peripheral regions of France (Brittany, the North-East, the Alps, the South-West). This model is mainly linked with Catholicism and/or social democracy.

Communal families (fraternal egalitarianism, Le Play's patriarchal families) are characterized by:

- equality between brothers laid down by the rules of succession;
- married sons and their parents living under the same roof.

In France, this type of family is found in the Nivernais and in Provence. It might be considered as typically giving rise to Communist ideology.

ENDOGAMOUS FAMILY STRUCTURES

These engender three structural categories, by dividing the communal family into two, by the absence of a differentiable model of authoritarian family, and by the lack of distinction, in the nuclear family, between the liberal and authoritarian aspects. We then have three types:

1 *Strict endogamous communal families* (preferred marriage with first cousins), based on the fraternal ideal, reducing the distinction between alliance and filiation to a minimum. These family structures are typical of Islam.
2 *Asymmetrical communal families*: the preferred axis is brother–sister, with a prohibition against a man's child marrying his brother's child (Indian family structures).
3 *Anomic families*: endogamous nuclear families; South East Asian families.

There is some uncertainty concerning the equality of brothers, equal in theory, fluid in practice. The living together of married children and their parents is rejected in theory but accepted in practice. Consanguineous marriages are possible.

AFRICAN FAMILY STRUCTURES

There is a wide range of anthropological systems according to ethnic background. Polygamy is common, as is divorce, which brings with it many domestic arrangements (including instability of the marriage line). It is estimated that at least 30 per cent of marriages are polygamous. Inheritance is often 'horizontal' rather than vertical. It passes from older brother to younger brother rather than from father to son. Paternal authority is weak. In polygamous structures, the father has several wives, each of whom has a hut which she occupies with her children. Paternal authority is less with the begetter than with the brother of the mother. The transplantation of African family systems to America has broken up the ideology of the original relationship systems, leaving the main link as the mother–child with the father becoming mobile and peripheral.

The value of this classification, suggested by Todd (1983), is to establish a first broad outline of the anthropological systems of the family, bringing to it social ways of organizing, on the one hand, and belief and religious systems, on the other.

THERAPEUTIC CONSEQUENCES

The identification of these major structural oppositions can only be arrived at statistically over a large number of families when the historical development of FAMILY LIFE-CYCLES is taken into account. The advantage of such a model is that it offers a backcloth against which one can put into perspective the perception one has of one's own system of family membership or those of the families who present themselves for therapy. The interest of such a model is thus that it prevents our regarding apparently unfamiliar traits as pathological when they are merely the expression of other anthropological systems.

In practice, we often observe these structures, which can in ideal terms be distinguished, actually being intermingled. Several stratifications may emerge within a single family group. Reality, as it is actually lived out, reveals the existence of marital break-ups, homosexual couples, adultery, the early death of children or parents, re-marriages etc. We thus find frequent examples of single-parent families, families where the children are brought up by the grandparents or by uncles and aunts, systems of 'common law relationship' etc. It is, therefore, necessary to distinguish the categories of the nuclear or extended family from those which are actually of relevance to clinical practice: PROCREATIVE FAMILIES, FOSTER FAMILIES, ADOPTIVE FAMILIES.

The relation between family and social structures, on the one hand, and individual and collective systems of belief, on the other, is thus based on a conflictual interaction. The family has as one of its functions that of stabilizing and reproducing systems of REALITY-definition. But it turns out at the same time to present a danger for the most solidly established social, religious and political institutions. Goody (1983) shows how the appearance of sects has its basis in the simultaneous destruction of existing family structures and the advocacy of the spiritualized model of a new family. The transformation of the sect into a church, in the next phase, seeks to re-establish new family rules which are to contribute to the consolidation of the new social structure thus instituted (see ALIENATION).

DELIRIUM, as a system of unshakeable belief, attempts to subvert the collective definition given to the reality of relationships, the reality of the order of the world, the reality of established material and spiritual territories. There are therefore good grounds for correlating it with the dysfunctioning of the family system within which it arises, though one must avoid the trap of trying to identify a linear type of causal relation. What is gained from confronting clinical and anthropological models is that it reveals the dynamic inter-relatedness of family structures and systems of belief, of the playing out of relationship systems in reality and their idealization in the form of PHANTASIES and MYTHS.

J.M.

O

Oedipus complex   See AGONISTIC BEHAVIOUR; COALITION; FAMILY MYTHS; FAMILY ORGANIZERS; FORCE FIELDS; IDENTIFICATION; METAPSYCHOLOGY; PERFORMATIVES; PHANTASY; POWER; PROCREATIVE FAMILIES; PSYCHOANALYSIS; REALITY; SECRETS; SELF-FULFILLING PROPHECY; SEXED BEHAVIOUR; TRIANGLES; UNCONSCIOUS, THE.

ontogenesis   See ACTUOGENESIS; ETHOLOGY; FAMILY ETHOLOGY.

open systems   The concept of an open system, which is applied to families in GENERAL SYSTEMS THEORY, assumes an exchange of matter, energy and information with the surrounding world. It is characterized by three essential properties: TOTALITY, relationship and EQUIFINALITY. Totality implies that the whole is greater than the sum of its parts. Relationship implies that one must grasp the articulations and interactions between the parts to understand the system. Equifinality implies that the final state of a system is independent of the initial conditions of the system under consideration. An open system is an evolving system, subject to a diachronic process.

In practice, the degree of openness of a family system makes possible the exchanges which are necessary with other social systems, leading to reversible processes and enrichments coming from the outside and making metabolic exchanges possible. A viable system cannot, however, be either totally open (unless it allowed itself to be totally invaded, leading to its destruction through lack of boundaries and defence systems) or totally closed (see CLOSED SYSTEMS).

The appearance of intervenors from outside the family system *ipso facto* creates openness in the system. Some 'muscular' interventions may very well create substantial damage, with irreversible FEEDBACK (by dint of reactional traumatic closures). Even where there is skilful intervention, the FAMILY SYSTEM can only react by developing mechanisms of protection and defence and hence movements of closure. Intervenors should respect these movements and therefore accept not knowing everything about a family and not exhausting all its material and spiritual resources. They should, rather, seek out localized openness at the technically functional point, in order to achieve a satisfactory therapeutic outcome.

(See also HOMEOSTASIS; TOPOLOGICAL SPACE.)

P.S.

order, disorder   The human mind constantly shows itself capable of rediscovering an order in apparent disorder and generating incomprehensible (if not indeed psychosis-inducing and lethal) disorder where there is perfect order. Though he or she is not able to resolve the epistemological and scientific problems of the age, which concern the problem of determinism and indeterminism, the therapist is none the less up against this problem in both his or her thinking and activity.

EPISTEMOLOGICAL CONFLICT BETWEEN ORDER AND DISORDER

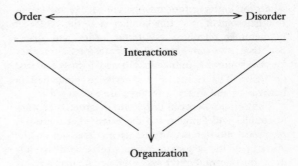

The situation might be described as follows, using a slightly modified version of the tetragram proposed by Morin (1977). For Morin, all that is real is the conjunction of order and disorder. However, light can only be cast on the relationship between order and disorder using intermediate notions:

- the idea of interaction, 'the Gordian knot of chance and necessity';
- the idea of transformation (of dispersive elements in an organized whole, of a whole into dispersed elements);
- the idea of organization.

Morin (1977) then sets about developing a theory based on chaos, namely the tetralogical loop in which order, disorder and organization occur in turn in interactions. Order and disorder would thus have to be seen as something relative. However, most importantly, 'One order is dead: the order based on the supra-temporal and supra-spatial principle of invariance, i.e. the order of the Laws of Nature' (Morin, 1977, p. 76).

Such a position unleashed a violent polemic with

Thom (1990a), whose project might be said precisely to consist in seeking to identify the structurally stable constraints to which living and non-living phenomena might be subject. A deterministic chaos does, in fact, exist (see ATTRACTORS; RANDOMNESS); a deterministic model may be perfectly non-predictable (see SENSITIVITY TO INITIAL CONDITIONS). Conversely, an indeterminist position is not incompatible with basic scientific discoveries (whether in quantum mechanics or molecular biology), even if the question of intelligibility remains open.

QUESTIONS AND ANSWERS IN THERAPY

Now, whether they like it or not, therapists are, implicitly or explicitly, exposed to this debate in their practice and theory. They need tools, even crude ones, with which to deal with both the ordered and disordered aspects of clinical realities. Since the epistemologists attest to the open and conjectural character of this problem, therapists are forced to step down a level and admit the limits of fundamental knowledge and scientific experiment. For this conflict is at the centre of inter-human relations. The terms 'order' and 'disorder' then lose something of their abstract aura; they become somewhat mundane, but new light is also cast on them. The reality they describe is embodied in behaviours and in the way these are accounted for.

The conflict between order and disorder is at work in couples and families. To the extent that there is a reciprocal interference of one partner's action on the other or of the actions of parents towards their children, the question of the way each person manages his or her order and disorder is going to be posed, both for him/herself and for others, for the couple or for the family.

To gain knowledge about objects, infants of only a few months put them in their mouths, then throw them away with all their might. Then they pick them up again, so that they can throw them once more. A few months later, the child spontaneously establishes its way of tidying up its things – or making them untidy. We then find conflicts of control occurring, conflicts which Freud pointed out were related to anality.

Within a couple, struggles for power often express themselves in the way one partner metacommunicates his or her control of the situation by tidying up the partner's disorder (or disturbing what the partner has tidied). Similarly, children often display opposition by refusing to tidy their things away. And, lastly, one even sees escalations of hyper-ordered or hyper-disordered behaviours in certain extreme situations (or even the juxtaposition of the former in the parents and the latter in the index patient for example).

Furthermore, the alternation of order and disorder is at the centre of therapeutic action. Two therapeutic attitudes are possible: (a) either the therapist starts out from a structured and ordered model of perception: his/her intervention will try to appeal to spontaneity and to push the system far from the equilibrium state; or (b) the therapist sets out from a disorganized, fragmented model of perception: his/her intervention will attempt to re-establish an adequately secure setting and therefore to avoid the system becoming even more destructured than it already is.

In either case, the intervention often turns out to be pertinent when the therapist, building upon a sufficiently solid framework, breaks free from pre-established algorithms and when his/her openness to the random is sufficient. It is at this point that unexpected events occur in the sessions, which can form a basis for therapeutic activity to take off. All change arises when a sufficient level of confusion appears, both in thought and in emotions. It is, however, difficult to accept the absence of an underlying determinism. The conscious perception of disorder may go together with an ordered unconscious dynamic. If change were totally open to chance, that would mean the total absence of therapeutic responsibility or of structurally stable factors against the background of which change would occur. It is true that for some families in schizophrenic transaction, a problem arises in respect of the often chaotic shifts with which the different professional interventions are confronted and the airframe clinical juxtaposition of equally absolute order and disorder. It is also true that indeterminism is not incompatible with a scientific approach and experimental results.

It would seem then to be desirable to attempt to find zones of continuity where cognitive and emotive breaks predominate. Psychoanalysis, psychotherapy, family therapy and systemic interventions derive their success from the discovery of hidden determinisms. The art of the therapist rests, in large part, upon his/her skill in bringing these out or allowing them to emerge.

(See also ENTROPY; INFANTILE AUTISM; INFORMATION; INTERACTIONS; SCHIZOPHRENIAS; SELF–ORGANIZATION; STOCHASTIC PROCESSES.)

J.M.

ordinal values See CARDINAL VALUES, ORDINAL VALUES.

oscillators, family oscillators An oscillator is a device which generates electrical or mechanical oscillations or oscillations of light or sound. The existence of oscillatory movements is also to be found in psychical activity and in interactions within a couple or family, and DOUBLE BINDS are the visible expression of these. The existence of virtual oscillators may therefore be postulated which perform a function of self-organization.

There are two categories of oscillation: those which remain in a single neighbourhood (pendulum, vibration of a string, a weight on a spring) and those which move (waves spreading along a taut string, the waves of the ocean). Sometimes a single phenomenon belongs to both categories, depending on the point of view of the observer (Boisot, 1985).

LINEAR HARMONIC OSCILLATOR

A linear harmonic oscillator is the simplest model of an oscillator. The movement of a point m on an axis $0x$, representative of the system, is defined by a return force proportional to the elongation (pendulum, weight on a spring). The second derivative of the angular momentum x obeys the equation $x'' = -\omega^2 x$, which induces a flow on the phase space R^2, the coordinates of which are the position x and the velocity x'. The orbits of this flow are concentric circles (a perturbation of the system causes a change of orbit, which renders the system structurally unstable). The position of point m is described either by its coordinates x, x' or by the angle θ. The angular frequency or pulsation is: $w = d\theta/dt$. It is possible to conceive structurally stable harmonic oscillators (tending towards a limit cycle or circular attractor) and structurally stable non-linear harmonic oscillators (whose flow is situated on a torus etc.) (see Zeeman, 1976; Thom, 1980b).

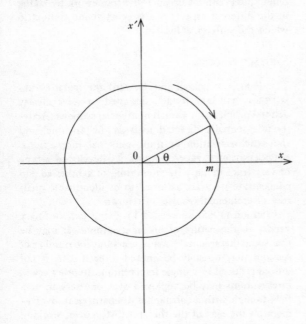

Whatever the case, a harmonic oscillator is characterized by (Boisot, 1985):

- its position or amplitude at a given moment;
- its phase (its angle with the horizontal);
- its pulsation or angular frequency;
- its period or time of cycle;
- its frequency, or the number of cycles per unit of time;
- its maximum amplitude (the radius of the circle).

CEREBRAL OSCILLATORS

Wiener, in his work *Cybernetics* (1975), advances the hypothesis that the electrical waves registered by electroencephalography are the product of cerebral oscillators. Cerebral oscillators would essentially be non-linear and would possess both a frequency of their own and a frequency provided by external variables. We could cite as an example the alternation between the rhythms of waking and sleeping. These depend on internal oscillators (the frequency of which may be demonstrated by sensory deprivation experiments or by speleological isolation) and on the constraints imposed by the alternation between night and day (nycthemeral rhythm). When these frequencies are in step, a phenomenon of resonance appears. The interaction of non-linear oscillators produces an attraction towards a specific new frequency and generates a self-organized system.

Zeeman (1976) has developed a topological model of brain activity and has further extended the oscillation theory. He sees the brain as being made up of a collection of strongly coupled oscillators directed towards one another. The stability of our INSTINCTS, of our habits and of our memories (see READ–WRITE MEMORIES), in his view, correlates with the strong stability of certain oscillators, while the rapidity of certain of our reactions is linked to an instability caused by strongly coupled oscillators. From this he derives an analysis of biological cycles of behaviour, the disturbances of which may throw light on various psychosomatic and psychical disorders: anorexia nervosa, manic–depressive psychosis, paranoia, schizophrenia etc.

FAMILY OSCILLATORS, SOCIAL OSCILLATORS

Interaction between two or more persons thus sets in play oscillatory phenomena. Interpersonal understanding and meaning can be seen as the product of an effect of dynamic resonance, on condition that a sufficient metric isomorphism exists between sender and receiver (Thom, 1980b). Hypotheses of this kind have also been developed by Foulkes (1964) and Anzieu (1975a) for the psychoanalysis of groups (see SEMANTIC RESONANCES). The existence of oscillators has been postulated at the level of family systems in their interferences with psychical and social spaces (Miermont, 1984c). Interaction between several oscillators produces attracting frequencies, and this leads to a self-organized system. The overall system functions as though it were under the influence of a virtual generator of oscillations.

Relations between family, institution and therapist can be seen as arising out of these phenomena in which two or more dynamic systems, having their own oscillatory dynamic, are brought into resonance, in a more or less sharp or fuzzy way. The sharper the resonances, the more the family/specialist service product will become indissociable. The institution then functions as a mirror or resonator of the family system. The relations between frequencies in the therapeutic encounters (daily, weekly, monthly etc.) induce relational resonances having very precise effects on the amelioration or aggravation of disorders (cf. Selvini Palazzoli et al., 1978). The objective of the therapeutic approach could be seen as one of regulating these resonance phenomena and of finding ways of disengaging from them which restore a maximum of autonomy to the family systems. To do this, one may try to appreciate, in an intuitive manner, the form of the cycles observed, their amplitude, the position of the system at a given moment, the periodicity and frequency of those events that are subject to oscillation. The propagation of waves in the family environment, from oscillators generating autonomy, makes its effects felt in the organization of RITUALS and FAMILY MYTHS and in the structuring of family memories and their activation.

(See also AGREEMENT AND DISAGREEMENT; ATTRACTORS; COUPLES; DYNAMIC SYSTEMS; FAMILY LIFE-CYCLES; FAMILY SELF-REFERENTIALITY; MARITAL BREAKDOWN; SEMANTICS OF COMMUNICATION.)

J.M.

outside time, in time In what way are the categories conceived as lying outside time (the unconscious, the family, the institution) capable of assuming concrete form in time? The various schools of psychoanalysis, psychotherapy and family therapy have given different answers to questions of this kind.

The figure of regulation of a structurally stable system may be provided by an organizing centre external to normal space–time. The way in which a patient designated as mad is excluded from space–time bears witness at one and the same time to a pragmatic disorder, a syntactic destructuring and a semantic questioning of family interactions. The objective of family therapy in this situation, whatever its time-scale, is to enable the various members of the family to re-engage semantically with one another, within the normal space–time coordinates.

PSYCHOANALYTIC PRACTICES

Freudian psychoanalysis, which emerged out of brief, intensive forms of psychotherapy, formalized the model of the typical psychotherapeutic course of treatment. This took the form of one-hour sessions four or five times a week. Practical constraints have substantially modified this ideal therapeutic framework, and this was the case even in Freud's own practice. This 'ideal' psychoanalytic framework is orientated towards the timeless dimension of the unconscious and seeks to put back 'into time' personal aptitudes which have, up until then, been inhibited.

Lacanian psychoanalysis introduced the idea of a scansion, determined by the analyst's perception of language effects (ambiguities of the 'signifier', puns, plays on words etc), leading to the practice of short – and even ultra-short – sessions, though these remain intensive in so far as there are still several sessions per week, the costs are still high and the duration long.

Winnicottian approaches have treated this framework as being equally malleable, in response to the requirements of treating borderline patients. Sessions remain generally long, with the 'setting' serving to maintain the connection with the classic model of analysis, in spite of modifications to the rhythm of the sessions. Here again, the overall duration of the analysis is long.

In 'micro-psychoanalysis', treatment lasts for several months in all, with a maximum concentration of therapeutic activity. Sessions last for several hours and the patient virtually 'lives' with the therapist during the course of the treatment.

All these approaches are essentially based on an intervention centred on the person of the patient. 'Systemic' interventions broaden the framework by taking in the different aspects of the ecosystemic context in which the sufferer is located.

SYSTEMIC PRACTICES

The Palo Alto school put forward the BRIEF INTERACTIONAL THERAPY model, designed to solve clearly defined problems in a small number of sessions. Activity is essentially directed towards the 'in-time' and the synchronization of multi-personal interactions. NEUROLINGUISTIC PROGRAMMING has developed a type of very brief therapy by attempting to synthesize and concentrate what are assumed to be identifiable qualities of eminent therapists of renown.

Erickson (1965) succeeded in giving extraordinary variety to the nature of his interventions. It may be that some therapies take many years but the number of sessions may possibly be limited in each case, if not indeed reduced to a single intervention. In other cases, interventions may be deployed over one session or a few, though with a substantial dramaturgical involvement on the part of the therapist. Moreover, working in the context of the family does not imply that the whole family has to be brought together to solve the problem facing it.

The Milan school (Selvini Palazzoli and colleagues) advanced the principle of monthly sessions in their therapeutic approach to family systems. The total number of sessions was limited to ten, though this could be further extended once. Several therapists have adopted this monthly rhythm, though without limiting the duration of therapy to one year.

In other cases, it is necessary to envisage more frequent consultations. The intensive family therapy approaches advocated by Boszormenyi-Nagy and Spark (1973) have been taken up by family therapists seeking to bring their practice as close as possible to the psychoanalytic model. It does, however, seem difficult to see the principle of between three and five weekly sessions being observed as a general rule for all the members of a family. It seems difficult to get beyond a maximum of one session per week and, in fact, the time-scales of the individual psyche and the family group are not identical.

The acceleration or deceleration of therapeutic processes leads to questions of a meta- or para-therapeutic order. Beyond the question of very, very brief and/or very, very long therapies, it is important to ask what family or institutional contexts will make a situation therapeutic or pathogenic.

(See also CONJUNCTION OF THERAPEUTIC AXES; DIACHRONIC AND SYNCHRONIC AXES OF A THERAPY; FAMILY THERAPIES.)

J.M.

P

paracommunication systems Several systems of communication may produce messages conjointly in a single sequence of interaction, without it being possible, or desirable, to take the view that one of the systems is hierarchically superior to the others, even if the messages produced seem to contradict one another (see diagram).

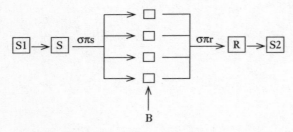

General paracommunication system: S1, source of information; S2, source of destination; S, sender; R, receiver; B, noise; $\sigma\pi s$, paracommunication signal sent; $\sigma\pi r$, paracommunication signal received, comprising *n* messages: body posture, body movement, gesture 1, gesture 2, tone, rhythm, linguistic representation etc.

Grinder and Bandler (1976) have suggested broadening Bateson's model of the distinction between content and relationship, which is supposed to establish a clear hierarchy in the levels of communication (see METACOMMUNICATION SYSTEMS; PRAGMATICS OF COMMUNICATION). In effect, in Bateson's model, non-verbal 'instructions' are based mainly on ANALOGIC CODING, forming metamessages for the verbal 'data', words being associated here with digital coding. In fact, Grinder and Bandler attempt to generalize Bateson's remark that, in the reality of communication, there is necessarily a confusion of logical types. It is then necessary to recognize the existence of paramessages situated on a single logical level. Three consequences then arise.

First, paramessages are not limited to binary oppositions, but are to be regarded as so many units of output per channel: the posture of the various parts of the body, body movements, sequences of gestures, intonation, voice rhythms, scenarios of verbal representation. Instead of being binary, the pattern is one of multiple messages (*n*-messages) of the same logical level, functioning in parallel.

Secondly, none of the paramessages recorded has to be considered a priori as more valid, true or representative than the others. The action of the therapist consists precisely in authenticating each of the systems which are paracommunicating, without seeking to introduce restrictions or subordinate a particular apparently masked (or particularly flaunted) expression to any other.

Thirdly, the recognition of systems of metacommunication could be said to remain necessary, in Grinder and Bandler's view, on two conditions. For message A to be in a 'meta' position in relation to message B: A and B have to be messages belonging to the same system of representation or the same output channel; and A has to be a message about B.

CRITICAL COMMENTS

Metacommunicative embedding is not to be limited either, in systematic fashion, to a binary distinction. Several media may thus be embedded one within another. However, there are probably topological constraints which limit the number of local regimes capable of expressing themselves in a single spatiotemporal unit to three or four.

It is necessary to recognize that a multi-channel coherence is achieved by a medium. To speak is to establish contact, to vocalize, to show oneself, to take one's place in a group, all these things creating a kind of 'interactional dance or dramaturgy'. Even if all these elements act in parallel, they none the less produce, in fortunate cases, a possibility of eliminating certain ambiguities and therefore of metacommunicating.

The recognition of metamessages and paramessages is achieved through analysis of the SYNTAX OF COMMUNICATION.

When a number of systems are paracommunicating, the underlying semantic archetype is a conflict catastrophe in which two or more attractors have the same minimum potential (see ELEMENTARY CATASTROPHES).

(See also COMMUNICATION SYSTEMS; SEMANTICS OF COMMUNICATION.)

J.M.

paradoxes In everyday parlance, a paradox is an extraordinary opinion which conflicts with the commonly accepted view (*para-doxos*). In the sciences, we find logical, topological, linguistic, psychological, semantic and pragmatic paradoxes.

In formal logic, a paradox is a proposition which contains a self-referential logic. A self-referential proposition is not necessarily a paradox, nor is a contradictory proposition. Most logical paradoxes appeared with the development of set theory (Cantor, 1932) and the archetypal paradox was the one of which Bertrand Russell made great play (concerning the set whose elements are the sets which are not elements of themselves). To eliminate any fundamental threats to set-theory definitions, Russell developed the THEORY OF LOGICAL TYPES with the aim of constructing a healthy mathematics from which 'any set that was an element of itself', i.e. all self-referentiality and all paradoxes, would be excluded.

In clinical practice, paradoxes abound in the structure of communication: PLAY, HUMOUR, DELIRIUM, DREAMS and PHANTASY are all situations which contain paradoxical elements. Similarly, benevolent neutrality in psychoanalysis or POSITIVE CONNOTATION are paradoxical attitudes. Family systems are connected to contexts which generate paradoxes that have life or death consequences. It was on the basis of the recognition of such pragamatic paradoxes in communication that Bateson and his school developed the theory of the DOUBLE BIND.

Linguistic and pragmatic paradoxes have exactly the same logical structure as the basic self-referential paradox. In both cases, there is an antinomy between two terms which are situated at different logical levels (e.g. the class and the element). Let us examine three exemplary paradoxes: that of Epimenides the Cretan, the linguistic paradox of heterological adjectives and, lastly, the pragmatic 'barber paradox'.

Linguistic paradox of epimenides the cretan: 'all cretans are liars'

This may be analysed in the following way: 'I am lying' is in fact a meta-statement which normally relates to all the statements I utter and thus relates to the class of all my statements. The paradox arises when the meta-statement (class) 'I am lying' is considered as a statement (element), which introduces self-referentiality. 'I am lying' is a member of the class of my statements and therefore refers to itself and, since, furthermore, it carries within it a negation (what I say is not true), it corresponds to the definition of a self-referential contradiction.

Linguistic paradox of heterological adjectives

Let us define two classes of adjectives. Autological adjectives will be all the adjectives which possess the property they express. For example, the adjective 'short' is short and therefore autological. Heterological adjectives will be all the adjectives which do not possess the property they express. For example, the adjective 'long' only has one syllable and, since it is not long, it is heterological, and so on. The paradox arises when one enquires whether 'heterological' is auto- or heterological. If the adjective 'heterological' were heterological, it would possess the property of heterology contained

within it and would therefore be autological. If the adjective 'heterological' were autological, it would not possess the property of heterology which it expresses and would therefore be heterological. Thus if it is heterological, it is autological and vice versa.

The analysis of this paradox is analogous to that of the paradox of Epimenides. The adjective 'heterological' is, in effect, a meta-adjective which relates to all adjectives, and thus to a class of objects which is the class of all English adjectives. The paradox arises when the meta-adjective (class) is considered as an adjective (element), a move which introduces self-referentiality. 'Heterological' is a member of the class of English adjectives and therefore refers to itself, and, since, moreover, it carries a negation within itself (not possessing the property it expresses) it meets the definition of a self-referential contradiction. By extension, we might ask whether all the signs which designate the arbitrariness of the sign are arbitrary. If they are, then they are not; if they are not, then they are. . . .

Pragmatic barber paradox

To save time, an officer orders the regimental barber to shave only those soldiers who do not shave themselves. The paradox arises when we come to the question of whether the barber will shave himself or not. He can, in fact, only shave himself if he does not shave himself and vice versa. The analysis of this paradox is the same as in the preceding cases. This barber is in fact a meta-soldier, a limit case of soldiery, if we can speak of such a being. He is a soldier who has to concern himself with all soldiers and thus he is involved with a class of human beings, the class of all the soldiers in the regiment. The paradox arises when the meta-soldier (class) is considered as a simple soldier (element), which introduces self-referentiality. This barber/meta-soldier is a member of the regiment and therefore belongs to the class of soldiers. He therefore has to look after himself and his beard and since, into the bargain, the definition of his task contains within itself a negation (not to shave those who shave themselves), he meets the definition of paradox as a self-referential contradiction. The barber paradox is a pragmatic paradox since the definition of the task the barber–soldier has to perform puts him in an impossible pragmatic situation. One cannot exist at the same time as both a soldier and as the concept of meta-soldier.

When a proposition is simply self-referential but contains no contradiction, at most it introduces intellectual confusion, but it is not a paradox. Self-reference or confusion of logical levels is a very commonplace phenomenon in the PRAGMATICS OF COMMUNICATION. Humour and the complementarity of digital and analog messages employ such self-reference constantly. Paradoxical impasses only arise where, alongside confusions of logical level, there are also contradictions.

PARADOXES AND SELF-REFERENTIALITY

Spencer-Brown's calculus (see SELF-REFERENTIAL CALCULUS), Gödel's INCOMPLETENESS THEOREM and probably a great deal of other work has shown that the ambition of the theory of logical types was vain. The definitive elimination of self-referentiality and paradoxes is impossible, both in human sciences and in the field of mathematics and formal logic. Moreover, since it is unavoidable, rather than attempting to eradicate it, Spencer-Brown has developed a calculus which makes it possible to work with the paradoxical element, conceived as a logical element in itself. This type of development is, in fact, quite similar to the process whereby imaginary numbers were conceived. There, the significant factor was the need to find a solution to the equation:

$$x^2 = -1.$$

Here, the need is to make sense of propositions such as:

- x is an element of x
- if x then not (x)
- if not (x) then x
- if x then not (x)
- and the propositions where the solution x that is being sought is a function of itself, which is written as $x = f(x)$. We should here note that these last propositions are not necessarily paradoxical, but are simply self-referential and may possibly lead to paradoxes if the function $f(x)$ contains a negation relating to x.

Once a sufficiently consistent abstraction has been conceived for resolving these propositions, it becomes possible to extend all logical operations to take account of the new conceptual entity, thus enabling Varela (1979) to apply this self-referential logic to the study of the SELF-ORGANIZATION of living organisms.

The following is an illustration which may help the reader to imagine how a self-referential proposition might be resolved. Let us take the following self-referential proposition which has to be completed:

Cette phrase a exactement . . . lettres ('This sentence has exactly . . . letters').

The dots here may be replaced by the letter x which will, from this point on, represent the solution sought. The exact number of the letters in the proposition is a function not only of the words *cette phrase a exactement . . . lettres*, but, in the last instance, of the number of letters the solution x possesses. This solution must therefore satisfy the equation $f(x) = x$, where f represents the number of letters in the sentence.

Let us try then with $x = 33$. *Cette phrase a exactement trente-trois lettres*. We get the result $f(33) = 40$. Let us try with $x = 40$. *Cette phrase a exactement quarante lettres*. We get the result $f(40) = 37$. Let us attempt with $x = 37$. We get $f(37) = 39$. Let us try with $x = 39$. We get $f(39) = 39$: *Cette phrase a exactement trente-neuf lettres*: 39 is therefore the solution we are looking for. If we continued indefinitely in this way, we would always obtain $f(39) = 39$. Thus 39 is the limit-value of f applied indefinitely to itself.

This example suggests two basic ideas:

1 The solution of a self-referential proposition for which the equation reads $f(x) = x$ is of the form $x = f(f(f(f \ldots = $ the limit value of f when it is applied indefinitely to itself.
2 If we had chosen a different initial value to come to the solution, the solution would have been different. A self-referential proposition may have several solutions. This is clearly expressed in the self-organization of living organisms, since living organisms possess both the property of SENSITIVITY TO INITIAL CONDITIONS and that of EQUIFINALITY: once the process has been begun, the result is equifinal and determinate.

The foregoing example turned out to have a simple solution. Some self-referential propositions do not produce such a happy solution and the method of approximation used does not produce a single and clearly determined limit value, but an oscillation between two (or sometimes more) values without either of the two being the solution that is sought. It is the oscillation itself between the two values which constitutes the solution to the problem and this is something which Spencer-Brown (1969) has successfully formalized. Self-referential propositions, which are paradoxes into the bargain, lead to this type of solution. In this, they are exactly like the question 'Is what I say true when I say "I am lying"?' which has, as its solution, the oscillation yes–no–yes–no. However, even non-paradoxical self-referential propositions sometimes produce this type of oscillating solution. Let us reconsider the example above: 'Cette phrase a exactement . . . lettres'; it is manifestly a self-referential proposition, but since it does not contain a contradiction it is not, therefore, paradoxical. However, if we begin the process of looking for a solution with $x = 3$, 12, 16, 20, 34, 41, 42, 43, 45, 46, 48 or 49, we do not get a determinate solution, but an oscillation between the value 41 and 42. Let us attempt with $x = 20$. We get the result *Cette phrase a exactement vingt lettres* or $f(20) = 34$. Let us try then with 34. We now get *Cette phrase a exactement trente-quatre lettres*, which gives the result $f(34) = 41$. With this, we get *Cette phrase a exactement quarante-et-une lettres* or $f(41) = 42$. With $x = 42$, we get $f(x) = 41$. And if we try again with $x = 41$, we get $f(x) = 42$. The solution is therefore in the oscillation between 41 and 42. A self-referential proposition may therefore have more than one solution, some of which are oscillating solutions.

Bateson was the first to theorize the relation between apparently absurd behaviour, with vital repercussions and the structuring of communication in double binds. The pragmatic effect of communication of this kind has been studied in detail by the Palo Alto school.

(See also ANCESTRAL RELATION; COUPLES; FAMILY SELF-BELONGING; FAMILY SELF-REFERENTIALITY; FORECLOSURE; IDENTIFICATION; METABINDING; NARCISSISM, 'NOTHING PLUS 10 PER CENT' PARADOX; OSCILLATORS; PARADOXICALITY; PROJECTIVE IDENTIFICATION; RESIDUAL RELATIONS; THERAPEUTIC DOUBLE BINDS; TRANSFERENCE; TRANSITIONAL OBJECTS.)

M.G. & J.M.

paradoxicality This concept, which is to be distinguished from that of 'paradoxical communication', was introduced by the psychoanalyst Racamier (1980, p. 152) to represent not only a mode of relating but also a psychical process: 'Paradoxicality is at one and the same time a form of mental functioning, a psychical regime and a relational mode.'

As a means of defence, paradoxicality functions at a narcissistic level. It subverts the secondary processes by subjecting them to the laws of the primary process. From the psychical point of view, it operates at the narcissistic level, is a continuous disqualification of the ego and prevents not only thinking but also phantasizing and dreaming since it disqualifies representations and 'by an indirect but pragmatic denial, short-circuits conflictuality and ambivalence' (1980, p. 153), whose normal or neurotic elaboration by the ego it prevents. It has its origins in an alternative which is offered to the subject of either believing its senses and trusting its ego or believing its object and privileging its love for the object, in such a way that all the activities of the ego – even the non-conflictual ones – become conflictual. Paradoxicality also appears as a defence: it denies ambivalence and is conflictual and anti-depressive since it enables the subject to evacuate conflict and to attack the object without losing it. Paradoxicality is simultaneously aggression and ego defence.

From the relational point of view, it sets up a relation which prevents both the recognition and the loss of the object. It makes possible the establishment of a 'denial of otherness'. It frustrates the psychoanalytic relationship: whatever the analyst does, says or thinks, he/she ought to do something else (paradoxical transference, Anzieu, 1975b). Paradoxicality is organized around a paradox relating to the existence of the object, the ego and the relationship between the two. 'Object, subject or relation only exist by not existing.'

In schizophrenics, paradoxicality is eroticized in the same way as the sensation of hunger may be in anorexics. 'It is the eroticization of paradoxicality which enables the schizophrenic to derive enjoyment from his mental activity, to preserve that activity and to follow a cure. And it is that eroticization which makes it so difficult for the schizophrenic to cease being schizophrenic' (Racamier, 1980, p. 158).

From the therapeutic viewpoint, we may cite the counter-paradox techniques of the Milan school of family therapy (Selvini Palazzoli et al., 1978) and the therapeutic double binds and prescription of paradoxical tasks of the Palo Alto school. Psychoanalytic techniques aim rather to bring to light the contradictions masked by paradoxicality and to arrive at awareness.

(See also NARCISSISM; PARADOXES.)

M.G.

paranoia In its everyday sense, paranoia is a state of querulousness and of the making of aggressive demands, both of these being of an unjustified nature. From a psychiatric point of view, paranoia appears as a type of characterological disposition structuring the personality and as a delusion concerning relationships: erotomania (the delusion of being loved), jealousy (delusional certainty of being deceived by one's partner), persecution (feeling one is being plotted against) and impassioned idealism (inventors, reformers). The nature of the relations between the personality and delusions remains, to a large extent, hypothetical.

STHENIC AND ASTHENIC POLES OF THE PARANOID PERSONALITY

On the personality level, there would seem to be two characterological poles, the *sthenic* and the *asthenic*. The paranoic disorder could be seen, then, as corresponding to a perturbation of the autonomous regulation mechanism relating to the intensity of motivations and how these are put to work socially, as a function of the perception of relations of force. The paranoic reaction can be seen as the product of an insufficient struggle for life; at the moment when vital challenges are posed, the paranoic withdraws and fails to match up to the demands. The result of this is a poor appreciation of the social relations of force and a disequilibrium between forces internal and external to the subject (see FORCE FIELDS). Paranoia derives from a pathology of family and social authority.

The two poles – the sthenic and the asthenic – can be seen in the combative character and the sensitive character (Kretschmer, 1927). The *combative* character is unbalanced towards a sthenic position which is continually stimulated by the weakness of the asthenic position; the *sensitive* character is unbalanced towards an asthenic position, which is continually stimulated by the weakness of the sthenic position. The autonomous centres which normally cause the sthenic and asthenic positions to oscillate become dysfunctional. What dominates, then, from a psychopathological point of view, is the reactive aspect of the disorder, through dysfunctioning of the oscillators generating autonomy which regulate the levels of emotional force of the personality. At that point, there is an all-or-nothing megalomaniacal explosion of omnipotence or impotence.

We therefore find the two characterological forms of self-realization – the combative and the sensitive – and these stand opposed to each other in the following respects:

- sthenia/asthenia;
- hypertrophy of the ego/hypercriticism of the ego;
- excess of mistrust/excess of confidence;
- psychorigidity/psychical laxity;
- absence of tenderness/hypersensitivity.

The relation between personality structure and delusional activity is neither linear, nor necessary. We may even consider the hypothesis of an indeterminacy principle between these two complementary points of view:

There is an opposition between the personality (static structural vision) and family interaction (dynamic systemic vision) such that if we study personality structure, the real contexts which give it a dynamic sense cannot be perceived and apprehended; and such that if we study the dynamics of the family system, the static positions taken up by the different actors become relative and interchangeable (with the risks of destabilization which follow from this).

PARANOIA AND IMBALANCES IN THE FAMILY LEDGER

In the view of Boszormenyi-Nagy and Spark (1973, p. 91), the paranoic personality may be based on a real imbalance in a person's familial merit LEDGER.

From his subjective vantage point of reciprocity, such a person may have been irreversibly emotionally exploited as a child. It is in the nature of the justice of the human world that if the parents remain in arrears in performing their parental obligations to a child, the child will tend to feel like a creditor in all his future relationships.

Mistrust or wariness are products of this instability in the merit balance. This produces the following fundamental position: 'Since I had not reason to learn to trust the world, the world has to prove itself trustable.'

Clinical experience with families shows the profound complementarity between the paranoid position taken up by one of the members and the position of counter-dependence enabling hostile feelings of all the other family actors to be projected towards the identified paranoic. In a family in schizophrenic transaction, it often happens that the father is placed in such a situation which may express itself either in the sthenic mode (more immediately perceptible) or in the asthenic mode ('absent father' who is terrorized and forced to take flight). In both cases, the paranoic feels his authority is disqualified and that he is scorned, if not indeed hated by those closest to him. And the more intense this feeling, the more those close to him feel themselves obliged to adopt an attitude of hostile counter-dependence. It is then necessary to authenticate the various different levels of communication, positively to connote the positions adopted by each person by showing their necessary interdependence, if not indeed their structuring oscillation.

PARANOID DELUSIONS

Paranoid delusions are relational delusions regarding the major social fulfilments of oneself. Hence the themes of jealousy, erotomania, great inventions and social reform. The paranoid delusion is based on the sense of persecution. A double polarity appears here too: the paranoic seeks to carry out justice himself/the paranoic punishes himself (Lacan, 1932). The persecutor, as Freud had rightly seen, is of the same sex as the patient. The paranoid delusion is based on a semiotic transformation which excludes the awareness of a homosexual passion (Freud, 1911). That semiotic transformation is based on a triple movement: rejection of the homosexual desire – negation – projection. Thus, in men, we have:

- *delusions of persecution*: the rejection of 'I love him, a man' is accomplished by negation of the predicate, which gives us: 'I hate him.' This is then projected by subject–object inversion into 'He hates me, he is persecuting me.'
- *erotomania*: negation of the object 'It isn't him I love, it's her I love.' Projection by subject–object inversion then gives 'It is she who loves me.'
- *delusional jealousy*: negation of the subject: 'It isn't me who loves the man.' Then, projection by modification of the subject: 'It is she who loves him.'
- *delusions of grandeur*: negation of any object: 'I don't love anyone.' Then, projection by object–subject modification: 'I only love myself.'

The delusion is, therefore, a means for the paranoic to live anew in a world which is as he himself creates it: 'The delusional formation, which we take to be the pathological product, is in reality an attempt at recovery, a process of reconstruction' (Freud, 1911). Paranoia thus reveals a narcissistic disorder, connected to the first phase of the anal stage. It is linked to rivalry of the fraternal type and corresponds to a non-differentiation of the sexes on the conjugal plane.

What the paranoic sets in motion in his delusion is the reproduction of the paternal complex:

> The model upon which paranoics base their delusions of persecution is the relation of a child to his father. A son's picture of his father is habitually clothed with excessive powers of this kind and it is found that distrust of the father is intimately linked with admiration for him. When a paranoic turns the figure of one of his associates into a 'persecutor', he is raising him to the rank of a father; he is putting him into a position in which he can blame him for all his misfortunes. (Freud, *Standard Edition*, vol. 13, p. 50)

Thus the paranoic exaggerates the importance of a particular person, attributes a boundless omnipotence to him, as if to make up in ideal terms for the emotional and intellectual exploitation of which he feels he has been a victim.

It is possible to get these relational delusions (see DELIRIUM) dynamically into perspective if one looks at the real relations the patient maintains with his present circle. Not only in shared delusions (e.g. delusions *à deux*), but also in family systems organized around paternal paranoia. By regarding everyone as in league against him/her and by delusionally seeking an external persecutor, the paranoic makes it possible in fact for everyone to be against him/her and for him/her to take on the role of SCAPEGOAT. Thus it has been possible for the case of President Schreber to be reconsidered in the light of his relationships with his parents. In bringing the family system into perspective, we are able to observe that there is no linear causality between the relational delusion and real relations, even though meaning effects appear. It is precisely the function of the delusion to prevent a direct causal link being made of the order of 'I'm mad because of my father's imposture.' From a semiotic point of view, such a delusion would rather signify 'It would be mad to think that the upbringing my parents received and the upbringing they gave me have anything to do with what is happening to us.' Hence the conjunction of the delusions and the interactions observed in reality enables us to grasp the situation in its dynamic, metabolic dimensions, where classical analysis is confronted with the static aspects of the problem. It turns out in practice that the two viewpoints are equally necessary if we wish to maintain coherence in our understanding of the situation and our action.

(See also ACCULTURATION; ANTI-THEATRE; COUPLES; FORECLOSURE; LAW; NARCISSISM.)

J.M.

parentification For Boszormenyi-Nagy and Spark (1973), parentification is a temporary or continuous reversal of role between parents and children. It leads to a distortion of the relation between two partners (child–parent or parent–parent), one of whom places the other in the position of parent. Children may thus become the father or mother of their own parents. Parentification must be distinguished from processes of identification or of projective identification, though it is a component in these processes. Its function is to prevent the emotional exhaustion of the person lacking sufficient parental qualities.

Parentification is a normal process of transmission of the parental roles and of regulation of transgenerational tensions. it is necessary for the emotional growth of the child, allowing him or her to identify with future roles of responsibility. When it becomes a habitual and prevalent mode of relating, parentification is a pathological process and the EXPLOITATION of the child by its parents may then lead to psychopathological disorders, preventing the maturation and rounded development of the parentified person.

The child is involved with parentification as soon as it comes into the world, and the partners in a couple become involved with it as soon as they form a relationship.

An infant, at birth, makes its parents dependent upon it, by the care, time and attention it requires. Parentification of the child occurs when the parents feel they are giving more than they can, that they are listening more than they are able and that their presence is required on a scale that exceeds the time they have available. The parents then demand, in an involuntary way, trust, gratitude and support from their child; he or she then assumes a parental attitude towards them. This temporary parentification has within it the seeds of identification, though it can be observed that the child does not identify, in the strict sense, with its parents (it does not have the means to do so); it identifies with a parental position, in an interaction where the parents are themselves confronted with an infantile position. It is, therefore, an *identification with the position of parent*, which becomes *de facto* a grandparental position, since the child is, in this way, the parent of its own parents. If the parents cannot assume their parental roles and if they systematically confer that position on the child, this becomes a crushing burden for him or her. Thus parentification is a system of equilibration of parent–child reciprocity over three generations: 'what remained unbalanced in one generation is expected to be balanced in the next' (Boszormenyi-Nagy and Spark, 1973, p. 86).

Falling in love reactivates the affective processes set in place during childhood. A more or less intense degree of relatively reciprocal imaginary parentification is created. The partner who imaginarily (and more or less really) parentifies his/her partner puts him or herself in an infantile position and re-establishes within the relationship a parent–child relation.

Parentification of this kind can also manifest itself in a phantasmatic form and/or through real dependent behaviour. The more parentification is actualized in behaviour, the more it sets up a pathological interaction. Parentified children possess a considerable degree of emotional responsibility, without having the codes with which to decipher the situations they are placed in charge of. They thus have very often to fight against depression in their mothers and the unavailability of their fathers. They then become loyal, hyper-mature children who exercise a considerable power of regulation within the family system.

(See also FAMILY CATASTROPHES; IDENTIFICATION; SOCIAL ORGANIZATION.)

A.L. & J.M.

parentified, parentalized or parental child This is a role assumed by a hyper-responsible child to whom has been ceded the power and authority which ought more normally to belong to the parents.

When, within a family, there is one or more parentified children, this usually indicates that there is a hyperflexible or inadequate generation boundary within the family system. Such a parentification is accompanied by a corresponding infantilization of the parents. One of the objectives of therapy will be to help to mark out these BOUNDARIES once again (Boszormenyi-Nagy and Spark, 1973; Minuchin, 1974).

(See also ANCESTRAL RELATION; FAMILY CATASTROPHES; IDENTIFICATION; PARENTIFICATION.)

P.S.

passions See FAMILY PASSIONS.

pathological communication One may establish a comparative typology of the individual styles of communication and symptoms encountered. There would thus be particular types of communication in schizophrenic, autistic, anorectic, alcoholic or delinquent transaction, in battered children or battered parent transaction etc., characterized by discriminative and distinctive features. From a more general point of view, we may envisage making the following distinctions:

Non-specific communication
This is a type of communication, described by Wynne (1978), which is so vague and ill defined that it cannot in any way be contradicted. Such communication lies at the origin of profound disturbances of the child's ego and renders therapeutic work extremely difficult, since all the members of the family are caught up in expectations which are only very vaguely definable.

Congruent communication
Several messages, of different logical levels, are directed toward a receiver, without any of these messages being in serious contradiction with one or more of the others. Conversely, a non-congruent communication is a communication in which the METACOMMUNICATION or non-verbal PARACOMMUNICATION accompanying the message does not coincide with the verbal content of the message and contradicts it in a more or less concealed way (Bateson, 1972).

Dysfunctional communication
This is an expression borrowed from communication theory and one that refers, in family therapy, to a collapse or malfunctioning of communication within a family. The members of the family can neither emit nor receive clearly definable messages.

Paradoxical communication
An expression frequently used by Haley (1963, 1973) to refer to the act of prescribing the symptom to a member of the family whom one expects, at that point, to enter into conflict with the therapist. This decision on the part of the 'rebel' to go against the therapist's orders is caused, at that moment, by the common resolve of the family that he/she should have control of his/her own situation, instead of allowing the therapist to exercise that control; the outcome of this manoeuvre in fact consists precisely in what the therapist really wished to see happen (see PRESCRIPTION).

(See also INTERACTIONAL TYPOLOGIES; INTERACTIONS; PRAGMATICS OF COMMUNICATION; TRANSACTIONAL TYPOLOGIES.)

P.S.

performatives (performative acts, behaviour and utterances) Behaviour is performative when its activation creates a new reality for one or more individuals. In this sense, animal and human rituals are performative in character, since they put to the test and realize, for two or more conspecifics, the nature of the relation, as this is displayed in the movements/signals they exchange. Rituals of seduction or combat and courtship, threatening or appeasement behaviour etc. thus have effects which modify the physical and psychical dispositions of the protagonists and transform the state of their reality. For Lorenz (1973), the transition from movement to the definition of the process that is the outcome of movement is a level of experience which lays the ground for the recognition of REALITY.

HOW TO DO THINGS WITH WORDS

As a ritualized act, language too has this characteristic. This makes the distinctions suggested by Austin (1962) between *locutionary* acts (saying something), *illocutionary* acts (the production of something by saying it – il-locution) and *perlocutionary* acts (the production of something further by the act of speaking – perlocution) rather abstract. To say 'It's a fine day' is a locutionary act, since it refers to the state of the weather, an illocutionary act because it establishes a certain contact at a level of superficial conviviality and, lastly, a perlocutionary act, since it establishes a singular relation which may possibly engender a new state of affairs (by signifying to someone that he can remove an article of clothing which is too warm or by indicating that this is an opportunity to go outside etc.).

PERFORMATIVE MODAL STRUCTURES GENERATIVE OF BEING AND DOING (CAUSING)

In this perspective, the performative character of speech acts is expressed in modal structures of the factitive type: 'causing-to-be' (cognitive performance) and 'causing-to-do' (manipulation), together with their variations on the SEMIOTIC SQUARE; these structures are the reflection of reciprocal interactions between father and mother, parents and children etc.

These modalities of communication are, in fact, set in place as soon as the child is born, creating a sexed human identity which will have the status of a shared reality. The way the parents look at the child, their mental attitudes, actions and words towards it will make it a boy or a girl. In some cases, distortions will arise between the anatomical sex and the symbolic sex that is produced in this way. Lebovici (1983), referring to one particular case, shows how the mother can even leave it to the child to make a mother out of her. We should also add, here, that the reciprocal interplay between the father, the grandparents, the infant and the mother *makes* the mother a mother for her child and *makes* the child the child of its parents etc.

Similarly, the human being cannot but manipulate – from the moment it comes into the world. It goes without saying that the baby *makes* its mother or its close relatives *do* a whole host of things (see NARCISSISM). Parental authority will only be performative if a minimum of intrafamilial consensus exists in the respective and complementary recognition of statuses and roles; this implies that the family turns heteroreferenced functions, such as the infantile, maternal and paternal functions – and the grandparental functions – into a self-referential system (see FAMILY SELF-REFERENTIALITY). Where there are serious communication disorders, then a disturbance of manipulatory functions exists. As Selvini Palazzoli et al. (1978) shows, all forms of action are disqualified in families in schizophrenic transaction; what each person does cannot be recognized as what has been done since no one is ever how he/she should be when he/she does it.

Given this state of affairs, it will be evident that the very construction of reality is particularly disturbed.

A meeting of several therapists to discuss a patient or the members of a family of a patient regarded as ill or delinquent carries within itself a positive or negative performative dimension, irrespective of the content of the communication considered. Similarly, communicating or not communicating the nature of these meetings to the various groups involved has undeniable effects in the PRAGMATICS OF COMMUNICATION.

SELF-REFERENTIAL PERFORMATIVE UTTERANCES

Certain speech acts do, however, lead to particular types of performative utterances, and these have a self-referential aspect if they refer to a reality which they themselves constitute. Proposing a psychoanalysis or a course of psychotherapy or family therapy are typically self-referential utterances. Such utterances are performative when the speaker is not free in the determination of the reference. They thus presuppose a hetero-reference, an AGREEMENT, a collective consensus which binds the sender of the message and the receivers and which fits into an anticipatory sequence (see SELF-FULFILLING PROPHECY). As Benveniste (1979) has pointed out, outside of its operational context (its 'operational closure' as Varela (1979) would say), a performative event becomes a piece of childish nonsense, an act of madness. We are speaking, then, of a unique act, occurring at one point in time and space, individual and historic, having a collective effect which authenticates its self-referential aspect and therefore its performative value ('We are going to begin', 'I leave my worldly goods to X' etc.). This is indeed a case of 'causing (something) to be done' which obviates the need for the person who makes the utterance to have to do that something him or herself. His/her utterance is only self-referential (for the person who utters it) to the extent that it has force of law for the collectivity which hears it (hetero-referenced consensus with regard to the self-referential utterance). We find this same property in PRESCRIPTIONS and INTERPRETATIONS, to the extent that they produce consequences.

Not all utterances or speech acts are necessarily followed by effects. If a parent orders a child to eat his/her soup, the child may reply: 'Yes, I'm eating my soup', without in fact touching it (Berrendonner, 1981). Balzac commented that love proved is superior to love expressed in words. In the same way, speaking of psychoanalysis or family therapy may be a supreme way of resisting a psychoanalytic or therapeutic process actually being set in train.

(See also INSTITUTIONS; LAW; MANIPULATION; RITUALIZATION; SYMPTOMATIC AND/OR AETIOLOGICAL TRANSACTIONS.)

J.M.

perverse triangles A specific form of dysfunction described by Haley (1967) concerning relations in certain families where the hierarchy and distribution of power are confused, causing reversals of position in respect of intergenerational boundaries.

These perverse triangles are created in relationships between the nuclear and the extended family. If, for example, a mother establishes a fusional relationship with her son in a horizontal mode and supports him against his father, such an alliance between two members of different generations (mother–son) against a third (father) constitutes a perverse triangle. It should be noted that these coalitions are often denied and may even not be perceived by those concerned.

In Haley's view, the characteristics of the perverse triangle are as follows:

1 The persons interacting in a triangle are not all of the same generation. There is, therefore, a transgression in the power hierarchy laid down by generational differences.

2 In the process of interaction, a person belonging to one generation forms a coalition with a person from another against his/her own peer or partner. A COALITION is by definition a union of two persons against a third (coalitions are to be distinguished from alliances which are established in pursuit of a common goal, without being negatively directed against a real third party).

3 A coalition between two persons is denied as soon as someone attempts to uncover it. It is present on the level of communication, but metacommunicative indices mask its importance and may even conceal its existence.

According to Haley, such perverse triangles seem to be repeated over several generations: the short-circuit between the child and one of the parents seems to go together with another short-circuit between one of the parents and one of the grandparents. One frequently then finds a coalition between the child who is the INDEX PATIENT and one of the grandparents.

(See also TANGLED HIERARCHIES; TRIANGLES.)

P.A., P.S., S.A. & A.C.

phantasy A psychical production based on the construction of a conscious or unconscious scenario in which the subject is present and in which he/she stages a conflict between the accomplishment of an unconscious desire and defensive processes. Phantasy was, for Freud, an alternative to the theory of infantile trauma. When it is possible for the phantasy to be structured, it is what founds psychical reality, as distinct from real events.

PHANTASY ACTIVITY

The theory of phantasy was for Freud a way of getting beyond the limitations of the theory of infantile trauma (actual violent seduction of a child by one of its parents). The phantasy theory has recently been criticized for being over-hasty in excluding real experiences of trauma (Bowlby, 1973; Masson, 1984). This debate has been re-opened with the practice of family therapy, which questions anew the opposition between real trauma and phantasized reality, and also puts in question the status of different *levels of reality*.

Phantasy differs from REALITY in the same way as a map differs from a territory. At the same time, however, phantasy cannot be regarded as the absolute opposite of reality, since the map establishes a new level of reality, psychical reality. It is the very nature of this state that is at the origin of the possible confusions between the two, which generate mythic narratives. The Oedipus myth is based on a collusion (of which Oedipus is the victim) between the reality of the phantasy and the phantasy of reality. The fiction created by Sophocles is the staging of the drama which prevented the construction of a phantasy in childhood: the reality of the phantasy is constructed on the basis of the relation Oedipus develops with his adoptive parents, Polybus and Merope – and not with his biological parents – during childhood; the phantasy of the reality is constructed once he has really killed Laius and has really slept with Jocasta. The doubling of parental figures in the experience of reality then leads to their being dramatically conjoined in the phantasy, an act which causes the sense of reality to teeter. When one is confronted with a psychosomatic or psychotic decompensation, the apparent poverty of the phantasy solution to the conflicts is a mark of the effraction of the psycho–affective territory of the personality. It is at this point that the map–territory confusion reaches its height.

Phantasy activity is based upon the circular organization of reality (Goutal, 1985). It serves both neurotic and normal subjects as a model for interpersonal relations and reveals, in the transference, the relational style they establish with those around them. For Bateson (1972), the phantasy is 'a kind of, a sort of'. The distinction between phantasy and non-phantasy is a function of secondary process. 'Psychotherapy itself is a context of multilevel communication, with exploration of the ambiguous lines between the literal and the metaphoric, or reality and fantasy' (Bateson, 1972, p. 196). A radical difference then emerges between the neurotic and the schizophrenic. The specific function of a phantasy is, normally, to protect the person from the realization of its content, internally to simulate situations experienced as traumatic in order to protect oneself from them. It enables us to divert the catastrophe into the sphere of mental elaboration. Neurosis intensifies the activity of the defence mechanisms (repression, projection/displacement, isolation, reaction formation etc.). The obsessional neurotic is caught up in an excess of protection from his/her phantasy activity, an excess which totally inhibits him/her. By contrast, the schizophrenic is confronted with the impossibility of labelling a phantasy as such. He/she thus takes a metaphor literally by acting it out in reality, which inevitably has unfortunate effects. One schizophrenic patient, for example, may not be able to bear anyone treading on his/her toes. Another, in the grip of mystical delirium, will strike a priest whom he/she suspects of insufficient faith, in order to see if he really will turn the other cheek. Schizophrenic relations attest to the (partial or total) difficulty the index patient has in acceding to the status of subject. He/she seems to remain a pure object of the observations and manipulations of others.

REALITY OF FAMILY INTERACTIONS

In a family group psychoanalytic perspective, the therapists will seek to work on the inter-phantasmic processes (Ruffiot, 1981a, b; Kaës et al., 1982; Eiguer, 1983). However, for there to be a phantasy, there must have been previously:

- a sufficient activation of the personality's instinctual potentialities and capacities for play;
- the ritualization of family relations;
- the construction of scenarios simulating reality and possible occurrences within it;
- processes of symbolization (deixis, naming);
- accession to the status of subject permitting psychical elaboration of the object relation.

Treatment of the most disturbed families shows that not all imaginary or dream productions, preconscious or unconscious phantasies can be interpreted as the fulfilment of an unconscious desire. In conditions of catastrophic experience, of extreme situations, the desiring function is supplanted by the attempt to protect the family from the danger of destruction both from within and without. In such cases, the ideas expressed are more like waking nightmares which have a premonitory dimension and seek to preserve the group from the anticipated danger.

The therapeutic attitude is therefore very different depending on whether the psychical representations are stabilized or not and whether the conflict is on the plane of personal phantasy or an interpersonal group plane. As Bateson (1972) shows, phantasy is no more able than the dream to introduce the idea of falsity, though this is a precondition for METACOMMUNICATION. It is one of the paradoxes of psychoanalysis that it calls for metacommunication regarding dreams and phantasies. The work of elaboration which such a process requires and the intensity of the resistance it

unleashes bear witness to the transformation which completely modifies their very nature. Therapeutic action with a schizophrenic patient and his/her family very often involves a completely opposite approach. The task here is to re-establish BOUNDARIES between different levels of reality – fact, PLAY, phantasy, DREAM, DELIRIUM etc. – to label metaphors and phantasies in order to distinguish them from acts, to differentiate stylistic figures from literal statements, territories from maps, the true from the false, external reality from psychical reality.

(See also AGONISTIC BEHAVIOUR; DEIXIS; FORECLOSURE, INCEST; METAPHORICAL OBJECT; PRESCRIPTION; SCHIZOPHRENIAS.)

J.M.

phase space of the family system On the level of family relations, the phase space of the family system will be defined by isolating certain parameters contributed by the GENOGRAM, COALITION systems, choices of career, values defended or abhorred by the system, preferential TERRITORIES, power and decision-making centres, FAMILY LIFE CYCLES etc.

An attempt will be made to specify the precise origins of the system and its evolution over time, by identifying the life cycles, recurrent trajectories and singular points of the system, and the point or multi-dimensional attractors with which the protagonists are confronted by virtue of the synchronization of their relations. In families with schizophrenic transactions, the number of dimensions of the phase space is very great, if not infinite. This explains the great difficulty involved in circumscribing the problem in time and space.

Such an evaluation cannot claim to arrive at a 'hard' and strict quantitative perception of the processes involved. We are dealing here rather with a 'soft' and qualitative evaluation, in which the subjective impression of the observer(s), therapists and other professionals not only cannot be invalidated, but must be considered as playing an integral part in the problem which is posed and has to be resolved.

(See also ACTUOGENETIC LANDSCAPE OF THE FAMILY; ATTRACTORS; DYNAMIC SYSTEMS; FAMILY MAPS; MAPS; POWER; STRUCTURAL STABILITY; TRIANGLES.)

J.M.

phylogenesis See ACTUOGENESIS; ETHOLOGY; FAMILY ETHOLOGY.

play A modality of communication based on a particular form of ritualization of relations. It is a fictive staging of behaviours that have a status of social reality (fighting, courtship behaviour, predation). It is constitutive of symbolic activity, of the structuring of the personality and of the learning of inter-human relations. For Gregory Bateson (1972, p. 158), MAPS and TERRITORIES are both equated and discriminated in play, whereas they are exclusively equated in the primary processes and exclusively discriminated in the secondary processes.

Play, in its different manifestations, is at the centre of therapeutic activity. In family clinical practice, the ability of the various members of the family to play on their relationships is an appreciable sign of detachment vis-à-vis the most dangerous forms of behaviour.

FUNCTION OF PLAY IN THE ONTOGENESIS OF RELATIONS

Play is a fundamental activity in higher animals: 'It is not because animals are young that they play but, on the contrary, they have a period of youth in which to play' (Groos, 1898). The animal complements its hereditary endowment with individual experience gained during play and prepares itself for the various tasks of adult life.

In the human infant, one can see the importance of motor interactions in playful mode for the construction of the relational system. Play is a ritual which humans share with other higher animals. It presupposes signals which metacommunicate about the relationship to indicate that what is going on is play (see MODE-IDENTIFYING SIGNALS). In the chasing games of young children, the partners alternate in the positions of hunter and hunted; they begin the movement of delivering blows, but stop before actually carrying out the attack. This game is accompanied by 'silent laughter'. These various behavioural traits function as signals, indicating that the fighting is not real fighting.

PLAY AND THERAPY

For Winnicott, it is the preoccupation and concentration which marks the importance of play for children, rather than the content of the play. This area of playing is not inner psychic reality, but neither does it belong to the external world. From a topological view, we might say that it is a non-orientated space (see TANGLED HIERARCHIES). Play has a creative potential dimension. Through play, the child is able to manipulate objects or fragments of objects from external reality, which are brought into contact with the exteriorization of internal personal reality. There is thus, in Winnicott's view, a progression from transitional phenomena to playing, from playing to shared playing and from this to cultural experiences. Winnicott (1971) here distinguishes between *play* and *games*. The transition from the one to the other is of great interest in family therapy, and precisely where modification of the 'rules of the game' is concerned. GAME THEORY relates explicitly to the rules of games, not to spontaneous play.

Play thus plays its part in the learning of social relations. It is a basic pillar of all therapeutic activity:

> Psychotherapy takes place in the overlap of two areas of playing, that of the patient and that of the therapist. Psychotherapy has to do with two people playing together. The corollary of this is that where playing is not possible then the work done by the therapist is directed towards bringing the patient from a state of not being able to play into a state of being able to play. (Winnicott, 1971, p. 54)

Therapeutic play thus conforms to a particular paradox, since 'there has to be play for there to be therapy.' In such a formulation, the 'there has to be' is as important as the play itself.

PLAY ABOUT INTERACTIONS, PLAY ABOUT PLAY

Play is not, however, merely a matter of personal development. The family, the school playground and informal social encounters are areas where play relates directly to collective interactions, the progressive learning of social rules and the permanent creation which these require. Worthwhile progress can be recorded when a family which has previously been prey to violent outbursts and symptoms expressed with no mediation succeeds in playing out its modes of relating, acting them out as if on stage. There is, in fact, total incompatibility between play and DELIRIUM: play activity 'requires a mental domain kept completely free and independent of any external coupling, in which the mind may realize high-codimensional chreods' (Thom, 1972, p. 317). Only access to family interactions makes it possible to grasp the redundancies within relations and enables progressive learning of shared play upon these interactions to develop.

On the basis of his ethological observations, Bateson has specified the semiotic structure of play and the hierarchical levels involved in it, together with the conditions which may, in some cases, cause it to break up. If one of the partners in play starts to metacommunicate about this ludic metacommunication, saying, 'this is play', he/she immediately changes the nature of the relationship and its meaning may then become undecidable: is this still play or must the relationship be changed? Play within play, or play about play, may thus lead to profound changes in communication, and it also brings with it risks of gratuitousness, insignificance and/or extreme danger, connected with the disappearance of a frame which would make it possible to define the relationship (see RESIDUAL RELATIONS).

When faced with particularly passive families, who have no outside relationships and are lacking in conceptual resources and whose only show of initiative is attending the sessions, therapists working in CO-THERAPY may come to play games about their own relationships, if not indeed the impediments within these relationships, during the sessions. This then appears as a first stage in the learning of role-playing.

(See also FAMILIODRAMA; PSYCHODRAMA; SOCIODRAMA.)

J.M. & P.G.

positive connotation   A therapeutic principle described by Selvini Palazzoli and colleagues (1978, pp. 55–66). It forms the basis of a strategy for conducting therapy with the most disturbed families. The principle consists in describing not only the symptom of the index patient, but also the symptomatic behaviours of the other members of the system, which are in direct resonance with the patient. It is thus a matter of confirming to the various family protagonists all their various modes of being and acting, which tend towards the homeostatic ideal of the family group to which they belong. Positive connotation consists in sustaining the HOMEOSTASIS of the family system rather than that of individuals in isolation.

Instead of seeking to put a brake upon the play of interactions, in their dysfunctional, aberrant and even perhaps outrageous aspects, efforts will be made to encourage this constraint to repeat which will then be considered as a stabilizing and 'reassuring' base for the transactions which bind the protagonists together. Where the family displays schizophrenic symptoms and attendant symptomatic behaviour, as provocative and threatening appeals, as solicitations of an imperative demand for change, if not indeed as a right to a cure, the therapeutic system, by contrast, emphasizes the necessary value of attempts made by all to maintain the present equilibrium of the system at all costs.

ADVANTAGES OF POSITIVE CONNOTATION

Positive connotation enables us to:

1   Reverse the moralizing valence which a negative designation of each person's activities would represent.
2   Gain access to the functioning of a system by reinforcing its regulatory and stabilizing tendencies.
3   Establish a system of therapeutic alliance, where the natural or spontaneous response would be disapproval and rejection.
4   Place each protagonist back at a level of full actor and thinker in his/her own right (symmetry of actants, from the patient to those who are well, including the therapist), while accepting the differential definition given by the system regarding the patient and the others (complementarily between patient and those around him/her who are not ill, between the patient and the family/therapists).
5   Transform the context which is perceived as inducing pathology into a situation which can produce care and potential change.

CRITICAL COMMENTS

Positive connotation is, at first appearance, a counter-manipulatory manoeuvre. It is employed in pathological situations in which disturbances appear in the manipulatory MODALITIES OF COMMUNICATION. Families with schizophrenic transactions do not betray a machiavellian tendency to manipulate unduly, but a dysfunctioning in what appears to be a component inherent in all communication.

Even if it includes a necessary dimension of artificial technique, positive connotation cannot be reduced to a mere recipe, in which it would be sufficient merely to tell each person how good his/her behaviour is in all circumstances. It implies deep investigation of the behaviour (ETHOS) and modes of thinking (EIDOS) of the members of the family, as well as a respect for the SINGULARITIES of the system perceived in this way.

This is to say that it fits into a spatiotemporal dimension in which the time factor has to be studied, in its own specific cycles and its irreducible time-spans, just as closely as the space factor. If strategy has to do with system modelling, positive connotation has to do with a set of tactical interventions.

Positive connotation corresponds to an inversion in the evaluation of the affective polarities of the family system. What will be explicitly designated in the uttering of the message (its denotative part) will have to be studied as being capable of contradiction or disqualification: the patient will be asked, for example, to listen more attentively to the voices persecuting him/her in order that he/she can try better to pinpoint their real origin. At the same time, the parents will be asked to reinforce their discreet – or even invisible – surveillance of the patient, so that they can better pin down the full range of his/her acts in the tiniest detail. Such a denotation will thus serve as a target and will protect the connoted dimensions of the message from an all-out attack from within by the family system. These connoted dimensions will relate to the reinforcement of the family's threatened structures, the stabilization of boundaries, the ritualization of messages and acts, and the recreation of interpersonal respect.

From the perspective of catastrophe theory, positive connotation makes it possible to activate the catastrophes which keep in being the 'figure of regulation' of the system, in order to improve its structural stability, the indispensable precondition for any possibility of real change.

(See also CIRCULARITY; FAMILY CATASTROPHES; FAMILY SYSTEMS; FEEDBACK; SYSTEMIC HYPOTHESIS; SYSTEMIC MODELLING AND INTERVENTION; NEUTRALITY; PRESCRIPTION; PROVOCATION.)

J.M. & P.S.

positive feedback in the family system See CY-
BERNETICS; FEEDBACK; HOMEOSTASIS; MULTI-LEVEL
HIERARCHIES; STRANGE LOOPS; TANGLED HIERARCHIES.

posturo-gestural exchanges See GAZE, EYE CON-
TACT AND POSTURO-GESTURAL EXCHANGES.

power The emergence of power presupposes the existence not only of communication but also of INTERAC-
TION. Visible power, 'the balance of net influence',
expresses itself in the dissymmetry of a relationship.

We speak of a power relation, where there is:

1   A relationship of belonging to a system and the
    hierarchical levels of regulation, control and sub-
    servience which such a relationship supposes. Be-
    ing in a relation of power means being located within
    a social hierarchy in which someone causes some-
    one else to do something or to be what they are. In
    this sense, power can be exercised from a lower
    position in the hierarchy as much as from a higher
    one.
2   A relation of forces which renders any system
    change illusory if the configuration of active forces
    and effective hierarchies is not studied and re-
    spected.
3   A capability to invest personal and social, material
    and psychical TERRITORIES, corresponding to the
    allocation of material or symbolic resources.

From the perspective of family relations, the OEDI-
PUS COMPLEX seems like assuming the myth of the con-
queror (Nathan, 1985b), a symbolic appropriation of
the organizing centre of the family unit. The understanding of power struggles also requires the interrogation of other mythic forms for which families provide
a theatre. The differences between the sexes and the
generations give rise to the oppositions of feminism
and machismo, on the one hand, and between parental
authority and filial revolt, on the other. Power has
effects upon the definition of the real. Clarifying the
power relations in the interactions between a psychotic
and the members of his/her family – and among those
treating him/her – has therapeutic effects.

Differences of opinion arose between Bateson and
Haley on the importance of power. For Bateson, if it
short-circuits the (individual, cultural and ecological)
biological systems, conscious purpose runs the risk of
destroying the great organic balances. The problem is,
therefore, not so much with power itself as with the
idea of power, which is incapable of taking into account the 'loop structure' which characterizes the whole
of the systemic structure, The total set of systemic
forces may be termed 'God', the 'Universe' etc. as

each person understands these things and believes in
them.

For Haley, symptoms can be seen as the expression
of power conflicts, stabilized in fixed coalitions and
revealing incongruity between the communicative and
metacommunicative levels of messages. They then become tactics aimed at maintaining or changing the
patterns of coalition, by way of threats, sabotage, promises, passive resistance or actual physical assaults. The
patient's symptomatic behaviour itself becomes an
instance of power which obliges the family system to
request aid from outside.

Bateson's preoccupation here deserves to be retained
so far as therapeutic action is concerned. On the one
hand, because it enables us to distinguish between
political and therapeutic power and, on the other, in
order to attempt to avoid both abuses of established
(political and therapeutic) power and the misrecognition of the effects of power, as the idea of therapeutic
power, whether 'systemic', 'psychoanalytic' or 'chemotherapeutic', runs the grave risk of destroying the very
purpose it sets itself: (a) if it conceals itself behind
scholastic oppositions; and (b) if it conceals the reciprocal skills of the intervening practitioners and the
circuits of responsibility which are effectively in play.

MANIPULATION, HIERARCHICAL POSITION AND
INFLUENCE

The way one person, by his/her actions, emotions and
thoughts, determines the destiny of another, by modifying that person's actions, emotions and thoughts, is
an explicit form of power. Such a relationship is a
product of the manipulatory (see MANIPULATION) and
DEONTIC modalities of communication: 'causing-to-do,
causing-to-be, having-to-do, having-to-be' and their
semiotic antitheses. It is correlated with the capacity to
make decisions and thus depends on the structure of
exchanges of information and the semantic values of
those exchanges.

Power is a matter of positions within a group, of the
investment of territory and social status and must be
viewed in relation to a balance of forces and the capacity to regulate conflicts seen as the overlapping of at
least two FORCE FIELDS. Power is not reducible, in
Lewin's view (1951, p. 40), to mere psychological force.
A's power may be greater than B's without A actually
exerting any pressure on B at a particular moment.
Power is, rather, 'the "possibility of inducing forces"
of a certain magnitude on another person' (1951, p.
40). Such a capacity may be linked to the creation of
COALITIONS or alliances with several other persons, leading to the formation of NETWORKS. As in military strategy, a relationship of authority, which establishes a
certain reality, functions as much as an immediately
realizable potential (threat) as it does as an actually
realized event.

POWER AND THE FAMILY

Power can thus be defined as the potential reciprocal influence of the members of the family in the development of an activity. It is a relative, not an absolute, datum which poses the question of its object – power over what? – and of its subject – power of whom? In Haley's view, every relationship needs to be defined which implies manoeuvres on the part of the protagonists. The definition given to the relationship – not the relationship itself – must be subject to a reciprocal implicit control, in such a way that this control issues in a shared agreement: friendly relations, working relations, love relations or no relations etc.

Various different forms of pathology appear. Instead of seeking to control the definition given to the relationship, partners will seek to control the relationship itself or to control each other in that relationship.

The analysis of family communication and its disorders shows that the statuses, roles and functions of father, mother, child and grandparent etc. depend on the nature of the interactions and definitions which each gives of him or herself and others in lived situations. It cannot leave out of account family systems nor cultural, intellectual and religious systems etc.

In this sense, power is not the individual action of a human being exerted on one or more other human beings. It is part of an exchange of complementarity, of symmetry and of reciprocity between them and thus presupposes the recognition of the power of the emergent system. In psychopathology, that system has been studied with particular attention in the epistemology of ALCOHOLISM, of SCHIZOPHRENIAS, of ANOREXIA NERVOSA and of delinquency. In all these cases, the starting point defined by Bateson as representing the first postulate of Alcoholics Anonymous may be generalized: 'There is a Power greater than the self' (1972, p. 302).

Depending on the particular case, that power is the relationship which the alcoholic and those around him have with the bottle and its contents, the relationship of the schizophrenic, monitored by his close relatives and his therapists, with his voices, the relationship the young offender has with laws that are stronger than any legality. But each case demands different specific responses.

We may suppose that the specific character of power in the family is connected with what differentiates it from other social groups and makes it a 'social envelope' of a particular kind. In Hoffman's (1981) view, that 'social envelope' constituted by the family is differentiated from other social groups by the regularity of the rhythm which impels individuals towards one another or tends to separate them from each other. Quoting Eliot D. Chapple, she describes a quota of daily interactions necessary to the well-being of each individual. 'At any rate, it is reasonable to hypothesize that any kind of satisfactory interaction between people in a family would involve a balance of giving and getting, and of being touched and being left alone' (Hoffman, 1981, pp. 192–3).

Power may therefore be seen as the capacity of one member of the family to control the frequency of intrafamilial interactions and moments of intimacy through the organization of daily activities. However, to get out of the ever-increasing escalation, which has no basis of any substance, of competing bids for power, it is necessary to delimit the reciprocal spheres of influence of each partner within a relationship over the others.

(See also COMMUNAL INDIVIDUALS; INSTITUTIONS; LAW; MANIPULATION; MULTI-LEVEL HIERARCHIES; PERFORMATIVES; SOCIAL ORGANIZATION; TANGLED HIERARCHIES; THERAPEUTIC STRATEGIES AND TACTICS.)

J.M. & A.L.

pragmatics of communication Has as its object the study of the actualization of the relations between organisms which are in a situation to communicate. It is concerned, therefore, with the concretization of events relating to behaviour, both manifest and latent. In fact, apragmatism ('doing nothing') is also of concern to the pragmatics of communication, by virtue of its being the realization of non-behaviour. Such a realization thus leads, in certain cases, to PARADOXES, having patent destructive and/or creative effects. 'Do not read this sentence' or ' "Will you answer me?" – "No!" ' are pragmatic paradoxes.

According to what has become the classic view, in the study of language, 'pragmatics' is distinguished from the SYNTAX and SEMANTICS OF COMMUNICATION, the three together forming semiotics within the framework of a general theory of signs. This distinction represents a difference of perspective, not of nature. Pragmatics concerns the users of signs and the way they act in the context of overall events, as these occur historically.

Combining the contributions of semiotics, information theory and cybernetics, the Palo Alto school radically renewed interest in the pragmatics of communication and the pathological, therapeutic and creative paradoxes it enables us to recognize and deal with.

AXIOMATICS OF COMMUNICATION

Communication produces meaning effects (semantic point of view), which arise out of creating interaction (pragmatic point of view) between interlocking structures of behaviour (syntactic point of view). The pragmatics of communication, which is founded on an *axiomatics of communication*, is based on five fundamental axioms (Watzlawick et al., 1967).

1   One cannot *not* communicate (see ALIENATION; AUTONOMY; DOUBLE BIND; MODE–IDENTIFYING SIGNALS; NARCISSISM; SCHIZOPHRENIAS).

2   All communication has two aspects, the content (report) and the relationship (command). The second of these subsumes the first and functions as metacommunication (see METACOMMUNICATION SYSTEMS).

3   The nature of a relationship depends on the punctuation of the sequences of communication between the partners (see PUNCTUATION OF SEQUENCES OF EVENTS).

4   Human beings employ two modes of communication: the digital and the analogic. Digital language is essentially syntactic, but lacks a semantics appropriate to relationship. Analogic language is essentially semantic, but lacks a syntax capable of suppressing the ambiguity and vagueness of relationships (see ANALOGIC CODING; DIGITAL (OR NUMERIC) CODING; MESSAGES).

5   Every exchange is symmetrical or complementary, depending upon whether it is based on equality or difference (see SCHISMOGENESIS).

Later contributors were to add corollaries and, indeed, modifications to these axioms. The following qualifications can be offered.

One cannot not *communicate*

Behaviour has no opposite. The human being, most particularly, cannot not behave: not to activate a behaviour is still to behave. Not saying 'Hello' to someone is to signify to that person that one does not recognize them or that one does not wish to see them or that one is depressed etc.

Every unit of behaviour has the value of a message. A message is therefore identifiable with a unit of communication, made up of units of behaviour activated by two or more persons. A series of exchanges of messages between two or more persons is called *interaction*. A set of series of messages exchanged produces *a model of interaction*. Identifying a set of this kind creates a MODEL OF A SYSTEMIC MODEL (a meta-model).

For example, the mother–child relationship is constituted by an interaction between complementary units of behaviour: attachment behaviour on the part of the child, caretaking behaviour on the part of the parent. This relationship is itself re-framed by multiple interpersonal exchanges (linked to the personality of the child, the parents, the grandparents etc.). The whole set of these creates a model of interaction.

Every interaction, every model of interaction, presupposes voluntary and involuntary, implicit and explicit *metacommunications* (communication about communication). A message will be the more intense, searching and complex, when the sender, consciously or unconsciously, seems totally isolated or refuses any

form of communication or metacommunication. In this sense, the schizophrenic is confronted with a continual instability of signals of metacommunication.

An organism possessing autonomy cannot be isolated. The isolation of an autonomous organism, outside its life context, destroys its autonomy. Its behaviour cannot but influence the behaviour of organisms around it. More exactly, an organism which succeeds in isolating its behaviour, and isolating the messages of its isolation, is confronted with paradoxes which are not only theoretical, semantic and linguistic, but, above all, pragmatic.

Metacommunication, paracommunication

All communication has a content aspect and a relationship aspect: the relationship aspect is of a more abstract level, subsumes the content aspect and produces a metacommunication, which is, in large measure, unconscious. Conversely, the content serves to define the relationship by secondary reinterpretation of the effects of the metacommunication.

Several units of communication may be juxtaposed without metacommunicating in respect of one another. They may thus co-evolve in synergy with or in opposition to one another or do so neutrally, creating PARACOMMUNICATION SYSTEMS.

A unit of communication leads to effective processing of the relationship and content of the communication. The content aspect serves as the report, the relationship aspect as the command. The content is a report of the nature of the unit of communication and corresponds to the bits of information. The relationship is information about the information or meta-information and provides instructions for processing the content data. In the nuclear sentence, the subject and object are reports; the verb functions as a command operating for the reports, subject and object.

Punctuation of sequences of events

An interaction or series of interchanges of messages forms an uninterrupted sequence of communication; the nature of the relationship depends on the punctuation of the sequence of events, which is established in a largely arbitrary way by the partners in the relationship and which leads to a self-referential coupling (see FAMILY SELF–REFERENTIALITY).

Codes and messages

Communication is based upon two types of analytic coding, the analogic and the digital. By means of digital coding a thorough syntactic and analytic processing is possible, conveying the content of the communication in ever more complex detail. It cannot, however, alone convey the semantic value of the interchange. It acts by dissociating syntax from semantics. Analogic coding, by contrast, contributes a particularly rich semantic processing, by constantly extending the relationship function of communication. However, messages which are only processed in this way remain ambiguous. Analogic coding couples semantics with syntax.

Communication is also based on holistic codings. Some signals have a holographic structure, each element of the message being isomorphic with the totality of the referent transmitted. Similarly, the totality of the message is isomorphic with each element of the referent (see HOLOGRAPHIC MEMORY). In complex organisms, systems of coding function at different levels and are subject to reciprocal transformations as an effect of ANALOG–DIGITAL and DIGITAL–ANALOG CONVERTERS, and of holographic processing of information. An elementary signal is the product of reciprocal interaction between several coding systems. A message is itself a set of signals.

Every message is made up of deictic, iconic and symbolic signals. A message is a superstructure which cannot be strictly reduced to a single type of coding.

Schismogenesis, symmetry, complementarity, reciprocity
Every structured interchange of communication produces phenomena of schismogenesis, of a complementary, symmetrical or reciprocal type. Complementary schismogenesis is based on the creation of difference, symmetrical schismogenesis on the creation of equality, and reciprocal schismogenesis on the creation of inter-level regulation. The dyadic differentiation which results from this is regulated and stabilized by the intervention of a third element (see TRIANGLES).

PRAGMATICS, BEHAVIOUR AND LANGUAGE

The pragmatics of human communication is concerned with the activation and de-activation of spoken and unspoken, verbal and non-verbal, expressible and inexpressible behaviour. These various levels of expression characterize communication in so far as they play a part in the definition of agreements and disagreements between partners. One may speak without saying anything and, by contrast, allowing someone else to speak and listening may be something active. One has the option not to utter a thought that is linguistically present in one's head ('to think before speaking'). Lastly, a part of the interaction which accompanies discourse cannot be subjected to linguistic transformation.

The pragmatics of communication therefore becomes indissociable from semantic and syntactic processes. Semantic processes presuppose an AGREEMENT, a resonance between users (with all the concomitant phenomena of discordance and disagreement). The problem is to find meaning in the apparent nonsense, to find purpose in situations which are apparently without meaning. Syntactic processes lead to the articulation of the grammar of language and the grammar of ATTITUDES. Syntactic morphologies possess a tree structure (see SURFACE STRUCTURES, DEEP STRUCTURES).

Between two or more levels of expression there can be synergy or antagonism. Language is a semantic unit capable of reflecting, up to a certain point, other semantic units. And yet a piece of music or a mathematical theorem is difficult to translate into everyday language. There are thus, in reality, breaks in meaning between two or more semantic units between which there is supposed to be correspondence.

The use of discourse, through speaking or generally bringing language to bear, may be a forceful and elegant way of confirming or denying the existence of behaviours which go to make up semiotic events. Verbal and non-verbal behaviours may stand in contradiction to one another, or there may be a contradiction between what one is saying and what one is thinking or between two or more levels of non-verbalizable behaviour. We thus find that a number of (posturogestural, vocal-linguistic) semantic units may simultaneously express wholly different and sometimes antinomic meanings.

An entire family in schizophrenic transaction may address a verbalized message to the therapists to the effect that they should do something. At the same time, their gestures, looks and postures (or, more subtly, certain details of these), as well as the patient's behaviour, may be informing the therapists that the family is terrified of the thought of any effective or significant action.

It follows from this that language – or, more precisely, languages (if we take into account the plethora of animal, computer and human languages) – are only one part of the phenomena involved in the pragmatics of communication. These languages are often clumsy when it comes to accurately describing the nature of what is really happening in communication between two persons, even when that communication lasts only for a few moments. The human being does not communicate only by way of the linear medium of words; he or she is caught up in a polyphony of interchanges, as well as in an orchestration of space. From a therapeutic point of view, the psychoanalytic ritual of couch and armchair deliberately channels all gestural manifestations (the 'dance of interactions') to centre attention on the effects of speech. Other rituals are, however, equally capable of meeting the demands of therapy. Each medium employed (groups, use of video, one-way screens, FAMILIODRAMA; GENOGRAM; SCULPTING etc.) in fact creates its own space of intervention and action.

(See also CIRCULARITY; COMMUNICATION THEORY; LEVELS OF COMMUNICATION; PERFORMATIVES; PRESCRIPTION; SELF–FULFILLING PROPHECY; SPEECH ACTS.)

J.M.

pregnance See FAMILY ACTANT; PROCREATIVE FAMILIES; SYMBOLIC REFERENCE.

prescribing (medical) drugs Psychotropic drugs have often been regarded as analysers of individual behaviour. The administration of these substances transforms the semiology and leads to a modification of certain psychopathological elaborations. It may also be observed that the prescription of a psychotropic drug modifies the nature of interactions between subjects and their various environments, in particular their families. The feedback observed after an input of medication should also be part of any evaluation of family dynamics.

In many cases, the context of the family interview succeeds in making intelligible behaviour which, up to that point, had seemed characterized by the most disconcerting illogicality. The systemic model enables us to set chemotherapeutic prescription, psychotherapeutic intervention and institutional work back in the whole spectrum of contexts under consideration.

The circulation of medical drugs within the family group sometimes constitutes an item of information which is crucial for grasping the dynamics of certain families which share a highly elaborate set of verbal and non-verbal codes. In many families where a psychosomatic, depressive or psychotic pathology is expressed, the index patient is not the only one who each day takes one or more forms of psychotropic medication. The case of the families of addicts seems to illustrate this point particularly well.

Consumption of psychotropic medical drugs in families of addicts

More than 60 per cent of drug addicts use psychotropic drugs in an addictive fashion. Amphetamines or barbiturates are the drugs most frequently cited. We wondered whether the lawful consumption of psychotropic drugs in the close environment of an individual may, by its high frequency, make their use seem routine, i.e. may modify the subject's perception of this type of product and make him/her more vulnerable to psychotropic drugs used both lawfully and unlawfully. Working with this hypothesis, with the team of Unit 185 of INSERM (Davidson and Angel, 1978), we researched the question whether subjects who have become addicts belong to families where the use of psychotropic drugs, whether issued by medical prescription or not, is more frequent than in the general population. Selecting treatments against insomnia, nervous states and anxiety, we obtained the results given below. In order to establish an order of magnitude, we indicate the regular consumption of the same medicaments by a population of 'all-comers' aged between 40 and 69, which was surveyed by INSERM in the Indre-et-Loire department of France (this age range is more or less comparable with that of the addicts' parents at the time of the research).

Consumption is higher among the population of parents of drug addicts than in the general population: one finds an excess of more than 40 per cent among the women and more than 80 per cent among the men. We should note here that the parents' consumption is reported by the subjects and they may have distant or non-existent relations with their parents either by virtue of deaths or of breaks with them and may therefore have no knowledge of their consumption of medical drugs. Moreover, the lower the educational level of the subjects or the more lowly their social origin, the more seldom do they report a consumption of psychotropic drugs in their parents (particularly in their mothers). The question therefore arises whether or not this represents the actual consumption of the parents.

In households where the head is a manual worker in industry or the service sector, the proportions of regular users of psychotropic drugs are reported as being 10 per cent for fathers, 13.3 per cent for mothers against figures of 16.9 per cent and 42.2 per cent respectively for the households of managerial staff, professionals and industrialists. This variation may be occasioned by the subjects not responding evenly across the various social backgrounds, the subjects' level of education and the frequency of their relations with their parents. It seems that both the parents' consumption and the proportion of young people reporting it play a part in giving this result. It would seem then that one can see particularly accentuated habits of drug consumption in the families of addicts from well-off backgrounds, particularly among the mothers.

A study by Smart and Fejer (1972), in which research was carried out on 8,865 Canadian school and university students, shows that the maternal consumption of tranquillizers has a marked effect upon drug-addicted subjects, particularly if that consumption is on a daily basis. The particular form of drug used by the father or mother (barbiturates, tranquillizers or stimulants) is often the one the child will use. Let us also add, lastly, that in 28 per cent of cases (a calculation made from a sample of 152 persons), the subject had taken one or more psychotropic medical drugs in their childhood, at a period when they were still in the care of their parents (or others responsible for their upbringing and education). This type of situation may have contributed to the transmission of a favourable attitude towards psychotropic drugs. We do not, however, have comparable data which would allow us to determine whether this frequency is abnormally high.

The description of the consumption of psychotropic drugs by parents of subjects who become users of serious drugs leads us to enquire into the conditions which cause parents to consume drugs in this way and about the relations which exist between their consumption and their children's addiction. The hypotheses may be suggested: either (a) the parents of addicts have been exposed to a particularly great number of traumatic events and, without presenting evidence of any major psychical disturbances, they could be more affected by various events (death, break-up, suicide attempts or alcoholism within their close circle etc.) than are the adults in the 'all-comers' population; or (b) they are less capable of facing up to the frustrations of existence, hence their recourse in both cases to medicinal drugs and to alcohol. During their childhood, addicts seem to experience major difficulties as their parents do and learn, by their example, to have recourse to psychotropic drugs as a means of dealing with these.

NEGATIVE CHEMOTHERAPEUTIC REACTIONS

Determining the mechanisms which lead to 'negative chemotherapeutic reactions' presents an interest for clinicians in so far as they are involved in elaborating STRATEGIES to make it possible to thwart sabotaging manoeuvres or to reduce rejection reactions to medicaments which have proved their effectiveness.

The abrupt abandonment of an appropriate therapy is something that is often encountered in clinical experience. The reasons advanced for this are many: secondary effects that are difficult to tolerate; finding it unbearable to be dependent on a drug; the restrictions imposed by having to take daily doses. Beyond these arguments, some of which seem justified, the prescribing doctor can sense that other factors are in play: attachment to the secondary gains from the symptom; nostalgia for the sense of manic elation suppressed by lithium; inability to tolerate the sense of emptiness created by the abrupt cessation of a delirium; an experience of having one's creative capacities amputated. One should, however, be careful not to overlook the resonances which psychotropic drugs create in a family group by abruptly modifying the rules of the game.

To prescribe a psychotropic drug for a member of a family is sometimes a way of expressing the summary character of these designation mechanisms. Moreover, one positively connotes the symptom by temporarily respecting its function. For example, how many times have we heard the complaint: 'It's not me who needs treatment, it's such and such a member of the family'? It does even happen that the patient designated by the family is not the one who seems to the therapist to be the most disturbed (see INDEX PATIENT). It is also rare for the therapist's view of what the symptoms are to coincide with the view of the family milieu. A prescription for drugs often becomes an object of discord. It is discussed by the family in terms of past experience and each person's medical knowledge. The prescription may also be evaluated in terms of the control it will allow over the patient. Within the family, the acceptance or rejection of a treatment is determined not only by rules, but also by meta-rules, i.e. rules governing the operation of the rules themselves.

These meta-rules are the product of a process of reciprocal adaptation and their structuring takes on a deeper significance within the framework of the mythology specific to each family. This observation should lead the clinician to take more account of the more or less implicit model which the family works out in respect of the psychopathological fact under consideration. Adopting a theoretical and practical position too far removed from this construction often leads to the failure of a therapeutic proposal.

CONCLUSIONS

Psychotropic drugs, as Maruani (1975a) has shown for lithium and we have hypothesized in a more general way with Miermont (1983), are multi-channel communicational vectors, whose inputs and outputs provide evidence of action at very different levels of the neurophysiological, psychical and interactional organization. The impact of psychotropic drugs ought to be recognized in the appreciation of sequences of communication.

This shows the positive value of heterogeneous models. The degrees of freedom rediscovered by the patients and their families are to be found more in the interstitial spaces surrounding the various fields of action, whether practical or theoretical. The limits to therapy often turn out to be therapeutic themselves. Our incapacity to conceive and think through certain aspects of the systems of a particular family, the emergence of an acute sense of failure, indeed of an authentically shared experience of catastrophe, between families and therapists, permit of creative redeployments which are often unexpected.

(See also ALCOHOLISM; DRUG ADDICTION; PSYCHOSOMATIC DOUBLE BINDS; SCHIZOPHRENIAS.)

P.A. & S.A.

prescription A level of communication which occurs in a legal, religious or therapeutic context. It has the status of an injunction (as has interdiction, which is its contrary from the semiotic point of view). Prescription is of the order of 'having to do', whereas interdiction is of the order of 'having not to do'. Injunction itself is a meta-modality which brings together the 'having to do' of prescription with the 'having not to do' of interdiction.

We may distinguish between several levels of intervention.

PRESCRIBING A SYMPTOM

Prescribing a symptom consists in using paradox in a therapeutic context. In psychoanalytic technique, the 'basic rule' is a technical prescription:

based on an extremely ambiguous message and, indeed, deriving its usefulness from that ambiguity. It is presented as a rule of communication and observation of mental events, but in reality constitutes more an end than a means. It is the resistance to compliance with it which enables the formations of the unconscious to be tracked down. Moreover, it implies a theory of mental functioning which takes into consideration the associative mechanisms governing the flow of thoughts and which supposes the existence of thoughts as objects of knowledge. (Widlöcher, 1986, pp. 25–6)

When dealing with very rigid family systems, where ACTING OUT is imminent or may indeed already have happened, the prescription of other technical rules, no less ambiguous and paradoxical, is necessary. It is very often impossible (if not indeed ethnically wrong) to ask all family members to engage in free association and to communicate the content of their thoughts when there are in fact serious disorders in the flow of thinking within the family. Prescription may in these cases be directed at the relations which exist between the act of thinking and the nature of the disorders directly expressed in action. But, here again, it would undoubtedly be necessary to recognize that, far from being an automatic recipe, prescription is an intervention which has to be used carefully. This leads us to a reconsideration of how we define what is termed the SYMPTOM. The symptom is not the same when viewed from the pure standpoint of psychiatric nosology as it is when seen from that of the police or the legal system. And it is different again if we focus on the index patient's dynamic and singular interactions with his/her family. One can easily imagine the havoc that would be caused by obliging the young offender to steal or to kill, the schizophrenic to be even more offensive to his close family, the anorectic to stop eating altogether, the drug addict to shoot up three times a day instead of once. We also know only too well, however, that prescribing simple antidotes, though it palliates the most immediate harmful effects, is not enough.

Prescription of the symptom is therefore based on the progressive recognition of the polysemic aspects of the symptom and therefore of the singularities of the contexts in which it arises. It is within a framework of this kind that prescriptions of tasks, prescriptions of rituals, the prescription of pretence and also the prescription of transactional structures can occur. Prescription is a therapeutic technique in which the therapist deliberately imagines a scenario, in such a way that the conflicts or other family problems may be expressed in action in the course of the family session, instead of merely being described. The therapist's task consists essentially in helping the family members to demonstrate concretely how they act, by using *in vivo* situations (Minuchin, 1974).

PRESCRIPTION OF THE STATUS QUO

This is made explicit in psychoanalysis, with the analyst asking the analysand to take no important decisions during the course of the analysis. It is a foundation of the strategy employed in dealing with the most destabilized family systems, where rigid forms of regulation are the only resource available for survival. The error is, then, merely to see it as a tactical technique, aimed at accelerating the process of change. Too often, the result obtained is an accentuation of the initial dysfunctioning.

MULTI-FOCAL PRESCRIPTIONS

To the extent that serious pathology most often derives from *group conflicts* (and not conflicts of internal representation, as in classic psychoanalysis), it becomes necessary to set up levels of intervention which are also multi-directional and also therapeutic teams where the roles are differentiated: accompanying the patient in everyday life, organization of time spent at home or within a particular institutional structure, specific intervention with the family, prescription of drugs, individual psychotherapy etc. The problem then arises of the effects which flow from the multiplication of therapies (see CO-THERAPY; THERAPEUTIC DOUBLE BINDS). Certain joint activities are likely to combine to good effect, but the risk of each of these therapies seeking to outbid the other also arises and there is some danger of iatrogenic effects (disorders which follow from therapeutic action). The merit of reflecting on phenomena relating to prescription lies, among other things, in the attention devoted to phenomena of dosing and overdosing, not only in matters pharmacological, but also in respect of psychotherapeutic measures, of family therapy and sociotherapy.

(See also INTERPRETATION; RITUALIZATION; SEMIOTIC SQUARE; SOCIAL ORGANIZATION; TASKS.)

J.M.

prescription of tasks See STRATEGIC THERAPY; TASKS, PRESCRIPTION OF TASKS.

primary process See METAPSYCHOLOGY; PLAY; UNCONSCIOUS, THE.

principle of complementarity A term created by the physicist Bohr and adapted by Ackerman (1958, 1966) for use in family therapy. Whereas in physics the term is used to resolve the dilemma of the particle that is also a wave, in family therapy it refers to the patterns of FAMILY ROLE relations through which the family members provide support and satisfaction for each of the others interdependently.

The term 'complementarity' refers to the family

actors' specific relational and role patterns which enable affection, care and loyalty to be expressed. Complementarity is the creative element which makes it possible to cope with the incompleteness and difference with which each family member is confronted. In Ackerman's (1966, p. 72) view, complementarity in family relations may be examined at five different levels:

- the support of self-esteem;
- cooperation in the quest for solutions to conflict;
- the satisfaction of needs;
- the support of needed defences against anxiety;
- support for the development and creative fulfilment of the individual family member.

(See also SCHISMOGENESIS; SOCIAL STATUS.)

P.S. & J.M.

procreative families, foster families, adoptive families The family fulfils three functions which can be separated out in reality: a procreative function, a caretaking function (feeding, upbringing) and a lineage function (adoption). In reality, these three functions of the family are combined or separated in varying degrees. Where there is a disjunction between them, particular problems arise and we are forced to recognize the home as one possessing 'multiple parenthood'. From a clinical point of view, it may be necessary to enquire into the degrees of PREGNANCE or salience of each of these family functions (see SYMBOLIC REFERENCE).

We may thus distinguish between three family functions, which may possibly be separated out in reality:

1 The *procreative family* function, is the 'natural' family, created by the birth of one or more children.
2 The *foster family* function is the family which sees that there is food, care and education, and nurture on a temporary basis until either return to the procreative family or inclusion into an adoptive family.
3 The *adoptive family* function is the family which gives the child full legal membership. It ensures that the child is a member of a 'line', offers him/her an identity and provides him/her with an inheritance.

The Oedipal myth derives its force from a dissociation/confusion of the procreative family and the foster/adoptive family. In reality, we do, however, find examples of a great many situations in which the different stratifications of family functions do not coincide, and this is something which leads to pragmatic paradoxes.

Some of these functional issues are highlighted in actuality. We shall cite here only the results from the detailed research into children living for long periods with foster families undertaken by Murphy (1974). He describes a syndrome with the following characteristics that is common to all children placed with foster families:

- fear that society will harm them, which is a compensation for their desire to attack society;
- excessive concern to defend themselves against aggression and hostile impulses;
- an over-hasty desire to marry and to have a home and children (above-average marriage rate) with a correspondingly high divorce and separation rate.

The difficulties experienced by those who have been foster children in adapting to adult life depend on several factors, some of which are related to the procreative family and others to the foster family:

1 The structure of the procreative family at the moment of the placement is a fundamental indicator for the subsequent prognosis.
2 The situation of being an illegitimate child, who could be adopted but has not been, in fact worsens the prognosis.
3 Financial participation by the procreative family, even where they do not visit, improves the proportion of cases where there is satisfactory development. By contrast, natural parents who do not contribute to the financial support of the child are an adverse factor, even if they visit their child.
4 Behavioural disturbances or alcoholism in both natural parents are more de-structuring than when only one parent suffers from these.
5 The influence of the foster family is apparently paradoxical: the prognosis is less hopeful for the child when attachment to the foster mother is intense and he/she identifies deeply with her.
6 Foster mothers succeed better when they are prepared to take several children, without showing preference as to age or number. In this case, they are seeking less to meet their own affective needs than are those mothers looking for a single child of preschool age.
7 For the child, the fact that he or she plays a role is only structuring for those foster children from a family milieu where there is no emotional deprivation, by contrast, for children who come from emotionally deprived or traumatizing environments, the imposition of too important a role or too much expectation accentuates the perception they have of their difficulties and reinforces their negative self-image.

(See also DISENGAGED FAMILIES; ENMESHED FAMILIES.)

J.M.

projection See FAMILY PROJECTION.

projective identification A concept developed by Melanie Klein (1946) and integral to her hypotheses on the early emotional development of the infant. It refers to a primary defence mechanism which, in its normal functioning, constitutes an important factor for the capacity of symbolization and human communication.

Projective identification is an omnipotent phantasy of the infant by which non-desirable parts of its personality and its internal objects may be dissociated, projected and controlled in an external object. Projective identification is therefore characterized by the fact that parts of the infant's ego, split and projected into an external object, cause it to feel this latter is controlled by the fragments it has projected into it.

PROJECTIVE IDENTIFICATION IN THE FIRST PHASES OF LIFE

This defence mechanism acts intensely during the first phases of life and, more particularly, during the phase Klein refers to in terms of the schizoparanoid position. In that phase, the infant, exposed to the impacts of external reality and the anxiety produced by its own death drive, splits external and internal objects into good and bad objects. The function of projective identification is to bring the ego relief from the bad parts and preserve the good parts by protecting them from a bad internal world while at the same time attacking and destroying the external object. The depressive position is a later phase, during which the bad parts projected into the external object may be reintrojected in a mitigated, elaborated, more bearable form, thus enabling the feeling of ambivalence to emerge.

It is this possibility of reintegrating the projected fragments, in a form which enables them to be represented psychically, which leads Bion (1961) to write that the origin of the activity which will subsequently become the capacity for thought has its basis in projective identification.

PROJECTIVE IDENTIFICATION AND PSYCHOTIC PATHOLOGY

There exists a pathological form of projective identification in certain forms of psychosis. The dissociation of the parts of the ego gives rise to a multitude of fragments projected outside and creates a bizarre reality, a reality which becomes increasingly painful and persecutory, and this intensifies projective identification. This latter, together with splitting, then bears on perception and judgement and creates an ever increasing withdrawal from reality on the part of the psychotic.

The function of pathological projective identification is to rid the psychotic of all the ego functions which would allow him/her to apprehend the reality principle and the establishment of relations and bonds. In fact, in the psychotic phantasy, fragments expelled by projective identification into real objects become encrusted in them and dominate them and the objects possessed in this way thus become persecutory, attacking the projected parts in their turn and robbing them of all vitality. If the reintegration of the dissociated and projected elements cannot take place, for want of a containing 'good breast' ready to pass back, in a disintoxicated and bearable form, the contents projected into it, one sees projective identification become hypertrophied, and subsequently everything relating to frustration being permanently expelled.

In Bion's view, the mechanism of projective identification distinguishes the psychotic personality from the non-psychotic. It is the mechanism used in the psychotic where the neurotic employs repression. The processes of incorporation of objects appear, then, as an 'inverted projective identification'; objects return by the same path along which they were expelled, with equal or greater hostility. In actual fact, when the schizophrenic attempts to think of or recall what has been expelled, he/she has recourse to inverted projective identification. Even if he/she reaches the depressive position, the frustrations which he/she tries to avoid rather than to work through force him/her to abandon that position by employing projective identification of the depressive anxieties into his/her analyst or other objects, and this causes depressive feelings in these latter.

To sum up, then, a 'normal' projective identification consists in expelling a 'bad object' into a real object. This latter, usually the mother, modifies the unpleasant sensations connected with the bad object and tries to soothe the baby, who then reintrojects a representation, a non-sensory elaboration of maternal love. When a new frustration occurs, a sense of the absence of an object will then be created which is the beginning, in Bion's view, of what is properly called thinking (See Grinberg et al., 1972). If the reintrojection of the expelled elements cannot take place, pathological projective identification is initiated, together with the construction of a bizarre reality made up of a part of the personality and various parts of the object. Between these a relationship is maintained that empties both of their meaning and vitality.

(See also ALIENATION; FORECLOSURE; IDENTIFICATION; SCHIZOPHRENIAS; SCOTOMIZATION; TRADING OF DISSOCIATIONS.)

M.G.

propaedeutic (function) See FAMILY SYSTEMS.

provocation, crisis provocation An expression used by Jackson (1957) to connote the idea that change within the family can only occur if the therapist deliberately provokes the crisis situation, in order to force the family to tolerate the parameters essential for the creation of a new equilibrium preferable to the previous one. Provocation is to be understood here as provocation of the homeostatic function and not as provocation of the family members, who, on the contrary, are to be supported.

Some therapists have observed how their efforts to bring about change within a family turn out to be unavailing when the family is not in a crisis period. For this reason, they have found it useful to act in such a way that the family system is pushed beyond its usual coping mechanisms. Thus Haley (1976) advocates intervention in a phase of disequilibrium. For Hoffman (1981), the object of therapy must be, most often, not to restore order, but, by contrast, to introduce a greater COMPLEXITY. According to Andolfi (1982, pp. 43–4) 'for there to be real improvement, the family's functioning must enter a crisis.'

The therapist's role is situated at the opposite pole from what the family desires. He/she will try to produce the disequilibrium the family wishes to avoid at any cost (Jenkins, 1989b). It will be the therapist's task, particularly in families in rigid transaction, to induce a crisis: 'the family wants stability and we are proposing to destabilize it; instead of patching it up, we are offering to throw a bomb into it' (Andolfi, 1982, p. 44).

Provocation is therefore used here as *crisis provocation*, inasmuch as this opens the way for therapeutic mobilization. In reality, in families in rigid transaction, the fear that one of the family members may threaten the habitual interactions by ceasing to obey the rules of the game creates a high degree of emotional tension. That tension and the anxiety which accompanies it force each individual to conform to all the injunctions which may reinforce the myth of family unity. 'That tension provides the energy that is required for the permanent effort to transform everything so that nothing changes' (Andolfi, 1982, p. 41). Though it fuels HOMEOSTASIS, such tension may reach such an intensity that it becomes an incitement to change, since it can no longer be contained by the function taken on by the INDEX PATIENT.

When the weight of conflict within the family has become too heavy to bear, the family calls in a 'professional' to preserve its structure and avoid crisis. However, this does not mean that the family is prepared to put into question the relationships established between its members, especially those with the index patient. On the contrary, it is hostile to the idea that it will have to renegotiate its rules of interaction and each person's space and functions. The danger of an uncontrolled transformation of each person's status which, previously, had created the need to find a SCAPEGOAT, reappears. Thus the family, feeling threatened once again, unites more than ever around the aim of avoiding this crisis which is both desired and feared.

If the regulative function taken on by the index patient is no longer sufficient to preserve the family structure, other resources have to be mobilized. For this the family uses an old tactic. It places an individual in a central position in order to make him/her soak up all the tension. By reproducing the manoeuvre already carried out with the index patient, the family can transfer the forces in conflict onto someone outside the family group. The presence of the therapist enables the family to off-load the tensions it can no longer contain within it. The family calls upon the therapist to manage these without putting in question the principles by which it functions.

If the therapist 'respects' the point of view of the family, which sees the patient as the sole source of its difficulties, then, like the 'patient', he/she becomes the repository of a malaise, the correlation of which with each person's problems it will then be more difficult to observe. Thus the designation of the patient and the request for a therapeutic intervention are two analogous moments in their functional meaning: the family seeks to avoid all tension between its members by designating an official repository for that tension. The family system, sensing danger, exacerbates its dysfunctional structure. Paradoxically, it has to make a show of strength at the point where it feels at its weakest. Thus at the moment when a request for therapeutic intervention is formulated, the family presents a greater rigidity. For fear of encountering pain, the family would like the therapist to limit his/her interventions and to content him/herself with attending to the most urgent matters, rather than confronting an uncontrollable crisis which threatens its structure.

To this request for assistance in resolving limited problems, the therapist responds by increasing the number of variables involved, offers a wider understanding of the problems and thus, by accentuating the pre-existing instability, brings about a loss of control of the established equilibria. For a real improvement to occur, he/she therefore induces a crisis within the family endeavouring to produce the disequilibrium that the family would rather avoid, and precipitating instability where it tries to maintain rigid stability.

The possibility of triggering a crisis depends on the nature of the intervention. In Andolfi's view, this must be a response to the inputs which the family communicates to the therapist and must be carried out in what is virtually a mimetic mode. Noting that certain messages addressed by the family are provocative, Andolfi has worked out a strategy of intervention which consists in privileging information of this type and responding to it by a counter-provocation. This consists essentially in using the index patient as the point of attack: the family provokes the therapist and controls the system through the index patient. The therapist must, in his or her turn, attempt to provoke the family and control the system through this same channel. The object is to provoke the system, not the members of the system. Instead of contesting the central position of the index patient, the therapist uses it. The index patient becomes the gateway to the system. Since the family has designated him or her as the obligatory intermediary of all interaction, the therapist acts in the same way and locks him/her into this function. The 'involuntary' behaviour of the patient must, progressively, appear voluntary to the family, in order to destabilize the family system and make it possible radically to redefine the problem and the relationship between the therapist and the family.

For provocation to be effective, the therapist must have already identified certain of the functions assumed by the various members of the family and have a picture of the relational tissue which unites them, particularly to the patient. He/she will thus be able to attack the index patient in his/her role as support of certain modalities of interaction. Provocation must not, in fact, be directed against an isolated individual, but at the individual in so far as he/she is an integral part of the wider system. And indeed, all provocation always has a dual thrust: to avoid confusion with aggression pure and simple, the symptom function must be provoked and, at the same time, the person must be supported. In other words, a family will not accept real change until it feels sufficiently structured and complexified to do so.

(See also CRISIS INTERVENTION; FAMILY CRISIS; ORDER.)

P.A., A.C. & J.M.

pseudo-hostility Defensive splits or ALIENATION within the family which remains merely superficial. Pseudo-hostility functions to mask the intense need for intimacy or affection which the family members cannot easily share with each other (Wynne, 1961).

(See also AGONISTIC BEHAVIOUR; MODE-IDENTIFYING SIGNALS; PSEUDO-MUTUALITY.)

P.S.

pseudo-mutuality Family situation in which the family members are concerned with reciprocal adaptation rather than with developing the differentiation of their own personal identities. Such a personal identity represents a threat to the whole family system. Pseudo-mutuality and PSEUDO-HOSTILITY are two ways of dealing with the observable phenomena of ALIGNMENTS and DISSOCIATIONS which, in reality, indicate to the therapist the dominant type of emotional system in the family (Wynne et al., 1958).

(See also AGREEMENT AND DISAGREEMENT.)

P.S.

pseudo-speciation, pseudo-species In Erikson's (1968) view, man survived as a species by dividing into pseudo-species by way of the distinctions introduced by language barriers and the tendency to reject outside groups as 'barbarians' excluded from humanity. Only the learning of cultural values enables him to differentiate himself from animal species. However, in so doing, he differentiates himself into groups, thus running the risk of rejecting as inhuman, animal or bestial the groups which do not share the same basic identity. Pseudo-speciation, by causing the sense of human specificity of every man to be lost, is one of the greatest dangers threatening humanity.

The collective identity of the horde, tribe, class, nation or religious community may lead to only regarding as truly human those who share the same identity. Now, the search for a pure identity is both a sign of alienation and a condition of historical evolution, through the necessary confrontation with confusions of identity.

Cultural pseudo-speciation may be seen to have its roots in tribal life. It seems to derive from man's neoteny (see DOMESTICATION), which leads the child to experience his/her human identity within his/her family group, clan or tribe. Cultural tradition is, in effect, the enforced and disguised prolongation of instinctual behaviour. In man, hereditary control mechanisms are insufficient. The control and regulation provided by acquired sociocultural experience are a biological necessity for the survival of the human species (Lorenz, 1973).

Man, with his ideal of pure identity, at times pushes too far the distinction between those who are familiar and those who are strangers. By a mechanism of projection of bad objects towards the outside, he perceives alien groups as made up of beings who are non-human since they do not possess the same cultural system of humanization (languages, myths, religions, ideologies). The sociocultural barriers contributed by language and the differential belief-systems conveyed in language, accentuate this process. This de-specification of man is linked, it seems, with a phenomenon of self-domestication.

In fact, the human species is not entirely a species like other animal species. It is a meta-species which contains in itself, by virtue of the effects of symbolic structures, certain behavioural variations observed within the plant and animal hierarchies. Hence the appearance of ethnic groups, clans and cultural groups, basing themselves on the diversity of languages to establish, upon the differentiations of collective identity, a sense of belonging to various organized social units. Hence, also, the falsification of signals, messages and representations, all of which necessarily interferes in the definition of the real (see REALITY) across the various cultures.

Racism is as much a product of cultural segregation

as of total non-differentiation of cultures. Lévi-Strauss (1961) courageously reminds us that not all cultures are equal. Six thousand years ago, on what is today the territory of France, *Homo sapiens sapiens* would eat his fellow man if he belonged to a different tribe. Contemporary totalitarianisms show no let up in their drive to exterminate styles of life which they do not understand. Even today, women are still stoned and men, women and children are mutilated and killed in the name of ideologies, moral and/or religious virtues and exlusive and devastating fanaticisms. As an obligatory micro-system, the family reveals, if it does not indeed generate, the experimental – physical and psychical – violence to which human beings may be subjected.

(See also INDEX PATIENT; RECIPROCAL VICTIMIZATION AND RESCUE; SCAPEGOAT; VIOLENCE.)

J.M. & P.G.

pseudo-static forms   See STATIC, PSEUDO-STATIC AND METABOLIC FORMS.

psychical apparatus   See FAMILY PSYCHICAL APPARATUS.

psychoanalysis   The first interdisciplinary model for understanding the human personality and therapeutic action in the twentieth century, and a theory of the psychical apparatus, showing the importance of UN-CONSCIOUS processes and the defence mechanisms by which they are structured (repression; isolation; undoing; denial; projection; PROJECTIVE IDENTIFICATION; FORECLOSURE; SCOTOMIZATION etc.). Psychoanalysis recognized the fundamental importance of infantile sexuality and the repression it undergoes during the latency period. It grasps the drama of the psyche as one that revolves around a triangulation structuring the normal and/or neurotic individual. The OEDIPUS COMPLEX appears as an organizer of – and a possible stumbling block within – family and social relations, on the basis of the desires and prohibitions of the child who is confronted, in REALITY and in PHANTASY, affectively and intellectually, with the parental figures. The Oedipus complex may thus be seen as a universal emotional invariant which structures, in a triangular manner, the individual's belonging to his/her nuclear family and the need he/she has to disengage him or herself from it.

Psychoanalytic theory has deeply transformed Western thought. In 1940, Bateson wrote:

as a matter of fact, *considerable contributions to science can be made with very blunt and crooked concepts*. We

may joke about the way misplaced concreteness abounds in every word of psychoanalytic writing – but in spite of all the muddled thinking that Freud started, psychoanalysis remains the outstanding contribution, almost the only contribution to our understanding of the family – a monument to the importance and value of loose thinking. (Bateson, 1972, p. 58)

Initially, Freud regarded the pragmatic coherence of psychoanalysis as being confined to the resolution of neurotic problems. That coherence derived from the discovery of an unconscious neurotic determinism, beneath the appearance of disorderly or chaotic phenomena. Subsequently, however, psychoanalysis has enabled us to cast theoretical light on other fields: madness, psychosomatic disorders, behaviour disturbances. It is not, however, certain that the application of psychoanalysis had been precisely appropriate in those fields. At the very least, we can say that Freud did not believe he had discovered the determinism of psychotic processes or behavioural disorders.

And yet, Freudian METAPSYCHOLOGY pertinently describes the modifications brought about by schizophrenic pathology: the secondary processes of thinking are invaded by the primary processes; words are taken for things; a single word may assume the function of a whole string of thoughts. Whereas object cathexes are abandoned, cathexis of word-representations of objects is maintained, but these word-representations are sundered from the thing-representations with which they are normally connected. Relationships between words become predominant over relationships between things: at the level of the linguistic sign, the signifier is split off from its signified. This explains the existence of a fundamental distinction between the dreamwork (see DREAMS) and SCHIZOPHRENIA.

In the latter, what becomes the subject of modification by the primary process are the words themselves in which the preconscious thought was expressed; in dreams, what are subject to this modification are not the words, but the thing-presentations to which the words have been taken back. In dreams there is a topographical regression; in schizophrenia there is not. In dreams there is free communication between (Pcs.) word-cathexes and (Ucs.) thing-cathexes, while it is characteristic of schizophrenia that this communication is cut off. (Freud, 'A metapsychological supplement to the theory of dreams', *Standard Edition*, vol. 14)

Whereas in dreams, the de-cathexis affects all the systems, it only affects the preconscious system in transference neuroses, only the unconscious system in schizophrenia and only the perception-consciousness system in amentia (psychosis of desire, reaction of denial in response to an unbearable loss).

This description seems both profoundly accurate

and incomplete. That it seems limited derives from its not being centred on the dynamics of the schizophrenic process. The question which remains concerns the conditions in which the unconscious system is de-cathected and, indeed, the conditions of structuring of that system. Bateson was to uncover part of that determinism by describing the learning contexts which preside over the organization of metacommunications, which are envelopes without which the unconscious system empties of all content, making the labelling of metaphors impossible.

As a self-referential theory, psychoanalysis cannot, of itself, establish all its limits and its own practical and theoretical coherence. It may give the impression of having made discoveries which it has not actually made. If it is believed that Freud conceived, in advance, the only methodology which enables us to grasp all future exploration, then the psychoanalytic project runs the risk of blinding researchers, its destiny here merging with that of Oedipus.

Family therapy would doubtless not have emerged, however, without the revolutionary contribution made by Freud's psychoanalysis and the many internal and external splits that ensued. These splits remain pregnant with questions for our own day: Jung and the 'collective unconscious'; Adler and the importance of social phenomena; Ferenczi and the introduction of active techniques; Anna Freud and the recognition of the psychopedagogical dimension in the child; Klein and the description of the psychotic positions; Hermann and consideration of the ethological myth; Winnicott and presymbolization; Lacan and the onto-logical status of the psyche; Bion and the structure of thought processes etc.

Within psychoanalysis, a great many writers have focused on the analysis of the family. Apart from the work of Anna Freud and child analysts, we should also mention the studies by Laforgue (1936) and Leuba (1936) on 'family neurosis', together with the important article by Lacan in the *Encyclopédie française* (Wallon, 1938). In the USA, the culturalist tendency within psychoanalysis played an even more direct role in the origins of family therapy. Particular mention should be made here of Sullivan (1953) who pointed out the correlation found between mental patients' relationships with the hospital medical team, on the one hand, and what occurred in their families, on the other, thus opening up the way for the systemic modelling of family-institution relations.

The discovery of the importance of the reality of familial and social interactions poses a number of new questions for psychoanalysis. In its methodological presuppositions, classic psychoanalysis assumes that the individual is already constituted and works on representations of psychically stabilized interpersonal relations. It perceives the real family as an obstacle to the full unfolding of the individual, which is true up to a point. How, then, is it to define the situations in which the real family must be supported and fortified if disorders of individuation are not to be aggravated?

How are non-Western family systems to be dealt with, for which the standard cure and the theorization which goes with it seem wholly inappropriate? (Todd, 1983, see NUCLEAR FAMILY, EXTENDED FAMILY).

How, more generally, is psychoanalysis to grasp (a) the reality of supra-individual structures – family and social organizations – in their specific dynamics; and (b) the biological underpinnings of these, on which systems of representation are based? In other words, what are the relations which exist between phantasmatic reality and the reality of events?

Is psychoanalysis an approach which excludes all other methodologies and which may possibly be threatened by the risks of heterodoxy or can it, on the contrary, theoretically confront other models (e.g. CYBERNETICS, GENERAL SYSTEMS THEORY, CATASTROPHE THEORY etc.)?

Is it possible to think of the effectiveness of the whole range of psychotherapies and sociotherapies in terms of a vision in which the psychoanalytic and systemic models are seen as complementary?

These are all pressing questions and, at the same time, family therapy has introduced a new conceptual and pragmatic revolution. Whether it likes it or not, psychoanalysis is now in direct contact with other models. The most uncompromising among the family therapists who define themselves exclusively as psychoanalysts (in France, Decobert, Ruffiot, Eiguer, Racamier etc.) refer at least once, in their approach, to the contributions of cybernetics and systems theory, either to reject it or to use it, in spite of everything, in a reinterpreted form. Lebovici (1985) has developed hypotheses on phantasmatic interaction and what he calls 'the transgenerational allegory'. Lemaire (1986) advocates integrating the psychoanalytic and systemic approaches.

The perspective proposed here is that we should recognize the need for a conflict between models of thought and action, the complementarity of the psychoanalytic and systemic approaches and the value of the confrontation between interpretative and prescriptive interventions in grasping family reality. The organization of levels of intervention presupposes the recognition of interfaces which should be sources of reflection and further elaboration rather than generating root-and-branch oppositions.

(See also ABSTINENCE, RULE OF; ALPHA AND BETA ELEMENTS; CONTEXT; COUPLES; DEMAND; DIFFERENTIATION OF SELF; DOUBLE BIND; FAMILIODRAMA; FAMILY PSYCHICAL APPARATUS; FAMILY THERAPIES; FAMILY TYPOLOGIES; FAMILY UNCONSCIOUS; FREE ASSOCIATION; IDENTIFICATION; INCEST; INCOMPLETENESS THEOREMS; INSTINCT; INTERPRETATION; LEARNING; LOVE; MARITAL BREAKDOWN; META-COMMUNICATION SYSTEMS; MULTI-LEVEL HIERARCHIES;

NARCISSISM; PARADOXICALITY; PRESCRIPTION; PSYCHODRAMA; SELF-REFERENTIAL CALCULUS; SOCIAL ORGANIZATION; TEACHING OF SYSTEMIC APPROACHES; THERAPEUTIC STYLES; TRANSFERENCE; TRUE SELF, FALSE SELF.)

J.M. & P.S.

psychoanalytic–phantasmatic typologies of the family The psychoanalytic school was the first to approach the understanding of psychopathology in terms of family configurations structured by a mythological organization. The OEDIPUS COMPLEX emerged in this way as the organizer of the neurotic questioning of life and the positioning of conflicts on the plane of PHANTASY. Confrontation with other clinical realities led both to a broadening of the initial psychoanalytic theories and to the development of other models of thought and action (see INTERACTIONAL TYPOLOGIES OF THE FAMILY; MORPHOGENETIC OR STRUCTURAL TYPOLOGIES OF THE FAMILY; TRANSACTIONAL TYPOLOGIES OF THE FAMILY).

The psychoanalytic model leads most often to making the following distinctions: character-neurotic families/symptom-neurotic families, neurotic/psychotic/perverse, objectal/depressive, narcissistic (cyclothymic, paranoiac, schizophrenic).

Richter (1970) distinguishes in this way between family symptom neuroses and family character neuroses. The *symptom-neurotic family* undergoes an internal split, one part of it being repudiated (Fleck in Richter, 1970). The repudiation leads either to a divorce or the placement of one or more children, to the exclusion of one or more young adults (sometimes in an asylum or the imprisonment of a delinquent member). If it does not go so far as repudiation, such a family organizes itself around an index patient or symptom-bearer, who may possibly vary from time to time, depending on the circumstances.

The *character-neurotic family* compensates an unsurmounted conflict by creating a neurotic world and behavioural and ideological defences that are stereotypical, but protective for each member with regard to internal and external tensions. The more acute its conflicts, the more it represents itself as a unified family. There could thus be said to be an over-identification of each person with the symptom-bearer, who is never excluded or repudiated. The style of such families might be paranoiac (the family fortress) or hysterical (the family theatre).

PHANTASMATIC OBJECT RELATIONS AND INTERACTIONS

Eiguer (1983) distinguishes between:

- the *normal family*, structured by castration;

- the *depressive family*, structured by absence of object (what systematic thinkers refer to as families with open systems and flexible boundaries);
- the *narcissistic family*, structured by emptiness and illusion (what systematic thinkers see as families with closed systems and rigid boundaries).

These distinctions refer to different modalities of object relations, genital or pregenital, as in sado-masochism which takes on a different tenor depending on the stages of sexual development. In psychoanalysis, sado-masochism is understood not as a perverse act but rather as a modality of structuring of the psyche. By contrast with the perverse act (in which the sadist and masochist, in their own satisfactions, do not meet), 'sado-masochism' can be seen as forming a phantasmatic pairing in which the two poles are indissociable and are the expression of the activity–passivity opposition in the constitution of sexual and psycho-affective life.

It appears here of little coherence epistemologically to apply such a concept directly to the real relations within a couple. The term 'sado-masochism' is already a metaphor taken from the literal description of perverse acts. To re-use it to describe behaviour necessarily gives rise to confusion between actual perversion and 'moral' perversion, implying that 'sado-masochistic' couples are made up of perverse or behaviourally perverse persons, which is not the case. The sado-masochistic dimension of the personality is constitutive, as we have seen, of the activity–passivity opposition. At the level of relationships, it takes on a dynamic character if we view it from the point of view of the oppositions between complementary and symmetrical relationships (see SCHISMOGENESIS).

PHANTASMATIC SCENES AND FAMILY MYTHS

Brodeur (1982) proposes a typology based on a mythic scene in which power is attributed to symbolic figures by all the real members of the family. Power is thus distributed symbolically around the maternal, paternal and fraternal mythic figures:

The *matriarchal family* would be organized around the pre-eminence of:

- the good mother (manic family);
- the bad mother (melancholic family);
- the split mother, good or bad (the manic-depressive family);
- the split mother, where the 'bad' mother sucessfully combats the father (paranoiac family);
- the coexistence/opposition of the good and bad mother (anguished family);
- the coexistence/opposition of a good and bad mother, with the presence of a father who does not succeed in counteracting the bad mother (character-neurotic family).

The *patriarchal family*: the symbolic father would, on this view, make his appearance on the mythic scene. All the members of the family would then be inscribed, from the mother down, under the primacy of the 'name of the father'.

The *fraternal family*: the real father, mother and children find themselves freed from the symbolic father, the patriarch, and belong to the assembly of brothers. By virtue of this, all the members of the fraternal family find themselves caught up in relations of opposition.

The *homosexual fraternal family*: there would here be a negation of the opposition between everyone and the communalization of a good or value, founding the primacy of the phallus.

The *heterosexual fraternal family*: here, the symbolic brothers find themselves separated, each possessing for their own part, confronted with the classical Oedipal myth, with castration anxiety and also with the difference of the sexes and generations which flows from it.

Other configurations referring back to even more archaic destructurings would seem to develop in relation to this model: that of ancestral families in which the mythic scene is not constructed, and in which the figures are not symbolic, or even structured:

1 The ancestral family in which the figures (and chiefly that of the 'singular mother' are merged with a universal prototype. The categories of good and bad, true and false etc. oscillate continually as in families in schizophrenic transaction.

2 The ancestral family in which universal human prototypes are systematically avoided, since they are too dangerous and cannot be created (autistic-like behaviour).

3 The ancestral family in which the mythic scene is rejected, on account of questioning the categories of good and bad, and situating itself beyond good and evil: delinquentogenic transactions.

Such a description seems more to reveal the phantasmatic grid of the therapist than to describe the processes specific to the families themselves.

(See also METAPSYCHOLOGY; PSYCHOANALYSIS.)

J.M.

psychodrama Introduced by Moreno (1934, 1965) and based on the improvised staging of scenarios, which have not previously been programmed and learned, for purposes of personal development. Psychodrama was used and developed for training and therapy, then reinterpreted in psychoanalytic and systemic terms. It is based on a paradoxical prescription, whereby the patient 'must act freely as things occur to him; that is

why he must be given all possible latitude to express his spontaneity in total freedom' (Moreno, 1934).

The psychodramatic technique was taken up by a number of psychoanalysts in the psychoanalytic approach to training groups and to groups of neurotic and psychotic patients (Anzieu, 1956, 1975a; Lebovici, 1973). A technique of this kind encourages the theatrical production of unconscious processes, develops the disposition to relational interplay which is specific to the human being confronted with an interactive situation.

Psychodramatic techniques are used in a number of ways in family therapy and for the training of therapists (including role-playing families and therapists). In therapy, it opens up exploration and activation of the intrafamilial roles of the protagonists, enabling the tendencies towards acting-in or acting-out of the patients and those close to them to be metabolized. In training, it enables the strategies and techniques used by the therapists to be simulated and also enables therapists to locate themselves emotionally and cognitively in relation to pathological family systems, as well as in relation to the family systems to which they themselves belong.

THEATRE AND PSYCHODRAMA

We may mention here the symbolic domains which connect Moreno's psychodrama, his 'theatre of spontaneity' with the theatre of Luigi Pirandello (Bouissy, 1977; see ANTI-THEATRE). In *Right you are (If you think so)*, *Six characters in search of an author*, *Each in his own way*, and *Tonight we improvise*, Pirandello explores the effects of 'theatre in the theatre' and the explosion of the theatrical frame which results. Apart from merely creating the term, in 'role-playing', Pirandello pushed to the point of tragic absurdity the identification of the protagonists of the husband–wife–lover trio with their abstract, disembodied roles. Finally, he put psychodrama itself on the stage in *Each in his own way*, the heroine, split between fiction and reality in the play itself making explicit reference to Moreno. The actress, who is presented in the play as a real actress, is called Amalia Moreno, to her great horror, sees her role being played in the play within the play by the 'actress' Delia Morello.

PRINCIPLES OF THERAPEUTIC PSYCHODRAMA

Intervention in family therapy is akin to the situation of group therapeutic psychodrama in which 'action avoids the frenzied nature of mere motor discharge and acquires an intersubjective structure and a psychological meaning' (Anzieu, 1956). The approach is, therefore, as far removed from the psychoanalytic cure as are group psychoanalytic therapies. Though it is, in fact, true that psychoanalysis has rarely tackled the problem of action in itself, and that there is almost no theoretical concept in which it is in any way implicated (Lagache, 1963), it remains fundamental that, in the terms in which the analysis is conducted, the rule of FREE ASSOCIATION is complemented by the rule of ABSTINENCE, which is defined by renunciation of action and the use, instead, of SPEECH. It is to these two rules that Ruffiot (1981b) and Caillot and Decherf (1984) refer in setting up their model of psychoanalytic family therapy. In an approach which takes into account the psychodramatic aspect of the psyche in its contact with group situations, action is not excluded, but it is not exclusive either. The therapeutic project is indeed a project of verbal therapy with the family group, but it turns out that the way to words can be opened up by making a detour through action.

It is thus possible for each member of the family to learn to play his or her own role, as well as other people's. For Anzieu, 'the principal lesson to be learned from the psychodrama is that a bodily activity – mime, the improvisation of a posture, an acting, a rhythm, a series of gurgles, singsong etc. – has the desired training or therapeutic effects only if it leads to verbalization' (Anzieu, 1975a, p. 56). It is thus particularly well suited to resolving the disequilibria which arise between disembodied words and instances of acting out which reflect a failure of phantasmatization. It also:

> strikes a mean between the error, familiar to psychoanalysts or psychotherapists treating individuals in a group, of concentrating exclusively on individuals and ignoring group phenomena and the error, familiar to group monitors and followers of Ezriel, of attempting a psychotherapy or psycho-analysis of the group without any concern for the individuals composing it. (Anzieu, 1975a, p. 56)

There follows from this, in Anzieu's view, what he terms 'the rule of imitative gesture': 'one acts by pretending to carry out actions, one does not really do anything' (1975a, p. 57).

PSYCHODRAMA AND FAMILY THERAPY

Such remarks are entirely valid in family therapy. Playing upon the different roles, statuses and functions of the family members and encouraging the simulation of the various LEVELS OF COMMUNICATION means recapturing degrees of freedom in the spontaneous expression of self. The advantage of this approach is that it enables us to be in direct contact with the real behaviour of each person in their life- and survival-group. The handling of such techniques should be done with sensitivity to the singularity of the persons grappling with relational impasses within their families. It is possible for the prescription of pretence to become part of the therapist's overall style, with the therapist being prepared to role-play his/her own part or the roles which the family forces him/her to adopt.

There are, however, 'wild' psychodramas, in the same way as there are 'wild' interpretations and 'wild' prescriptions. In families in schizophrenic – or delinquent – transaction, confronted with dangerous acting out, one finds insufficient mechanisms for the simulation of relations. Such fragility deserves clinical attention, though the dynamic evolution of the therapy, the evaluation of its contexts and the imminent risks of acting out must all be taken into account. Premature role-playing may precipitate dangerous acting out, whereas at critical moments of the therapy, it enables the node of the group conflict, which had not previously been accessible to phantasy, to be simulated.

(See also FAMILIODRAMA; SOCIODRAMA.)

P.G. & J.M.

psychosomatic double binds Patients presenting with a psychosomatic symptom are immersed in family, conjugal and socio-professional contexts which cut off the possibility of retreat into a territorial or psychic space. The coronary patient is compelled to continue to rise in a hierarchy which continually and increasingly crushes his personal aptitudes. The sufferer from hypertension regulates the emotional tensions of those around her, whom she contributes, in spite of herself, to keeping under pressure. The asthmatic reduces his anxiety level by crises of asthma which worry those around him, thus increasing their proximity which generates crises. In the discharge of a crisis, the epileptic resynchronizes the breaks in the interactions of those close to her; the terror she spreads around her accentuates the desynchronizations which bring on crises. The schizophrenic in an acute phase will swing over into somatic decompensations which present discordant signs. This may lead to one-sided (biological or psychological) therapeutic responses, which will aggravate the observed psychosomatic discordance.

These double binds will express themselves in the diagnostic, prognostic and therapeutic encounter. Depending upon the therapeutic attitude adopted, they will either (a) generate an aggravation that is sustained either by the patient him or herself or by others (for example, by medication being stopped or escalated; by a total 'parentectomy'; or by the enforced maintenance of the patient in his milieu); or (b), on the contrary, produce a reorganization of family or social interactions. Several double binds have been described by Maruani (for example, 1976, 1977a, b, 1978a, b).

TREATMENT OF CORONARY PATIENTS

The object is to get the patient to give up his or her hyperactivity which, to the patient, is a refuge from anxiety, but which is, in fact, one of the causes of his/her illness! A monitoring of the condition based solely on so-called objective data (electrocardiograms, pulse rate, blood pressure etc.) could only reinforce the patient's anxiety.

HIGH BLOOD PRESSURE

Abandonment of medication

The implicit transmission of an attitude to the patient by the doctor modulates the therapeutic response. When first prescribing medication for high blood pressure, the doctor very often adopts a firm attitude to explain to the patient the vital importance of the treatment and more or less willingly creates an image of the medication as vicarious in its effects. If the patient neglects to take the medication for a few days and feels none the worse for it, he or she will have discovered the falsity of that image and from that point on will be much more prepared to give up his/her protective pills. This may be an aggressive reaction against the doctor and an assuaging of guilt by taking a risk, a genuine risk which often comes on top of family, social and work problems which the subject encounters in reality.

PROSPECTIVE DIAGNOSIS OF HIGH BLOOD PRESSURE

The subject who becomes an idiopathic sufferer from high blood pressure will be found, ten years before this, to have had a blood pressure which, when measured by the cuff method, was higher than a normal subject or than one who would later suffer high blood pressure as a result of kidney damage. This means that in the situation where he/she is passively awaiting a medical assessment, the psychological reactions of the future high blood pressure sufferer are accompanied, in spite of him or herself, by reactions of the cardiovascular system. The patient is constantly subject to conflicts from which he/she cannot, will not or does not know how to free him or herself.

AETIOLOGICAL DIAGNOSIS OF CEPHALALGIAS

All the best writers insist on the need, when faced with a cephalalgic, for detailed, if not indeed 'police-style' questioning of the patient, in order to discover a cause. However, in half of the cases, no aetiology is discovered. It can hardly be denied that such a session must have an effect of mental suggestion on the patient, and conjure up for him or her all the various forms his/her pain might assume and the multiple complications he/she may justifiably expect. Very often it will be preferable to listen patiently to the sufferer rather than subject him/her to interrogation.

INTERVIEW WITH AN ALLERGIC PATIENT

The person suffering an allergy is a person who is made ill by a situation and his/her symptom expresses a conflict whose resolution, in one way or another, is costly. Often the allergy-sufferer is someone who feels the world to be a thorny place. If it is established

that this is the case, one may interpret the positive effect of a desensitization treatment as that of a behavioural 'de-conditioning' treatment, the sufferer becoming accustomed to his/her fear as much as he/she is to the allergen. If this hypothesis is correct, the doctor who simply injects will not be any less successful than the doctor who injects and speaks.

PELVIC ALGIAS

Theories relating to reproduction and human sexuality have followed quite a typical course of development. We have moved first from the register of the sacred (or the predestined) to that of positivism or experimentation and have then returned, in cases where science's resources seem insufficient, to the modern and sophisticated conception of fate, namely the unconscious as defined by psychoanalysis.

The clinical treatment of pelvic algias illustrates this process. The classic approach runs as follows: all the resources of the most complicated (hormonological, radiological, endoscopic) examinations are used, and when nothing is found, the doctor announces that 'It's psychogenic' and the woman is advised to consult a psychiatrist. Currently the majority of gynaecologists acknowledge the existence of psychogenic pelvic algias which, in effect, are treated as pains without known cause.

The fact is that it is the psychological structure of a woman and her conjugal interaction which determine the place the pain symptom will occupy in the picture she presents to the gynaecologist, not the virulence of a germ or the size of a patch of endometrial tissue, whether the illness is seen as somatic or psychosomatic. By situating the symptom at the level of the pain and the genital apparatus, the doctor–patient relationship is being placed at the outset within a field which has, as its instinctual backdrop, a sado-masochistic dimension. We can see here all that determines the specificity of the doctor–patient interaction where pelvic algias are concerned, from the point where the doctor fails to discover a cause which seems sufficient to him to explain them:

- 'I am the one who is hurting you' (and this will mean an escalation of increasingly aggressive surgery or complementary examinations);
- or 'I'll calm you down' (and this will mean an inflation of analgesic medication, tranquillizers and hypnotic drugs);
- or 'You are mad' (and this will mean referral to the psychiatrist).

It is up to him, in the last resort, to restore to the symptom its meaning in the woman's sexual life, its function within the couple and its value as a commentary on her relationship with her gynaecologist. A psychoanalysis takes longer to do this than a paradox-based intervention.

OBESITY

Mothering is the preliminary form of all inscription within culture. Through maternal care a whole mode of life is expressed and passed on. The fact that the baby is given the bottle when he/she asks for it or at fixed times represents a basic difference regarding the place which it is intended the child will occupy and the way it is intended that he/she will accept external reality.

Every family environment thus selects from among a certain number of innate behaviours in the child and from the hypothalamic, endocrine and metabolic circuits underlying them. This imprinting occurs at an early stage and has a lasting effect. Three obese children out of four will grow up to be obese adults, more or less with their family's complicity. This occurs by way of two varieties of unconscious strategy: (a) providing alimentary gratification (a sweet or chocolate) every time the child poses a problem, including problems related to the normal necessities of his/her learning; (b) considering eating to be anxiolytic by a diverting of aggression on to food.

Obese people, who display to the whole world the area in which they transgress the ideology of the control of desire (while paying homage to the ideology of consumption) are, in general, socially open, determined people and as far as can be from 'the idle rich'. Eating too much will be their (disastrous) way of fighting tiredness and inhibitions and they may persist in this for a long time. Obese people will complain to their doctor of their aesthetic failings. However, at the same time as they implicitly admit to having forfeited their capacity for sexual seduction, they will attempt to seduce the doctor by tempting him or her to use his/her demiurgic power to make them thin.

SCHIZOPHRENIAS

With some extremely serious acute decompensations, one sees the appearance of physical syndromes: eschars, hyperthermia (acute delirium, if not indeed malign syndrome of neuroleptics), phlebitis with a risk of pulmonary embolism, aggravation of the general state by a refusal to take food etc. Given the extent of the somatic symptoms, a danger then arises that meetings with the family milieu will be neglected. When these are possible, family interviews then often reveal a complete destructuring of exchanges, rendering illusory any well-codified technique of intervention. In conflicts within the team, the risk then arises that the somatic emergency will be put before the family emergency, or the reverse (these conflicts may possibly be aggravated by the need for simultaneous interventions on the part of several hospitals). Let us note also the less serious matter of the dyskinesias of neuroleptics which arise when the prescription is reduced or stopped, the treatment of which consists in paradoxically administering the drug which caused them.

Coherent therapeutic action consists here in establishing, then reinforcing, the connection between these exploded semiotic expressions.

(See also DOUBLE BIND; FAMILY DOCTOR; PSYCHOSOMATIC ILLNESS; PSYCHOSOMATIC MEDICINE; SCHIZOPHRENIAS; THERAPEUTIC DOUBLE BINDS AND MULTIPLE BINDS.)

G.G.M. & J.M.

psychosomatic illness: personality and/or interaction? A class of illnesses which are judged to be the product of psychical factors, acting, to a greater or lesser extent, as relays for causes of harm in the human environment.

The best known studies devoted to the interactional family approach to psychosomatic disorders centre mainly on certain forms of pathology: ANOREXIA NERVOSA in adolescents and diabetes and asthma in children (Selvini Palazzoli, 1963; Weblin, 1963; Minuchin, et al., 1978; Dare et al., 1990). Even though the number of publications in this field is still low, we find a growing interest with regard to a very varied range of illnesses. These include illnesses which are classically defined as psychosomatic such as gastroduodenal ulcers and ulcerative colitis and somatic disorders in which a possible psychopathological component has been suggested, such as the appearance of a CANCER.

DEFINITION OF THE PROBLEM

For Groddeck, who saw in '*das Es*' (the 'it' or the 'id') 'the totality of what is living in the individual being from conception onwards', all illness was psychosomatic (cf. Le Vaguerese, 1985). The physiologists inspired by work on the neuro-vegetative and neuro-endocrine systems around Selye's notion of *stress* have aligned themselves with most of the researchers of a psychoanalytic persuasion to elaborate a nosography which distinguishes between psychosomatic syndromes and psycho-affective participation in an infectious or accidental aggression.

For example, for the Chicago school of Alexander, the gastroduodenal ulcer, haemorrhagic rectocolitis, asthma, high blood pressure, rheumatoid arthritis, eczema and hyperthyroidism are psychosomatic syndromes. In effect, each of these syndromes is thought to derive from a localization in a single system of one of the 'normal' somatic manifestations of anxiety which has then become chronic in a non-mentalized form, in reaction to a conflict. The choice of organ here is thought to conform to an erotic or aggressive symbolism (see Fernandez-Zoila and Sivadon, 1986).

For many authors, however, the conflict situation is not in itself sufficient. Some believe that a personality predisposed to psychosomatic illness is also required, while others believe that there is need of a significant interaction.

PSYCHOSOMATIC ILLNESS: PERSONALITY AND/OR INTERACTION?

THE PSYCHOSOMATIC PERSONALITY

Though it is clearly the case that systemic epistemology leads to the treatment of patients rather than illnesses, it does not have any truck with the concept of a particular style of personality being exposed to psychosomatic ailments. All the more so as many psychoanalytic and behaviourist studies have sought to refine their procedures by distinguishing between an allergic personality, a hypertense personality, a Basedow personality and a coronary personality (Freidman's Type A) etc. Jackson (1966, p. 329) pointed out the limits to the notion of personality in connection with Friedman's type A: 'the coronary prone individual may be considered by family members as the main "mover" or "power" in the family, whether it relates to finances, disciplinary action, social activities, or whatever . . . [He] considers it his duty to accept the responsibility.'

We shall merely mention here the contribution of the 'psychosomatic school of Paris' which regards the process of somatization as being linked with a mentalization deficiency with attendant impoverishment of the powers of imagination. A mode of thinking termed 'operative' sets in, in which the representation of concrete actions takes the place of symbolization. The preconscious is empty and has lost its functional value, allowing movements of disorganization of the psychosomatic unity and unbinding of the death instinct to come into play.

This theorization is only convincing when it is applied to the study of the very special psychosomatic unit formed by the mother–infant dyad. The book by Kreisler et al. *L'enfant et son corps* (1974) is typical of this need to think interaction, to which psychoanalytic thinking submits well when it rediscovers the dynamic equilibria between parents' family histories, the personalities of the father and mother, and the somatic and psychical development of the child, the functional disorders of which (colics, insomnia, mericism, anorexia etc.) constitute possible breakdowns of these equilibria. American writers use the term *alexithymia* to describe the *absence of verbalization of emotions*.

Some have sought to make 'environmental' dwarfism – which is also called 'retardation of growth of psychoaffective origin' – the paradigm of psychosomatic disorders in children. In this condition, we in fact observe the following:

1 A specific character of interaction. According to Bouras et al. (1980, p. 630): 'From birth, the mother treats this child as a thing which is not expected to show signs of an existence of its own, but to depend totally on her desire and her will.' The child shows an 'absence of attachment to the mother as an elective object of cathexis and, particularly, an absence of anxiety in the presence of strangers'.

2 Behavioural disorders: 'Extreme physical violence of the mother towards the child, with the father looking on, powerless.' The child displays a bulimic voracity: 'He eats anything that comes his way: a whole loaf of bread, half a dozen eggs, the dog's food, the dishwater . . . This aberrant eating behaviour disappears as soon as he is hospitalized.'

3 Precise physiopathological manifestations: curtailment of the child's REM sleep with attendant absence of secretion of the growth hormone.

4 *Paradoxical therapeutic prescription* (and one that is urgent for the child if he/she is to grow without waiting for the family's rules to be modified): 'The person who is the mother of this child must accept separation from him rather than seeing him destroyed'. This means the child being placed with a foster family far away from the mother, a step which results in the child beginning to grow in stature again and the recommencement of pubertal development.

It now appears that well-conducted family therapies make it possible to re-start the child's growth without separating him/her from his/her parents, while putting the child out with a foster family secondarily aggravates the problem. A case example describes the process. A pre-pubertal child of 12 is seen by a paediatrician who has known the child and the family for several years. The conflict between the parents is plain to see; the curve of the child's growth has been stagnating for several months, leading to fears of an irreversible halt to the development of his height and weight at the critical moment of pubertal mutation. The nuclear family has never been properly established, both as a couple, in transgenerational conflicts, and in the establishment of a family territory that is capable of ensuring a stable home. In the family therapy interviews, the parents and the child are seen, with sessions where the parents are seen alone. The interviews are directed towards the structuring of interpersonal functions, the re-valorization of roles and the child's re-entry into the family milieu.

One is struck by the parallels that exist between this affliction and Gisela Pankow's theory of the importance of the structuring of the body image. In certain psychosomatic patients, as in psychotics, we find, in her view, a dissociation of the 'way-of-being-in-one's-body', a dissociation explaining on the analytic level that the world of desire is destroyed (Pankow, 1977), the lacunae in the body image corresponding to the gaps in the family structure.

IN SEARCH OF INTERACTIONAL SPECIFICITY (FAMILIAL OR SOCIAL)

Drawing on the work of Jackson (1966) and Hoebel (1974), Watzlawick (1978a) emphasized that the risk of heart attack in a man who is hyperadapted to competitive society, and incapable of stopping working and following his doctor's advice, diminishes markedly when his wife is included in the description and the doctor stops asking her to persuade her husband to rest. He also pointed out the existence of psychosomatic families which have a peculiar rule which states that there is no such thing as a permissible mood. Similarly, Jackson, studying families with a child suffering from ulcerative colitis, found them to be the victims both of a restriction of their mutual exchanges and of the social exchanges on offer in their cultural milieu, unlike 'ordinary families' where 'there appeared to be much larger exchanges of spontaneous behaviour, such as laughter, critical comments, sarcasm, irony etc.' and also 'involvement in a wide range of activities' (Jackson, 1966, p. 331).

In the systemic perspective, dysfunctional relations between a subject and his various (family, professional, community) environments may cause what are termed secondary psychosomatic illnesses. More often, we find that a somatic impairment is aggravated by contextual factors.

Meissner (1966) has drawn up a list of illnesses (tuberculosis, cancer, arthritis, ulcers) whose aetiological factors he proposes to determine in an interactional manner. In his view, gastroduodenal ulcers result from the patient's inability to cope with stress and, conversely, high blood pressure causes symptomatic manifestations which are likely to aggravate the stressful character of family interactions.

Meissner (1966) proposes a description of the psychosomatic processes in the family context. According to him,

1 The patient is less than mature and his/her immaturity is directly proportional to the degree of his/her involvement in family interactions.
2 The family constellation functions as an undifferentiated ego and the patient is caught up in the emotional turmoil of the family group.
3 Interpersonal exchanges are structured in a complementary manner. The 'deficiencies' of some members are compensated by the 'strengths' of others.
4 The fragile emotional equilibrium of these families is easily disturbed by any change and any disorganizing event.
5 It is in response to family difficulties that the patient decompensates on the somatic level.

In the view of Grolnick (1972), there are certain models of interaction that are privileged in families where one of the members suffers from a psychosomatic illness. He stresses that in these families, tensions are hidden and interaction is rigid. He notes that there are more psychosomatic disorders in families where, in spite of marital discord, the home has remained united, than there are in broken families. Among the pathogenic factors, Grolnick quotes changes in role or status which occur at the various stages of the life-cycle (puberty, death of a parent, separation, marriage etc.).

Repression of affects increases the risks of decompensation in the psychosomatic mode. Several studies carried out with groups of young offenders show that those subjects who give free rein to the expression of their affects – even where these are hostile – only rarely suffer from psychosomatic illnesses.

Minuchin et al. (1978) have isolated five modes of interaction which are found, in their view, in all psychosomatic families, whatever the set of symptoms presented. The management of conflict in these families is carried out on several models. Pathological triangulations and privileged coalitions express themselves in stable alliances between one of the parents and the patient. The other parent is placed in a marginal position. For the children, the strategy of 'detouring' consists in short-circuiting parental conflicts and mobilizing the parental couple so that it satisfies their essential needs in their rivalry with their other siblings. Marital tensions are eliminated and the psychosomatic illness becomes the family's only problem.

Minuchin et al. advocate the structural approach as the best treatment for psychosomatic disorders. Individual psychopathological difficulties are not denied, but Minuchin's considerable experience leads him to assert that an approach to the system within its eco-system often enables the patient to be released from incapacitating, if not indeed lethal, pathologies. However, many practitioners remain cautious on this subject, noting that 'family somatics' still remains, to use Weakland's (1974) expression, a 'neglected edge'. Lask (1979), stresses the lack of controlled studies and warns family therapists against a reductive, linear vision which might seek to tie in a particular type of family dysfunctioning too closely with a specific psychosomatic illness. Bloch (1989) none the less attests to the interest of the systemic model in research and medical practice.

It can hardly be by chance that it is in Chicago that a school of human ecology has developed which stresses the role of factors relating to urban life, the constraints of production-line work and the pressures of hierarchical organizations in the adaptive disorders of which psychosomatic illness is one aspect. We should remember that, in this field, the systemic model must not stop at the family, but must also include the office, workshop or factory where the subject sells his/her labour power or, in other words, the wearing out of his/her body.

An example: the diabetic child
By way of example, we shall mention the studies on diabetes in children, which too often neglect

overdetermination of family interactions by schooling. Several studies concern themselves with identifying the reciprocal influences between the diabetic child and the family around him or her. Minuchin et al. (1978) have shown that there are certain specific features in hyperlabile diabetics. In these families, the parents' attention is essentially focused on the child who performs a regulatory function in the couple's interpersonal relations. The avoidance of conflicts is ensured by very varied strategies in which the child participates actively (Compernolle, 1980).

Auslander and Anderson, quoted by Simeon (1983), express severe reservations about this work, since, among other things, they criticize the criteria for the inclusion of patients in the research and the analysis of the results. And there is a further omission, in that Minuchin's study does not take into account the role of the medical personnel in the family dynamics of diabetics. The object of Simeon's research is to differentiate between families that are organized on psychosomatic, neurotic and borderline lines. This clinician stresses the advantages of a transdisciplinary approach to diabetes which brings together paediatricians and psychologists within the therapeutic team. Masson (1985) takes up this same working perspective, taking account, 'at the first evaluation, of the overall ecosystem' and looking, at the outset, for 'the possible presence of pathological relational interplay, whether symmetrical or complementary, between the parents and the therapists'.

(See also CANCER; FAMILY DOCTOR; PRESCRIBING (MEDICAL) DRUGS; PSYCHOSOMATIC DOUBLE BINDS; PSYCHOSOMATIC MEDICINE; SYSTEMIC MODELLING OF CARCINOGENESIS.)

G.G.M., P.A. & S.A.

psychosomatic medicine In medicine, the adjective 'psychosomatic' refers to matters relating to the union (or, more precisely, the articulation) between the mind and the body, the *psyche* and the *soma*.

HISTORICAL AND PHILOSOPHICAL PERSPECTIVES

In its understanding of health and illness, psychosomatic medicine connects with the Hippocratic tradition, considering the sick subject as a microcosm whose exchanges with the environment are perturbed in a manner that reflects an adverse change in the macrocosm: 'disease is not simply disequilibrium or discordance; it is, and perhaps most importantly, an effort on the part of nature to effect a new equilibrium in man' (Canguilhem, 1943, in 1984 edn, p. 12).

This is a systemic vision which is opposed to the other great – ontological – tradition which, from Egyptian theogonic medicine to the Pasteurian revolution,

identifies an external (and ideally curable) cause of the illness which is conceived as a morbid species attacking the patient. This quarrel was given further reinforcement by the repercussions of the philosophical debate between Cartesian dualism and Spinozist monism, which both equally lay at the origin of modernity with their autonomization of the material from the spiritual, Descartes consigning to metaphysics a merged mind–spirit totality and Spinoza legitimating all action on nature.

yet because, on the one side, I have a clear and distinct idea of myself inasmuch as I am only a thinking and unextended thing, and as, on the other, I possess a distinct idea of body, inasmuch as it is only an extended and unthinking thing, it is certain that this I (that is to say, my soul, by which I am what I am) is entirely and absolutely distinct from my body, and can exist without it. (Descartes, *Sixth meditation*)

mind and body are one and the same individual conceived now under the attribute of thought, now under the attribute of extension . . . The mind does not know itself, except in so far as it perceives the ideas of the modifications of the body. (Spinoza, *Ethics*, part II, prop. XXI, note)

Men are mistaken in thinking themselves free; their opinion is made up of consciousness of their own actions, and ignorance of the causes by which they are conditioned. (Spinoza, *Ethics*, part II, prop. XXXV, note)

Spinoza thus opens up a space for reflection on the correlations between body and mind in response to a non-conscious causality. That space is very precisely that of psychosomatic medicine which is today attempting to integrate the Hippocratic notion of terrain and the Pasteurian notion of pathogenic agent. The term 'psychosomatic' can be applied to an illness or a patient or to a form of medical practice.

PSYCHOSOMATIC MEDICAL PRACTICE

This is, *par excellence*, the field of activity of the FAMILY DOCTOR, who is ideally positioned to identify interactional models in the sequences of symptoms that are presented to him or her by various members of the family over the course of time. Jackson (1966) attempted a first topology of these. On the whole, we may say that we can observe various phenomena such as the 'communicating vessel', 'SCAPEGOATING' or 'identified harbinger' phenomena depending upon whether the somatic disorders slide from one member of the family to another, always affect the same person or spare the person who actually comes for a consultation to relieve the others who are incapable of grasping their suffering.

We cannot, of course, speak of psychosomatic practice without referring to Balint who, in his classic work of 1957, *The Doctor, his patient and the illness*, laid down the terms of the doctor–patient relationship in a definitive manner. The patient's offer of his symptoms is answered by the doctor who prescribes himself as remedy. The 'apostolic function' of the general practitioner too often prevents him or her from perceiving that, at the same time as being a somatician, he/she is always a psychotherapist. The progressive spread of Balint's ideas, and the psychological training groups for doctors which he launched, very certainly contributed to making the practice of a great many doctors more effective and relaxed. And this is so even though the fact of tranquillizers coming on to the market after the initial publication of his writings has too often led to doctors – even those who follow Balint – reacting to any impression that the patient is presenting a psychological problem by the prescription of anxiolytic or hypnotic drugs.

Though he is not unaware of the circulation of disorders within families (he quotes the case of 'the wife as presenting symptom of the husband's illness' (1957, p. 69), Balint devoted himself chiefly to the study of interaction between doctors and patients. One of his main lessons is that the communication which is set up between doctors – and particularly between somaticians and psychiatrists – is, very precisely, a metaphor for the psychosomatic status of the patient and the possibilities of his/her benefiting from psychotherapy rather than treatment for functional disorders or a developing illness.

In conclusion to his research into *Neurosis in the ordinary family*, which was based on 112 families in the London suburbs, Ryle (1967), a disciple of Balint, confirmed that the interpersonal experiences within the family in childhood were of crucial importance for a child's stability and maturation and that the general practitioner, in the course of his/her practice, was best placed to observe emotional disturbances and family problems. If this is the case, rather than multiplying specialist services (remedial teaching, child guidance, paediatric hospitals, health education and social work) which merely increase the number of individual demands on those services, it would be sufficient to disseminate psychiatric knowledge to the full range of professionals concerned and to organize their team work around the family doctor as a pivot of the system.

In the years 1972–82, influenced by his experience as leader of a Balint group which brought together gynaecologists and psychiatrists, as a consultant psychoanalyst in the medical service of a large Parisian hospital and as a disciple of Paul Watzlawick, Guy Maruani published many articles attempting to establish the principles of an interactional psychosomatic practice.

PROBLEM OF THE STATUS OF THE PSYCHICAL

What is the place of the psyche in psychosomatic illnesses, whether or not the cause of these is clinically clear cut? Illness brings about objective signs and subjective symptoms. In other words, in the last resort, for the doctor, it only exists in the form of communication, whether that communication takes the path of language (the most frequently encountered) or that of behaviour (which is most sensitive to cultural influences). Given this state of affairs, the psyche is always totally involved where there are symptoms which are repeated, since the subject is necessarily confronted with his/her capacities of adaptation, adaptation here consisting in assigning various interchangeable indices to the depression and anxiety which unfailingly accompany the symptoms, so as to conquer, accept or intensify his/her suffering. These indices or co-efficients are denial, repression, displacement, conversion, obsessive mentalization, hypochondriacal somatic conversion, masochistic eroticization and narcissistic depression, all of them defence mechanisms in the psychoanalytic sense of the term. Now, and it is this point which is important for our discussion here:

- these mechanisms are brought into play without any proportional relationship with the degree of organicity or seriousness of the initial symptoms;
- these mechanisms are brought into play as a function of the prior personality of the patient, of his/her family constellation and the relational style of the doctor.

In general, the medical approach consists in seeking out objective – preferably visual – signs, drawing on all the resources of medical technique, setting in train a course of somatic therapy and only troubling with the psyche where the diagnosis and treatment break down. Such a style of reasoning repeats some of the traditional errors of medical thinking and disregards the foundations of an authentically psychosomatic attitude, since:

1 One must not become a prisoner of the body–mind dualism with which, in the tradition of Thomism and Cartesianism, medical ideology is imbued. A morbid disorder does not have its origin either in the soma (the body) or the psyche (exact translation: the soul). It is always at one and the same time indissolubly somatic and psychological and there is nothing to be gained by introducing a cause-and-effect relation between the two. On the contrary, the symptom must be seen from the outset from the perspective of its physical consequences and its psychical repercussions.

2 It is quite possible that progress in the sphere of physiology (particularly where the large field which

is opening up for the neuroendocrinology of the diencephalon is concerned) will enable us to isolate the biochemical mechanisms adopted by those illnesses which we term psychosomatic because we do not know their cause.

3 By attributing the status of an object of study to the disorders observed, the doctor forgets that he or she is not merely a spectator, but an actor. What doctors observe is not a fact in itself, but a fact for them. Their own activist or wait-and-see attitude conditions symptomatic expressiveness. Similarly, every subsequent examination is not merely a search for anomalies in the bodily functioning of the patient, but is also suffering and hope for one of the people involved and appropriation and curiosity for the other (Maruani and Atlan, 1981).

COLLABORATION BETWEEN PSYCHIATRIST (OR PSYCHOLOGIST) AND SOMATICIAN

Whether in outpatient practice or in a hospital, the astute somatician often sends his or her patients to see a psychiatrist, either for a specialist opinion or with the firm advice that they should begin a course of therapy. This necessary acceptance of the freedom of the patient to take up a psychotherapeutic relationship or not is slightly shocking for the somatician who, precisely when he/she believes in the curative effects of a psychotherapy for certain disorders, cannot understand that the patient can refuse to undergo therapy and continue to complain. For, deep down, what is expected of the psychiatrist, with his/her mysterious, non-scientific and unfounded knowledge? An opinion, a remedy, a way of being rid of something awkward? One has the impression that often what is asked of the psychiatrist is a conjuring trick. All in all, he/she is expected to pull a rabbit out of his/her apparently empty hat. And in fact, when the team's demand is sufficiently strong for the patient to be properly prepared and conditioned for this effect, then the conjuring trick comes off. There is, of course, nothing magical in this, but simply the utilization of the following three procedures: catharsis; changing the punctuation of events; and the unconscious transaction.

Catharsis
The situation of a prolonged one-to-one interview in a quiet office, contrasting as it does with the workaday, animated atmosphere of a hospital room, achieves a degree of emotional closeness for the patient which makes it possible for him/her to bare his/her soul. It thus becomes possible to relate the symptom to its more or less conscious symbolic meaning in a 'sudden moment of empathy' in Balint's sense. That meaning will often be sexual in nature, though just as often a case of unperformed mourning will be involved.

On other occasions, the patient will express his/her own intimate convictions as to how his/her illness is to be explained. Admittedly, this may take the form of a delusion of persecution or hypochondria, but, in general, one encounters the relics – or the living presence of – beliefs in a supernatural causality integrated into a cultural universe where they play a precise role.

It is of no avail, in these cases, to attempt to substitute our scientific mythology for the older mythology of superstition. On the contrary, one may lean upon these ideas (without, however, expressing an opinion about the degree of truth embodied in them) to set in place an effective treatment, which is in general constructed on the model of the treatment of reactive depression. Sometimes this cathartic effect only occurs after the patient has come to acquire confidence in the treatment, i.e. only at the third or fourth session.

Changing the punctuation of events
In general, the medical world takes the view that there is a patient, who is the bearer of symptoms and probably also of lesions. In so doing, it is neglecting two orders of fact. First, it is forgetting that sometimes a symptom only exists in relation to an interaction. And, secondly, before a consultation with the doctor, there is no patient, but merely a person who is suffering. In other words, the patient only assumes his/her status in his/her encounter with the doctor, whose status as a doctor is itself only established by the demand of the patient or the social group.

The most banal example of the failure of the medical institution to accommodate to the patient is that of alcoholism. When one confines oneself merely to the alcoholic's own case, one finds oneself faced with an individual who is inexplicably destroying his/her health in exchange for a few hours of intoxication. By contrast, when one involves the alcoholic's partner in the description of the process, one is dealing with two people who play perfectly complementary roles to form a pathological entity: the couple, like an egg-timer turned first one way up and then the other, alternates between two types of attitude. The woman, for example, who is an obsessional character of the 'perfect housewife' type and who is, ultimately, 'castrating', is matched by the sober husband who faithfully hands over his wage to her and puts his slippers on before entering the dining room. The frigid wife, who is incapable of abandoning a maternal position, is matched by the drunken, dionysiac, violent, violating husband. It should therefore be the rule that the couple is always seen in such cases and one should ask what benefits will be offered to the alcoholic in place of alcohol if he/she gives up drinking.

Changing the PUNCTUATION OF SEQUENCES OF EVENTS (also known as RE-FRAMING) sometimes means approaching problems at this level without beginning by looking for a somatic ailment. It also sometimes means beginning the investigation by perceiving the psychological structure of the patient, establishing a new mode of communication not only between him or herself and his/her family or those around him/her but also between the different agencies of his/her personality. In sum, this means never looking at the meaning of a symptom without looking at its intra- and interpersonal function.

The unconscious transaction

The psychiatrist in the general hospital must accept the language of organs. He/she must even collude with it. That is to say that in some cases he/she is presented with a choice between aggravation of the iatrogenic somatic dangers, decompensation in a psychotic mode and flight into health. By this latter we understand from a psychoanalytic perspective the disappearance of symptoms without any deep modification of the conflicts which gave rise to them. For our part, we admit that we prefer this solution to what are most often ill-fated attempts to bring about an awareness of the meaning of the symptom through a long psychotherapy to which the patient is not committed.

The fact is that the psychoanalytic model is valid for hysterical conversion in which symbolization precedes the symptom; it has revealed itself to be inoperative in somatic conversion where the symptom short-circuits mentalization. How, then, are we to establish with the patient that transaction which, at bottom, far from removing repressions, will intensify them for him or her, but will do so through a curing of the symptom? First, by using drugs as much for their placebo as their pharmaco-dynamic effects, the whole creating a specific biological symbol (Miermont, 1988, 1993). The reader will bear in mind that the placebo power of medication is higher where the pharmacodynamic properties are greater. In the early days of atropic disorders, a perfusion of anti-depressants offered an honourable way out. Antibiotics, corticoids, insulin and, most especially, the key remedies for psychosomatic syndromes (anti-epileptics, bronchodilators in asthma, per-oral anxiolytics, anti-uratics in gout and even neuroleptics in psychotic states) function as real substitute protecting persons, with which patients and those around them have to come to terms.

What will also be positive is any apparently active treatment which has had a time limit irrevocably fixed in advance, where the psychiatrist has shown the patient, by the quality of his/her listening, that the message has been received. It is therefore not necessary for the psychiatrist to believe in the medication and it is even preferable that he/she does not. Since this treatment is applied by the therapeutic team, this has itself to be placed in a paradoxical situation in such a way that it will call upon the patient to stop suffering from his/her symptoms. Quite an art of letter writing or informal discussion about the patient comes into play here, the ultimate substance of the message transmitted being either 'There's nothing wrong with him, so

treat him!' or 'He's too sick for us to be able to do anything for him!' In this way, the team is relieved of the crushing guilt it would feel if it were not to live up to its ideal image of unfailingly putting everything right (Maruani et al., 1978).

(See also PRESCRIBING (MEDICAL) DRUGS; PSYCHOSOMATIC DOUBLE BINDS; PSYCHOSOMATIC ILLNESS.)

G.G.M.

punctuation of sequences of events The punctuation of sequences of events determines the nature of a relationship between two or more persons. A disagreement (see AGREEMENT) on how events are to be punctuated is the source of many conflicts for couples and families and within society in general (Watzlawick et al., 1967).

In human interaction, a certain number of communications may at times create self-referential circuits between the protagonists (see FAMILY SELF-REFERENTIALITY). In these cases, all sending of INFORMATION is itself a receiving of information and all receiving of information is itself a sending of information. The way each protagonist arranges the order in which events occur therefore becomes arbitrary. To ask 'Who began?' or 'Who is acting, who reacting?' is to pose questions to which there is no answer. *'To an outside observer*, a series of communications can be viewed as an uninterrupted sequence of interchanges' (Watzlawick et al., 1967, p. 54). Let us take the example of a jealous husband, displaying his jealousy (*x*) and his wife who, in making a show, in response, of her fidelity (*y*) unconsciously sends messages which further whip up her husband's jealousy (*x*). The more she tries to show how faithful she is, the more jealous he will feel. And the more jealous he feels, the more his wife will try to show how faithful she is. . . . Thus we arrive at an oscillation (see OSCILLATORS). Depending upon its amplitude, frequency and periodicity, that oscillation will regulate the boundaries of the couple in a functional way or will, by contrast, lead to violent explosions.

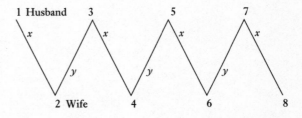

The husband only sees the sequences 2–3–4, 4–5–6 and 6–7–8, while the wife only sees 1–2–3, 3–4–5, 5–6–7 etc. Each one thinks they are only reacting to the other's behaviour, but in fact the partners do not succeed 'in metacommunicating about their respective interaction models', which leads to a distortion of the shared definition of reality (Watzlawick et al., 1967). The punctuation of sequences of events becomes particularly discordant between two persons when one of the partners does not possess the same quantity of information as the other, without knowing that this is the case. This can be seen clearly in pathological communication: in marital conflict, alcoholic, psychotic or drug-addiction behaviour where each protagonist has an absolute need of information about the other(s) in his/her existence, and where his/her survival may even depend on this.

(See also CIRCULARITY; COUPLES; MARITAL BREAKDOWN; PRAGMATICS OF COMMUNICATION.)

J.M.

Q

quantifiers In classic formal logic, a distinction is made between two types of quantifier: existential quantifiers and universal quantifiers. The theory of 'fuzzy sets' adds a further type: the 'fuzzy quantifier'.

- existential quantifiers are of the type: there is an x, such that . . .
- universal quantifiers are of the type: for any x – or whatever x may be – there is . . .
- fuzzy quantifiers are of the type: for an x between a and b, there is . . .

If existential quantifiers establish the possibility of reference, universal quantifiers often reveal paradoxical propositions in everyday language: I'm not thinking about *anything*, I've tried *everything*, he doesn't do *anything*, he *never* has any luck etc. In therapy, it is necessary both to find the differences contained within these asserted totalities and the differences of level which are conflated within them. For example: 'Can you try not to think of the thought inspired in me by the fact that you aren't thinking of anything?' or 'What energy must he expend to be sure he really doesn't do anything?' or 'Has it occurred to you that there was no solution to the problem in the way that you posed it?' or 'What is the really serious catastrophe that would be certain to occur in his life if he had any luck?'

We shall note the existence, in language, of 'fuzzy' quantifiers which attenuate the digital, all-or-nothing effects of the arbitrariness of the sign. Among these quantifiers we may cite 'a little', 'much', 'certain/some', 'perhaps', 'in a way' or 'somewhere'. These have been interpreted within the framework of the logic of FUZZY SETS. They occur as attenuators and regulators of speech-based therapeutic interventions (for example: 'He is very very *very* nervous' or 'He is a little bit happier than usual' or 'He is really rather boring' etc.

(See also DOUBLE BIND; LAW; 'NOTHING PLUS 10 PER CENT' PARADOX.)

J.M.

quid pro quo In Jackson's COMMUNICATION THEORY, the quid pro quo (literally: something for something) is another term for referring to the family rules or norms. The quid pro quo is 'a descriptive metaphor for a relationship based on differences, and expression of the redundancies which one observes in marital interaction' (Jackson, 1965b, p. 25). The marital relationship is based on a kind of bargain or contract which defines the rights and duties of each partner. The definition on which they are agreed, which is necessary for the couple to be viable, may be considered a quid pro quo. That definition is, in fact, never made explicit as such, but experienced, tested out in the redundancies of the couple's interactions.

Among the examples of quid pro quo, Jackson quotes some which appear to be viable. For example, the husband is an instrumental type of an intellectual and logical cast of mind who is realistic and practical, while the wife is a sensitive and 'feeling' person who understands people better than things (a common quid pro quo in white middle class American families). Or, the husband stays at home while the wife brings home the money: such a situation should be evaluated in terms of the quid pro quo on which the couple is established rather than whether such an arrangement is classic or corresponds to the norms of the society.

Other quid pro quos are unlikely to be lasting, either because of internal escalation or because of the presence of children. The 'Big Daddy–Baby Doll' arrangement leads to an escalation which ultimately exhausts itself. While the husband's gifts can only be finite in number, the woman's satiation will unbalance the original premise on which the relationship was built so that it will either end or have to be established on a new level. Conversely, the quid pro quo of total independence has to be re-worked when a child is born.

QUID PRO QUO AS THE PRODUCT OF THE COUPLE'S RELATIONSHIP

In Jackson's view, the quid pro quo theory is an alternative to the classic understanding of the marital couple in terms of sexual differences. Individual differences become products of the schismogenetic process which enables that relationship to develop – exceptional and difficult as it is – not the cause of relational phenomena. More precisely, sexual differences which exist between partners do not play a part in the agreement which binds those partners or in the differentiation which comes about as a result of the couple's relationship. The rules and conventions which govern how the quid pro quo is worked out are often unconscious or hidden; in therapy, these have to be made conscious to the family.

In Jackson's perspective, the quid pro quo is, then, an *agreement*. Yet, like any other AGREEMENT, it cannot be perfect. Reality introduces some modifications into the definition of the agreement. In cases of crisis, the quid pro quo will reveal the different assumptions on which the agreement was implicitly established. In the most extreme cases, the ending of the quid pro quo leads to full-blown MISUNDERSTANDINGS and ultimate MARITAL BREAKDOWN.

Seen from this point of view, the quid pro quo, like SECRETS, misunderstandings and NOSTALGIA etc., is one of the processes of communication structuring through which FAMILY MYTHS are organized.

(See also COUPLES; FAMILY ROLE; FAMILY RULES; LAW; SOCIAL STATUS.)

J.M. & P.S.

R

randomness   A process is random when its outcome is a matter of chance. The idea of unpredictability is closely linked to the concept of randomness. Such a process cannot be simulated by any mechanism, nor described by any formalism, whose rules of construction one might possess. Put more rigorously, a random process cannot be described by any mechanism whose description is shorter than the description of the process itself.

The random event is unpredictable on the local level, but at the same time predictable on the global level; a random process is based upon a limited number of possible occurrences, and on the frequencies of appearance of these occurrences which, it is presumed, can be evaluated.

RANDOMNESS AS AN EPISTEMOLOGICAL AND PRAGMATIC PROBLEM

Chaitin shows that one may define chance as algorithmic incompressibility (see ALGORITHM), and also that one can prove the random character of a phenomenon. We do not in fact know whether the uncertainty brought about by a phenomenon that is seemingly random has to do with the inadequacy of the resources of the human mind – an inadequacy which prevents the mind from finding the hidden ORDER or law behind the apparent disorder – or whether it has to do with the objective character of reality itself. Recent developments in chaos theory (Gleick, 1988) attest to the existence of periodic behaviour and the phenomenon of scaling, and of patterns within patterns.

The clinician (psychotherapist, psychoanalyst, systemic practitioner, family therapist) runs up against this uncertainty on a daily basis. To cope with it, he/she possesses theoretical grids which indicate to him/her the types of hypotheses which he/she can make about the psychic organization of the patient or the systemic order which governs the functioning of the presenting family. Though the theory provides reference points for structuring the therapeutic framework and selecting the pertinent elements within the session, to that extent decreasing the degree of randomness, a genuinely therapeutic process cannot begin without the therapist renouncing the certainties and the hypotheses which would account entirely for the wealth of information which comes out of the clinical situation. The space left for the unpredictable, for the random in the subjective perception that the therapist has of the situation is also the place where something new may emerge.

DETERMINISM AND INDETERMINISM

Confronted with these systems whose future behaviour, in apparently identical circumstances, it is impossible to predict, and within which we do not know which of the fluctuations to which they are subject will be amplified to the point of leading to the emergence of a new state, some writers (Atlan, 1972, 1979; Morin, 1980a, 1986; Prigogine, 1980), by extending the field of observation to include in it the environment, introduce randomness into the heart of morphogenetic processes; others (Petitot-Cocorda, 1977; Thom, 1981b), believers in a determinism governing the dynamic overall landscape of phenomena, suppose the existence of hidden parameters, of a law which organizes them, without however seeking to make these explicit. They consider that a random system is the product of a very general phenomenon of statistical degradation of determinism.

MANAGEMENT OF RANDOMNESS AND DETERMINISM

In family therapy, clinical practice brings us up against this frontier of contemporary science. We do not have the requisite theoretical tools for conceptualizing the association between – and complementarity of – randomness and determinism in the emergence of new modalities of family behaviour. The effects which the environment, the site of stable or changing events and objects, triggers off within the family, may be considered as random, unpredictable acts of aggression. But this only remains true if the therapist perceives the disturbances as lacking any coherent link with what constitutes the evolutive history of the family. Now, among these fluctuations in the environment, the family system operates a selection. A selection imposed at every point by its history, its myths, its operating rules, in short its own organization (just as the therapist him or herself operates a selection within what he/she is able to see and hear). The disturbances are to some extent assimilated, used as opportunities for new connections and for increases in the degree of its organization. This predisposition to take in certain privileged fluctuations of the environment makes its history dependent on the very existence of these external events. Determinism and randomness are here intimately connected. The families which are called 'rigid' select the events they will be able to assimilate very narrowly. Therapy might consist in reinjecting randomness, in getting the family system to exploit fluctuations which were not 'recognized', where, up until then, repetition and homeostatic mechanisms had prevailed. Events such as lateness or absence of one of the members will be considered significant (or otherwise) depending on whether the selective structure of the therapist has been sufficiently enriched with similar, redundant events which enable him or her to situate what he/she has hitherto perceived as random within a dynamic that is more specific to this particular family. The paradox is that to reach a goal, it is often necessary not to seek to take the path that is apparently the most strongly indicated and direct.

It is sometimes necessary to accept a number of elements continuing to appear random, in order to leave a space for other less reductive hypotheses to emerge. There is a maturation period for the therapist's selective grid just as there is a time-scale specific to each family: the time it takes to broaden the range of events it is capable of integrating into its history as significant and determining experiences. The paradox is that to reach a goal, one very often increases predictability and determinism by accepting the appearance and the danger of the random: human thought processes (mainly unconscious processes) are good at reacting to apparently random situations, to the breaks in a pre-established algorithm, to the conjunction of two heterogeneous random series, without our being able to say, however, the order is born out of chance as such.

(See also ENTROPY; HEURISTICS; STOCHASTIC PROCESSES.)

M.G.

ratio   The etymology of this term, which means 'computation' in Latin, must not be allowed to conceal the mythical and ritual origin of rational thought. The logic of opposition and complementarity, in particular, is simply a Greek continuation of the tradition of the myths of opposition (*polemos*) and attraction (*eros*), a tradition which is itself related to social structures: clan divisions and exogamy.

What, then, distinguishes reason (ratio) from MYTH is a mode of exposition: the move is made from mythic narrative to logical questioning. Hence we can understand the fragility of the bar separating myth from reason, a bar which all dogmatisms dissolve, suppressing the interrogative dimension and thus restoring myth. Myth is, however, of use to us, in psychotherapeutic practice, for example, since it enables us to take upon ourselves the ordeal of the other's suffering. It is useful in this regard, but pathological when it presents itself as theory. The bar is currently the more fragile as a result of the questioning of the ideological foundations of classical rationality. That questioning, which is a profoundly rational process, has thrown into relief the distinction which progressively came to be made between two spheres of ideas which were not, originally, dissociated in the Greek tradition.

Initially *reo*, *ruein* meant 'to flow, run, stream, gush' and referred to production, creation, generation, origin and becoming; gradually a distinction came to be made (see MAIEUTICS), in connection with the development of the function of the artisan and, subsequently, of production for the market. The concept of reason brought this development to a close, aiming to understand the play of a mechanism instead of defining the operation of an agent. This concept was situated wholly within the sphere of production, which was dissociated from (human) reproduction, a sphere which soon came to be defined as one of consumption.

In its critique of productivist ideology (thinking based on the energy model), systems theory restores a humanism (stresses the role of the agent) but deprives itself, by so doing, of the convenient division between producing and giving birth. By bringing to its conclusion the process by which that scansion of /producing/giving birth, origin/birth/ etc. was suppressed, it reintroduces the risk of ambiguity between myth and theory. Hence the increased need for conceptual rigour, the importance of which is often poorly understood by impatient sorcerer's apprentices.

(See also FAMILY MYTHS; INSTITUTIONAL MYTHS.)

D.C.

read–write memories, read–only memories, bulk memories and auxiliary memories   In computing, these terms refer to various different information storage media and various practical modalities of access, read-out and transformation of the information stored. Read–write memory (or random access memory, RAM) is a processing medium that can be both consulted and modified. The two operations – reading and writing – are both possible with a read–write memory, so that the information stored can be deleted, modified or preserved as desired. Read–write memories may be components internal to the machine which are activated when the machine is switched on and lose their information when it is switched off. The storage media (magnetic tape, cassettes, floppy disks, hard disks etc.) are not the same as read–write memories. They constitute auxiliary memories whereas the specific character and the advantage of read–write memories are that their content can be modified immediately in the course of working. Read–only memory (ROM) is an information medium which can only be consulted. Data is etched into it definitively and irreversibly and cannot be changed. Read–only memories are components internal to the machine.

STRUCTURES OF STORAGE MEDIA

The various types of media have different advantages and disadvantages. This is best illustrated by the example of debugging a programme. A programme is a series of instructions written in a special language, the objective of which is to carry out a task. Debugging consists in having the programme instructions carried out and modifying them until the result is satisfactory. It is therefore necessary that the instructions, which are a certain type of information, should be stored in a *read-write memory* so that they can be consulted, modified or deleted. However, as soon as debugging is finished and the programme is completely reliable, it very often becomes necessary, especially for micro-computers, whose main characteristic is that they possess a low capacity read-write memory, to economize on space available for read-write memory. The solution regularly employed, when a programme is frequently used, is to write the set of instructions – once these have been debugged – on a *read-only memory storage medium* or, in other words, an integrated circuit. When the programme is less frequently used, it is found preferable to write it on to an *external storage medium* such as a floppy disk etc. and, when the programme is run, the computer loads that external memory into its central RAM. The central RAM is indispensable to the machine when the quality required is flexibility, the possibility of introducing new data, adaptations etc. ROM is indispensable to the machine when the quality required is a saving of memory space. However, what the ROM gains in saving of memory space it loses in rigidity and, conversely, what RAM gains in flexibility, it loses in available memory space.

COMPUTER MEMORIES AND BIOLOGICAL MEMORIES

Let us note here, by way of an analogy, that nothing is more like a stalled computer system – or one that seems to be repeating the same recursive loops – than a system that is working flat out. Only time makes a difference from the point of view of the outside observer. A very strong analogy exists between this description of the functioning of computers and phenomena of *phylogenetic acquisition* (instinctive acts) and *ontogenetic learning* (made possible thanks to the appearance of parental care in vertebrates), as well as processes of unlearning, morphological and behavioural modifications in animals and humans. The passing of information from read-write memories into read-only memories is, above all, a supra-individual process, leading to the stabilization of hereditary coordinations (instinctive acts and hereditary LEARNING programme sequences). The human being, in its learning capacities, is, in spite of everything, obliged to follow obligatory paths, semantic CHREODS. For from moving towards an ever greater range of its adaptive possibilities, its evolution is, by contrast, narrowed down towards an increasing specialization without which it could not survive in its ecological environment. Bateson quotes the case of vision to illustrate the absolutely

indispensable role of repression. In effect, we are not consciously aware of the mechanisms of visual perception and, if we were, it is most probable that that awareness would take away from us a substantial quantity of our capability to think of other things. The repression of this type of information may very well be compared with the act of putting completely reliable data in read-only memory, which then no longer needs monitoring. This repression is, in fact, comparable with Freud's 'primary repression' which establishes the non-accessible data of the unconscious.

There would thus seem to be different stratifications of memorization, varied degrees of accessibility and non-accessibility of unconscious information. To bring a family together is to reactivate collective read-only memories having effects of rearrangement of read-write memories (hence the importance of festivals, collective rituals and ceremonies). Family read-only memories preserve the data which allow a family to define its cohesion, identity and specificity. This may involve FAMILY MYTHS, the history of an ancestor, genealogy, religion or membership of a particular social class. The periodicity of certain FAMILY LIFE-CYCLES may thus stretch over centuries or longer, though naturally this enters into resonance with the populational and familial read-only memories of phylogenesis on the one hand, which set the constraints of the open programmes of social learning and, on the other, the redefinitions proposed by the family cycles with each new generation. In this perspective, the patient who is designated schizophrenic would seem to have been deprived of certain programmatic sequences which are usually coded in read-only memories. Hence the necessity of synchronically reactivating his/her familial and institutional psycho-affective entourage and constructing or reconstructing life programmes functioning as safety barriers (prescription of TASKS in family therapy; establishment of frameworks, life scripts and stable reference points in institutional therapy).

The equivalence between flexibility and losing space or that between rigidity and gaining space was particularly well demonstrated by Bateson when he described the phenomena of habit acquisition. The acquisition of a habit in fact represents a considerable gain in time and energy, but if one then has to adapt to another context, the difficulty of changing makes itself felt on account of the rigidity of this mechanism. Habits are in effect 'hard programmed' and out of consciousness. And the rigidity is even greater if the genotype is modified to register a definitive adaptation. It is very fortunate that the genotype cannot easily be modified, as the specialization which would result would impoverish us irremediably.

(See also IMPRINTING; INSTINCT; TRANSGENERATIONAL MEMORIES.)

M.G. & J.M.

reality, the real The definition of reality is based on the individual arbitrariness of the linguistic sign which contrasts with its socially determined, and therefore collectively agreed, character ('calling a spade a spade'). Reality therefore presupposes a socially shared and stabilized AGREEMENT regarding the relations between signifier and signified. PHANTASY and DREAMS throw that signifier/signified agreement into question at the individual level, while delusional states throw it into question at a collective inter-group level.

Rosset (1977) argues that the real is the singular fact, the fact without an image and without a double. As SINGULARITY, the real is paradoxical, being at once random and determinate, unstoppable and possessed of its own dynamic, banal and surprising. It is what is happening in the here and now. In this sense, the real is the singularity of reality.

From a pragmatic point of view, the real is what exerts pressure on the clinical event, what acts efficiently upon it, defying meaning and representation. It is the accident, the unexpected which arises in the everyday-ness of experience. And it is, just as much, that everyday-ness itself. The real is distinct from the other categories of communication, whereas reality integrates these in their particular rhythms: dreams, nightmares, sleep, wakefulness, DELIRIUM, PLAY and phantasy (Miermont, 1986a).

The real is both a call for help and a calling to order which we are brought up against by persons, institutions and families. There is an obligation to do something (which may be to defer action, to mark out metaphors or to mark the bounds of delusions and phantasies). In this regard, family therapy proceeds from a bio-psycho-social construction of the real.

THE REAL AS PERCEIVED REAFFERENCE OF ACTUALIZED MOVEMENTS

The real may be defined as what is current, what is given at the present moment. It is related to the 'actual' and to 'actuality' and to what is contained in the German concepts *wirklich* and *Wirklichkeit*. The etymology of these terms has as a core meaning the idea of 'acting' and connects also with the idea of 'fact'. As Lorenz (1973, p. 196) explains: 'These reafference mechanisms in the learning of motor patterns are of decisive importance for the development of the central representation of space, the faculty which underlies all higher kinds of insight-controlled learning.' The experience of the perception of internal and interpersonal movements in INTERACTIONS plays a crucial role in our representation of reality and in the definition we may give of it. The interpersonal recognition of that experience is an essential therapeutic lever.

PLEASURE PRINCIPLE, REALITY PRINCIPLE

The distinction made by Freud between the 'pleasure principle' and the 'reality principle' is swept away in the reorderings characteristic of psychosis. Can we, however, gain access to the conditions which actually lie at the basis of reality? We can only have knowledge of drives by way of their psychical representatives. The psychotic loses 'an intimate sense of an essential familiarity between the ego and reality (Widlöcher, quoted in Racamier, 1978, p. 930). What is important here is the question of the sense attaching to that familiarity (see DEIXIS). This presumes there is an equivalence, a sufficient isomorphism between the real and the ego: 'The real is a hallucination of desire which has worked for the ego' (Racamier, 1978, p. 930). The psychotic is disturbed in his/her sense of the real. In fact, he/she questions it as a transgenerational datum which has lost its self-evident quality.

Similarly, for Lacan, 'the real is the impossible' which the psychotic runs up against, in so far as a signifier, foreclosed from the symbolic, disintegrates the imaginary and makes its return in the real. (For opposition between the realist real and the symbolized real, see FORECLOSURE.) We might add here that it is also the 'impossible' of psychoanalysis if that science lapses into idealism and confines itself to the study of self-referring representations, excluding from its purview the referential situations which construct and deconstruct those representations. It is the case, in fact, that a considerable proportion of these referential situations arise out of the ACTUOGENESIS of behaviour and deictic phenomena. For delirium is, precisely, what puts the definition of reality to the test.

THE REALITY OF REALITY

Watzlawick et al. (1974) stress the fact that the real is seldom, in psychopathology, the real of a thing in itself (if indeed such a thing can be apprehended), but rather the referent, as demonstrated and understood. It is thus made up of *opinions*, i.e. of the meaning the situation has for a group of persons. 'Real is what a sufficiently large number of people have agreed to call real (Watzlawick et al., 1974, p. 96).

In *How real is real?*, Watzlawick (1976) draws a distinction between a first- and a second-order reality: *First-order reality* is based on a consensus about perceptions: 'It is daytime', 'Gold is a yellow metal', 'The light is red' etc. *Second-order reality* rests on the symbolic or sociocultural value of the events of first-order reality.

THE FACTORS WHICH MAKE UP REALITY

It appears, clinically, that first-order reality is already in question for the autist or the schizophrenic: night is not necessarily perceived as such; gold is not necessarily a metal; the red light may be a wood fire etc. Moreover, collective convention is a necessary but insufficient condition. Submission to arbitrary authority, false rumours, illusions or collective delusions are counter-examples which show the importance of other parameters in the constitution of reality. Among these, we should recognize:

First, the *impact of sociopolitical events*: effects of LAW, POWER and war (see THERAPEUTIC STRATEGIES AND TACTICS). There is a relationship between potential relations of force and the actualization at a particular point of certain of those forces in the construction of reality. In this sense, one might say, for example, that, in paranoid delirium, there is a misrecognition of a potential reality which the subject is forced to reconstruct by himself at each moment.

Secondly, the *structure of the media which construct the levels of collective consciousness*. Concentration camps only became an indisputable social reality when they were mediated by cinema and television. Before that, they were only known about by certain individuals or certain well-informed groups.

Thirdly, the *state of science and technology at a particular moment*: hence the need for a comparative study of models. Scientific paradigms provide the basis for the definition of reality in a particular society. Macrocosmic and microcosmic exploration and intervention in biological reproduction throw into question what seemed to be the most solidly established definitions concerning humanity's relationship with itself and its environment.

BEHIND THE MIRROR AND FAMILY REALITY

The cognitive apparatus is, in itself, an element of reality which only acquired its present form through confrontations with and adaptation to equally real elements. It is therefore a mirror, whose back reflects nothing, but whose structure is at the same level of reality as all the real beings which it reflects (Lorenz, 1973). In this sense, family therapy is part of an anthropo-ethology. It advances a step further than objectivist ethology by the metaphorical construction of that 'back of the mirror' which makes it possible to avoid the snares of individualism. Its instruments (two-way mirror, VIDEO, CO-THERAPY, SUPERVISION) enable it to actualize the simulation of family interactions as the reflection of a reality to be determined. The real is thus constructed at each moment by virtue of interactions as these arise and are perceived. Thought can only know itself at the moment when it knows itself in action. To do so, it needs sensory input, i.e. things (Largeault, 1985). In this sense, family therapy participates in the (re)construction of that 'family thing' which has not come to be.

Thus processes of interaction draw on an interpretation of reality which takes place on various levels. Delirium corresponds to a singular kinship relation, which is its semantic expression rather than its cause. Hence the need to identify that structure of communication, in order to bring out the reality effects it puts

in question. Moreover, the nature of the interactions between therapists and various other professionals modifies the real with which patients and families are confronted. Restructuring these relations between families and therapists in itself means re-elaborating part of the reality which emerges out of the real, as this occurs spontaneously.

(See also ACTION; CONSTRUCTIVISM; DOUBLE BIND; METAPSYCHOLOGY; NARCISSISM; PARANOIA; PERFORMATIVES; PSEUDO-SPECIATION; SCHIZOPHRENIAS; SELF-FULFILLING PROPHECY; SEMIOLOGY AND SEMIOTICS OF COMMUNICATION; SYMBOLS.)

J.M.

reciprocal structural coupling See AGREEMENT AND DISAGREEMENT; COUPLES; FAMILY SELF-REFERENTIALITY; OSCILLATORS; SELF-REFERENTIAL CALCULUS; SEMANTIC RESONANCES; SEMANTICS OF COMMUNICATION.

reciprocal victimization and rescue An expression used by Wynne et al. (1958) to refer to the idea that, particularly in the families of schizophrenics, all the members – children and parents together – are caught up in a game in which each makes the other a victim and tries to come to their aid and rescue them.

Fear and hostility to what is perceived as alien, bringing with it feelings of hatred and even behaviour of aggression, expulsion or destruction, are likely to appear in the very bosom of the family in many situations. The autistic, handicapped or dysharmonic child and, equally, the 'idiot' (the singular child who differs from the norm) or the 'very gifted' child bring about 'victimizations' and compensatory rescues. In effect, the INDEX PATIENT develops symptoms in an attempt at reparation of the family's suffering and to regulate its most dysfunctional aspects, while the family may make the index patient into a victim or a SCAPEGOAT for the same reason.

In many species of animal, the mother becomes aggressive towards – and may even kill – her offspring if it does not send out certain characteristic signals (for a review of the literature, see Miermont, 1978a). The experiments carried out by Harlow (1972) on rhesus monkeys show the existence in 'motherless mothers' (isolated at an early age from any contact with their own species) of violent and abusive behaviour towards their young, when they manage to have any. In fact, their behaviour is often ambitendent: they may shift suddenly from rocking them to being violently aggressive towards them: bites, laceration of the hands and face, and throwing them to the ground. So long as the young monkey survives this abuse, this ambivalent phase tends to fade away. On the birth of a second infant, these mothers tend to be hyper-protective, as if the first had had a therapeutic function for the mother. We may conclude, following Seay and Harlow, that early social deprivation may disrupt the pattern of maternal behaviour in certain primates. This does not mean that this pattern is learned during ontogenesis, but rather that it may be blocked and destructured by inadequate environmental conditions.

Soulé (1977) shows the effects an autistic child may produce in his or her mother: pathological symbiotic fusion, persecution, over-intense frustration on the libidinal plane (each confrontation reactivating the narcissistic wound and tending to cause the incestuous phantasy to swing over into its opposite in the face of the possibility of its realization), desire to destroy the child to protect her own life, and exacerbation of the repetition automatism leading to repetition of the automatic.

Sacrificial or hyper-protective attitudes are attempts to regulate dysfunctions which relate to certain systems of personal behaviour as much as to the state of the transactions resulting from them. Similarly, the morphological configuration of the family, as a global system, is not without its influence upon behaviour and transactions. It is, then, necessary to recognize the inadequacy of linear causality as intuitively perceived, according to which the parents could be seen as the cause of their child's state or the child the cause of the parents' or the family's distress.

Related processes appear at all stages of FAMILY LIFE-CYCLES, as soon as a collective danger to life exists. The schizophrenic adolescent or the demented old person also bring about disturbances of RITUALIZATION, destructure tolerable human relations, threaten collective survival and give rise to antinomic reactions in DOUBLE BIND form, in which the aggressor is victim and the victim aggressor. The 'black sheep of the family' may also be a child of normal height in a family of dwarfs, a hearing child in a family of deaf-mutes, a 'contemplative' child in a milieu where action is encouraged (or the opposite). Each, in his or her way, threatens the adaptations found by the family to survive with its singularities.

(See also DEMENTIA; INCEST; INFANTILE AUTISM; SACRED; SCHIZOPHRENIAS.)

P.S. & J.M.

redundancy For Bateson, following on from the work of Weaver and Shannon (1949), redundancy is synonymous with 'the internal structure of message material', which helps the receiver to distinguish between signal and noise, and ensures that the 'singular' MESSAGE to be transmitted is not a pure artefact. The regularity of the signal–noise relationship is a special case of redundancy. Redundancy stands opposed here

to 'camouflage' and has, in the same way as this latter, become a technique of therapeutic intervention (see HYPNOSIS).

Redundancy in a message is the repetition of identical INFORMATION. Repetition marks the importance of this information in the message, and confirms the absence of error in the expression of the message. Weaver and Shannon (1949) define redundancy in terms of the dependency of symbols. Redundancy in the most general form, they say, represents the fact that symbols are not transmitted by the source in such a way that they are totally independent of one another. According to Weaver and Shannon, if we are dealing with repetition pure and simple, then the sending of repeated symbols is determined as soon as they have been sent the first time; the same is true in the case of extra symbols whose function is to enable errors to be recognized. This is why, in a very general way, it is the non-dependency of symbols in a message which Weaver and Shannon (1949) use to define redundancy.

It is, however, with another form of dependency that we are concerned here, namely the dependency of information upon redundancy. Watzlawick et al. (1967) described this paradox in their turn. A series of events in which each element, at any moment, possesses an equal chance of appearing is termed random (this, according to Weaver and Shannon, is the field of maximum information). One can draw no conclusion from this and make no prediction as to the future course of events. This is another way of saying that it transmits no information. Only redundancy, permitting predictability, produces a 'pattern . . . which connects' (Bateson). Because of the surrounding noise, the message must be organized in such a way as to reduce the frequency of transmission errors. The method which occurs most immediately to the human mind is to repeat the message. That technique is, in itself, revealing of what Morin (1977, p. 348) refers to as an 'ever-implicit, ever-hidden, ever-present and ever-dominant paradigmatology'.

In fact, this is present in us from earliest times, since it is connected with our oldest experiences at the ontogenetic, if not indeed, the phylogenetic, level of language organization. Jakobson (1957) stresses that the acquisition of language comes about by way of learning the notion of articulation, since in all languages the transition to the second linguistic period is marked by the opposition between closure (m) and opening (a). We shall note here that it is the repetition of this first phonological or phonemic group which ensures that it becomes established as something distinct from a mere noise. We find this again in the naming of more distant kin (e.g. French 'tata', 'tonton' etc.).

Redundancy, then, makes sense. It is the precondition for information to have meaning. It is this process which Bateson stresses:

Telegraphist A has a written message on his pad and sends this message over wire to B, so that B now gets the same sequence of letters on his message pad. This transaction (or 'language game' in Wittgenstein's phrase) has created a redundant universe for an observer O. If O knows what was on A's pad, he can make a better than random guess at what is on B's pad. (Bateson, 1972, p. 104)

This can be verified, in music, in the serial compositions of Schoenberg; in literature, in Joyce's *Finnegans Wake*; and, in painting, in Kandinsky's lyrical abstraction. The only way of apportioning meaning to these works is to increase the number of times one listens to, reads or sees them again. A similar verification can be found in the most disturbed families, where meaning only emerges after a sufficient prescription of the status quo, i.e. after setting in place sequences of repetition which establish sufficient redundancy.

(See also COMMUNICATION THEORY.)

D.C. & J.M.

reference   Searle (1969) defines reference as a 'speech act' (see SPEECH ACTS) used to isolate or identify an 'object' or an entity or a 'particular' to the exclusion of other objects about which the speaker is able to say something, ask a question etc. This referential function is particularly badly damaged in psychotic or psychosomatic pathology or in behavioural deviance.

In these situations, the only reference initially (and sometimes finally) offered by the family system has, as its FAMILY ACTANT, the index patient, as its predicate the set of his/her activities, and as its circumstances the contexts in which these activities occur. One may hypothesize that this polarization on the index patient is connected with a disturbance of FAMILY SELF-REFERENTIALITY.

(See also DEIXIS; REALITY; SHIFTERS.)

J.M.

re-framing, re-labelling   Expressions, first used in the work of Haley (1963) and Jackson (1968), referring to an attitude on the part of the therapist whereby he/she responds to an assertion from a different angle. For example, a situation which is initially negatively labelled is re-labelled in a positive mode. The therapist might, for example:

- say of a mother who is apparently hyper-protective toward her child that she is devoted to him body and soul;
- re-frame a father's criticisms of his son by stressing that such a paternal attitude is a mark of interest and of a desire to ensure his son will do well in life;

- re-label a violent sibling conflict as a way of testing out closeness and the sharing of solidarity in difficult conditions.

The objective is to reorientate the family by a re-framing of reality, towards a new way of seeing their interactions in a more positive way, to communicate something of this to them and thus to leave them more open to change. Re-framing of this kind is closely related to POSITIVE CONNOTATION.

(See also MODEL OF THE SYSTEMIC MODEL.)

J.M.

relational archetypes   The difference between the sexes and between the generations, the concepts of child, father, mother, grandparents, ancestors and collaterals refer back to archetypal categories of perception, thinking and feeling which ground the very possibility of a diversity of FAMILY SYSTEMS between different civilizations and human cultures.

Studies in comparative anthropology show us – if such demonstration were needed – that each family group is different from every other in its concrete realization. Such a diversity is only made possible by the existence of constraints which ultimately enable an alliance to be formed between two families from different cultures, for the purpose of starting a new family. The possibility of such an alliance presupposes that there are common structures of reference, which we shall here, in a perspective deriving from the work of Jung (1933), Lorenz (1954), von Uexküll (1956) and Thom (1972), term 'family archetypes'.

We may throw some light upon the concept of archetype by looking at what von Uexküll has to say about it. In the predator–prey relationship, the predator has no concrete knowledge of a particular prey; it acts in conformity with an 'original script', an archetypal pattern, which brings together the essential, habitual and average characteristics of the figure of regulation of prey. 'Behind the screen of phenomena, the various original images or the various original melodies are joined together in terms of an overall plane of meaning.' Thus the spider's web is not the copy of a concrete physical fly, but it is structured in such a way that it takes into account all the properties which describe the morphogenetic characteristics of the fly in so far as these are pertinent to predation (the strands of the web have to be sufficiently invisible, solid and tight for the population of flies to be statistically caught in the trap).

For Freud (1915), the conscious–unconscious opposition does not apply to drive (or INSTINCT). A drive can never enter consciousness; only the representative which represents it can do that ('Observations on transference love'). It is on this point that Jung felt the need, as a result of his regular dealings with psychotic patients, to postulate the existence of levels of an archetypal, collective unconscious devoid of content. For Jung, archetypes might be described as the stock of the collective unconscious. This is made up of innate typical forms, even though no inheritance of individual memories exists. In his 'Introduction to the Tibetan Book of the Dead', he writes:

So far as I know, there is no inheritance of individual, pre-natal or pre-uterine memories, but there are undoubtedly inherited archetypes, which are, however, devoid of content because, to begin with, they contain no personal experiences. They only emerge into consciousness when personal experiences have rendered them visible. (Quoted in Gordon Montagnon, 1984, p. 56)

In other works, archetypes will be described as empty structures devoid of all content, being purely formal, 'a possibility of representation which is given *a priori*', 'an irrepresentable, unconscious, pre-existent form that seems to be part of the inherited structure of the psyche' (Chomsky, 1980, p. 228).

As we can see here, Jung's position is a fluctuating, oscillating one, as befits a problem of this complexity. As regards the question of the inaccessibility of certain unconscious processes – and not merely their practical, but also their theoretical inaccessibility – one might assume that the Freudian position is a clearer one, since the instinct as such, as we have seen, lies beyond psychical categories; the only thing that enters the psyche is the *representative* of the instinct.

For Gordon Montagnon (1984), the Jungian archetype is seen as being akin to the innate releasing mechanism described by the ethologists. However, Lorenz, for his part, is quite clear on this point:

Experiments show that there is no foundation for the immediate assumption that an organism of a given species innately possesses a 'species-specific memory picture', as postulated by C. G. Jung in his theory of the 'archetype'. An enormous amount of observational and experimental material which has accumulated in recent years . . . shows quite convincingly that the innate releasing mechanism – in contrast to a conditioned Gestalt responding to a complex quality – does not respond to the overall total or even a large proportion of the stimuli accompanying a certain relevant situation. Instead, the mechanism selects relatively few of the great number of stimuli and permits these to act as a 'key to the response'. (Lorenz, 1954, p. 136)

The very term 'schema' is also to be criticized here, since it gives the impression that there might be an innate overall picture of an object or a situation: 'It is misleading to talk of a releasing schema of "the sexual partner", of "the prey", of "the offspring", and so on,

since each of the different responses elicited by one of these objects possesses its own releasing mechanism' (Lorenz, 1954, p. 137). There is, in fact, little resemblance between the optimal lure imposed by the perception of the form that triggers an instinctive movement and the natural object of the reaction. This 'arbitrariness' of the lure is perhaps the prototype of SYMBOL construction at the phylogenetic level. It cannot be the case that the functions of parental care and filial attachment are performed as a consequence of a mere decision – a decision which would confront mother, father and child anew in each generation – culturally to reconstruct them *ex nihilo*. The necessary insertion into the weft of a differentiated culture presupposes the existence of phylogenetic threads interwoven with a sufficient degree of sophistication to allow variations to be compared.

Lorenz (1954, p. 430) defines the properties of the 'symbolic motor patterns' observable in animal communication: differentiation of the stimulus-transmitting motor pattern accompanied by an equivalent development of the receiving innate 'schema'; the motor pattern is rendered more effective by certain exaggerations of the visually effective components; it is also simplified by the omission of certain details, and there are material morphological differentiations of form and colour which further increase the visual effect; thus the simplification of movements and the exaggeration of the gestural effect are associated; these symbolic motor patterns are no longer connected with the initial movements from which they are derived (catastrophe jump). In fact, the concept of archetype becomes of greater heuristic value if it is conceived as a set of morphogenetic invariants, of which the elementary catastrophes of Thom and Zeeman are the universal prototypes.

Thom (1972) gave a new direction to this debate by suggesting that there were *archetypal morphologies*, present in the structure of ELEMENTARY CATASTROPHES, formalizing the structurally stable configurations of the dynamic processes of change (or, in other words, the stable attractors of morphological change); these morphologies do not need to be written into the genetic code to possess a character of archetypal universality; their algebraic and geometric properties ensure that this is the case (theory of UNIVERSAL UNFOLDING).

There follow from this *graphs of interaction* (graphic representations of a function or a relation) enabling us to determine the level of isomorphy possible between the behavioural manifestations of organisms and the structural properties of semiotic systems (which in practice, in Thom's theory, means language).

What then are these archetypal morphologies? In the form of apparently very simple and highly abstract graphs, they describe morphologies of interaction; these are present in the most common verbal syntagms; we shall propose the hypothesis that they enter directly into resonance with what family morphologies transmit to their offspring: being–existing, beginning–being born, ending–dying, uniting–attaching, separating–detaching, becoming–changing, capturing–incorporating, emitting, failing, committing suicide, agitating–stirring, rejecting–repulsing, crossing–piercing, giving, sending–communicating, taking, fastening, cutting (Thom, 1972; Wildgen, 1982). The hypothesis proposed here is that these archetypal morphologies only stabilize their meaning for a person if family interactions have sufficiently explored in concrete terms the universal unfolding from which they result.

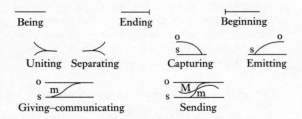

Examples of archetypal morphologies deriving from structurally stable attractors of elementary catastrophes (after Thom, 1972). s, subject; o, object; M, messenger; m, message.

We shall therefore propose to define relational, intrafamilial and interfamilial archetypes in the following way. The human family is underpinned by archetypes which structure its reproduction above and beyond all the contrasting cultural forms which can be envisaged. These archetypes are materialized in the individuation of each human being, but they only take on form and meaning in transpersonal actions by being used in a complementary, symmetrical and reciprocal way by the various family protagonists (see SCHISMOGENESIS); they are non-conscious and totally inaccessible to preconscious representation, yet at the same time they serve as morphogenetic matrices for family imagos (child, parent, grandparent, husband, wife etc.) and for the psychical representatives which derive from them.

It is therefore possible for their individual stabilization not to be acquired, so that they do not enable the transition to take place between the great 'biological pregnant forms' and the pregnant forms of socialization (language, means of expression through epistemology, art, sport etc.) There exists an emergent supraindividual quality in the activation of behaviour, whether actual or phantasized, which is covered by the very concept of family system; the properties of the family system derive from the personal embodiment of family archetypes and, in return, influence the differentiated structuring of the individual psyches.

Lastly, all family interaction would be rendered impossible if there did not exist ideal schemas of recognition and regulation of the positions of child, mother,

father, brother, sister etc. (ATTRACTORS). The innate schema of the child is the best known and most 'caricatural' example of this. But other archetypes operate too: that of the 'angry father' (Hermann, 1943), that of the 'murderous, mortiferous, mortified mother' (Soulé, 1977); and the archetype which is to the fore in the phantasy construction of the primal scene (Freud, 1900, 1918).

(See also SYMBOLIC REFERENCE.)

J.M.

relational stagnation May be defined as the consequence of attempts invalidated from an ethical point of view to resolve the difficulties of existence. Relational exchanges, pre-programmed to maintain the state of equilibrium of the family LEDGER, lose their flexibility and variety and tend to become confined to rigid patterns.

The concept of stagnation is intimately connected to the notion of growth. For Boszormenyi-Nagy, 'the major purpose of families is the child-rearing function; a family system may be considered alive, healthy, and growing to the extent that it fulfils that aim, and developmentally stagnant if it fails in this most important function' (Boszormenyi-Nagy and Spark, 1973, p. 114).

(See also ETHICS; FAMILY SYSTEM; SEMANTICS OF COMMUNICATION.)

A.L.

residual relations, relations of absence of absence A relation based on absence of absence (of attachment, love, quantum of effect or of representations) is a self-contradictory relation. If it is present, it is absent and if it is absent, it is present.

This paradox underlies Bateson's observations regarding structures of communication based on representations of representations. Let there be a relation R between two conspecifics A and B. The relation of combat is metacommunicated by the index C.

$$A \longleftrightarrow R \longleftrightarrow B \quad \text{Conspecific relation}$$
$$\longrightarrow C \longleftarrow \quad\quad \text{Combat relation}$$

PLAY is typically a relation of type T which exists when combat, R, is no longer in relation with the relation, S, established between two conspecifics A and B.

$$A \longleftrightarrow R \longleftrightarrow B \quad \text{Conspecific relation}$$
$$\longrightarrow T \,(C) \longleftarrow \quad \text{(Play relation)}$$

When two apes play, or two young children, they express a behaviour which is derived from a fight that does not in fact take place; the exchange of signals indicates that the residue of fighting, marked by the indices T, is a non-fight and therefore a game. (Ethologists have shown that the indices are rapid alternation between hunter and hunted, the 'pulling' of attacking arm movements, 'silent laughter' etc.)

A ⟵⟶ T (C) ⟵⟶ B   Play relation

⌐⟶ T (C) ⟵⌐   Relation of playing on play

⌐⟶ T (T(T)) ⟵⌐   'This is play'

The paradox appears clearly when play behaviour is denoted by the linguistic expression: 'This is play' or 'We are playing.' The verbal expression takes the place of play which, from that point, is no longer happening. We then have an absence of absence of fighting, with the risks of oscillation that entails. It is then that play may effectively degenerate (see also Bateson, 1972: 'A theory of play and fantasy').

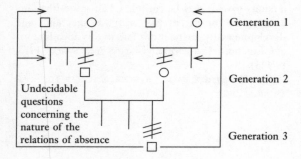

Relation of paradoxical attachment on the basis of a schematization over three generations.

The paradox of residual relations appears with families expressing experiences of early affective deprivation over several generations. If the parents have already undergone the ordeal of a pathology in the formation of the bond between them, with a defect in the relation of attachment (pathology of the forming of the bond, rather than of its breaking), the experience of MOURNING in later life will become particularly dangerous, if not indeed downright impossible. The choice of partner will be made in adult life (among the parents of the future patient) in the mode of a residual attachment, with defective introjection of the primary love object. The children, in the course of their development, will be confronted with an experience of absence of absence of affectionate ties. The most exposed child will have to perform multiple parenting functions for his/ her own parents, the mechanisms of PARENTIFICATION then taking on an exacerbated character. He or she will

become a conglomerate of multiform parental relations, having to provide for the affective needs of the whole of the family group (Miermont, 1986a).

(See also AGONISTIC BEHAVIOUR; SCHIZOPHRENIAS.)

J.M.

restructuring   Therapeutic interventions which aim to confront and even challenge a family in an attempt to bring about a therapeutic change: setting TASKS for the family members, escalating the stress within the family group or setting rules of behaviour during the therapy session (Minuchin, 1974, see also PROVOCATION).

Restructuring techniques include all interventions aimed at changing the structure of family transactions or other systems which are part of the problem.

They are distinguished from joining operations by the challenge they pose. Joining operations do not challenge; they decrease the distance between family and therapist, helping the therapist to blend with the family . . . In restructuring . . . he uses his position of leadership within the therapeutic system to pose challenges to which the family has to accommodate. (Minuchin, 1974, p. 138)

Restructuring techniques can be grouped in three basic categories: interventions to reshape the system; utilization of the symptom; and structural modifications.

RESHAPING THE SYSTEM

These techniques are based on adding or subtracting sub-systems from the system in question, in order to achieve change. In Minuchin's view (1974, p. 135):

with some families, the therapist always works with the total group. In others, he selects the group that he feels is most appropriate, alternating different groupings depending on the developing dynamics . . . the therapist can divide members of a coalition. He can see two members who have been in a stable coalition for some sessions . . . opposing members can be seen together to alter their pattern of transactions.

At the level of the family interview itself, for example, it may be important to work with the two parents alone at a particular stage, to allow them to work on a latent conflict between them. Or, alternatively, a grandparent or some other member of the extended family who seems to be playing a decisive role in the family's current difficulties may be included in the session. In Minuchin's view, this technique can also be applied in the context of the wider ecosystem. Thus, the therapist may suggest or request the intervention of a social, ethnic or religious community to break down the isolation of a single mother etc. Even when he or she is working intensively with a subgroup, or even with a single family member, the overall restructuring of the family always remains the therapist's objective. And always the therapist 'works with his map of the total family in mind' (Minuchin, 1974, p. 147).

UTILIZING THE SYMPTOM

The SYMPTOM is a consequence of the dysfunctioning of the family structure. It may be the most direct route to solving the problem or, by contrast, the chief obstacle to its solution. In Minuchin's view, in every case and whatever the strategy chosen by the therapist, he/she must decide on his/her attitude towards the symptom. Interventions focused upon the symptom may make it possible, by modifying the function it performs in the system, to achieve its elimination.

By *exaggerating the symptom*, the therapist accentuates its importance to the point where it can no longer fulfil its regulative role. *Prescribing the symptom* (see PRESCRIPTION) is a very similar technique. *De-emphasizing the symptom* sometimes makes it possible to reduce the energy that is mobilized by the symptom and necessary to its function. This is often associated with a displacement on to a new symptom which temporarily refocuses the therapy on another member of the family. In the *re-labelling of the symptom*, the difficulties are reformulated in interpersonal terms and thus acquire a new meaning within the family. For example, anorexia nervosa may sometimes be redefined as an act of disobedience (Minuchin, 1974). We may compare the technique of *changing the symptom's affect*.

STRUCTURAL MODIFICATIONS

For Aponte and Van Deusen (1981), the explicit project of modifying the family structure is what distinguishes structural therapy from other forms of family therapy. These techniques are aimed at modifying ALIGNMENTS, BOUNDARIES and the division of POWER within the structure of the system directly at the level of the primary locus.

Disassembly
Disassembly aims to eliminate and break down inadequate transactional patterns (Aponte and Van Deusen, 1981). As a necessary stage in every durable structural modification, this covers several types of intervention:

- the blocking of certain relational models, by stopping the 'communication flow' when it is passing through its habitual channels;
- the emphasizing of differences by bringing out the divergences which the family members tend to gloss over to maintain a mutual lack of differentiation;
- developing implicit conflict.

Construction of transactional patterns
This type of intervention brings together the use of techniques more or less directly derived from learning theory to compensate for the non-acquisition of the structures required for conflict resolution etc.

Reinforcement of transactional patterns
The therapist seeks to bring out and amplify transactional patterns which exist within the family in order to increase the part they play in the various family functions and operations. For example, he/she may underscore the affectionate words or gestures of a mother who is, in other respects, most often aggressive toward her children.

Reorganization of transactional patterns
It is possible by means of these interventions to render operational potential structures present in the family, by removing the obstacles opposing them.

Put simply, these different restructuring techniques are directed at two types of problems: the existence of a conflictual system or a structural insufficiency. The notion of *conflictual system* refers to the existence of a conflict between contradictory needs, either in a single individual or between several family members or subsystems, a conflict which it does not prove possible to resolve without dysfunction. A *structural insufficiency* may be defined as the absence or lack of structural resources in the family to respond to the system's functional needs. It may be the consequence of an absence of family or social support during the formation and development of the system.

The various restructuring interventions may be grouped, in a non-specific way, according to the type of difficulty being confronted by the family. In the case of a conflictual system, the techniques of disassembly and reorganization seem more appropriate. By contrast, techniques of reconstruction and reinforcement seem more pertinent where there is structural insufficiency.

(See also AFFILIATION OR JOINING; FAMILY STRUCTURES; NETWORKS; STRUCTURAL FAMILY THERAPY.)

A.L.

'revolving slate' See LEDGER.

ritualization, rituals A ritual is an organizer of interpersonal relations which structures both small (couples, dyads, triads, nuclear families) and large groups (extended families, clans, social organizations). Ritualization is a formal schematization of an encounter (by containment, canalization and derivation of behaviours), which permits of a maximally clear definition of the nature of the relations which form within the family or social unit thus created. It is capable of removing the ambiguity that is inherent in any communication, by providing information on its characteristics. In so doing, it enables us to make a choice between two or more equally possible alternatives, which leads to a decision being made in which the protagonists participate equally, either to continue with the same style of encounter, as formalized, or to halt it or transform it.

Rituals function as structures accompanying the symbolic changes in communication between individuals (changes of level of REALITY: relations within a couple, professional relations; or changes of levels of metareality: sacraments, religious ceremonies, celebrations). They channel the process of change by establishing new facts, acknowledged and shared by the parties; hence the importance of rites of passage which, for example, enable adolescents to gain access to the adult world, i.e. the transgenerational transmission of modalities of communication. Rites of passage thus function on the premiss: 'Is this still a game?' The indicator of this nuance is a certain dose of pain, linked to the mild persecution of the person undergoing the rite. Such a prescription of pain is an index of the registering of entry into a particular level of social reality.

Ritualization thus avoids the encounter degenerating in the form of a material de-structuring and/or excessive release of energy. Psychotic and psychosomatic accidents or behavioural disorders attest to a breakdown of this kind. A pathological communication marks the non-regulated escalation of suffering and complete confusion between MAP and territory. In effect, if the ritual is a relatively stable channel, metacommunication about rituals ('This is ritual') like metacommunication about play ('This is play') is profoundly unstable: it runs the risk of degenerating into direct aggression. De-ritualization destroys the METACOMMUNICATION SYSTEMS and is accompanied by family and/or social violence.

Therapeutic action leads to the establishment, and even the PRESCRIPTION, of singular rituals (Selvini Palazzoli et al., 1978), adapted to each family context as a function of the reconstitution of the anamnesis. It is possible, through these rituals, to make a tangential approach to situations which would be totally explosive if they were approached head on. The framework of psychoanalytic psychotherapy of family therapy is already a ritual through and through, laying down a spatial and rhythmic structure for encounters. Therapeutic ritualization can call upon a wide variety of forms of media, as well as hybrid combinations of these (words, drawings, letters, METAPHORICAL OBJECTS, technical equipment, acoustic and video recordings, rooms equipped with one-way mirrors, the persons of the therapists, relational games, inter-institutional games etc.).

DE-RITUALIZATION AND CONFLICT BETWEEN RITUALS

In pathology, we see many disorders of ritualization. Rituals may lose their initial function, become emptied of all content and degenerate as time erodes them. In the obsessional, they take on a purely defensive function of struggle against anal-sadistic instincts; they then lose their social dimension and become transformed into strictly individual and internal ceremonial. As for the schizophrenic, he/she utilizes para-rituals and metarituals as a mode of existence; these are made up of all the waste-material which is usually rejected when conventionally ritualized interchanges take place (Laing, 1961). Now, these troubled forms of ritualization not only concern the INDEX PATIENT, but all those in his/her immediate circle. But confusions between levels of ritualization are also found in normal human beings in moments of transformation or in groups at critical moments of their development. There may then also be *conflicts between rituals*, connected with the multistratified aspect of ritualizations in mankind. One may, in fact, distinguish between two complementary and overlapping modalities of ritualization in the human species, which share a common function of enabling the individual to anticipate the partner's actions.

Phylogenetic ritualization, studied by ethologists, is formed through the canalization of instinctive movements (relating to predation or the satisfying of hunger, sexuality or aggression) which are reorientated toward purposes of communication between conspecifics. These display, courtship, threat and combat rituals have an invariant character within any particular species and enable the individuals to assess one another, to discover the complex morphology of their behaviours, by way of a synchronization of their reactions; this may lead to specific, lasting bonds. Such sequences, having an invariant character and one that is typical of humans, have been observed in interactions between children (Blurton-Jones, 1972; Montagner, 1978), between adults (Darwin, 1872; Eibl-Eibesfeldt, 1973; Ekman, 1973) and also in parent–child interactions (Ambrose, 1961; Erikson, 1965; Bowlby, 1969, 1973, 1980) or in situations of courtship and seduction (Eibl-Eibesfeldt, 1973).

Cultural ritualization characterizes human nature in a more radical way than the phylogenetic, interacting with it continually in the form of transcultural REFRAMINGS. In the case of cultural re-framings, signal movements and receivers of signals are not fixed hereditarily, but are acquired, most often at an early stage, and may thus come into question in interactions. These re-framings come into play at particularly critical moments. Writing of the peace-making ceremonials of the Andaman Islands, where each side is given freedom to strike a final ritual blow against the other, Bateson (1972, p. 155) notes that 'the discrimination between map and territory is always liable to break down': the ritual blows of peace-making are then liable to be taken for real blows of combat and the peace-making ceremony becomes a brawl. One sees the same phenomenon in family conflicts.

FUNCTIONS OF NATURAL AND CULTURAL RITUALIZATION

At least five functions are fulfilled by natural and cultural ritualizations. First, there is the *function of communication*, by containing and canalizing behaviours which may possibly become dangerous. From a cybernetic point of view, in ritual, analogic communications are digitalized and make up a 'complex set of meta-linguistic (but non-verbalized) rules' which subsequently determine the relations between, on the one hand, words and sentences and, on the other, objects and events (Bateson, 1972). From a topological point of view, a biological pregnance runs up, in a sense, against a salience which stands in its way and serves to protect the invasive aspect of the pregnance (see SYMBOLIC REFERENCE). The information contained in the various rituals has an anti-entropic effect which makes it possible to avoid a dissipation of energy linked to the risk of direct aggression. The levels of intrafamilial and extrafamilial violence indicate the selective pressures which lead to the maintenance and constitution of ever more elaborate rituals. Words are, in a sense, micro-rituals, semantic CHREODS which strictly control the invasion of pregnances (secondary processes of thinking).

This function of communication is directly used in family therapy and corresponds to the exploration of the phenomenological level described by Caillé (1985) (see MODEL OF THE SYSTEMIC MODEL). Thus the therapist will attempt, for example, to:

- reactivate the rituals of the first encounters between the members of a couple in difficulty;
- set in place substitutive mourning rituals where deaths have not been worked through on the symbolic level;
- set up rituals of separation and differentiation where relationships are breaking up.

Secondly, there is the *function of creating motivations and the autonomization of social units*. In man, ritualizations serve as supports for the autonomization of couples, families and the various social organizations. Cultural ritualizations integrate and re-frame phylogenetic ritualizations, with all the variations and interpretations which the 'choices', norms and laws of the various human subgroups represent. However, the PSEUDO-SPECIATION of civilizations increases distinctly more quickly than the modification of species (Lorenz, 1973). Civilizations would collapse if pseudo-speciation were to become totally cut off from its

natural foundations and to mask them completely. This is what also seems to happen to the neurotic who is prey to his/her internal struggles (the obsessional's ceremonials) or the psychotic, in resonance with the fractures within his/her family milieu.

Thirdly, there is a *performative function*: rites lead to the effective constitution of relationships and to the construction of reality which follows from this. Love, work and friendship are experienced in ritualized encounters, which enable the nature of the relationship to be defined in the very process of the experience. It is ritualization which enables the phenomenological model of reality to be defined, as specified by Caillé (1985). Following an observation by Michael Houseman (personal communication), we may say that the performative function of rites leads to the differentiation of the two following polarities:

1 The necessary and the contingent: this covers the distinction between what is essential for life and survival and what is superfluous, but also the distinction between determinism and indeterminism in interactions and therefore the definition of their causality by the partners.
2 The reversible and the irreversible: rites of passage secure a change of state while maintaining continuity of being (choice of a profession, partner etc.); the so-called 'irreversibility' of schizophrenias probably has to do with a natural process of evolution which has not received a satisfactory ritualization.

Fourthly, there is the *function of maintenance of the cohesion of groups*, with isolation of one from another, for purposes of protection and survival. Cultural ritualization is quite close to what Bateson called the ETHOS of a culture. It enables BOUNDARIES to be marked by setting in place barriers or separations which ensure an equilibrium which provides a sense of security in the sub-units thus constituted. This is to stress the importance of intra- and interfamilial rituals and of rites of passage at the critical moments when the jump is made from one cycle to another. There is a difference – and there may possibly be a conflict – between interpersonal rituals (rituals of mothering, fathering, seduction of adolescents, transmission of 'stories' by the grandparents, mourning etc.) and the inter-group rituals marking the stages of the FAMILY LIFE-CYCLE in institutional fashion: (marriage ceremonies, religious rituals around birth, rites of passage of adolescents, wakes or vigils etc.).

Fifthly, there is the *function of marking life-cycles and transmitting values across generations*. Every stage of life gives rise to religious and/or pagan festivals, leading to the synchronic meeting of two or more generations.

When mourning early deaths, certain disturbed families will avoid the display of the ritualizations connected with death (vigils, rituals inherent in burial), which leads to what are sometimes considerable distortions of reality for the children who are, consequently, not informed of what has happened. Rites of passage thus ensure the conservation of religious and social structures and stabilize MODE-IDENTIFYING SIGNALS. They mark the precedence of the older generations over the younger. They have an initiatory function, through the inscription of TRANSGENERATIONAL MEMORIES. Where MYTHS express the eidonomy (see EIDOS) of a social group, rites stabilize their ethonomy.

This is how the establishment of the SACRED, the constitution of collective and FAMILY MYTHS and the organization of beliefs functions. It is only through the activation of rituals that it is possible to ground the reality of reality. The inscription of the individual in the socius leads to the setting in place of RITUALS OF BELONGING and rituals of inclusion.

(See also ANALOG–DIGITAL, DIGITAL–ANALOG CONVERTERS; ARTIFICIAL CODES; HOLOGRAPHIC MEMORY; INSTITUTIONAL MYTHS; MESSAGES; PERFORMATIVES; PRAGMATICS OF COMMUNICATION; SEMANTICS OF COMMUNICATION; STATIC, PSEUDO-STATIC AND METABOLIC FORMS; SYNTAX OF COMMUNICATION.)

J.M.

rituals of belonging (or membership), rituals of inclusion   Human groups seem to be constituted in two radically different ways, through rituals of belonging and rituals of inclusion. The function of rituals of belonging is to play a part in the maintenance and cohesion of groups. Some are rituals of passage (rites of passage) to belonging (competitive examinations, religious conversions, entry into analytic schools, entry into sects, clubs, political parties). Others are rituals ensuring the maintenance and permanence of the group and they consist in giving pledges of loyalty, such as, for example, ritual participation in meetings or ceremonies, conformity to a model or to communicational, linguistic, vestimentary, ideological or other particularisms.

The function of rituals of inclusion is to select subjects, then to obtain their 'express' acceptance of being defined as a member of a predetermined category. We may here speak of reification of the subject in the sense that the invidividual is subsequently represented only by a partial characteristic or even merely by a number. Examples of 'rituals of passage to inclusion' might be the court judgment, which makes the person a condemned criminal, or the psychiatric certificate which recognizes a particular 'sick person' as dangerous for him or herself or others, and who has to be interned under the law. One may also cite rituals of induction into military service, compulsory schooling or the life of a worker/taxpayer.

BELONGING

Belonging simply indicates the relation between an element or individual and the set which contains it or him/her and to which it or he/she belongs. A single element may belong to several sets.

Examples of groups which may be described as ones 'to which people may belong' (or 'membership groups') are legion. We may mention clubs, sects, sporting, religious or political associations, political parties, gangs, families. The metaphors and vocabulary used in relation to these groups stress the discontinuity between the individual and the group as an entity. We speak of members, and of the group as a body or 'corps', as in the expression 'esprit de corps'. This is an image which is often used and which we find as early as Pascal in *Pensées*: 'Etre membre est n'avoir de vie, d'être et de mouvement que par l'esprit de corps' (1991 edn, p. 1305) ('To be a member is to have neither life, being, nor movement save by the spirit of the body').

Lastly, the difference of logical level between an individual and the membership group is illustrated perfectly by Groucho Marx's famous quip that he could never join any club which would have him as a member. The constitution of a group of this kind imposes a solidarity on its members quite apart from any feelings of antipathy or sympathy which the members may feel for one another. What the individual gains in return for that effort of solidarity is a differentiation from the general run of society: the group gives the individual a group-related identity which satisfies what Freud called 'the narcissism of minor differences'.

INCLUSION

Inclusion isolates on the basis of an already constituted set, which may be a 'membership group', a subgroup or subgroups of elements having common characteristics. Examples of human groups structured by inclusion would be a barracks, a school class, a town, the class of disabled, certain human groups subject to racist laws, women subject to sexist laws, inclusion in a family lineage. This relationship is, to some extent, imposed on the subject, but, curiously, he/she is not targeted personally. Unlike the relationship of belonging (or membership relation), the relation of inclusion demands no solidarity between the members of the group. Most often, indeed, it forbids it (soldiers may be prohibited from forming a trade union, the formation of closely knit subgroups within a particular group may be forbidden).

RESPECTIVE FUNCTIONS OF RITUALS OF BELONGING AND RITUALS OF INCLUSION

To sum up, then, belonging to a group implies a certain conformism, whether ideological or of some other nature but, paradoxically, it serves to valorize the individual by virtue of his/her membership of the group, preserving him or her from becoming just another run-of-the-mill person, like the rest of society. Rituals of belonging or membership formalize integration into the group and reinforce solidarity between its members. The relation of inclusion, on the other hand, suppresses the differences between individuals and attaches itself to a partial characteristic which, alone, is used to represent them, thus promoting their classification into 'categories'; rituals of inclusion are intended to impose an order, to promote the assimilation of a subject into a category, to prevent the formation of a solidarity between the members so included that might be directed against the guardians of a pre-established order.

Groups formed by membership or belonging and those formed by inclusion do, of course, involve the same individuals. The family is typically sited at the point where these two types of group overlap, as is evidenced in the contradictory diversity of its rituals. Most often, the rituals which set the rhythm of the family's life-cycles are combinations of rituals of belonging and rituals of inclusion. Baptism, for example, is a mark of the child's belonging to its family, but, at the same time, it is also the sign of its inclusion in the world of believers.

PATHOLOGY OF RITUALS OF BELONGING AND
RITUALS OF INCLUSION

The relation of belonging seems acutely over-developed in families in psychotic transaction; it is, by contrast, virtually absent from disengaged families presenting delinquency-related or psychopathic disorders. The former are as resistant to any attempt to include them in the social body as the latter are intent upon infiltrating or working their way into external groups (placements, residential 'homes', thefts, breaking and entering etc.). The symptoms of the two groups also reveal themselves in different ways. In the first type of family, they occur at the point of inclusion in school, an occupation or the military, whereas, with the second type, they occur at the point of recognition of belonging. *In extremis*, the social body defends itself in the former case by the in-closing of the excluded (the asylum) and, in the latter, by the exclusion of the in-closed (prison).

(See also CLAN; EVOLUTIONARY SURVIVAL UNIT; FAMILY MYTHS; FUZZY SETS; MYTH; NETWORKS; RITUALIZATIONS; SEMANTIC UNIT OF MIND; SYMPTOMS; THEORY OF LOGICAL TYPES; TRANSGENERATIONAL MEMORIES; UNIT OF CHANGE.)

R.N. & J.M.

role   See FAMILY ROLE, SOCIAL ROLE.

role play   A technique from PSYCHODRAMA used in family therapy practice and in training family therapists. This allows the participants in an interaction to experience a particularly difficult or conflictual situation, and appreciate the effects on themselves and on others, as well as seeing what might be the eventual relational consequences.

During a training session in family therapy, a participant who is stuck with a therapeutic intervention in respect of a family may be asked to take the place of the family member whom she or he finds it most difficult to understand or the most difficult to appreciate. Other trainees are asked to play the parts of the other family members and of the therapist. Such a technique allows trainees to develop skills in being in touch with their fantasies, with simulating feelings of others, and of developing alternative possible stories. These skills are drawn out by the concrete realization of the situation through play. The participants become aware of emotions and the ways people think when they are caught up in pathological processes which are often unfamiliar to the ways in which therapists experience their worlds. Role play therefore allows the development of empathy and therapeutic abduction.

The setting up of role play can be done progressively and in an almost imperceptible way during a session of family therapy. The therapeutic process appears when family members who are stuck in repetitive patterns of behaviour begin to develop the ability to play with their own roles and the roles of others, thereby acquiring a level of freedom with each other. The playful re-framing leads to the recognition of reciprocal attitudes and expectations. It encourages the learning of rules of interaction and of the constraints linked to the rules of behaviour of the system which become evident through the phenomenon of repetition and the transformation of the boundaries between play and reality. Role play functions as a preparation for the demands which come with the shared understanding of the real.

(See also INFORMATION; PLAY; THERAPEUTIC ABDUCTION.)

J.M.

rubber fence   See BOUNDARIES.

S

sacred, sacraments, sacrifice   The sacred is a universal modality of communication between human beings. The basis of the sacred lies, in fact, in a changing of the nature of certain symbols within the framework of a system of religious belief. The symbols which are sacralized in this way are separated off, placed in a forbidden realm and become subject to a respect which establishes a union between persons bound together by the same system of transcendental belief. The realm of the sacred stands opposed to that of the profane, marking off the identity of spiritual communities.

The sacred provides a meeting point for antinomic realities and maintains a complex relationship with violence, origins, art and the social bond (religion). Sacrifice is a ritual which makes it possible to circumscribe, by prescription, the violence of the sacred. The ritual of sacrifice is translated into metaphor in the sacrament. This is how an object, animal or person may become sacralized. As totems, they are bearers and vehicles of taboos. The metaphor then leads to a symbol which is no longer simply metaphorical or phantasmatic but creates a real bond between participants, though no delusional state is, in fact, involved.

The sacrament is the manifest expression of the sacred, 'the outward and visible sign of an inward and spiritual grace' (Bateson, 1979). It is the performative symbolization of the sacrifice, a ritual marking the spirituality of personal and familial life-cycles. Birth, adolescence, marriage and death are sacralized in this way, as are daily, weekly and yearly temporal rhythms.

We can say with certainty that the signs of religious activity appeared some 50,000 years ago in the history of humanity (Leroi-Gourhan, 1965). The sacred function can be clearly seen with the appearance of the cult of the dead and of ritual cannibalism and in the relations ensuring his life and survival which man maintained with his environment. Thus, cave paintings reveal the existence of true sanctuaries between 30,000 and 8,000 years before our own era, marking a fundamental bond between art and sacred. However, the sacred is also related to the beautiful and the folly of reductionism could be said to be to wish consciously to circumscribe the nature of the beautiful and the sacred (Bateson, 1979). At most we might note that there is a mysterious relation between the two.

For Girard (1972), the sacred is intimately connected with 'generative violence' and the sacrifice of victims which enables savage violence to be transformed into beneficent and civilizing violence. Thus the sacred is based upon profoundly paradoxical rituals: 'Because the victim is sacred, it is criminal to kill him – but the victim is sacred only because he is to be killed' (Girard, 1972, p. 1). Sacrifice is thus criminal violence, but that violence is, by that very sacrifice, seeking to found a sacred order. Now the sacred 'shake[s] loose the violence between [men] . . . to make of it a separate entity' (Girard, 1972, p. 135). VIOLENCE, like the sacred, is a genuine contagious 'pregnancy' which diffuses and seeks to invest itself in saliences which will channel it (see SYMBOLIC REFERENCE).

The sacred is, in fact, at the meeting point of the following pairs of opposites: order and disorder, peace and war, good and evil, beauty and ugliness, separation and diffusion (Girard, 1972). In the sacrificial rite, Girard sees two substitutions: (a) generative violence substitutes a single victim for the whole community; (b) ritual substitutes a sacrificial victim (from outside the community) for the surrogate victim. The surrogate victim is generally destroyed, and always expelled from the community. As the violence subsides it is thought to have departed with the victim, to have somehow been projected outside the community. In the sacrifice, the victim absorbs the difference between inside and outside, while at the same time ejecting the destructive violence from the group.

Clinical practice with families shows us, first and foremost, the terrifying, savage aspects of the violence which damages the psychical, if not indeed physical, integrity of the index patient and directly threatens that of those close to him. Hence the importance of the victim-creating process, which leads to the 'totemization' of the index patient (Neuburger, 1984). The 'mental illnesses' reveal that it is the functions of sociality or reproduction and symbolization which are directly impaired in the family group. The 'victim' of the group here performs a function of attraction/expulsion of group violence which he/she manages, one way or another, in his/her symptoms.

The art of the therapist consists, to a certain extent, in finding the right dose of the antinomic aspects contained in the transition from violence to the sacred. It was from the *pharmakos* and the *catharma*, human surrogate victims, the bearers of the sins of the group who were ritually sacrificed in Ancient Greece, that the prescription of the *pharmakon* and *catharsis* appeared. Poisons and remedies were intrinsically linked together:

A cathartic remedy is a powerful drug which causes the humours or matter whose presence is considered harmful to be evacuated. Remedies are frequently regarded as being of the same nature as the illness or at least being likely to aggravate the symptoms and, by so doing, to bring about a salutary crisis from which a cure will emerge. (Girard, 1972, p. 399)

We find a similar process in the inducing of the transference neurosis in psychoanalysis and in the prescription of the symptom in systemic intervention. The contemporary therapist must also come to terms with phenomena of this order. His/her function is to assess the dosage at which his/her action will transform a maleficent state of affairs into a beneficent one. Hence the ambiguity and ambivalence of his/her social status.

This sacred dimension must therefore be sought out, preserved and recreated in family groups which are hurting. Beyond the technical artifices involved, the ritualization of exchanges between families confronted with mourning or with intense levels of sacrifice may make it possible to recover modalities of communication which might be situated beyond PHANTASY and delusion. It is necessary to respect the sacred dimensions of family exchanges, whether or not these fit into clearly established religions. 'The sacrament is the traditional strategy for bringing together the energy-based and the communicational, for management of the rupture between the everyday and the sacred' (Christian, 1985).

The present-day Western world had fragmented the constituents of the sacred by splitting up its various different aspects: established religions have emptied out the artistic dimension from their rites. Contemporary ALIENATION, in the Marxian sense, leads to the desacralization of exchange, since, as Marx put it, quality (use-value) becomes strictly transformable into quantity (exchange-value). This was not the case in traditional societies where a prestation was given, accepted and re-given. Similarly, a person became sacred when that person underwent a ritual investiture and was invested with charismatic powers. The sacred person then functioned as an intermediary between the natural order and the social and established the cohesion and perpetuity of the group.

It was in music that the sacred reappeared, doing so paradoxically in what were apparently the most profane works: Stravinsky's *Rite of spring*, Schoenberg's *Gurrer lieder* and *Pierrot lunaire* and Boulez's *Marteau sans maître* and *Répons* (the Middle Ages had its *Messe des fous* more recently reproduced by the Berry Hayward Consort). As for violence, it is, precisely, hived off into the mental illnesses which show, in *statu nascendi*, how it spreads and explodes within family systems. However, whether we like it or not, we are all members of religions of which we are unaware (Porte, 1980).

(See also ACCULTURATION; DELIRIUM; DREAMS; MIMESIS; REALITY; RECIPROCAL VICTIMIZATION AND RESCUE; SCAPEGOAT.)

J.M.

salience See FAMILY ACTANT; PROCREATIVE FAMILIES; SACRED, SACRAMENTS, SACRIFICE; SYMBOLIC REFERENCE; VIOLENCE.

scaling questions See SOLUTION–FOCUSED THERAPY.

scandalmongering A modality of communication in which one person expresses a negative judgement to another about a third person. This judgement may be based on objective facts or derived from information which, when taken together, lead to the establishment of a negative opinion.

The comment thus made about the person who is the subject of the scandalmongering possesses a dimension of denigration, if not indeed of defamation. Scandalmongering is, from the point of view of content, intermediate between CALUMNY (or slander) and mere gossip (see TRIADIC QUESTIONING). It may have particularly powerful group effects, if not indeed noxious effects in the designation of scapegoats and by creating rumours (Morin, 1973) which are amplified by self-maintenance (the phenomenon of percolation in which, beyond a certain threshold, all the communication pathways of a group of mutually trusting persons are invaded by the same opinion).

(See also DISCLOSURE; FAMILY MYTHS; FORGETTING; INFORMATION; NOSTALGIA; TRANSGENERATIONAL MEMORIES.)

J.M.

scapegoat The member of the family deemed responsible for the distress or the malfunctioning of the whole of the family system. A person becomes the active recipient of an affect which is collectively perceived as negative – and even perceived as such by him or herself. There exists an active (though in large measure involuntary) role of the scapegoat in the concentration of negative vectors (Epstein and Bishop, 1981). The scapegoat stands in a circular relationship to others, as attacker and attacked (Lewin, 1947a). The mechanism by which scapegoating appears draws on the phenomenon of PROJECTIVE IDENTIFICATION (Boszormenyi-Nagy and Spark, 1973).

This colourful term, which is taken from the Bible, has in the past been employed in group psychology and, more especially, in sociometry to indicate a function or a particular role within a group (Lewin, 1947a; see FORCE FIELDS). It has recently served as a paradigm for a reinterpretation of biblical texts (Girard, 1982). Girard sees the Gospels as revealing the scapegoating mechanism and allowing it to be transcended, by unveiling the unconscious nature of the process: 'Father, forgive them for they know not what they do' (Gospel according to St Luke).

This is why it would seem inadequate to employ the term 'scapegoat' as though it were synonymous with INDEX PATIENT, since it is only one particular modality among others of the process of patient designation and victimization. A scapegoat may very well not be recognized as sick or psychopathic etc. He or she will, however, be induced to sacrifice a more or less important part of him or herself, in order to expiate a collective crime, the origin of which may be transgenerational and the conscious memory of which may be completely lost.

It is the view of Boszormenyi-Nagy and Spark (1973) that this role or this group function implies the need socially to penalize the negative aspects, of which the scapegoat is supposed to be the bearer, which necessitates there being at least a triadic relational structure in existence. It is in fact important that the negative designation of one subject by another and the exposure of his or her 'bad identity' (or negative identity) should be socially sanctioned by the validation of a third party. This process can frequently be observed in the treatment of young marginals where a double validation often appears very markedly, first provided by the family itself ('He's always been difficult'), then by the neighbourhood ('He's the terror of the neighbourhood') only to be ratified, ultimately, by the judiciary.

For Ackerman (1964), the scapegoat can be seen as participating in a family pattern of interdependent roles which have the function of *neutralizing the antagonistic forces* within the family:

- the destroyer–persecutor;
- the victim, scapegoat of the attack;
- the family healer, therapist, family doctor; he/she neutralizes the destructive powers of the attack and, to a certain degree, brings aid to the victim.

The reader will note the interest there may be in regarding the function of the 'therapist' as a function which arises, first and foremost, spontaneously within the organization of the family. The scapegoat is the victim of prejudice and this is connected with the negative VALENCY attaching to certain characteristics which differentiate him/her from other members of the family. The characteristic in question may be related to sex, youth or old age, to a physical or intellectual quality, to a behavioural attitude (enterprising character or stargazer, etc.).

The state of affairs which results may be open or veiled, simple or complex, salient or amorphous. At some future date, the respective roles may prove to be interchangeable. The most disturbed families break into several factions: each member allies with one faction; each faction competes to gain the dominant position by defending a preferred family identity with distinct aims;

each faction gives itself a leader who will attack a designated scapegoat in the other faction.

Whitaker and Keith (1981) stress that in dysfunctional families, there is a limited sense of the totality; the person who electively adheres to the FAMILY MYTH, whether in a positive or negative manner, is the scapegoat who may be either the 'black sheep', delinquent or sick person or, by contrast, the 'knight in shining armour', the family hero, hyper-adapted and set upon a pedestal.

(See also MIMESIS; RECIPROCAL VICTIMIZATION AND RESCUE.)

A.L., P.S. & J.M.

schismogenesis This process described by Bateson refers to one of the possible outcomes of cultural contact between two human groups, clans or communities, which is characterized by the appearance of a dynamic equilibrium differentiating the two groups under consideration.

The possible outcomes of cultural contact between two groups are in effect:

1 The complete fusion of two groups which were initially different. Since the differentiation of each group was based on relations of reciprocity, this leads to homogeneous behaviours.
2 The elimination of one or even both of the groups.
3 The persistence of the two initial groups, which maintain an interface between them and then establish a dynamic equilibrium within a wider community which unites them. Each subgroup acts and reacts to the behaviours of the other by the establishment of either symmetrical or complementary differentiations, leading to heterogeneous behaviours; it will be possible to attenuate and correct these latter by reciprocal differentiation.

A 'successful' schismogenesis corresponds to the succession of several phases: a phase of fusion–symbiosis, a phase of opposition and a phase of differentiation–reciprocity.

SYMMETRICAL DIFFERENTIATION

This is characterized by the appearance of the same aspirations and attitudes in the two groups. Behaviours A, B and C, within one group will refer to the same behaviours A, B and C, within the other group; similarly, behaviours X, Y and Z serving as interchanges for one group will release similar behaviours X, Y and Z as a response in the other group, that response possibly going on to reinforce the initial behaviours X, Y and Z. One can see that ideally a symmetrical schismogenesis leads to 'symmetrical escalations' which may lead to collapses, explosions or open conflicts, if regulative mechanisms or configurations of another nature do not halt that evolution. The critical moments which ensue are also likely to lead to the discovery of new dynamic equilibria.

Symmetrical relations lead to the building up of clans, villages, nations and enterprises and bring out attitudes of competition, rivalry and combativeness; boastfulness gives rise to boastfulness, hostility to hostility and despair to despair. In a purely symmetrical relationship, there is competition in the mirrored attitude, as if each protagonist or group were trying to keep control of the situation.

In psychoanalysis, the genital, phallic and Oedipal stages are the symbolic and psychical expression of the pursuit of symmetry (acting like the same-sex parent). In psychopathology, the excess of symmetrical relations corresponds to narcissistic relations and its disorders; the pursuit of differentiation, by the attenuation of differences, leads in effect to the exacerbation of 'the narcissism of minor differences' and to the escalation being pushed even further when differences are attenuated. Phenomena of rupture, rejection, exclusion – and even of symmetrical violence – ensue.

COMPLEMENTARY DIFFERENTIATION

This is based on the expression of radically distinct attitudes and aspirations. The behaviours internal to the first group will be of the type L, M, N, whereas their external attitudes will be of the type O, P, Q. In resonance with this, the internal behaviours of the other group will be of the type R, S, T, whereas their external behaviours will be of the type U, V, W. Now, to the extent that these two groups form part, *de facto*, of a wider community, subject to unique economic, cultural and affective constraints, the activation of these totally different behaviours leads to increasingly complementary expressions. One therefore finds an accentuation of inter-group differences, between attitudes of domination, activity, assistance and affirmation of identity on the one hand and attitudes of submission, passivity, dependence and negation of identity on the other. That accentuation may lead to another form of schismogenesis, which may be marked by manifestations of inter-group hostility, implosions and repression of the 'weak' by the 'strong'. Complementary relations lead ultimately to distinctions between social classes, age groups, sex differences, generations, spheres of competence, statuses and roles.

In psychopathology, complementarity is expressed in the oppositions between voyeurism and exhibitionism, sadism and masochism, activity and passivity, speaking and listening. The erogenous zones of the body, as Bateson pointed out, following Erickson, and particularly those which play a part in the constitution of the pregenital sexual stages, are ordered in complementary fashion: introjection, incorporation, projection, retention and evacuation are the psychical expression of the creation of bonds that are complementary to other people (representations). Complementary interaction brings into opposition the attitudes of two partners or two groups: the warm dynamism of the one is matched by the depressive attitude of the other or one may find oppositions between dominant and dominated, talkative and silent, scruffy and smart etc.

RECIPROCAL DIFFERENTIATION

This is based on the isolated appearance of asymmetrical responses in fundamentally symmetrical relationships and of anti-complementary responses in complementary relationships. A relationship is never wholly symmetrical or complementary, except where there are destructive escalations. It fits into a symbolic context which regulates the beginning or end of the symmetrical or complementary exchange. In a sports match, the game consists in establishing the most symmetrical possible conditions of confrontation. The context of the rules does, however, allow of a complementary differentiation of players and teams. All the tension of games arises out of the *de jure* equivalence between players and this *de facto* hierarchy acquired by the dramatic setting of the game.

Reciprocity makes the affirmation of inter-group difference possible, but it reduces the exponential risks of schismogenesis and therefore stabilizes the nature of the differences without destroying the identity that arises out of their expression. We shall note here that in every interaction there are hierarchical levels of communication and that complementary or symmetrical 'runaway' can be situated on one level while the other levels give the appearance of flexibility and reciprocity. A person in a complementary one-down position may very well re-frame the situation by controlling his or her partner's complementary one-up position. A silent partner may 'let' the other partner speak, while still retaining power. Some human activities derive their 'spice' from the tension between these hierarchical levels of interaction. An example of this is sport, where pure symmetrical competition leads on 'dramatically' to complementary levels of differentiation.

SCHISMOGENESIS AND MARITAL AND FAMILIAL INTERACTIONS

Following Bateson, the Palo Alto school generalized the concept of schismogenesis, studying the nature of the relations existing within the marital pair (see COUPLES), the family and, also, the interactions between the family containing a patient designated as 'ill' or 'deviant' and an institution. On a structural plane, one may suppose that the marital couple is based on the hierarchized product of symmetrical and complementary behaviours. These categories are themselves the result of multiple biological and cultural stratifications.

In the same way, the parent–child relationship seems essentially complementary in nature. The mother dispenses care to her newborn baby or infant, while the child expects to receive such care; the child appears totally dependent on his/her mother. However, from the outset, their relationship at the same time supposes the establishment of corrective mechanisms whereby the child possesses the means of calling upon his/her mother in such a way that it is she who is also dependent on him or her. These corrective mechanisms are in part innate and in part acquired in the very earliest phases of ontogenesis. The discontinuity associated with birth is 'compensated' by many behavioural parameters: IMPRINTING, the multi-sensory processes of 'BECOMING ACCUSTOMED' and the child's innate releasing mechanisms.

This problem of reciprocal, symmetrical and complementary interactions, like that of the temporal and spatial constraints to which couples, families and groups are subject, may lead us to some reflections of a topological nature. From that point of view, the conclusion will be that complementary schismogenesis corresponds to a bifurcation catastrophe whereas symmetrical schismogenesis corresponds to a conflict catastrophe (see ELEMENTARY CATASTROPHES). However, to the extent that it is successful, the terminal phase of differentiation-reciprocity corresponds to a GENERALIZED CATASTROPHE of the anabolic type.

(See also DIACHRONIC AND SYNCHRONIC AXES OF A THERAPY; MARITAL BREAKDOWN; PRAGMATICS OF COMMUNICATION; SCHIZOPHRENIAS.)

J.M.

schizophrenias Defined by Bleuler (1911) (from the Greek *skhizein*, to split, to separate; and *phrēn*, the mind) as a set of chronic psychoses occurring in adolescents or young adults which develop either gradually or by sudden surges in such a way that the state of illness is, in appearance, irreversible (the possibilities of ameliorating the condition do not extend so far as a *restituo ad integrum*).

Bleuler distinguishes between (a) 'fundamental' and (b) 'accessory' symptoms. The *fundamental* irreversible symptoms disturb:

- the elementary functions: disturbances of association (logical syncretism, incoherent associations), emotional deterioration, parathymia, paradoxical and discordant affective reactions, ambivalence;
- the complex functions: autism (detachment from reality, retreat into a world of one's own); loss of active attention, passive attention focused on apparently random events; persistent blockings of the will; lacunae in the expression of thoughts and intelligent behaviour (rather than dementia).

These fundamental symptoms are compatible with social life.

Accessory symptoms include hallucinations, paranoid delusions, catatonic psychomotor disturbances; these generally require hospitalization, but are theoretically reversible, depending upon events relating to changes of context.

The four main forms are:

1 *Schizophrenia simplex* (in which only the fundamental signs of the disorder are expressed). Such cases are rarely met with in asylums. 'The simple schizophrenics vegetate as day labourers, peddlers, even as servants' (Bleuler, 1911: 1950 edn, p. 236). Bleuler goes on to say that 'there are many simple schizophrenics among eccentric people of every sort who stand out as world saviours and world reformers, philosophers, writers and artists, beside the "degenerated" and deteriorated' (Bleuler, 1950 edn, p. 237). He further stresses that 'there is also a latent schizophrenia and I am convinced that this is the most frequent form' (Bleuler, 1950 edn, p. 239).
2 *Hebephrenia*: a form in which various incapacities are the most evident signs, together with apragmatism, indifference and apathy, as met with in young adolescents.
3 *Hebephrenia–catatonia*: loss of motor initiative, negativism, complete refusal of work.
4 *Paranoid schizophrenia*: vague, poorly systematized delusions, with a low degree of commitment to the delusional beliefs.

The Palo Alto school (Bateson, Haley, Jackson and Weakland, from 1956 onwards) suggested a dynamic understanding of schizophrenia through the discovery of the DOUBLE BIND and the therapeutic possibility of a positive re-framing of the irreversibility of the condition, as observed in clinical practice (THERAPEUTIC DOUBLE BIND). That re-framing is centred on the PRAGMATICS OF COMMUNICATION between the patient and his/her family and social circle, which enables meaning to be discovered out of what initially seems to be nonsense. The basic paradox of the schizophrenic patient is that he/she does not communicate that he/she is not communicating (non (non communication)), which amounts to a collapse of the METACOMMUNICATION SYSTEMS (communication about communication); it consequently becomes impossible to label metaphors and there is confusion in the identification of modes of communication; friendly, professional, sexual, playful, loving and humorous interchanges become unstable, confused and impossible to differentiate.

A discovery of this kind enables interest to be shifted from the personality disorder (static expression) to the interactional disorder (metabolic expression) while at the same time showing what is none the less the necessary interdependence of the two points of view (see UNCERTAINTY PRINCIPLE).

DIAGNOSIS OF SCHIZOPHRENIA

The diagnosis of schizophrenia is a source of therapeutic discord: personality disorder or illness? structure or position? dissociation or discordance?

DSM-III Classification

In the view of the American Psychiatric Association, if we follow the DSM-III-R classification (1987), the term 'schizophrenia' covers a set of disorders which probably have different aetiologies. The diagnostic criteria are six in number:

1 At least one of the following during one of the episodes of the illness: bizarre delusions such as delusions of being controlled, thought broadcasting, thought insertion or thought withdrawal; somatic, grandiose, religious or nihilistic delusions; delusions with persecutory or jealous content accompanied by hallucinations; auditory hallucinations with a running commentary on the patient's thought or behaviour by one or more voices; incoherence, loosening of associations, illogical thinking and poverty of content of speech, if any of these three are accompanied by blunted, flat or inappropriate affect, delusions or hallucinations, catatonic or other grossly disorganized behaviour.
2 Deterioration from a previous level in such areas as work, social relations and self-care.
3 Continuous duration of illness for at least six months, with prodromic or residual phases in which some of the aforementioned symptoms were present.
4 The possibility of a full depressive or manic syndrome, but arising secondarily or in the context of psychotic disorders.
5 Onset of illness before age 45.
6 Not due to any organic mental disorder or mental retardation.

In this perspective, disorders not including manifest psychotic symptoms, which were grouped by E. Bleuler under the head of schizophrenia simplex, are excluded. Here they are regarded merely as personality disorders ('schizotypal personality disorder'). In DSM-III, the other clinical forms become:

- the disorganized type (formerly hebephrenia);
- the catatonic type;
- the paranoid type;
- the undifferentiated type (the symptoms of which cannot be classified or represent a mix of the types referred to above;
- the residual type (a form developing in a low-key manner, after a manifest expression of schizophrenic disorder).

Bleuler's conception of dissociation

The shift of accent from Bleuler's inaugural writings on this subject is thus very marked. For Bleuler, in fact, the most manifest symptoms (those which are most striking such as delusions, hallucinations, catatonic manifestations etc. which lead to patients being admitted to a mental hospital) are, in fact, *accessory symptoms*, whereas the *fundamental symptoms* (disturbances of association, modifications of affectivity conceived as emotional degeneration which is in fact connected with an initial hypersensitivity leading to a withdrawal from all external dealings, autism involving the insertion of internal imaginary productions into external reality) may vary very greatly in their intensity. These fundamental symptoms, characteristic of the illness, in fact show no break in continuity from the normal state:

> it is extremely important to recognize that they exist in varying degrees and shadings on the entire scale from pathological to normal; also the milder cases, latent schizophrenics with far less manifest symptoms, are many times more common than the overt, manifest cases. Furthermore, in view of the fluctuating character which distinguishes the clinical picture of schizophrenia, it is not to be expected that we shall be able to demonstrate each and every symptom at each and every moment of the disease. (Bleuler, 1950 edn, p. 13)

Such an opinion prompted Henri Ey, who translated an abridged version of, and wrote an introduction to, Bleuler's book (1926), to write that 'This rather vague and approximate side to Bleuler's descriptions can be constantly seen as implying a reference to the concrete reality of clinical practice.' In fact, the advantage of Bleuler's description is that he does not try to skirt around the conceptual paradox which is necessary for the description of the disorders. It is perhaps insulting to Bleuler to refer to his vague and fuzzy approximation as 'descriptive' when it is in fact presented as a specific theoretical abstraction. All Bleuler's successors who were to attempt to clarify the description or the theory were to fall more or less one side or the other of the dichotomy thus identified, leading to apparently greater conceptual comfort, but doing so at the cost of more or less totally losing sight of the problem posed. It was not until the arrival of Bateson and his school that, from a perspective external to that of psychiatry, the epistemological and pragmatic need for the principles of logical antinomy and the confusion of contraries in the very description of the illness was recognized.

Let us, then, summarize Bleuler's position. The expression of the fundamental disturbances of the illness lies on a continuum running from the normal state, even though it corresponds, on a latent plane, to a point of irreversible break in respect of that 'normal state'; schizophrenia simplex is therefore the prototype of all the other morbid manifestations. As regards the most distressing signs – the ones that are most difficult to cope with on the individual, family and social levels – these are regarded merely as accessory signs which are often relatively unspecific. Though leading to hospitalization, they are most often reversible, remission occurring unexpectedly and being dependent upon parameters which are most often not identified. In other words, the expression of accessory signs appears as a break-off point in relation to the other manifestations of the illness, whereas the underlying process leading to the appearance and disappearance of accessory disturbances is thought to be continuous in nature.

If we scrutinize it closely, in spite of appearances, DSM-III is no more precise in its definition of the schizophrenias. The clarity it seems to achieve by making a sharp distinction between 'simple schizophrenia' as a personality disorder and the other clinical forms which are perceived as schizophrenic disorders, may well obscure the debate and cause therapeutic attitudes to rigidify. The advantage of Bleuler's model is that it shows that, in the last resort, all forms of schizophrenia are potentially reducible to a socially acceptable personality disorder.

In fact, DSM-III (1987) acknowledges that 'the limits of the concept of Schizophrenia are unclear'. What are we to make, then, of the further specification of an unclear concept within a framework in which it is rightly said that the notions of physical or mental disorder, together with those of physical and mental health, do not have well-defined limits (see CONJUNCTION OF THERAPEUTIC AXES)? The limits of the clinical picture merge with the limits of other clinical pictures, while the walls of the galleries housing these pictures merge with other buildings. In actual fact, only the walls of the asylum, the communicational boundaries worked out by family therapies and the labellings of metaphor made possible by psychotherapies are reminders to us that therapeutic strategies and tactics aim to create new spaces by constructing material and fictive dividing walls where these were previously non-existent or inadequate.

Following Maurel et al. (1983), we shall note that Bleuler pinpointed the negative, deficient aspects of the schizophrenic catastrophe. However, that is as far as we shall go with that author, for Bleuler's terms and those of others, cruel as they may be, are attempting to describe a no less cruel reality. Merely to declare that the terms of a reality are 'unacceptable', as Maurel et al. do, is not sufficient actually to recognize that cruelty, attempt to describe it and make efforts to remedy it. Among these 'unacceptable' terms we find the retention of a large number of earlier ones, some of them from the work of Kraepelin: '*Verblödung*' (literally: 'stupefaction') found in some forms of schizophrenia

and '*läppische Verblödung*' (which Kraepelin's English translator rendered as 'silly dementia') found in hebephrenia. But we also find terms coined by Bleuler: 'deterioration', 'affective deficiency' (*Affective Verblödung*), though this might equally well have been translated as affective stupefaction, and 'affective indifference', referred to as *Würstigkeit*: 'what the French call "*je-m'en-fichisme*" and the English "I don't give a damn!"' (Bleuler, 1950 edn, p. 42), which has cruder connotations in German, where *Wurst* means sausage. As for schizophrenic dementia, this relates to an 'intellectual defect' ('*der schizophrene Blödsinn*'), which might more literally have been translated as schizophrenic stupidity, folly or silliness.

There can be no doubt that Bleuler's terms bear the clear mark of a tragic – and apparently pejorative and destructive – perception of the object of study which seems also to extend to the sick person himself, the subject of the illness. Bleuler writes, however, that 'in no other disease is the disturbance of intelligence more inadequately designated by the terms "dementia" and "imbecility" than in schizophrenia' (Bleuler, 1950 edn, p. 71). It seems that the discredit into which Bleuler's thought has fallen in France is more than merely terminological in nature.

Can we not, in a sense, see the history of words in psychiatry as the history of the creation of euphemisms, themselves sooner or later found to be to some degree contaminated by the terrible reality underlying them. Have we not in France seen the 'asylum' become first the 'psychiatric hospital', then, more recently, the 'departmental hospital', the 'specialized hospital centre', if not indeed – and can hypocrisy go much further? – the 'psychotherapeutic centre' (as though some psychotherapies were not in danger of having effects every bit as devastating as abusive prescription of drugs)? Moreover, the frequentation of the families of schizophrenics shows that verbal aggression and the most shocking insults seem to correspond to a relatively typical system of de-ritualization of communication.

CHASLIN'S CONCEPT OF DISCORDANCE

Chaslin, creator of the concept of discordance (for a contemporary review of this concept, see Lanteri-Laura and Gros, 1984), had, without doubt, identified some fundamental points. These patients simulate dementia and stupidity without, however, showing the least sign of intellectual deterioration, loss of memory or error of judgement. It is the case, however, that any of these three signs alone would allow one to speak of dementia. For Chaslin, dementia is rarely *praecox* (i.e. 'early'). It usually occurs only 'late in life' and is not 'profound'. The specific characteristic of these patients is, in his view, that they take on the *appearance of a vegetative or automatic life* and are liable to resemble idiots for years, without, however, really being in that state. In the view of Maurel et al. (1983), the schizophrenic is not a schizophrenic, but *resembles a schizophrenic*, just as our psychiatric institutions resemble Bleuler's (and also Pinel, Esquirol and Chaslin's) institution, a pure artefact, which could thus be seen as the perpetually reduplicated analog of what the 'bad and maleficent' neologism of 'schizophrenic' had engendered. 'Discordance', by contrast, could be said to refer to the idea of a discord between the patient and another person, always permitting of negotiation and dialectical resolution: 'discordance is a dialectical discord, a faux-pas in the relationship for which either of the parties may be seen as responsible' (Maurel et al., 1983, p. 59). Let us note here that for Chaslin, discordance corresponds to an 'intrapsychic ataxia', an 'intrapsychic disharmony'. Let us note also that the French psychiatrist agrees with the Kraepelinian classification which groups together the various clinical forms – hebephrenic, paranoid, catatonic etc. – adding to them 'verbal discordant madness', characterized by pure verbal incoherence without delusions.

The fact of 'dissociating' is a profoundly natural and healthy process, an essential act for thinking. If dissociation is not pathological, why does this same term imply invalidation when we are speaking of schizophrenics? Is not their problem that they do not actually manage to dissociate, that deep down they have failed to perform the processes of splitting and separation? Fragmentation could then be seen as the image of fragmentation, a caricature of the differentiation function of thought. Such an analysis seems to connect with what Bateson identified as the *non-labelling of metaphors among schizophrenics*. The problem is not, therefore, to set discordance off against the 'schizze', hypersensitivity against affective de-afferentation (Bleuler had very correctly identified the extreme sensitivity of these patients at the onset of their illness), apparent dementia against the maintenance of all intellectual functions. The point is, rather, to explain these phenomena of appearance and simulation, these symptoms with an extremely pejorative, unbearable, inconceivable connotation. It is to recognize that the image of the worst decay is possible, even though all the accessory disturbances are at any moment reversible and the fundamental signs of the illness are merely the compensatory exaggeration of a normal attitude of the human mind. It is to accept that the simulation of states that are apparently horrific may, in reality, have horrific effects.

THE EPISTEMOLOGICAL REVOLUTION OF BATESON AND HIS SCHOOL

Critiques of Bateson
Many writers have criticized the double bind theory for referring to the THEORY OF LOGICAL TYPES of Bertrand Russell when that theory is, in fact, obsolete, or for

basing itself on CYBERNETICS when that is outmoded or for tying the clinical description to a psychiatry which is no longer valid. Lastly, it has been said that the only consequence of bringing logico–mathematical and pragmatic paradoxes together in this way has been a therapeutic activism with no basis in theory.

It is in such terms, for example, that Maurel et al. (1983) denounce Bateson's terminology as being made up of 'words' which are allegedly as harmful as those of the psychiatric tradition: psychotic collapse, annihilation of the system of metacommunication, incapacity to judge with precision what the other is really trying to say. The worst of all this would be contained in what follows: thus deprived of his powers of judgement, 'the human being is like a potentially self-governing system which has lost its regulator and is spinning in a spiral, in endless, but always systematic distortions.' We should note in passing that certain nineteenth-century clinicians stressed the way in which the mentally 'alienated' resembled automata or machines.

Yet three non-psychiatrists (Bateson, Haley and Weakland) were able with one psychiatrist and psychoanalyst of genius (Jackson) effectively to design a possible approach to a symptomatology that was previously unintelligible. The product of all this is an accumulation of clinical documents and theoretical propositions, the full richness of which still remains to be explored. We may here remind ourselves that only a non-psychiatric neurologist like Freud was able to bring illumination to a field in which he too was not originally a specialist.

The schizophrenias as learning disorders in respect of relations to oneself and to others
If one takes the view that the function of the ego (see METAPSYCHOLOGY; NARCISSISM) is to distinguish between modes of communication, whether within the SELF or between the self and others, the schizophrenic is dysfunctional on this level. In effect, he/she has difficulties assigning the correct mode of communication to different types of message or distinguishing between those modes. These messages are:

- the ones he/she receives from other people;
- the ones he/she sends out verbally or non-verbally;
- the ones he/she addresses to him or herself (perceptions, feelings, thoughts).

The schizophrenic thus displays difficulties in the handling of the signals which enable the various modes of communication to be identified (see MODE-IDENTIFYING SIGNALS). He/she cannot *label metaphors*, tell PHANTASY from REALITY or friendly from hostile behaviour. He/she almost systematically eliminates everything which refers to the relationship between him or herself and others or, indeed, his/her relationship to him or herself. This is particularly clearly seen in institutions. A schizophrenic patient expects the various therapists encountered to be able, first of all, to define the relationships which exist between them in respect of him or her.

Forms of schizophrenia as pragmatic responses to double binds

Watzlawick et al. (1967) set out to investigate the way in which the various symptomatic forms of schizophrenia are attempts to respond to contexts offering no possibility of choice, where every liveable outcome is sealed off:

Paranoid delusions: the patient is likely to conclude that he/she must be overlooking vital clues essential to the understanding of his/her environment; those around him or her might be withholding these from him/her. The goal then has to be to reconstitute these at whatever cost, using every fragment of communication from the most absurd to the most insignificant.

Hebephrenia: in this case, the patient tries to conform to all the mutually contradictory injunctions to which he/she is subject, taking these literally, and avoiding all individual thought.

Catatonia: the patient withdraws from the game, blocking all input channels of communication. That blocking may be effected by 'perceptual defence' (akin to what Laforgue termed SCOTOMIZATION) or by an attitude of intense and sustained hyperactive behaviour which drowns out all the messages received.

The schizophrenias as expression of dynamic group conflict

The concept of 'dynamism' is used here in a non-thermodynamic sense (Bateson, 1972). Where Freud interpreted the neurotic symptom as a compromise solution in a conflict of psychical representation, Bateson et al. (1956) identify schizophrenic symptomatology as a compromise solution in a group conflict, particularly in intrafamilial or family–society conflict. To be even more precise, the conflict involved is one between the family institution and the social institutions with which the *real family* is confronted. That conflict can only be pinpointed in a roundabout way, through analysis of the nature of the discords which emerge between the therapists confronted with the patient and his/her family (METABINDING).

Why is the structure of communication in families in schizophrenic transaction essentially based on pathological double binds? Bateson advanced a hypothesis based on John von Neumann and Oskar Morgenstern's GAME THEORY (1942). The patient and his or her close relatives seem to be caught up in a zero sum game in which there is no gain or loss in information, matter or energy between them. Families in schizophrenic interaction are apparently confronted with certain peculiar game configurations (configurations which appear from the point where there are 5–7 players), in which there are at least two types of coalition which seem perfectly equivalent as regards each individual's apparent interest. That equivalence leads to a situation where, as soon as a coalition is established, at least one player will be able to make it tip over at any instant into the opposite state. It is thus impossible for any two members of the family to establish a stable relationship.

For his part, Bowen (1978b) advanced the hypothesis that what is involved is an absence of multi-generational transmission with an increasingly massive undifferentiation of self over at least three generations (see DIFFERENTIATION OF SELF, TRANSGENERATIONAL MEMORIES). Clinically, in fact, it appears that the more intense the schizophrenic symptomatology, the more the (even casual) mention of relations with ancestors or the extended family is experienced as an intolerable intrusion or as an improper subject.

Clinically, it seems that the schizophrenic state is an attempt to maintain an equilibrium in a family that is in the process of breaking up or in one that is already subject to a deflagration that has already affected all the members of the group. That deflagration often occurs when the INDEX PATIENT has suffered a setback in love or at work. The parental couple becomes the focus of a destabilization of relations (Lidz et al., 1965), without it being possible to analyse that destabilization as a pure conflict between the partners (see MARITAL SCHISM; MARITAL SKEW). The destabilization itself occurs when the grandparents are either old or dead. The family's safety barriers are then broken down, as though hit by a shock wave arising at a critical point in the development of the FAMILY LIFE–CYCLE. Disorders of thinking and emotional disturbances invade all the members of the group (Wynne et al., 1958; Lidz et al., 1965), leading to interchanges characterized by apparent inauthenticity (relations in pseudo-mutual or pseudo-hostile form; see PSEUDO-MUTUALITY; PSEUDO-HOSTILITY). In this sense, the index patient reflects in his or her symptoms his or her family's state of disorganization and its incapacity to deal with the conflicts of reality which threaten to destroy it even more if no benevolent assistance is forthcoming from outside.

PROVISIONAL CONCLUSIONS

It thus seems necessary to seed out the articulation between an internal (psychiatric-psychoanalytic) model and an external (eco-etho-ethnological) model of the problem. These two models are in effect strictly compatible with one another, even though they *seem* to be mutually exclusive (see UNCERTAINTY PRINCIPLE). If Bateson was a pioneer, it was in exploring those uncertain and none the less fundamental zones where these articulations occur. It was also in allowing us to work through his writings and to work *with* his writings with sufficient apparent disorder for us to have some chance of finding our feet in them.

(See also ACTUOGENESIS; ALIENATION; ANCESTRAL

RELATION; DELIRIUM; ELEMENTARY CATASTROPHES; FAMILY CATASTROPHES; FAMILY–THERAPEUTIC INSTITUTION DIFFERENTIATION; FAMILY SELF-BELONGING; FAMILY SELF-REFERENTIALITY; FORECLOSURE; GENERALIZED CATASTROPHES; GENETICS AND THE FAMILY; GENETICS AND PSYCHOPATHOLOGICAL HEREDITY; INFORMATION; INTERFACTIONAL TYPOLOGIES OF THE FAMILY; MAP AND COUNTER-MAP OF A FAMILY SYSTEM; MENETIC THEORY; 'NOTHING PLUS 10 PER CENT' PARADOX; OSCILLATORS; PARADOXES; PARADOXICALITY; POSITIVE CONNOTATION; PSYCHOSOMATIC DOUBLE BINDS; RESIDUAL RELATIONS; SELF-REFERENTIAL CALCULUS; SEMANTIC SPECTRUM OF THE PROPER NAME; SYMBOLS; SYMPTOMATIC AND/OR AETIOLOGICAL TRANSACTIONS; SYMPTOMS; TANGLED HIERARCHIES; TRANSACTIONAL TYPOLOGIES OF THE FAMILY; TRANSFERENCE; UNCONSCIOUS, THE.)

J.M.

scotomization A defensive process described by Laforgue in a letter to Freud (10 May 1925) in SCHIZOPHRENIAS. It consists in the refusal to accept an actual fact, by means of a compromise between two incompatible tendencies: love and hatred towards the mother, a compromise which extends secondarily to all those in the subject's circle. Scotomization resembles a blindness of the mind, which enables the subject to compensate for certain failures and a fall in self-esteem.

In Laforgue's conception, scotomization is the opposite of repression, since, by contrast, it is the saturated expression of a quest for unattainable objects. 'We believe we can put down the misrecognition of reality to scotomization, which corresponds to the infantile – and thus unrepressed – desire not to acknowledge the outside world but rather to set one's own ego in its place' (letter of Laforgue to Freud, 10 May 1925, quoted in Lilamand, 1980). All the attention, instead of being concentrated on the chosen subject or the persons present is, by contrast, dispersed over events, signals and indices perceived outside the situation currently being experienced.

J.M.

sculpting, family sculpting An active, non-verbal therapeutic technique, which was conceived by David Kantor and developed at the Boston Family Institute. It is also used in the training of therapists. It was, in fact, in that training and treatment centre that F. and B. Duhl contributed to the development of this mode of intervention which is increasingly used today (see Kantor and Duhl, 1973).

Sculpting is a therapeutic game based on a confrontation of the pseudo-static and dynamic forms of attitudes and behaviour. The members of a family are represented and physically modelled during the sessions in positions symbolizing the mode of relations between them, as perceived by one or more members of the family. Thanks to this sculpting process, past events and attitudes, as these affect the present, may be perceived and tested out. Family sculpting inevitably gives rise to new meanings and a new picture of family relations, such as could not be produced by mere verbal expression (Kantor and Duhl, 1973).

Papp et al. (of the New York Nathan Ackerman Institute) describe it as

a form of therapeutic art within which each family member arranges the other members in a sculpture which physically symbolizes their interpersonal relations. Each person creates a portrait by placing the members together in terms of posture and spatial relations which represent action and feeling. The essentials of family experience are projected into a *tableau vivant*. (Papp et al., 1973)

This tableau is often as good as words, since it uses some aspects of family life which had until then remained hidden. Verbalization, in fact, only occurs in a second phase to comment on the affects in play in the interpersonal relations, as expressed in the family sculpture.

Andolfi (1980) defines sculpting 'as the symbolic representation of a system which uses the dimensions of space, time and energy, which are common to all systems. It enables the participants simultaneously to represent and test out relations, feelings and change.' The 'sculptor', whether he/she is a volunteer or a person designated by the therapist (or trainer) metaphorically sets out his/her representation of the family group by way of the postures he/she chooses.

Sculpting of this kind is carried out in various different modalities. Duhl et al. (1973) distinguish between three types of sculpting depending on the number of persons involved at a given moment. Sculpting may be:

- individual;
- boundary or dyadic;
- family or group.

Beyond such categorization, all share a common feature: the gaining of an awareness of representations by way of a dynamic, non-linear process carried out in the here-and-now.

The therapist encourages the sculptor and helps him/her to arrange the actors in space. A *static phase* is usually followed by a *dynamic phase* in which the sculptor carries out readjustments as a function, for example, of his/her desires for change or in response to suggestions from the therapist.

Sculpting essentially accords greater importance

to motor expression than to verbal exchanges in the representation of emotional situations. It is an opportunity for families to try out new channels of communication and to redefine modalities of interaction on new bases. Triangulations, alliances and conflicts are represented in concrete form and situated in a symbolic register which gives the participants an opportunity to express their emotions without the constraints of rationalization.

Testing out new movements and positions tends to open up new communication channels and brings out the connections between family sculpting (represented by the *spatial position* of its members, the *static form* of the family system), family interactions (represented by the *movements* of each person in relation to the initial sculpture, the *metabolic form* of the family system) and emotional states (the *feelings aroused* by the different movements and positions assigned to each person, giving rise to SEMANTIC RESONANCES).

Papp et al. (1973) have stressed that a technique of this kind avoids rationalization, resistance and guilt feelings. Since people are deprived of their customary channels of verbalization, they are induced to communicate at a more meaningful coenaesthetic level. Triangulations, alliances and conflicts are represented in concrete form and situated in a symbolic, visible and sensory sphere which gives the participants the opportunity to communicate their emotions to one another at all levels. Another advantage of sculpting is the cohesive effect it produces within the family. The members begin to view themselves as a systemic unit in which each person plays an integral part and influences each of the others. At the same time, to represent oneself as, or to be represented as, part of a system is a way of promoting greater individualization. Family sculpting is often a 'different', effective experience in enmeshed families, in which phenomena of symbiosis and absence of identity and personal space are a permanent source of suffering.

Family sculpting is both a *diagnostic* and a *therapeutic* tool. One may, for example, ask the family members to use it to represent the problem which prompted the request for therapy. It thus offers each person the opportunity to test out the degrees of mobilization which exist around static positions imposed by the constraints of the family system, by setting these in direct contact with their emotional correlatives. In particularly rigid family systems, representing dysfunctional relations spatially may have the same pragmatic effect as a paradoxical prescription (Andolfi, 1980). Behaviours which are, by definition, involuntary, spontaneous and uncontrollable are made voluntary and may be reproduced.

In the framework of TRAINING in family therapy, family sculpting is often used. Representing families encountered in clinical practice or their own families with this technique better enables novice therapists to analyse their negative attitudes, to identify their emotional place in family systems, to differentiate out their family allegiances and the impacts received in clinical practice and to extricate themselves from zones of suffering and relational dead-ends.

(See also ACTUOGENETIC LANDSCAPE OF THE FAMILY; ELEMENTARY CATASTROPHES; FAMILIODRAMA; FAMILY CATASTROPHES; STATIC, PSEUDO–STATIC AND METABOLIC FORMS.)

P.A., S.A. & A.C.

secondary process See METAPSYCHOLOGY; PLAY; UNCONSCIOUS, THE.

secrets In most families, there are secrets of greater or lesser significance, shared by some members of the family. There are things which everyone knows but which no one speaks about and which are not revealed in any circumstances to outsiders. There are, by contrast, secrets which are not known by all members of the family, but only by some, and which are not shared: this is often the case where events in the childhood or adolescence of the parents are concerned or, alternatively, certain events surrounding the birth or childhood of an adolescent (a problem of filiation, for example).

Ausloos (1980), who has developed this 'family secret' notion extensively, thinks that it may be the quality of the content of the secret which makes the difference in the mode of expression of family 'pathology'. He takes the view, for example, that some cases of acting out by an adolescent (delinquency) represent a way of staging outside the family what cannot be spoken or put into words within it. Such cases of acting out can be seen as making it possible, while keeping the secret within the family, to reveal its meaning to the outside world in a symbolic mode, without that meaning becoming comprehensible to the members of the family or the extrafamilial members of their circle.

Ausloos (1980) points out the sequence of secrets which attended the Oedipal drama, in the form of a series of transgressions of laws over several generations. Laius, the father of Oedipus, commits a double crime: he transgresses the laws of hospitality by abducting Chrysippus, the son of Pelops, and by having homosexual relations with him while he is an adolescent. Out of despair, Chrysippus commits suicide and his father, Pelops, casts a curse upon the descendants of Laius. When Oedipus is born, the secret of the curse is not revealed. Oedipus is sent away from his natural parents and entrusted to his adoptive parents, Polybus, king of Corinth and his wife, Merope. These adoptive parents will not reveal to Oedipus that they are not his natural parents. Oedipus kills his father, Laius, and sleeps with his mother, Jocasta, not knowing his relationship to them. Carrying his investigations through to a conclusion, he then discovers that he is the guilty party, as much as he is the plaything of repeatedly maintained secrets and defective memories which are vehicles of a retribution operating over several generations.

More generally, the secret represents one of the mythic structurings of communication, in the same way as MISUNDERSTANDING, mix-ups, DISCLOSURE, NOSTALGIA and SCANDALMONGERING etc. The same morphologies are also found in social and FAMILY MYTHS.

(See also CALUMNY; FORGETTING; INFORMATION; INSTITUTIONAL MYTHS, SOCIAL MYTHS; TRANGENERATIONAL MEMORIES.)

P.S. & J.M.

seduction behaviour See SEXED BEHAVIOUR, SEDUCTION BEHAVIOUR, SEXUAL BEHAVIOUR.

self The self is what enables an individuated person to refer to him- or herself and therefore to acquire the subject/object distinction. We may thus speak of an immunological self (which lies almost totally outside the representative levels of mental activity) and a psychical self (representation of self).

A human 'self' is naturally structured by the incorporation of 'objects' (human persons, institutions, clothing, cars, mass media etc.) It is in the nature of man also to construct his self with a host of artificial prostheses which cannot be disconnected from the self without bringing about a de-symbolization and a collapse of meaning. 'The wheel is an extension of the foot, the book is an extension of the eye, clothing an extension of the skin, electric circuitry an extension of the central nervous system' writes Marshall McLuhan is *The Medium is the Message* (McLuhan and Fiore, 1967).

To speak of a 'false self' engages a relationship between the 'sick' person and the 'therapist'. The self is, therefore, 'false' for the therapist whose help has been sought, who declares him- or herself ready to re-establish the TRUE SELF in accord with the patient. Similarly, a DOUBLE BIND directly engages the person describing it and thus reveals the deadlock – or even total lack of a solution – with which the describer is confronted.

(See also AUTONOMY AND HETERONOMY OF A SYSTEM; DIFFERENTIATION OF SELF; FAMILY SELF-REFERENTIALITY; NARCISSISM; SELF–ORGANIZATION.)

J.M.

self-domestication See DOMESTICATION; PSEUDOSPECIATION.

self-fulfilling prophecy Defined by Watzlawick (1981) as a 'self-fulfilling prophecy', a performative prophecy is a thought, hope or prediction which, by the mere fact of having been uttered, brings about what had been thought, hoped or predicted. A concretization of this kind reinforces the initial movement of thought, hope or prediction and seems to validate it thus bringing about a sort of self-confirmation of the psychical movement. The present is here determined not by the past but by the future, as it is anticipated by the person or group concerned. Thus a purely psychical, mental construct creates reality in advance.

The implicit or explicit mode of thinking of neurotic patients or of families in psychotic, psychopathic or psychosomatic transaction will reveal the way in which symptomatic events, which may possibly be catastrophic, are all the more likely to occur in that they are mentally pre-programmed. We shall here note that such events only happen in circumstances of FAMILY SELF-REFERENTIALITY: the sensitive, jealous paranoic will preferentially meet a partner who is likely to stoke his/her jealousy and mistrust; a cyclothymic person will, similarly, choose a partner who will counterbalance and possibly maintain, in complementary fashion, the excesses of his/her thymic oscillations. In such a perspective, the perception of a phantasy or dream may very well have a premonitory effect several years in advance or, indeed, ranging over a whole lifetime.

The Oedipus myth may be reconsidered in this light: it was the very mechanisms which were supposed to avert the incestuous catastrophe which enabled it to come about. It is, however, difficult to go along with those who assert that the explanation in terms of the experience of earliest childhood is no longer pertinent. It is precisely because Oedipus was separated from his biological mother at birth that she, as an 'exogamous' woman, was able to give in to his advances.

(See also LAW; PERFORMATIVES.)

J.M.

self-organization Theories of self-organization have developed at the crossroads of a great number of diverse disciplines apparently far removed from each other, such as cybernetics, the thermodynamics of irreversible processes and far-from-equilibrium systems, biochemistry and biophysics, neurophysiology, immunology, artificial intelligence, natural and experimental epistemology and the sciences of organization, information, communications and complexity. In spite of the scattered nature of these disciplines, the various theories of self-organization are difficult to dissociate one from another and form a whole which may be isolated on the strength of epistemological criteria. These theories have become associated with the established disciplines, but they have also created a kind of meta-scientific field.

HISTORICAL SURVEY

It was CYBERNETICS (Wiener, 1948) which was the crucible of the first theories of self-organization. A second flowering came at the beginning of the 1970s with the thermodynamics of far-from-equilibrium processes and the growing interest in the dynamics of singular points (strange attractors, chaotic dynamics). The discovery of the 'genetic programme' gave a new impulse to research into self-organization.

We should point out that the notion of self-organization has been around ever since the point when the GENERAL SYSTEMS THEORY of von Bertalanffy (1947) appeared. In fact, this author emphasizes repeatedly in his work that a specific characteristic of the living organism is its capacity to grow towards higher and higher levels of organization. He remarks upon the apparent contradiction with the findings of the thermodynamics of isolated systems, which state that the development of an isolated system is irrevocably doomed to a state of maximum disorder and levelling down of differences (the second principle of classic thermodynamics). According to von Bertalanffy, this capacity of the living system to grow towards higher levels of organization and complexity is due to the 'openness' of the system, i.e. to the incessant exchanges of energy, information and matter taking place between the living system and its environment. His view is that it is the importing of energy from the outside which enables the living system to 'self-organize'.

In 1944, the physicist, Schrödinger, in a famous paper entitled '*What is life?*' formulated a first theory of self-organization by openness: the 'order from order' principle. He showed how the assemblage of the molecules of the living organism were akin to an aperiodic crystal.

Systemic modelling of the family uses this conceptualization to explain the capacity of a family system to alter its operating rules to adapt to the growth of its members. At each stage of growth, a stage often symbolized by an event such as a marriage, birth, a child starting school or entering adolescence, a new state of the system commences, characterized by new modes of operation and representing a higher level of organization in relation to the preceding organization of the system. These stages are organized in cycles whose periodicity is complex.

Von Foerster (1960) suggested that we add to the 'order from order principle' an 'order from disorder or noise principle'. The main idea here is as follows: for there to be self-organization, there must be openness to noise and at the same time redundancy.

Von Neumann in the 1950s ('The general and logical theory of automata', 1951) noted a fundamental difference between natural and artificial automata; the paradox is that the former are based on an apparently unreliable substrate, which is rapidly degradable, namely biochemical molecules, whereas the latter call upon more reliable constituent parts. Now, the least error in these apparently dependable parts brings the artificial automaton to a total stop, while the degradation of molecules is subject to re-adjustment, and is indeed a precondition for the survival and renewal of the natural automaton.

To remedy this lack of reliability of artificial automata, some writers (Winograd and Cowan in Atlan, 1972) have sought to determine the conditions necessary for the construction of automata more dependable than their own component parts. These conditions are a redundancy of components, redudancy of functions, complexity of components, the de-localization of functions (Atlan, 1979).

In *Cybernetics* (2nd edn, 1961), Wiener proposed the hypothesis that brain waves, as recorded by electroencephalography, are the product of *cerebral oscillators*, created by self-maintenance and operating at frequencies which can interfere with one another. The nonlinear interaction of these frequencies brings about an attraction of frequencies, capable of generating self-organizing systems. We may therefore hypothesize that the interaction between two or more persons is similarly based on the attraction of precise frequencies, creating fictive, familial and social OSCILLATORS and leading to the autonomization of the levels under consideration.

OPERATIONAL CLOSURE, COMPLEXITY THROUGH NOISE

As biologists, and starting out from the principle stated by von Foerster, Atlan (1972, 1979) and Varela (1979) have proposed theories of the self-organization of living systems by developing different points of view depending upon the position of the observer.

Operational closure of systems (Varela)

Varela (1979) poses questions about the identity and autonomy of the living being and its capacity to maintain itself thanks to operations which are produced by itself. Varela's basic thesis is that *every autonomous system is organizationally or operationally closed*. According to Varela, the idea of operational closure generalizes the classic notion of system stability. In certain examples, the stability of a DYNAMIC SYSTEM may be considered as a representation of the organizational closure of an autonomous system. However, the notions of dynamic stability and of organizational closure must not be confused with one another; the former is merely a particular case of the latter, since stability is only one case of invariance among others. The notion of operational closure is quite close to, but none the less distinct from, that of FEEDBACK. Feedback requires an external source which is completely absent in the notion of organizational closure. A network of mutually interconnected feedback, without inputs or outputs, is organizationally closed.

The fundamental thesis, which states that every autonomous system is organizationally, operationally closed is somewhat dangerous if taken literally. Such internal coherence pushed to the extreme, ends up imploding and invading the surrounding world in a degraded fashion (see AUTONOMY AND HETERONOMY OF A SYSTEM).

Complexity through noise

Atlan (1972, 1979) concentrates on the no less surprising aptitude of living systems to produce, in and through their exchanges and their interactions with their environment, ever new forms or, in other words, to *complexity*. Atlan's fundamental thesis is the idea of *complexity through noise*, i.e. the capacity of a living system to increase its complexity as an effect of the random disturbances which it receives from its milieu. Atlan takes the point of view that not everything can be known about the elements and relations which constitute a living system. The observer is necessarily external to the system.

The phenomenon of self-organization is then considered a process of increase in complexity – both structural and functional – resulting from a series of disorganizations caused by random perturbations of the milieu, followed in each case by a re-establishment at a higher level of diversity, as though the perturbation had been incorporated as new information inherent in the specificity of the system, at a weaker level of redundancy. The 'noise' caused in the system by random factors in the environment becomes a factor of organization. The external factors both are and are not random: it is the reaction of the system itself which causes events to be considered random or, by contrast, become part of the organization.

From the moment when the system is capable of reacting in such a way not only that it does not disappear, but that it modifies itself and integrates them [the events] into its own organization in a sense which ensures its survival, they lose their character as noise to some extent. They only retain that character from a point of view external to the system when they no longer correspond to any programme that is destined to organize the system. By contrast, from a point of view internal to the system, they are factors of organization. (Atlan, 1979, p. 57)

The effects of noise become events in the history of the system and of its process of organization.

The theories of self-organization should be critically evaluated and compared, on the one hand, with the self-referential models of the family proposed by a variety of therapists and, on the other, with the models of catastrophe theory.

(See also AGREEMENT AND DISAGREEMENT; ALIENATION; ELEMENTARY CATASTROPHES; FAMILY CATASTROPHES, FAMILY SELF-REFERENTIALITY; GENERALIZED CATASTROPHES; SELF-REFERENTIAL CALCULUS.)

M.G. & J.M.

self-referential calculus   Whereas it had been the project of Whitehead and Russell (1910–13, see 1978 edn) to establish mathematics upon a logical basis and to eradicate the paradoxes by the THEORY OF LOGICAL TYPES, it was to be the aim of Spencer-Brown (1969), a disciple of Russell, to reintroduce logic into a mathematical perspective, by seeking a mathematical treatment of logical paradoxes (see PARADOXES).

The interest of such an attempt is that it leads to a new appreciation of the signs, forms and categories of formal logic, by integrating them into a wider framework in which self-reference and the 'third value' are not excluded (Varela, 1979; Le Moigne, 1983, 1984) such a procedure is of interest when one is considering the problems of uncertain and/or multiple relations of kinship and, more generally, disturbances of family autonomy and FAMILY SELF-REFERENTIALITY, and when one is looking to generalize the theory of the DOUBLE-BIND. The self-referential calculus thus suggests a possible means for modelling those phenomena which are perceived as complex.

The self-referential calculus is an attempt at a response to the Russellian theory of logical types. Rather than trying to eliminate the confusion of logical levels, this calculus brings it in right at the outset, so to speak, by proposing a symbol which is at the same time the operator (act) and the operand (result). It makes it possible to deal with transformations and hierarchical equivalences, and to engender forms which self-reproduce; it ultimately makes possible the modelling of the possible destiny of the 'third value', when it is apparently excluded from the alternative of true or false, presence or absence, belonging or not-belonging, existence or non-existence. It also ultimately makes possible the description of the formal properties of autonomy. It enables the processes which underlie the defensive transformations of the psychical representatives (displacement–condensation, denial–disavowal, introjection–foreclosure etc.) to be represented symbolically.

THE ELEMENTARY ARITHMETIC

Spencer-Brown (1969) thus defines an elementary arithmetic which has the surprising property of being both discrete and non-numerical. To do this, he uses an elementary, minimal form to distinguish an object from its environment, a figure from its ground, a structure from its context, an index from its configuration. This elementary form also permits of the distinction between inside and outside, surface and depth, hierarchy and equivalence. Such an elementary form is represented by a mark, in the form of two lines meeting at a right angle, which is called a 'cross'. The cross is the minimal form which marks the distinction between an inside and an outside, a surface and a depth. A mere line is not sufficient. This right-angle symbol has a dual meaning: it represents the act of distinction and it marks the space which contains it.

When a space contains a cross, the space is said to be marked. When a space does not contain one, it is said to be unmarked. Two initial axioms will make it possible to resolve all the possible configurations by reducing them to these two fundamental states: the marked state and the unmarked state. These two axioms define the procedural rules which transform the marks of distinction, as a function of the positions they occupy within the space they distinguish.

These two axioms are the axiom of condensation–iteration and the axiom of cancellation–compensation.

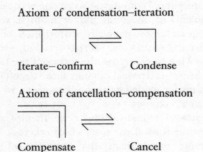

Axiom of condensation–iteration

Iterate–confirm   Condense

Axiom of cancellation–compensation

Compensate   Cancel

The axiom of condensation–iteration signifies that any number of crosses situated at the same depth are equivalent to a single cross (and vice versa). This may be translated into ordinary language by the words 'to remark is to mark'. These two axioms reflect two fundamental properties of living things: the reduplication of marks of distinction, the disappearance–reappearance of hierarchized spaces.

The axiom of cancellation–compensation states that an even number of crosses situated hierarchically in relation to one another are reducible to the unmarked state (reciprocally, the unmarked state may be indicated by a hierarchically arranged even number of crosses). This may be translated into ordinary language by the words to over-mark or under-mark is to unmark, to cancel the mark.

The two axioms of the primary arithmetic engender a whole calculus based on theorems connecting together the various formal arrangements of the marked and unmarked states. The value – marked or unmarked – of the state may thus become an independent variable in what Spencer-Brown calls the primary algebra.

THE PRIMARY ALGEBRA

Let p. q. r be expressions which may take the value of the marked or unmarked state. On the basis of the axioms and theorems of the primary arithmetic, the two following theorems called the *theorem of position* and the *theorem of transposition* can be demonstrated.

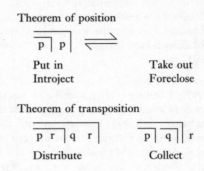

Theorem of position

Put in   Take out
Introject   Foreclose

Theorem of transposition

Distribute   Collect

The theorem of position is of particular interest in one respect, as it is the transcription of the excluded third value at the logical level (one may in fact interpret it as 'not (p implies p) = false'; or again 'p cannot imply other than itself'. It will be necessary to introduce the 'imaginary' or 'complex' value of the autonomous calculus for another solution to appear and the obstacle of the excluded third value to be removed.

From these two theorems, a whole series of consequences and other theorems follows. Among other things, the existence of a form, f, capable of reproducing itself indefinitely can be demonstrated. Let there be that form f, characterized by a hierarchy of three levels containing two variables a and b at depth levels 2 and 3.

$$f = \overline{\overline{a}\,b}$$

Spencer-Brown also demonstrates the following generative process:

$$f = \overline{\overline{a}\,b} = \overline{\overline{\overline{a}\,b}\,\overline{a}\,b}$$

$$f = \overline{\overline{\overline{\overline{a}\,b}\,\overline{a}\,b}\,\overline{a}\,b}$$

Since this operation is capable of reproducing itself indefinitely, the form f is both the initial cell which reproduces itself and the indefinite totality of its development. The total structure reincorporates its own representation or copy at its deepest level. This gives us:

$$f = \overline{\overline{\dots a}\,b} = \overline{\overline{f}\,a\,b}$$

in which a and b determine the value of f. The structure generated in this way is the most pared down and abstract formalization of a self-referential and self-reproducing configuration. It can also be represented by a mark of re-entry of a form into itself such as is proposed by Varela (1979, p. 122).

$$f = \overline{\boxed{a} \boxed{b}}$$

The expression f thus makes it possible to introduce the existence of re-entrant forms.

THE DISTINCTIVE VALUES OF SELF-REFERENTIAL STATES

One may study the value of f (marked or unmarked state) as a function of the values of a and b. In order to facilitate the formulation of this, and by convention, we shall also represent the marked state by the letter m and the unmarked state by the letter n.

It can then be shown that:

$$f = \overline{\overline{f\ m}\ n} = m$$

$$f = \overline{\overline{f\ n}\ m} = n$$

$$f = \overline{\overline{f\ m}\ m} = n$$

$$f = \overline{\overline{f\ n}\ n} = m \text{ or } n$$

The self-referential form f assumes a strictly determinate value when the variables a and b do not together assume the value of the unmarked state. By contrast, it assumes a value that is, of itself, indeterminate – marked or unmarked – when the variables a and b together have the value of the unmarked state.

Illustrations of the self-referential state may be given starting out from the following examples (Miermont and Gross, 1985):

- f = communication system (CS), where a = communication, b = metacommunication.
- f = kinship system (KS), where a = parental relationship, b = grandparental relationship (see ANCESTRAL RELATION).
- f = system of ACTUOGENESIS (SA), where a = ontogenesis, b = phylogenesis.

One may, for example, consider that a kinship system is indistinct if the parents and grandparents both keep power within the system at the same time (a and b = m). Similarly, the kinship system will be indistinct if the grandparents, having the position b (hierarchical 'meta' position in relation to the kinship system), preserve power while the parents, in position a (level of self-reference of the kinship system) are in an unmarked state. By contrast, there exist systems in which the grandparents preserve the 'parental' position a, marked, while the parents are placed in the 'parentified

position' b which is, however, unmarked. The self-reference of the kinship system is then ensured by the grandparents. The nuclearization of kinship systems implies that the parents take the marked position a and that the grandparents delegate their powers by assuming the unmarked position b, so that the self-reference of the family system is marked.

Self-reference is, in a sense, put in question when a and b together take on the value of the unmarked state. The form f, being able to take either value m or n equally, comes into contradiction with the starting point of Spencer-Brown's calculus, which stated that the value of an expression had to be unique, marked or unmarked.

It is at this point that self-reference becomes paradoxical. Spencer-Brown's hypothesis, taken up again and developed by Varela, is that a new calculus may be founded on the basis of this apparently indeterminate state. Varela suggests the name 'autonomous state' for the paradoxical self-referential states (still called imaginary states by Spencer-Brown).

The autonomous state makes its appearance when one considers the following re-entrant form:

$$f = \overline{f}$$

Now, if $\quad f = \overline{f}$ then $f = \overline{\overline{}} =$

and if $\quad f = $, then $f = \overline{}$

The autonomous state formalizes the notion of paradox and makes it possible to treat it symbolically rather than avoid it.

AUTONOMOUS STATES AND FORMS OF EXTENDED CALCULUS

Everyday common sense bases itself on the fact that an event either happens or it does not, that a thing or property exists or does not. In semiology a sign is either present or absent. It may, at a pinch, appear or disappear, be intense or weak, depending on the state and development of the illness, for example. But it cannot be both present and absent at the same time . . . unless one is looking at what is in a sense the prime problem of SCHIZOPHRENIA where this question is posed quite dramatically. It also arises in the stunning first sentence of Franz Kafka's *Metamorphosis*: 'When Gregor Samsa awoke one morning from agitated dreams, he found he had been transformed in his bed into a monstrous, verminous creature.' One misses something of the brilliance of that sentence if one takes the view either that a real or a metaphorical transformation is involved. It was Kafka's stroke of genius to bring what passes for an imaginary state into a fictional story told in the most realistic manner possible, or to present as real a transformation which, as is quite plainly announced, is the product of a kind of nightmare.

Spencer-Brown and, following him, Varela, define an imaginary or autonomous self-referential form whose solution is neither the marked nor the unmarked state. This form is defined thus:

$$f = \overline{f}$$

This imaginary of autonomous form symbolizes the structure/dynamic or space/time complementarity. Its temporal unfolding rests upon the oscillation between the marked and unmarked state. We then find the following *fixed point* theorem:

$$f = \overline{f} = \overline{\overline{\cdots\cdots}} = \overline{\overline{\cdots\cdots}} = \square$$

The autonomous state thus created may be represented in the form:

$$\square = \text{either}$$

I propose to make the distinction between the two opposing positions of the autonomous state

$$\square = \quad , \quad , \quad , \quad , \quad ,$$

$$\square = \quad , \quad , \quad , \quad , \quad ,$$

This reflects the arbitrary punctuation of the facts as soon as an autonomous state is established within a relation.

As Spencer-Brown stresses, the value represented by the autonomous state, being indeterminate in space, may be called imaginary in relation with the form, but it is real in relation with time. In the extended calculus, the marked, unmarked and autonomous states are regarded as being elementary expressions, unique resolutions of all the others.

The main original theorems which appear as a consequence of the axioms of the primary arithmetic are the theorems of constancy, iteration and the autonomous third value:

Constancy

Autonomous particle   Autonomous wave

Iteration

Self-production   Self-reproduction

Autonomous third value

Ejection   Autonomization

THERAPEUTIC ACTIVITY RESTS UPON A PHENOMENON OF SELF-REFERENTIAL COUPLING

I thus propose the distinction between *retrospective* autonomous forms and *anticipatory* autonomous forms:

(a) The symmetrical self-referential coupling of two autonomous forms of the same nature (retrospective or anticipatory) leads to the unmarked state.

(b) The complementary self-referential coupling of two autonomous forms which are different in nature (a retrospective autonomous form within an anticipatory autonomous form, or the contrary) leads to the marked state.

Resolution: Two autonomous states, situated at two hierarchical levels of depth n and n + 1 have the following 'real' solutions, depending upon their reciprocal arbitrary positions:

Resolution toward the unmarked state:

Resolution toward the marked state:

in effect:

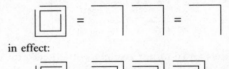

which amounts to unmarking the symptom

and:

which amounts to re-marking the context

The art, in therapy, consists in coupling these two complementary movements.

We shall note here, schematically, that the standard form of psychoanalytic treatment prescribes the injection of a retrospective autonomous state (analysis of childhood) into an inhibiting anticipatory autonomous state (neurotic phantasies). By contrast, family therapy prescribes the injection of an anticipatory autonomous state (foreseeing catastrophes) when dealing with an inhibiting retrospective autonomous state ('pregenital' fixations and regressions which are insuperable from a psychoanalytic point of view).

When faced with a pathology of autonomy, the demarcation of the symptom (its 'prescription') consists in cancelling its autonomy. This amounts to putting an end to the autonomy of a relation or state. The therapeutic intervention consists in injecting an autonomous state or re-framing by an autonomous state, whose re-entry has the same sense as the autonomous state which creates the symptom (the prescription apparently agrees entirely with the self-referential sense of the symptom).

The re-marking of the context presupposes an autonomous redefinition of its autonomy (transformation of a negative connotation into a positive connotation; one injects an autonomous state or one re-frames by an autonomous state whose re-entry is opposite in meaning to the autonomous state which creates the context). This amounts to transforming the autonomous state into a marked state.

The difficulty for the therapist is to combine the establishment of several autonomous systems of re-framing or re-injection at the same time: the system of the symptom or symptoms, so that they cease; the system of the context of the persons involved (that of the groups to which they belong or within which they are included), so that they become coherent stimuli.

Without seeking here to make a systematic application of the extended calculus to autonomous systems and sub-systems, it is possible to see the phenomena of paradoxical self-reference, which are particularly clearly to be seen in families with pathological transactions, in a new light. We shall note for example that the runaway of a pathological autonomous state (an escalation in the violence within a couple, or in schizophrenic symmetry etc.) may find its resolution by the setting in place of a therapeutic autonomous state which 're-frames' that pathological autonomous state. Widlöcher (1986, p. 16) rightly emphasizes the fact that psychoanalytic communication rests upon a basic tautology: 'The psychoanalytic cure is designed to treat the neuroses (i.e. the discovery of the conflict linked to the existence of unconscious representations). But neurosis is precisely defined as the expression of those unconscious representations.' The Lacanian tautology for its part rests on the use of the 'signifier' conceived in a self-referential manner, in a sense which at one and the same time attaches it to linguistics and detaches it from that field: the signifier is what represents the subject for another signifier; but the subject only comes into being from the disengagement of the unconscious chain of signifiers. And all of this is based upon the postulate that the unconscious is structured like a language (the expression 'structured like' allowing oscillation between a linguistic and non-linguistic understanding of the signifier).

What was true of psychoanalysis, suited as it is to deal with neurotic conflict, may be generalized to cover different pathological and therapeutic contexts, on condition that tautologies are constructed which enter into resonance with the epistemology of the symptom and suffering under consideration. The theory of the double bind in relation to families with schizophrenic transactions, problems of delinquent behaviour, addiction or psychosomatic illness, is one example. the self-referential calculus of the autonomous state precisely explains the structure of the double bind: setting several 'meta' levels at the same level. However, though the tautological character of theory and practice is necessary, it is not sufficient adequately to treat all the problems encountered in reality. An autonomous state continues to follow its own path until it meets an adequate autonomous state which frames or re-frames it.

(See also HOLOGRAPHIC MEMORY; RESIDUAL RELATIONS; INCOMPLETENESS THEOREMS.)

J.M.

self-referential coupling, reciprocal structural coupling See AGREEMENT AND DISAGREEMENT; COUPLES; FAMILY SELF-REFERENTIALITY; OSCILLATORS; SELF-REFERENTIAL CALCULUS; SEMANTIC RESONANCES; SEMANTICS OF COMMUNICATION.

self-regulation See CYBERNETICS; FAMILY SELF-REFERENTIALITY; FEEDBACK; GENERAL SYSTEMS THEORY; HOMEOSTASIS; SELF-ORGANIZATION.

semantic resonances A sense of meaning relies on the phenomenon of coupling between a referent and a sign, this latter itself being made up of a signifier and a signified. That coupling is itself the product of stabilized resonances between OSCILLATORS.

For Foulkes (1948, 1964), the concept of resonance puts the emphasis on the selective and specific character of unconscious communications (termed METACOMMUNICATION SYSTEMS by Bateson and his school).

We all know of examples of people who unite, say in marriage or friendship or hostility, a relationship which turns out to be extraordinarily and intricately fitting, quite often in a negative sense – in the sense of clashing, on deep instinctive levels. The idea behind the concept of resonance is that an individual exposed to another individual and his communications in behaviour and words seems instinctively and unconsciously to respond to them in the same coin as it were. (Foulkes, 1964, p. 290)

These resonances are, therefore, either attractant or repellant. In certain cases, we find a complex combination of the two.

Following Esriel, Anzieu (1975a) developed the hypothesis that these resonances are essentially phantasmatic in nature. It would seem more prudent here to view these interpersonal resonances as being established on very varied strata of exchanges: instinctive, ritualized and representational. Phantasmatic activity could be seen as marking particularly elaborate scenarios of representations, possibly indeed thwarting more elementary and more profound resonances. In other cases, phantasy organizations are literally 'disintegrated' by virtue of the potency of certain unconscious resonances.

In a topological perspective, one might view behaviour, whether verbalized or otherwise, and instinctive, oneiric, phantasmatic and symbolic activities as DYNAMIC SYSTEMS bringing into resonance oscillators which regulate family and social morphologies. A word, a gesture or a posture can be seen as possessing a characteristic semantic spectrum (see SEMANTIC SPECTRUM OF THE PROPER NAME). Bringing together two or more dynamic systems brings about couplings of variable intensity, whose product-frequencies will lead to more or less 'hooked up' resonances.

There would seem to be a pathology of these coupling phenomena (of which human couples are probably a particularly frequent and complex example), connected with topological characteristics. It may happen that, for certain frequencies, unstable regimes establish themselves and lead to chaotic regimes. In these situations, mathematicians have spoken of strange ATTRACTORS (Gleick, 1988), which entrain catastrophic BIFURCATIONS where the regulation of the system is concerned. The best known example in physics is the destruction of a bridge by soldiers marching in step at a period which is a sub-multiple of the resonating frequency of the bridge. In the pathology of the couple, one finds, with the drift of time, and the birth and development of children, the appearance of desynchronizations connected to the erosion of rituals and the weight of transgenerational traditions.

(See also AGREEMENT AND DISAGREEMENT; FAMILY SELF-REFERENTIALITY; SYMBOLIC REFERENCE; SEMANTICS OF COMMUNICATION.)

J.M.

semantic spectrum of the proper name   The most complex semantic spectrum is that of the human individual, localized in the product of a surname and a forename. There is here a semantic double articulation in which the singularity of an individual is secured by the combination:

(a)   of a family name which is not interchangeable or decidable at the family level and which, for the individual, marks the differentiation of his/her family identity within the body of society;

(b)   and of an interchangeable forename, which may be decided for the child at the level of the parental 'myth' (from within a limited pool of socially acceptable names), and which is a mark of intrafamilial differentiation of identity and of a relation of intimacy.

In some schizophrenic situations, one finds total indeterminacy as regards the patient's forename, with the parents still trying to come to some agreement about what name to give the child. In one particular case, many of the members of an institution had actually adopted the name 'imposed' by the mother, while the choice of another name by the father came out in a family therapy session. In practice, there was an oscillation between these two names, the composite name having no particular stability. In other cases, one may find a paranoiac refusal of the forename given to the child by its mother.

(See also HOLOGRAPHIC MEMORY; SCHIZOPHRENIAS; SEMANTICS OF COMMUNICATION.)

J.M.

semantic unit of mind   The unit of mind is defined by Bateson (1972) as a global cybernetic system which brings a process of trial and error to its conclusion and processes the information. A unit of mind is made up of a hierarchy of sub-systems and may be identified with an EVOLUTIONARY SURVIVAL UNIT. In Bateson's perspective, the mind is, in effect, immanent in the biological system of the ecosystem.

Pathological phenomena demonstrate a possible dissociation between units of mind and survival units. When faced with a family group in which one or more members are designated as symptom-bearers, it is necessary to identify the semantically pertinent units of mind of the group in question, even though the symptoms indicate that meaning has been thrown into question here. A semantic unit is based on the dynamic interconnection between two or more sub-systems brought together with a view to achieving a particular goal. Such a unit is based upon the coupling of two or more metabolic forms, or metabolic and static forms. It is possible, through the way in which each person occupies his or her mind and the state of mind which emerges from the analysis of the relationships, to begin a semantic understanding of the system. Similarly, where there are unpleasant symptoms, the way each person defines the symptom ('I don't have any personal problems, apart from my partner, or my family') will delineate the UNIT OF CHANGE with which one may envisage working. The definition given by a particular actor in the system may be in open or latent conflict with the perception the therapists have of the situation. The therapeutic process will only begin if there is a mutual transformation of points of view between the family members and the therapists.

Such units assume the integration of the individual or group concerned in its ECOSYSTEM, i.e. its material and human life context. A schizophrenic patient rarely constitutes, in him- or herself, a semantically pertinent unit, either of survival or of mind. The evaluation of his/her interactions with his/her family group, as well as the recognition of his/her ties to social organizations (clans, tribes, school, company etc.) will define various units of mind, from which a meaning may possibly spring, in the very process of the reconstitution of these various units. For example, traditionally, the 'village idiot' was able, in certain cases, to be a messenger of the 'spirit' or 'mind' of his village. In other cases, the unit of mind may very well be located in an individual person, provided that they are in a sufficiently structured connection with their environment. Such a concept leads us to define more precisely the notions of unit, mind and meaning, and to articulate these with the notions of body, psyche and soul.

For von Uexküll (1956), it is *signification* that is the directing thread by which biology should be guided, not the mere rule of causality which is much too partial and blind to the 'great structural relations'. It is 'harmony' that corresponds to signification in the orderliness of nature, while the 'counterpoint' is the theme of development and morphogenesis. harmonic and contrapuntal phenomena are at work at all levels of communication (the art of music is a privileged site of knowledge of these phenomena, since it explores, almost in the pure state, vibratory phenomena and their combinations).

Organism and ecosystem are interdependent, as point and counterpoint, in communication: the subject, the receiver of signification, is the organism, while the bearer, the creator of signification, is the ecosystem in which the organism lives. If the human being is the harmonic subject of signification, the family and social ecosystem is the contrapuntal bearer of signification. More precisely, the family is the creator of semantization of differentiated interpersonal relations.

For Bateson, the unit of mind presupposes a connection between the bearer and the subject of meaning: of man in his environment; of the blind man with his stick and the pavement when he goes for a walk; of the woodman, the blow he gives with his axe and the tree when he chops it down. In other words, the elementary unit of mind is the set of messages registered in the circuit of a cybernetic system, i.e. of a system regulated in terms of an elementary goal to be achieved. An elementary idea in that unit is the minimum transform of a difference moving around the circuit to create another difference. If, then, such a unit of mind processes differences of differences in the circuit thus travelled, the reader will see that, for certain complex problems, huge areas of the network of thought are situated outside the body. The mental characteristics of the system are immanent, not in some parts, but in the whole system. Lorenz (1973, 1978b) specifies the basic difference between the mind and the psyche (*Seele*). The life of the mind is supra-individual, made up of products of collective conceptual thought, nourished by languages, semiotic productions, transmissions of skills and knowledge by cultural inheritance. The ecological niche of man is made up, for a large part, of multiple units of mind identifiable in the high-level ritualization of languages, beliefs and values. These supra-individual units of mind function like very closely related pseudo-species (see PSEUDO-SPECIATION), to which the psyche adapts itself more or less successfully. In effect, the emotional and cognitive systems of the *Seele*, which make up the psychical apparatus, have a phylogenetic history that is much older than that of the mind which is born out of the products of culture.

One of the current debates in family therapy reflects the conflictual aspect of the relations between units of mind and psychical processes of thought. In some cases, culture may act as a veritable straitjacket on a family system and accord no place for the harmonious development of its members. In other cases, access to the spirit of the time and space into which the family is trying to insert itself in order to survive is rendered very difficult by a great degree of psychical undifferentiation. Such conflicts arise acutely when there are substantial distortions between units of mind, evolutionary survival units and units of change.

(See also AGREEMENT AND DISAGREEMENT; CHREOD; EIDOS; ETHOS; LOCUS; MIND; OSCILLATORS; SEMANTIC RESONANCES; SEMANTICS OF COMMUNICATION; STATIC, PSEUDO-STATIC AND METABOLIC FORMS.)

J.M.

semantics of communication The study of the meaning assumed by messages exchanged in interactions between people, together with the messages a person sends to him- or herself. It therefore relates to systems of belief and the systems explaining the origin, destiny and meaning of life. FAMILY and INSTITUTIONAL or SOCIAL MYTHS and rites are vehicles of meaning in so far as they seek to remove the ambiguity from the messages inherent in every system of communication. This suppression of ambiguity is at the centre of activity in family therapy.

Semantics complements the syntactic and pragmatic analysis of communication. Syntax studies the distinctions and oppositions between forms (see SYNTAX OF COMMUNICATION). It studies the structure of the signifier, where the semantics of communication concerns itself with the morphology of the signified. Pragmatics studies the concrete conditions in which the structuring of meaning is impossible (see PRAGMATICS OF COMMUNICATION).

In the view of Watzlawick et al. (1967). Semantics arises out of analogic communication. These analogic properties structuring the semantic function of messages are the product:

- of acquisitions linked to the evolution of species (phylogenetic memories);
- and of auto-domesticated simulations of the human mind (arts and languages: cultural memories, symbolic functions).

Meaning arises out of the existence of differentiated forms; these forms become SEMANTIC UNITS OF MIND when they are:

- endowed with a position in space–time;
- actuated by impulses regulated in function of certain goals to be achieved;
- structurally stable (see STRUCTURAL STABILITY);
- identifiable by other semantic units (reciprocal representations).

There is an intrinsic ambiguity in every action possessing meaning, so long as its objective is not achieved. If the objective short-circuits the action along the way, then the meaning will be destroyed and will lead to epistemological errors (Bateson, 1972). The objective is what removes the ambiguity in the meaning of the semantic unit under consideration. Meaning effects often function retrospectively, when the process has been completed.

The semantics of communication depends upon the dynamic interaction between persons and groups, who are capable of feeling and thinking, by creating contact between metabolic forms (memories) which come into resonance with one another (biological and symbolic OSCILLATORS). The meaning effect is thus a relative effect, dependent on the movements and directions of the various units in relation to one another, and on mutual recognition between these units. In this perspective, the family may be a semantic unit with various ultimate objectives: reproduction (the birth of children), protection and education, differentiation of persons and cultural groups.

Humanity's quest for meaning leads to (a) the study of systems of religious belief, philosophical systems, family and social myths and mystical experience; and (b) the familial and social definition of the true and the false, good and evil, the sacred and the profane, life and death, the necessary and the contingent, the reversible and the irreversible.

The paradox is that the discovery of the meaning of life is inexpressible. As Wittgenstein (1921) points out: 'The solution of the problem of life is seen in the vanishing of this problem. (Is not this the reason why men of whom after long doubting the sense of life became clear, could not then say wherein this sense consisted?)' This is no doubt the reason why it is difficult to transmit the authentic meaning assumed by a therapeutic measure, whereas the meaning of madness can be reconstituted from identification of the contexts in which it arises.

BIOLOGY OF SEMANTIC UNITS

Meaning is produced through the creation of a relationship between prehistoric and historic levels.

Elementary semantic unit of communication
An elementary semantic unit of communication is the product of one or more FUNCTIONAL CIRCLES defining a subject and object made up of a perception–action loop in contact with an environment. A functional circle is, for example, a circuit of predation (cat–mouse, man–animals/edible plants), courtship behaviour, a spiritual quest. The psychical integration of the functional circles of conspecifics/relatives, children, companions, prey and predators leads to the construction of more or less differentiated selfs. The family ecosystem becomes a complex unit leading to multi-semic processes of symbolization (see SYMBOLS).

Circuits of predation
Circuits of predation realize goal-directed sequences that are highly significant if the evolution of species. The spider's web possesses a certain degree of knowledge of the archetype of the fly (von Uexküll, 1956), to the point that its texture is programmed not to communicate its presence to the fly! Similarly, the cat is, to a large extent, the mouse it has to capture to feed itself (Thom, 1972). The more complex living organisms are, the more hetero-referent knowledge of the environment presupposes auto-referenced and interiorized constructions of the environment, namely the transformation of the ectoderm by the environment (the nervous system). And the more they are alienated by the forms whose capture, in communication, ensures their autonomy. ALIENATION is thus one of the parameters which contribute to the construction of meaning.

Semantics of symbolic movements
Animal rituals (see RITUALIZATION), which originate in instinctual movements whose normal course they deflect, are the phylogenetic prototypes which channel interchanges between semantic units by accession to a function of representation.

The value of ethology is that it shows us the semantic framework within which the phylogenetic learning processes of symbolic communication are carried out. The strata of learning built up in this way enable psychical hierarchies to be constructed, in turn enabling a host of unconscious metacommunications and paracommunications to be made. If human communication cannot be reduced to the semiotics of animal 'symbolic movements', as it obviously cannot, this is true in so far as that communication rests on psychical mechanisms of cultural simulation, regulation, amplification or inhibition of these symbolic movements, constructing the human self. In this sense, human rituals are symbolic sequences which resolve pragmatic and theoretical paradoxes.

Lorenz describes the differentiation of the movement

emitting excitation side by side with that of the innate 'schema' which perceives it. The movement is made more effective by the exaggeration of the parts exerting an optical effect. Simplification by ignoring extraneous detail and by material differentiation of structure, in shape and colour, is thus arrived at, increasing optical effect. There is, then, an association between simplification of movements and the exaggeration of mimetic effect. These symbolic movements have become something quite separate from the initial movements from which they derived.

The following one examples of animal symbolic movements:

- the symbolic gift of fish in the courtship behaviour of the blackheaded gull: here, the fish is not for eating, but the archeo-symbolic representative of a courtship ritual;
- the exhibiting of the erect penis in some species of primates, having a function of phallic intimidation, for purposes of group or territorial defence or as a symbolic threat of mounting the enemy;
- mounting a conspecific as a mark of hierarchical precedence (Lorenz, 1978b). Sometimes, the 'leader' simply touches the anus of the hierarchical inferior. Some insults in humans recall the threats of territorial infringement or hierarchical precedence ('bugger', 'homo' etc.). These are also found in the form of voices in mental automatism or obsessional ideas in obsessional neurosis.

Considering certain disorders of human behaviour, one might view enuresis and encopresis as protosymbolic manifestations of questing for a lost territory or one that has never been achieved, rendering the conquest of an imagined territory illusory so long as the actual 'nest' has not been acquired. Such phenomena are particularly meaningful in so-called disengaged families where the children are fostered out to families or institutions and moved around between multi-parental agencies.

In man, self-referentiality becomes duplicated, since he becomes a universal predator, a meta-predator, being able to capture his own conspecific as prey. In fortunate cases, this 'capture' is governed by cultural rules which are not too alien to his nature. The relation between nature and culture is, however, conflictual here. It is of the essence of symbols to allow this articulation over several levels; hence the protean character of symbols: plant, animal, human 'object': idea, word, musical sound, line in a picture, concept, mathematical equation – so many supports mediating symbolic activity, to the extent that they refer back one to another.

TOPOLOGY AND MORPHOLOGY OF THE SIGNIFIED

Conjecturing of meaning
Unlike the reality of a behaviour which cannot but be what it is (see PRAGMATICS OF COMMUNICATION), its meaning is not self-evident. It may degrade or take a long time to appear and is born out of ambiguity. The systems which make it possible to canalize meaning and eliminate ambiguity may be termed semantic CHREODS. Rituals, both phylogenetic and cultural, or the words and sentences of language are an example.

Conditions of intelligibility
Meaning arises out of a representation in space; it presupposes forms inscribed within spatiotemporal limits. These forms:

- possess structural stability;
- have a position on an orientated trajectory;
- are actuated by movements and cycles of regulation;
- recognize one another;
- co-memorize; and
- are regulated as a function of the goals to be achieved.

The meaning of schizophrenic symptoms only appears with the recreation of artificial boundaries, as is seen most starkly in the case of confinement in an asylum. Similarly, the ritualization of meetings with the family, for purposes of therapy, leads to new meaning effects for patients, families and their therapists.

Transmission of meaning
In Thom's (1972) view, the semantic transmission of information can only take place through the free interaction of two metabolic systems or in interaction between a pseudo-static system and a metabolic one (see STATIC, PSEUDO-STATIC AND METABOLIC FIRMS), where the reciprocal attractors of the systems have oscillatory periods capable of entering into resonance and where the product of the two systems leads to an intermediate shared field (see SEMANTIC RESONANCES). In other words, the sender and the receiver must be dynamic systems actuated by oscillators whose own frequencies are induced to interfere and to create characteristic product resonances. There then exists a more or less complex coupling between the oscillators of the sender and the receiver. In interaction between two persons, the expressions 'being (or not being) on the same wavelength', 'vibrantly feeling the same emotions' and 'experiencing an intellectual or emotional resonance' are doubtless less metaphorical than they seem. In some cases, pseudo-static forms serve as supports or as AUXILIARY MEMORIES (the alcoholic's bottle, behaviours that are perceived as rigid and repetitive etc.). The formation of a couple or a family presupposes a sufficient synchronization of thoughts, emotions, activities and attitudes. That synchronization is commonly produced by phenomena of ritualization.

The semantics of 'parole'
Human language derives its meaning from the relations it maintains with the prelinguistic and paralinguistic communication known as 'non-verbal' communication.

There may be match or mismatch between the meaning of words and the sense of non-verbalized actions. The interaction between these levels cannot be described better than it is by the metaphor suggested by Thom:

> In certain conditions of excitation, the concept will produce a 'gamete' bearing the 'logos' of the concept. This gamete is simply the word, uttered by the speaker. In the mind of the hearer, the word, which is nothing other than the seed of the concept, provided that it encounters an appropriate context, germinates and bursts open: the logos of the concept unfolds and it reconstitutes the figure of regulation of the concept and, hence, its signification. (Thom, 1980b, p. 184)

Rites and family myths as morphologies conveying meaning

Thom emphasizes that the term 'information' refers, so far as the psychical and mental fields are mainly concerned, to the powers of form and the topological constraints to which the morphologies conveying signification are subject. Hence, phyolgenetic and cultural rites are semantic chreods which enable the meaning of a relationship to be established. They determine the distinction between what is vital (indispensable, necessary) and what is superfluous (contingent), as well as the transition between reversible (cyclical forms) and irreversible processes (birth, death, the formation of couples and families by the establishing of myths). Similarly, family myths are semantic morphologies the formal constraints of which appear at the points of maximum distortion in the transmission of information (excess/lack, truth/falsehood, oneself/others, good/bad).

THERAPY AND SYMBOLIC DISCOVERY OF MEANING

Symbolization of the subject–object relation

The semantics of comunication leads into the symbolic constitution of subject–object relations. Winnicott (1965, pp. 179–80) writes:

> Looking directly at communication and the capacity to communicate one can see that this is closely bound up with relating to objects. Relating to objects is a complex phenomenon and the development of a capacity to relate to objects is by no means matter simply of the maturational process. As always, maturation (in psychology) requires and depends on the quality of the facilitating environment.

Winnicott suggests the concept of *subjective object* to describe the subjective phenomenon which precedes the objective constitution of the other subject as object. 'It is the destruction of the object that places the object outside the area of the subject's omnipotent control' (1971, p. 90). The subject is the object's predator. Access to the symbol presupposes a meta-predation (for male and female gulls, 'this fish is not destined to be eaten, but is a gift ritualizing a relation of couple-formation').

Psychoanalytic communication

The analysis of a dream, 'psychoanalytic communication' (Widlöcher, 1986, pp. 25–40) and the family meeting may possibly have hermeneutic effects; semantics cannot therefore be dissociated from the pragmatics and syntax of communication. The behaviour of a psychotic patient, which has no obvious meaning, will assume semantic content by the mere fact of his/her encounter, at the appropriate time, with the members of his/her family. The inscription of a pragmatic event in time has the effect of restructuring the syntax of behaviour and language and bringing semantic communication back into play. One observes, at that point, more or less substantial incongruities between speech acts and posturo–gestural attitudes (the 'verbal' and the 'non-verbal'). These incongruities are precisely the expression of the quest for a new meaning.

Family communications

Family therapy is directly concerned with the constitution of object relations, which takes place via the state of the relation of subjection. In contact with his or her family, the mental patient clearly shows the failure to set in place such a relation. Access to the symbolic relation comes via this alienating movement of subjection by the family group.

The paranoic, the schizophrenic and the delinquent are, on a strictly structural plane, without apparent meaning. Seen from the perspective of family dynamics, their 'structures' begin to enter into resonance with those of their close relatives. That resonance only comes to bear meaning if it leads to structurally stable morphologies, capable of symbolization, which may then be termed morphologies of the signified.

A communication becomes symbolic between two 'subjects' when an internal and/or external agency occupies a third position in relation to these two and permits a certain objectivation of them. The triangulation function of the OEDIPUS COMPLEX was identified by Freud as constitutive of the difference between the sexes and the generations and as the matrix of the family nucleus. Approaches centred on the family ecosystem have led to the recognition of other forms of triangulation (see TRIANGLES), which have considerable importance in regard to the definition which may be given to REALITY (Haley, 1967; Bowen, 1978a).

(See also MYTH; SEMANTIC SPECTRUM OF THE PROPER NAME.)

J.M.

semiology and semiotics of communication To comprehend symbolic phenomena, within the framework of inter-human communication, one is obliged to situate these concisely in relation to the other forms of signalling. The two great founding models of the twentieth century were Saussurian semiology, on the one hand, and Peircian semiotics, on the other.

SAUSSURIAN SEMIOLOGY

It is in France that Saussurian theory has been most extensively developed, both in its linguistic and psychoanalytic strains (the two being radically opposed in character). The theory is based on the recognition of the self-referential and systemic dimension of the linguistic sign, which is self-defined in the signifier–signified opposition independently of the structure of the referent. The Saussurian project was to establish a general semiology, with linguistics as its 'master-pattern'.

In the development of his work, the Saussurean perspective has been subjected to a variety of criticisms.

First, the structure proposed is essentially dyadic and neglects the density of the referent of the signified, as well as the mental structure linking together acoustic image and concept (Peirce was to distinguish between the primary, secondary and tertiary aspects of signs).

Secondly, the arbitrariness of the sign, as a fundamental element of language (admittedly relativized by the secondary analogic motivations of the signifier) radicalized the emphasis on the effects of the signifier and caused social motivation to be correspondingly downplayed. The semantic problem of the morphology of the signified was thus fundamentally excluded.

Thirdly, symbolic acts, the processes of production of symbols – linguistic, musical, pictorial etc. – were reduced to their strict dimension of arbitrary rupture and were supposed, in the last resort, to be analysable in terms of verbal signifiers. In *Theories of the symbol*, Todorov (1977) relates the fabulous pathology of 'Miss Helene Smith' who lived at Geneva at the turn of the twentieth century, involving both somnambulism and her activities as a medium. During her trance states, she spoke Sanskrit or Martian depending on whether she was in India or on the planet Mars. Now, the surprising properties of these two languages, totally hermetic and idiosyncratic, defied Saussure's understanding and did not begin to disclose their secret until the tropic processing underlying the creation of these neo-languages was identified. If the letter F was absent, this was not because of a supernatural knowledge of the absence of F in Sanskrit but because F symbolized the French language which had to be concealed at any price. (We refer the reader here to the *traitements symboliques* of Jean-Pierre Brisset, on the one hand, and to Joyce's *Finnegans wake* on the other.) In Todorov's view, Saussure could be seen to have 'missed' the interpretation of what was happening here on account of having reduced the symbol solely to its arbitrary part, thus eliminating its creative, productive, self-engendered dimension (which may, in some cases, career madly out of control) and hence its meaning.

Lastly, the 'symbolic' which resulted from this was, then, practically synonymous with numerical or digital coding. In psychoanalysis, Lacan was to affirm the supremacy of the symbolic over the imaginary and the real, and the primacy of the signifier over the signified. Now, it is not a question of denying the importance of the arbitrary structure of signifiers, of their articulation in a systematically structured chain and of their reference to a law-giving agency of the order of the superego, but their supremacy, one might say, is merely a matter for the neurotic. The psychotic will, by contrast, use symbols to question the real, and to attempt, at a danger to himself, to modify its sense. The symbol is already a sublimated solution of real and imaginary flows; and the LAW only functions as an effective source of arbitrary authority if the context authorizes it, which is something with which all work with families in schizophrenic or delinquent transaction is precisely confronted.

PEIRCIAN SEMIOTICS

To the same degree that de Saussure's semiology is clear, explicit and relatively simple – though operationally effective to a high degree in linguistics – so the semiotics of Peirce is complex and proliferating and seeks to adapt itself of a host of different forms of sign systems. So far as we are concerned here, Peirce's semiotics resituates the symbol in broader contexts, attempting to take all semiotic systems into account.

Benveniste (1979–80) has pointed out that its application to linguistics is much less straightforward and apparently limited, even though is enables a triangulation with the referent of the sign to be re-established. In fact, it permits a much more all-inclusive evaluation of semiotic systems and lays the ground for fruitful etho-linguistic, psychoanalytic and topological developments. From among a highly complex grid of trichotomies, Peirce proposes the following fundamental distinctions:

- representamen, object, interpretant;
- indices (see DEIXIS), ICONS, SYMBOLS.

The *representamen* is quite close to the ideational representative described by Freud. It is what takes the place of something for someone. It therefore assumes a topological displacement of one thing, replaced by another (capture of one attractor by another in Thom's perspective), in order to bring out a primary difference, creating a distinctive categorial perception, generating a significant feature. This *primary sign* that is the representamen is *secondarily* connected with the object of the relation, this latter being deciphered by an interpretant in a *third* position. Neither the representamen nor the interpretant are persons, but rather relations between persons sharing the same significant object. Peirce (1935, vol. 1, p. 215) writes, for example:

A sign, or *representamen*, is something which stands to somebody for something in some respect or capacity. It addresses somebody, that is, creates in the mind of that person an equivalent sign, or perhaps a more developed sign. That sign which it creates I call the *interpretant* of the first sign. The sign stands for something, its *object*. It stands for that object, not in all respects, but in reference to a sort of idea, which I have sometimes called the *ground* of the representamen.

In even more condensed fashion, Peirce introduces this triangulation of the sign as follows: 'A representamen is a subject of a triadic relation. To a second, called its object, for a third, called its interpretant, this triadic relation being such that the representamen determines its interpretant to stand in the same triadic relation on to the same object for some interpretant' (Peirce, 1935, vol. 1, p. 285). In other words, this triangular relation of the representamen of the object determines the interpretant to be a representamen of the same object. The following is an example: a musical score is the representamen of the composer's creation, the object of which is the work to be played, such that the interpretant, constituted by the relation between the performer, the score and the public becomes the representamen of the work played. The composer is thus represented by his work.

Peirce then makes the following distinctions which I shall not go into in detail here: representamen, (mediate) dynamical and immediate objects, (effective) dynamical, (intended) immediate and explicit (final, normal, possible, logical and ultimate) interpretants.

(See also SYMBOLIC REFERENCE.)

J.M.

semiotic square Fundamental semiotic structure described by Greimas and Courtes (1979), which makes it possible to describe the configuration of the signs present in the various modalities of human communication, as they are reflected by and conveyed in language.

A semantic axis is created from a term A when it is connected to:

- its absence, A* (two terms A and B cannot be present together; a term cannot be both present, A and absent, A*). This is termed a contradictory relation.
- its opposite (not-A). This is termed relation of contrariety.
- the absence of its contrary: absence of not-A.

An assertion gives us the following square:

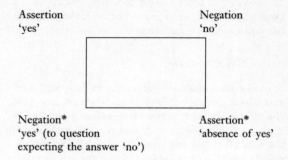

Assertion 'yes' — Negation 'no'

Negation* 'yes' (to question expecting the answer 'no') — Assertion* 'absence of yes'

The relation which runs from A* to A, from A to A* from −A to −A*, and from −A* to −A is termed complementary. The relation which runs from A to −A* (e.g. from 'yes' to 'yes') is termed positive deixis (from the Greek for 'exhibiting', the act of showing). The relation which runs from −A to A* (from absence of assertion to negation) is termed negative deixis.

Greimas's semiotic square is somewhat reminiscent of the square in classical scholastic logic known as the Square of Apuleius:

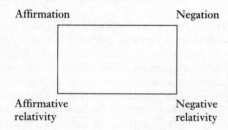

Affirmation — Negation

Affirmative relativity — Negative relativity

which itself follows on from Aristotle's positing of the four modalities:

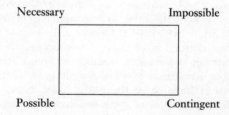

Necessary — Impossible

Possible — Contingent

(see Grangeon, 1986). One is equally reminded of Piaget's (1949) INRC group of transformations (identity, negation, reciprocity, complementarity), and the procedures of musical composition from Bach to Schoenberg.

Let us note at this point that these values distinguished here are only distinguished by differences. These differences are, however, conceived as engendering positive demarcations: the absence of a term Y is the necessary counterpart of the presence of a term Y*. The absence of negation is a value which reinforces the initial assertion. Haley (1959) and Selvini

Palazzoli et al. (1978) have shown that this is not the case in schizophrenic messages: the negation of the expression and the content – of what is said and the person who speaks – leads to a radical disqualification of the message, including the sender and receiver (see SCHIZOPHRENIAS). It is true that in this case, every manifestation of difference is usually erased.

Let us return, however, to normal semiotic functioning: there is a hierarchy in the exposition of categorial terms: at an immediately higher level, 'meta-terms' may be observed, produced by the relations between the terms, taken in pairs:

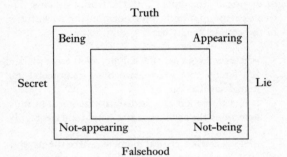

Truth

Being   Appearing

Secret   Lie

Not-appearing   Not-being

Falsehood

According to Greimas, 'truth' and 'falsehood' are contradictory meta-terms, while 'secret' and 'lie' are contrary meta-terms. One can see the interest of this semiotic description if one considers the deontic modalities, the semiologies of power, manipulation, belief, knowledge etc. Let us, first of all, take the case of DEONTIC MODALITIES, which are the foundation for prescription. This will give the following semiotic square:

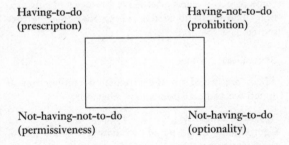

Having-to-do (prescription)   Having-not-to-do (prohibition)

Not-having-not-to-do (permissiveness)   Not-having-to-do (optionality)

It will be clear here that the semiotics of interpretation is not on the same plane as that of prescription. To interpret is to promote understanding, and the contradictory of this is to 'promote lack of understanding' (misunderstanding); the contrary, 'not to promote understanding' is to say nothing (silence); the double negation, 'not to not promote understanding' (not to say nothing) will have two possible bifurcations in psychopathology: either to reinforce the interpretation, to render it inescapable (which presupposes that the semiotic functions of the square leave an operative trace), or to render it eternally impossible by speaking at the

wrong moment and hence producing scrambling or noise. Within this perspective, the analyst's interpretations and silences will be seen as a matter of striking the right prescriptive balance. The pragmatics of interpretation will only be functional, then, in a prescriptive context (prescription of the framework and modalities of the cure), while every form of psychotherapeutic prescription will have direct or indirect interpretative effects in terms of the way the patient comes to understand what is happening to him or her (Watzlawick et al., 1974, stresses that it is preferable for insight to come after change and not the other way about).

(See also ALETHIC (MODALITIES); MANIPULATION.)

J.M. & G.G.M.

sensitivity to initial conditions It currently appears that not all open systems meet the requirements of EQUIFINALITY. In some cases, we observe phenomena of sensitivity to initial conditions such that a variation – even an infinitesimal one – of one or more parameters at point t_i of a system may lead to considerable modifications of that system at point t_{ii}. In such cases, the determinism which underlies this sensitivity to initial conditions is not incompatible with the impossibility of predicting the nature of the bifurcation. Sensitivity to initial conditions is better suited to accounting for fixations in ontogenesis (the theories of IMPRINTING and FAMILY ORGANIZERS.)

Family therapists are becoming attentive to sensitivity to initial conditions. Singular events and small perturbations are likely to bring about profound changes in family and personal functioning. Thus, determinist models may be unpredictable in their long-term effects. The accumulation of effects of ontogenesis in several members of the same family may, over several generations, produce perturbations which apparently break out quite suddenly without any unilateral aetiological explanation being possible. Periodic phenomena associated with FAMILY LIFE-CYCLES may thus lead to apparently chaotic movements, related to the systems concerned being drawn towards strange ATTRACTORS.

(See also DYNAMIC SYSTEMS; GENERAL SYSTEMS THEORY; HOMEOSTASIS.)

J.M.

sexed behaviour, seduction behaviour, sexual behaviour Sexual behaviours are extremely variable, running, as active behaviours, from the single encounter to intermittent relations, and right through to the exclusive relationship between lovers. They lead, in correlation with loving ATTACHMENT BEHAVIOUR, to monogamous or polygamous relations, depending on the culture. But these behaviours can only be intelligible if one takes into account:

- the totality of manifest behaviour (appetitive behaviour: courtship, seduction, display, consummatory behaviour);
- the phantasmatic representations and resonances of these behaviours. As a system of behaviour, human sexuality is the complex resultant of instinctive, ritual, phantasmatic and symbolic behaviours.

ADVANTAGES OF CONFRONTATIONS BETWEEN ETHOLOGICAL, PSYCHOANALYTIC, COGNITIVISTIC AND SYSTEMIC THEORIES

The recognition of infantile sexuality has made it possible to discover the importance of the experiences of the child, which are structured in the course of the sexual phases (Freud, Abraham); these phases show the connection which exists between the erogenous zones of the body, representations and affects and characteristic styles of relationship. At the level of representations, these phases stabilize sequences set in motion during childhood (phenomenon of RITUALIZATION, anaclisis of the sexual drives on the self-preservative ones): *oral phase* (sexual derivation of incorporation–introjection); *anal phase* (derivation of possession and mastery from the establishment of territory and power relations); *phallic phase* (derivation of relations of hierarchical display). Fixation at one particular prevalent mode of satisfaction lays the ground for the sexual difficulties of the adult.

The importance of negative imprinting in the course of childhood for the constitution of the sexual object will also be noted. The child's sexual games lead to the structuring of sexual desire. Later, however, desire becomes orientated towards objects different from those towards which the sexual games of childhood were directed. Family and social constraints may bring about perturbations in the unfolding of these experiences and later promote the behaviour which was supposed to be avoided at all costs (adultery, homosexuality).

The OEDIPUS COMPLEX is a dramatic structure which is superimposed upon these experiences. It brings together attachment and sexuality, is based on the distinction between the sexes and the generations by the symbolic inscription of filiation. The phantasy of the death of the same-sex parent/rival, and the sexual phantasy directed toward the opposite-sex parent, enable the distinction between REALITY and the imaginary, between MAP and TERRITORY to be made.

One must in this connection emphasize how pointless it is to attempt the sexual eduction of the child (in the sense of bringing to it objective concepts relating to sexuality), whether this is carried out by parents or teachers. The child will only believe what he/she wants to believe according to the phantasmatic sexual theories which his/her libidinal stage allows him/her to believe or which he/she is able to believe depending on his/her level of cognitive maturation in Piaget's sense. 'The child's interest in sexuality, as a phenomenon, is permanent (which is allowed for in a theory of intelligence), but "desexualized" or, rather, libidinally de-cathected at certain periods of the child's development (which only Freudian theory can currently explain)' (Jagstaidt, 1984).

FAMILIES AND SEXUALITY

Sexual behaviours are determined by the symbolic and mythic structure of the family. These may be openly or cryptically in conflict with the family systems. The two extreme mythic formulations, in the constitution of the couple, might be:

- whatever happens, the stability of the couple and the family take precedence over sentimental and sexual satisfaction;
- it is sentimental and sexual satisfaction that must determine the stability of the couple and the family.

Adolescence is a critical moment where the psycho-affective realization of sexuality is concerned, re-activating infantile experiences, on the one hand, and putting to the test the early experiences of the parental couple. Within the organization of married couples, Porot (1954) notes 'the crucial importance and relative rarity of permanent sexual harmony'. A great variety of compensatory activities will arise to make up for a failure to renew sexual activity within the couple: work, play, alcoholism, drug-taking, Platonic sentimental relationships, adultery, homosexuality, recourse to religiosity (adoption of a saintly position) etc. will thus come to play a role as defensive strategies of substitution. The break-up of the COUPLE may then be presented as a solution.

SEXUAL BEHAVIOURS

These are based on the articulated conjunction of appetitive and consummatory behaviour.

Appetitive behaviour
Courtship is made up of invariant elements and of codes (or rather algorithms) which vary according to culture, fashions and habits (see EIDONOMY; ETHONOMY).

We may note here the importance of *seduction behaviour* in the adolescent, which is indispensable for the maturation of adult sexual activity.

young people must overcome personal inadequacies, they must be able to associate with people their own age, they must achieve adequate status in their social network, they must have become disengaged from their family of origin, and they require a society stable enough to allow the steps of courtship to go to their completion. (Haley, 1973, p. 65)

Within this perspective, Erickson works both on the external appearance of the adolescent or young adult and the internal image he/she has of him- or herself and others in relation to sexual attraction.

Consummatory behaviours

These bring together instinctual sequences and sequences connected to phantasy activity. They presuppose a sufficient climate of trust, security and tenderness, a synchronization of the ritualizations of courtship and seduction and a self-abandonment to erotic imaginary, which stands in an anaclitic relation to the body and its erogenous zones, which are integrated into an overall genitality.

SEDUCTION BEHAVIOUR, SEXUALIZATION OF SOCIAL RELATIONS AND CULTURAL ALGORITHMS

Sexuality in man is not restricted to behaviours centred on the pursuit and realization of the sexual act. Phantasy representations, which enable social relationships to be structured and learned, are cathected with libidinal energy. The comparison of the contributions of psychoanalysis and ethology is fruitful here. It is necessary to distinguish between:

- hetero- and homosexuality, relating to object choice;
- sexed identification (feeling oneself to be a man for a man, for example, while identifying with women);
- sexed identity (feeling oneself to be a man for a woman, and vice versa: trans-sexualism).

The phallus as symbol of hierarchical rank and mark of a threat

The phallus is a representative of the penis, this latter having a triple function in the evolution of the species: copulation, urination and the marking of territory. This last-mentioned function is effected by the emission of urine on to territory, excrement, defeated conspecifics and courted females by the male of higher rank in the hierarchy. The erect penis thus becomes a signal of threat. Enuresis and exhibitionism in man may be regarded as dysfunctions of these rituals of power, threat and phallic display. The exhibitionist seeks not so much to accomplish the sexual act as to frighten his victim, to threaten that victim symbolically and to signal his relational distress.

Homosexuality

Homosexuality also comprises a semiotic dimension. It is then a signal of social hierarchy: males mount other males and females mount other females not so much to accomplish a sexual act as to signal hierarchical superiority, a power relation. A defeated male adopts behaviour which resembles feminine behaviour.

The behaviour of men and women is in part dictated by social archetypes: virility/femininity (anima/animus in Jung's terms). Sexual identity plays a role in the formation of couples; a study of the search for partners among homosexuals shows differences between male and female homosexuals. Among men, there is often a distinct divide between sexuality and fondness while this divide is much less marked among women.

Trans-sexualism

Trans-sexualism has been studied from a systemic perspective by Neuburger (1984). In his view, the trans-sexual's penis is reduced to being a sign of belonging to the genus 'man', without reference to the sexual identification of the phallus. Such an attitude has to be seen in relation to the determination of the gender of the child at his/her birth by the choice and desire of the parents. The child's conviction of belonging to his/her own sex is very closely connected to its own parents' convictions concerning its sexed identity. A father or a mother who expresses a preference for having a boy instead of a girl (or the opposite) shows precisely by so doing that he or she has recognized the sexed identity of the child. In Neuburger's view, the identity of the trans-sexual is linked to a desire for parental twinning, determined by the position of the parents and of the whole of the family. 'The constitution of a precocious and stable narcissistic dyad poses a defiant challenge to the symbolic order. It is an apparently stable and solid solution. It is complementary and therefore non-conflictual, narcissistic and impenetrable, hence the absence of Demand' (Neuburger, 1984b, p. 85).

(See also AGONISTIC BEHAVIOUR; FAMILY MYTHS; IDENTIFICATION; INCEST; LOVE; MARITAL BREAKDOWN; METAPSYCHOLOGY; NARCISSISM; RELATIONAL ARCHETYPES.)

J.M., M.G., G.G.M. & P.G.

shifters A linguistic term used by Jespersen (1922) and adopted by Jakobson (1950, 1957, in *Selected writings*, vol. 2, pp. 130–47). A shifter (synonymous with 'deictic', see DEIXIS) is a class of words with a general meaning which can only be defined exactly and individually by reference to the message. The prototypical shifters are among the first words uttered by the child: 'Daddy', 'Mummy'. If we accept that the code, C, and message, M, are the two vehicles of linguistic communication, which can function in 'a duplex manner' (Jakobson, *Selected writings*, vol. 2, p. 130), meaning that they can be both 'utilized and referred to', then the shifter establishes a circulation between a code and the message to which it refers. A 'shift' does, in fact, occur, due to the code being used, from the message on to the situation.

Each shifter possesses a general meaning of its own, such as the personal pronouns 'I', 'you', 'he', which underlie the process of triangulation; or 'you', 'we', 'they', which are the vehicles of a sense of collective belonging etc.; the impersonal pronoun 'one' being by contrast the practical vehicle of indifferentiation of SELF and of the mechanism of PROJECTIVE IDENTIFICATION which necessarily refers to the message to establish its precise meaning. Shifters combine the symbolic and deictic functions. They are symbolic in so far as they associate a sign with a represented object according to a convention, but in a socially motivated way. They are deictic (i.e. they are indices) in so far as the referent (what Peirce called the 'dynamic object') is connectable to the sign-object (Peirce's 'immediate object'), as, for example, in the act of pointing something out.

The ontogenesis of shifters is complex since it begins with the most rapidly acquired 'indexical symbols' ('Daddy', 'Mummy') and runs through to those that are the most fragile, i.e. the last ones to be learned, and the most likely to be damaged in cases of pathology (personal pronouns). For Jakobson, this complexity is explained by the fact that, in the shifter, code and message overlap. The complexity is already present in the connection between the generic symbols 'Daddy', 'Mummy' and their coincidence with the indices which secure the connection with the precise persons within the family. The mother points out 'Daddy' to the child not as her own father, but as the father of the child. One can observe, even at this level, many levels of deictic undecidability which make the functioning of the shifter difficult, if not, in some cases, impossible. At the most extreme level, a particular deeply backward, self-mutilating child says 'Daddy', but has never pronounced the word 'Mummy', his mother having died a few months after his birth, after which he was cut off from his family roots and placed with a wet-nurse far from his family. The family says that he cannot pronounce the word 'Mummy' since he never knew her (which shows a collusion between real facts and the FAMILY MYTH).

At a level that is much more culturally integrated, we know that the designation of the child's father, the father acknowledged as such by the mother, may pose a problem. However, the whole range of family members – and the positions of generation, affiliation and consanguinity they may occupy – are subject to a more or less precise deixis. This may be disturbed by a great number of factors which we encounter in clinical practice. These include an absence of information between the parents or grandparents and the children, an absence of knowledge of certain facts as a consequence of the family myth (SECRETS, MISUNDERSTANDINGS etc.), the collapse of transgenerational and/or sexual barriers preventing all perception of categories, disturbances of thinking, distortions in the designation of words and things by parents and grandparents, the messages thus transmitted being rather odd in character.

Forenames are the shifters which enable personification to occur within the family group. In an initial phase, the child appropriates the forename given by its parents by using it, as though from outside, to objectivize him- or herself and refer to him- or herself as someone distinct from Daddy, Mummy and his/her brothers and sisters etc. We can again observe here a specific pathology which might be connected, for example, to the absence of agreement about the name given by the parents. Thus a hyphenated Christian name of a schizophrenic patient continued to be a site of violent conflict between the parents, each of them becoming attached to one part of the name (the mother seemed to win out in this case, since the institution used only the part of the name which she favoured), the patient here playing out the oscillatory undecidability of the problem. In other cases, it is the child who refuses the name he or she has been given and is thus placed in a paranoid position.

The most developed shifters in ontogenesis – and hence the most fragile ones – are personal pronouns. Before a child is able to handle personal pronouns in all their subtlety and flexibility, we observe the phenomenon of pronoun inversion in which he/she refers to him- or herself in the third person. This inversion continues for a prolonged period in cases of childhood autism. The dialectic between 'I' and 'you' leads to the assertion of particular attitudes, depending upon the prevalent pathological tendencies. An ethology of deixis can be derived from this.

(See also IMPRINTING; PERFORMATIVES; SEMIOLOGY AND SEMIOTICS OF COMMUNICATION; SYMBOLS.)

J.M.

shock waves Murray Bowen (1978a, b) describes the existence of emotive shock waves as chain reactions (symptoms, accidents, sudden changes) which will affect different members of a family group, who may possibly be far removed from one another, and will do so over a varying time-scale, following the death or change of position of a key family member.

This key person may be the founder of a dynasty, or a special child who is particularly cathected, or a group member with a particular aura, power or prestige. A modification of that initial arrangement, such as death, the physical or symbolic exclusion of someone, may, over several months or years, lead to the triggering of various symptoms: disaffection with school, abortions, separations, the appearance of a manic or melancholic crisis etc. Usually, the members of the family recognize no cause–effect relation between the initial event and the incidents or accidents which follow.

We may reasonably postulate that there is, in fact, no material or efficient causality here, whether it be linear or circular, but rather a formal causality which is linked to the morphogenetic constraints to which the group is subject or to what Thom (1988, pp. 39 and 197) calls 'propagation of pregnance'. Drawing on

ELEMENTARY CATASTROPHES, we can develop a model of this: the family, as a system of biological and cultural reproduction is the interference space between the wave fronts of two reproduction processes and the product of this manifests itself in shock waves. Such a hypothesis enables us to view the contexts in which psychotic or psychosomatic symptoms arise in a new light. In certain cases, the shock wave strikes social organizations:

- educational and legal organizations in the case of families which reproduce biologically but which are deficient in the organization of their cultural reproduction (DISENGAGED FAMILIES);
- health organizations in the case of families which reproduce culturally, but which place rigid constraints upon the emotional and 'biological' development of their members (ENMESHED FAMILIES).

(See also DIFFERENTIATION OF SELF; FAMILY SYSTEMS; MOURNING; SOCIAL ORGANIZATION; SYMBOLIC REFERENCE.)

J.M.

sibling position profiles An expression coined by Toman in 1961 and used by Bowen (1978a) in an attempt to understand the immediate insight that is likely to precipitate a particular member of the family into the position of generally recognized symptom-bearer. This profile involves both the position within the family (firstborn, youngest etc.), certain physical characteristics and features of character and sex and assumes meaning in the context of the perception of all these characteristics (Wynne et al., 1958; Bowen, 1978a).

P.S.

'siding' See MULTI-DIRECTIONAL PARTIALITY.

singularities From the topological point of view, a singularity is the point on a curve for which a derivative of order n comes to equal zero. The singularities or critical points of a curve qualitatively describe that curve and the functions it represents.

One may thus define a singularity as a function describing the specific 'logos' of an organism or a group of living organisms. The singular points or critical points of the system describe its particular, unique qualitative aspects which differentiate it from equivalent systems. Size, tone of voice, the metaphors employed and the unique function of the symptom are thus the singularities of a given family system. Similarly, the unique

way that each family structures its eating habits, its management of money and its symbolic values enables one to describe the singularities of the system.

Thus a symptom possesses general features (insomnia, anorexia, schizophrenia) and singularities characteristic of a given situation. 'Prescribing the symptom' (see PRESCRIPTION) relates not to the common, generic aspect, as revealed by the medical or social diagnosis, but to the singularities specific to a given patient and family. For example, 'prescribing the symptom' to an insomniac consists not in telling him or her not to sleep, but, for example, in telling him/her to accomplish an activity, in a determinate period of time, at certain moments when he/she cannot get to sleep. The singularities of prescription arise out of the clinical understanding which emerges from the patient's story and emotions, as these are taken on board, in an equally singular way, by the therapist.

Very often the singularities of the system that are pertinent for an intervention reveal themselves through incidents in the interaction between family and therapist. An absent member, an apparently aberrant temperamental reaction, a bizarre idea or an original perception are capable of illuminating the functional singularities of the family group and the critical points at which change can occur.

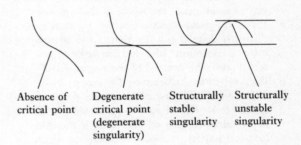

| Absence of critical point | Degenerate critical point (degenerate singularity) | Structurally stable singularity | Structurally unstable singularity |

Example of the appearance of a symptom with a structurally stable singularity and a structurally unstable singularity.

Elkaim (1985) describes a singularity as an ASSEMBLAGE made up of unique and singular elements. He distinguishes between:

- the level of intrinsic and general rules;
- signifying singularities (which belong to the intrinsic rules but are specific to the members of the system under consideration);
- non-signifying singularities (which are heterogeneous to the system under consideration and refer only to themselves).

(See also DYNAMIC SYSTEMS; FAMILY MYTHS; REALITY; SYMPTOMS.)

J.M. & M.G.

sleep See DREAMS, NIGHTMARES, SLEEP AND THE WAKING STATE.

social myths See INSTITUTIONAL MYTHS, SOCIAL MYTHS.

social organization A human group presenting a set of common features:

1 It possesses a specific structure in which statuses and roles are allotted to persons having different qualifications and belonging to distinct familial and social backgrounds.
2 It is characterized by the combination of cooperation and hierarchy, which brings with it horizontal divisions (division of labour) and vertical ones (hierarchy enabling a distinction to be made between executive and administrative tasks).
3 It is made up of a multiplicity of decision centres. Each person may, in effect, be looked upon as a decision centre to the extent that, from the bottom to the top of the hierarchy, he/she can cause his/her behaviour to vary, even minimally, in such a way as to influence the whole of the organization.
4 It seeks to attain objectives, which are more or less distinctly defined as a function of the interplay of internal constraints (the decision centres) and external ones (the demand of the rest of society and the competition confronting the group).
5 It has an officially established part, which corresponds to its formal operational framework and a non-established part which makes it possible, by informal activity, to deal with situations which are not foreseen by the framework within which it is established.

A great deal of work has been devoted to the theory of organizations (Simon, 1945–7; March and Simon, 1958; Boudon and Bourricaud, 1982; Handy, 1985). Systemic intervention-based studies have also been proposed (see, for example, Selvini Palazzoli et al., 1978, 1981). We shall confine ourselves here to examining a number of points relating to the organizational contexts of family interventions, in relation to the social organizations on which they are officially dependent.

IDENTIFICATION WITH THE ORGANIZATION

The advantage of the theory of organizations is that it identifies factors playing a part in processes of identification which had escaped the grasp of the classic psychoanalytical approach (see IDENTIFICATION). In fact,

in *Group psychology and the analysis of the ego*, Freud saw too direct a relationship in the individual's identification with the leader of an undifferentiated mass, thus leaving himself unable to grasp the intermediate levels of organization and the multiplicity of specific identifications which result from these.

Simon (1945–7) distinguishes between personal motivations, which lead to identification with oneself and one's own family, and impersonal motivations which lead to identification with a social organization. He thus defines identification with an organization as 'the process whereby the individual substitutes organizational objectives . . . for, his own aims as the value-indices which determine his organizational decisions' (Simon, 1945–7, p. 218).

In this latter case, identification concerns an abstract entity, namely identification with the goals of – or protection of – a given organization. To speak of 'the French' or 'the Americans', of 'the psychiatric hospital' or the 'district clinic', or of 'psychoanalysis' or 'family therapy' amounts to identifying with collective organizations in their formal and informal, official and unofficial aspects.

Such identification with the organization does, however, lead sooner or later to a confusion. The clients of an organization are, in effect, members of that organization, whether that membership is explicit or not. We might add that, in the fields of health, education and treatment, the families of 'clients' are also full members of the organizations which take care of them, whence the METABINDINGS with which the professionals in these fields are irretrievably confronted (see FAMILY–THERAPEUTIC INSTITUTION DIFFERENTIATION).

Family therapy is thus most peculiarly confronted with this disjunction between personal and impersonal motivation in the identificatory processes of the patients and their close relatives and in the identificatory processes of the various professionals involved.

HEALTH, EDUCATION AND JUDICIAL ORGANIZATIONS

These are non-profit-making organizations (outside the economic market), which have within them, in the public sector, a considerable bureaucratic element, emphasizing the importance of rules, of the authority of the state, of hierarchies, of the executive role of the directors and of relative insensitivity to personal motivations.

Social organizations are founded on a basic myth which might be spelled out as follows: 'The professionals, by their status, must take on and resolve all the people's problems, for which they are held to be responsible, whatever the difficulties encountered and even where there is no technical solution at the level at which the problem is posed.'

By the division of labour it implies, social organizations are necessarily faced with a number of contradictions.

First, public health is based on the prevention of ill-nesses, the maintenance of good sanitary conditions and the treatment of actual disorders. It has no direct access, however, either to the control of health in schools, or to the control of pathological disorders which entail the involvement of the legal system.

Secondly, the modern school is based on the care and education of children, their acquisition of a certain level of culture and the development of their person-alities. It is, however, unable to cope as soon as serious schooling problems arise when these are connected with pathological phenomena or medico-legal incidents.

Thirdly the judicial system is based on the applica-tion of the LAW which creates a framework for the education and socialization of children and it inter-venes in various cases where the family fails in its mission (abandonment, temporary fostering of abused children, marital conflict, divorce etc.). In carrying out their tasks, however, neither judges nor residential social workers have any legal authority to intervene at a therapeutic level, as is attested by a great deal of thinking which relates precisely to family therapy (see DEMAND; FAMILY DOCTOR; PSYCHOSOMATIC MEDICINE; SYSTEMIC MODELLING AND INTERVENTION).

The following point deserves attention: the family brings together in a single entity the functions and objectives peculiar to its organization; by contrast, society is obliged to separate these, in order to pro-pose a collective synthesis for each function and each objective.

All coherent thinking on the interaction between family organizations and social organizations is thus based on a twofold approach.

1   Differentiating out the levels referred to above within the consulting families in order to help them to reorganize themselves in response to their spe-cific difficulties. The intervenor offers a framework, establishes boundaries, seeks to define the problem better, to distinguish the functions and statuses of the various family members and to clarify their modes of thinking, perception and action.
2   Combining levels in the organization of social inter-ventions (police, judges, social workers, residential social workers, psychologists, nurses, psychiatrists, paediatricians, general practitioners, speech thera-pists, psychometricians etc.) in order to enable them not to fall into the traps of therapeutic ALIENATION. In practice, combining levels in this way leads to networking, to meetings between professionals with differing responsibilities, which modifies the con-tacts with the families being received for therapy and improves the levels of response to the symp-toms that are expressed.

We shall note here that the most productive forms of training for family therapy are based on multi-occupational groups. We shall also note that the organ-ization of social interventions which may result from this remains, to a great degree, an open programme.

ORGANIZATION OF SYSTEMIC INTERVENTIONS

We shall only deal here with a number of matters relating to the organization of treatment involving the activities of family therapy and systemic intervention. In actual fact, it is not sufficient simply to model fam-ilies and intervene with them. The question very soon arises of the changes which arise in the overall pattern made up by all the treatment activities relating to the particular patient concerned.

Some observations
Selvini Palazzoli et al. (1986) offer several observations, which are, allegedly, valid for different types of social organization: hospitals, schools, enterprises. First, when a psychologist is called in, it is often on the initiative of a person or group who is in a losing position, in order to establish an implicit coalition against someone who is assumed to be winning. Secondly, depending upon the sociopolitical circumstances, an organization shows a desire for change by setting in place costly struc-tures; within these structures, unrealized projects and factional struggles proliferate, with the appearance of symptoms in one or more persons. Lastly, a manifest disagreement at the top of a decision-making hierarchy may serve as a means of controlling the situation from that very point. This disagreement is resolved as soon as the need to do so is felt.

Specialization and unity of command
This last point connects with the thinking of Simon, who stressed (1945–7) the mutual contradiction be-tween the two principles to which any administrative organization is subject: the need for specialization and the need for unity of command.

The problem of specialization: there is a horizontal specialization, which leads to a division of labour, and a vertical specialization which leads to a hierarchy of decision centres. Though the question of decision-making is unavoidable, the real problem is to know how it is to be organized. Should one, for example, have geographical or functional specialization? Should inter-institutional family therapy units be created for a particular geographical area, for example, or should a large number of micro-units be set up within each existing specialist service?

The problem of unity of command: this is as unavoid-able as the question of specialization. A man cannot obey two contradictory orders at the same time in response to demands arising from different specialist interventions. From a systemic point of view, the symptom is precisely a solution to this problem. The problem is an obvious one in schizophrenic or psycho-somatic pathology (see PSYCHOSOMATIC DOUBLE BINDS;

THERAPEUTIC DOUBLE BINDS), when hospitalization, the taking of medication and consideration of the patient's family organization all have to be managed at the same time. In Simon's view, it appears that the imperative of specialization takes precedence in such cases over the need for unity of command.

There can be no theoretical solution to this contradiction since the problem is the solution. Hence the need to recognize double binds which generate confusion and irresponsibility and which are, precisely, the mainsprings of creativity and decision-making.

There is a further contradiction which concerns the span of control of the administrators responsible for each functional unit in the hierarchy. The narrower that span of control, the greater the extent of bureaucracy, with a concomitant loss of identification with the whole organization. The broader the span of control, however, the weaker the span of control of each administrator (Simon, 1945–7).

Family intervention unit
The creation of a family intervention unit within an organization poses various problems. A minimal functional unit is based on an alliance between at least two persons within the organization who are ready to organize themselves with a view to achieving their goal. This is the minimal level at which a set-up for cooperation (CO-THERAPY) in, and hierarchization (SUPERVISION) of, interventions can be established. These two minimal persons will have to manage the contradictions inherent in these two imperatives, which generate the myth of their alliance.

This alliance will bring about resistance on two fronts: on the front of the consulting family systems and on that of the organization to which the functional unit thus created is answerable. The myths of organization (see above) and of the family will then support each other mutually in parrying the threat of change which is now present: an important part of the work consists in sustaining and indeed in encouraging these respective myths instead of trying to destroy them. Another part of the work consists in differentiating between them as a function of the myth of systemic intervention.

This myth might, for example, be spelled out in the following way: 'We shall not take the decisions which are the responsibility of the professionals who have to consider your problem (judges, psychiatrists etc.), but we propose to help you and to help them to find more satisfactory solutions than those currently available.'

In spite of all this, a problem of loyalty to the overall organization will arise. Identifications with the various different levels of the organization will inevitably be conflictual. But the conflict is likely to be a lever for change, if it is accompanied by mutually recognized reciprocal skills and a sharing of authority, it being possible to define authority as the capacity to take decisions accepted by others who may possibly belong to

positions which are not all lower in the hierarchy (a person in a high position may very well recognize the authority of a person in a lower position).

The intervenors with the family will have to take care not to seek to treat the organization as such or to act as its systemic consultant.

A frequent difficulty arises out of the collusion which exists between the organization and the institution of which the family therapy unit is officially a part. Reducing thinking on therapeutic interventions to the problems of the institution reveals a peculiar reduction of the work to its 'organizing canvas'. The officially instituted organization becomes a self-generating end in itself, not a means enabling certain ends to be achieved. Hence the surprise at recognizing the 'institution' as hyper-rigid or hyper-homeostatic, which is precisely its function. The institution must be a static form; the organization, for its part, is a metabolic form. To speak only of the institution is equivalent to reducing the study of the human organism to its anatomy, without taking any account whatever of its physiology.

(See also COMMUNAL INDIVIDUALS; FAMILY ROLE; INSTITUTIONS; MULTI-LEVEL HIERARCHIES; POWER; SELF-ORGANIZATION; SOCIAL STATUS; TANGLED HIERARCHIES.)

J.M.

social role   See FAMILY ROLE, SOCIAL ROLE.

social status, legal status   Social status is the semi-official position which an individual occupies within a group or a group occupies within a society (the latter being understood as a group of groups). It has a horizontal dimension, i.e. the network of contacts at the same level and a vertical dimension, i.e. contacts and exchanges up and down the hierarchical scale.

(Social) status articulation concerns the decisions a person must make as to which of his/her role-sets to give priority to. When status articulation does not become routine, or when that routine is broken, a role conflict appears (Laub Coser and Rokoff, 1974).

Legal status is, by contrast, defined by the body of laws governing all a person's relationships, both egalitarian and hierarchical, within a legally recognized familial or social group. It corresponds to the official legislation regarding positions in a role-set. Legal status is the set of behaviours which an individual may legitimately expect on the part of others in the social positions which are institutionally allotted to them. Legal status contributes to giving a sense of security and confidence in the performance of one's role (Stoezel, 1978). It implies the clarification of hierarchical positions and of the processes governing movement up and down the various hierarchies.

More or less conflictual oppositions may thus exist between family and social status (who is the most competent, most popular, most devoted, the decision-maker etc?) and legal status (who is authorized to act, think and make decisions?).

SOCIOLOGY OF INSTITUTIONS AND RELATIONAL SOCIOLOGY OF THE FAMILY

The distinction between legal status and social status corresponds to a difference between two points of view on the family (Bastide, 1965).

First, the *institutional* point of view, defended by Durkheim and French sociology, views the family as a social institution, the organization of which is regulated and controlled by church and state. Thus divorce is subject to laws and the marital bond cannot be broken in the eyes of the church. In this institutional perspective, a marriage is seen as an affective group engaged in social cooperation. This point of view, which is also favoured by Bastide, has dominated French psychiatry down to the present and doubtless explains the various forms of institutional 'reticence' toward the family therapy movement in France.

Secondly, the *relational* point of view, as represented in the work of Talcott Parsons, is, essentially, the Anglo-Saxon perspective. It stresses conjugal relations, parent/child relations, the relations between siblings and grandparent/parent/child relations. It is, broadly, the conception which underlies the family therapy movement. To give an example quoted by Bastide (1965), we may note that the paranoid forms of schizophrenia seem to develop more in families where the patient is rejected, whereas catatonic forms seem to appear in families where the patient is overprotected. This observation would be perfectly compatible with the correlations proposed by Jackson (1977) between the forms of SCHIZOPHRENIAS and the structure of family relations.

THE DISTINCTION BETWEEN HOME AND WORK

The distinction between HOME and work is a basic element in the understanding of the organization of statuses and roles in Western societies. The separation of the systems of family and professional activity and the way in which emergency situations are regulated, both within the family and in respect of work, make it possible to identify the status differences between men and women (Laub Coser and Rokoff, 1974).

Cultural mandate establishes the normative priorities in routine and emergency situations. It allows the temporary abandonment of an anticipated role. When a routine is broken, status articulation makes it possible for family and professional functioning to be regulated. If a child falls ill, status articulation will indicate, for example, that it is the mother (and not the father) who will stay at home and look after him/her; this will cause a break in the mother's occupation of her place at work. If some professional task has to be urgently accomplished, status articulation may very well indicate that it is the father who has to do it (not the mother), which will bring about a temporary break in his presence within the family. These examples have more to do with customs than with norms and are subject to wide variation in actual clinical experience.

LEGAL STATUS AND ROLE OF THE MENTAL PATIENT

As Bastide (1965) stresses, the mental patient has a particular legal status. The price to be paid upon hospitalization is a heavy one and this may become particularly iatrogenic when hospitalization lasts for a long time. The processes of everyday interaction disappear in hospital:

the patient no longer has may familial relations, and even sexual relations are theoretically forbidden; he is deprived of his professional life, and even if he takes part in occupational therapy he is not paid for the work he does. He also enters a new, strongly hierarchical society where mobility is blocked and communication is structured. (Bastide, 1977 edn, p. 191)

By seeing the families of hospitalized patients, one is able to modify this apparently clear-cut picture and evaluate the compromise situations between the pathological state and problems of material and psychical space which are at the centre of mental alienation; continuing with family interviews in outpatient treatment confirms the analysis which Bastide, following Davis et al. (1957), made of the family structure of hospitalized patients:

it is important to differentiate between the conjugal family and the parental family. It is only the former that refuses to take back the patient until he is able to work; the parental family accepts the patient who cannot readjust to an occupation, since his role as the dependent and assisted 'child' is the only one his parents expect. (Bastide, 1977 edn, p. 193)

The definition of this problem by families in schizophrenic transaction is, in fact, essential for the conduct of treatment.

(See also FAMILY MYTHS; FAMILY ROLE, SOCIAL ROLE; FAMILY RULES; INSTITUTIONAL MYTHS; INSTITUTIONS; LAW; SOCIAL ORGANIZATION.)

J.M.

sociodrama   Defined by Moreno (1934) as a method of research into, and action upon, collective ideologies and the relations which form between groups. Whereas PSYCHODRAMA is centred on the individual and the resonances he/she creates in the audience, sociodrama has as its protagonist the group as such.

Sociodramatic techniques may be adopted to study the interface between a family and the social groups on which it is dependent. In training groups, the conjoint simulation of a family *in situ* and its various members involved in their social and institutional relationships may possibly be undertaken.

(See also ANTI-THEATRE; FAMILIODRAMA.)

J.M.

sociogenetics of family schisms   Maruani (1982a) proposed a sociogenetic model of family schisms applying the laws of Gregor Mendel to cultural rather than biological traits, each such trait being provided by the endowments of the parents, who are themselves either culturally homozygotic or heterozygotic.

The development of mores and, in particular, ACCULTURATION introduce a dynamic dimension, modifying the dominant or recessive quality of a cultural trait. Myth can then be seen as corresponding to a cultural genotype and behaviour to a cultural phenotype (Maruani, 1985b). The competence in behaviour transformation that is necessary for adaptation to a developing environment (i.e. for a socially acceptable performance) will be dependent upon the fit between inherited mythemes and the demands of acculturation. The emphasis is thus placed on temporality as a motor of family equilibrium. Berenstein (1976) and, after him, Eiguer (1983) distinguish an unconscious mythical time in which past and present are conflated in a debt towards the preceding generation, particularly where the giving of the bride by her family has not been met by a reciprocal gift on the part of the husband to form the bond of alliance. On the other hand, mythic time, though it orders the unconscious structure of the family, is the product of thinking by individuals *en famille*. 'Family myths provide information about present needs and circulate to resolve insoluble contradictions' (Berenstein, 1976, in Eiguer, 1983, p. 68).

(See also DECULTURATION; FAMILY MYTHS.)

G.G.M.

sofa-bed syndrome   A term proposed by Maruani (1982a) for the logical impasse observed in families of schizophrenics as a result of a generational grammar of schismatic behaviours.

In an article of 1976, devoted to the everyday life of adult psychotics treated as hospital outpatients, Verbizier et al. noted the frequency (two cases in three) with which they lived with their parent(s) and slept in the same room as another adult. In this context, the concept of fusional relation finds its image in the cases where sofa-beds are unfolded for sleeping on, preventing either person from getting up individually, particularly where a mother and child are involved. According to Verbizier et al. (1976), the problem for the families consists in getting the schizophrenic patients out of bed. It is not that they are asleep, but they have great difficulty getting moving and need to be stimulated or even threatened each day.

A sofa-bed is an ambiguous object: is it for sitting or lying on? And what are we to say about the analyst's couch? (a question taken up by Anzieu, 1983). The schizophrenic will attempt to flesh out the two meanings of the sofa-bed *at the same time*. What better way to do this, given the situation, than not to sleep at night and not to get up in the daytime, or, in other words, to produce the symptoms of insomnia and apragmatism? Rougeul has published a highly revealing case-study (1983) in which the inability to leave a psychiatric hospital stands in direct relation to the myth and rules of a family in which the patient's bed is not the one one thinks it is, in which she stresses the context-revealing function played by the bed which also serves as an element of temporal reinforcement of double binds. It very frequently occurs, in fact, in clinical practice, that one only discovers after a great number of interviews with the family that the indicating patient has no bed of his/her own or indeed may even have no pillow when he/she shares a bed with another member of the household.

Admittedly, the child's bed is the container and metonymic representative of the parental bed, the symbolic *anchoring point* which is necessary for instinctive–affective development. We also know, however, the degree to which psychosis reactivates conflicts connected with cultural changes of a historical order. According to Philippe Aries (1977), in the Middle Ages, in Western Europe, the site of marriage was the *bed*. Not the bedroom, but the bed. There is nothing more symbolic in this regard than the place of the bed in the bedroom, in a dark corner, far from the heat and light of the hearth, the site of sociability. Then there was a shift, without any brutal transition from vigilant, extra-marital sexuality, which avoided coitus, from medieval courtly love and the pre-marital sexuality of modern peasant cultures, to coitus interruptus, the dark secret which served the industrial societies of the nineteenth century and the beginning of the twentieth as a highly effective means of contraception. The internal walls by which marriage was compartmentalized were taken away, as were the panels or curtains which enclosed the bed: The function of the bed was extended to the whole of the bedroom. The old places of refuge of wild sexuality, like the box bed, became sites of domestication.

The schizophrenic's clinophilia (i.e. 'love of his/her bed') therefore appears both as incarnation of the primal scene over-territorialized and placed outside time, and as metacommunication that the sexuality of the parental couple has been unable either to confine itself to the closed space of the bed or to conform to a temporal, technical form of organization. The sofa-bed, with its dual use contested, is the best metaphor for this.

(See also DISTANCE; MAPS; MULTI-CHANNEL COMMUNICATION SYSTEMS; TERRITORY.)

G.G.M.

solution-focused therapy An approach which has developed over the past decade out of the traditions of the interactional approach to brief therapy (Watzlawick et al., 1974; Weakland et al., 1974; Watzlawick and Weakland, 1977; Bodin, 1981; Fisch et al., 1982) and the work of the psychiatrist/hypnotist Milton H. Erickson (Haley, 1973, 1985; Erickson et al., 1976; Erickson and Rossi, 1979; Rossi, 1980; Rosen, 1982; O'Hanlon, 1987). The approach has been developed primarily by the members of the Brief Family Therapy Center, Milwaukee (de Shazer and Molnar, 1984; de Shazer, 1985, 1988, 1991; de Shazer et al., 1986; Berg, 1991; Berg and Miller, 1992). However, it has had a significant impact on the work of brief therapists throughout the world and an increasing number of books and papers are being published describing the application of the ideas (O'Hanlon and Weiner-Davis, 1989; Durrant and Kowalski, 1990; Dolan, 1991; Furman and Ahola, 1992; Walter and Peller, 1992).

In 1984, de Shazer and Molnar described a routine first-session task given to clients, couples or families regardless of the problem with which they presented.

Between now and the next time we meet, we (I) want you to observe, so that you can tell us (me) next time, what happens in your (life, marriage, family, or relationship) that you want to continue to have happen. (de Shazer and Molnar, 1984, p. 298)

They found that concrete and significant changes had often occurred by the following session that could then be built upon. This first-session task was empirically tested by Adams et al., who found that it 'was an effective intervention in the initial stages of treatment for gaining family compliance, increasing the clarity of treatment goals, and initiating improvement in the presenting problem' (Adams et al., 1991, p. 288).

In *Keys to solution in brief therapy* (de Shazer, 1985), it was suggested that solutions are not necessarily as closely related to the problems they address as is usually assumed. Several 'formula interventions' were described through which the process of developing solutions could be started, often without knowing very much, or sometimes anything, about the nature of the problem to be solved. The analogy of a skeleton key

was used. Many doors can be opened with such a key without the need to find the correct key that fits the exact shape of the lock. In 1986, the Milwaukee team described the principles of the solution-focused approach (de Shazer, 1986) which concentrates on what is working or beginning to work in a client's or family's life, rather than on the exploration, clarification or categorization of a pathology with its origins seen as located in the past or the present.

As summarized further in *Clues: investigating solutions in brief therapy* (de Shazer, 1988), the approach is based on the certainty that there are invariably exceptions to the behaviours, ideas, feelings and interactions that are, or could be, associated with the problem. There are times when a depressed person feels less sad, when an obsessive person can relax, when a couple will resolve rather than escalate a conflict, when a bulimic resists the urge to binge, when a child does not have a tantrum on being asked to tidy a room, when an 'alchoholic' does contain drinking to within sensible limits. Yet, as de Shazer observes,

Problems are seen to maintain themselves simply because they maintain themselves and because clients depict the problem as always happening. Therefore, times when the complaint is absent are dismissed as trivial by the client or even remain completely unseen, hidden from the client's view. Nothing is actually hidden, but although these exceptions are open to view, they are not seen by the client as differences that make a difference. (de Shazer, 1991, p. 58)

Clients are invited to recognize and to build on what they are already doing that can be seen as dealing more effectively with the problem. Of course, to be persuaded to consider these 'successes', it is clearly important that these exceptions are, or can be made, meaningful to the client or family. It is not enough that the therapist considers them significant.

Another technique central to the approach is the *miracle question*.

Suppose that one night there is a miracle and while you are sleeping the problem that brought you into therapy is solved: How would you know? What would be different?
What will you notice different the next morning that will tell you that there has been a miracle? What will your spouse notice? (de Shazer, 1991, p. 113)

And de Shazer asserts, 'Clients frequently are able to construct answers to this "miracle question" quite concretely and specifically' (p. 133). Thus, the process of how the problem will be solved, and therefore many of the client's doubts, can be bypassed. The client, couple or the family members are encouraged to imagine, in as concrete a way as possible, what the many differences will be. The technique is a development of Milton Erickson's, hypnotic technique of pseudo-orientation in time (Erickson, 1954). O'Hanlon and Weiner-Davis contend, 'It appears that the mere act of constructing a vision of the solution acts as a catalyst for bringing it about' (O'Hanlon, 1987, p. 106). Tasks and suggestions are then put forward to help create a climate in which the behaviours which have been described can be carried out in reality.

Careful use is made of language to presuppose the inevitability of change. 'When' is used rather than 'if': 'what else will be different?' rather than 'what else would be different?'. 'As you become less inhibited' rather than 'If you were to become less inhibited'. 'When you stop hearing voices' rather than 'If you were to stop hearing voices'. Language is seen as highly important as is the frame through which people construe their difficulties. de Shazer describes the rapid resolution of a case of nymphomania through its being re-framed as the more easily addressed problem of insomnia. Each 'problem' had enough behavioural and emotional overlaps that could be highlighted such that either could become the legitimate area of focus (de Shazer, 1991, pp. 63–84).

Another important technique is that of asking *scaling questions*, used in a variety of ways. 'On a scale ranging from zero to ten where zero represents things at their worst, and ten represents how things will be when these problems are resolved, where would you place yourself today?' Built on the assumption of the inevitability if change, such scales can be used to look at any aspect of a person's life or of the process of therapy.

> scaling questions can be used to assess the client's self-esteem, self-confidence, investment in change, willingness to work hard to bring about desired changes, prioritizing of problems to be solved, perception of hopefulness, evaluation of progress, and so on – things considered too abstract to concretize. (Berg, 1991, p. 88)

Traditionally, therapies have been concerned with the past or with the present and with attempting to effect changes through the process of re-examination. The solution-focused approach assumes that the future exists in our anticipation of how it will be and thus is also open for re-examination even though it has not yet occurred. As Furman and Ahola summarize:

> Since the future is often connected to the past, people with a stressful past are prone to have a hopeless view of their future. In its turn a negative view of the future exacerbates current problems by casting a pessimistic shadow over both past and present.
>
> Fortunately, the converse is also true; a positive view of the future invites hope, and hope in its turn helps to cope with current hardships, to recognize

signs indicating the possibility of change, to view the past as an ordeal rather than a misery, and to provide the inspiration for generating solutions. (1992, p. 91)

de Shazer reports follow-up results of 'an 80.4 per cent success rate (65.6 per cent of the clients met their goal while 14.7 per cent made significant improvement) within an average of 4.6 sessions. When recontacted at 18 months, the success rate had increased to 86 per cent. In addition, 77 per cent reported no new problems had developed' (de Shazer, 1991, p. 161).

This approach, as with other brief approaches, has been criticized for being manipulative, over-simplistic and superficial as well as for failing adequately to address either the inner world of people or their wider sociopolitical context (Luepnitz, 1988; Flaskas, 1992). Alternatively, the results have been dismissed as 'transference cures' or 'flights into health'.

(See also BRIEF INTERACTIONAL THERAPY; COMMUNICATION; CONTEXT; MILAN SYSTEMIC THERAPY; POSITIVE CONNOTATION; STRATEGIC THERAPY; SYSTEMIC MODELLING AND INTERVENTION; THERAPEUTIC STRATEGIES AND TACTICS.)

B.C.

space–time Recording in space and time (territory) is one of the three basic axes of anthropology, alongside the maintenance of life (i.e. the need for food) and the reproduction of the species (essentially the sexual urge). 'What may be called an individual's ego space-time thus preserves the social topology of his childhood surroundings as well as the outline of his body image' (Erikson, 1968, p. 60).

As with the other axes, play and variations upon this constraint will be a source of pleasure. Though a certain number of strategies have been developed to disturb this spatiotemporal inscription in its spatial dimension (the myth of Icarus, the race for the moon, a week in the Seychelles), a certain modernity attaches to the disturbances of the temporal dimension. The vogue for 'face-lifts' and other 'youth-restoring' treatments is well known, but it is another 'skin game' I shall be focusing on here, a game which consists in trying to get *out* of one's skin. That game is drug use, since this is a practice which demonstrates, in a simple, unsophisticated way, the foundations of pleasure.

This is a perturbation of localization in time because it entangles the levels of absence. Absence in the real (privation), imaginary absence (frustration) or absence of the symbolic (castration): the drug addict has lost (or has not acquired) the art of discriminating between different levels. The first consequence of this will naturally be his incapacity to situate himself in a simple way in a specific relationship to settle a particular level of a problem. More profoundly, however, this mixing of levels will disturb the chronological ability which is developed through the organization of the different absence–repetition cycles. A one-dimensional incoherence sets in, instead of a multi-dimensional complexity. This – regressive – incoherence only produces pleasure if the spatial pole is guaranteed or fixed. The apparent 'trips' of drug addicts, which are searches for extremes, should not deceive us. The attempt of many observers to describe drug-takers as 'voyagers' is mere sleight of hand. All this is maybe arrived at intuitively from the fact of weight and dependence having a common etymology and the connection between the chemical 'high' and free fall reveals the importance of the humoral in spatiotemporal games.

(See also BOUNDARIES; DISTANCE AND ORGANIZATION OF TERRITORY; FAMILY MAPS; MAPS; OUTSIDE TIME, IN TIME; TOPOLOGICAL SPACE; TERRITORY.)

D.C.

speech acts The pragmatic nature of language has been studied by the British philosopher, Austin (1962). He distinguishes between three types of speech act:

1 *The locutionary act* is the mere fact of saying something, leaving out of account its intrinsic (illocutionary) and extrinsic (perlocutionary) effects.
2 *The illocutionary act* is the effect which the utterance produces in the act of saying something, as opposed to the mere fact of saying something: thus an utterance will have the status of a question, an opinion, an order etc.
3 *The perlocutionary act* is the effect which the utterance produces, by the fact of saying something to someone. Questions, opinions and orders are not just received by an interlocutor but produce in him or her respectively an effect of being questioned, of reflection and of obedience.

It is possible to distinguish between the different effects produced by speech acts by virtue of the different media employed: speech acts proper, written speech acts, telephone calls, interviews recorded on video etc. The therapeutic impact of each in clinical practice merits careful evaluation.

Saying 'It is fine today' is a *locutionary* act in so far as it provides information about the weather; it is an *illocutionary* act in so far as it strikes up conversation at a sufficiently informal and superficial level or suggests to one's interlocutor that he or she come out for a walk; it is a *perlocutionary* act if the interlocutor in fact joins in the conversation at the superficial level at which it has been initiated or if he/she is willing to go for a walk. Understanding a statement means, then, going beyond its communicational content to identify its pragmatic intention, i.e. its illocutionary value and force,

and also its perlocutionary effects (Kerbrat-Oerchioni, 1980, p.185). The hypothesis is that 'to speak is undoubtedly to exchange INFORMATION', but it is also to perform an act, governed by precise rules which claims to transform the situation of the hearer and modify his/her system of belief and/or his/her behavioural attitude in a verbal exchange. Remaining silent may be a way of getting someone else to speak or in other cases silence may take on overtones of aggression or pacification in reference to the particular context of verbal exchanges.

In family therapy, the following questions may be asked: 'Who is speaking and with what intent?' 'Who is speaking for whom?' 'Who is making whom speak?' Are the words spoken performative or are they, rather, seeking to disinform or to fill a relational void? A statement by any speaker is an act in the full sense; that act fits into the flow of communication; its uttering requires an expenditure of energy; the performative level of the speaker depends on his/her position in the relational, family and social systems within which he or she is inscribed. Certain speech acts have a particularly powerful effect in human relations, causing others to do what they decree; they thus possess the force of law.

What the different actors of the family group and the team of therapists do is thus expressed not only in enactments but also in the language transmitted and received within a particular context and conceived as a 'network of regularities governed by strategies' (Parret, 1980). The sign is put in relation to the context in which the language is produced. The nature of the media employed possesses specific intrinsic effects: the spoken word and direct visual monitoring enable one flexibly to modulate and nuance the contents of speech. A written letter may have, a priori, more lasting effects, but its very potency risks being disqualified in the most disturbed family systems; written style has to be quite distinct from spoken style.

The performative effects of speech acts are thus very much bound up with their metacommunicative functions and with the implicit messages to which these latter refer. Bateson makes a distinction between *metacommunicative messages* ('I was joking', 'this is play', 'don't get me wrong') and *metalinguistic messages* ('this sentence contains five words', 'the word "cat" does not scratch' etc.) (Bateson, 1972, pp. 150–66). The different linguistic media thus, each in their particular way, prescribe contextual modifications, the effects of which must, in practical use, be drawn on in varying doses.

(See also FAMILY SPOKESPERSON; LAW; MANIPULATION; METACOMMUNICATION SYSTEMS; PARACOMMUNICATION SYSTEMS; PERFORMATIVES; PRAGMATICS OF COMMUNICATION; SELF-FULFILLING PROPHECY.)

J.M. & P.G.

sphere See BALL; DISTANCE AND ORGANIZATION OF TERRITORY; MAPS; TANGLED HIERARCHIES; TERRITORY.

split double bind A concept developed by Ferreira (1960) to describe antinomic messages belonging to distinct and contradictory logical types, emanating generally from two parental figures whom the child regards as being of equal importance.

In Ferreira's view, the conditions necessary for it to be effective are as follows:

- two 'binders' A and B, usually the parents in a complementary one-up position (dominance);
- a 'victim', usually a child of the family in a complementary one-down position (dependence);
- series of messages from A and B to C, connected in time and yet, at the same time, of different logical levels in terms of their – verbal and non-verbal – content, so that A's message, for example, is a commentary on B's message, implying condemnation or destruction of that message.

Furthermore, the victim C must be in a position to attribute a relatively equal value to the two messages (emanating from two equally vital sources) and finds him- or herself exposed to the full force of the affective-logical conflict produced by their interaction. The messages involved are often contradictory negative injunctions of the type:

1 *A to C*: 'You mustn't. . . .'
2 *B to C*: 'You mustn't (obey, listen to etc.) that message of A's.' When faced with such a contradiction, the victim C can only obey the one by disobeying the other and finds him/herself, by that token, 'in the wrong' or 'rebelling' and thus at constant risk of being punished by the one or the other.

Such a mode of interaction has frequently been observed in family systems in which delinquent conduct arises among the young, though this type of communication cannot be considered as the simple explanation of delinquency, any more than the DOUBLE BIND can account for the whole aetiology of schizophrenia. In both cases, we are dealing with pathogenic situations, the scope of which is distinctly wider than the triggering and maintentenance of a single type of behaviour (see SYMPTOMATIC AND/OR AETIOLOGICAL TRANSACTIONS).

It will be noted that the concept of double bind processes may be further extended in two different directions. First, the split may occur between more than two persons: a grandparent, uncle or dead ancestor may continue to send more or less concealed messages, which totally contradict those coming from the parents (see LOYALTY). Secondly, one and the same person may generate and transmit to another person *n* messages which are mutually antinomic.

We ought, following Hoffmann (1981), to distinguish between paradoxical injunctions and double binds properly so called; paradoxical injunctions do, in fact, represent a pressure for change. They are also known as 'simple binds', when the communicational paradox is an open one: a parent's paradoxical injunction to a child may be, 'I want you to be independent, but I also want you to want this independently of my wanting it!' The *simple bind* at one and the same time accepts the confusion of levels (desire for independence) and resolves it. By contrast, pathological double binds block off any possible leap forward and generate escalating confusion, without any reward appearing when progress is registered.

The concept of double bind may therefore be extended, so that we may speak of multiple binds or *n*-binds (*n* possibly varying from 0 to infinity). On the plane of therapy or the resolution of problems, it is possible to conceive of THERAPEUTIC DOUBLE BINDS or MULTIPLE BINDS as responses to the antinomic logic of psychotic or delinquent symptoms.

(See also ANTI-THEATRE; LAW; METABINDINGS; PSYCHOSOMATIC DOUBLE BINDS.)

P.S. & J.M.

split loyalties See LOYALTY, SPLIT LOYALTIES, INVISIBLE LOYALTIES.

splitting, individual and family For Freud in *Outline of psychoanalysis* (1938), splitting is a phenomenon which comes to light in psychoses and fetishism: in respect of a given behaviour, on a manifest plane, the subject adopts two opposed psychical attitudes, which are independent of each other. Thus an attitude which takes account of reality coexists with an attitude which detaches the ego from that reality. The difference from neurosis is topographical and structural in nature: neurotic 'splitting' pushes back the unreal alternative to the level of the id.

The term was taken up again in family therapy to describe the existence of split families, which are distinct from binding families, on the one hand, and from families in a state of dissolution, on the other (Stierlin, 1977). Family splitting is dependent upon particular modalities of COALITION within a family. Splitting designates the experiences of opposition, ALIENATION, distancing and denial leading to the isolation–interdependence of subsystems within the family.

From an individual point of view, Winnicott (1952) extends the theory of the splitting of the personality using the TRUE SELF/FALSE SELF distinction. Splitting is seen as arising as a result of the lack of an active adaptation of the environment which the child expects. 'Where there is a high degree of the tendency to split at this early stage, the individual is in danger of being seduced into a false life, and the instincts then come in on the side of the seducing environment' (Winnicott, 1952, p. 225).

Clinical experience shows that these splits are also produced between different members and different sub-systems of certain families. Only part of the family feels the need to consult, with the active and apparently agreed exclusion of one or more members of the family. For example, the mother may consult with her psychotic/autistic son or daughter (who may be an adult), forming a fusional and functional dyad, while the father is excluded from all initiative and decision-making. He is then isolated, disqualified and may possibly be described as an alcoholic refusing to receive attention. The split structure of the family may be repeated over several generations (Stierlin, 1977). It is the product of an initial reciprocal idealization of the partners, which has tipped over into total disparagement as soon as the first phases of enamourment have faded. The family split seems to rest on an internal–external explosion of individuals, cut off from their authentic functioning and from satisfactions which they none the less seek desperately within the family group. It is then impossible to separate the various members of the family, even though attention is noisily drawn to oppositions, break-ups and estrangements. While the separation and subsequent coming together again is both internal and external to each person, the autonomous cores, the ideal attractors which have brought them together continue fundamentally to be in resonance. The family split thus appears as a particular modality of family structuring, which has to be distinguished from the process of SCHISMOGENESIS (Wynne, 1961).

(See also PRINCIPLE OF COMPLEMENTARITY; UNCERTAINTY PRINCIPLE.)

J.M. & P.S.

stalemate, 'deadly embrace' 'Stalemate' is an expression borrowed from the game of chess by Stierlin (1977) to denote the extreme form of negative reciprocity that has degenerated into a struggle for power. It is equivalent to the term 'deadly embrace' employed in computer science. In a case of stalemate, the system in question becomes completely frozen. In spite of what may possibly be dramatic surface agitation, nothing evolves inside the relationship, in which the partners are trapped in a kind of bodily combat. Such a stalemate may also arise in the absence of any symmetrical conflict when the relationship develops in a totally complementary way.

The alliances one finds in such a stalemate may either be blocked or shifting. Bowen writes

When tensions are very high in families and available family triangles are exhausted, the family system triangles in people from outside the family, such as police and social agencies. A successful externalisation of the tension occurs when outside workers are in conflict about the family while the family is calmer. (Bowen, 1978a, p. 201)

The structure of TRIANGLES in families depends on two variables: the level of DIFFERENTIATION OF SELF and the levels of anxiety and emotional tension in the system. The higher the level of anxiety or the lower the levels of differentiation of self, the more automatic triangulation intensifies. During periods of calm, a triangle is in constant movement. Therapy looks to modify the central triangle of the family which will modify other triangles within the family system.

(See also AGONISTIC BEHAVIOUR; COALITION; PERVERSE TRIANGLES; POWER.)

J.M.

static, pseudo-static and metabolic forms It is important, from a morphological point of view, in assessing an individual or a family or social group, to be aware which are the fixed and which the mobile components of the system under consideration, as well as the structure of the system's articulations. It is possible to formulate this perception precisely, taking a lead from the study of DYNAMIC SYSTEMS, by distinguishing between what Thom (1972, pp. 121–49) has termed static, pseudo-static and metabolic forms.

A *static* form is a form which has a punctual ATTRACTOR and rigid, geometrically simple boundaries, insensitive to variations. The dynamic of the system is a gradient dynamic and its structurally stable forms can be described in terms of ELEMENTARY CATASTROPHES. A very great variation of environmental conditions leads to the destruction of the system. A static form is, for example, an inorganic object, a tree trunk, an animal skeleton, a fixed sequence of behaviour, an interaction ritual. Very often the static character of an object can only be determined approximately. Such a form is most often *pseudo-static* in that it possesses, in spite of appearances, parts that are capable of being set in motion and can enter into resonance with metabolic forms. A book for a reader, a chair and a table for a person eating, a stick for a blind person etc. take on meaning in the dynamic interaction these objects enter into with their users.

A *metabolic* form is characterized by attractors with a high number of dimensions, evolving in a periodic or aperiodic manner and creating phenomena of resonance. The system possesses a dynamic in which there is recurrence (circular phenomena); the forms assumed by the system are GENERALIZED CATASTROPHES. Their boundaries are complex, developing as a function of the state of the internal and external environment. Examples of metabolic forms are fires, the neuromuscular systems of animals, learnt sequences of behaviour, the individual dimension of an interaction.

The interaction of several metabolic forms is capable, through coupling, of creating new forms and generating meaning effects. The greater the number of dimensions possessed by the attractors, the more complex the resonances and the more nuanced the meaning effects. The interaction of two persons or two groups engenders a social unit of change which may be regarded as a metabolic form, with its own frequencies relating to the cyclical movements that regulate it. The product of this is a unit of mind, as formed for example by the interaction between a writer, a book and readers.

When generalized catastrophes occur, metabolic forms may perform like static forms and thus lose their semantic potentialities. Families termed 'families with rigid transactions' are typically static forms, their form of organization being reduced to that of a 'survival unit'. Their attractors (superego functions, collective ideals) are reduced to punctual minima of potential. The behaviour of others is then perceived in a linear and Manichaean manner. On the level of family and social organization, the greater the critical risk, the more the units fall back into rigid interactions of stereotyped hierarchies or symmetrical escalations. Many neurotic, psychosomatic, psychotic or perverse symptoms are an expression of static forms. The obsessional's ritual, the apragmatism of the hebephrenic, the loss of independent motor activity of the catatonic are the most visible manifestation of the static forms of the families of which they are members. In fact, a unit with rigid transactions, is never static, but corresponds to a pseudo–static form: attractors continue to oscillate to a greater or lesser degree. The DOUBLE BIND may thus be conceived as an oscillatory residue of degraded symbols.

The advantage of a model of this kind is that it takes into account the morphological constraints to which systems are subject. Causality is not merely linear or circular. It is also formal. Meaning is a by-product of the topological properties of the interacting morphologies. A static or pseudo–static form can only possibly acquire a meaning if articulations with meta-bolic forms are sought out. A meaning cannot simply be found by desperate efforts to mobilize their internal structures. This is to say that, in an interaction, perception and intuition on the part of the protagonists are essential for meaning effects to be derived. Whence the interest of a therapeutic technique such as SCULPT-ING, which brings out the fixed and mobile components of interactions.

(See also AGREEMENT AND DISAGREEMENT; CHREOD; EVOLUTIONARY SURVIVAL UNIT; FAMILY CATASTROPHES; SEMANTIC RESONANCES; SEMANTIC UNIT OF MIND; UNIT OF CHANGE.)

J.M.

stochastic processes A sequence of events is described as 'stochastic' when it combines a random component with a selective process so that certain outcomes are preferred to others.

In several of his works (*Mind and nature, Steps to an ecology of mind*), Bateson advances the hypothesis that biological evolution (genetic change) and learning (somatic change) are stochastic processes. He thus views evolution and the process of thought as two double stochastic processes functioning alternately: 'In each case there is, I believe, a stream of events that is random in certain aspects and in each case there is a non-random selective process which causes certain of the random components to "survive" longer than others' (Bateson, 1979, p. 147).

Genetic change and somatic change are fundamentally similar by dint of their stochastic nature. The one extends over several generations and operates through heredity for a whole population and is termed evolution. The other extends over one life only, is located within an individual and is known as learning.

In both these types of change, the processes at work create a considerable number of possibilities and, from among these, selection eliminates the ones which would not be favourable from the point of view of survival. The difference resides in the way in which these possibilities are stored. The random mutations which constitute the possibilities of genetic change are stored in the genetic heritage of the population, whereas the possibilities of learning and somatic adaptation are stored in the individual.

Bateson believes that these two great stochastic systems, operating at different logical levels, are both autonomous and interacting, this latter point being essential to life. Genetic change is, in his view, a stochastic process of a higher logical level than the stochastic process relating to somatic change. He notes that genetic change represents an economical solution to a situation that has become chronic and that it may avoid the price of imposing rigidity on the system by being delayed until the circumstance which was coped with by the soma at a reversible level is indeed permanent. Moreover, genetic change probably does not operate directly on phenotypic variables, but on the homeostatic control of these variables, i.e. by modifying their tolerance limits and by broadening their scope for variation and change.

The random element, genetic change, is produced either by mutation or by the reshuffling of genes among the members of a population. However, the degree of change is limited:

1 Somatic adaptations cannot rashly become genetic changes. They remain reversible thanks to the Weissmannian barrier between soma and gene plasma.
2 Sexual reproduction provides a guarantee that the new genetic blueprint will not be too incompatible with the old. What is new in the ovum must meet with what is old in the spermatozoon and vice versa.

Somatic change has its origin in external adaptation, in interaction between the individual (the phenotype) and its environment. The random element resides in that interaction: 'Between them, environment and physiology *propose* somatic change that may or may not be viable, and it is the current state of the organism as determined by *genetics* that determines the viability' (Bateson, 1979, p. 178).

These two stochastic systems are therefore very closely related in so far as, if, ultimately, the random element which proposes change is the combination of the phenotype and the environment, it is, none the less, the genetic state which disposes, which prohibits certain changes and permits others. The individual, like the population, possesses a bank of available potentialities for adaptation. For the individual, this is the genome. For the population, it is the collective genetic inheritance. In the individual, most of these possibilities remain unused, just as in the population, not all of the possible genetic combinations are realized. The population and the individual are therefore always ready for change, but it is the selective element which orientates these changes.

Bateson compares the processes of thought with the double stochastic system of biological evolution. He stresses the fact that all creative thought must contain a random component and that empiricism and trial-and-error processes only achieve the new by embarking upon pathways presented by chance. Moreover selection processes also exist in the mental field. When a new idea appears, it is subjected to a test of coherence: does it make sense in terms of what is already known or believed? These tests of coherence are analogous to the tests of genetic compatibility in sexual reproduction. The acceptance of new notions is dependent upon the reshuffling of ideas we have already. 'In the process of thought, *rigor* is the analogue of *internal coherence* in evolution' (Bateson, 1979, p. 183).

The other mental process, which is called LEARNING, which involves not only the individual's brain, but also the world about him/her, is the equivalent of the process of evolution which we call adaptation and which imposes somatic changes. Just as somatic changes are ultimately regulated by the current genetic constitution, what can be learned at a particular moment is limited or facilitated by what has previously been learned.

(See also CIRCULARITY; COMPLEXITY; ENTROPY; EVOLUTIONARY SURVIVAL UNIT; ORDER; PSEUDO-SPECIATION; RANDOMNESS; SEMANTIC UNIT OF MIND; UNIT OF CHANGE.)

M.G.

strange loops Defined by Hofstadter (1979) as the phenomenon which occurs when, moving downwards or upwards through the levels of some hierarchical system, we find ourselves back at the starting point. Such loops exist in biological systems, in certain works of music or the visual arts and in interactions between individual, family and social systems. When a strange loop appears in such a system, we may then speak of a TANGLED HIERARCHY. A strange loop is the 'levelling out' of an observed level and the observing meta-level (Le Moigne, personal communication).

Within an institutional therapeutic system, a nursing assistant may possess the relevant information which would enable the consultant to take the appropriate decisions. Similarly, in a therapeutic context, the most alienated index patient controls the course of the therapeutic process at least as much as the most 'qualified' and active therapist. The interactions between the institutional and family levels are also subject to regulation in the form of strange loops.

J.M.

strategic model See BRIEF INTERACTIONAL THERAPY; HYPNOSIS; MILAN SYSTEMIC THERAPY; POWER; SOLUTION-FOCUSED THERAPY; STRATEGIC THERAPY; THERAPEUTIC STRATEGIES AND TACTICS.

strategic therapy Haley (1963) first used the term 'strategic therapy' to describe the work of Milton H. Erickson. The term was, for a considerable time, used synonymously with the tactical and pragmatic focus of the brief therapy approaches of, for example, the Mental Research Institute (Watzlawick et al., 1974; Weakland et al., 1974). More recently, the term has come to be associated with the approach developed by Haley and Madanes (Haley, 1976, 1980; Madanes, 1981, 1984, 1990). This approach concentrates predominantly on hierarchy and structure.

Some confusion still remains, however. Haley was an original member of the Gregory Bateson project studying the paradoxes of abstraction in communication. His earlier concerns were very much with process and his earlier writings, especially his seminal work *Strategies of psychotherapy* (1963), had a profound influence on the development of the brief approaches. After nearly a decade with the MRI, Haley moved to the Philadelphia Child Guidance Clinic in 1967 and joined Salvador Minuchin and Braulio Montalvo. He became increasingly concerned with structure and hierarchy, with form rather than process. He began less and less to use the hypnotic and the more indirect and paradoxical techniques that had been a major feature of his earlier work and his earlier writings. This is not to say that they are never used in his more recent work, but their use is always subordinate to the primary goal of organizational restructuring (see the use of paradox and pretending as described in Madanes, 1981).

> Just as a person cannot not communicate . . . he cannot not organize. Every message between people defines a relationship and each message defines a person's hierarchical position in the organization. The members of an organization are not equal but of differing status, authority and precedence. Each message the people exchange indicates a position in relation to others; if that hierarchy is confused, the messages will be conflicting and confused. (Haley, 1981, p. 197)

The strategic approach is based on the notion that SYMPTOMS are the sign of a family, or other human system, in which the hierarchy is either constantly ambiguous or involves a constantly repeated COALITION across the natural generational or organizational boundaries (Haley, 1967, 1976, 1980; Madanes, 1981). For example:

> a parent may be exasperated by, yet continually protecting, a child from a spouse's attempts to help impose discipline, whilst at the same time expressing anger or desperation and demanding such help. Alternatively, a grandparent can constantly be colluding with a child against, or protecting it from, its parents, thus undermining their attempts to encourage or enforce what they consider to be appropriate behaviors. At the same time, he or she can be blaming the child's disturbed behaviors on the parents' incompetence or indifference. (Cade and O'Hanlon, 1993, p. 6)

The more the ambiguity or coalition remains covert and is denied, the more serious symptoms are likely to be. The ambiguity or confusion is mapped by observing the repeating sequences that reflect the way family members deal with, or avoid dealing with, each other, particularly in respect of the problem.

Therapy, from this perspective, involves changing sequences such that the hierarchy is ultimately corrected and the ambiguity or confusion diminished. It is therefore based on clear normative ideas as to how a well-functioning family's structure ought to be. This is one area in which the approach significantly differs from BRIEF INTERACTIONAL THERAPY and SOLUTION-FOCUSED THERAPY. However, the ideas are very consistent with

those underpinning the structural approach of Salvador Minuchin (Minuchin, 1974; Minuchin and Fishman, 1981) (See STRUCTURAL FAMILY THERAPY).

Symptoms are also seen as a metaphorical communication about a more fundamental problem in the family and also often as a dysfunctional solution to that problem. They are seen as tactics in interpersonal and intergenerational power struggles. As Madanes comments:

> In the case of a depressed man who does not do his work, it would be assumed that this is the way that the man and his wife (and/or his mother, father, children, and others) communicate about some specific issues, such as whether the wife appreciates her husband and his work, or whether the husband should do what his wife or his mother wishes, or so on. It is possible that the couple could become unstable over the presenting problem and that then a child might develop a symptom which will keep the father actively involved taking care of the child rather than depressed and incompetent. (Madanes, 1981, p. 21)

Symptoms are thus seen as having a protective or stabilizing function. The function of a symptom is seen as either defending the family against changes or, alternatively, helping such changes to be negotiated by forcing the family to reorganize.

The approach also requires the therapist to see the basic unit of therapy as a triad, as involving three persons or three subgroupings (in marital therapy, the third person can be the therapist). The therapist must therefore be particularly careful not to become caught up in an unhelpful hierarchical position in his or her dealings with a family. For example, a therapist can help a woman deal more effectively with a child, give her problems a sensitive hearing, and remain unaware that the role of her husband has thus been inadvertently usurped, both as a parent and as a spouse. His response to this will possibly tend further to entrench the hierarchical incongruity that underpinned the original problem such that the difficulties may ultimately become more profound. It can also be easy, particularly where scapegoating or the potential for violence occurs, to take the part of a child against its parents. As Madanes comments:

> Parents are expected to be in charge of their children, and cross generational coalitions, such as one parent siding with a child against another parent, are blocked. There is also a cautious concern about where the therapist is in the hierarchy, so that he or she does not inadvertently form coalitions with members low in the hierarchy against those who are higher. (Madanes, 1981, p. 22)

Madanes has also shown how more than one incongruous hierarchy can exist at the same time. For example, a husband's symptoms may render him apparently helpless and thus low in a hierarchy in relation to his wife, who appears both healthy and competent. Yet his symptoms may be extremely powerful in defining what may or may not happen in the family such that he has a kind of status against the influence of which his wife may be totally powerless. A child's symptoms can also be seen as having the function of caring for a parent. Thus, in both of these situations, each of the members are simultaneously both high and low in a hierarchy such that change can be impossible (Madanes, 1981). It is also not difficult to see how easy it would be for a therapist to become snarled up in such structures.

Symptoms are also seen as an indication that a family is failing to move successfully from one stage in the FAMILY LIFE-CYCLE to the next. Therapy is focused on helping families negotiate that transition and to re-organize more appropriately for the next stage. Symptoms are seen as particularly likely to occur where someone is either being added to or is leaving the system; for example, as a result of a birth, a marriage, a divorce or a death, or when children grow up and begin to move towards leaving home, first of all emotionally and then physically (Haley, 1973, 1980). Many of the problems of young people are seen as reflecting the difficulties a family is having with the normal process of growing up and their failure to negotiate separation. The young person's symptoms or failures in life are seen as attempts to protect the parents from having to face difficult issues such as their bankrupt marriage, for example. Therapy thus becomes a process of moving the young person out from between his or her parents and getting on with life, leaving them ultimately to confront their own problems themselves (with or without the therapist's help).

Therapy is addressed directly at the presenting problem. As Haley observes:

by focusing on the symptoms the therapist gains the most leverage and has the most opportunity for bringing about change. It is the presenting problem that most interests the client: when the therapist works with that he can gain great cooperation . . . The goal is not to teach the family about their malfunctioning system, but to change the family sequences so that the presenting problems are resolved. (Haley, 1976, p. 129)

Therapy tends to be planned in stages and will be focused directly onto the family's dysfunctional organization. The family will often be given directives that move it to a different dysfunctional organization as the first step towards a more functional one. For example, as an initial step, the tendency of a parent to be over-involved with a child will be blocked and the more peripheral parent required to make all of the important decisions about the child. Both parents will then be helped to act together more effectively.

Although strategic therapists give directives for how a family should operate between sessions, they will also often direct families to do something different during the interviews. A parent might be directed to control a disruptive child there and then, the therapist interrupting any attempt to intrude by an over-involved parent, grandparent or a parentified child. Sessions are used to rehearse changes that the family will be directed to carry out at home. Clearly, these sessions can sometimes become very dramatic. When task assignments are given to families, the outcomes of the directives tend to be followed up in the next session with some vigour. Madanes (1981, p. 23) observes: 'The approach assumes that all therapy is directive and that a therapist cannot avoid being directive, since even the issues he chooses to comment on and his tone of voice are directive.' Strategic therapists must therefore develop skills at influencing people, thus maximizing the likelihood that directives will be accepted and carried out.

The work of Madanes (1990) with families in which sexual abuse has taken place has found favour with some and outraged others. Her insistence that the perpetrator kneel and beg forgiveness has been seen by some as appropriate and others as an abusive 'be-spontaneous' paradox. Two abuses, as with two wrongs, are not seen as making a right. Haley's claims that schizophrenia/psychosis in young persons is essentially a leaving home issue has received much criticism. As with the brief interactional approach, strategic therapists have also been criticized for being superficial, for being manipulative, and for showing little interest either in the inner world of the client or in the sociopolitical context (Luepnitz, 1988; Flaskas, 1992). Also, along with the structural family therapy approach, strategic therapy has been criticized for its normative stance which is seen as supportive of the traditional status quo, particularly in respect of gender issues.

(See also ABSENT MEMBER MANOEUVRE; AGONISTIC BEHAVIOUR; MANIPULATION; MILAN SYSTEMIC THERAPY; POWER; PSYCHOANALYSIS; THERAPEUTIC STRATEGIES AND TACTICS.)

B.C.

strategies and tactics See THERAPEUTIC STRATEGIES AND TACTICS.

structural family therapy This approach occupies a particularly important place in the development of family therapy. A criticism of traditional psychotherapy as a talking cure is its reliance on the articulate client having time to explore his or her own internal processes and relationships in a protected setting, and with the ability to pay for treatment. Clearly, this is not an option for the majority of people who come into contact with the mental health and other professions in practice in the public sector, and represents a danger for the future of family therapy if the profession moves in this direction (Jenkins, 1990).

Minuchin and his colleagues recognized this in their work with an immigrant and socioeconomically deprived population at the Wiltwyck School for Boys. Their seminal text, *Families of the slums* (Minuchin et al., 1967), remains as relevant today as it was then. These researchers and therapists noted that these families 'share with each other a style of thinking, coping, communicating, and behaving, aspects of which can be directly traced to the structure and processes of the family systems of which they are, or were, a part' (Minuchin et al., 1967, p. 193). The techniques developed with this population have been further described by Minuchin and Montalvo (1967) and Aponte (1976).

The model of therapy which came from this group is called 'structural family therapy'. It directs the therapist to pay attention to the structure and organization of the family, and therefore to the ways in which sub-systems of the family relate to each other. By focusing on sub-systems, the therapist must look at the nature of the boundaries between these sub-systems or family subgroups.

Minuchin described three main characteristics of these boundaries: disengaged, permeable and enmeshed. It is important to remember that there is nothing inherently pathological in these descriptions, since high levels of enmeshment are functional and have high survival value for the relationship between a newborn infant and its primary care-giver, but that the same levels of involvement in latency and ADOLESCENCE would be problematic. Equally, there need to be degrees of disengagement so that there can be maturation and individuation, but there will be difficulties if this comes to characterize all aspects of the relationship between an individual and other family members. This leads to an appreciation of what is appropriate at different stages of individual and FAMILY LIFE-CYCLES. It will also be mediated by ETHNICITY, since what pertains for a Western family will be different, for example, from that of a traditional Chinese family. There will be differences where an immigrant family is attempting to come to terms with the new host culture, while retaining the core values of the culture of origin.

Structural family therapy has been criticized for apparent GENDER and culture blindness. That is, for seeming to suggest that there is only one way in which healthy families should organize, with parents in control, and adolescents and children in hierarchically lower positions. As with most new ideas, the originality of the innovator frequently becomes stifled by the perceived orthodoxy of the followers, true as much for the followers of Freud as for those of Minuchin.

What structural family therapy focuses on is the organization of the family and the ways in which, when that structure becomes skewed, the family is no longer able to carry out its tasks of socializing and preparing its members to cope in society. If the structure can be changed, then the problems which brought the family for help will no longer be necessary, and they will disappear. In working within this model, the therapist will look for alliances and coalitions within the family; the therapist will pay attention to COMMUNICATION patterns, especially as they involve different triangular relationships. This is most clearly described by Minuchin (1974). The therapist will be active, making alliances at different times with family members, being respectful of hierarchy, having family members show how they attempt to deal with problems and then finding ways to deal with them more effectively within the body of the session.

Minuchin does not rely on homework tasks between sessions as do some other approaches, but rather will leave the family to try out their new-found skills in their own ways between meetings. In that the model is active and enactive, it does not rely primarily on high levels of verbal skill, and is particularly effective in work with families with young children, adolescents, and families where skills in abstract thought are low. This does not make it a way of working that is somehow inferior to other models, since it demands considerable skill in the therapist, and the ability to tolerate high levels of intensity in the sessions. A sense of what is involved is given in Minuchin's later co-authored book, *Family therapy techniques* (Minuchin and Fishman, 1981).

While the overt focus of structural approaches is on organization and the family, it is clear that if a clinician does not have a firm grounding in human growth and development and an understanding of the internal processes of individual functioning, there is a danger of therapy becoming mechanistic and manipulative. In so far as Minuchin does not make clear the complexity of understanding on which he draws in his own work and his own experience, he has left the model vulnerable to these kinds of criticism.

Structural approaches have been developed in work with treatment populations other than impoverished groups, including: psychosomatic problems (Aponte and Hoffman, 1973; Minuchin et al., 1978; White, 1979); children (Carpenter and Treacher, 1982); children and divorce (Kaplan, 1977); psychogenic pain (Liebman et al., 1976); and consultation (Dare et al., 1990).

(See also FAMILY STRUCTURES; MULTI-LEVEL HIERARCHIES.)

H.J.

structural model   See AFFILIATION OR JOINING; FAMILY STRUCTURES; RESTRUCTURING; STRUCTURAL FAMILY THERAPY.

structural stability A DYNAMIC SYSTEM defined by a vector field X on the manifold M is structurally stable if, for every field X' sufficiently close to X, there is a homeomorphism of M onto itself which throws every trajectory of X on to a trajectory of X'. There is equivalence between all the perturbations of the system, the set of perturbations being situated in an open set.

To define the property of structural stability, it is necessary to specify the definition of the equivalence between two forms X and Y. That equivalence may be looser or tighter:

1 *Metric definition*: displacement in R^3 with identity of all distances: valid for the STATIC OR PSEUDO-STATIC FORMS (solid bodies): isomorphic identity.
2 *Projective definition:* homothetic displacement accounting for effects of perspective: homomorphic identity.
3 *Topological definition:* homeomorphism, i.e. biunivocal or bicontinuous mapping f of a form X on to a form Y. This definition would cover objects without any static parameter, i.e. completely 'shapeless' objects, deformable in a continuous manner, on condition that there be no break in the deformation: homeomorphic identity.

Now, every biological organism possesses metric, projective and topological aspects. Moreover, there may be an overlapping of folia. We shall agree to an approximation by speaking of a pseudo-equivalence-group G.

If, then, we consider a TOPOLOGICAL SPACE E, a form F will be an equivalence class of closed sets of apace E, subject to the laws of the pseudo-group G. This form F will be structurally stable if every form F' close to F in space E is equivalent to F. That is to say, that the totality of the points of E of that equivalence class forms an open set in space E.

In other words, a form, as a catastrophe set, is subject to variations corresponding to a class of closed sets. If that class of closed sets is an open set, the form in question is structurally stable.

(See also CHANGE; ELEMENTARY CATASTROPHES; UNIVERSAL UNFOLDING.)

M.G.

structural typologies See MORPHOGENETIC OR STRUCTURAL TYPOLOGIES OF THE FAMILY.

subject–object See ALIENATION; AUTONOMY AND HETERONOMY OF A SYSTEM; DEIXIS; DEMAND; DIFFERENTIATION OF SELF; FORECLOSURE; FUNCTIONAL CIRCLE; IDENTIFICATION; INDEX PATIENT; MANIPULATION; NARCISSISM; PHANTASY; PROJECTIVE IDENTIFICATION; RECIPROCAL VICTIMIZATION AND RESCUE; SCAPEGOAT; SELF; SEMANTICS OF COMMUNICATION; SHIFTERS; SPLITTING; SYMBOLS; SYNTAX OF COMMUNICATION; TRADING OF DISSOCIATIONS; TRUE SELF.

sucking-in by the system From a systemic point of view, sucking-in by the system is the process developed by families or institutions to render attempts by the therapist inoperative at the moment when the risk of change poses too great a threat for the system concerned.

In this case a part of the family (or institution) sucks the therapist (or therapists) into an ever-increasing degree of incorporation into the system and into more and more action and care, while at the same time restricting, if not indeed entirely destroying, his or her means of carrying out that action or delivering that care, together with his/her objectivity and his/her capacity to provide assistance. From a dynamic point of view, the system is then confronted with strange ATTRACTORS (vortices, complex forms) obliging the therapists, so far as is possible, to distance themselves sufficiently to intervene in an appropriate way.

(See also AGREEMENT AND DISAGREEMENT; DYNAMIC SYSTEMS; SEMANTIC RESONANCES.)

P.S.

suicide See ADOLESCENT SUICIDE.

supervision The family therapy team is a small SOCIAL ORGANIZATION, a system made up, possibly, of just a therapist and a supervisor. Supervision denotes hierarchical interdependence and has, as its complement, work in CO-THERAPY which denotes a horizontal interdependence.

The function of the supervisor is to amplify the creativity of the therapeutic system. It is necessary to distinguish between the supervision provided by a member of the team and supervision as part of teaching. The supervisor who is a member of a team is, by virtue of his/her belonging to that team, subject to a certain number of constraints. He or she has, however, the opportunity of participating in a word of therapeutic co-creation. He or she makes it possible to propose alternative images specific to the family and the therapist, in such a way that these contribute to restoring the creativity of the therapeutic process: a difference which makes a difference.

DIRECT AND INDIRECT SUPERVISION

One may distinguish between *direct* supervision (behind a one-way mirror and/or a video camera) and *indirect* or deferred supervision (consisting in the reviewing of recorded sessions).

The value of direct supervision is that it can deal with the most labile, least palpable and least reproducible singularities of interactions, as they are occurring, in the immediacy of the emotional exchanges. Through it, the therapist can be rapidly freed from blocks which, otherwise, would lead to the establishment of unanalysable vicious circles. Now, this type of 'paralysis' is in itself an important piece of information which one can possibly base oneself upon in pulling in wider contexts to help the therapeutic system to progress. Indirect supervision, by contrast, allows one to step back from what is going on, to evaluate the technical, tactical or strategic choices adopted for the therapy as a whole.

POTENTIAL PITFALLS OF SUPERVISION WITHIN A TEAM

The supervisor cannot take on the identity of a teaching supervisor; such a 'supervisor' runs the risk of very soon being disqualified if he/she seeks to dispense teaching to the therapist or tries to refine his/her technique. Nor can the supervisor substitute him- or herself for the therapist. Such a mistake can be seen when the therapist is continually called upon by his/her supervising colleague 'to correct errors'. Each correction, in fact, brings about the amplification of the initial error. The family may then become intrigued by all this and wonder what game is going on between the therapist and his/her colleague tucked away in the shadows. Moreover, the supervisor cannot take the place of the family either, pointing out to the therapist all the sufferings he/she is inflicting on such and such a member by his/her attitude. The risk then would be that the therapist would be disqualified, in a collusion between the family system and the supervisor.

Nevertheless, the supervisor can fulfil an essential role. If one takes the view that the therapeutic process depends on the image of the family with which the therapist is working, the supervisor may, before it is too late, assure him- or herself of the therapist's creativity, i.e. of his/her ability to move within the system in such a way as to take information (CIRCULARITY) from outside the system to change it (SYSTEMIC HYPOTHESIS). The supervisor may therefore ensure that the therapist is not confusing the images of the family which have imposed themselves upon him/her in the therapeutic framework, and the images he/she may phantasize about the family and its functioning outside the therapeutic setting.

QUESTIONS POSED TO THE THERAPIST BY THE SUPERVISOR

The supervisor may then pose a certain number of questions:

- with what image of the family is the therapist working?

- has he/she alternative images or the possibility of creating these?
- what image does the family have of the therapist? Is it an image shared by all the members of the family or, alternatively, is the image of the therapist neutral in the Selvinian sense of the term (See NEUTRALITY)?

After which, the supervisor may pose four levels of question to the therapist:

1 What does the therapist think of the different members of the family descriptively?
2 What does the therapist think of the family descriptively?
3 What does the therapist think about how the family regards the systems of aid and therapy in general?
4 What does the therapist think that the family thinks of him/her in particular?

The descriptive approach makes it possible to ensure that the therapist is not alienated by the immediate image he/she has of the family. In such a perspective, supervisor and therapist may then work together and not impose from the outset hypotheses imparted overhastily to the family, which are then likely to block the process that is underway.

(See also FAMILY–THERAPEUTIC INSTITUTION DIFFERENTIATION; INSTITUTIONS; MAP AND COUNTER-MAP OF A FAMILY SYSTEM; METABINDING; THERAPEUTIC DOUBLE BINDS; THERAPEUTIC STYLES.)

R.N. & J.M.

support An indispensable function in every therapeutic process and one that requires expenditure of energy on the part of the therapist(s). Too often relegated to the rank of a minor technique, support remains the essential precondition for the deployment of more specialized methodologies and techniques.

One of the ontogenetic foundations of support is the process of 'holding' described by Winnicott (1960b), i.e. the physical and psychical supporting of the infant by its maternal environment, as a preliminary to the development of a shared life together.

J.M.

surface structures, deep structures The distinction between surface and deep structures was propounded by Chomsky (1957) in transformational generative linguistics. It was introduced into clinical practice by Grinder and Bandler (1976). These writers proposed that the distinction be widened, in the SYNTAX OF COMMUNICATIONS, to embrace the whole of sensory-motor behaviour (kinaesthetic, gustatory, olfactory, visual and auditory) in the theory of NEUROLINGUISTIC PROGRAMMING.

Transformational linguistics may serve as a frame of reference for the study of the different levels of human communication. We shall here note the following points:

DERIVATION FROM DEEP STRUCTURE TO SURFACE STRUCTURE

Surface structure may derive from various layers of deep structure; conversely, a deep structure may give rise to various versions of surface structure.

STUDY OF PATIENT MODELS

Patient's models, which are usually impoverished and reduced as regards the range of options they offer, can be studied. Modelling leads to transformations in the representation of the world. Therapeutic action makes use of meta-models. The transition from deep structures to surface structure gives rise to three types of process.

Deletion–selection
There are gaps in the surface structure articulated by the patient: 'My mother detests me' (in what way? what are the signs of that? in what situations do you perceive that? etc.).

Distortion
The surface structure sometimes designates as a finished, limited event a situation which only exists in the form of continuing process in the deep structure. Grinder and Bandler (1976) give the following example:

> Surface structure: I regret my decision to return home.
> Deep structure: I regret having to decide to return home.

This phenomenon is particularly active in individual psychotherapy, psychoanalysis and family therapy, it being possible for the anticipation of change and the a priori perception of the 'treatment' to prevent the process itself actually being set in train.

Generalization
The models human beings construct of their environment (representation of nature, of themselves, their relations to others, the image of their families etc.) tend to be generalizations from particular, precise events. 'Gertrude doesn't love me' becomes 'Women don't love me.' Generalization gives rise to an impoverishing of representations and to a loss of detail and fine distinctions. It is particularly active in conflict within couples.

Such an attitude may cause the therapist to act in the same way and the words of family therapy, psychoanalysis, systemic therapy and brief therapy may short-circuit the processual levels of the deep structure. Such words generalize an experience before it has even been experienced in a specific manner; they name a continuing process, fixing it in advance; they effect a considerable deletion of what is really going on in a therapy. The more serious the pathology, the more the patients hold – indeed, cling – on to an impoverished surface structure.

RECONSTITUTION OF DEEP STRUCTURE BY THERAPIST

The deep structure may be more complete, but remain fuzzy, unclear and unfocused Grinder and Bandler (1976) show that three basic therapeutic options are possible:

1 To accept the unfocused model and leave it to the patient to complete and investigate the missing elements for him- or herself by successive clarifications.
2 Asking a question which requires the clarification of the model presented.
3 Guessing what the clarified model must be.

In the two latter cases, it is assumed that the therapists have a sufficient knowledge of the underlying systemic characteristics, with the requisite acceptance of risk of error. It is to the credit of Haley and Erickson that they specified the critical points in family life-cycles. The danger which then arises, however, is thinking that a standard path exists for not falling ill (conformity of thought, morality and behaviour). The first case refers essentially to psychoanalytic methodology, where the opposite risk exists, namely that the 'therapist' will never be in a position where he/she can commit errors (not only errors in the content of interpretation, but in the utilization of the framework created by the methodology employed).

SOME OBSERVATIONS

These choices probably depend as much on the structure of the therapist as on that of the patient, if not indeed on the context of events in which the patient–therapist interaction takes place.

A paradox may be observed here. By seeking to make such a clarification, such an approach seems less synthetic and holistic than psychoanalysis which, to some extent, 'prescribes the symptom' of fuzziness by propounding the rule of FREE ASSOCIATION. To what degree, most importantly, is it possible to give an accurate account in words of what precisely lies beyond their grasp? Is not information-gathering more pertinent and multi-dimensional precisely when the use of the surface structures of language is not taken literally? The therapist works at least as much with his/her coenaesthetic resonances, in an intersensory synergy, in a vibration of the different parts of his/her body as with mere manipulation of language.

Grinder and Bandler (1976) show that distinctions between 'paramessages' involve all the channels of communication and are not purely binary, as in the Batesonian version of analogical levels (non-verbal meta-messages) and digital levels (verbal messages) of communication. They distinguish between the visual, auditory, kinaesthetic, olfactory and gustatory channels and stress intersensory connections and their ANCHORING in founding experiences.

The integration of these into a diffuse general sensibility does, however, leave something to be desired, precisely because that integration is very difficult to describe with words (and even more difficult to experience through their agency). Freud referred to this by the term 'coenaesthesia' and showed that its potent action really only made its effects felt at night as a source of dream images (as stimuli and sources of dreams in the *Interpretation of dreams*). Now, these coenaesthetic phenomena which are also foregrounded in psychotic experiences, at the very surface of communications, are very difficult to transmit and transcribe in the terms of the perception-consciousness system. They are, however, of great importance in communication from unconscious to unconscious (META-COMMUNICATION SYSTEMS).

Language has a function of non-communication (Chomsky, 1957); it is not certain that the precision sought through language necessarily leads to the provision of the most pertinent information and the establishment of the most well-anchored communication: everything doubtless depends here on precision of wording.

Deep structures are in fact relatively shallow transformations, quite some way removed from the dynamics which generate the complex modalities of communication (ritual and mythic levels, for example). The derivations of which they permit seem relatively reversible, though without any particular censorship barriers. The development of Chomskian theory has gone in the direction of a superficialization of the deep structures.

(See also ATTITUDES, CONSCIOUS AND UNCONSCIOUS; PARACOMMUNICATION SYSTEMS; PRAGMATICS OF COMMUNICATION.)

J.M.

survival See EVOLUTIONARY SURVIVAL UNIT.

symbolic reference An axiomatic of association (or conditioning) proposed by Thom (1981a), who distinguishes between:

- *salient forms or saliences*: material objects, elementary particles, distinctive features of perception or language, the properties of which are strictly local and 'punctual'; and
- *pregnant forms or pregnances*: movement, energy, temperature, physical and microphysical fields, communication between living organisms, the properties of which are trans-locality, diffusion and the profound transformation of the invested saliences.

In animals, symbolic reference arises through an invading influence (pregnance) investing perceived forms (saliences). The number of such pregnances is small, but they have a highly propagative and labile character. These pregnances have a metabolic (semantic) signification: of hunger–feeding, sexual differentiation, development–reproduction. These semantic metabolisms are syntactically realized: in relations between prey and predator, between sexual partners or lovers, parents and children, brothers and sisters and between peers.

As Petitot-Cocorda (1977, 1983) points out, through predation, sexuality etc., animal regulation brings about catastrophes with actants. In predation, an actant (the prey) is devoured by another actant (the predator). As an internal object, the prey (its archetype) alienates the predator so long as he does not recognize it as an external object, a biologically pregnant form. The predator rediscovers his identity in the very act of predation. In this perspective, the linear character of language could be seen as reflecting these prelinguistic semantic achievements of prehistory. There would thus exist a 'phyletic unconscious structured like a prelanguage' (Thom, 1986).

The source-forms of these great biological pregnances are 'black holes' filled up by early learning experiences, such as IMPRINTING, leading in this way to stabilized target-forms. One may thus say that the maternal pregnance spreads from the source-form (the unfilled potential well of the ectodermic tissue) to the target-form (the maternal imago structured neurodermically).

In man, social RITUALIZATION has created a great number of pregnances (concepts) but their propagative character is strictly limited to the neighbouring semantic concepts (satellite concepts). This ramification of an undifferentiated initial pregnance into concepts occurs in childhood, essentially through parent–child deictic behaviour.

The phenomena of imprinting, BECOMING ACCUSTOMED and HABITUATION are structured in sensitive periods which connect with embryological inductions. The ectoderm–neuroderm division passes from the real to the virtual state by virtue of the encounter with the mesodermic tissue. The interest of such a theory lies in its viewing the process of exfoliation of linguistic forms in terms of these great pregnances of animal origin.

The acquisition of the words of language seems to be made, then, in sensitive periods, structurally similar to the sensitive periods in which it is possible for the ability to recognize familiar persons to be acquired, together with the capacity to distinguish them from strangers. The potential well of the neuroderm wins out from the thermodynamic point of view by virtue of the existence of the inductor at the right moment and in the right position. The acquisition of parental figures is only possible if the internal and familial contexts permit this specific spatiotemporal disposition. Similarly, the maternal – and subsequently the paternal – pregnance divides and ramifies (GENERALIZED CATASTROPHES) to issue in indices of the parental figures: 'breast', bottles, transitional objects, the infant's own body, toys. The naming, by deixis, of these derived pregnances leads to a coupling which stabilizes signifiers and signifieds.

The various types of connection between salient forms and pregnant forms establish phenomena of conversion and determine the great semantic fields of the living and non-living:

Collision	salient form — salient form
Obstacle	pregnant form — salient form
Investment	salient form — pregnant form
Semantic coupling	pregnant form — pregnant form

Saliences and pregnances are either objective or subjective. The sun is an objective pregnance for all living or non-living beings, whereas a mouse is a subjective pregnance for a cat.

Thom stresses that in quantum mechanics, the salience–pregnance distinction is abolished. Quantum theory is both irrefutable at the level of its experimental predictions and 'unintelligible' at the conceptual level. The same phenomenon seems to occur in family therapy. There is a quantum indetermination at the root of the most serious family disturbances, as in INFANTILE AUTISM, SCHIZOPHRENIAS, delinquent transactions and PSYCHOSOMATIC ILLNESS.

However, receiving the family for a consultation leads to re-establishing figures of regulation, to staging catastrophic events. Catastrophe theory then appears as a condition of intelligibility of the 'symbolic references', but does not enable us to describe or understand the unintelligible, indeterminate part of the psychotic or psychosomatic symptoms. It enables the nature of changes to be formalized, together with the structure of interpersonal configurations and the topological constraints which bear upon family morphologies. It makes it possible to conceive the symbolic processes in a bio-sociological continuum by the semantic relation established between phylogenesis and ontogenesis, embryology and language.

(See also CHREOD; ELEMENTARY CATASTROPHES; FAMILY ACTANT; FAMILY CATASTROPHES; PROCREATIVE FAMILIES; RELATIONAL ARCHETYPES; SACRED; STATIC, PSEUDO-STATIC AND METABOLIC FORMS; VIOLENCE.)

J.M.

symbols, symbolism, the symbolic Though symbols are what make it possible to think, communicate and process information, there is no general theory of the symbol which has been able to present itself as such without generating a counter-theory.

How, then, are we to make sense of this multiplicity of theories of the symbol? Is the symbol a unique entity or, by contrast, a series of different realities, reflecting the variety of personal and collective mental productions? We may note that dreams, myths, behaviours, phantasies, customs, drawings, images, shapes, plants, animals and parts of the body are all media that are constantly being employed in symbolic activity.

Etymologically, the 'symbol' is an object separated into two parts, each of these being kept by a person. The cutting up of the object is the mark of a transaction, ritualization or continuing event such as a debt, an expression of friendship, hospitality, love. The rejoining of the two separated parts represents mutual recognition.

As Chevalier and Gheerbrant (1982, xiii) point out in their *Dictionary of symbols*, 'every symbol has a "broken sign" aspect; the sense of the symbol is to be found in what is simultaneously the breaking and reconnection of its separate terms.' This is to say that there is no trans-spatial connection without a symbolic system which connects together sender and receiver; the difference of the sexes – biological, anatomical, psychical and cultural – is the multi-stratified prototype, a precondition of connection and reproduction.

FUNCTIONS AND SEMIOTIC STRUCTURE OF SYMBOLS

Chevalier and Gheerbrant identify a certain number of functions connected with the dynamic activity of symbols: an exploratory function, a function of open anticipation, of cryptic substitution, of mediation, of integration and unification, a pedagogic and therapeutic function, a socializing function, a function of vibratory resonance, a function of energy transformation and, indeed, a transcendence function (see ACTOGENESIS). For his part, McLuhan (1964) stresses the symbol's functions of collocation (position of the object in relation to the context and hence topological form) and parataxis (juxtaposition of elements, with absence of an intermediate linkage).

We shall note, from the perspective of Peirce, that the symbol is a particular type of *representamen* (see SEMIOLOGY), made up of indicial and iconic signs. In effect, the sign, in conjunction with the dynamical object (i.e. the object which provides effective mediation between representamen and interpretant), maybe an icon, an index or a symbol.

The *icon* is a representamen whose representative quality derives from its properties of resemblance; the icon is a simulacrum, the first image of its object, isomorphic with the thing which constitutes it.

An *index* presupposes a dynamic spatiotemporal connection providing a punctual contact with the object to be interpreted, in a dyadic relation, such that there is no resemblance between index and object: 'indices assert nothing'; they merely say: 'See there!' This intersection which unites and detaches is a fact of a unique, singular type. The index directs the gaze or the attention on to the object being designated.

A *symbol* presupposes (both in its phylogenetic and ontogenetic construction) an icon and an index. The symbol is a conventional sign which depends on (acquired or innate) habit. It is defined by Peirce as a representamen whose representative character determines its interpretant: words, sentences and books are thus symbols, made up of icons and indices, but fundamentally artificial and conventional, referring to a law established by men. Unlike the icon and the index, the symbol generates symbols. Peirce writes, for example:

A Symbol is a law, or regularity of the indefinite future. Its Interpretant must be of the same description; and so must be also the complete immediate Object, or meaning . . . But a law necessarily governs, or is 'embodied in' individuals, and prescribes some of their qualities. Consequently, a constituent of a Symbol may be an Index, and a constituent may be an Icon. (Peirce, 1935, p. 166)

We may compare this definition of the symbol with the concept of ritual (as a canalized derivation of an instinct for signalling purposes) and with the concept of semantic CHREOD proposed by Waddington (1977).

The articulation between symbols, indices and icons is specified as follows: 'A *Symbol* is a sign naturally fit to declare that the sets of objects which is denoted by whatever set of indices may be in certain ways attached to it is represented by an icon associated with it' (Peirce, 1935, p. 167). Moreover, 'A symbol, as we have seen, cannot indicate any particular thing; it denotes a kind of thing. Not only that, but it is itself a kind and not a single thing' (Peirce, 1935, p. 169). One should add: it admittedly denotes a kind of thing in a general way, but always in a particular situation, a specific context or a unique position. But if the symbol is a law which channels the future, which gives a meaning to participation in a human community, how are we to explain that people believe they are understanding each other when they use the same word in different senses and that they think they are constructing

different theories when they use different words to say the same thing?

From what point, in the history of phylogenesis, is it possible to speak of symbolic activity? The rituals of the animal world appear not as symbols supported by other symbols but as goal-seeking actions, bearing meaning, a necessary condition for symbolization. They are, in a sense, the prototype of symbolization since they make it possible to differentiate the modes of relations and to link conspecifics in shared communication (see RITUALIZATION; SEMANTICS OF COMMUNICATION). Symbolization properly so-called seems related to the reorganization introduced by the linear sequence of language.

Writers as divergent as von Bertalanffy and Lacan see symbolization as the specific quality of humanity. The learning of rudimentary languages by higher primates has, to some degree, thrown into question the point at which that absolute break occurs, as a result of which the linguist Hagège (1985) has drawn a distinction between animal 'symbolism' and human 'semiotics':

The way in which the two chimpanzees Washoe and Sarah seem, during their training, to master the code they are learning, indicates that they are capable of symbolization, and that they can even use symbols in the absence of their corresponding physical objects. Better still, they can isolate features through analysis. As long as symbols rather than arbitrary signs are involved, the chimpanzees can use them to abstract, i.e. to classify different objects according to some common feature: for example, apple and banana, a series from which they can abstract the symbol for 'fruit'. (Hagège, 1985, p. 77)

We see here the gap which may exist between the symbol, the product of icons and indices, and the symbolic, which is based on the arbitrary nature of the sign. Chimpanzees certainly do not possess the capacity for assertion, interrogation and injunction (Hagège, 1985, p. 78), the essential modalities of verbal communication. Moreover, as Vidal (1985, p. 94) points out, invective, scornful rejection and the deliberate ignoring of another's presence are forms of aggression which have no counterpart in the aggressive rituals of animal dissociation. Vidal describes these attitudes as 'symbolic procedures'. One might equally well see them as corresponding to an absence of symbolization or of conceptual resources. However this may be, we see here again that the symbol is subject to being understood in contradictory ways.

Symbols then appear, in communication, as a system of OSCILLATORS whose product resonances stabilize the arbitrary and motivated aspects of communication. Such a system assumes an already highly elaborated integration of the ANALOGIC and DIGITAL CODINGS which transcribe messages. Symbols bring together and, at the same time, disjoin many levels of communication. Among these levels, that of human interchange with computers opens up new perspectives, leading to the creation of veritable 'meta-symbols' (see below).

ONTOGENESIS OF SYMBOLIZATION

Early stages of symbolization

The main currents of psychoanalysis have explored in detail the most diverse aspects of symbolic phenomena, to the extent that they structure phantasmatic activity, and the possibilities of sublimation. The field of study is essentially the relationship of the sexed body to the psyche, inasmuch as there is a break between the two, in the dimension of the representation of the drives (Freud, Abraham, Klein). Each psychosexual stage (oral, anal, urethral, phallic) generates its own symbolic constellation. Winnicott was subsequently to describe the phenomena of *pre-symbolization* in ontogenesis, phenomena of internal/external transition between the child and the mother by way of transitional objects, in a 'potential space', while Lacan placed greater emphasis on the subject's inscription in the symbolic by way of language. We shall attempt here to identify the relations between this symbolic activity and the way in which communication structures or destructures it. In other words, we shall try to track down how the activation of behaviours in interaction gives form and meaning to psychical activity, in a complex counterpoint between pre-linguistic and linguistic communication.

The starting point for symbolization in the child may be the impulse with which the structuring of incorporation and projection begins. When only a few months old, children explore objects by putting them in their mouths or throwing them away with all their might (coming as near as is possible to the Greek etymology of the word *sumballo*, which signifies both throwing together and bringing together, and also exchanging, comparing, interpreting, placing in common and meeting with). The basic effect of PLAY is 'to attract the child's attention to communication itself and to the structure of the acts in which communication plays a part' (Bruner, 1983, p. 223).

Some objects lose their purely utilitarian functions (as tools) to become the supports of activities of thinking and non-contextual affect, functioning as veritable pivotal-symbols (Vygotsky). If one sits astride it, a stick can become a horse or a witch's broom; or it can be a tree or a sword. Out of this activation, the space of the imagination is born, and the construction of iconic representations. At around three years of age, the *Fort-Da* game (Freud) or its equivalents will lay the ground for the elaboration in phantasy of the existence of the absence of the love object.

Symbols and deixis: reference, co-reference

We shall distinguish between:

1 *Designation:* the mother's gaze follows the child's. From 4 to 9 months onwards, the child will look towards the point being looked at by the experimenter facing him. In other words, the mother orientates her child's gaze toward third objects.
2 *Deixis properly so-called,* by the co-localization of the referent and its representative: the use of the spatial, temporal and interpersonal characteristics of a situation as tools of co-reference.
3 *Naming:* development of standard lexical items which 'designate' the extra-linguistic events in the common universe shared by the child and an available person close to him (Bruner, 1983, p. 178).

The deictic, indicating function is 'coloured' by the structure of the parental pregnance. In this sense, the first DEIXIS is that 'imprinting' which designates the mother for the child and the child for the mother, the precondition for which is that the mother should be presented as mother – and the child as child – by the family and social system.

Symbols and associative breaks

In Freud's view, in the *Interpretation of dreams*, symbolic interpretation has a role to play where the dreamer's associations leave the analyst in the lurch. Symbols comprise a small number of contents, whose meaning is constant, enabling abstract thoughts to be transposed from formal canvases into visual images. There is here an associative break, an entry into the social field. In his *New introductory lectures on psychoanalysis*, Freud writes

We have not yet finished with symbols. There are some which we believed we recognized, but which nevertheless worried us because we could not explain how *this* particular symbol had come to have *that* particular meaning. In such cases, confirmations from elsewhere – from philology, folklore, mythology, ritual – were bound to be especially welcome. (*Standard Edition*, vol. 22, p. 23)

Now, in schizophrenics, sexual, epistemophilic and social metaphors are no longer labelled. There is a disturbance of the dissociative bond. All the sciences drawn upon by Freud should be examined again here, though they should be examined *in statu nascendi*, so to speak, on the terrain of etho-anthropology.

SCHIZOPHRENIC COMMUNICATION AND PHENOMENON OF DE-TRIBALIZATION

In approaching the question of symbols, von Bertalanffy (1981) starts out from an anthropological analysis of schizophrenia. He observes that this corresponds to a 'loosening of associational structure', 'splitting of personality', a 'losing of ego-boundaries and self-identity'. These characteristics are perceived as pathological in terms of a particular sociocultural context, namely that of the West (1981, p. 39). In fact, the phenomenon of schizophrenia is an expression of a distortion of culturally accepted symbolic interpretations. Now, 'a concretistic incapacity to symbolize' or 'loss of symbolic capacity', together with reification of concepts and dissociative activity, are phenomena which occur in normal thinking without it being possible clearly to establish a borderline between this and pathology. There would appear to be a symptomatic relatedness between the Western hospitalized schizophrenic and the genius or mystic of primitive tribes. This analysis is shared by Devereux and McLuhan.

In the opinion of Devereux (1970), schizophrenic symptoms are not found in authentically primitive societies and would seem to be the product of a violent phenomenon of ACCULTURATION. The schizophrenic could thus be seen as an insistent witness to detribalization, and this justifies NETWORK-style approaches and the search for the concealed tribal units which now, in our societies, have only symptoms through which to express themselves.

There is thus in schizophrenia a subversive activity which radically throws into question the existing forms of symbolic consensus. This shows that the stakes in 'therapy' are essentially symbolic stakes, which concern the redefinition of words and things, and, hence, of REALITY. The schizophrenic is, in fact, in his or her person, the split-off symbol of a family junction that has to be re-established, beyond the fragmentation linked to the intense process of splintering nuclearization.

For Marshall McLuhan, schizophrenia might be the consequence of literacy (1962, pp. 21–2). The translation of sounds into a visual code arises from alphabetic and phonetic writing (which is extended to a perfect correspondence between the two by the Greek alphabet). It is impossible with pictographic, hieroglyphic or ideographic script.

From the magical, resonating world of simultaneous relations that is the oral and acoustic space, there is only one route to the freedom and independence of detribalized man. That route is via the phonetic alphabet, which lands men at once in varying degrees of dualistic schizophrenia. (McLuhan, 1962, p. 22)

Thus, the development of the visual sense alone, to the detriment of the others, leads to a 'division of the faculties'. Whereas the tribal world is based on the magical, dynamic and highly ritualized power of spoken words and the simultaneous perception of events, the de-tribalized world, by freezing the word in a stereotyped, de-personalized form in the visual world of the written text, renders it static and creates in itself a visual imagery that is completely distinct from the synaesthetic perception of reality (the 'other scene' of the Freudian unconscious).

HUBRIS might be seen as being linked to this exacerbated dichotomy which arises between phenomena pertaining to the passions and cognitive phenomena (Russell), and which has its origins in the ancient Greek world.

ARTIFICIAL INFORMATION-PROCESSING AND META-SYMBOLIZATION

We shall note the importance of the 'cannoning' of words one against another and the explosive interpenetration of metaphorical levels, leading to a 'schizophrenian' language which *simulates* a computer-style symbolization and indicates the level of de-ritualization of interpersonal communication in the family group.

Just as man possesses mechanisms for the simulation of systems of ineraction and communication (a feature of schizophrenic illness is the inability to play on all these metacommunicative levels), the computer can simulate the non-animal properties of the human brain. This electrical extension of mental activity is merely in its infancy. Such a development cannot but have an impact, once again, upon the very definition of the concept of symbol.

The computer is not merely subject to syntactic rules, any more than it is confined to analogic or digital processing of reality. It is now capable of handling hierarchically more complex symbolic units. It is capable of manipulating or processing 'physical symbol systems', which are bearers of meaning. These processes, by creating new symbols, are capable of manipulating them, storing them, comparing them in terms of identity or difference and giving commands to read or rewrite them. An important point is that these physical symbol systems have a material base, whether physical (interconnections between transistors, micro-processors) or biological (macro-molecules, neuronal networks). The symbol quality is, however, independent of the substrate which produces it.

We may note here a surprising point of convergence with Thom's morphogenetic theory which also stresses the independence of the substrate in the biological morphogenesis of symbols, even though the viewpoints and levels of research of Simon (for example, 1984a) and Thom are fundamentally opposed. The models of cybernetics and artificial intelligence seek to simulate the functioning of biological organisms by proposing comparison-based models (in terms of identification–differentiation) and approximations, relating to precise functions (information-processing, understanding/production of language, recognition of forms, games, expert systems etc.). Thom's morphogenetic project aims, by contrast, to study the ontological identity (the *logos*) which makes a biological organism, whose organizing parameters presuppose a space of a very high number of dimensions, none the less deploy itself in the four dimensions of space–time in an individuated unit.

As Hofstadter et al. have so well described (1980), one basic property of symbols is that they create TANGLED HIERARCHIES which produce the illusion that there is no inviolate level (see BLACK BOX). Now, the tangled hierarchy of symbols is based on the material levels which produce it, which, for their part, are not based on a tangled hierarchy.

HUMANIZING FUNCTION OF SYMBOLIZATION

von Bertalanffy (1967, 1981) placed the question of the symbol at the centre of his GENERAL SYSTEMS THEORY. In his view, the danger facing humanity is one of robotization, and the concept of 'symbol' enables us to stand out against the dangers of behaviourism, positivism and the closed mechanistic conceptions of cybernetics. He writes, in 'On the definition of the symbol' (1965), that the use of the term derives essentially from Germanic philosophy and is practically excluded from Anglo–Saxon neo-positivist philosophy, except in its logico–mathematical sense. The term is also not identified as a concept by Bateson. It could, however, make possible an interesting bridge within the current debates between the various different – analytic and systemic – currents of family therapy, as has been pointed out by Goutal (1985). Goutal has made a close analysis of the Bertalanffian and Freudian positions as regards what can be seen as the 'specific nature of man', his relations to symbolization, to happiness and the dangers of massification threatening him, as well as the dangers of robotizing mechanism (even if it be 'circular'). The analysis yields a surprising area of agreement between the founder of psychoanalysis and the inventor of systems theory so far as the phenomena of symbolization is concerned, and the relationships maintained by man as an individual attached to a totality. From von Bertalanffy's standpoint, symbols are:

- freely created (no biologically reinforced connections between the sign and the thing connoted);
- representative;
- transmitted by tradition.

In *A systems view of man* (1981), von Bertalanffy adds three other characteristics. Symbols are also:

- productive;
- possessed of an autonomous life;
- discursive and non-discursive.

We may criticize the idea of a totally free creation here, even if we accept the fact that the symbol is independent of the substrate which produces it. It would also seem necessary to recognize that symbolic transmission presupposes an interaction between phylogenetic and cultural 'traditions'. Yet it is, in effect, most important to emphasize the creative, productive character of symbolic systems. A symbol is, in a sense, richer than its premises might suggest; moreover, it obeys autonomous laws which are not reducible to the laws of biology, psychology or sociology. This autonomous character connects with the hypothesis advanced above, namely that it might be regarded as the product of a system of oscillators, ensuring the creation of spontaneous impulses within a metasystemic ensemble. Lastly, it is important to recognize that an important dimension of symbolic activity is not reducible to phenomena of discourse and that a great quantity of what is ineffable underlies essential symbols (inexpressible function of myths, rituals, arts and religions). And yet is it absolutely necessary that only the symbol be seen as being in play in the break which separates man from the world which surrounds and constitutes him? Let us, here again, accept the paradoxical ambiguity of the schism which joins, the break which unites, the other side of which is the union which permits splitting, the continuous form which generates the 'catastrophe' jump.

The point is not to say that the human symbol is pure animality or purely computer-processable. It is, rather, to try to emphasize its inhuman and para-human roots and extensions. How could man communicate with nature and its artificial excrescences if he did not share interconnected forms with them or possess varied and differentiated vehicles which brought these forms into contact? From the earliest times, robotics seems to have been at the heart of mankind. Ancient democracy was only able to set itself up on the basis of slavery. And the subjugation of man by man does not seem especially exceptional in the history of humanity. The opportunity we have today is that of identifying and artificially simulating, as far as is possible, the algorithms which assail, shape and alienate us, which are the minimal preconditions for true liberation. For this reason, symbolic activity, as the social inscription of the human being capable of judgement and desire, will not reject as lying outside itself the constraints of subjection. Reduced to a homeostatic function, the schizophrenic can neither desire nor phantasize. Access to the status of desiring subject does not come about through the disavowal of repetitive constraints or zones of rarefaction of the affects, but through the exploration of their survival value.

ANTHROPOLOGY AND THERAPEUTIC SYMBOLIZATIONS

For Lévi-Strauss, communication operates on several levels at once. There is communication of men and women, governed by the kinship systems; communication of goods, services and technologies; and communication of media and messages. Lévi-Strauss shows that these communication systems do not function on the same scale or at the same rate.

For most men, language represents without falsifying. But modern psychology has refuted this simplistic conception: Language does not enter into a world of accomplished objective perceptions merely to give purely external and arbitrary signs or 'names' to individual given objects . . . it is itself a mediator in the formation of objects . . . This more accurate view of linguistic fact is not a discovery or new invention . . . it emerges that the conception of the spoken word as communication, as power, and as action represents a universal feature of human thought. (Lévi-Strauss, 1969, p. 494)

We shall note that psychopathology directly confronts us with clashes between these levels which are much less separate than one might think. The effectiveness of symbols, which Lévi-Strauss sees at work both in shamanism and psychoanalysis, and which is extended in both a specialized and generalized manner in family therapy, comes into play when the patient has a lived – and indeed vital – experience of a myth to be constructed, reconstructed or transformed. The symbol here is an expression of the interconnections between biological, organic functions and the conscious and unconscious structuring of the mind. 'The effectiveness of symbols would consist precisely in this "inductive property", by which formally homologous structures, built out of different materials at different levels of life – organic processes, unconscious mind, rational thought – are related to one another' (Lévi-Strauss, 1973, p. 201). The symbolic function is, then, no longer the prerogative of the classic psychoanalytic cure alone, regarded as the underlying model for every therapeutic situation, but has to be worked out case by case, as different patients are encountered in different contexts. What takes precedence here is the form of the myth over the content of the discourse, the structure of the context over the data of expression, the morphology of the 'fit' between the various media over the themes expressed.

(See also SCHIZOPHRENIAS; SYMBOLIC REFERENCE.)

J.M.

symmetry   See COUPLES; NARCISSISM; SCHISMOGENESIS.

symptomatic and/or aetiological transactions
We may define a 'transaction' as an INTERACTION stabilized, implicitly or explicitly, by a process of deuterolearning. A transaction is termed 'symptomatic' when it refers to a state whose origin lies beyond its grasp (see SYMPTOMS). Hence the expressions: schizophrenic,

delinquent, incestuous, sadomasochistic or anorectic transaction etc.

A transaction is termed 'aetiological' when it may be considered that it generates pathological manifestations, at sub- or supersystemic levels. Hence the expressions: pathogenic reverberating circuits (see INFANTILE AUTISM; DOUBLE BINDS; the ACOUSTIC FEEDBACK EFFECT; the SOCIOGENETICS OF FAMILY SCHISMS; SCHISMOGENESIS, delinquentogenic transactions; PERVERSE TRIANGLES; schizophrenogenic transactions etc. Thus the paradoxical nature of a transaction prejudges neither of its form, its gravity nor its aetiology.

PERSONALITY STRUCTURE AND TRANSACTION

Traditional biological psychiatry was based on the analysis of the person recognized as being ill and is currently based on the search for internal biological causes and essentially pharmacological treatments. Antipsychiatry proposed that this attitude be reversed, identifying the factors external to the patient, whether these be parental or social. Within this perspective, the patient found him- or herself in a sense freed from any participation – active or passive – in the nature of his or her disorder. Writers were thus able to describe the 'schizophrenogenic mother', the 'castrating' wife of the alcoholic, the non-affective parents of autistic children and, in the majority of situations, the physically or emotionally absent or paranoiac father.

The model of family therapy consists in recognizing the specificity of relationships in the understanding of disorders; designating someone a patient or accusing a person in his/her close circle amounts to an arbitrary punctuation of a sequence of interactions which loops back on itself in a circular manner. For example, to say of a relationship that it is sadomasochistic amounts to leaving out of account a possible third person who fuels it.

By the same token, it is just as dangerous to view the relationship or even the family as the cause or origin of the disorders observed without closely analysing the notion of causality and the complex problem of how psycho-pathological disorders are determined. It seems, fundamentally, that the parameters in play in the definition of causality are multiple: linear, circular, systemic and formal. Biological factors do not simply relate to a single person, but may concern the whole group. They may be subject to pressure from intense sociocultural constraints. Conversely, however, these latter may be an expression of biological systems of regulation. One then comes to see how the different states observed are formally, topologically determined.

SCHIZOPHRENIC TRANSACTIONS, SCHIZOPHRENOGENIC TRANSACTIONS

The DOUBLE BIND concept has displaced aetiology by freeing the persons involved from the responsibility or even guilt that is linked to linear causality and shifting attention to contexts and relationships. A great temptation then arises to identify FAMILY TYPOLOGIES. Schizophrenia becomes a *symptomatic transaction* if one accepts Bateson's hypothesis that the index patient can be said to be suffering from a manifest schizophrenia and his or her close relatives from a latent schizophrenia.

Thus 'families in schizophrenic transaction' present typical patterns of interaction (Haley, 1959; Selvini Palazzoli et al., 1978). These involve the systematic negation of their own and others' statements, the negation of the very existence of the person speaking, the disqualification of every attempt at leadership, the impossibility of decision-making, and the impossibility of a confirmed alliance. Every attempt at the establishment of a rule by one member of the family is countered by another member, the rule being that there can be no rules and it is forbidden to define the relationship. All the family members criticize themselves and criticize the others for what they do, since no one in the family is as they should be. In this process, there inevitably arises an aetiopathogeny: the self-maintenance of a positive FEEDBACK which, in Bateson's view, is comparable to the death instinct described by Freud. The human being tends, in effect, to wish to verify his sensation of the unpleasant by attempting to repeat the experience in the necessary transition from play to reality which characterizes the transition from the childhood to the adult state. Thus the overall malaise activates a positive feedback which reinforces the behaviour which preceded the malaise. Similarly, in schizophrenic transactions, HUBRIS exacerbates the pseudo-symmetry, which exacerbates hubris (Selvini Palazzoli et al., 1978). In the process, these transactions become aetiological or even schizophrenogenic.

DELINQUENT TRANSACTIONS, DELINQUENTOGENIC TRANSACTIONS

By analogy with the notion of 'schizophrenic transactions', to which much research has been devoted since the beginnings of family therapy (and an attempt to examine this concept with epistemological rigour would be profitable), the expression 'families in delinquent (or even delinquentogenic) transaction' is beginning to appear in the literature. Apart from the fact that prudence commands that one should not forge a new nosology which, though it does not label individuals, stigmatizes families, the scope of this formulation should be carefully defined since it may lead to confusion and even create the risk of returning us to the linear and, occasionally, even genetic explanations of Lombroso and his disciples. (In avoiding the old 'dangerous classes', or the later 'public enemies' and 'born delinquents', we may fall into the trap of a preventive identification of 'dangerous families' or, more simply, of 'at-risk families'.) What is to be done, moreover, with families presenting a poly-symptomatology, with one member designated schizophrenic, another delinquent and a third 'borderline' (see 'multiple problem families' in INTERACTIONAL TYPOLOGIES OF THE FAMILY)?

To term certain modalities of communication delinquent amounts to emphasizing that such transactional modes appear with a relative frequency that is statistically significant in families where one or more members have been identified as 'delinquent' by the various agencies of social control. We should not forget that beneath the label 'delinquent' are grouped individuals with extremely varied personalities and diverse histories, who have in common only one characteristic (but one which often screens out the differences between them), namely that they have not only broken the laws in force in a particular society, but that they have also been 'caught'. One should therefore beware of over-reductive simplifications. There can no more be a purely systemic model of understanding of a deviant behaviour which, like any human behaviour is rooted in the complexity of circular multi-causalities, than there is – or can be – a pure and unambiguous economico-political, sociological or psychological model for explaining delinquency. Moreover the quasi-constant absence of comparative samples, other than those made up of families presenting 'another dysfunctionality' (since by definition 'happy' families have little dealing with therapists or the law) makes it necessary that we observe great prudence in every aetiological approach to juvenile delinquency.

It is none the less true that family therapists who regularly have to carry out interviews with families in which one child is designated as 'delinquent' have observed particular modes of verbal and non-verbal transaction with a certain clinical frequency, though these are not necessarily specific to this type of family alone, nor are they inevitably 'delinquentogenic' in the absence of other reinforcing factors. The modes of transaction concerned include SPLIT DOUBLE BINDS; CONTRARY INJUNCTIONS in parent–child messages; processes of DELEGATION; early emotional deprivation; SCAPEGOATING; systems of transgenerational fidelity with underlying 'invisible' LOYALTIES; the existence of family SECRETS; disengaged boundaries leading to triangulations external to the family (recourse to institutions, placements etc.); the acting out of conflicts rather than their inscription in phantasy.

(See also DELINQUENT ACTING OUT; DYNAMIC SYSTEMS; LEARNING; PERVERSE TRIANGLES; SYMPTOMS; TRANSACTIONAL TYPOLOGIES OF THE FAMILY; TRANSFERENCE; UNCERTAINTY PRINCIPLE.)

J.M. & P.S.

symptoms The symptom is a process linked to a pathogenic factor, an illness. Unlike illness, however,

Three levels for understanding the meaning of symptoms.

Level of understanding	Linear causal level	Circular causal level	Systemic causal level
Definition	The symptom is a problem: what is experienced as a symptom	The symptom is a message: the effect of the symptom on the relationship	The symptom is a solution: function of the symptom in and for the system
Logical modelling	[A] ⟶ [B] The symptom [B] is linked to a pathogenic cause, an 'illness', [A]	A, C, B circular diagram. (A) and (B) and . . . are both symptoms of a pathogenic cause and causes of the symptom	(nested circular diagrams) A, B are both symptoms, causes and elements of a solution in and for the system
Models of therapy and intervention	1 Symptomatic treatment: remove, eradicate the symptom or its cause; modifications here and now 2 Modifying causalism: circularity places symptom and cause on analogical planes	1 Blocking the process of repetition: prescribing the symptom or semblance. Split double binds 2 Changing logical level: positive connotation of the system	Beyond the symptom: challenging belief in the inevitable existence of rigid recursive loops, circular alienation processes which block the development of the system
Treatment indicated	1 Symptomatic treatment: if there are risks of acting out within an institution or the family Otherwise 2	1 Blocking the specific process: if the symptom and/or the cause is serious Otherwise 2	

the symptom never contains its own causality. The Greek etymology casts light on the meaning of the term: *sumptōma* (literally: 'that which falls with') means casualty, coincidence, chance event, mishap, misfortune and . . . symptom.

The detail provided by the *Littré dictionary* casts light on the distinction between symptom and illness. The symptom is an 'unusual phenomenon in the material constitution of the organs or in their functions which is linked to the existence of an illness and which one can observe while the sufferers are alive: the symptoms of pleurisy, of plague etc.' As *Littré* sees it, the term *symptomatic* is applied to 'what is the effect or symp-tom of some other ailment: e.g. a symptomatic fever'. A symptomatic illness is 'one which is merely a symptom of another disease and which, when that other disease ends, itself ceases immediately.' Symptomatic medicine is the 'method which consists in attacking the symptoms and not the illness itself.' A symptom is a phenomenon linked to the existence of an illness, of a pathogenic factor. This distinction between symptom and illness seems to be an essential one.

Illness is a state which is self-explanatory and which thus contains its own cause: examples might be diphtheria, a whitlow or, in the view of some, SCHIZOPHRENIA. By contrast, the symptom is an index/indication/clue:

its cause is external to itself: a whitlow may be a symptom of diabetes, schizophrenia a symptom of family dysfunction etc.

In this sense, to speak of a symptomatic dimension may constitute a considerable advance. Freud's discovery suggested a shift from illness to symptom. This change of logical level displaced what had up to that point been known as syndromes or illnesses – phobia or hysteria – and made these the marks of a structural process involving the rest of the personality – the symptoms. In family therapy, the most important discovery has consisted in this transition from illness to symptom, as for example with schizophrenia, which has come to be seen as a 'sign' or, in other words, the symptom of a particular family structure (see table).

In practice, it is not enough for the therapist to be convinced by a particular theory for an element to be considered as a symptom or an illness. The type of therapeutic approach selected will depend essentially on the content of the DEMAND of the subjects or families, i.e. on what is experienced as an illness or a symptom. How the demand expresses itself is not an irrelevant matter. This may take the form: 'He's mad. On account of him, everyone in the family is suffering.' Here the illness is the patient and the 'symptoms' the suffering of the family (situation 1). Or it may take a different form: 'We don't know what's going on, but we can't communicate any more and we don't understand each other.' This makes the patients out to be the 'symptoms' of an 'illness' which is thought to be a communication problem (situation 2). In general, it seems to be of little use to determine what constitutes a symptom in a situation without taking into account the context of the demand underlying it. To do so is to risk misunderstandings. It is clear that, in situation 1, nothing is to be expected of a meeting at which the therapist decided, against the views of the family, that the behaviour of the family group is, in fact, the illness and the INDEX PATIENT or, alternatively, a symmetrical conflict, the symptom. These problems are not merely incidental, since they determine the pathology itself.

The work of Selvini Palazzoli has enabled us to go beyond a reading of the relations between illness and symptom in terms of linear causality. The technique of CIRCULARITY she introduced has brought about an acceptance that what is experienced as an 'illness', or, in other words, as alien to oneself, may also be a symptom of one's own functioning. The various therapeutic approaches summarized in the table are the consequences of specific hypotheses concerning not the symptoms or the illness themselves, but the particular way in which they are interconnected.

(See also DOUBLE BIND; FUNCTION OF THE SYMPTOM; GENERAL SYSTEMS THEORY; PRESCRIPTION; SINGULARITIES; SYMPTOMATIC AND/OR AETIOLOGICAL TRANSACTIONS.)

R.N.

synchrony See AGREEMENT AND DISAGREEMENT; DIACHRONIC AND SYNCHRONIC AXES OF A THERAPY; RITUALIZATION.

syntax of communication The study of:

1 The disposition of the lexical, kinetic and linguistic structures which mediate sequences of INTERACTIONS (Birdwhistell, 1970). It is based on an analysis into discrete, discontinuous constituents, enabling the different sequences to be discriminated one from another.
2 Algorithms and heuristics which transform the deep structures into surface structures; on the level of the pathology of communications, the analysis of character and symptoms is of the order of a syntactic study.
3 The disposition and movement of the protagonists in relation to one another – and in relation to the contexts – in a situation of interaction which issues in a certain synchronization of gestures and speech.

The syntax of communication is the complement to the PRAGMATICS and SEMANTICS OF COMMUNICATION. Through it one can specify clinically (a) *the paradigmatic axis*: the set of sequences potentially present at a particular moment in the unfolding of the interaction, irrespective of the one that is effectively activated; and (b) *the syntagmatic axis*: the whole disposition of the sequence in its actual unfolding.

DIFFERENT MEDIA OF COMMUNICATION

A distinction can be made here between mediate and immediate contexts:

Mediate contexts: the environment in which a given exchange occurs
The nature of the life-context – town or countryside, characteristics of the means of travel, structure and nature of the habitat, public or private, family house, school, courtroom, hospital, welfare centre etc. – may influence the collective nature of the problems encountered.

One should take into account the journeys made by the various participants in an interchange. In the context of specialist interventions (whether we are speaking of general medicine, psychiatry, the police or the courts), the problem arises of whether the specialists should make visits to the homes of the persons concerned or whether 'clients' should be received for consultations in specific professional spaces.

Immediate contexts: the natural and cultural parameters operating in the interchange
The territorial and proxemic behaviour of the various participants: DISTANCE AND ORGANIZATION OF TERRITORY during interactions, which are linked to the levels of contact, are: tactile (the to-ing and fro-ing of children

around their parents, children sitting on knees, arm-entwining gestures or physical distancing on the part of marriage partners); olfactory (natural smells or perfumes); visual (strategies of establishing visual contact or avoiding the other's eyes) or acoustic (ambient sound level, intensity of vocal interchanges).

Corporal, vestimentary and cosmetic habitus: this is characterized by size, corpulence, tonus, general mobility, the intensity of neuro-vegetative reactions, respiratory rhythms, colouring of the skin, tears, laughter etc.; but also the style of dress, hairstyle and make-up etc. These link together natural and cultural parameters in a continuum.

Posturo–voco–gestural attitudes: a sequence of interaction will be influenced by fundamental postures: standing position; seated position, slumped back in the chair or sitting upright or sitting forward, with arms folded and legs crossed; lying flat for the patient in psychoanalysis; in a listening or speaking position. The development of the sequence can be broken down into sub-units, marked by partial modifications of posture functioning as 'actonic points' used as signals (Scheflen, 1973).

These 'point units', which mark changes of posture, punctuate the different parts of the interaction and structure the articulation of interchanges:

- *contentless actonic points* which maintain attention and the orientation of interchanges: for example, stroking the throat, reciprocal eye contact maintaining a bond, the nodding of the head, carried out instinctively by the receiver when listening to a speaker;
- *actonic points used as signals*: for example, smoking a cigarette, taking out a handkerchief, partially modifying one's posture, crossing and uncrossing one's legs;
- *representational points that suggest more complicated activities*: marking positions of dominance–submission or symmetry, quasi–courting behaviour etc. (see below).

These behaviours as a whole have a non-linear character. They function essentially by contiguity and by analogical adjustments, producing a kind of interactional dance or even an orchestration of messages evolving in parallel. (For a discussion of the analogy between the ritual of communication and orchestral performance, see Winkin, 1981, p. 103). The structure of interchanges thus has paracommunicative and metacommunicative aspects.

Paralinguistic behaviour

Posturo-gestural positions structure paralinguistic behaviours which can be differentiated, according to Ekman (1977), into body manipulators, illustrators, emotional expressions and emblems.

Emblems are symbolic actions which have a specific verbal meaning within a given sub-culture or culture. Nodding or shaking the head to indicate 'yes' and 'no' are emblems. The emblem for suicide in the USA consists in pointing the index finger at the temple, whereas in Japan it is a symbolization of sticking an imaginary dagger in the stomach and in New Guinea a depiction of strangling. Emblems stand in the place of direct verbal expression. They are, therefore, the bodily activities that are closest to linguistic expression.

Body manipulators are similar to the displacement activities described in ethology. One part of the body acts on another: blowing one's nose, scratching oneself, running one's hand through one's hair, brushing some dirt from one's clothing. They have a meaning in global terms and are interpreted as expressing a situation of discomfort linked to a motivational conflict or an ambiguity in communication.

Illustrators and regulators are intimately tied to the content and/or flow of speech: 'batons' and 'underliners' enabling a word, phrase, clause, sentence or group of sentences to be accentuated; 'ideograph' which sketch the path or direction of thought; 'kinetographs' which depict a bodily action or a non-human action; 'pictographs' which draw the shape of the referent in the air; 'rhythmics' which depict the pacing of an event; 'spatials' which depict a spatial relationship; 'deictics' which point to the referent. Illustrators have no direct semantic content. They arise within speech. They increase with enthusiasm and appear more in neurotic than in psychotic depressions. They make it possible to express in gesture what speech does not manage to render easily. They have a function of self-priming of the speech-making process and punctuate the flow of speech.

Emotional expressions have been extensively studied, both in ethological terms and in the context of intercultural comparisons. The ethological studies stress universals (joy, sadness, anger, fear, scorn, disgust, flirtation etc.), while the intercultural work points to expressions that are typical of a particular culture. In Ekman's view:

The contradictory observations of the relativists and universalists can be resolved, in part, if we presume that the relativists were describing the cultural variations in emblems, illustrators and regulators and not distinguishing these from the universals in emotional expression. Conversely, the universalists may have focused on the emotional expressions to the exclusion of recognizing cultural variations in the facial actions which function as emblems, illustrators or regulators. (Ekman, 1977, p. 53)

Linguistic behaviour

Human language is based on the double articulation: phonemes (discriminative units without intrinsic meaning) and monemes (structured sets of phonemes, bearers of intrinsic meaning). The disposition of monemes on a sentence is provided by the process which transforms deep structures into surface structures.

The linear, one-dimensional forms of language grammars reflect the irreversible flow of time and the substructure of efficient causality. They enable information to be transmitted over a distance. The chain of verbal discourse, the linear sequencing of books with a beginning and an end are examples of one-dimensional morphologies which enable precise information to be transmitted in large quantities and, in some cases, over very large distances from their point of departure.

Sentence-order – the ordering of subject, verb and object (S, V, O) – varies between the world's languages: SVO is found is 36 per cent, VSO in 15 per cent and SOV in 39 per cent. The remaining 10 per cent are split between OSV, OVS and VOS (Hagège, 1985). This reveals the fundamental conception which prevails in each of the linguistic systems under consideration. Whatever the sentence-order, however, that conception is based on a linear and orientated, one-directional development, reflecting the effects of efficient causality. We find this same conception in the recognition of the INDEX PATIENT ('He hit his mother', 'He committed suicide').

SYNTAX OF FAMILY COMMUNICATION

It will also be possible, on the plane of family relations, to observe a double articulation between, on the one hand, the expression of characters and symptoms, which are discrete, but not necessarily successive units; and, on the other, intrafamilial and suprafamilial sequences of interaction leading to the existence of tree-patterns structuring the hierarchy of occurrence of different behaviours and the establishment of FAMILY RULES.

Family behaviours obey largely implicit rules which set the rhythm for the nature of interactions between members of a single family. Pathological communications reveal *a contrario* more or less complete destructurings of these rules which may lead to entropic drifts which are expressed in physical or mental 'illnesses'.

The structure of the family rules can be determined from the following questions: who has the right to speak, who must speak and who has to be silent depending on the particular circumstances? What are the taboo subjects, the ones everyone knows but which they must keep quiet about? What are the possible COALITIONS and which ones are prohibited? What is the structure of the dyads and triads? How are the processes of triangulation set in place? (see TRIANGLES)

SYNTAX OF PATHOLOGICAL COMMUNICATION

In pathological communication, the differential analysis of characters (schizoid, paranoid, hysterical, obsessional, phobic etc.) and symptoms (systematized or non-

systematized delirium, alcoholism, drug addiction, autism, epilepsy, schizophrenia, encopresis, delinquency etc.) contributes to the recognition of typologies of interaction. The recognition of family interactions leads to the structure of characters no longer being considered as pure static forms, but enables one to see their 'metabolic' value in the dynamics of live exchanges.

Let us take as an example a mother who appears at a family therapy consultation with her two children, having been referred by a house physician during a period of hospitalization. She prefers her elder son of seven to stay in the waiting room. She explains her intimate problems in the presence of her three-year-old daughter, manifestly assuming she is too young to understand. Her face bears the marks of alcohol consumption. This is the principal factor prompting her consultation. She regards the whole of her problem as having to do with her husband: she describes him as very kind, but rejects him sexually. He was supposed to come with her, but she thinks he would not be able either to understand or even hear what she has to say. It seems, moreover, that she remains very close to her own parents. There is a distortion between the surface structure of the immediate context (organizing the distances between herself and her children) and the active power of the deep structure of the contexts of the couple and the family of origin. The pragmatic dimension of the situation is gradually revealed: she comes to family therapy to speak alone, but she has already consulted a psychiatrist who has asked her husband to see him too, having described to him the couple's symmetrical games where once temporary sobriety is achieved, it can only be confirmed by a return to the bottle. (cf. Bateson, 1972). The restoration of meaning to these double-bind relations can only occur in CO-THERAPY work, with collaboration between the various intervenors, prescribers and consultants involved.

(See also AGREEMENT AND DISAGREEMENT; DISTANCE AND ORGANIZATION OF TERRITORY; GAZE; MAP AND COUNTER-MAP OF A FAMILY SYSTEM; METABINDING; MULTI-CHANNEL COMMUNICATION SYSTEMS; PATHOLOGICAL COMMUNICATION; TERRITORY.)

J.M.

systemic analysis See SYSTEMIC MODELLING AND INTERVENTION.

systemic approach See BRIEF INTERACTIONAL THERAPY; CONTEXT; FEEDBACK; MILAN SYSTEMIC THERAPY; NEUTRALITY; STRATEGIC THERAPY; SYSTEMIC HYPOTHESIS; SYSTEMIC MODELLING AND INTERVENTION.

systemic hypothesis A tool which enables therapists or other professionals to conduct their interviews, to ask the questions which will bring them pertinent information and thus to have a directing thread. It is an 'unproved supposition, accepted provisionally as a basis for subsequent investigation' (Selvini Palazzoli et al., 1980a). It may be confirmed or refuted. Refutation brings with it new elements and enables the therapist to formulate another hypothesis (trial and error technique).

The hypothesis is neither true nor false, but more or less useful. It acts to underwrite therapists' activities, their exploration of sequences of interactions. In the absence of hypotheses, the danger is that the family will impose its own linear hypotheses which very often consist in finding a particular person or persons guilty of causing its current suffering.

A systemic hypothesis covers each of the members of the family and offers a theoretical assumption as to how the SYMPTOM functions for the family system as a whole. It defines the FUNCTION OF THE SYMPTOM for each of the members and the gain each derives from it.

(See also DATA GATHERING; THERAPEUTIC ABDUCTION.)

M.G.

systemic modelling of carcinogenesis In 1962, Smithers wrote:

> The behaviour of individual cells is, in fact, the result and not the origin of organised living. Organisms contain vastly more information than any one of their cells: the amount of information in a system is a measure of its organisation . . . Organismal organisation and its disturbances can no more be tied down solely to the laws of individual cell action than everything which happens in society can be attributed to the direct design of individuals within that society (or even of powerful groups) . . . Cancer is a disease of organisation, not a disease of cells. (*The Lancet*, 10 March 1962)

Though he was later knighted for his work, little attention was paid to Smithers's 'attack on cytologism', since it took twenty years for a systemic approach to be timidly set on foot in the realm of oncology, by concealing itself inside the Trojan horse of pure theory (Maruani, 1982b).

Admittedly, in 1963, Weiss had already attempted to think in terms of networks of cellular interactions, but the implicit dogma which dominated oncology for twenty years more remained that of cytocentrism, i.e. the idea that a cancer derived from a single cloning of cells, developed by direct filiation and local extension and then by metastatic migration. In the light of this assumption, treatment was directed exclusively at destroying 'monstrous' cells, even though it was known that, under certain conditions, cells could become subject

once again to the normal regulation of the organism. As a result, the question posed for the advocates of a theoretical oncology is the following (Salomon, 1985); is cancer a local illness which becomes generalized or a general illness which becomes localized? And this, of course, created a space for systemic hypotheses seeking to comprehend and curb the mechanisms by which neoplastic cells escape from homeostatic control in this way. Though, in actual fact, what is involved here is, more exactly, homeorhesis (see HOMEOSTASIS).

Moreover, in *Structural stability and morphogenesis*, Thom (1972) had suggested that the events by which cancers developed followed upon a perturbation of the genetic cycle which led to a jump on the part of germinal cells towards a zone reserved for mature cells; according to the mathematical model known as the 'inundated terrain' hydraulic model, this would result in a self-sustaining oscillation with an increasingly shorter period.

Thom (1986) produced a more detailed account of his thinking on this subject, drawing on a classic article by Waddington, which appeared in *Nature* of 20 April 1935, which was devoted to cancer and the theory of organizers by comparison with the development of embryonic tissues at certain limited moments of competence and under the influence of an 'evocator' determining an 'individuation field'.

However, the model defined by Maruani (1982b, 1985d) claims to bring about the epistemological break which makes it possible to bring order into the complexity and multiplicity of the experimental and clinical arguments. First, it is not a model of carcinogenesis, but of all illnesses of cellular equilibrium, both quantitative and qualitative. In effect, by virtue of the systemic principle that complicated phenomena become simpler if one introduces supplementary data (i.e. if one does not simply stop at certain limits), this model attempts to represent the cybernetic processes of exchange of humoral information which preside over the normal functioning of the organism and over illnesses of the system, over benign tumours and malignant ones (cancers). It ascribes the totality of communications within a cell (R1), a tissue (R2) and the organism (R3) to different logical levels. However, as the organism is a multi-tissual being and therefore multi-cellular, the molecules exchanged belong by definition to several logical levels. The needs of homeorhesis imply that these have contradictory informational values at two contiguous levels, the double bind appearing to be a necessary mechanism of biological regulation. The 'concert' of hormones shows, for example, how the same substance may convey different messages depending upon the level of complexity under consideration and the particular context. In this sense, hormones are not paradoxical but symbolic molecules. They enable a jump in signification to be made from one level of regulation to another.

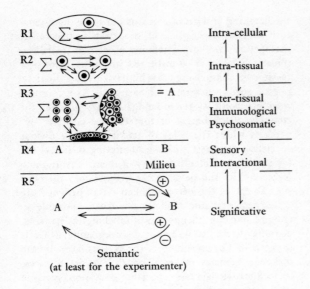

R1   Intra-cellular

R2   Intra-tissual

R3   = A   Inter-tissual
Immunological
Psychosomatic

R4   A   B   Sensory
Milieu   Interactional

R5

A   B   Significative

Semantic
(at least for the experimenter)

For toxic, physical, chemical or microbiological reasons, the genetic programme of a cell may be degraded in various ways (see diagram):

- it becomes incapable of synthesizing one or more proteins, i.e. of emitting a precisely determinate message: in this case, the neighbouring cells will compensate for it at R2 and R3, unless they have the same lesion;
- or it becomes incapable of stopping synthesizing one or more proteins because it has been rendered 'deaf' to the habitual feedback mechanisms at R2: from that point on it will reduce the healthy cells of the tissue to silence, but will itself continue to develop clonally at accelerated speed;
- or it combines the two faults and sets itself free not only from R2 but also from R3.

The first of these configurations describes the phasic evolution of viral illnesses and the emergence of be-

nign tumours in cases of metabolic or viral damage to a substantial part of the tissue. The second configuration describes system illnesses of the type in which there is overall regression of the tissue contrasting with centres of hyperactivity. The third configuration describes cancerization as a cybernetic effect of a double problem of self-regulated command (neoplastic R3).

The paradox resulting from the double-bind structure of homeorhesis is that when the healthy cells of the affected tissue halt the production of proteins and hormones (fall silent), they receive an order from the organism to emit once again, which in fact stimulates the mitoses of the degraded clone, which is not inhibited by this production of messages to which it is deaf.

All in all, cancerization occurs when the double-bind structure of inter-cellular and inter-tissual regulation is endangered by a lack of the usual negative feedback.

(See also CANCER; PSYCHOSOMATIC DOUBLE BINDS; PSYCHOSOMATIC ILLNESS; PSYCHOSOMATIC MEDICINE.)

G.G.M.

systemic modelling and intervention Systemic modelling, a methodology based on GENERAL SYSTEMS THEORY within the framework of the pragmatics of communication, is here conceived as bio-, familio- and sociosystemic.

Psychoanalysis offered the first systemic models of mental activity and its structuring in terms of family relations (see FAMILY PSYCHICAL APPARATUS; METAPSYCHOLOGY; PSYCHOANALYSIS; UNCONSCIOUS). Its unit of study is essentially the individual personality, from which starting point it is, in some cases, possible to grasp group realities. New models seem necessary which take account not only of individuated mental activity, but also of the reality of family and social systems which contribute to that individuation or impede it. Systemic modelling goes beyond the therapeutic field properly so-called and is found at the most varied levels of the investigation of reality.

The terms 'systemic modelling', 'systemic analysis', and 'systemic intervention or approach' are becoming increasingly widespread and are tending to resituate the notion of family therapy within a wider context (this being most particularly obvious in the fields of social, medical and psychiatric work) for epistemological, methodological and interdisciplinary reasons. We note here the vague character of the expression 'systemic approach'. One may, strictly speaking, take the view that a systemic intervention presupposes an 'approaching' of the persons or families concerned, but it is, nevertheless, desirable that it should arrive at a minimum of methodological and conceptual clarification. Similarly, the expression 'systemic analysis' is incoherent, since the object is to study, within a particular reality, what cannot be reduced to the analysis

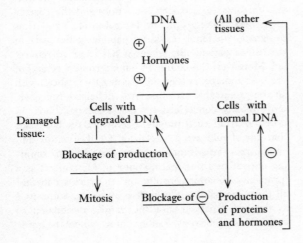

DNA

(All other tissues

⊕

Hormones

⊕

Damaged tissue:

Cells with degraded DNA   Cells with normal DNA

Blockage of production   ⊖

Mitosis   Blockage of ⊖   Production of proteins and hormones of its component parts. We may thus distinguish three interconnected planes: the *plane of modelling*, the *plane of intervention* and the *plane of organization* (see MULTI-LEVEL HIERARCHIES).

If, then, the term 'modelling' permits us to expect a minimum of methodological coherence, it is also right that some care should be exercised over its use in actual practice. We cannot proceed by identifying with misleading 'models', whether these be charismatic leaders or ready-made ideologies. Such identifications, which were undoubtedly necessary in a first phase, rapidly become obsolete. Modelling operates in a process of alternation with systemic intervention. One can only determine how the interrelationship between the two is to be regulated through contact with the persons, families and groups one actually encounters, and with the capacity to organize functional units of intervention.

Systemic modelling and intervention tend increasingly to refer to a specific field of theorization and intervention, only part of which coincides with the domain of therapeutic interventions proper and/or of interventions with families. And we have, of course, already seen the snares and confusions thrown up by the very concept of FAMILY THERAPY. Systemic modelling enables us to cast some light on these indistinct, obscure areas of therapy, though it also produces other traps of its own. Various modalities of intervention are, in effect, brought together under this head, bearing both on the family system and on other life systems: collective family interviews, family therapies in the strict sense, systemic interventions bearing on institutions (educational, academic, professional and health institutions), on a particular district or on large-scale units (such as NETWORK interventions). Onnis (1980) defines it as a 'practical theoretical orientation which, referring for its conceptual model to systems theory, relates above all to interpersonal systems', focusing in particular on 'the process of interaction and communication currently occurring between the different members of a system rather than on the intra-psychic dynamics or the psychogenetic reconstruction of individual problems, whence the many possibilities of applying it to all human interactive systems'. From the epistemological point of view, as Daigremont et al. (1979) point out, following Bateson, that approach includes 'the dialectical relation of the phenomenon under investigation with the context in which it appears and develops'.

THE SOCIOEDUCATIONAL MILIEU

The conceptual framework delimited in this way by systemic modelling reveals a potential for the deployment of an interdisciplinary methodology. Having the advantage of being medically 'neutral' or de-centred, this point of view turns out to be less stigmatizing than the flaunting of what often turns out to be the premature advance description of an action as necessarily therapeutic. It allows a genuine process of interdisciplinary dialogue to be instituted within teams of professionals comprising psychiatrists, psychologists, nurses, social workers, sociologists etc. As a common reference point, systemic modelling may promote the concrete establishment of contacts and creative connections where the fields of activity of these diverse specialists interface, without attempting to cancel out the professional identity of any of them. A re-framing of hierarchies and fields of competence may then ensue. So far as the persons 'taken on as patients' are concerned, systemic modelling makes it possible to enquire into the phenomena of labelling (as patients, delinquents etc.) while avoiding scapegoating, as far as is possible. The ascription of the various labels by the different agencies of social control (social services, socioeducative agencies, specialist education, juvenile courts etc.) may lead to diagnostic over-emphasis: 'dangerous alcoholic', 'problem individual', 'educationally sub-normal', 'delinquent' etc. Without denying the importance of such categories, the systemic approach makes it possible to remove some of these labels, by recognizing both the process which generates them and their relation to the particular contexts in question; in some instances, one observes that the labels cease, to a certain extent, to be embodied definitively in statuses of pathology or delinquency, with all the associated primary and secondary gains. The roles and functions of specialists and institutions are thus better defined and better delimited as regards their reference to the medical, judicial and educational order.

In effect, as Selvini Palazzoli (1983) stresses, it would be dangerous, in the case of a 'first-level' health service consultation to replay to a request for assistance with a referral for family therapy. Apart from the fact that coherent therapeutic action can only be conceived within a context where indications and therapeutic choices are carefully weighed up, such a referral, right at the outset, amounts to 'accusing the family and the parents of at best being stupid or incapable etc.' and thus designates the family as 'index patient' in the place of the 'index patient' for whom it has come to request aid. Moreover, this could not but engender a refusal of the indication or, at least, its 'passive acceptance', with all the predictable accompanying defensive reticence, only flimsily concealing a secret defiance. Thus, in order to avoid such pitfalls, Selvini Palazzoli advises that one should avoid 'declaring' family therapy and emphasizes the advantages to be gained from confining oneself to a minimal marking of the context as a 'problem-evaluation consultation', to which are invited all those 'co-habitants' who live under the same roof as the index patient, not the 'family designated as such'. This public consultation context, where the transdisciplinary team takes its bearings from the systemic approach, presupposes that not all the members will be identified as 'family therapists' or even, more correctly, as 'family consultants'. In this first stage, the object is to assess together a situation which seems difficult and ultimately to arrive at a definition of the problem and suggest ways it might be resolved.

Such a non-declaration of family therapy appears even more strictly pertinent in the context of an intervention with 'non-voluntary families' referred in France by a Children's Judge for a *Consultation d'Orientation Educative* or *Consultation d'Education en Milieu Ouvert*, whether the problem be one of a minor exposed to moral or physical danger or of a juvenile delinquent. In such a context, it is even more important to be certain that it is then epistemology of the SYSTEMIC APPROACH that is likely to be operative in the work undertaken with the family group (which is often restructured by the presence of a socioeducational or institutional system which is preliminarily involved in the new intervention).

The stakes are too high here to sacrifice them for the satisfaction in terms of prestige that may be gained from the ambiguous title of 'family therapist', a title which, as we know, may be highly regarded in the professions connected with social work. These professions are often ensnared by an 'imaginary capture by the medical model', which is defined by a function out of the common run of the therapeutic function and as 'representing the prototype of an aristocratic position'. The fascination of such a model may lead to the pursuit of 'emblematic remuneration', as has been so well demonstrated by Fustier (1983). In chasing after such narcissistic compensations, it is not only the index patients and their families that are the losers, but the social workers too.

Within this perspective, systemic modelling may serve as an effective pivot for determining the concrete orientations to be adopted in respect of the disorders and needs that are found (whether these be intrafamilial or institutional), on condition that its outlines be clearly determined:

- systems theory, as such, is a theory of general systems which has a self-referential dynamic. While it grounds its own fields of validity, it can only validate its pertinence as a function of the situations it encounters (see INCOMPLETENESS THEOREMS);
- as a methodology, it cannot therefore (any more than psychoanalysis) determine by itself the limits of its own validity, since all the fields of reality are susceptible of systemic modelling;
- certain assertions, which provide its foundations, only derive their truth and pertinence from data external to the systemic model under consideration; the territory of the family is distinct from the map which makes it possible to model it;

- systemic modelling is thus a metasystemic modelling, a metasystem of intervention (Caillé, 1985), which has a duty to respect the various spheres of competence of the practitioners intervening.

THE PSYCHIATRIC TREATMENT OF CHILDREN

In his article, 'Towards a theory of schizophrenia', Bateson states that a psychiatric institution, whose function consists as much in satisfying the needs of the hospital personnel as those of the patients, tends to recreate dysfunctional modalities of communication. This thought leads us to seek out the distortions of exchanges which take place between the members of a specialist resident medical staff and the families of children admitted to the hospital.

When home-based treatment has failed, a request to admit the child is usually made, either in the period following a critical episode or at a point where intrafamilial relations are rigidifying. In most therapeutic establishments, admissions are carried out according to a relatively strict procedure. The parents are received by a therapist, who performs the history taking and the child is then examined to assess whether his/her problems may benefit from residential treatment. The child or adolescent is often offered an observation period in order to confirm or disconfirm the conclusions arrived at at the admission visit. The cooperation of the parents is usually explicitly desired and is often confined to a few episodic interviews with a therapist. Parallel with this, the child's admission into the institution proceeds, punctuated by case conferences and, when indicated, sessions of individual psychotherapy.

This procedure is faithful to the teaching of Bruno Bettelheim, who explains that, when dealing with a family which presents a disturbed child to him, he indicates to the parents that this is the youngster's personal problem. If the child is admitted, Bettelheim tries to convince the parents that they must derive consolation from the thought that they have done all they could for him. They are advised to strive to reconstruct their own lives which have probably been sorely tested by the presence among them of someone who is mentally ill.

Many psychiatric institutions elaborate complex 'parentectomy' strategies, placing ever more obstacles between the hospitalized child and his/her family. The family is then seen by a doctor away from any other member of the socioeducational team: he/she thus receives only fragmentary information, which increases the phenomena of exclusion and competition. Thus what is happening here, in good faith, is the protection of the child from the family environment which a permanent disqualification made depressive, guilt-ridden, indifferent or even demanding and hostile. The catastrophic effects of these attitudes can be seen in the repeated placements of several siblings.

It is, however, the aim of the institutional structure, which is hierarchical and clearly defined spatially, to reassure the child and the family. Every decision is supposed to be taken for the good of the children and adolescents concerned, without any mention of the increased staff well-being to be expected from it. We are dealing here, then, with a form of pathogenic communicative behaviour, which, in Bateson's view is typical of many double-bind situations created in and by the very framework of the hospital milieu.

Very often, the hospitalized child is not in a position to comment on the contradictory situation in which he/she is placed both by the medico-educational team and within his/her own family group. Over-rigid partitioning off of the exchanges between index patient, family and hospital staff restricts the child's access to the metacommunicative level. Moreover, the residential social worker's lack of understanding of the intrafamilial pathological interactions generally leads to the reproduction within the hospital 'life-group' of a dysfunctional repetition of the family's relational models. (Jenkins, 1984). This is why it becomes necessary to integrate the residential treatment of the child into the systemic analysis of the family–institution ensemble along the lines of the model proposed by Siegi Hirsch (in Schouten et al., 1974). Therapeutic interviews are organized in a contractual manner with the family in its entirety and several of the staff members most closely concerned with the child. As Bruggen (Byng-Hall and Bruggen, 1974; Bruggen and O'Brian, 1982) demonstrates, it is essential that this process begins at the very first contact between family, outside professionals and the in-patient unit.

These family therapies are different from the interventions of the same order carried out in the community. In effect, the placement of a single member of the family reinforces his/her labelling as index patient, while the first consultations often reveal intense collective suffering and the presence of psychical or somatic disorders in several members of the family group.

In families in psychotic transaction, the parents falsify their messages more or less consciously by flaunting their impotence in the face of their children's behavioural difficulties. Nothing and no one can induce some of them to give up their demand for absolute control.

How many parents, after generously praising the devotion of the residential workers, go into a long string of disqualification manoeuvres. These families throw out a challenge to the team: 'Treat my child, but don't change him.' We may cite as an example parents who were scandalized by the appearance of certain swear words in the vocabulary of their previously silent daughter.

The techniques of family therapy save the parents from becoming involved in an endless game with a psychiatric institution promoting intrafamilial readjustments which progressively make it impossible for the scapegoat to return home. By stifling any possibility of a hidden symmetrical escalation in the competition between the parents and the residential staff for a monopoly on the definition of the relation to the child, the therapists free the index patient from a conflict of loyalty. In effect, it is up to the young person to remain faithful to his/her family group's rigid rules while at the same time respecting the institution's codes.

When dealing with a large number of psychopathic adolescents who privilege motor discharge over verbal elaboration, the non-congruence of the messages they simultaneously receive from their parents is striking. These SPLIT DOUBLE BINDS, to use Ferreira's (1966) expression, increase in number when the adolescent is subject to bi-polar messages of different logical types within the family and in the institutional living group.

This brief evocation of the pertinence of the systemic model in the treatment of families in pathological transaction would be incomplete without a mention of its use as a model for the analysis of the institutional macro-system (see also INSTITUTIONS). Taking into account the objectives of the institution in which the therapists practice, and identifying the 'games without end' in which the various practitioners are involved, and the potency of the centrifugal tendencies produced by divergent or contradictory personal strategies, must not lead us to overlook the regulative mechanisms ensuring each person's integration in that collective structure. The understanding of a functional organization cannot be reduced to any kind of rationality, even a systemic one. However, within a paradoxical therapeutic organization which, to satisfy its goal, must distance itself from it, systemic analysis provides the foundation for pragmatic interventions which free the institution from its rigid homeostatic tendencies.

THE PSYCHIATRIC TREATMENT OF ADULTS

There are many features in common between the placement of young children, as referred to above, and the hospitalization of young adults in psychiatric hospitals. It was, in fact, through contact with adult schizophrenic hospital patients that Bateson formulated his cybernetic hypotheses on schizophrenic interactions. One can only receive the families of hospitalized patients if one respects the institutional context, while at the same time sensitizing the institution to the therapeutic advantage that is to be gained from not entering into symmetrical escalations with the family systems of hospitalized patients in a game of mutual disqualification.

The most sharply significant point concerns the extra degree of a-topia of the adult mental patient: his/her place seems to be nowhere, least of all in these contexts of hospitalization, though, for very serious forms of disorder, it is very difficult, if not impossible, to dispense with them. At the height of the crisis, families will direct messages in DOUBLE BIND form towards the staff of the institution, bringing considerable intellectual and emotional pressure to bear on them.

A double trap lies in wait for the team when faced with these challenges from the family:

1 Contempt, directed toward those 'manipulative' families, who are apparently uncooperative. This leads to the patient's close circle being viewed as instrinsically pathogenic, if not indeed to the family being considered 'sick' and then being treated 'as a single person'. Such attitudes run the risk of reinforcing the vital individual and collective defences which the patient and those close to him/her put up as a last-ditch measure.
2 Hyperactive interest, seeking at all costs systematically to turn every form of family meeting with the therapists into an enterprise of collective control. Collective interviews with the family have a sense as institutional therapy if they enable the levels of (factual and fictive) demand to be differentiated and with them the style of intervention of each of the professionals, whether nurses, social workers, psychologists, psychiatrists, or even family therapists.

Not everyone in the institution can (nor in fact wants to) take the responsibility for carrying out sustained work with the family group. A nurse who is both competent and sensitized to the value of such interviews with the family in the case of a particular patient, to whom he/she dispenses the most attentive care, will not necessarily be able to attend all the family interviews on account of clashes with other pressing duties. A bifurcation can be seen here between institutional therapy and family therapy and it is of value both to identify this in practice and in theory in order to increase the degree of responsibility in a genuine CO-THERAPY undertaking.

(See also FAMILY DOCTOR; FAMILY–THERAPEUTIC INSTITUTION DIFFERENTIATION; MAP AND COUNTER-MAP OF A FAMILY SYSTEM; METABINDINGS; PSYCHOSOMATIC MEDICINE; SOCIAL ORGANIZATION; SUPERVISION.)

P.S., P.A. & J.M.

systemic work with individuals The interface between individual and family therapy may be thought of as different ways of understanding the locus of therapeutic space. Individual psychodynamic therapy places particular emphasis on the influences on individuals of relationships in the person's internal world. Family therapy (the systemic approach) emphasizes the interpersonal and relational contexts of individuals and their various social groupings. Neither approach denies the importance of the other perspective and both are concerned with the nature of space. The wider perspective in individual psychodynamic work becomes the 'ground'

against which the 'figure' of practice occurs; in systemic work, it is the relational system which is the figure in the figure–ground dimension, while the internal world of the individual is emphasized less. Psychodynamic approaches are concerned primarily with the spaces within, while systemic approaches are concerned primarily with the space in between.

Both models can be conceptualized systemically. Family therapy uses the frameworks of GENERAL SYSTEMS THEORY and CYBERNETICS. Psychoanalytic theory constructs models which are also 'systemic': the construct of super-ego, ego and id is an internalized system of checks and balances; the OEDIPUS COMPLEX is a triadic system for understanding a particular set of relationships; and the description of TRANSFERENCE and counter-transference in cybernetic terms may be seen as a recursive FEEDBACK LOOP.

Systemic work with individuals provides an opportunity to work with the individual, focusing both on individual internal processes and on the impact of change by the individual on the wider social system. Systemic work with individuals is concerned with the spaces in between people and therefore with their relationships, but must also attend to how the spaces within organize and are organized by the individual's social contexts, as well as by their internal experiences.

The position of the therapist is significantly different in systemic work with individuals. He or she works with the 'door open', in that the patient's family members or social world may be involved in treatment at any stage (Jenkins and Asen, 1992). Such individual work may have as one of its goals that various significant others will participate in sessions at a later stage. The therapist does not work in the transference where similarity is experienced as sameness, so that previous experience and related feelings from the past are transferred to the present in actuality by the patient (Casement, 1988). Instead, the systemic therapist working with individuals focuses on connections and relationships, and the feedback loops between the individual and the context(s) in which the problems occur, whether past, present or future, and not on a person's individual characteristics (Papp, 1983).

The thinking that has greatly influenced these developments can be traced to the early work of the Milan group (Selvini Palazzoli et al., 1980; Penn, 1982; Boscolo et al., 1987; Cecchin, 1987) and the styles of therapeutic questioning described by Tomm (1987a, b, 1988) as 'interventive interviewing'. This approach allows the therapist to interview in a way which helps and challenges the patient to re-examine his/her position in relation to the problem, in relation to others involved, and to view the difficulties from a multiple range of perspectives of time and place. It focuses on introducing new information to the system, to the way the individual perceives his/her situation and to changing previously held belief systems.

By maintaining what in effect is a therapeutic meta-perspective, the patient is discouraged from investing past experiences in the therapeutic relationship. Instead, the patient constantly examines feelings, beliefs and behaviours in real time and real life contexts. By ensuring that the therapist does not become too central to the life of the patient, it is possible for treatment to be relatively brief in many instances, although no less intense a therapeutic experience.

Such an approach is powerful where family members are not available because of geographical distance, death or because of potential harm to the individual for reasons such as physical or sexual abuse or domestic violence. Systemic work with individuals can be powerful when working transgenerationally (Lieberman, 1979a). It is congruent with the important work of Bowen (1978a) and Boszormenyi-Nagy and Spark (1973), drawing on transgenerational, psychodynamic and systems theory approaches. As the field has become more flexible in drawing from a range of models, so descriptions of systemic work with individuals have

increased (Carter and McGoldrick Orfanidis, 1976; Weakland, 1983; Weber and Simon, 1988; Jenkins, 1989c; Jenkins and Asen, 1992).

While the emphasis here is on developments in thinking and practice in methods of working with individuals from a systemic perspective, Haley (1987) warns of the dangers of diluting the advances made in theory and practice by reverting to approaches which do not engage with all the people involved in the problem(s). However, a recognition among family therapists of the importance of focusing on the individual, without losing the advantages of a systemic perspective, is important. In this way, some of the earlier blindness among the pioneers and their followers, which resulted in the individual's relegation to a powerless unit subject to the rules of the system, is being reversed (Nichols, 1987).

(See also CONTEXT; FAMILY SYSTEMS; INTERPRETATION; MILAN SYSTEMIC THERAPY; SELF.)

H.J.

T

tangled hierarchies Two or more hierarchies, joined together in such a way that the coupling is formed of STRANGE LOOPS, in which the lower level of a hierarchy reacts back upon the higher level of another, while the higher level of the latter reacts back upon the lower level of the former. Let H1 and H2 be two hierarchies and A and B two coupled sub-systems belonging to H1 and H2. We then have A below B in H1 and B below A in H2.

If we view the system as a whole, something internal to the system 'moves out' of it to act 'upon' the system. Such configurations appear in non-orientated topological spaces such as the Möbius strip or the Klein bottle. Hofstadter et al. (1980) argue that, in every self-organized system, there exists a 'protected' level which cannot be affected by the rules of the other levels, however tangled their interactions. A tangled hierarchy is based on 'self-modifiable software' and 'inviolate hardware'.

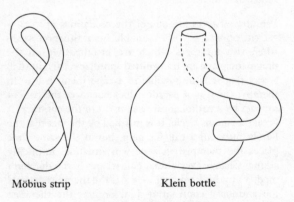

Möbius strip   Klein bottle

Non-orientated topological forms.

'A writer A is writing a book x in which a writer B is writing a book y in which a writer C is writing a book z in which a writer A is writing a book x etc.' is an elementary example of a tangled hierarchy. The inviolate level is that of the writer who conceives the story that loops back on itself in this way.

There is no shortage of tangled hierarchies in clinical practice. For example, an alcoholic may drink because his wife is overbearing and rejecting, while the wife is overbearing and rejecting because he drinks. Or the psychotic feels his thoughts are being stolen because he finds that, around him, those closest to him are attentive to the very faintest of his expressions, but they behave that way because, in the very faintest of his expressions, he lets it be seen that he believes his thoughts are being stolen.

Adding a family therapy unit to an organization providing psychiatric care or an inter-institutional complex also creates tangled hierarchies. The institution includes this new therapy in its therapeutic arsenal and the family therapy, in its working model, includes the institution as a part of the family's problem. In the same way, the family therapist is a member of the institution, but also one who leaves it when he or she receives the family in a place that is sufficiently private and confidential. If the index patient is faced with serious pathology, he/she will be called for a consultation, together with his/her family, at the outpatient department of another institution. This work will react back upon family therapy no. 1. Experience reveals the existence of tangled hierarchies which may be even more complicated than this.

(See also COMMUNAL INDIVIDUALS; FAMILY SYSTEMS; FAMILY—THERAPEUTIC INSTITUTION DIFFERENTIATION; GENERAL SYSTEMS THEORY; INSTITUTIONS; MULTI-LEVEL HIERARCHIES; PARADOXES; SELF-REFERENTIAL CALCULUS; THEORY OF LOGICAL TYPES.)

J.M.

tasks, prescription of tasks The assigning of tasks is used to promote change, i.e. to provoke new transactional patterns. Therapeutic tasks are of two types: those carried out during the session and those developed for the family to carry out outside the sessions. The first type includes the diagnostic techniques used to identify dysfunctional interactions and pathological behaviour in the context of the session, as well as the therapeutic interventions which invite the family to adopt new behaviour. The second type of task aims to amplify the therapeutic process far beyond the session. Andolfi (1977) divides tasks into three types: restructuring tasks, paradoxical tasks and metaphorical tasks.

RESTRUCTURING TASKS

Restructuring is a process in which the usual transactional patterns of the family are modified by employing the elements and energies that are present, at least partially, in the system. As a result, the system acquires new characteristics. It changes, even though the elements making it up remain the same. This also applies in the case of paradoxical tasks. The difference consists in the fact that, in paradoxical tasks, the

401

restructuring is produced indirectly, as a consequence of the changes brought about by the use of a therapeutic paradox. Restructuring, by contrast, produces immediate changes. Restructuring tasks are of several types.

Counter-systemic tasks

This mode of intervention often reflects lack of experience on the part of the therapist rather than the choice of an appropriate strategy. The therapist, who bases his/her judgement on the content rather than on the underlying interactional patterns, may seek to stand out against the homeostasis of the family system. Such tasks are the product of a simplistic view of the situation. They include, for example, all those types of therapeutic advice which aim to bring about a change in the index patient, calling on him/her to draw on an energy which he/she feels he/she does not possess. Such an approach leads to the creation of a 'blaming' context or to unhelpful competition.

Contextual tasks

These are executed in the session and used to promote the formation and maintenance of a therapeutic context with a view to bringing about change. For example, these tasks serve to encourage respect for the autonomy of each individual and to show that each person in a family is responsible and occupies a specific place.

Displacement tasks

These are aimed at artificially displacing the scapegoat's problem on to another family member. When the index patient has been removed from his/her central position, and the symptomatic register has been displaced, it is easier to set in place a process of change. These tasks transitorily create a new situation, by breaking down the homeostatic equilibrium of the family system and increasing the number of possible alternatives. To create a displacement, the therapist may, for example, amplify a minor disorder mentioned by a family member.

System-restructuring tasks

The objective of these is to offer new habits in the modes of communication. Restructuring is obtained by the substitution of more functional communication patterns, drawn out from exploration of the elements and forces existing in the system.

Reinforcement tasks

These are used to reinforce movements already begun within the family system which one believes will serve to bring about change. They are aimed at consolidating the changes which have taken place and at promoting other changes. It is during the last phase of family therapy that one most has recourse to this type of task.

Tasks using the symptom

With tasks attacking the symptom, the therapist confronts the behaviour of the index patient and stresses its dysfunctional character. According to Andolfi (1977), one should simultaneously also seek out the zones of autonomy to be protected or reinforced. The therapist may achieve this by modifying the interactional significance of the symptom.

Conversely, tasks allying with the symptom are particularly useful with families comprising adolescents or pre-adolescents in the process of achieving autonomy and separation from the family. This process engages the family system in a situation of accelerated transformation and constitutes one of the most delicate phases of its existential cycle.

Often the appearance of symptoms (phobias, anorexias, tics etc.) functions to keep the adolescent in the home precisely at an age when he/she should normally be creating greater spaces of personal autonomy and socio-professional integration for him or herself. It is useful to make a pact with the child and to encourage the behavioural disorders in order to attempt to modify their relational meaning. The therapist may choose several methods, but he/she always intervenes at two levels simultaneously. On the one hand, the therapist provokes the child with regard to his/her symptomatic behaviour and, on the other, he/she develops the adolescent's potential.

PARADOXICAL TASKS

Paradoxical tasks are one of the modalities of THERAPEUTIC DOUBLE BINDS. A double bind situation arises when two messages which are incompatible on the pragmatic plane are transmitted simultaneously, in such a way that it is impossible to escape them in life. In therapy, the use of paradox does not force the patient to react by a pathological response. On the contrary, it breaks a vicious circle. It is justified by the fact that the family puts out a call for help, but at the same time places the therapist in a no-win situation, implicitly asking 'Change everything, but, whatever you do, don't modify anything relating to us.' If the therapist accepts the antinomy confronting him or her, the therapist sets him/herself against what the family apparently expects of him/her. His/her response to the family's demand takes the form of a counter-paradox (Selvini Palazzoli et al., 1978) because he/she recreates a mode of communication of the double-bind type by prescribing the symptom and prescribing the family rules (see PRESCRIPTION).

METAPHORICAL TASKS

Metaphorical language is a particularly potent means for re-establishing multi-level transfers of meaning by modifying the relations between signifier and signified and the zones of clarity and obscurity of interchanges. The therapist speaks metaphorically or stimulates the metaphoric potential of the family members and, as a result, new information on the particular features of the family is obtained which would have been difficult to glean otherwise from families that are often reticent or stuck in very defensive and fixed positions. Such a task may possibly be facilitated by play with a real object that has particular affective and cognitive connotations for the family relating to a specific or interpersonal relationship (see METAPHORICAL OBJECTS). Metaphorical tasks are also prescribed in cases where the family members do not wish to follow directives, even if they recognize their usefulness. Generally, these families are more willing to accept tasks which they do not consciously recognize as such.

(See also HYPNOSIS; THERAPEUTIC STRATEGIES AND TACTICS.)

S.A., P.A. & A.C.

teaching of systemic approaches   If the TRAINING of family therapists is limited to the mere teaching of a theory or a technique, then there is a danger it will lead only to the creation of sects or working groups. It is, however, highly desirable that practitioners should learn to cast off their knowledge and keep open the question of the conflicts between therapeutic myths in order to promote their dynamic development within the families they encounter.

This raises a great number of problems, the first of course being the problem of the sense of vocation. Why does someone wish to become a therapist?

The role of the imaginary as the engine of training is a crucial one, when one sees . . . the effect of something which revolves unconsciously around the notion of reparation: reparation of the child one has been, the child one would have liked to be; reparation of a handicap one has experienced in one's own family or in one's immediate vicinity. (de Martino, 1984)

As a direct corollary of this, we must ask whether a selection should be operated. Is this admissible when teaching leads to an academic diploma and is it legitimate (or even possible) when teaching is carried out by private associations authorized only by themselves? The current response to these questions is that the teaching of family therapy is reserved for the training of people who are already professionals in the field of social, medical and educative work. Behind this lies an idea that once these professionals have finished their training, they will gradually influence the institutions employing them in the direction of 'systemic intervention', a term which Caillé (1985) prefers to that of 'family therapy'.

The point is that what is involved in this teaching is not merely the acquisition of a new skill, but the awakening to a different epistemology which redefines individual problems or symptoms as by-products of interpersonal relations. Once this is accepted, three points must be noted:

- the students begin their training with a professional identity and their own specific techniques;
- it is essential that they be given a precise theoretical orientation;
- they must, however, acquire 'forms of learning rather than contents' (Lang and Lang, 1986).

Defining the objectives is, however, rather more tricky. Is the object to enable the future therapist to develop his/her capacity to come to the aid of troubled families or to teach him/her effective procedures for creating change, to teach manoeuvring skills?

This is all the more a problem as the student has acquired a first layer of ATTITUDES from his/her profession. These attitudes come, in general, from idealized social and cultural images formed through identification with teachers and peers. Very often, the first encounter with the reality of work, e.g. the first hospital appointment for a doctor or the first work at 'street level' for a social worker, marks his/her professional behaviour with its imprint (almost in the ethological sense) and influences him or her for years.

The second layer of attitudes comes, particularly in France, from psychoanalysis and the personal therapy which the student has often experienced as part of earlier training in order to discover what neurotic limitations he/she may have, though also to accomplish a rite of passage. Now, most of the major figures in family therapy who are regarded as prestigious trainers (a) have themselves been analysed, and may, indeed, have been analysts; and (b) claim that it is not necessary to have had this radical individual experience to become family therapists and that it is even less necessary in the case of 'systemic practitioners'.

In my view, this position is both demagogic and dangerous. A valuable argument in this regard is to be found among family therapists from the countries of Eastern Europe (Poland, Czechoslovakia) where psychoanalysis was banned. When they are confronted with the enormous affective charge represented by immersion in family interactions, they are themselves in genuine psychic danger. As the Polish therapist Maria Orwid put it at the International Congress in Jerusalem in June 1986, 'we had not a psychoanalytic paradigm, but a holistic psychiatric paradigm which made the systemic model seem an obvious one, but which exposed the therapists to heavy emotional involvement which we have attempted to counter through the use of training groups inspired by the work of Balint.' The use of such Balint groups in the training of doctors in the family therapeutic approach has, in fact, been shown to be of little value (Gillieron, 1982). However this may be, usually in France, prior professional experience has taught therapists how to get results, while psychotherapeutic experience has put the emphasis on abstinence and verbalized interpretation.

The benefit of ageing is that one eventually comes to acquire a certain wisdom. One notices, for example:

- that family therapy is not all powerful and cannot perform miracles every time;
- that the best results are achieved early in one's career. After a few years one realizes that, to obtain a cure, repetition is required;
- and that no psychotherapeutic method is, in itself, better than any other.

If the majority of studies evaluating therapies are to be believed, then efficacy actually depends on non-specific factors which seem to be related to the personality of the therapist.

I deduce from this that the object of the teaching of family intervention is to enable the student to make the best use of his/her personality. I would add that, in terms of logical types, the personality is a set or class, of which the therapist's attitudes are members or elements. We can see immediately that a communicational double bind may arise if one of the therapist's attitudes runs counter to his/her personality as perceived by his/her clients. Which means that factors of a transferential order will have their part, but also that this double bind, this paradox in the communication may, when it arises, be a powerful therapeutic instrument if it is logically consistent though, if it is not, it will engender noise and confusion. Thus I believe that the most important theoretical objective of training should be to try to get the students to think in terms of levels of communication. Levels of communication between therapist and family, between the members of the family during the session and between the team of therapists and therapists in training.

Boscolo et al. (1986) state that the mere fact of thinking as a team has therapeutic virtues. But, in that case, who thinks the system? Must one include what goes on inside each individual? Doubtless the processes are repeated at each level. Attention must, however, be paid to individuals and not only to their interfaces (Lang and Lang, 1986). The question of the technical framework – the use of the two-way mirror or a video circuit – has to be reformulated in this context. Caillé (1985) speaks of an 'intruder' in the family and an 'observer' on the other side of the mirror to distinguish between the co-therapists.

Let us say that the one has to give an account of his/her attitudes and that the other does not. In fact, once communication has been established and structured, any behaviour on the part of the therapist becomes a kind of signifying unit functioning as a metonym or metaphor of his/her attitude towards the members of the family and is received by them as an expression of his/her personality. We have, therefore, three different levels:

- a unit of (verbal or non-verbal) behaviour;
- an attitude (a behaviour pattern unconsciously orientating responses, or, to use Piaget's terms, a mental image);
- the perceived personality.

If we wish to enable the family members (and the students in training) to metacommunicate (i.e. to be capable of moving from one communicational level to another), then we have to be alive to the different messages that we are directing towards them in what is multi-channel communication.

In a sense, teaching aims to show how to be spontaneous and creative without effort, and that is something which obviously requires hours of work! Moreover, the problem of the relations between (operational) intelligence and (figurative) creativity is not an unequivocal one. The trainer in family therapy has recourse almost exclusively to analogy as a teaching method, and draws on the similarities with what goes on between him- or herself and the students as illustrations of his/her interaction with a family. All in all, he/she demonstrates operational procedures, but in so doing he/she teaches the creation of figures.

Rieben (1978) believes that the role of operationality should not be looked for in modifications produced by the appearance of a particular operation, but that it has to do rather with the progress in mobility of thought and in the balancing mechanisms between assimilation and accommodation which govern exchanges between individuals and their environment. Every therapist has his or her own style which depends on the particular balance of these two aspects which applies in his/her case. However, inventiveness seems indispensable to the extent that when one is confronted with a family, part of the task consists precisely in formulating the task itself. This is why, ideally, training must both extend the repertoire of the person receiving it and stimulate his or her personal development.

Should marital therapy (see COUPLES; MARITAL BREAKDOWN) be thought of as merely a form of family therapy or does it require a special tactical approach of its own? We find in it:

- the importance of the dialectic between the object-orientated and the narcissistic;
- the tendency to throw back upon one's children the traumatic impact of sexuality through attempts at seduction of them when young ('the confusion of language' which Ferenczi spoke of in 1932 between the language of affection and the language of passion);
- the ease with which transference feelings arising from the Oedipal triangle are projected on to the therapist.

By contrast, family therapy is more concerned with the life-cycle and the necessary adjustments to it, the oscillation between diachrony and synchrony. It demands of one that one has experienced and formulated that oscillation.

In conclusion, rather than a clearly defined theoretical indoctrination, teaching 'in the field' seems desirable for training in systemic approaches. Four basic points will have to be taken on board by the candidate:

1 *There are no independent phenomena* that can be observed from outside. Observation is part of the reality observed and created.
2 *The solution is already in the problem.* If one can acquire an understanding of the appropriate facts, the solution seems obvious. It is arrived at through a high degree of attention to the messages received and emitted in context. 'The system knows better than we do what the solution is' (Caillé, 1985).
3 *It is essential to respect the feedback* one finds in the system. Very often (and particularly in somatic medicine), it will be enough simply to do nothing very significant but allow the regulatory mechanisms to express themselves.
4 *It is essential not to confuse logical levels.* As Lang and Lang (1986) ask with some humour, 'Would you eat a sandwich which a paranoiac claims has been poisoned?'

(See also COACH; FAMILY THERAPIES; GENERAL SYSTEMS THEORY; PSYCHOANALYSIS; SYSTEMIC MODELLING AND INTERVENTION.)

G.G.M.

territory, territoriality A territory is the expanse of the earth's surface on which a human group lives. It is the material and real space providing vital resources (food, energy) on which a collectivity imposes its laws and asserts its authority.

The cross-cultural study of territoriality forms the subject-matter of proxemics (Hall, 1966, 1968). That discipline identifies 'the complex of behavioural activities and their extensions', essentially dealing with the notion of 'distance outside the field of consciousness'. For Hall, territorial structure varies between cultures as a result of a different interconnection of sensory channels. The organization of space by architecture is fundamental to this. Depending on the culture, space is structured in static forms, semi-mobile forms and dynamic forms. Thus furniture may be either fixed or semi-fixed (chairs, doors), its degree of mobility varying between peoples.

A territory is apprehended and constructed by means of MAPS which are more or less isomorphic in their relation to it. As a result of its value for sustaining life and survival, it gives rise to biological and symbolic behaviours which tend to mark its boundaries by signals and by the establishment of intersensory connections. If, then, the territory is identifiable by the unconscious maps which represent it, it remains an asymptotic entity, distinct from those maps. It is by means of maps that the organism seeks to invest the territory those maps have helped to delimit. The map/territory distinction is constitutive of psychical space, of the organization of representations, of the structuring of the various modalities of communication.

TERRITORY AS ECOSYSTEM OF LIFE AND SURVIVAL

In ethology, the nature of territory is determined by:

- the means of subsistence it offers (natural resources, prey);
- the means of subsistence of neighbouring species;
- the conspecifics pursuing the same means of subsistence;
- the predators from whom it is necessary to protect oneself.

An animal's territory is the larger where resources are scarce and conspecifics are predators of the same kinds of resources. The defence of the territory is regulated by intra-species ritualized aggression behaviour.

The territory of an animal is very closely linked to the space in which a sequence of actions unfolds (Tinbergen, 1947). If the habitual space is no longer present, the sequence of actions breaks down and the animal is forced to go back to the beginning of the sequence. In the view of Spitz (1959), for man, there would seem to be specific volumes, without which the psychical organizers would, at critical moments, no longer fulfil their roles. The affinity between the stereotypies and self-mutilation of wild animals in captivity and of psychotic patients who have been locked up for a long time reinforces this observation.

Wild animals keep strictly to their territories which they ritually mark with their dejecta. Domestication brings with it the construction of new boundaries or frontiers which hem the animal into various closed spaces, bringing about considerable changes by comparison with territories 'in the wild'.

In man, the stress of overpopulation and/or of very tiny territories leads to the reappearance of behaviour of a 'wild' type. Enuresis and encopresis may be interpreted as phylogenetic residues, vestigial signs of behaviours occurring in systems where the establishment of symbolic BOUNDARIES is uncertain. Schizophrenic forms of behaviour are an expression of fundamental disturbances of the organization of the material and symbolic territories of the family (see DYNAMIC SYSTEMS; SOFA–BED SYNDROME).

TERRITORY, WAR AND LAW

The establishment of a territory presupposes protection and defence behaviour when the established territory is threatened. It gives rise to threatening and aggressive behaviour. The regulation of territories is thus based on intra-species aggressive behaviour. We may distinguish between predation territories, family territories and social territories, which, in man, are subject to power struggles and symbolic struggles, the extreme expression of which occurs in war.

The human race becomes an element of the territory which is to be domesticated (see DOMESTICATION). Maps are thus transformed as advances occur in the symbolic territories to be created (the arts) and to be discovered (the sciences). Laws define the rules inherent in the behaviour permitted on the territories they control. They establish the distinction between public and private territories.

OCCUPYING THE HOME AS TERRITORY

The articulation between territory and map is a continuation of Freudian theory which distinguishes between (unconscious) thing-presentations and (preconscious) word-presentations. It establishes a connection between the instinct and its representation. Bateson shows that the map and the territory are mingled at the level of primary processes, differentiated at the level of the secondary processes and simultaneously mingled and differentiated in play. The construction of personal and collective territories and their modification as a function of the maps subtending that construction is a founding element of the definition of REALITY.

The phenomenological description of behaviour already depends to a great extent on proxemics. Transcultural variations between partners generate conflicts which cannot be grasped on the basis of the theory of the psychical apparatus alone. In effect, intersensory structuring establishes a selective grid in regard to the investment of space. That structuring is contained more in unconscious attitudes relating to territoriality than in unconscious representations capable of being directly verbalized by subjects.

Techniques of tidying (putting order into one's own disorder or the disorder of those close to one) are one of the ways employed by humans to mark territory. Which are the shared spaces and the spaces specific to each person? Who controls the tidying of the house, the organization of its fittings and furniture? Where and how are these things carried out? The organization of the different territorial spaces and of interpersonal and inter-group distances contributes to the structuring of psychical representations.

(See also DISTANCE AND ORGANIZATION OF TERRITORY; ORDER, DISORDER; SPACE–TIME.)

J.M.

theatre   See ANTI-THEATRE.

theory of logical types   A part of the *Principles of mathematics* (1903) elaborated by Russell, whose aim was to give a sure foundation to set theory, arithmetic and metric theory. Set theory (Cantor, 1932) gave rise to a series of contradictions and paradoxes. The theory of logical types attempted to establish a 'healthy' axiomatics excluding paradox and eliminating any self-referentiality in the definition of sets. Once that axiomatics had been set in place, all mathematical objects could be expressed in terms of set theory.

The fundamental postulate of the theory of logical types, a postulate which in itself alone sums up the prohibition applying to self-referentiality in the logical-mathematical world, is the following: 'A class cannot be a member of itself.' This postulate implies the existence of an infinite hierarchy of logical levels or types. At the lowest level of this hierarchy come the members. At the next level up, we have classes of members or sets. At the next level, we find 'meta-classes', i.e. the class whose members are themselves sets. And so on. This hierarchy may be conceived as infinite.

As an example, an individual is a child (level 1 element) of a nuclear family (level 2). The nuclear family is a member of an extended family (level 3). The extended nuclear family is a member of a clan (level 4) etc. The theory of logical types very clearly formalizes the fact that concepts concerning objects of different logical levels are necessarily different.

The theory of logical types is the source of very many applications. The systems approach to communication, the family, living systems and change has drawn extensively on that theory. In communication one finds different logical types, depending on whether one is looking at the content of a message or its context (the metacommunicational level). Systemic modelling of the family has revealed the existence of family rules specific to each family situated at a higher logical level than the level of the family members. Second-order changes constitute changes of a higher logical level in the sense that what are involved are transformations of the rules which previously governed (first-order) change. As a general rule, everything relating to the framework or the context is of a higher logical level.

The theory of logical types may, however, be criticized in the following respects. It assumes an absolute discontinuity between the different logical levels and forbids the confusion of those levels. The application of the theory of logical types comes up against its limits in human interaction where just such a confusion of logical levels is very frequent, without, for all that, being systematically pathological.

Humour and creativity are phenomena which the

theory of logical types cannot handle. New mathematical developments, such as category theory, in part enable the structure of hierarchical systems to be formalized while taking account of inter-level links (Ehresmann and Vanbremeersch, 1985, 1986a, b).

The DOUBLE BIND theory provides a theoretical and practical response to the theory of logical types. The sciences of living organisms cannot merely be content with an infinite hierarchy of names and classes, all perfectly distinct from one another and never entering into zones of hierarchical confusion and turbulence. As Bateson writes in *Mind and nature*, 'We are trying to deal with an interlocking or interaction of digital (i.e. naming) and analogic steps. *The process of naming is itself nameable*, and this fact compels us to substitute an *alternation* for the simple ladder of logical types that *Principia* would propose' (1979, p. 185).

This alternation will occur, in Bateson's view, between the two stochastic processes which found our existence: the processes of evolution and mental processes. There must first be a generative process which establishes a class, making it possible, secondarily, for it to be named. The double bind is the first clinically identifiable elementary sequence of an impediment-to/creation-of new relations between analogic and digital communication, between evolutionary and psychical processes, between phenomena of denomination and occultation. It should also be remembered that Russell himself was never satisfied with the theory of logical types and that he recognized the creation of the SELF-REFERENTIAL CALCULUS proposed by his disciple Spencer-Brown as an interesting alternative. The recognition by Bateson of structures of communication which, over the same unit of time, convey perfectly antinomic, mutually incompatible messages involving the family protagonists in a 'life and death' contest is, henceforth, an epistemological fact with undeniable therapeutic consequences.

(See also INCOMPLETENESS THEOREMS; MULTI-LEVEL HIERARCHIES; PARADOXES, SCHIZOPHRENIAS.)

M.G. & J.M.

therapeutic abduction When dealing with a new or incomprehensible situation, we are frequently obliged to process information or take decisions on the basis of intellectual presuppositions, i.e. of models of thinking which do not enable us to make either sure deductions or quasi-certain inductions. We tend, in these cases, to step back from our immediate intuitions and suggest relatively probable hypotheses in order to understand the strange situation with which we are faced. This mode of hypothetical reasoning on the basis of uncertain premises is called *abduction*. Abduction depends on our taking an intellectual risk, which consists in surmising or guessing at regularities and similarities by comparing the immediate situation with situations which may be far removed from it. These are orders of phenomena which defy immediate intuition or the usual system of reference and which force us to widen the field of our thinking by resorting to new frames of reference.

In therapy, abduction operates on two planes: first, a communicational and organizational plane, on which we bring together persons affectively and cognitively involved in vital relationships who are no longer able spontaneously to regulate the distances between them; and, secondly, a cognitive plane, on which we engage in hypothetical reasoning of a kind likely to promote the knowledge that the partners to the interactions may develop of each other. We are thus looking not so much for 'the truth in itself', nor to reveal the total state of family functioning, but to re-establish viable functioning between the ritual, mythic and epistemic operators at play in the family system.

HISTORIC SURVEY OF THE THEORY OF ABDUCTION

The theory of abduction is an ancient one. In his *Prior analytics* (II, 25), Aristotle mentions it alongside 'induction', 'argument by example', 'objection' etc. as a form of reasoning which is akin to the syllogism (deduction).* Abduction provides not certain, but merely approximate, knowledge. If, for example, we accept that science can be taught, we will also admit that justice can be, even though it is uncertain that justice is a science.

At the turn of the twentieth century, the mathematician, logician, philosopher and semiotician Charles Sanders Peirce was to develop the theory of abduction (still known then as hypothesis or reduction) in minute detail, distinguishing it both from induction and deduction. An abduction, for Peirce, is a judgement which, on the basis of a given situation, infers a hypothetical general rule which one assumes will be valid in the particular case in question. Normally, this inference is not directly verifiable. Of abduction, Peirce writes that:

in very many questions . . . we shall do better to abandon the whole attempt to learn the truth . . . unless we can trust to the human mind's having such a power of guessing right that before very many hypotheses shall have been tried, intelligent guessing may be expected to lead us to the one which will support all tests, leaving the vast majority of possible hypotheses unexamined. (Peirce, 1935, 6.530)

Starting out from a surprising fact – one that is incomprehensible in terms of accepted models of thinking –

*While French translations of Aristotle refer to 'abduction', English translations refer to 'reduction' (*Editor*).

and by making an inference which is reasonable, even though there is no logical connection between premises and conclusion, thought conceives a new, unexpected model which better explains this surprising fact.

However, this aptitude for guessing the relevant hypothesis is not simply a matter of chance. It would seem that the human mind has an instinctive capacity for restricting the number of hypotheses that have to be considered and for hitting on the one which will be validated by experience. Curiously, the plausibility of a hypothesis is most often deceptive, as is the force of the arguments which lead to the viable hypothesis. By nature, abductive arguments are weak. Abduction enables us to choose, for preference, the least probable hypotheses, except where these are easily refutable by experience.

> An abduction is a method of forming a general predic-
> tion without any positive assurance that it will succeed
> either in the special case or usually, its justification
> being that it is the only possible hope of regulating our
> future conduct rationally, and that induction from past
> experience gives us strong encouragement to hope that
> it will be successful in the future. (Peirce, 1935, 2.270)

Abductive reasoning must meet the following validation criteria:

- starting out from the hypothesis in question, it must be possible to propose a deductive argument which accounts for the observed facts;
- the choice of the hypothesis must increase our knowledge;
- the hypothesis must submit to the verdict of experience.

Gregory Bateson seeks to give the concept of abduction general application within the framework of the theory of evolution. Anatomy and physiology may be regarded as forming one vast abductive system having its own coherence within itself at any given time (Bateson, 1979, p. 143): the doubling of brain activity (left and right sides of the brain), of psychomotor activities (voluntary and involuntary), of sensory experience (binocular vision etc.) and of the processes of thought (primary and secondary) enables a constant process of comparison to take place between perceptions and experiences. Similarly, the environment within which an organism evolves can also be seen as functioning like an internally coherent abductive system. Among the possible doublings, we may cite the distinctions between matter and anti-matter, wave and particle, energy field and material object, prey and predator, male and female. Yet, argues Bateson, the coherence of the environment and that of the organism do not coincide. As a cognitive process, abduction is based on a separation of the flow of thought, a separation which can be seen as enabling experiences of

representation to be doubled and the organism to see the possibility of a more appropriate life-context by successive adjustments. Abduction presupposes the double or multiple description of an object, event or sequence. 'It thus comes about that what I have called *double description* becomes double requirement or double specification' (Bateson, 1979, p. 144). The splitting of the subject, the comparison of consciousness with its own doubling and with the hypothesis of unconscious processes seems to be the *sine qua non* for reality-testing. The distancing of thinking from itself enables the distance between the organism and the environment from which it differentiates itself to be reduced. It would also seem to be abduction that makes it possible to glue back together the experiences duplicated in this way by that comparative process which connects disunited forms and brings together entities which are mentally perceived as heterogeneous.

For an organism to change in a viable way, the new elements must satisfy two demands: the demand for intra-organismic coherence and the external exigencies of the environment. Comparing the cognitive process to the evolutionary process produces a metaphor, a 'syllogism in embryo', which casts light on the organism's capacity to find adequate responses to its evolution in the environment. Abduction allows us to glimpse some congruence between the doublings of the abductions internal to the mind and the abductions of the environment.

Abduction and therapy

It is well known that the formulation of hypotheses is of primary importance in the research conducted by Selvini Palazzoli and her team. The therapists should not, in her view, arrive 'empty-handed' at the sessions and it should be their aim to learn by trial and error, i.e. to proceed by the formation of hypotheses. This hypothesis formation can be given concrete form in the production of a chart to serve as a guide in the orientation of the specific family game. In *Paradox and counterparadox* (Selvini Palazzoli et al., 1978) the point was, essentially, to 'imagine an intervention which modifies' (see SYSTEMIC HYPOTHESIS). In *Family games* (Selvini Palazzoli et al., 1989) the general pattern pursued is more of a cognitive than a pragmatic, interventionist kind.

The elaboration of hypotheses may, however, be carried out in a more flexible, less systematic way. This presupposes, in fact, a sufficient impregnation of the therapist(s) by the family, a capacity to 'fantasize' family interactions (Hirsch, personal communication), a progressive synchronization between therapist(s) and family members. Following the Batesonian theory of abduction, I shall accept that therapeutic abduction is both a process of communication and a process of cognition. In the dynamics of TRANSFERENCE and counter-transference between patient and psychoanalyst, the co-presence of each enables a person-to-person comparison to be made, it being understood that each 'person' is often the expression of several unconscious *personae*. In family – and/or network – therapy, the comparison operates group-to-group by SCHISMO-GENESIS, conjunction/disjunction of the categories of the familiar and the strange, the familial and the social. Therapeutic abduction operates simultaneously on several planes: the ritual, the mythic and the epistemic (Miermont, 1993).

Meeting the family in a therapeutic context makes it possible for new modalities of RITUALIZATION to be tried out, modalities which can usefully be compared with the spontaneous forms of ritualization (or de-ritualization) with which the family members are normally confronted. There is, also, a gap between the belief systems structuring family ties and those shared by the therapists. Distortions in the transmission of information can be seen operating in the framework of a neo-mythology shared within the therapeutic setting. By virtue of the fact that each person, when confronted with the group's episteme (see EPISTEMOLOGY), deploys their own modes of knowledge, learning and skill, it is possible to bring the different appreciations of a single complex situation into perspective in a relational climate which does not *ipso facto* end in a breakdown of exchanges. Each participant is likely to compare the spontaneous modalities of exchanges, beliefs and knowledge with those artificially arrived at in the sessions. The family members then find themselves faced with a choice.

In interpersonal relations, the reciprocal need to deal with teleological behaviours (Le Moigne, 1990) obliges us to identify with others up to a certain point. The capacity to put oneself in the place of others is a function of an abductive distancing. The presence of a therapist with a patient or a family enables a doubling of perceptions and judgements about the situation presented to be achieved. The therapist must experience this distancing and propose new adjustments which make possible the learning of play, of a balance between communication and metacommunication, of humour.

A mother who shows an aggressive and restrictive attitude towards her autistic son might connote a very worried parent making enormous efforts to come to his aid. The therapist frees him or herself from the immediate impression that the mother is doing all she can to do him down. By emphasizing the necessary attention with which she seeks to render her son autonomous, the alarm function which she feels is lacking in him is recognized, and this makes her better able to judge how she can disentangle herself from the mutual grasp in which they are held. Abduction therefore modifies the nature of the relations between immediate, common sense and good sense.

There is a see-saw relationship between the generality and the singularity of a situation. Patients or families sometimes express this to us as a form of resistance to the therapeutic process: 'Is it normal for nothing to be happening?', 'Have you had cases like this before?', 'Isn't it all down to genetic factors?', for example. The reasoning is then typically inductive and leads to therapeutic dead-ends.

ABDUCTION AND AUTONOMY

We may thus take the view that the organism is an abduction of the environment, concentrating within itself autonomous organization processes endowed with cognition; the cognitive processes 'mentally' reproduce this distancing, which makes it possible to re-establish a 'join' between these autonomous organisms and the environment on which their autonomy depends. Abductive reasoning enables the organism to explore the contexts in which behaviour which has already been observed in the past is likely to be repeated, on the basis of certain regularities. That exploration leads to selecting the common features which characterize cognitive processes and the evolutionary processes of the environment (Bateson and Bateson, 1987). The internal rules and the laws of the milieu are separate and yet, at the same time, admit of a comparative evaluation. Starting out from a singular behaviour, it is possible to explore the contexts in which such a behaviour is likely to be repeated and to infer a general rule from this (Bateson, 1979, p. 142).

The coupling of two autonomous systems implies a co-evolution of their capacity to remain viable. This principle also applies to therapeutic procedures. Viability, AUTONOMY or hermeneutic capacity are never properties which are acquired once and for all. This presupposes that an autonomous system not only has a very rich dynamic, in order to obtain an excellent hermeneutic capacity, but that it also has a sufficiently broad metadynamic to cause that hermeneutic capacity to evolve. It is this richness which is expressed in the idea of a system that is auto-determined and open to the test of reality. 'It is entirely as though the living unit knew its field of viability' (Bourgine, 1991). Therapeutic activity seeks to broaden the fields of pertinent knowledge for patients and those close to them. In the view of Demailly (1993), the researcher observes reality on the basis of good questions, i.e. by constructing reality as a plausible model, and then sees whether that construction can resist refutation (confronting the MAP with the TERRITORY). Exploring fields apparently far removed from the one actually being studied is a spur to the discovery of new paradigms (or models of the situation) which can be usefully compared to the one habitually employed. Now, in my view, this knowledge corresponds to the development of the capacity to get inside 'the skin of things', to empathize with the situation under consideration. By identifying the subject one has to know and identifying with him, one arrives at a doubling of oneself and one comes to observe, or even to promote, a similar development in the clinical process. As a paradigm shift, abductive reasoning moves our perception, apprehension and conception of reality forward.

(See also CONSTRUCTIVISM; MILAN SYSTEMIC THERAPY; RATIO.)

J.M.

therapeutic abstention In confronting a complex clinical situation, the paradox is that one runs the risk of being summoned all the more insistently to intervene precisely where no solutions exist and where indeed one may not even be able to apprehend the nature of the problem.

Thus it is that the more impossible the mission, the more the members of a family will seek to put their demand to a great number of practitioners, whose responsibility is disqualified from the outset. The escalation from therapeutic devotion to aggravation of the problem, the two reinforcing each other mutually, presents similarities with the 'NOTHING PLUS 10 PER CENT' PARADOX. Identifying that such a mechanism is operating enables one to escape from this original circle and create a new space for development.

The attitude of therapeutic abstention is an attitude which is particularly difficult to apply in the so-called 'serious conditions', but one which may serve as a paradoxical prescription both for therapeutic teams and for a family group embroiled in outbidding each other in their devotion and the provision of a multiplicity of therapies.

(See also ADMISSION OF IMPOTENCE; ZEAL.)

J.M.

therapeutic contract and therapeutic consensus By definition, a contract presupposes two equal parties. A family is made up of human beings who request aid (even paradoxical aid) from other human beings. Before it can be regarded as being a particular technical procedure, a therapeutic intervention presupposes the establishment of a personalized bond between the various parties involved, the proposing and mutual acceptance of the rules of the therapeutic game.

In family therapy, the contract differs from the classic therapeutic contract in so far as the therapist must extend its terms to take in the CONTEXT of family interactions and of their institutional implications, as an integral part of what he/she is aiming to change, alongside the aim of changing the index patient or other individuals in the family. Such a contract aims to bring

about a change not merely at the individual level, but at the level of the system as a whole.

The term 'contract' is in fact ambiguous. At most, one might speak of consensus around a therapeutic and/or didactic project, which is partly explicit and partly implicit. The process in itself will reveal MISUNDERSTANDING, SECRETS, DISCLOSURE etc. which precisely make impossible, at the very outset, any clearly established 'contract'. Change only becomes a real possibility at the point when the family members give up illusory objectives or purely normative changes. In other words, as soon as the contract is perfectly clarified, the therapeutic objective is practically achieved.

J.M. & P.S.

therapeutic double binds and multiple binds When faced with the polysemic complexity of certain symptoms, behavioural disorders, somatic impairments, acts leading to the involvement of the medicolegal authorities etc., it is necessary to adopt methods of intervention which take into account the specificity of each systemic sphere under consideration (the pharmacological, educative, psychotherapeutic, sociotherapeutic etc.). It is the role of therapeutic or propaedeutic action to re-frame the nature of the DOUBLE BINDS and multiple binds with which the various specialists are confronted. It then becomes necessary to coordinate approaches which belong to apparently contradictory and opposed, if not indeed antinomic, levels (see PSYCHOSOMATIC DOUBLE BINDS).

This type of problem appears as soon as a complex symptom requires the application of a range of different skills. This often leads to the treatment being based in different institutions, thus making its overall management difficult. These may include hostels for delinquent adolescents, psychiatric hospitals or day centres for schizophrenic patients or structures for profoundly 'backward', bedridden patients etc.

Ausloos (1983) shows, for example, how difficult it is to apply a 'family therapy' model within the framework of a residential setting with education on the premises for delinquent adolescents. Upon analysis, it emerged that these difficulties were very much related to the partial overlap which necessarily exists between the three systems involved in the relationship which centres upon the question of the index patient: the basic family system, the institutional educational system and the therapeutic system. such a situation inevitably leads to tensions, such as loyalty conflicts, symmetrical escalations, reciprocal disqualifications etc.

In a situation of this type, it appears that the therapeutic context implies the presence of two co-therapists with highly differentiated roles: one therapist (T1) works more specifically on the aspects of the patient–institution relationship: he/she speaks to the patient on behalf of the institution; the other (T2) will have to work more specifically with the family and the index patient in his/her relations with the family (see CO-THERAPY).

On the basis of such a treatment context, in which the roles of each therapist are carefully stipulated and accepted mutually and in which the different systems involved are precisely delimited both in their specificity and their zones of contact, the thinking was extended with reference, on the one hand, to the concept of SPLIT DOUBLE BIND defined by Ferreira (1960) and, on the other, to the work bearing on the therapeutic use of the double bind in paradoxical prescriptions. What is involved is the relaying to the family and to the index patient of a double connotation of the symptom, the one expressed by T1 on the basis of the problems of the institution, the other expressed by T2 on the basis of an analysis of its function in the family system: this double connotation, which is contradictory in appearance, is worked out in common by the two co-therapists and has to be announced without show of disagreement, while metacommunicating, in analogical fashion, the mutual approval which binds T1 and T2 in spite of the 'contradictions' between their messages. The therapeutic split double bind (Ausloos, 1983, p. 212) verbalizes inside what has been acted out outside, thus reversing the pathogenic effect: its efficacy:

> is a product of the dialectical confrontation of two propositions, the first of which prescribes that the behaviour should be continued for the good of the individual in the name of the institution, whilst the second prescribes the opposite for the good of the family system; whatever the patient does, 'he will be right' and 'it will be alright' whereas in the split double bind he is always in the wrong.

So far as schizophrenic transactions are concerned, it also seems necessary to identify the responsible persons who have to be involved on the basis of the index patient's behaviour. Thus a number of intervenors will be selected, I1, I2, I3 ... In, the series varying in length. The prescribing psychiatrist (I1) cannot deny his/her specific role by seeking to evade his/her necessary role of prescribing neuroleptics and his/her paradoxical conjoint relation with the patient, and possibly with members of the patient's close circle, when they ask for an 'explanation about the treatment'. The social worker (I2) is called upon to respond to possible claims for invalidity benefits or for specific institutional aid which the patient may be able to receive. The approach to the patient and his/her family may also require a team (I3–I4) ready to undertake specific work at the level of inter-family communication. These multiple interventions very often give rise to METABINDINGS between the intervenors themselves; the patient will request individual therapy from the 'family therapists', psychoanalysis from the prescribing physician and medication from the social worker. The confusion is further increased when the various intervenors are involved in ideological conflicts ('systemic approach', 'collective interviews', 'psychoanalysis', 'drug therapy', 'institutional analysis' etc). This phenomenon of ALIENATION of the intervenors is manifestly one of the crucial points posed by the patient and his/her family. The family system seems to map the nature of its functioning and dysfunctioning on to the institutional and therapeutic systems from which it seeks help (see MAP AND COUNTER-MAP OF A FAMILY SYSTEM).

A pertinent family approach will consist first of all in deciphering the nature of the metacommunications which are mapped on to the actions of the intervenors in order the better to identify the singularity of the dysfunctioning to which the intervenors are subject in relation to the family in question. It will then be a question of offering the members of the family appropriate metacommunications in which therapeutic paradoxes or therapeutic metabindings emerge. It is to the extent that the intervenors – medical personnel, social workers and therapists – are able to play on these metabindings, to handle them with humour and restore them to the family group, that a propaedeutics of metacommunication may emerge for the patient and his/her family. It will be noted that in the prescription of symptoms, the number of intervenors with principal roles (I3, I7) and secondary ones (I'25 or I'53) may become one of the aspects of the question posed, an aspect in which the question is itself the solution.

It is possible that other situations may involve different levels of medical intervention. Some retarded patients, bedridden patients and patients with cerebral infirmities require a form of care in which nursing is to the fore. This deserves to be recognized for its full value, above and beyond the mechanisms of denial, shame, rejection or self-sacrificing devotion to which these situations invariably give rise. A certain specific relational approach is to be sought here, and the possibility of meetings with the family should also be pursued, on condition that therapeutic impulses be strictly controlled and that they form a complementary pattern of care with the nursing work. More than elsewhere, prudence in action and planning is essential here.

(See also FAMILY–THERAPEUTIC INSTITUTION DIFFERENTIATION; SYSTEMIC MODELLING AND INTERVENTION; SUPERVISION.)

P.S. & J.M.

therapeutic strategies and tactics Thinking along strategic and tactical axes in psychotherapy has been carried out by Haley, Erickson and Guntern: a therapy may be termed 'strategic' when the therapist accords him- or herself the resources to begin his/her action and bring it to a conclusion as a function of his/her assessment of the situation to be changed and the forces at his/her disposal. Within this perspective, the symptom is a tactic which reveals the stakes of a power conflict. It is, however, easier to describe the tactical means (the 'technique') than the strategy properly so-called.

Hierarchies of human behaviour may be considered from the perspective of strategic and tactical choices and the implementation of these (Guntern, 1986).

- strategy: the coordination of therapeutic actions towards objectives beyond immediate success and failure;
- tactics: the deployment of particular therapeutic actions using the appropriate techniques.

It may seem questionable a priori to view therapeutic interventions from the perspective of a military metaphor. The goal of a therapeutic activity is, admittedly, to combat illness and unpleasant symptoms. In reality, however, that combat occurs in the context of an existing conflict: a conflict of representations in neurotic symptoms, more complex conflicts in psychosomatic and psychotic illnesses or behavioural disorders. If there are conflicts, they relate to events which are already spontaneously present, i.e. loyalty conflicts and the pursuit of more appropriate rules or laws.

Taking this military metaphor literally may thus lead to curing the illness, but disposing of the patient and/or destroying his/her survival contexts! If every therapeutic action contains an aggressive dimension, its dosing should be carefully evaluated in terms of the vital forces present (polarity of hard and soft medicines).

The war and politics model

War may be defined as the means a people employs to impose its LAW on another people, either by force or deception. As an event, it has its part in the definition human groups give of REALITY.

Strategy is the theory which relates to the use of engagements to achieve the objectives of the war. It coordinates and directs engagements and uses them for ulterior purposes. It establishes the general plan of the war, determines a series of actions as a function of the objective to be attained and organizes the various engagements. It intervenes just as much in the details of action as in the general plan. Strategic qualities are: force of character, clarity of mind and firmness: 'in Strategy everything is very simple, but not on that account very easy' (von Clausewitz, 1955, p. 182).

Tactics is the theory relating to the use of armed forces in an engagement. It is the study of the form of particular engagements. As in warfare, it is easier to study tactical aspects (the therapeutic techniques) than the strategic goals (the evaluation of the well-foundedness of the results obtained). Victory is due to tactical success; it is the goal of tactics. For strategy, victory is a means, not an end.

In the view of Carl von Clausewitz, strategy determines the place, time and nature of combat, as well as the forces required to conduct it. Thus strategy coordinates the circumstances of time, place and form of combat. In strategy, it is preferable to do just what has to be done to achieve one's goal, to put one's own resources to the best use, especially if they are limited (a paradox which every apprentice therapist comes up against). Moreover (von Clausewitz, 1955, p. 186), 'By virtue of their consequences, possible engagements have to be regarded as actual.'

If, for von Clausewitz, strategy was essentially the decisive engagement of armed forces at the opportune moment, for the Chinese strategist Sun Tzu (500 BC), it was, above all, *the art of deception, the total war of lies*: 'All warfare is based on deception. Therefore, when capable, feign incapacity; when active, inactivity. When near, make it appear that you are far away; when far away, that you are near' (Sun Tzu, 1993 edn). The important thing for Sun Tzu is to attack the enemy strategy. Keeping the state against which one is fighting intact and capturing its army is an outcome preferable to total annihilation. Hence the importance of spies, double agents and disinformation agents (spreading false news). Watzlawick (1976) has shown the importance of these mechanisms in the very *definition* we may give of *reality*; the manipulation of double agents is able to create any kind of 'reality' in the mind of the enemy, so long as the mystification contains verifiable elements. Paranoid mechanisms are similar to such fictions when there are lures and mystifications in the unconscious metacommunications between two or more persons (an implicit change in the contract between two partners, for example, including signals implying that there is 'something fishy going on').

The basic strategic virtues are *perseverance* (von Clausewitz) and *swiftness of action at the opportune moment* (Sun Tzu). Intrepidness is a secondary virtue. It is essential that it be present in the troops involved in engagements, but as one rises through the hierarchy, its importance diminishes. By contrast, perseverance, the capacity to remain constant in adversity, is what is needed in the higher reaches of the hierarchy.

Strategy consists in massing the greatest number of forces at the decisive points of an engagement at the most opportune moment. It thus seeks to obtain a relative superiority. Once tactics has given battle and the result – victory or defeat – is achieved, strategy makes use of it as it is able, in conformity with the final object of the war.

Strategy unfolds slowly. It has to accept periods of

tension and rest. Periods of inactivity are often longer than the engagement properly so-called. Strategy must incorporate all tactical reverses, everything which, in reality, comes to obstruct the simplicity of the overall plan. Elements playing a role in strategy are:

- moral (intellectual resources);
- physical (available forces, quantity and quality of weapons);
- mathematical (nature of angles of attack, of convergent or divergent movements, or of the trajectories adopted);
- geographical (terrain);
- statistical (means of supply).

STRATEGIES AND TACTICS AS SYSTEMIC INTERVENTIONS

Strategic choices
For Guntern (Family Therapy Congress on 'Autonomy', February 1985), man has several hierarchical levels of strategies at his disposal, from the most elaborate and normal to the most deviant:

- normal strategies: eating, drinking, working, living etc.;
- neurotic strategies;
- psychosomatic strategies;
- strategies of addiction (drugs, addiction to toxic substances, pursuit of success etc.);
- psychotic strategies;
- aggressive-destructive strategies (auto/hetero-aggression).

Implementation of strategy
The thing is to give chance a chance: wars are lost in the heads of generals. There are thus a certain number of rules which are valid, both in therapy and in the pursuit of any goal to be attained:

- the best strategy may fail completely when it is not pursued to its end;
- strategies which are not mature are the cause of many difficulties;
- strategies differ in quantity and in quality.

Where communication is concerned, it is necessary for each party to take the other into account. There is no single strategy in therapeutic approaches. In the choice of weapons, one must seek to adopt the techniques best adapted to one's capabilities. When someone drowns himself, the elegance of the style is of little moment; it is efficacity which is most important, in terms of the means at his disposal, whatever the apparent and formal beauty of the gesture.

A certain number of parameters must be taken into consideration:

- necessary redundancy in the instrument employed;
- economy of means;
- intensity of space–time used;
- the importance of a good beginning and an ability not to miss the mark at the opportune moment;
- the value of persevering: 'we've done everything, tried all there is', except perhaps persevering longer;
- good strategists do not seem to be hurried, but the pertinent action is carried out without delay, almost instantaneously when the right moment arrives.

A harmonious frequency or rhythm is required just as an experienced walker walks slowly, without jerking, at a very steady rhythm. It will be observed that the unfolding course of a family's life is subject to a variety of different rhythms. Some cycles are relatively slow (see FAMILY LIFE-CYCLES) and therefore subject to inertia mechanisms ensuring the relative stability of the system. Other cycles are infinitely slower, involving stabilizations extending over centuries or even millennia (the transmission of religion, for example, with apparently wholly unexpected cyclical returns). Other periodicities have an accelerated character, linked to phenomena of ACCULTURATION. Strategic choices have to take account of these different time-scales that may be involved in the achieving of particular goals.

Tactical interventions
Haley (1969) had shown how power tactics, based on surrender and the display of weakness, may have paradoxical effects of domination in the long term. In this connection, he compares the teachings of Jesus, the psychoanalytic attitude and the art of the schizophrenic. The latter is a particularly virtuoso performer when it comes to generating power struggles around him/her.

Many techniques have been proposed in therapy for treating symptoms: management and interpretation of the TRANSFERENCE; INFORMATION gathering; prescription of TASKS or RITUALS; admissions of impotence; encouragement of resistance, HYPNOTHERAPY; PROVOCATION; word salad etc. However, these techniques are all of no avail if, in the detail of each action undertaken, the overall strategic project does not come into give meaning to a particular intervention, or even to a particular active refusal to intervene. The most difficult thing, in therapy, is to elaborate the most pertinent strategies at the outset for the particular problem to be dealt with.

(See also PERFORMATIVES; POWER; SOCIAL ORGANIZATION; SYSTEMIC MODELLING AND INTERVENTION.)

J.M.

therapeutic styles The development of family therapy in France, the pace of which has appreciably quickened in recent years, has led to the assertion and accentuation of a solid dichotomy between the psychoanalytic and the systemic (or, more precisely, sociosystemic) model. That dichotomy is shared by psychoanalysts who believe that they can wholly maintain their identity as analysts while receiving families for consultation (Lebovici et al., 1972; Ruffiot, 1979, 1981b; Lebovici, 1981, 1985; Eiguer, 1983; Decobert, 1985) and by family therapists who believe that the systemic model constitutes an epistemological break in relation to classic psychoanalysis (Jackson, 1957, 1968; Haley, 1959, 1963; Watzlawick et al., 1967; Minuchin, 1974; Andolfi, 1977, 1982; Bowen, 1978a; Selvini Palazzoli et al., 1978, 1978; Elkaim, 1979b, 1980; Ausloos, 1980; Benoit, 1981, 1982, 1984; Colas, 1984).

Other therapists are prepared to take on board the epistemological break and to assume levels of identity corresponding to the nature of the particular practice they are engaged upon: the rigour of the protocol of the classic psychoanalytic cure in treating neuroses, systemic intervention, with its equally rigorous protocol in dealing with grave behavioural pathologies. New alternatives then arise, in which the methodologies employed (analytic or systemic) are each subject to the influence of the other and in which they are regarded as necessarily complementary, both in practical and theoretical terms. Lastly, the question of the personal styles of therapists and families arises.

CLASSIFYING THERAPISTS

This pure dichotomy between psychoanalytic and systemic models has been qualified a little in the writings of Lebovici (1981, 1985): family psychoanalysts take into account systems theory, double binds, interaction and interdisciplinarity in their conceptions and practice. For their part too, many family therapists have extensive psychoanalytic experience: the cybernetic, systemic and catastrophe-theory models can do none other than base themselves on the major contributions of the psychoanalytic movement, as can be seen in the contributions of Bateson or Thom to a theory of play, phantasy, delusions or dreams. Haley and Jackson have proposed a communication interpretation of the phenomena of TRANSFERENCE and COUNTER-TRANSFERENCE which are conceived as paradoxical transactions, providing external confirmation, in the process, of their theoretical validity and practical pertinence. In seeking to ground a 'metapsychology of meaning, Widlöcher (1986) shows how the prescription of the 'fundamental rule' in 'psychoanalytic communication' generates meaning in its very ambiguity (see PRESCRIPTION; SEMANTICS OF COMMUNICATION).

At a congress, Watzlawick once said there are two kinds of people, those who think there are two kinds of people and those who think the opposite. Le Moigne has shown that the real epistemological shift rests on logics other than those of the excluded (or included) middle. We shall suggest, then (Miermont, 1984c),

that there are two kinds of family therapist: those who think there are two kinds of family therapist and those who think the opposite. Among these latter, it is necessary to consider various examples, which have implications for thinking and practice; either there is only one kind of family therapist or there are a great many – an infinite number even – or else there is no such thing as a family therapist.

This last option carries within it the double bind which makes it possible to begin a 'family therapy': the only way that a process can begin between a 'therapist' and a family obliges one not to fix beforehand the definition of what a therapist or a therapy must be. Systematicians and analysts would here agree that the therapeutic dimension is not to be stressed; it is an indispensable condition for setting a process in train, but it is not a sufficient condition.

The option which says there is only one kind of family therapist is less incongruous than it may seem. Is not the main thing, in the last instance, the result obtained (both for the therapists and for the families), whichever way one goes about achieving it? Over-rigid models might actually function to mask the results actually achieved (the reeling off of case histories is not always such a good sign as it seems since, most often, the therapists involved in the therapy alone act as judge and jury).

The idea that there are a great number of different family therapies is one that has gained in acceptance as this form of therapy has become more widespread. Membership of the various psychoanalytic and systemic schools cannot easily be laid down by pre-established programmes. The non-linearity of personal approaches reflects the complexity of family processes. For example, rather than wishing at all costs that a psychoanalysis should be a precondition for training, it may seem best as the terminal phase of that training. And who can decide in advance at what point a training supervision will be most fruitful for a particular therapist?

The idea of an infinite range of family therapies becomes a paradox that can be very happily entertained if one believes that the real family therapists are the members of the families themselves and the family as a system. In this perspective, every human being possesses and spontaneously utilizes therapeutic ritualization, the 'official' therapists being in a meta-therapeutic position (from the theoretical point of view of hierarchical systems); or in a position of regulating the flow of channels of communication or of changes in the force fields (from a topologico-dynamic point of view: Lewin, 1947b); or even having a function of hetero-referential junction for contradictory self-reference (from the point of view of autonomy theory, in relation to self-referential calculus).

Thirty years of practice in the USA have led to certain practical and stylistic distinctions between family therapists. In 1969, Beels and Ferber (1972) offered an assessment of 'What family therapists can do', by describing the styles of intervention of the great pioneers. Though they took the theoretical references of these therapists into account, they did not use these as a basis for classification. More recently, Gurman and Kniskern (1981) pulished the *Handbood of Family Therapy* where the many currents which contribute to the overall map of the field are enumerated in detail; this was further developed in a second volume (Gurman and Kniskern, 1991).

CONDUCTORS AND REACTORS

Beels and Ferber (1972) distinguish between the 'conductors' and the 'reactors'. Even if all therapists necessarily have to play both these roles, notable differences emerge from their interventions concerning the position the therapist takes up towards the family group.

The *conductors* basically remain on the 'dominant' side of dominance–submission complementarities. They assume a leadership role, taking control of and directing the therapy. In the hierarchy of the generations, they place themselves on the side of maturity and experience, on the side of the senior generations, at the top of the pyramid of interactions. The conductors seem to have particularly strong, marked personalities and are able to serve as models (to be adopted or rejected) by the families. Beels and Ferber uninhibitedly state that 'Some of them are regarded by their critics as sadistic, manipulative, exhibitionistic and insensitive' (Beels and Ferber, 1972, p. 175).

The *reactors* seek less to influence the family by direct intervention than to respond to its calls upon them, as expressed in the messages it sends out. They are able to move outside the group boundaries from time to time (taking a position against the family system, consulting co–therapists, interrupting the sessions) and join in symmetrical same-generation relationships with members of the family or adopt one-down complementary positions in respect of the direction of operations. Their personalities are less forceful and 'irresistible', less useful as a working model; they will be led to change roles in response to tactical demands; they stress the dangers of being swamped, invalidated, digested, disqualified or excluded by families.

Beels and Ferber subdivide the reactors into two groups: the psychoanalysts and the 'system purists'. In their view, the analysts view the family as interaction and see in the behaviour of families and therapists processes identifiable in psychoanalytic terms: transference and counter-transference, unconscious processes, acting out etc. Interaction is seen as much in terms of internal processes as external ones. The 'system purists' view the family as a system of rules which shape and constrain the behaviour of each member towards the others. The attitudes of all the members

influence those of the others in a succession of interactions; any scansion of those interactions is purely arbitrary. Moreover, the set of rules is more than, or at least other than, the mere summation of personal attitudes; emergent properties arise which have a further impact upon these attitudes.

In practice, this distinction is far from being quite so obvious. What do the systematician working in the here and now, studying the definition of rules, and a 'historicist' systematician delving into the transgenerational dynamics and the articulation of the emotional, intellectual and sentimental systems have in common? And is the prescription of the 'fundamental rule' of psychoanalysis compatible with psychodramatic acting out. On the other hand, should such a clear distinction be made between interpretative work (see INTERPRETATION) and the elaboration of SYSTEMIC HYPOTHESES, between the family unconscious and metacommunications, between the superego and family rules? In practice – and in theory – analytic and systemic methodologies interpenetrate in understanding – and acting upon – the family group.

Among the main conductors, Beels and Ferber (1972) cite Ackerman, Satir, Bowen, Minuchin, Tharp, Paul and Bell. It is interesting to note that, though Ackerman was the pioneer of the psychodynamic conception of the family, Satir was a member of the Palo Alto group, while Bowen developed a systemic conception highly influenced by the work of Freud. Overall, the conductors stress their teaching function: Bowen presents himself as a researcher teaching the members of the family to become researchers themselves. Satir, through the clarity and apparent simplicity of her interventions, offers the family a new language. Minuchin transmits a non-verbal, iconic, experience which enables the members of the family to find new ways of functioning in an emotional mode. Paul assumes the role of a transferential substitute and empathetic model, making possible, within the framework of therapy, the abreaction of emotions, the experience of mourning not previously worked through etc.

Beyond the technical and theoretical differences between them, the conductors have in common that they offer a reference model, thus forcing families to situate themselves in relation to that model. The behaviour the families are to adopt is laid down clearly in advance, in terms of ethical criteria and value judgements enabling the family members to see what is good and bad, desirable and undesirable, a source of maturation or regression, of differentiation or undifferentiation.

Within this same theoretical strand, such European authors as Selvini Palazzoli et al. (1978), Andolfi (1977, 1980), Andolfi et al. (1982) and Caillé (1985) set out with a clearly affirmed directive, propaedeutic intention. For his part, Lebovici (1981, p. 573) reveals the dynamic and active coherence of his interventions, writing:

In fact there are radical differences between the study of family communication and interrelation on the one hand and psychoanalytic communication on the other. Psychoanalysts, within the framework of the individual cure, follow the principle of not responding to efforts at interaction and not intervening in the description given by the patient of his family circle.

Lebovici (1981) thus sharply criticizes those psychoanalysts who merely content themselves with extending the metapsychological concepts that originated in the traditional psychoanalytic cure to the study of the family and putting those concepts to use in the family therapies they practise. He, for his part, will thus attempt, as a psychoanalyst, to 'mobilize communication and encourage transaction to broaden the interactive and interpersonal space, thus allowing a relative freedom in the patient's intrapsychic interactive space' (Lebovici, 1981, p. 580).

Among the *reactors*, Beels and Ferber (1972) distinguish the 'analysts' from the 'system purists'. Among the 'reactor-analysts', we might mention Whitaker, Wynne, Boszormenyi-Nagy and Framo. In France, writers like Eiguer and Ruffiot have pursued the principle of intensive family psychotherapies with a Kleinian and post-Kleinian theoretical corpus. System purist reactors like Zuk, Haley, Jackson, Watzlawick, Weakland, Fisch and Hoffmann are not merely reactors; or, rather, the fact of being a reactor is, in their case, a somewhat paradoxical way of being active, with perhaps a gain in efficacy by comparison with immediate and direct intervention. The notions of action and reaction provide a relatively arbitrary way of punctuating the uninterrupted sequence of events and interactions. For their part, psychoanalysts have very often shown up in reality the defensive aspect of certain demonstrative forms of activity or activism, which is simply a form of struggle against passivity. The very principle of psychoanalysis is the opposite of non-directiveness.

There are thus discrepancies between what therapists think and what they do – or between what they show and what they do. And between the level of their active intervention and their real influence. As Framo (1972) pointed out in response to Beels and Ferber's paper, every therapist to varying degrees uses the modes of intervention enumerated by all the others. Similarly, Wynne (1980) stresses the effect on his practice of the types of persons and families the particular family therapist is meeting, as well as the nature of the symptomatology being treated.

(See also ABSTINENCE, RULE OF; BRIEF INTERACTIONAL THERAPY; BRIEF THERAPIES; CO-THERAPY; FAMILY THERAPIES; FAMILY STRUCTURES; HYPNOSIS; METAPSYCHOLOGY; MODEL OF THE SYSTEMIC MODEL; SUPERVISION; TEACHING OF SYSTEMIC APPROACHES; THERAPEUTIC ABSTENTION; THERAPEUTIC STRATEGIES AND TACTICS; TRAINING.)

J.M.

therapeutic tactics   See PSYCHOANALYSIS; THERAPEUTIC STRATEGIES AND TACTICS.

time   See OUTSIDE TIME, IN TIME.

topological space   Topology may be defined in terms either of open or of closed sets. The term 'topological space' is applied to any pairing make up of a set E and a set 0 of parts of E which are together called open sets, having the three following properties:

1   Every union, finite or not, of open sets is an open set.
2   Every finite intersection of open sets is open.
3   The set E and the empty set are open sets.

A topological space may have one dimension (straight line, curve), two dimensions (surface, plane), three dimensions (volume) or more (hyperplane, hyperspace). It may be a space of curves or a space of functions or of mappings. The straight line R, the surface R^2, the sphere S^1 (circle), the sphere S (the normal sphere) and spaces with n dimensions, R^n, S^n, are open sets.

The notions of open and closed set can be seen as representing the perception of the world from a dual perspective: the continuous and the discontinuous. In three-dimensional space, a set will be open if every point belonging to that space is the centre of a sphere of radius r (not zero), however small, included in that set. Conversely, a set will be closed if it possesses some points which are not the centre of a sphere of radius r included in that set (or if its radius is zero). The points of a closed set may therefore be the centre of a closed sphere of radius r (of a sphere which therefore contains the hypersurface which constitutes its limit or which, in other words, possesses a boundary). The points of a closed set situated on the boundary will therefore be the centre of a sphere whose radius is zero. The inside of a set is defined in the following way: the spheres of zero radius contained in the set.

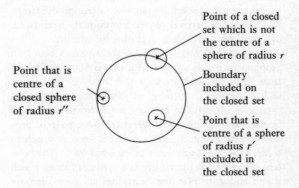

Point of a closed set which is not the centre of a sphere of radius r

Boundary included on the closed set

Point that is centre of a sphere of radius r' included in the closed set

Point that is centre of a closed sphere of radius r''

Closed set of a topological space.

Intuitively, the notion of open set refers to that of continuous space, the notion of closed set to that of discontinuous space.

If, therefore, as we have seen, every finite or infinite union is an open set, every finite or infinite intersection of closed set is a closed space. Similarly, if every finite intersection of open sets is an open space, every finite union of closed sets is a closed space.

A topological space is therefore a set S on which is defined a set 0 of parts of S, called 'open sets' and having the following properties:

1 Every finite or infinite union of open sets is open.
2 Every finite intersection of open sets is open.
3 The total space S and the empty set are open.

An open set is a locus with finite or infinite limits, but in which the (asymptotic) limit itself is never reached. An open set is therefore a continuous space. A sub-set A of the topological space S is termed closed if its complement in S is open. The topological properties of the closed space will be defined in the following manner:

1 Every finite or infinite intersection of closed sets is closed.
2 Every finite reunion of closed sets is closed.
3 The total space S and the empty set are closed.

A closed set is thus a discontinuous space which contains its own limits.

Closed and open sets are therefore complementary. How does passage from the one to the other occur? Let us note, first of all, that the topology of space S, of the sub-sets and of the empty set may be defined as open or closed. A topology is, therefore, a set whose elements are sets, these latter being open or closed.

The infinite intersection of open sets may be a closed set (when that infinite intersection of open sets is a point which is not the centre of any sphere, it is closed. This is not always true, however, and such an intersection may also be open. Reciprocally, the infinite union of closed sets may be an open set if the points of the boundary are at infinity, therefore asymptotic. Otherwise such an infinite union of closed sets is a closed set if the points of the boundary situated at infinity are part of the union.

We shall call neighbourhood N of a point x of space S every sub-set N of S which contains an open set containing x. This definition implies, therefore, that the point x has many neighbourhoods, one of which is the space S itself.

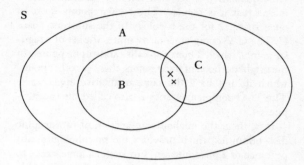

A, B and C are neighbourhoods of x in the topological space S.

The notions of open set, closed set and topological space may also be defined starting out from the notion of neighbourhood. An *open set* is a set of points such that each of those points possesses a neighbourhood contained within that set. In other words, one can approach, in continuous fashion, as near as one wishes to the edge of the set, since one will always find a point closer to that edge. An open set has no flagrant discontinuities in its morphology, even in the neighbourhood of its limits. On the other hand, a *closed set* has an edge, a clearly delineated boundary where one can observe notable morphological and functional singularities and it introduces the notion of discontinuity. The notion of closed set is an ideal notion. If one examines an orange, one may at first think that it forms a closed set. But if one examines its surface at the microscopic level, one perceives molecules which are in constant interaction with the outside. In other words, the notion of closed set introduces a perceptual idealization of forms (see below the Thomian concept of 'catastrophe set').

The definition of a topological space on the basis of the notion of neighbourhood also follows from this. As we have seen, a topological space is a space possessing a topology. To endow a space S with a topology is to provide for every point of that space a set of parts of the space which are neighbourhoods of that point. In other words, a topology on a space S is a set of neighbourhoods of the points of S.

It is on the basis of these initial, abstract definitions that Thom (1976b) has advanced the idea of a catastrophist idealization of morphologies. He defines a substrate space U as a Euclidian topological space R^4 (the three dimensions of space plus the dimension of time) equipped with two types of points: regular or irregular. In our perspective, the substrate space may be a family, an informal or institutionalized group, a person etc.

A point u of the substrate space U will be regular if it is not differentiated, from a qualitative point of view, from a point v situated in its neighbourhood N. The same qualitative appearance holding between u and v means that u is regular. The regular points form an open space Ω for the topology of the substrate space U. The U-Ω complementarity unites the set of irregular points, which Thom also calls catastrophe points. In the neighbourhood of these points, there are other points which do not have the same qualitative appearance. This U-Ω complementarity is also called the catastrophe set.

It is, then, the qualitative perception of catastrophic discontinuities which provides the morphological appearance of a phenomenon. For such an appearance to be susceptible of study, it has to be structurally stable (see STRUCTURAL STABILITY). In other words, a structurally stable catastrophe corresponds to an item of information in Bateson's sense, since a quantitative difference in a reality creates a qualitative difference in the mind of the observer.

What may we gain from such an abstraction in identifying psychopathology and the spaces in which it is registered? May we legitimately speak of the 'topological properties' which characterize the impenetrability of the schizophrenic patient's mind? How are we to understand how the relational barriers in schizophrenic families can be described as impermeable or as 'rubber fences' while the morphologies of interaction appear rigid? How are we to understand the contrastingly extremely diffuse and invasive character of the thought of such a patient for all those around him/her? How are we to understand the degrees of neuroleptic, family, psychical, hospital or institutional closure which may be prescribed in such situations?

Psychology is no more reducible to topology than it is to logic. The advantage of this detour through topology is precisely that it prevents us from making overhasty assimilations, from thinking that the ontology of the subject or family structure can be easily described. Thus, it enables a genuine confrontation to take place between clinicians and topologists with a complete awareness of what is at stake. In itself, the concept of topological space is both too reductive and too broad accurately to specify the real properties of individual, family and social morphologies. Compared with catastrophe theory, for which it provides one of the foundations, it enables the constraints which govern the genesis and viability of animate and inanimate forms to be brought out. It offers a partial insight into the complexity of the modalities of openness and closure of systems encountered in reality. The evaluation of these remains, for the moment, in the realm of the intuition of the observer, intervenor or therapist. The 'naturalistic' perception of the boundaries, inputs and outputs of a concrete system is, to some extent, the poetic counterpoint of the theorems of pure topology.

Schizophrenic impenetrability thus has to do essentially with the field of thought. It goes together with extreme penetration into the thinking of persons around one, schizophrenics offering their behaviour to be thought by others, while at the same time being subject to mechanisms of the theft or divination of thoughts. What they are describing in this kind of delusion perhaps has a topological reality, which is connected with disturbances in the co-localization of systems of thought. They will be particularly vigilant and bewildered when it comes to logical contradictions in the personal relationships between those with whom they come into contact and thus in the localization of the effects that this communication may have in the definition of reality. In other words, the field of their thought is hermetically closed as regards their interiority, while at the same time it is opened up to all the fissures and breaches of the psychical apparatuses of the members of their close circle. On the plane of family organization, this goes together with what is often a total absence of free access to transgenerational information. Access to the inscription of the parents in the grandparents' history – and in an ancestral lineage – is impossible.

So far as delinquency is concerned, we shall note the theft of affects, the usurping of the law and the importance of invisible loyalties or recondite systems of law-giving. It then becomes necessary to imagine the paths of synchronic and diachronic connection, territorial and transgenerational, which seem lost, hidden or broken off. The prison and the asylum are the two traditional systems of de-tribalized societies which mark a closed social catastrophe set (thus social morphology is characterized by a state of closure).

(See also ATTRACTORS; BOUNDARIES; CONNECTEDNESS; DYNAMIC SYSTEMS; ELEMENTARY CATASTROPHES; FAMILY CATASTROPHES; FORCE FIELDS; FRACTALS; GENERALIZED CATASTROPHES; MAPS; PHASE SPACE OF THE FAMILY SYSTEM; SPACE–TIME; TERRITORY; UNIVERSAL UNFOLDING.)

J.M.

totality of a system A property of an open system, corresponding to the emergent quality of a system (von Bertalanffy, 1947), irreducible to the mere summation of the properties of its component parts. Every change in a sub-system leads to modifications in all the other sub-systems and therefore modifies the emergent quality which results.

As a system, communication within a couple or a family is not reducible to the characterological, behavioural or symptomatic properties of each of the members taken individually. As a totality, the family group possesses a spirit, an inner life, a particular existence different from the sum of individual personalities making it up.

(See also FAMILY SYSTEMS; GENERAL SYSTEMS THEORY; HOLISM; HOLOGRAPHIC MEMORY; SYMPTOMATIC AND/OR AETIOLOGICAL TRANSACTIONS; SYMPTOMS.)

P.S.

tracking   See AFFILIATION OR JOINING.

trading of dissociations   An expression coined by Wynne (1965) to describe the unconscious figures and procedures which consist, for each partner in a family, in exchanging the perception he/she has of another for a rigid perception of him- or herself by the latter. The effect of this is to make it possible to confront ideas and feelings which would not otherwise be tolerable.

In this process, each partner keeps out of his/her own consciousness those characteristics of his/her own which seem difficult to cope with by 'localizing' these in his or her partner by means of an unconscious process of dissociation. In other words, each person perceives his or her own problem as coming from another member of the family who is the only one who can put matters right. Thus no one acknowledges that he or she is contributing to the problem in question. The underlying psychic mechanism in this process is that of PROJECTIVE IDENTIFICATION in Klein's sense and, in Bateson's terms, corresponds to an error in the appreciation of the ECOSYSTEM.

P.S.

training   Training models have emerged – and been further elaborated – as the various systemic theories and different schools of family therapy have developed.

In the years 1945–60, the systemic movement spread throughout the United States. Informal systems for the transmission of this new clinical practice and original conceptual field emerged at that time. Lectures, seminars and workshops came to be organized around personalities like Nathan Ackermann, Donald Jackson, Murray Bowen, Carl Whitaker, Virginia Satir, Jay Haley and Salvador Minuchin.

Fully fledged training programmes were created in the 1970s and took on diverse forms reflecting the various schools and institutes spread throughout the United States (for example, the Mental Research Institute of Palo Alto, the Family Institute of Chicago, the Philadelphia Child Guidance Clinic, the Ackerman Institute and the Boston Family Institute) and in the UK at the Institute of Family Therapy, London and the Family Institute, Cardiff.

As Bloch (1985a, p. 16) explains:

An important step in the development of the field of family therapy in the USA was the creation of an accreditation commission which is authorized by the Federal Government to decide, on the basis of a certain number of rules and procedures, what are the training institutions which will be recognized, that is to say which ones meet the criteria fixed by the commission. Two types of programme have been approved in this way; programmes for beginners (akin to the social work diploma) and post-professional programmes in which professionals already qualified in the mental health field are trained in family therapy.

In Europe, where the family therapy movement has developed since the 1970s, there are many centres offering training along lines compatible with their particular practice. Thus the original trainers of the Milan School (Selvini Palazzoli, Prata, Boscolo, Cecchin) sensitize their students to the elaboration of hypotheses. The essential tool is teamwork which enables them to acquire a circular and systemic point of view. On the basis of this systemic work, the team works out an intervention (a re-framing or a ritual) which the therapist communicates to the family. In Boscolo's view, the therapist and the student create a learning context in which the fact of 'learning to learn' is of vastly greater importance than the learning of ready-made solutions. In other words, process is given precedence over content. Andolfi, Menghi and their colleagues (Rome School) see the training group as an experimental family unit. On the basis of their interpersonal experiences within the group, the students analyse the systemic dimensions of their functioning (definition of leadership, internal coalition processes, attempts at alliance with the trainer etc.). The learning of the provocative approach represents one of the chief teaching objectives. The balance between provocation and support is gradually worked out and articulated between trainers and students.

In fact, the various trainers offer models which have many aspects in common, even if certain technical particularities are more developed in one model than another. We shall focus here on the following basic functions.

SENSITIZATION AND TRAINING

The work is carried out in groups, the dynamic potentialities of the group serving as an engine for the learning and conceptualization of models. Courses usually last for three years and comprise 120 learning hours per year. Training is generally based on clinical experience of family therapy and theroretical research activity conducted in parallel with this.

The *Centre d'Étude et de Recherche sur la Famille* forcuses its training work on six points in such a way as to bring together various models on offer in Europe.

1 Personal reflection on the nature and characteristics of human family systems.

2 The learning of various practical modalities of intervention with families; working out genograms, role-playing, sculpting, prescription of tasks and rituals, the quest for a therapeutic language on the basis of a work of modelling and simulation of concrete situations.

3 Progressive confrontation with the personal impacts produced by therapeutic activity, working from clinical examples.

4 Elucidation of the interactions occurring between the pathological family systems and the family systems to which the therapist belongs; the use of video material to this end is precious since it can be used to log the verbal and non-verbal attitudes of therapists.

5 Gradual entry into therapeutic work with direct or deferred supervision.

6 Linking up with various institutional practices.

COMPLEMENTARY COURSE OF TEACHING

Based on clinical supervision, this may extend over several years and is organized in two ways:

- through video recordings of sessions (indirect supervision);
- by direct supervision: the family attends at the training site and the therapist is supervised through a two-way mirror.

What is involved here is a new form of pedagogical relationship using varied models and the personal involvement of the students and trainers. Training is aimed not only at the transmission of a body of knowledge and a technique, but seeks to free up the personal creativity of future therapists. Training in family therapy is directed mainly to mental health practitioners, such as psychiatrists, psychologists, specialist teachers, social workers and nurses. However, other professions where complex family processes are encountered may benefit from this training: lawyers, magistrates, paediatricians, marriage guidance counsellors, teachers etc. For homogeneous professional groups working in specific contexts, more specific forms of training are generally offered.

TRAINING IN THE UK

The development of family therapy in the UK originally centred on a small number of urban areas. The establishment of the Association for Family Therapy (AFT) in 1976 greatly facilitated the spread of interest and training programmes. Centres of excellence in family therapy have developed, such as the Institute of Family Therapy and the Tavistock Clinic in London, and the Family Institute in Cardiff, along with training programmes in Manchester, Leeds and Newcastle among others, based in academic centres. In the UK there has been less of a need to establish specific schools of therapy around each centre, unlike the Italian training centres. Much of the impetus to develop models came from the influence of visiting American trainers in the 1970s and early 1980s, followed by the Italians, especially Boscolo and Cecchin.

At first, a structural model found favour, but more recently developments from the original Milan approach have gained ground, with a greater attention to GENDER and ETHNICITY. This has helped moderate the claims make by the more extreme proponents of the various schools.

One of the important characteristics of family therapy in the UK has been the attention paid to the application of theory in the public sector where, among others, practice may be constrained by the LEGAL CONTEXT. Two influential texts have been published in the UK which draw attention to these developments (Treacher and Carpenter, 1984; Carpenter and Treacher, 1993). This differs from the direction of much family therapy in the USA and in some parts of mainland Europe.

In the early years of the family therapy movement in the UK there was strong resistance to its professionalization. The fear was that a fifth mental health profession would be formed, one which would exclude from practice all those who had not undergone a formal training programme. This was in the spirit of developing family therapy practice within the main mental health disciplines. Against this background, the United Kingdon Council for Psychotherapy (UKCP) was established in 1993, after a gestation period of over fifteen years. This has a brief to regularize the whole field of psychotherapy training and practice. The process of contributing to this registering body has further helped family therapists and the main training programmes clarify what are the central tenets of good practice, recognizing the importance of protecting clients from abuse (Peterson, 1992). The dilemma for the future in the UK will be how, on the one hand, to continue to develop and monitor standards of training and practice, while, on the other, to keep alive the sense of excitement and openness which has so far characterized the movement.

(See also CIRCULARITY; MILAN SYSTEMIC APPROACH; SYSTEMIC HYPOTHESIS; TEACHING OF SYSTEMIC APPROACHES.)

S.A., P.A. & H.J.

transactional patterns   See ACTUALIZING FAMILY TRANSACTIONAL PATTERNS.

transactional typologies of the family   There is often an empirically observable correlation between a type of individual pathology and the particular form of transactions observed. One may then consider the symptomatic aspect of the relations as dynamic modalities of personality-realization, without prejudging the origin of the disorder (whether single-factor or, more probably, multi-factor, individual and relational). Within this perspective, one may, drawing on the work of Haley, Lidz, Wynne, Stierlin, Ferreira and Selvini Palazzoli, propose a comparative table of the structuring of symptomatic family transactions. That table might usefully be completed by describing the structure of perceptions and the psychical organization by reference to the work of Searles, Rosen, Racamier, Kestenberg and Decobert, Brusset etc. We shall here make a distinction between families in schizophrenic, anorexic and delinquent transaction: FST, FAT and FDT.

MYTHS

FST: of unity;
FAT: of harmony;
FDT: of autonomy.

EXPERIENCE OF CONSENSUS

FST: concerned to achieve consensus. Glosses over not only the opinions of each individual, but also personal identity; the index patient's symptoms express the conjunction of irreconcilable positions.

FAT: also concerned to achieve consensus, with recognition of identity, but intolerant of each person's opinions and feelings, these giving rise, most often, to mutual opposition and negation.

FDT: concerned to maintain interpersonal distance, the family members develop a sense of the 'ego centred on self' with personal opinions stubbornly defended by each member.

STRUCTURE OF ROLES

FST: pseudo-mutuality, pseudo-hostility, with defective reciprocity. The family members are withdrawn and close themselves off from the outside world as if behind a 'rubber fence' which is presumed to be tacitly understood. Each person's roles are fundamentally disqualified and are not constituted as such. Symmetrical competition is not based on any possible conflictual confrontation of stabilized roles.

FAT: all attempts at child–parent confrontation are avoided which would challenge roles and might possibly destroy them. Roles exist, but they are fragile in their constitution.

FDT: roles are loosely defined and competitive, with a tendency to be always one step ahead of the others. The parents disregard other people's rules about relations with children and punish their unsatisfactory behaviour arbitrarily. The family members are 'detached' from one another and align themselves with outside groups.

TRANSMISSION

FST: irrationality, repeated transgenerational breaks, rendering any evocation of the past beyond the pale or dangerous and transgenerational confrontation illusory.

FAT: gap between emotional satisfactions and moral demands.

FDT: weakness of the 'superego' related to the existence of invisible loyalties and secret allegiances to persons and systems that are officially forgotten.

COMMUNICATION

FST: partialized, split double binds; the generalized sacrifice of ties prevents one from leaving the field.

FAT: unified and personified double binds, with localized sacrifice of behavioural relations.

FDT: split double binds, with the consequence that the ties exclude 'sacrifice' and force one to leave the field.

PERCEPTION OF RELATION BETWEEN THE ALIEN AND THE FAMILIAR

FST: distortion, deformation of mode-identifying signals, with adaptation to the reality of the 'strongest'. Exacerbated sensitivity, with an imprecise grasp of what are familiar and what are alien elements.

FAT: paradoxical maintenance of a pseudo-sexualized exterior.

FDT: 'each against all', with hyper-acuity for outside perceptions.

QUALIFICATION OF THEIR OWN MESSAGES BY MEMBERS OF THE FAMILY

FST: disqualification of the various levels of one's own messages, both as regards the content and the relationship itself. Each member implicitly invalidates what he/she is saying, together with the very fact of speaking: self-disconfirmation.

FAT: congruent qualification of one's own levels of messages, but disconfirmation of the sexed body.

FDT: enactment by others of the incongruence of one's own message levels.

QUALIFICATION OF OTHER PEOPLE'S MESSAGE LEVELS BY MEMBERS OF THE FAMILY

FST: disqualification of other people's different message levels both in terms of content and of relationship. Each person is invited to speak on condition that they are neither heeded nor even listened to; refutation covers both what is said and the fact of speaking; disconfirmation of the very existence of others.

FAT: rejection of the other person's message, apparently relating only to the message received, but in fact also attacking the way the other person defines the relationship.

FDT : disqualification by each parent of the other's messages demanding obedience, with a conformist attitude on the part of the child, obeying the one while disobeying the other, and vice versa.

THE PROBLEM OF LEADERSHIP

FST : every attempt to assert leadership is annihilated, both where intrafamilial relations are concerned and the relations established between the family and outside institutions. No one can therefore explicitly declare who exerts leadership within the family nor, even less, can they take any kind of decisive initiative.

FAT : similarly, no one is prepared to assume or assign leadership within the family. That leadership is, however, delegated to some degree to outside social agencies.

FDT : the attempt to exert leadership is very clearly displayed, but is regularly thwarted by the SPLIT DOUBLE BIND structure of parental communication.

ALLIANCES

FST : all alliances are unstable and it is impossible to triangulate the least dyadic relationship. In extreme forms, the parents, brothers and sisters do not even appear united in their convergence towards the index patient, even when they assert the opposite; transgenerational coalitions seem non-existent at all levels; the mere statement that they exist may be experienced as a totally irrelevant incongruity.

FAT : declared alliances are unthinkable, except that of the parents making a stand against the index patient's attempts at rebellion; transgenerational coalitions, which may be observed at one level, are denied at another level.

FDT : the alliances which are overtly displayed are inevitably betrayed at some point in the name of systems of invisible loyalty, most often situated on transgenerational axes.

(See also COMMUNICATION; INDEX PATIENT; PARADOX; PSEUDO-MUTUALITY; SPLIT DOUBLE BIND; SYMPTOMATIC AND/OR AETIOLOGICAL TRANSACTIONS.)

J.M. & P.S.

transference, counter-transference Transference is a process of actualization of unconscious desires, representable in the form of object relations, with persons met in certain precise contexts (amorous relationships, psychotherapeutic relationships, teacher–pupil relations).

As 'false connection' (Freud, *Studies on hysteria*), the transference appears as a love relation displaced from the first objects known during childhood (parents, acquaintances) to persons met in the present. During psychoanalytic treatment, the transference

appears as an erotic artefact. It is this arteficial aspect which has to be identified and analysed.

The counter-transference refers to the whole of the analyst's unconscious reactions to the patient's transference (Freud, 'The future prospects of psychoanalytic therapy', 1910). It is a kind of 'mirror concept of transference' (Stierlin, 1977, p. 303).

The meaning of these two concepts remains ambiguous and controversial: that meaning is either (a) limited to the rigorous conditions of the appearance of transference during psychoanalytic treatment, where it is understood as a 'transference neurosis'; it is, then, an operational tool; or (b) extended to every psycho-affective movement from one person to another and the counter-movement induced by this. Its heuristic and pragmatic aspect is, then, much more limited. The semantic ambiguity is even greater in its application to family therapies, in so far as many situations reveal dislocated, disorganized, impossible or non-existent transferences.

For Bateson, the transference is deutero-learning or level 2 LEARNING relating to interpersonal relationships. It is based on a certain number of fundamental PARADOXES which characterize the cognitive and emotional dispositions of the human mind, which makes it akin to a paradoxical transaction in DOUBLE BIND or, rather, multiple-bind form. These paradoxes are not the same, depending on whether one looks at the structuring of a neurotic, perverse, psychosomatic, delinquent, psychopathic or demented person etc.

The paradoxes of transference will be all the more obvious where narcissistic phenomena are in the foreground (see NARCISSISM). This fact may be related to the first axiom of the PRAGMATICS OF COMMUNICATION: 'one cannot not communicate'. By virtue of this, the extension of the concept is unlimited in character.

Thus, depending on the writer and the point of view, transference in family therapy will be regarded as intense, immediate and violent (Hirsch, 1980) or as an obsolete concept which is inappropriate to the context of the family approach (post-Batesonian system theorists). Transference and counter-transference have been studied in family therapy by, for example, Framo, Whitaker, Ruffiot, Eiguer etc. Transference may be both an aid and an obstacle in the unfolding of the therapeutic process.

INDIVIDUAL TRANSFERENCE: PARADOXES OF TRANSFERENCE AND PARADOXICAL TRANSFERENCE

Many writers have devoted attention to the double binds constitutive of transference phenomena. Jackson and Haley (1963) studied the paradoxes of transference as these appear in the analyst–analysand relationship which underpins the standard form of psychoanalytic treatment of the neurotic. Anzieu (1975b) explored the paradoxical transferences of some borderline patients when they seek to obtain two mutually incompatible results. de M'Uzan (1976) discovered the existence of a paradoxical system in counter-transference when the psychoanalyst is suddenly invaded by incongruous thoughts which neither seem connected to the patients' associations nor to his/her own. McDougall (1978) mapped out the functioning of the anti-analysand in analysis. Kohut (1971) described the narcissistic transference of borderline personalities. Searles (1965, 1979) showed the interaction between the delusional transference of the patient and the therapist's counter-transference, and the way in which the psychotic seeks to treat the therapist by the very efforts he/she deploys to drive him/her mad. The interest of such researches resides, it must be conceded, in the discovery of paradoxes, but also in the specific study of each of them.

A risk of extension does, however, exist, in the name of the very limits of transference. Referring to articles devoted to autism, erotomania, bulimia, acting out etc., Nasio (1985, p. 11) writes, for example, 'Thus, "*at the limits of transference*", is more a way of asserting the primacy of the analytic experience, than a way of designating another space beyond it.' If one follows the analysis proposed by Martine Gross (see INCOMPLETE-NESS THEOREMS), such an attitude amounts to extending the theory by reducing the model.

PARADOXES OF THE CONCEPT OF TRANSFERENCE IN FAMILY THERAPY

LOVE or hate, as they are expressed in the transference, are invariably structured or destructured by the organization of the family interactions which play a part in the construction or destruction of the personality.

Freud (*Lectures on psychoanalysis*, 1933) pointed out how the psychoanalysis of children led to considerable modifications of technique from the classic model of adult analysis. It is evident that all Freud's remarks are precursors of an approach directed towards the family context. The child is a different object from the adult, one as yet without a superego and the FREE ASSOCIA-TION method does not get one far. Since the parents intervene in reality, the transference plays a different role, in so far as resistances which are internal in the adult are here replaced by external difficulties. It then becomes necessary concretely to involve the parents, since they are the bearers of resistance (Montalvo and Haley, 1973). Moreover, when adult patients are confronted with infantile character traits, the distinction between adult and child analysis becomes hazy, so that the analyst must adapt him/herself to the object and use techniques more usually employed in child analysis. As Stierlin emphasizes (1977, p. 307), 'transactional phenomena in families, whatever their specific content and source, reflect chiefly one fact – that transferences originate within families. It is family transactions which give rise to those relational patterns which

later, inappropriately and repetitively, are transferred to non-family contexts.'

It is, then, desirable to distinguish between transference and ALIENATION as two complementary but different processes. In alienation, non-family contexts (social, ideological, mythological etc.) are transported into family contexts, influence the nature of the interactions and unconscious metacommunications and play a part in building up the individual and collective identity. In other words, it is much more difficult to displace a love relationship on to persons encountered in the present, if the experiences of childhood have not enabled either the formation of a bond or the structuring of its unconscious representations. In such cases, the movement, constitutive of the transference, which enables the transition from the intrafamilial to the extrafamilial to be made, does not take place. A family member will concentrate upon him/herself all the emotional and intellectual affects of his/her close circle, either as SCAPEGOAT or as INDEX PATIENT.

OTHER TYPES OF TRANSFERENCE

Dissociated transferences, central and lateral transferences, collective transferences, group transferences, transferences of transferences: there is no lack of adjectives for attempting to characterize the affective and representative impulses which drive the family members and the intervenors who come to their assistance.

In dealing with situations of family SPLITTING, one sees lateral transference and counter-transference phenomena appear. A transference is lateral when it is directed to an analyst other than the original psychoanalyst, who is the object of the central transference. Such situations appear when what is in question is a search for 'mirror' relations (relations of inverted symmetry or anti-symmetrical relations). In such cases, Rubinstein and Weiner (1967) have applied the term 'double transference' or 'transference of transference' and these may be deciphered and used in CO-THERAPY. The whole of the situation thus created may lead to highly entangled, if not totally befogged and inextricable, interactions. Following Oury's terminology (1985), the transference then becomes dissociated; a 'group to group' analysis is then required.

With regard to transference, Freud could not envisage the nature of the problems posed by behavioural disturbances, or of psychotic states, in which the components of the transference are affected. It is then necessary to have recourse to systemic modelling of the supra-individual contexts. The point is not so much to analyse the transferential movements as to create situations in which they can appear, so that one can structure, consolidate and synthesize them.

(See also ABSTINENCE, RULE OF; FAMILY SELF-BELONGING; FAMILY–THERAPEUTIC INSTITUTION DIFFERENTIATION; INTERPRETATION; MAP AND COUNTER-MAP OF

A FAMILY SYSTEM; METABINDING; METASYSTEMS; PARADOXICALITY; RESIDUAL RELATIONS; SUPERVISION; THERAPEUTIC ABSTENTION; THERAPEUTIC DOUBLE BINDS AND MULTIPLE BINDS.)

J.M.

transgenerational memories, family memories

INFORMATION storage devices which, for living organisms, are linked to the acquisition of data from the environment as this is transmitted and modified from one generation to another. Within this data, transgenerational memories incorporate more or less reliably certain characteristics of the co-evolving organisms, as well as models of the relationships between them. Family memories are the part of transgenerational memories which ensure cultural transmission from antecedents to descendants by way of individual learning processes. Memories make it possible to simulate the behaviour, thoughts and emotions of others, and also the models of interpersonal relations within family and social units. The structure of memories is influenced by rites and myths which function as FAMILY ORGANIZERS. VIOLENCE arises out of the quantitative and qualitative destruction of memories.

Transgenerational memories are structured as a function of various parameters:

- of the function of the storage medium: phylogenetic 'read-only' memories; cultural 'READ-WRITE' memories;
- of the group unit under consideration: individual, family, social memories;
- of the nature of the process memorized: affective memories of the emotional systems constructing the ETHOS of a group; memories representative of intellectual systems constructing the EIDOS of a group.
- of the coding of information: ANALOG, DIGITAL, HOLOGRAPHIC.

Transgenerational phenomena have been studied by Bowen (1978a) and Boszormenyi-Nagy and Spark (1973) in particular. The family is the necessary intermediate agency in the reproduction of supra-individual memories and cultural traditions as embodied to some degree in each person. If unconscious memories, stored as engrams by the normal or neurotic individual in the form of phantasies, inevitably stamp their effects on family groups, family memories are also made up of spaces which escape an individual mental representation, whether unconscious or preconscious. Only the simultaneous presence of several members of the family will activate certain types of memory. Family therapy treatment of psychoses reveals the disintegration of phantasy organization and the importance of multi-generational 'all-or-nothing' ruptures between affective and representative memories. Faced with the family's defective memories, the therapeutic system functions as auxiliary, palliative or substitutive memories, having effects of construction or reconstruction and capable of being reinforced by the use of recordings (written records, video tapes etc.). This activation in the 'here and now' can possibly be potentiated by the therapists leaving the consulting room and by thinking through, restoring and elaborating information in the real time of the session.

MEMORY AND PHYLOGENESIS

As Atlan (1972, p. 224) stresses,

The algorithms of the living world cannot initially be algorithms of reproduction of equilibrium states, but are, rather, algorithms of departures from that equilibrium and of return to that state by detours, during which, in a dynamic way, the characteristics of an integrated organization may be constituted and manifest themselves ... The mechanisms of reproduction would seem rather to be memories added to systems in a non-equilibrium state, in such a way that the systems preserve the properties of that state in a more economical way.

Thus the mechanisms of the evolution of species are those of self-organized systems with a very great resistance to random change by virtue of the addition of high-fidelity memories to self-organizing structures. These memories produce a very high level of reliability in the transmission of information.

Phylogenetic memories function as ATTRACTORS, invisible traces serving as rules of procedure for the organization of behaviour. When a pair of greylag geese lose their brood, the young who were born in the previous year return to their parents if they have not already formed couples. Similarly, a goose which has lost its partner returns to its parents or to its 'unmarried' brothers and sisters. The human species has elaborated these biological forms of regulation which are present in the animal kingdom, though it has not done away with them altogether. These forms of regulation call upon *affective memories of the family group*, structured on the basis of instinctive attachment behaviour, fear and rejection, and phenomena of IMPRINTING and early parent–child, child–parent habituation. These phenomena are akin to the primal repression described by Freud. Though the object of the INSTINCT is 'presented' as such in the psyche, and though the psyche possesses an elementary level of representation, it is not the same with the instinctive movement properly so-called, which is registered as affective memory. The regulative schema of the whole sequence is thus present and may possibly be activated, but the meshing-in of memories of symbolic representation of the parent–child relation is secondarily superimposed on this affective memory.

So far as groups are concerned, the quantity of information possessed by a group may be greater or less than the quantity of information possessed by the members of the group (Wiener, 1948). Man is capable of alternating between anonymous group behaviour (in public transport or crowds) and extremely elaborate interpersonal behaviour. There are variable capacities of individual memorization of group memories and of collective memorization of individual memories. In the most disturbed families, the family members seem to take up forms of functioning characterized by anonymity and misrecognition. Schizophrenic behaviour seems to reveal a cultural memory that is either practically emptied of all content, regarded with derision or experienced as a source of terror, while the phylogenetic memory functions insistently to remind of the incongruence of the founding myth of the family unit: the unconscious is, to some extent, emptied of all substance, of all content.

MEMORY AND ONTOGENESIS

Thus very varied forms of memory exist:

Individual memories
In his letters to Fliess, Freud attempts to formalize the various forms of registration of these:

> our psychical mechanism has come into being by a process of stratification: the material present in the form of memory-traces being subjected from time to time to a rearrangement in accordance with fresh circumstances – to a re-transcription. Thus what is essentially new about my theory is the thesis that memory is present not once but several times over, that it is laid down in various species of indications . . . I cannot say how many of these registrations there are: at least three, probably more. (*Standard Edition*, vol. 1, p. 233)

The first registration was assumed to be at the level of the perceptual sign which is incapable of becoming conscious. The second was inscribed at the level of the UNCONSCIOUS and its traces might correspond to conceptual memories. The third transcription was related to the verbal representations of the preconscious system. 'The psychical apparatus possesses the unlimited gift of being able to receive new impressions and yet creates durable, if not unchangeable, memory traces in a continuous way.' This is how the hysteric suffers from reminiscences, whose repressed offshoots in the unconscious return by way of 'conversion'.

Family and social memories
The structuring of family memories is indispensable for the organization of individual memories and therefore for accession to the status of subject and stabilization of object relations. Freud pinpoints an incapacity for unconscious registration of memory in psychosis. If the unconscious memory cannot be produced in the psychotic patient, this is because it does not exist as such; it is possible for a sense of guilt or shame to freeze transmissions of identity over several generations by preventing access to the ancestral 'crime'. However, the problem then posed is not only the question of true and false memories or the relation between real trauma and phantasy organization. It concerns the processes which stabilize the definition of REALITY – or do not – and make it possible to distinguish between true and false, i.e. the ritual and mythic organizers of multigenerational memories.

MULTIGENERATIONAL MEMORIES

The family is both the container and the content which enables biological and symbolic reproduction to take place. Rites and myths have a performative function which structures the modalities of communication and enables these to be transmitted from generation to generation. This transmission superimposes biological and cultural memories and knocks them up against one another. Family trees are, in the strong sense, mechanisms transmitting and supporting the reproduction of emotive and intellectual norms, the origins of which may be situated over extremely broad time-scales.

The multigenerational transmission of attitudes lays the foundations of the cultural traditions which are set in place very early on in ontogenesis by the prodigious capacities of observation and active imitation of the child, who in this way enriches his/her own potentialities. These processes of observation/imitation are of two types which succeed one another in the earliest years, in the different cycles of imprinting (and may possibly go on right through a lifetime):

- non-verbal, gestural, vocal imitation of the non-verbal behaviours of parents and grandparents, transmitting the identity of ancestors;
- the acquisition of language by way of DEIXIS.

Parents thus transmit the varied levels of their maturity and immaturity to their descendants, which leads to a variation in the DIFFERENTIATION OF SELF over several generations, a condition of access to the 'I' ('I feel', 'I think': Bowen, 1978a). The grandparents also have an essential role in this transmission. In a family, an old person may very well lose a large part of his/her faculties of memory, but the resurgence of his/her earliest memories, which are particularly durable, often has a precious transmission value for grandchildren, far beyond the mere content of what is then expressed. The identity of deceased parents will remain the more alive in their descendants if they have been successfully introjected, this being an indispensable condition for the elaboration of mourning.

In schizophrenic transaction, there is a non-differentiation of selfs which prevents access to the status of subject and prevents stabilization of the subject–object relation. The more 'marked' the schizophrenic symptoms, the more the evocation of preceding generations gives rise to very lively defences, panic reactions of rejection, all-or-nothing emotional discharges and the more likely it is to lead to the immediate halting of therapy. All the events within the family then seem frozen, clenched and fossilized and cannot be re-used or re-cast to reconstruct new mythologies. The point then becomes not so much to remember the past as to synchronize the present. A loss of information concerning previous generations, which is connected to emotional ruptures due to painful affective traces, brings about an accumulation of ancestral hatreds which produce quantitative and qualitative defects in the vital memories indispensable for psycho-affective individuation.

In DELIRIUM or psychotic deterioration, there is a falsification of the falsification of messages; the transmission of information over several generations thus leads to ever-increasing blanks or noise, which leave the messages totally disconnected from their initial referents. This is reminiscent of the game in which a message which is initially whispered by someone has to be passed from person to person through a group, again as a whisper. The message the last person receives in no way resembles what the first person said. Where there is multigenerational transmission of a sense of guilt or a feeling of unconscious guilt, the *report aspect* of the messages may be preserved, but not the *command aspect* which would render the reports operational in an appropriate context (the initial contexts being lost). The degrees of freedom and flexibility are counteracted by punitive experiences: the nature of the transgression is no longer accessible, but the principle of that transgression is, and this makes its expiation the more formidable since it is the cruellest and most skeletal dimension of the superego that is expressing itself here. In critical or fertile moments, schizophrenics thus attempt to recreate the command aspect of the relation in a system marked by a refusal to refer to the lineage. The recall of this latter often occurs in a way that is terrifying for those close to the schizophrenic, who find themselves suddenly confronted with the unbearable and aberrant return of the ancestor, prophet, totem or divinity (or rather of combined images of the two parental lineages which are characterized by the failure to achieve a satisfactory combination-differentiation; see Miermont, 1981a; Miermont and Angel, 1982). In such cases, the very foundations of the ritual and mythic levels of the family are directly put in question.

(See also FAMILY MYTHS; FAMILY SELF-REFERENTIALITY; FORECLOSURE; INSTITUTIONAL MYTHS; LEARNING; LEDGER; LOYALTY; RELATIONAL ARCHETYPES; RITUALIZATION.)

J.M.

transgenerational therapies   There have been two main strands in the development of family therapy: that which remained within the psychodynamic model and that which moved much more towards here-and-now and behavioural/cognitive and task-orientated approaches. Transgenerational approaches draw primarily on psychodynamic frameworks. In recent years there has been a greater cross-over between the two traditions, representing a degree of maturity within the field with practitioners open to integrating different models in order to provide a more holistic therapeutic service (Jenkins, 1985). However, even those pioneers in the field who are more associated with the approaches that stress current interactions and family structure acknowledge the importance of family history in so far as it affects current family functioning (Minuchin, 1974).

Important in the development of transgenerational approaches is the work of Boszormenyi-Nagy who describes his ideas about the family LEDGER and debts (Boszormenyi-Nagy and Spark, 1973). Although his writing is often not easy to follow, his ideas are important and the metaphor of family book-keeping is an elegant one. It is as if in the early stages of life the dependent infant incurs psychological, emotional and even financial debts which, later on when the parents become dependent, they in their turn can 'call in'. Where debts are repaid within the current life-cycle of the family, the family ledger can be ruled off, and each generation starts as if with a clean slate. However, in families where debts are not honoured, there will be a carry over.

The analogy of the balance sheet is useful. In accounting practice, a business must have a balancing figure in the end of the year accounts: literally, the balance sheet. If the business is running in deficit, the balancing figure which is carried forward to the next accounting period will be a debt representing creditor liabilities. If the business continues to function in this way over a number of years it will use up all its reserves of capital and ultimately become bankrupt. In the interim, after two or more years of deficit trading, the published balance sheet will no longer reflect the origins of how the debts were incurred, and employees and shareholders alike will not easily know how or why the company is so impoverished. Similarly in families, as debts are carried forward to the next generation(s), members will know in some way that there are roles to be fulfilled but no longer why or how. The tensions which arise around such issues then become involved in the negotiations within the family without members understanding to what these relate. In addition, social, economic and cultural circumstances will have changed from the circumstances of the past, further complicating the process. It is within this framework of thinking that family SECRETS also develop (Pincus and Dare, 1978).

The main tenets of transgenerational approaches are therefore that:

- current difficulties stem from attempts to master earlier conflicts (or debts) in families of origin;
- these conflicts and transference distortions are being lived out through the spouse, children and other important relationships;
- when people can return and deal directly with the people involved to resolve previously avoided issues, there is an opportunity for reconstructive changes to come about between the individual and the family of origin; current marital relationships can more effectively be dealt with; and adult(s) and child(ren) are better able to renegotiate their relationships.

Framo (1976, 1981) lays particular emphasis on encouraging people to go back to, or to bring in, their family members from older generation(s). He believes that most children's problems are metaphors about the quality of the relationship between the parents. Therefore, in his therapy, parents are seen with the child and grandparents are seen for the parents. He believes in the importance of recognizing that 'family members collusively carry psychic functions for each other' (Framo, 1981), both horizontally and vertically.

His particular interest is in how individuals 'solve' their psychic distress and their relationship problems through their choice of partner and in the role and functions that children come to fulfil as part of an intergenerational dance. The importance of a transgenerational approach to therapy is that the focus is on the interpersonal aspects of relationships. Family members have the opportunity to test reality rather than focus on internalized figures. Framo says: 'The original transference figures can also be the objects of transference today; few adults ever get to see their parents as real people' (Framo, 1981, p. 138). In marital work, by going backward in time, it is more possible for the individual to relate to his or her partner in an appropriate fashion, as a person in his/her own right, since the transference meaning will have changed.

Within this framework, the FAMILY LIFE-CYCLE is an important perspective to hold, since it links current family life experience with developments over time (Carter and McGoldrick, 1989). Not only will parents deal with difficulties in ways which are seen as culturally appropriate in the present, but they will be influenced by myths and beliefs which are brought from their respective, and sometimes conflicting, family histories. The life-cycle of any family has a shape both in the present and one which stretches over generations.

Murray Bowen's work (Bowen, 1978a) has been influential in the field, although it is often not taught explicitly on many family therapy training programmes. The main tenets of his theory are of the importance of the DIFFERENTIATION OF SELF in order to achieve emotional and intellectual integration. From his own family experiences, Bowen became interested in the importance of what he described as triangulation in families and cross-generational alliances (see TRIANGLES). He characterized the main aspects of SELF as having two parts; the solid self and the pseudo-self, that part which is modified in relationships. Where there are high levels of pseudo-self, one witnesses high fusion and enmeshment, a word also used frequently by Minuchin (1974). The opposite of fusion is emotional cut-off. Both extremes indicate the existence of maladaptive solutions to intimacy in relationships. Wynne et al. (1958) have described the implications of extreme PSEUDO-MUTUALITY in families having a schizophrenic member.

Bowen (1978a) described the nuclear family as an emotional system where partners choose each other based on levels of differentiation. Where poor differentiation and high fusion are passed on from parents to children this is expressed in the new family's relationships. Clinicians frequently witness what he describes as a family projection process. Members in their adult relationships and in their turn as parents project onto their members material brought forward from previous relationships and generations. Where this is too painful, a possible solution is one of emotional cut-off as a pathological way of separating the past in order to live in the present. Where such painful issues remain unresolved Bowen describes a MULTI-GENERATIONAL TRANSMISSION process which can be identified across three or more generations.

Bowen's therapy aims to reverse emotional cut-off, detriangulate the individual and achieve differentiation of self. A technique which is useful clinically in this and all approaches to transgenerational work is the GENOGRAM.

Analysis of genogram material will include looking at sibling positions in the family, the timing of entries and exits, and the similarity or repetition of names and 'replacements' in families. Similarity or difference in FAMILIES OF ORIGIN of the parents, such as culture, ETHNICITY, GENDER roles and socioeconomic status, will be of importance. The meaning of psychiatric illness, the early deaths of females or males will be addressed as well as looking for patterns which are observable through each generation or which skip a generation.

Transgenerational approaches have been developed by a number of practitioners, including Ferreira (1963); Byng-Hall (1973, 1980, 1986, 1988); Lieberman (1978, 1979a,b,c, 1987); Jenkins and Donnelly (1983); Heinl (1985); and Friedman et al. (1988).

(See also ANCESTORS; FAMILY MYTHS; LOSS AND GRIEF; MYTH; PROJECTIVE IDENTIFICATION.)

H.J.

transitional objects, transitional phenomena In the work of Winnicott, these terms refer to the zone of experience intermediate between thumb-sucking and playing with a doll or furry animal. They are thus intermediate between oral eroticism and object relations properly so-called. It may be the corner of a blanket that is involved, or a rag or even the child's babbling or the undifferentiated area of play between child and mother. The transitional object has a pre-symbolic function.

Winnicott (1951) further specifies that the value of the transitional object lies in what it actualizes or realizes, rather than in what it in fact symbolizes:

> It is true that the piece of blanket (or whatever it is) is symbolical of some part-object, such as the breast. Nevertheless, the point of it is not its symbolic value so much as its actuality. Its not being the breast (or the mother) is as important as the fact that it stands for the breast (or mother). (Winnicott, 1958 p. 233)

Technical use is made of these phenomena in family therapy in situations in which the family runs up against a pathology of transitional zones and comes up against objects that are bearers of symptoms and pathology (the alcoholic's bottle, the addict's syringe, the pervert's fetish object etc.). We may see METAPHORICAL OBJECTS as a secondary elaboration of transitional phenomena.

(See also SYMBOLS; TRUE SELF, FALSE SELF.)

J.M.

triadic questioning A technique of intervention proposed by Selvini Palazzoli et al. (1980a) and Caillé (1985), based on the comments, actively solicited by the therapist, which a family actor may make on the relationship he/she perceives between two other family actors. Triadic questioning is the artificial activation of a behaviour which arises naturally in family interactions.

Talking about others is a spontaneous behaviour which occurs within families and groups. It consists in speaking to one person in the family about the doings of other members of the family, the relationships between them and the events which have occurred among them, when they are no longer present. It may in some cases make it possible to elaborate behavioural strategies, to resolve certain conflicts or to fuel others. It functions as a 'safety valve', allowing people to let off steam.

This tendency to talk about others may be used in an artificial, paradoxical manner, by soliciting, for example, a mother's comments on what she perceives of the relationship between her husband and one of her children, or a father's comments on the style of his wife's relationship with her mother etc. The information gathered in this way is often more instructive than what one acquires by trying to find out how each of the family members perceives their own relationships with others.

In the most destabilized families, this type of research may mobilize more or less lively resistance. In some cases, family members are incapable of transcribing verbally the nature of the relationships they perceive, or else they will report a total absence of relationship. The patient diagnosed as psychotic may be the first to react very brusquely, turning the question back on the therapist, asking him/her what business it is of his/her and, in the process, revealing the function of the symptom: his or her state as psychotic patient allows him or her to avoid precisely such questions being posed. It is advisable in that case to accompany this defensive move or indeed to prescribe it, asking each person not to try to give a particular meaning to the communication which is established – or not established – in the family.

(See also CALUMNY; CIRCULAR QUESTIONS; DISCLOSURE; MILAN SYSTEMIC THERAPY; SCANDALMONGERING.)

J.M.

triads See COALITION; PERVERSE TRIANGLES; TRIANGLES.

triangles The triangle is an emotional configuration of three persons: it is the smallest of the stable systems of relations.

A family may be conceived as a complex network of triangles, some rigid and constant, the others flexible and changing. These triangles occupy a central or peripheral position. Their structure may or may not be pathogenic.

In Bowen's theory, triangles are seen as lying at the base of the construction of every emotional system within the family. It commonly occurs that the tension between two persons in a system (for example, the parents) reaches such a level that it is too uncomfortable to bear. A third person, usually the parents' child is 'triangulated' to reduce that tension within the system to a more tolerable level. The outcome of such a dysfunctional triangulation is usually the appearance of inadequate COALITIONS (inside or outside the family) and an undesirable behavioural symptom in the child (Ackerman, 1966; Haley, 1967; Satir, 1967; Minuchin, 1974; Minuchin et al., 1978; Bowen, 1978a).

From the psychoanalysis of neurotic patients, Freud discovered in the OEDIPUS COMPLEX a universal emotional invariant which structures the child's relationship with its parents in triangular fashion. That triangulation functions by shifting intensely felt affective impulses on to the plane of unconscious PHANTASY: for the boy, desire for the mother and the lethal rivalry of the father; for the girl, desire for the father and the lethal rivalry of the mother. The existence of non-neurotic pathologies revealed the inadequacy of the Oedipal model and led to the discovery of other founding myths and other types of triangulation.

A triangle usually comes about through the establishment of a stable coalition between two persons (dyad) such that a third person finds him or herself involved in that dyad, performing the peripheral function of regulating the dyadic coalition. In the absence of conflict, the person in the peripheral – or third – position is placed in a state of emotional insecurity or even suffering. In the case of conflict, the trouble or suffering is transferred on to the members of the dyad and the third person is relieved of it. Where intrafamilial regulation proves impossible, one or more persons or institutions are brought in to perform this triangulation function. The suffering is thus reduced within the family and transferred to the chosen external agencies.

In family therapy, the hypothesis is often advanced that a child–parent coalition camouflages underlying marital conflicts and prevents the resolution of the marital discord. In consequence, the task of therapists often consists in consolidating the boundary around the couple and attempting to resolve the marital conflict.

THE FUNCTIONAL FAMILY TRIANGLE

In a father–mother–child triangle of this kind, the partners are confident in their own marital relationship and are thus capable of allaying the child's fears of abandonment. The mother is capable of allowing the child to maintain a good relationship with his/her father. The father encourages a harmonious mother–child relationship. Each of the partners thus authenticates the other's status and role.

In cases of father–child or mother–child conflict, the peripheral partner, while accepting that the conflict has a genuine foundation, will attempt to regulate the aggressive dimension of the interchange in a flexible way. However, the two partners make it clear to the child that he or she can never be included in the intimacy of their conjugal relationship.

THE DYSFUNCTIONAL FAMILY TRIANGLE: TRIANGULATION OR THE RIGID TRIAD

In a family, a child may find itself locked into a situation where its behavioural symptoms mask the conflict existing between its parents. That behaviour is reinforced by the parents as a way of keeping their own conflicts buried and the child thus remains stuck in a role which serves to protect the parents (Minuchin, 1974).

The partners have no confidence in their own marital relations. These are threatened, if not indeed damaged, by parental relations which reactivate the transgenerational conflicts not resolved by the parents. The parents each feel shut out by the other, to the point that they turn to the child seeking compensation for the needs that are not satisfied by their conjugal relationship. Disappointed with each other, caught up in conjugal warfare and not accepting loss of face, they both, paradoxically, call on the child to be on their side, i.e. to side with them against the other parent. The child thus becomes caught up in a conflict of loyalty and ends up distancing him or herself from one of his/her parents, unless he/she is capable of the kind of skilful tightrope act that will reassure both.

A child who comes to be designated the 'identified' or INDEX PATIENT by a dysfunctional family takes on the onerous task of keeping his/her parents together. He/she learns that he/she can unite them by concentrating all their attention upon him/her. However, a procedure of this kind for uniting the parents does not totally relieve their conjugal suffering nor does it really include the index patient in that conjugal relationship. The patient suffers from the unfortunate illusion that he/she is 'on the outside' (in a functional triangulation, such an illusion would be dismantled in the course of time). The index patient is not an integral part of the conjugal relationship. That relationship is a system that is closed on the organizational and operational plane, both physically and psychologically. This is a precondition for the structuring of the 'primal scene' phantasy. The child is not the equal of his/her parents: he/she does not know what they know, he/she cannot do what they do. The boy cannot really be his mother's lover because she shows she is disappointed with his father, any more than the girl can be her father's lover. In the other preferential coalition, father–son, mother–daughter, the therapists become spectators in an all-out pseudo-war of the sexes.

Although the index patient does not succeed in completely relieving his/her parents' pain, they allow him/her to think that he/she can and that he/she is essential to the marital relationship. The child thus falls victim to another illusion: he/she believes himself to be omnipotent.

THE FATHER–DAUGHTER, MOTHER–SON RELATIONSHIP IN THE DYSFUNCTIONAL TRIANGLE

In a dysfunctional family, one very often sees the establishment of overdeveloped father–daughter or mother–son relations. In the opinion of Satir (1967), Oedipal development only becomes Oedipal conflict when the individual is incapable of integrating a compatible image of the other sex. To avoid such an impasse, the parents have to be clear, direct and specific about their sexual differentiation and their unity as a couple.

Children are faced with various taboos, the most important of which, the INCEST taboo, has come about as a means of protecting children's psycho-affective maturation and adult sexual relations. The children of functional families receive clear messages and acquire the notion that neither of their parents is a suitable object for their sexual drives. In dysfunctional families, the other-sex parent encourages incestuous feelings by expectations and demands expressed openly. The same-sex parent increases the degree of guilt attaching to such feelings if he/she does not interpose him/herself between his/her partner and the child. At the same time, this parent denigrates and rejects the child and forces him/her to turn even more to the attracting parent.

The incest taboo in itself only gives rise to minor conflicts in the child. It is the parents' ambivalence towards the taboo which both stimulates the child's sexual desires and increases the sense of guilt.

When tensions are very great within the family, the triangulation occurs with persons outside the family.

(See also PERVERSE TRIANGLES.)

P.A., P.S., J.M., A.C. & S.A.

true self, false self This conceptual opposition originates in the work of Winnicott. A detailed description of it is to be found in his article 'Ego distortion in terms of true self and false self' (1960a). According to Winnicott, there is a parallel between the distinction between the true self and the false self and the distinction drawn by Freud between a part of the self that is central and powered by pre-genital and genital sexuality and a part that is turned outwards and related to the world.

The psyche-soma system forms the basis of the SELF. The self is a unit that is both physically contained within the body and psychologically integrated. That unit is the place where the sense of self and the richness of the individual's personality reside, a richness which develops as a result of the simultaneous experience of love and hatred. The split between true and false self arises in all individuals to varying degrees since a certain quality of obedience is necessary and reflects a tendency on the part of the infant to comply and not expose itself.

Periodically, the infant's gesture expresses a spontaneous drive. The source of this gesture is the 'true self'. Winnicott connects the idea of the true self to a spontaneous gesture. The good-enough mother responds to the infant's omnipotence and, to a certain extent, makes sense of it. A true self then begins to come into being. If she is not a good-enough mother, instead of meeting the infant gesture, she substitutes her own gesture which will only acquire meaning through the compliance of the infant. This is the

earliest stage of the 'false self'. The true self only becomes a living reality as a result of the mother's repeated success in meeting the infant's spontaneous gesture or sensory experience. When the mother's adaptation is not good enough, the infant gets seduced into a compliance and a compliant false self reacts to environmental demands and the infant seems to accept them.

The function of the false self is a defensive function. Its object is to hide and protect the true self, whatever it might be. Winnicott classifies possible false self organizations in the following way:

1 *At one extreme*: the false self sets up as real. It is confused with the real person. In work relationships and friendships, this false self may fail; it has something essential lacking. The true self is completely hidden.
2 *Less extreme*: the false self defends the true self. This latter is acknowledged as a potential and is allowed a secret life.
3 *More towards health*: the false self is mainly concerned with a search for the conditions which will make it possible for the true self to come into its own. In this context, suicide may occur as a means of avoiding, by destruction of the total self, annihilation of the true self.
4 *Still further towards health*: the false self is built on identifications.
5 *In health*: the false self is represented by the social attitude, polite manners and a certain reserve etc. 'Much has gone to the individual's ability to forgo omnipotence and the primary process in general, the gain being the place in society which can never be attained or maintained by the True Self alone' (Winnicott, 1960a, p. 143).

When a false self is built up in an individual with a high intellectual potential, there is a tendency for the mind to become the location of the false self. In this case, intellectual activity and psychosomatic existence become dissociated. When a false self is built up to hide the true one and the individual tries to resolve his/her personal problem by using his/her intellect, the clinical picture may easily become deceptive. The world may observe a high degree of academic success and find it difficult to believe in the very real distress of the individual concerned, who feels increasingly 'phoney' the more he or she is successful.

(See also DIFFERENTIATION OF SELF; NARCISSISM.)

M.G.

trust A term used by Boszormenyi-Nagy and Ulrich (1981) to define the necessary quality of relations within a group. A climate of trust is, in the long run, more significant for the future of the quality of family relations than any transactional pattern. The disappearance of this climate of trust may give rise to symptoms and endanger the growth – or even the survival – of the group.

The creation of a climate of trust among the members of the family and the therapist is one of the essential parameters for building the therapeutic setting. It takes a varying amount of time to develop. Therapists are in effect the guarantors of the respect for secrecy that is necessary in any therapeutic act. They must

also guarantee adequate safety barriers for each person who consults them and they must establish both the limits of their actions and the commitment to offer their services within these limits. The establishment or re-establishment of a relationship of trustworthiness between the members of the family is, for Boszormenyi-Nagy, one of the main aims of contextual therapy.

(See also CONTEXT; FAMILY THERAPIES; LEDGER; LOYALTY; MULTI-DIRECTIONAL PARTIALITY; TRANSGENERATIONAL THERAPIES.)

A.L.

U

uncertainty principle In family therapy an uncertainty principle may be stated in the following terms: it is impossible to apprehend at the same moment, *t*, the personality of two or more people with whom one is speaking and the nature of the interaction between them.

One cannot simultaneously know the individual structure of the personality, its static position (the psychopathological diagnosis), and its relational dynamics within the system (its evolutive metabolic function). A fundamental uncertainty arises from this – and it is one which cannot be removed – as to whether one should treat the patient with his/her family or treat the family as a relational group.

(See also ALCOHOLISM; INTERACTIONS; PSYCHOSOMATIC ILLNESS; SCHIZOPHRENIAS; SPLITTING; SYMPTOMATIC AND/OR AETIOLOGICAL TRANSACTIONS.)

J.M.

unconscious, the The transition from pragmatic effects (slips, parapraxes, dream interpretation and symptoms) to the theory of the unconscious is one of the most fundamental and most disputed of epistemological issues and it has given rise to a great number of exhaustive debates. After the inaugural works of Freud (*The interpretation of dreams*, 1900; *The psychopathology of everyday life*, 1914b; *Jokes and their relation to the unconscious*, 1960a; the metapsychological writings etc.), we may mention the following works which form part of these discussions: George Politzer's *Critique des fondements de la psychologie* (1967); The Sixth Bonneval Colloquium on the subject of 'The Unconscious', edited by Henri Ey (1966); Henri Ellenberger's *The discovery of the unconscious* (1970); and Philippe Bassine's *Le problème de l'inconscient* (1973). When the family perspective comes to be taken into account, the problem takes on a new form and becomes more complicated. Other unconscious registers have been explored and utilized by Milton Erickson within the framework of hypnotherapy (see HYPNOSIS).

Within a family, the levels of consciousness and unconsciousness cannot easily be superposed on the individual structuring of the psyche. One person may make another person dream of him/her or may seek to metacommunicate by relating a dream. Another will make someone think or force someone to act. The nature of the ISOMORPHISMS between the psychical apparatus and family and social structures still remains in large part to be studied. As a preliminary, it would require further mathematical understanding of the operational concepts involved in this work of differentiation–comparison. It certainly cannot be reduced to a pure and simple opposition, or a generalized confusion.

THE UNCONSCIOUS AS DESCRIBED BY FREUD

The unconscious described by Freud is intra-system and inter-systemic:

1 *Intra-systemic*, in the first topography, which provided a meta-neurophysiology–metapsychology connection, on the basis of levels of consciousness (perception-consciousness system) and structures of thought (preconscious and unconscious systems properly so-called).
2 *Inter-systemic*, in the second topography, which provided a bio-psycho-sociological connection: id (biological source), ego (individual integration/differentiation) and superego (prohibitions, parental and social ideals).

Some psychoanalysts, following Freud, have studied the unconscious phenomena which are to be found neither within nor outside a totally circumscribed psyche. This topologically non-orientated part of the unconscious processes has been explored in different ways by a variety of authors:

1 The collective unconscious (Jung, with his concept of archetypes).
2 Lacan's topological representations: tangled topological figures (Borromean knots) interweaving the symbolic (the Freudian superego), the imaginary (the ego) and the real (the id); the non-orientated topological figures of the Möbius strip, the Klein bottle (see TANGLED HIERARCHIES) and the cross-cap.
3 The TRANSITIONAL OBJECT, Winnicott's potential space, also describing zones of interchange which leave the categories of inside and outside indistinct, zones of creative potentiality which are also preliminaries to symbolization.

THE UNCONSCIOUS IN COMMUNICATION THEORY

In communication theory, the unconscious is a property which arises out of the necessary hierarchization of psychical processes (Bateson, 1972). Following from the ideas of Samuel Butler, Bateson (1972) emphasizes that the more an organism knows something, the less it is conscious of that knowledge. That is to say that there is a process whereby knowledge (or habit or perception or thought) is buried at deeper and deeper levels of the mind. Bateson (1972) makes this point in 'Style, grace and information in primitive art'. For him, it was inconceivable that a system be completely conscious, but that all organisms must be content with a field of consciousness which is relatively restricted.

It has been observed that METACOMMUNICATION SYSTEMS are, to a considerable degree, unconscious. Freud himself observed the phenomenon of reciprocal influence between one unconscious and another. The child's superego is structured, in an essentially unconscious way, out of the parental superego.

There is a risk of reifying the concepts of unconscious and the psychism. Whereas the term 'unconscious' was intended to denote the property of an object or a thought process, it has become an object which is supposedly localizable and definable. By its nature, an unconscious thought or affect is a particular – metacommunicative – mode of exchange of messages between two or more persons. One may therefore always say of a person that he/she is not conscious of something or that the members of a family are not conscious of their family functioning or their problems. The 'unconscious' refers to a set of trans-local properties, like white or green, size or agility.

In a letter to Fliess, Freud made the following remark:

in the most deep-going psychosis the unconscious memory does not break through, so that the secret of childhood experiences is not betrayed even in the most confused delirium. If in this way we see that the unconscious never overcomes the resistance of the conscious, then, too we lose our expectation that in treatment the opposite will happen, to the extent of the unconscious being completely tamed by the conscious. (*Standard Edition*, vol. 1, p. 260)

If the unconscious memory does not break through, this is because it does not exist or that it is not to be found in the individual in whom the psychotic symptoms are lodged. The memory (conscious or unconscious) is not localizable in the mnemic systems of the sick individual. The problem becomes further complicated when one takes into account the thought disturbances to which those in his/her close circle are subject.

UNCONSCIOUS PROCESSES IN FAMILIES WITH PSYCHOTIC TRANSACTIONS

Within a family suffering schizophrenia, the effects of the primary processes of thought of the various participants are manifest and no longer in any way latent. What then, after that point, is the nature of what is latent? Freud reminds us that, in a case of chronic paranoia, it is DREAMS which reveal the correct version

of the facts, while jealousy is delusional. Asking the protagonists of a family drama to tell their dreams confronts them not with the reality of their phantasies but with the often very fragile phantasy which they have of an impossible reality. Henceforth, what is latent no longer has the properties of the unconscious system (in the Freudian sense of the term), but of the preconscious system. And this preconscious system relates directly to the often simple description of the relations which individuals perceive of their interactions and their family systems.

Erikson rightly emphasizes the gulf which separates Freudian psychoanalysis, which is based on 'a situation strictly *à deux*' (Erikson, 1968, p. 46), from the sociological model: 'The resulting methodological divergence has perpetuated in psychoanalytic thought an artificial overdifferentiation between the isolated individual forever projecting his infantile family constellation on the "outer world," and the "individual-in-the-mass," submerged in what Freud calls an "indistinct aggregate" of men' (Erikson, 1968, p. 46). Thus, for Erikson, the 'Oedipal trinity' cannot be regarded as an irreducible explicative schema. Social forms also co-determine the structure of the family through the – largely unconscious – organization of the superego. We have to recognize today that family structures themselves co-determine the structuring of the individual's unconscious processes, and the systems of belief and collective ideology.

Hence the unconscious as formalized and clinically identified by Freud, and as worked upon and pragmatically transformed by Erickson, calls upon different properties of the psyche and involves equally dissimilar therapeutic effects.

(See also FAMILY PSYCHICAL APPARATUS; FAMILY UNCONSCIOUS; METAPSYCHOLOGY; MULTI-LEVEL HIERARCHIES; PARACOMMUNICATION SYSTEMS; PHANTASY; RELATIONAL ARCHETYPES; SECRETS; TRANSGENERATIONAL MEMORIES.)

J.M.

unit of change   A unit of change is the product of a coupling between several EVOLUTIONARY SURVIVAL UNITS capable of creating a SEMANTIC UNIT OF MIND. From a morphological point of view, it is a metabolic form.

In therapy, a unit of change presupposes interaction between:

- a person or group in a state of DEMAND or consultation;
- and a person or group of intervenors, normally differentiated and organized professionally.

The unit of change it is possible to create clinically depends on the nature of the symptom in question and the way in which the suffering groups and the therapists define the threatened survival unit. An individual person, the marital couple, the parental couple, the mother–child dyad, the father–mother–child TRIAD, the NUCLEAR or EXTENDED FAMILY, the CLAN and the NETWORK may all be perceived, depending upon the circumstances, as the sub-system, system or meta-system with which a therapeutic relationship is to be established. The pertinent unit of change will also include the therapist or therapists involved.

In classic psychoanalysis, one may take the view that the threatened survival unit is the individual patient. The pertinent unit of change is made up of analysand and analyst, whereas the semantic unit of mind is much wider than the dyad that is directly involved: it includes the symbolic interaction between the family and social backgrounds of the two protagonists. Some psychoanalytic family therapists define their protocols by requiring from the outset the simultaneous presence at the sessions of at least two generations. Other family therapists prefer not to intervene – or to cancel the session – if all the family members are not present (see ABSENT MEMBER MANOEUVRE).

It seems necessary to us to introduce some nuances into these oppositions and to broaden the modes of intervention. Hence the distinction we propose between unit of change, unit of mind and survival unit. In dealing with complex psychotic situations, whereas the survival unit includes the family with all the children, some of whom may have left home, it is sometimes necessary to create differentiated sub-units of change.

Viewed schematically, one may take the following as sub-units. First, there is the *index patient–therapist interaction*. Secondly, there is the *family–therapist interaction*. In some cases, the therapist will see only the parental couple, not to conduct couple therapy, but to set up a therapeutic change in the index patient and his/her family through his/her parents. Every forced definition of the situation by the therapists (such as, for example, a problem within the marital pair in schizophrenic situations), like every interpretation of the content of relationships, seems to run the risk of calling forth a 'meaning' which is, apparently, all the more obvious for not taking account of the family's demand and resistances, and for actually threatening the homeostasis of the system and the survival of its members.

Thirdly, there is the *family–systemic intervenors–network interaction*. The family may, for example, be made up of several index patients, each with their mental health workers, and living in different specialized units (day hospitals, hostels etc.). These different units may possibly be involved in an overall approach to the family group. In other cases, the unit of change will be created when it has become possible to recognize the group or clan to which the index patient belongs and its secret rules of operation.

(See also STATIC, PSEUDO-STATIC AND METABOLIC FORMS.)

J.M.

universal unfolding   The universal unfolding of a germ function (which is called the organizing centre of the unfolding) is the function which generates the set of variations leading to morphological creations and transformations in such a way that this morphological creation is structurally stable. The theory of the universal unfolding of a function is based on a set of theorems. It is by building on these that Thom has developed the theory of ELEMENTARY CATASTROPHES. What is interesting about the universal unfolding is that it lays the ground for the theory of morphogenesis and change.

One may represent a natural phenomenon or system in terms of the development of n internal variables which describe the state of the system at any given moment. In the absence of any external perturbation, this system is in a state which is dependent upon its internal variables. We may express this by saying that the state of the system is a function f of the n internal variables of the system. Within the framework of catastrophe theory, a stable state of the system is a state for which the function f takes the minimum value. The number of possible stable states of a system depends therefore on the topological properties of the function f, i.e. the number of minima it presents.

An unfolding is therefore nothing but a function of n internal variables and r external parameters. But only stable unfoldings are of interest, i.e. those which resist perturbations and which retain their topological properties. Not all unfoldings are stable. It is not enough to add control parameters to a function to ensure that a neighbouring unfolding, i.e. one taking into account other deformations of the initial function, will be an equivalent unfolding.

The universal unfolding is a stable unfolding in which the number of external parameters is as low as possible. It is therefore the most economical means – in terms of the number of parameters that have to be taken into account – for describing all the possible deformations of a function. 'It is a way of parameterizing all the possible actualizations of the virtualities contained in an unstable situation' (Thom, 1983b, p. 70). What Thom shows is that, for a number of control parameters less than four, once the notion of stability has been appropriately formulated for an unfolding, one can establish a finite list of standard potentials (i.e. of universal unfoldings) to which all the stable deployments are equivalent. Stable regimes of phenomena and their conflicts (when several minima exist for certain values of the external parameters) may therefore be described by the singularities and minima of one of these universal unfoldings or of combinations of them.

(See also CHANGE; FAMILY CATASTROPHES, GENERALIZED CATASTROPHES.)

M.G.

V

valence An interaction between two or more persons in a family will be regarded as having a positive, negative or neutral valence depending upon:

- the number of connections those persons are capable of establishing among themselves and with others within or outside the family (great number of relationships or, by contrast, significant degree of withdrawal, without interchanges);
- the quality of those connections (conversational partners, affective interchanges, tolerance of conflict etc.);
- the power of attraction or repulsion created by those connections;
- the way the system allots them, congruently or incongruently, the place corresponding to this *de facto* state (see NETWORKS).

It will be possible, through this valence, to identify the interdependence of interactive roles between family actants:

- intrusive–indifferent parents/hallucinated terrorizing patient;
- SCAPEGOAT/persecutor/carer;
- father 'absent', without contact, alcoholic/mother–autistic child symbiosis;
- pseudo-omnipotent parentified child/impotent parents/grandmother providing control etc.

We shall note here that very often one and the same person is a bearer of both positive and negative, aggressive and sacrificial, selfish and altruistic valences. It will be necessary to evaluate the congruencies and incongruencies between the way that these valences are translated into action and the way that they are expressed in the syntactic and semantic morphologies of spoken language:

- monovalent intransitive verbs of state and action: he is good, Paul sleeps all the time, James won't sit still etc.;
- bivalent transitive verbs with two actants: John struck his mother with a knife;
- trivalent transitive verbs with three actants: verbs of communication and giving.

The way these narratives are formulated reveals particular tonalities of communication (ludic, phantasmatic, oneiric etc.) which are themselves underpinned by modalities of communication (deontic, alethic, veridictory etc.), all of which taken together structure the categories of communication (professional, friendly, loving etc.).

(See also FORCE FIELDS; LOVE; MODE-IDENTIFYING SIGNALS; SEMIOTIC SQUARE.)

J.M.

variety See LAW OF REQUISITE VARIETY.

vector fields See FORCE FIELDS, VECTOR FIELDS, MORPHOGENETIC FIELDS.

vectors A vector is an element of a vector space. It may be defined as a jet of order n, or as 'germs of curves' (Thom, 1983b). A vector is a multi-dimensional variable, possessing a direction, which may characterize the position of an organism or system moving in a vector space.

The postulate of the existence of vector fields (see FORCE FIELDS) must be linked with that of differentiable manifolds and ATTRACTORS, enabling us to define the family and its sub- and super-systems as DYNAMIC SYSTEMS. It is also associated with an approach to therapy, 'vector therapy', described by Howells (1979).

Identifying the dynamics of the family in this way requires, on the part of the therapists, that the action of the family members be resituated in complex trajectories and movements, whose deployment in time and space can only be apprehended in a manner that is, to a large degree, intuitive. Beyond the appearance of the verbal and non-verbal messages exchanged, the more or less unconscious SEMANTIC RESONANCES, as well as the intensity of the agitation and collisions between families and therapists, will give precise indications as to the dynamic aspect or these paths and trajectories, without however 'freezing' these continuing processes into precise definitions.

(See also MORPHOGENETIC OR STRUCTURAL TYPOLOGIES OF THE FAMILY.)

J.M.

video The use of video occupies a special place in family therapy. In the field of research, the work of

Scheflen (1973) and Birdwhistell (1981), among others, has shown how much can be gained from a 'micro-analytic' approach to human interaction. Stoller (1968) and Alger (1972) have shown how useful video can be in group therapy.

We are indebted to Milton Berger (1970) for a detailed and critical inventory of video techniques used in psychiatry. We shall mention only some of these here which are sometimes used in family therapy (Geffroy et al., 1980).

The use of video is especially helpful in certain precise circumstances: where there is great distortion between visual and verbal messages, grave psychotic pathology requiring an effort of distancing and reflection, or intense narcissistic disturbance, requiring an 'objectification' of the sessions. It may be contraindicated when, by contrast, the therapeutic parameters call for intimacy, when families wish to undertake essentially introspective work. As with any use of technical equipment, the use of video depends on the clinical intuition and sensitivity of the therapist.

FEEDBACK

The VCR is used here during the course of the session. The therapist selects a sequence from the present interview or an edited compilation from previous sessions in order to induce a change in the family interaction. This is an opportunity for the family to grasp the complexity of the exchange of non-verbal messages and to gain awareness of certain privileged modes of communication.

REPEATED PRESENTATION OF A SEQUENCE

The therapist helps the family to analyse a set of significant interactions by using the slow-motion facility of cutting the sound in order to concentrate attention on the picture. Some therapists have no qualms about handing the camera over to a member of the family at some points. Alger sometimes suggests that a family view a videotape between two family interviews (1979).

Naturally, these protocols are only effective thanks to the clinical skills of those who implement them. This is very much the case when video is used to back up CO-THERAPY or SUPERVISION. The continuous recording of all the family interviews is only of interest if the recording is analysed at the end of each session. Video is actually most useful in enabling the analogical modes of communication within a family and within a therapeutic system to be studied. The technique of confrontation may also be enhanced by the use of close-up shots of sequences of interaction.

VIDEO AND TRAINING

Video occupies a key place in the TRAINING of family therapists. Thanks to video libraries, the trainer has available recordings made by clinicians of repute. He/she can also present his/her own video tapes, at times, to illustrate a theoretical or technical point. The disadvantage of using video in this way is that it puts the students in a passive position and does not help them to create their own therapeutic model.

Filming role-play or therapeutic interviews conducted by the trainee can also be a stimulating phase in the training process. It is an opportunity for future family therapists to gain awareness of their styles of intervention, of their attitudes and their non-verbal behaviour.

(See also MIMESIS; NARCISSISM; REALITY; TEACHING OF SYSTEMIC APPROACHES.)

P.A. & S.A.

violence   A daily occurrence which each of us hears about: acts of war, road accidents and great catastrophes. We may distinguish between physical violence, which is only patent when bodily marks can be seen connected with the brutality suffered, and moral violence, the destructive and/or structuring effects of which are much more difficult to assess. The state of war arises when one human group attempts to subject another to its rule by force or deception.

Violence corresponds to a diffusion of power, capable of invading a whole family group, as the prevalent tone of communications. The loss of the integration of his/her family model releases great social violence in an individual.

Following Freud, psychoanalysts have been tempted to conceptualize the notion of violence by reference to the death drive, to aggressivity. In his book *La violence fondamentale*, Bergeret draws on those studies which are psychoanalytic in inspiration in an attempt better to grasp the psychogenetic foundations of violent phenomena. Bergeret is particularly interested in adolescence, in so far as the violent phenomena encountered during that period of life constitute one of the alarming characteristics of our times (Bergeret, 1984). He thus puts the emphasis on the awakening of fundamental violence at the moment of adolescence; in his work he mentions the contribution of Girard (1972). Primal violence resolves itself with the putting to death of a representative victim, the SCAPEGOAT. This is also a concept we have used to describe the transactional dynamics of the families of drug addicts (see Sternschuss and Angel, 1983). Initial, individual violence is transformed and metabolized into a particular form of rationalization which is transferred into the cultural order.

From a historical point of view, Chesnaies (1981) shows that the family is the site of paradox. Violence is more intense there than in any other milieu. He quotes American studies showing that one homicide in four occurs within the framework of the family. In Britain the statistics are the same. It is within the bosom of the victim's family circle or, more broadly, the circle of those close to him, that his/her murderers are recruited. Other American studies show that one couple in six fights at least once a year, resorting to throwing things, wielding knives or even using firearms. According to Chesnaies, one runs a greater risk of being killed within one's own family group than in any other social group, except perhaps in the army or the police.

It is, currently, rare for family violence to go so far as murder in Western society. Family conflicts manifest themselves more often in veiled hatred or bottled-up tension than in brutal, bloody outbursts. Patricide and infanticide only subsist now in cases of pathological distress in which the role of alcohol (see ALCOHOLISM), drug abuse and grave mental pathology are frequently important factors.

The family is the only place where behaviour is not codified in a definitive manner. It is the only space where a certain state of nature still exists. Apparently, anything is permitted, with the exception of INCEST, which is harshly condemned but exists none the less. One implicit rule persists: that of the mutual right of intervention and punishment. Parents hit their children, the children fight among themselves. Such violence is legitimate and is considered healthy and educative. There is an element of PLAY in this, forestalling real aggression or violence by the ritualization of blows, delivered within limits which normally indicate the boundary that is not to be overstepped. Brutal corporal punishment is no longer the norm and severe corporal punishment only persists among marginal groups or in deprived milieus.

With the development of the family, as represented essentially by its nuclear kernel: parents and children, individuals, are increasingly thrown back upon themselves: emotions are concentrated within the narrow family group and crystallize there. The extended family can scarcely serve as mediator. The nuclear family either becomes despotic or breaks up and scatters.

We shall here distinguish between: violence within couples; battered women (or men); battered children; battered parents; other forms of intrafamilial violence. We shall not refer here to the effects of violence directed against the self (suicide, drug addiction, self-mutilation etc.), but confine ourselves to the violence arising from aggression directed against others.

VIOLENCE WITHIN COUPLES

Certain exogenous factors (alcohol or drugs) may increase the level of that violence, but we shall not go into these matters here. Everstine and Everstine (1983) propose two interactional models which are most frequently found when such violence occurs. First, the symmetrical couple, in which an escalation of aggression leads to acting out. That escalation will vary depending on whether family rules are transgressed consciously or not. Relations with the family systems of origin are projected into the couple's interactional pattern. In other cases, what will be involved are pathological relations of a complementary type: this model is found in couples in which one of the members is 'battered'.

BATTERED WOMEN

It must be conceded that battered men do exist, but they are in a minority for at least two reasons: (a) men are stronger than women; (b) men are quicker to leave the marital home.

Violence by men is accepted at times in certain cultures and may be regarded as evidence of love: for some women, the extent of violence is masked by subsequent demonstrations of affection expressed by their partner after household 'scenes'. Remorse and tenderness lead to fragile reconciliations. In general, the partners come from families where there was also violence. As in other subgroups, the factor of transgenerational repetition is significant.

Some examples of interaction are quoted by Everstine and Everstine (1983). The man is attracted by a gentle, naïve woman, but that naïvety and passivity frustrate him. The woman tries to be more and more cooperative and only increases her husband's annoyance. In other cases, the husband feels threatened by his wife's abilities; he would like her to take care of him more. The feelings he has for his wife are ambivalent and he feels threatened in his autonomy. In general, pathological complementary relations are involved, where the two partners are excessively attached to each other with an irrational fear that they could not go on living without one another. Generally, battered women belong to socially underprivileged groups. They are isolated and have neither emotional nor financial resources to escape. Finkelhor (1983) describes women's sense of emotional and psychological 'entrapment' which makes it even more difficult to escape an abusive relationship. Only recently is our society coming to recognize the seriousness of domestic violence as a result of feminist campaigning.

BATTERED CHILDREN OF 'SILVERMAN'S SYNDROME'

This is a symptomatology which is very familiar to the pediatric services, where children are hospitalized after 'repeated falls'. The team gradually discovers that the injuries are caused by the parents. These situations are characterized by a significant degree of disavowal on the part of the family. In general, the parents involved have themselves been beaten in their childhood, have suffered emotional deprivation at an early stage and project their frustrations on to their children. They often look upon them as adults. Depression and marital problems are frequently found in such families.

BATTERED PARENTS

In recent years, we have seen an increase in the number of violent acts by adolescents or young adults against their parents. This kind of violence appears in the families where the generational barriers are virtually non-existent. Transgenerational relationships are the 'true psychological marriages' in such families and we might assume that the violence breaks out when the incestuous pact between the adolescent and the over-involved parent breaks down (Chartier and Chartier, 1982).

Physical violence (blows, illegal restraint etc.) appear after a succession of conflicts in what is most often a highly eroticized context. This apparent generational reversal of violence echoes the physical violence experienced by the young person in childhood and also factors of repetition revealed by a family anamnesis.

OTHER FORMS OF FAMILY VIOLENCE

We have written here of the matters relating to physical violence, without enumerating the forms of sexual violence, one of which is incest. In fact, violence may express itself in other forms – action to cause abortion, abandonment, giving a child to be fostered – and more subtly. We shall mention here, for example, lethal processes found in certain family configurations (Angel et al., 1985). Bourguignon (1984) has attempted a psychosociological approach to families in which a child had violently died young. Her conclusions were that there were pathogenic interactions.

In contemporary forms of violence, we may mention the abuse of psychotropic drugs (see DRUG ADDICTION), which allows conflict to be temporarily avoided. Although violence is mainly visited on children, it also exists towards grandparents. However, this is less well documented (temporary hospitalization for holidays, placement in old peoples' homes).

THERAPEUTIC PROTOCOL

The systems-based approach has made it possible to open up a range of treatments for these families, though the work is often difficult. Consultations frequently take place at the request of a social worker and the families are not highly motivated by a therapeutic process of any kind. These are extremely rigid families. Some therapists have specifically advocated a paradox model as advocated by Selvini Palazzoli et al. (1978). Others prefer strategic family therapy approaches or, more recently, the solution-focused work of de Shazer (1985, 1988; de Shazer et al., 1986).

We have to be able to offer different treatment models, depending on the specific character of families, and to organize systemic work in a network with the various organizations and social workers concerned.

(See also INDEX PATIENT; RECIPROCAL VICTIMIZATION AND RESCUE; SACRED; SCAPEGOAT.)

P.A. & S.A.

W

waking state See DREAMS, NIGHTMARES, SLEEP AND
THE WAKING STATE.

Z

zeal When faced with messages meeting the criteria of the DOUBLE BIND from patients and their families, therapists may feel inclined to respond to the most immediate demands and may embark on a series of initiatives in an effort to repair the irreparable. This situation usually leads to forms of therapeutic escalation in which therapeutic teams enter into symmetrical competition with the patients and their families.

Therapeutic escalation usually manifests itself in an excess of zeal on the part of the therapists, who seek to 'do something' at whatever cost. Rather than improve the situation, this in fact accentuates the various phenomena of repetition, violence and acting out, in forms destructive both to self and others. A self-maintaining cycle is set up in which the exacerbation of the disorders and excess of zeal feed off each other, producing exhaustion among the therapists and teams and a potentially negative outcome for the patients.

The therapeutic response may continue to reintroduce complementary feedback into family interactions and between the family and the therapeutic team. Absolute THERAPEUTIC ABSTENTION may also lead to dangerous forms of escalation. By taking account of the COMPLEXITY of the situation, which is characterized by the absence of a total solution to the demands expressed in immediate reality, it becomes possible to propose a programme of care spread out over time, to coordinate multi-focal interventions (drug treatment, institutional psychotherapy, family therapy, temporary changes of living space etc.) and to regulate empirically the various prescriptions envisaged.

(See also STALEMATE.)

J.M.

BIBLIOGRAPHY

Abraham, K. (1913–25) *Développement de la libido, formation du caractère. Etudes cliniques. Oeuvres complètes*, 2 vols. Trans. I. Barande and E. Grin. Paris: Payot, 1966.

Abraham, N. (1978) L'écorce et le noyau. In *Notules sur le fantôme*, pp. 426–33. Paris: Aubier-Flammarion.

Ackerman, N.W. (1958) *The psychodynamics of family life. Diagnosis and treatment of family relationships*. New York: Basic Books.

Ackerman, N.W. (1962) Adolescent problems: a symptom of family disorder. *Family process* 1, 202.

Ackerman, N.W. (1964) Prejudicial scapegoating and neutralizing forces in the family group, with special reference to the role of the family 'healer'. *International journal of social psychiatry* Congress Issue.

Ackerman, N.W. (1966) *Treating the troubled family*. New York: Basic Books.

Ackerman, N.W., Beatman, F.L. and Sherman, S.N. (eds) (1961) *Exploring the base for family therapy*. New York: Family Service Association of America.

Ackermans, A. and van Cutsem, C. (1987) Le labyrinthe de la supervision. *Thérapie familiale* 8 (3), 275–85.

Ades, J. (1985) *Alcoolisme, états névrotiques et troubles de la personnalité*. Cerm: Riom Laboratoires.

Acworth, A. and Bruggen, P. (1985) Family therapy when one member is on the death bed. *Journal of family therapy* 7, 379–85.

Adams, J.F., Piercy, F.P. and Jurich, J.A. (1991) Effects of solution focused therapy's 'formula first session task' on compliance and outcome in family therapy. *Journal of marital and family therapy* 17, 277–90.

Alberoni, F. (1979) *Innamoramento e amore*. French trans. *Le choc amoureux*. Paris: Ramsay, 1981.

Aleksandrowicz, R. (1974) Les enfants des survivants des camps de concentration. In E.J. Anthony and C. Koupernik (eds), *L'enfant dans sa famille*, vol. 2, pp. 315–21. Paris: Masson.

Alger, I. (1972) Television image confrontation in group therapy. In C.J. Sager and H. Kaplan (eds), *Progress in group and family therapy*. New York: Brunner Mazel.

Alger, I. (1979) Techniques audio-visuelles en thérapie familiale. In D.A. Bloch (ed.), *Techniques de base en thérapie familiale*. Paris: Delarge.

Alliot, M. (1968) Ethnologie générale: l'acculturation juridique. In J. Poirier (ed.), *Encyclopédie de la Pléiade*, pp. 1180–236. Paris: Gallimard.

Allyn, G. (1974) Mammalian socialization and the problem of imprinting. *La terre et la vie* 28, 209–71.

Allyn, G. (1993) Désir et souffrance: approche bouddhique et approche psychanalytique. In F. Chenet (ed.), *Nirvana*, pp. 347–70. Paris.

Ambrose, J.A. (1961) The development of the smiling response in early infancy. In B.M. Foss (ed.), *Determinants of infant behaviour*, vol. 1. London: Wiley.

American Psychological Association (1987) *Diagnostic and statistical manual of mental disorders*, 3rd rev. edn, p. 107. Washington, DC: APA.

Amiel, C., Garapon, A., Gruenais, M.E., Hamadi, M., Le Roy, E. and Yacoub, S. (1985) *La justice des mineurs en région parisienne*, pp. 40–94. Laboratoire d'Anthropologie Juridique de Paris, Université de Paris 1, Centre d'Etudes Juridiques Comparatives.

Andersen, T. (1987) The reflecting team: dialogue and meta-dialogue in clinical work. *Family process* 26, 415–28.

Andolfi, M. (1977) *La thérapie avec la famille*. Trans. A-M. Colas and M. Wajeman. Paris: ESF, 1982.

Andolfi, M. (1980) Formation en thérapie familiale. *Thérapie familiale* 1 (3), 195–221.

Andolfi, M. and Angelo, C. (1980) Le thérapeute comme metteur en scène du drame familial. *Réseaux, systèmes, agencements* 3, 55–62. Paris: Gamma.

Andolfi, M., Angelo, C., Menghi, P., Nicolo, A-M. and Giacometti, K. (1982) *La forteresse familiale*. Trans. M. Rives. Paris: Dunod, 1985.

Andolfi, M., Menghi, P., Nicolo, A-M. and Saccu, C. (1979) L'interaction dans les systèmes rigides. In *L'approche systémique en thérapie familiale. Réseaux, systèmes, agencements*. Cahiers critiques de thérapie familiale et de pratiques de réseaux 1, pp. 25–42. Paris: Gamma.

Andreasen, N., Scheftner, W. et al. (1986) The validation of the concept of endogenous depression. A family study approach. *Archives of general psychiatry* 43, 246–51.

Angel, P. (1979) Le rôle des parents dans la formation de l'enfant. A propos de thérapies de famille. *Gazettes médicales de France* 86 (41), 4885–8.

Angel, P. (1981) Usage et mésusage de l'épidémiologie dans le champ de la toxicomanie. In *Adolescence et toxicomanie. Journées nationales des intervenants en toxicomanie* 1, 24–30.

Angel, P. (1982) Approche systèmique et cure institutionelle en psychiatrie infantile. In G. Maruani and P. Watzlawick (eds), *Hommage à Bateson*, pp. 53–6. Paris: Erès.

Angel, P. (1983) Adolescence et psychothérapie familiale. *Adolescence* 1 (1), 81–5.

Angel, P., Angel, S. and Couture, F. (1985) La mort dans les familles de toxicomanes. *Thérapie familiale* 6 (3), 203–8.

Angel, P., Geberowicz, B. and Sternschuss Angel, S. (1982–3) Le toxicomane et sa famille. Présentation Mony Elkaim. *Réseaux, systèmes, agencements* 6. Paris: Editions Universitaires.

Angel, P., Miermont, J. and Schlee, M. (1985) Ethologie humaine et thérapie familiale. *Bulletin de psychologie* 38, 431–7.

Angel, P. and Neuburger, R. (1980) Les thérapies familiales systémiques. *Psychanalyse à l'université* 6 (21), 159–64.

Angel, P., Robbe, G. and Sternschuss Angel, S. (1984) *Violence et toxicomanie.* Cahiers de Beaumont, Actes du Colloque National. Paris.

Angel, P. and Sternschuss, S. (1981) Les survivants de l'holocauste et leur famille. *Revue de médecine psychosomatique et de psychologie médicale* 2, 147–55.

Angel, P. and Sternschuss Angel, S. (1983a) La famille du toxicomanie. Revue critique de la littérature. *Psychiatrie de l'enfant* 26 (1), 237–56.

Angel, P. and Sternschuss Angel, S. (1983b) La toxicomanie au féminin. *Adolescence* 1 (2), 247–58.

Angel, P., Taleghani, M., Choquet, M. and Courtecuisse, N. (1978) Abord épidémiologique de la tentative de suicide de l'adolescent: quelques réponses de l'environnement. *Evolution psychiatrique* 42, 351–67.

Angel, P., Valleur, M. and Chauvel, J. (1977) Le généraliste et le toxicomane. *Gazette médicale de France* 86 (2), 101–6.

Anthony, E.J., Chiland, C. and Koupernik, C. (1980) *L'enfant dans sa famille. L'enfant à haut risque psychiatrique.* Paris: PUF.

Anthony, E.J. and Koupernik, C. (eds) (1974) *The child and his family: Yearbook of the International Association for Child Psychiatry and Allied Professions,* 3 vols. New York: Wiley.

Anzieu, A. (1983) Lit ou divan? *Dialogue* 82, 43–4.

Anzieu, D. (1956) *Le psychodrame analytique chez l'enfant.* Paris: PUF.

Anzieu, D. (1974) Le moi-peau. In *Le dehors et le dedans. Nouvelle revue de psychanalyse* 9, 195–208. Paris: Gallimard.

Anzieu, D. (1975a) *Le groupe et l'inconscient.* Paris: Dunod-Bordas.

Anzieu, D. (1975b) Le transfert paradoxal. De la communication paradoxale à la réaction thérapeutique négative. In *La psyché. Nouvelle revue de psychanalyse* 12, 49–72. Paris: Gallimard.

Anzieu, D. (1985) *Le moi-peau.* Paris: Dunod.

Anzieu, D. and Martin, J.-Y. (1968) *La dynamique des groupes restreints.* Paris: PUF.

Aponte, H.J. (1976) Underorganisation of the poor family. In P. Guerin (ed.), *Family therapy: theory and practice,* pp. 432–48. New York: Gardner Press.

Aponte, H.J. and van Deusen, J.M. (1981) Structural family therapy. In A.S. Gurman and D.P. Kniskern (eds), *Handbook of family therapy,* pp. 310–60. New York: Brunner Mazel.

Aponte, H.J. and Hoffman, L. (1973) The open door: a structural approach to a family with an anorectic girl. *Family process* 12, 1–44.

Apostel, L. (1967) Syntaxe, sémantique et pragmatique. In J. Piaget (ed.), *Logique et connaisance scientifique. Encyclopédie de la Pléïade.* Paris: Gallimard.

Aries, P. (1977) A propos de 'la volonté de savoir'. *L'arc* 70, 'la crise dans la tête', pp. 27–32.

Aristotle (1986) *De anima.* Trans. H. Lawson-Tancred. Harmondsworth: Penguin.

Asen, K.E. and Tomson, P. (1992) *Family solutions in family practice.* Lancaster: Quay.

Ashby, R. (1952) *Design for a brain.* London: Chapman and Hall.

Ashby, R. (1956) *An introduction to cybernetics.* London: Methuen, 1979.

Atlan, H.L. (1972) *L'organisation biologique et la théorie de l'information.* Paris: Herman.

Atlan, H.L. (1979) *Entre le cristal et la fumée. Essai sur l'organisation du vivant.* Paris: Seuil.

Atlan, H.L. (1981) Sur le déterminisme. Réponse à René Thom. Postulats métaphysiques et méthodes de recherche. *Le débat* 14, 83–9.

Attneave, C.L. (1976) Social networks as the unit of intervention. In P.J. Guerin (ed.), *Family therapy: theory and practice,* pp. 220–32. New York: Gardner Press.

Audisio, M. (1978) *Psychisme et biosystèmes*. Toulouse: Privat.

Auerbach, E. (1946) *Mimésis. La représentation de la réalité dans la littérature occidentale*. Trans. C. Heim. Paris: Gallimard, 1968.

Ausloos, G. (1979) Adolescence, délinquance et famille. Paper presented to the Congress on Juvenile Deliquency and Deviant Behavior, Milan 4–8 May. Reprinted in G. Ausloos and P. Segond (eds), *Marginalité, système et famille: l'approche systèmique en travail social*. Vaucresson: CFRES–IES.

Ausloos, G. (1980) Secrets de familles. In *Changements systémiques en thérapie familiale*. Paris: ESF.

Ausloos, G. (1983) Adolescence, délinquance et famille (expériences de thérapie familiale). In G. Ausloos and P. Segond (eds), *Marginalité, système et famille: l'approche systémique en travail social*. Vaucresson: CFRES–IES.

Ausloos, G. and Segond, P. (eds) (1983) *Marginalité, système et famille: l'approche systémique en travail social*. Vaucresson: CFRES–IES.

Austin, J.L. (1962) *How to do things with words*. Oxford: Oxford University Press.

Bahnson, C.B. (1978) Stress psychologique familial et problème des antécédents psycho–affectifs du cancer. In *Psychologie et cancer*, pp. 7–12. Paris: Masson.

Baillet, J. (1982) L'indispensable opératif. In G. Maruani and P. Watzlawick (eds), *L'interaction en médecine et en psychiatrie*, pp. 110–14. Paris: Erès.

Baker Miller, J. (1976) *Towards a new psychology of women*. Harmondsworth: Penguin.

Balandier, G. (1971) *Sens et puissance. Les dynamiques sociales*. Paris: PUF, 1981.

Balandier, G. (1974) *Anthropologiques*. Paris, 1985.

Balint, M. (1957) *The doctor, his patient and the illness*. London: Pitman.

Baltat, F. and Smagghe Floc'h, M-F. (1980) La guerre des mondes. *Réseaux, systèmes, agencements* 3, 71–3. Paris: Gamma.

Bandler, R. and Grinder, J. (1975) *The structure of magic*, vol. 1. Palo Alto: Science and Behavior Books.

Bandler, R. and Grinder, J. (1979) *Frogs into princes*. Utah: Real People Press.

Barel, Y. (1985) L'institution dans tous ses états. In *Y-a-t'il une théorie de l'institution?*, pp. 18–103. Paris: Centre d'Etude de la Famille Association.

Barthes, R. (1970) Pour une psychologie de l'alimentation. *Cahier des annales* 28.

Bassine, P. (1973) *Le problème de l'inconscient. Les formes non conscientes de l'activité nerveuse supérieure*. Trans. E. Bronina, revised by M. Rouze. Moscow: MIR.

Bastide, R. (1965) *Sociologie des maladies mentales*. Paris: Flammarion, 1977.

Bastide, R. (1968) Psychiatrie sociale et ethnologie. In J. Poirier (ed.), *Ethnologie générale. Encyclopédie de la Pléiade*, pp. 1655–79. Paris: Gallimard.

Bastide, R. (1990) Acculturation. *Encyclopedia universalis*, vol. 1, pp. 114–19.

Bateson, G. (1958) *Naven*, 2nd edn. Stanford: Stanford University Press.

Bateson, G. (1961) *Perceval's narrative*. Stanford: Stanford University Press.

Bateson, G. (1969) Metalogue: what is an instinct? In T.A. Seboek and A. Ramsay (eds), *Approaches to animal communication*, pp. 11–30. Mouton: The Hague.

Bateson, G. (1971) Communication. In H. MacQuovn (ed.), *The natural history of an interview*. Chicago: Chicago University Library, microfilm collection of manuscripts on cultural anthropology 95, 1991, pp. 1–40.

Bateson, G. (1972) *Steps to an ecology of mind*. London: Intertext Books. 1973 edn, London: Paladin.

Bateson, G. (1978) The birth of a matrix or double bind and epistemology. In M.M. Berger (ed.), *Beyond the double bind: communication and family systems*, pp. 41–64. New York: Brunner Mazel.

Bateson, G. (1979) *Mind and nature: a necessary unit*. New York: E.P. Dutton.

Bateson, G. and Bateson, M.C. (1987) *Angels fear: towards an epistemology of the sacred*. New York: Macmillan.

Bateson, G., Jackson, D.D., Haley, J. and Weakland, J.H. (1956) Towards a theory of schizophrenia. *Behavioural science* 1 (4). Reprinted in Bateson (1972), pp. 173–98.

Bateson, G., Jackson, D.D., Haley, J. and Weakland, J.H. (1963) A note on the double bind. *Family process* 2, 154–61. Reprinted in D.D. Jackson (ed.), *Communication, family and marriage. Human communication*, vol. 1, pp. 55–62. Palo Alto: Science and Behavior Books, 1974.

Beels, C. and Ferber, A. (1972) What family therapists can do. In A. Ferber, M. Mendelsohn and A. Napier (eds), *The book of family therapy*, pp. 168–232. Boston: Sentry.

Behling, D.W. (1979) Alcohol abuse as encountered in 51 instances of reported child abuse. *Clinical pediatrics* 18 (2), 87–91.

Benghozi, P., Girard, C. and Lelu, F. (1986) Formation, action, recherche et supervision: le réseau RASTA. *Thérapie familiale* 8, 315–27.

Ben-Ishay, Y., Rattock, J. et al. (1985) Neurophysiologic rehabilitation: quest for a holistic approach. *Seminars in neurology* 5 (3), 252–9.

Benjamin, J. (1988) *The bonds of love*. London: Virago.

Benoit, J.-C. (1981) *Les doubles liens*. Paris: PUF.

Benoit, J.-C. (1982) *Angoisse psychotique et système parental*. Paris: PUF.

Benoit, J.-C. (1984) *Les thérapies systémiques et la thérapeutique institutionelle en psychiatrie de l'adulte*. Paris/New York: Masson.

Benoit, J.-C. and Roume, D. (1986) *La désaliénation systémique. Les entretiens collectifs en institution*. Paris: ESF.

Bentovim, A., Elton, A., Hildebrand, J., Tranter, M. and Vizard, E. (eds) (1988) *Child sexual abuse within the family*. London: Wright.

Benveniste, E. (1979–80) *Problèmes de linguistique générale*, 2 vols. Paris: Gallimard.

Berenson, D. (1976) Alcohol and the family system. In P.J. Guerin (ed.), *Family therapy: theory and practice*. New York: Gardner Press.

Berenstein, I. (1976) *Familia y enfermedad mental*. Buenos Aires: Païdos.

Berezin, M.A. (1965) *Geriatric psychiatry: grief, loss and emotional disorder in the aging process*. New York: International Universities Press.

Berg, I.K. (1991) *Family preservation: a brief therapy workbook*. London: BT Press.

Berg, I.K. and Miller, S.D. (1992) *Working with the problem drinker: a solution-focused approach*. New York: Norton.

Berger, M.M. (1970) *Videotape techniques in psychiatric training and treatment*. New York: Brunner Mazel.

Berger, M.M. (ed.) (1978) *Beyond the double bind: communication and family systems. Theories and techniques with schizophrenics*. New York: Brunner Mazel.

Berger, P., Pomeau, Y. and Vidal, C. (1984) *L'ordre dans le chaos. Vers une approche déterministe de la turbulence*. Paris: Hermann.

Bergeret, J. (1974) *La personnalité normale et pathologique. Les structures mentales, le caractère, les symptômes*. Paris: Dunod.

Bergeret, J. (1984) *La violence fondamentale*. Paris: Dunod.

Bergeret, J. (1985) Post adolescence et violence. In A.M. Alleon, O. Morvan and S. Lebovici (eds), *Adolescence terminée, adolescence interminable*. Paris: PUF.

Bernard, C. (1865) *Introduction à la médecine expérimentale*. Paris: Garnier-Flammarion, 1966.

Berrendonner, A. (1981) *Eléments de pragmatique linguistique*. Paris: Editions de Minuit.

Berquez, G. (1983) *L'autisme infantile. Introduction à une clinique relationelle selon Kanner. Le fil rouge*. Paris: PUF.

Bertalanffy, L. von (1947) *General systems theory*. Harmondsworth: Penguin, 1968.

Bertalanffy, L. von. (1965) On the definition of the symbol. In J.R. Royce (ed.), *Psychology and the symbol: an interdisciplinary symposium*. New York: Random House.

Bertalanffy, L. von (1967) *Robots, men and minds. Psychology in the modern world*. New York: George Braziller.

Bertalanffy, L. von (1981) *A systems view of man*. Edited by P.A. Laviolette. Boulder, Colorado: Westview Press.

Bertrand, J. (1986) Plusieurs médecins soignent un même malade. Une tentative d'examen des interactions. *Documents de recherches en médecine générale* 15, 5–24.

Bettelheim, B. (1962) *Dialogue avec les mères*. Trans. T. Carlier. Paris: Robert Laffont, 1973.

Bettelheim, B. (1966–7) Aliénation et autonomie. In T. Carlier (trans.), *Survivre*, pp. 392–411. Paris: Laffont, 1979.

Bettelheim, B. (1967) *La forteresse vide. L'autisme infantile et la naissance de soi*. Trans. R. Humery. Paris: Gallimard, 1969.

Bettelheim, B. (1982) *Freud and man's soul*. New York: Alfred A. Kopf.

Bion, W.R. (1961) *Experiences in groups, and other papers*. London: Tavistock.

Bion, W.R. (1962) *Learning from experience*. New York: Basic Books.

Bion, W.R. (1963) *Elements of psycho-analysis*. London: Heinemann Medical.

Bion, W.R. (1965) *Transformations. Change from learning to growth*. London: Heinemann Medical.

Bion, W.R. (1970) *Attention and interpretation*. London: Tavistock.

Birdwhistell, R.L. (1970) A kinesic-linguistic exercise: the cigarette scene. In *Kinesics and context: essays on body motion communication*, pp. 227–50. Philadelphia: University of Pennsylvania.

Birtchnell, J. (1970a) Early parent death and mental illness. *British journal of psychiatry* 116, 282–8.

Birtchnell, J. (1970b) Depression in relation to early and recent parent death. *British journal of psychiatry* 116, 299–306.

Black, D. (1981) Mourning and the family. In S. Walrond-Skinner (ed.), *Developments in family therapy*, pp. 189–201. London: Routledge and Kegan Paul.

Black, D. (1982) Handicap and family therapy. In A. Bentovim, G. Gorell Barnes and A. Cooklin (eds), *Family therapy: complementary frameworks*, vol. 2, pp. 417–39. London: Academic Press.

Bleuler, E. (1911) Dementia praecox or the group of schizophrenias. Trans. J. Zinkin. New York: International Universities Press, 1950.

Bloch, D. (ed.) (1973) *Techniques of family psychotherapy: a primer*. New York: Grune and Stratton.

Bloch, D. (1985a) Modèles de traitement et modèles de formation en thérapie familiale. In M. Elkaim (ed.), *Formations et pratiques en thérapie familiale*. Paris: ESF.

Bloch, D. (1985b) Thérapie familiale et formation. In M. Elkaim (ed.), *Formations et pratiques en thérapie familiale*. Paris: ESF.

Bloch, D. (1989) The dual optic: researchers and therapists. *Family systems medicine* 7, 115–19.

Bloch, D. and La Perriere, A. (1973) In D. Bloch (ed.), *Techniques of family therapy: a primer*, pp. 1–19. New York: Grune and Stratton.

Blurton-Jones, N.G. (1972) *Ethological studies of child behaviour*. London: Cambridge University Press.

Bodin, A.M. (1981) The interactional view: family therapy approaches of the Mental Research Institute. In A.S. Gurman and D.P. Kniskern (eds), *Handbook of family therapy*, pp. 267–309. New York: Brunner Mazel.

Boisot, M. (1985) Introduction à la physique des phénomènes vibratoires. CERF Conference, 24 May 1985.

Bolton Finley, C. and Wilson, D.C. (1951) The relation of the family to manic-depressive psychosis. *Diseases of the nervous system* 12, 39–43.

Bompart, A. (1972–86) *L'événement psychique collectif*. Compte-rendu du séminaire. Première Edition HC. Paris.

Bonnafe, L. (1948) Le personnage du psychiatre (étude méthodologique). *Evolution psychiatrique* 13 (3), 23–56.

Bonnefoy, Y. (ed.) (1981) *Dictionnaire des mythologies*, 2 vols. Paris: Flammarion.

Boscolo, L. and Bertrando, P. (1992) The reflexive loop of past, present and future in systemic therapy and consultation. *Family process* 31, 119–30.

Boscolo, L., Caillé, P.H., Lang, M., Maruani, G. and Wertheimer, D. (1986) Training and supervision in family therapy. Fifth International Congress of Family Therapy, Jerusalem, 24 June 1986.

Boscolo, L., Cecchin, G., Hoffman, L. and Penn, P. (1987) *Milan systemic family therapy: conversations in theory and practice*. New York: Basic Books.

Boszormenyi-Nagy, I. and Framo, J.L. (1965) *Intensive family therapy*. New York: Harper and Row.

Boszormenyi-Nagy, I. and Spark, G.M. (1973) *Invisible loyalties: reciprocity in intergenerational family therapy*. New York: Harper and Row.

Boszormenyi-Nagy, I. and Ulrich, D.N. (1981) Contextual family therapy. In A.S. Gurman and D.P. Kniskern (eds), *Handbook of family therapy*, pp. 159–86. New York: Brunner Mazel.

Bott, E. (1968) *Family and Social Network*. Thetford.

Bouchard, R., Lorilloux, J., Guedeney, C. and Kipman, D. (1975) *L'épilepsie essentielle de l'enfant*. Paris: PUF.

Boudon, R. and Bourricaud, F. (1982) *Dictionnaire critique de la sociologie*. Paris: PUF.

Bouissy, A. (1977) Réflexions sur l'histoire et la préhistoire du personnage 'alter ego'. Lectures pirandelliennes, Université de Paris 8, 101–290.

Bouras, M., Bourneuf, H. and Raimbault, G. (1980) Le nanisme 'psycho-social': point de vue psychanalytique. In L. Kreisler (ed.), *L'abord psychosomatique en pédiatrie. Génitif* 2 (10), 629–31.

Bourgine, P. (1991) Heuristique et abduction. Rapport de synthèse en vue de l'habilitation à diriger des recherches. CEMAGREF, Université de Caen, Laboratoire d'informatique.

Bourguignon, O. (1984) *Mort des enfants et structures familiales*. Paris: PUF.

Bovet, P. and Schmid, F. (1985) Phénomènes répétitifs et pathologie du deuil dans les généalogies des schizophrènes. Brussels Congress, September 1985.

Bowen, M. (1978a) *Family therapy in clinical practice*. New York: Jason Aronson.

Bowen, M. (1978b) Schizophrenia as a multi-generational phenomenon. In M.M. Berger (ed.), *Beyond the double bind: communication and family systems*, pp. 103–233. New York: Brunner Mazel.

Bowlby, J. (1969) *Attachment and loss. Vol. 1: Attachment*. London: Hogarth Press and the Institute of Psychoanalysis.

Bowlby, J. (1973) *Attachment and loss. Vol. 2: Separation, anxiety and anger*. London: Hogarth Press and the Institute of Psychoanalysis.

Bowlby, J. (1980) *Attachment and loss. Vol. 3: Loss, sadness and depression*. London: Hogarth Press and the Institute of Psychoanalysis.

Bowlby-West, L. (1983) The impact of death on the family system. *Journal of family therapy* 5, 279–94.

Box, S., Copley, B., Magagna, J. and Moutstaki, E. (eds) (1981) *Psychotherapy with families: an analytic approach*. London: Routledge and Kegan Paul.

Bracinha-Vieira, A. (1982) Ethologie et psychiatrie. Phylogenèse des comportements et structure des psychoses. *Evolution psychiatrique*, vol. 47, pp. 1001–17.

Braudel, F. (1969) *Ecrits sur l'histoire*. Paris: Flammarion, 1985.

Braverman, L. (ed.) (1987) *Women, feminism and family therapy*. New York/London: Haworth Press.

Bretherton, I. (1974) Making friends with one-year olds: an experimental study of infant–stranger interaction. Unpublished doctoral dissertation. Baltimore, MD: The Johns Hopkins University.

Bretherton, I. and Ainsworth, M.D. (1974) Responses of one-year olds to a stranger in a strange situation. In M. Lewis and L.A. Rosenblum (eds), *The origins of fear*. New York: Wiley.

Breton, A. (1939) *Anthologie de l'humour noir*, 3rd edn. Paris: Jean-Jacques Pauvert, 1966.

Bridgman, F. (1986) Les systèmes familiaux à parentés multiples. Communication à la journée de l'ATSF, 15 November 1986.

Brillouin, L. (1949) Life, thermodynamics and cybernetics. *American scientist* 37, 554–67. Reprinted in W. Buckley (ed.), *Modern systems research for the behavioral scientist*, pp. 147–56. Chicago: Aldine.

Brillouin, L. (1950) Thermodynamics and information theory. *American scientist* 38, 594–9. Reprinted in W. Buckley (ed.), *Modern systems research for the behavioral scientist*, pp. 161–5. Chicago: Aldine.

Brillouin, L. (1956) *Science and information theory*. New York: Academic Press.

Brodeur, C. (1980) Peut-on éviter de passer par l'inconscient? *Thérapie familiale* 1 (23), 109–16.

Brodeur, C. (1982) *Portraits de famille. Une typologie structurale du discours familial*. Editions France-Amérique, Montreal.

Brouwer, L.E.J. (1975) *Collected works*, ed. A. Heyting. Amsterdam/Oxford: North Holland.

Brown, G.W., Harris, T. and Copeland, J.R. (1977) Depression and loss. *British journal of psychiatry* 130, 1–18.

Bruch, H. (1975) *Les yeux et le ventre*. Paris: Payot.

Bruch, H. (1979) *L'énigme de l'anorexie*. Paris: PUF.

Bruggen, P. and O'Brian, C. (1982) An adolescent unit's focus on family admission decisions. In H.T. Harbin (ed.), *The psychiatric hospital and the family*, pp. 27–47. Lancaster: MTP.

Bruner, J.S. (1983) *Savoir faire, savoir dire*. Paris: PUF.

Brusset, B. (1977) *L'assiette et le miroir. L'anorexie mentale de l'enfant et de l'adolescent*. Paris: Privat.

Brusset, B. (1985) L'anorexie mentale des adolescentes. In S. Lebovici, R. Diatkine and M. Soulé (eds), *Traité de psychiatrie de l'enfant et de l'adolescent*, vol. 2, pp. 467–85. Paris: PUF.

Bruter, C.P. (1974) *Topologie et perception*, 2 vols. Paris: Doin-Maloine.

Bruter, C.P. (1982) *Les architectes du feu*. Paris: Flammarion.

Buckley, W. (ed.) (1968) *Modern systems research for the behavioral scientist*. Chicago: Aldine Publishing.

Burck, C. and Daniel, G. (1990) Feminism and strategic therapy. In R.J. Perelberg and A. Miller (eds), *Gender and power in families*, pp. 82–103. London/New York: Tavistock/Routledge.

Burck, C. and Daniel, G. (1993) Gender, power and subjectivity. Paper delivered at the Fifth World Family Therapy Congress, Amsterdam.

Burck, C. and Daniel, G. (1994) *Gender and family therapy*. London: Karnac.

Byng-Hall, J. (1973) Family myths as defence in conjoint family therapy. *British journal of medical psychology* 46, 239–50.

Byng-Hall, J. (1980) Symptom bearer as marital distance regulator: clinical implications. *Family process* 19, 355–65.

Byng-Hall, J. (1986) Family scripts: a concept which can bridge child psychotherapy and family therapy thinking. *Journal of child psychotherapy* 12, 3–13.

Byng-Hall, J. (1988) Scripts and legends in families and family therapy. *Family process* 27, 167–79.

Byng-Hall, J. and Bruggen, P. (1974) Family admission decisions as a therapeutic tool. *Family process* 13, 443–59.

Cade, B.W. (1985) Unpredictability and change: a holographic metaphor. In G.R. Weeks (ed.), *Promoting change through paradoxical therapy*, pp. 28–59. Illinois: Dow-Jones Irwins.

Cade, B.W. and O'Hanlon, W.H. (1993) *A brief guide to brief therapy*. New York: Norton.

Caillé, P. (1985) *Familles et thérapeutes. Lecture systémique d'une interaction*. Paris: ESF.

Caillé, P. (1989) L'intervenant, le système et la crise. *Thérapie familiale* 8 (4), 359–70.

Caillé, P., Abrahamsen, P., Girolami, C. and Söye, B. (1979) Utilisation de la théorie des systèmes dans le traitement de l'anorexie mentale. *Cahiers critiques de thérapie familiale* 1, 15–23. Paris: Gamma.

Caillot, J.P. and Decherf, G. (1984) Le cadre de la thérapie familiale psychanalytique. In *Variations du cadre. Revue française de psychanalyse* 58, 6. Paris: PUF.

Cameron, D. (1985) *Feminism and linguistic theory*. London: Macmillan.

Campbell, D. and Draper, R. (eds) (1985) *Applications of systemic family therapy: the Milan approach*. London: Grune and Stratton.

Campbell, D., Draper, R. and Huffington, C. (1988) *Teaching systemic thinking*. London: DC Associates.

Campbell, D., Draper, R. and Huffington, C. (1989) *A systemic approach to consultation*. London: DC Associates.

Cancrini, L. (1977) *Esperienze di una vicerca sulla tossicomane giovanili in Italia*. Milan: Mondedori.

Canguilhem, G. (1943) *Le normal et le pathologique*, 5th edn, 1984. Paris: PUF.

Cannon, W.B. (1929) Organization for physiological homeostasis. *Physiological review* 9, 397.

Cannon, W.B. (1932–9) *The wisdom of the body*. New York: Norton.

Cantor, G. (1932) *Gesammelte Abhandlungen mathematischen und philosophischen Inhalts*. Edited by E. Zermelo. Berlin: Springer Verlag.

Caplow, T. (1968) *Deux contre un. Les coalitions dans les triades*. Trans. P. Cep. Paris: ESF, 1986.

Carnap, R. (1937) *The logical theory of syntax of language*. Trans. A. Smeaton. London: Routledge and Kegan Paul, 6th edn, 1964.

Carnap, R. (1942) *Introduction to semantics*. Cambridge: Cambridge University Press.

Carnap, R. (1947) *Meaning and necessity*. Chicago: Chicago University Press, 2nd edn, 1956.

Carpenter, J. (1992) What's the use of family therapy? *Australian and New Zealand journal of family therapy* 13, 26–32.

Carpenter, J. and Treacher, A. (1982) Structural family therapy in context: working with child focused problems. *Journal of family therapy* 4, 15–34.

Carpenter, J. and Treacher, A. (eds) (1993) *Using family therapy in the '90s*. Oxford: Blackwell.

Carpenter, J., Treacher, A., Jenkins, H. and O'Reilly, P. (1983) 'Oh no! Not the Smiths again!' An exploration of how to identify and overcome 'stuckness' in family therapy. Part II: Stuckness in the therapeutic and supervisory systems. *Journal of family therapy* 5, 81–96.

Carrer, P. (1983) *Le 'matriarcat psychologique des Bretons'*. Paris: Payot.

Carter, E.A. and McGoldrick, M. (eds) (1980) *The family life cycle: a framework for family therapy*. New York: Gardner Press.

Carter, E.A. and McGoldrick, M. (eds) (1989) *The changing family life cycle: a framework for family therapy*, 2nd edn. Boston: Allyn and Bacon.

Carter, E.A. and McGoldrick Orfanidis, M. (1976) Family therapy with one person and the therapist's own family. In P. Guerin (ed.), *Family therapy: theory and practice*, pp. 193–218. New York: Gardner Press.

Carton, M., Desclaux, B. and Roumagnac, M. (1984) Devenir social, familial et psychologique de l'adolescent après cancer. *Revue de médecine psychosomatique et de psychologie médicale*, 5.

Casement, P. (1988) *On learning from the patient*. London: Routledge.

Cassiers, L. (1982) La fonction familiale de l'alcoolisme. *Thérapie familiale* 3 (4).

Cassiers, L. (1983) Prescriptions et aliénation. In *L'aliénation. Journée de psychanalyse et de thérapie familiale systémique* 3, 5–16. Paris: CEFA.

Cassiers, L. (1985) Rites et psychosomatique. Une hypothèse. In *Fonction du rituel. Journée de psychanalyse et thérapie familiale systémique* 5, 95–130. Paris: CEFA.

Cassou, B., Schiff, M. and Stewart, J. (1979) Génétique et schizophrénie: réévaluation d'un consensus. *Evolution psychiatrique* 4, 733–48.

Cauchois, E. (1985) Intervention à la journée du Centre d'Etude et de Recherche sur la Famille. In J. Miermont (ed.), *Mythes et modèles scientifiques en psychothérapie individuelle et en thérapie familiale. Actualités psychiatriques* 9.

Cauffman, L. and Igodt, P. (1984) Quelques développements récents dans la théorie des systèmes: les contributions de Maturana et de Varela. *Thérapie familiale* 5 (3), 211–26.

Cayrol, A. and Saint Paul, J. de (1984) *Derrière la magie. La programmation neuro-linguistique*. Paris: Interéditions.

Cazeneuve, J. (1976) *Dix grandes notions de la sociologie*. Paris: Seuil.

Cecchin, G. (1987) Hypothesizing, circularity and neutrality revisited: an invitation to curiosity. *Family process* 26, 405–13.

Chaltiel, P. (1981) Eléments pour une éthique systémique. In *Journée psychanalyse et thérapie familiale systémique* 2, 25–43. Paris: CEFA.

Chaltiel, P. (1983) Relation d'interdépendance dynamique et changement du système thérapeutique. In M. Elkaim (ed.), *Psychothérapie et reconstruction du réel. Réseaux, systèmes, agencements* 7, 57–69. Paris: Editions Universitaires.

Chartier, J.P. et al. (1982) *Les parents martyrs*. Paris: Privat.

Chemama, R. (1983) Identifications paternelles, rôles parentaux. In *L'aliénation. Journées de psychanalyse et de thérapie familiale systémique* 3, 19–27. Paris: CEFA.

Chertok, L. (1965) *L'hypnose*. Paris: Payot.

Chertok, L. (1979) *Le non-savoir des psych. L'hypnose entre la psychanalyse et la biologie*. Paris: Payot.

Chesnaies, J-C. (1981) *Histoire de la violence*. Paris: Pluriel.

Chevalier, J. and Gheerbrant, A. (1982) *Dictionnaire des symboles*. Paris: Robert Laffont-Jupiter.

Chiland, C. and Becquart, P. (eds) (1974) *Traitement au long cours des états psychotiques*. Toulouse: Privat.

Chodorow, N. (1978) *The reproduction of mothering*. Berkeley: University of California Press.

Chomsky, N. (1957) *Syntactic structures*. The Hague: Mouton.

Chomsky, N. (1976) *Reflections on language*. London: Fontana.

Chomsky, N. (1980) *Rules and regulations*. New York: Columbia University Press.

Christian, D. (1985) La profondeur des effets de surface. *Cahiers dispatch* 6.

Clausewitz, C. von (1955) *De la guerre*. Trans. D. Naville. Paris: Editions de Minuit. English trans: *On war*, Harmondsworth: Penguin.

Cloutier, J. (1978) *La communication audio-scripto-visuelle*. Montreal: Didier.

Cohen, Y. and Emerique, M. (1979) Les effets psychologiques de l'acculturation chez les juifs traditionnalistes d'Afrique du Nord immigrés en France. *Compte-rendu de la journée médico-psychologique franco-israélienne*, 24 April, pp. 60–101. Paris: COFRISEMS.

Colas, Y. (1984) L'approche systémique des démences. *Thérapie familiale* 5 (1), 22–38.

Coleman, S., Myers Avis, J. and Turin, M. (1990) A study of the role of gender in family therapy training. *Family process* 29, 365–74.

Colin, M. (1984) Le temps du divorce, passage critique et entre-deux. *Dialogue* 86 (4), 3–14.

Collier, A. (1987) The language of objectivity and the ethics of reframing. In S. Walrond-Skinner and D. Watson (eds), *Ethical issues in family therapy*, pp. 118–26. London: Routledge.

Collonge, M. (n.d.) Unpublished manuscript. Mémoire de psychologie clinique.

Compernolle, T. (1980) Eco-psychosomatique: influence de la famille sur l'enfant malade et vice versa. *Thérapie familiale* 2 (3).

Coogler, O.J. (1978) *Structured mediation in divorce settlement*. Lexington, Mass.: Lexington Books.

Cook, M. (1977) Regard et regard réciproque dans les interactions sociales. In J. Cosnier and A. Brossard (eds), *La communication non verbale*, 1984.

Cooper, D. (1967) *Psychiatry and anti-psychiatry*. London: Tavistock.

Cooper, D. (1970) *The death of the family*. New York: Pantheon Books. 1972 edn, London: Pelican.

Copi, I.M. (1971) *The theory of logical types*. London: Routledge and Kegan Paul.

Corraze, J. (1980) *Les communications non-verbales*. Paris: PUF.

Cosnier, J., Berrendonner, A., Coulon, J. and Orecchioni, C. (1982) *Les voies du langage. Communications verbales gestuelles et animales*. Paris: Dunod-Bordas.

Cosnier, J. and Brossard, A. (1984) *La communication non verbale*. Neuchâtel/Paris: Delachaux et Niestlé.

Costa de Beauregard, O. (1980) Cosmos et conscience, pp. 57–76. In *Colloque de Cordoue*. Paris: Stock.

Cottet, A. (1984) Familles et pathologie du troisième âge. *Thérapie familiale* 5 (1), 7–22.

Couffignal, L. (1972) *La cybernétique*, 4th edn. Paris: PUF.

Course Registration Evaluation and Development (CRED) (1992) Training criteria for qualified family therapists. *Context* 10, 37–9.

Crowe, M. and Ridley, J. (1990) *Therapy with couples: a behavioural systems approach to marital and sexual problems*. Oxford: Blackwell.

Crowther, C., Dare, C. and Wilson, J. (1990) 'Why should we talk to you? You'll only tell the court!' On being an informer and a family therapist. *Journal of family therapy* 12, 105–22.

Cuisenier, J. (ed.) (1977) *The family life cycle in European societies*, pp. 9–38. New Babylon Studies in the Social Sciences 28. Paris: The Hague.

Cyrulnik, B. (1983) *Mémoire de singe et parole d'homme*. Paris: Hachette.

Cyrulnik, B. (1989) *Sous le signe du lien*. Paris: Hachette.

Cyrulnik, B. (1991) *De la parole considerée comme une molécule*. Paris: ESHEL.

Cyrulnik, B. and Leroy, R. (1977) Ethologie de la famille. Modèles naturels de physiologies familiales. *Annales médico-psychologiques* 135 (1), 15–42.

Daigremont, A., Guitton, C. and Rabeau, B. (1979) *Des entretiens collectifs aux thérapies familiales en psychiatrie de secteur. Collection méthodes de cas*. Paris: ESF.

Dare, C., Eisler, I., Russell, G.F.M. and Szmukler, G.I. (1990) The clinical and theoretical impact of a controlled trial of family therapy in anorexia nervosa. *Journal of marital and family therapy* 16, 39–57.

Dare, J., Goldberg, D. and Walinets, R. (1990) What is the question you need to answer? How consultation can prevent professional systems immobilizing families. *Journal of family therapy* 12, 355–69.

Darwin, C. (1872) *The expressions of emotions in man and animals*. London: Murray.

Daumezon, G. and Bonnafe, L. (1946) L'internement, conduite primitive de la société devant le malade mental. *Documents de l'inf. psychol.* 1.

David, P. (1976) *Psychanalyse et famille*. Paris: Armand Colin.

Davidson, F. and Angel, P. (1978) Prévoir et prévenir le suicide des adolescents. *Cahiers médicaux* 3 (38).

Davidson, F. and Choquet, M. (1981) *Le suicide de l'adolescent*. Paris: ESF.

Davis, D.I., Berenson, D., Steinglas, P. and Davis, S. (1974) The adaptive consequences of drinking. *Psychiatry* 37, 209.

Davis, J.A., Freeman, H.E. and Simmons, O. (1957) Rehospitalisation and performance level of former mental patients. *Social problems* 5, 37–44.

Debray, Q., Caillard, V. and Stewart, J. (1974) Schizophrenia: a study of genetic models. *Human heredity* 29, 27–36.

Debray, Q. and Lalouel, J.M. (1981) Définition des facteurs d'environnement par rapport au facteur génétique: leur contribution à la ressemblance familiale. In P. Fedida, J. Guyotat and J.M. Robert (eds), *Génétique clinique et psychopathologie*, pp. 117–29. Lyon: Simep, 1982.

Decobert, S. (1985) Spécificité de la thérapie familiale psychanalytique. Clancier-Guénod (ed.), *Psychanalyse familiale. Revue de psychanalyse groupale*, pp. 87–102.

Decobert, S. and Soulé, M. (1971) La notion de couple thérapeutique. (A propos de l'expérience d'un couple de thérapeutes dans un groupe de couples.) *Revue française de psychanalyse* 1 (36), 83–110.

Delay, J., Deniker, P. and Green, A. (1957) Le milieu familial des schizophrènes. 1: Position du problème. *Encéphale* 3, 187–232.

Delay, J., Deniker, P. and Green, A. (1960) Le milieu familial des schizophrènes. 2: Méthodes d'approche. *Encéphale* 1, 1–21.

Delay, J., Deniker, P. and Green, A. (1962) Le milieu familial des schizophrènes. 3: Résultats et hypothèses. *Encéphale* 1, 5–73.

Deleuze, G. and Guattari, F. (1972) *L'Anti-Oedipe*. Paris: Editions de Minuit.

Dell, P. (1989) Violence and the systemic view: the problem of power. *Family process* 28, 1–14.

Demailly, A. (1993) Apprendre à boire: une approche psychosociale inspirée du paradigme de l'autonomie. Equipe de Recherche de Psychologie Sociale, Université Paul Valéry, Montpelier.

Demailly, A. and Le Moigne, J.L. (eds) (1986) *Sciences de l'intelligence, sciences de l'artificiel. Avec Herbert A. Simon*. Lyon: Presses Universitaires de Lyon.

Demaret, A. (1979) *Ethologie et psychiatrie. Valeur de survie et phylogenèse des maladies mentales*. Brussels: Pierre Mardaga.

Deniker, P. (1957) Hibernothérapies et médicaments neuroleptiques en thérapeutique psychiatrique. *Encéphale* 3, 281–398.

Deputte, B.L. (1985) L'évitement de l'inceste chez les primates non-humains. Nouvelle revue d'ethno-psychiatrie. *Inceste* 3, 41–72.

Derrida, J. (1978) Cogito and the history of madness. In *Writing and difference*, pp. 31–63. London: Routledge and Kegan Paul.

Descartes (1639–47) *Méditations métaphysiques*. Paris: Garnier-Flammarion, 1979.

Deshaies, G. (1968) Du délire. *La revue de médicine neuro-psychiatrie. Délires*. October 24, 1565–70.

Dessoy, E. (1985) Autisme et organisation familiale. In R. Depuydt-Berte and M. Legrand (eds), *Psychiatrie, autisme, infantile et société*. Louvain La Neuve: Cabay.

Devereux, G. (1970) *Essais d'ethnopsychiatrie générale*. Paris: Gallimard.

Dewey, J. (1938) *Logic: the theory of inquiry*. New York: Holt.

Doane, J.R., Goldstein, M.J., Miklowitz, D.J. and Falloon, I.R.H. (1986) The impact of individual and family treatment on the affective climate of families of schizophrenics. *British journal of psychiatry* 148, 279–87.

Dolan, Y.M. (1991) *Resolving sexual abuse: solution-focused therapy and Ericksonian hypnosis for adult survivors*. New York: Norton.

Donzelot, J. (1980) *The policing of families*. London: Hutchinson.

Doucet, P. and Laurin, C. (eds) (1971) *Problems of psychosis*. Amsterdam: Excerpta Medica.

Dreyfus, H.L. (1984) *Intelligence artificielle: mythes et limites*. Paris: Flammarion.

Dumas, A. (1982) Le chrétien et la mort. *Bulletin de l'Association française de psychiatrie et de psychopathologie sociales. La mort* 14, 14–18.

Dumont, L. (1966) *Homo hierarchicus. Le système des castes et ses implications*. Paris: Gallimard.

Dumouchel, P. and Dupuy, J.-P. (1983) *L'auto-organisation*. Paris: Seuil.

Durand, G. (1969) *Les structures anthropologiques de l'imaginaire*. Paris: Dunod-Bordas, 1983.

Durand, G. (1979) *Figures mythiques et visages de l'oeuvre*. Paris: L'Ile Verte–Berg International.

Durrant, M. and Kowalski, K. (1990) Overcoming the effects of sexual abuse: developing a self-perception of competence. In M. Durrant and C. White (eds), *Ideas for therapy with sexual abuse*, pp. 65–110. Adelaide: Dulwich Centre Publications.

Durrant, M. and White, C. (eds) (1990) *Ideas for working with sexual abuse*. Adelaide: Dulwich Centre Publications.

Dutrenit, J.-M. (1976) Ethos du service social et enfance en danger. *Revue française de sociologie* 17, 615–32.

Ehresmann, A.C. and Vanbremeersch, J.P. (1985) Systèmes hiérarchiques évolutifs: une modélisation des systèmes vivants. *Prépublication* 86 (1).

Ehresmann, A.C. and Vanbremeersch, J.P. (1986a) Systèmes hiérarchiques évolutifs: modèle d'évolution d'un système ouvert par interaction avec des agents. *Prépublication* 86 (2).

Ehresmann, A.C. and Vanbremeersch, J.P. (1986b) Un modèle mathématique pour un système vivant évolutif et hiérarchique, fondé sur la théorie des catégories. *Présentation à l'Accadémie des Sciences par J.P. Changeux*. Paris: Académie des Sciences, vol. 302, series 3, no. 13.

Eibl-Eibesfeldt, I. (1967) *Ethology: biology of behaviour*. New York: Holt, Rinehart and Winston, 1975.

Eibl-Eibesfeldt, I. (1973) *Der Vorprogrammierte Mensch*. Vienna/Munich/Zurich: Verlay Fritz Molden.

Eibl-Eibesfeldt, I. (1976) *Par delà nos différences. Etude de 5 tribus dites primitives*. Trans. T. Strub. Paris: Flammarion, 1979.

Eichenbaum, L. and Orbach, S. (1982) *Outside in, inside out*. Harmondsworth: Penguin.

Eiguer, A. (1983) *Un divan pour la famille. Du modèle groupal à la thérapie familiale psychanalytique*. Paris: Paidos/Le Centurion.

Eiguer, A. and Litovsky de Eiguer, D. (1981) Contribution psychanalytique à la pratique de la psychothérapie familiale. In A. Ruffiot (ed.), *La thérapie familiale psychanalytique*, pp. 99–148. Paris: Dunod.

Eisenring, J.J. (1985) Bibliographie analytique de thérapie familiale francophone 1980–1984. *Thérapie familiale* 6 (2), 61–169.

Eisler, R. (1988) *The chalice and the blade: our history, our future*. San Francisco: Harper and Row.

Ekeland, I. (1984) *Le calcul, l'imprévu. Les figures du temps de Kepler à Thom*. Paris: Seuil.

Ekman, P. (ed.) (1973) *Darwin and facial expression: a century of research in review*. London: Academic Press.

Ekman, P. (1977) Biological and cultural contributions to body and facial movement. In J. Blacking (ed.), *The anthropology of the body* (ASA Monograph 15), pp. 39–84. London: Academic Press.

Ekman, P. (1985) *Telling lies*. New York: Norton.

Ekman, P. and Friesen, W.V. (1975) *Unmasking the face: a guide to recognizing emotions from facial expressions*. Englewood Cliffs, NJ: Prentice Hall.

Elder, G.H. (ed.) (1985) *Life course dynamics: trajectories and transitions, 1968–1980*. Ithaca: Cornell University Press.

Elkaim, M. (1979a) Une approche systémique de quelques cas d'anorexie mentale. L'approche systémique en thérapie familiale. *Réseaux, systèmes, agencements* 1, 43–51. Paris: Gamma.

Elkaim, M. (1979b) Système familial et système social. Agencements, pratiques de réseaux. Cahiers critiques de thérapie familiale et de pratique de réseaux. *Réseaux, systèmes, agencements* 1, 55–63. Paris: Gamma.

Elkaim, M. (1980) Défamiliariser la thérapie familiale. De l'approche familiale à l'approche sociopolitique. Cahiers critiques de thérapie familiale et de pratique de réseaux. *Réseaux, systèmes, agencements* 2, 6–29. Paris: Gamma.

Elkaim, M. (ed.) (1985) *Formations et pratiques en thérapie familiale*. Paris: ESF.

Elkaim, M. (1986) *Assemblages. Présentation à la journée de rencontre des écoles belges de formation à la psychothérapie systémique*. Brussels.

Elkaim, M. (1987a) Constructions mutuelles du réel, assemblages et thérapie familiale. In A. Ackermans and C. von Cutsem (eds), *Histoires de familles*. Paris: ESF.

Elkaim, M. (ed.) (1987b) *Les pratiques de réseau: santé mentale et contexte social*. Paris: ESF.

Elkaim, M. (1989) *Si tu m'aimes, ne m'aime pas: approche systèmique de la psychothérapie*. Paris: Seuil.

Elkaim, M., Goldbeter, A. and Goldbeter, E. (1980) Analyse des transitions de comportement dans un système familial en termes de bifurcations. *Réseaux, systèmes, agencements* 3, 18–34. Paris: Gamma.

Ellenberger, H. (1970) *The discovery of the unconscious*. (*A la découverte de l'inconscient. Histoire de la psychiatrie dynamique*. Trans. J. Feisthauer. Villeurbanne: SIMEP, 1974.)

Engelberg, S. and Symansky, J. (1989) Ethics and the law. *Family therapy networker* 13, 30–1.

Epstein, N.B. and Bishop, D.S. (1981) Problem-centered systems therapy of the family. In A.S. Gurman and D.P. Kniskern (eds), *Handbook of family therapy*, pp. 444–82. New York: Brunner Mazel.

Erickson, M.H. (1939) Experimental demonstration of the psychotherapy of everyday life. *The psychoanalytic quarterly* 8, 338–53.

Erickson, M.H. (1954) Pseudo-orientation in time as a hypnotherapeutic procedure. *Journal of clinical and experimental hypnosis* 2, 261–83.

Erickson, M.H. (1965) The use of symptoms as an integral part of hypnotherapy. *American journal of clinical hypnosis* 8, 57–65.

Erickson, M.H. (1981) *My voice will go with you*. New York: Norton.

Erickson, M.H. (1983) *Healing in hypnosis*. New York: Irvington.

Erickson, M.H. and Rossi, E.L. (1979) *Hypnotherapy: an exploratory casebook*. New York: Irvington.

Erickson, M.H., Rossi, E.L. and Rossi, S.I. (1976) *Hypnotic realities: the induction of clinical hypnosis and forms of indirect suggestion*. New York: Irvington.

Erikson, E.H. (1965) *Childhood and society*. Harmondsworth: Penguin.

Erikson, E.H. (1968) *Identity, youth and crisis* (Austen Riggs Monograph, no. 7). New York: Norton.

Everstine, D. and Everstine, L. (1983) *People in crisis. Strategic therapeutic interventions*. New York: Brunner Mazel.

Everstine, D. and Everstine, L. (1985) L'inceste et la thérapie familiale systémique. *Génitif* 5 (4), 45–60.

Everstine, D. and Everstine, L. (1989) *Sexual trauma in children and adolescents*. New York: Brunner Mazel.

Ewing, A. and Fox, J. (1968) Family therapy with alcoholism. In J.H. Massermann (ed.), *Current psychotic therapy*, vol. 8, pp. 86–91. New York: Grune and Stratton.

Ey, H. (ed.) (1966) *L'inconscient*. Sixth Colloquium of Bonneval. Paris: Desclée de Brower.

Ey, H. (1977) *Défense et illustration de la psychiatrie*. Paris: Masson.

Falletta, N. (1983) *Le livre des paradoxes*. Trans. J-F. Hamel. Paris: Pierre Belfond, 1985.

Fedida, P. (ed.) (1986) *Communication et représentation*. Paris: PUF.

Ferenczi, S. (1920) Prolongements de la 'technique active' en psychanalyse. In *Psychanalyse 3. Oeuvres complètes*, pp. 117–33. Paris: Payot, 1974.

Ferenczi, S. (1926) Contre-indications de la technique active. In *Psychanalyse 3. Oeuvres complètes*, pp. 362–72. Paris: Payot, 1974.

Ferenczi, S. (1932) Confusion de langue entre les adultes et l'enfant. In *Psychanalyse 4. Oeuvres complètes*, pp. 124–35. Paris: Payot, 1982.

Fernandez-Zoila, A. and Sivadon, P. (1986) *Corps et thérapeutique*. Paris: PUF.

Ferrari, M. (1983) The family with child epilepsy. *Family process* 2, 53–9.

Ferreira, A.J. (1960) Double bind and delinquent behaviour. *Archives of general psychiatry* 3, 359–67.

Ferreira, A.J. (1963) Family myth and homeostasis. *Archives of general psychiatry* 9, 457–63.

Ferreira, A.J. (1966) Family myths. *Psychological research reports* 20. American Psychological Association. Reprinted in P. Watzlawick and J.H. Weakland (eds), *The interactional view*, pp. 49–55. New York: Norton, 1977.

Feyereisen, P. and de Lannoy, J.-D. (1985) *Psychologie du geste*, ed. P. Mardaga. Brussels.

Finkelhor, D. (1983) Common features of family abuse. In D. Finkelhor, R.J. Gelles, G.T. Hotaling and M.A. Straus (eds), *The dark side of families: current family violence research*, pp. 17–28. Beverly Hills, CA: Sage.

Finley, C.B. and Wilson, D.C. (1951) The relation of the family to manic–depressive psychosis. *Diseases of the nervous system* 12, 39–43.

Fisch, R., Weakland, J.H. and Segal, L. (1982) *The tactics of change: doing therapy briefly*. San Francisco: Jossey-Bass.

Fischer, C. (1979) Gastronomie et gastro-anomie. *Communications*, 31. Paris: Seuil.

Fisher, T. (ed.) (1992) *Family conciliation within the UK: policy and practice*. Bristol: National Family Conciliation Council with Family Law/Jordans.

Flandrin, J.-L. (1984) *Familles: parenté, maison, sexualité dans l'ancienne société*. Paris: Seuil.

Flaskas, C. (1992) A reframe by any other name: on the process of reframing in strategic, Milan and analytical therapy. *Journal of family therapy* 14, 171–5.

Flaubert, G. (1850) *Dictionnaire des idées reçues. Oeuvres complètes*, 2 vols. Paris: Seuil, 1964.

Flaubert, G. (1881) *Bouvard et Pécuchet. Oeuvres complètes*, 2 vols. Paris: Seuil, 1964.

Flavigny, C. (1980) L'approche familiale après les gestes suicidaires des enfants. *Neuropsychiatrie de l'enfance* 28 (9), 387–91.

Florence, J. (1984) *L'identification dans la théorie freudienne*. Saint Louis, Brussels: Publications des Facultés Universitaires.

Flugel, J.C. (1921) *The psycho-analytic study of the family*. London: The Hogarth Press and the Institute of Psychoanalysis, 1972.

Foerster, H. von (1960) On self-organizing systems and their environments. In A. Yovitz and J. Cameron (eds), *Self-organizing systems*, pp. 31–50. London: Pergamon.

Foerster, H. von (1972) Notes for an epistemology of living objects. In E. Morin and M. Piatelli-Palmarini (eds), *L'unité de l'homme*, pp. 139–55. Paris: Seuil.

Foerster, H. von (1985) Machines triviales, machines non-triviales. Conference of 15 February, St Etienne.

Foley, V.D. (1974) *An introduction to family therapy*. New York: Grune and Stratton.

Forrester, J.W. (1968) *Principles of systems*. London: Wright Allen Press.

Foucault, M. (1954) *Maladie mentale et personnalité*. Paris: PUF.

Foucault, M. (1961) *Madness and civilisation (Folie et déraison. Histoire de la folie à l'âge classique*, rev. edn, 1964. Paris: UGE.)

Foucault, M. (1962) *Maladie mentale et psychologie*. Paris: PUF.

Foucault, M. (1980) *Power/knowledge: selected interviews and other writings*. New York: Pantheon.

Foulkes, S.H. (1948) *Introduction to group analytic psychotherapy*. London: Heinemann.

Foulkes, S.H. (1964) *Therapeutic group analysis*. London: Allen and Unwin.

Framo, J. (1972) Comments on C. Beels and A. Ferber, 'What family therapists can do'. In A. Ferber, M. Mendelsohn and A. Napier (eds), *The book of family therapy*, pp. 210–14. Boston: Houghton Mifflin.

Framo, J. (1976) Family of origin as a therapeutic resource for adults in marital and family therapy: you can and should go home again. *Family process* 15, 193–210.

Framo, J. (1981) The integration of marital therapy with sessions with family of origin. In A.S. Gurman and D.P. Kniskern (eds), *Handbook of family therapy*, pp. 133–58. New York: Brunner Mazel.

Freeman, D.S. (1981) *Techniques of family therapy*. New York: Jason Aronson.

French, M. (1986) *Beyond power: on women, men and morals*. London: Abacus.

Freud, S. (1900) *The interpretation of dreams*. Trans. J. Strachey, ed. A. Richards. London: Penguin, 1991.

Freud, S. (1905) *Jokes and their relation to the unconscious*. Trans. J. Strachey, ed. A. Richards. Harmondsworth: Penguin, 1991.

Freud, S. (1910–24) *Three essays on the theory of sexuality*. Trans. J. Strachey. London: Hogarth Press, 1949.

Freud, S. (1911) Psychoanalytic notes on an autobiographical account of a case of paranoia. *Standard edition*, vol. 13. Trans. J. Strachey. London: Hogarth Press.

Freud, S. (1914a) Pour introduire le narcissisme. In *La vie sexuelle*. Trans. D. Berger and J. Laplanche. Paris: PUF, 1969.

Freud, S. (1914b) *The psychotherapy of everyday life*, ed. A.A. Brill. London: Unwin.

Freud, S. (1914c) Remembering, repeating and working-through. In *Further recommendations on the technique of psychoanalysis. Standard edition*, ed. J. Strachey. London: Hogarth Press.

Freud, S. (1915) Observations sur l'amour de transfert. In *La technique psychanalyse*. Trans. A. Berman. Paris: PUF, 1967.

Freud, S. (1918) Extract of a case of infantile neurosis. In *An infantile neurosis and other works*. London: Hogarth Press.

Freud, S. (1919) The 'Uncanny'. *Standard edition*, vol. xvii. *An infantile neurosis and other works*, pp. 217–56. London: The Hogarth Press.

Freud, S. (1929) *Introductory lectures on psychoanalysis*, 2nd edn. London: Allen and Unwin.

Freud, S. (1933) *Introductory lectures on psychoanalysis*. Trans. J. Rivière. London: Allen and Unwin.

Freud, S. (1936) *Inhibitions, symptoms and anxiety*. Trans. J. Strachey. London: Hogarth Press.

Freud, S. (1938) The technique of psychoanalysis. In *An outline of psychoanalysis. Standard edition*, ed. J. Strachey, vol. 23. London: Hogarth Press.

Freud, S. (1955) *An infantile neurosis and other works*. London: Hogarth Press.

Freud, S. (1960a) *Jokes and their relation to the unconscious*. London: Hogarth Press.

Freud, S. (1960b) *Totem and taboo: some points of agreement between the mental lives of savages and neurotics*. Trans. J. Strachey. London: Ark Paperbacks.

Freud, S. (1966) *The complete introductory lectures on psychoanalysis*. Trans. J. Strachey. New York: Norton.

Freud, S. (1991) *The interpretation of dreams*. Trans. J. Strachey, ed. A. Richards. London: Penguin.

Freud, S. and Breuer, J. (1895) *Etudes sur l'hystérie*. Trans. A. Berman. Paris: PUF, 1956.

Fried, M. (1962) Grieving for a lost home. In L.J. Dahl (ed.), *The environment of the metropolis*. New York: Basic Books.

Friedman, H., Rohrbaugh, M. and Krakauer, A. (1988) The time-line genogram: highlighting temporal aspects of family relationships. *Family process* 27, 293–303.

Fromm, E. (1942) *The fear of freedom*. London: Kegan Paul.

Froussart, B., Borek, A. and Esteve, M. (1985) La réapparition des âges dans le système familial. *Systèmes humains* A, 4. Quebec: Trois-Rivières.

Froussart, B. and Esteve, M. (1986) L'écart d'âge entre époux comme organisateur familial temporel. *Dialogue* 93 (3), 89–101.

Froussart, B., Lecamp, M., Louis, V., Borek, A. and Esteve, M. (1986) Essai sur l'organisation du temps familial. *Génitif* 7 (3), 15–42.

Furman, B. and Ahola, T. (1992) *Solution talk: hosting therapeutic conversations*. New York: Norton.

Furniss, T. (1983) Family process in the treatment of intrafamilial child sexual abuse. *Journal of family therapy* 5, 263–78.

Fustier, P. (1983) *L'enfance inadaptée: repère pour des pratiques*. Lyon: Presses Universitaires de Lyon.

GAP (1980) *Committee on the family divorce, child custody and the family*, vol. 10 (106), pp. 849–911. New York: Mental Health Material Center.

Garapon, A. (1985) *L'âne portant des reliques. Essai sur le rituel judiciaire. 'Justice humain.'* Paris: Le Centurion.

Gardner, M. (1964) *The ambidextrous universe*. Harmondsworth: Penguin, 1982.

Garmezy, N. and Rutter, M. (1985) Acute reactions to stress. In M. Rutter and L. Hersov (eds), *Child and adolescent psychiatry: modern approaches*, 2nd edn, pp. 152–76. Oxford: Blackwell Scientific.

Garrigues, P., Maurin, M., Castella, A., Aussilloux, Ch. and Gabbai, Ph. (1973) Naissance et développement d'un groupe de psychodrame dans un hospital psychiatrique. Report of the Fifth International Congress on Group Psychotherapy, Zurich 19–24 August. Berne: Edition Scientifique Echtenhagen, Battegay et Friedman, Hans Huber Verlag.

Gear, M.C. and Liendo, E.C. (1976) Ernesto César. Psychanalyse, sémiologie et communication familiale. *Evolution psychiatrique* 2, 239–72.

Gear, M.C. and Liendo, E.C. (1981) Psychanalyse, sémiologie et communication familiale. In A. Ruffiot (ed.), *La thérapie familiale psychanalytique*, pp. 149–79. Paris: Dunod.

Gear, M.C. and Liendo, E.C. (1984) Vers une classification systématique et une conception rigoureuse du plan d'action thérapeutique. *Psychothérapies* 4, 247–54.

Geffroy, Y., Accola, P. and Ancelin Schutzenberger, A. (1980) *Formation et thérapie*. Epi.

Gelcer, E. (1983) Mourning is a family affair. *Family process* 22, 501–16.

Gervet, J. (1986) Les fonctions de relations sociales. In J. Piaget, P. Mounoud and J.-P. Bronckart (eds), *Psychologies*, pp. 229–73. *Encyclopédie de la Pléiade*. Paris: Gallimard/NRF.

Gillieron, E. (1982) Groupe Balint et thérapie familiale. In Missenard et al. (eds), *L'expérience Balint: histoire et actualité*, pp. 223–46. Paris: Dunod.

Gilligan, C. (1982) *In a different voice*. Cambridge, Mass.: Harvard University Press.

Girard, R. (1972) *La violence et le sacré*. Paris: Grasset.

Girard, R. (1978) *Des choses cachées depuis la fondation du monde*. Paris: Grasset.

Girard, R. (1982) *Le bouc-émissaire*. Paris: Grasset.

Glaser, D. (1991) Neutrality and child abuse: a useful juxtaposition? *Human systems: the journal of systemic consultation and management* 2, 149–60.

Glaser, D. and Frosh, S. (1988) *Child sexual abuse*. Houndmills: BASW/Macmillan.

Glaserfeld, E. von (1984) An introduction to radical constructivism. In P. Watzlawick (ed.), *The invented reality*. New York: Norton.

Gleick, J. (1988) *Making a new science*. London: Sphere.

Gleser, G.L., Green, B.L. and Winget, C. (1981) *Prolonged psycho-social effects of disaster: a study of Buffalo Creek*. New York: Academic Press.

Glick, D. and Kessler, D.R. (1980) *Marital and family therapy*. New York: Grune and Stratton.

Gödel, K. (1931) On formally undecidable propositions of *Principia mathematica* and related systems. In S. Feferman, J.W. Dawson jr, S.C. Kleene, G.H. Moore, R.M. Solovay and J. van Heijenoort (eds), *Kurt Gödel: Collected works. Vol. 1: Publications 1929–1936*, pp. 145–95. Oxford: Clarendon Press.

Gödel, K. (1986) *Collected works. Vol. 1: publications 1929–1936*. Edited by S. Feferman, J.W. Dawson jr, S.C. Kleene, G.H. Moore, R.M. Solovay and J. van Heijenoort. Oxford: Clarendon Press.

Gödel, K. (1990) *Collected works. Vol. 2: publications 1938–1974*. Edited by S. Feferman, J.W. Dawson jr, S.C. Kleene, G.H. Moore, R.M. Solovay and J. van Heijenoort. Oxford: Clarendon Press.

Goffman, E. (1961) *Asylums*. New York: Anchor Books.

Goldner, V. (1985) Feminism and family therapy. *Family process* 24, 31–47.

Goldner, V. (1988) Generation and gender: normative and covert hierarchies. *Family process* 27, 17–31.

Goldner, V. (1991a) Feminism and systemic practice: two critical traditions in transition. *Journal of family therapy* 13, 95–104.

Goldner, V. (1991b) Toward a critical relational theory of gender. *Psychoanalytic dialogues* 1 (3), 249–72. Hillsdale, NJ: Analytic Press.

Goldner, V., Penn, P., Sheinberg, M. and Walker, G. (1990) Love and violence: gender paradoxes in volatile attachments. *Family process* 29 (4), 343–64.

Goldstein, K. (1934) *(Der Aufbau des Organismus) The organism*. Boston: Beacon Press.

Gonin, A. (1983) L'importance de la loi dans l'éducation. In 'Action éducative spécialisée'. *Cahiers de l'UNAEDE*, 97 'La famille et la loi', pp. 30–39.

Goodman, N. (1992) *Lire Goodman. Les voies de la référence*. Combas: Editions de l'Éclat.

Goodrich, T., Rampage, C., Ellman, B. and Aalstead, K. (1988) *Feminist family therapy: a case book*. New York: Norton.

Goody, J. (1983) *L'évolution de la famille et du mariage en Europe*. Trans. M. Blinoff. Paris: Armand Colin, 1985.

Gordon, S.B. and Davidson, N. (1981) Behavioral parent training. In A.S. Gurman and D.P. Kniskern (eds), *Handbook of family therapy*, pp. 517–55. New York: Brunner Mazel.

Gordon Montagnon, R. (1984) Jung: fils rebelle ou prophète? In M. Cazenave (ed.), *Carl Gustav Jung*, pp. 53–63. Paris: Les Editions de l'Herne.

Goutal, M. (1985) *Du fantasme au système. Scènes de famille en épistémologie psychanalytique et systémique*. Paris: ESF.

Graham, H. (1991) Family interventions in general practice: a case of chronic fatigue. *Journal of family therapy* 13, 225–30.

Grangeon, M. (1986) Du nécessaire au pas-tout. In *Situation de la psychanalyse en 1986*, 5–7 December, pp. 63–85. Paris.

Granon-Lafont, J. (1985) *La topologie ordinaire de Jacques Lacan*. Paris: Point Hors Ligne.

Green, A. (1957) Le milieu familial des schizophrènes. Unpublished thesis, University of Paris.

Green, A. (1963) Remarques méthodologiques sur l'interprétation des modes d'expression de certaines drogues psychotropes. In *La relation médecin-malade au cours des chimiothérapies psychiatriques par P.A. Lambert et CLRTP*. Paris: Masson.

Green, A. (1970) Répétition, différence, replication. *Revue française de psychanalyse* 34, 461–502.

Green, A. (1983) *Le langage dans la psychanalyse. Confluents psychanalytiques*. Paris: Les Belles Lettres.

Greenberg, G.S. (1980) Problem-focused brief family interactional psychotherapy. In L.R. Wolberg and M.L. Aronson (eds), *Group and family therapy*, pp. 307–22. New York: Brunner Mazel.

Greimas, A. and Courtes, J. (1979) Sémiotique. *Dictionnaire raisonné de la théorie du langage*. Paris: Classiques Hachette.

Grimal, P. (1951) *Dictionnaire de la mythologie grecque et romaine*, 5th edn. Paris: PUF.

Grinberg, L., Sor, D. and Tabak de Bianchedi, E. (1972) *Introduction aux idées psychanalytiques de W.R. Bion*. Paris: Dunod.

Grinder, J. and Bandler, R. (1976) *The structure of magic*, 2 vols. Palo Alto: Science and Behavior Books.

Grolnick, L. (1972) A family perspective of psychosomatic factors in illness. *Family process* 11, 457–86.

Groos, K. (1898) *The play of animals*. London: Chapman and Hall.

Guedeney, N. (1986) In M.C. Mouren-Simeoni (ed.), *La maladie dépressive chez l'enfant et l'adolescent*, pp. 235–54. Paris: Ciba.

Guerin, P.J. (ed.) (1976) *Family therapy: theory and practice*. New York: Gardner Press.

Guillaumaud, J. (1971) *Norbert Wiener et la cybernétique*. Paris: Seghers.

Guillaume, P. (1979) *La psychologie de la forme*. Paris: Flammarion.

Guir, J. (1983) *Psychosomatique et cancer*. Paris: Points Hors Ligne.

Guitton Cohen Adad, C. (1980) Réalité systémique familiale et dépsychiatrisation. *Thérapie familiale* 1, 367–79.

Guitton Cohen Adad, C. (1981a) Analyse du système familial d'un cas de psychopathie. In *Passions de famille. Génitif* 3, 59–66.

Guitton Cohen Adad, C. (1981b) Comment et pourquoi démarrer des thérapies familiales en institution. *Thérapie familiale* 2, 257–63.

Guitton Cohen Adad, C. (1982) Aliénation, réalité, virtualité. Paris Conference. *Journées du CEFA. Psychanalyse et thérapie familiale*, pp. 29–44.

Guitton Cohen Adad, C. (1987) L'interaction thérapeute-famille. L'éphémère de la séance. Conference 12 March 1987. Brussels: Institut d'Etudes de la Famille et des Systèmes Humains.

Guntern, G. (1986) Eco-anthropologie et thérapie systémique: une nouvelle image de l'homme. *Thérapie familiale* 7 (1), 15–40.

Gurman, A.S. (1978) Contemporary marital therapies: a critique and comparative analysis of psychoanalytic, behavioral and systems theory approaches. In T.J. Paolino and B.S. McCrady (eds), *Marriage and marital therapy: psychoanalytic, behavioral and systems theory perspectives*, pp. 445–566. New York: Brunner Mazel.

Gurman, A.S. and Kniskern, D.P. (eds) (1981) *Handbook of family therapy*. New York: Brunner Mazel.

Gurvitch, G. (1962) *Dialectique et sociologie*. Paris: Flammarion, 1977 edn.

Gutheil, T.G. and Avery, N.C. (1977) Multiple overt incest as family defence against loss. *Family process* 16, 105–16.

Guyotat, J. (1963) Remarques sur les relations entre les chimiothérapies et psychothérapies individuelles. In *Actualités de thérapeutique psychiatrique (CLRTP)*. Paris: Masson.

Guyotat, J. (1972) Recherche sur l'action psychodynamique de certains médicaments psychotropes (neuroleptiques – antidépresseurs). *Confrontations psychiatriques* 9.

Guyotat, J. (1985) Famille et cancer, famille et psychose. *Psychologie médicale* 17 (6), 695–7.

Guyotat, J. and Marie-Cardine, M. (1975) Médicaments psychotropes et psychothérapies. *Encyclopédie médico-chirurgicale* 37820 B 90 10.

Hagège, C. (1985) *L'homme de paroles. Contribution linguistique aux sciences humaines*. Paris: Fayard.

Haley, J. (1958) An interactional explanation of hypnosis. *American journal of clinical hypnosis* 1 (2), 41–57.

Haley, J. (1959) The family of the schizophrenic: a model system. *Journal of nervous and mental diseases* 133, 357–74.

Haley, J. (1961) Control in brief psychotherapy. *Archives of general psychiatry* 4, 139–53.

Haley, J. (1963) *Strategies of psychotherapy*. New York: Grune and Stratton.

Haley, J. (1967) Toward a theory of pathological systems. In G.H. Zuk and I. Boszormenyi-Nagy (eds), *Family therapy and disturbed families*, pp. 11–27. Palo Alto: Science and Behavior Books.

Haley, J. (1969) *The power tactics of Jesus Christ and other essays*. New York: Grossman.

Haley, J. (ed.) (1971) *Changing families: a family therapy reader*. New York: Grune and Stratton.

Haley, J. (1973) *Uncommon therapy: the psychiatric techniques of Milton H. Erickson*. New York: Norton.

Haley, J. (1976) *Problem-solving therapy. New strategies for effective family therapy*. New York: Jossey-Bass, 2nd edn, 1978.

Haley, J. (1980) *Leaving home: the therapy of disturbed young people*. New York: McGraw-Hill.

Haley, J. (1981) *Reflections on therapy and other essays*. Washington, DC: The Family Institute of Washington.

Haley, J. (ed.) (1985) *Conversations with Milton H. Erickson*. New York: Triangle Press.

Haley, J. (1987) The disappearance of the individual. *Networker* March/April, 39–40.

Hall, A.D. and Fagen, R.E. (1956) Definition of system. In L. von Bertalanffy and A. Rapoport (eds), *General systems: yearbook for the advancement of general systems theory*, vol. 1, pp. 18–28.

Hall, E.T. (1966) *The hidden dimension*. New York: Doubleday.

Hall, E.T. (1968) Proxemics. *Current anthropology* 9 (2–3), 83–108.

Hall, E.T. (1976) *Beyond culture*. New York: Anchor Books.

Handy, C.B. (1985) *Understanding organisations*. Harmondsworth: Penguin.

Harburg, F., Davis, D. and Kaplan, R. (1982) Parent and offspring alcohol use. Imitative and adversive transmission. *Journal of studies on alcohol* 43 (5), 497–516.

Hare-Mustin, R. (1978) A feminist approach to family therapy. *Family process* 17 (2), 181–94.

Hare-Mustin, R. (1987) The problem of gender in family therapy theory. *Family process* 26, 15–27.

Hare-Mustin, R. and Maracek, J. (eds) (1990) *Making a difference*. New Haven/London: Yale.

Hare, J. and Shaw, R. (1965) A comparison of the health of fathers, mothers and children. *British journal of psychiatry* 111, 467.

Harlow, H.F. (1972) Love created, love destroyed, love regained. In *Modèles animaux du comportement humain*, pp. 13–60. Paris: CNRS.

Harper, J.M., Scoresby, A.L. and Boyce, W.D. (1977) The logical levels of complementary, symmetrical and parallel interaction classes in family dyads. *Family process* 16 (2), 199–209.

Harthong, J. (1992) Le continu ou le discret, un problème indécidable. In J.-M. Salanskis and H. Sinaceur (eds), *Le labyrinthe du continu. Colloque de Cerisy*, pp. 350–65. Paris: Springer Verlag.

Haynes, J. and Haynes, G. (1989) *Mediating divorce: casebook of strategies for successful family negotiations*. San Francisco/London: Jossey-Bass.

Heinl, P. (1985) The image and visual analysis of the genogram. *Journal of family therapy* 7, 213–29.

Heinroth, O. (1910) Beiträge zur Biologie, namentlich Ethologie und Psychologie der Anatiden. *Verhandl. d. V. Intern. Ornithçol.* Kongress, Berlin.

Henry, J. (1961) L'observation naturaliste des familles d'enfants psychologiques. *La psychiatrie de l'enfant* 4 (1), 65–203.

Henry, M. and Pical, D. (1984) *Protection judiciaire de la jeunesse. Textes et commentaires*. Vaucresson: Service d'Etudes CFRES.

Héritier, F. (1981) *L'exercice de la parenté*. Paris: Gallimard/Seuil.

Hermann, I. (1943) *L'instinct filial*. Trans. G. Kassai. Paris: Denoël.

Herz, F. (1980) The impact of death and serious illness on the family. In E.A. Carter and M. McGoldrick (eds), *The family life cycle: a framework for family therapy*, pp. 223–40. New York: Gardner Press.

Hilbert, D. and Ackermann, W. (1928) *Grundzüge der Theorischen Logik*. Berlin: Springer.

Hill, R. (1972) *The strengths of black families*. New York: Emerson-Hall.

Hill, R. (1977) Social theory and family development. In J. Cuisenier (ed.), *The family life cycle in European societies*, pp. 9–38. New Babylon Studies in the Social Sciences. Paris/The Hague: Mouton.

Hinde, R.A. (ed.) (1972) *Non-verbal communication*, pp. 313–44. Cambridge: Cambridge University Press.

Hirsch, S. (1981) La famille, répertoire émotionnel spécifique. Interview 14 April 1980 with Guy Maruani and Jacques Miermont. In *Passions de familles. Génitif* 3 (1–3), 7–11.

Hochmann, J. (1971) Pour une psychiatrie communautaire. *Collection esprit: la cité prochaine*, pp. 137–88. Paris: Seuil.

Hoebel, F.C. (1974) Maladie de l'artère coronaire et interaction familiale. In P. Watzlawick and J.H. Weakland (eds), *Sur l'interaction*, pp. 440–55. Paris: Seuil.

Hoffman, L. (1975) 'Enmeshment' and the too richly cross-joined system. *Family process* 14, 457–68.

Hoffman, L. (1981) *Foundations of family therapy: a conceptual framework for systems change*. New York: Basic Books.

Hoffman, L. (1985) Beyond power and control: toward a 'second order' family systems therapy. *Family systems medicine* 3, 381–96.

Hoffman, L. (1988) A constructivist position for family therapy. *Irish journal of psychology* 9 (1), 110–29.

Hoffman, L. (1992) A reflexive stance for family therapy. *Journal of strategic and systemic therapies* 10 (3/4), 110–29.

Hofstadter, D.R. (1979) *Gödel, Escher, Bach: an eternal golden braid. A metaphorical fugue on minds and machines in the spirit of Lewis Caroll*. New York: Basic Books.

Hogan, P. (1963) The content-context syndrome. *Newsletter of the Society of Medical Psychoanalysts* 4, 1 & 6.

Hollis, P. (1987) The management of adolescent overdose: a systems approach. *Journal of family therapy* 9, 161–75.

hooks, b. (1982) *Ain't I a woman: black women and feminism*. London: Pluto Press.

Howells, J.G. (1968) *Theory and practice of family psychiatry*. Edinburgh: Oliver and Boyd.

Howells, J.G. (1979) Vector therapy. In J.G. Howells (ed.), *Advances in family therapy*, pp. 457–63. New York: International Universities Press.

Huxley, J. (ed.) (1971) *Le comportement rituel chez l'homme et l'animal*. Trans. P. Vielhomme. Paris: Gallimard.

Ionesco, E. (1954) *Théatre*. Paris: Gallimard.

Irigaray, L. (1985) *Speculum of the other woman*. Ithaca, NY: Cornell University Press.

Jackson, D.D. (1957) The question of family homeostasis. In D.D. Jackson (ed.), *Communication, family and marriage. Human communication*, vol. 1, pp. 1–11. Palo Alto: Science and Behavior Books, 1968.

Jackson, D.D. (1965a) The study of the family. *Family process* 4, 1–20.

Jackson, D.D. (1965b) Family rules: marital quid pro quo. *Archives of general psychiatry* 12, 589–94.

Jackson, D.D. (1966) Family practice: a comprehensive medical approach. *Comprehensive psychiatry* 7, 338–44.

Jackson, D.D. (ed.) (1968) *Communication, family and marriage. Human communication*, 2 vols. Palo Alto: Science and Behavior Books.

Jackson, D.D. (ed.) (1968) *Therapy, communication and change*. Palo Alto: Science and Behaviour Books.

Jackson, D.D. (1975) The question of family homeostasis. *Psychiatric quarterly supplement* 31, 79–90.

Jackson, D.D. (1977) Schizophrenia: the nosological nexus. In P. Watzlawick and J.H. Weakland (eds), *The interactional view*, pp. 193–207. New York: Norton.

Jackson, D.D. and Haley, J. (1963) Transference revisited. *Journal of nervous and mental diseases* 137, 363–71.

Jackson, D.D. and Satir, V. (1961) A review of psychiatric developments in family diagnosis and family therapy. In N.W. Ackerman, F.L. Beatman and S.N. Sherman (eds), *Exploring the base for family therapy*, pp. 29–51. New York: Family Service Association of America. Republished in D.D. Jackson (ed.), *Therapy, communication and change*, pp. 249–70. Palo Alto: Science and Behavior Books, 1968/69.

Jagstaidt, V. (1984) *La sexualité et l'enfant*. Neuchâtel: Delachaux et Niestlé.

Jacobson, D. and Matheny, A. (1962) Mate selection in open marriage systems. *International journal of comparative sociology* 3, 98–123.

Jakobson, R. (1957) Les embrayeurs, les catégories verbales et le verbe russe. In *Essais de linguistique générale*. Paris: Editions de Minuit, 1963.

James, K. (1991) Paper delivered at the International Womens' Colloquium, Copenhagen.

James, K. and McIntyre, D. (1983) The reproduction of families. *Journal of marital and family therapy* 9 (2), 119–29.

Jankelevitch, V. (1977) *La mort*. Paris: Flammarion.

Jenkins, A. (1990) *Invitations to responsibility*. Adelaide: Dulwich Centre Publications.

Jenkins, H. (1984) Family therapy with adolescents in in-patient psychiatric units. In A. Treacher and J. Carpenter (eds), *Using family therapy: a guide for practitioners in different professional settings*, pp. 33–46. Oxford: Blackwell.

Jenkins, H. (1985) Orthodoxy in family therapy practice as servant or tyrant. *Journal of family therapy* 7, 19–30.

Jenkins, H. (1986) Loss: bereavement, illness and other factors. In G. Horobin (ed.), *The family: client or context?*, pp. 97–120. London: Kogan Page.

Jenkins, H. (1989a) Family therapy and child sexual abuse: a treatment of choice? *Psihoterapija* 18, 1–11.

Jenkins, H. (1989b) Precipitating crises in families: patterns which connect. *Journal of family therapy* 11, 99–109.

Jenkins, H. (1989c) Family therapy with one person: a systemic framework for treating individuals. *Psihoterapija* 19, 61–74.

Jenkins, H. (1989d) The family and loss: a systems perspective. *Palliative medicine* 3, 97–104.

Jenkins, H. (1990) Poverty, state and the family: a challenge for family therapy. *Contemporary family therapy* 12, 311–25.

Jenkins, H. and Asen, K. (1992) Family therapy without the family: a framework for systemic practice. *Journal of family therapy* 14, 1–14.

Jenkins, H. and Donnelly, M. (1983) The therapist's responsibility: a systemic approach to mobilizing creativity. *Journal of family therapy* 5, 199–218.

Jespersen, O. (1922) *Language, its nature, development and origin*. London: Allen and Unwin.

Jolivet, B. (1985) L'héritage de Dieu. In *Y-a-t'il une théorie de l'institution?*, 6th edn, pp. 71–83. Paris: Centre d'Etude de la Famille Association.

Jones, E. (1953) *The life and work of Sigmund Freud. 1: The formative years and the great discoveries, 1856–1900.* New York: Basic Books.

Jones, E. (1955) *The life and work of Sigmund Freud. 2: Years of maturity, 1901–1919.* New York: Basic Books.

Jones, E. (1957) *The life and work of Sigmund Freud. 3: Last years, 1919–1939.* New York: Basic Books.

Jones, E. (1990) Feminism and family therapy: can mixed marriages work? In R.J. Perelberg and A. Miller (eds), *Gender and power in families*, pp. 63–81. London/New York: Tavistock/Routledge.

Jones, E. (1991) *Working with adult survivors of child sexual abuse.* London: Karnac.

Jones, E. (1993) *Family systems therapy.* Chichester: Wiley.

Jung, C.G. (1916) Les sept sermons aux morts. In M. Cazenave (ed.), *Carl Gustav Jung*, pp. 152–63. Paris: Les Editions de l'Herne.

Jung, C.G. (1933) *Dialectique du moi et de l'inconscient.* Trans. R. Cahen. Paris: Gallimard, 1964.

Jung, C.G. (1964) *L'homme et ses symboles.* Paris: Robert Laffont.

Jung, M. (1984) Structural family therapy: its application to Chinese families. *Family process* 23, 365–74.

Kaës, R., Missenard, A., Ginoux, J.C., Anzieu, D. and Bejarano, A. (1982) *Le travail psychanalytique dans les groupes*, 2 vols. Paris: Dunod.

Kaës, R., Missenard, A., Kaspi, R., Anzieu, D., Guillaumin, J. and Bleger, J. (1979) *Crise, rupture, dépassement. Analyse transitionelle en psychanalyse individuelle et groupale.* Paris: Dunod.

Kafka, F. (1916) *Die Verwandlung. La métamorphose.* Trans. A. Vialatte. Paris: Gallimard, 1938.

Kafka, F. (1926) *Der Prozess (Le procès).* Trans. A. Vialatte. Paris: Gallimard, 1933.

Kafka, F. (1934) Vor dem Gesetz. Devant la loi. In *La métamorphose.* Trans. A. Vialatte. Paris: Gallimard.

Kafka, F. (1953) *The trial.* Harmondsworth: Penguin.

Kahn, L. (1978) *Hermès passé, ou les ambiguïtés de la communication.* Paris: François Maspéro.

Kanner, L. (1942) Autistic disturbances of affective contact. *Nervous child* 2 (3), 217–30.

Kant, I. (1973 edn) *Critique of pure reason.* Trans. N. Kemp Smith. London: Macmillan.

Kantor, D. and Duhl, B.S. (1973) Learning, space, and action in family therapy: a primer of sculpture. In D. Bloch (ed.), *Techniques of family psychotherapy: a primer*, pp. 47–63. New York: Grune and Stratton.

Kaplan, S. (1977) Structural family therapy for children of divorce. *Family process* 16, 75–84.

Kaslow, F. (1986) *Divorce around the world.* Fifth International Congress of Family Therapy. Jerusalem, 23 June.

Kaufman, E. and Kaufmann, P. (eds) (1979) *The family therapy of drug and alcohol abusers.* New York: Gardner Press.

Kaufmann, J-C. (1986) Les habitudes ménagères. *Dialogue* 91 (1), 19–31.

Kerbrat-Orechioni, C. (1980) *L'énonciation de la subjectivité dans le langage.* Paris: Armand Colin.

Kerr, M.E. (1981) Family systems theory and therapy. In A.S. Gurman and D.P. Kniskern (eds), *Handbook of family therapy*, pp. 226–64. New York: Brunner Mazel.

Kestemberg, E., Kestemberg, J. and Decobert, S. (1972) *La faim et le corps. Une étude psychanalytique de l'anorexie mentale.* Paris: PUF.

Kestenberg, J.S. (1974) Les enfants de l'holocauste. In E.J. Anthony and C. Koupernik (eds), *L'enfant dans sa famille*, pp. 297–9. Paris: Masson.

Kingston, P. (1987) Family therapy, power and responsibility for change. In S. Walrond-Skinner and D. Watson (eds), *Ethical issues in family therapy*, pp. 127–37. London: Routledge.

Kleckner, T., Frank, L., Bland, C., Amendt, J.H. and DuRee Bryant, R. (1992) The myth of the unfeeling strategic therapist. *Journal of marital family therapy* 18, 41–51.

Klein, H. (1970) Survivor families in kibbutzim. Paper presented at the Seventh Congress of the International Association of Child Psychiatry, Jerusalem, August.

Klein, H. (1974) Les enfants de l'holocauste: deuil et perte d'un être cher. In E.J. Anthony and C. Koupernik (eds), *L'enfant dans sa famille*, pp. 322–35. Paris: Masson.

Klein, M. (1921–45) *Contributions to psycho-analysis.* London: Hogarth Press.

Klein, M. (1946) Notes on some schizoid mechanisms. In J. Riviere (ed.), *Developments in psycho-analysis.* London: Hogarth Press.

Kluckhohn, F. (1953) Dominant and variant values orientations. In F. Kluckhohn and J. Murray (eds), *Personality in nature, society and culture*, pp. 342–57. New York: Knopf.

Knight, R. (1937) The dynamics and treatment of chronic alcohol addiction. *Bull. Menniger clin.* 1, 233.

Kohut, H. (1971) *The analysis of the self.* New York: International University Press.

Korzybski, A. (1941) *Science and sanity. An introduction to non-Aristotelian systems and general semantics.* New York: Science Press.

Korzybski, A. (1951) The role of language in the perceptual processes. In R. Blake and G. Ramsay (eds), *Perception: an approach to personality.* New York: Ronald Press.

Koudou, K.R. (1983) La crise de la famille ivoirienne traditionelle et le problème de la délinquance juvénile en Côte d'Ivoire. Homo XXIII Toulouse. *Famille imaginaire et famille réelle,* pp. 59–73.

Kreisler, L. (1985) Les enfants victimes de sévices. In S. Lebovici, R. Diatkine and M. Soulé (eds), *Traité de psychiatrie de l'enfant et de l'adolescent,* pp. 53–70. Paris: PUF.

Kreisler, L., Fain, M. and Soulé, M. (1974) *L'enfant et son corps.* Paris: PUF.

Kreisler, L. and Raimbault, G. (eds) (1980) L'abord psychosomatique en pédiatrie. *Génitif* 2 (10). In particular, R. Rappaport, Réflexions à propos du retard de croissance d'origine psycho-affective, pp. 625–7; M. Bouras, H. Bourneuf and G. Raimbault, Le nanisme 'psycho-social', point de vue psychanalytique, pp. 629–31; L. Kreisler, Commentaires sur le nanisme psycho-social, pp. 632–3.

Kretschmer, E. (1927–50) *Paranoïa et sensibilité. Contribution au problème de la paranoïa et à la théorie psychiatrique du caractère.* Trans. S. Horinson and D.J. Duche. Paris: PUF, 1963.

Kristeva, J. (1981) Women's time. *Signs* 7, 13–35.

Laborit, H. (1978) Ecologie et physiopathologie humaines. *Evolution psychiatrique* 1, 9–25.

Lacan, J. (1932) *De la psychose paranoïaque dans ses rapports avec la personnalité.* Paris: Points-Seuil, 1980.

Lacan, J. (1938) La famille. *Encyclopédie française VIII.* Paris: Larousse.

Lacan, J. (1954–5) *Le moi dans la théorie de S. Freud et dans la technique de la psychanalyse.* Paris: Seuil.

Lacan, J. (1961–2) *L'identification.* Unpublished seminar.

Lacan, J. (1966) *Ecrits.* Paris: Seuil.

Lafargue, P. (1880) Le droit à la paresse. *Introduction de Maurice Dommanget.* Paris: François Maspero, 1969.

Laforgue, R. (1936a) A contribution to the study of schizophrenia. *International journal of psychoanalysis* 17, 147–62.

Laforgue, R. (1936b) La névrose familiale. *Revue française de psychanalyse* 9 (3), 327–55.

Laforgue, R. (1939) *Psychopathologie de l'échec.* Paris: Payot.

Lagache, D. (1963) *De la fantaisie à la sublimation.* Paris: PUF.

Laing, R.D. (1960) *The divided self.* London: Tavistock/Routledge.

Laing, R.D. (1961) *Self and others.* Harmondsworth: Penguin.

Laing, R.D. (1965) Mystification, confusion and conflict. In I. Boszormenyi-Nagy and J.L. Framo (eds), *Intensive family therapy,* pp. 343–63. New York: Harper and Row.

Laing, R.D. (1970) *Knots.* New York: Random House.

Laing, R.D. and Cooper, D. (1964) *Reason and violence.* London: Tavistock.

Laing, R.D. and Esterson, A. (1964) *Sanity, madness and the family.* London: Tavistock. 1970 edn, London: Pelican.

Lalande, A. (1985) Immanence. In *Vocabulaire technique et critique de la philosophie,* 15th edn, pp. 469–70. Paris: Presses Universitaires de France.

Lamb, M.E. (1976) Interactions between eight-month-old children and their fathers and mothers. In M. Lamb (ed.), *The role of the father in child development.* New York: Wiley.

La Mettrie (1745–7) *L'homme machine. Coll. libertés,* no. 40. Paris: J.J. Pauvert, 1966.

Lane, M. (1970) *Introduction to structuralism.* New York: Basic Books.

Lang, T. and Lang, M. (1986) *Corrupting the young and other stories of a family therapist.* Victoria: René Gordon.

Langsley, D.G. and Kaplan, D.M. (1968) *The treatment of families in crisis.* New York: Grune and Stratton.

Lanteri-Laura, G. and Gros, M. (1984) *La discordance.* UNICET.

Laplanche, J. and Pontalis, J-B. (1967) *Vocabulaire de la psychanalyse.* Paris: PUF. English edition 1973: *The language of psycho-analysis.*

Laqueur, H.P. (1976) Multiple family therapy. In P.J. Guerin (ed.), *Family therapy: theory and practice,* pp. 405–16. New York: Gardner Press.

Laraby, A. (1983) Science et magie en concurrence dans le droit constitutionnel du XVIIIème siècle. *Cahiers systema* 11, 5–28.

Largeault, J. (1985a) *Principes de philosophie réaliste.* Paris: Klincksieck.

Largeault, J. (1985b) *Systèmes de la nature.* Paris: Librairie Philosophique J. Vrin.

Lasegue, Ch. and Falret, J. (1877) *La folie à deux*. Paris: P. Asselin.

Lask, B. (1979) Family therapy outcome research 1972/8. *Journal of family therapy* 1, 87–91.

Lask, B. (1982) Physical illness and the family. In A. Bentovim, G. Gorell Barnes and A. Cooklin (eds), *Family therapy: complementary frameworks in theory and practice*, pp. 441–61. London: Academic Press.

Lau, A. (1988) Family therapy and ethnic minorities. In E. Street and W. Dryden (eds), *Family therapy in Britain*, pp. 270–90. Milton Keynes: Open University Press.

Lau, A. (1990) Psychological problems in adolescents from ethnic minorities. *British journal of hospital medicine* 44, 201–5.

Laub Coser, R. (ed.) (1974) *The family: its structures and functions*. New York: Macmillan.

Laub Coser, R. and Rokoff, G. (1974) Women in the occupational world: social disruption and conflict. In R. Laub Coser (ed.), *The family: its structures and functions*, pp. 490–511. New York: Macmillan.

Lautman, F. (1977) Cycle de vie domestique et incidences de l'hétérogamie religieuse: les cas de mariages mixtes entre juifs et catholiques en France. In J. Cuisenier (ed.), *The family life cycle in European societies*, pp. 189–205. New Babylon Studies in Social Sciences, no. 28. Paris/The Hague: Mouton.

Lawick-Goodall, J. van (1970) *In the shadow of man*. London: St James's Place.

Lazarus, A.A. and Fay, A. (1990) Brief psychotherapy: tautology or oxymoron? In J.K. Zeig and S.G. Gilligan (eds), *Brief therapy: myths, methods and metaphors*, pp. 36–51. New York: Brunner Mazel.

Leach, E. (1970) Du nouveau sur 'papa' et 'maman'. In R. Needham (ed.), *La parenté en question*, pp. 168–90. Paris: Seuil.

Leach, E. (1972) L'influence du contexte culturel sur la communication non-verbale chez l'homme. In *L'unité de l'homme*. Paris: Gallimard, 1980.

Lebovici, S. (1973) Une association du psychodrame et de la psychothérapie de groupe. In S. de Schill (ed.), *La psychothérapie de groupe*, pp. 331–59. Paris: PUF.

Lebovici, S. (1981) A propos des thérapeutiques de la famille. *Psychiatrie de l'enfant* 24 (2), 541–83.

Lebovici, S. (1983) *Le nourisson, la mère et le psychanalyse. Les interactions précoces*. Paris: Paidos, Le Centurion.

Lebovici, S. (1985) Approche familiale. In S. Lebovici, R. Daitkine and M. Soulé (eds), *Traité de psychiatrie de l'enfant et de l'adolescent*, vol. 1, pp. 17–43. Paris: PUF.

Lebovici, S., Diatkine, G. and Arfouilloux, J.-C. (1972) A propos de la psychothérapie familiale. *Psychiatrie de l'enfant* 12 (2), 447–536.

Lebovici, S., Diatkine, R. and Soulé, M. (1985) *Traité de psychiatrie de l'enfant et de l'adolescent*, 3 vols. Paris: PUF.

Lebovici, S. and Soulé, M. (1970) *La connaisance de l'enfant par la psychanalyse*, 4th rev. edn, 1983. Paris: PUF.

Le Bras, H. (1981) Le cycle de la vie familiale: une nouveauté déjà périmée? In *Les cycles de la vie familiale. Revue dialogue* 72, 5–10.

Leclaire, S. (1975) *On tue un enfant*. Paris: Seuil.

Lederer, W. and Jackson, D.D. (1968) *The mirages of marriage*. New York: Norton.

Ledermann, S. (1956–64) *Alcool, alcoolisme et alcoolisation*, 2 vols.

Leighton, A.H. (1981) Culture and psychiatry. *Canadian journal of psychiatry* 26 (8), 522–9.

Lemaire, J.G. (1979) *Le couple: sa vie, sa mort. La structuration du couple humain*. Paris: Payot.

Lemaire, J.G. (1986) Utilisation des rituels familiaux en thérapie de famille et en thérapie de couple. *Dialogue* 91 (1), 5–18.

Lemaire-Arnaud, E. (1983) Le lit de papa-maman. *Dialogue* 82 (4), 8–15.

Le Moigne, J.-L. (1977) *La théorie du système général. Théorie de la modélisation*. Paris: PUF.

Le Moigne, J.-L. (1982) *Formalisations systémiques de la théorie de l'organisation*. GRASCE Aix-en-Provence. ERA CNRS, 640.

Le Moigne, J.-L. (1983) Science de l'autonomie et autonomie de la science. In *L'auto-organisation. De la physique au politique*. Paris: Seuil.

Le Moigne, J.-L. (1984) Notes sur les paradoxes de l'autonomie. In *Analogies. Psychanalyse et thérapie familiale systémique*, pp. 69–74. Paris: Revue du Centre d'Etude de la Famille.

Le Moigne, J.-L. (1986a) L'intelligence de la complexité. In *Science et pratique de la complexité*, pp. 47–77. Paris: La Documentation Française.

Le Moigne, J.-L. (ed.) (1986b) *Intelligence des mécanismes, mécanismes de l'intelligence*. Paris: Fayard/Fondation Diderot.

Le Moigne, J.-L. (1988) Représentation des processus d'auto-information de l'organisation sociale. Note de recherche 88–03 April 1988. GRASCE URA CNRS Université de droit et d'économie et des sciences d'Aix-Marseille, Faculté d'Economie Appliqué.

Le Moigne, J.-L. (1990) *La modélisation des systèmes complexes*. Paris: Dunod.

Le Moigne, J.-L. (1992) La modélisation systémique des processus cognitifs. In PISTES, no. 3, Sciences dures, sciences humaines. Paris.

Le Moigne, J.-L. (1993) Contributions aux épistémologies constructivistes. Repères épistémologiques pour le développement des nouvelles sciences de l'ingénierie (sciences des systèmes, science de la complexité). Cahiers no. 2–3, GRASCE, March 1993.

Leroi-Gourhan, A. (1964) *Le geste et la parole. Technique et langage*. Paris: Albin Michel.

Leroi-Gourhan, A. (1965) *Le geste et la parole. La mémoire et les rythmes*. Paris: Albin Michel.

Lesourd, J. (1984) La dépression post-divorce vue à travers le déroulement d'un groupe 'divorçants-divorcés'. *Dialogue* 86 (4), 21–7.

Lesser, R., Ashkenazi, N. and Ayal, H. (1986) Family therapy with head injured patients. *Proceedings of the Fifth International Family Therapy Congress*, Jerusalem, 22–25 June 1986.

Leuba, J. (1936) La famille névrotique et les névroses familiales. *Revue française de psychanalyse* 9 (3), 360–413.

Le Vaguerese, L. (1985) *Groddeck, la maladie et la psychanalyse*. Paris: PUF.

Levick, S.E., Jalili, B. and Strauss, J.S. (1981) Onions and tears: a multidimensional analysis of a counter-ritual. *Family process* 20, 77–83.

Lévi-Strauss, C. (1961) *Race et histoire*, ed. Gonthier. Paris: UNESCO.

Lévi-Strauss, C. (1969) *The elementary structures of kinship*. Boston: Beacon Press.

Lévi-Strauss, C. (1973) Mythologie et rituel. In Plon (ed.), *Anthropologie structurale deux*, pp. 137–315. Paris.

Lévi-Strauss, C. (1983) La famille. In Plon (ed.), *Le regard éloigné*, pp. 65–92. Paris.

Lewin, K. (1935) *A dynamic theory of personality*. New York: McGraw-Hill.

Lewin, K. (1936) *Principles of topological psychology*. New York: McGraw-Hill.

Lewin, K. (1939) Field theory and experiment in social psychology: conceptual methods. *American journal of sociology* 44, 868–9.

Lewin, K. (1947a) Frontiers in group dynamics. *Human relations* 1 (1), 2–38.

Lewin, K. (1947b) *Psychologie dynamique*. Presented by C. Faucheux. Paris: PUF, 1959.

Lewin, K. (1951) *Field theory in social science: selected theoretical papers*. New York: Harper.

Lewis, E. (1976) The management of stillbirth: coping with an unreality. *The Lancet* 2, 619–20.

Leyhausen, P. (1974) Aspects phylogénétiques, ontogénétiques et actogénétiques du concept de l'agressivité. In Entretiens de Rueil 1974, L'agressivité, pulsion ou réponse à l'environment? *Cahiers Sandoz* 28.

Lidz, T. (1970) La famille, cadre du développement. In E.J. Anthony and C. Koupernik (eds), *The child and his family*. Yearbook of the International Association for Child Psychiatry and Allied Professions. New York: Wiley.

Lidz, T., Cornelison, A.R., Fleck, S. and Terry, D. (1956) Marital schism and marital skew. In T. Lidz, S. Fleck and A.R. Cornelison (eds), *Schizophrenia and the family*. New York: International Universities Press, 1965.

Lidz, T., Fleck, S. and Cornelison, A.R. (1965) *Schizophrenia and the family*. New York: International Universities Press.

Lieberman, S. (1978) Nineteen cases of morbid grief. *British journal of psychiatry* 132, 159–63.

Lieberman, S. (1979a) *Transgenerational family therapy*. London: Croom Helm.

Lieberman, S. (1979b) Transgenerational analysis: the genogram as a technique in family therapy. *Journal of family therapy* 1, 51–64.

Lieberman, S. (1979c) A transgenerational theory. *Journal of family therapy* 1, 347–60.

Lieberman, S. (1987) Going back to your own family. In A. Bentovim, G. Gorell Barnes and A. Cooklin (eds), *Family therapy: complementary frameworks*, pp. 205–20. London: Academic Press.

Lieberman, S. and Black, D. (1982) Loss, mourning and grief. In A. Bentovim, G. Gorell Barnes and A. Cooklin (eds), *Family therapy: complementary frameworks in theory and practice*, vol. 2, pp. 373–87. London: Academic Press.

Liebman, R., Honig, P. and Berger, H. (1976) An integrated treatment program for psychogenic pain. *Family process* 15, 397–405.

Lilamand, M. (1980) *René Lafforgue (1894–1962). Fondateur du mouvement psychanalytique français. Sa vie, son oeuvre. Mémoire de CES de psychiatrie*, Créteil.

Lin, T.Y. (1986) Multiculturalism and Canadian psychiatry: opportunities and challenges. *Canadian journal of psychiatry* 31, 681–90.

Lindemann, E. (1944) Symptomatology and management of acute grief. *American journal of psychiatry* 101, 141–8.

Lindley, R. (1987) Family therapy and respect for people. In S. Walrond-Skinner and D. Watson (eds), *Ethical issues in family therapy*, pp. 104–17. London: Routledge.

Littlewood, R. and Lipsedge, M. (1982) *Aliens and alienists*. Harmondsworth: Penguin.

Lodeon, J., Van Dyck, R. and Erickson, M.H. (1986) Histoires d'Erickson. *Génitif* 7 (1).

Lord, C. and Rutter, M. (1994) Autism and pervasive developmental disorder. In M. Rutter, E. Taylor and L. Hersov (eds), *Child and adolescent psychiatry: modern approaches*, 3rd edn, pp. 569–93. Oxford: Blackwell Scientific.

Lorenz, K. (1954) *Studies in animal and human behaviour*. Trans. C. and P. Fredet: *Essais sur le comportement animal et humain*. Paris: Seuil, 1970.

Lorenz, K. (1966) *Evolution and modification of behaviour*. London: Methuen.

Lorenz, K. (1973) *Die Ruckseite des Spiegels (Behind the mirror)*. Munich: Piper.

Lorenz, K. (1975) *Ecrits et dialogues avec Richard I. Evans*. Trans. J. Etoré. Paris: Flammarion, 1978.

Lorenz, K. (1978a) *L'homme dans le fleuve du vivant*. Trans. J. Etoré. Paris: Flammarion, 1981.

Lorenz, K. (1978b) *Vergleichende Verhaltensforschung: Grundlagen der Ethologie*. Trans. J. Etoré: *Les fondements de l'éthologie*. Paris: Flammarion, 1984.

Lorenz, K. (1983) *L'homme en péril*. Trans. J. Etoré. Paris: Flammarion, 1985.

Louttre du Pasquier, N. (1981) *Le devenir d'enfants abandonnés. Le tissage et le lien*. Paris: PUF.

Lowie, R. (1969) La famille. In *Traité de sociologie primitive*. Trans. E. Metraux. Paris: Payot.

Luepnitz, D.A. (1988) *The family interpreted: feminist theory in clinical practice*. New York: Basic Books.

Luepnitz, D.A. (1992) Nothing in Common but their first names: the case of Foucault and White. *Journal of Family Therapy* 14, 265–79.

Luria, A.R. (1963) *Recovery of function after brain injury*. New York: Macmillan.

Lussato, B. (1979) *Introduction critique aux théories d'organisation*. Paris: Dunod.

McCulloch, W.S. and Pitts, W. (1943) A logical calculus of the ideas immanent in nervous activity. *Bulletin of mathematical biophysics* 5, 115–33.

McDougall, J. (1978) *Plaidoyer pour une certaine anormalité*. Paris: Gallimard.

McGoldrick, M. (1980) The joining of families through marriage: the new couple. In E.A. Carter and M. McGoldrick (eds), *The family life cycle: a framework for family therapy*, pp. 93–119. New York: Gardner Press.

McGoldrick, M. (ed.) (1989) *Women in families: a framework for family therapy*. New York/London: Norton.

McGoldrick, M., Pearce, J. and Giordano, J. (eds) (1982) *Ethnicity and family therapy*. New York: Guilford Press.

MacGregor, R., Ritchie, A.M., Serrano, A., Schuster, F.P., McDonald, E.C. and Goolishian, H.A. (1964) *Multiple impact therapy with families*. New York: McGraw-Hill.

MacKinnon, L. (1983) Etude comparative des thérapies stratégiques et du modèle milanais. *Family process* 22, 425–41. Trans. M.T. Matras. ANTFAS.

MacKinnon, L. and Miller, D. (1987) The new epistemology and the Milan approach: feminist and sociopolitical considerations. *Journal of marital and family therapy* 13, 139–55.

McLuhan, M. (1962) *The Gutenberg galaxy*. Toronto: University of Toronto Press.

McLuhan, M. (1964) *Understanding media*. New York: McGraw-Hill.

McLuhan, M. (1973) *Essays, processus and media*, ed. Hartbuise. Canada: Montréal Québec.

McLuhan, M. and Fiore, Q. (1967) *The medium is the massage*. New York: Bantam Books.

McLuhan, M. and Fiore, Q. (1968) *War and peace in the global village*. New York: McGraw-Hill.

McNamee, S., and Gergen, K. (1992) *Therapy as Social Construction*. London: Sage Publications.

Machiavelli (1983) *The discourses on the first decade of Livy*. Harmondsworth: Penguin.

Madanes, C. (1981) *Strategic family therapy*. San Francisco: Jossey-Bass.

Madanes, C. (1984) *Behind the one-way mirror: advances in the practice of strategic therapy*. San Francisco: Jossey-Bass.

Madanes, C. (1990) *Sex, love and violence*. New York: Norton.

Madigan, S.P. (1992) The application of Michel Foucault's philosophy in the problem externalizing discourse of Michael White. *Journal of Family Therapy* 14, 265–79.

Mahler, M. (1968) *On human symbiosis and the vicissitudes of individuation. Vol. 1: Infantile psychosis*. New York: International University Press.

Mairlot, F.E. (1982) *La nouvelle cybernétique, essai d'épistémologie des systèmes dynamiques*. Brussels: Chabassol.

Maisondieu, J. (1984) La démence: un excès de (la) raison? *Thérapie familiale* 5 (1), 39–52.

Maisondieu, J. (1985) Approche familiale de la démence: des démences précoces aux démences tardives. *Thérapie familiale* 6 (3), 287–94.

Maisondieu, J. (1986) Les déments ne sont pas fous. *Synapse* 22.

Malan, D. (1976) *The frontier of brief psychotherapy: an example of the convergence of research and clinical practice*. New York: Plenum.

Malarewicz, A. and Godin, J. (1986) *Milton H. Erickson. De l'hypnose clinique à la psychothérapie stratégique*. Paris: ESF.

Mandelbrot, B. (1975) *Les objets fractals*. Paris: Flammarion.

March, J.G. and Simon, H.A. (1958) *Organizations*. New York: Wiley.

Marchais, P. (1983) *Les mouvements psychopathologiques*. Toulouse: Erès.

Margalef, R. (1984) Les écosystèmes: la diversité et la connectivité comme composantes mesurables de leur complication. In *Science et pratique de la complexité*, pp. 263–82. Actes du Colloque de Montpelier. Paris: La Documentation Française, 1986.

Martino, J. de (1984) *Formation paradoxale et paradoxes de la formation*. Toulouse: Privat.

Marty, P. (1976) *Les mouvements individuels de vie et de mort. Essai d'économie psychosomatique*. Paris: Payot.

Maruani, G. (1975a) La relation médecin-malade au cours des traitements au lithium. *Actualités psychiatriques* 4, 53–7.

Maruani, G. (1975b) Abandon du traitement et sujétion aux médicaments: raisons et solutions. *Revue des sciences médicales* 214, 95–8.

Maruani, G. (1976) Psychosomatique des douleurs thoraciques. *Revue des sciences médicales* 219, 29–35.

Maruani, G. (1977a) Douleur et psychosomatique. *Revue des sciences médicales* 225, 19–24.

Maruani, G. (1977b) Psychologie de l'hypertendu. *Revue des sciences médicales* 226, 15–20.

Maruani, G. (1978a) L'entretien avec un malade allergique. *Revue des sciences médicales* 232, 91–3.

Maruani, G. (1978b) Fatigue et obésité. *Quintessence* special issue, 16–17.

Maruani, G. (1982a) Sociogénétique des schismes familiaux. In G. Maruani and P. Watzlawick (eds), *L'interaction en médecine et en psychiatrie*. Paris: Erès.

Maruani, G. (1982b) Pour une médicine théorique. Vers une épistémologie du cancer. In G. Maruani and P. Watzlawick (eds), *L'interaction en médecine et en psychiatrie*. Paris: Erès.

Maruani, G. (1985a) Attitude et psychothérapie. *Psychothérapies* 5 (3), 135–7.

Maruani, G. (1985b) Family myths and acculturation. Paper delivered at the symposium on Analysis of the Structure and Effectiveness of Mental Health Care in a Metropolis, New York, 13 June.

Maruani, G. (1985c) Le couple, une déviation sexuelle désuète? *Génitif* 6 (1), 45–53.

Maruani, G. (1985d) Levels of communication and cancerogenesis. *Fundamenta scientiae* 6 (1), 47–64.

Maruani, G. and Atlan, P. (1981) La place de psychiatrie. In Société française de gynécologie, *Algies pelviennes chroniques sans cause cliniquement évidente*, pp. 395–402. Paris: Masson.

Maruani, G., Le Quintrec, Y., Gendre, J.P. and Verbizier, J. de (1978) Une expérience d'antenne psychiatrique en service hospitalier de médecine générale. *Annales médico-psychologiques* 6 (8), 867–76.

Maruani, G. and Miermont, J. (eds) (1981) *Passions de famille*. *Génitif* 3 (1–3).

Maruani, G. and Watzlawick, P. (1982) *L'interaction en médecine et en psychiatrie*. Paris: Erès.

Maruyama, M. (1968) The second cybernetics. Deviation-amplifying mutual causal processes. In W. Buckley (ed.), *Modern systems research for the behavioral scientist*, pp. 304–16. Chicago: Aldine Publishing.

Marx. K. (1867) *Capital*. London: Allen and Unwin, 1928.

Mason, B. and Mason, E. (1990) Masculinity and family work. In R.J. Perelberg and A. Miller (eds), *Gender and power in families*, pp. 209–17. London/New York: Tavistock/Routledge.

Masson, J. (1988) *Against therapy*. London: Fontana.

Masson, J.M. (1984) *Le réel escamoté. Le renoncement de Freud à la théorie de la séduction*. Trans. C. Monod. Paris: Aubier.

Masson, O. (1981) Mauvais traitements envers les enfants et thérapies familiales. *Thérapie familiale* 2, 269–86.

Masson, O. (1985) Thérapie des syndromes psychosomatiques en pédopsychiatrie. *Thérapie familiale* 6 (3), 295–303.

Masud Khan (1974) *The privacy of the self*. London: The Hogarth Press.

Matthews-Simonton, S. (1984) *The healing family. The Simonton approach for families facing illness*. New York: Bantam Books.

Maturana, H. (1972) Cognitive strategies. In E. Morin and M. Piatelli-Palmarini (eds), *L'unité de l'homme*, pp. 156–80. Paris: Seuil.

Maturana, H. (1987) Représentation et fonctions de communication. In J. Piaget, P. Mounoud and J-P. Broucquart (eds), *Psychologie. Encyclopédie de la Pléïade*, pp. 1442–75. Paris: Gallimard.

Maturana, H. and Varela, F. (1980) *Autopoiesis and cognition: the realization of the living*. Boston Studies in the Philosophy of Science, vol. 42. Dordrecht: D. Reidel.

Maturana, H. and Varela, F. (1988) *The tree of knowledge: the biological routes of human under-standing*. Boston: Shambala.

Maurel, H., Pujol, B., Boudet, M. and Berne, A. (1983) La schizophrénie instituée. *Les schizophrénies. Etude psychopathologique, clinique, thérapeutique. L'information psychiatrique*, vol. 59, special issue, 45–62.

Mead, M. (1935) *Sex and temperament in three primitive societies*. London: Routledge and Kegan Paul.

Mead, M. (1957) Changing patterns of parent-child relations in an urban culture. *International journal of psychoanalysis* 38, 369–78.

Meissner, W.W. (1966) Family dynamics and psychosomatic processes. *Family process* 5, 142–61.

Mendel, G. (1968) *La révolte contre le père. Une introduction à la sociopsychanalyse*. Paris: Payot.

Mendel, G. (1969) *La crise de générations. Etude sociopsychanalytique*. Paris: Payot.

Mendell, D. and Fisher, S. (1956) An approach to neurotic behavior in terms of a three generation family model. *Journal of nervous and mental diseases* 123 (2), 171–80.

Mendlewicz, J. (1981) Données génétiques récentes sur la maniaco-dépression. In *Génétique clinique et psychopathologie*, pp. 71–6. Lyon: Simep, 1982.

Menghi, P. (1981) La supervision provocatrice. *Thérapie familiale* 2 (4), 287–92.

Mesarovic, M.D., Macko, D. and Takahara, Y. (1970) *Theory of hierarchical, multilevel systems*. New York: Academic Press.

Miermont, J. (1975) Vers une nouvelle connaisance de l'inconscient? A propos d'une théorie soviétique. *Actualités psychiatriques* 2, pp. 49–56.

Miermont, J. (1976a) Le comportement instinctif d'attachement selon J. Bowlby. *Actualités psychiatriques* 2.

Miermont, J. (1976b) L'apport de J. Bowlby à l'étude ontogénétique de l'anxiété: introduction et discussion. *Perspectives psychiatriques* 2.

Miermont, J. (1976c) Vie et mort dans la demande d'interruption de grossesse. *Actualités psychiatriques* 6, 45–8.

Miermont, J. (1978a) Aberrations instinctives dans les comportements maternels animaux. Con-tribution à une journée scientifique de Michel Soulé sur le thème: *Mère meurtrière, mère mortifière, mère mortifiée*. Paris: ESF.

Miermont, J. (1978b) Phylogénèse, ontogénèse et comportement humain: l'attachement humain, ses origines et ses avatars. *Evolution psychiatrique* 43, 1.

Miermont, J. (1979a) Histoire d'un attachement atypique. *Génitif* 1, February.

Miermont, J. (1979b) Schizophrénie et souffrance familiale. *Evolution psychiatrique* 46 (3), 525–35.

Miermont, J. (1979c) Acculturation et communication. *Compte-rendu de la journée médico-psychologique franco-israélienne*, pp. 102–29. Paris: COFRISEMS.

Miermont, J. (1980a) Thérapie familiale et acculturation. *Revue transition* 4, 106–17.

Miermont, J. (1980b) La communication entre l'enfant et l'animal. In M. Soulé (ed.), *L'animal dans la vie de l'enfant*, pp. 26–53. Paris: ESF.

Miermont, J. (1980c) Problèmes épistémologiques posés par l'apparition de la pensée abstraite à la puberté. *Génitif, puberté et adolescence* 2, 4–5.

Miermont, J. (1981a) Inconscient individuel et mémoire familiale. *Etudes psychothérapiques* 43 (1), 17–23.

Miermont, J. (1981b) Cybernétique des ritualisations normales et pathologiques. In *Passions de familles. Génitif* 3 (1–3).

Miermont, J. (1982a) Double bind, pathologie, thérapie et créativité. In G. Maruani and P. Watzlawick (eds), *L'interaction en médecine et en psychiatrie*, pp. 61–83. Paris: Génitif-Erès.

Miermont, J. (1982b) Familles de catastrophes, catastrophes de familles. In G. Maruani and P. Watzlawick (eds), *L'interaction en médecine et en psychiatrie*, pp. 153–75. Paris: Génitif-Erès.

Miermont, J. (1983) Aliénation thérapeutique, autonomie schizophrénique. *Revue transition* 14 (2), 61–72.

Miermont, J. (1984a) Jean-Pierre Brisset ou l'archéologie des savoirs. In *Entre folie et folie: catachrèse du signifiant et des pulsions*. Paris: Génitif.

Miermont, J. (1984b) Intérêt de l'approche familiale comme instrument de connaissance en éthologie de l'homme, et de l'éthologie humaine à la thérapie familiale. *Bulletin d'écologie et éthologie humaines* 3 (1–2), 83–92.

Miermont, J. (1984c) L'auto-référence familiale. *Revue psychiatrie de l'enfant* 27, 127–73.

Miermont, J. (1985a) Ethologie et développement de l'enfant. In S. Lebovici, R. Diatkine and M. Soulé (eds), *Traité de psychiatrie de l'enfant et de l'adolescent*, vol. 1, pp. 121–41. Paris: PUF.

Miermont, J. (ed.) (1985b) Mythes et modèles scientifiques en psychothérapie individuelle et en thérapie familiale. *Actualités psychiatriques* 9, pp. 8–80.

Miermont, J. (1986a) Métacommunication. In P. Fedida (ed.), *Communication et représentation*, pp. 113–53. Paris: PUF.

Miermont, J. (1986b) Pragmatique des communications. In J.L. Le Moigne (ed.), *Intelligence des mécanismes, mécanisme de l'intelligence*, pp. 293–312. Paris: Fayard.

Miermont, J. (1988) Le corps, l'âme et l'écosystème. Pour une éthologie de l'esprit. In CEFA (eds), *Approche familiale des troubles psychosomatiques*, pp. 135–62. Paris: CEFA.

Miermont, J. (1993) *Ecologie des liens*. Paris: ESF.

Miermont, J. and Angel, P. (1982) De la résurgence de schémas phylogénétiques dans les systèmes familiaux humains pathologiques. *Journal de médecine de Lyon* 63, 339–50.

Miermont, J. and Angel, P. (1983) Pratique, formation et recherche en thérapie familiale: en pratique, faut-il accorder les violins? *Revue psychothérapies* 2, 87–94.

Miermont, J. and Gross, M. (1985) Les formes auto-référentielles: modélisation élémentaire de l'autonomie d'un système de communication. In J. Miermont (ed.), *Actualités psychiatriques* 9.

Miermont, J. and Neuburger, R. (1989) *René Thom expliqué par lui-même*. PISTES, no. 1, Paris.

Miermont, J. and Sternschuss, S. (1981) Thérapies familiales. *Encyclopédie médicale chirurgicale, Paris: psychiatrie*, 37819 F10 2.

Miller, J.G. (1978) *Living systems*. New York: McGraw-Hill.

Minuchin, S. (1974) *Families and family therapy*. London: Tavistock.

Minuchin, S. (1979) Constructing a therapeutic reality. In E. Kaufman and P.N. Kaufmann (eds), *Family therapy of drug and alcohol abuse*, pp. 5–18. New York: Gardner Press.

Minuchin, S. (1984) *Kaleidoscope*. Cambridge, Mass.: Harvard University Press.

Minuchin, S. and Fishman, H.C. (1981) *Family therapy techniques*. Cambridge, Mass.: Harvard University Press.

Minuchin, S. and Montalvo, B. (1967) Techniques for working with disorganised low socio-economic families. In J. Haley (ed.), *Changing families*, pp. 202–11. New York: Grune and Stratton.

Minuchin, S., Montalvo, B., Guerney, B.C., Rosman, B.L. and Schumer, F. (1967) *Families of the slums: an exploration of their structure and treatment*. New York: Basic Books.

Minuchin, S., Rosman, B. and Baker, L. (1978) *Psychosomatic families: anorexia nervosa in context*. Cambridge, Mass.: Harvard University Press.

Mitscherlich, A. (1969) *Vers la société sans pères: essai de psychologie sociale*. Paris: Gallimard/NRF.

Moles, A.A. (1986) *Théorie structurale de la communication et société*. Paris: Masson.

Montagner, H. (1978) *L'enfant et la communication: comment des gestes, des attitudes, des vocalisations deviennement des messages*. Paris: Pernoud/Stock.

Montaigne, M. (1967) *Oeuvres complètes*. Bibliothèque de la Pléiäde. Paris: Gallimard/NRF.

Montalvo, B. and Haley, J. (1973) In defense of child therapy. *Family process* 12, 227–44.

Montesquieu, C. (1748) *The spirit of the laws*. Trans. Cohler et al. Cambridge: Cambridge University Press, 1989.

Morel, D. (1984) *Cancer et psychanalyse*. Paris: Belfond.

Moreno, J.L. (1934) *Who shall survive?*, 2nd edn, 1953. New York: Beacon House.

Moreno, J.L. (1965) *Group psychotherapy and psychodrama*. New York: Beacon House.

Morin, E. (1973) *La rumeur d'Orléans*. Paris: Seuil.

Morin, E. (1977) *La méthode. 1: La nature de la nature*. Paris: Seuil.

Morin, E. (1980a) Au-delà du déterminisme: le dialogue de l'ordre et du désordre. *Le débat* 6, 105–22.

Morin, E. (1980b) *La méthode. 2: La vie de la vie*. Paris: Seuil.

Morin, E. (1986) *La méthode. 3: La connaisance de la connaisance/ 1. Anthropologie de la connaisance*. Paris: Seuil.

Morin, E. and Piatelli-Palmarini, M. (eds) (1972) *L'unité de l'homme*. Paris: Seuil.

Mottron, L. (1983) Contraintes communes à l'acquisition, la théorisation et la pathologie de la déixis. Unpublished PhD thesis, University of Paris.

Mottron, L. (1986) Renvoi symbolique et renvoi comportemental: l'observable du sens. *Journées d'éthologie théorique et d'épistemologie*. Montpelier, 19–20 April.

Mrazek, P.B. and Kempe, C.H. (eds) (1981) *Sexually abused children and their families*. New York: Pergamon Press.

Murphy, H.M.B. (1974) In E.J. Anthony and C. Koupernik (eds), *The child and his family, 3: Children at psychiatric risk*. Yearbook of the International Association for Child Psychiatry and Allied Professions. New York: Wiley.

Murstein, B.I. (1961) The complementarity need hypothesis in newly weds and middle-aged married couples. *Journal of abnormal and social psychology* 63, 194–7.

Murstein, B.I. (1971) Self-ideal/self-discrepancy and the choice of marital partner. *Journal of consulting and clinical psychology* 37 (1), 47–52.

M'Uzan, M. de (1967) Expérience de l'inconscient. In *L'inconscient, revue de psychanalyse*, 4, pp. 35–54. Paris: PUF.

M'Uzan, M. de (1976) Contre-transfert et système paradoxal. *Revue française de psychanalyse* 40 (3), 575–90.

Nahas, G. (1982) La fréquence d'utilisation du cannabis chez les adolescents. *Bulletin national médecine* 166, 509–13.

Nasio, J.-D. (ed.) (1985) *Aux limites du transfert*. Paris: Rochevigne.

Nathan, T. (1985a) L'enfant ancêtre. *Nouvelle revue d'ethnopsychiatrie, 4: La pensée sauvage*.

Nathan, T. (1985b) L'inceste. *Nouvelle revue d'ethnopsychiatrie, 3: La pensée sauvage*.

Needham, R. (ed.) (1971) *Rethinking kinship and marriage*. London: Tavistock/Association of Social Anthropologists of the Commonwealth.

Neuburger, R. (ed.) (1981) *Pratique, théorie de la pratique*. Paris: Centre d'Etude de la Famille Association, 1982.

Neuburger, R. (ed.) (1982) *L'alienation*. Paris: Centre d'Etude de la Famille Association, 1983.

Neuburger, R. (ed.) (1983) *Analogies*. Paris: Centre d'Etude de la Famille Association, 1984.

Neuburger, R. (ed.) (1984a) *Fonction du rituel*. Paris: Centre d'Etude de la Famille Association, 1985.

Neuburger, R. (1984b) *L'autre demande*. Paris: ESF.

Neuburger, R. (1985a) Rituels d'appartenance, rituels d'inclusion. *Fonction du rituel*. Paris: Centre d'Etude de la Famille Association.

Neuburger, R. (1985b) *Y-a-t'il une théorie de l'institution?* Paris: Centre d'Etude de la Famille Association, 1986.

Neuburger, R. (1987) *Lectures du symptômes*. Paris: Centre d'Etude de la Famille Association.

Neumann, J. von (1951) The general and logical theory of automata. In W. Buckley (ed.), *Modern systems research for the behavioral scientist*, pp. 97–107. Chicago: Aldine.

Neumann, J. von (1979) *The computer and the brain*. New Haven/London: Yale University Press.

Neumann, J. von and Morgenstern, O. (1944) *The theory of games and economic behavior*. Princeton, NJ: Princeton University Press.

Newell, A. (1983) Intellectual issues in the history of artificial intelligence. In F. Machlup and U. Mansfield (eds), *The study of information: interdisciplinary messages*, pp. 187–228. New York: Wiley.

Newell, A. and Simon, H. (1972) *Human problem solving*. London: Prentice Hall.

Nichols, M. (1987) *The self in the system: expanding the limits of family therapy*. New York: Brunner Mazel.

Nicholson, L. (ed.) (1990) *Feminism/post-modernism*. New York/London: Routledge.

Nicolo, A-M. (1980) L'emploi de la métaphore en thérapie familiale. *Thérapie familiale* 1, 4.

Niederland, W.G. (1959) Le 'monde miraculé' de l'enfance de Schreber. In *Le cas Schreber*. Paris: PUF, 1979.

Noel, J. and Soulé, M. (1985) L'enfant 'cas social'. In S. Lebovici, R. Diatkine and M. Soulé (eds), *Traité de psychiatrie de l'enfant et de l'adolescent*, vol. 3, pp. 23–51. Paris: PUF.

Noller, P. (1980) Gaze in the married couple. *Journal of nonverbal behaviour* 5, 115–29.

O'Hanlon, W.H. (1987) *Taproots: underlying principles of Milton H. Erickson's therapy and hypnosis*. New York: Norton.

O'Hanlon, W.H. and Weiner-Davis, M. (1989) *In search of solutions: a new direction in psychotherapy*. New York: Norton.

Olson, D.H., Sprenkle, D.H. and Russell, C. (1980) Circumplex model of marital and family systems. I: Cohesion and adaptability dimensions, family types and clinical applications. *Family process* 18, 3–28.

Onnis, L. (1980) La thérapie familiale dans les institutions et dans les services territoriaux. Utilité et limites. *Réseaux, systèmes, agencements* 2, 39–49. Paris: Gamma.

Orwid, M. (1986) Family therapy in Poland. Paper presented to the Fifth International Family Therapy Congress, Jerusalem, June 1986.

Oury, J. (1985) Existe-t'il une théorie de l'institution? In R. Neuburger (ed.), *Y-a-t'il une théorie de l'institution?*, pp. 39–52. Paris: Centre d'Etude de la Famille Association, 1986.

Padovani, P., Porot, D. and Portelli, C. (1986) La rupture du lien conjugal. Aspects psychopathologiques. Rapport de la Société Latino-Méditerranéenne de Psychiatrie.

Pankow, G. (1969) *L'homme et sa psychose*. Paris: Aubier-Montaigne.

Pankow, G. (1977) *Structure familiale et psychose*. Paris: Aubier-Montaigne.

Papert, S. (1981) *Jaillissement de l'esprit. Ordinateurs et apprentissage*. Paris: Flammarion.

Papp, P. (1983) *The process of change*. New York: Guilford Press.

Papp, P., Silverstein, O. and Carter, E. (1973) Family sculpting in preventive work with 'well' families. *Family process* 12, 197–212.

Parkes, C.M. (1965a) Bereavement and mental illness. Part I. A clinical study of the grief of bereaved psychiatric patients. *British journal of medical psychology* 38, 1–12.

Parkes, C.M. (1965b) Bereavement and mental illness. Part 2. A classification of bereavement reactions. *British journal of medical psychology* 38, 13–26.

Parret, H. (1980) Les stratégies pragmatiques. In *Les actes du discours. Communications.* Paris: Seuil.

Pascal, B. (1991) *Pensées.* Edition de la Pléiade. Paris: Gallimard/NRF.

Pasini, W., Bydlowski, M., Papiernik, E. and Beguin, F. (1984) *Relation précoce parents–enfants.* Lyon-Villeurbane: SIMEP.

Paul, N. (1967) The role of mourning and empathy in conjoint marital therapy. In G.H. Zuk and I. Boszormenyi-Nagy (eds) *Family therapy and disturbed families*, pp. 186–205. Palo Alto: Science and Behavior Books.

Peirce, C.S. (1935) *Collected papers*, ed. C. Harsthorne and P. Weiss. Cambridge, Mass.: Harvard University Press.

Peitgen, H.-O. and Richter, P.H. (1986) *The beauty of fractals.* Heidelberg: Springer Verlag.

Pelicier, Y. (1980) Maladie et système. *Journeé de psychologie, biologie et thérapie* 1 (1), 5–12.

Penn, P. (1982) Circular questions. *Family process* 21, 267–80.

Pennachionni, I. (1986) *De la guerre conjugale.* Paris: Mazarine.

Perelberg, R.J. and Miller, A. (eds) (1990) *Gender and power in families.* London/New York: Tavistock/Routledge.

Peseschkian, N. (1986) *Positive family therapy.* Berlin/Heidelberg: Springer.

Peterson, M.R. (1992) *At personal risk: boundary violations in professional–client relationships.* New York: Norton.

Petitot-Cocorda, J. (1977) Identités et catastrophes. In *L'identité. Séminaire dirigé par Claude Lévi-Strauss*, pp. 109–56. Paris: PUF.

Petitot-Cocorda, J. (1983) Théorie des catastrophes et structures sémio-narratives. In *Sémiotique et théorie des catastrophes. Actes sémiotiques-documents* 5, 47–8.

Petitot-Cocorda, J. (1985a) Les catastrophes de la parole de Roman Jakobson à René Thom. *Collection recherches interdisciplinaires dirigée par Pierre Delattre.* Paris: Maloine.

Petitot-Cocorda, J. (1985b) *Morphogenèse du sens. Pour un schématisme de la structure.* Paris: PUF.

Petitot-Cocorda, J. (1992) *Physique du sens. De la théorie des singularités aux structures sémio-narratives.* Paris: Editions du CNRS.

Pheline, C. (1986) Prise en charge personnalisée du coma traumatique grave. *Revue de médecine psychosomatique de psychologie médicale* 18 (8), 1257–61.

Philippe, A. and Davidson, F. (1981) Epidémiologie-statistiques. In J. de Vedrinne, O. Quenard and D. Weber (eds), *Suicide et conduites suicidaires*, pp. 105–41. Paris: Masson.

Piaget, J. (1949) *Traité de logique. Essai de logique opératoire.* Paris: Armand Colin.

Piaget, J. (1967a) *Biologie et connaisance.* Paris: Gallimard.

Piaget, J. (1967b) *La construction du réel chez l'enfant.* Neuchâtel/Paris: Delachaux and Niestlé.

Piaget, J. (1967c) Les problèmes principaux de l'épistémologie des mathématiques. In *Logique et connaissance scientifique. Encyclopédie de la Pléïade*, pp. 554–96. Paris: Gallimard/NRF.

Piaget, J. (1976) *Le comportement, moteur de l'évolution.* Paris: Gallimard. Trans. D. Nicholson-Smith, *Behaviour and evolution*, 1979.

Piaget, J. and Inhelder, B. (1963) *Les images mentales, les opérations intellectuelles. Traité de psychologie expérimentale.* Paris: PUF.

Pichot, A. (1983) *Etude théorique des rapports du biologique et du psychologique chez l'animal et chez l'homme.* Louvain La Neuve: Cabay.

Pierce, R. and Pierce, L.H. (1985) The sexually abused child: a comparison of male and female victims. *Child abuse and neglect* 9, 191–9.

Pilat, J. and Jones, J.W. (1985) Identification of children of alcoholics: two empirical studies. *Alcohol health and research world* 9 (2), 27–33.

Pincus, L. and Dare, C. (1978) *Secrets in the family.* London: Faber.

Pinson, G., Demailly, A. and Favre, D. (1985) *La pensée. Approche holoscopique.* Lyon: Presses Universitaires de Lyon.

Pirandello, L. (1977) *Théatre complet*, 2 vols. Bibliothèque de la Pléïade. Paris: Gallimard.

Pittman III, F.S. (1977) In J.H. Massermann (ed.), *Current psychiatric therapies*, vol. 17, pp. 129–34. New York: Grune and Stratton.

Poincaré, H. (1963) *Dernières pensées.* Nouvelle Bibliothèque Scientifique. Paris: Flammarion.

Politzer, G. (1928) *Critique des fondements de la psychologie.* Paris: PUF, 1967.

Pollak-Cornillot, M. (1986) Freud traducteur. Une contribution à la traduction de ses propres oeuvres. *Revue française psychanalyse* 4, 1235–45.

Porot, M. (1954) *L'enfant et les relations familiales*, 8th edn. Paris: PUF.

Porte, M. (1980) Naissance d'une science: regard sur la communauté scientifique de langue allemande à la fin du XIXème siècle. Unpublished thesis, University of Paris.

Porte, M. (1987) *Mémoire de la science.* Paris: Ouvrage hors collection des cahiers de Fontenay, 2 tomes.

Prigogine, I. (1980) Sur le déterminisme. Réponse à René Thom. Loi, histoire et désertion. *Le débat* 6, 122–30.

Prigogine, I. and Stengers, I. (1979) *La nouvelle alliance: métamorphose de la science.* Paris: Gallimard.

Rabkin, R. (1977) *Strategic psychotherapy: brief and symptomatic treatment.* New York: Basic Books.

Rabkin, R. (1980) The midgame in strategic therapy. *International journal of family therapy* 2, 159–68.

Racamier, P.C. (1978) Les paradoxes des schizophrènes. In *Psychoses et états limites. Revue française psychanalyse* 42 (5–6), 877–969.

Racamier, P.C. (1980) *Les schizophrènes.* Paris: Payot.

Racamier, P.C. (1982) La paradoxicalité comme défense intra-psychique. In G. Maruani and P. Watzlawick (eds), *L'interaction en médecine et en psychiatrie.* Paris: Erès.

Racamier, P.C. (1985) Dépression, deuil et alentour. *Revue française de psychiatrie* 3 (1).

Rakoff, V. (1966) Long term effects of the concentration camp experience. *Viewpoint* March, 17–21.

Rao, A.V. (1986) Indian and Western psychiatry: a comparison. In J. Cox (ed.), *Transcultural psychiatry.* London: Croom Helm.

Recanati, F. (1981) *Les énoncés performatifs.* Paris: Les Editions de Minuit.

Reiger, K. (1981) Family therapy's missing question, why the plight of the modern family. *Journal of family therapy* 3, 293–308.

Reiss, D. (1971) Varieties of consensual experience. 1: A theory for relating family interaction to individual thinking. *Family process* 10, 1–28.

Revel, J.-F. (1976) *La tentation totalitaire.* Rev. edn, 1986, pp. 149–363. Paris: Robert Laffont.

Revel, J.-F. (1977) *La nouvelle censure.* Paris: Robert Laffont.

Richter, H.-E. (1970) *Psychanalyse de la famille. Naissance, structure et thérapie de conflits conjugaux et familiaux.* Paris: Mercure de France.

Rieben, L. (1978) *Intelligence et pensée créative.* Neuchâtel/Paris: Delachaux et Niestlé.

Roberts, S. (1988) Three models of family mediation. In R. Dingwall and J. Eekelar (eds), *Divorce mediation and the legal process.* Oxford: Clarendon Press.

Robinson, M. (1991) *Family transformation through divorce and remarriage: a systemic approach.* London: Routledge.

Robinson, M. (1993) A family systems approach to mediation. In J. Carpenter and A. Treacher (eds), *Family therapy in the '90s,* pp. 87–110. Oxford: Blackwell.

Rodgers, R.H. (1977) The family life cycle concept: past, present, future. In J. Cuisenier (ed.), *The family life cycle in European societies,* pp. 39–57. New Babylon Studies in the Social Sciences 28. Paris/The Hague: Mouton.

Rosen, S. (1982) *My voice will go with you: the teaching tales of Milton H. Erickson, MD.* New York: Norton.

Rosenberg, L. (1974) Les enfants des survivants. In E.J. Anthony and C. Koupernik (eds), *L'enfant dans sa famille,* p. 308. Paris: Masson.

Rosenblueth, A., Wiener, N. and Bigelow, J. (1943) Behavior, purpose and teleology. *Philosophy of science* 10, 18–24. Reprinted in W. Buckley (ed.), *Modern systems research for the behavioral scientist,* pp. 221–5. Chicago: Aldine, 1968.

Rosenthal, M.K. and Bergman, Z. (1986) A flow-chart presenting the decision-making process of the MRI Brief Therapy Center. *Journal of strategic and systemic therapies* 5, 1–6.

Rosolato, G. (1976) Le narcissisme. In *Narcisses. Nouvelle revue de psychanalyse* 13, 7–36.

Rosset, C. (1977) *Le réel. Traité de l'idiotie.* Paris: Les Editions de Minuit.

Rossi, E.L. (ed.) (1980) *The collected papers of Milton Erickson.* New York: Irvington.

Rougeul, F. (1983) Le lit fantôme d'Aurélie B. *Dialogue* 82 (4), 45–52.

Roussel, L. (1986) Du pluralisme des modèles familiaux dans les sociétés post-industrielles. In *Les familles d'aujourd'hui.* Colloque de Genève 17–20 September 1984. Association Internationale des Démographes de Langue Française. AIDELF, no. 2, pp. 143–51. Paris.

Roussel, L. (1989) *La famille incertaine.* Paris: Editions Odile Jacob.

Roustang, F. (1986) *Lacan, de l'équivoque à l'impasse.* Paris: Les Editions de Minuit.

Roy, A. (1985) Early parental separation and adult depression. *Archives of general psychiatry* 42, 987–91.

Rubinstein, B. and Wiener, D.R. (1967) Co-therapy teamwork relationships in family therapy. In G.H. Zuk and I. Boszormenyi-Nagy (eds), *Family therapy and disturbed families,* pp. 206–20. Palo Alto: Science and Behavior Books.

Ruesch, J. (1953) Social factors in therapy. In *Psychiatric treatment* (ARNMD/31), pp. 59–93. Baltimore: Williams and Wilkins.

Ruesch, J. and Bateson, G. (1951) *Communication, the social matrix of psychiatry*. New York: The Norton Library.

Ruffiot, A. (1979) La thérapie familiale analytique: technique et théorie. *Perspectives psychiatriques: psychothérapie psychanalytique de groupe* 71 (2), 121–43.

Ruffiot, A. (1981a) Deux modèles en thérapie familiale: la conception 'systemique' interactionelle et la conception psychanalytique 'groupaliste'. In *Passions de familles. Génitif* 3, 13–22.

Ruffiot, A. (ed.) (1981b) *La thérapie familiale psychanalytique*. Paris: Dunod.

Rushen, J. (1982) La hiérarchie sociale chez les animaux. In P.O. Hopkins (ed.), *La recherche*, 1983, vol. 14, no. 145, pp. 826–8.

Russell, B. (1903) *Principles of mathematics*. New York: Norton.

Russell, B. (1919) *Introduction to mathematical philosophy*. London: George Allen and Unwin.

Rutter, M. (1985) Infantile autism and other pervasive developmental disorders. In M. Rutter and L. Hersov (eds), *Child and adolescent psychiatry: modern approaches*, pp. 545–66. Oxford: Blackwell Scientific.

Ryle, A. (1967) *Neurosis in the ordinary family*. London: Tavistock.

Sabatini, M.R. (1985) Les enfants victimes de sévices ou de privations. Législation-juridiction. In S. Lebovici, R. Diatkine and M. Soulé (eds), *Traité de psychiatrie de l'enfant et de l'adolescent*, vol. 3, pp. 71–86. Paris: PUF.

Sabourin, P. and Ferenczi, S. (1985) *Paladin et grand vizir secret*. Paris: Editions Universitaires.

Sager, C.J. (1976) *Marriage contracts and couple therapy*. New York: Brunner Mazel.

Salomon, J.-C. (1985) Personal communication.

Sandler, J., Dare, C. and Holder, A. (1992) *The patient and the analyst*. London: Karnac Books.

Sartre, J.P. (1943) *L'être et le néant*. Paris: Gallimard.

Sartre, J.P. (1971) *L'idiot de la famille*. Paris: Gallimard.

Satir, V. (1967) *Conjoint family therapy*. Palo Alto: Science and Behavior Books.

Satir, V. (1972) *Peoplemaking*. Palo Alto: Science and Behavior Books.

Saussure, F. de (1906–11) *Cours de linguistique générale*. Paris: Payot.

Schaffer, L., Wynne, L., Day, J., Ryckoff, I. and Halperin, A. (1962) On the nature and sources of the psychiatrist's experience with the family of the schizophrenic. *Psychiatry* 25, 32–45.

Schappi, R. (1984) Soins paternels et organisations sociales dans le règne animal: faits et hypothèses. In W. Pasini et al. (eds), *Relation précoce parents–enfants*. Lyon-Villeurbanne: SIMEP.

Schatzman, M. (1973) *Soul murder: persecution in the family*. London: Allen Lane.

Scheff, T.J. (1979) *Catharsis in healing. Ritual and drama*. Berkeley, California: University of California Press.

Scheflen, A.E. (1965) Systems in human communication. Conference of the American Association for the Advancement of Science, Society for General Systems Research, 29 December. Berkeley, California: University of California Press.

Scheflen, A.E. (1972) *Body language and social order*. Englewood Cliffs, NJ: Spectrum Books.

Scheflen, A.E. (1973a) *Communicational structure: analysis of a psychotherapy transaction*. Bloomington: Indiana University Press.

Scheflen, A.E. (1973b) *How behaviour means*. New York: Gordon and Breach.

Scherrer, P. (1985) L'inceste dans la famille. Nouvelle revue d'ethno-psychiatrie. *Inceste* 3, 21–34.

Schouten, J., Hirsch, S. and Blankstein, H. (1974) *Garde ton masque*. Paris: Fleurus.

Schrödinger, E. (1944) *What is life?* Cambridge: Cambridge University Press.

Searle, J.R. (1969) *Speech acts*. Cambridge: Cambridge University Press.

Searles, H. (1959) The effort to drive the other person crazy. An element in the aetiology and psychotherapy of schizophrenia. *British journal of medical psychology* 32: 1–18.

Searles, H. (1965) *Collected papers on schizophrenia and related subjects*. New York: International University Press.

Searles, H. (1979) *Countertransference and related subjects. Selected papers*. New York: International University Press.

Segal, L. (1990) *Slow motion: changing masculinities, changing men*. London: Virago.

Segalen, M. (1981) *Sociologie de la famille*. Paris: Armand Colin.

Seghers, A. (1982) Thérapie familiale chez les maniaco–dépressifs. Luxe et nécessité? *Pratique, théorie de la pratique. 2ème journée psychanalyse et thérapie familiale systèmique*, pp. 103–19. CEF.

Seghers, A. (1984) Etude d'un cas de psychose maniaco–dépressive traité en phase aigüe par médicaments et psychothérapie familiale. *Acta psychiatrica belgica* 84, 38–49.

Selvini, M. (1985) *Mara Selvini Palazzoli, histoire d'une recherche. L'evolution de la thérapie familiale dans l'oeuvre de Mara Selvini Palazzoli*. Paris: ESF, 1987.

Selvini Palazzoli, M. (1974) *Self-starvation*. London: Human Context Books.

Selvini Palazzoli, M. (1975) Le barrage du conditionnement linguistique dans la thérapie de la famille du schizophrène. *Evolution psychiatrique* 40 (2), 423–30.

Selvini Palazzoli, M. (1983) La naissance d'une approche systémique globale. Conférence donnée au Congrès Internationale du MRI 24–27 June 1982, Nice, 'Innovations in psychotherapy and family therapy'. Published in *Thérapie familiale* 4 (1), 1983.

Selvini Palazzoli, M. (1984) Behind the scenes of the organisation: some guidelines for the expert in human relations. *Journal of family therapy* 6, 299–307.

Selvini Palazzoli, M., Anolli, L., Di Blasio, P., Giossi, L., Pisano, I., Ricci, C., Sacchi, M. and Ugazio, V. (1986) *The hidden games of organisations*. New York: Pantheon.

Selvini Palazzoli, M., Boscolo, L., Cecchin, G.F. and Prata, G. (1978) *Paradox and counterparadox*. New York: Jason Aronson.

Selvini Palazzoli, M., Boscolo, L., Cecchin, G.F. and Prata, G. (1980a) Hypothesising–circularity–neutrality: three guidelines for the conductor of the session. *Family process* 19, 3–12.

Selvini Palazzoli, M., Boscolo, L., Cecchin, G. and Prata, G. (1980b) The problem of the referring person. *Journal of marital and family therapy* 6, 3–9.

Selvini Palazzoli, M., Cirillo, S., d'Ettorre, L., Garbellini, M., Ghezzi, D., Lerma, M., Lucchini, M., Martino, C., Mazzoni, G., Mazzuchelli, F. and Nichele, M. (1976) *Le magicien sans magie*. Trans. B. Sommacal, A. Wery and P. Segond. Paris: ESF.

Selvini Palazzoli, M., Cirillo, S., Selvini, M. and Sorrentino, A.M. (1989) *Family games: general models of psychotic processes in the family*. London: Karnac Books.

Selvini Palazzoli, M. and Viaro, M. (1988) The anorectic process in the family: a six stage model as a guide for individual therapy. *Family process* 27, 129–48.

Serrano, A.C. and Wilson, N.J. (1963) Family therapy in the treatment of the brain damaged child. *Diseases of the nervous system* 24 (12).

Serrano, J.A. and Dipp, C. (1986) La famille du migrant: adaptabilité et cohésion. *Thérapie familiale* 7 (1), 73–85.

Serre, J.L., Jacquard, A. and Maruani, G. (1979) Schizophrénie, héritabilité et génétique. *Evolution psychiatrique* 4, 749–55.

Shands, H.C. (1971) *The war with words: structure and transcendance*. Paris/The Hague: Mouton.

Shazer, S. de (1982) *Patterns of brief family therapy: an ecosystemic approach*. New York: Guilford Press.

Shazer, S. de (1984) The death of resistance. *Family process* 23, 11–17.

Shazer, S. de (1985) *Keys to solution in brief therapy*. New York: Norton.

Shazer, S. de (1988) *Clues: investigating solutions in brief therapy*. New York: Norton.

Shazer, S. de (1991) *Putting difference to work*. New York: Norton.

Shazer, S. de, Berg, I.K., Lipchik, E., Nunnally, E.. Molnar, A., Gingerich, W. and Weiner-Davis, M. (1986) Brief therapy: focused solution development. *Family process* 25, 207–22.

Shazer, S. de and Molnar, A. (1984) Four useful interventions in brief family therapy. *Journal of marital and family therapy* 10, 297–304.

Shepher, J. (1971) Mate selection among second generation kibbutz adolescents and adults: incest avoidance and negative imprinting. *Archives of sexual behaviour* 4.

Shorter, E. (1975) *The making of the modern family*. London: Fontana Books.

Sieber, F.M. (1979) Social background, attitudes and personality in a three-year follow-up study of alcohol consumers. *Drug/alcohol consumers* 4, 407–17.

Signer, P., Chaperon, C. and Masson, O. (1982) La violence dans la dynamique familiale. *Génitif* 4 (5–6), 43–55.

Simeon, M. (1983) L'enfant diabétique, sa famille, ses soignants. *Thérapie familiale* 4 (3), 269–86.

Simon, F., Stierlin, H. and Wynne, L.C. (1985) *The language of family therapy. A systemic vocabulary and sourcebook*. New York: Family Process Press.

Simon, H.A. (1945–7) *Administrative behavior. A study of decision making processes in administrative organization*. New York: Free Press.

Simon, H.A. (1969) *The sciences of the artificial*. Cambridge, Mass.: MIT Press. 2nd edn, 1982.

Simon, H.A. (1979) *Models of thought*. New Haven and London: Yale University Press.

Simon, H.A. (1984a) *Les nouvelles sciences: comprendre les sciences de l'artificiel*. Paris: AFCET.

Simon, H.A. (1984b) *L'unité des arts et des sciences: la psychologie de la pensée et de la découverte*. Paris: AFCET Interfaces 15, pp. 3–16.

Simonton, S.M. (1984) *The healing family: the Simonton approach for families facing illness*. New York: Bantam Books.

Singer, M.T. and Wynne, L.C. (1965) Thought disorders and family relations of schizophrenics. IV: results and applications. *Archives of general psychiatry* 12, 201–12.

Sivadon, P. (1983) Histoire des réactions aux médicaments de 1950 à 1980 en psychiatrie. *Génitif* 5 (1), 9–15.

Sivadon, P., Mises, R. and Mises, J. (1954) Le milieu familial du schizophrène. *Evolution psychiatrique* 1, 147–57.

Sjögren, A. (1986) Le repas comme architecte de la vie familiale. *Dialogue* 93 (3), 54–61.

Skinner, B.F. (1969) *Contingencies of reinforcement: a theoretical analysis.* Meredith Corporation.

Skinner, B.F. (1971) *Beyond freedom and dignity.* New York: Alfred A. Knopf.

Skynner, A.C.R. (1981) An open-systems, group-analytic approach to family therapy. In A.S. Gurman and D.P. Kniskern (eds), *Handbook of family therapy*, pp. 39–84. New York: Brunner Mazel.

Sluzki, C.E., Beavin, J., Tarnopolsky, A. and Vernon, E. (1967) Transactional disqualification: research on the double bind. *Archives of general psychiatry* 16, 494–504. Reprinted in P. Watzlawick and J.H. Weakland (eds), *The interactional view*, pp. 208–27. New York: Norton, 1977.

Sluzki, C.E. and Ransom, D.C. (ed.) (1976) *Double bind: the foundation of the communicational approach to the family.* New York: Grune and Stratton.

Smart, R.G. and Fejer, G. (1972) Drug addicts and their parents: closing the generation gap in mood modification. *Journal of abnormal psychology* 79, 153–60.

Smart, R.G., Fejer, G. and White, J. (1972) Drug use trends among metropolitan Toronto students: a study of changes from 1968 to 1972. Unpublished manuscript of the Addiction Research Foundation, Toronto.

Smithers, D.W. (1962) An attack on cytologism. *The Lancet* 10 March, 493–9.

Snakkers, J., Ladame, F.G. and Nardini, D. (1980) La famille peut-elle empêcher l'adolescent de se suicider? *Neuropsychiatrie de l'enfance et de l'adolescence* 28 (9).

Soulé, M. (ed.) (1977) *Mère meurtrière, mère mortifère, mère mortifiée*, 2nd edn, 1979. Paris: ESF.

Soulé, M. (ed.) (1978) *Les grand-parents dans la dynamique de l'enfant.* Paris: ESF.

Soulé, M. (ed.) (1980) *Frères et soeurs*, 2nd edn, 1981. Paris: ESF.

Speck, R. (1987) L'intervention en réseau social: les thérapies de réseau, théorie et développement. In M. Elkaim (ed.), *Les pratiques de réseau: santé mental et contexte social*, pp. 21–40. Paris: ESF.

Speck, R. and Attneave, C.L. (1973) *Family networks.* New York: Pantheon.

Spencer-Brown, G. (1969) *Laws of form.* New York: E.P. Dutton, 1979.

Spender, D. (1980) *Man made language.* London: Routledge and Kegan Paul.

Spiegel, J.P. (1968) Cultural strain, family roles patterns and intrapsychic conflict. In J.G. Howells (ed.), *Theory and practice of family psychiatry*, pp. 367–89. Edinburgh: Oliver and Boyd.

Spinoza (1665–75) *Ethique.* Paris: Flammarion, 1965.

Spitz, R.A. (1957) *No and yes. On the genesis of human communication.* New York: International University Press.

Spitz, R.A. (1959) *A genetic field theory of ego formation. Its implications for pathology.* New York: New York Psychoanalytic Institute, The Freud Anniversary Series.

Spitz, R.A. (1965) *The first year of life. A psychoanalytic study of normal and deviant development of object relations.* New York: International University Press.

Stanton, M.D. (1977) The addict as savior. Heroin, death and the family. *Family process* 16, 191–7.

Stanton, M.D. (1981) Strategic approaches to family therapy. In A.S. Gurman and D.P. Kniskern (eds), *Handbook of family therapy*, pp. 362–402. New York: Brunner Mazel.

Stanton, M.D. and Todd, T. (1979) Structural family therapy with drug addicts. In E. Kaufman and P. Kaufmann (eds), *Family therapy of drug and alcohol abuse*, pp. 55–69. New York: Gardner Press.

Stanton, M.D., Todd, T., Heart, D.B., Kirxchner, S., Kleiman, J.I., Mowatt, D.T., Riley, P., Scott, S.M. and van Deusen, S.M. (1978) Heroin addiction as a family phenomenon: a new conceptual model. *American journal of drug and alcohol abuse* 5, 125–50.

Stanton, M.D., Todd, T., Steier, F., van Deusen, S.M., Marder, L.R., Rosoff, R.J., Seaman, S.F. and Skibinski, E. (1979) Family characteristics and family therapy of heroin addicts: final report 1974–1978. Report prepared for the Psychological Branch, National Institute of Drug Abuse.

Steinglass, P. (1979) Family therapy with alcoholics: a review. In E. Kaufman and P. Kaufmann (eds), *Family therapy of drug and alcohol abuse*, pp. 147–86. New York: Gardner Press.

Steinglass, P., Davis, D. and Berenson, D. (1977) Observations of conjointly hospitalized 'alcoholic couples' during sobriety and intoxication: implications for theory and therapy. *Family process* 16, 1.

Sternschuss, S. and Angel, P. (1983) In J. Bergeret (ed.), *Précis des toxicomanies*, pp. 193–200. Paris: Masson.

Stierlin, H. (1975) Countertransference in family therapy with adolescents. In M. Sugar (ed.), *The adolescent in group and family therapy.* New York: Brunner Mazel.

Stierlin, H. (1977) *Psychoanalysis and family therapy.* New York: Jason Aronson.

Stierlin, H. (1979) *Le premier entretien familial.* Trans. J. Jeudy. Paris: Delarge.

Stierlin, H. (1981) *Separating parents and their adolescents.* New York: Jason Aronson.

Stierlin, H., Wirsching, M., Haas, B., Hoffmann, F., Schmidt, G., Weber, G. and Wirsching, B. (1986) Médecine de la famille et cancer. *Thérapie familiale* 7 (1), 41–59.

Stoezel, J. (1978) *La psychologie sociale.* Paris: Flammarion, 1984.

Stoleru, S. (1979) Sept jours dans la famille d'un patient psychologique. *Evolution psychiatrique* 44 (3), 537–61.

Stoller, F.H. (1968) Use of videotape in group counseling and group therapy. *Journal of research and development in education* 1 (2).

Stone, L. (1979) *The Family, Sex and Marriage in England 1500–1800.* Harmondsworth: Penguin Books.

Sullivan, H.S. (1953) *Interpersonal theory of psychiatry.* New York: Norton.

Sun Tzu (1993) *The art of war.* Trans. J.H. Huang. New York: Quill, William Morrow.

Szasz, T. (1972) *The myth of mental illness.* London: Paladin.

Tabary, J.-C. (1991) Cognition, systémique et connaissance. In E. Andrewsky et al. (eds), *Systémique et cognition,* pp. 51–99. Paris: Dunod.

Tamura, T. and Lau, A. (1992) Connectedness vs. separateness: applicability of family therapy to Japanese families. *Family process* 31, 319–40.

Tansley, A.G. (1935) In *Science et pratique de la complexité. Actes de Colloque de Montpelier.* Paris: Documentation Française, 1986.

Tatossian, A. (1977) Les structures existentielles chez les cancéreux. *Revue de médecine psychosomatique et de psychologie médicale* 19 (2), 135–43.

Tharp, R.B. (1963) Psychological patterning in marriage. *Psychological bulletin* 60, 97–117.

Thom, R. (1972) *Stabilité structurelle et morphogénèse,* 2nd edn, 1977. Paris: Interéditions.

Thom, R. (1976a) Crise et catastrophe. In *La notion de crise. Communications,* 25, pp. 34–8. Paris: Seuil.

Thom, R. (1967b) Stabilité structurelle et catastrophes. In A. Lichnerowicz, F. Perroux and G. Gadoffre (eds), *Structure et dynamique des systèmes,* pp. 51–88. Paris: Séminaires Interdisciplinaires du Collège de France.

Thom, R. (1978) Morphogénèse et imaginaire. *Circé, Cahiers de recherche sur l'imaginaire.* Paris.

Thom, R. (1980a) Halte au hazard, silence au bruit. *Le débat* 3, 119–32.

Thom, R. (1980b) *Modèles mathématiques de la morphogénèse.* Paris: Christian Bourgois.

Thom, R. (1981a) Morphologie du sémiotique. *Semiotic inquiry* 1 (4), 301–7. Reprinted in *Apologie du logos. Histoire et philosophie des sciences,* pp. 53–65.

Thom, R. (1981b) Sur le déterminisme, en guise de conclusion. *Le débat* 15, 115–23.

Thom, R. (1983a) *Animal psychism versus human psychism. Glossogenetics: the origin and evolution of language,* ed. de Grolier. Harwood Academic Publishers.

Thom, R. (1983b) *Paraboles et catastrophes.* Paris: Flammarion.

Thom, R. (1983c) Structures cycliques en sémiotique. Complément à la thèse de Jean Petitot. *Actes sémiotiques – Documents 'sémiotique et théorie des catastrophes'* 5, 47–8.

Thom, R. (1985) Description et explication. In *Analogies. Psychanalyse et thérapie familiale systémique,* pp. 37–48. Paris: Centre d'Etude de la Famille Association.

Thom, R. (1986) Cancer and the theory of the organizer: editorial introduction. *Cancer journal* 1 (1), 38.

Thom, R. (1988) *Esquisse d'une sémiophysique. Physique aristotélicienne et théorie des catastrophes.* Paris: Interéditions.

Thom, R. (1989) Théorie des systèmes et théorie des catastrophes. In J. Miermont and R. Neuberger (eds), *René Thom expliqué par lui-même,* vol. 1, pp. 5–81. Paris: PISTES.

Thom, R. (1990a) In K. Pomian (ed.) *La querelle du déterminisme. Le débat.* Paris: Gallimard.

Thom, R. (1990b) Morphologie du sémiotique. In *Apologie du logos,* pp. 53–9. Paris: Hachette.

Thom, R. (1992) *Esquisse d'une sémiophysique,* 2nd edn. Paris: Interéditions.

Tinbergen, E.A. and Tinbergen, N. (1972) Early childhood autism: an ethological approach. *Zugleich Beiheft zur Zeitsch für Tierpsychologie* Berlin/Hamburg: Parey.

Tinbergen, N. (1947) *L'étude de l'instinct.* Trans. B. de Zelicourt and F. Bourliere. Paris: Payot, 1971.

Todd, E. (1983) *La troisième planète. Structures familiales et systèmes idéologiques.* Paris: Seuil.

Todd, E. (1984) *L'enfance du monde. Stuctures familiales et développement.* Paris: Seuil.

Todd, E. (1990) *L'invention de l'Europe.* Paris: Seuil.

Todd, E. and Le Bras, H. (1981) *L'invention de France.* Paris: Pluriel.

Todorov, T. (1977) *Théories du symbole*. Paris: Seuil. English trans. C. Porter. Oxford, Blackwell, 1982.

Toman, W. (1961) *Family constellation: its effects on personality and social behaviour*. New York: Springer.

Tomm, K. (1987a) Interventive interviewing. Part 1. *Family process* 26, 3–13.

Tomm, K. (1987b) Interventive interviewing. Part 2. *Family process* 26, 167–83.

Tomm, K. (1988) Interventive interviewing. Part 3. *Family process* 27, 1–15.

Treacher, A. (1987) 'Family therapists are potentially damaging to families and their wider networks': discuss. In S. Walrond-Skinner and D. Watson (eds), *Ethical issues in family therapy*, pp. 87–103. London: Routledge and Kegan Paul.

Treacher, A. and Carpenter, J. (1982) 'Oh no! Not the Smiths again!' An exploration of how to identify and overcome 'stuckness' in family therapy. Part I: Stuckness involving the contextual and technical aspects of therapy. *Journal of marital and family therapy* 4, 285–305.

Treacher, A. and Carpenter, J. (eds) (1984) *Using family therapy*. Oxford: Blackwell.

Trillat, E. (1986) *Histoire de l'hystérie*. Paris: Seghers.

Tseng, W. (1975) The nature of somatic complaints among psychiatric patients: the Chinese case. *Comparative psychiatry* 16, 237–45.

Trossman, B. (1968) Adolescent children of concentration camp-survivor. *Journal of the Canadian Psychiatric Association* 13 (2), 121–3.

Turing, A.M. (1937) On computable numbers, with an application to the *enscheidungsproblem*. *Proceedings of the London Mathematical Society* 43, 544.

Turing, A.M. (1950) Computing machinery and intelligence. *Mind* 59 (2236), 433–60. Reprinted in M.A. Bodem (ed.), *The philosophy of artificial intelligence*, pp. 40–66. Oxford: Oxford University Press, 1990.

Uexküll, J. von (1956) *Mondes animaux et monde humain, suivi de théorie de la signification*. Trans. P. Muller. Paris: Gonthier.

Valéry, P. (1973) *Cahiers 1919. Edition de la Pléïade*, p. 562. Paris: Gallimard.

Vappereau, J.M. (1985) *Essaim, le groupe fondamental du noeud*. Paris: Point Hors-Ligne.

Varela, F. (1979) *Principles of biological autonomy*. New York/Oxford: North Holland.

Verbizier, J. de, Maruani, G., Arbousse-Bastide, H. and Gosselin, Ph. (1976) Quelques aspects de la vie quotidienne des psychotiques en hospitalisation partielle. *Annales médico-psychologiques* 2 (1), 153–64.

Vernant, J.-P. (1965) *Mythe et pensée chez les Grecs: études de psychologie historique*. Paris: François Maspéro.

Vickers, G. (1968) *Value systems and social processes*. New York: Basic Books.

Vidal, J.-M. (1976a) L'empreinte chez les animaux. *La recherche* 63.

Vidal, J.-M. (1976b) *Empreinte filiale et sexuelle. Réflexions sur le processus d'attachement d'après une étude expérimentale sur le coq domestique*, 2 vols. Rennes: University of Rennes.

Vidal, J.-M. (1985) Explications biologiques et anthropologiques de l'interdit de l'inceste. Nouvelle revue d'ethno-psychiatrie. *Inceste* 3, 75–107.

Vidal, J.-M. (1986) Les fonctions visant à la satisfaction des besoins primaires. In J. Piaget, P. Mounoud and J.P. Brounckart (eds), *La psychologie. Encyclopédie La Pléïade*, pp. 160–228. Paris: Gallimard.

Vogel, G. and Angemann, H. (1967) *Atlas zur biologie*. Munich: Deutscher Taschenbuch Verlag.

Waddington, C.H. (1957) *The strategy of the genes*. London: Allen and Unwin.

Waddington, C.H. (1975) *The evolution of an evolutionist*. Edinburgh: Edinburgh University Press.

Waddington, C.H. (1977) *Tools for thought*. St Albans: Paladin.

Wallon, H. (ed.) (1938) *Encyclopédie française, vol. 8: La vie mentale*. Paris: Larousse.

Walrond-Skinner, S. (1976) *Family therapy: the treatment of natural systems*. London: Routledge and Kegan Paul.

Walrond-Skinner, S. (1978) Indications and contra-indications for the use of family therapy. *Journal of child psychology and psychiatry* 19, 57–62.

Walrond-Skinner, S. (1986) *Dictionary of psychotherapy*. London: Routledge and Kegan Paul.

Walrond-Skinner, S. (1987) Introduction. In S. Walrond-Skinner and D. Watson (eds), *Ethical issues in family therapy*, pp. 1–6. London: Routledge.

Walter, J.L. and Peller, J.E. (1992) *Becoming solution-focused in brief therapy*. New York: Brunner Mazel.

Walters, M. (1988) *The invisible web: gender patterns in family relationships*. New York/London: Guilford Press.

Walters, M. (1990) A feminist perspective in family therapy. In R.J. Perelberg and A. Miller (eds), *Gender and power in families*, pp. 13–33. London/New York: Tavistock/Routledge.

Watzlawick, P. (1963) A review of the double bind theory. *Family process* 2 (1), 132–53.

Watzlawick, P. (1976) *How real is real? Communication, disinformation, confusion*. New York: Random House.

Watzlawick, P. (1978a) *The language of change. Elements of therapeutic communication*. New York: Basic Books.

Watzlawick, P. (1978b) *Séminaire de thérapie familiale*. Grenoble: IREC, no. 36.

Watzlawick, P. (1981) Les prophéties à coup sûr. *Passions de familles. Génitif* 3 (1–3), 35–6.

Watzlawick, P. (ed.) (1984) *The invented reality*. New York: Norton.

Watzlawick, P., Beavin, J. and Jackson, D.D. (1967) *Pragmatics of human communication. A study of interactional patterns, pathologies and paradoxes*. New York: Norton.

Watzlawick, P. and Weakland, J.H. (eds) (1977) *The interactional view: studies at the Mental Research Institute, Palo Alto, 1965–1974*. New York: Norton.

Watzlawick, P., Weakland, J.H. and Fisch, R. (1974) *Change: principles of problem formation and problem resolution*. New York: Norton.

Weakland, J.H. (1974) 'Somatique familiale': une marge négligée. In P. Watzlawick and J.H. Weakland (eds), *Sur l'interaction*, pp. 456–72. Paris: Seuil, 1981.

Weakland, J.H. (1977) Schizophrenia: basic problems in sociocultural investigation. In P. Watzlawick and J.H. Weakland (eds), *The interactional view*, pp. 163–92. New York: Norton.

Weakland, J.H. (1983) Family therapy with individuals. *Journal of strategic and systemic therapies* 2, 1–9.

Weakland, J.H., Fisch, R., Watzlawick, P. and Bodin, A. (1974) Brief therapy: focused problem resolution. *Family process* 13, 141–68.

Weakland, J.H. and Jackson, D.D. (1958) Patient and therapist observations of the circumstances of a schizophrenic episode. *Archives of neurology and psychiatry* 79, 554–74.

Weaver, W. and Shannon, C.E. (1949) *The mathematical theory of communication*. Illinois: University of Illinois Press.

Weber, G. and Simon, F.B. (1988) Systemic individual therapy. In J. Hargens (ed.), *Systemic therapy: a European perspective*, vol. 1, pp. 33–53. Borgman. Broadstairs: Kent.

Weblin, J.E. (1963) Psychogenesis in asthma: an appraisal with a view to family research. *British journal of medical psychology* 36, 211–25.

Weiselberg, H. (1992) Family therapy and ultra-orthodox Jewish families: a structural approach. *Journal of family therapy* 14, 305–30.

Weisman, A.D. (1970) The psychiatric and the geriatric patient. Partial grief in family members and others who care for the elderly patient. *Journal of geriatric psychiatry* 3, 65–9.

Weiss, P. (1963) Cells interactions. *Proceedings of the 5th Canadian Cancer Conference*, pp. 241–86. New York: Academic Press.

Whan, M. (1983) Tricks of the trade: questionable theory and practice in family therapy. *British journal of social work* 13, 321–37.

Whitaker, C.A. (1962) First stage techniques in the experiential psychotherapy of chronic schizophrenic patients. In J.H. Masserman (ed.), *Current psychiatric therapies*, vol. 2. New York: Grune and Stratton.

Whitaker, C.A. (1973) Psychotherapy of the absurd: with special emphasis on the psychotherapy of aggression. *Family process* 14 (1), 1–16.

Whitaker, C.A, (1978) Co-therapy of chronic schizophrenia. In M.M. Berger (ed.), *Beyond the double bind: communication and family systems*, pp. 155–75. New York: Brunner Mazel.

Whitaker, C.A., Felder, R.E. and Warkentin, J. (1965) Le contre-transfert dans le traitement familial de la schizophrénie. In I. Boszormenyi-Nagy and J.L. Framo (eds), *Intensive family therapy*. New York: Harper and Row.

Whitaker, C.A. and Keith, D.V. (1981) Symbolic-experiential family therapy. In A.S. Gurman and D.P. Kniskern (eds), *Handbook of family therapy*, pp. 187–225. New York: Brunner Mazel.

Whitaker, C.A. and Malone, T.P. (1953) *The roots of psychotherapy*. New York: Blakston.

White, M. (1979) Structural and strategic approaches to psychosomatic families. *Family process* 18, 303–14.

White, M. (1989a) The externalising of the problems. *Dulwich Centre newsletter*, Summer 1988–9, pp. 3–21. Adelaide: Dulwich Centre Publications.

White, M. (1989b) *Literate means to therapeutic ends*. Adelaide: Dulwich Centre Publications.

Whitehead, A.N. and Russell, B. (1910–13) *Principia mathematica*. Cambridge: Cambridge University Press.

Whitman, C.O. (1919) The behavior of pigeons. *Publications of the Carnegie Institute* 257, 1–161.

Wickler, W. (1967) Les signaux socio-sexuels et leur imitation intra-spécifique chez les primates. In D. Morris (ed.), *L'éthologie des primates*. Brussels: Complexe, 1978.

Wickler, W. (1971) *Les lois naturelles du mariage*. Trans. P. Leccia. Paris: Flammarion.

Widlöcher, D. (1970) *Freud et le problème du changement*. Paris: PUF.

Widlöcher, D. (1983a) *Les logiques de le dépression*. Paris: Fayard, Les temps des sciences.

Widlöcher, D. (ed.) (1983b) *Le ralentissement dépressif. Psychiatrie ouverte*. Paris: PUF.

Widlöcher, D. (1986) *Métapsychologie du sens*. Paris: PUF.

Wiener, N. (1948) Cybernetics. *Scientific American* 179, 14–18.

Wiener, N. (1971) *Cybernétique et société*. Union générale d'édition. Paris: Christian Bourgois Dominique de Roux.

Wiener, N. (1975) *Cybernetics or control and communication in the animal and the machine*, 2nd edn. Cambridge, Mass.: MIT Press.

Wiener, P. (1983) *Structure et processus dans la psychose*. Paris: PUF.

Wilden, A. (1972) *System and structure. Essays in communication and exchange*. London: Tavistock.

Wildgen, W. (1982) *Catastrophe theoretic semantics*. Amsterdam/Philadelphia: John Benjamins Publishing Company.

Willi, J. (1982) *La relation du couple. Le concept de collusion*. Trans. R. Monjardet. Neuchâtel-Paris: Delachaux et Niestlé.

Williams, M. (1974) A propos de la psychanalyse d'un enfant de survivants. In E.J. Anthony and C. Koupernik (eds), *L'enfant dans sa famille*, pp. 303–5. Paris: Masson.

Wilson, E.O. (1975) *Sociobiology: the new synthesis*. Cambridge, Mass.: Belknap Press of Harvard University Press.

Winch, R.F. (1958) *Mate selection: a study of complementary needs*. New York: Harper and Row.

Winkin, Y. (ed.) (1981) *La nouvelle communication*. Paris: Seuil.

Winnicott, D.W. (1951) Objets transitionnels et phénomènes transitionnels. In D.W. Winnicott (ed.), *De la pédiatrie à la psychanalyse*, pp. 109–25.

Winnicott, D.W. (1952) Psychosis and child care. In D.W. Winnicott, *Collected papers*. London: Tavistock.

Winnicott, D.W. (1958) *Collected papers: through paediatrics to psychoanalysis*. London: Tavistock.

Winnicott, D.W. (1960a) Ego distortion in terms of true self and false self. In D.W. Winnicott, *The maturational process and the facilitating environment*. London: Hogarth Press, 1965.

Winnicott, D.W. (1960b) The theory of parent–infant relationships. *International journal of psychoanalysis* 41.

Winnicott, D.W. (1963) Communicating and not communicating. In D.W. Winnicott, *The maturational process and the facilitating environment*. London: Hogarth Press.

Winnicott, D.W. (1965) *The maturational process and the facilitating environment*. London: Hogarth Press.

Winnicott, D.W. (1971) *Playing and reality*. London: Tavistock.

Winokur, G. (1974) The division of depressive illness into depression spectrum disease and pure depression disease. *Pharmacopsychiatry* 9, 5–13.

Wittgenstein, L. (1921) *Tractatus logico-philosophicus*, trans. D.F. Pearce and B.F. McGuiness. London: Routledge, 1974–89.

Wittgenstein, L. (1951) *On certainty*. Oxford: Basil Blackwell.

Wolin, S. and Bennett, L.A. (1984) Family rituals. *Family process* 23, 401–20.

Woodcock, A.E.R. and Poston, T. (1974) *A geometrical study of the elementary catastrophes*. Berlin: Springer Verlag.

Wynne, L.C. (1961) The study of intrafamilial alignments and splits in exploratory family therapy. In N.W. Ackerman, F.L. Beatman and S.N. Sherman (eds), *Exploring the base for family therapy*. New York: Family Service Association of America.

Wynne, L.C. (1965) Indications and contra-indications for exploratory family therapy. In I. Boszormenyi-Nagy and J.L. Framo (eds), *Intensive family therapy*. New York: Harper and Row.

Wynne, L.C. (1978) Knotted relationships, communication, deviances and metabinding. In M.M. Berger (ed.), *Beyond the double bind: communication and family systems*, pp. 179–88. New York: Brunner Mazel.

Wynne, L.C., Ryckoff, I.M., Day, J. and Hirsch, S.I. (1958) Pseudo-mutuality in the family relations of schizophrenics. *Psychiatry* 21, 205–20.

Wynne, L.C. and Singer, M.T. (1963) Thought disorders and family relations of schizophrenics. *Archives of general psychiatry* 9, 191–8.

Yankelevitch, V. (1982) In *Bulletin de l'association française de psychiatrie et de psychopathologie sociales. La mort* 14, 215.

Young, M. and Wilmot, P. (1962) *Family and Kinship in East London*. Harmondsworth: Pelican Books.

Yung-Chen Lu (1976) *Singularity theory and an introduction to catastrophe theory*. Berlin: Springer Verlag.

Zadeh, L. (1965) Fuzzy sets. *Information and control* 8, 338–53.

Zadeh, L. (1976) Fuzzy logic and approximate reasoning. *Synthèse* 30, 407–28.

Zeeman, E.C. (1976) Duffing's equation in brain modelling. In *Catastrophe theory: selected papers*. London: Addison Wesley, 1980.

Zeeman, E.C. (1980) *Catastrophe theory: selected papers*. London: Addison Wesley.

Zeeman, E.C. (1985) La théorie des catastrophes en psychiatrie et en psychologie. In J. Miermont (ed.), *Mythes et modèles scientifiques en psychothérapie individuelle et en thérapie familiale. Actualités psychiatriques*, 9.

Zinoviev, A. (1976) *Les hauteurs béantes*. Trans. W. Belerowitch. Lausanne: L'âge d'homme, 1977.

Zinoviev, A. (1980) *Nous et l'Occident*. Trans. W. Belerowitch. Paris: Gallimard, 1982.

Zinoviev, A. (1980–1) *Ni liberté, ni égalité, ni fraternité*. Trans. J. Lahana. Lausanne: L'âge d'homme, 1983.

Zinoviev, A. (1981) *Le communisme comme réalité*. Trans. J. Michaud. Paris/Lausanne: Juillard/L'âge d'homme.

Zygmond, M. and Boorhem, H. (1989) Ethical decision making in family therapy. *Family process* 28, 269–80.

INDEX

abduction, therapeutic 407–10
Abraham, K. 259
absence of absence relations 258, 327–8
absent member manoeuver 1
abstention, therapeutic 130, 410, 440
abstinence, rule of 1–2, 307
abstraction 48–9
absurd, psychotherapy of the 2
abuse 15, 16, 119, 157–8, 174, 192–3
accommodation 11, 239
acculturation 2–4, 31, 90, 109, 256, 368, 386
accustomed *see* becoming accustomed
Ackerman, N. W. xvii, xli, 8, 148, 223, 298–9, 336, 415, 428
Ackermann, W. 194
acting out 4–5, 93, 298, 437
action 5
activation 144
actualizing techniques 6
actuogenesis 6–7, 43, 322, 349
Acworth, A. 233
Adams, J. F. 369
adaptation 302, 375
addiction, drugs 40–1, 108–10
Ades, J. 15
adjectives, paradoxical 281
admission, of impotence 7–8
adolescence 8–9: aggression 14; boundaries 378; psychopathic 398; sexuality 360; suicide 9–10; tasks 402; violence 436
adoptive families 299
adults, psychiatric treatment 398–9
affects 234, 250
affiliation 10–11, 239, 271
ageing 234, 404
aggression 12, 13–14
agonistic behaviour 11–14, 136
agreement 14–15, 62, 145
Ahola, T. 370
Ainsworth, M. D. 10
Alberoni, F. 241
Alcoholics Anonymous 17
alcoholism 9, 15–19, 40–1, 55, 109, 314
Aleksandrowicz, R. 58
alethic modalities 19–20, 232
algebra, primary 348
Alger, I. 436

algorithms 20–1, 71, 179, 227, 236, 390
alienation 21–6: and autonomy 22, 25; bio-ethology 22; desacralization 335; and differentiation 98; and identity 33, 188; intervenors 411; and meaning 354; and narcissism 267; and networks 269; paradox 24–5; pseudo-hostility 302; psychopathology 21–2; social 23–5; splitting 372; and systemic modelling 159; therapeutic 25–6, 238, 365; and transference 22–3, 423
alignment 26
allergies 308
alliances 26, 422
Alliot, M. 2
Allyn, G. 40, 78, 191
alpha elements 26–7, 147
Ambrose, J. A. 330
American Association of Marital and Family Therapy 120–1
Amiel, C. 224, 225
amnesia, partial 163–4
anaclitic object choice 82
analogic coding 27–8, 280
analogic reasoning 245
ancestors 28–9
anchor 29, 368
Anderson, T. 237
Andolfi, M. xli, 2, 127, 184, 248, 301, 343, 344, 401, 402
Andreasen, N. 177
Angel, Pierre xxxvi (n25), xli, 9, 109, 170–1, 177, 296, 426, 436, 438
Angel, Sylvie xxxvi (n25), xli
Angelo, C. 2, 127, 248
Angemann, Hartmut 137
anorexia nervosa xxix, 29–32, 309
anthropology 79, 272–3, 325, 387–8
Anti-Oedipus (Deleuze and Guattari) xxviii
anti-psychiatry xxvii–xxviii
anti-theatre 32–4
Anzieu, D. 102, 145–6, 269, 277, 283, 306, 307, 351, 368, 422–3
Aponte, H. J. 6, 26, 100, 153, 232, 329, 378
Apostel, Léo 68–9

appeasement 12, 255
appetitive behaviours 211, 212, 360–1
archetypes: couples 83–4; relational 113, 114, 154, 268, 325–7
Aries, Philippe 368
Aristotle 258–9, 358, 407
arithmetic 347–9
art, and the sacred 334
artificial intelligence xix, 386–7
Asen, K. E. 131, 399, 400
Ashby, R. xvi–xvii, xix, 43, 45, 132, 154, 227
assemblage 35, 363
Association for Family Therapy (UK) 120, 420
asylum 213
Asylums (Goffman) xxi–xxii
Atlan, H. L. 207, 314, 319, 346, 424
attachment behaviour 35: autism 203; in couples 150, 359–60; and cybernetics 88; and ethology 136; imprinting 35, 191; and narcissism 268; smile 145
attitudes 35–6, 392, 403
Attneave, C. L. 269, 270
attractors 37, 57: coupling of resonances 15; in elementary catastrophes 112; family interaction 327, 359; forms of organization 373, 374; in information 208; in machine 237; in memory 424; metabolic form 175–6; metacommunication 246–7; reciprocal 355; strange 37, 57, 352, 379
Audisio, M. 175
auditory communication 260
Auerbach, E. 253
Augustine, Saint 258
Ausloos, G. 27, 80, 93, 112, 344–5, 410
Austin, J. L. xxii, 69, 286–7, 371
authority 272–3, 287
autism 201–4: boundaries 46; differentiation 99; mother's attitude 324; victimization 323; withdrawal of gaze xxi, 172
auto-imprinting 192
automata xix, 346

autonomy 37–8: and abduction 409–10; and alienation 22, 25; differentiation 97–8; individual 119
Avery, N. C. 234

Bachelard, Gaston 65
Bahnson, C. B. 54
Baillet, J. 133
Baker Miller, J. 173
Balandier, G. 3
Balint, M. 133, 313, 403
ball, topology 39–40
Baltat, F. 226
Bandler, R. 270, 271, 280, 380, 381, 382
Barel, Y. 213
barriers *see* boundaries
Barthes, Roland 30
Bassine, Philippe 432
Bastide, R. 2, 3, 367
Bateson, Gregory xl–xli: abduction 408, 409; acculturation 2; alcoholism 15, 16, 17; algorithms 20, 21; alienation 24; brief interactional therapy 48–51; change 56–7; codes 34; communication theory xx, xxiii, 67, 69, 432–3; context 79; cultural relativism 65; 'Culture contact and schismogenesis' 14; 'Cybernetic Explanation' 69; determinism, circular xxxix; double bind xvi–xvii, 41, 104–7, 341–2; eco-etho-anthropology 79; ecosystem and mind 111, 352; eidos/ethos 111–12; epistemology 64, 117; ethos 111–12, 124–5; evolution 125, 375; 'Form, substance and difference' 239; game theory 169, 170; gender 172; genetics 176–7; heuristics 180; information 204, 209; learning levels 228–9; map and territory 290, 330–1, 406; metacommunication 246, 258, 289, 290, 371; metaphor 247; metapsychology 250; *Mind and nature: a necessary unity* 54, 253–4, 374, 407; mother's role xvi; negentropy 116; neurolinguistic programming 271; paradox 283; Perceval, John xxvii; phantasy 288; play 5, 290; power 174, 292, 293; psychoanalysis 303; redundancy 244–5, 324–5; repression 321; residual

relations 327–8; sacrament 334; schismogenesis 97, 216; schizophrenia 197, 339; *Steps to an ecology of mind* 374; system flexibility 184; 'Towards a theory of schizophrenia' 185, 397; unit of mind 353
Bateson, William 176
battered children 437
battered parents 438
battered women 437
Baudrillard, J. 207
becoming accustomed 12, 35, 40–1, 136, 179, 192, 382
Beels, C. 415
behaviour: agonistic 11–14, 136; analogic 27; and domestication 103; hierarchies 212, 411; instinctive 211–12, 360–1; linguistic 392–3; mediation 5–6; paralinguistic 392; performative 286; periodic 37; profiles, child 138–40
behavioural disorders 310
behaviourism 41–2, 88
Behling, D. W. 16
belief systems 121–2
belonging rituals 332–3
Ben-Ishay, Y. 48
Benghozi, P. 270
Benjamin, J. 173
Bennett, L. A. 123
Benoit, J.-C. 25, 213–14
Bentovim, A. 193
Benveniste, E. 69, 287, 357
Berenson, David 18
Berenstein, I. 368
Berezin, M. A. 234
Berg, I. K. 370
Berger, M. M. 46, 436
Bergeret, J. 267, 436
Bergman, Z. 50
Berkeley, George 75
Bernard, C. 61
Bernard, Claude 180–1, 183
Berquez, G. 203
Berrendonner, A. 69, 287
Bertalanffy, Ludwig von: general systems theory xix, 68, 117, 174–5, 346; homeostasis 183; isomorphisms 219; living systems 115–16; open systems 118, 418; symbols 385–6; *Systems view of man* 387
Bertrando, P. 252–3
beta elements 26–7
Bettelheim, Bruno 22, 147, 397
bifurcation 42–3, 101, 399
bifurcation catastrophe 43, 113, 114, 246–7, 352
bijection 219

binds *see* double binds
Bion, W. R. 26–7, 46, 234, 300
Birdwhistell, R. L. xx, 390, 436
Birtchnell, J. 233
Bishop, D. S. 335
Black, D. 234
black box 43–5, 236, 237: family system 153; general systems theory 174–5; in generalized catastrophes 176
Bleuler, E. 46, 106, 338, 339–40, 341
Bloch, D. 72, 160, 311
blood pressure, high 308
Blurton-Jones, N. G. 330
body manipulators 392
Boisot, M. 277
Bolton Finley, C. 257–8
Bompart, A. 152
bonding 12
Bonnafe, L. 25
Bonnefoy, Y. 264
Boorhem, H. 120, 121
Boscolo, L. 252, 399, 404, 419
Boston Family Institute 343
Boszormenyi-Nagy, Ivan: alignment 26; contextual therapy xli, 121; fairness 127; family emotional oneness 134; intensive therapy 279; ledger 198, 229, 284, 327; legacy and merit 92–3; loyalty 142, 235; multi-directional partiality 261; parentification xvii, 125–6, 285–6; projective identification 335; scapegoat 336; systemic work 400; transgenerational memories 424, 426; trust 430–1
Boudon, R. 148, 364
bound families 54
boundaries 1, 45–8, 378: communication 160; and fusion 166; parentification 286; phantasy 289; quality 68, 256; ritual 331; and territory 153, 405
Bouras, M. 310
Bourgine, P. 409
Bourguignon, O. 438
Bourricaud, F. 148, 364
Bovet, P. 244
Bowen, Murray: ancestral relations 29; autism 202; boundaries 46; catastrophes 130; co-therapy 80, 81; differentiation of self 18, 97, 98–9, 166, 233, 425, 427; eidos 112; ethos 125; family emotional oneness 133–4; family life-cycles 141; family projection 146; family

system xli, 62; genogram 178; global theory of marriage 85; instinctive behaviours 211; memory 424; shock waves xxxix, 362–3; sibling position 363; systemic work 400, 415; triangles 96, 217, 356, 428; undifferentiation 342

Bowlby, John: aggression 13; attachment behaviour 35, 88, 145, 191; mourning 257, 258; phantasy 288; ritualization 330

Bowlby-West, L. 233

Box, S. 216

brain, model of xvi–xvii

brain damage 48

Braverman, L. 174

Bretherton, I. 10

Breton, André 185

Breuer, J. 165

Bridgman, F. 127

Brief Family Therapy Center xxiii, 50, 369

brief therapies 20, 48–52, 108, 278, 369

Brillouin, Léon 115

Brodeur, C. 159, 305–6

Brossard, A. 258

Brouwer, L. E. J. 75

Brown, G. W. 233

Bruch, Hilde 30, 31

Bruggen, P. 233, 398

Bruner, Jérôme 117, 385

Brusset, B. 30, 32

bulimia 30

Burck, C. 173, 174

butterfly catastrophe 114–15, 129–30

Byng-Hall, J. 232, 258, 265, 398, 427

Cade, B. W. 51, 182, 376

Caillé, P. xli: anorexia nervosa 32; couples 86; intervention 251; psychiatric institution 214; reality and ritual 331; self-referentiality 150, 151, 255; systemic modelling 397, 404, 405; triadic questioning 428

Caillot, J. P. 307

calculus 349–50

calumny 53, 204

Cameron, D. 173

Campbell, D. 253

cancer 53–5, 394–9

Canguilhem, G. 312

canonical representation 152

Cantor, G. 220, 281, 406

Caplow, Theodore 62–3

carcinogenesis 394–5

cardinal values 55, 223

caretaking behaviour 137

Carnap, R. 68

Carpenter, J. xiv, 118, 271, 378, 420

Carrer, P. 90

Carter, E. A. 141, 178, 233, 400, 427

Carton, M. 55

Casement, P. 399

Cassiers, L. 18–19

Cassou, B. 177

catastrophe theory xiv, xl, xlii: bifurcation catastrophes 43, 113, 114, 246–7, 352; butterfly catastrophes 114–15, 129–30; change 57; conflict catastrophes 114; crises 87; cusp catastrophes 113–14, 128, 129; double bind 128; elementary catastrophes 42–3, 44, 112–15, 129–30, 161, 326, 363, 373–4, 434; family catastrophes 128–30; family systems 128–30; fold catastrophe 113; generalized catastrophes 130, 175–6, 338, 374; and holism 181; homeostasis 184; and meaning 250; messages 245; metapsychology 250–1; mind 254; models 30–1; swallowtail catastrophes 114; symbolic references 383; and topology 417–18

catatonia 342

categories theory 262

catharsis 314, 334–5

cathexis 188, 249, 303

Cauchois, E. 128, 130

Cauffman, L. 151

causality xxxix, 362–3, 374

Cayrol, A. 29, 270

Cazeneuve, J. 148

Cecchin, G. 119, 252, 271, 399

Centre d'Étude et de Recherche sur la Famille 419–20

Centre de Traitement et de Réadaptation Sociale xxvii

cephalalgias 308

change 56–7: and conflict 366; and crisis 88; dynamics 159; first-order and second-order 49–50, 87; genetic 374–5; interactional 167; non-change 102; provocation of 301; qualitative 68, 70; unit of 125, 352, 433–4

Change: Principles of Problem Formation and Problem Resolution (Watzlawick) 49, 51

channel theory 171

chaos theory 65, 134, 164–5, 275–6, 319

chaotic families 57

Chartier, J. P. 438

Chaslin 340–1

Chemama, R. 163

chemotherapy xxv–xxvi: *see also* drugs

Chesnaies, J.-C. 436–7

Chevalier, J. 383

Chicago school 309

child abuse 57–8

Child Support Act, UK (1991) 243

children xvi: battered 437; behaviour profiles 138–40; growth 310; psychiatric treatment 397–8; seduction 77; sexual development 360; survivor parents 58–60; *see also* parents

Children Act, UK (1989) 243

Children's Panel, Scotland 231

Chodorow, N. 173

choice of love object 82–4, 146, 328

Chomsky, N. 69, 249, 326, 380, 382

Choquet, M. 9

chreods 60, 246, 290, 321, 331, 355, 384

Christian, D. xli, 335

circular questions 54, 60, 61

circularity 60–2: communication theory 68; generalized catastrophes 130; illness 390; interactions 161; networks 269; neutrality 271; scapegoat 161; self-referentiality 155; systemic concept, Milan 172–3, 252

Clausewitz, Carl von 412

clinophilia 368–9

closed set 417

closed systems 62, 174

closure 65, 149, 324, 346–7

Cloutier, J. 66

Clues: investigating solutions in brief therapy (de Shazer) 369

coach 62

coalition 26, 62–4, 288, 292, 328–9, 372, 376, 428

codes xx, 34–5, 244, 294–5

coding 27–8, 34, 94, 99–100, 280, 384

coenaesthesia 69–70, 382

Cohen, Y. 3

Colas, Yves 95

Coleman, S. 174

Colin, M. 241

collective unconscious 219, 220, 432

Collier, A. 120

Collingwood, R. G. xxii

Collonge, M. 30

command, unity of 365–6

commensalism 30

communal families 273

communal individuals 65–6

communication 66, 232, 309:
auditory 260; axiomatics
293–4; boundaries 160;
calumny 53, 204; chaos
65; circularity 68; content
and relationship 14;
day-to-day 69; delinquent
modalities 25, 389; deontic
modality 96; disturbed 201;
family 145, 356, 393;
hierarchy 33; human xxii;
iconic 81, 188; and
information xxii, 206;
interrupted 164; language
and interpretation 122–3,
260; and manipulation 238;
McLuhan xxiii; memory 66;
non-verbal xx, xxi, 28;
object as 248; paradoxes
48–9, 246, 286; pathological
286, 393; play 289–91;
prescription 297–8; and
projection 55; and ritual 66,
331; scandalmongering 335;
schizophrenic xx, 106, 295;
self-performative utterances
118; semantics 353–6;
semiotics of 68–9, 356–8;
social 67–8, 70, 150; syntax
of 280, 380–1, 390–3;
systemic modelling 406;
transactions 421; verbal
246; visual 172, 260; see also
metacommunications;
paracommunication;
pragmatics of
communication
communication media
391–2
communication systems 66–7,
69–70, 254–5, 258–61
communication theory
xvi–xvii, 39–40, 67–70,
84–5, 104–5, 317–18,
432–3
communicational-systemic
therapies 157
Compernolle, T. 312
competence 122, 209–10, 214
complementarity 24, 223,
298–9, 337, 338
complex systems 71–2
complexity xix, 70–2, 116,
181, 227, 264, 301, 347
computers xix, 249, 321, 386
conditioning, operant 41
conductors and reactors
415–16
conflict catastrophe 114
conflicts: and change 366;
contextual 79; couples 97,
123, 315–16; and
intervention 298; leadership
81; loyalty 412, 429; marital
256; transgenerational 93
confusion technique 186

conjugal relations 13, 84:
see also couples; marital
breakdown; marriage
connectedness xxii–xxiii, 73
consensus 421
constricted families 216
constructivism 73–9
consummatory behaviour
211–12, 361
contexts 28–9, 79, 93, 178,
234–5, 391–2
contextual therapy xli, 121
contracts, between partners 82
contrary injunction 80
conversion, centripetal /
centrifugal 27
Coogler, O. J. 242
Cook, M. 171–2
Cooper, D. xxxv (n19), 32
cooperative therapies 157
coronary patients 307–8
corporal habitus 392
Corraze, J. 258
cosmetic habitus 392
Cosnier, J. 69–70, 258
Costa de Beauregard, A. 68
co-therapy 80–2, 290–1
Cottet, A. 95
Couffignal, Louis 88, 131
counter-transference 8–9, 414,
422, 423
couples 82–7: attachment
behaviour 150, 359–60;
conflicts 97, 123, 315–16;
lack of complementarity
223; marital breakdown 240;
schismogenesis 337–8;
violence 437; see also
marriage
Courtes, J. 19, 69, 114, 232,
238, 358
creatura 117
CRED guidelines 120
crisis 87–8, 300–2, 335
crisis intervention 87–8,
130–1, 157, 301
Crowe, M. 86
Crowther, C. 231
Cuisenier, J. 140–1
cultures 121, 260, 330–1:
see also acculturation;
deculturation
cusp catastrophe 113–14, 128,
129
cybernetics xviii–xx, 34, 49,
68, 69, 88–9, 131, 159, 346
Cybernetics (Wiener) 277
Cyrulnik, B. 136

Daigremont, A. 396
Daniel, G. 173, 174
Dare, Christopher xiii, 309,
426
Dare, J. 115, 378
Darwin, Charles 330
data gathering 90

Daumeson, G. 25
Davidson, F. 3, 9, 296
Davidson, N. 41, 42
Davis, D. I. 15, 18
Davis, J. A. 367
death 232–3; cult 334: fear
of 95–6; rituals 232–3,
331–2
Death of the family (Cooper)
xxxv (n19)
death instinct 210–11, 267
Debray, Q. 147, 177
debt 198, 426
Decherf, G. 307
decision process 262–3
deculturation 90–1, 109
deep structures 380–2
deixis 91–2, 171, 199, 226,
362, 385
delegation 92–3
Deleuze, Gilles xxviii
delinquency 25, 93, 189, 389
delirium 77, 93–4, 274, 285,
323, 426
Dell, P. 253
delusions 284–5, 339
Demailly, A. 67, 70, 409
demand 94–5, 390
Demaret, A. 30
dementia 94–5, 340–1
Deniker, P. xxv
deontic modality 19–20, 96,
232, 292, 359
dependancy, and redundancy
324
depression 177–8, 186–7,
256–8
deritualization 330–1
Derrida, Jacques xxxiv (n16)
desacralization 335
Descartes, R. 312, 313
desire 94, 225, 253, 289, 387
Dessoy, E. 202, 203
determinism xxxix, 319–20,
359
detouring 26, 96
de-triangulation 96
de-tribalization 385–6
Deusen, J. M. van 6, 153, 232,
329
Devereux, G. 386
Dewey, J. 77
diabetes, childhood 311–12
diachronic therapy 96–7, 153,
154–5, 405
Dictionary of Symbols
(Chevalier and Gheerbrant)
383
Dictionnaire de la sémiotique
(Greimas and Courtes) 69
differentiation of self 97–9:
alcoholism 18;
complementary 337; couples
85; and fusion 166; and
identification 188;
information 205; loss 233;

reciprocal 337; symmetrical 336–7; transgenerational memories 425–6, 427; triangles 97, 373
Dipp, C. 31
disagreement 14–15
disanchoring 29
disassembly 329
disclosure 100, 204, 254
discordance concept 340–1
disengaged families 47, 64, 94–5, 100, 162, 255–6, 355, 363
dislocated families 54
disorder 116, 176, 275–6
disqualification 33, 100–1
dissipative structures 101–2, 115
dissociation 83, 339–40, 419
distance 102–4
Divided self (Laing) xxviii
divorce 239, 241, 242–3
doctor, general practitioner 131–3
Doctor, his patient and the illness (Balint) 313
doctor–patient relationship 131–2, 313
domestication 103–4, 210, 405
Donnelly, M. 427
Donzelot, Jacques 118
double bind xvi–xviii, xxx–xxxi (n1), 104–7: anti-theatre 32–3; catastrophes 128; cybernetics 88; desire 253; experimental 41; family and institution 214, 399; hypnosis 186; law 225–6; learning 105, 176, 422; multiple binds 410–11; oscillators 276–7; paradox 105, 281; paradoxical tasks 402; pragmatics of communication 105–6, 176; psychosomatic 307–9; schizophrenia 105–6, 309, 338, 341–2, 388–9; self 345; split 372, 411; therapeutic 410–11; topology 160; zeal 440
Draper, R. 253
dreams 107–8, 432, 433
dreamwork 107, 303
drugs: addiction 40–1, 108–10; prescribing 296–7, 315; use 3, 370–1; values 55; and violence 438
Duhl, B. 343
Duhl, F. 343
Dumas, A. 95
Dumont, Louis 261, 263
Durand 264, 265
Durrant, M. 174
Duval, Evelyn 140–1
dwarfism 136, 310

dyads, typology 84
dynamic system 42, 110, 346–7, 352, 373–4, 379

eating disorders 30, 260, 309
ecosystem 76–8, 111, 352–3, 405
education, law 224
educational organizations 364–5
ego 56, 145, 185, 249–50, 268, 432
Ehresmann, A. C. 262, 407
Eibl-Eibesfeldt, I. xx, 136, 210, 330
Eichenbaum, L. 173
eidos 64–5, 111–12, 127, 154, 291
Eiguer, A. xli: family organizers 82, 143, 146; family schisms 368; family system 238; family therapy 200; interpretation 217; marital breakdown 239–40; narcissism 268; phantasmic objects 289, 305; phantasy 44–5; self-referentiality 150
Einstein, Albert 206
Eisler, R. 173, 174
Ekman, P. 91, 255, 330, 392
Elder, G. 178
elementary catastrophes 112–15, 129–30: archetypal morphologies 326–7; bifurcation 42–3; black box 44; force fields 161; shock waves 363; static forms 373–4; universal unfolding 434
Elkaim, M. xli: absurd, the 2; anorexia nervosa 32; assemblage 35, 363; communication theory 67; dissipative structures 101, 102; family dynamics 43; identification 189; networks 269; self-referentiality 151
Ellenberger, Henri 432
emblems 392
Emerique, M. 3
emotional systems 234–5
encopresis 355, 405
endogamy 225, 272, 273
Enfant et son corps (Kreisler) 310
Engelberg, S. 121
enmeshed families 47, 54, 64, 115, 255–6, 363, 427
entropy 101, 115–16, 207, 254
enuresis 355, 361, 405
Epimenides the Cretan 194, 195, 198, 281
episteme 116–17
epistemic modality 232
epistemology 64–5, 73–9, 116–17

Epstein, N. B. 335
equifinality 117–18, 124, 155, 275, 359
equilibrium 101, 102, 112
Erickson, Milton H.: family life-cycles 381; family spokesperson 152; hypnosis 49, 185, 370, 432; metaphor xxiii, xli, 247–8; sexual behaviour 361; strategic therapy 375–7; systemic practices 278
Erikson, E. H. 213, 302, 330, 370, 433
Eros and Thanatos 267
erotomania 283, 284
Erriau, Gilles xxxvi (n25)
errors, compounding 72–3
Esterson, A. xxviii
ethical issues, family therapy 118–21
ethnicity, family therapy 121–4
ethnology, family 134–5
etho-anthropological organizers xlii, 145
ethology 124, 135–40: anorexia nervosa 30; and autism 202; black box 45; cybernetics 88; and law 224; and metapsychology 250; objectivist 79; ritualization 330; and semantics 354
ethonomy 124–5
ethos 124–5: and eidos 111–12; familiodrama 127; family system 154; marital conflicts 256; metacommunication 246; myths 143; positive connotation 291
euphemisms 340
Europe: drug addiction 109; family therapy training 419
Everstine, D. 185, 192–3, 437
Everstine, L. 185, 192–3, 437
Evolution and modification of behaviour (Lorenz) 42
evolutionary survival unit 125, 154, 181, 352
Ewing, A. 18
exhibitionism 361
exogamy 272, 273
exploitation 125–6, 285
expressions, emotional 392
extended family 272–4
Ey, Henri xxix, 33–4, 339, 432
eye contact 171–2

Fagen, R. E. 175
failure, recognition of 7–8
fairness 127, 229
Falret, J. 30, 94
families of origin 127, 427

Families of the slums (Minuchin et al.) 378
familiodrama 127–8
family xvi, xxxii (n9), xxxvii–xxxviii, xl, 47, 140: as black box 45; coalitions 63–4; as dynamic system 43, 110; histories 59–60, 229, 426; and institutions 155–7, 214, 399; interactional typologies 215–16; morphogenetic or structural typologies 255–6; phylogenetic origins 136–7
family actant 128, 325
family assessment guidelines 123–4
family catastrophes 128–30
family crisis 130–1
family doctor 130–3, 131–3, 312–13
family emotional oneness 133–4
family ethnology 134–5
family ethology 135–40
Family games (Selvini Palazzoli) 408
family interactions 97–8, 102, 216–17, 326–7, 359
family intervention unit 366
family life-cycles 140–3: adolescence 8; critical points 381; death 233; hierarchies 264; marital breakdown 239; memory 321, 424–6; myths 141; nuclear family 274; rituals 141, 331; transgenerational therapy 427
family maps 143
Family Mediators' Association 243
family myths 143–5, 265, 305–6: acting out 93; couples 85; disclosure 100; family life-cycles 141; forgetting 163–4; information 204; memories 321; resemblance 147, 177; scapegoat 336; shifters 362
family network 269–70
family organizers 62, 82, 143, 145–6, 244, 329–30
family oscillators 150–1, 277–8
family passions 146, 241
family psychical apparatus 146–7, 158–9
family resemblance 147, 177
family role 148, 263, 298–9
family rules 148–9, 393
family schisms 368
family self-belonging 149
family self-referentiality 149–52, 155, 263, 267, 345, 347

family structures 122, 137–8, 152–3, 305–6
family system xli, 62, 153–5: actuogenic and morphogenetic landscapes 43; catastrophe theory 128–30; ethos 154; feedback 160; hierarchies 263; map and counter-map 238–9; mediation 242; nuclear family 272–3; positive connotation 291; self-belonging 149; and unconscious 219
family therapy xxx, xxxvii, xxxviii, 304: alcoholism 18–19; boundaries 46; conductors and reactors 415–16; diachronic and synchronic 96–7, 153, 154–5, 405; Eastern Europe 403; feminist critiques 172–3; in the home 157–8; indications and contraindications 200–1; intervention 158, 306–7; transference paradoxes 423
Family therapy techniques (Minuchin and Fishman) 378
family typologies 158, 215–16, 255–6, 305–6, 389, 420–2
family unconscious 158–9, 219
father 163, 189–90, 284: *see also* parents; paternity
Fay, A. 49
fear-withdrawal 12
feedback 4, 159–60: brief interactional therapy 50; circularity 61, 68; equifinality 117; family systems 160; general systems theory 174; homeostasis 159, 174, 183; open systems 275; and operational closure 347; positive 15, 389; reactions 90; video 436
Fejer, G. 296
Ferber, A. 415
Ferenczi, S. 1, 165
Fernandez-Zoila, A. 309
Ferrari, M. 234
Ferreira, A. J. xli, 143, 150, 232, 265, 372, 411, 427
Feyereisen, P. 171, 172
Finkelhor, D. 437
Fiore, Q. 206, 345
Fisch, Richard 49, 50
Fischer, C. 30
Fisher, S. 3, 242
Fishman, H. C. 6, 173, 376, 378
fixation 227
Flandrin, J.-L. 140
Flaskas, C. 51, 370, 377
Flaubert, Gustave 149–50, 180

Flavigny, C. 9
Florence, J. 188
Foerster, H. von xix, 67, 68, 236, 237, 346
fold catastrophe 113
Foley, V. D. 223
Folie et déraison: histoire de la folie à l'âge classique (Foucault) xxvii
food-related disorders 30, 31, 59, 171: *see also* anorexia nervosa
force fields 42, 56, 160–2, 200, 234, 292
foreclosure 162–3
forestalling 186
forgetting 163–4
formalism 75
foster families 299
Foucault, Michel xxvii, 174
Foulkes, S. H. 277, 351
Fox, J. 18
fractals 130, 164, 176, 208, 209, 239
Framo, J. L. 134, 416, 427
France: chemotherapy xxv–xxvi; drug addiction 109; family therapists xxiv–xxvii; family therapy 229–31, 413–14
free association 165, 307, 381–2, 423
French, M. 174
Freud, Sigmund: abstinence 1; acting out 4; alienation 24; anachronistic plagiarism 213; anaclisis 13; cancer 54; change 56; coenaesthesia 382; delirium 94; dreams 107–8; drive 325–6; forgetting 163; free association 165; hysteria 262, 422; identification 188, 364; infantile stages 259; instinct 210; *Interpretation of dreams* 107–8, 196, 249, 382, 385; *Jokes and the relation to the unconscious* 184–5; memory 425; metapsychology 263; *Moses and monotheism* 159; mourning and melancholia 256–7; narcissism 198, 267; Oedipus complex 428–9; paranoia 284–5; phantasy 288; psychical apparatus 146–7, 248–9; psychoanalysis xiii–xiv, 278, 303, 372, 423; reality 76–7; resistance xiv; symbolism 385; uncanny 25; unconscious xxxviii–xxxix, 184–5, 432
Fried, M. 234
Friedman, H. 427
Fromm, Erich 234

Fromm-Reichmann, Frieda xxiii
Frosh, S. 193
Froussart, B. 243
function of symptom 20, 90, 165–6, 394
functional circles 166, 354
functions theory 26–7
Furman, B. 370
Furniss, T. 234
fusion 166, 167
Fustier, P. 397
fuzzy sets 167

Gabor, Dennis 182
game theory xix, 168–71, 290, 342
games 1, 7, 252, 259, 342
Garmezy, N. 234
Garrigues, P. xli, 203
gatekeeper 171
gaze xxi, 171–2
Gear, M. C. 4, 84
Geffroy, Y. 436
gender 172–4, 361, 378
general systems theory xix, 68, 117, 174–5, 275, 346, 395
generalized catastrophes 130, 175–6, 338, 374
generation gaps 64
genetics 176–8, 374–5, 395
genogram 143, 178, 270, 427
Gervet, Jacques 136
Gheerbrant, A. 383
Gillibert, Jean 188
Gillieron, E. 403
Gilligan, C. 173
Girard, R. 253, 334, 335–6, 335, 436
Glaser, D. 193, 252, 253
Glaserfeld, Ernst von 76, 78
Gleick, J. 319, 352
Gleser, G. L. 233
Godel, K. 105, 194–8, 282
Godin, J. 186
Goffman, E. xxi–xxii, 171
Goldner, V. 119, 172, 173, 174, 252
Goldstein, K. 106, 128, 181, 210
Goodman, N. 78
Goodrich, A. 174
Goody, J. 23, 140, 223, 274
Gordon, S. B. 41, 42
Gordon Montagnon, R. 326
Goutal, M. 288, 387
Graham, H. 133
grandeur, delusions 284
grandparents 234–5, 425: see also transgenerational memories
Grangeon, M. 358
Green, André xxxiv (n14) xxv, 4, 163, 267
Greenberg, G. S. 51

Greimas, A. 19, 69, 96, 114, 232, 238, 358, 359
grief 232–4: see also mourning
Grimal, P. 265
Grinberg, L. 300
Grinder, J. 270, 271, 280, 380, 381, 382
Grolnick, L. 311
Groos, K. 290
Gros, M. 340
Gross, M. 6, 349, 423
Guattari, Félix xxviii
Guir, J. 55
Guitton Cohen Adad, C. 23, 152
Guntern, G. 411
Gurman, A. S. 86, 415
Gurvitch, G. 181
Gutenberg galaxy, The (McLuhan) xxiii
Gutheil, T. G. 234
Guyotat, J. 55

habit formation see becoming accustomed
habituation 35, 179, 192, 382
habitus 392
Hagège, C. 384, 393
Haley, Jay xvi, xxiii, xli: acting out 5; adolescence 8, 360; brief therapy 49, 51; communication 356; couples 85, 86; double bind 105; errors 72; family life-cycles 141, 142, 381; feedback 160; hypnosis 185–6; marital breakdown 240; metagovernor 247; metaphor 248; mirrors 268; paradoxical communication 286; power 292, 293, 413; provocation 301; re-framing 325; schizophrenia 389; semiotics 356, 358; strategic therapy 49, 375–7; systemic approach 400; transference 422, 423; triangles 288, 428
Hall, A. D. 175
Hall, E. T. xx, xxi, 102, 103, 260, 405
hallucinations 339
Handbook of Family Therapy (Gurman and Kniskern) 415
Handy, C. B. 263, 364
Harburg, F. 16
Hare-Mustin, R. 172, 173
Harlow, H. F. 323
Harper, J. M. 84
Harthong, J. 78
hatred 234–5, 423
Haynes, G. 242
Haynes, J. 242
head injuries 48
health organizations 364–5
hebephrenia 338, 340, 342

Hegel, Georg Wilhelm Friedrich 23
Heidegger, Martin 65
Heinl, P. 427
Heinroth, O. 191
Henry, Jules xxxii (n9)
Henry, M. 231
Héritier, F. 176
Hermann, I. 259, 327
Hermes myth 25, 265–6
Herz, F. 233
Hestia 266
heteronomy 37–8
heuristics 20, 67, 179–80, 227, 390
hierarchies: behaviour 212, 411; multi-level 155, 250, 261–4; social 138–40; tangled 23, 181, 214, 251, 264, 375, 387, 401
Hilbert, D. 194, 197–8
Hill, R. 122, 140–1
Hirsch, S. xxxvi (n25), 82, 213, 398, 408, 422
Hochmann, J. 167
Hoffman, L.: complexity 301; enmeshed family 47, 64; errors 72; gender 172; injunctions 80, 372; legal context 229; mediation 242; power 253, 293; structural approach 378
Hofstadter, D. R. 149, 219, 375, 387, 401
Hogan, P. 79
holism 180–1
Hollis, P. 10
holographic memory 27, 34–5, 181–2
holoscopic memory 181–2
home 182–3, 367
homeorhesis 159, 183–4, 394–5
homeostasis 183–4: chemotherapy xxv–xxvi; family system 148, 155, 198; feedback 159, 174, 183; function of symptom 166; and myths 2, 144; positive connotation 291; provocation 301; systemic modelling 117; variety 227
homosexuality 361
hooks, b. 173
Houseman, Michael 331
Howells, J. G. 162, 435
hubris 184, 258, 386, 389
Hume, David 75
humour 184–5, 255, 281
Husserl, Edmund 64–5
hypertension 308
hypnosis 49, 185–7, 370, 432
hypnotherapy 185–7, 432
hypokalaemia 30
hysteresis cycles 30–1, 114, 128, 129, 203

icon 188, 384
id 56, 249, 250, 432
idealism 74, 283
identification 188–90, 300,
   364: *see also* projective
   identification
identity, and alienation 33, 188
Igodt, P. 151
illegitimacy 299
illness, and symptoms 390
illustrators and regulators 392
imaginary 249–50
imagos, parental 258
immanence 190
imprinting 190–2: and
   attachment 35, 191;
   becoming accustomed 40;
   deixis 91; identification
   189; and imaginary 250;
   narcissism 268; negative
   360; symbolic reference 382
incest 192–4, 225, 430
inclusion rituals 332–3
incompleteness theorem 105,
   194–8, 282
indebtedness 198
indeterminism 319
index 384
index patient 146, 198–200:
   alienation 21–2; ancestors
   29; distance 102;
   provocation 301–2;
   scapegoat 336; symptoms
   390; totemization 334;
   victimization 323
indifference 234–5
infants: autism 201–4;
   dreaming 107; neurosis 96;
   psychosexual stages 259
information 70, 72, 204–9: and
   communication xxii, 206;
   cybernetics 88; data 90; and
   learning 227; and memory
   424; myths 145; processing
   34, 386; and punctuation
   315; repressed 321; and
   speech 371
information theory xix,
   115–16, 206
injunction, contrary 80, 106,
   372
inputs–outputs 256
instinct 209–12: algorithms
   21; as behaviour xxi,
   211–12; and holism 181;
   and imprinting 190;
   oscillators 277; and psyche
   424
institutions 144–5, 212–15, 367
interaction xxx (n1), xxxix:
   circularity 161; familial and
   social 215–17, 310–12;
   graphs 326; phantasmic
   305–6; psychosis xvii; and
   reality 322; rules xxii;
   schismogenesis 337–8;

syntax 390; and transactions
   388–9
interpersonal relations 129–30,
   169–71, 186, 251–2, 409
interpretation 217
Interpretation of dreams (Freud)
   107–8, 196, 249, 382, 385
intersensory structuring 260–1
intervenors 411
intervention: conflicts 298;
   crisis 87–8; family therapy
   158, 306–7; metasystems 86,
   251, 255; network 270;
   systemic modelling 365–6,
   395–9, 413; unit of change
   434
intimacy 217–18
intime 278–9
intuitionism 75
Ionesco, Eugène 32–3
Irigaray, L. 173
irreversible processes 101
isomorphism 45, 219–20, 432

Jackson, D. D. xxiii, xli:
   circularity 60;
   communication theory
   317–18; couples 84, 85;
   family relations 367; family
   role 148; family therapy xxx
   (n1); family typologies 215;
   homeostasis xvi, xxxiv (n13),
   183; Mental Research
   Institute 49; paradox of
   transference 422;
   provocation 300–1;
   psychosomatic medicine
   312–13; psychosomatic
   personality 310; quid pro
   quo 85, 254, 317–18;
   re-framing 325
Jacobson, D. 83
Jagstaidt, V. 360
Jakobson, R. 91, 244, 324,
   361–2
James, K. 172, 173
jealousy 56, 94, 221, 283, 284,
   433
Jenkins, H.: autism 204;
   crisis intervention 88, 301;
   feedback 160; hospitalized
   child 398; legal context
   231; loss 233, 257; sexual
   abuse 193; structural
   family therapy 378;
   systemic therapy 252, 399,
   400; transgenerational
   therapies 426, 427; violence
   174
Jespersen, O. 361
joining 10–11, 221
*Jokes and the relation to the
   unconscious* (Freud) 184–5
Jones, E. 54, 119, 174
Jones, J. W. 16
judicial organizations 364–5

Jung, C. G. 17, 220, 325–6, 432
Jung, M. 123
juridical acculturation 2–3
justice, and law 224–5

Kaës, R. 289
Kafka, Franz 104, 225–6, 349
Kahn, L. 265
Kanner, L. 201–2
Kant, Immanuel 75
Kantor, David 343–4
Kaplan, S. 378
Kaslow, F. 241
Kaufmann, J.-C. 31
Keith, D. V. 336
Kempe, C. H. 193
Kerbrat-Oerchioni, C. 371
Kerr, M. E. 46
Kestemberg, E. 30, 212
Kestenberg, J. S. 58
Keys to solution in brief therapy
   (de Shazer) 369
Kingston, P. 118
kinship 28, 62, 125, 134, 176,
   222, 268–70, 349
Kleckner, T. 51
Klein, H. 59
Klein, M. 188, 259, 300
Kluckhohn, Florence xvii
Knight, Robert 18
Kniskern, D. P. 415
knowledge 74–5, 77, 117, 222,
   234–5
Kohut, H. 267, 423
Korzybski, A. xviii, xxxi (n2),
   77, 239
Koudou, K. R. 90
Kraepelin, E. 340, 341
Kreisler, L. 310
Kretschmer, E. 283
Kristeva, J. 173

La Perriere, A. 160
Laborit, H. xxv, xxvi
Lacan, Jacques xxv: demand
   94; family 304; foreclosure
   162–3; identification 188,
   189; law 225; narcissism
   267; paranoia 268, 284;
   psychoanalysis 278; real
   322; sphere 39; symbolic
   250, 357, 385; topology 249;
   unconscious 432
Lafargue, Paul 23
Laforgue, R. xxiv, xli, 215,
   304, 343
Lagache, D. 307
Laing, R. D. xxviii, xxxiv
   (n18), xxxv (n19), (n20), 33,
   106, 264, 330
Lalande, A. 190
Laloue, J. M. 147
Lamb, M. E. 10
Lane, M. xxi, 152
Lang, M. 403, 404, 405
Lang, T. 403, 404, 405

language: communication 122–3, 260; metacommunication 246; micro-imprinting 191–2; non-communication function 382; as ritualization 70, 286–7; and semantics 295, 355–6; semiotics 68, 69
language acquisition 324, 383
Lannoy, J.-D. de 171, 172
Lanteri-Laura, G. 340
Laplanche, J. 82, 147, 165, 188, 210
Laraby, A. 225
Largeault, J. 323
Lasègue, Ch. 30, 94
Lask, B. 234, 311
Lau, A. 121, 122, 123
Laub Coser, R. 366, 367
Lautman, Françoise 142
law 223–7: and father 163; and institution 213; Kafka 104; and reality 323; social organization 365; and symbolic 357; territory 406
Lawick-Goodall, J. van 257
Lazarus, A. 49
Leach, E. xxi, 143
leadership 81, 422
learning 227–9, 375: and change 56; and double bind 105, 176, 422; game theory 170; and instinct 211; social 136
Lebovici, S. 107, 287, 304, 306, 414, 415–16
Le Bras, Hervé 142–3
Leclaire, S. 198
Lederer, W. 84
Ledermann, S. 16
ledger 229, 261, 426: debts 198, 426; loyalty 235; and disease 55; paranoia 284; relational stagnation 327
legacy 92–3, 229
legal context 229–32
legal status 366–7
Leighton, A. H. 121
Lemaire, J. G. 31, 82–3, 86, 304
Le Moigne, J.-L.: cognitive epistemology 64; constructivism 77, 78; general systems theory 175; interpersonal relations 409; memories 150; self-referential calculus 347; social communication 67, 70, 150; strange loops 375
Le Play, P. G. F. 272, 273
Leroi-Gourhan, A. 238, 334
Lesourd, J. 241
Lesser, R. 48
Leuba, John xxvi, 304
Le Vaguerese, L. 309

Lévi-Strauss, Claude 134–5, 143, 193, 204, 264, 265, 272, 303, 387–8
Levick, S. E. 123
Lewin, Kurt xxx (n1), 55, 160–2, 171, 335, 414
Lewis, E. 233
Leyhausen, P. 6
liberty 272–3
Lidz, T. xvii, xli, 45, 64, 189, 190, 215, 242, 342
Lieberman, S. 234, 400, 427
Liebman, R. 378
Liendo, E. C. 4, 84
Lilamand, M. 343
limits see boundaries
Lin, T. Y. 121–2
Lindemann, E. 233
Lindley, R. 120
linearity 60–2
linguistic behaviour 392–3
linguistic paradoxes 281
linguistics, transformational 381–2
Lipsedge, M. 122
Litovsky de Eiguer, D. 268
Littlewood, R. 122
living systems 115–16
Locke, John 74–5
locus 232
logical types theory 56, 104–5, 194, 254, 262, 281, 406–7
loops, strange 375, 401
Lord, C. 203
Lorenz, K.: aggression 12; archetypes 325, 326; becoming accustomed 40; constructivism 76; death instinct 210; domestication 103; ethology 79, 136, 224; *Evolution and modification of behaviour* 42; habituation 179; imprinting 190; instinct xxi, 20–1; learning 228; mind/psyche 254, 353; mirror 323; mourning 257; pseudo-speciation 302; reality 286; ritualization 331; symbolic movement 354–5
loss 232–4, 256, 257
Loutre du Pasquier, N. 35
love 234–5, 285–6, 423
love object 82–4
Lowie, Robert 134
loyalties 93, 94, 142, 162, 235, 412, 429
Luepnitz, D. A. 51, 173, 370, 377
lure 250, 326
Luria, A. R. 48

McCulloch, W. S. xix
McDougall, J. 423
McGoldrick, M. 123, 141, 174, 178, 233, 240, 427

McGoldrick Orfanidis, M. 400
McIntyre, D. 172
MacKinnon, L. 119
McLuhan, Marshall xxiii, 70, 206, 259, 260, 345, 383, 386
Machiavelli, Niccolò 53, 224
machines xix, 43, 88–9, 236–7
Madanes, C. 49, 375–7
Mahler, M. 97
maieutics 42, 237
Mairlot, F. E. 243–4
Maisondieu, J. 95
Malarewicz, A. 186
Malone, T. P. 97
Mandelbrot, Benoit 164–5
Manhood of humanity (Korzybski) xviii
mania 256–8
manic-depressive families 177–8, 257–8
manipulation 120, 237–8, 292
manipulative families 399
mapping 75
maps 11, 143, 165, 238–9, 290, 330–1, 406
Maracek, J. 173
March, J. G. 364
Marchais, P. 175
marital breakdown 85, 138, 239–41
marital schism 31, 242
marital skew 242
marital therapy 404–5
marriage: aggression 13; differentiation of self 99; endogamy 225, 272, 273; exogamy 272, 273; global theory 85; mixed 123; monogamy 135, 137; natural laws 224, 225; polygamy 137; polygyny 137; types 240–1; see also couples
Martin, J.-Y. 269
Martino, J. de 403
Maruani, G. xxxvi (n25), xli: acoustic feedback 4; couples 83; double binds 307; drugs 297; family passions 146; family resemblance 147; psychosomatic illness 313, 314, 315; sofa-bed syndrome 110, 368–9; systemic modelling 394
Maruyama, M. 89
Marx, Karl 23–4, 213, 335
Masaud Khan 1
Mason, B. 174
Mason, E. 174
Masson, J. 119, 120
Masson, J. M. 77, 288
Masson, O. 57, 58, 312
mastery polarity 150
Matheny, A. 83
Maturana, H. xix, 76, 119
Maurel, H. 44, 213, 340, 341
Mead, M. 3, 173

meaning: alienation 354; catastrophe theory 250; conjectured 355; and morphology 374; and myth 143–4, 356; and rites 356; and semantics 354
mediation 5–6, 242–3
Medium is the message (McLuhan and Fiore) 206, 345
Meissner, W. W. 311
melancholia 256–8
memories: auxiliary 320–1, 355; multigenerational 425–6; read-only 249, 320–1; read-write 320–1; transgenerational 213, 332, 424–6; register of 150
memory: communication 66; holographic 27, 34–5, 181–2; holoscopic 181–2; and learning 424; and ontogenesis 425; and phylogenesis 424; unconscious 425; and violence 424
Mendel, Gregor 104
Mendell, D. 3
Mendlewicz, J. 177
menetic theory 243–4
mental alienation 21–2
mental illness, law 224–5
mental patient, legal state 367
Mental Research Institute 49: *see also* Palo Alto school
merit 92–3, 229, 244, 261
Mesarovic, M. D. 261–3
mesnie 244
message 112, 244–5, 250, 324
metabindings 238, 245, 258, 364, 411
metabolic forms 175–6, 373–4
meta-change 57
metacommunication: attractors 246–7: autism 202; language 246; and learning 227; and metapsychology 250–1; μ-function 258; and pathological communication 286; phantasy 289; play 290; and ritualization 246, 330; speech acts 371
metacommunication systems 67, 70, 245–7, 294, 351, 433
metagovernor 247
Metamorphosis (Kafka) 349
metaphor xxiii, xli, 186, 247–8
metaphorical objects 247–8, 268–9, 428
metaphorical tasks 402–3
metapsychology 89, 248–51, 263, 303
meta-symbolization 386–7
metasystems xxxvi–xxxviii, 86, 227, 250, 251, 255
meta-theory 196, 197–8

Miermont, Jacques xiv, xxxvi (n25), xli: absurd 2; acculturation 3; actuogenesis 6; alienation 25; catastrophe theory 128, 130; constructivism 76; drugs 297, 315; family passions 146; family self-belonging 149; game theory 170–1; genetics 177; incest 194; mourning 258, 328; oscillators 150, 277; real 322; self-referential calculus 349; therapeutic abduction 409; transgenerational therapy 426; victimization 323
Milan school xxix, 119, 278–9, 283, 399, 419
Milan systemic therapy 173, 251–3
Miller, A. 119, 173, 174
Miller, D. 119
Miller, J. G. 67, 206
mimesis 11, 253
mimicry 253
mind 67, 125, 189, 253–4, 352–3, 354
Mind and nature: a necessary unity (Bateson) 54, 253–4, 374, 407
Minuchin, S. xli: acculturation 3; anorexia nervosa 31–2, 309; boundaries 45–8, 286, 378; coalitions 328–9, 428; as conductor 415; detouring 96; disengaged families 100; enmeshed families 64, 115, 427; *Families of the slums* 378; family history 426; family life-cycles 141; family maps 143; family structures 152; family typologies 255–6; gender 173; interaction 311, 312; joining 10–11; legal context 231; mimesis 253; prescription of symptom 298; *Psychosomatic families* 26; questioning 60; systemic therapy 252; transactional patterns 6; triangles 428, 429
miracle question 369–70
mirror, family 268–9, 323
Mises, J. xxvi
Mises, R. xxvi
misunderstandings 204, 254
Mitscherlich, A. 90
Moles, Abraham 88
Molnar, A. 369
mono-therapy 81
monogamy 135, 137
Montagner, H. 12, 138–40, 330
Montaigne, M. E. de 74

Montalvo, B. 378, 423
Montesquieu, Charles de Secondat 223–4
Morel, Denise 54–5
Moreno, Jacob Levi xxx (n1), 127, 128, 306, 367–8
Morgenstern, Oskar 342
Morin, E. xxx, 38, 70–1, 180, 275–6, 319, 324, 335
morphogenetic theory 27, 145, 162, 255–6, 386–7
morphologies 205, 374
Morris 68
Moses and monotheism (Freud) 159
mother: alpha function 147; autism 324; blamed 173; and child 31, 91–2, 323–4; role in family xvi
motivation 211
Mottron, L. 92, 192, 202
mourning 232–4, 256–8: context 178; divorce 239; injuries 48; marital breakdown 241; rituals 331–2; schizophrenics 244; survivor parents 59; unfinished 254, 272, 328
Mrazek, P. B. 193
multi-generational transmission 144, 427
multi-laterality 261
multi-problem families 215–16, 230
multiple binds 410–11
multiple family therapies 157, 158
multiple parenthood families 127
Murphy, H. M. B. 299
Murstein, B. I. 83
music, sacred 335
M'Uzan, M. de 423
mystification 33, 106, 264
myth 158, 264–5: acculturation 2–3; as analog-digital converter 264; communication 66, 232; and death 232–3; and episteme 116; ethos 143; Hermes 25, 265–6; homeostasis 2, 144; institutional 144–5, 212–13; and learning 145; and meaning 143–4, 356; and misunderstanding 254; Narcissus 267; Oedipus 192, 288, 299, 344–5; performative 425; and ritual 143, 264; and schisms in family 368; self-referentiality 150; social 212–13; systemic model 255; *see also* family myths
Myth of mental illness (Szasz) xxvii, 143

Nahas, G. 16
names 352, 362, 407
narcissism 198, 267–9: and disqualification 101; filiation 55; humour 185; object choice 82; and paranoia 284–5
Nasio, J.-D. 423
Nathan, T. 29, 291
natural selection 125
Needham, R. 193
negation 33
negentropy 115–16, 207, 254
neoteny 104, 302
networks 158, 238, 269–70, 292
Neuburger, Robert xiv, xxxvi (n25), xli, 25, 272, 334, 361
Neumann, J. von xix, 34, 342, 346
neurolinguistic programming 270–1, 278, 381
neutrality 119, 261, 271
New York Nathan Ackerman Institute 343
Newell, A. 34, 180
Nichols, M. 400
Nicholson, L. 173
Nicolo, A.-M. 248
Niederland, W. G. 163
Noel, J. 225
noise 207–9, 324, 347
Noller, P. 172
non-voluntary families 271–2
normal families 216
nostalgia 204, 272
nothing plus ten per cent paradox 272, 410
nuclear family 90, 125, 127, 140, 155, 272–4

O'Brian, C. 398
O'Hanlon, W. H. 51, 370, 376
obesity 309
object, as communication 248
object relations 166, 305
objectivist school 12
Oedipus complex 197, 305, 356, 360: aggression 14; identification 188; incest 193; power 292; repression 163; triangles 428–30
Oedipus myth 192, 288, 299, 344–5
old age theory 132
Olievenstein, Claude 108–9
Olson, D. H. 31
On narcissism: an introduction (Freud) 198
oneness, emotional 133–4
Onnis, L. 396
ontogenesis 6–7, 46, 91, 145, 250, 268, 425
open sets 416–18
open systems 275: and closed systems 62, 174; equifinality

117, 118; and equilibrium 101; family structure 153; homeostasis 183; totality 418–19
openness 149, 346
operational closure 346–7
Orbach, S. 173
order 275–6, 319
ordinal values 55, 223
organization theory 364, 365
organizations 72, 365, 373, 374
organizers, psychical 145–6: see also family organizers
Orwid, Maria 403
oscillators 150–1, 276–8, 315, 346, 354, 384
Outline of psychoanalysis (Freud) 372
outside time 278–9

Padovani, P. 239–40
Palo Alto school xxiii, xxx–xxxi (n1), xxxiii (n11), 49: anti-theatre 32; brief therapies 51–2, 278; change 56; cybernetics 159; double bind xvi, xviii; family typologies 215–16; manipulation 237–8; pragmatics of communication 293; schismogenesis 84–5, 337–8
Pankow, Gisela 310
Papp, P. 118–19, 174, 343, 344, 399
paracommunication 67, 70, 227, 280, 286, 294
Paradox and counterparadox (Selvini Palazzoli) 408
paradoxes 280–3: communication 48–9, 246, 286; double bind 105, 281; Epimenides the Cretan 194, 195, 198, 281; ethics 120; and identification 188–9; and information 208–9; linguistic 281; logico-pragmatic 188–9; and metacommunication systems 246–7; nothing plus ten per cent 272, 410; pragmatics of communication 293; of relations 258; social alienation 24–5; and transference 422–3
paradoxicality 283
paralinguistic behaviour 392
paranoia 94, 268, 283–5, 342
paranoid schizophrenia 338
parentectomy 213, 397
parentification 126, 139, 148, 154, 188, 285–6, 328
parents: battered 438; and children xxxvi (n24), 97, 136–7, 233–4, 268, 338; psychotic families 234, 256;

schizophrenics 238; as survivors 58–60; see also father; mother; parentectomy; paternity
Parkes, C. M. 233
parole, semantics 355–6
Parret, H. 371
partiality, multi-directional 261
partner, choice of 82–4
paternity 90, 137, 138
pathological communication 286, 393
Patient and the analyst, The (Sandler) xiii
patient-therapist relationship xiii
Patients have families (Richardson) xxxi (n1)
Paul, N. 233, 234, 415
Peirce, C. S. 91, 188, 357–8, 383–4, 407–8
Peitgen, H.-O. 164, 165
pelvic algias 308
Penn, P. 252, 399
Pennachionni, I. 13
Perelberg, R. J. 119, 173, 174
performative utterances 53, 118, 213, 287, 371
performatives 286–8, 425
persecution 283, 284
person, familial and social creation 264
personality 372–3, 388
perverse triangle see triangle, perverse
Peseschkian, N. 123
Peterson, M. R. 420
Petitot-Cocorda, J. 114, 250, 319, 382
phallus 150, 266, 361
phantasmic interaction 289, 305–6
phantasy 288–9, 305–6: alpha elements 27; and black box 44–5; constructivism 76–7; in psychoanalysis 303; and reality 255, 288, 303; and schizophrenia 341–2
pharmakon 334–5
phase space 161, 176, 289
Pheline, C. 48
phenomenology 64–5
Philippe, A. 3
phylogenesis 6–7, 136–7, 384–5, 424
Piaget, J. 11, 75–6, 152, 358
Pical, D. 231
Pichot, A. 61, 107
Pierce, L. H. 193
Pierce, R. 193
Pilat, J. 16
Pincus, L. 426
Pinson, G. 34, 182
Pirandello, Luigi 33, 306
Pittman, F. S. 234
Pitts, W. xix

plagiarism, anachronistic 213
Plato 74
play 5, 168, 254–5, 288–91, 437
pleasure principle 322
pleroma 117
Poincaré, H. 42, 69–70
Policing of families (Donzelot) 118
Politzer, George 432
Pollak-Cornillot, M. 147, 210
poly-therapy 81
Polya, G. 179–80
polygamy 135, 273–4
polygyny 137
Pontalis, J.-B. 82, 147, 165, 188, 210
Porot, Maurice 182–3, 360
Porte, M. 335
positive connotation 102, 148, 281, 291, 325
post-modernism, therapy and gender 173
posturo-voco-gestural attitudes 392
power 292–3: abuse 119; in family 305–6; and gender 174; index patient 199–200; and reality 323; systemic therapy 251, 252–3; tactics 413; and violence 436
pragmatic barber paradox 281
pragmatics 68–9, 232
pragmatics of communication xx–xxii, 293–5: alethic modalities 19–20; change 56; communication theory 69; double bind 105–6, 176; information 204; myths 264–5; narcissism 267; re-framing 338; self-reference 281–2; transference 422
Pragmatics of human communication (Watzlawick et al.) xxiv
predation 12–13, 78, 129, 325, 354
pregnance 27, 91–2, 250, 331, 334, 362–3, 382, 383
prescribing symptom 363
prescription 297–8, 330
Prigogine, I. 43, 101, 115, 207, 319
Principia mathematica (Whitehead and Russell) xvi, 194, 196
prison 213
Prisoner's Dilemma 169
problem-solving 180, 369–70
procreative families 299
programming, neurolinguistic 270–1
projection 55
projective identification 105, 300, 335, 419

prophecy, self-fulfilling 345
Proust, Marcel 29
provocation 142, 300–2
proxemics xx–xxi, 102–4, 391–2, 405
pseudo-hostility 302
pseudo-mutuality 302, 427
pseudo-speciation 11, 302–3
pseudo-static forms 373–4
psuedo-speciation 331
psyche 258–9, 313, 424
psychiatric treatment 397–9
psychiatrist, and somatician 314–15
psychiatry, conferences xxviii–xxix
Psychiatry and anti-psychiatry (Cooper) xxxv (n19)
psychical apparatus 146–7, 248–9
psychoanalysis xlii, 157, 278, 303–5, 356: *see also* Freud
psychodrama 33, 127, 306–7, 333, 367–8
psychodynamic model xli
psychopathology xli, 21–2, 398
psychosis: alienation 21–2; and deixis 92; foreclosure 162–3; interactional pattern xvii; manic-depressive 177–8; metabinding 245; narcissism 267; parents 234, 256; projective identification 300; reality 322; symbolic reference 357
Psychosomatic families (Minuchin et al.) 26
psychosomatic illness 115, 307–15
psychotic transaction 398, 433
punctuation 294, 314, 315–16

quality 68, 256
quantification 106
quantifiers 317
questionable families 216
questions: circular 54, 60, 61; miracle 369–70; scaling 370; therapeutic 399; triadic 428
quid pro quo 85, 254, 317–18

Rabkin, Richard 50
Racamier, P. C. xli, 28, 198, 268, 283, 322
racism 302–3
Rakoff, V. 58
random events 71, 116, 319–20
Rao, A. V. 121–2, 123
ratio 320
read-only memories 249, 320–1
read-write memories 320–1
reafference mechanisms 322

reality 322–3: antinomic 334; constructivism 77–9; and family 274; and humour 185; and idealism 74; and madness 158; mathematics 197; and mediating behaviour 5–6; performatives 286; and phantasy 255, 288, 303; psychical 76–7; and ritual 331; and symbolism 250, 386; and territory 406
reality principle 249
reason: and law 224: and myth 320
Reason and violence (Laing and Cooper) xxxv (n19)
Recanati, F. 69
reciprocity 336
redundancy 69, 207, 244–5, 324–5
reference 325
referent, and signified 91
referral process 252, 271
reflex 41, 181
re-framing 198, 314–15, 325, 330–1, 338, 370
reification 106
Reiger, K. 118
Reiss, D. 134
relatedness 124
relational archetypes *see* archetypes, relational
relations xxvi: absence of absence 258, 327–8; interpersonal 129–30, 169–71, 186, 251–2, 409; paradox 258; and play 290; residual 327–8; resonances 278; stagnation 327; symmetrical 336–7; transgenerational 234–5; triadic 62, 85, 376–7
relativism, cultural 65
religion 117, 334
repetition 324–5
representamen 357–8, 383–4
represented, and signified 250
repression 163, 321
reproduction 129, 137–8
rescue 323–4
resonances: coupling 14–15; relational 278; semantic 344, 351–2, 435
restructuring 328–9, 401–2
Revel, J.-F. 53
Richter, H. E. 86–7, 305
Richter, P. H. 164, 165
Ridley, J. 86
Rieben, L. 404
rites 150, 356, 425
rites of passage 3, 330, 332
ritualization 329–33: analogic behaviour 27; constructivism 78; deritualization 330–1; episteme 116; gaze 171;

hierarchies 261; and instinct 210; and language 70, 286–7; metacommunication 246, 330; schizophrenia 330; semantics 354, 355; sleep 107–8; social 382; victimization 324
rituals: actions 5; appeasement 12; of belonging 332–3; communication 66, 331; death 232–3, 331–2; divorce 241; family life-cycles 141, 331; food 30, 31; mourning 331–2; and myth 143, 264; performative 331; phylogenetic 188; and religion 334; seduction 286
rivalry 13, 63
Roberts, S. 243
Robinson, M. 242
robotics 387
Rokoff, G. 366, 367
role play 205, 333
role structure 421
Rome school 248, 419
Rosen, John xxxiii (n11)
Rosenberg, L. 58
Rosenthal, M. K. 50
Rosset, C. 322
Rossi, E. L. 49
Rougeul, F. 368
Roume, D. 25
Roussel, L. 240
rubber fence 421
Rubinstein, B. 81, 423
Ruesch, J. xx, 67, 204
Ruffiot, A. xli, 1, 108, 146, 147, 165, 238, 289, 307
rules xxii, 85, 226–7
Rushen, J. 261
Russell, Bertrand xvi, 29, 49, 104–5, 189, 194, 281, 406
Rutter, M. 203–4, 234
Ryle, A. 313

Sabourin, P. 1
sacraments 255, 334–5
sacred 332, 334–5
sacrifice 334–5
sado-masochism 305
Sager, C. J. 82
Saint Paul, J. de 29, 270
salience 27, 250, 331, 334, 382, 383
Salomon, J.-C. 394
Sandler, J. xiii
Sanity, madness and the family (Laing and Esterson) xxviii
Sartre, Jean-Paul xxviii, xxxv (n19), xxxv–xxxvi (n24), 34
Satir, V. xxiv, 128, 141, 229, 415, 428, 429–30
Saussure, F. de 91, 100, 246, 357
Saussurian semiology 357
scaling questions 370

scandalmongering 204, 335
scapegoat 335–6: and circularity 161; constricted family 216; crisis 301; and hierarchy 261; paranoia 285; psychosomatic illness 312–13; transgenerational 93; or victim 199, 323; violence 436
Schaffer, L. 242
Schappi, R. 137, 138
Schatzman, M. 163
Scheff, T. J. 123
Scheflen, A. E. xxii, 21, 255, 392, 436
Scherrer, P. 193
schismogenesis 84–5, 97, 216, 295, 336–8, 373
schizophrenia xxviii, 197, 338–43; anti-theatre 32; black box 44; Bleulerian/ ontological; boundaries 46; communication modes xx, 106, 295; and de-tribalization 385–6; differentiation 99; discrimination xvi, xvii; double binds 105–6, 309, 338, 341–2, 388–9; and dreamwork 303; DSM-III 95, 339, 340; genetics 177; identification 190; impenetrability 418; imprinting 192; memory 425; mourning 244; mystification 264; and narcissism 268; paradoxicality 283; phantasy 341–2; play-like exchanges 247; ritualization 330; and self-referentiality 151; transactions 287, 359, 388–9, 411, 426
schizophrenia simplex 338, 339
schizophrenic dementia 340
schizophrenics xxviii, xxix: desire 387; love of bed 368–9; non-verbal communication xxi; parents of 238; victimization 323–4
Schmid, F. 244
Science and sanity (Korzybski) xviii
scotomization 342, 343
sculpting 127, 130, 248, 343–4, 374
Searle, J. R. 69, 325
Searles, H. 97, 423
secrets 55, 59, 204, 254, 258, 344–5, 426
seduction 77, 286, 359–61
Seele 353
Segal, L. 174
Seghers, A. 257, 258
Segond, Pierre xxxvi (n25), xli

self 24, 65, 341–2, 345, 372–3, 427, 430: see also differentiation of self
Self and others (Laing) xxviii
self-domestication 103–4
self-organization 116, 117–18, 282, 345–7
self-referential calculus 7, 347–51, 407
self-referentiality xl, xlii, 149–52: and actuogenesis 6; circularity 155; and equifinality 118; institutions 213; learning 229; and logic 194; mythic level 255; and paradox 281, 282–3; semantics 355
Selvini Palazzoli, M. xxix, xli, 251–3: anorexia nervosa 31, 251, 309; autism 202; circularity 390; context markers 79; Family games 408; function of symptom 20, 90; hubris 184; index patient 198; interventions 365; legal context 230; Paradox and counterparadox 408; paradoxical tasks 402; positive connotation 291; questioning 54, 60, 61, 428; referral 271; relational resonances 278; ritualization 330; schizophrenic transaction 287, 359, 389; systemic therapy 251–3, 394, 396, 399; transgenerational relationships 234–5; violence 438
semantic resonances 344, 351–2, 435
semantics xviii–xix, 68; communication 353–6; ethology 354; gaze 171–2; language 295, 355–6; naming 352; unit of mind 352–3, 354
semiology 349–50, 356–8
semiotic square 19, 114, 232, 358–9
semiotics 4, 19, 124, 237–8, 239
semiotics of communication 68–9, 356–8
sensitivity 359
sensitization, training 419–20
separation 8
Serrano, A. C. 48
Serrano, J. A. 31
Serre, J. L. 177
set theory 75, 153, 167, 194, 406
sexual abuse 174, 192–3
sexual behaviour 191, 359–61
sexual dimorphism 138

sexual instinct 210, 212, 217–18
sexual reproduction 375
sexuality 82–3, 129, 360–1
Shannon, C. E. xix, 34, 66, 67, 68, 204, 206, 207, 208, 324
Shazer, Steve de 50, 51, 52, 369–71, 438
Shepher, J. 191
shifters 91, 361–2
Shorter, E. 140
siblings 63, 109–10, 363
Sieber, F. M. 15
signals xx: mode-identifying 254–5, 332; and noise 324; play 290
signification 353
signified: and signifier 162–3, 250, 322, 351, 357; topology and morphology 355–6
signs, classified 91, 100, 258
Silversten, O. 174
Simeon, M. 312
Simon, F. xv, 400
Simon, H. A.: complex systems 71–2; heuristics 179, 180; identification 189; information processing 34, 386; manipulation 237, 238; organization theory 364, 365
Simonton, S. M. 54
Singer, M. T. 65, 134
singularities 106, 144, 192, 291, 363
Sivadon, P. xxvi–xxvii, 309
Sjögren, A. 31
Skinner, B. F. 41, 42, 236
Skynner, A. C. R. 46
sleep 107–8
Sluzki, C. E. 33
Smagghe Floc'h, M.-F. 226
Smart, R. G. 296
smell 260
smile 145
Snakkers, J. 9
social alienation 23–5
social communication 67–8, 70, 150
social network therapy 158
social organization 189, 263, 364–6
social status 263, 366–7
sociodrama 127, 367–8
sociogenetics 368
Socrates 237
sofa-bed syndrome 110, 368–9
solution-focused therapy 369–70
Soulé, M. 107, 202, 225, 324, 327
space-time 73, 183, 258, 278–9, 370–1
spacing xx–xxi, 102–4
Spark, G. M.: alignment 26; contextual therapy 121; fairness 127; intensive

therapy 279; ledger 198, 229, 284, 327; legacy and merit 92–3; loyalty 142, 235; multi-directional partiality 261; parentification 125–6, 285–6; projective identification 335; scapegoat 336; systemic work 400; transgenerational memories 424, 426
Speck, R. 269, 270
specular interactions 268–9
speech act 287, 325, 371
Spencer-Brown, G. 282, 347–9, 407
Spender, D. 173
sphere, topology 39–40
Spiegel, J. P. xvii, 3
Spinoza, B. 312
Spitz, R. A. 40, 145, 405
split double bind 372, 411
split families 54, 372–3, 423
spoken word 260, 264
spokesperson, for family 152
spouse, choice of 82–4: see also couples; marriage
stalemate 373
Stanton, M. D. 51, 108, 162
static forms 215, 373–4
statistical theory, entropy 115
Steinglass, Peter 18
Stengers, I. 101, 115, 118, 207
Steps to an ecology of mind (Bateson) 374
Sternschuss, S. 436
Stierlin, H. xli: cancer 54; counter-transference 8–9, 422, 423; delegation 92; myths 150; self-referentiality 151; split families 372–3; suicide 10; vectors 162
stochastic processes 374–5
Stoezel, J. 366
Stoller, F. H. 436
strange loops 375, 401
Strategic Psychotherapy: Brief and Symptomatic Treatment (Rabkin) 50
strategic therapy 49, 120, 173, 375–7, 411–13
Strategies of psychotherapy (Haley) 375–6
Strauss, Pierre 192, 193
stress 309
structural family therapy xli, 173, 232, 377–8
structural historicism 181
structural stability 112, 379
Structural stability and morphogenesis (Thom) 394
Structure of magic (Bandler and Grinder) 271
structures, dissipative 101–2
Studies on hysteria (Freud) 422
subject-object relation 356
sucking-in by the system 379

suicide 9–10, 90
Sullivan, H. S. 304
Sun Tzu 412
superego 56, 249, 432
supervision 379–80
support 380
surface structures 380–2
survival unit 125, 154, 181, 352
survivors, parents and children 58–60
swallow-tail catastrophe 114
Symansky, J. 121
symbolic movement 354–5
symbolic reference 27, 203, 254, 264, 357, 382–3
symbolism 121–2, 250, 383–8
symbols 186, 326, 383–8
symptom 389–90: function 20, 90, 165–6, 394; prescribing 297–8; and singularity 363; utilizing 329
synchronic therapy 96–7, 153, 154–5
syntax 68, 295, 353, 390
syntax of communication 280, 380–1, 390–3
systemic hypothesis 393–4
systemic modelling xlii, 403–5: alienation 159; carcinogenesis 394–5; communication 406; homeostasis 117; immanence 190; incompleteness theorems 197–8; interpretation 217; and intervention 395–9, 413; model of 255, 294; myth 255; self-organization 346
systemic therapy 251–3, 278–9, 415; anorexia nervosa 31–2; individual 399–400; neutrality 173; socio-educational 396–7
systems: autonomy and heteronomy 37–8; closed 62, 174; complexity 70–2; dynamic 42, 110, 346–7, 352, 373–4, 379: see also open systems
systems theory xix, 147, 172, 320: see also general systems theory
Systems view of man (von Bertalanffy) 387
Szasz, T. xviii, xxvii, 143

Tabary, J.-C. 77, 78
taboo 192, 225, 334, 430
tactics 412
Tamura, T. 123
tangled hierarchies: see hierarchies, tangled
Tansley, A. G. 111

tasks 5, 6, 321, 328–9, 370, 401–3
taste 259–60
Tatossian, A. 55
territory 405–6; cultural comparisons 260; family system 153; hierarchy 261; and intimacy 217–18; and map 239, 290, 330–1, 406; organization of 102–4, 391–2; and paternity 138
Thanatos 267
thanatoses 95
Tharp, R. B. 83
theatre 32–4, 306
Theories of the symbol (Todorov) 357
therapeutic abduction 407–10
therapeutic abstention 130, 410, 440
therapeutic axes 73, 96–7
therapeutic consensus 410
therapeutic contract 410
therapeutic double binds 410–11
therapeutic strategies and tactics 411–13
therapeutic styles 413–16
therapists xiii, xxxvii, 36, 120, 251, 414–15
thermodynamics, entropy 115
Thom, R. xiv: admission of impotence 7; archetypes 325; ball topology 39; catastrophe theory xiv, 42–3, 87, 112, 175, 250, 417; causality 362–3; chaos 276; chreod 60, 290; communication 68, 259; determinism 319; dynamic systems 110, 313–14; elementary catastrophes 112, 129, 326–7, 434; homeostasis 183; imprinting 191; information 208; metacommunication 245; morphogenetic theory 386–7; mother and child 91–2; oscillators 277; parabolic-umbilic 115; predation 78, 354; salience/pregnance 382, 383; semantics 355–6; space-time 73; *Structural stability and morphogenesis* 394; symbolic reference 254; topology 39, 153; universal unfolding 72, 112, 434; vectors 435
time: intime/outside time 278–9; reflexive nature 252–3
Tinbergen, E. A. xxi, 202
Tinbergen, N. xxi, 20, 79, 202, 210, 212, 224, 405
Todd, E. 140, 213, 272, 304

Todd, T. 108
Todorov, T. 357
Toman, W. 363
Tomm, K. 242, 252, 399
Tomson, P. 131
topology 160, 416–18: ball 39–40; black box 175; connectedness 73; double binds 160; dynamic systems 110; family system 153–4; information 208; and marital breakdown 240; metacommunication 246–7; semantic resonances 352; structural 249
totality xxviii, 117, 155, 275, 418–19
totems 62, 334
touch 258–9
tracking 11
trading of dissociations 419
training 128, 205, 344, 403–5, 419–20, 436
trans-sexualism 361
transactional patterns 6, 329, 388–9
transactional typologies, family 420–2
transcendence 190
transference 414, 422–4; and abduction 408; and alienation 22–3; and change 56; double 81; learning 228; and love 234; narcissistic 267
transformational linguistics 381–2
transgenerational allegory 304
transgenerational contexts 28–9, 93, 234–5
transgenerational memories 213, 332, 424–6, 427
transgenerational therapies 157, 426–7
transitional objects 247, 428, 432
transitional phenomena 428
Treacher, A. xiv, 51, 120, 271, 378, 420
triad 62, 85, 376–7
triadic questioning 428
triangle 26, 356, 428–30: de-triangulation 96; and differentiation 97, 373; dysfunctional 429–30; interlocking 217; perverse 14, 57, 192–3, 288
Trossman, B. 58
trust 127, 430–1
truth 19–20, 78, 232
Tseng, W. 123
Turing, Alan 236
Turing machine xix
typologies of family 158, 215–16, 225–6, 305–6, 389, 420–2

Uexküll, J. von 72, 166, 325, 353, 354
UK: divorce 242–3; family therapy training 120, 420; legal context 231–2
Ulrich, D. N. 430–1
umbilics 115
uncanny 25
uncertainty principle 432
unconscious xxxviii–xxxix, 432–3: collective 219, 220, 432; family 158–9, 219; and jokes 184–5; and memory 425; transaction 315
unconscious processes 303, 306
undifferentiation 99
unit of mind 125, 352–3, 354
unity of command 365–6
universal unfolding 112, 113, 326, 434
unpredictability law 117
USA: drug addiction 108–9; family therapy 231, 304, 414–15, 419
utterances xxii–xxiii, 19, 53, 118, 213, 287, 371

vagabond feeding 30
valence 270, 336, 435
Valéry, P. 5
values 55, 121–2, 223
Vanbremeersch, J. P. 262, 407
Varela, F. 37–8, 119, 282, 287, 346–7
variety, requisite 71, 227
vectors 43, 161–2, 435
Verbizier, J. de 368
veridictory modality 232
Vernant, J.-P. 237
vestimentary habitus 392
Vickers, G. 111
Vico, Giambattista 74
victimization 199, 323–4
Vidal, J.-M. 40, 190–1, 192, 193, 384
video 100, 268, 269, 435–6
violence 436–8: agonistic behaviour 11; and alcoholism 18; and law 224; and memory 424; sacrifice 334, 335; sexual abuse 174; systemic therapy 253
Violence fondamentale, La (Bergeret) 436
visual communication 172, 260
Vogel, Günter 137
Vygotsky, L. S. 385

Waddington, C. H. 60, 183, 384
Walrond-Skinner, S. xv, 80, 81, 120, 201, 242
Walters, M. 172, 173, 174
war 224, 406, 412–13
Watzlawick, P. xxiii, xxiv, xxix, xxxiii (n11, n12), xli:

agreement 14; alienation 24; axiomatics of communication 293–4; change 49, 50, 56; circularity 60, 61; conflicts 315–16; digital coding 34; double bind xvii, 106; errors 72; gender 172; general systems theory 175; holism 180; hypnosis 185, 186; interactions 310–12; interpretation 217; manipulation 120; metaphor 247; paradoxical communication 246; paranoia 94; reality 76, 77–8, 197, 322; redundancy 324; schizophrenia 342; semantics 353–4; strategy 412

Weakland, John H. xvi, xxiii, 49, 50, 311, 400

Weaver, W. xix, 34, 66, 67, 68, 204, 206, 207, 324

Weber, G. 400

Weblin, J. E. 309

Weiner, D. R. 81, 423

Weiner-Davis, M. 370

Weiselberg, H. 123

Weisman, A. D. 234

Weiss, P. 183, 394

Whan, M. 120

Whitaker, C. A. xli, 2, 97, 248, 336

White, C. 174

White, M. 174, 378

Whitehead, A. N. xvi, 49, 104–5, 194

Whitman, C. O. 191

Wickler, W. 224, 266

Widlöcher, D. 56, 188, 256, 257, 267, 298, 322, 351, 414

Wiener, N.: coding 34; communication 204; complexity xix; cybernetics 49, 68, 88–9, 159, 277; general systems theory 175; homeostasis 183; information 205–6, 425

Wilden, A. 34, 206

Wildgen, W. 327

Willi, J. 83, 84

Wilson, D. C. 258

Wilson, E. O. 125, 137

Wilson, N. J. 48

Winch, R. F. 83

Winkin, Y. 392

Winnicott, D. W.: differentiation 97; functional circle 166; games 1; holding 380; identification 188; play 290; psychoanalysis 278; self, true/false 24, 65, 372–3, 430; self-referentiality 151; subject–object relation 356; transitional objects 247, 428, 432

Winokur, G. 177

wirklich 322

Wirklichkeit 322

Wittgenstein, Ludwig 189, 354

Wolfe, Tom xxxv (n22)

Wolin, S. 123

wordplay 186

Wynne, L. C. xvii, xli: alignment 26; boundaries 45, 46, 48; collective cognitive chaos 65, 134; communication, non-specific 286; dissociation, trading of 419; family typologies 215; marital skew 242; metabinding 238, 245; pseudo–hostility 302; pseudo–mutuality 427; as reactor 416; schismogenesis 373; schizophrenia 342; separation problems 8; siblings 363; victimization 323

Yankelevitch, V. 95

Zadeh, L. 167

zeal 440

Zeeman, E. C. 1, 112, 114, 277, 326

zero sum game 342

Zinoviev, A. 22, 24, 65–6, 209

Zygmond, M. 120, 121